# Praise for the *Dickson Baseball Dictionary*

"A book that whets your appetite as much as a ballpark hot dog."
—*Washington Post Book World*

"A dinger of a read!"
—*People Magazine*

"A Babe Ruth of an undertaking . . . Fascinating reading as well as a valuable reference work."
—*Chicago Sun-Times*

"A monumental job."
—*Red Barber*

"Delightful and informative . . . concise and engaging . . . comprehensive. . . . All in all, this treasure trove of information and lore that should be as indispensable to armchair managers, owners, and umpires as it is to serious students of the game."
—The Society of American Baseball Researchers (SABR) *Review*

"God dwells in the details. So do all real baseball fans. This wonderful book has every lexico-graphical nuance and detail associated with our most beautiful and complex sport. Neophytes will learn and experts will simply enjoy."
—Stephen Jay Gould

"A reference resource, an argument settler, a map of our richest sporting language—and, most of all, a delight."
—Daniel Okrent

# THE NEW DICKSON
# BASEBALL
# DICTIONARY

# THE NEW DICKSON

# BASEBALL DICTIONARY

## PAUL DICKSON

*A cyclopedic reference to
more than 7,000 words, names, phrases,
and slang expressions that define the game,
its heritage, culture, and variations*

A HARVEST ORIGINAL
HARCOURT BRACE & COMPANY
SAN DIEGO   NEW YORK   LONDON

*Special acknowledgment is offered here
to the mammoth contribution made to this work
by Skip McAfee. His skills as a lexicographer
and baseball scholar are formidable.*

Copyright © 1989, 1999 by Paul Dickson

Requests for permission to make copies of any part of the work should be mailed to: Permissions Department, Harcourt Brace & Company, 6277 Sea Harbor Drive, Orlando, Florida 32887-6777.

Library of Congress Cataloging-in-Publication Data
Dickson, Paul.
The new Dickson baseball dictionary/Paul Dickson.—1st Harvest ed.
p.    cm.
Rev. ed. of: The Dickson baseball dictionary.  1991.
Includes bibliographical references (p.    ).
ISBN 0-15-100380-7—ISBN 0-15-600580-8 (pbk.)
1. Baseball—United States—Dictionaries.  I. Dickson, Paul.
Dickson baseball dictionary.  II. Title.
GV862.3.D53  1999
796.357'0973'03—dc21   98-40700

Text set in AGaramond with Gill Sans Bold
Designed by Linda Lockowitz
Printed in the United States of America

First Harvest edition 1999
C E F D B

*To Nancy Hartman Dickson,*
*who has given me the time, consideration,*
*constant help, and encouragement to create*
*and then re-create this dictionary.*

# CONTENTS

## THE JARGON OF THE DIAMOND

The diamond has a language all its own;
If a player makes an error, it's a "bone";
    If he attempts the "squeeze"
    And strikes out, it's a "breeze";
A play at which the fans belch forth a groan.

A safe drive to the field is called a "bingle";
If good for one base only, it's a "single";
    If the hurler throws a "cripple"
    And the batter clouts a "triple,"
The swat will put the nerves of fans a-tingle.

When a runner's left on base, 'tis said he "died."
If he goes out on a high fly, he has "skied";
    A one-hand stop's a "stab";
    The pitcher's mound, the "slab";
Successful plays are certainly "inside."

When a player's making good his work is "grand."
But let him boot just one and he's "panned";
    If he comes up in a "pinch"
    And he "whiffs"—well, it's a cinch,
The fickle fans will yell, "He should be 'canned.'"

—*Baseball* magazine, October 1916

# PREFACE

Before the ink had dried on the first edition of this book, good people—fans of baseball, and both professional and self-taught lovers of American words—began to call and write with their lists of omissions from what I had deemed to be a work that defined the national game one entry at a time. I had thought that the dictionary pushed the whole business of baseball terminology and slang to its logical conclusion.

I was wrong for two reasons: first, the language of the game is, as a roster of •readers pointed out, more varied, complex, and fraught with subtle distinctions than I had originally thought—sort of like the game itself.

Second, the game has continued to change, occasioning the need for terms like "wild card," "realignment," "Executive Council," "interleague play," and "acting commissioner." Old terms that had worked a decade ago are being supplemented or even replaced as baseball's oldest and most revered working scribe, Shirley Povich, writing in the *Washington Post* in 1996, summed it up: ". . . almost gone from the language is the 'curveball' that was such a staple for so many generations. It's the play-play orators who have substituted with the 'sidearm' and 'forkball.' The 'screwball,' too, has all but vanished from the lexi-

con of baseball. But the fastball has taken on multiple identities. Play-by-play men talk now of a 'four-seam fastball,' 'a two-seam fastball,' and 'a cut fastball,' whatever that is."

Povich then goes to his favorite New Wave term: "They now also talk of a 'semi-slider.' What is a 'semi-slider,' and how does the play-by-play man know that it is a semi-slider? Half the time the batter himself confesses he doesn't know what kind of pitch he hit or whiffed at, but the men with tube microphones from their vantage points in the sky pretend to know the full nature of the pitch."

Clearly there was work to be done.

By early 1997, the project was up and running again with new vigor and many, many helpers whose names can be found in the acknowledgments. Before we go on, however, a quick flashback into what got this project going in the first place—in a bygone and simpler era when Milwaukee was still in the American League, they didn't give ballparks names like 3Com Park at Candlestick Point, and teams that came in second place did not get to play after the regular season.

People are always asking writers how they got the idea for their latest book. It is a ritual as familiar to an author as the question "What does the baby weigh?" is to a new mother. I'm not sure whether others really care exactly how an idea was hatched, just as they really only pretend to care about the exact weight of a baby, but both rituals are important for the simple reason that they express friendship for and interest in the proud author and parent.

Having said that, I will tell you how I got the idea for this book.

## 1: On Seeing a Three-Year-Old Watch Rickey Henderson Steal Second

On September 5, 1981, our family went to see the Oakland Athletics play the Baltimore Orioles in Memorial Stadium in Baltimore. Among other things, it was the first time our younger son, Alex, had ever been to a baseball game. He was still a few weeks short of turning four, and we had almost left him home with a baby-sitter.

With breathtaking suddenness he was taken with it all. You could hear it in his voice, see it in his eyes, and realize it when he chose to stay in his seat rather than leave for food and souvenirs. The moment of his hooking came within minutes of our arrival: Rickey Henderson stole second. And later in the game, as if the Commissioner's Office itself engineered it in order to guarantee one more die-hard fan, Henderson stole again. Needless to say, a big Henderson poster hung above Alex's bed for many years.

This got me thinking about the game in a new way; not because getting hooked by Henderson was novel, but because it was, perhaps, so predictable. I had seen this earlier with my older son, Andrew, whose hooking had come in the same stadium during a doubleheader.

I thought back to my own hooking, which had been in 1946 when my father took me to Yankee Stadium to see what he called the whole game. His idea of the whole game meant getting there early enough to see the batting practice, the horseplay, and the preparation of the field. We had, in fact, gotten there so early that we ran into outfielder Tommy "Old Reliable" Henrich, who was still in his street clothes. Then I remembered the night three summers later when I first saw something that I had only dreamed of: Johnny Mize in a Yankees—not a Giants—uniform.

I began to realize that the old cliché of fathers taking sons to baseball games as a rite of initiation was flawed. In reality it is the child who often brings the parent back to the game. If the youngster is hooked, his father is re-hooked in the process.

Part of this process, I soon learned, had to do with getting reacquainted with baseball tradition, a very specialized body of wisdom and ritual. Being able to give a perfect, yet seemingly off-the-cuff description of the infield fly rule, knowing how to keep score and how the teams got their names, being able to recite the right aphorism at the proper moment—these are all important. So is remembering the feel of the ball itself.

## 2: On Getting a New Mitt at Age 47

I have had three baseball gloves in my lifetime. The first was bought by my grandmother when I was 11. It was technically a fielder's glove, but I always called it a mitt after the custom in my neighborhood by which all gloves were called mitts. Gloves were for boxing and snowball fights.

That first mitt was a Spalding, bought on a special train trip to New York City. I still have it, a #197 Young Star. It's a mess: a laceless, lifeless, stubby-fingered pancake with padding long ago pounded into so much dust. I hang onto it because it is a source of wonder to me. It has outlasted a dozen bats, bikes, and family sedans, as well as Presidents Truman, Eisenhower, Kennedy, Johnson, Nixon, Ford, Carter, Reagan, and Bush.

It was deployed for hardball, softball, and countless games of catch. It baked in the sun, rotted in the rain, and once fell out of a rowboat and had to be retrieved from the muck at the bottom of a lake. It was oiled, tortured into various shapes depending on the needs of the moment and, until my dog chewed off a lion's share of the lacing, had a pocket so deep it could devour a regulation hardball.

I outgrew that mitt and didn't feel the need for another until my two sons came along. My second mitt turned up at a flea market. A decent enough piece of leather, it carried the autograph of Wayne Causey, a journeyman infielder who played for the Orioles, Kansas City A's, and White Sox from 1955 through 1968. It had a marvelous snap to it when a ball hit the pocket, but the pleasure diminished considerably when the padding began migrating to the outer edge of the glove. The snap then correlated so directly with pain that I found I couldn't even hear anybody field a hot one without emitting a small Pavlovian wince.

I started making plaintive noises about needing a new mitt about the time my 47th birthday hove into view. I could have bought one myself but somehow never got around to it, perhaps because it didn't seem quite right for a man who is 20 months and two weeks older than Pete Rose to walk into a store alone and buy a mitt for himself. Then my wife announced that she was buying me one for my birthday. We'd go together and pick one out.

The choices were overwhelming and a far cry from the homely work gloves of my childhood. There were Spaldings, Wilsons, Mizunos, Rawlings, and Louisville Sluggers at prices ranging from $35 to more than $100. Most were signed by stars except for those priced at $100 and up. These expensive models are termed "pro" models, so if you're a pro I suspect it is "bush" to have somebody else's moniker on your mitt. I have since learned that while a player may autograph and authorize a glove, that is not the actual model he uses.

There was much trying on, fist pummeling, and posing. The reflected image is important and I'm sure is one reason why sporting goods stores, like bridal shops, always have mirrors. I wound up with a Rawlings 1445 Darryl Strawberry "fastback." I took the tan model rather than the "strawberry"-hued version. As much as I love puns, I was not ready to wear one for my baseball reentry. A number of magic words and copyrighted phrases are stamped into its surface, including the "deep well" pocket, "edge-U-cated heel," and "holDster" fastening band. The webbing is an immense, supple leather network large enough for trapping and comforting small furry animals.

The glory of a brand-new mitt is the glory of leather without a memory. *My* Darryl Strawberry "fastback" had never committed an error or a flub of any sort. It offered the new start that middle age needs, all but begging to be shaped to my hand. Add to this the fact that for pure consumer pleasure the sweet aroma of a new baseball glove ranks with the smell of a new car, and it is easy to see why I couldn't put it down the day it came home.

On its first outing it proved to be a magnet. Not once did I have to apologize for its newness or my oldness. Second time out, a very serious catch with a man my own age, I booted a couple. The first time I used its newness as an excuse—"Still breaking it in"—and the next time I just muttered, "The old back!" But despite a few gaffes here and there, the magic of the new glove had become a given. Soon it was eliciting comments and compliments in words and phrases I had not heard since I was in high school. I jumped up and pulled down a high one that just barely stuck in the top of the webbing. "Nice snowcone," said my companion as I examined the proof of what had happened—I had violated the law of gravity.

All this glory did not come without a price tag. What I found, I had to admit openly and often, was that the glove, not me, was making the difference. My abilities in the field had not improved over time. I also began to understand one of the reasons why there might not be another big-league .400 hitter during my lifetime. Larry McClain, vice president for baseball at Rawlings in St. Louis, puts it in perspective: "Today's gloves are not only superior to those of the 1920s but also the 1950s." He believes that men like Willie Mays and Mickey Mantle might have fared even better in the field with some of today's models. He does, however, acknowledge that Ozzie Smith, a spectacular fielder, uses what is essentially a '50s-style glove.

My last few comments on glove evolution are not a digression but are added testimonial to the power of the present I got at age 47. Simply put, the new mitt put me back in touch with the feel of the game of baseball. To describe such a gift as marvelous is to dabble in understatement.

A dozen years after the great glove purchase, the passion for baseball has only been cooled during shutouts and strikes. Despite the Dark Age that followed August 1994, March continues to be the month of hope and anticipation, October the time of hope and the months in between a steady stream of box scores, scorecards, and ticket stubs.

The act of acquiring the glove also had to do with history. To buy into baseball this way is to buy into the history of the game: children born after Watergate know about the Black Sox and the Babe, but draw a blank when the National Recovery Act or Harry Truman are mentioned. Football and basketball seem to date back a couple years at most; but baseball is a realm where players of the past die but never seem to age, where records are recalled even if they were set in 1933, where Ty and Cy are household names, and where half the people who "recall" Bobby Thomson's home run of the century weren't even born when it happened. Roger Angell put it this way in *Late Innings* (1982): "I have read so much about the old-timers and heard older players and writers and fans (including my father) talk about them so often that they are almost as visible to me as the stars I have watched on the field."

If there is an intergenerational glue that holds all of this together, it is composed of numbers, stats and records, and words—the motley vocabulary of baseball, which is a mix of slang, nicknames, metaphors, and official terminology. What were the Miracle of Coogan's Bluff and Merkle's Boner? What is a "can of corn" or a "cup of coffee" and what are they doing on the field? Why is K the scorecard symbol for strikeout? What and when was the "live-ball era"? The list goes on and on, but the point is made that baseball is intensely verbal.

It is, in fact, verbal on many levels. Tom Boswell has written that for a minor leaguer, talk is the staple of sanity and that the man who cannot spin a yarn, tell a joke, or create an epigram is "condemned to be an outsider." He adds, "This rich verbal tradition—the way the game has taken on the ambiance of the frontier campfire or the farmer's cracker-barrel stove and moved it into the dugout—is what marks baseball so distinctively. . . ." On another occasion he wrote, "Conversation is the blood of baseball."

Paul Dickson
Garrett Park, Maryland

# INTRODUCTION

Baseball needs a Webster and a standing-Revision Board to keep the dictionary of the game up to date. The sport is building its own language so steadily that, unless some step soon is taken to check the inventive young men who coin the words that attach themselves to the pastime, interpreters will have to be maintained in every grand stand to translate for the benefit of those who merely love the game and do not care to master it thoroughly.
　　—Hugh S. Fullerton, "The Baseball Primer," *The American Magazine,* June 1912

Reading the baseball news in some of the daily papers is like reading a totally unfamiliar language. Some of the terms used awaken a faint comprehension in my doubtless dull brain, but others leave me simply gasping for breath.
　　—English visitor quoted in the New York *Sun,* October 9, 1929

A people who are prosperous and happy, optimistic and progressive, produce much slang; it is a case of play; they amuse themselves with the language.
　　—W. Sumner, A. Keller, M. Davie (sociologists), 1927

Back in 1913, an odd movement started in Chicago. Time has obscured some of the details, but what it amounted to was a movement away from baseball slang. The *Chicago Record-American* began covering games two ways: one in the slang of the time and, next to it, a description of the game in "less boisterous" terms. A Professor McClintock of the English department at the University of Chicago brought the matter to national attention when he suggested that the Republic would be better served if baseball slang were dropped and

that, for starters, the newspapers would start describing the sport in dictionary English.

This call came at a time when, for example, the *Washington Post*'s Joe Campbell, "the Chaucer of baseball," would write: "And Amie Rusie made a Svengali pass in front of Charlie Reilly's lamps and he carved three nicks in the weather," to say that Rusie had gotten Reilly to strike out.

A few managers and players actually agreed with McClintock, but there was little sympathy expressed by the press, which whipped

McClintock's notion into something big. "The question has assumed the importance of a national issue," said an editorial in the *Charleston News and Courier.* "It has received editorial discussion in the columns of the most influential newspapers, and it has aroused interest from end to end of this baseball-loving land." Calling the notion the "injury which is now proposed," the paper went on to say, "It is to be hoped, and it may reasonably be expected, that the movement will not accomplish the results which its more radical advocates desire. Baseball stories told in conventional English are dull reading indeed; and it is a pertinent fact that the decadence of cricket in England is attributed by many British newspapers to the failure of the press to put brightness or 'ginger' into the descriptions of the game."

The *Washington Post* chose to make fun of McClintock by describing play using dictionary English. Sample: "Johnson gave the batter a free pass to first" becomes "Mr. Johnson pitched four balls that in immediate sequence made a detour of the plate, which, according to the rules of the game, entitled the batter to go to first base, despite the fact that he had not even aimed his bat at the baseball in any one instance." After a thorough roasting, the *Post* concluded, "Much of the English used by Professor McClintock himself was once regarded as slang."

On the other hand, *The Nation* saw the threat as a serious one and wrote about it as if it were a disease: "One of the most puzzling problems of this puzzling era is the effect wrought upon our native speech by contact with the national pastime."

All of this was, of course, a passing controversy that amounted to little; but it did serve

to drive home a point: Baseball had its own ever-changing language, and it was not to be meddled with. Ironically, not too many years would pass before men and women with Ph.D.s would be making names for themselves not by decrying slang but by collecting it—not only that of the diamond, but also of the carnival, the hobo jungle, the railroad yard, the soda fountain—and publishing it in *American Speech,* that superb journal, then as now, devoted to the riches of American English.

It also served to underscore another point: The baseball language of the daily press was sometimes different from that of the participants in the game.

Sometimes lost in all of this discussion of the propriety of slang is the fact that it was a remarkably rich and effective way of writing that could allow the drama of nine innings to be compressed into one socko, lung-straining sentence. Such sentences tend to retain their vitality for many years. An example from the *San Francisco Examiner* for April 13, 1932: "Greeting big George Ernshaw like a long lost 'cousin,' Babe Ruth and the New York Yankees fell upon the right-handed act of the Athletics this chilly afternoon, blasted him off the field in four innings and outslugged the American League champions 12 to 6."

If baseball is a game of slang, it is also a game of heaped-on modifiers. A word like *single* seldom stands naked. Listen, as one is described in a sentence by Richard Justice of the *Washington Post:* "The only California run scored after Davis had wild-pitched rookie Wally Joyner (three for four) into scoring position and then given up a broken-bat, opposite-field bloop single to Brian Downing" (May 22, 1986).

When one combines the formal language of the rule book, the technical terms of a sport obsessed with mechanics and statistics, the journalese, *and* the slang, the results are remarkable. If someone had told me at the very beginning of this project that I would be able to find some 7,000 words, terms, names, and phrases to define, I would have said this was impossible. That I did is not an accomplishment to be credited to the author, but rather one to be scored to the game itself, with an assist to that rich and flexible entity known as the English language. (While I was working on the book, I occasionally thought that the game might have an entirely different tone and presence if it had evolved in, say, France or Germany. This is impossible to prove, of course.)

It also came as a surprise to realize that a number of terms had more than one meaning in the context of this game. There are ten baseball meanings of *hook,* seven for *hole,* six for *pick up* and *option,* and four or five for dozens of terms all of which have distinctly different meanings.

Despite this dazzling total, a number of terms have been purposely left out of this work—some having to do with collective bargaining, strikes, lockouts, and the legalities of labor contracts, others having to do with the collecting of baseball cards and statistical notions which are limited to a small, ardent group of "statistorians." Also excluded are the names of dozens of annual awards in baseball for public relations, traveling secretaries, and more. Only the most important awards are here.

Countless terms were rejected because there was only a single citation attesting to their use. I am convinced that from time to time someone sits down and cranks out a list of terms native to the national game that may or may not have ever been uttered by an actual player. For instance, the terms listed below appeared in the *Sporting News* November 27, 1897, as part of a glossary of baseball terms:

*A whistling triplet:* a three-base hit

*Hugging a musty:* catching a swift ball

*Had Tabasco sauce in his arms:* a vigorous batter

*Unchaining a cyclone with the willow:* to bat a ball that moves off very swiftly, pursuing a course near the earth

*Ambled to the bag:* made a base by easy stages

*Embezzling the plate:* when strategy temporarily takes the place of leg talent

*Popping a mushy one:* hitting a ball which lacks momentum

Nestled in among well-used terms, these appear to be ones that only lasted for only a moment and leave no evidence that they had application beyond the glossary itself. This compiler will gladly stand corrected if someone can show him that the mouthful *unchaining a cyclone with the willow* actually got used within twenty feet of home plate.

The fact that I have limited this work to terms for which I have a minimum of two citations has yielded a much slimmer book.

Some of these terms were appealing and interesting and on numerous occasions I wished I had more citations. For instance, I was able to find only one instance of *David Harums,* the eponym used to describe owners and managers, and it does not appear in the dictionary. A recent example of the ephemeral is the line, "Elvis has left the building," for an out-of-the-park home run. It was created, puckishly, by television comedian David Letterman who told his audience that baseball announcers needed a new means of announcing a home run. It was used by announcers, but always explained in terms of Letterman's humor of the absurd.

By holding to this rule of citations, I was forced to leave out those wonderful, colorful terms uttered by one or a handful of individuals. Lest it be lost forever, here is one term that did not make the cut:

*bowel locker.* A powerful pitch that overwhelms the pitcher. Coined by pitcher Glenn Abbott, it appears in Roger Craig's *Inside Pitch* (1984).

There were also several words that have appeared elsewhere than in lists of baseball terms and seemed so general to American English that I left them out. A few examples follow: *blunder, boo, break even, dark horse, discard, fast one, hoist* (to hit high), *lift one, mogul* for a team owner, *nook, shake up, shoulder-high, shine* (to perform well), and *toss up.*

Then there were those tantalizing one-citation mysteries like the *Cincinnati base hit,* raised by baseball researcher Norman Macht, who found the reference in an old baseball guide next to the date January 13, 1974: "Baseball writers declare against the Cincinnati base hit scoring rule." Macht reported, "None of the experts on Cincinnati baseball history that I asked knew anything about it."

Some terms seem to be so intensely regional they have no broader application, such as this one from Robert Perkins:

*pig tail.* In elementary school team play, a "back-up catcher" to help keep the ball in play and to allow as many kids as possible to play at one time.

He adds: "[T]his was eons ago when I was a first through third grader in Kansas. I never knew of it to be used when I lived in Texas."

A few conclusions derived from the study of baseball language are in order.

I. *Baseball is a metaphoric circus.* The game has a particular infatuation with what one critic of sportswriters termed, "the incorrect use of correct words." There are hundreds of examples, but the point can be made by simply listing a selection of synonyms for the hard-hit ball or *line drive.* It is variously known as an *aspirin,* a *BB,* a *bolt,* a *clothesline,* a *frozen rope,* a *pea,* a *rocket,* and a *seed.* A player's throwing arm seems to be called everything but an arm: *gun, hose, rifle, soupbone, whip,* and *wing,* to name just a few. The arm is not the only renamed body part. From top to bottom, players have *lamps* (eyes), a *pipe* (neck or throat), *hooks* (hands), *wheels* (legs), and *tires* (feet).

So many allusions are made to food and dining—including pitches that seem to fall off the table—that a fairly well-balanced diet suggests itself in terms like *can of corn, cup of coffee, fish cakes, banana stalk, mustard, pretzel, rhubarb, green pea, juice, meat hand, grapefruit league,* and *tater.* Among the many terms for the ball itself are *apple, cantaloupe, egg, lemon, orange, pea, potato,* and *tomato.* Implements? There is the *plate* (also known as the *platter, pan,* and *dish*) and, of course, the *forkball.* Dessert? The red abrasion from a slide into base is a *strawberry* and the fan's time-honored sound of disapproval is a *raspberry.*

II. *Ballyard slang comes back from obscurity.* Slang, we are always being told, is ephemeral. This is only somewhat borne out by baseball slang because, for every seemingly fleeting term or phrase, there seems to be one that hangs on for several generations. Many terms that began as slang have been so widely accepted and are used so routinely that they are no longer considered slang. This point was first made in an article in the *Saturday Review* in 1933 in which the author, Murray Godwin, pointed to the permanence of such "slang" as *sacrifice* and *wind up*. Compare this, for example, to the slang of popular music or the high school, which seems to change constantly.

Etymologist Peter Tamony put it much more strongly. In his essay on the term "Dick Smith" (a name assigned to a loner in both baseball and horse racing slang) he wrote: "It is always amusing to be able to run down the history and origin of a real slang word. Real slang always laughs at the professors and others who hold that it is ephemeral. They mistake mere metaphor and simile for slang. To hold that slang is largely ephemeral is to say that dress is ephemeral because women's fashions change four times a year. A large part of our slang has a long, long history, but records of it are short. It is only since the advent of the modern sports page, about 1900, that this vital and human aspect, this color of our speech, has been properly recorded."

Baseball slang is in fact hard to kill, and specific terms have a way of asserting themselves after being written off as archaic. While researching this book, I encountered many articles that declared dead terms that are still very much alive today. For example, a 1964 article in *Baseball Digest,* written by Tim Horgan of the *Boston Traveler,* tells us, "There are no more bleachers. They are now 'porches.'" The same article reported that "No pitcher today . . . throws a fastball or, as our forefathers knew it, 'a high hard one.'" In 1933, Damon Runyon described a hit that "used to be called" a Texas Leaguer, and in 1937, sportswriter Curley Grieve of the *San Francisco Examiner* told his readers, "A left-handed hurler is no longer a southpaw. He's a cock-eyed hurler.'"

Similarly, a 1982 article on baseball slang

that appeared in the USAir inflight magazine listed the term *wheelhouse* (for the area of the batter's greatest hitting strength) as one of a number of bygone words that had "gone down swinging." If the term is dead, no one has bothered to tell the many writers and sportscasters who use it regularly. Then there is the term "can of corn," which is annually declared dead but comes back as surely as Opening Day. Some recent obituaries follow:

1986. "For starters, one phrase that's out is can of corn," wrote Scott Ostler in the *Los Angeles Times,* ". . . several players warned me to stay away from that one."

1987. Mets catcher Gary Carter deems the term "ancient history" in an article in the *St. Petersburg Times* on the latest in baseball slang.

On the other hand, consider another vegetable. There are a number of writers who have reported the term *pea* (for a ball batted or pitched so fast that it can hardly be seen) as an example of the very latest in baseball lingo, even though it can be traced back at least to 1910. To fill out the platter, there is *rhubarb,* which never seems to have gone out of vogue since it made its baseball debut in the 1930s.

III. *The game proudly displays its rustic roots.* There is a tone to the language of the game that is remarkably pastoral. If any imagery dominates, it is that of rural America. Even under a dome, it is a game of *fields* and *fences,* where *ducks sit on the pond* and pitchers sit in the *catbird seat.* New players come out of the *farm system* and a *farm hand* who pitches may get to work in the *bullpen.*

It is also low key. Although some of the terms for whacking the ball with the bat are strong (to *crush, smash, powder*) and *base stealing* is aptly named, other actions are described in absurdly mild terms. The most glaring example can be heard when the pitcher throws the ball at the batter in an attempt to intimidate or injure him. Terms associated with this act include *bean* and *beanball, dust* and *duster, brush* and *brush back, shave* and *barber.* It is sometimes called a *purpose pitch* or *chin music* that can be used to *flip* a batter. Such behavior may lead to a noisy and sometimes violent confrontation that is called a *rhubarb.*

Compare this to a headline run over a *Washington Post* interview with New York Giants linebacker Lawrence Taylor a few days before Super Bowl XXI: "Taylor: 'Kill Shots' Make the Game." Comedian George Carlin has a routine in which he compares the pastoral game of baseball to football, which is played on a *gridiron* where there is *blitzing, red-dogging, drives* into *enemy territory,* and where *bombs* are thrown. Baseball is played in a *park,* and the offensive plays include the *free pass, homer,* and *sacrifice fly.* In football you *spear, march,* and *score;* in baseball you *walk, stretch,* and *run home.* In an op-ed piece in the *New York Times* (September 6, 1987) Steve Palay points out that the language of arms control is very close to that of football (*throw weight, end run, hammering out* an agreement, etc.) but that it would be better served if it was taken from baseball. "Arms control is not won," Palay concludes, "it is played. And going into 'extra innings' sounds so much better than 'sudden death.'"

All of this is not to say that baseball terminology is without its dark side. A letter from Jim Land of Felton, California, published in the October 5, 1987, *The Sporting News* makes the point: "Baseball terminology, steeped in tradition, pays tribute to chicanery. For example, stealing bases, stealing signs, cheating toward the lines, robbing homers and hits, stabs, swipes, bluffs and suicide

squeeze are all part of the game. There are hidden ball tricks, faked tags and in-the-vicinity plays."

IV. *Clubhouse chatter defies logic.* For reasons that are unclear, baseball seems driven to come up with its own terms for things that are used widely in other sports. Everywhere else teams are piloted by head coaches but baseball insists on *managers* (and with rare exception dresses them like players) and all the referees are called *umpires.* If other sports had to deal with discrimination and segregation, baseball dealt with the *color bar.* Substitutes are good enough for most sports, but not for baseball, which insists on loading its benches and bullpens with *firemen, pinch hitters, pinch runners,* and *platoon players.* Baseball players never seem to turn, they always *pivot.* In realms as diverse as bowling and bombing, a strike is a hit; but in baseball alone it is a *miss.* Out of bounds works for everyone else, but baseball insists on *foul territory.* If the same facility is used for football on Sunday and baseball on Monday, it is transformed overnight from a stadium to a *ballpark.* And the locker rooms used by the football players become *clubhouses* for the baseball players.

V. *The major influence on baseball language was British.* If one person had to be singled out for having the most influence on the *official* language of the game, it is a pioneering Englishman named Henry Chadwick, but this may be only because he came along so early that he was essentially given the opportunity to fill in blanks. He wrote the first rule book, created the first box score, and served as one of the game's first journalists. He also created many of the early instructional baseball manuals that were used during the latter half of the 19th century.

Beyond Chadwick, there have been several attempts to assign somebody the title of father of baseballese (baseball jargon). Among the contenders is the school of midwestern and western baseball writers who appeared in the late 19th century and had a great impact in building the vocabulary needed to describe the game. This assertion is made in John Allen Krout's 1929 *Annals of American Sport,* where he gives some of their names: "Shortly after 1883 Leonard Washburn, Finley Peter Dunne, who earned national fame as the creator of Mr. Dooley, and Charles Seymour began to write their entertaining stories of Anson's White Stockings for the Chicago papers."

But all of this is somewhat misleading because so many people have had a continuing impact on the language of baseball. A very small and incomplete list would have to include Branch Rickey, Casey Stengel, Earl Weaver, Red Barber, Yogi Berra, Ring Lardner, Red Smith, Dizzy Dean, Jim Murray, Gaylord Perry, Theodore A. "TAD" Dorgan, Alexander Cartwright, Pierce Egan, Jim Brosnan, Satchel Paige, Willard Mullin, Leo Durocher, and Babe Ruth.

VI. *The influence of baseball on American English at large is stunning and strong.* In that great work on the lore of baseball, *The Old Ball Game,* Tristram Potter Coffin writes, "No other sport and few other occupations have introduced so many phrases, so many words, so many twists into our language as has baseball. The true test comes in the fact that old ladies who have never been to the ballpark, coquettes who don't know or care who's on first, men who think athletics begin and end with a pair of goal posts, still know and use a great deal of baseball-derived terminology. Perhaps other sports in their efforts to replace baseball as 'our national pastime,' have two strikes on them before they come to bat."

Perhaps the best way to drive this home is to present a partial list of terms and phrases that started in baseball (or, at least, were given a major boost by it) but that have much wider application, to wit: "A" team, ace, Alibi Ike, Annie Oakley, back-to-back, ballpark figure, bat a thousand, batting average, bean, bench, benchwarmer, Black Sox, bleacher, bonehead, boner, box score, the breaks, breeze/breeze through, Bronx cheer, bunt, bush, bush league(r), butterfingers, "call 'em as I see 'em," catch flat-footed, caught in a squeeze play, charley horse, choke, circus catch, clutch, clutch hitter, curveball, doubleheader, double play, extra innings, fan, fouled out, gate money, get one's innings in, get to first base, go to bat for, grandstander, grandstand play, ground rules, hardball, heads up, hit and run, "hit 'em where they ain't," hit the dirt, home run, hot stove league, hustler, in the ballpark, in a pinch, in there pitching, "it ain't over 'til it's over," "it's a (whole) new ball game," jinx, keep your eye on the ball, ladies day, Louisville Slugger, minor league, muff, "nice guys finish last," ninth inning rally, off base, on-deck, one's licks, on the ball, on the bench, out in left field, out of my league, phenom, pinch hitter, play ball with, play the field, play-by-play, pop up, rain check, rhubarb, right off the bat, rookie, rooter, Ruthian, safe by a mile, "say it ain't so, Joe," screwball, seventh-inning stretch, showboat, shut out, smash hit, southpaw, spitball, squeeze play, Stengalese, strawberry, strike out, sucker, switch hitter, team play, Tinker-to-Evers-to-Chance, touch all bases, two strikes against him, "wait 'til next year," warm up, whitewash, "Who's on first?", windup, "you can't win 'em all," "you could look it up."

Elting E. Morison, writing in *American Heritage* (August/September 1986), asks: "Why is baseball terminology so dominant an influence in the language? Does it suggest that the situations that develop as the game is played are comparable to the patterns of our daily work? Does the sport imitate the fundamentals of the national life or is the national life shaped to an extent by the character of the sport? In any case, here is an opportunity to reflect on the meaning of what I think I heard Reggie Jackson say in his spot on a national network in the last World Series: 'The country is as American as baseball.'"

# HOW TO USE THE DICTIONARY

Having long thought that *I* needed a baseball dictionary, I imagined what one would look and feel like well before the first word of this one was put down on paper. From the outset the idea was that it had to be useful to a nine-year-old looking for a clear definition of the infield fly rule, but it also had to be a book that would appeal to two of the toughest audiences for the printed word: the baseball fanatic and the lover of language.

First and foremost, this is a dictionary meant for these three users. But it is also a book for browsing, and for that reason there is a flexibility in the presentation of entries. If, for example, a good story begs to be told as a digression, it gets told.

Nonetheless, a general format was adopted for the first edition and is used, with minor adjustments, in the second edition:

**entry 1.** *part of speech (when there is more than one definition or when there could be confusion)/usage* first definition. **2.** *part of speech/usage* second definition. Referrals: *Synonyms (Syn.,)* Compare, See, See also.

Following the part of speech, either *arch.* for archaic or *obs.* for obsolete may be indicated. Great restraint has been exercised in using the archaic label because, as was pointed out in the Introduction, certain terms have had a way of making a comeback at the very moment they are deemed to be dead. (I had been convinced that *yakker* [for curveball] was archaic until I heard Jim Palmer use the term twice during a baseball telecast. I had already labeled *twirler* [for pitcher] as archaic when I read this line in the July 1, 1987, *Lewiston* [Maine] *Daily Sun* in an account of a game in Jay, Maine: "The Litchfield twirler had a shutout until the seventh inning.")

A term is labeled obsolete only when it refers to a rule, practice, or element of the game that is no longer a part of it and that seems unlikely ever to stage a comeback.

A term appearing in italic letters within a definition or at the end of a definition indicates a synonymous cross-reference. If the cross-reference appears as a term's first definition, the reader should turn to that term's entry for a full definition.

When it appears useful to the reader, the term is illustrated as it appears in the context of an attributed, dated quotation. I have also included, as part of the definition, the historic background of the concept or object in question.

Following each definition, any or all of the following elements are likely to appear.

**1st Use.** A dated reference often accompanied by a display of a term as it appears in that reference. In most cases it is, of course, impossible to cite the very earliest example that appears in print, so this feature is really meant to give the reader a feel for the relative antiquity and early use of the word or phrase. Lest there be any question, the citation given will be the earliest found.

Most of these citations are marked with the names of the researchers who found them— primarily Edward J. Nichols, Peter Tamony, David Shulman, Gerald Cohen, Peter Morris, Barry Popik, or the late Charles D. Poe.

For reasons of space, not every citation will be followed by the actual reference. Most of those without the actual quote are from Nichols's 1939 doctoral thesis, "An Historical Dictionary of Baseball Terminology." These were omitted as they have been known through the Nichols thesis for some years. Nichols relied heavily on the A. G. Spalding collection of baseball material at the New York Library, which includes the scrapbooks of Henry Chadwick, and on the multi-volumed records of the Knickerbocker Club beginning in 1845. These records contain rulings, discussions, and other material that have never been published, so a reference to the Knickerbocker Rules of 1845 (or any other year) refers to these records. For instance, Nichols finds that the first use of the term "catcher" appears on page 154 of the *Rules of the Original Knickerbocker Club.*

**Etymology.** When possible, the history of the term is given. If there are several theories about the origin of a term, all will be given and often they will be followed by a discussion of their relative merit. Such explanations are not attempted when the term itself appears to suggest its origin, as in the case with terms like *out* and *fly ball.*

Some terms will have more than one etymology and these may be in conflict with one another. The principle at work in this dictionary is that *all* the claims should be presented. If there is a bias lurking in this book, it is that words and phrases can have a motley assortment of etymologies that have acted corroboratively to give the term momentum and popularity. One of them may, in fact, be the original, but that does not mean the others did not have important influence.

**Usage Note.** Comment on a special context in which a term may be used as well as when, in the author's opinion, it should not be used.

**Extended Use.** Use of the term in the English language at large. It is through these subentries that one gets to see the immense influence of baseball on the American language. Interestingly, there are many terms, which no longer sound like baseball terms, that appear to have first sprung from the diamond.

**Cross-reference.** Terms italicized at the end of an entry may be consulted as separate entries.

**Notes.**

*Abbreviations.* The following are used throughout this dictionary:

| | |
|---|---|
| Abbrev. | Abbreviation |
| Co. | Company |
| esp. | especially |
| Pron. | Pronounced |
| specif. | specifically |
| Syn. | Synonym |
| Var. | Variation |

An exhaustive list of abbreviations used in baseball is enclosed as an appendix.

*Expert authority.* In certain cases an expert has been asked to contribute a detailed definition of a term. In these cases the name of the individual is listed with the definition.

*Softball terms.* It has long been assumed that the vocabulary of softball and that of baseball are identical or almost so. This assumption is wrong and commonly made by those who think of softball as a pale reflection of baseball.

Folks who play the game and spend odd hours with their heads poked in rule books or the latest issue of *Balls and Strikes* know bet-ter. More than one hundred softball terms occur here, all of which are clearly marked [softball term]. These are terms unique to softball or are definitions of baseball terms with significantly different meanings.

*Deanisms.* Every attempt has been made to give the source of the quotes used in the book. However, quotes attributed to Dizzy Dean have proven elusive because they have appeared in several versions of often undated pamphlets and ballpark handouts named "Dizzy's Definitions," "Dizzy Dean's Dictionary," and the like.

# A

**A 1.** See *Class A.* **2.** Scoreboard abbrev. for *assist,* 2. **3.** Box score abbrev. for *attendance.*

**AA 1.** See *Class AA.* **2.** Abbrev. for *American Association,* 1. **3.** Abbrev. for *American Association,* 2.

**AAA** See *Class AAA.*

**AAABA** Abbrev. for *All-American Amateur Baseball Association.*

**AAGPBL** Abbrev. for *All-American Girls Professional Baseball League.*

**AB** Scorecard and box score abbrev. for *at-bat.*

**ABC** Abbrev. for *American Baseball Congress.*

**ABCA** Abbrev. for *American Baseball Coaches Association.*

**Abner Doubleday Field** A small ballpark (capacity 10,000) near the National Baseball Hall of Fame and Museum in Cooperstown, N.Y. It has been used since 1940 as the site for the annual Hall of Fame Game. It is named for Civil War officer Abner Doubleday, who, according to the traditional but erroneous story, invented baseball in Cooperstown in 1839.

**aboard** On base; e.g., "Smith hit a home run with two men aboard." **1st Use.** 1907. (*McClure's Magazine,* Apr.; Edward J. Nichols). **Usage Note.** The term is one of several long-standing nautical allusions in baseball terminology.

**above the hands** Said of a high pitched ball. The term has come into common play since the 1990 World Series.

**abroad** Playing away from one's home field. A schedule card may have two columns: one for the team "at home" and the other for the team "abroad."

**accept the offering** To swing at the pitch.

**accessories** A collective term for pine tar rag, bat weight, rosin bag, and other items used by players. "Accessories Give Players Extra Edge" (*Baseball Digest* article title, Sept. 1969).

**accordion act** Collapsing in a pennant race. "Anybody who's waiting for the New York Yankees to pull an accordion act and fold is in for both a surprise and a long wait" (*Baltimore Sun,* June 1, 1994).

**ace 1.** *n./obs.* A run or score in the earliest era of baseball, so called in the 1845 rules of the original Knickerbocker Base Ball Club. In that original version, the first team to score 21 aces was the winner regardless of the number of innings played. Syn. *count,* 3. **1st Use.** 1845. (*New York Morning News,* Oct. 21): An account of a game in Hoboken, N.J., at the Elysian Fields describes a game in which "four aces" were scored off a single hit (Fox Butterfield, *New York Times,* Oct. 4, 1990) **2.** *n.* A team's best pitcher, usually a starter; the "rock of the rotation." Wilson Alvarez signed with the Tampa Bay Devil Rays in Dec. 1997 to be the number-one starter: "That's every pitcher's dream—to be the ace. That's why I'm here." (*Baltimore Sun,* Dec. 4, 1997). See also *number 1,* 2. **1st Use.** 1902. "The work of McCreedie has been watched closely too, and he gives promise of being an Ace." (*The Sporting*

*News,* Nov. 15; Peter Tamony). David Shulman has dated the term as applied to tennis, for a serve that is not touched by the receiver and that scores for the server, to 1885. **Etymology.** Baseball lore and tradition have always laid the origin of this term to one man. In 1869, pitcher Asa Brainard won 56 out of 57 games played by the Cincinnati Red Stockings, baseball's first professional team. From then on, according to lore, any pitcher with a dazzling string of wins was called an "Asa," which later became "ace." But lexicographer David Shulman (letter, Feb. 24, 1989) is not convinced that the term applied to Brainard: "This pitcher was active 1871–1874 in the big leagues and he was nicknamed 'Count.' I have seen no attestation of 'ace' during his time." This strongly suggests that the name was applied to Brainard after his time as an ace. The fact that the ace is the most valuable card in a deck of cards certainly helped the term evolve. Lexicographer Eric Partridge and others have traced the term "flying ace," an outstanding fighter pilot of World War I, to cards. **3.** *n.* The "star" of any baseball team. **4.** *n.* A low-percentage, tough-to-hit pitch used in a two-strike situation. **5.** *adj.* Best, or foremost; e.g., "Smith threw his ace fastball."

**across the body** Said of a defensive play when a fielder either catches a ball by extending the gloved hand to the opposite side of his body or expeditiously throws the ball over or across his body rather than with his arm extended straight away from his body.

**across the letters** Said of a pitched ball that passes across the batter's chest at the approximate location on the uniform of the letters spelling out the team's name.

**across the shirt** Said of a pitched ball that is close to the batter, chest high. **1st Use.** 1937. (*Pittsburgh Press,* Jan. 11; Edward J. Nichols).

**acting commissioner** Interim commissioner. It is the official term used to describe the reign of Bud Selig as "temporary commissioner" from the time that Fay Vincent was given his walking papers in Sept. 1992 to Summer 1998.

**action pitch** The pitch thrown when the count is full (three balls and two strikes) with two outs and

men on base. The situation calls for the baserunners to start running just before the ball is delivered.

**activate** To return a player to the team's active roster after injury, illness, or suspension.

**active list** A list of those players on a team's playing roster, excluding those inactive due to illness, injury, or some other factor. Abbrev. *AL.*

**active player** A player who is regularly and actively engaged in playing baseball.

**activity** A relief pitcher or pitchers warming up; e.g., "There's activity in the Cardinals bullpen."

**adios** *v.* To hit a home run; e.g., "Smith adios-ed that one." The term is Spanish for "good-bye" and this bit of "Spanglish" is in keeping with the traditional penchant of sportscasters to say "goodbye" to the baseball as it is heading into home run territory.

**adjudge** For an umpire to make a decision.

**adjustment** The reaction of a player upon leaving the game of baseball which he may have begun to play at the age of seven or eight. "He's made the Adjustment. He doesn't *like* it, but he's made the Adjustment." (Dock Ellis, quoted in Donald Hall & Dock Ellis, *Dock Ellis in the Country of Baseball,* 1976).

**admire a third strike** To be called out on strikes while watching the third one.

**advance** For a batter to move a baserunner ahead one or more bases because of a hit, groundout, or sacrifice.

**advance sale** The number of tickets sold before the actual day of a baseball game.

**advance scout** A scout who looks for the strengths and weaknesses of the team that the scout's team will be playing next. **Etymology.** The term was first used by Casey Stengel, according to Tony Kubek (in George F. Will, *Men at Work,* 1990). The practice dates to the early 1950s when the Brooklyn Dodgers began sending an advance man to the Polo Grounds or to Philadelphia to scout the teams on their way to Ebbets Field. Peter Schmuck (*Baltimore Sun,* May 22, 1994) wrote: "Former Dodgers executive Al Campanis claims some credit for the concept, which he said sprang from a conversation in 1950 with then general manager Buzzie Bavasi." Campanis told Bavasi that he had scouted for a college football team and thought that the practice could be extended to baseball. The Dodgers felt it was a success and the Chicago Cubs were the next to adopt the practice.

**afterpiece** *arch.* The second game of a double-header.

**agate** A baseball. **Etymology.** The term may have derived from "marble," another name for the ball. Agates or aggies were popular forms of marbles.

**agent** An individual who negotiates a player's salary with a professional ball club and also makes other business arrangements in the player's inter-est, such as commercial endorsements. It was not until 1970 that the team owners agreed to let agents represent players in contract negotiations.

**aggregation** A baseball team. **1st Use.** 1898. (*New York Tribune,* June 17; Edward J. Nichols).

**aggressive** Said of a team or player who plays heads-up, all-out baseball.

**aggressive hitter** A hitter who habitually swings at pitches delivered out of the strike zone.

**aggressive in the strike zone** Said of a pitcher who throws quality pitches over the plate without trying to be too precise with the location of the pitches. Pete Smith (quoted in the *Baltimore Sun,* July 4, 1998): "I've got to learn this new strike zone and learn the hitters. Over in the National League you get those corners. Over here [in the American League] you don't. I'm learning I have to be more aggressive in the zone."

**agreement 1.** See *Tripartite Agreement.* **2.** See *National Agreement,* 1. **3.** See *National Agreement,* 2. **4.** See *Basic Agreement.* **5.** See *Major League Agreement.* **6.** See *gentlemen's agreement.*

**ahead** At an advantage; e.g., said of a team that is winning or of a pitcher with a count of more strikes than balls. Compare *behind,* 1.

**ahead in the count 1.** Said of a pitcher when there are more strikes than balls on the batter. Compare *behind in the count,* 1. Syn. "ahead of the count." **2.** Said of a batter with more balls than strikes. Compare *behind in the count,* 2. Syn. "ahead of the count."

**AIBS** Abbrev. for *all-important box score.*

**AILC** Abbrev. for *all-important loss column.*

**aim** To try to pinpoint a pitch in the strike zone; to work too hard to put the ball over the strike zone. When pitchers aim the ball, they may devi-ate from their natural motion.

**"ain't the beer cold!"** An expression used by Baltimore Orioles broadcaster Chuck Thompson, originally as an announcer for the National Brew-ing Company, but later for anything good that oc-curred on the field, such as a home run or defeating an opponent. Thompson picked up the expression from Bob Robertson, who spotted for Thompson at Baltimore Colts games.

**air ball** *arch.* A fly ball. **1st Use.** 1862. (*New York Sunday Mercury,* July 13; Edward J. Nichols).

**airhead** A zany or spacey player; one with little brainpower.

**air it out 1.** For a batter to unwind and hit the ball for a long distance. **2.** For a pitcher to give it all he has when throwing the ball. **3.** For a pitcher to test himself coming off an injury. "Plans call for [disabled pitcher Rocky] Coppinger to air it out on Wednesday" (pitching coach Ray Miller, quoted in *Baltimore Sun,* April 7, 1997).

**airmail** To throw the ball over another player's head. "A catcher who throws one into center field on an attempted steal air mails the second baseman." (Joe Falleta, quoted in *Baseball Digest,* Dec. 1983). President Ronald Reagan "airmailed" his 1986 cer-emonial Opening Day pitch. Asked how a team keeps its errors low, infielder Billy Ripken told *Wash-ington City Paper* (June 12, 1992): "You try to elim-inate plays like the two-hopper that you grab and airmail into the dugout." Also spelled "air mail."

**air out 1.** To lecture (Orel Hershiser, *Out of the Blue,* 1989). **2.** See *air it out.*

**air pocket** A mythical air current that causes a fielder to drop a fly ball.

**airtight** Said of a great defense; e.g., an "airtight infield" rarely allows batted balls to get through. **1st Use.** 1910 (*Baseball Magazine,* Sept.; Edward J. Nichols).

**airway** [softball term] The path that a ball goes through in underhand pitching.

**AK** Abbrev. for *ant killer.*

**AL** **1.** Abbrev. for *American League,* 1. **2.** Abbrev. for *active list.*

**alabaster blaster** Announcer Bob Prince's term for a ball hit sharply down in front of the batter and intended to bounce over the head of the pitcher and other infielders. See also *Baltimore chop.*

**a la carte** Said of fielding a ball with one hand. The term was sometimes corrupted to "aly carte" by Dizzy Dean.

**Alaskan Summer League** A league of high school and college players who play summer baseball to gain experience.

**ALCS** Abbrev. for *American League Championship Series.*

**Alibi Ike** A player who has an excuse for every fault and mistake. **1st Use.** 1914. (Ring W. Lardner, short story "Alibi Ike," later published in *Round Up: The Stories of Ring W. Lardner,* 1929). In the story, the nickname "Alibi Ike" is given to a baseball player. The introductory passage: "His right name was Frank X. Farrell, and I guess the X stood for 'Excuse me.' Because he never pulled a play, good or bad, on or off the field, without apologizin' for it." The name gained further recognition in the 1932 movie *Alibi Ike* starring Joe E. Brown. Traced back to 1743, the work "alibi" took on a new life with Lardner's characterization. **Extended Use.** One who excuses all of his faults and mistakes. A condition: "Alibi Ikes Can be Cured" (*San Francisco Examiner,* "Teen-Age Date Line," March 19, 1966; Peter Tamony). John Ciardi (*Good Words to You,* 1987) notes that after Lardner created the term, "it became an established Am. slang idiom almost at once and remains so."

**alive** **1.** Said of a fastball that seems to have its own animation; one that appears to speed up and take a sudden hop or rise as it nears the plate. Such a ball is often said to "move." **2.** Said of an inning that is prolonged by timely hits; e.g., "Smith and Jones kept the inning alive by hitting back-to-back doubles." **3.** See *stay alive.*

*Alibi Ike. Joe E. Brown in the title role of the oafish Ike in the 1932 film, with leading lady Olivia de Havilland.*

**All-American** A high school or college player voted as the best player in the country in his position at his level. **Etymology/1st Use.** 1888. "Ere these lines meet the eyes of *Sporting Life*'s readers the members of the Chicago and All-American teams will have departed upon their great trip to Australia and the greatest baseball invasion upon record thus inaugurated. . . . Van Hailiren will play short for the All-Americas." (*Sporting Life,* Oct. 24; Barry Popik). This establishes the first use of the term in baseball, not in football, which lexicographer Popik has verified as 1889.

**All-American Amateur Baseball Association** An organization based in Johnstown, Pa., that helps advance, develop, and regulate baseball at the amateur level. Abbrev. *AAABA.*

**All-American Girls Professional Baseball League** A league that began playing in 1943 and ended in 1954. The brainchild of Chicago Cubs owner Philip K. Wrigley, the game originally was a hybrid of baseball and softball (the ball was 10.5 inches in circumference, making it an exact split between the two games and pitchers had a choice of overhand or underhand delivery). At its height, the league had as many as 15 teams, all in the Midwest. It was intended to serve as a substitute entertainment to baseball during World War II, but it survived the war and was probably a casualty of television. Some 556 women played in such places as Rockford, Ill. (the Peaches), Racine, Wis. (the Belles), Milwaukee, Wis. (the Chicks), Fort Wayne, Ind. (the Daisies), and Kalamazoo, Mich. (The Lassies). The league was celebrated in the film *A League of Their Own* (1992). Abbrev. *AAGPBL*. **Usage Note.** According to Morris A. Beale (*Softball Story,* 1962), Wrigley originally named his circuit the "All-American Women's Professional Baseball League." The term "Girls" apparently replaced "Women's" in popular usage.

**All-American out** A poor hitter.

**All-American team** An honorary team com-posed of the best players from the two major leagues. Based on his research, Edward J. Nichols noted: "All Star teams may actually play, whereas All-American teams are mere honorary selections." **1st Use.** 1905. (*Sporting Life,* Sept. 2; Edward J. Nichols).

**All-City Series** A World Series between two teams from the same city or next-door neighbors. In 1989, the Oakland Athletics played the San Francisco Giants in what was called the Bay Bridge World Series. See also *subway series,* 1.

**all–New York Series** A World Series between the New York Yankees and either the New York Giants, Brooklyn Dodgers, or New York Mets. **1st Use.** 1934. "As you know, there is an ancient tradition, or let me say axiom, in baseball that the team in the lead on July 4 is the team that will win

**All-American team.** *Composite photograph showing a touring team. Despite the fact that most All-American teams have been honorary, this one went on the road.*

the pennant. New York fans are sure that this situation is a true augury of an all–New York World Series." (*The Sporting News,* July 12; Barry Popik).

**alleged flinger** A derogatory term for a pitcher who does not measure up to expectations.

**alley 1.** One of the two areas between the outfielders in left-center field and in right-center field. "Rickey Henderson's average continues to dwindle as he swings for the fences instead of the alleys" (*St. Petersburg Times,* Apr. 3, 1987). See also *power alley.* **2.** The center or "heart" of home plate. **3.** *arch.* The dirt path between the pitcher's mound and home plate that was common to most ballparks in the first half of the 20th century. This skinned area began disappearing from major-league ballparks in the late 1940s. The reason why it first appeared and why it disappeared are both mysteries. **4.** The approximate middle space between first base and second base or between second base and third base. See also *slot,* 4.

**alley hitter** A hitter who drives the ball into the alleys.

**alley softball** [softball term] An urban form of softball played in alleys. It has rigid rules, as described by Fred Ferretti (*The Great American Book of Games,* 1975): "A . . . ball hit off the wires and caught is an out. A ball that hits or even grazes a house wall and is caught before hitting the ground is an out. A ball that lands atop any shed, house, or garage roof is an out. So is a ball landing in any yard. And what was safe, you ask? Any line drive to dead center (straight down the alley), so long as it isn't caught. Pull hitters shun alley softball."

**all-group team** An amateur baseball all-star team that is selected from teams playing at different levels and in different leagues. An area all-group team may include high school players from various levels of public and parochial school competition; e.g., the All-South Jersey All-Groups All-Star Team.

**alligator mouth** *arch.* A loud or noisy person; a loudmouth.

**all-important box score** The newspaper box score that adds so much to the fans' enjoyment of the game. Bob Brown (*Orioles Gazette,* July 30, 1993) used the initialism *AIBS:* "We live only 20 minutes from downtown but if the Orioles are playing at night a time zone away, the paper dropped in our driveway probably won't have that AIBS (all-important box score)."

**all-important loss column** The column in the league or division standings that records the number of losses incurred by a team in relation to the number of games played or to be played or games a team is ahead or behind another team. The term points to the fact that there is more to a club's standings than the column in which wins are counted. This is because standings are based on the number of wins and losses, not on the winning percentage. Also, because teams will have played different numbers of games at any given point, the true measure of a team's performance is the number of losses it has posted. The loss column is also "all-important" because the losses cannot be "made up" or overcome. Abbrev. *AILC.*

**all-injured team** A facetious and mythical team of players who, because of injuries, played the least but made the most money in a season.

**all-money team** A mythical team composed of players making the most money at each position.

**all over the plate** Wild; said of a pitcher who cannot deliver the ball in the strike zone.

**allow 1.** To give up hits and/or runs; e.g., "Smith allowed five hits and three runs in the fifth." **2.** To make an error; e.g., "Jones allowed the hot grounder to go between his legs."

**all-rookie team** A mythical team composed of the best rookie players at each position.

**all runners breaking** Said of all baserunners advancing to the next base during the pitcher's windup. It occurs when there are two outs and the count on the batter is three balls and two strikes. The baserunners break during the pitcher's windup because the pitch must result in a batted ball, walk, or the final out of the inning; i.e., there is no risk in sending the runners.

**all star** A player selected at almost any level of baseball to a team comprising the best players from a league or geographic area.

**All Star** A player chosen to play in the All-Star Game.

**All-Star balloting** The act of voting for players to appear in the All-Star Game. Various methods have been used: beginning in 1933 and 1934, fans voted for the players through ballots printed in the *Chicago Tribune;* from 1935 through 1946, the managers voted; from 1947 through 1957, fans voted; from 1958 to 1969, the players, managers, and coaches voted; and since 1970, the fans voted. The decision to turn the balloting over to the fans has, according to the critics of nonprofessional voting, turned selection of the game's starting players into more of a popularity contest than a true contest based on merit. Even with spaces for write-ins, the number of names on the ballot has risen regularly. In 1979 the number went up from 128 to 144. On the 1986 ballot, 208 names appeared. Balloting has been an activity sponsored by a company willing to put up a million dollars a year for the privilege. The Gillette Safety Razor Co. conducted the voting from 1970 to 1986, and *USA Today* and its parent, Gannett Co., Inc., picked it up beginning in 1987.

**All-Star berth** A selection to play in the All-Star Game.

**All-Star break** The three-day, mid-July break in the schedule of major-league baseball to accommodate the All-Star Game. It represents the midpoint in the season and is an important point of reference when charting a team's fortunes; e.g., a manager may say that his team will be in fine shape if it is within three games of first place by the time of the All-Star break.

**All-Star Game 1.** The annual interleague game played each July between players selected as the best at their position in the American League and the National League. The starting players are selected by fan balloting, but the pitchers, coaches, and substitutes are selected by the respective managers. At least one player must be selected from each team.

The first All-Star Game was played on July 6, 1933, at Comiskey Park in Chicago. It was the brainchild of *Chicago Tribune* sports editor Arch Ward, who saw it as a one-shot "dream game" to go along with the 1933 Century of Progress Exposition going on in the city. Though opposed by

**All-Star Game.** *Souvenir pin from the 1951 game.*

some owners, the idea appealed to the presidents of the two leagues and Commissioner Kenesaw Mountain Landis. A third-inning, two-run home run by Babe Ruth led the American League to a 4–2 win. Because of World War II, the game was not played in 1945. There were two All-Star Games in 1959 through 1962, but this idea was scrapped as it became clear that two games lacked the impact of one. The only game to be postponed was the one scheduled for July 14, 1981, which was moved to August 9 because of a players' strike. Syn. *dream game; midseason classic; summer classic; midsummer classic; summer spectacle.* **2.** Any similar contest at other levels of play and in softball.

**All-Star team** A team participating in an All-Star Game. **1st Use.** 1905. (*Sporting Life,* Sept. 2; Edward J. Nichols).

**All-Star Week** The week of festivities surrounding the All-Star Game. An editorial in the *Baltimore Sun* (July 15, 1993) entitled "An All-Star

Week to Remember" discusses FanFest, an old-timers game, a tribute to black baseball players, the home run derby, an architectural forum on stadium architecture, and the game itself.

**all-time 1.** Describing a player past or present who is considered the best or one of the best in baseball history. **2.** Describing the best of baseball for all time, up to and including the present. **3.** Describing baseball records that are the best for any particular player, team, or league. **4.** Describing an outstanding event; e.g., "Whereas, sports fans everywhere are celebrating the outstanding accomplishment of [Boston Red Sox pitcher] Roger Clemens as one of the all-time great individual performances in the history of baseball." (Sen. Edward Kennedy [D-Mass.], resolution commending Clemens for striking out a record 20 batters in a single, nine-inning game, *Congressional Record,* May 1, 1986).

**all-time all-timer** One of the greatest of the great baseball players.

**all-timer** One of the all-time great players of baseball.

**all to the mustard** In good physical condition. **1st Use.** 1907. (*New York Evening Journal,* Apr. 18; Edward J. Nichols).

**Alphonse and Gaston** *adj.* Said of an act, play, error, or fielding situation in which one or more players defer to another, often allowing the ball to drop to the ground in the process. **Etymology.** Alphonse and Gaston, two cartoon characters created by Frederick B. Opper, deferred to one another to the point where they were unable to get anything done: "After you, my dear Alphonse." "No, after you, my dear Gaston." They have become symbolic of exaggerated politeness.

**altered bat** [softball term] A bat whose physical structure has been changed; e.g., attaching a flare or cone grip to the bat handle, replacing the handle of a metal bat with a wooden or other type of handle, inserting material inside the bat, applying excessive tape (more than two layers) to the bat grip, or painting a bat at the top or bottom for other than identification purposes. Compare *doctored bat; illegal bat.*

**alternative pitch** An illegal pitch of any sort. **Usage Note.** The term is an obvious euphemism and tends to be used with tongue firmly in cheek.

**alto queso** Spanish for *high cheese.* The term is often used to describe a high fastball delivered by a pitcher from Latin America.

**aluminum bat** A piece of tubular aluminum closed at both ends and shaped like a conventional baseball bat. Aluminum bats have been used by college players since 1972 (they were approved by the National Collegiate Association of America in 1974) and at virtually all levels of amateur baseball, but not in the professional leagues, where they are prohibited. Aluminum bats are widely used in softball. Some aluminum bats have wood cores.

Although initially more expensive than wooden bats, aluminum bats break or become damaged with far less frequency; hence, they are appealing in terms of cost. Generally speaking, they are said to help weak hitters drive the ball farther and give an extra edge to sluggers. However, aluminum bats are opposed by the professional baseball establishment for several reasons, including their potentially devastating effect on batting records and fielders' safety and to the fact that they ping rather than crack when coming in contact with a ball. See also *graphite bat.*

**amateur** Any player who is not a professional.

**amateur draft** Syn. of *free-agent draft.*

**Amateur Softball Association of America** [softball term] The governing body of American softball, headquartered in Oklahoma City, Okla. This group first met in 1933 in conjunction with the Century of Progress Exposition in Chicago. Its purpose was to establish a standard set of rules for a game to be played at the exposition. With 101 local associations, 5,000 local administrators, and more than 260,000 teams, the association directs slow pitch, fast pitch, and modified pitch programs for male, female, and coed (co-recreational) leagues with players aged 9 through 70 and over. Abbrev. *ASA.*

**Amazing Mets** A description that has been used for the New York Mets from its beginning in 1962 to the present. Mets manager Casey Stengel ex-

**Amazing Mets.** *Souvenir pin from the Mets' amazing 1969 season.*

claimed after watching the team win its first exhibition game: "They're amazing!" But before long, Stengel turned that sentiment into a lament: "They're amazing. Can't anybody here play this game?" No matter how good or bad they have been in the intervening years, the Mets have been amazing, albeit for different reasons. The term shows up in book titles, newspaper headlines, and even a record album, *The Amazing Mets,* made by members of the team in 1968 and featuring such selections as "We're Gonna Win" and "Green Grass of Shea." Also spelled "Amazin' Mets." See also *Amazin's.*

**Amazin's** A variation on *Amazing Mets* and the term that manager Casey Stengel himself often used to refer to the New York Mets. "The Amazin's amazed us so often that almost every one of the 2,175,373 fans who saw them at home this year . . . must be convinced that he was there on that one special afternoon or crucial evening when the Mets won *the* big game that fused them as con-

tenders and future champions" (Roger Angell, *The Summer Game,* 1972; Charles D. Poe).

**ambish** Ambition on the part of a player or team. **1st Use.** 1908. (*New York Evening Journal,* Apr. 13; Edward J. Nichols).

**American Association 1.** A major league that existed from 1882 to 1891 as a rival to the National League. It played ball on Sundays, sold beer at the park, charged half the National League price for admission, and had a permanent core of umpires. The association floundered due to financial and leadership problems. Four of its teams (St. Louis, Baltimore, Washington, and Louisville) were absorbed by the National League. Full name: American Association of Professional Base Ball Clubs. Abbrev. *AA,* 2. Syn. *Beer and Whiskey League.* **2.** A minor league since 1903, with cities primarily in the Midwest. It was a Class A league from 1903 to 1907, a Class AA league from 1908 to 1945, and a Class AAA league from 1946 to 1962 and since 1969. Abbrev. *AA,* 3.

**American Baseball Coaches Association** An organization based in Hinsdale, Ill., with more than 5,000 members who coach at various levels of the game. It originated the NCAA College World Series and holds national clinics. Abbrev. *ABCA.*

**American Baseball Congress** An organization, founded in 1935 and headquartered in Battle Creek, Mich., that supports amateur baseball in the United States, with affiliates in many foreign countries. It has seven divisions named for former major-league players: Minor Willie Mays (8 & under), Willie Mays (10 & under), Pee Wee Reese (12 & under), Sandy Koufax (14 & under), Mickey Mantle (16 & under), Connie Mack (18 & under), and Stan Musial (19 & over). Abbrev. *ABC.*

**American Baseball Guild** A players' union organized in 1946 by Robert Murphy, a Boston lawyer with the National Labor Relations Board, as a means of airing the players' grievances, which primarily concerned the lack of financial security. The Guild won concessions that included payment of spring training expenses (Murphy money) and the first player pension plan. A failed strike in June 1946 signaled its end.

**American League 1.** One of the two major leagues, founded in 1901 by former sportswriter Byron Bancroft "Ban" Johnson. The teams that were charter members were Boston, Baltimore, Chicago, Cleveland, Detroit, Milwaukee, Philadelphia, and Washington, D.C. Currently, the American League has 14 teams divided into three divisions: East (Baltimore Orioles, Boston Red Sox, New York Yankees, Tampa Bay Devil Rays, Toronto Blue Jays); Central (Chicago White Sox, Cleveland Indians, Detroit Tigers, Kansas City Royals, Minnesota Twins); and West (Anaheim Angels, Oakland A's, Seattle Mariners, Texas Rangers). Since it came into being after the National League, it has always been called the *junior circuit.* One of the immediate differences between the older league and the new was that Johnson gave the umpires stronger authority over the game; a current difference is the existence of the designated hitter in the American League. Abbrev. *AL.* **2.** See *Negro American League.*

**American League Championship Series** The *Championship Series* in which the two American League teams that won divisional titles (and since 1995, the Division Series) play for the American League pennant and the right to play the National League champion in the World Series. Abbrev. *ALCS.*

**American League East** The East Division of the American League, consisting of teams grouped around eastern cities, created in 1969 when the American League expanded from 10 to 12 teams. The division consisted of six teams from 1969 to 1976 (Baltimore Orioles, Boston Red Sox, Cleveland Indians, Detroit Tigers, Milwaukee Brewers from 1972 to 1976, New York Yankees, and Washington Senators from 1969 to 1971), seven teams from 1977 (with the addition of the Toronto Blue Jays) to 1993, and five teams since 1994 (Baltimore Orioles, Boston Red Sox, New York Yankees, Toronto Blue Jays, Detroit Tigers from 1994 to 1997, and Tampa Bay Devil Rays beginning in 1998).

**American League Central** The Central Division of the American League, created in 1994, consisting of five teams grouped around midwestern cities (Chicago White Sox, Cleveland Indians, Kansas City Royals, Minnesota Twins, Milwaukee Brewers from 1994 to 1997, and Detroit Tigers beginning in 1998).

**American League style** The real and imagined style of play and officiating in the American League, accentuated since 1973 when the league adopted the designated hitter. The strike zone is supposedly higher in the American League, where there is supposedly less emphasis on the running game. Compare *National League style.*

**American League West** The West Division of the American League, consisting of teams grouped around western cities, created in 1969 when the American League expanded from 10 to 12 teams. The division consisted of six teams from 1969 to 1976 (California Angels, Chicago White Sox, Kansas City Royals, Minnesota Twins, Oakland A's, Seattle Pilots in 1969, Milwaukee Brewers from 1970 to 1971, and Texas Rangers from 1972 to 1976), seven teams from 1977 (with the addition of the Seattle Mariners) to 1993, and four teams since 1994 (California/Anaheim Angels, Oakland A's, Seattle Mariners, and Texas Rangers).

**American Legion Baseball** A national program for 15- to 18-year-olds that culminates in an annual eight-team World Series tournament. It was founded in 1926 and sponsored by the American Legion, a national veterans' organization.

**America's pastime** The game of baseball, more commonly termed *national pastime.*

**America's Team** A name that the Atlanta Braves have tried to give itself, presumably because of the fact that so many people can see the team play on Ted Turner's television station (TNT), which is carried by many cable systems. The precedent for the name was the Dallas Cowboys, which has been long known as America's Team in football.

**Anaheim Angels** The name of the American League West Division team in Anaheim, Calif. The team formerly was known as the Los Angeles Angels (1961–64) and California Angels (1965–96).

**anchor** *v.* To be at the base of; e.g., "Smith anchors the team's pitching rotation."

**anchorage** A base. **1st Use.** 1915. "Having reached the middle anchorage in this manner, the local base runner was amazed on getting a sign from the manager to steal third" (Burt L. Standish, *Covering the Look-in Corner;* David Shulman).

**anchor man** Syn. of *leadoff batter.*

**ancient mariner** A poor infielder. Art Hill (*I Don't Care If I Never Come Back,* 1980; Peter Morris) writes: "In recent years it has become fairly general to say of a poor infielder that he plays like the Ancient Mariner. That is, 'he stoppeth one of three.'"

**anemic** Weak; e.g., "The Blue Jays hoped the addition of [Roger] Clemens would make them a pennant contender, but an anemic offense short-circuited that quest" (*Milwaukee Journal Sentinel,* 1997).

**angel** **1.** A cloud that comes to the aid of a fielder by blocking out the sun and therefore making it easier for him to catch a high fly ball. Syn. *guardian angel.* **1st Use.** 1909. "Pitilessly, the sun beats down from a sky, broken only by the fleecy-white clouds that the players call 'angels' because they afford so benevolent a background for the batted ball" (*Baseball Magazine,* Aug.; David Shulman). **2.** One who invests money in a team with scant hope of financial reward; a "starry-eyed owner who thinks baseball is a sport" (Bert Dunne, *Folger's Dictionary of Baseball,* 1958). This use of the term comes from the theatrical angel who is the financial backer of a play.

**angler** A player or his agent who "casts" about looking for testimonials, product endorsements, speaking engagements, and other off-field sources of income.

**annex** To win a game.

**Annie** See *Baseball Annie.*

**Annie Oakley** **1.** A free pass to a baseball game. See also *machine-gun ticket.* **2.** A base on balls; a "free pass" or "free ticket" to first base. "[Bob] Lemon's No-Hitter Lift to Tribe, Only Three Tigers Get On—All Via Annie Oakleys." (*San Francisco News-Call Bulletin* headline, July 1, 1948; Peter Tamony) **Etymology.** Obviously named for

**Annie Oakley.** *Sharpshooter whose name became part of baseball and theatrical slang.*

the legendary star of Buffalo Bill's Wild West Show who used to show off her sharpshooting skills by putting bullets through the suit symbols of playing cards. Since free passes to baseball games have traditionally had holes punched in them, the jump to baseball was a natural one.

While the inspiration for the term is easily traced to the famed sharpshooter, its transfer has been a matter for much conjecture. The most commonly repeated version appeared in her biography (Courtney Ryley Cooper, *Annie Oakley, Woman at Arms,* 1927). The full Cooper account:

"And by one of her tricks, Annie Oakley achieved a form of notoriety which she did not expect. The feat was to place a playing card, the ace of hearts, as a target at a distance of twenty-five yards. Then, firing twenty-five shots in twenty-seven seconds, she would obliterate that ace of hearts in the center, leaving only bullet holes in its place. A card thus shot by Annie Oakley formed quite a souvenir in the Eighties.

"There came into being a baseball magnate who looked with some disfavor upon passes—as all baseball managers look upon these avenues of free admission. It is the custom, that the door-tender may know the ticket to be free, to punch a hole or two in the card, this saving a miscount when the proceeds of the day were checked. One day a card came through to the gate which had been thoroughly perforated. The magnate remarked laconically:

"'Huh! Looks like Annie Oakley'd shot at it!'

"The remark was repeated—and re-repeated. Soon along Broadway, a new name came into being for a free ticket of admission. It was an Annie Oakley, and passes remain Annie Oakleys to this date. The surprising thing being that Annie Oakley herself denied ever having had one of the things.

"'I always pay my way,' she averred."

Oakley herself established that the baseball magnate was none other than Ban Johnson, longtime American League president. In an interview in the *World* (New York) for June 28, 1922—reproduced in *American Speech* (Feb. 1933) along with the letters mentioned below—she told of Johnson looking at a pass "and suggested that the man has been letting me use it as a target. Now the term is in use in Australia and England, as well as America."

Several readers of the *World* were not happy with this explanation and in the following days the newspaper published their letters. One man insisted that it came from Oakley's first appearance with the Barnum and Bailey Circus at Madison Square Garden when "a number of her pictures, ticket size, were scattered throughout the streets of the city. Finders were entitled to free admission to 'the greatest show on earth.' You can imagine the resultant eagerness of small boys and their equally boyish fathers, to find an 'Annie Oakley.'"

A second writer insists that virtually all slang comes from the underworld and its fringes. He insists that the term in question "originated among the hangers-on of circuses and street fairs and was, like so many bits of argot, an opprobrious word, usually accompanied with profanities and obscenities. If you have ever experienced the mood of circus people on a rainy day, when the paid admissions were few and passes many, you will understand how the expression in question came to be used."

The final letter insisted that the term originated when a man walked through the gates at Madison Square Garden and was asked to produce a ticket. "Don't need one," he said, "I'm Annie Oakley's brother." He was let in free and the next evening 37 of Miss Oakley's brothers showed up to see her act.

More recently, another version has come into being in the form of a letter to the *Smithsonian* magazine (Nov. 1990) from Roe Fowler (Fresno, Calif.) who wrote: "In 1912 or 1913 my father took me to see Annie Oakley's last touring show, 'The Young Buffalo Wild West,' in Herrin, Ill. In her final stunt her assistant, probably Frank Butler, tossed her loaded rifles with full magazines. She emptied each one at a sheet of tin, firing as fast as she could pull the trigger and recock the rifle, spelling out her name in bullet holes. While the audience applauded wildly, she took a bow, then grabbed the rifle and fired backward, dotting the 'i.' That brought down the house."

Fowler wrote that it was this name-spelling act, not the playing-card shoot, that gave the name "Annie Oakleys" to complimentary tickets. The theater's name, spelled out in tiny perforations like the bullet holes Annie shot into the tin sheet, made counterfeiting of comps more difficult. He added: "As a reporter on the *Chicago Tribune* in the 1920s I got many an Annie Oakley from the theater critics, and all were perforated in that manner."

Despite these alternative theories, it is the Ban Johnson version that seems to have the greatest credibility (probably because this is Oakley's own version). When Johnson died on March 28, 1931, the obituary carried in many newspapers noted that he had coined the term when he "likened a well-punched baseball pass to a discarded Annie Oakley target" (*San Francisco News,* March 30, 1931; Peter Tamony).

**announced for** A term used in a box score for a pinch hitter who was denied an opportunity to bat because he was removed by another pinch hitter.

**answer the bell** For a relief pitcher to be warmed up and ready to pitch when summoned by the manager. The bell alludes to the telephone connecting the dugout and the bullpen.

**ant** *arch.* A baseball fan. **Etymology.** According to Patrick Ercolano (*Fungoes, Floaters and Fork*

*Balls,* 1987), the term "dates from the early 1900s and stems from the observation that fans in the stands often appear as small as ants to the players (and to some players, as insignificant as ants)."

**ante-over** An early variation of baseball, similar or identical to one old cat.

**Anthem Annie** A nickname given to Donna Greenwald (Columbia, Md.) who has sung the national anthem at most major-league ballparks. She was dubbed "Anthem Annie" by the Toronto media even though her first name is Donna (*Washington Post,* Sept. 23, 1997).

**antitrust exemption** The 1922 U.S. Supreme Court opinion that removed baseball from the antitrust laws because, in the words of the Court, the sport "would not be called trade or commerce in the commonly accepted use of those words." Often derided, the exemption is a legal aberration that is not enjoyed by other professional sports and U.S. businesses: it covers team relocations, league expansion, broadcasting contracts, and protection of minor-league markets. The Curt Flood Act of 1998 revoked part of the exemption for labor relations.

**ant killer** A hard-hit ground ball or one pounded into the dirt in front of home plate; one that appears to be hit so hard that it will kill insects in its path. Abbrev. *AK.* **1st Use.** 1874. (Chicago *Inter-Ocean,* July 7; Edward J. Nichols). Despite this early first appearance, the term is listed by the *Los Angeles Times* (May 15, 1994) as current "baseball lingo."

**Aparicio double** A walk and a stolen base. **1st Use.** 1959. "When larcenous Luis Aparicio, a .260 hitter, stole fifty bases in his first sixty-one tries, an 'Aparicio double' became renowned throughout the league as a walk and a stolen base" (*New York Times Magazine,* Sept. 27; David Shulman).

**APBA** A tabletop baseball board game that takes its name from the original American Professional Baseball Association. It has been said that more than 500,000 Americans play the game, including David Eisenhower, George Bush, and New York Mayor Ed Koch. It was created in 1931 by J. Richard Seitz and is now popular as a computer game. Pron. "app-bah" (the term is seldom stated in letters).

**APBPA** Abbrev. for *Association of Professional Baseball Players of America.*

**appeal 1.** *n.* An official notice by the defensive team that a rule has been broken or a request that a call be reexamined; specif., when: a) the fielding team claims that a member of the batting team has violated a rule or that an umpire has made a decision that is in conflict with the rules; and b) the fielding team asks the plate umpire to seek the help of the umpires at first base or third base in determining if the batter took a full swing at the ball for a strike or only took half a swing (not a strike) for a ball (such an appeal is made after a pitch that was called a ball). **2.** *v.* To make an appeal. **3.** *v.* To ask the league president to review the suspension of a player, manager, or coach.

**appeal play** A play made in conjunction with and as a part of an appeal; e.g., if a baserunner neglects to touch a base when running, it is the responsibility of the defensive team, not the umpire, to claim the violation. To make an appeal play in a dead-ball situation, the pitcher must first put the ball back in play by stepping on the pitching rubber, then stepping off the rubber and throwing the ball to a teammate who tags the base in question. At this point the umpire decides if the runner is safe or out. The appeal play and the appeal must be made before the next pitch is delivered. If the ball is still in play at the time of the appeal, the ball may be thrown directly to the base.

**appear** To play in a baseball game; e.g., "Smith appeared for the first time in eight weeks."

**appearance 1.** Playing in a baseball game. **2.** See *plate appearance.*

**appearance clause** A clause in a pitcher's contract that stipulates he is to be given a bonus if he appears in at least *x* games and an additional bonus if he appears in *y* games.

**appearance game** An exhibition game played to show the talents of certain stars or to pair two teams that do not play normally. "The All-Stars met little resistance from the Elite Giants. It was the Giants' second game of the day, an 'appearance' game as they called it, a game set up for the fans instead of the players." (William Brashler,

*The Bingo Long Traveling All-Stars and Motor Kings,* 1973; Charles D. Poe).

**apple** The baseball **1st Use.** 1922. (*Saturday Evening Post,* Oct. 28; Edward J. Nichols).

**apple comes up** Failure to accomplish a desired result in a key situation. The term is a reference to one's Adam's apple; to choke. See also *feel the apple.*

**apple-knocker** A batter. **1st Use.** 1937. (*The Sporting News Record Book;* Edward J. Nichols).

**apple tree** A verbal symbol for choking, and an allusion to the Adam's apple. When Dick Young once wrote that "the tree that grows in Brooklyn is an apple tree," he was using what George Vecsey (*New York Times,* Sept. 2, 1987) later wrote was "the ultimate sports phrase for choking in the clutch."

**apply the whitewash** To shut out; to keep the opponent from scoring. **1st Use.** 1888. (Chicago *Inter-Ocean,* July 3; Edward J. Nichols).

**appreciation day** A celebration dedicated to a particular player, held in conjunction with a baseball game. **1st Use.** 1942. "It is 'Gehrig Appreciation Day' at Yankee Stadium, July 4, 1939" (*Baseball Magazine,* June; David Shulman).

**April Cobb** *arch.* A spring whirlwind; a rookie who looks like the next Ty Cobb for a short period of time.

**aqueous toss** Syn. of *spitball.* **1st Use.** 1920. (*New York Times,* Oct. 7; Edward J. Nichols)

**arbiter** An umpire. See also *arbitrator,* 1. **1st Use.** 1859. Peter Morris reports that in early baseball, each club usually brought an umpire who was a club member; in fact, the umpire was an elected official in some clubs. Sometimes an arbiter also officiated. In the first-ever intercollegiate game between Amherst and Williams, according to the *Pittsfield* (Mass.) *Sun* (July 7, 1859): "William R. Plunkett . . . was chosen arbiter or referee, and it is somewhat remarkable, that his services were required to decide every point, the Umpires not being able to agree upon any question proposed for their decision."

**arbitration** An action requested by a baseball player with less than six years of seniority when he and his team are unable to reach agreement on the terms of a new contract, by which the player's salary is determined by a third party, an independent labor arbitrator. This custom has been employed since 1974 to settle salary disputes between players and the team owners, and represents an opportunity for a player to obtain a salary approximately equal to what he would earn without a reserve clause in his contract. The arbitrator holds a hearing to decide whether the player is being fairly paid. If not, a raise can be granted by the arbitrator. Salaries for arbitration players are determined on the basis of comparability to other players. Each side files a proposed salary and the arbitrator selects one or the other; no compromise is allowed in the process. The judgment made is binding and not subject to further appeal. The results of the off-season hearings are often tallied like a game. After reporting a player win and an owner win, *USA Today* (Feb. 12, 1986) added: "The split gave the players four victories and the owners six in the ten arbitration decisions this year." Until 1990, players had to have at least three years of service to be eligible, but since then some selected players (the most senior 17% of those with more than two, but less than three, years of service) are eligible as well. Prior to the end of the 1986 season, the pre-arbitration period was only two years. Free agents are not eligible for arbitration.

**arbitrator 1.** An umpire. Famous umpire Bill Klem was known as the "Old Arbitrator." See also *arbiter.* **2.** An individual who conducts salary arbitration.

**Arby's RBI Award** An annual award first given in 1986 for the hitter in each major league who drives in the most runs. The prize is a coproduction of Major League Baseball and the Arby's fast-food chain. For each run batted in by the winners, $1,000 is donated to the Big Brothers/Big Sisters of America. The actual prize given to the players is known as the *Hank Aaron Trophy.*

**arc** [softball term] The point at which the ball reaches its highest point in its trajectory from the pitcher's hand to the plate in slow pitch softball. It is measured in feet from the ground to that high point. The prescribed arc is between 6 feet and 12 feet in the Amateur Softball Association of America and between 3 feet from the release point and 10 feet from the ground in the United States Slo-Pitch Softball Association. See also *minimum arc; maximum arc; unlimited arc.*

**arcade card** Syn. of *exhibit card.*

**"aren't your hands bleeding yet?"** Traditional taunt to a player spending too much time at the plate during batting practice.

**Arizona Diamondbacks** The National League West Division expansion team in Phoenix, Ariz., that began play in 1998.

**Arizona Fall League** An *instructional league* based in Arizona during the autumn. Michael Jordan played here during his brief baseball career.

**Arlie Latham** 1. *n./arch.* An infielder who makes a futile attempt to field a ground ball. The term, used rarely today, was once a major eponym among baseball players and writers. **2.** *n.* A player or coach who makes a lot of noise. **3.** *v./arch.* To yell and gesticulate in the coach's box to distract the opposing pitcher; to pull an Arlie Latham. **1st**

**Arlie Latham.** *Walter Arlington Latham poses for a tobacco card (1888).*

**Use.** 1907. (*New York Evening Journal,* Apr. 24; Edward J. Nichols). **Etymology.** Named for Walter Arlington "Arlie" Latham, a major leaguer in the 1880s and 1890s. Toward the end of his career, Latham's arm had become so weak that his name became synonymous with making a weak or halfhearted attempt at fielding a grounder. His arm had been injured in a contest with Doc Bushong, a St. Louis Browns (American Association) teammate, to see who could throw a ball the farthest. Latham won the contest—and the $100 put up by their manager, Charles Comiskey—but had neglected to warm up, thus causing the injury. The second definition of the eponym—to distract the pitcher from the coach's box—dates from his coaching days with John McGraw's New York Giants when, according to Fred Lieb (*Comedians and Pranksters of Baseball,* 1958), "he amused New York fans by dancing jigs in the coaching box and performing other acrobatic gyrations."

**Arlie Latham hit** *arch.* A grounder that evades the infielder. For etymology, see *Arlie Latham.*

**arm** 1. A player's throwing or pitching arm. **1st Use.** 1863. (*New York Sunday Mercury* clipping; Edward J. Nichols). **2.** Throwing ability, usually applied to a fielder who makes fast, accurate throws. **3.** A euphemism for a pitcher; e.g., "Any baseball team can use a good arm." See also *arms.* **4.** A euphemism for a fielder with ability to throw a baseball a long distance and with accuracy; e.g., "Smith is a good arm from right field to third base."

**arm fake** A deceptive defensive move in which the player with the ball simulates throwing the ball to one base in the hope of drawing a runner off another base. Compare *head fake.*

**arms** A team's *pitching staff.* "Young Arms Have Rangers Riding High in the AL West" (*USA Today* headline, May 30, 1986). "We have a lot of good young arms" (Baltimore Orioles manager Johnny Oates, quoted in *Baltimore Sun,* Sept. 10, 1994). See also *arm, 3.*

**arm speed** The velocity with which a pitcher throws the ball. "The last three innings I got more comfortable, more in sync. The arm speed got a little better." (Kevin Appier, quoted in *Baltimore Sun,* Apr. 3, 1996).

**arm thrower** A fielder who fails to coordinate his stride or body momentum with arm motion in the act of throwing. An arm thrower is often said to have poor mechanics.

**arm trouble** Any physical problem with a pitcher's throwing arm, such as muscle soreness, elbow stiffness, or rotator cuff injuries. Although the term is usually applied to pitchers, any player can have arm trouble.

**army ball** [softball term] An early name for softball. The term probably derives from the fact that an early form of softball was played on army bases before, during, and after World War I.

**around the horn 1.** *adj.* Describing a force double play in which a ground ball is fielded by the third baseman who throws to the second baseman who then throws on to the first baseman; e.g., "The Seals pull a twin killing around the horn" (San Francisco Seals telecast, July 19, 1956; Peter Tamony). Many modern writers, however, drop the "a" in the word "around"; e.g., "[Ray] Knight started two 'round-the-horn double plays both of which required hard-nosed, low-bridge pivots by [Rick] Burleson with spikes aimed at his knees" (Thomas Boswell, *Washington Post,* Apr. 7, 1987). **Usage Note.** This would appear to be the older and more traditional of two current meanings of the term (see below). **2.** *adv.* Pertaining to throwing the ball around the infield for practice and/or show, or during a game after the first or second out has been made and nobody is on base. **3.** *n./arch.* A "side-arm curve to batter when count is 3 and 2" (*Sporting News Record Book,* 1937). **Etymology.** The term is an old nautical one referring to the long voyage between the Atlantic Ocean and the Pacific Ocean, which, before the opening of the Panama Canal, required a vessel to go around the tip of South America at Cape Horn. Robert Hendrickson (*Salty Words,* 1984) notes: "Cape Horn, incidentally, isn't so named because it is shaped like a horn. Captain Schouten, the Dutch navigator who rounded it in 1616, named it after Hoorn, his birthplace in northern Holland."

The custom of throwing the ball around the infield is an old one. In 1970, Lenny Anderson of the *Seattle Post-Intelligencer* asked Casey Stengel about the custom: "They were doing it in the fall of 1912 when I went to the big leagues. They did it in '13 and '14. Then later on they started to say it took too long. I'll tell you why they changed. One reason was they doctored the ball. The second reason though was the games were too long when they started at 3:30 and when they went too long it got very dark."

**around the plate** Said of a pitcher who consistently throws strikes or near strikes; said of a pitcher who is not wild.

**arson squad** An effective bullpen that appears "to throw gasoline on a fire." The term was used to describe the California Angels bullpens of the 1980s.

**artificial grass** Syn. of *artificial turf.*

**artificial turf** A synthetic playing-field surface textured and colored to resemble grass. The first such surface was installed in the Houston Astrodome in 1966. It can be installed both indoors and outdoors. See also *Astroturf; Tartan Turf.* Syn. *artificial grass; fake grass; synthetic turf;* "artificial surface." **Usage Note.** Although the term is a perfectly good one, the concept is not without its strong critics who will let you know what they think of it when they hear it. Leonard Koppett (*New York Times,* March 30, 1986): "artificial turf spoils all the formulas and ruins the rhythms of the game, especially in the outfield." Even its supporters will grant the point that artificial turf changes the nature of the game. It is generally agreed that balls hit along artificial turf move faster and that the turf produces more injuries than its natural and more forgiving counterpart.

**artillerist** A pitcher. **1st Use.** 1910. (C. M. Klump, *Who's Who and What's What in Baseball*).

**artillery** A team's most powerful hitters. **1st Use.** 1912. (*New York Tribune,* Sept. 6; Edward J. Nichols). **Etymology.** Perhaps inspired by "battery," a much older term for the pitcher and catcher as a unit.

**artist 1.** An accomplished baseball player in the late 1800s and early 1900s. "The most experienced players of a nine come under this head, viz., such as are not only physically active and expert but mentally quick, and shrewd in judgment of the 'points' in the game" (Henry Chadwick, *The Game of Baseball,* 1868). **2.** A skilled pitcher; e.g., "Artist [Greg] Maddux Brushes off O's" (*Baltimore Sun* headline, June 8, 1998).

**art of misdirection** A pitcher's ability to throw strikes effectively by confusing batters with breaking balls of all types. Red Barber (National Public Radio, "Morning Edition," Nov. 14, 1986) said that this was the quality that had enabled Mike Scott to win the 1986 National League Cy Young Award.

**A's** A nickname used frequently for the Philadelphia, Kansas City, and Oakland Athletics.

**ASA** [softball term] Abbrev. for *Amateur Softball Association of America.*

**ascend** *arch.* To become nervous or rattled. **1st Use.** 1901. (Burt L. Standish, *Frank Merriwell's Marvel;* Edward J. Nichols).

**ash** A baseball bat. Most bats are made of northern white ash *(Fraxinus americana),* which grows in Pennsylvania, Canada, and the Adirondack Mountains of New York. **1st Use.** 1872. "The Unas handled the ash more vigorously" (*Detroit Advertiser and Tribune,* July 17; Peter Morris).

**ash-handle** The smaller end of the bat. "You ain't never goan hit that bawl if you don't choke up on the ash-handle, Horsefoot" (Stephen King, *It,* 1986; Charles D. Poe).

**ash heap** *arch.* A derogatory term for a hard and rocky infield. See also *contractor's back yard; Hogan's brickyard.* **Etymology.** The reference is to the hard, flinty residue of burned coal that is piled in ash heaps. Before World War II, bad infields and ash heaps were much more common sights.

**aside** In reserve.

**aspirin** The baseball; esp., the ball thrown by a fastball pitcher, in which the ball appears smaller than it really is. Dizzy Dean referred to it as "a fast ball that shrank up to the size of a aspirin when it reached the plate" and Jim Brosnan called it "the best way for a pitcher to cure his manager's headache." Compare *balloon,* 1. Syn. "aspirin tablet."

**assigned to the bench** Kept out of the game.

**assist 1.** *n.* Any throw or deflection of the ball by one fielder to another contributing to a putout. **1st Use.** 1865. (Chadwick Scrapbooks; Edward J. Nichols). **2.** *n.* A credit that is given in the scoring to a fielder who throws or deflects a batted or thrown ball and who contributes to a putout or would have resulted in a putout except for a subsequent error by another fielder. No assist is credited to a catcher (or anyone else) on a strikeout, unless the catcher drops the third strike and has to throw the batter out. A putout is credited to the catcher on all other strikeouts. Abbrev. *A, 2.* **3.** *v.* To make the play in which an assist is registered.

**Assisto glove** A special training glove that uses a strap to keep the batter's hand on the bat when he swings.

**Association of Professional Baseball Players of America** A nonprofit organization that assists handicapped, ill, or impoverished former players. Abbrev. *APBPA.*

**assortment** The mixture of different pitches that a pitcher throws during a given outing. Syn. *repertoire.* **1st Use.** 1898. (*New York Tribune,* June 7; Edward J. Nichols).

**asterisk 1.** A figurative symbol to indicate a special achievement. In the context, the asterisk is used in conjunction with entering an event or achievement in the official baseball record. Because the record book merely portrays things in a numerical or statistical fashion, the historical context in which an event occurs or an achievement is accomplished can be lost. The inclusion of an asterisk, along with a verbal explanation to which it refers, is felt to be a way to retain the historical context of an item entered into the record book. "An asterisk should be placed on [Dwight] Gooden's start that game, since his removal was due to a rain delay" (*New York Daily News,* July 6, 1987). See also *Year of the Asterisk.* **2.** Specifically, the long-held and sometimes bitterly disputed asterisk that was thought to have been attached in the record book to an accomplishment by Roger Maris when he was with the New York Yankees. The asterisk was allegedly affixed by commissioner Ford C. Frick when, in 1961, Maris topped Babe Ruth's single-season home run record. Because Maris broke the record during a 162-game schedule—giving him eight more games than the 154-game schedule in which Ruth set the record—some fans and sportswriters felt that Maris's achievement should only be entered in the record book with an asterisk, calling attention to these extra games. In fact, no asterisk was ever affixed to Maris's achievement. It was suggested at one point, but it never appeared in the official record. For eight years there were separate records kept for 154- and 162-game seasons.

In 1968, the Special Baseball Rules Committee ruled that baseball would have one set of records and that "no asterisk or official sign shall be used to indicate the number of games scheduled." In Sept. 1991, baseball's statistical accuracy committee took it even further, listing his 61 home runs in 1961 as the highest recorded—or as Shirley Povich (*Washington Post,* Sept. 7, 1991) put it: "[The] challenged home run record belongs to Maris—no asterisk, no notations, no nothing."

Yet, the myth of Maris's asterisk persists. Tony Kubek (*USA Today,* July 2, 1986) is quoted supporting the idea of putting asterisks next to the names of teams setting hitting records with designated hitters: "If . . . Frick put an asterisk by Roger Maris' name, which was ridiculous, then you should do the same here." Frank Robinson (*Baltimore Sun,* Apr. 30, 1996) was quoted about one of his hitting records being eclipsed: "You know what they say, put an asterisk by it. They did it when Maris broke Ruth's record."

In his autobiography, Ford C. Frick (*Games, Asterisks and People,* 1973) notes that the asterisk was discussed at a press conference: "Oh yes, during the conference the word 'asterisk' was mentioned; not by the commissioner but by Dick Young, one of the outstanding baseball writers of his time. Dick remarked kiddingly, 'Maybe you should use

an asterisk on the new record. Everybody does that when there's a difference of opinion.'"

**Astrodome** The home field of the Houston Astros since 1965. The first domed sports arena, the Astrodome was originally called the Harris County Domed Stadium, and was termed the *Eighth Wonder of the World* by its promoters.

**Astroturf** The brand name for one of the earliest and most popular forms of *artificial turf.* It received its name from the Astrodome, where it was first installed. Originally, transparent panels on the Astrodome's roof allowed adequate sunlight to grow real grass, but this made conditions too bright for the players, and two of the eight panels had to be painted to control the sun's glare. This killed the real grass and by June 1966 the artificial turf had been laid. The first visiting team to play on the rug was the Philadelphia Phillies whose third baseman that night was Dick Allen, who was quoted as saying, "If cows don't eat it, I ain't playing on it"; a later version (*Esquire,* Mar. 28, 1978) had Allen saying, "If a horse won't eat it, I don't want to play on it."

**at bat** *adv.* Taking one's turn in the batter's box for the purpose of batting; e.g., "Smith was at bat with the bases loaded" or "Jones had another productive season at bat." Syn. *at the plate.*

**at-bat** *n.* **1.** A turn at the plate; e.g., "Smith walked in his last at-bat" or "Jones had seven at-bats in the doubleheader." **Extended Use.** Referring to a person "in the spotlight"; e.g., a jazz reviewer commenting on the soloist in a big band concert wrote: "I can't tell which one is at bat" (*San Francisco Call Bulletin,* Sept. 24, 1960; Peter Tamony). **2.** An official statistic for the batter coming to the batter's box, excluding those appearances when the batter walks, sacrifices, is hit by a pitched ball, or is interfered with by the catcher. Abbrev. *AB.* Compare *plate appearance.* **1st Use.** 1861. (*New York Sunday Mercury,* Aug. 10; Edward J. Nichols).

**at bat, on deck, in the hold** The sequence of terms traditionally used in reference to the current batter and the player scheduled to bat next, fol-

**At bat, on deck, in the hold.** *The original deck of "on deck" as depicted in a Civil War issue of* Harper's Weekly.

lowed by the subsequent player in the lineup. In the modern era it is usually given as "at bat, on deck, in the *hole*," 3, but this is a corruption of "in the hold," a reference to the interior of a ship, below decks. **Etymology.** Few borrowings are as evident as these words, except for "at bat," which came directly to the baseball field from a ship, where to be on deck is to be on the main deck (or floor) and the hold is the area of the ship below the main deck. That these terms have obvious roots in nautical language is made clear by Joanna Carver Colcord (*Sea Language Comes Ashore,* 1945): "The newspaperman's dogwatch, the baseball player's on deck and in the hole (hold), the contractor's wrecking crew, the bus-driver's and the soda-fountain clerk's double-deckers, are also sea-borrowings."

According to one important source, the term can be traced to an official scorer of a game played in Belfast, Maine, a town with both a rich baseball and nautical history. The source is a short, unsigned story that appeared in *The Sporting News* (Mar. 24, 1938) and was based on a report sent to its offices by Robert P. Chase, a nonagenarian from Belfast. According to *The Sporting News* report, the Boston team was making a tour of Maine in 1872 and played, among others, The Pastimes of Belfast on August 7 of that year. The scorer for each team was called upon to announce the batters. The Boston scorer simply announced: "G. Wright at bat; Leonard and Barnes next." To quote from the original story: "But when the Belfast team had its turn, the Belfast scorer would say, 'Moody at bat, Boardman on deck, Dinsmore in the hold,' using nautical terms which made such a hit with the Boston scorer that he carried them back to Boston, after which they became general." *The Sporting News* added that the final outcome of the game was Boston 35, Belfast 1.

"So all the Maine town got out of that contest was the distinction of being a contributor to the lexicon of the game."

Further investigation of this claim was made by the compiler of this dictionary on a visit to Belfast in Aug. 1987. The investigation revealed the following:

1) The game in question did occur, on the 6th (not the 7th) of Aug. 1872, according to the *Republican Journal,* which came out on the 8th. It said in part: "The visit of the famous Boston Red Stocking Baseball Club to our city on Tuesday the 6th was an unusual treat to the lovers of the national game."

2) According to the *Republican Journal,* the pitcher for the Pastimes was named Chase. No other name or initial is given, but it suggests that the man who gave the report to *The Sporting News* may have been more than an observer but a participant. He would have been 25 at the time of the game and was the only Chase in the local city directory who seemed to have been of playing age in 1872. Chase was a well-known and respected resident of Belfast who died when he was nearly 100.

3) Ironically, the story was known locally in Belfast, but had been largely forgotten until after a local Belfast reporter picked up the story on vacation when he read it in the scorecard at the Astrodome in Houston. Jay Davis, editor of the local *Waldo* (County) *Independent,* published in Belfast, says that his paper then reinvestigated the story and while it could not prove it conclusively, it could not find anything to cause him to doubt its authenticity.

All of this is well and good, but it underscores one of the central premises of lexicography, which is that one needs citations to prove or disprove a theory on the origin of a term. In this case, David Shulman convincingly eliminates the Belfast story as the origin of the term "on deck"—although it was almost certainly used there and may, in fact, have sounded new to people at the game. Shulman has found a Sept. 26, 1867, citation from *Ball Players Chronicle:* "Well I went on deck and took up a bat."

Meanwhile, the sequence "at bat, on deck, in the hold" did not show up in print (yet) until after the Belfast game.

**A team** A group composed of a club's top players by position. The term is used figuratively to refer to a team's best players (as in "he's potential A team material") as well as literally, such as during spring training, when the assembled players are divided into an A team and a *B team* for the purpose of practice play. **Extended Use.** Any elite grouping.

**at 'em ball** A ball hit right at a defensive player ("at him"), often resulting in a double play because of the extra time it gives to make a second out. Syn. *atom ball.*

**athletic hose** Syn. of *sanitary socks.*

**athletic supporter** An elastic undergarment worn to protect the genitals and to hold the protective cup in place. An old Philadelphia gag (which lost its punch when the city's American League Athletics moved to Kansas City): "Are you a Phillie fan?" "No, I'm an Athletic supporter."

**at home** *adj.* **1.** Played at a team's home ballpark; e.g., "The Cubs played three games at home." Compare *away,* 3. **2.** Said of a play at home plate; e.g., "Smith was out at home on Jones's strong throw from left."

**Atlanta Braves** The name of the National League East Division team in Atlanta, Ga. The name Braves has followed the team since its inception in Boston in 1912, stayed with the franchise when it moved to Milwaukee in 1953, and then on to Atlanta where the team has been located since 1966.

**Atlantic luck** *obs.* Good fortune. **Etymology/ 1st Use.** 1870. (*New York Tribune,* June 1, 1870; Edward J. Nichols). Nichols has written that luck was characteristic of the early Atlantic League clubs.

**atom ball** A punning variation of *at 'em ball.* See also *nuclear fission ball.*

**attaboy** A congratulation given to a long reliever before a *hold,* 4, was awarded. Jim Henneman (*Baltimore Sun,* July 22, 1994) commented: "After a good performance they got a pat on the back, ac-

***Atlantic luck.*** *The Brooklyn Atlantics (bottom row) pose with the original Philadelphia Athletics. The image is a wood engraving from a photograph that appeared in* Harper's Weekly, *Nov. 3, 1866.*

companied by a congratulatory 'attaboy.' At the end of the season the pitcher with the most 'attaboys' was long reliever of the year."

**attack** Syn. of *go after.*

**attack point** A point tallied for each total base and steal earned by a team in the Japanese Central League, used to determine the victor of a game that ends in a tie, with the team earning the most attack points being declared the victor (*Washington Post,* Apr. 5, 1993).

**attempt 1.** *n.* Trying to steal a base; e.g., "Smith has 26 steals for 47 attempts." **2.** *v.* To try to steal a base.

**attendance 1.** The number of spectators actually present at a baseball game. **2.** The number of tickets actually sold ("paid attendance") for a baseball game. Abbrev. *A,* 3.

**attendance clause** A provision of some modern contracts that promise a bonus to a player if the home attendance for a season goes above a certain number. The assumption here is that the player in question is a draw who will help the gate. Howard Smith (*Cleveland Plain Dealer,* Aug. 27, 1978) on Harry Caray, who then announced for the Chicago White Sox: "Caray supposedly even has an attendance clause in his contract." Jerry Howarth (*Baseball Lite,* 1986) defines the word "attendance" as "formerly a noun of interest to major league owners, it is now an adjective for 'clause' when players negotiate salary bonuses."

**at the plate** Syn. of *at bat.*

**audible signal base** A base that emits sound when it is touched. The idea of such a base had been discussed for decades, but never attracted much interest. Consider this description by Lester

L. Sargent (*Baseball Magazine,* Mar. 1914): "A step toward the dawn of universal peace has been taken in the audible Signal-Base for Baseball Fields, which is the invention of Stephen H. Wills. Those terrible things that are said about the umpire will be said no more. Everybody will know for sure whether or not the runner reached the bag safe, for when he does touch base an electric bell will be rung by the base itself."

**Aunt Susie** A curveball. David Halberstam (*The Summer of '49,* 1989) writes that "Aunt Susie" was the name used by New York Yankees pitchers in the era (1947–53) of Vic Raschi, who lacked one, and Allie Reynolds, who had one.

**authority** An attribute of a hitter who swings the bat with power and purpose; e.g., "Smith hits with authority."

**autographed ball** A baseball with a player's signature. A long-standing baseball tradition has been the autographing of baseballs by players. Autographs themselves have become a baseball commodity, with stars getting up to several hundred dollars to sign their names at baseball-card collector conventions. A 1987 UPI story reported that Mickey Mantle received a flat $10,000 for four hours of autographing.

**automatic out 1.** A batter who most likely will make an out at the plate or be retired. **2.** An out made by such a batter. **Usage Note.** There are many, including the compiler of this dictionary, who believe that such an out is a great pitching feat which is anything but automatic and do not like the term.

**automatic pitcher** A *pitching machine.* Lee Allen (*The Hot Stove League,* 1955) reports that the first automatic pitcher was demonstrated by Princeton professor Charles E. Hinton at that institution's gymnasium on December 15, 1896.

**automatic strike** A pitch delivered when the count on the batter is three balls and no strikes. It is so called because, in the hope of receiving a base on balls, the batter will not swing at the next pitch. The manager of the batting team sometimes will order a batter to take a pitch. Knowing this tendency of batters and managers, pitchers are more likely to put the ball in the strike zone. Keith Hernandez (*Pure Baseball,* 1994) notes the term "semiautomatic strike" is used. **1st Use.** 1937. (Red Barber, World Series broadcast, Oct. 6).

**automatic take** Not swinging in an automatic strike situation. The batter is ordered to take the next pitch (i.e., not swing at it), hoping for a fourth ball and a base on balls.

**autumn classic** Syn. of *World Series.* **Usage Note.** The term is a cliché of such magnitude that it is commonly capitalized; e.g., "But if the Autumn Classic is baseball's prime-time ode, opening day is when baseball's fans are born and reborn, when hope springs eternal for all teams" (*USA Today,* Apr. 7, 1987).

**average** One of the general classes of statistics of baseball; e.g., *batting average, earned run average, fielding average,* and *slugging average.* Abbrev. *AVG.*

***Autographed ball.*** *Goose Goslin of the Washington Senators autographing a ball for a flapper fan during the 1925 World Series.*

**Averill shift** A defensive ploy used to defend against the left-handed, pull-hitting Earl Averill of the 1930s by placing the shortstop to the batter's right of second base. Before his passing in 1983 Averill recalled: "I played five or six seasons before I found out there were three fields to hit the ball to." See also *Williams shift*.

**AVG** Abbrev. for *average*.

**"a walk is as good as a hit"** A colloquialism urging a batter to get on base by not swinging at bad pitches.

**away 1.** Syn. of *out*, 1; e.g., "two away" is two out. **1st Use.** 1881. (*New York Herald*, July 15; Edward J. Nichols). **2.** Said of a pitch outside the strike zone. A strategy called "pitch him away, play him away" is one in which the pitcher consistently pitches a batter outside and the defense overshifts to the opposite field, where the batter is more likely to hit the ball. **3.** Played in another team's ballpark; e.g., "The Cubs played three games away." Compare *at home*, 1.

**away game** A game played on the other team's field, as opposed to a *home game*. The 162-game major-league schedule comprises 81 away games and 81 home games.

**away team** A visiting baseball team.

**awful** A *Texas Leaguer*.

**AWOL** Absent. The term is usually applied to a fielder who is not present when a fly ball or foul ball comes down in his territory. **Etymology.** Time-honored military acronym for "absent without official leave," which has been in use since before the Civil War. Confederate soldiers caught while AWOL were made to walk about the camp carrying a sign bearing these letters. The term was brought back from World War II by players who had been in the armed forces.

# B

**B** **1.** See *Class B.* **2.** Abbrev. for *bunt.*

**BA** Abbrev. for *batting average.*

**Babe** **1.** The most famous nickname in baseball, the one given to George Herman Ruth. The 1933 edition of *Who's Who in Baseball* gives this explanation: "The nickname 'Babe' was originally applied to him when he joined the Baltimore Orioles in 1914. Coach Steinam, who was owner [Jack] Dunn's right hand man, greeted the big fellow when he came into the ball yard, shouting to the other Baltimoreans: 'Boys, here's Jack's New Babe!'" In his autobiography, *The Babe Ruth Story* (1948), Ruth pointed out that the "clincher" came a few days later when he was playing with the controls of a hotel elevator. After almost decapitating himself, Ruth was chewed out by Dunn. One of the older players, taking pity on him, called him a "babe in the woods." "After that," said Ruth, "they all called me Babe."

Ruth was not the only player to be called Babe. Probably the most famous was Floyd C. "Babe" Herman, who was also known as "the other Babe." The importance of the names "Babe" and "Babe Ruth" is underscored in Eleanor Gehrig's book *My Luke and I* (1976). At various points she mentions that her late husband, Lou Gehrig, is deemed "the Babe Ruth of the high schools" and the "college Babe Ruth."

Ruth may have been able to claim a record for the most aliases in the history of baseball. Though some of the names only existed in the vocabulary of sportswriters, he was called, at various times: Bam, Bambino (Italian for little baby), Behemoth of Biff, Big Bambino, Caliph of Clout, Colossus of Club, Colossus of Sport, Goliath of Grand Slam, Home Run King, Jidge, King of Clout, King of Swat, Monk, Monkey, Prince of Pounders, Slambino, Sultan of Swat, and Wizard of Whack. **2.** Any big, fat player. The term was used only after Babe Ruth began showing the effects of excessive drinking and eating. **3.** An element of infield chatter, as in *"humm-babe."*

**Babe Ruth** A home run. **Etymology.** As a player, Babe Ruth hit so many home runs, his name actually became synonymous with a home run. In the 1930s, when Ruth did his greatest slugging, his name was a common sports page eponym.

**Babe Ruth, the** Ultimate compliment to a baseball player or any athlete; e.g., Clay Carr is "the Babe Ruth" of rodeo riders (*Sports Illustrated*, May 16, 1994) or "Josh Gibson is the black Babe Ruth" or "Sadaharu Oh is the Babe Ruth of Japan" or "Billy Haughton is the Babe Ruth of harness racing."

**Babe Ruth Baseball** A nonprofit organization founded in 1951 and located all over the United States that supports summer leagues for age groups 9–12, 13–15, and 16–18.

**Babe Ruth curse** The cloud under which the Boston Red Sox have toiled since owner Harry Frazee sold Babe Ruth in 1920. There are many aspects to the curse, but one of them is that the Sox have a penchant for losing the seventh and deciding game of the World Series (which they did in 1946, 1967, 1975, and 1986). "The Red Sox Have Babe Ruth Curse" read the headline for a George Vecsey column (*New York Times,* October 28, 1986) after the Sox were beaten by the Mets in Game 7 of that year's World Series. See also *curse of the Bambino.*

**Babe Ruther** One who plays Babe Ruth Baseball. "Knox Babe Ruthers Place Third in State" (*Camden* [Maine] *Herald* headline, July 31, 1986).

**"Babe Ruth is dead"** Advice given to a pitcher who is nibbling the corners and getting behind every hitter. The full thought here is: "Babe Ruth is dead; throw strikes to this guy!"

**baby act** *obs.* Term used by Adrian "Cap" Anson and other late 19th-century ballplayers to describe the bunt. They felt that the strategy of the bunt could potentially ruin the game. See also *baby hit.* **Etymology.** The clear point made by Anson and others is that the bunt was a weak and pitiful act that might be fine for infants and youngsters but not for grown men.

**baby boomer** A nickname for a strong, young power hitter of the mid-1980s. **Etymology.** The term refers to a child of the period after World War II when the birthrate skyrocketed. In the 1980s the baby boomers were seen as coming into a time of great influence. The baseball baby boomers were born much later but the term fit because they were young (babies) and could hit the long ball (boomers).

**baby hit** *arch.* A name for the bunt in the late 19th and early 20th century. See also *baby act.*

**Baby Ruth** The name of a candy bar that many have long assumed was named after Babe Ruth, the baseball player. The manufacturer has long insisted that its product was so named in 1917, when the candy bar came out, for the daughter of President Grover Cleveland. Regardless, the closeness of "Baby Ruth" to "Babe Ruth" had the effect of tying the candy bar to the slugger. Robert Hendrickson (*The Facts on File Encyclopedia of Word and Phrase Origins,* 1987) has been able to shed additional light on the situation: "In fact, when another company got Babe Ruth to endorse Babe Ruth's Home Run Candy in 1926, Baby Ruth's manufacturer appealed to the Patent Office on the grounds of infringement and won, the Babe's candy bar never appearing."

**backdoor slide** A slide in which the runner touches the base with his hand as he slides beyond the bag with his body. Something of a rarity, this slide is performed when an advancing baserunner sees that he is about to be tagged out. He fakes a conventional slide, throws himself beyond the base, and reaches back to the bag with his hand. It is a desperation play that only works when it confuses the fielder.

**backdoor slider** A slider that comes in front of the outside of the plate but crosses the plate on the inside, or vice versa; e.g., a slider thrown by a right-handed pitcher to a left-handed batter will cross the plate moving away from the hitter. George F. Will (*Men at Work,* 1990) used the term for a slider that starts outside but at the last instant slices in over the outside corner of the plate. See also *backup slider.*

**back end** The trailing runner in a double steal. "Garrett Jenkins scored on the back end of a double steal" (*Tampa Tribune,* Apr. 23, 1990).

**back foot** The batter's foot away from the pitcher. Compare *front foot.*

**backhand** To field a batted or thrown ball by extending the gloved hand across the body.

**back into** To clinch a championship despite the team's poor play when the nearest contender mathematically eliminates itself by losing. "For awhile it seemed as if the Padres might back into the division title, losing seven of 11 games while the second-place Astros kept a similar pace" (*Tampa Tribune,* Sept. 29, 1989).

**backlot** A sandlot; an amateur or semipro baseball field. **1st Use.** 1908. (*Baseball Magazine,* Dec.; Edward J. Nichols).

**back off** To pitch inside to a batter so that he

moves away from the plate, thus giving the pitcher more room for his delivery.

**back of Podunk** Said of a team that is very low in the standings or is out of contention. Syn. "back of Squeedunk."

**backspinner** A pitch thrown with a backward, rotary motion so that the ball, when struck by the batter, will hit the ground and bounce backward, recoil, stop dead, or roll forward only a short distance.

**backstop 1.** A screen behind and extending over the home plate area to keep the ball in the playing area and protect spectators from foul balls. In the major leagues, the backstop must be at least 60 feet from home plate. **1st Use.** 1872. "There was no back-stop for the catcher" (*Boston Daily Globe*, Mar. 27). **2.** Syn. for *catcher*, 1.

**backstopper** Syn. for *catcher*, 1.

**backswing** The return movement of the bat after a batter swings at a pitch.

**back them up** To hit a pitched ball hard enough to force the outfielders back to the fences to play the ball.

**back through the box** Said of a ball that is hit sharply through the pitcher's box. Such hits often end up as hits to center field.

**back-to-back** Said of two events of the same kind, usually performed by the same individual on consecutive occasions; e.g., Johnny Vander Meer pitched "back-to-back no-hitters" on consecutive starting dates in 1938 and Mark McGwire in 1997 became the first player with "back-to-back 50-homer seasons" since Babe Ruth did it in 1927 and 1928. Two homers, or any other hit, in a row are invariably called "back-to-back." **1st Use/Extended Use.** About 1900. John Ciardi (*Good Words to You*, 1987) reports that this term started in baseball about the turn of the 20th century and long ago generalized to the language at large. He also notes that the term can become absurd in a sentence such as "Remember when Reggie Jackson hit three back-to-back homers in one World Series Game?" Ciardi's answer: "I do as a matter of fact, but after the third, what was his position relative to the other two, and after the second, what was his position relative to the first and third?"

**"back to the mines!"** "A cry from disgruntled spectators to a player to take himself back to the job with pick and shovel that he held before disgracing his Club and themselves by playing ball" C. M. Klump (*Who's Who and What's What in Baseball*, 1910).

**back up** *v.* To play in such a way to help another player in a difficult situation; e.g., to move into a supporting position to help the player who is fielding or receiving the ball in the event it is missed, dropped, or overthrown, such as when the pitcher gets behind ("backs up") the third baseman on a throw from the outfield or behind the catcher on a throw to home.

**backup 1.** *n.* A player who fills in for a regularly assigned player when the latter is unable to play; a substitute. **1st Use.** 1869. (*DeWitt's Base Ball Guide*; Edward J. Nichols). **2.** *adj.* Said of a reserve or substitute player; e.g., a "backup catcher."

**backup slider** A slider in which the catcher sits on one side of the plate, but the ball is thrown over the middle of the plate. See also *backdoor slider*.

**backward runner** A baserunner who, having advanced one or more bases, is forced to return to a previous base. If such a runner has tagged a new base while advancing, he must retouch that base before returning to the original one; e.g., a runner, leaving first base as a ball is hit to the outfield and thinking it will hit the ground, crosses second base and advances toward third, then realizes that the ball is caught, must return to first, making sure to retag second base on the way.

**back yard** A team's home field; e.g., "We know they are not going to beat us three in a row in our own back yard."

**backyarder** A World Series played by two teams from the same geographic area; for instance, the 1989 Series between the Oakland Athletics and the San Francisco Giants.

**bad actor** A player who is difficult to deal with.

**bad ball** A pitched ball thrown outside the strike zone in hopes of enticing the batter to swing.

**bad-ball hitter** A hitter who willingly swings at pitches outside the strike zone. Such a practice is usually a deficiency because the hitter tends to swing and miss or hit fly balls, but some players have turned it into an asset. Roberto Clemente, Joe Medwick, Yogi Berra, and Hank Aaron were all considered excellent bad-ball hitters. "I swing at everything. I'm always one to swing the bat." (Joe Carter, a self-described bad-ball hitter, quoted in *USA Today,* Mar. 6, 1998).

**bad bounce** A batted ball that bounces and then unexpectedly deflects in a direction contrary to what the fielder anticipates; e.g., "The grounder took a bad bounce and hit Smith in the face." See also *bad hop; base on stones.*

**bad call** An umpire's decision that is felt to be an incorrect ruling on a play. The term is commonly used by the real or imagined victim and applied to a ball crossing the plate (was it a ball or a strike?) or a runner arriving at a base (safe or out?). **Extended Use.** Any perceived misjudgment.

**bad hands** A player with poor fielding ability, especially one who has difficulty holding on to the ball; one who has trouble with short hops. "A physical affliction common to ball players with poor fielding averages. There is no known cure." (Jim Brosnan, *The Long Season,* 1960). Syn. "bad paws."

**bad head 1.** A player with an ugly face. **2.** A player with a bad psyche.

**bad hop** A batted or thrown ball that suddenly changes direction because it hits an object or irregularity on the field. Marian Edelman Borden (*New York Times,* n.d.) defined a bad hop as "any ball that comes toward your son and doesn't roll into his glove." See also *base on stones; bad bounce.*

**bad hose** The poor throwing arm of a player.

**bad lamps 1.** The poor eyesight of a player. **2.** The lighting of a poorly lit field.

**Bad News Bears** The name of an unruly, motley Little League team in three movies: *Bad News Bears* (1976); *The Bad News Bears in Breaking Training* (1977); and *The Bad News Bears Go to Japan* (1978). The name has been used to characterize a club in decline or in the midst of a losing streak.

**bad wood** Poor contact between the bat and ball.

**bag 1.** A square canvas sack filled with light material used to mark first base, second base, and third base since the earliest days of baseball. **1st Use.** 1857. "The first, second, and third bases shall be canvas bags, painted white, and filled with sand or sawdust" (*Spirit of the Times;* David Shulman). **2.** The base itself. **3.** A stolen base. "What if I go 4-for-4 with three bags?" (Jeffrey Hammonds, quoted in *Baltimore Sun,* Mar. 8, 1996).

**bagger 1.** *arch.* A one-base hit; a single. **1st Use.** 1880. (Chicago *Inter-Ocean,* June 3; Edward J. Nichols). **2.** The extent of a hit; e.g., "two-bagger" for a double and "three-bagger" for a triple. **Extended Use.** Famed money manager Peter Lynch borrowed from baseball slang to describe how he tried to find "two-baggers" or "three-baggers," i.e., stocks that would quickly double or triple in price. Many have aped Lynch in this application. **3.** A first baseman, second baseman, or third baseman, who can be a first bagger, second bagger, or third bagger, respectively.

**bagman** *arch.* Syn. of *baseman.* **1st Use.** 1880. (Chicago *Inter-Ocean,* June 3; Edward J. Nichols).

**bag of bones** An extremely thin player.

**bag of peanuts** A broken or misshapen hand, like that of a veteran catcher. **1st Use.** 1963. "His hand looked like a bag of peanuts" (Leonard Shecter, *Baseball Digest,* June 1963).

**bag puncher** *arch.* A term used in the National League for a player who talks too much (*American Speech,* Apr. 1930). Compare *barber,* 1.

**bagel** See *go for a bagel.*

**bags clogged** Syn. of *bases loaded.* **1st Use.** 1913. (*Harpers' Weekly,* Sept. 6; Edward J. Nichols).

**bags full** Syn. of *bases loaded.*

**bail out 1.** For a batter to step back or fall away from a pitch. This act is seldom voluntary and usually takes place when the ball is, or appears to be, coming at the batter. A common situation in which the batter bails out is when he is expecting a fastball and the pitcher serves him a breaking pitch. Some batters are said to "bail out slightly." **2.** To win or save a game as a relief pitcher.

**bait 1.** To lure the pitcher into throwing a good pitch; e.g., for a good hitter who is often "semi-intentionally walked" to swing at two bad pitches to draw the pitcher into throwing a "half-good" pitch in hope of a strikeout. **2.** To lure the batter into swinging at a bad pitch by throwing the ball just outside the strike zone. **3.** To upset an umpire by making uncomplimentary remarks to him.

**Baker** *obs.* A home run. Before Babe Ruth came along, Frank "Home Run" Baker was the most dominant home run hitter in baseball. As with Ruth, Baker's name was synonymous with "home run." **1st Use.** 1912. (*New York Tribune,* Oct. 15; Edward J. Nichols).

**balance point** [softball term] The moment in the underhand pitching delivery in which the pitching hand is at its highest point above the head and the opposite foot is at its highest point above the ground.

**balance the budget** To tie the score, a term which may have been introduced in the 1989 All-Star Game by Vin Scully.

**balata ball** The baseball used during the 1943 major-league baseball season when supplies of rubber were rationed during World War II. Balata, a nonstrategic, rubberlike gum obtained from the milky juice or latex of a tropical American tree (*Manilkara bidentata*) and most commonly used for golf-ball covers, machinery belts, and telephone cable insulation, was used by Spalding as a binder in the manufacture of baseballs. Red and black layers of balata substituted for the traditional layer of rubber surrounding the cork center. The balata ball used ground cork instead of high-grade cork and the cover of the ball came from domestic horsehide. Initially, the balata ball was much less resilient than the traditional baseball; later in 1943, Spalding made balls containing rubber cement that remained soft and sticky.

**balk 1.** *n.* Any illegal act or motion by the pitcher that the umpire deems to be an attempt to deceive a baserunner into making a move that may get him picked off base. The ball becomes dead when a balk is called and all runners advance one base. Most balks are called as the pitcher shows a move that appears to be a delivery to the plate; specif., failure by a pitcher to complete the delivery of the ball to home plate once his foot has made contact with the rubber. It is a departure from the pitcher's regular delivery that is, ostensibly, designed to deceive the baserunner. A common balk occurs when the pitcher does not come to a stop after his stretch. The rules spell out 14 specific balk situations while the pitcher is in contact with the rubber; e.g., making any motion naturally associated with his pitch and failing to make such delivery, or feinting a throw to first base and failing to complete the throw, or failing to step directly toward a base before throwing to that base.

Even without a change in the balk rule, the degree to which balks are called changes, depending on the strictness with which the rule is being interpreted. Scores of balks were called at the beginning of the 1988 season, which probably would have been ignored the previous year. Bob Considine once termed the balk "a misdemeanor which permits runners to advance a base under the protection of a temporary armistice" (*The Saturday Evening Post,* Apr. 9, 1938; Peter Tamony). See also *foul balk.* **Usage Note.** In 1978, a year in which the balk rule was being strongly enforced, Ira Miller wrote: "It is one of baseball's least understood rules. It even sounds funny. Say 'balk' and people hear 'ball.' It's pronounced 'bawk' as in the first syllable of 'awkward,' which is how umpires are making pitchers feel about it." (*San Francisco Chronicle,* May 16, 1978; Peter Tamony). **1st Use.** 1845. (Knickerbocker Rules, rule 19). **Etymology.** From "balca," the Anglo-Saxon word for "beam." Balcas were put across the doors of huts in the days before locks and keys to thwart or stop intruders. Tracing the term through "baulk" for a "false shot or mistake," Peter Tamony wrote: "The sense of this word seems in general to be to stop short, to frustrate, to disappoint. In billiards, the balk-line is a line drawn a certain distance from the cushion, and used in connection with certain methods of playing billiards. In baseball, a feint or false motion made by the pitcher in the delivery of the ball to the batter, which is penalized." **2.** *v.* To commit a balk. **Extended Use.** To recoil; to fail to deliver, such as a politician "balking" on tax reform. **3.** See *catcher's balk.*

**balkamania** The furor during the early weeks of the 1988 season when the balk rule was reinterpreted along stricter lines. During the first 11 days of the season, 88 balks had been called in the American League and 36 in the National League, a situation which caused *The Sporting News* (Apr. 25, 1988) to headline its article on the subject "Balkamania Unchecked."

**balk move** A pitcher's move that suggests a balk. **Usage Note.** This is a highly subjective notion as a "balk move" is something alleged by the team at bat. A pitcher charged with making a balk move to first base will insist that it is nothing more than his regular move.

**ball 1.** A pitch that is not swung at by the batter and that is judged outside the strike zone by the umpire. **2.** The baseball itself. **1st Use.** 1845. (Knickerbocker Rules). **3.** The game of baseball, as in, "he plays good ball." In some childhood circles this term actually overwhelms the proper one. In his autobiography (*The Education of an American*, 1938), Mark Sullivan wrote: "We did not know our game as baseball but merely as 'ball,' and in other respects we failed to conform to the orthodox formula." **4.** A type of pitch; e.g., fastball, screwball, spitball, and curveball.

**ball-and-strike umpire** The *plate umpire* who is responsible for judging whether a pitch was in or out of the strike zone. In cow-pasture games, schoolyard games, and in other fields not major or minor, the ball-and-strike umpire may stand behind the pitcher.

**Ballantine blast** A home run. The term was made popular by Mel Allen, whose New York Yankees broadcasts were sponsored by Ballantine beer and ale. Other product-inspired names for the home run used by radio and television announcers to please their sponsors include White Owl Wallop, Case of Wheaties, and Case of Lucky Strikes, which, respectively turned long balls into ads for cigars, breakfast cereal, and cigarettes. A 1988 example is given by New York Yankee announcer Phil Rizzuto linking the home run to one of his broadcast's sponsors, Budweiser beer: "Hey, Yankee fans, you know what happens every time a Yankee hits a home run: Dave Winfield, this Bud's for you."

**ball boy** A young man whose job is to retrieve and/or collect foul balls. See also *ball girl.*

**ball club 1.** *arch.* A baseball bat. **2.** A baseball team; an organization whose prime activity is the building up and support of a baseball team. Sometimes spelled "ballclub." **1st Use.** 1845. (Chadwick Scrapbooks clipping, Oct. 13; Edward J. Nichols).

**ball dog** Syn. of *ball hound.* Linguist Kelsie Harder (Potsdam College) reported (letter of Feb. 25, 1989): "I heard it used in Perry County, Tenn., where I used to play baseball hour after hour and never gained much ability. I remember hearing: 'Young boys dog them balls out there in them corn middles.'"

**balldom** The realm of baseball; e.g., *Balldom: "The Britannica of Baseball"* by George L. Moreland (1914). See also *baseballdom.* **1st Use.** 1905. (*Sporting Life,* Sept. 2; Edward J. Nichols).

**ball field** An area for playing baseball. **1st Use.** 1864. (*Brooklyn Daily Eagle,* Sept. 20; Edward J. Nichols).

**ball game 1.** A baseball game. See also *new ball game.* Sometimes spelled "ballgame." **2.** The moment or event that determines the outcome of a game. "That one at-bat was the ball game" (Earl Weaver on a key out, quoted in Thomas Boswell, *How Life Imitates the World Series,* 1982). The term is often used as an expression of a loss, as "there goes the old ball game." **Extended Use.** A coherent event or set of circumstances, such as the movement of a bill through Congress. "Duncan's only comment on the close vote yesterday was 'The ball game isn't over yet'" (AP dispatch, May 30, 1986; Peter Tamony). During the Vietnam War, the term "ballgame" meant a military operation, according to Leonard B. Scott in the glossary to his novel about the war (*Charlie Mike,* 1985). **3.** A baseball player; e.g., Ted Williams referred to himself as "Teddy Ballgame."

**ball game is at first, the** The notion that if the runner on first base scores, his team will win the game. Similarly, "the ball game is at second" and "the ball game is at third" allude to the game-winning potential of runners at second and third bases, respectively.

**ball girl** A young woman whose job is to retrieve and/or collect foul balls. See also *ball boy.*

**ball hawk 1.** An especially fast and adept outfielder; one who covers a lot of ground. Willie Mays was always regarded as being in this elite group. Ducky Medwick was one of the first, if not the first, players to be linked to this honorific term. Harry Grayson (*They Played the Game,* 1944) described Turkey Mike Donlin: "He was a ball hawk in center field and a strong and accurate arm swung from his shoulder." See also *hawk; flyhawk.* Sometimes spelled "ballhawk." **1st Use.** 1920. (*New York Times,* Oct. 10; Edward J. Nichols). **2.** A person who collects as souvenirs balls that are hit outside a ballpark. Ball hawks are common at the smaller major- and minor-league parks and at those that are used for exhibition games during spring training because more balls land out of the park at such sites.

**ball hound** One who will chase and return stray baseballs. Syn. *ball dog.* **1st Use.** 1935. "A couple of 'ball hounds,' youngsters not quite old enough for the team yet loyally interested in it, should be relied upon to rescue balls going out of the grounds" (Ralph H. Barbour, *How to Play Better Baseball,* 1935; David Shulman).

**"ball in"** A command to throw the practice ball(s) to the dugout at the start of a half inning.

**ballist** A 19th-century baseball player. See also *baseballist.*

**ballite** *arch.* A baseball fan. Also spelled "ball-ite."

**balloon 1.** A ball that looks big to the batter because it is moving slowly and gives the illusion of being oversized. Compare *aspirin.* **2.** A fly ball.

**1st Use.** 1920. (*New York Times,* Oct. 6; Edward J. Nichols). **3.** An umpire's portable *chest protector* worn outside the uniform. "Although 'the balloon' was difficult to master, it did provide more protection" (Ron Luciano, *Strike Two,* 1984; Charles D. Poe). The balloons were abandoned by American League umpires in 1985. Syn. *bubble,* 1. **Etymology.** The name is an allusion to the puffy, bloated look of the outside chest protector.

**balloon ascension** *arch.* An occurrence when a pitcher loses his effectiveness or control. The term was commonly framed in terms of spectators witnessing a balloon ascension. **1st Use.** 1907. (Burt L. Standish, *Dick Merriwell's Magnetism;* Edward J. Nichols).

**balloon ball** A slowly thrown pitch that arches high in the air and drops precipitously as it passes through the strike zone. It is a rarely thrown pitch that can be effective when the odd trajectory is enough to throw the batter's timing off. See also *eephus.* **1st Use.** 1913. "My team had their batting eyes along, but that balloon ball fooled us every time" (Alan Douglas, *Fast Nine;* David Shulman).

**balloon flier** *arch.* A high fly ball. **1st Use.** 1919. "Horatio Juggins was an elongated chap whose specialty, besides capturing balloon fliers out in right field, consisted in great throwing" (Donald Ferguson, *Chums of Scranton High Out for the Pennant;* David Shulman).

**ballpark 1.** An enclosed baseball field including its seating areas; a stadium. It is a short form of *baseball park.* Also spelled "ball park." **2.** An honorific term for a classic baseball venue. Roger Angell (*Five Seasons,* 1977) writes: "Wrigley Field is one of the few remaining enclosures that still merit the title of ball park." The home of the Texas Rangers since Apr. 1994 is aptly named The Ballpark in Arlington. **1st Use.** 1908. (*Baseball Magazine,* June; Edward J. Nichols). **Etymology.** The first such enclosed playing area was Union Grounds in Brooklyn, N.Y., which opened on May 15, 1862. The enclosure was invented and designed by William Cammeyer. **Extended Use.** A given realm; a field of activity. "Senators Knock FmHA [Farmers Home Administration] All Over

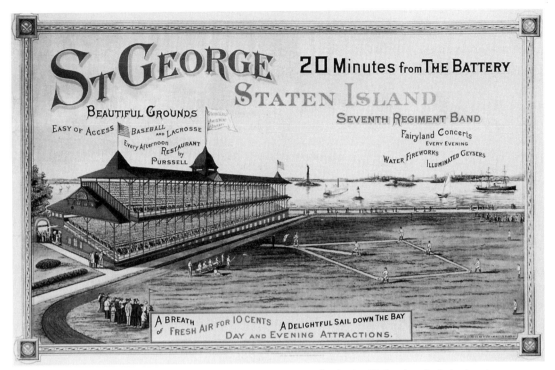

**Ballpark.** *An 1886 lithograph of the St. George Grounds on Staten Island, New York, where both the American Association Metropolitans and the National League Giants played in the 1880s.*

the Ballpark" (*Washington Post* headline, Sept. 10, 1986). By extension, "in the ball park" refers to something (a cost estimate, a plan, etc.) that is within the realm of consideration, while "out of the ballpark" is something that is beyond negotiable limits.

**ballpark figure** A rough estimate. **Extended Use.** The term has a decidedly odd connection to baseball given that most figures having to do with the game (such as batting averages and earned run averages) are relentlessly precise. Lexicographer Stuart Flexner is quoted by William Safire (*I Stand Corrected*, 1984) on its evolution: "Our Random House dictionary citation files show the term first started out as 'in the ballpark' (1962), as when talking about figures, estimates, etc., with 'I hope that's in the ballpark.' Then, in 1968, we first recorded 'ballpark figure' from the *Seattle Times*."

**ballpark frank** A *hot dog*, 2. Possibly the most

beloved food sold by vendors at baseball games, it is often felt that it tastes better there than elsewhere. At some parks hot dogs are given local nicknames, such as the Fenway Frank (Boston) and the Dodger Dog (Los Angeles). On the other hand, not everyone is convinced that these franks are superior. "I ask you, is there anything in the world tastier than a ballpark frank?" writer Rick Horowitz asked himself in a *Washington Post* (Apr. 8, 1987) article on ballpark food. "Are you kidding?!" he answers, "Hot dogs steamed since the 1958 World Series? Buns carved out of broken bat handles?"

**ballplayer 1.** A professional baseball player. See also *baseballist*. Also spelled "ball player." **2.** Any individual who plays baseball. Syn. *baseball player.* **Usage Note.** This term carries its own honor. Donald Honig (*Baseball America*, 1985) quotes Smoky Joe Wood on his phenomenal 1912 season when he had a 34-5 pitching record and a batting average of .290: "I wasn't just a pitcher, I was a ballplayer." **1st Use.** 1862. (correspondence of the Knickerbocker Base Ball Club; Edward J. Nichols). In James Fenimore Cooper's *Home as Found* (1838) there is discussion of apprentice boys amusing themselves with a "game of ball," whom he later refers to as "ball-players." This is certainly an earlier use of the term, but it is not known precisely what game of ball they were playing.

**balls and strikes** The count on a batter.

**ball-shoe** Baseball footwear. **1st Use.** 1909. ". . . and most of all I'll want my glove and ball-shoes" (Zane Grey, *The Short-Stop*).

**ball team** See *team.* **1st Use.** 1902. (*Sporting Life,* Apr. 26; Edward J. Nichols).

**ball town** A city that supports baseball, such as one that keeps a team in the black. "Time was when the name of Toledo as a ball town was one to conjure with, but that time has passed." (National Association of Professional Baseball Leagues, *Official Guide,* 1905; David Shulman) **1st Use.** 1883. "Detroit is one of the best playing ball-towns in the country" (*Sporting Life,* July 22).

**ball with eyes on it** A batted ball, usually a grounder, that barely gets past the outstretched gloves of two fielders. It is so described because it would seem to need "vision" to chart such an evasive course. See also *seeing-eye single; eyes on it.*

**ballyard** A ballpark. **1st Use.** 1940. "But a possible reason for the maintenance of this attendance level may be that the commercial plugs those announcers drop in are driving people . . . into the ballyards for protection" (*Golf,* July 6; David Shulman). **Usage Note.** The term is used by some sportswriters, but far from universal. In fact, it would seem to be something of a taboo or red flag to traditionalists. After Dave Kindred (*Washington Post*) called Baltimore's Memorial Stadium a "ballyard," the paper printed a letter from a reader named Caroll Beaulac, which said in part: "Since the birth of baseball, the area where the game is played has been called the ball*park.* Will Kindred grow tired of calling that area the ball*yard* by next year and start calling it the ball*patio* or the ball*lot*

or perhaps the ball*arena?*" (*Washington Post,* Oct. 16, 1982). Nonetheless, there are those who seem able to get away with it, especially if they are affecting a gushy style. Writing about Candlestick Park at the beginning of the 1987 National League Championship Series, Thomas Boswell (*Washington Post,* Oct. 11, 1987) said: "Oh, thou loveliest of ball yards, how have you been maligned."

**Baltimore bounce** Syn. of *Baltimore chop.*

**Baltimore chop** A batted ball that hits the ground close to home plate and then bounces high in the air, allowing the batter time to reach first base safely. It is occasionally described as a ball that hits the plate. See also *alabaster blaster; butcher-boy stroke; Pittsburgh chopper.* Syn. *Baltimore bounce.* **Etymology/1st Use.** 1910. Despite the fact that the term did not begin to show up in print for sev-

**Baltimore chop.** *The innovative Wilbert Robinson, a former Baltimore batsman, shown here as the manager of the Brooklyn Dodgers, who were also known as the Robins in his honor.*

eral decades (*Baseball Magazine,* Apr. 1910; Edward J. Nichols), it got its name, by all accounts, in the 1890s when the tactic was perfected by Wee Willie Keeler of the old Baltimore Orioles. Two other Baltimore batsmen (John McGraw and Wilbert Robinson) also used it as a method to get on base. Evidence suggests that at the Orioles' field, the dirt near home plate was purposely hardened to make the ball bounce higher. A description of the tactic from an 1896 edition of the *Baltimore News* appears in Dan Schlossberg's *Baseball Catalog* (1975): "A middle-height ball is picked out and is attacked with a terrific swing on the upper side. The ball is made to strike the ground from five to ten feet away from the batsman and, striking the ground with force, bounds high over the head of the third or first baseman." Although Mike Whiteford (*How to Talk Baseball,* 1983) notes that "today's Baltimore chops, however, are almost always accidental," the term is very much alive as this kind of hit occurs frequently on artificial turf.

**Baltimore farewell** The collective act by fans of waving handkerchiefs in a derogatory fashion on the departure of an opposing pitcher who has been removed from the game. **Etymology.** Murray Wieman (*Baltimore Evening Sun,* Apr. 12, 1955) reveals that the custom was spawned in Baltimore, back when the Orioles were a team in the Class AAA International League: "In spite of critics who called it 'small town' the farewell blossomed again last season [1954] as the Orioles went big league."

**Baltimore Orioles** Traditional name for several baseball teams that have played in Baltimore, Md. The original Baltimore Orioles played during the 19th century and the first two years of the 20th century in the American Association, the National League, and the American League. That team was followed by the Class AAA International League team. The current Orioles of the American League East Division moved to Baltimore in 1954 from St. Louis where they had been the Browns. The Orioles of the present era are also known as the "Birds" and the "O's". **Etymology.** The black-and-orange Baltimore Oriole is the Maryland state bird and has always been linked to the city because of its name.

According to legend, the bird was named by Cecilius Calvert, the second Lord Baltimore.

**Bambi** A meek or extremely mild-mannered player, manager, or coach, from the name of the fictional deer. "Though he [Cal Ripken Sr.] never kicked dirt on an umpire or turned his cap around to argue nose-to-nose as [Earl] Weaver is famous for, Ripken says he will be no Bambi with the umpires" (*USA Today,* Jan. 28, 1987).

**banana 1.** *n.* A good player; a prospect that makes the team. "There isn't a scout in the business who hasn't touted more lemons than bananas" (Dick Friendlich, *Relief Pitcher,* 1964; Charles D. Poe). **2.** *n.* A thrown baseball that sails off to one side and misses its mark. **3.** *v.* To throw a banana ball; e.g., "Smith's throw to second bananaed and pulled Jones off the bag."

**banana boat** A player who has played winter ball in Latin America. Joseph C. Goulden recalls: "A derisive name for minor leaguers who played Central American and Mexican baseball during the off-seasons in the late 1940s, employed chiefly by bench jockeys of opposing teams. This was the period when a three-year man in Class C baseball might earn upwards of $225 monthly during the regular season, so he went south for both the money and the experience. The next summer, however, he would hear the growl, 'banana boat, banana boat, TOOT TOOT TOOT!' from the other team's dugout."

**banana oil** A mythical solver of all problems on and off the field. **1st Use.** 1943. "But the old banana oil of psychology would be the right lubricant" (*Baseball Magazine,* Jan.; David Shulman).

**banana stalk** A bat of inferior wood or low quality. "This banana stalk won't crack an aspirin" (Ad in *Time* magazine with a theme of baseball slang, Nov. 22, 1948; Peter Tamony). Syn. "banana stick." **1st Use.** 1937. (*The Sporting News Record Book;* Edward J. Nichols).

**bandbox** A ballpark whose small dimensions make it easier to hit home runs; e.g., Baker Bowl in Philadelphia in the early 1930s and Ebbets Field in Brooklyn in the 1950s. Today the term is most likely to attach itself to Fenway Park (which John Updike termed a "lyric little green bandbox") in Boston and Wrigley Field in Chicago. Among the newer ballparks, the term has been applied to Oriole Park at Camden Yards, The Ballpark in Arlington, and Coors Field. The term is sometimes used to suggest that a batter's numbers are less impressive because of the dimensions of his home field. At the end of the 1988 season, Jose Canseco (Oakland A's) said that the record posted by Mike Greenwell (Boston Red Sox) was diminished "because he plays in a bandbox" (*The Sporting News,* Oct. 10, 1988). "The best moments of my life were spent in the old [San Francisco] Seals Stadium at 16th and Potrero, a beautiful little bandbox of a ball park" (*Anderson Valley Advertiser,* Boonville, Calif., May 21, 1986). See also *crackerbox.* Also spelled "band box." **1st Use.** 1906. (*Sporting Life,* Feb. 10; Edward J. Nichols). **Etymology.** A reference to the bandstands and band boxes that were common in small towns at the turn of the century.

**bang** A base hit. **1st Use.** 1888. (*New York Press;* Edward J. Nichols).

**bang-bang play 1.** An attempted tag or force play at a base when the runner and the ball arrive simultaneously. The action happens in quick succession, making it difficult for the umpire (and spectators) to determine whether the runner is safe or out. "I blew a play at first base. I admit it. I was wrong. But I wasn't *that* wrong. It was a bang-bang play and I anticipated the throw arriving before it did and I called the runner out." (Ron Luciano, *The Umpire Strikes Back,* 1982; Charles D. Poe). Compare *tap-tap play.* **2.** Any defensive play accomplished with precision and speed.

**banger** A big hitter in the heart of a team's lineup.

**bangup game** *arch.* A well-played, exciting baseball game. **1st Use.** 1914. (*New York Tribune,* Sept. 27; Edward J. Nichols).

**banish** For an umpire to eject a player, coach, or manager from a game. **1st Use.** 1912. (*New York Tribune,* Apr. 21; Edward J. Nichols).

**banjo eyes** The wide-eyed look of a batter attempting to steal a sign from the catcher while at the plate. J. G. Taylor Spink attributes this term to Chicago Cub second baseman Billy Herman (Fred Lieb, *Comedians and Pranksters of Baseball,* 1958).

**banjo hit 1.** A weak hit as the result of a poor swing or accidental contact with the ball, such as one made on a check swing. **2.** A hit that falls between the infield and outfield; a *Texas Leaguer.* **Etymology/1st Use.** 1937. According to both Tim Considine (*The Language of Sport,* 1982) and Lee Allen (*The Hot Stove League,* 1955), the term was coined in 1924 by Jersey City second baseman Ray "Snooks" Dowd for the way the ball "plunks" off the bat. Edward J. Nichols first found the term in print in the *Pittsburgh Press* (Jan. 11, 1937).

**banjo hitter** A hitter who cannot hit the long ball. When basketball legend Michael Jordan tried his hand at baseball in 1994, he was widely described as a banjo hitter. On his leaving, Dave Kindred (*The Sporting News,* Mar. 20, 1995) wrote: "The woods are full of banjo hitters. But Jordan's leaving is important for what it says about baseball." **Usage Note.** Although it underscores the inability to hit for distance, the term is not necessarily derogatory as it can be applied to an effective place hitter. "As a baseball player, little Bert Campaneris dreams of powering the ball over distant fences such as Hank Aaron or Willie Mays, but he is happy at being a banjo hitter with a pair of speedy legs" (Associated Press dispatch, Oct. 17, 1973; Peter Tamony). **1st Use.** 1943. "A 'banjo hitter' is one who hits pop flies over the field" (*Baseball Magazine,* Jan. 1943; David Shulman).

**Banks' dictum** The name given to Chicago Cubs Ernie Banks' famous line, "It's a great day for a ball game. *Let's play two!*" The line is quoted often and widely and tends to be uttered when the weather is mild and the players are primed. To many, the line captures the spirit and joy of the game of baseball. It could never, for instance, be

**Barnstorm.** *A National League troop that barnstormed from Chicago to Honolulu in the off-season. This undated photograph was sent to the National Baseball Hall of Fame and Museum by Fred C. Snodgrass, one of the players depicted.*

major-league players as Bob Stanley, George Foster, Tug McGraw, and Ferguson Jenkins.

**barrage** Many hits and/or runs in close succession; e.g., "[Scott Erickson] left the Rangers' third [inning] shell-shocked by a six-run, seven-hit barrage" (*Baltimore Sun*, Apr. 18, 1998).

**barrel** The top, thick, or heavy part of the bat, often referred to as *good wood.*

**barrelhoop curve** A sweeping curveball. **1st Use.** 1910. (*American Magazine*, June; Edward J. Nichols).

**Bart Giamatti Award** An annual award, named for 1989 Commissioner A. Bartlett Giamatti, given to the game's model citizens. The first award in 1991 was given to Cal Ripken Jr.; the second was given to Glenn Davis (who founded the Glenn Davis Home for Boys).

**base 1.** One of the four corners or points of the baseball diamond, each 90 feet from the next. Each base is an incremental unit used in reaching

the fourth unit and scoring a run. Only one runner is allowed on any base at one time. **2.** A marker representing a base. The home base is a rubberized plate; the other three are canvas bags measuring 15 × 15 inches. See also *bag,* 1; *cushion; hassock; pillow; sack; station.* **1st Use.** 1845. (Knickerbocker Rules, rule 4). **Extended Use.** To "touch base" is to make contact, to "touch all the bases" is to be thorough, to be "off base" is to be wrong, and to be "off one's base" is to be out of one's mind. In the language of teenage sexuality, knowing your way "around the bases" was (is?) to know that first base was kissing, second base was petting above the waist, third base was petting below the waist, and a home run was sexual intercourse. **3.** Syn. of *stake,* 1. **4.** An early term for the game of baseball.

**base ball** *arch.* An earlier spelling of "baseball" that is seldom used today but was dominant in the 19th century. **1st Use.** 1817. "It was not very wonderful that Catherine [Morland], who had by nature nothing heroic about her, should prefer cricket, base ball, riding on horseback, and running

**Baseball.** *Woodcut showing a precursor of baseball. It first appeared in the book* Children's Amusements, *published in New York in 1820.*

about the country, at the age of fourteen, to books" (Jane Austen, *Northanger Abbey,* written in 1798 but not published until 1817).

**base-ball 1.** *arch.* An earlier spelling of "base-ball." The term was commonly hyphenated around the turn of the 20th century; e.g., the 1896 rules and specifications of the Government Printing Office call for it to be written in this manner. **2.** The traditional British game of *rounders.* **1st Use.** 1744. "B is for/Base-ball/The Ball once struck off,/Away flies the Boy/To the next destin'd Post,/And then Home with Joy" (John Newberry's *A Little Pretty Pocket-Book,* published in London in 1744, republished in the United States several times between 1762 and 1787). The earliest citation of the hyphenated term in the United States is *Porter's Spirit of the Times* (May 29, 1858) in an article on the Massachusetts game (Fred Ivor-Campbell).

**baseball 1.** The game itself, comprising a body of rules, records, and traditions and played at many levels from that of young children to the seasoned professionals. *Official Baseball Rules* (rule 1.01): "Baseball is a game between two teams of nine players each, under the direction of a manager, played on an enclosed field in accordance with these rules, under jurisdiction of one or more umpires." Baseball also has been defined many ways in many quarters, including this Freudian interpretation: "The pitcher-father tries to complete a throw into the mitt of his mate crouched over home plate. A series of sons step up and each in turn tries to intercept the throw. If any of them is successful, he can win 'home' and defeat the pitcher—if he is able first to complete a hazardous journey out of the adult world of the father's allies." (Thomas Gould, *The Ancient Quarrel between Poetry and Philosophy,* quoted in *New York Times Magazine,* Sept. 11, 1983). Abbrev. *BB.* **2.**

The leather-covered ball (horsehide until 1975, then cowhide) used to play the game of baseball, being not less than nine nor more than 9¼ inches in circumference. "Save that old Spalding major league baseball. It'll soon be a collector's item" (*Washington Star,* June 21, 1975). **3.** The organized game in its entirety; the "industry." "Baseball has never answered any charges directed against it by anyone regarding the war records of its players" (*Springfield* [Mass.] *Union,* May 5, 1954). **4.** [softball term] See *indoor baseball.* **5.** [softball term] Women's fast pitch softball; specif., "baseball modified." It is of some significance that despite the title, in Viola Mitchell's *Softball for Girls* (1942), the terms "softball" and "baseball" were used interchangeably. **1st Use.** 1877. "The present Board of Directors forming the Cincinnati Ball Club Association have already begun their arrangements for a brilliant season of baseball in Cincinnati next year" (*Cincinnati Enquirer,* Aug. 7, 1877; Fred Ivor-Campbell). **Extended Use.** 1. A general metaphor for other organized activities relying on teamwork. "R. Sargent Shriver, Jr., director of the Peace Corps, said today the Corps will be operated like a baseball team, with the manager empowered to yank out a player before he ruins the game" (Associated Press dispatch, May 18, 1961; Peter Tamony). 2. A method of wagering; e.g., in dog racing: "And the most popular method of selecting quinellas is called, by golly, a 'baseball.' Since there generally are eight greyhounds in each race, students of the sport have noticed there can be a problem in forecasting the two which will run best. So, in a 'baseball' you select three lean pooches, which means you're betting on three combinations. With this baseball though, there are more wild pitches than two-baggers" (Harry Jupiter, *San Francisco Examiner,* Mar. 20, 1967; Peter Tamony). 3. Any of several children's games that ape the scoring of baseball but that do not involve other elements of the game; specif., a mumblety-peg-like jackknife game played under flexible rules by two or more children who toss a pocketknife with two open blades and depending on how the knife sticks in the ground, the thrower is credited with a single, double, triple, or home run, or if the knife lands

flat, the thrower is out (*The Dictionary of American Regional English,* under the heading for "baseball"). 4. A baseball-shaped grenade, 2.5 inches in diameter, used during the Vietnam War. Also, "baseball grenade," a nickname for a handheld explosive device which is baseball-shaped and meant to be thrown in the manner of a baseball. "Pieces of a 'baseball grenade' that sent half a dozen policemen scurrying from Taraval station will be turned over to Army ordnance experts" (*San Francisco News,* Mar. 25, 1954; Peter Tamony).

**baseball age** An attempt to appear younger. Dave Anderson (*New York Times,* Feb. 1, 1990): "Through the years, many baseball players have lied about their ages. Their 'baseball age' is always a year or two younger than their real age." Jim Bouton (*Ball Four,* 1970) writes: "Most baseball people have two ages, real and baseball. The older they get the greater the discrepancy between their numbers."

**Baseball Annie** A generic name for an unattached woman who favors the company of baseball players. The phrase was given prominence after the Phillies's Eddie Waitkus was shot without provocation on June 15, 1949. "He sat up in bed and tolerantly described Ruth [Steinhagen, a 19-year-old] as a 'Baseball Annie,' one of an army of hero-worshiping teen-age girls who follow the players around" (*Time* magazine, June 17, 1949; Peter Tamony). Although the term is not as commonly used as it once was, it is still used in special situations; e.g., "Margo Adams, who has filed a $6 million palimony suit against [Wade] Boggs, has been categorized by some as a Baseball Annie, a woman attracted to ballplayers" (Ira Berkow, *New York Times,* Aug. 12, 1988). See also *Baseball Sadie; Chicago Shirley.*

**baseball arm** A nonmedical term for a painful throwing arm that can take a pitcher out of the rotation or hamper a fielder; any sore arm produced from playing baseball. See also *baseball pitcher's arm.* **Extended Use.** The term can be applied to players in other sports as well. "Baseball arm will be the long-range football problem at Stanford during the interim until plans start for the next big game" (*San Francisco Call Bulletin,* Nov. 24, 1952; Peter Tamony).

**Baseball Assistance Team** An organization that raises money for indigent and needy retired ballplayers and others associated with baseball. Abbrev. *BAT.*

**baseball bat** See *bat,* 1.

**baseball bedroom** A room in a boardinghouse without sink or toilet, so called because it featured "a pitcher on the dresser and a catcher underneath the bed."

**baseball bet** A bet on a baseball game. **Extended Use.** A horse-racing bet involving a parlay on three or more horses.

**baseball bride** The wife of a baseball player. **Extended Use.** One's ninth wife, after the fact that there are nine players on a baseball field. "Bandleader Charlie Barnett breezed into town last night with his 'baseball bride'" (*San Francisco News,* Aug. 18, 1955; Peter Tamony).

**baseball bug** *arch.* An earlier term for *baseball fever.* "Just as eagerly is the baseball bug watched these days as the proverbial ground hog" (*Daily Argus* [Mount Vernon, N.Y.], March 13, 1911). A 1940s-vintage Bugs Bunny cartoon entitled "Baseball Bugs" may be a play on this term.

**baseball cage** Syn. of *batting cage,* 1.

**baseball camp** A commercial enterprise, usually operated by former major-league players and dedicated to teaching beginning and semiexperienced youths the fundamentals of baseball. The periods of instruction vary from camp to camp. Not to be confused with *fantasy baseball camp.* Syn. *baseball school.*

**baseball cap** The billed hat worn by baseball players. It was once rigid custom for a player to doff or touch the peak of his cap when crossing home plate after hitting a home run. **Extended Use.** The term is just as likely to show up in a news story as on the sports pages: "Two gunmen wearing black baseball caps escaped with an estimated $2,500 from the Gary Federal Savings and Loan . . . this morning" (*Gary Post Tribune,* Aug. 12, 1967). A *Washington Post* (Feb. 28, 1993) edi-

**Baseball bedroom.** *The elements of a baseball bedroom comically depicted in a turn-of-the-century postcard.*

torial entitled "Hail to the Cap" noted: "The baseball cap, an item once worn almost exclusively by young boys . . . has come quite a distance in recent years. This week the President of the United States was wearing one on his travels, and he wasn't doing it in the consciously folksy way some past presidents have but rather as part of the standard all-business garb of a chief executive: hard shoes, suit, tie, dignified topcoat . . . baseball cap."

**baseball card** A piece of cardboard depicting a baseball player, a group of players, or a team; a *trading card* with a baseball motif. Approximately the size of a playing card, most feature a picture of a baseball player, past or present, on one side and appropriate biographical data and career statistics on the other side. Baseball cards are collected and

**Baseball Card.** *This small photographic depiction of the Brooklyn Athletics, with an 1865 copyright, is exactly the size of a modern baseball card (3½ × 2½ inches).*

traded, and many are collectors' items. They have been included as a premium with tobacco and chewing gum, as well as such widely diverse products as soft drinks, bread, potato chips, candy, and breakfast cereals. They have been produced in many shapes and sizes.

There are no rules as to what can or cannot appear on a baseball card, but the established format is to feature a portrait or action photograph of the player on one side of the card and statistics and biographical information on the flip side. The growing variety of baseball cards is suggested in these lines from a Topps Chewing Gum Inc. press release: "The 1988 card series will consist of 792 cards. This will consist of 700 regular cards, 26 team cards, 26 manager cards, 22 All-Star cards, 7 record-breaker cards, 6 checklists and 5 Turn-Back-The-Clock cards. Included among the 700 regular

player cards will be five cards designated as 'Future Stars' and ten cards designated as 'Topps All-Star Rookie.'" See also *bubble-gum card.*

**Baseball Chapel** An organization of religious major- and minor-league baseball players based in Bloomingdale, N.J., and dedicated to spreading Christian gospel to players throughout North America.

**baseball club** See *club,* 1 and 2.

**baseball code** Preordained behavior; unwritten rules. Ross Atkin (*Christian Science Monitor,* May 5, 1997) writes: "If an opposing pitcher knocks down one of his teammates, a player expects his pitcher to get even and knock down the other pitcher, or one of the opposition players. It's part of the baseball code."

**baseball diamond** See *diamond.*

**baseballdom** The domain of baseball, especially professional baseball. "Current Gossip From Baseballdom" was once a typical name for a column on the sport. See also *balldom.*

**baseballeer** *arch.* A rarely used term for a baseball player or fan in the earlier days of the 20th century. The most recent example of its use is by Frank G. Menke (*New Encyclopedia of Sports,* 1944): "The report was like some heaven-sent gift which arrived for the harassed baseballeer."

**baseballer** A baseball player. "And Mr. Clarke sadly advises all golfers, cricketeers and baseballers that the moon, with its reduced gravitational pull, is no place to swat a ball" (*New York Times Book Review,* Apr. 25, 1955). Although the term has a certain anachronistic whiff to it, citations are still made: "Equally sleek are the customers at Rusty's Restaurant, 1271 Third Ave., owned by baseballer Rusty Staub" (*Harpers Bazaar,* Feb. 1981). **Extended Use.** Those who freebase cocaine, smoking it as a pure powder through a water pipe. A comment about Hollywood: "There are a lot of baseballers in those hills" (*Newsweek,* June 23, 1980).

**baseballese 1.** The overall language of baseball, comprising official terminology, slang, and jargon. "They liked his language—some of it authentic American baseballese, but most of it just plain Dizzy Dean" (Norman Cousins, *Saturday Review,* Aug. 2, 1946). **1st Use.** 1912. "Some writers call it 'baseballese'; you call it either one you please." (Edmund Vance Cooke, *Baseballogy*) **2.** The language of baseball players as distinguished from that of those who write about the game. This distinction is made forcefully by William G. Brandt (*Baseball Magazine,* Oct. 1932): "That Unrecognized Language—Baseballese." After giving some authentic examples, Brandt writes: "That's baseballese. [*You Know Me Al* author] Ring Lardner's half-wit bushers don't talk that way. Nor any of the sluggers in the baseball yarns you read in 'Flimsy Stories.' In fact you won't read baseballese anywhere."

**baseball farm** A minor-league team. "The San Jose Bees, a very minor league team, almost won a championship in 1973, providing a semi-dramatic framework for a determinedly undramatic overview of life on the modern, mechanized baseball farm" (Robert Lipsyte, *New York Times,* Apr. 6, 1975). See also *farm,* 1.

**baseball fever** Passion for the game of baseball. It usually starts with spring training and ends after the World Series. The motto of organized baseball in television ads in the early 1990s was "Baseball fever—catch it!" See also *baseball bug.* **1st Use.** 1881. "Violent attack of Base Ball Fever at the Central Market" (*Detroit Free Press,* May 21; Peter Morris).

**baseball field** The surface on which a baseball game is played, usually located in a park or stadium. "A baseball field is found on the edge of the settlement and baseball seems to be the favorite sport" (*Harper's Magazine,* June 1902).

**baseball finger** Digital syndrome defined as a "disruption of the tendon to the tip of a finger caused by the ball striking the finger" (*Annals of Western Medicine and Surgery,* 1952). **1st Use.** 1889. "Then, can you tell me what a base-ball finger is?" "A WHAT?" "A base-ball finger! I heard an American lady use that term." (A. C. Gunter, *That Frenchman;* David Shulman).

**baseball fingers** "Thickened, distorted fingers caused by injuries received in excessive playing of baseball" (Erle Fiske Young, *The New Social Worker's Dictionary,* 1941). **Extended Use.** The term also shows up as a generic name for distorted fingers. "Fingers distorted at the joints by accident are called 'baseball fingers' and are frequently marks of identification" (*New York Daily Tribune,* Dec. 20, 1903).

**baseball grenade** See *baseball* (**Extended Use,** 4).

**baseball grip** The general manner in which the bat is held firmly by a batter, with one's two fists touching but not linked. **Extended Use.** A method for holding a golf club that was made popular by professional golfers Bob Rosberg and Art Wall in the late 1950s. It bears some resemblance to the grip used by a baseball player in holding a bat, although the left thumb is not tucked in but extends along the shaft.

**Baseball fever.** *Fans climbing the fences at the Huntington Avenue Baseball Grounds in Boston for a view of the first modern World Series between Boston and Pittsburgh.*

**baseball gum** The thin piece of aromatic, pink bubble gum included in certain packages of baseball cards. The practice of pairing gum and baseball cards began in 1933 when the Goudey Gum Co. of Boston issued a set of cards depicting 239 famous players. Though paper and latex shortages during World War II brought production to a halt, some companies began issuing gum and cards as soon as the war ended. When the Topps Co. (Brooklyn, N.Y.) began manufacturing its own cards in 1951, the collecting and trading of baseball cards became a fad. "Just chew it like baseball gum" (Hunter S. Thompson, *Fear and Loathing in Las Vegas,* 1971).

**Baseball Hall of Fame** See *Hall of Fame.*

**baseballia** Materials concerning or characteristic of baseball and the culture of baseball; collectible baseball Americana.

**baseballically** Relating to the game of baseball. "The Babe was one of my children, you know, baseballically speaking. First Lou [Gehrig] and now the Babe." (Edward G. Barrow, retired Yankee president and the man who converted Babe Ruth from a pitcher to an outfielder, quoted at the time of Ruth's death, *Washington Star,* Aug. 17, 1948).

**baseball immortal** Any of the greatest and most influential players to play the game, an individual who presumably will never be forgotten. The title is totally subjective and seems to be bestowed on one who has had an effect on the very nature of the game. It is bestowed by common and repeated usage; e.g., if almost all of the nation's sportswriters call Ty Cobb a "baseball immortal," he is one. Caption for a *New Yorker* cartoon (Aug. 16, 1982) in which two angels eye a uniformed New York Yankee with a halo and wings: "I don't care if he *is* a baseball immortal, he should wear a robe and carry a harp like the rest of us." See also *immortal; eleven immortals; Hall of Famer.*

**baseballism** An expression or custom peculiar to the game of baseball. Calling a team's locker room a "clubhouse," as is the practice, is a baseballism. Another is that the manager of a baseball team customarily dresses in the team uniform (unlike the coach in other sports who wears street clothes).

**baseballist** *arch.* One who plays or is in some other way closely associated with the game of baseball. It was a term of honor, as can be heard in a speech by Rep. J. M. Glover of Missouri (*The Congressional Record,* Apr. 2, 1886): "[He is well known] as a baseballist among constitutional lawyers, and a constitutional lawyer among baseballists." Sometimes spelled "base-ballist." **Usage Note.** The term was fairly common in the 19th century for a person who would be termed a "ballplayer" today. A headline in *National Police Gazette* (Sept. 20, 1890): "Young Lady Baseballists." **1st Use.** 1866. "That illustrious base-ballist, Mr. Blindman, was appointed umpire" (*The Galaxy;* David Shulman).

**baseballistics** Baseball statistics. The term was used by Bert Randolph Sugar for the title of his 1990 book.

**baseballite** *arch.* A baseball fan; a person with an enthusiasm for the sport. The term seems to have been in vogue in the 1930s and may have been a poke at the word "socialite."

**baseballitis** A mock-disease name for infatuation with the game of baseball. "Since early childhood I've been afflicted with a near-fatal illness known as diamond fever or, to call it by its medical term, baseballitis" (Frank Barnicle, *Clearwater* [Fla.] *Times,* Apr. 4, 1986). "Baseball-itis" is the title of V. H. Smalley's one-act comedy (1910). **1st Use.** 1909. (*Baseball Magazine,* Sept.).

**baseball jacket** A coat designed to keep the upper body and arms warm, often worn by a player when he is warming up or practicing before a game, or in the dugout during a game, but never when actually playing the game. **Extended Use.** An outer garment of the same style. "He [a rock star] wears a baseball jacket piped in red" (*New Times,* Nov. 1973).

**baseball jackknife** See *baseball* (**Extended Use,** 3).

**baseball leather** The outer skin or cover of a baseball, made from fronts of horsehides until 1975 when cowhide was used. Sheepskin is used for inexpensive baseballs.

**baseball lifer** See *lifer.*

**baseball man** A professional who knows, loves, and understands the game of baseball, whether he be an owner, manager, coach, scout, player, or trainer; e.g., Charles S. "Chub" Feeney was "the very definition of the vanishing species known as Baseball Men" (Ron Fimrite's obituary of Feeney, *Sports Illustrated,* Jan. 24, 1994). Syn. *baseball person.* **Usage Note.** To be called a "baseball man" is a major compliment, and to be told that one is not is to be marked as an outsider to the game. "[Maine Guides owner Jordan] Kobritz is a good businessman, but no matter how much research he did and how many books he read he could not turn himself into a baseball man" (*Maine Sunday Telegram,* Aug. 31, 1986).

**baseball martini** A drink composed of four parts gin and one part cigar smoke, a staple of the winter banquet circuit, which, according to Arnold Hano (*Willie Mays,* 1966), "never done anything to a player except make him fat and acquaint him with a baseball martini."

**baseball mother** A dedicated woman who, in the process of ferrying her children to baseball practice and games, becomes a dedicated supporter. "In her case she is a baseball mother. So even though she was due at a class reunion one recent evening and perhaps should have been at home washing her hair or on her way to the Detroit airport to pick up her husband, Lou, there she was in the bleachers, watching her 14-year-old son Ken play in a Babe Ruth League game." (*New York Times,* July 3, 1976).

**baseball movie** A feature film that includes baseball in a major portion of its fictional scenario with actors playing ballplayers; e.g., *The Natural* (1984), *Bull Durham* (1988), and *Field of Dreams* (1989).

**baseball mud** A special composition of earth used to rub up a baseball to give it a uniform gripping surface. In practice it removes the sheen from new baseballs. See also *rubbing mud.*

**Baseball Network, The 1.** An organization formed to find jobs for minorities in baseball. It was founded in the late 1980s by Frank Robinson when he was the only black manager in baseball. **2.** A short-lived (1994–95) joint venture by ABC, NBC, and Major League Baseball to create regional television coverage for the last 12 weeks of the regular season and the first round of the playoffs by sharing network advertising revenues (in lieu of broadcast rights fees), production facilities and costs, and corporate sponsorship.

**baseball nut** A baseball fan who is unusually exuberant about the game.

**baseballogy** A term used by Edmund Vance Cooke for the title of a collection of baseball ballads (1912) incorporating the mention of prominent players.

**baseball parachute** Extended Use. A parachute used by the Navy during World War II for mine-laying and precision deliveries of delicate cargoes. "Unlike conventional chutes, which swing their loads in pendulum fashion, the baseball chute has a hemispheric canopy cut like a baseball cover and deposits its burden gently and vertically on the ground" (*Life* magazine, Jan. 7, 1946).

**baseball park** *arch.* Syn. of *ballpark.*

**baseball pass** Extended Use. A one-handed, overhead basketball pass that requires making a motion similar to that when throwing a baseball. It is used to pass to a teammate cutting downcourt and is essential to the repertory of members of fast-breaking teams.

**baseball person** Syn. of *baseball man.*

**baseball pitcher's arm** A malady often caused by throwing a baseball; "a condition of sprain, with pain and soreness over the points of insertion of the muscles, occurring sometimes as a result of overuse by base-ball players" (*Century Dictionary,* 1909). See also *baseball arm.*

**baseball pitcher's elbow** A "fracture of bone or cartilage from the head of the radius at the elbow due to strenuous baseball pitching" (*Journal of the American Medical Association,* 1930).

**baseball player** Syn. of *ballplayer.*

**Baseball Player of the Year** Formerly an annual award made by Seagram's Distillers and based on fan voting, but since 1988 an award given by the Associated Press (AP) based on balloting by sportswriters and broadcasters. In 1995 Greg Maddux became the first pitcher to win the AP award with all previous titles bestowed on position players.

**baseball poker** Extended Use. A form of seven-card stud. According to Albert A. Ostrow (*The Complete Card Player),* it varies from the conventional game of seven-card stud through these exceptions: a) a three of any suit dealt faceup makes a player's hand dead, and he must drop out of play; b) a three of any suit dealt face down is wild; c) a four of any suit dealt faceup entitles the player to have an extra card dealt faceup; and d) all nines are wild. The fact that it is called "baseball poker" probably derives from the fact that a face card with a three on it puts one in the manner of three strikes being an out in baseball.

**baseball pool** An illegal lottery in which one wagers on the appearance of a certain set of winning numbers taken from the box scores of different baseball games. It is a form of gambling that has been popular since about 1900 and is a variation on the numbers game or numbers pool, which gets its winning number from horse racing or stock market totals. It has existed in many variations, including, it seems, crooked ones: "It's anybody's guess as to how much money fans have tossed into a bottomless well playing phony baseball pools" (*Easy Money* magazine, July 1936).

**baseball-rounders** *obs.* A largely forgotten hybrid game of American baseball and British rounders (J. M. Walker, *Rounders and Quoits,* 1892).

**baseball rule** A legal concept that bars spectators who are injured by flying baseballs from suing teams for injury. A court in Milwaukee ruled that the Admirals hockey team was protected by the baseball rule even though the offending object was a hockey puck. (*Milwaukee Journal Sentinel,* Sept. 9, 1997).

**Baseball Sadie** A woman whose weakness is ballplayers. See also *Baseball Annie.*

**baseball's attic** Nickname for *National Baseball Library and Archives* in Cooperstown, N.Y. "A Library Known as 'Baseball's Attic'" (*New York Times* headline, July 31, 1984). The term was probably inspired by "nation's attic," the old nickname for the Smithsonian Institution.

**baseball scholarship** A scholarship given to an outstanding high school baseball player to play on a college team. Often, the recipient is optioned by a major-league club toward the end of his college years.

**baseball school** Syn. of *baseball camp.*

**baseball score** The outcome of a baseball game. **Extended Use.** The term is used in football for a low-scoring game, such as winning by a baseball score of 6–3 or 3–0.

**baseball sense** Instinct for making the correct move, whether it be in a play on the field or an advantageous trade.

**baseball shoe** A special shoe designed for and worn by baseball players that features cleats for traction and a full set of laces for support. Harold R. Quimby (*The Shoe Dictionary,* 1955): "A shoe built of leather for the sport indicated with sole having cleats or plugs to prevent slipping. Usually laced to the toe." Syn. *cleats,* 2; *spikes,* 2.

**baseball shot Extended Use.** An attempt to score in basketball by throwing the ball with a motion similar to that of throwing a baseball. Boston Celtics head coach Red Auerbach forecast that this technique would have a major impact on the future of basketball (*The Sporting News,* Dec. 23, 1959): "It can't miss. Some kid with unusually big hands will come along and wind up like a baseball pitcher, or a football passer, and throw the ball in."

**baseball shoulder** A painful and debilitating shoulder of a player, usually a pitcher, that expresses itself medically with calcific deposits and fraying of the tendons (*Journal of* the *American Medical Association,* Nov. 21, 1959).

**baseball sleeve Extended Use.** Short (usually ¾ length), cuffless sleeve common to the shirts worn under the short-sleeved uniform shirt. "[The baseball sleeve is] the important detail of jersey blouses worn under dresses, jackets and jumpers which have short sleeves of their own and a cutaway neckline which reveals turtle neck, cowl-drape or two-inch band of the jersey neckline" (*Women's Wear Daily,* June 4, 1952).

**"Baseball's Sad Lexicon"** Title of a 1908 poem by Franklin P. Adams that appeared in the *New York Globe* and featured the double-play combination of *Tinker to Evers to Chance.*

**baseball stitch** A sewing stitch, worked under and over from the inside, for meeting the two edges of the leather cover being sewed on a baseball. The sewing technique makes two edges meet exactly, rather than overlap. No machine has yet been devised to sew baseballs, which are all produced by hand. **Extended Use.** This sewing technique is often used when mending sails. It is also likely to show up in other areas, such as tent repair: "Better way still is to sew large tears with a baseball stitch using greased thread" (Joe Godfrey Jr. & Frank Dufresne, *The Great Outdoors,* 1949).

**baseball strike** See *strike.*

**Baseball's Valhalla** Syn. of *Cooperstown,* 1.

**baseball swing** A swing used in activities other than baseball, but resembling a batter's attempt to hit a pitched ball, such as a golfer when driving the ball.

**baseball team** See *team.*

**baseball throw** A field event, now rare, in which individuals throw a baseball for distance.

**baseball toss** A contest to determine the ability to throw a baseball for distance and accuracy.

**baseball widow** A woman who loses her husband to the ballpark, television set, or radio during the baseball season. The husband spends so much time watching and listening to the games that the wife is virtually abandoned.

**baseball widower** A man who loses his wife to the ballpark, television set, or radio during the baseball season. The wife spends so much time watching and listening to the games that the husband is virtually abandoned.

**baseball wife** A wife whose baseball-player husband is away from home often and for extended periods of time and therefore often carries the burden of family life.

**baseballwise** In a manner pertaining to baseball. **1st Use.** An early use was recorded on the radio broadcast of the first game of the 1946 World Series (Oct. 6) when it was observed "baseballwise the day is perfect."

**baseball with cards** A game in which the various situations and events from the game of baseball are evoked by turning over playing cards from a shuffled deck.

**baseball with dice** A game in which the various situations and events from the game of baseball are evoked by throwing dice. The complete rules of the game (*Foster's Complete Hoyle,* 1928): "Each side has 3 dice, to represent 3 strikes. Only aces count as runs, and as long as a side scores it continues to throw. Nine turns in a game."

**Baseball Writers Association of America** An association of writers and beat reporters who cover a major-league team for an accredited news organization on a daily basis. It was founded in 1908 by two dozen disgruntled writers infuriated by their treatment during the pennant races and World Series: they demanded and received permanent press box facilities in all parks. The Association provides official scorers, consults on rule changes, and participates in Hall of Fame elections. Abbrev. *BWAA* or *BBWAA.*

**basebally** Quintessentially baseball; characteristic of the game. Miss Manners (columnist Judith Martin) on spitting in baseball (*Baltimore Sun,* Oct. 21, 1993): "If it's properly done (not aimed at anyone or anyone's shoes) it's part of the charm. It's a terribly basebally thing to do."

**baseball year** A period of 184 days (Jim Palmer, telecast, Apr. 12, 1989).

**base-ballyhoo** *arch.* Hyperbole and boosterism sometimes associated with the game of baseball; bunkum baseball-style.

**basebrawl** A fight among baseball players, triggered by an event such as a batter charging the mound after being hit by a pitched ball. Steve Wulf (*Sports Illustrated,* Aug. 16, 1993) characterized Nolan Ryan's pummeling of Robin Ventura as a "basebrawl," epitomizing "a baseball season marred by bench-clearing incidents."

**base clogger** A slow runner. Mickey Mantle on New York Yankee teammate Elston Howard: "We called him 'base clogger' because if you hit a double you had to stop at first and wait up for him" (*The Mick,* 1985; Charles D. Poe).

**base coach** One of the two uniformed team members positioned in the coach's box at first base and third base to direct the batter and baserunners and to relay signs. Syn. *wig-wagger.*

**base-getter** *arch.* One who achieves a base and advances with regularity. **1st Use.** 1911. "But Arthur has made him into a great field captain and a base-getter of remarkable skill" (Zane Grey, *The Young Pitcher;* David Shulman).

**base hit 1.** A batted ball on which the batter advances safely to, but no farther than, first base; a *single.* **2.** A batted ball that permits the batter to get on any base safely with no error being made and no baserunner being forced out on the play. See also *hit,* 1. Syn. *base knock.* **1st Use.** 1874. (Henry Chadwick, *Baseball Manual;* Edward J. Nichols).

**base jockey** A runner who, when on first base, yells derisive comments to the opposing pitcher.

**base knock** Syn. of *base hit,* 2. See also *knock,* 2.

**baseline** One of four lines connecting the bases; specif., the white chalk marking between home plate and first base and between home plate and third base and the imaginary line between first base and second base and between second base and third base. Compare *basepath*. Also spelled "base line." **1st Use.** 1869. (*New York Herald,* Aug. 5; Edward J. Nichols).

**baseman** A defensive player assigned to cover first base, second base, or third base. Syn. *bagman; sacker; station keeper.* **1st Use.** 1891. (*New York Evening Post,* July 9; Edward J. Nichols).

**basement** Syn. of *cellar.* **1st Use.** 1911. *(Baseball Magazine,* Oct.; Edward J. Nichols).

**basement troop** A team at the bottom of the standings.

**base on balls** An advance to first base awarded to a batter who, while at bat, accepts four pitches outside the strike zone. In 1889, it was ruled that, in the course of one at-bat, four balls would result in a walk. In the years preceding 1889, the rule changed with confusing regularity: before 1880 (9 balls for a walk); 1880–82 (8 balls); 1882–84 (7 balls); 1884–86 (6 balls); 1886 (7 balls); 1887–89 (5 balls); and 1889 to the present (4 balls). Abbrev. *BB.* Syn. *walk,* 1; *Annie Oakley,* 2; *casualty pass; four wide ones; free check; free pass; free passage; free ride; free ticket; free transit; free transportation; free trip; furlough; gift,* 1; *handout; life,* 2; *pass,* 1; *ticket to first.* **1st Use.** 1858. (Chadwick Scrapbooks; Edward J. Nichols). **Extended Use.** To "wait for a base on balls" is to forgo action in the hope that something will happen or to assume a passive posture in an attempt to force one's opponent to make a false move. "U.S. Should Stop Waiting for Bases on Balls" (*San Francisco News* headline for article concerning diplomatic relations with Bulgaria, Feb. 22, 1950; Peter Tamony).

**base on stones** A base hit in which a ground ball strikes a pebble or other impediment causing it to bounce away from a fielder. The use of the term has declined in direct proportion to steady advances in groundskeeping and use of artificial turf. See also *bad hop.* **1st Use.** 1937. (National League Service Bureau, clipping files; Edward J. Nichols).

**base open** Said of a base that is not occupied by a baserunner; esp., said of first base when second base and/or third base are occupied but first base is not.

**basepath** The six-foot-wide lane that connects the four bases and serves as the path along which the baserunner runs and which he cannot leave to avoid a tag. Compare *baseline.* Also spelled "base path." Syn. *runway.* **1st Use.** 1910. (*Baseball Magazine,* Dec.; Edward J. Nichols).

**baseplayer** *arch.* A ballplayer.

**baser** A single. **1st Use.** 1880. (Chicago *Inter-Ocean,* May 19; Edward J. Nichols).

**baserunner** A player on the team at bat who occupies a base or is attempting to reach or return to a base. See also *runner; batter-runner.* Also spelled "base runner." **1st Use.** 1875. (*DeWitt's Base Ball Guide;* Edward J. Nichols).

**baserunning 1.** *n.* The integral facet of the game by which one travels from one base to the next. It includes such skills as leading, sliding, and stealing. Also spelled "base running." **2.** *adj.* Pertaining to one's ability as a baserunner.

**bases bulging** Syn. of *bases loaded.*

**bases choked** Syn. of *bases loaded.*

**bases-clearing** Said of a hit that brings all baserunners home; e.g., "Smith hit a bases-clearing double."

**bases crowded** Syn. of *bases loaded.* **1st Use.** 1912. (*New York Tribune,* Sept. 5; Edward J. Nichols).

**bases drunk** Syn. of *bases loaded.* **1st Use.** 1943. "'Bases drunk' is Jimmie[sic] Dykes' favorite phrase for a 'full house' or three men aboard" (*Baseball Magazine,* Jan.; David Shulman).

**bases empty** Said of a game situation when there are no runners on base.

**bases-empty home run** A home run with no runners on base, thereby scoring no additional runs. Compare *bases-loaded home run.* Syn. *solo home run.*

**bases full** Syn. of *bases loaded.* **1st Use.** 1894. (*Spalding's Official Base Ball Guide;* Edward J. Nichols).

**bases jammed** Syn. of *bases loaded.*

**bases juiced** Syn. of *bases loaded.*

**bases loaded** Said of a game situation when there are runners on first base, second base, and third base. Syn. *bags clogged; bags full; full house; sacks full; sold out,* 1; and various words used with "bases," such as bulging, choked, crowded, drunk, full, jammed, juiced, tenanted, and waterlogged.

**bases-loaded home run.** A home run with runners on each base, resulting in four runs; a *grand slam,* 1. Many regard a bases-loaded home run to be the game's most spectacular offensive play. Compare *bases-empty home run.*

**bases-loaded walk 1.** A base on balls that will put runners on first base, second base, and third base. **2.** A base on balls with the bases loaded.

**base stealer** A runner who advances from one base to the next without the aid of a hit, error, balk, passed ball, wild pitch, base on balls, hit by pitch, outfield throw to another base, or defensive indifference. Generally, a base stealer is a fast runner with an ability to judge the pitcher's attention and reflexes. Sometimes spelled "base-stealer." Syn. *burglar,* 2; *thief.* **1st Use.** 1892. (*New York Press,* Aug. 7; Edward J. Nichols).

**base stealing** The act of a runner advancing a base without the aid of a base hit, putout, error, force out, fielder's choice, balk, passed ball, or wild pitch. Syn. *larceny; petit larceny, thievery.*

**bases tenanted** Syn. of *bases loaded.* **1st Use.** 1908. (*Baseball Magazine;* Edward J. Nichols).

**base-sticker** A baserunner who takes either a short lead off a base or no lead at all.

**bases waterlogged** Syn. of *bases loaded.* **1st Use.** 1910. (*New York Tribune,* July 10; Edward J. Nichols).

**basetender** Syn. of *staketender.*

**base-to-base** Syn. of *station-to-station.*

**base umpire** An umpire stationed at first base, second base, or third base. See also *field umpire.*

**bash** To hit the ball with great power.

**basher** A hitter with great power, such as Mark McGwire.

**Basic Agreement** The overarching labor contract between the owners (Player Relations Committee) and players (Major League Baseball Players Association) that contains virtually all conditions of employment, including pension benefits, minimum salary for major-league players, salary arbitration, rules that govern free agency, and working conditions such as scheduling, discipline, and travel. It was attained as a result of the 1981 baseball players' strike and is renegotiable every three years. Syn. *Collective Bargaining Agreement.*

**basket catch** A catch in which a defensive player cups his glove and bare hand together, close to his body and belt-high, to trap the ball. Although several prominent players (starting with Rabbit Maranville and including Willie Mays) used the technique, Morris A. Shirts (*Warm Up for Little League Baseball,* 1976) advises: "It is not a very good way . . . to catch the ball." See also *vest-pocket*

**Basket catch.** *Walter "Rabbit" Maranville demonstrates the catch that he made famous.*

*catch.* **Etymology.** A likely shortening of *bread-basket catch.*

**basket glove** Syn. of *orange crate.*

**bass-ball** **1.** A variant form of rounders. **2.** Syn. of *rounders.* **1st Use.** 1825. "The undersigned, all residents of the new town of Hamden . . . challenge an equal number of persons of any town in the County of Delaware, to meet them at any time at the house of *Edward B. Chace,* in said town, to play the game of BASS-BALL, for the sum of one dollar each per game" (*Delhi* [Hamden, N.Y.] *Gazette,* July 13, 1825).

**bastard pitch** An unhittable pitch; e.g., a pitch down and away and out of the strike zone.

**bastard play** A baseball play that, if it works, "it's a real bastard for the other team" (Don Wilson, quoted by Jim Bouton, *Ball Four,* 1970). The actual play as described by Wilson occurs in a bunt situation: the first baseman and third baseman charge in for the ball, the shortstop sneaks to third, and the second baseman sneaks over to cover first. "Then whoever fields the ball, fires it to third base. The guy on third fires to first and maybe we get the double play. If we don't, we at least get the lead runner."

**baste** *arch.* To hit a ball hard. **1st Use.** 1891. (*Chicago Herald,* May 12; Edward J. Nichols).

**baste ball** An early form of baseball played on the campus of Princeton University in 1786.

**bat** **1.** *n.* The wooden implement that is used to hit a pitched ball. There are different regulations for bats at various levels of organized baseball and softball, but the major leagues require that it be made of a single piece of wood, which cannot be longer than 42 inches or thicker than 2¾ inches at its thickest point. It is usually made from mountain ash, but originally from hickory. Metal bats are increasingly used at lower levels of the game and almost exclusively in softball. **1st Use.** 1845. (Knickerbocker Rules, rule 9). **2.** *v.* To take a turn as a batter. **1st Use.** 1875. (*DeWitt's Base Ball Guide;* Edward J. Nichols). **3.** *v.* To hit a pitched ball. **4.** *n.* One's hitting ability; e.g., "Ozzie Smith

bulks up in hopes of improving his bat" (*St. Petersburg Times,* April 2, 1987) and "Off-season focus takes nothing from [Eric Davis's] bat" (*Baltimore Sun,* Mar. 10, 1998). **5.** *n.* A player seen in his role as a hitter; "We're looking for a left-handed bat" (Brewers manager Tom Trebelhorn, quoted in *St. Petersburg Times,* Feb. 29, 1988). **Extended Use.** This baseball term has long been borrowed by the greater language:

"Right off the bat": from the start, or immediately. "The producers got the verdict right off the bat, and they are wise enough to fold up and depart when the decision is thumbs down" (*National Police Gazette,* Jan. 14, 1928).

"To go to bat for": to take up someone else's cause or argument. "When Morgenthau went strongly to bat for [the new tax bill], Roosevelt turned on him sharply" (Drew Pearson, *San Francisco Chronicle,* May 23, 1939; Peter Tamony).

"To not get the bat off one's shoulder": not given a chance. On an attorney not being able to make his case: "Being well-known as a Wall Street attorney he didn't even get his bat off his shoulder" (*San Francisco News,* June 8, 1933; Peter Tamony).

"To bat two for three," "to bat three for four," etc.: to be successful but not altogether successful. "Mayor Bats Two for Three on the Washington Circuit" (*San Francisco Call-Bulletin* headline, June 17, 1960; Peter Tamony).

**BAT** Abbrev. for *Baseball Assistance Team.*

**bat around** *v.* To have all nine batters in a team's lineup come to bat during an inning.

**bat-around** *n.* The occasion when all nine batters in a team's lineup come to the plate in an inning. **1st Use.** 1880. (Chicago *Inter-Ocean,* May 19; Edward J. Nichols).

**bat a thousand** See *bat one thousand.*

**bat bag** A canvas or leather duffel bag in which bats are carried. **1st Use.** 1892. (*Brooklyn Daily Eagle,* Aug. 22; Edward J. Nichols).

**batboy** A young man employed by a team to take care of its players' personal equipment before, during, and after games. Traditionally, the most important responsibility of the job is to retrieve each player's bat from home plate where it has been dropped or tossed and put it back in its proper place in the bat rack. The bat boy is also responsible for keeping the home plate umpire supplied with baseballs. "The New York Yankees . . . forgot to vote World Series money to their bat-boys, but rectified the problem the other day by tapping the fine fund and sending each the grand sum of $100" (Melvin Durslag, *San Francisco Examiner,* Feb. 28, 1977). See Neil D. Isaacs, *Batboys and the World of Baseball,* 1995. Abbrev. *BB.* Also spelled "bat boy." **1st Use.** 1909. (*Baseball Magazine,* July; Edward J. Nichols).

**batboy shot** A home run of such clear and immediate magnitude that the batter is simply able to hand his bat to the batboy because he has the time for such a ritual. **Etymology.** According to Joe Goddard (*The Sporting News,* Mar. 6, 1982): "This is the brainchild of Yankee Oscar Gamble, who says he knows when he hits one well and it's out of the park. 'I don't even look at it,' Gamble says. 'I know it's gone. I just turn around and hand my bat to the batboy.'"

**bat breaker** A hard hitter who swings the bat with tremendous force; one whose powerful swings often result in a broken bat.

**bat-burning ceremony** A mostly metaphoric ritual during which the useless bats of a baseball team are burned in a bonfire.

**bat cleanup** To bat in the cleanup position.

**bat control** The ability to use the bat as a tool. Good bat control involves getting a piece of the ball, executing the hit and run, fouling off pitches, and hitting the ball where it is pitched.

**bat day** A promotion at which fans are given a souvenir bat at a baseball game.

**Bates** *arch.* A worn-out or declining player; a veteran player who has seen his best days. Var. "Batesy."

**batfest** Syn. of *batting fest.* **1st Use.** 1913. "For some reason his teammates were beginning to hit Merriwell and Needham wanted his share in the batfest" (Burt L. Standish, *Frank Merriwell, Jr.'s Athletic Team;* David Shulman).

**batgirl** A young woman engaged by a team to take care of the players' bats and other equipment during a game. Also spelled "bat girl." **1st Use.** 1942. "She's the only batgirl in major-league baseball" (*Baseball Magazine,* June).

**bat grip** A sleeve or coating that is placed over the bat handle to give the batter a firmer grip when swinging. It also protects the handle, the thinnest part of the bat, from chipping.

**bat-handle blooper** A ball hit on the slender end of the bat, which lacks power but nevertheless falls in for a hit. "But a bat-handle blooper into right drove both men home" (Dick Friendlich, *Relief Pitcher,* 1964; Charles D. Poe).

**bat head** The thick end of a baseball bat.

**bat in** To get a hit by which one or more runners are able to score.

**bat night** A promotion at which fans are given a souvenir bat at a night baseball game.

**bat one thousand** To be perfect at the plate. Because an average of 1.000 is a virtual impossibility after a dozen or so at-bats, the term finds greater application in baseball fiction (e.g., Bob Allison & Frank Ernest Hill, *The Kid Who Batted 1.000,* 1951) than in real life. Syn. *bat a thousand.* **Extended Use.** To be absolutely correct; to perform flawlessly.

**baton swinger** *arch.* A batter. **1st Use.** 1915. "Only when I use baseball terms—about . . . fanning the baton swinger . . . you say you don't like to hear me talking slang" (Burt L. Standish, *Covering the Look-In Corner;* David Shulman).

**bat production** The ability to make base hits; e.g., "Smith gave the team a boost with his bat production."

**bat rack** An open, slotted box located in front of the dugout or hung from the dugout wall that holds a team's supply of bats during a game. Syn. *lumberyard,* 1.

**Batsman.** *Boy posed with bat circa 1865.*

**bat ring** [softball term] A metal or plastic ring for measuring the diameter or circumference of a legal bat. If the head of the bat will not fit through the ring, the bat is deemed to be illegal and is disallowed for play.

**bats left** Said of a left-handed batter. Abbrev. *BL.*

**batsman** *arch.* Syn. of *batter.* This term was commonly used in the early days of baseball for "the striker at the bat." **1st Use.** 1856. "He who strikes it fairly must be a fine batsman" (*Porter's Spirit of the Times,* Dec. 6; Peter Morris).

**batsmanship** A player's ability as a batter.

**bat speed** The velocity of the bat as the batter swings at the pitch. The greater the bat speed, the greater the velocity of the batted ball. It is generally regarded that, to be successful, a hitter must generate good bat speed; e.g., Ken Griffey Jr.'s bat speed is greater than 100 mph, and Jose Canseco has been described as having "awesome bat speed."

**bats right** Said of a right-handed batter. Abbrev. *BR.*

**batted ball** A ball that has been struck by the batter, as distinguished from a *thrown ball* in interpreting the rules of baseball.

**batter** An offensive player with a bat who is positioned in the batter's box. The main focal point of the game of baseball is the contest between the batter and the pitcher. Compare *hitter.* Syn. *batsman; sticker; stickman; sticksmith; striker.* **1st Use.** 1869. (*DeWitt's Official Base Ball Guide;* Edward J. Nichols).

**batter-runner** A *baserunner* who has just completed his time at bat but before he is put out or until the play on which he became a runner is completed.

**batter's box** One of the two rectangular 6-foot-by-4-foot areas in which the batter must stand. Each box is positioned six inches on either side of the plate, for right- and left-handed batters. Though the boundary for each box is lined with white lime before the game, batters have been known to scrape away the back line with their feet to distort the umpire's ability to determine if they have stepped out of the batter's box.

**batter's circle** Syn. of *on-deck circle.*

**batter's eye** A screen in the outfield that makes it easier for the batter to see an incoming pitch.

**batter's wheelhouse** See *wheelhouse.*

**"batter up!"** Umpire's call to the batter that it is time to step into the batter's box and for play to start. Traditionally, the call is made at the beginning of the game, at the start of each half inning, and after a long time out, such as that taken for a change of pitchers. **Extended Use.** The term is used in the military as a call to get aircraft airborne.

**battery 1.** The pitcher and catcher collectively. In Steve Kluger's novel *Changing Pitches* (1984), a successful battery is described as one in which the pitcher and catcher could switch brains and nobody would know the difference. **1st Use.** The explanation offered by Richard G. Knowles &

**Batter's box.** *The batter's box is evident in this scene from the 1944 World Series; Don Gutteridge of the St. Louis Browns is shown striking out.*

Richard Morton (*Baseball,* 1896) is that the term "has its origin in telegraphy, the pitcher being the transmitter, and the catcher the receiver." However, Henry Chadwick (*Technical Terms of Baseball,* 1897) clearly implies a military borrowing when he gives this definition: "This is the term applied to the pitcher and catcher of a team. It is the main attacking force of the little army of nine players in the field in a contest." Most later attempts to pin a history on the term have alluded to this comparison to a military artillery unit. Metaphorically, it fits nicely with "firing line," a now dated, but once popular term for the "pitcher's mound," and "powder" and "smoke," two synonyms for "fastball."

Perhaps the most contrived attempt to explain the exact origin of the term appeared in a letter in response to an appeal for clues to the origin of the term. Frank J. Reiter of Kenmore, N.Y. (*The Sporting News,* Jan. 18, 1940) wrote: "It may possibly have arisen as follows: General Abner Doubleday, the founder of baseball, being a military man, may have originated the phrase, or someone in the army so named it in honor of General Doubleday. As the word 'fire' is a military command, and as the pitcher literally 'fires' the ball to the plate much in the same manner as a field artillery battery fires a cannon, this may have prompted the name of a military unit to be applied to the pitcher and catcher." **2.** A term commonly used before the 1880s for the pitcher alone. **1st Use.** 1868. (Chadwick Scrapbooks; Edward J. Nichols).

**battery mate** The pitcher or the catcher. Also spelled "batterymate."

**batting** Attempting to hit a pitched ball; the act of coming to home plate with a bat in an attempt to become a baserunner. **1st Use.** 1861. (*Sunday Mercury,* Aug. 10; Edward J. Nichols).

**batting average** The standard numerical measure of a hitter's ability. It is the ratio determined by dividing the number of hits made by a batter by the number of official at-bats and is expressed in thousandths (three decimal places). A batting average can be carried beyond three places; e.g., in 1982 Robin Yount ended the season with a .3307 average, which was .0009 short of that of Willie Wilson, who won the batting title. The standard of excellence is an average of .300 (three hundred) or better, while .400 has been achieved by only eight batters since 1900, the last of whom was Ted Williams (.406 in 1941). Abbrev. *BA.* Syn. *plate record.* **1st Use.** 1880. (*Brooklyn Daily Eagle,* Aug. 16; Edward J. Nichols). **Extended Use.** Success or failure in other realms is often measured in terms of "batting a thousand" or "batting zero." An ad from an investment corporation (*Forbes,* Oct. 6, 1986) opens: "If the S&P is hitting .333, then our top two hitters are batting over .630."

**batting bee** A succession of hits. **1st Use.** 1905. (*Sporting Life,* Oct. 7; Edward J. Nichols).

**batting cage 1.** A portable, wire-enclosed framework, open on one side, that is wheeled behind home plate during batting practice to prevent foul balls from being hit into the stands. A time-honored prank is to ask a rookie or batboy to go back to the clubhouse and pick up the "keys" to the batting cage. Syn. *baseball cage.* **2.** An enclosed indoor framework used for batting practice and instruction. It can be used in bad weather, in the off-season, or when a batting coach wants to work with a batter in private. See also *indoor cage.*

**batting champion** The player who wins the batting title. Syn. *batting king.*

**batting championship 1.** The figurative crown and real title that are given to the player with the highest batting average over the course of a season. **2.** The race for the title of batting champion.

**batting circle** Syn. of *on-deck circle.*

**batting clothes** The clothes worn by a player who is hitting well. It is a figurative term for a period of good hitting and does not refer to a special uniform (although batters have been known to wear the same uniform during a batting streak). Syn. *batting togs.* **1st Use.** 1890. (*New York Press,* July 28; Edward J. Nichols).

**batting coach** Syn. of *hitting coach.*

**batting crown** Syn. of *batting title.*

**batting eye** The visual judgment by a batter of the pitches affecting the batter's ability to hit safely. **1st Use.** 1905. "Carr . . . would be a fixture if he could get his batting eye" (*Sporting Life,* Apr. 27; David Shulman).

**batting fest** A hitting spree, often celebrated at the expense of a single pitcher. Syn. *batfest.* **1st Use.** 1916. "After turning the enemy down in one, two, three order, High School proceeded to indulge in another battingfest" (Christy Mathewson, *First Base Faulkner;* David Shulman).

**batting glove** A thin leather or vinyl glove used by a batter to gain a better grip of the bat. It was introduced by Ken "Hawk" Harrelson in 1964 when he was with the Kansas City A's. Bobby Thomson of the New York Giants wore golf gloves in spring training as early as 1949, but he never wore them during the regular season.

**batting helmet** A protective headgear made of hard, shatterproof plastic, worn while at bat and on the bases. Designed to fit over a player's cloth baseball cap, the latest version of the helmet includes a flap to cover the ear and the temple. Batting helmets are mandatory at all levels of organized baseball, including (since 1971) the major leagues. A light plastic liner was first adopted experimentally for a whole team by the 1941 Brooklyn Dodgers; however, they had been used by individual batters before then. Research conducted by the National Baseball Library at Cooperstown and reported in 1969 by Librarian

John Redding concluded: "[On] January 24, 1905 the A. J. Reach Co., patented and later manufactured the Reach Pneumatic Head Protector, which served the same purpose as today's helmet. The head protector was not widely accepted, but some players, amongst them Roger Bresnahan, did wear it." In more recent times, the 1953 Pittsburgh Pirates was the first team to adopt them permanently. Syn. *beanie; skuller.*

**batting king** Syn. of *batting champion.*

**batting lineup** Syn. of *batting order.*

**batting-list** *arch.* Syn. of *lineup card.* **1st Use.** 1907. "The head of the batting-list came up again, and now by using his combination ball Merriwell succeeded in fanning Strothers" (Burt L. Standish, *Dick Merriwell's Salvation;* David Shulman).

**batting order** The official listing of the order in which batters will come to the plate. The batting order must be submitted to the home plate umpire before the game begins and cannot be changed. Substitutes must be inserted in the batting order in the position of the player being replaced. See also *batting rotation.* Syn. *batting lineup.* **1st Use.** 1901. (*Frank Merriwell's Marvel* by Burt L. Standish; Edward J. Nichols).

**batting out of order** The act of a player who appears at the plate out of the proper place in the batting order. On appeal by the defensive team, the proper batter is declared out by the umpire. Syn. "batting out of turn."

**batting practice** 1. That period of pregame time set aside for hitters to improve the swings, speed, and timing of their batting habits. The batting practice period has its own rituals and traditions; e.g., it is customary for each batter to take the same number of practice pitches and some teams have established cycles of batting, such as starting each practice plate appearance with a bunt. It is also a time for a batter to work on his timing and adjust for the wind, lights, and other environmental factors. Mark McGwire and Jose Canseco are two sluggers who attract fans to batting practice because they put their power on display. Abbrev. *BP.* **1st Use.** 1908. (*Baseball Magazine;* June, Edward J. Nichols). **2.** The offensive production of a team having a field day against a particular team or pitcher.

**batting-practice fastball** A fastball thrown during a game whose speed is a little less than that of a normal fastball and thereby can be hit more easily; a fastball with "nothing on it." The term can be used derogatorily.

**batting-practice pitcher** An individual who regularly pitches to the team during batting practice. There are no rules on who performs this chore but it is commonly a member of the club staff who is not on the roster.

**batting-practice screen** A protective screen placed in front of the batting-practice pitcher. Barry Landers (1973 letter on file at the National Baseball Library and Archives) notes: "It is obvious as to why it [the screen] is there; however, back in 1927, there was no screen. An incident involving my father, who pitched batting practice for the New York Yankees in spring training of that year, sparked the use of the screen. He was pitching to

**Batting-practice screen.** *A young Ted Williams pitching batting practice behind the protection of the screen.*

the immortal Babe Ruth, when 'the Babe' slapped a hard line drive back at him, striking him in the face and knocking out all his teeth in front. From that day to this, a screen is used to protect the batting-practice pitcher."

**batting rotation** The *batting order,* which may be changed daily.

**batting slump** A period of at-bats during which a batter fails to get a hit or gets only a few hits. See also *hitting slump.*

**batting stance** The set position taken by the batter at the plate as the ball is about to be delivered by the pitcher. Not only do different batters have different stances, but the same batter may change stances during the course of a game. See also *closed stance; open stance; square stance.*

**batting tee** A large, adjustable pole on which the ball rests allowing a batter to hit without the services of a batting-practice pitcher. It is used to help a batter adjust his stance, grip, and other elements of his swing. It is also used for playing T-ball. Syn. *tee.*

**batting title** The honor earned by the hitter in each major league with the highest batting average at the end of the regular season. A hitter must have at least 502 (3.1 times 162, the number of games scheduled) official plate appearances to be eligible. Syn. *batting crown.*

**batting togs** Syn. of *batting clothes.*

**Battle of Broadway** The intense rivalry between the New York Giants and the New York Yankees in the 1920s.

**battlin' backstop** A tough, combative catcher. "[Thurman] Munson was a seeming throwback to the 'battlin' backstops' of old, establishing an identity as one of the toughest catchers in the game" (Associated Press obituary for Munson, Aug. 3, 1979).

**bat weight** A metal or plastic, doughnut-shaped ring that is slipped onto the barrel of a bat to make it feel heavier than normal. The purpose of the weight is to strengthen the batter's arm and wrists and to make the bat feel lighter in the batter's box. The bat weight is used by the on-deck batter while limbering up and replaces the method of swinging two bats simultaneously. See also *doughnut.*

**Bauer and Black player** One who is always playing with a lot of bandage tape, from the name of a company that makes such tape. The term appears in Fred Lieb's *Comedians and Pranksters of Baseball* (1958) along with the traditional comment for such a player: "As long as the tape and baling wire hold up, you ought to have a hell of a year."

**Bay Bridge World Series** Nickname for the 1989 World Series between the San Francisco Giants and the Oakland Athletics.

**bazooka 1.** The strong throwing arm of a pitcher, catcher, or fielder. **2.** A mechanical device used to shoot fly balls and line drives for fielding practice.

**Bazooka.** *Los Angeles Angels coach Jack Paepke (assisted by Bob Lemon) gets ready to fire the club's bazooka during spring training. The picture was taken in the early 1960s, before the team became known as the California Angels and then the Anaheim Angels.*

**BB 1.** A ball thrown with such speed that it seems as small as a ball-bearing (BB) pellet when it crosses the plate. **2.** Abbrev. for *base on balls.* **3.** Abbrev. for *batboy.* **4.** Abbrev. for *baseball.*

**BBWAA** Abbrev. for *Baseball Writers Association of America.*

**beachhead** Getting a batter to reach first base to start an inning. **Etymology.** A term brought back from World War II by players who had been in the armed forces.

**bean 1.** *n./arch.* A player's head. **1st Use.** 1910. "A 'bean' you ask? Why, bean is baseball language for head." (Frank Chance, *The Bride and the Pennant*). Peter Tamony noted that T. A. Dorgan used the term in a cartoon (*San Francisco Examiner,* June 19, 1910) in which a man is hit in the head with a ball, which causes another character to remark, "right on the bean." **Etymology.** An explanation that appeared in 1920 when the term was still novel: "The slang expression 'bean' was derived from descriptions of pitchers throwing the ball at the heads of batsmen. This was originally described as a 'bean ball' and from that the word 'bean' became synonymous with 'head.'" (Sid Mercer, *San Francisco Call & Post,* July 2; Peter Tamony). **Extended Use.** The head (as in, "use your bean"). **2.** *v.* To hit a batter in the head with a pitched ball. **Extended Use.** To hit someone in the head.

**beanball** A pitch thrown intentionally at a batter's head for the purpose of either moving the batter away from home plate or to punish him, his team, or another player for something he has done. Pitchers who throw beanballs are supposed to be ejected from the game, but it is usually difficult for the umpire to determine that the act was premeditated. "Another Epidemic of Beanballs" (*New York Daily News* headline, June 20, 1964). The only player ever to be killed in a major-league game was Ray Chapman of the Cleveland Indians who was hit in the head by a pitch thrown by Carl Mays of the New York Yankees on Aug. 16, 1920. But there have been others at other levels of the game. A chilling headline (*San Francisco Call-Bulletin,* Sept. 23, 1947): "'Bean Ball' Is Fatal To S.F. Sandlotter" (Peter Tamony). Compare *brushback pitch; knock-down pitch.* Also spelled "bean ball." Syn. *beaner; Rawlings lobotomy.* **1st Use.** 1905. "While pitching, Mr. [Chief] Bender places much reliance on the bean ball" (Charles Dryden, *The Athletics of 1905;* David Shulman). **Extended Use.** A direct shot meant to do damage, often verbal. "Wallace Winds Up to Pitch Bean Ball at Truman Doctrine" (*San Francisco News* headline, Apr. 16, 1947).

**beanball war** *n.* Games between two teams characterized by potentially lethal retaliatory pitches thrown at batters' heads and bodies, often spread over several days. "Baseball must act to defuse beanball war" (*Christian Science Monitor* headline, Aug. 3, 1987). Compare *brushback war.*

**Beaneaters** *arch.* A nickname for various professional teams from Boston; e.g., the Boston Braves were called the Beaneaters from 1891 to 1906. **1st Use.** 1880. (Chicago *Inter-Ocean,* June 29; Edward J. Nichols).

**beaner 1.** Syn. of *beanball.* **2.** One who throws the beanball. Carl Mays is described as a "beaner with little regard for the consequences of his actions" (Mike Sowell, *The Pitch That Killed,* 1989). **1st Use.** 1912. "Bing! Up comes another 'beaner.'" (Christy Mathewson, *Pitching in a Pinch,* 1912; David Shulman).

**beanie** Syn. of *batting helmet.*

**beany** Said of a player who is a bit off mentally, a condition attributed to being hit in the head by a ball. "[A] condition similar to 'The Dance,' a disease among prizefighters struck on the head often" (Hugh S. Fullerton, *American Magazine,* June 1912).

**Bearded Wonders** A generic name for a renegade team. Franklin P. Huddle (*American Speech,* Apr. 1943) explained: "One occasionally sees references to barnstormers or non-league traveling teams. These are, quite often, pretty disreputable outfits, since they are likely to be made up of men who have been thrown out of organized baseball. Many of these gentry grow beards and call themselves (in imitation of the real thing) *House of David* teams or 'Bearded Wonders.' The beards serve the twin purpose of advertising and disguise."

**bear down** To exert total concentration and maximum effort in any aspect of the game; esp., for a pitcher to give his all and use his last ounce of energy. See also *get naked*. **1st Use.** 1931. (*The World* [New York], Feb. 26; Edward J. Nichols).

**bear's nest** A shabby hotel. **Etymology.** This term may have been a bit of slang common to the Los Angeles Dodgers: it is part of the baseball language that Dodger rookies learn on arriving at the team's spring training camp at Vero Beach, Fla. (Fresco Thompson, *Every Diamond Doesn't Sparkle*, 1964).

**Beasts of the East** The best teams in the eastern divisions of the American League and the National League. Compare *Best of the West*.

**beat a tag** To reach a base before being touched by the ball in the gloved or bare hand of the fielder covering that base.

**beat a throw** To reach a base ahead of the ball. **1st Use.** 1892. (*Brooklyn Daily Eagle*, Feb. 26; Edward J. Nichols).

**beat out** To reach a base slightly ahead of the fielded ball thrown to that baseman. It is implied

"BEATING OUT THE BALL TO FIRST"

*Beat out.*

that the batter-runner was fast enough to beat the throw. See also *leg out*, 1. **1st Use.** 1896. (*Frank Merriwell's Schooldays*; Edward J. Nichols).

**beat reporter** A journalist who writes about a particular subject on a daily basis; specif., a sportswriter who covers a major-league team on a daily basis. One must be a beat reporter to become a member of the Baseball Writers Association of America.

**beat the bushes** To look for baseball talent in the minor (or bush) leagues.

**beauty** A called strike that should have been hit out of the park.

**beaver-shooting** Ogling the opposite sex from the field. This crude term is discussed by Maury Allen (*Bo: Pitching and Wooing*, 1973), Sparky Lyle (*The Bronx Zoo*, 1979), and Jim Bouton (*Ball Four*, 1970).

**beball** A neologism used by Satchel Paige for the "only type" of pitch he threw because "it be where I want it to be."

**Beckett** Short for *The Baseball Card Price Guide* by Dr. James Beckett and Dennis W. Eckes, the leading and most reliable price guide in baseball card collecting. The name "Beckett" has become an important point of reference in pricing cards; e.g., one card that is particularly hot may sell for "50% over Beckett" while run-of-the-mill cards sell "under the Beckett price."

**beef 1.** *n.* A loud and prolonged protest. **2.** *v.* To make such a protest; to have a dispute with. **1st Use.** 1908. (*New York Evening Journal*, May 27; Edward J. Nichols). **Etymology.** According to Hy Turkin (*Baseball Almanac*, 1955), the term sounds "as if noises come from lowing [mooing] cattle or beef."

**bee liner** *n.* A batted ball that travels fast and straight, not far from the ground; a low *line drive*.

**beep ball** [softball term] A sound-emitting ball used in a form of softball played by the blind.

**Beer and Whiskey League** A nickname for the *American Association*, a major league from 1882 to 1891. The term referred to the league's tolerance of alcohol in its parks and several of its prominent backers were connected to the beverage industry. See David Nemec, *The Beer and Whisky League,* 1994.

**Beer Night** A promotional event where beer is sold at a game at a greatly reduced price. On June 4, 1974, the Cleveland Indians let their fans drink all the beer they could hold for ten cents a cup. Predictably, the fans became intoxicated and unruly, forcing umpire Nestor Chylak to forfeit the game.

**bees in the hands** An expression for the stinging sensation a batter's hands feel when a pitch strikes the handle or end of the bat. Atlanta Braves pitcher Jim Nash explained that it "usually happens on a cold day against a pitcher throwing heat" (quoted in Wayne Minshew, *Atlanta Constitution,* 1972). Keith Hernandez (*Pure Baseball,* 1994) wrote about pitchers like Tom Henke who throw "heavy" balls that one must hit "in the sweetest part of the sweet spot to get any results. Otherwise, it's 'bees in the hands.'" Syn. "bees in the bat."

**behind 1.** *adj.* At a disadvantage; e.g., said of a team that is losing or of a pitcher with a count of more balls than strikes. Compare *ahead.* **2.** *n.* The catcher, per 1845 Knickerbocker Rules.

**behind in the count 1.** Said of a pitcher when there are more balls than strikes on the batter. Compare *ahead in the count,* 1. **2.** Said of a batter with more strikes than balls. Compare *ahead in the count,* 2.

**behind the bat** Said of the catcher's position.

**behind the plate** Said of the area of operation for the catcher and the plate umpire.

**béisbol** Spanish for "baseball." The term is often used when Latin baseball is discussed. "People of Cuba have serious case of 'beisbol' fever" (*USA Today* headline, Apr. 29, 1987). See Michael M. Oleksak and Mary Adams Oleksak, *Beisbol: Latin Americans and the Grand Old Game,* 1996.

**belabor a pitcher** For a team to get several hits off a pitcher.

**bellcow** Syn. of *bellwether.*

**bells on** Said of a ball that has been hit hard. **1st**

**Use.** 1908. (*New York Evening Journal,* June 19; Edward J. Nichols).

**bellwether** The leader of a pitching staff. Syn. *bellcow.*

**belly slide** Syn. of *headfirst slide.*

**belly whopper** A *headfirst slide,* characterized by a long, airborne dive into the base. Dizzy Dean's definition (*Dizzy's Definitions*): "Hittin' the dirt head first on your stummick. Pepper Martin was the last great belly-whopper."

**belt 1.** *v.* To hit a ball hard. **1st Use.** 1891. (*Chicago Herald,* Aug. 25; Edward J. Nichols). **2.** *n.* A ball that has been hit hard. **1st Use.** 1907. (*Harper's Weekly,* Dec. 14; Edward J. Nichols). **3.** A home run. "Two Belts Tie Sosa, McGwire" (*Baltimore Sun* headline, Sept. 26, 1998), describing the occasion when Sammy Sosa and Mark McGwire each hit his 66th home run on Sept. 25, 1998. **4.** *v.* To win a baseball game decisively; e.g. "The Tigers belted the Yankees, 14 to 1."

**belt-buckle ball** A pitched ball that has been scratched or cut on the pitcher's belt buckle. The defacing of the ball makes it curve unnaturally, putting the batter at an unfair disadvantage. The umpire, detecting such a pitch, can eject the pitcher from the game.

**belt high** Said of the location of a called strike at the batter's belt.

**bench 1.** *n.* The seating area in the dugout for a team's players, substitutes, and coaching staff. **1st Use.** 1891. (Chicago *Inter-Ocean,* May 5; Edward J. Nichols). **2.** *n.* Syn. of *dugout.* **3.** *n.* Collectively, the players a team holds in reserve. Even though they don't sit on the bench, pinch hitters are part of the "bench" in this metaphorical sense. **Extended Use.** The figurative location of those who are not participating or have been taken out of participation. "Blonde Miss North Gets Off Bench for First of Monroe Roles" (*Life* magazine subheadline on Sheree North getting a Marilyn Monroe role, March 21, 1955). **4.** *v.* For a manager to remove a player from the lineup for one or more games; to demote a starting player to the role of a substitute player. **1st Use.** 1902. (*Sporting Life,* July 12; Edward J. Nichols). **Extended Use.**

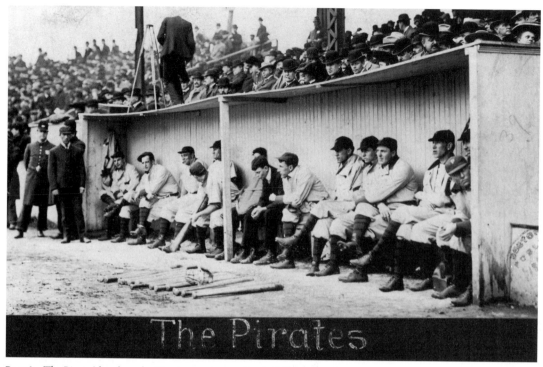

**Bench.** *The Pirates' bench at the Huntington Avenue Baseball Grounds in Boston, 1903, during the first modern World Series between the Boston Pilgrims and Pittsburgh.*

To get rid of or demote. A letter to the *Washington Post* (June 22, 1996) that argued for the removal of a popular advice columnist was headlined: "Bench Ann Landers."

**bench blanket** Syn. of *benchwarmer.*

**bench-bound** Said of a player who is unable to play because of having been removed earlier from the lineup; e.g., "Smith was bench-bound when his spot came up in the ninth."

**bench brigade** The full roster of a baseball team.

**bench clearing** *n.* A quick emptying of the dugout, leaving an empty bench in its wake. It can be prompted by a brawl on the field or by the umpire who can clear the bench to retain control over the game.

**bench-clearing** *adj.* Said of an incident in which players come out of the dugout. "George Foster hit his 13th career grand slam, triggering a benches-clearing melee" (*USA Today,* May 28, 1986).

**bench coach** A coach who assists the manager from the bench. Such a coach is often a "manager in waiting."

**bench jockey 1.** A player who verbally abuses or yells derisive comments at opposing players or umpires from the safety of the dugout. Bruce Catton (*American Heritage,* Apr. 1959) called him "the man who will say anything at all if he thinks it will upset an enemy's poise." See also *jockey,* 1. **2.** A substitute who rides the bench or seldom gets to play; a *benchwarmer.* **1st Use.** 1939. "The doctor's orders were soon grapevined around the league, and all the bench jockeys on the circuit were quickly counting ten [i.e., keeping quiet] on every pitch Lefty made" (Gordon S. "Mickey" Cochrane, *Baseball: The Fans' Game,* 1939; David Shulman).

**bench performer** An exceptionally good utility player who is always ready to replace another player whose performance is faltering during the course of a game; e.g., "Smith was one of the best bench performers in the game because it took some pretty good offensive players to keep him there."

**bench player** A player who spends much of the time on the bench rather than starting. "Bench players can keep a team flying high when injuries or batting slumps strike the regulars" (William Gildea, *Washington Post,* Aug. 29, 1997).

**bench polisher** A substitute player whose constant presence on the bench is said to "polish" it.

**bench strength** An array of competent players on the bench who are available for play if and when needed.

**benchwarmer** A substitute player whose constant presence on the bench is said to "warm" it. Sometimes spelled "bench warmer." Syn. *bench blanket; bench jockey,* 2; *rider of the lonesome pine.* **1st Use.** 1889. "Jack Doke's 'dead cold duck' will spring from some bench warmer as a batsman with a good eye and cold head walks up the plate" (*Cincinnati Times,* Feb. 8; David Shulman). "The days for 'bench warmers' with salaries are also past" (*Sporting Times,* Jan. 9, 1892). "A certain rich man offered a manager $10,000 if the manager would carry his son as a combination of mascot and bench-warmer" (*Saturday Evening Post,* 1912). **Extended Use.** A judge (who also sits on a bench) is sometimes called a "benchwarmer." A book on judges by Joseph C. Goulden is entitled *The Benchwarmers* (1974).

**benchwarming** *n.* Sitting in the dugout. "The most unplayed, but not unpaid, athlete of his time, Charlie [Silvera], as Yogi Berra's stand-in with the Yankees, collected over $50,000 in bonus pelf for six World Series, during which he did nothing but practice the gentle art of bench warming" (Jack McDonald, *San Francisco Call-Bulletin,* Sept. 23, 1960). Sometimes spelled "bench warming." **1st Use.** 1916. "Bench-warming for a week or so, and then a trial" (*Redbook,* Apr.; David Shulman).

**bender** *arch.* A curveball. "A term not often used in modern times" (Parke Cummings, *The Dictionary of Baseball,* 1950). **1st Use.** 1901. (Burt L.

Standish, *Frank Merriwell's Marvel;* Edward J. Nichols).

**Bengals** A nickname for the Detroit Tigers. The term was commonly used before about 1950.

**Ben-Gay League** Baseball players who use Ben-Gay to relieve sore muscles early in spring training.

**bent-leg slide** A slide in which a runner bends both legs when approaching a base. Sliding with straightened legs can cause serious injury if the runner's spikes get caught in the dirt.

**Bermuda triangle** A place in the infield where batted balls are "lost" (become base hits). "Blue Jays leadoff man Otis Nixon bunted the ball into a Bermuda triangle between pitcher Jose Mercedes, first baseman David Nilsson and second baseman Fernando Vina" (Drew Olsen, *Milwaukee Journal Sentinel,* July 25, 1997).

**Berraism** Syn. of *Yogiism.*

**berth 1.** A player's position on a team. **2.** A team's position in the standings. **1st Use.** 1908. (*Baseball Magazine,* Sept.; Edward J. Nichols).

**best** To defeat. The term is one of many for one team winning a game from another. Here is a list of such terms collected in the space of a week's newspaper reading in the summer of 1987: down, trim, trounce, blast, fend off, thump, spank, outlast, stun, shock, tame, foil, defeat, beat, nip, upset, clobber, spill, pound, wallop, edge, roll past, whip, rout, unplug, shade, stop, upend, tip, trip, drill, claw, drop, top, win, stifle, dump, take, hold off, shake down, halt, haunt, quell, power over, and sweep. **1st Use.** 1912. (*New York Tribune,* Sept. 6; Edward J. Nichols).

**best interest** The legal empowerment that gives the commissioner of baseball the jurisdiction to determine that which is and is not good for baseball or "in the best interests of the game." (Major League Agreement, article 1, section 2).

**best-of-five** Describing the means of determining the modern Division Series playoff format in which the first team to win three games advances to the Championship Series.

**best-of-seven** Describing the means of determining the modern League Championship playoff and World Series format in which the first team to win four games is the champion.

**Best of the West** The best teams in the western divisions of the American League and the National League. Compare *Beasts of the East*.

**Best Tools Award** One of several awards given each year by the publication *Baseball America* for performance in several areas, ranging from best changeup to best defensive third baseman.

**be-there play** Syn. of *"I'll be there" play*.

**Betsy** See *Black Betsy*.

**between-innings commentator** A baseball announcer who fills in with baseball talk and trivia between innings.

**between the lines** Syn. of *between the white lines*.

**between the seams** The location, on the surface of a pitched ball, of the spot most advantageous for the batter to hit. **1st Use.** 1910. (*American Magazine*, July; Edward J. Nichols).

**between the white lines** On the field of play; the location of the action of the game, itself, as opposed to off-the-field activity. The "white lines" are the foul lines, which both physically and symbolically mark the realm of the actual game itself. Players have been known to say that what another player does off the field is his own business and that all that matters is what goes on "between the white lines." Television critic Ken Hoffman criticized announcer Vin Scully: "If it's not between the white lines, Scully pretends it doesn't exist" (*Houston Post*, June 27, 1987; Charles D. Poe). Probably the most famous line using the phrase was uttered by pitcher Early Wynn: "That space between the white lines—that's my office. That's where I conduct my business." See also *white lines*. Syn. *between the lines*.

**B game** A game played by team aspirants during spring training. "B games are games that the clubs occasionally schedule so they can give some playing time to second-stringers and also get a look at rookies up from the minors for a tryout" (William Zinsser, *Spring Training*, 1989).

**Bible hitter** One who receives very few bases on balls ("thou shalt not pass").

**biff** To bat a ball hard. **1st Use.** 1888. Gerald Cohen found several examples of this term in *The World* (New York) for 1888, with the earliest being on June 7. One example: "It was biff! bang! from the start, and Cleveland was not in it." **Etymology.** Coined by William T. Hall, a Chicago sports reporter, according to H. L. Mencken (*The American Language*, 1919).

**biffer** *arch*. A hard-hitting batter. **1st Use.** 1908. (*New York Evening Journal*, Feb. 24; Edward J. Nichols).

**biff stick** A baseball bat. **1st Use.** 1908. (*New York Evening Journal*, Mar. 16; Edward J. Nichols).

**big as a balloon** Said of a pitched ball that is very easy to hit. **1st Use.** 1910. (*American Magazine*, June; Edward J. Nichols).

**big ball** [softball term] An early name for softball.

**big bang theory** The assumption that, in a majority of games, the winning team scores as many or more runs in one inning than the loser scores in nine innings; the notion that baseball is a game of *big innings*. The name was given to the theory by Thomas Boswell (*How Life Imitates the World Series*, 1982).

**big bat** A club's leading hitter. "Von Hayes . . . has become the big bat in the Philadelphia lineup after the retirement of Mike Schmidt" (*St. Petersburg Times*, Mar. 24, 1990).

**Big Bertha 1.** The *cleanup hitter;* the fourth player in the batting order. **2.** A vastly oversized catcher's mitt that was designed by Baltimore Orioles manager Paul Richards to make it easier for Gus Triandos to handle Hoyt Wilhelm's most unpredictable knuckleball. The mitt (Wilson model #1050 CL) was 45 inches around and would be illegal today because of a 1964 rule stipulating that no glove can have a circumference of more than 38 inches. **3.** A favorite bat; e.g., in 1927, Babe Ruth referred to one of his bats as "Big Bertha." **4.** A colossal base hit. When Babe Ruth became the first and only player ever to hit a home run into the old, wooden center field bleachers at the Polo Grounds on July 13,

1921, the *New York Times* wrote: "The Babe had had it upon his mind to perpetrate this Big Bertha shot for some time, but never seemed to get around to it." **Etymology.** Big Bertha was the nickname for the German Army's mammoth 420-millimeter gun of World War I. It was named for Bertha Krupp, the sole heir to the Krupp armament empire.

**big bill** A long, easy bounce, particularly the last bounce of a batted ball before it reaches the fielder. It is an easy bounce to catch and tends to make the fielder catching it look good. See also *charity hop; bounder.* **1st Use.** 1932. (*Baseball Magazine*, Oct.; Edward J. Nichols). **Etymology.** It has been suggested that the term comes from the fact that on such a bounce, the ball often reaches the fielder at head level and is named for the bill of the baseball cap (Mike Whiteford, *How to Talk Baseball*, 1983). However, Edward J. Nichols cites a letter (*The Sporting News*, Apr. 15, 1937) that asserts that the term is named for Bill Bradley (who played for several teams between 1899 and 1915), who hit many such bounders.

**big bounce** Syn. of *bounder.*

**big classic** A nickname for the *World Series.* **1st Use.** 1915. (*Baseball Magazine*, Dec.; Edward J. Nichols).

**big cut** A full swing for power as though trying to hit a home run.

**big E** Short for *earned run average.*

**big fly** A home run. "They [1990 Toronto Blue Jays] have a lot of guys who can go 'big fly'" (Tom Yantz, *Hartford Courant*, June 25, 1990). Keith Hernandez, on his thoughts on going to the plate with the idea of hitting a home run (quoted in Davey Johnson, *Bats*, 1986): "I'm looking in. I'm looking in. If I get it, I'm going big fly." The term is clearly a players' term of the mid-1980s. In 1986, R. J. Reynolds explained that the long ball is no longer called a "dinger" or "tater" but the "big fly."

**biggies** Syn. of *major leagues.*

**big guns** A team's best batters; the sluggers in the lineup. **1st Use.** 1902. (*Sporting Life*, Sept. 27; Edward J. Nichols).

**big hit** **1.** A key hit; a hit in the clutch. **2.** A

home run. **1st Use.** 1922. (*Spalding's Official Base Ball Guide;* Edward J. Nichols).

**big hop** A batted ball that takes a high bounce and is easy to play, as it allows the fielder to watch the ball and predict where the bounce will take it.

**big inning** An inning in which at least three runs are scored by one team. Often it occurs as the result of home runs being hit with runners on base. As a bona fide statistic, the big inning has started to show up with some regularity in newspapers. Prior to the 1986 World Series, *USA Today* was looking for a number or statistic that tipped off a winner: "Big innings are excellent indicators. Teams that have had 'big innings' are 40-7 (.851)." See also *big bang theory.* **Etymology.** "Ruth Originator of the Big Inning" (Frederick G. Lieb, *The Sporting News*, July 12, 1950) is the title of an article in which Lieb asserts that Ruth's ability to hit the home run "revolutionized" baseball, creating what seemed to be an entirely new game. He compares the third-place 1908 Chicago White Sox to the fourth-place 1947 New York Giants: the White Sox had only three home runs all year, but the Giants hit 221. "That's what the Ruthian influence did to baseball," concluded Lieb.

The term comes into play in a well-worn baseball riddle: Where is baseball mentioned in the Bible? Answer: Genesis ("In the beginning . . .").

**big knock** A home run; e.g., "he is going to a ballpark where big knocks are a way of life" (*Tampa Tribune*, Dec. 11, 1988).

**big league** *n.* Syn. of *major league,* 1. **1st Use.** 1884. "The Union clubs are offering big inducement to big pitchers. The only way that some pitchers can be kept in the big League next year is by paying them big money." (*Sporting Life*, Oct. 15; Barry Popik). **Etymology.** Under the heading "Baseball Language in the 1890s," Bill James (*Bill James Historical Baseball Abstract*, 1986) states: "The term 'big league' apparently referred originally to the size of the one major league [National League], which had twelve teams in it. But . . . 'big league' came to stand for . . . 'major league,' and 'big leagues' became a synonym for 'majors.'"

**big-league** *adj.* Syn. of *major-league.* **Extended**

**Use.** Said of the highest level in any given field; major, large, important; e.g., "a big-league appetite." Compare *bush-league.*

**big leaguer** Syn. of *major leaguer.* **1st Use.** 1911. (*Baseball Magazine,* Oct.; Edward J. Nichols).

**big leagues** Syn. of *major leagues.*

**Big Mac 1.** Affectionate nickname for *Macmillan,* from the popular McDonald's hamburger. **2.** Nickname for St. Louis Cardinals slugger Mark McGwire during 1998 as he established a new season record for home runs with 70.

**big mitt 1.** The large padded glove worn by the catcher. **1st Use.** 1905. (*Sporting Life,* Oct. 5; Edward J. Nichols). **2.** Any oversized catcher's glove that was designed to reduce the frequency of passed balls.

**big-name player** A baseball star; e.g., "Babe Ruth was a big-name player."

**big one 1.** The third strike, especially in a key situation. **1st Use.** 1907. (*New York Evening Journal,* n.d.; Edward J. Nichols). **2.** A putout at first base. **3.** The last out of an inning.

**big out** A putout at an important or crucial time in a game. It has been said there are a couple of big outs in each game.

**Big Red Machine** A nickname for the Cincinnati Reds in the middle to late 1970s. The moniker is more commonly used when the team is playing well, such as when the Reds won back-to-back World Series in 1975 and 1976.

**Bigs, the** Syn. of *major leagues.* "Winterport's [Mike] Bordick headed for the Bigs?" (*Waldo* [Maine] *Independent* headline, Dec. 3, 1987).

**big series** Syn. of *World Series.*

**big show** Syn. of *major leagues.*

**big stick** A heavy hitter; one given to hitting home runs and extra-base hits. **1st Use.** 1908. "The Giants suddenly got out the 'big sticks' and swatted the ball with such continuity and vigor that they piled up an even dozen runs" (*New York Herald,* May 5; Peter Morris). **Etymology.** The term probably entered baseball in the wake of

Theodore Roosevelt's line delivered on Sept. 2, 1901, at the Minnesota State Fair: "Speak softly and carry a big stick."

**big swat** A home run.

**big team** The parent major-league club as viewed by a minor leaguer.

**big tent** Syn. of *major leagues,* an obvious reference to the circus.

**big time 1.** Syn. of *major leagues,* 1. **2.** A player who has a major impact on the game. Thomas Boswell (*Washington Post,* Oct. 11, 1988) used the term to describe the likes of Reggie Jackson, Pete Rose, Willie Stargell, and Kirk Gibson.

**big Van Heusen** See *Van Heusen.*

**big W** A victory, based on the abbreviation "W" for a win achieved by a team or a pitcher. Jim Bouton (*Ball Four,* 1970): "I ended up with my first big W, as we baseball players call it. It was my first major-league win earned with a knuckleball."

**bill 1.** *n.* A game in the schedule; e.g., "Tomorrow we play a twin bill." **1st Use.** 1912. (*New York Tribune,* Sept. 8; Edward J. Nichols). **2.** *v./ arch.* To schedule a game. **1st Use.** 1902. (*Sporting Life,* July 12; Edward J. Nichols). **3.** *n.* The visor of a baseball cap.

**Bill Hassemer Bounce** *n./arch.* A batted grounder that jumps neatly into a fielder's glove, named presumably for a man known for hitting such ground balls. **1st Use.** 1937. (*Pittsburgh Press,* Aug. 4; Edward J. Nichols). **Etymology.** Although the term was current baseball slang in the 1930s, it does not seem to be named for a player of that era. The only major-league player with a name close to Hassemer was William Louis "Roaring Bill" Hassamaer (1894–96).

**billiard** A ball that, when batted, hits the ground in front of the plate and rolls back toward the batter, similar to the "reverse spin produced with a billiard ball" (Edward J. Nichols). **1st Use.** 1937. (*Pittsburgh Press,* Jan. 4; Edward J. Nichols).

**Bill Klem** Any person in baseball who is never wrong. **Etymology.** An eponym for infallibility inspired by Hall of Fame umpire Bill Klem, who is

**Bill Klem.** *The Hall-of-Fame umpire, who earned the nickname "the Old Arbiter," worked in 18 separate World Series.*

credited with several statements in which he never admits a bad call; e.g., "It ain't nothin' till I call it" and "Gentlemen, he was out . . . because I said he was out."

**Bill Klem Award** An award for service as an umpire, named in honor of one of baseball's greatest umpires.

**Billy Ball** The style of aggressive, alert, and fan-pleasing baseball practiced by Alfred Manuel "Billy" Martin in his various terms as manager for five major-league teams; "old-fashioned baseball" (Billy Martin, quoted in *Houston Post*, May 10, 1987).

Red Smith (*New York Times,* Apr. 22, 1981) wrote: "In Billy Ball, the players run. Rickey Henderson stole 100 bases last year, breaking Ty Cobb's American League record. They work the double steal, they squeeze and they steal home. They sacrifice and they hit behind the runner.

They worry runs out of the opposition, while their pitchers hold the varmints off at the pass." For all of its successes, Billy Ball has also been characterized by controversy and dissension: "Feuding Rips Away Facade of Billy Ball" (*San Francisco Examiner* headline, March 7, 1983).

Martin's baseball philosophy combined speed, daring, fundamentals, and aggressive style. It was based on a willingness to intimidate (including throwing at batters) as well as executing the fundamentals (such as hit and run, stealing, and bunting to reach base). "It was about establishing an aggressive and unpredictable approach to the game, throwing fear and uncertainty into the heads of opponents and into the minds of opposing managers" (David Falkner, *The Last Yankee,* 1992).

The term was introduced as one word ("Billyball") in 1981 when Martin was manager of the Oakland Athletics. See also Billy Martin (*Billyball,* 1987).

**Billy Martin Rule** The practice by which umpires go out of their way to make calls against a certain individual. The term is facetious because the "rule" is seldom observed, although certain players and managers sometimes are subject to extra scrutiny. Named after Billy Martin, a manager for five teams between 1969 and 1988.

**bing** To hit a ball hard. An "onomatopoetic term" (Edward J. Nichols), based on the sound of the bat solidly meeting the pitched ball. **1st Use.** 1909. "Bing one, Cap!" (Zane Grey, *The Short-Stop*).

**bingle 1.** *n.* A *single,* usually a "clean one." **2.** *v.* To hit safely. **Etymology/1st Use.** 1902. David Shulman (*American Speech,* Feb. 1937) conjectured: "If it is not an erroneous reading of 'single,' perhaps it may be a blend of 'bang' or 'bing' with 'single.'" Responding to Shulman's suggestion, Peter Tamony did not doubt that the term was based "on the onomatopoetic 'bing,'" but posed an alternate theory (*American Speech,* Oct. 1937) by asking: "Was such a hit first called 'bingo,' from the exclamation in use, and later blended with 'single'?" Tamony cited an example of bingo in use: "Truck Egan is showing his form of other seasons, playing a swell short and getting his timely bingoes as of yore" (*The Sporting News,* Nov. 15, 1902). But Tamony is quick to note that "bingle" was in use in 1901: "You must give him credit for being good on ground balls, but he is not a good ground coverer, loses bingle after bingle near second base and is a light hitter" (*Sporting Life,* Sept. 6, 1902).

**bingo** A single.

**bird cage** *arch.* A slang nickname for *catcher's mask,* so-called because of its resemblance to a small, wire cage. "So in 1875 Fred W. Thayer hit upon the nose-saver we call a mask, but which people then called a 'bird cage'" (Roger Kahn & Al Helfer, *Mutual Baseball Almanac,* 1954; Charles D. Poe). **1st Use.** 1906. (*Sporting Life,* March 3; Edward J. Nichols).

**bird dog** *n.* A friend or associate of a scout who tips him off to high schoolers and other young players with major-league potential; an assistant scout. A bird dog is not paid, but occasionally a small bonus is given if the player eventually becomes a major leaguer.

Bird dogs are the first people one meets in Pat Jordan's *A False Spring* (1973): "The bird dogs came first. They just appeared one spring day in your sophomore year of high school as if drawn by the odor of freshly cut outfield grass.... They were called bird dogs because they sniffed out talent, although the name does not do justice to the men. The bird dogs were kindly old men in plaid shirts and string ties. They owned taverns and hardware stores, and had even played ball with Kiki Cuyler and Georgie Cutshaw. Now in their last years, they measured out the weekday afternoons at an endless succession of high school baseball games." After the bird dogs, wrote Jordan, "came the full-time scouts." See also *commission scout.* **1st Use.** 1950. (Sam Nisenson, *Handy Illustrated Guide to Baseball,* glossary; David Shulman).

**bird-dog** *v.* To play close to a base in an attempt to catch a runner off that base; e.g., "Smith was bird-dogging Jones at third but Jones did not fall for it." **Etymology.** An obvious reference to the dog used by a hunter to hunt and retrieve birds. "To bird-dog" is also general slang for "to watch closely."

**Bird Land** Baltimore Orioles and the geographic area from Delaware and Pennsylvania through Virginia where the team has a broad fan base.

**Birds** A nickname for the present-day Baltimore Orioles. For some reason the sobriquet has not worked for the other avian teams, the Toronto Blue Jays and the St. Louis Cardinals. However, the term is used from time to time in print for other teams, such as an article on the Toronto Blue Jays in *Sports Illustrated,* entitled "Birds on the Wing."

**bite 1.** *v.* To swing at a bad or unexpected ball, as a fish bites at a baited hook. The term has usually been applied to a hapless batter who cannot resist swinging at and missing the elusive slow curve. "The message 'he will bite' passed through the league among the players generally means the end of the usefulness of that player" (Hugh S. Fullerton, *American Magazine,* June 1912). **1st Use.** 1905. (*Sporting Life,* Sept. 2; Edward J. Nichols). **2.** *v.* To hit a batter with a pitch, as if to take a "bite" out of him. **3.** *n.* The tight spin applied by the pitcher on a breaking ball. "[Armando Benitez's] slider had bite, buckling the knees of Ray Durham and Barry Lyons" (*Baltimore Sun,* Apr. 23, 1995).

**bite the dust** To slide. **1st Use.** 1910. (*New York Tribune,* July 9; Edward J. Nichols). **Etymology.** Since approximately 1870 this term has been slang for dying or being killed violently. It is also used as an expression of defeat (as in "my idea bit the dust"). Baseball uses the term literally, as a player sliding is likely to send up a cloud of dusty soil.

**BK** Abbrev. for *balk.*

**BL** Abbrev. for *bats left.*

**black** The black borders of home plate; the perceived inside and outside edges of the strike zone.

**Black and Decker** A player used for odd jobs, such as warming up bullpen pitchers. **Etymology.** From the Black and Decker tool manufacturer. The term originated in Kansas City, where the Royals's bullpen applied this tag to bullpen catcher John Wathan: "A weak tool, less than human" (Dan Quisenberry, quoted in *The Sporting News,* March 6, 1982).

**blackball** Baseball as it was played in the Negro

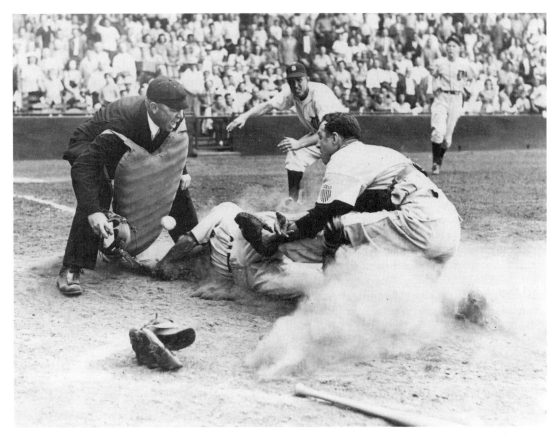

**Bite the dust.** *Paul Richards of the Detroit Tigers raises a cloud as he slides safely into home in a game against the Philadelphia Athletics on July 1, 1945.*

leagues. See *Blackball Stars* by John B. Holway (1988).

**Black Betsy** A large, fearsome-looking baseball bat, usually painted black, first popularized by Shoeless Joe Jackson and used by other sluggers, including Babe Ruth. The name was originally given to the bat by its manufacturer, A. G. Spalding and Co. (Edward J. Nichols).

   Donald Gropman (*Say It Ain't So, Joe!,* 1979) writes that Jackson's bat, called "Black Betsy," was 36 inches long and weighed about 40 ounces. "But she was more than just a bat; she was Joe's talisman, his trademark, the handmade tool of his profession. She fit the grip of his big hands so perfectly and sliced through the air so smoothly when he cut loose at the plate that it seemed as if some of the sweeping power came from her, seemed as if

Black Betsy was alive and eager to whack the baseball as it came whistling in over the plate." **1st Use.** 1922. (*Spalding's Official Base Ball Guide;* Edward J. Nichols).

**blackboard** Syn. of *scoreboard*. **1st Use.** Peter Morris found two citations of this term during the 1881 season (e.g., "people now began to cast affectionate glances at the blackboard"), but is unsure whether a blackboard was actually used or it was just a metaphor.

**black out** *v.* To keep a game off television or radio for any number of reasons, usually economic; e.g., a team may have an agreement with a local television station or cable system that a game cannot be shown unless a certain number of tickets are sold in advance of the game.

**blackout** *n.* The act of blocking the television broadcast of a game. When a Boston Red Sox game versus the New York Yankees was kept off a New England cable-TV system, the *Boston Globe* (June 27, 1986) ran an explanation under the headline: "Light Shed on Blackout."

**black seats** Empty bleacher seats such as those in dead center field in Yankee Stadium and for which tickets are not sold. Reggie Jackson (*Reggie,* 1984) wrote: "He threw me a knuckler. Didn't knuckle. I crushed it nearly 500 feet into those beautiful empty black seats in dead center."

**Black Sox 1.** A derogatory name for the 1919 Chicago White Sox team on which eight players illegally conspired with gamblers to lose the World Series to the Cincinnati Reds. "Black Sox" was a nickname coined to bring shame to the team. The whole incident became known as the Black Sox scandal and the 1921 trial of the players was known widely as the Black Sox trial. To bring respectability back to the sport, the powerful office of Commissioner of Baseball was created, and Judge Kenesaw Mountain Landis became the first commissioner. **2.** A derogatory name for the eight 1919 Chicago White Sox players who were initially indicted for throwing the 1919 World Series. In W. P. Kinsella's novel *Shoeless Joe* (1982), the narrator muses: "Instead of nursery rhymes, I was raised on the story of the Black Sox Scandal, and instead of Tom Thumb or Rumpelstiltskin, I grew up hearing of the eight disgraced ballplayers: [Buck] Weaver, [Eddie] Cicotte, [Swede] Risberg, [Happy] Felsch, [Chick] Gandil, [Lefty] Williams, [Fred] McMullin, and, always, Shoeless Joe Jackson."

See also *"say it ain't so, Joe."*

**Blade** A commonly used nickname for a thin, wiry player; specif., Mark Belanger during his days with the Baltimore Orioles.

**blank 1.** *v.* To allow no runs in an inning or

**Black Sox.** *The 1919 Chicago White Sox, including the eight men who were indicted for throwing the World Series.*

game. The term is beloved of headline writers. **1st Use.** 1862. (*New York Sunday Mercury,* June 29; Edward J. Nichols). **2.** *n.* A scoreless inning. "Relaxed [Dwight] Gooden Throws Three Blanks" (*New York Daily News* headline, Mar. 14, 1987).

**blast 1.** *v.* To hit a home run; to hit the ball with a hard blow. **2.** *n.* A hard-hit ball, usually a home run. **3.** *v.* To cause a pitcher to be removed from the game by making too many hits; e.g., "The Tigers blasted Smith out of the box in the second inning."

**blaze** To hit a ball hard. **1st Use.** 1912. (*New York Tribune,* Oct. 13; Edward J. Nichols).

**blazer** A fastball.

**bleacher** See *bleachers.*

**bleacher bugs** *obs.* Syn. of *bleacher bums.*

**bleacher bums** Horde of boisterous, often shirtless fans who inhabit the bleachers of such places as Wrigley Field in Chicago (where the term originated). The term appears to have been in use since the late 1960s when it replaced the earlier *bleacher bugs.*

**bleacher critic** A critical fan sitting in the bleachers. **Extended Use.** A critic who, to use another sport's terminology, sits on the sideline. "But Secretary of State Cordell Hull, speaking directly over the Columbia network, was performing primarily for the home folks answering bleacher critics of his foreign policy pitching" (*Newsweek,* Apr. 17, 1944).

**bleacher entrance** An admission gate at a ballpark reserved exclusively for the bleachers. "The tickets will be sold at the bleacher entrances, not at the main box office" (*St. Petersburg Times,* Mar. 14, 1987).

**bleacherite** A spectator who sits in the bleachers. "Another Brooklyn first baseman earned the jeers of the bleacherites by being picked off base, after singling, on a version of the hoary hidden-ball trick" (Bennett Cerf, *Shake Well Before Using,* 1948). Certain popular players of the past (such as Zack Wheat) have been referred to as an "idol of the bleacherites." A later example of the term in use appeared in the "Jocks" column of *People* (June 24, 1974): "In Cincinnati, bleacherites poured beer on Houston outfielder Bob Watson as he lay stunned after running into the left field fence."

When Hugh S. Fullerton (*American Magazine,* June 1912) defined the term, he gave it a certain nobility with lines like this: "The bleacherites usually are much better posted on the game than those patrons who occupy the grand stand boxes and seats and are much more dreaded by the players because of their caustic criticism." **1st Use.** 1890. (*New York Press,* July 10; Edward J. Nichols).

**bleacheritis** The name of a mock disease for the deteriorated physical conditioning of those who have given up active participation in athletics and become more spectators: "The active athlete of the teens succumbs to bleacheritis by 30 and is interested only because he has money on the Giants" (C. C. Furnas, *The Next Hundred Years,* 1936).

**bleachers 1.** Originally, the uncovered, unreserved, backless benches for spectators at a ballpark; currently, the most distant and inexpensive seats, which are beyond the outfield wall and may be covered, in the case of domed stadiums.

The bleachers carry with them a certain rowdy, romantic image: "The democracy of the game is at its best on the bleachers and in the grandstand. There the wealthy banker, straight from downtown by the 'Wall Street subway special,' hobnobs with the office-boy for once, on terms of perfect equality." (*New York Evening Post,* Sept. 14, 1911).

One appeal of the bleachers has always been their relative cheapness. *The Sporting News* (July 14, 1954) reported that "Ebbets Field prices will continue to be $3 for lower boxes, $2.50 upper boxes, $1.75 grandstand, and 50 cents bleachers." Another draw has been the party atmosphere that exists in some parks. A report from Fenway Park (*Boston Globe,* June 25, 1986): "Beachballs are only the newest, and most visible, of the bleacher game-time activities. But while beer-spilling, Frisbee-throwing and marijuana-smoking are time-honored traditions in the cheap seats, this season seems to have brought, if anything, an improved situation." Syn. *scorchers.* **2.** The spectators in the

"ON THE BLEACHERS"

*Bleachers.*

bleachers. "The bleachers nursed their wrath until the game was over when they swarmed into the field and started to mob the offending official" (*Sporting Life,* May 13, 1905; Peter Tamony). **Etymology/1st Use.** 1888. Derived from *bleaching boards,* a jocular reference to people bleaching in the sun (Thomas W. Lawson, *The Krank: His Language and What It Means,* 1888). Hugh S. Fullerton (*American Magazine,* June 1912) added this racial twist to the etymology of the term when he announced that the term "originated in the south where the colored spectators were forced to sit in the sun, and were 'bleached.'" **Extended Use.** The term that originated in baseball is now applied to the cheaper backless seats in football stadiums, gymnasiums, and even nightclubs. Bleacher seats are offered for rock concerts and religious revival meetings. Every four years they become inaugural fixtures in Washington: "A mile of tiered board bleachers flanked Pennsylvania Avenue from the Treasury to Capitol Hill" (*New York Times,* Jan. 19, 1969).

Foreign affairs conducted in an aloof manner is "bleachers diplomacy." "In that part of the world [southeast Asia] Washington seems to practice 'bleachers' diplomacy, as a non-participating spectator of events" (Blair Bolles, *Headline Series—78 of Foreign Policy Association,* Nov.–Dec. 1949).

**bleaching boards** *obs.* A term that evolved into *bleachers* but also coexisted with it. "The horny handed sons of toil made a brave show upon the bleaching boards, where they were jammed and crowded without a seat to spare, so that they overflowed the grounds and crowded in upon the players" (*Illustrated American,* May 10, 1890).

Thomas W. Lawson (*The Krank: His Language and What It Means,* 1888) defined the term as "the resting place for the kranks [fans] who are not acquainted with the doorkeeper of the grandstand." O. P. Caylor (*Cincinnati Enquirer,* 1877, and later reprinted in *The Sporting News,* May 16, 1956): "The bleaching boards just north of the north pavilion now hold the cheap crowd which comes in at the end of the first inning at a discount." (Peter Tamony) **1st Use.** 1836. "His antics on the field prove a source of amusement to the boys on the 'bleaching boards'" (*Sporting Life,* May 24; David Shulman).

**bleeder** 1. A batted ball that, as the result of an erratic roll, pop, bad bounce, or overall slowness, becomes a base hit. Dizzy Dean once described it as "a weak scratch hit that is just slow enuff so the runner can beat it out to first base." A typical bleeder is a ground ball that slows to a stop about halfway down the baseline (with a possible assist from the infield grass), but it can also be an underpowered fly ball that drops unexpectedly. **Etymology/1st Use.** 1937. "A bleeder aptly describes a scratchy single" (Curley Grieve, *San Francisco Examiner,* March 11; Peter Tamony). Mike Whiteford (*How to Talk Baseball,* 1983) states: "The term is a sarcastic one, suggesting the ball was hit so hard that it's bleeding. Following such a hit, players often say, 'Wipe the blood off it.'" A tad more logical, perhaps, is Bert Dunne's (*Folger's Dictionary of Baseball,* 1958) explanation that the term grew out of the phrase "that hit had blood on it!" Dunne further notes that "while the ball was hit on the handle, the batter's fists were figuratively responsible, bled in the process, and left blood on the ball." Thomas P. McDonald (letter, Apr. 13, 1991) suggests that the term might also derive from the speed of the ball, in conjunction with the term "trickler": "Blood trickles from a superficial cut, as opposed to gushing or spurting from a slashed artery, and I think the term 'bleeding' is usually associated more with the former. Thus the *trickler* is also a 'bleeder.'" 2. *obs.* A sharply hit ball "threatening to split the first finger that's laid upon it" (William G. Brandt, *Baseball Magazine,* Oct. 1932). This meaning appears to have been totally canceled out by the first.

**blind** *arch.* A club's scoreless inning. Henry Chadwick (*Technical Terms of Base Ball,* 1897) noted that the term was already considered of historic interest only: "An old-time term used to indicate the retirement of a side in a game without their being able to score a single run."

**blinder** *arch.* "The provincial term in the Middle States for a blank score in a game" (Henry Chadwick, *The Game of Base Ball,* 1868).

**blind mice** A derogatory term for a group of umpires. See also *three blind mice.*

**blind staggers** Awkward maneuvering of a fielder positioning to catch a high windblown fly ball.

**blind tom** An *umpire.* The term refers to an umpire's faulty judgment because of poor eyesight. Robert Hendrickson found this bit of typical and traditional doggerel: "Breathes there a fan with soul so dead, who never to the ump hath said: Yer blind, you bum!" **Usage Note.** Although the term is an affront, it can be used affectionately. "Bill Engeln [is] about to start his fourth season as a National League umpire and his twentieth as a blind tom" (Jack McDonald, *San Francisco Call-Bulletin,* Jan. 25, 1955; Peter Tamony). **1st Use.** 1912. "I get me a newspaper, so I can keep me lamps off that high-ball sign, and right there at the top o' the page is a spiel printed in letters that Blind Tom could read" ("The Wise Guy," *Bonehead*; Peter Tamony). **Etymology.** It is quite likely that the term originated with and was appropriated from Old Blind Tom, a popular black musical prodigy of the period just after the Civil War.

**block** 1. *n.* An action by a defensive player (commonly performed by the catcher) to prevent a runner from tagging a base, accomplished with the aid of the defensive player's body. A block is illegal and can be ruled an obstruction if it occurs without the blocker having the ball or being in the process of fielding it. **1st Use.** 1902. (*Sporting Life,* July 12; Edward J. Nichols). 2. *v.* See *block the plate.* 3. *n.* See *trading block.* 4. *n./arch.* Syn. of *blocked ball.*

**blocked ball** A batted or thrown ball in play that is touched, stopped, or handled by a person not engaged in the game, or that touches any object that is not part of the official equipment or official playing area. Such an occurrence causes a dead ball. This was not so during the early 1880s. Peter Morris has researched this point: *Spalding's Official Base Ball Guide* for 1884 stated that a *block* is "a batted or thrown ball that is stopped or handled by any person not engaged in the game" (rule 31) and whenever a block occurs "the Umpire shall declare it, and Base Runners may run the bases without being put out, until after the ball has been returned to and held by the Pitcher standing in his position" (rule 60). One can imagine the chaos created by this rule: "The ball went into the crowd and became a block[ed] ball. Connolley went to field it, and as a small boy tossed it to him, Weiss of the Cass [the visiting team] struck it with his bat, allowing Shaughnessey to reach third before the ball could be sent to center. This was not exactly right, but as there is no rule covering such work, it was passed by." (*Grand Rapids Daily Democrat,* Aug. 18, 1882).

**blocker 1.** A catcher or other defensive player who blocks either a base or home plate. See also *plate blocker.* **1st Use.** 1905. (*Sporting Life,* Sept. 2; Edward J. Nichols). **2.** A baserunner who throws himself into ("takes out") the second baseman or shortstop to prevent a double play.

**block the plate** For a catcher (or a pitcher, if he is covering the plate) to stand in the way of the runner and use his body to prevent the runner from scoring while attempting to tag him out. It is only legal when the fielder has the ball or is in the process of fielding it.

**blood bounty** Money paid for retaliatory action on the field. "Money irate manager offers to player who will drag ball down first, cause pitcher (who has been throwing at hitters) to cover, offering opportunity to 'run up his back' and spike pitcher" (Bert Dunne, *Folger's Dictionary of Baseball,* 1958).

**bloomer 1.** A player who looks good in spring training, but is a failure when the regular season starts. The term is probably a corruption of "early bloomer." **2.** An erratic player who "blows hot and cold."

**bloop 1.** *n.* A poorly hit ball that drops between the infielders and the outfielders for a hit; a *Texas Leaguer.* The term is onomatopoetically named for the "bloop" sound that is suggested when the bat hits the ball, such as the sound "of a soft tomato struck by a broomstick" (Jim Brosnan, *The Long Season,* 1960). Syn. *blooper,* 1. **2.** *v.* To hit a bloop. "I made a pretty good pitch, but that's how you hit .350. You hit one hard, then bloop one in." (Mike Flanagan, quoted in *Washington Post,* Sept. 25, 1986).

**bloop and a blast** Battle cry of the Pittsburgh

Pirates during announcer Bob Prince's heyday. The cry was used most often in the bottom of the ninth when the Pirates were one run down. Clifford Jordan (letter of Aug. 5, 1989) explained: "It started in 1959, I believe, when so often the Pirates would pull out a victory by getting a bloop single from Dick Groat or Bill Virdon, then a home run blast from Roberto Clemente or Dick Stuart."

**blooper 1.** A *bloop* hit; a *Texas Leaguer;* a *flare,* 1. **1st Use.** 1937. (*New York Times,* Oct. 8; Edward J. Nichols). **2.** Syn. of *blooper ball.*

**blooper ball** A pitch that is lobbed into a high arc, which, when thrown correctly, drops precipitously through the strike zone, tantalizing the batter in the process. It has also been termed a "glorified slow ball" thrown with a high arc. See also *eephus; folly floater; freaky floater.* Syn. *blooper,* 2.

**bloop single** A bloop that allows the batter to reach first base safely. "[Jackie] Gutierrez moved him to third with a bloop single to center" (*Boston Globe,* Aug. 11, 1984).

**blow 1.** *v.* To fail in any of several ways; e.g., lose a game, relinquish a lead, misplay a ball, lose a save opportunity, or make a bad umpiring call. **2.** *n./arch.* A base hit. The term is probably what Babe Ruth and his Yankee teammates called a "single" as it is the only alternative to single offered in *Babe Ruth's Own Book of Baseball* (1928). **3.** *n.* A clutch hit; e.g., "Smith hit the big blow that won the game in extra innings." **1st Use.** 1907. (*New York Evening Journal,* Apr. 27; Edward J. Nichols). **4.** *v.* To hit a baseball hard. **5.** *v.* To throw a fastball with such speed that it cannot be hit; e.g., "Smith could just blow the ball past the hitters" or "Jones blew it by him." **6.** *v.* To pitch strikes. **7.** *n.* A respite, rest, or breather. After being taken out of a game for two innings, Cal Ripken Jr. told the *New York Times* (July 17, 1989): "It was an opportunity with the heat and everything else to get a two-inning blow."

**blow away** To retire a batter when he swings and misses a third strike.

**blow by** See *blow,* 5.

**blow-down pitch** A rarely used synonym of *brushback pitch.* "A pitched ball high and close to the batsman designed to drive him away from the plate" (Ralph H. Barbour, *How to Play Better Baseball,* 1935; David Shulman).

**blower** A fastball pitcher. "I'm not a blower who can throw 95 miles per hour, but I think I've been throwing real well" (Damon Allen, quoted in *Baltimore Sun,* Mar. 30, 1994).

**blown call** A bad judgment or incorrect decision by an umpire. "He had another homer in the game but it was ruled a double on a blown call by umpire Dan Morrison" (*Tampa Tribune,* Mar. 30, 1986). Memory for blown calls can survive long after the act: "[Bob] Feller Can't Forget Blown Call" (*USA Today* headline, Oct. 19, 1990), an allusion to a pickoff play in the first game of the 1948 World Series.

**blown save** A statistic charged to a relief pitcher who enters the game in a save situation but departs with the save situation no longer in effect because he gave up the lead. The statistic was introduced by the makers of Rolaids antacid tablets in 1988. Abbrev. BS.

**blow out** *v.* **1.** To defeat overwhelmingly. "They're not just getting beat, they're getting blown out" (George Steinbrenner on the 1987 New York Yankees, quoted in *Tampa Tribune,* Aug. 13, 1987). **2.** To injure oneself, esp. a pitcher who hurts his arm; e.g., "Smith blew his arm out by pitching a doubleheader."

**blowout** *n.* **1.** A leg or foot injury. The term is a play on "bad wheel." **2.** A one-sided game, such as one in which a team outscores its opponent by a wide margin; e.g., a "16–4 blowout." See also *laugher.*

**blow smoke** To throw a fastball; to throw a ball so hard it "blows the lid off."

**blow up** To lose one's ability to throw strikes; to come unglued. Calvin T. Ryan (*Word Study,* Feb. 1952) noted that the term "is one of those rare examples of slang which just about hits the nail on the head." **1st Use.** 1908. (*Brooklyn Daily Eagle,* May 27; Edward J. Nichols).

**bludgeon 1.** *n.* A baseball bat. **1st Use.** 1908. (*New York Evening Journal,* Mar. 18; Edward J. Nichols). **2.** *v.* To hit the ball.

**bludgeon wielder** A batter. **1st Use.** 1913. (*Harper's Weekly,* Sept. 6; Edward J. Nichols).

**blue** Syn. of *umpire,* in reference to the color of the umpire's uniform. **Usage Note.** The term may have been derogatory at one time, as if it referred not to the color of the umpire's uniform but to someone who "blew it." However, it is common to hear coaches, scorers, spectators, and players at Little League, high school, and college games use the term whenever they address the umpire, even on friendly terms, such as "What's the count, blue?"

**Blue Book** The rules governing Major League Baseball as distinguished from the rules of the game itself. Tom Verducci (*Sports Illustrated,* Aug. 25, 1997) describes one section of the work: "To find the height of arcane verbiage look no farther than Rule 10 of the rules governing Major League Baseball, in what is known as the Blue Book. The corresponding entry explains the waivers system—the procedures that pertain to certain player transactions—in a way that makes the Magna Carta look like part of the Jackie Collins oeuvre. Not even those in the know profess to fully understand it."

**bluecoat** Syn. of *umpire.* "The ball game went on—fortunately, without any especially difficult calls to challenge the bush-league bluecoats" (Roger Angell, describing a game during an umpires' strike, *The Summer Game,* 1972; Charles D. Poe).

**blue dart** A hard, low *line drive,* often difficult to field. "And how about Billy Hunter? I never saw a shortstop make the play he did on Joe Astroth's blue dart. If that wasn't a hit, I never saw one." (Alva "Bobo" Holloman, quoted in *San Francisco News,* May 7, 1953; Peter Tamony). See also *blue darter.* **1st Use.** 1933. (Honus Wagner, *Baseball Grins*).

**blue darter** A low *line drive* "that speeds viciously through the air, as though it were propelled by a blue gas flame" (Mike Whiteford, *How to Talk Baseball,* 1983). The term was used by Donald Gropman (*Say It Ain't So, Joe!,* 1979) for the line drives often hit by Shoeless Joe Jackson. See also *blue dart; darter.* **Etymology.** "Big Blue Darter" is another name for Cooper's hawk, a bird that "will dash into the farmyard like a bolt, passing within a few feet of individuals and carrying off a young chicken with incredible swiftness" (R. I. Brasher, in T. Gilbert Pearson, *Birds of America,* 1936).

**board 1.** *n.* A flat and/or stiff glove or mitt from which balls are likely to bounce, as if it were a board or plank. The term is used less often today than it once was because modern gloves come with deep, preformed pockets and break in quickly. **2.** *v.* To get on base; e.g., "The Rangers boarded two baserunners against Smith." **3.** *n.* Short for *scoreboard;* e.g., "We got on the board early tonight."

**bob-and-weave** The *knuckleball,* so-called because of its erratic nature. "The bob-and-weave became [Al] Nipper's bread-and-butter pitch yesterday" (*Boston Globe,* June 21, 1987).

**bobble 1.** *v.* To mishandle, drop, or lose control of a batted or thrown ball, often resulting in an error. See also *juggle.* **2.** *n.* A ball that has been mishandled. **Etymology.** The term was first used in the early American West as slang for "mistake" or "blunder"; it is listed in 1893 in a "Texas Vocabulary" by F. K. Wister, which appears in the 1968 collection, *Owen Wister Out West* (David Shulman). "Sal, I'm mighty afeerd you'll make a bobble of it" (William C. Campbell, *Colorado Colonel,* 1901; David Shulman).

**bobo** A fan, usually of a manager. Followers of Los Angeles Dodgers manager Tommy Lasorda sat in an area known as "Bo-bo Row." Roger Bresnahan was known as New York Giants manager John McGraw's bobo (Bill James, *The Politics of Glory,* 1994). Also spelled "bo-bo." See also *little bo-bo.*

**Bobby ball** The kind of heads-up baseball played in 1983 by the Toronto Blue Jays, managed by Bobby Cox.

**Bob Fishel Award** An annual award given for excellence in baseball public relations.

**boiler** The stomach of a player, manager, or coach, esp. when upset. A gastric ailment such as an ulcer or an upset stomach is known as a "bad boiler."

**boiling-out place** *arch.* A spring training camp, usually situated in a hot climate. **1st Use.** 1908. (*New York Evening Journal,* Feb. 11; Edward J. Nichols).

**boing ball** A facetious, onomatopoetic term used to describe baseball played on an artificial surface because of the tendency of the ball to bounce erratically and make odd synthetic noises. It apes the boing sound of animated cartoons.

**Bolshevik League** A nickname for *Players League* of 1890. **Etymology.** The term was applied after the fact because the Bolshevik party did not emerge until 1903 in Russia; it seized power in that country in Nov. 1917. In the United States, the term "Bolshevik" and its variations (including the slangy "Bolshie" or "Bolshy") were applied to that which was wild-eyed, radical, and anticapitalistic. The application of the term by conservative sportswriters to a group of baseball players was clearly meant to be derogatory. (Charles D. Poe)

**bolt** *n.* A *line drive.*

**bomb 1.** *v.* To surrender many hits during a finite period (e.g., an inning or game). "Bombed" is said of "pitchers whose pitches return from the plate traveling faster than they were going when they arrived" (Jim Brosnan, *The Long Season,* 1960). **1st Use.** 1905. (*Sporting Life,* Sept. 2; Edward J. Nichols). **2.** *v.* To defeat decisively with many hits; e.g., "The Reds bombed Smith with five extra-base hits." **3.** *n.* Syn. of *home run.* When Ken Griffey Jr. decided to forgo his pursuit of Roger Maris's single-season home run record during the late stages of the 1997 season, he said: "I've got six bombs to go. There ain't no way I'm going to reach it." (E. J. Dionne Jr., *Washington Post,* Oct. 19, 1997).

**bombard** To get many hits off a pitcher.

**bombardment** A rash of hits.

**bomber** A home run hitter.

**Bombers** Short for *Bronx Bombers.*

**bone 1.** *v.* To rub the maximum hitting point or "sweet spot" of one's bat with a soupbone to harden the bat. It is perfectly legal to bone a bat; such noted hitters as Frank Howard and Joe DiMaggio boned their bats. Even Roy Hobbs, the tragic main character of Bernard Malamud's novel *The Natural* (1952), took care of his bat (Wonderboy) in such a fashion: "Hadn't used it much until I played semipro ball, but I always kept it oiled with sweet oil and boned it so it wouldn't chip." **2.** *n.* A heedless or foolish play, often stated as "pulling a bone." Syn. *boner,* 1. **1st Use.** 1915. "Among the spectators not a few expressed the belief that Ganton had 'pulled a bone' by his failure to try for Runyan instead of Schmidt" (Burt L. Standish, *Covering the Look-In Corner;* David Shulman). **3.** *n.* The fist-to-fist congratulatory gesture between a player and a teammate, sometimes coupled with a look of intimidating indifference. This celebratory ritual of the 1990s has replaced the *high five* of the 1980s. The origin of the gesture and term have been claimed by Jose Canseco and Mark McGwire (when they were Oakland A's teammates) and by Brady Anderson in 1989 (*Sports Illustrated,* Sept. 14, 1998).

**bonehead 1.** *n.* A dumb player. **2.** *adj.* Said of a dumb play or dumb player. **1st Use.** 1916. "He took his place in baseball history along with Bonehead Harry, the mythical player who is supposed to have made all the foolish, rattle-brained plays of the game" (*New York Times,* Oct. 16; David Shulman). **Etymology.** This "sweet word" we are told by lexicographer Gretchen Lee (*American Speech,* Apr. 1926) began in baseball as a term of ridicule for a particularly unintelligent player or action. Many sources agree that the origin and certain initial popularity of both "bonehead" and "boner" stem from a single incident. Describing an event that took place on Sept. 23, 1908, Mark Sullivan (*Pre-War America,* volume III of *Our Times,* 1930) stated: "At the Polo Grounds, New York, a dispute historic in baseball, which enriched the language with two exceedingly forceful words, 'bonehead' and 'boner,' arose over whether Frederick Charles Merkle did or did not touch second base." The incident in question occurred under the most dramatic circumstances. It was the last half of the ninth inning in a 1–1 game between the New York Giants and Chicago Cubs. Tied for first place, the winner of the game would take the lead in the National League. New York had two out, Moose McCormick on third, and Merkle on first. Al Bridwell singled to

center field and McCormick crossed the plate with what appeared to be the winning run. The play, however, would not be complete until Merkle touched second base ahead of the ball. If Merkle did not touch second, he could still be retired by a force at the base. With two outs, no runs can score until a possible force play has been completed.

Although there were claims to the contrary on the part of Merkle and others (including 8,000 fans who signed a petition that said they had seen him touch the bag), Merkle apparently veered right toward the clubhouse in center field before touching second. He presumed the game was over when McCormick crossed the plate, causing him to stop short of the bag. At this point, Cubs second baseman Johnny Evers signaled for the center fielder to throw him the ball so he could tag second. Jubilant with their apparent victory, fans and Giant players rushed onto the field, creating mass confusion. Before Evers could retrieve the ball and record the out at second base, a spectator grabbed the ball and threw it into the stands. The Giants pushed Merkle back to the base, as the ball, recovered by a Chicago fan, was tossed back to Evers. But all this took place after the umpires had left the field. Despite the fact that the New York papers credited the Giants with the win, it was decided by National League President Harry C. Pulliam that the game be recorded as a tie. The drawn game was replayed a day after the season ended, and Chicago won both the game and the pennant.

As to the origin of "bonehead" and "boner" in their modern sense, Sullivan reported: "In their wrath at Merkle, an excellent player, the New York fans fixed upon a previously anemic and almost meaningless word, and gave to it a significance with which every reader is familiar. For more than twenty years, there has been rarely a game when from some part of the stands there did not arise from time to time, in shrill falsetto or hoarse bellow, the cry 'bonehead' directed at any player disapproved, not always justly, by a 'fan.'" The sad part of the story is that Merkle is remembered for this one play, but he had an otherwise respectable career playing for four teams from 1907 to 1926.

As Sullivan suggests, there is evidence to hint that "bonehead" (but not "boner") predates the Merkle play. Alfred H. Holt (*Phrase Origins,* 1936) reports that the term has been spotted in print as early as 1903 for a person who acts stupidly (presumably with bones where there should be brains) and that it was popularized by the 1908 incident; however, the earliest Edward J. Nichols can date the term is Mar. 9, 1908 (*New York Evening Journal*), five and a half months before the Merkle affair. A specific point of origin was suggested by Hy Turkin when he noted that manager George Stallings first used the term to describe the "brainless play" of his 1898 Phillies. Lee Allen (*Hot Stove League,* 1955) agrees but insists that the term was applied mainly to Phillies owner Col. John I. Rodgers, who released Stallings in 1898.

Still one more piece of the puzzle: Norman Macht noted in the necrology section of the 1913 *Spalding's Official Base Ball Guide* that Edward Aschenbach, manager of teams in the New York State league, "coined the term 'bonehead.'"

As is often the case with American slang, researchers are faced with conflicting claims that are long past the point of being sorted out; however, what is clear and conclusive in this case is that the term was a slang rarity until the 1908 error. **Extended Use.** Stupid or foolish. "I don't like ta knock ya, but when ya pull a bonehead stunt like ya did yesterday, y're in love, or else y're getting balmy in the bean" (*Railroad Man's Magazine,* Aug. 1916; Peter Tamony).

**bonehead play** A blunder; an error; a dumb play. **1st Use.** 1912. "I don't know as I'd call it a vice so much as a bonehead play" (Alfred H. Lewis, *The Apaches of New York;* David Shulman).

**boner 1.** A dumb play, usually as the result of an error of judgment or lack of concentration as opposed to a mere physical mistake, such as a baserunner taking off on a catchable fly thinking that there are two outs when, in fact, there is only one; specif., *Merkle's boner.* "A mental blunder—or fit of absentmindedness, a sudden blanking out, a momentary wandering—that brings on dreadful consequences" (Ron Fimrite, *Sports Illustrated,* Oct. 15, 1990). Syn. *bone,* 2; *bull; Merkle.* **2.** Any stupid move on or off the field. "Bill Sullivan the old White Sox catcher talked to me and told me not to pull no boner by refusing to go where they sent me" (Ring W. Lardner, *You Know Me Al,*

1914). **Usage Note.** Historically, the term has not been used lightly in baseball and tends to be reserved for only the most serious gaffes. In its most extreme case (the infamous Merkle's boner) it hung on Fred Merkle for the rest of his life. "Fred Merkle, Of 'Boner' Fame, Dies" (Associated Press obituary headline, Mar. 2, 1956; Peter Tamony). **Etymology.** Gretchen Lee (*American Speech,* Apr. 1926) noted: "The sweet word 'Bone-head' began with ball players, and from it has sprung the useful term 'boner,' meaning an error in judgment." The full etymology from the Fred Merkle play of 1908 is discussed under *bonehead.* **Extended Use.** An error, but without the sting it carries in the context of baseball. The term has also specifically come to mean a hilarious classroom gaffe or howler.

**boneyard** The imaginary dying grounds for washed-up pitchers.

**boneyard aggregation** A team made up of old or worn-out players.

**bonk** A lightly hit ball.

**bonus 1.** A cash incentive given to a draft choice for signing with a team; e.g., Gregg Olson received a $200,000 bonus from the Baltimore Orioles in 1988. See also *signing bonus.* **2.** A special incentive or reward payment built into a player's contract, based on a particular aspect of that player's performance, such as innings pitched, games played, or selection to the All-Star team.

**bonus baby** A free-agent player signed under the *bonus rule* of 1953–57. Such players were usually 18 or 19 years old, so full of promise and talent that they overshadowed their high school or college teammates and had professional teams scrambling to sign them; however, many bonus babies had failed careers as they were not ready for baseball at the major-league level and their talent rusted in idleness on the bench. The first bonus baby was Vic Janowicz, who signed out of Ohio State Univ. with the Pittsburgh Pirates for $25,000. Three bonus babies are in the Hall of Fame: Al Kaline, Harmon Killebrew, and Sandy Koufax. Syn. "bonus kid."

Pat Jordan (*False Spring,* 1975) wrote: "The term 'bonus baby' is usually applied to any player receiving more than $10,000 upon signing a contract. Naturally, whenever a team invests such money in a player they treat him more tenderly than they would a player in whom they invested little money. A bonus baby had only to hint at improvement in order to advance in the minors. But a non-bonus baby had to fashion a record of unquestionable success before he advanced."

**bonus player** A prospective player who is given a cash bonus as an extra incentive to sign with a major-league team. The first bonus player was pitcher Charlie Devens who signed with the New York Yankees for $20,000 in 1932. The first bonus player to capture popular attention was outfielder Dick Wakefield who received $52,000 and a new car to sign with the Detroit Tigers upon his graduation from the Univ. of Michigan in 1941. Sportswriter Jimmy Cannon defined "bonus player" as one "who is paid a fortune to watch ballgames" as many such players fail to live up to expectations. The term did not attract attention as a new term until after World War II; e.g., "bonus player" is listed as new in 1947 in Kenneth Versand's *Polyglot's Lexicon 1943–1966* (1973).

**bonus rule 1.** A rule in effect from shortly after World War II to 1952 by which a player signed to a contract of more than $6,000 had to be placed on the major-league roster at the end of his professional season. **2.** A rule in effect from 1953 to 1957 by which a player who signed a professional contract with a major-league team for more than $4,000 had to remain on the team's roster as an active player for a period of two full seasons. A player given a bonus contract by a minor-league team had to go through an unrestricted draft before his contract could be assigned, sold, or traded to any other club. The rule was instituted at the Dec. 1952 winter meetings to discourage paying large amounts of money to untried players. See Brent Kelley, *Baseball's Biggest Blunder* (1996). See also *bonus baby*.

**boob** A fool; a dolt. **Etymology.** David Shulman (*American Speech*, Feb. 1951) noted that the term is not baseballese, but seems to have originated with baseball players. The earliest use that Shulman could find was in Christy Mathewson's *Pitch-*

*ing in a Pinch* (1912): "There's a poor 'boob' in the hospital now that stopped one with his head." The term may have been inspired by the much older term "booby," for a fool.

**boo bird** A fan given to jeers, boos, and catcalls when the home team falters. "The boo birds in the Cleveland stands were in full voice. Even Earl Averill, a star for eight years and one of the great hitters of all time, came in for his share of sour notes from the fans." (Bob Feller, *Strikeout Story,* 1947; Charles D. Poe).

**book 1.** *n.* The official rules of the game. **2.** *n.* The philosophy of the game; the unwritten code of baseball tenets that "everyone knows" are true; the collection of assumptions and percentages used to make baseball decisions; the compilation of baseball's conventional wisdom. It is often referred to as *The Book.* These unwritten but widely observed rules and assumptions are followed by the game's managers, players, and fans. Perhaps the most often-cited example of a tenet of the book is that left-handed batters face right-handed pitchers and vice versa. Other tenets include not intentionally walking the potential winning run and playing for a tie on the road and a win at home. "The book says you've got to run through the bag [rather than diving headfirst into first base] because it's quicker" (Ray Miller, quoted in *Baltimore Sun,* Apr. 19, 1998). But the book is not universally followed, as manager Dick Williams noted in 1980: "I never play by the book because I never met the guy that wrote it." A manager who makes an unconventional move is said to be "going against the book." **3.** *n.* The information that a team has on the specific strengths and weaknesses of an opposing pitcher, batter, or manager. Clubhouse food, out-of-town restaurants, umpires, and practically any other variable may have a book. Ken Singleton (quoted in *The Sporting News,* June 13, 1981): "You keep a book on umpires the way you do with pitchers." **4.** *n.* A scouting report; the sum of facts on how to pitch or hit against a certain player. Jim Henneman (*Baltimore Sun,* June 7, 1994) wrote: "While constantly aware of his speed, the opponents' 'book' on [Brady] Anderson is that he no longer relies on the bunt as a primary offensive weapon." **5.** *n.* The record book of baseball. The term is often used in the plural. **6.** *v.* To move very fast or with maximum speed; e.g., "Smith was really booking around the bases for a stand-up triple."

**book-crazed** Being overly obsessed with baseball statistics.

**bookends** A pair of defensive players positioned on opposite sides of the playing field; specif., the left fielder and right fielder collectively, and the first baseman and third baseman collectively. The term was used to describe first baseman Don Mattingly and third baseman Mike Pagliarulo of the New York Yankees (ca. 1986).

**boom** To hit the ball hard. **1st Use.** 1909. (*Baseball Magazine,* July; Edward J. Nichols).

**boomerang ball** A batted ball that comes back to the pitcher.

**boost** *arch.* To hit the bottom half of the ball, causing it to pop up in the air. **1st Use.** 1908. (*New York Evening Journal,* Aug. 26; Edward J. Nichols).

**boot 1.** *n.* An error, such as one made while handling a ground ball. Typically, the ball bounces off the fielder's glove, as if it were kicked or booted. Originally, a booted ball was (and still is on occasion) one that had actually been kicked ("booted") in error, but the term has long since been generalized to any fielding error. "Why does he waste his efforts booting baseballs, when Yale is mourning the lack of a punter?" (Hugh S. Fullerton, *American Magazine,* June 1912). **2.** *v.* To commit a boot. See also *kick,* 3. **1st Use.** 1907. (*New York Evening Journal,* May 2; Edward J. Nichols). **Extended Use.** To err; to mishandle. **3.** *v.* To remove from a game; e.g., "The umpire booted Smith for kicking dirt on him."

**booth** The area in a ballpark where radio and television announcers work, usually from an elevated position behind home plate. "Booth" is a traditional baseball term that is often used when the work area bears no resemblance to a booth. "This spring, after dreaming of it for years, I finally entered 'the booth.' Actually, it's not a booth at all; it's more like a pen, open to the elements ex-cept for some light wire mesh designed to protect the announcers from irate fans." (J. Anthony Lucas, *New York Times,* Sept. 12, 1971).

**bopper** A player who makes many hits. "We don't have many big boppers, but every once in a while it gets contagious" (Jeromy Burnitz, quoted in *Wisconsin State Journal,* July 19, 1997).

**Borough Hall** A sidearm pitch in Brooklyn when that borough was Dodger territory.

**Bosox** A nickname of the Boston Red Sox.

**Boston ball** Syn. of *Massachusetts game.*

**Boston Bees** A temporary name for the Boston Braves. In 1936, a contest was held among fans of the Braves to rename the team (this came after a disastrous 1935 season). From some 1,327 entries the name "Bees" was selected as the new official team name. It lasted only five seasons, when the name reverted to Braves. If nothing else the Bees were a headline writer's dream. Not only could the team's name be abbreviated as "B's," but stories could be introduced with lines like "Bees Swarm South" and "Bees Sting Again." The old name was brought back in the 1941 season as a new group of owners took over the team and concluded that the fans much preferred the old name; in fact, many fans persisted in calling them the Braves during the Bees' years.

**Boston Braves** A National League team from 1876 to 1952, after which it moved to Milwaukee in 1953 and later to Atlanta for the 1966 season, each time retaining the nickname "Braves." The team had several nicknames (including Red Stockings, Red Caps, Beaneaters, Doves, and Rustlers) before it became the Braves in 1912 after James E. Gaffney bought the team. Gaffney was a contractor and Tammany Hall chieftain. The name, suggested by John Montgomery Ward, one of Gaffney's partners, came from the fact that members of the Tammany machine were often referred to as "braves." The Tammany Society, which had been formed in New York City in 1789, was named for a Delaware Indian chief (Tammany) known for his sagacity. Tammany Hall was the most famous of the big-city political machines and had a major influence (often corrupt, sometimes effective) in New York politics for about 100 years (roughly from the middle of the 19th century to the middle of the 20th century).

**Boston game** Syn. of *Massachusetts game.*

**Boston Massacre 1.** The widely used nickname for the 1978 fade by the Boston Red Sox. "Red Sox rooters have known heartbreak. They haven't forgotten the Boston Massacre in 1978 and the 14½-game lead that vanished like an apparition." (Tom Pedulla, *The Gannett Westchester Newspapers,* June 25, 1986). Also recalled as "the Collapse," "the Fade," and "the Fold." **2.** The four-game sweep of the Boston Red Sox by the New York Yankees at Fenway Park in Boston, Sept. 7–10, 1978, by scores of 15–3, 13–2, 7–0, and 7–4. Recalled by Joseph St. George: "Yankees came to town four games behind, left town tied for first." **Etymology.** The name comes from the event that took place on Mar. 5, 1770, when British soldiers fired on a crowd of Colonists in Boston; five people died. The word of the Boston Massacre spread rapidly and served to strengthen the spirit of revolution.

**Boston Red Sox** The name of the American League East Division franchise in Boston, Mass. The nickname originated in Ohio with the Cincinnati Red Stockings, baseball's first professional team. When the Red Stockings broke up in 1871, many team members headed to Boston to form a new National Association team, and they carried with them both the name and the red stockings for which they were famous. The name was gradually dropped in the 1880s but revived and reapplied in 1904 for a new American League team that had come to town in 1901. The Boston Americans had been called the Somersets (in honor of owner and American League vice president Charles W. Somers), the Puritans, Pilgrims, Plymouth Rocks, and Speed Boys, and became the Red Sox under the ownership of the Taylor family, which also owned the *Boston Globe.* The team is sometimes called the Bosox, the Carmine Hose, and the Rouge Hose.

**"both feet on the rubber"** [softball term] A point often made by the coach or other players to the pitcher to remind him that both feet must touch the pitcher's rubber before the ball can be delivered.

**bottle** To contain an opponent. To "bottle a game" is to win it or make certain of winning it.

**bottle bat** A baseball bat with an especially large barrel, a short taper, and very small handle, which gives it a bottlelike appearance. The bat was made famous by Heinie Groh, who used it with great effectiveness from 1912 to 1921 when he played for the Cincinnati Reds. A bottle-shaped bat would be legal today as long as it was not more than 2¾ inches at its thickest and not more than 42 inches in length. Syn. *fat bat.*

**bottom 1.** The *second half* of an inning. The home team's scoring always appears on the bottom line of the scoreboard. **2.** The last few players in a

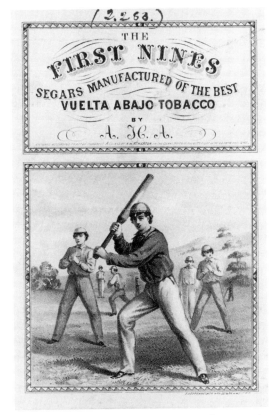

**Bottle bat.** *A tobacco wrapper from 1867 illustrating the classic bat with the large barrel.*

team's batting order, usually comprising the weaker hitters, and, in the National League, including the pitcher.

**bottom falls out** Said of a pitched ball that drops sharply as it crosses the plate. Syn. "bottom drops out."

**bottom half** The *second half* of an inning.

**bottom of the order** The last three batters in the batting order, almost always a club's least effective hitters.

**Boudreau shift** Syn. of *Williams shift.*

**bounce a beauty** To make a safe hit with a well-directed ground ball.

**bounce back** 1. To hit the ball so that it bounds back to the pitcher. 2. To recover quickly; e.g., "After losing the first game of the doubleheader, the Giants bounced back to take the second game."

**bounce out** *v.* To hit the ball so that it bounces and is fielded for an easy out.

**bounceout** *n.* A batted ball that promptly starts to bounce and is fielded immediately for the out.

**bouncer** A ground ball that takes a series of moderate bounces.

**bounce target** *arch.* Syn. of *cutoff man.* **1st Use.** 1935. A "bounce target" is "provided by a player placing himself in line between the home base and an outfielder making a throw-in to indicate the length and direction of the throw and to intercept it if advisable" (Ralph H. Barbour, *How to Play Better Baseball;* David Shulman).

**boundary belt** A home run.

**bounder** A high-bouncing, easy-to-field ball. See also *big bill.* Syn. *big bounce.*

**bow and arrow** An umpire's technique in calling a third strike by punching one arm forward while jerking the elbow of the other arm backward, aping the movements of an archer (*Sports Illustrated,* Apr. 16, 1990).

**Bowery, the** Row of lockers reserved for players who are past their prime. **Etymology.** The term dates from the middle 1930s and is a direct reference to the Bowery, a street running diagonally across the east side of lower Manhattan. The street and the area around it have long been associated with grim poverty and human dereliction. Metaphorically, it stands for the end of the road. The name comes from the Dutch word "bouwerji," for farm.

**bow tie** A term used by Satchel Paige for a pitch at the batter's throat.

**box** **1.** *n.* A designated area on the playing field within which a player or coach is obliged to stand; e.g., *batter's box, catcher's box, pitcher's box* (or mound), and *coach's box.* However, in the 19th century it was all but exclusively a reference to the pitcher's position (originally a box-shaped area) or, as one reference put it, "the little square in the middle of the diamond." **1st Use.** 1883. (*Sporting Life,* May 20; Edward J. Nichols). **2.** *n.* Short for *box seat.* **3.** *n.* Short for *box score;* e.g., "Give me a few minutes to look at yesterday's boxes." **4.** *v.* To get in front of the ball to prevent it getting past; e.g., a catcher who blocks a pitch is said "to box it." **5.** *v.* To field a ground ball awkwardly.

**box artist** A pitcher. **1st Use.** 1908. (*Brooklyn Eagle,* May 20; Edward J. Nichols).

**boxcar town** *arch.* A small town. **Extended Use.** In the derogatory talk of players, the term suggested a sleepy town whose main feature was a siding where the railroad stored boxcars.

**boxman** *arch.* A pitcher. "[Carl] Mays has a lot less 'stuff' than a whole raft of other boxmen, whom he outlasts in winning results" (*Baseball Magazine,* 1917).

**box score** A condensed statistical summary of a baseball game, traditionally a feature of newspaper sports sections. For years it was believed that the first box score appeared in the *New York Clipper* (July 16, 1853): however, historian Melvin Adelman located a newspaper account of a baseball game in the *New York Herald* (Oct. 25, 1845), accompanied by a sort of proto–box score that qualifies as a "condensed statistical summary" of the game. Box scores did not appear with regularity until 1876 and the founding of the National League. Henry Chadwick is given credit for the creation of the shorthand ("phonographic") box

**Box score.** *The Hall-of-Fame plaque acknowledging Henry Chadwick's contribution to the game.*

score, although some have insisted that *New York Herald* writer Michael J. Kelly deserves the credit. Syn. *box*, 3. **1st Use.** 1908. (*Baseball Magazine*, June; Edward J. Nichols). **Etymology.** According to Edward J. Nichols, the term is derived "from the old newspaper custom of placing the data in a boxed-off section on the page." **Extended Use.** The term has long been used for statistical summaries in other sports and as a metaphor for results in other areas. A headline in the *New York Herald Tribune* (Oct. 4, 1936) proclaimed "Republicans See Errors in 'Box Score' of New Deal"; the story under the headline read in part: "Arthur M. Curtis, assistant to the chairman of the Republican National Committee, Friday issued a statement calling attention to 'five errors' and one 'deliberate misplay' which belong in the 'box score' brought to the nation by President Roosevelt's Pittsburgh address." Roosevelt had talked of "the

box score of the government of the United States" in his speech. This political use of the term continued: when Harry Truman became President he issued periodic "box scores" scoring Congressional action on his legislative program. "Truman 'Box Score' Hits Congress Again" (*San Francisco Call-Bulletin* headline, Aug. 12, 1948; Peter Tamony).

**box seat** A choice and most expensive seat at the ballpark, located near home plate, first base, or third base. Syn. *box*, 2. **1st Use.** 1871. "[New York Mutuals president William H.] Cammeyer has installed a platform [at the Union Grounds in Brooklyn] in front of and above the dressing rooms of the Mutual Club to which persons who wish to be exclusive can obtain admission by the payment of an extra quarter" (*New York Clipper*, June 3, 1871).

**box-work** *arch.* Syn. of *pitching*, 1. **1st Use.** 1888. (*New York Press*, Apr. 2; Edward J. Nichols).

**boy blue** Syn. of *umpire*. **Etymology.** Almost certainly inspired by the horn-blowing "Little Boy Blue" of nursery rhyme fame and a tie-in to the traditional blue umpire's uniform.

**boys in blue** The umpires. See also *men in blue*. **1st Use.** 1937. (*New York Daily News*, May 6; Edward J. Nichols). **Etymology.** An obvious borrowing from the nickname of both the Union soldiers of the Civil War and police forces of modern times, who have both been recognized by their blue uniforms.

**Boys of Summer 1.** A retrospective nickname for the Brooklyn Dodgers of the 1950s, created by Roger Kahn in his 1972 book on the Brooklyn Dodgers, *The Boys of Summer*. The book, according to Kahn, was "not on sports but on time and what it does to all of us." **2.** A term used by broadcasters and writers to connote all baseball players. An Opening Day story from *USA Today* (Apr. 7, 1987) begins: "The Boys of Summer are back—at last." There has been some play on the term; e.g., players in spring training are called the "Boys of Spring," and popular broadcaster Jon Miller is called the "Voice of Summer" (*Washington Post*, July 31, 1988). **Etymology.** The term itself comes from a Dylan Thomas poem entitled "I

See the Boys of Summer," which Kahn quotes at the beginning of his book.

**Boys of Zimmer** The 1989 Chicago Cubs under manager Don Zimmer.

**BP** Abbrev. for *batting practice*. It is also used as a term; e.g., "Mark McGwire and Ken Griffey Jr. can put on great shows in BP."

**BR** Abbrev. for *bats right*.

**Brabender's Law** A facetious "natural law" of postseason play that states: "The most inactive player during the World Series will be the most active during the clubhouse follies." Discovered by George Vecsey (*New York Times*), the law is named for pitcher Gene Brabender of the Baltimore Orioles who drenched the clubhouse after spending all of his time in the bullpen as his team swept the Los Angeles Dodgers in the 1966 World Series.

**brace of homers** Two home runs, such as when a player hits two home runs during a game.

**braille-man** *arch.* A coach skilled at sending signs and hand signals to baserunners. Most signs involve use of the hands.

**brain cramp** A mental error. "The Red Sox lost more than a game to the Yankees last night, more than an argument with an umpire who admitted afterward that he had suffered a 'brain cramp'" (Gordon Edes, *Boston Globe*, Sept. 16, 1997). See also *vapor lock*. **Etymology.** Buster Olney (*San Diego Union-Tribune*, Apr. 11, 1994) wrote that if former San Diego Padres pitching coach Pat Dobson did not originate the term, "then he was responsible for popularizing its use."

**brains** The manager of a baseball team.

**brain surgeon** A ballplayer. When Leonard Shecter (*Baseball Digest*, June 1963) asks what is easier to become than a successful ballplayer, a disgusted pitcher replies: "I think I'll take up something simple, like brain surgery."

**Branch Rickey Award** An award presented by the Rotary Club of Denver to a major-league player, manager, or executive who epitomizes outstanding community service. It is named for a Hall of Famer who served as player, manager, and executive.

**brander** *arch.* A hard-hit ball that dents or "brands" the ground. **1st Use.** 1869. (*New York Herald*, Sept. 16; Edward J. Nichols).

**Brannigan** A brawl. "Don't start a Brannigan. But if somebody else does, give 'em hell." (Ty Cobb, *My Life in Baseball*, 1961). Not to be confused with *pull a brenegan*.

**brass** A team's management, including the owner, general manager, and field manager. "[Dwight] Evans takes [verbal] shot at Red Sox brass" (Associated Press dispatch, July 4, 1987). **1st Use.** 1946. "Manager Frankie Frisch is the 'CO,' the 'Old Man,' or 'The Brass,' and he and his coaches have come to be known as 'GHQ'" (Chester L. Smith, *Baseball Digest*, May). **Etymology.** The term originated during World War II and was a reference to the decorative metal insignias (usually made of brass) worn by officers. It established itself as service-wide military slang for officers as a class. It was brought back and reapplied by baseball players returning from the war.

**bravery suit** The protective gear worn by the plate umpire. "On occasion an umpire will forget to wear part of his 'bravery suit'" (Ron Luciano, *Strike Two*, 1984; Charles D. Poe).

**bread-and-butter pitch** A pitcher's most effective pitch; the specific pitch by which the pitcher "earns a living." Bert Dunne (*Folger's Dictionary of Baseball*, 1958) noted: "When pitcher is denied right to dust off batter, he cries, 'You're taking away my bread and butter.'"

**breadbasket catch** A catch of a high fly ball with the glove held just above the waist as opposed to one's arms over one's head. "Breadbasket" has been a slang word for "stomach" since the 16th century. See also *basket catch*.

**breadwinner** A player who brings home the most in terms of wins, saves, or winning runs.

**break 1.** *v.* To deviate along the trajectory of a pitched ball; e.g., "Smith's curveball breaks sharply." **1st Use.** 1905. "The deceptive feature of this delivery [spitball] is the fact that it is nothing but a straight ball until just as the batter swings at it, then it 'breaks' sharply" (*Sporting Life*, May 13;

Peter Tamony). **2.** *n.* The deviation in the trajectory of a pitched ball. **3.** *n.* A runner's start toward the next base. **4.** *n.* A lucky or unlucky event; e.g., "To make your own breaks is to create your own luck." See also *breaks, the.* **5.** *n.* The turning point in a game; a crucial play—often a mistake—on which a team capitalizes. "Time and again these two have kept the score board clean as far as the sixth or 'lucky seventh' and then would come the break for which each team was working" (William Patten & J. W. McSpadden, *The Book of Baseball,* 1911; Peter Tamony). **6.** *v.* To end something; e.g., to "break" a hitting streak or to "break" another player's record. **7.** *n.* A prompt movement by a fielder to a batted ball; e.g., "Getting a good break to the ball involves knowing the pitcher's habits, the batter's manners, and the pitch being thrown." **8.** *v.* To react promptly to a batted ball; e.g., "Smith breaks toward second as the ball was hit to right field." **9.** *v.* To run toward a batted ball; e.g., "Smith breaks to the ball as soon as it is hit." **10.** *n.* An interruption; e.g., the *All-Star break.*

**breaker** Syn. of *breaking ball.*

**break his dishes** To break a batter's bat handle; e.g., "The pitcher got in his kitchen [inside] and broke his dishes." Phil Pepe (*The Encyclopedia of Sports Talk,* 1976) reports: "The term has been refined as in, 'He got in his refrigerator and broke his eggs.'"

**break in 1.** To make good with a club; to make the team. **2.** To condition or soften a glove or mitt to fit a player's hand or for game use.

**breaking** Deviating. Curveballs are variously described by the manner of their deviation; e.g., high-breaking, low-breaking, fast-breaking, slow-breaking.

**breaking ball** Any pitched ball (curveball, slider, sinker, knuckleball, screwball) that deviates from a relatively straight and natural trajectory. The generic nature of the term was underscored when announcer Brooks Robinson (telecast, Aug. 18, 1987) admitted that this was the term broadcasters used when they were not sure what kind of pitch had just been thrown. Robinson is not alone in this perception. Jerry Howarth (*Baseball Lite,*

1986) noted: "A term used by radio and television sportscasters who have difficulty detecting the difference between a slider and curve." Syn. *breaker; hammer,* 5. **1st Use.** 1905. (*Sporting Life,* Oct. 7; Edward J. Nichols).

**breaking stuff** An assortment of breaking balls.

**break into** To make one's professional debut at a particular level of the game; e.g., to "break into" the minors or to "break into" the majors. **1st Use.** 1906. (*Sporting Life,* Mar. 10; Edward J. Nichols).

**break off the table** To drop suddenly. The term is used to describe the motion of a curveball that falls precipitously. Syd Russell (*San Francisco Examiner,* Feb. 26, 1961) on 16-year-old prospect Frank Bertaina: "He has a variety of serves, but is primarily a curve baller. In the jargon of the trade, his downer is described as one that 'breaks off the table.' In other words, it drops all of a sudden—just like a round object rolling off the edge of a flat surface."

**break one off** To throw a breaking ball.

**break on top** To score first in a game.

**break open 1.** To get the first run(s) in a game. **2.** To establish a commanding lead in a game.

**breaks, the** Luck and good fortune, often created by another's mistake or miscue. **1st Use.** 1908. (*American Magazine,* June). The term was identified as a baseball term by Edward J. Nichols. V. Samuels (*American Speech,* Feb. 1927) noted: "The player of the side favored by luck 'gets the breaks' or the 'lucky breaks.'" The term appears to have been regarded as exclusive to baseball as late as 1943: Franklin Faskee (*Baseball Magazine,* Jan. 1943), in an article entitled "The Breaks," reported: "Some call it fate. The old-time player called it the jinx. And players and fans now call it 'the breaks.'" **Extended Use.** The breaks and the breaks of the game are common ways of connoting luck in many realms of modern life.

**break the wrists** To bring the top hand over the bottom hand when taking a full swing at a pitched ball. The term and concept come into play when a batter starts to swing at a pitch and then attempts to stop. If, in the view of the umpire, the batter has turned or rolled ("broken") his wrists, the pitch will be called a strike; if not, the pitch will be judged (as a ball or called strike) as if the bat had not moved at all.

**break up 1.** To score the game-winning run(s) with a flurry of hits. **1st Use.** 1905. (*Sporting Life*, Oct. 7; Edward J. Nichols). **2.** To dismantle a winning team by trading or releasing players. **3.** See *break up the double play*.

**break-up slide** A slide that is made to prevent a double play or triple play. The baserunner who is about to be forced out attempts to slide into the infielder making the play so that he will not be able to relay the ball.

**break up the double play** To prevent a second out with the break-up slide.

**breeze 1.** *v.* To work with ease, whether it is to run the bases without interference or to win against easy competition; e.g., "Smith breezed through the lineup by retiring nine batters in a row." **2.** *n.* An easy victory; e.g., "Smith won it in a breeze." **1st Use.** 1910. (*Baseball Magazine*, Sept.; Edward J. Nichols). **3.** *v.* To throw the fastball. **4.** *n.* A strikeout (*Baseball Magazine*, Oct. 1932). **Extended Use.** Baseball's popular term of ease has been long applied to other easy conquests, such as "breezing" through an examination or "it was a breeze."

**breezer** A fastball.

**breeze through** See *breeze*, 1.

**brenegan** See *pull a brenegan*. Not to be confused with *Brannigan*.

**Brew Crew** A nickname for the Milwaukee Brewers, so named after its 13-game winning streak at the beginning of the 1987 season.

**brick 1.** An inexpensive ball; a rocklike ball. See also *nickelbrick*. **2.** A ball thrown by a pitcher or infielder that feels heavy to the fielder catching it. **3.** A lot of 50 or more baseball cards sold as a unit and packed like a solid brick. A brick usually contains cards of one type (e.g., a "Mariners brick") and do not normally contain rarities.

**bridge** To give up a home run. "When a pitcher is 'bridged' he has allowed a home run" (*Sports Illustrated*, Sept. 13, 1982).

**Briggs Stadium** The name of the home field of the Detroit Tigers from 1938 to 1960, when it became known as Tiger Stadium.

**bring along** To expose a player to increasingly difficult learning situations.

**bring in 1.** To score a runner; e.g., "Smith's single brings in Jones from second." **1st Use.** 1865. (Chadwick Scrapbooks; Edward J. Nichols). **2.** To move the infielders and/or outfielders closer to home plate in an attempt to prevent the opposing team from scoring a run on a batted ball.

**bring it** To throw a pitch with great velocity.

**bring up** To promote a player from a minor-league team (usually a farm club). If such a player fails, it is often said that "he was brought up too soon."

**Broadway 1.** The middle of the plate; e.g., "Smith threw the ball right down Broadway." **2.** *arch.* "A flashy dresser, loud talker" (*Sporting News Record Book*, 1937). Once a popular baseball catchall nickname, it may have been last widely used to describe pitcher Charlie Wagner of the Boston Red Sox (1938–42, 1946). Lyn Lary, whose major-league career extended from 1929 through 1940, served as the epitome of the player who attracted the name. Today it is hard to find his name in print without an adjective like "dapper" or "snappy." When Lary and Leo Durocher, another snappy dresser, were both with the New York Yankees in 1929, Durocher got nicknamed "Fifth Avenue" presumably because he was a bit less flashy than Lary. **Extended Use.** The term may have made a permanent transfer to football with the dubbing of "Broadway" Joe Namath of the New York Jets.

**broken-bat** *adj.* Said of a hit achieved in spite or because of a bat that breaks when it comes in contact with the ball; e.g., "Smith hit a broken-bat single just beyond the infield."

**broken play** A play, such as a hit and run or a steal, that began but was stopped because the umpire called a time out or the batter fouled a pitch, thereby revealing the strategy of the team at bat.

**Bronx Bombers** A nickname for the New York Yankees that first became popular in the 1930s when heavyweight boxing champion Joe Louis was known as the Brown Bomber. The term connotes a team that hits many home runs and is still in common use when referring to the Yankees. Syn. *Bombers.* **Etymology/1st Use.** The term was coined by *New York World-Telegram* writer Daniel M. Daniels in July 1936, after Louis's Yankee Stadium fight against Max Schmeling in June 1936. It displaced "Ruppert's Rifles" and "McCarthymen" as nicknames for the Yankees. (Barry Popik)

**Bronx Bummers** A nickname for the New York Yankees when the team is not doing well. Mike Downey (*The Sporting News,* Sept. 12, 1988): "These guys are not the Bronx Bombers. They are the Bronx Bummers."

**Bronx bunnies** A nickname for the New York Yankees. The term was used in Roger Angell's *The Summer Game* (1972).

**Bronx cheer** A contemptuous razzing sound making by sticking the tongue between the closed lips and expelling air; a *razzberry.* Long associated with New York baseball fans who have never been shy about criticizing players in disfavor: "Bronx Cheers Hit [Joe] DiMaggio at Failure to Clout Ball" (*San Francisco News* headline, May 13, 1946; Peter Tamony). Although there is no direct evidence to support the connection, the term may have been created in reference to the Bronx-based New York Yankees. **1st Use.** 1931. "The Bronx cheer has even invaded Forest Hills. During tight tennis matches there this last summer the gallery with increasing frequency undertook to line the matches." (*San Francisco News,* Dec. 31; Peter Tamony).

**Bronx Zoo** A derogatory nickname for the New York Yankees during the ownership of George Steinbrenner, taken from the name of the famous zoo of the same borough. The clear implication is that of a motley assortment of wild animals. "Not for nothing are the New York Yankees of George Steinbrenner known as the Bronx Zoo" (William Gildea, *The Washington Post,* Apr. 27, 1986). **1st Use.** 1979. In that year Sparky Lyle and Peter Golenbock published an account of the Yankees' 1978 season called *The Bronx Zoo.* According to Golenbock's preface

**Brooklyn Dodgers.** *A pin celebrating the team that belonged to Brooklyn from 1890–1957.*

the title was the "masterstroke" of the book's editor, Larry Freundlich of Crown Books.

**Brooklyn Dodgers** The name of the National League franchise that played in Brooklyn, N.Y., from 1890 to 1957 (in Ebbets Field from 1913 through 1957). The nickname "Dodgers" was originally used by baseball writers in the late 1890s when the team was known as The Bridegrooms and it was customary to refer to the residents of Brooklyn as trolley dodgers. Trolley-dodging was a term for jaywalking in Brooklyn, where pedestrians had to avoid being hit by numerous streetcars that crisscrossed the borough. The team was known as the Superbas (from the name of a popular Broadway play) from 1899 to 1905 and as the Robins when Wilbert Robinson took over as manager (1914–31), but always seemed to revert to the name Dodgers. The name went with the team when it moved to Los Angeles in 1958.

**Brooksian** Characterized by adroit fielding, especially in play at third base, in the manner of Brooks Robinson of the Baltimore Orioles (1955–77). "[Wade] Boggs has been semi-Brooksian at third base" (Tony Kornheiser, *Washington Post,* Oct. 25, 1986). **Etymology.** Named for Brooks Robinson who won virtually every possible award and accolade for defensive play during his 23-year

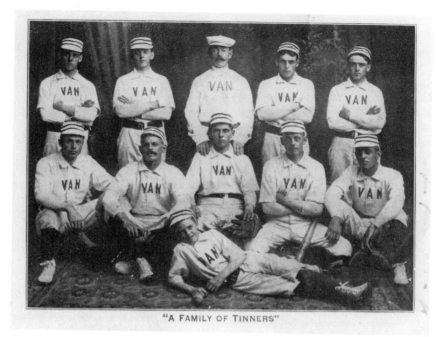

"A FAMILY OF TINNERS"

**Brother Act.** *Postcard depicting father Tinner and his ten sons playing as one team.*

career. In 9,196 chances he made only 264 fielding errors. Along with *Ruthian* and *Koufaxian,* this is one of those rare cases where a player has been honored with an eponymous adjective.

**broom** See *ump's broom.*

**brother act** An occasion when two or more brothers play for the same team. "Over the years baseball has known a number of brother acts, prominent among them being Dizzy and Paul Dean, Paul and Lloyd Waner, Morton and Walker Cooper, and Wes and Rick Ferrell" (Douglas Wallop, *Baseball: An Informal History,* 1969).

**Brotherhood of Professional Base Ball Players** First players' union, organized by John Montgomery Ward and a few New York Giants teammates in 1885 to protect and promote the rights of players. It eventually created its own league, the Players League, in 1890. The Brotherhood challenged the reserve clause and attempts to restrict players' salaries. The union was hailed as "the greatest move in the history of the National Game" by *The Sporting News.* Usually referred to as "the Brotherhood."

**brown** *adj./arch.* Inept. **1st Use.** 1889. "Some of the brownest work ever seen on a baseball field characterized the home team's play in the second. It was enough to drive a baseball man to drink. . . . It was one complete jumble of uncanny mistakes, high-salaried muffs and skyscraping throws. . . . People who can't play any better than they did here shouldn't be allowed to eat." (*New York World,* Aug. 18).

**Brownies** A nickname for the St. Louis Browns of the American League (1902–1953). The term tended to be used to underscore the chronic ineptitude of the team: a play on "brown" as a term for imperfection.

**brown spitter** A *spitball* moistened with chewing tobacco juice. Gaylord Perry (*Me and the Spitter,* 1974) admits that it was one of the few variations on the spitball that he did not throw: "I couldn't take to the tobacco." (Charles D. Poe)

**Bruins** A nickname for the Chicago Cubs. **Etymology.** "Bruin" is a synonym for "bear"; it originated in the character of Sir Bruin, a bear in the medieval German epic, *Reynard the Fox.*

**brush** Syn. of *ump's broom.*

**brush back** *v.* To move a batter away from the plate with the aid of a *brushback pitch.* Syn. *buzz;* "brush aside."

**brushback** *n.* Syn. of *brushback pitch.*

**brushback ball** Syn. of *brushback pitch.*

**brushback pitch** A pitch that comes so close to the batter's chest that he is forced to step backward, thereby keeping him from digging in at the plate. When a batter crowds the plate, taking away some of the pitcher's target area, a pitcher may decide to throw a pitch close to the batter's body to encourage him to move back. Or, as Jim Brosnan (*The Long Season,* 1960) put it: "To let the batter know the pitcher may, occasionally, lose control and to keep him from digging in at the plate with confidence." The brushback pitch is not to be confused with a *beanball,* which is intentionally thrown *at* the batter's head. Red Smith once wrote that the brushback pitch, coming after two strikes, was, "in the classical pattern, as rigidly formalized as the minuet." Others are less understanding. "That is what they call a ball thrown 90 miles an hour in the general direction of someone's nose—a 'brushback pitch'" (Mike Royko, *Houston Chronicle,* Aug. 6, 1987; Charles D. Poe). Bob Gibson (*From Ghetto to Glory,* 1968) wrote: "One of the most valuable weapons at a pitcher's command is the brushback pitch. First let me clear something up. A brushback pitch is not to be confused with a deliberate knockdown. There is a difference. A world of difference." Compare *knockdown pitch.* Syn. *brushback; brushback ball; brush-ball; brush-off pitch; blow-down pitch; buzzball; face ball,* 1; *rib roaster.*

**brushback pitcher** A pitcher who uses the ball to keep the batter away from the plate. When Boston Red Sox manager Billy Herman was asked who was the best brushback pitcher in baseball, he replied: "Freddie Fitzsimmons is my man. He once hit me in the on-deck circle." However, the distinction is sometimes blurred. Bill Lee (*The Wrong Stuff,* 1984), referring to Boston Red Sox manager Don Zimmer, wrote: "He constantly encouraged his pitchers to loosen batters up with a brushback. One pitcher turned to me and asked, 'How bright can this guy be? Here he is walking about with a

plate in his head, the souvenir of a serious beaning, and he's talking about knocking guys down.'"

**brushback war** Baseball games in which opposing pitchers employ excessive brushback tactics. "[Joe] Torre remembered when there were some brushback wars with other teams" (*New York Times,* Aug. 1, 1987). Compare *beanball war.*

**brush-ball** Syn. of *brushback pitch.*

**brush-off pitch** Syn. of *brushback pitch.*

**Brush Rules** The basic set of rules for staging the World Series, established in 1905 by John T. Brush, owner of the New York Giants. Many important features of these rules are still followed today, including the best-of-seven-games format. The Brush Rules also established the principle of a date after which no new players could be added to a team in anticipation of postseason play.

**BS** Abbrev. for *blown save.*

**B team** A second team created from a club's roster for the purpose of playing an *A team,* composed of the best players at each position. In the major leagues such teams are created to play each other in practice games and are a fixture of spring training, especially during the first week or two.

**bubble** 1. Syn. of *balloon,* 3. **2.** See *on the bubble.*

**bubble-gum ball** A *spitball* pioneered by Orlando Peña, who is quoted by Gaylord Perry (*Me and the Spitter,* 1974): "I mix tobacco with a piece of gum and chew it good. . . . Tastes like sweet tobacco. When you blow a bubble with that mixture, anybody who sees it wants to throw up. I knew guys playing winter ball in Cuba who would put a spot of gum right on the ball. Every time the umpire found it, he would throw out the ball. But you could win a ball game in a tight spot with it."

**bubble-gum card** A baseball card sold with bubble gum. For many years the cards have become far more important than the gum, and in reality the gum is now the premium and the cards are the prime product being sold. "When someone asked Doug Rader what advice he would give a kid, he suggested that they eat bubble-gum cards. 'Not the gum,' he said, 'but the cards. They have a

*Bug.*

lot of good information on them.'" (*Sports Collectors Digest,* Nov. 26, 1982).

**Buccos** Var. of *Bucs.*

**buck** A batting average of .100. The batter who is not "hitting a buck" is failing miserably. See also *dollar; Interstate.*

**Buck Canel Award** An annual award presented by the Latin American Press Organization to the best Latin American major-league baseball player. It is named for a well-known broadcaster of baseball games to Latin America.

**bucket** See *foot in the bucket; step in the bucket.*

**bucket hitter** A hitter who often steps back from the pitch; one who "steps in the bucket."

**buck-fifty** A batting average of around .150; e.g., "Smith is batting about a buck-fifty."

**Bucs** A nickname for the Pittsburgh Pirates. The term is short for "Buccaneers," which has tended to be used interchangeably with "Pirates." In 1986, the club came up with a new slogan: "The New Bucs: We Play Hardball." Syn. *Buccos.*

**budder** Syn. of *rookie,* 1.

**buffalo 1.** To bluff. **2.** To intimidate. **1st Use.** 1905. (*Sporting Life,* Sept. 2; Edward J. Nichols).

**bug** *arch.* A baseball enthusiast; a fan. **1st Use.** 1907. (*New York Evening Journal,* May 10; Edward J. Nichols). Also: "The streets were thronged with cheering 'bugs.'" (Harry Ellard, *Base Ball in Cincinnati*).

**bugaboo** *arch.* Syn. of *sore arm.* **1st Use.** 1935. "'Bugaboo' or sore arm necessitates the application of dry heat" (Ralph H. Barbour, *How to Play Better Baseball;* David Shulman).

**bug bruiser** *arch.* A hard-hit ground ball. **1st Use.** 1874. (Chicago *Inter-Ocean,* July 7; Edward J. Nichols).

**bug crawler** "A ball that when hit has a lot of over-spin, eliminating the usual hop" (Carol R. Gast, *Skill on the Diamond,* 1953).

**bug on the rug** Originally, a ground ball that eludes one or more fielders and gets into the outfield, usually into one of the corners. The term has been around for decades, but became more popular with the advent of ruglike artificial playing surfaces, after which announcers tended to use the term to describe a ball bouncing on plastic grass. It has been attributed to Pittsburgh Pirates announcer Bob Prince, who supposedly introduced it about 1970, but it appears in much earlier listings of baseball slang.

**bulb** *arch.* The baseball. **1st Use.** 1908. (*New York Evening Journal*, Mar. 5; Edward J. Nichols).

**bulge 1.** *arch.* A slow curveball. **1st Use.** 1907. (*New York Evening Journal*, Apr. 25; Edward J. Nichols). **2.** The advantage, or lead, in runs made or games won; e.g., "The Yankees have a five-game bulge over the Tigers."

**bull** *arch.* Syn. of *boner*, 1. **1st Use.** 1902. (*Sporting Life*, July 5; Edward J. Nichols).

**bulldog** A tenacious pitcher; e.g., Orel Hershiser, whose nickname is "Bulldog."

**Bull Durham** See *bullpen*.

**bullet** A hard-hit line drive.

**bullpen 1.** The area of a ballpark where the relief pitchers and warm-up catcher are situated during the game. There are two bullpens, one for each team, located outside of fair territory, usually either at opposite ends of the outfield or along each foul line. The appointments differ, but all major-league bullpens contain mounds and home plates. The primary purpose of the bullpen is as a place where relief pitchers can prepare and warm up for entry into the game. Joe Garagiola (*The Sporting News*, May 16, 1956) commented: "A bull pen is supposed to be a place for warming up pitchers. That's what it is a little bit of the time. Mostly it's a place for eating peanuts, trading insults with the fans, second-guessing the manager and picking all kinds of silly all-star teams, like the all-screwball team or the all-ugly team or the all-stackblowing team." Sometimes spelled "bull pen"; "bull-pen." Syn. *pen*, 2. **2.** The relief pitching staff of a team. **3.** Pitchers appearing in relief in a given game. "Bullpen Collapses after Ron's [Darling] Seven No-Hit Innings" (*New York Post* headline after a stunning Mets loss, June 29, 1987). **Usage Note.** Currently, the bullpen is the realm of high-priced

specialists rather than a place for pitchers who simply couldn't pitch for a full game or were out of favor. The degree to which the situation has changed is underscored by the fact that as recently as 1966, Jack McDonald (*San Francisco Chronicle*) defined the bullpen as "a group of ex-starting pitchers in the manager's doghouse." The term is variously written as "bullpen," "bull pen," and "bull-pen"; however, it is mostly written as one word (*USA Today, Sports Illustrated, The Sporting News,* and *New York Post*) but *New York Times* uses two words. Player-turned-broadcaster John Lowenstein has used the term "bully" for "bullpen," which has infuriated some purist fans, but it shows no signs of growing. **1st Use.** 1915. The earliest use of "bullpen" for a place where pitchers warm up was discovered by Edward J. Nichols in *Baseball Magazine* (Dec.). David Shulman found three uses in Lester Chadwick's *Baseball Joe in the Big League* (1915); e.g., "He took a ball, and nodding to Rad, who was not playing, went out to the bullpen." Another early example shows up in the Tamony collection, which includes a line from T. A. Dorgan's "Indoor Sports" in *San Francisco Call and Post* (June 7, 1917): "I been out here in the bull pen all season warming up—I ain't been in one game yet." **Etymology.** The origin of the term has long been debated in baseball. Joseph Durso (*New York Times*, Mar. 10, 1967) provided two interesting theories. Writing during spring training, Durso quoted New York Mets manager Casey Stengel: "You could look it up and get 80 different answers, but we used to have pitchers who could pitch 50 or 60 games a year and the extra pitchers would just sit around shooting the bull, and no manager wanted all that gabbing on the bench. So he put them in this kind of pen in the outfield to warm up, it looked like a place to keep cows or bulls." Stengel's quote was followed by this contrasting opinion from Johnny Murphy, who spent 11 years in the bullpen for the New York Yankees: "It came from Bull Durham tobacco, I was always told. All the ball parks had advertising signs on the outfield fences and Bull Durham was always near the spot where the relief pitchers warmed up."

Murphy's explanation has been given various twists. Michael Gartner in his nationally syndicated column on language (*Newsday*, Apr. 27,

**Bullpen.** *Spectators draped over a mammoth Bull Durham sign. The picture was taken on Aug. 9, 1911, at the old Huntington Avenue Baseball Grounds in Boston when a record crowd of 33,904 came to see Boston play Detroit.*

1986) asserts that the bullpen/Bull Durham connection originated in the days when all games were day games and when "pitchers warming up for relief duty often chose to limber up in the shade of those big signs."

In the early days of the 20th century, the Bull Durham name was, indeed, closely associated with the ballpark. In fact, by 1910, the big bull-shaped signs were on the outfield fences of almost every park in the country. As part of its advertising campaign, Bull Durham drew minor- and major-league attention to the 40-foot-long, 25-foot-high signs by offering a reward to any batter who could hit a ball off one. Quoting from the 1911 edition of *The 'Bull' Durham Base Ball Guide:* "Any player who hits the bull with a fairly-batted fly ball, during a regular scheduled league game on any of the grounds where these 'Bull' Durham signs are located on the field will receive $50.00 in cash." In addition, any player hitting a home run in a park with a bull on the fence got a carton containing 72 packs of the tobacco.

In 1909, the first year of the hit-the-bull contest, there were 50 signs in place and 14 players won. The next year with nearly 150 Bull Durham signs being hit 85 times, Blackwell's Durham Tobacco Co. gave out $4,250 in cash and more than 10,000 pounds of tobacco. According to *The 'Bull' Durham Base Ball Guide,* the sign promotion scheme was expanded because "interest in the National Game was then waning in various parts of the country" and this was seen as a way to stimulate interest, which it apparently did.

While there is significant merit to the Bull Durham theory (particularly because the term hadn't been used in baseball until after the signs were in place), the term "bull pen" had long been used in the United States to denote either a log enclosure for holding cattle or a holding area for prisoners. A reader from Deer Trail (Colo.) wrote an unsigned letter to *The Sporting News* (Nov. 2, 1939) that sided with the jail theory: "The place in most jails where prisoners exercise is known as the bullpen. I just remembered, when a young boy, I asked the policeman where he was going with two drunken men and he said to the bullpen and sober them up to be good men." Lexicographer David Shulman (letter, 1997) attests to the fact that "bullpen" was criminal slang for a "prison yard" before it shows up applied to baseball.

This concept of the bullpen as an enclosure where, in the words of Shulman, "pitchers were confined ... for warming up until called on to pitch" may have strongly influenced and helped corroborate the notion of the bullpen as an enclosure for pitchers, perhaps giving an assist to the influence of Bull Durham. In fact, it was in use as early as 1877 for an area in foul territory beyond first base and third base where spectators could stand penned in like bulls. O. P. Caylor (*Cincinnati Enquirer*, May 7, 1877; Peter Tamony) wrote: "The bull pen at the Cincinnati grounds with its 'three-for-a-quarter' crowd has lost its usefulness." Tamony theorized that this use of the term came from the Civil War when soldiers on both sides used the term "bull pen" for a roped-off corral where prisoners of war were herded like cattle. Tamony believed that the Bull Durham signs reinforced and redefined the term "bull pen" in baseball. Early bullpens for pitchers were almost always placed along the outfield foul lines (as some still are), which would suggest how this term developed.

One other theory, which is published from time to time, likens the relief pitchers to the reserve bulls in bullfighting, who are penned near the arena should the starting bull be found to be lacking. There is a certain neatness to this idea, but it would appear to be pure conjecture.

Incidentally, the first area set aside for major-league relief pitchers was probably at the Polo Grounds in 1905.

**Extended Use.** The term has several specialized meanings for defined spaces and enclosures outside baseball, which may or may not have been inspired by the baseball bullpen. These include the barracks in a lumber camp, a used-car lot, a cashier's cage in a bank, the box in some courtrooms where defendants sit during trials, a room for railroad crewmen, a work area in a large company, the sale ring at a horse auction, a smoking area for oil refinery workers, the penalty box in ice hockey, the area in a jazz club where a youngster can pay to sit without being bothered by a waiter, an area where prisoners are kept during a riot, an enclosure for prostitutes, and a flophouse for men only.

**bullpen ace** A team's best relief pitcher; one who can "close" games.

**bullpen boss** A *bullpen coach*. "Birds' bullpen boss Elrod Hendricks claims his boys are into each pitch. But every so often he jolts them with his favorite pastime, a pop quiz on the count." (*The Washington Weekly*, June 21, 1985).

**bullpen by committee** A relief staff with no prominent member or closer. The term was used by manager Whitey Herzog for the 1985 St. Louis Cardinals bullpen staff in which he used everybody, but is now applied widely to relief staffs from which different pitchers are used depending on the game situation.

**bullpen catcher** A catcher assigned to duty in the bullpen to warm up relief pitchers.

**bullpen coach** A *pitching coach* who spends all or most of his time in the team's bullpen, advising and preparing the relief pitchers. Most major-league teams have such a coach. Syn. of *bullpen boss*.

**bump 1.** *v.* To hit a ball squarely; e.g., "Smith really bumped the ball." Not nearly as common today as it was when reported in *American Speech* in 1927. **1st Use.** 1908. (*Brooklyn Daily Eagle*, May 23; Edward J. Nichols). **2.** *n.* A fastball; e.g., "He has good bump tonight" (Relief pitcher Mark Davis, quoted in *San Diego Union-Tribune*, April 11, 1994). **3.** *n./arch.* An overwhelming defeat. "A pitcher gets his 'bumps' when his delivery is hit hard, a team 'gets its bumps' when it is badly beaten" (Hugh S. Fullerton, *American Magazine*, June 1912). **1st Use.** 1910. (*Baseball Magazine*, Sept.; Edward J. Nichols).

**bumper** The thick pad attached to walls in modern ballparks. Many bumpers now carry advertising.

**Bums** A nickname for the Brooklyn Dodgers, more commonly *Dem Bums*.

**bun** *arch.* The baseball. One 1918 scrapbook

clipping from a Detroit paper talks of a batter "banging the bun in goodly fashion."

**bunched hits** A cluster of base hits that come in one inning. **1st Use.** 1880. (*New York Herald,* July 23; Edward J. Nichols). Syn. of *flock hits.*

**bungle 1.** *n.* An error or misplay. **2.** *v.* To make an error. **1st Use.** 1898. (*New York Tribune,* May 29; Edward J. Nichols).

**bunt 1.** *n.* A batted ball that is intentionally met with a loosely held bat and tapped softly into the infield. The purpose of a bunt is to advance a baserunner (sacrifice bunt) or get the batter to first base on the element of surprise. Its success depends to a large degree on the placement of the ball on the infield. An ideal bunt is one that proves difficult for infielders to reach. The bunt is performed as the batter loosens his grip, flexes his knees, and squares around to face the pitcher. The hands are separated along the handle of the bat and it is presented as if the batter wants the pitcher to read the bat label. The bat is not swung at the ball, rather the ball is tapped with the bat. Credit for introducing the bunt goes to Dickey Pearce of the original Brooklyn Atlantics in 1866, but the practice did not become common until after 1876 when Tim Murnane of the Boston Red Stockings started "butting" the ball with a special flat-sided bat. Gerald Secor Couzens (*A Baseball Album,* 1980) adds: "The bunt was referred to as a freak play in accounts of 1888 and did not take on its importance in game strategy until much later." This is confirmed in a profile of Pearce written by Sam Crane (*New York Journal,* Dec. 20, 1911): "It was not known as a bunt at that time and Dickey himself had no idea that he was making baseball history." Compare *swinging bunt.* Abbrev. *B.* **2.** *v.* To execute a bunt. Syn. *put the ball on the ground.* **1st Use.** 1886. "Arlie Latham quite captured the great crowd presented by his good-natured antics, and was cheered as he left the field. Every one knows Latham's great feat is to 'bunt' the ball and beat it to first." (*Sporting Life,* June 2; Barry Popik). **3.** *n.* [softball term] A legally tapped ball in fast pitch softball. It is not swung at, but intentionally met with the bat and tapped within the infield. It is, however, illegal in slow pitch softball: if it occurs, the batter is called out and all runners return to their bases. **Etymology.** The term is a nasalized variation or corruption of the term "butt," which comes from the batter butting at the ball with his bat in the manner of a goat butting. Michael Gartner (*Newsday,* Apr. 27, 1986) suggested the original butt "quickly became known as a 'bunt,' probably because somebody misheard the word in Brooklyn." But *Merriam-Webster's Collegiate Dictionary* (10th ed., 1993) notes that "bunt" as an alternative term for "butt" can be dated back to 1584. The term itself may have come into baseball by rail. In railroading, to "bunt" was to "shove" a car onto a side trench or (and this may be even more to the point) to "nudge" an uncoupled freight car to get it moving. **Usage Note.** Knowing what a bunt is has long been a test of whether one knows anything about baseball. A character in a 1952 *Boy's Life* story is ridiculed for not knowing "a bunt from a Buffalo." A story by Jerome Beatty (*McClure's* magazine, Mar. 1917) contains the following incident: "An' another thing I asks him. I used to be the greatest sacrifice hitter in baseball. So I asks him, 'Young man, can you bunt?' 'Mister Ryan,' says he—Jake fairly yelled his protest

RICHARD J. PEARCE,
The Veteran Base Ball Player, and Short Stop of the Mutual Nine.

**Bunt.** *Richard J. "Dickey" Pearce, father of the bunt.*

against such disgusting incompetence—'Mister Ryan, I don't like to brag about myself, but I can bunt farther than any other man on the team!' Them's his very words! Can you beat it?"

**bunt along** To advance a baserunner by making a bunt.

**bunt and run** 1. *n./arch.* Syn. of *squeeze play.* 2. *v.* To effect a squeeze bunt.

**bunting** 1. The art of making bunts. 2. *arch.* The flag or banner that represents winning a pennant; the *pennant,* 2, itself. **1st Use.** 1892. "The first round in the fight for the little piece of bunting that represents so much to base ball teams and to baseball patrons is over" (*Cleveland Plain Dealer,* Oct. 18; Peter Morris).

**burglar** 1. A quick-thinking player who takes advantage of the breaks; one who is said to "steal" opportunities. 2. Syn. of *base stealer.*

**burn a hole** To pitch or throw a ball with great velocity; e.g., "Smith's pitch burned a hole in Jones's mitt." **1st Use.** 1907. (Burt L. Standish, *Dick Merriwell's Magnetism;* Edward J. Nichols).

**burn ball** A variant of baseball in which a baserunner can be put out ("burned") by being hit with a ball. **1st Use.** 1888. "The boys used to play 'burn ball,' if you were hit by the ball before reaching the base, you were out." (Michael J. Kelly, *"Play Ball";* David Shulman). **Etymology.** The "burn" in burn ball is an overt reference to the fact that an object of the game was to inflict pain and leave bruises.

**burn off** To run close behind another baserunner, thereby forcing (or "burning") him to advance or be put out.

**burnout** A baseball game for two players who throw to each other at a given distance and then, advancing on each other, throw the ball as hard as they can until one of them backs away.

**burn over** To throw a hard fastball; e.g., "Smith burned over three called strikes."

**burn up the circuit** To win routinely and decisively on the road. The term is applied to teams, pitching staffs, individual pitchers, and, on rare occasions, to dominant hitters (such as one with a string of game-winning runs batted in).

**bury** To strike out or retire a batter.

**bush** 1. *adj.* Unprofessional, unsportsmanlike, amateurish. The term is used to refer to both crude play on the field and poor behavior off the field. It can be applied at any level of the game; e.g., it is "bush" to talk too much on the field, wear your uniform incorrectly, show too much enthusiasm, or steal a base when your team is way ahead. Syn. *bushie,* 2; *bush-league.* **Usage Note.** Scornful to the point that this is one of the labels that a player at any level of play strives to avoid. **Extended Use.** Amateurish or inferior, such as an actor who is accused of a "bush performance." 2. *n.* Exile; a low rung of the minor leagues at the end of a baseball career. "The 'bush' with its sadness of cheap hotels, rancid food, and fetid dressing-rooms; of inferior craftsmanship and memories of gone glories" (William Patten & J. W. McSpadden, *The Book of Baseball,* 1911; Peter Tamony). Plural *bushes.* **1st Use.** 1905. "Manager [Bill] Armour has gone out into the bushes and signed two twirlers" (*Sporting Life,* Sept. 2; Edward J. Nichols). 3. *n.* A college player. See also *Joe Bush.*

**bushel basket** An oversized fielder's glove with a deep pocket. Compare *pancake,* 2.

**busher** 1. A *rookie,* just up from the bush leagues. "Jerome Dean reported to Joe Schultz who managed Houston that season. 'What's your name, busher?' asked Schultz. 'Just call me Dizzy,' replied Dean." (Undated player biography for Dizzy Dean issued by the St. Louis Cardinals). The term was given a boost with the publication of Ring Lardner's novel *You Know Me Al* (1914), which is the tale of Jack Keefe: the term "busher" is key to the book (Keefe has a fight with one of his girlfriends because he thinks she called him one), and each of the six chapters has the word in its title (e.g., "A Busher's Letter Home," "The Busher Comes Back," and "The Busher's Honeymoon"). Syn. *bushie,* 1; *bush leaguer,* 1. **1st Use.** 1908. "Had [Hughie] Jennings held onto the busher long enough to give him a trial he would have recognized in him a player who is almost a perfect duplicate of Ty Cobb" (*Detroit Free Press,*

Mar. 3; Peter Morris). A slighter later quotation is illuminating (Hugh S. Fullerton, *Collier's*, Sept. 11, 1909): "In the major leagues there are three classes of players designated in the picturesque language of the game as 'bushers,' 'bone-heads,' and 'topnotchers.' The 'busher' is the freshman, inexperienced but promising and derives its name from the fact that he recently graduated from the 'bush' or minor league." **2.** A player in the bush leagues. Syn. *bush leaguer,* 2. **3.** Any professional baseball player who lacks class. Syn. *bush leaguer,* 3.

**bushes** Plural of *bush,* 2. Syn. *woods.*

**bushie. 1.** *n.* Syn. of *busher,* 1. **2.** *adj.* Syn. of *bush,* 1.

**bush league** *n.* A lesser minor league consisting of teams in small cities or towns, usually composed of players who are too old or lacking in experience or ability to compete in the major leagues. **Etymology.** From the nickname for the lower levels of the minor leagues, which were traditionally typified as "out where the bushes grow" or where the land has not been cleared.

**bush-league** *adj.* Syn. of *bush,* 1. **1st Use.** 1908. (*Baseball Magazine,* July; Edward J. Nichols). **Extended Use.** Having to do with a group or class of things that is at best mediocre, but more likely inferior. Compare *big-league.*

**bush leaguer 1.** Syn. of *busher,* 1. **1st Use.** 1906. "Consider the bush leaguer on the bench!" (*Sporting Life,* Feb. 10; Edward J. Nichols). **2.** Syn. of *busher,* 2. **3.** Syn. of *busher,* 3.

**bushness** Inexperience. "'Dobie, I hate to bug your ointment,' said Tommy, 'but there is a distinct chance your bushness is showing'" (Steve Kluger, *Changing Pitches,* 1984; Charles D. Poe).

**businessman's special** A weekday baseball game, played in the mid- to late afternoon, that caters to a salaried, white-collar clientele that, presumably, can get out of work for a few hours or wants to entertain clients. As day games have become less common, there are fewer businessman's specials every year. St. Louis Cardinals manager Whitey Herzog (*Village Voice,* Sept. 2, 1986) stated that Chicago Cubs reliever Lee Smith had the biggest advantage in baseball because he gets to pitch "those damn three o'clock businessman specials" at Wrigley Field, adding "it's hard enough to hit that guy in the daylight, much less the twilight."

**bussie** A players' nickname for the team bus driver. This term was popular among major leaguers before teams started traveling by plane. Today the term is used by players during spring training and in the minor leagues where bus travel is still common. According to an item in *Comedians and Pranksters of Baseball* (edited by Fred Lieb, 1958), the ritualistic joke is to ask the bussie if the regular driver is off. Jim Bouton (*Ball Four,* 1970) says that the way you tell a driver that he is going too slowly is to call out, "Hey, bussy, there's a dog pissing on your rear wheel."

The term has stayed alive through new incarnations. Leonard Shecter (*Baseball Digest,* June 1963) reported: "Once this meant simply bus driver. But times change and now it's applied to those in charge of vehicles of any sort, from bus driver to pilots of jet aircraft." Tim Horgan (*Baseball Digest,* June 1964) added that the term also applied to "the park employee who drives the relief pitcher in from the bullpen."

In one odd case the "bussie" label has been used as a nickname. Devon White picked it up in the minors when he tried to turn on the air-conditioning in a hot bus while waiting for the driver to show up. White accidentally got the bus rolling and it ran through a fence. The label stuck with him when he came up to the majors with the California Angels. Also spelled "bussy."

**bust 1.** To hit the ball hard. **1st Use.** 1938. "He busted the fences down with line drives" (J. I. Rodale, *The King's English on Horseback;* David Shulman). **2.** To throw a pitch close to the batter's body in an effort to move the batter away from home plate; e.g., "Smith busted the batter inside" or "Jones busted one on the batter's hands."

**butcher** A bad defensive player; one who has a difficult time holding onto the ball.

**butcher-boy** *v.* To swing at a pitched ball with a downward chopping motion. **1st Use.** 1959. "I know what Casey's [Stengel] telling him. He's telling him, 'Don't swing hard now. Just butcher-boy the ball. Just butcher-boy it.'" (Phil Rizzuto, quoted in John Lardner, *The New Yorker,* July 18; Peter Tamony).

**butcher-boy stroke** A batter's downward chopping swing to ensure a high-bounding ground ball. In situations calling for a ground ball, manager Casey Stengel (who coined the term) told his players to use the butcher-boy stroke, likening the motion to that which a boy in a butcher shop would use when chopping meat. See also *Baltimore chop.*

**buttercup** *arch.* A weak hitter, one without power. Syn. "buttercup hitter." **1st Use.** 1937. (*The Sporting News Record Book;* Edward J. Nichols).

**butterfingered** Clumsy, inept, error-prone. "The ancient 'butterfinger[ed]' plague is making itself a factor in the major league pennant races" (Howard Sigmand, *San Francisco Call & Bulletin,* Aug. 25, 1952). **Etymology.** "Butter-fingered" is cited as early as 1615 by J. F. Farmer & W. E. Henley (*Slang and Its Analogues,* 1890) for a person who is likely to let things drop. It is clearly old English slang that appears to have entered both cricket and baseball.

**butterfingers** A derogatory term for a player who drops the ball. **1st Use.** 1888. "The buttercups I gather/While the batsman waits and lingers,/And now you know the reason/Why they call me 'butter-fingers'" (Thomas W. Lawson, *The Krank: His Language and What It Means*). As late as 1927, *American Speech* (Apr.) reported the term

as peculiar to baseball rather than the language at large. **Extended Use.** The term, which saw its early American popular use in baseball, has since been used for anyone who is clumsy and drops things.

**butterfly** *arch.* Syn. of *knuckleball,* 1. The term was more common in the earlier days of 20th century. It first shows up in a list of players' terms in the 1937 edition of *The Sporting News Record Book,* but is rare after about 1950. **Etymology.** The erratic flight of a knuckleball is similar to that of a butterfly.

**butterfly ball** A knuckleball that seemingly floats on its way to the plate.

**buzz** Syn. of *brush back;* e.g., "The inside pitches were no accident: we buzzed his tower." **Etymology.** From the practice of playful pilots who use aircraft as instruments of expression.

**buzzball** Syn. of *brushback pitch.*

**buzzer** A fastball that asserts itself by the noise it makes as it passes a batter's ear. It is presumably louder than a *hummer,* 1.

**BWAA** Abbrev. for *Baseball Writers Association of America.*

**"bye-bye baby"** Trademark home run call of New York/San Francisco Giants broadcaster Russ Hodges.

**bye-bye ball** A home run.

# C

**C** 1. See *Class C.* 2. Abbrev. for *catcher.*

**cabbageball** [softball term] The 16-inch softball, so-called because it resembles a head of cabbage.

**cackle clout** A foul ball, a play on the homonym "fowl."

**Cactus League** Commonly used nickname for the major-league teams that conduct spring training and play exhibition games against each other in the Southwest. Formerly known as the Arizona State League (when Arizona had four teams training in the state), the terms "Cactus League" and "Cactus Loop" began appearing in newspaper articles in 1954. The name seemed to solidify at the end of the 1954 spring training season when an American Legion post sponsored a trophy (immediately dubbed the Cactus Cup) for the team with the best training record in the Southwest. Cactus League clubs of the 1990s include the Anaheim Angels, Chicago Cubs, Cleveland Indians, Milwaukee Brewers, Oakland A's, San Diego Padres, San Francisco Giants, Colorado Rockies, Seattle Mariners, and Arizona Diamondbacks. Compare *Grapefruit League.* **Etymology.** The term comes from the cacti that are common to the southwestern area of the United States.

**caddie** 1. A reserve player who generally is used as a substitute in the late innings of a game. "As a rule, the 'caddie' is younger, quicker, but has less experience and makes less money than the player for whom he is substituted." (Jim Brosnan, *The Long Season,* 1960) 2. Alternate spelling of *caddy.*

**caddy** Syn. of *setup man.* "[Roberto] Hernandez has pitched four times in his new role as caddy for incumbent closer Rod Beck" (*Milwaukee Journal Sentinel,* Aug. 7, 1997). Also spelled *caddie,* 2.

**Cadillac trot** A *home run trot* by a high-salaried slugger, often staged to show up a high-priced pitcher or other opponent. During the 1986 National League Championship Series, CBS radio announcer Johnny Bench said that the term should now be called the "Mercedes trot." An interesting variation of "Cadillac trot" was collected by Peter Tamony who noted that, during a June 1966 interview of John Roseboro by broadcaster Vin Scully, Roseboro thought he had hit a home run and said, "I was just Cadillac-ing along"; however, the ball did not go out of the park and Roseboro should not have been trotting around the bases. **Etymology.** The term certainly can be traced to a famous line uttered by slugger Ralph Kiner in the 1950s: "Hitters of home runs drive Cadillacs, single hitters jalopies." On another occasion Kiner told a reporter that he never choked up on the bat because the Cadillacs were down at the end of the bat.

**cage** 1. See *batting cage.* **1st Use.** 1910. (*Baseball Magazine,* Sept.; Edward J. Nichols). 2. See *bird cage.* **1st Use.** 1908. (*Baseball Magazine,* July; Edward J. Nichols).

**cake 1.** Something done easily; e.g., a pitcher who tells a manager "it's cake" means he is fired up to retire the side. See also *piece of cake.* **2.** *arch.* A player of little skill. The term appears in the third stanza of Ernest L. Thayer's 1888 poem, "Casey at the Bat": "And the former [Flynn] was a lulu and the latter [Jimmy Blake] was a cake."

**cake and coffee** Low pay, a long-established player slang, usually said in reference to the salaries of minor-league players. Syn. *coffee and cake.* **1st Use.** 1934. "How would you feel if you'd been playing the cakes and coffee route for years and somebody suddenly dropped you in soft on the champagne and caviar circuit" (Pat Robinson, *Fort Worth Star-Telegram,* Feb. 5). **Etymology.** Presumably, a reference to the fact that the player got something to eat and drink and little else.

**cakewalk** An easy, lopsided victory. **Etymology.** From the dances and promenades (or walks) that were once staged as contests. Popular among 19th-century black Americans, the couple who won the contest often got a cake as its prize, hence the name. The idea of being able to win with a set of fancy steps no doubt conveyed the idea of an easy win in baseball.

**California Angels** The former name of the American League West Division franchise in Anaheim, Calif., now known (since the 1997 season) as the Anaheim Angels. Joining the American League as an expansion team in 1961, the Angels, then based in Los Angeles, took its name from the Pacific Coast League's Los Angeles Angels. The name is derived from Los Angeles, Spanish for the "angels." When the team moved to Anaheim in 1966, the name of the city was replaced by that of the state. The name allows some nice wordplay; e.g., calling the general manager the "Archangel."

**call 1.** *n.* An umpire's stated or signaled ruling on a pitch (ball, strike, balk, foul ball, or hit batsman) or a play (safe or out). **2.** *v.* To make an umpiring decision. **3.** *n.* The catcher's signal for a specific pitch. **4.** *n.* The manager's decision on a starting pitcher, or his signal to the bullpen for a relief pitcher or for a relief pitcher to begin warming up.

**call a game 1.** For an umpire to officiate or control a baseball game. An accolade for an umpire is that he "calls a good game." **2.** For an umpire to cancel, suspend, postpone, or terminate a baseball game due to bad weather or other problems. **3.** For a catcher to signal to the pitcher the pitches to be thrown to specific batters and to control the positioning of defensive players.

**called ball** *arch.* A pitched ball delivered outside the strike zone and which is not swung at. It is deemed to be a ball by the umpire. Compare *called strike.*

**called game** A game that has been terminated, for any reason, by the umpire-in-chief. Games are most commonly called for rain, but they have also been called for fog, wind, sleet, snow, and darkness. In the American League, games can be called for going past the curfew time. If a game is called before the trailing team has batted in five innings, the game is replayed from the beginning. If the losing team has had its five innings and the game is called, it is recorded as a *shortened game.* **1st Use.** 1866. (Henry Chadwick, *Base Ball Player's Book of Reference;* Edward J. Nichols).

**called out looking** To get a called strike for not swinging with two strikes on the batter.

**called shot** A hit whose destination is predicted in advance; specif., the called shot allegedly made by Babe Ruth on Oct. 1, 1932, in the fifth inning of the third game of the World Series when he hit a home run against Charlie Root of the Chicago Cubs, a blast over the bleacher screen in deep center field at the base of the flagpole in Wrigley Field. When Ruth died in 1948, the story of the "called shot" appeared in almost every newspaper in America, and some even made it the central anecdote of his life. *The Evening Star* (Washington, D.C., Aug. 17, 1948) headlined a huge 98-paragraph article on the Babe, "Ruth Climaxed Fabulous Career By Calling Shot on Homer in '32." The article opened:

"As long as baseball is played, the memory will live of a bulbous man on matchstick legs pointing in eloquent gesture to Wrigley Field's faraway centerfield barrier, the jibes of 50,000 Chicago fans searing his ears.

"There were two strikes on George Herman 'Babe' Ruth . . . like there had been . . . many times during his career. The score was 4 to 4 in the fifth inning and Ruth's Yankees were gunning for their third straight win.

"Two called strikes and there stood baseball's greatest hitter in the sunset of his career, majestically drawing a bead on a spot 400 feet away. Contemptuously, the Babe held up two fingers, then pointed to the centerfield flagpole.

"Charlie Root pitched. He shouldn't have done it. Like a projectile the ball left the Ruthian bat to scream on a line over the right centerfield wall."

Depending on the source, the story is likely to be embellished with any of several extra details, such as these two: 1) that one of those who witnessed the called shot was New York Governor Franklin Delano Roosevelt, who would be elected President a month later (in fact, FDR was in the stands, as was President Herbert Hoover, both on the campaign trail); and 2) that Ruth pointed to the sky with one finger after the first strike, and with two fingers after the second, as if to show the assembled multitude that a singular event was taking place.

Furthermore, there are those who witnessed all of Ruth's motions. Tom Fleming (*American Heritage,* Nov. 1990) tells of going to the game with his father. "How lucky we were to be on the third-base side. As a left-handed batter Ruth faced us, and we could see his every move and gesture. Root was very careful. After each strike the Babe raised his right arm, showing one finger for a strike, then two to keep the stands posted on the duel between him and the pitcher. The crowd reacted wildly. When the count stood at 2 and 2, Ruth stepped back a bit and then pointed grandly to the outfield, making a big arc with his right hand."

The issue of whether Ruth actually called his shot is still being argued. When old-timer Bill Wambsganss was interviewed by *Sports Collectors Digest* (June 24, 1983), he was asked about Joe Sewell (who grounded out just before Ruth's home run): "Sewell is fine. He and Riggs Stephenson are still in Alabama fighting over whether Babe Ruth called his shot in 1932."

When the debate was sparked again in the letters columns of the *Washington Post* in 1988, an Alexandria (Va.) man wrote to point out that he seemed to be one of the few survivors of the year 1932 who was not present at Wrigley Field that day. He then put his tongue firmly in cheek and concluded (Sept. 9): "I find it most interesting, however, that while the capacity of Wrigley Field is 39,008, to this date (by my count) 55,603 living witnesses from the Washington area alone have written to the *Post* to verify that the Babe did in fact predict his blast."

Jerome Holtzman (*Chicago Tribune,* June 29, 1991) concluded that Ruth had not pointed and even quotes Ruth's denial the following spring when broadcaster Hal Totten asked him if he had made the gesture: "Hell, no. Only a damn fool would do a thing like that." As the legend grew, however, Ruth became more and more convinced that he had called his shot.

The first "called shot" (although it was not referred to by such a term) may have occurred in 1881. Bryan DiSalvatore (*Nineteenth Century Notes,* Summer/Fall 1995) cited the *New York Clipper* (Jan. 28, 1882), which recalled that Providence Grays outfielder Paul Hines, prior to the game against Buffalo on Sept. 30, 1881, took a reporter's score book, wrote "home run" in it, and indicated the fifth inning with a mark over that column of the sheet; sure enough, Hines knocked the ball over the left-field fence in the fifth inning. William D. Perrin (*Days of Greatness,* 1928, repr. 1984) reported the story in his history of the Grays: "Hines drove the ball over the left fence for a home run, 'a terrific drive.' The previous day he had halted a newspaper man and, after telling him a yarn about dreaming he made a home run in the final game, marked the home run on the score book just where it actually occurred." Providence won the game, the season finale, 10–1.

**called strike** A pitched ball that a batter does not swing at, but which is judged to have passed through the strike zone by the umpire. Compare *called ball.*

**call for the ball** To yell a claim to a ball to prevent a misplay or a collision. When two players are headed for the same batted ball, one or the other, usually the one in the best position, takes command and claims it. **1st Use.** 1888. "The necessity of 'calling' for a fly hit applies with particular force to the centre fielder. As soon as he has seen that he can get to a hit and has decided to take it, he calls out loudly so that every one must hear, 'I'll take it,' and all other fielders near him respond, 'Go ahead.'" (John Montgomery Ward, *Base-Ball: How to Become a Player;* Peter Morris).

**calling card** A pitch thrown intentionally close to a batter. Syn. *wakeup call.*

**call off** For a defensive player to alert a teammate not to approach a batted ball that the defensive player will handle.

**call time 1.** For an umpire to create a temporary cessation of play; to take time out. **2.** For a player to request a time out from the umpire.

**call up** *v.* To bring to the major leagues a player from a minor-league club when the parent team needs his services during the season. See also *come up,* 1.

**callup** *n.* **1.** The act of bringing up a minor-league player to the majors; e.g., "Smith was expecting a July callup." Sometimes spelled "call-up." **2.** A player who has been called up; e.g., "The team plans to rely on recent callups." Sometimes spelled "call-up."

**cambio** "Changeup" Spanish for, used increasingly by nonspeakers of Spanish.

**camera day** A promotional event at the ballpark in which fans are allowed on the field to take photographs of the players.

**camp** A team's spring training home. News from spring training is often reported in the newspapers under the headings "Around the camps" or "News from the camps."

**camp under** To position oneself and wait for a fly ball to drop into the fielder's glove.

**can 1.** *v.* To be removed; e.g., to be taken out of service by an umpire or manager, or to be released or discharged from a team. **1st Use.** 1908. (*New York Evening Journal,* May 30; Edward J. Nichols). **2.** *n.* Removal from the game. In Harry Stein's novel *Hoopla* (1983), a character in the 1910s says: "He went ahead and issued five passes in a row, be-

fore the Tall Tactician finally figured it out to give him the can." **3.** [softball term] The literal name (not slang) for home plate in Over the Line play.

**Candlestick Park** Home field of the San Francisco Giants since 1960, now known as 3Com Park at Candlestick Point. Candlestick Point, which overlooks the park, is named for the rocks and trees that poke up from the surrounding area like giant candles. It is known for its inhospitable winds and chilliness. New York Mets broadcaster Fran Healy's response to the question of whether a dome would improve conditions at the park was that someone told him it "would be like putting lipstick on a pig." Nicknamed *The Stick.*

**cannon 1.** A strong throwing arm, almost always applied to outfielders and catchers. "You talk about a cannon; you could've had a 30:30 and you wouldn't have gotten him" (San Diego Padres announcer Jerry Coleman, quoted on the speed of a runner, *Baseball Digest,* Dec. 1983). **2.** A hitter who hits the ball hard, often referred to as a "big cannon."

**cannon ball** A ball pitched or thrown with great velocity, as if it were fired out of a cannon. **1st Use.** 1891. (*Chicago Herald,* May 7; Edward J. Nichols).

**cannon shot 1.** An exceptional fastball. **2.** An exceptionally long-hit ball; e.g., "The original dimensions of the park called for a 460-foot cannon shot to reach the bleachers."

**cannon's mouth** An infielder's location when positioned close to the batter during a probable bunt situation. Implied is the danger that the batter may unexpectedly take a full swing and imperil the fielder with a hard-hit ball.

**can of corn** An easily caught fly ball; a high fly ball that allows a defensive player time to stand under the ball and catch it easily. Of a Wade Boggs drive to center held up by the wind, Jerry Remy (New England Sports Network, June 11, 1990) commented: "A big can of corn tonight." Ron C. Judd (*Seattle Times,* Mar. 26, 1997) defined the term as "the only product in your home not personally endorsed by Ken 'I (Once) Drove a Chevy' Griffey, Jr." Var. "can o' corn." **1st Use.** 1896. (Burt L. Standish, *Frank Merriwell's Schooldays;*

Edward J. Nichols). **Etymology.** The phrase has long been assumed to have come from the old-time grocery store where the grocer used a pole or a mechanical grabber to tip an item, such as a can of corn, off a high shelf and let it tumble into his hands or his apron, which was held out in front like a fire net. An alternate theory is suggested by Mike Whiteford (*How to Talk Baseball,* 1983) in which he quotes Pittsburgh Pirates announcer Bob Prince who said "it's as easy as taking corn out of a can." Still another, suggested by Bert Dunne (*Folger's Dictionary of Baseball,* 1958), is that the "can of corn" ball is hit with a "kerplunk" sound, presumably that of a can being hit with a stick.

Peter Tamony developed a separate theory that was published in the form of a letter appearing in Bucky Walter's "Mail Bag" (*San Francisco Examiner,* Aug. 24, 1977): "'Can of corn' no doubt developed out of the complex of usage surrounding 'cornball,' a confection made of pop corn and molasses, munched by the young for over a century. Popped corn flies wildly, of course, making a handy word association with a light pop-up to the outfield." Tamony, incidentally, determined that the term was in use in the early to mid-1920s, based on a series of interviews in 1953 with semiprofessional players. **Usage Note.** "We still have to hear even one player refer to . . . a 'can of corn' . . . a high, lazy fly to the infield." (*Baseball Magazine,* Jan. 1943). From time to time, the term is deemed to be an archaic bit of slang, but it is still used by sportscasters with regularity; e.g., "that's a can of corn for [John] Shelby" (ABC telecast, June 8, 1986). **Extended Use.** An easy accomplishment. The term also underscores the degree to which a bit of baseball slang can work its way into other realms; e.g., note the term "can of corn decision," a court decision in San Francisco that made the sponsor of a semiprofessional baseball team responsible for an injury to a bystander. In the case, a player for a team sponsored by the Double Play Tavern dropped an easily catchable fly ball (i.e., a can of corn) with two out and the bases loaded in the bottom of the ninth inning during a scoreless tie. The player who dropped the ball was so angry that he threw it across the street, accidentally hitting a woman at a gas station. The woman sued and won the case, which was reported in full under the headline, "Can of Corn Decision" (*San Francisco News,* May 12, 1959; Peter Tamony).

**cantaloupe** A pitched ball that looks big to the batter.

**"can't anybody here play this game?"** A lament and backhanded rallying cry, first uttered by Casey Stengel after taking over as manager of the inept 1962 New York Mets. The phrase became the title of a 1963 book by Jimmy Breslin.

**can't buy a hit** Said of a player or team having difficulty in getting out of a batting slump.

**can't catch cold** *arch.* Said of a poor defensive player, who is unable to catch anything, from a baseball to a common cold. **1st Use.** 1915. (*Baseball Magazine,* Dec.; Edward J. Nichols).

**can't hit a balloon** *arch.* Said of an inept hitter. **1st Use.** 1908. (*Baseball Magazine,* Sept.; Edward J. Nichols).

**can't-miss** Said of a young player who appears headed for baseball success, whether to the majors or for stardom. "In 1983, that heaviest of burdens—'can't-miss' status—was conferred upon a dozen or so major-league rookies" (Bruce Lowitt, *St. Petersburg Times,* Mar. 30, 1988).

**canto** *arch.* Syn. of *inning,* 1. The term is likened to a division in poetry to connote the divisions of a baseball game. See also *stanza.* **1st Use.** 1915. "During the nine cantos just three Dodgers reached the initial hassock." (Describing a Rube Marquard no-hitter, *Newark Evening News,* Apr. 16).

**can't pitch hay** *arch.* Said of an ineffective pitcher. **1st Use.** 1915. (*Baseball Magazine,* Dec.; Edward J. Nichols).

**can't teach that** A flare that drops into the shallow outfield. **Etymology.** David A. Markiewicz (*Fort Worth Star-Telegram,* Mar. 26, 1998) quotes Texas Rangers manager Johnny Oates: "Last year, Mike Simms broke a bat on a little flare. He points to a spot near the right-field foul line about 15 yards from the edge of the infield. It dropped in for a hit and someone said, 'Can't teach that.'"

Markiewicz added that the phrase has since become a staple of the Rangers clubhouse.

**cap 1.** *n.* The visored hat that is a standard element of a player's uniform at all levels of baseball. It is usually decorated with the team's initials or insignia. **2.** *n.* The last play, of whatever kind, by a player or team in any baseball game, series, or season. **3.** *v.* To score a run to end an inning or game; e.g., "Smith capped a 4–2 ball game with a home run."

**capacity crowd** Spectators who fill all seats in a ballpark.

**cap day** An event when young fans come to the ballpark wearing, or to receive (free), the caps of the home team.

**Cape Cod League** An amateur, wooden-bat summer league on the Cape Cod (Mass.) peninsula featuring college ballplayers. Graduates include such major leaguers as Carlton Fisk, Will Clark, Jeff Bagwell, Jeff Conine, Scott Erickson, and Mel and Todd Stottlemyre.

**captain 1.** An honorary title bestowed on a player to acknowledge leadership. Such an appointment is rare: "First baseman Eddie Murray, clearly the most respected man on the Orioles, was named the first captain in the history of the franchise by manager Earl Weaver yesterday during a team meeting" (*Baltimore Sun,* Feb. 28, 1986). Sometimes, but not always, the team captain will wear a small letter "c" on his uniform sleeve. **2.** A player in the early days of baseball who handled the functions currently assumed by the manager. "[The Unions] only have one captain, whose name is law" (*Detroit Free Press,* Aug. 4, 1868).

**cap-tipper** *arch.* A *showboat,* 2, in the 1930s.

**cardboard** *arch.* An admission ticket to a baseball game. **1st Use.** 1912. (*New York Tribune,* Sept. 26; Edward J. Nichols).

**Cards** A long-established nickname for the St. Louis Cardinals.

**career record 1.** The statistical data accrued by a baseball player during his playing career. **2.** The achievement for the most or best lifetime total in a particular category; e.g., Hank Aaron holds the "career record" for home runs (755).

**career year** The best season of a player's career; a season as statistically good as a particular player can expect to have during his playing years. Tom Verducci (*Sports Illustrated,* Sept. 9, 1996) defined the term as "when a player exceeds his well-established statistical norms."

**caress** *arch.* To hit the ball. **1st Use.** 1912. (*New York Tribune,* Sept. 7; Edward J. Nichols).

**Carmine Hose** A nickname for the Boston Red Sox.

**carnage** A clobbering during which many runs are scored.

**carom** A batted ball that bounces or ricochets off a wall or fence in the manner of a carom shot in billiards. **1st Use.** 1908. (*Spalding's Official Base Ball Guide;* Edward J. Nichols).

**carpet** The infield playing surface, whether it be real or artificial grass. Mike Whiteford (*How to Talk Baseball,* 1983) applies the term to a surface made of synthetic material, but the term also shows up in print for the natural surface as early as 1908. **1st Use.** 1908. (*New York Evening Journal,* Aug. 21; Edward J. Nichols).

**carry 1.** *v.* To go a long distance. The term is used in the context of such atmospheric factors as humidity, fog, and wind. The question of whether the presence of fog affects the ability of the ball to carry was raised by sportscasters during the final game of the 1986 World Series, but back-to-back hits by the Red Sox had Vin Scully conclude that the fog was not a factor. **2.** *n.* The way a batted ball travels away from home plate. **3.** *n.* The distance traveled by a fly ball. "They [new bats] last far longer than any other bat I've tried and I get more carry from them" (David Segui, quoted in *Sports Illustrated,* Oct. 8, 1995).

**carry a club** To be able singlehandedly to hit and score enough to keep a team playing winning baseball. "When Jack Clark is hot, he can carry a club for three or four weeks at a time." (Kevin Horrigan, *St. Louis Post-Dispatch,* May 29, 1987)

**carry a safe** *arch.* To run slowly; to run as if weighed down by a heavy object.

**carry the mail** *arch.* To run swiftly. "He is a fellow who can 'carry the mail,' or get from here to there in a hurry, and frequently it is said he 'can high tail it' or is a 'deer'" (Herbert Simons, *Baseball Magazine,* Apr. 1943). **1st Use.** 1937. (*New York Daily News,* Feb. 14; Edward J. Nichols)

**Cartwright myth** The belief that Alexander Cartwright (1820–92) had more to do with the creation of baseball than is actually the case. John S. Bowman (letter, Sept. 18, 1989), who created the term (Joel Zoss and John S. Bowman, *Diamonds in the Rough,* 1989), lays to rest the belief that Cartwright "almost singlehandedly organized the Knickerbockers, set down the rules of modern baseball, and then set about to convert many teams and individuals to 'his' game. Harold Peterson was greatly responsible for promoting this new

**Cartwright myth.** *Alexander Cartwright, a New York bank teller who helped organize the Knickerbocker Base Ball Club in 1845.*

myth, and it still permeates many articles and books. Well-informed people know that Cartwright doesn't deserve all this priority."

**carve nicks in the weather** *arch.* To swing at pitches without making contact. **1st Use.** 1912. (*American Magazine,* June; Edward J. Nichols).

**casaba** A baseball.

**Casey 1.** *n.* A player who strikes out at the crucial moment in a game; one who fails in the manner of Casey, the figure in Ernest L. Thayer's 1888 poem, "Casey at the Bat." Usually stated as *do a Casey* or "pull a Casey," the term recalls the last stanza of the poem:

"Oh, somewhere in this favored land the sun is
    shining bright;
"The band is playing somewhere, and somewhere
    hearts are light,
"And somewhere men are laughing, and some-
    where children shout;
"But there is no joy in Mudville—mighty Casey
    has struck out."

**2.** *v.* To strike out.

**Casey act** A strikeout; esp., one occurring at a crucial moment in a game and in the manner of "Casey at the Bat." **1st Use.** 1912. (*New York Tribune,* Oct. 15; Edward J. Nichols).

**"Casey at the Bat"** A poem by Ernest L. Thayer (*San Francisco Examiner,* June 3, 1888) that gives epic quality to a single strikeout. The poem is probably the most popular ever written by an American; it is almost certainly the most recited, most parodied, and most sequeled. It was termed "the nation's best known piece of comic verse" by Martin Gardner (*The Annotated Casey at the Bat,* 1967, a book that contains, among other things, 27 variations and updates in the style of the original). The poem attracted little attention until it was recited by a vaudevillian and comic actor named De Wolf Hopper (1858–1935) later in 1888. Hopper went on to recite the poem more than 10,000 times during his lifetime.

**cashew** An undisciplined, zany nonconformist; a "nutty" player. "The [Philadelphia Phillies] roster included such cashews as Richie Allen, who liked

*"Casey at the Bat."* In this 1927 Paramount version of the famous 1888 poem, the players were (l. to r.) Wallace Beery as Casey, Sterling Halloway as Putnam, and Ford Sterling as O'Dowd. In this rendition Casey is framed by gamblers, among other things.

everything about a ball park except getting there" (Bob Uecker, *Catcher in the Wry,* 1982; Charles D. Poe).

**castoff** A player who has been let go or dismissed by a team. Occasionally, a castoff from one team goes on to become successful with another. **1st Use.** 1900. (*New York Tribune,* July 4; Edward J. Nichols).

**casualty pass** *arch.* Syn. of *base on balls.* **1st Use.** 1922. (Ernest J. Lanigan, *Baseball Cyclopedia;* Edward J. Nichols). **Etymology.** This is almost certainly a reference to the pass given to a wounded soldier to allow him to retreat from the front lines to seek medical attention.

**cat 1.** A great fielding pitcher; one with feline agility, such as Harry "The Cat" Brecheen. **2.** Syn. of *catball.*

**catball** A simple game of ball, which, according to the number of batters available, was known as "one old cat," "two old cat," etc. Syn. *cat,* 2. **1st Use.** 1866. "The game was 'cat ball,' or what is called in some parts of New England 'Two Old Cat'" (Charles A. Peverelly, *The Book of American Pastimes;* David Shulman).

**catbird seat** A position of control and mastery, often stated as "sitting in the catbird seat." The term was popularized by Brooklyn Dodgers announcer Red Barber, who would use it, for example, to describe a batter with a count of three balls and no strikes. The term is often used to describe a team's first-place position in the standings; e.g., "Twins, Giants in Catbird Seat," as those two teams were on the verge of clinching playoff berths (*The Sporting News* headline, Oct. 5, 1987). **Etymology.** The term has long been attributed to Red Barber. Though he denies having created the term, he does explain how he once "bought" it. In his biography (*Rhubarb in the Catbird Seat,* 1968), Barber tells the story of how, while playing penny ante poker in Cincinnati with friends, he sat for hours unable to win a hand. Then he relates: "Finally, during a round of seven-card stud, I decided I was going to force the issue. I raised on the first bet, and I raised again on every card. At the end, when the showdown came, it was between a fellow named Frank Cope and me. Frank turned over his hole cards, showed a pair of aces, and won the pot. He said, 'Thank you, Red. I had those aces from the start. I was sitting in the catbird seat.' I didn't have to be told the meaning. And I had paid for it. It was mine."

One question that has never been satisfactorily answered is why the catbird? James Rogers (*The Dictionary of Clichés,* 1985) commented: "The catbird commands a good view from its lofty perch, but then, so do many birds. Why the catbird's vantage point was signaled out is beyond explaining." **Extended Use.** The term is used to describe anyone finding himself or herself in an advantageous situation: "[Israeli Foreign Minister Shimon] Peres in the Catbird Seat" (*Newsweek* headline, Sept. 29, 1986). The phrase eventually became so popular that James Thurber wrote a short story for *The New Yorker* (which also appears in a collection of stories called *The Thurber Carnival,* 1945) entitled "The Catbird Seat." In the story a mild-mannered chap is driven to distraction by a woman in his office who asks questions in the colorful, metaphoric Barber manner: "Are you tearing up the pea patch?" "Are you hollering down the rain barrel?" "Are you sitting in the catbird seat?" "Are you lifting the oxcart out of the ditch?" Another employee must explain that the woman, named Ulgine Barrows, is a Brooklyn Dodgers fan who has picked up these Barberisms from the radio.

**catch 1.** *v.* To retrieve and control a thrown or batted ball, usually with the aid of a glove or mitt. The term is most commonly applied to a ball that has not hit the ground. **1st Use.** 1883. (*Sporting Life,* Apr. 22; Edward J. Nichols). **2.** *v.* To play the position of catcher. "Bo [Belinsky] is starting tomorrow and, Ron [Brand], you will catch him" (Maury Allen, *Bo: Pitching and Wooing,* 1973). **3.** *n.* The act of a fielder in receiving and controlling

or securing firmly in his hand or glove a batted or thrown ball before it hits the ground. To be a valid catch, the fielder must hold the ball long enough to prove that he has complete control of the ball and that his release of the ball is voluntary. **1st Use.** 1862. (*New York Sunday Mercury,* June 29; Edward J. Nichols). **4.** *n.* A game in which two or more people throw a ball back and forth; e.g., "Smith and Jones are playing catch or having a game of catch." **5.** *v.* To rise in the standings and overtake a higher-ranked team. **6.** *v.* To hit a ball well. "I hit all my homers in batting practice. Every now and then I catch one in a game" (Lance Johnson, quoted in *Baltimore Sun,* Oct. 10, 1993). **7.** *n.* Short for *catcher,* 1.

**Catch, The** The over-the-shoulder catch in deep center field at the Polo Grounds, 460 feet from home plate, made by Willie Mays of the New York Giants on Sept. 24, 1954, during the eighth inning of the first game of the World Series, off a long drive hit by Vic Wertz of the Cleveland Indians. "When baseball heads into the 22nd century, they'll still be talking about The Catch" (*Time* magazine, special insert on the 1981 World Series).

**catcher 1.** The player behind home plate to whose mitt the pitcher aims the ball. The role of the catcher is relatively complex and extends far beyond being a target for and receiver of pitched balls; e.g., the catcher orders (calls) the pitches to be thrown through the use of signals, backs up throws to first base, attempts to field pop fouls, sets defensive alignments, attempts to tag out baserunners trying to score, and attempts to throw out would-be base stealers. Abbrev. *C.* Syn. *catch,* 7; *backstop,* 2; *backstopper; receiver; wind paddist.* **1st Use.** 1854. (Knickerbocker Rules; Edward J. Nichols). **2.** The position played by the catcher. Abbrev. *C.*

**catcher's balk** The correct but rarely used term for *catcher's interference.*

**catcher's box** The four-by-six-foot rectangular area at the rear edge of the batter's box in which the catcher must remain until the pitch is delivered.

**catcher's earned run average** The earned run

average of a team's pitchers with a given catcher. Abbrev. *CERA.*

**catcher's equipment** The protective gear worn by the catcher, consisting of a catcher's mask, mitt, chest protector, and shin guards. The equipment is designed to protect the catcher from being injured by the baseball (and to a much lesser extent, the bat). In the early days of baseball there were catchers who chose to work without this equipment. George Ellard, a nonprofessional catcher, protested the wearing of protective gear with the poem "The Red Stockings" (1880s), which contains these lines: "We used no mattress on our hands,/No cage upon our face;/We stood right up and caught the ball,/With courage and with grace." Syn. *fernalia.*

**catcher's interference 1.** An act by the catcher that hinders the batter; e.g., pushing the batter, touching the batter's bat, or running in front of the batter to catch a pitched ball. The batter is awarded first base (he is not charged with an official at-bat) but the catcher is charged with an error. Syn. *catcher's balk.* **2.** An act by the catcher that hinders a baserunner; e.g., blocking home plate without holding or attempting to field the ball. The runner is awarded the base to which he was advancing. Syn. *catcher's balk.*

**catcher's mask** A padded metal grate that protects the catcher's face from the baseball (such as errant pitches and foul tips) and the bat. Invented by Fred Winthrop Thayer, a Harvard coach and player of the 1870s, the mask was first worn by a Harvard catcher named James Alexander Tyng in a game on April 12, 1877, against the Live Oaks, a semiprofessional team from Lynn, Mass. Not only did the new invention protect the catcher's face from the ball and bat, it also allowed him to move closer to the plate and pay greater attention to the runners on base.

The catcher's mask attracted quick criticism. An article on Thayer by John Hanlon (Portland [Maine] *Sunday Telegram,* June 1, 1896) recounted several critics, including a sportswriter who commented: "There is a great deal of beastly humbug in contrivances to protect men from things which do not happen. There is about as much sense in putting a lightning rod on a catcher as there is a mask."

But as the demand for masks grew steadily, Thayer realized that he had come up with a good idea. On Jan. 15, 1878, he applied for a patent (no. 200,358), which was granted less than a month later. One of the three "original" models used in conjunction with the patent application has been silvered and is on display at the Harvard Varsity Club in Cambridge, Mass. See also *face mask.* Syn. *bird cage; wire cage.* **1st Use.** 1877. (*Harvard Crimson,* April 20). The term was first mentioned in print eight days after its debut. The *Harvard Crimson* deemed the mask "a complete success, since it entirely protected the face and head and adds greatly to the confidence of the catcher, who need not feel that he is every moment in danger of a life-long injury."

**catcher's mitt** The large padded glove worn by catchers since the 1890s. In *The Sporting News* (Feb. 23, 1939), a claim is made that the "Father of the Catching Glove" was "Mother" Joe Gunson, whose invention was prompted by an injury when he was performing for Kansas City in 1888. He never realized any gains from his idea, as others soon devised similar aids for themselves.

**catch leaning** To pick off a baserunner who has moved or is moving too far from the base occupied toward the next base. One is said to have been "caught leaning" when picked off by the pitcher or catcher after leading and trying to get a jump on the next base.

**catch looking** To fool or deceive a batter with a pitch that crosses the plate for a called third strike. See also *strike out looking.*

**catch napping** To surprise a less-than-alert baserunner with the result that he is picked off or suddenly caught between bases; also known as "being asleep at the switch" or "catch asleep." A quaint but accurate early definition of "baseball napping": "When a player through carelessness or sleepy-headedness is caught off his base" (Mrs. John A. Logan, *Home Manual,* 1889). **1st Use.** 1862. (Chadwick Scrapbooks; Edward J. Nichols).

**catch stealing** See *caught stealing.*

**catch up 1.** To bring the bat around to hit the ball. **2.** To try to overtake a team higher in the standings.

**catch-up game** A game in which one team comes from behind to lead or win.

**caught leaning** See *catch leaning.*

**caught looking** See *catch looking.*

**caught stealing** Tagged out while attempting to steal a base. The *Official Baseball Rules* (rule 10.08) provides that a runner shall be charged as "caught stealing" (an official statistic) when he a) tries to steal a base, b) is picked off a base and tries to advance (any move toward the next base is considered an attempt to advance), or c) overslides while stealing. In 1982 when Rickey Henderson set the all-time single-season steal record of 130, he was also caught stealing a record 42 times. Abbrev. *CS.*

**CBA** Abbrev. for *Collective Bargaining Agreement.*

**cellar** The position in league or divisional standings held by the team with the worst won-lost record. Syn. *basement.*

**cellar championship** A facetious term for the efforts of two or more teams to determine which one will end up in last place in the final standings. **1st Use.** 1905. "With a team which never had a look-in for anything better than cellar championship . . . the club made money" (National Association of Professional Base Ball Leagues, *Official Guide–1905;* David Shulman).

**cellar dweller** A team with the worst won-lost record in the standings at any given moment during the season. Syn. "cellar tenant."

**cello pack** A set of baseball cards packaged in transparent cellophane. The term is used by collectors to distinguish cellophane-packed cards (which collectors tend to prefer because the top and bottom card in each pack are exposed) from those in a *wax pack.*

**center** Short for *center field.*

**center field 1.** The area beyond second base, which is not regularly covered by either the right fielder or the left fielder; the center of the outfield. Syn. *center.* **2.** The position of the player who defends center field. Abbrev. *CF* or *cf.* Syn. *center.* **1st Use.** 1854. (Knickerbocker Rules; Edward J. Nichols).

**center fielder** The defensive player who is positioned in center field. Because of the size of the area the center fielder must patrol, the player in this position is usually quite fast and has a strong, accurate arm. Sometimes spelled "centerfielder." Abbrev. *CF* or *cf.*

**Central Division 1.** See *American League Central.* **2.** See *National League Central.*

**CERA** Abbrev. for *catcher's earned run average.*

**ceremonial first pitch** The traditional tossing of a baseball by an honored person to the catcher of the home team to open the first game of the season in the home team's ballpark or for some other noteworthy event.

**CF 1.** Abbrev. for *center field,* 2. Sometimes *cf.* **2.** Abbrev. for *center fielder.* Sometimes *cf.*

**CG** Abbrev. for *complete game.*

**chaffing** *arch.* **1.** Complaining about an umpire's decision. **1st Use.** 1863. (Chadwick Scrapbooks; Edward J. Nichols). **2.** Sarcastic allusions to, or irritating comments on, opposing players' weaknesses or style of play. See also *chin music,* 2.

**chain-store baseball** *arch.* The system by which a team obtains first option on the players on certain minor-league teams. The system later was known as *farm system.* Syn. "chain baseball."

**chair position** "The right position for a catcher to catch the ball as the pitcher throws it; he looks almost as if he is sitting on the edge of a chair" (Morris A. Shirts, *Warm Up for Little League Baseball,* 1971).

**chalk** The white powder that is spread on the playing field to mark the foul lines, baselines, on-deck circles, coach's boxes, catcher's box, and batter's boxes. Lime is often used as a substitute for chalk.

**chalker** A hand-operated piece of equipment used to mark the white lines needed on a baseball field.

**chalk line** Any line drawn on a baseball field, although it usually refers to one of the foul lines.

**chalk raiser** A batted ball that is ruled fair because, in hitting the chalked foul line, it raises a corroborating puff of white-line dust.

**chalk up 1.** To record a baseball feat as if on a blackboard, such as "chalking up" a no-hitter or a victory. **1st Use.** 1912. (*New York Tribune,* Sept. 12; Edward J. Nichols). **2.** To hit a ball off the end of the bat, in allusion to billiards where the end of the cue is "chalked up." Players once commonly hollered "chalk up" when a batter hit the ball off the end of the bat.

**challenge 1.** To pitch one's best pitch to a batter, daring him to hit it, usually expressed as "challenge the hitter"; to pitch to that area of the strike zone where the batter displays his greatest strength, as opposed to avoiding it. This is most likely to occur when the pitcher's strength seems to match that of the batter. Art Hill (*"Don't Let Baseball Die,"* 1978) comments: "When a pitcher 'challenges' a hitter, he throws him the pitch he's looking for because it is also the pitcher's best pitch; he pits strength against strength." See also *go after.* **2.** To test the throwing capability of an outfielder by a runner who attempts to advance an extra base.

**Chalmers Award** An award presented by the Chalmers Motor Co. from 1911 through 1914 to one player in the American League and one player in the National League who "should prove himself as the most important and useful player to his club and to the league at large in point of deportment and value of services rendered." A commission of baseball writers (one writer from each city in each league) decided the winner of the award. The players selected for the award received a Chalmers automobile. The Chalmers Award was a precursor to the Most Valuable Player Award. In 1910, a Chalmers automobile was presented to the batting champions in each league.

**champagne celebration** A postgame clubhouse ritual in which a victorious team celebrates by spraying and drinking champagne. It usually occurs when a team clinches its division or the pennant, or wins the World Series; but not exclusively—in 1950, the St. Louis Browns held a champagne celebration upon winning their 55th game, which (under the former 154-game schedule) meant that it was impossible for them to lose 100 games.

**championship season 1.** The regular season, during the course of which the divisional championships are established. Before there were divisions, the term referred to the period between Opening Day and the winning of the pennant. **2.** A specific season in which a particular team wins the championship.

**Championship Series** A set of playoff games (best four of seven games) between the two division (and since 1995, the *Division Series*) winners in each of the major leagues (National League and American League) to determine the two pennant winners to play in the *World Series.* The series was the best three of five games from 1969 to 1984. See also *League Championship Series; American League Championship Series; National League Championship Series.*

**champions of the world** A resplendent title claimed annually by the winner of the World Series. Many have commented on this all-embracing title, including linguist Peter Tamony (*News Letter and Wasp,* Oct. 13, 1939) who wrote: "That baseball . . . is played only in the United States, and that the game is not international is of little moment in the excitement attending the outcome of the series. Whichever team wins holds the Championship of the World, and is thus, in our scheme of things entitled to a place just to the right of that of the gods."

**chance 1.** A reasonable opportunity for a defensive player to field a batted or thrown ball with the opportunity of making or assisting a putout or an error. Generally the first baseman accepts the most chances in a game since he ends most infield outs. A fielder's *total chances* are determined by adding putouts, assists, and errors. **1st Use.** 1867. (Chadwick Scrapbooks; Edward J. Nichols). **2.** An opportunity to perform well. Baltimore Oriole manager Earl Weaver once said: "I gave Mike Cuellar more chances than my first wife."

**change 1.** *adj./arch.* Said of a relief or substitute player or players; e.g., a "change pitcher" or a "change battery." **1st Use.** 1883. "The Athletics pitted their change battery against the amateur Hartville Club" (*Sporting Life,* Apr. 15; David Shulman). **2.** *n.* Syn. of *changeup.*

**change livery** *obs.* To change teams.

**change of pace** A once commonly used term for *changeup*. It is a slowly pitched ball, thrown in an effort to deceive the batter into thinking it is a fastball, thereby throwing off the batter's timing; "a slow ball throwed with a fast ball motion" (Dizzy Dean). Rogers Hornsby (*My Kind of Baseball*, 1953) wrote: "The change of pace can be achieved by dragging the back foot across the mound or by holding the ball deeper in the hand and gripping it tighter, and like the curve, the ball should be kept low." Formerly, it was known simply as a *slow ball*. The term "change of pace" has gone out of style because of the tendency to use the term "changeup" to describe the same pitch. **1st Use.** 1868. (Chadwick Scrapbooks; Edward J. Nichols). The term also appears in an 1889 baseball glossary where it defines the strategy of a pitcher who "alternates in his delivery between a slow and swiftly pitched ball." This would indicate that when the term was first used it was applied to both fast and slow pitches.

**change of scenery** The opportunity afforded a player to rejuvenate his career by being traded to another club. When it was reported that Los Angeles Dodgers pitcher Hideo Nomo had requested a trade, he said it was true that he "definitely needed a change of scenery, a change of environment" (*Baltimore Sun*, June 2, 1998). See also *new life*, 1.

**changeup** A modern term for *change of pace*; specif., a slow ball thrown after one or more fastballs, or a *letup pitch* thrown to look like a fastball to upset the batter's timing. It is thrown with the same windup and arm speed of a fastball but with reduced velocity and the intention of deceiving the batter making it, in the opinion of some, the most difficult pitch to master. To do so requires a different grip, usually either a "choke" hold, in which the ball is shoved back into the hand, or a "circle" configuration (see *circle change*). "The slow pitch that follows the fast breaking curve is the change-up off the curve ball" (Arthur Mann, *How to Play Winning Baseball*, 1953). See also *off-speed pitch*. Also spelled "change-up." Syn. *change*, 2. **1st Use.** 1948. "He's got everything—speed, curve, change-up and

plenty of heart" (*Birmingham News*, May 7). **Usage Note.** The term is still a pretentious way of saying "slow ball" to older ears. In his essay "The Grand Old Game," Jim Murray (*The Best of Jim Murray*, 1965) quotes veteran writer Jack Olsen: "Know what they call a 'slow ball' nowadays? A 'changeup'! Now, I ask you!"

**chapter** Syn. of *inning*, 1.

**charge 1.** *n.* A player on a team. **2.** *v.* See *charge the ball*. **3.** *v.* See *charge the mound*.

**"CHARGE!"** *v.* A rallying cry bellowed in unison by many a modern fan after a bugle (which is usually on a tape recording) sounds the cavalry charge. Such cries are often prompted by instructions appearing on electronic scoreboards. Despite the fact that it seems more appropriate to football or a sport where players charge down the field, it has become a very popular form of baseball fan participation. See also *"we want a hit!"*

**charge the ball** To rush forward to field a batted ball in an effort to reduce the time it takes to reach the ball and make a play. The time that is saved by charging a ball (often fractions of a second) may be crucial.

**charge the mound** For a batter to run to the mound after being hit or knocked down by a pitch and to start a fight with the pitcher. The batter is often ejected and suspended; e.g., in 1994, Reggie Sanders of the Cincinnati Reds received a five-game suspension for charging the mound.

**charity hop** A batted ball that bounces waist-high, making it easy to field; a gift to an infielder. See also *big bill*.

**charley horse** A muscular cramp or pain, especially one in the legs or quadriceps, usually produced as a result of physical exertion or a strain or bruise. See also *"here comes Charley."* Syn. "Charlie horse." **Etymology/1st Use.** 1886. "Joe Quinn is troubled with 'Charley-horse'" (*Sporting Life*, Sept. 15; Barry Popik).
   "Charley horse" is one of those wonderful terms that has fascinated many, all of whom seem to have come up with a different theory of its origin.

This may be one of those cases in which several stories, seemingly contradictory, contributed to give a term the momentum it needed to become popular.

H. L. Mencken (*The American Language: Suppl. II,* 1948) cites Bill "Boileryard" Clarke, an original Baltimore Oriole of the 1890s, who argued that the term had come "from the name of Charley Esper, a left-handed pitcher, who walked like a lame horse." This theory was discredited when it was learned that the term was already in use by the time Esper joined the Orioles in 1894.

Another version involving members of the same Orioles team appears in Forrest C. Allen's *My Basket-ball Bible* (1930) and was repeated in *American Notes and Queries* (Apr. 1947). One day at a local racetrack, several players put money on a horse called Charlie who, winning throughout the race, pulled up lame in the final stretch. The following day a player pulled a tendon in his leg and was likened by one of the coaches to "our old Charlie horse."

Hy Turkin (*Baseball Almanac,* 1955) relates a similar story with the Chicago Cubs, asserting the term was "coined by either Billy Sunday or Joe Quest in the 1880s after a horse backed by the Chicago players had pulled up lame in the stretch." A note written by Peter Tamony in the Tamony collection, attributed to "Baseball Slang and Origins" (but not further identified), agrees with Turkin, but taps Sunday as the one who coined the term. It reads: "When George Gore hit what should have been an inside-the-park homer and strained a thigh muscle rounding second, so that he had to limp into third, Billy cried, 'Here comes the Charley horse.'"

Lee Allen (*The Sporting News,* May 2, 1962), on the other hand, insisted that it was Quest who coined the term in 1882. Allen reported: "Son of a blacksmith from New Castle, Pa., Quest noticed that players hobbling around with a peculiar muscle injury of the legs reminded him of an old white horse, Charlie, employed at his father's shop." (Peter Tamony)

Peter Morris found a much earlier and more detailed account of this version in the form of a note in the Grand Rapids (Mich.) *Daily Democrat* (June 28, 1889): "A Newcastleman gives the origin of Charley horse. Years ago Joe Quest was employed as an apprentice in the machine shop of Quest & Shaw in Newcastle, his father, who was one of the proprietors of the firm, had an old white horse by the name of Charley. Doing usage in pulling heavy loads had stiffened the animal's legs so that he walked as if troubled with strained tendons. Afterwards, when Quest became a member of the Chicago club, he was troubled, with others, with a peculiar stiffness of the legs, which brought to his mind the ailment of the old white horse Charley. Joe said that the ball players troubled with the ailment hobbled exactly as did the old horse, and as no one seemed to know what the trouble was, Quest dubbed it 'Charley horse.' The name has spread until today it has become part of the language of the national game."

A letter (June 1, 1957) on file at the National Baseball Library and Archives in Cooperstown, N.Y., from Henry R. Viets, curator of the Boston Medical Library, begins: "I have been trying to trace for some months the derivation of the term 'Charley horse' and have gotten back to the year 1889 where we have found a reference in the *Cincinnati Commercial Gazette* for March 17 of that year stating that one of the players 'was affected with a "Charley horse"' and that ended his ball-playing for 1888."

Tim Considine (*Language of Sport,* 1982) came up with this unreferenced explanation: "Often in the 1800s, old workhorses kept on the grounds of ballparks were called Charley. The movements of the injured, stiff-legged ballplayers were likened to the labored plodding of these old horses, and the injury itself eventually became known as a 'charley' or 'charley horse.'"

Gerald Secor Couzens (*A Baseball Album,* 1980) traces the term back to the Sioux City (Iowa) team of 1889 and an old white horse named Charley. Couzens attributes this version to a minor-league coach named Walter McCredie. This same story appears in an unsigned article in *San Francisco Chronicle* (July 2, 1934), but the old white horse in this version inspired the coinage in 1890, not 1889.

The earliest attempt to explain the term was located by lexicographer Barry Popik (*St. Louis*

*Post-Dispatch,* July 15, 1887) in which it is stated: "The name is said to owe its origin to the fact that a player afflicted with it, when attempting to run, does so much after the fashion of a boy astride of a wooden horse, sometimes called a 'Charley horse.'"

**Extended Use.** The leap from the slang of ballplayers to standard English is described by Tristram Potter Coffin (*The Old Ball Game,* 1971) as being so complete "that most people would have trouble describing the ailment if the phrase were taken [away] from them." Coffin notes that the *Journal of the American Medical Association* (Nov. 30, 1946) published a letter to the editor entitled "Treatment of Charleyhorse" rather than "Treatment of Injury to Quadriceps Famoris"; such a usage indicates "the phrase to have been a part of even the most formal American English for a quarter of a century."

**chart** To keep a detailed record of each pitch in a game; to record pitches on a *pitching chart.* It is an old and widely observed custom in baseball that the next day's pitcher charts the game.

**chase 1.** To force the removal of a pitcher by the offense getting hits, literally chasing the pitcher out of the game. **2.** To eject from the game by the umpire. Beans Reardon (quoted in Larry R. Gerlach, *The Men in Blue,* 1980): "I never chased very many ballplayers. I didn't believe in chasing them." **3.** To pursue first place in the standings. **4.** To swing at a pitch out of the strike zone; e.g., "Smith chased a bad pitch." Compare *lay off.*

**chase card** A baseball card that is so desirable or rare that people buy packs of baseball cards searching for them. Once occurring naturally and randomly, chase cards are now produced in more limited numbers, inserted sparingly, and have brought an element of lottery to the hobby. *Sports Illustrated* (July 29, 1996) reported that premium cards, often of exotic design, are inserted at a "ratio that varies from one card to every two boxes to one card to every case to stimulate interest."

**chase flies** To play the outfield. **1st Use.** 1905. (*Sporting Life,* Feb. 10; Edward J. Nichols).

**chatter** Lively, often meaningless, talk spoken for team morale. Infield chatter is intended to keep everyone alert and on his toes and to encourage the pitcher, while chatter from the bench or dugout is meant to inspire the batter. Writer Courtland Milloy tried to capture some chatter from the Continental League of the District of Columbia (*Washington Post,* May 26, 1987): "'Dada boy. Dadda boy, baby,' the catcher yelled out to the pitcher's mound during a recent game. 'Make him think. Pick 'em up. Lay it on 'em, baby. [Ball one, above the strike zone] Too high, but no damage done. [The next pitch strike one] Dada boy, baby. That's the one. Do it for me two mo' times.'" **1st Use.** 1891. (*New York Post,* June 8; Edward J. Nichols).

**Chavez Ravine** The location of Dodger Stadium in Los Angeles, Calif. The ravine itself is on a hill overlooking downtown. When the Angels played there from 1962 to 1965, it was only referred to as Dodger Stadium when the National League club was in residence. When the Angels were at home, it was called Chavez Ravine so as not to refer to the Dodgers.

**chaw** Chewing tobacco; a smokeless form of the weed that has long been common in baseball circles. Dizzy Dean: "A cud of tabaccer. Some pitchers can't even start warmin' up without at least one good chaw."

An article on a campaign to battle smokeless tobacco among Little Leaguers contained this line on antichaw pitcher Nolan Ryan: "After his two sons began playing Little League baseball, Ryan said he saw youngsters as young as 10 years of age using dip [snuff] and chaw" (*Houston Post,* Sept. 29, 1987; Charles D. Poe).

As of this writing the day of the chaw is limited. In 1997, Sen. Frank Lautenberg (D.-N.J.) persuaded the players' union to make the All-Star Game tobacco-free. In 1993, tobacco in all forms was banned at all levels of the minor leagues.

**cheap hit** A ball that is batted into fair territory for a hit, but that lacks power and relies on an odd bounce, fortunate placement, or some other "lucky" factor; e.g., a hit made as the result of a poor swing, such as one that tips off the end of the bat and rolls too slowly to be fielded promptly.

**cheap seats** The bleachers and other areas distant from home plate. The term is not used to comment on the spectators or their chosen seats, but on the distance of a home run or deep foul ball; e.g., "Smith just put one in the cheap seats." The seats are cheap because they are far from most of the action. See also *nosebleeds*. **1st Use.** 1912. (*American Magazine,* Aug.; Edward J. Nichols).

**cheap win** A victory in which the winning team did nothing spectacular, but the losing team did even worse (fewer hits or more errors).

**cheater** An illegal bat (Roger Angell, *Late Innings,* 1982).

**cheating** Any action of a fielder playing the percentages as to what he thinks the batter or baserunner will do; e.g., infielders positioning themselves closer to the bases than normal so as to prevent a stolen base or to take part in a double play.

**check 1.** *v.* To hold a swing after it has begun. **2.** *n.* A *check swing.* **3.** *v.* See *check the runner.* **4.** *v.* To stop a rally.

**checked swing** *n.* Syn. of *check swing.*

**checked-swing** *adj.* Said of that created by a check swing; e.g., "Smith hit a checked-swing grounder."

**checker 1.** A batter who is able to keep his wrists from breaking and his bat from crossing the plate when a pitch is not to his liking. **2.** See *cross-checker.*

**checklist card** A baseball card that does not feature a player but rather lists the numbers and names of other cards in the set; e.g., all the Red Sox in a set may appear on a Boston Red Sox checklist card.

**check swing** A half or partial swing of the bat; one stopped midpoint before the batter's wrists break or turn. If a ball is thrown outside the strike zone and the batter checks his swing, the pitch will be called a ball by the umpire. But if the batter swung the bat across home plate, or, in the opinion of the umpire, intended to hit the ball, it would be called a strike. Often when the umpire rules "no swing" the catcher or pitcher will appeal the decision, at which time the umpire at first base (for a right-handed batter) or the umpire at third

base (for a left-handed batter) will verify or overrule the plate umpire's call. See also *half swing.* Sometimes called *checked swing.* Syn. *check,* 2.

**check the runner** For a pitcher to glance at the baserunner to dissuade him from taking too long a lead.

**cheddar** A fastball; a contemporary player's term for *cheese.* "Doc [Gooden] blew some big-league cheddar" (Lenny Dykstra, quoted in *Newsday,* Mar. 1, 1988). Keith Hernandez discussed "the high, rising cheddar" in *Pure Baseball* (1994).

**cheer leader** The loudest bench jockey on a team.

**cheese** A fastball. Bill Lee (*The Wrong Stuff,* 1984) translates Dennis Eckersley's "cheese for your kitchen" as meaning "a fastball up and in" and added that Eckersley also called himself the "Cheese Master." See also *cheddar; good cheese; hard cheese; high cheese.* **Etymology.** Even though the term is relatively new to baseball, it may have a much older basis. *London Guide* (1818) defined "cheese" as standing for "the best thing of its kind." The term appears in most 19th-century slang dictionaries as meaning anything first rate in quality (as in "that's the cheese") and is usually traced to the word "chiz," which means "thing" in Hindustani and Anglo-Indian, rather than the food. James Rogers (*The Dictionary of Clichés,* 1985) traces the term "chiz" to an origin in Persian and Urdu and notes that it is also the source of "the big cheese."

**chemistry** A distinct sense of teamwork, cooperation, and friendship created by a mix of individuals on a team; instant support, morale, and esprit de corps of like-minded people on a team, often stated as "good chemistry." Keith Moreland (*Vineline,* Aug. 1987) offered this formula: "The makeup of an organization—the players, coaches and the fans. And the talent. The total ingredients that go into a team's makeup."

The term has created its own set of clichés: e.g., "chemistry or lack thereof may be the problem"; "chemistry is attitude"; and "chemistry starts with the manager and coaches." The moral: good chemistry is good for a team.

**cherry** A pitch that a batter can hit well; an "unconvincing" pitch. New York Mets manager Davey Johnson (quoted in George F. Will, *Men at Work*, 1990): "If a guy is a first-ball, fastball, high-ball hitter, and you are a fastball pitcher, give him a first-ball fastball a little higher than he likes it and see if he'll bite on it rather than hook him and miss, hook him and miss, and then give a cherry fastball."

**cherry pie** A poor hitter, an easy out. **Etymology.** An unflattering term created and used almost exclusively by Casey Stengel, it is probably a play on "easy as pie" applied to an easy out.

**chestiness** *arch.* Conceit. **1st Use.** 1909. (*New York Evening Journal*, July 14; Edward J. Nichols).

**chest pad** Syn. of *chest protector.*

**chest protector** A pad used by catchers and home-plate umpires to protect the body from the shoulders to the waist from pitched and fouled-off balls, esp. foul tips. Most are worn but some umpires' models are held like a warrior's shield. See also *balloon, 3; West Vest.* Syn. *chest pad; mattress; protector; wind pad.* **1st Use.** 1889. "[When] he sprained the bosom of his pants . . . it was worth a gold medal to see Jim shift his chest protector around to his rear" (*Cincinnati Commercial Gazette*, Mar. 17; cited in Mitford M. Mathews, *Americanisms*, 1966). **Etymology.** A small item entitled "A Woman's Gift to Baseball" in the popular *Leslie's Weekly* (Oct. 15, 1914) gives this account of the origin of the protective device:

"Charles Bennett, famous as a catcher for the noted Detroit team of 1886–1887, delights in telling the story of how his wife made the first catcher's breast protector. It was a constant source of worry to Mrs. Bennett to watch her husband acting as a target for the speedy twirlers of 30 years ago, and she determined to invent some sort of an armor to prevent the hot shots from the pitchers playing a tattoo on the ribs of her better half. After much planning, assisted by practical suggestions from her husband, she shaped a pad which answered the purpose and which bore some resemblance to the 'protector' of the present day. In a private tryout it worked well and Charles, after

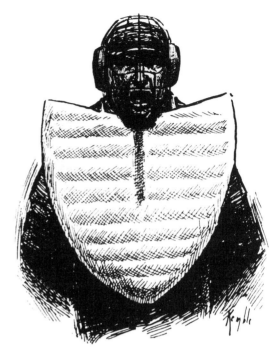

THE UMPIRE: "S-S-STRIKE ONE!"

*Chest protector.*

permitting the ball to strike him repeatedly without feeling a jar, decided to use it in public. The innovation created almost as great a sensation as Bresnahan's shin guards, but it made a hit with the catchers and they were quite ready to follow Bennett's lead."

**Chicago** *v./arch.* To shut out the opposing team. To have been "Chicagoed" (or "Chicago'd") was to be shut out. Most recent use that could be found was in the slang section of Fred Lieb's *Comedians and Pranksters of Baseball* (1958) where it is listed as an "old term." Arthur "Bugs" Baer (*San Francisco Examiner*, Jan. 19, 1953; Peter Tamony) wrote a column on the term, which he opened with the line: "Baseball word you never hear any more is 'Chicagoed.'" **1st Use.** 1870. "Each party was 'Chicagoed.'" (*Cleveland Leader*, July 30; Peter Morris).

George L. Moreland (*Balldom: "The Britannica of Baseball,"* 1914) concluded: "The word was coined by some wag when on July 23, 1870, the

Mutuals of New York shut out the Chicago [White Stockings] team by a score of 9 to 0. Shutouts prior to that date had been few and far between, for previous to this game but five shutout games had ever been played." *DeWitt's Base Ball Guide* (1876) confirms the 1870 game, adding: "From that time on all contests in which one side has failed to score a run have been known as Chicago defeats, the nine so beaten being said to have been 'Chicagoed.'" *The Sporting News* (May 10, 1886) notes that "Chicago," as a less derogatory term, replaced *skunk* (for a whitewash).

A contrary theory suggests a later coinage and says that it is based on the effectiveness of the Chicago White Stockings of the 1880s. Patrick Ercolano (*Fungoes, Floaters and Fork Balls*, 1987) argues that a more likely theory is that it came from the 1876 Chicago team featuring their ace, Al Spalding, who pitched eight shutouts. **Extended Use.** The term was applied to a shutout in card playing.

**Chicago Cubs** The name of the National League Central Division franchise in Chicago, Ill. The team was founded in 1876 as the White Stockings, and was also known as the Colts and the Orphans. Reflecting the number of young players on the team, the *Chicago Daily News* (Mar. 27, 1902) suggested the team be called the Cubs, which became the official team name in 1907. With an eye on the team's generally lackluster standing, former manager Herman Franks once commented: "The Chicago Cubs fans are the greatest fans in baseball. They've got to be."

**Chicago Shirley** A *Baseball Annie* (Bill Lee, *The Wrong Stuff*, 1984).

**Chicago slide** The original *hook slide,* which was invented and first employed by Mike "King" Kelly when he played for the Chicago White Stockings from 1880 through 1886. See also *"Slide, Kelly, Slide."* **1st Use.** 1911. (*American Magazine*, May; Edward J. Nichols).

**Chicago White Sox** The name of the American League Central Division franchise in Chicago, Ill. Originally the Invaders, the club took the name

*Chicago Cubs. A pin commemorating the Cubs who, before 1907, had also been known as the White Stockings, the Colts, and the Orphans.*

White Stockings and turned it into White Socks after it had been discarded by their National League neighbors (Chicago Cubs). The name was used when the club entered the American League in 1901. Sportswriters Carl Green and Irving E. Sanborn shortened the name to White Sox. Sometimes known as *Chisox* for short.

**chief of staff** Syn. of *umpire-in-chief.*

**chief of umpires** The administrator of umpires in each major league.

**chill a bat** For a hitter in a slump to discard his regular bat and borrow a bat from a player who is in the midst of a hitting streak; to take the "heat" out of a bat.

**Chinese blow** A lucky hit; a *fluke hit.*

**Chinese home run 1.** A derogatory term for a home run hit over the portion of the outfield fence closest to home plate, often one that lands just inside (or hits) the foul pole in a ballpark with small dimensions. The most famous locale for Chinese homers was the Polo Grounds, which had 280- and 258-foot foul lines. Pinch hitter Dusty Rhodes's three-run home run at the Polo Grounds that won the opening game of the 1954 World Series for the New York Giants was described as a "260-foot pop fly."

The term is not to be used lightly as a letter from Phil Harmon (New York City) in *Sports Illustrated* (Aug. 21, 1971) attests: "Shame on you for calling Bobby Thomson's historic sudden-death home run [Aug. 9, 1971] against the Dodgers in the 1951 National League playoff a 'Chinese home run.' It is the first time I ever heard it characterized in such a demeaning way, and I can only conclude that the writer, Larry Keith, is an anguished Dodger fan who still doesn't believe it happened."

Common in the 1950s, the term has been used sparingly since the demolition of the Polo Grounds. It did come into play, however, when the Dodgers relocated to the Los Angeles Memorial Coliseum in 1958 and home runs began landing in the left-field seats, which were only 250 feet from the plate. Cartoonist Willard Mullin labeled the Coliseum "Flung Wong O'Malley's Little Joss House in Los Angeles." Syn. "Chinese homer"; *Pekinese poke*.

**2.** A long foul ball, perhaps used mostly in sandlot baseball. In Stephen King's *Skeleton Crew* (1985), there is a story called "The Monkey," which contains this line: "Hal was too small to play, but he sat far out in foul territory, sucking his blueberry Popsicle and chasing what the big kids called 'Chinese home runs.'" This use may very well be limited to New England. A query to King about his use of the term brought this reply: "I first heard the term 'Chinese home run' in Stratford, Conn., learning to play the game. When I moved back to Maine in 1958, the term was also used—in both cases, a Chinese home run was a foul ball, usually over the backstop."

**Usage Note.** A note in Herb Caen's column (*San Francisco Chronicle*, May 18, 1981; Peter Tamony) underscores why the use of the term is now an invitation to controversy and charges of racial insensitivity: "Bill King, the Oakland A's announcer, got off a racist line Thurs. night, but he'll learn. After describing Bobby Murcer's homer as 'not a Chinese home run'—meaning it was well hit—I'm sure he has heard from militant Oriental groups, all of which hit hard." This point was made obliquely by Jimmy Cannon (*Baseball Di-*

*gest,* Apr. 1956) when he gave "Chinese home run" this definition: "A cheap homer which would be called something else if the Chinese had enough influence."

**1st Use.** 1954. When Dusty Rhodes hit his aforementioned Chinese home run, Joseph H. Sheehan (*New York Times,* Oct. 1, 1954) attempted to trace the term: "According to Garry Schumacher of the Giants' front office, who in his baseball writing days was a noted phrase-coiner, 'Chinese homer' was one of the numerous Thomas Aloysius (Tad) Dorgan contributions to the lexicon of American slang." Sheehan concluded that the connotation of a cheap homer came from the association in Dorgan's era of the name "Chinese" with coolies and cheap labor. "The term carried the added connotation of a homer of little account, in line with the cynical observation of a colorful political leader who reportedly once stated, 'Why should we care about the Chinese. There ain't a vote in a million in them.'"

**Etymology.** The debate over the Chinese Exclusion Law in the 1910–20 era served as the motivation for Dorgan's term for an insubstantial home run. David Shulman commented: "The idea was to express a cheap home run as Chinese then represented what was cheap, such as their labor." Dorgan used his cartoon "Indoor Sports" to introduce, or popularize, slang; such terms as "dumbbell," "skimmer" (for hat), and "hot dog" have been traced to Dorgan's cartoons.

Dorgan's coinage fit in with a larger group of Chinese terms, such as a "Chinese Rolls-Royce," which is a Ford according to Abraham Roback (*Dictionary of International Slurs,* 1944), and probably was not intended to be especially disparaging. Sheehan noted that Dorgan was a "benign and gentle" satirist with two adopted sons of Chinese ancestry.

J. G. Taylor Spink (*The Sporting News,* May 7, 1958) did an exhaustive search for the origin of the term and came to the same conclusion that Sheehan did. However, the Spink article was reprinted in the *Los Angeles Times* and inspired several letters to the newspaper, including one from a retired San Francisco sportswriter named Travis McGregor. His thoughts appeared in *The Sporting News* (May 28, 1958) and are repeated here in part:

"The use of the term 'Chinese homer' goes far beyond the answers given in Mr. Spink's article, and I think you will find it originated in San Francisco prior to World War I. There was a young China boy there at about 1912 or 1913, if my memory is correct, who had an unpronounceable name, keen sense of humor, a degree from Stanford and a great yen to be a newspaperman. . . . The typewriter jockeys gave up on spelling his name and renamed him Mike Murphy, and he was a one-man show at the ball games. . . . While Mike was educated beyond any trace of an accent his quips were all in Chinese dialect, and made with a perfectly straight face. 'Ow,' he would wail, 'look the way he bat. Wave at ball like Mandarin with fan.' The old Oakland park's short fence caught the most of it from Mike and his 'Mandarin fan' waving balls out of the park were knocked back to 'Chinese homers.'"

Later in the letter McGregor gets to Dorgan. "For two or three seasons Mike was a riot—an Oriental Fred Allen, and Tad Dorgan drew a number of cartoons featuring Mike's comments." McGregor adds that several writers picked up and used the term, including Ring Lardner and Damon Runyon, and he thought that the first writer to put it into print was either Ed Hughes or Harry Smith of the *San Francisco Chronicle.*

While not disputing the Dorgan story, Dan Schlossberg (*The Baseball Catalog*, 1980) notes that the term was used in the 1920s by *New York Tribune* sports editor Bill McGeehan to describe the right-field wall at the Polo Grounds, which looked "thick, low, and not very formidable—like the Great Wall of China."

But this seems to be one of those terms that has attracted a fascinating collection of explanations. Russ Hodges, longtime Giants announcer, gave this explanation to the *San Francisco Call-Bulletin* (Apr. 21, 1958; Peter Tamony): "Years ago in the Polo Grounds, Chinese gamblers were wont to gather in the left-field stands at the foul line, a little over 250 feet. Any hit that went out at that point was followed by cries of: 'There goes one for the Chinese.'"

Other explanations, such as those that appeared in Joe Falls's *The Sporting News* column, which solicited etymologies from readers, seem to be purely conjectural: that a short homer is so named because the Chinese are a shorter people; that the outfield seats in the Polo Grounds used to stick out like a pagoda; and that it was inspired by the "short jump" of Chinese checkers. Without question, the wildest of all the theories was one suggested by Tom Becket (St. Louis). As far-fetched as it sounds, however, it does offer an explanation, even as an elaborate pun, for the fact that, in New England, Chinese homer may refer to a long, foul ball. In this version, the term harks back to the turn of the 20th century and a game in Salem, Mass., between teams of Irish and Polish immigrants. The game lasted into the 17th inning at which point there was only one ball left to use because the others had been lost. Becket explains: "A shortstop named Chaney fouled a fast ball into the high grass deep beyond the backstop. After 20 minutes of searching for the ball, the umpires declared the victory for the Irish. They ruled that the Polish team, which was the home team, had failed to furnish the necessary amount of baseballs to complete the game. . . . So the cheer went up, 'Chaney's home run won the game.' From then on, any foul ball clearing the backstop was heralded as another Chaney's home run. Various misunderstandings as to dialects eventually brought it to the now-familiar 'Chinese home run.'"

**Chinese line drive** *arch.* A pop fly. **1st Use.** 1930. "The sports writers call those little flies over the infield . . . 'chinese line drives'" (*Country Home,* Aug.; David Shulman). **Usage Note.** This term carries the same derogatory implications as "Chinese home run" and was probably inspired by it.

**chink** To hit a ball weakly; to squeeze out a hit. **Usage Note.** The term is widely used but subject to offensive interpretation; e.g., "steal bases, advance runners, chink in some hits" (New York Yankees manager Dallas Green, quoted in *Hartford Courant,* Apr. 5, 1989). Although it has been argued that this is the "chink" defined as "a short metallic sound," it was interpreted in an angry letter to the *Hartford Courant* (Apr. 8, 1989) "as a demeaning metaphor about people of Chinese extraction."

**chinker** Syn. of *chink hit.*

**chink hit** A batted ball that is not hit squarely,

the bat making a "chink" sound on contact. The term is widely used but subject to offensive interpretation as demeaning to people of Chinese extraction. Syn. *chinker.*

**chin music** **1.** A beanball or knockdown pitch that passes close to the batter's jaw. Brent Musberger (broadcast of 1986 National League Championship Series, Oct. 14) said of Houston Astros pitcher Nolan Ryan: "He served [Lenny] Dykstra a little chin music. It almost set his hat spinning." **2.** *arch.* Impudent back talk from a player or umpire, or from the grandstand or bleachers (V. Samuels, *American Speech,* Feb. 1927). See also *chaffing,* 2. **3.** *arch.* Shouting. **1st Uses.** 1875. "Last season an element of weakness . . . prevailed in the form of 'chin-music' and 'chaffing'" (*New York Clipper,* Jan. 30; Tom Shieber). Gerald Cohen (*Comments on Etymology,* 1986–87) cited the following from *The World* (New York, Sept. 4, 1888): "Nearly 10,000 people witnessed the game, each one of whom wasted an inordinate amount of chin-music in the general effort to brace the Giants up to victory or death." Peter Morris found this example from the *Detroit Free Press* (May 5, 1883): "The Clevelands have been hearing some chin music that sounded like the mother tongue to them. It was Schaffer's." ("Schaffer" is George "Orator" Shaffer, so nicknamed because of his ceaseless chatter; the correct spelling of his last name is unknown, according to Morris.) David Shulman notes that the term was in general use as early as 1836 and he, for one and for this reason, does not consider it a baseball term.

**chipmunk** A punning, self-deprecating name for a sportswriter who, in the words of Milton Gross, is so called "because in the long run all we do is nibble around the edges." Gross is quoted calling himself the first chipmunk of sportswriters in Pat Jordan's *Suitors of Spring* (1973; Charles D. Poe) in this interchange on the subject: "But what about the heart of a story?" says the novice. "Don't you ever try to get to the heart of the matter?" Gross smiles and shakes his head: "Kid, when you've been in the game as long as I have you'll learn there is no heart."

**chip** A calcium deposit, such as one that some-

times develops in a pitcher's elbow and that can be debilitating.

**chirp** To make complimentary remarks about an opposing player.

**Chisox** A nickname of the Chicago White Sox.

**choke** **1.** *v.* To play badly in a crucial situation or lose one's resolve; e.g., "Smith choked in the clutch." Players, managers, coaches, and umpires have all been accused of choking. See also *olive in his throat.* **2.** *n.* A bad showing, especially in a pinch. When in 1978 the Boston Red Sox blew a 14½-game division lead it was labeled "The Great Choke." **Usage Note.** According to baseball tradition, the term is not to be used lightly, esp. when emotions are running high. "In fact, so strong is the feeling concerning the word 'choke' that a player needs only to hold his hand to his throat after an umpire's decision to get thrown out of the game" (Tristram Potter Coffin, *The Old Ball Game,* 1971). **1st Use.** 1937. (National League Service Bureau clipping; Edward J. Nichols). **Extended Use.** The choke is a factor and a term in most every sport and in situations outside baseball, from business to military conflict. **3.** *v.* See *choke up.*

**choke grip** A method of holding the bat several inches from the narrow end.

**choke hitter** **1.** A hitter who does badly under pressure. Babe Ruth (*Babe Ruth's Own Book of Baseball,* 1928; David Shulman) commented: "The other division is the 'choke hitters' . . . [where they] stand flatfooted and take half a swing." Syn. *choker.* **2.** A hitter who chokes up on his bat; one who uses the choke grip.

**choker** Syn. of *choke hitter,* 1.

**choke up** To grip the bat above the customary lower end; to move one's hand up the handle of the bat to achieve greater control (but also reducing the power of the swing). **1st Use.** 1909. (Zane Grey, *The Short-Stop;* Edward J. Nichols). **Etymology.** From the impression that the bat is being grabbed by the neck and choked.

**choose up** **1.** *v.* To form sides for an informal game of baseball, softball, or their variations. Usu-

*Choose up.*

ally two captains are decided on and alternate in picking players for their teams. **2.** *n.* An early form of baseball.

**choose-up game** A contest between two teams formed by choosing up.

**chop 1.** *v.* To swing down on the ball, a move that often results in a grounder. **1st Use.** 1902. (*Sporting Life,* July 12; Edward J. Nichols). **2.** *n.* The motion of swinging down on the ball. **3.** *n.* A ground ball resulting from a chopping motion; e.g., "Smith hit a chop to the infield."

**chop one off the high limb** To swing at a ball that is pitched above the strike zone.

**chopper 1.** A batted ball that hits the ground sharply and bounces high. See also *high chopper.* **2.** A ball hit with a chopped stroke.

**chopstick** A baseball bat. **1st Use.** 1908. (*New York Evening Journal,* Apr. 25; Edward J. Nichols).

**chuck 1.** *v.* To pitch for a baseball team; e.g., "Smith chucked for the home team for seven sea-

sons." **2.** *v.* To throw a baseball; e.g., "Jones fielded the grounder and chucked it to first." **1st Use.** 1907. (*New York Evening Journal,* May 7; Edward J. Nichols). **3.** *n.* A pitch.

**chucker 1.** A pitcher, usually a fastballer. The term originally referred to a pitcher who threw only fastballs and no breaking balls. **1st Use.** 1937. (New York *Daily News,* Jan. 31; Edward J. Nichols). **2.** Syn. of *inning,* 1. Also spelled "chukker." **Etymology.** A borrowing from polo in which a chukker is a discrete period of play usually lasting for 7½ minutes. **1st Use.** 1934. (*Journalism Quarterly*).

**chump** A dupe or stupid person. David Shulman noted the term is not strictly a baseball term but because of its original context "seems to have been originated by ballplayers." **1st Use.** 1883. "Maybe Manager [Frank] Bancroft isn't regarded as a chump by baseball people" (*Sporting Life,* May 27).

**church ball** [softball term] An early name for softball.

**chute** The area over home plate where it is easiest for the batter to hit the ball; the middle of the strike zone. "He threw Rick nothing but fastballs down the chute, and Manning got two base hits" (Bill Lee, *The Wrong Stuff,* 1984; Charles D. Poe). See also *down the chute.*

**cigar box** A small ballpark, such as Old Oriole Park in Baltimore which burned to the ground on July 4, 1944. **1st Use.** 1937. (*New York Daily News,* Jan. 17; Edward J. Nichols).

**cigarette card** A baseball card that came in a cigarette pack. Eleanor Gehrig (*My Luke and I,* 1976) wrote that husband Lou saved and traded "the cigarette cards that carried pictures of Ty Cobb, Zack Wheat and Christy Mathewson" when he was a boy of 12. (Charles D. Poe)

**cinch 1.** *n.* An easy victory. **2.** *v.* To win or wrap up, such as a pennant. **1st Use.** 1905. "This cinches the pennant for the White Sox" (*Sporting Life;* David Shulman).

**Cincinnati base hit** A proposed scoring rule

change that would give a batter credit for a base hit on reaching first by a fielder's choice. The origin of the name is unclear, possibly because Cincinnati scorers used it during the 1913 season or it was proposed by them. The Baseball Writers Association of America rejected the proposal by a mail vote in 1914.

**Cincinnati Reds** The name of the National League Central Division franchise (since 1890) in Cincinnati, Ohio. The team is a direct descendant of the Cincinnati Red Stockings, who became known as the Red Legs or, simply, the Reds in 1876. During the early days of the Cold War, there were some who were disturbed by the name "Reds." In the early 1960s, a justice of the Pennsylvania Supreme Court admonished the team for its unpatriotic name. "Let the Russians change," was the altogether proper response of *Cincinnati Enquirer* sports editor Lou Smith. "We had it first."

**Cincinnati Red Stockings** The name of the first professional baseball team, formed in 1869. Named for the color of their hose, the original team won 130 games over two seasons before suffering its first loss.

**Cinderella** A team that emerges from the lower level and becomes a contender in the manner of the Cinderella fairy tale. "The game pitted two Cinderella teams making their state tourney debuts" (*Bangor* [Maine] *Daily News* account of a state American Legion tournament, Aug. 11, 1986).

**Cinderella Softball Leagues** [softball term] An association based in Corning, N.Y., that seeks to promote national and international softball for girls and women.

**circle 1.** *v.* To run around the bases and reach home plate. **2.** *n.* Short for *on-deck circle.*

**circle change** A *changeup* in which the pitcher uses his thumb and index finger to form a circle around one side of the ball, with the outside three fingers atop the ball sitting deep in his palm. The overhand motion causes the ball to tumble out of the circle, acquiring a rotation that causes it to run down and in (when thrown by a right-handed

**Cincinnati Red Stockings.** *The original Red Stocking Club (1869) with a mutton-chopped Asa Brainard in the upper-right-hand corner.*

pitcher to a right-handed batter). The purpose of the grip is to force the middle finger to exert more pressure on the ball at release, thereby giving the pitch more down-and-away movement. Paul Richards tried to popularize the pitch; Frank Viola and Tom Glavine threw it.

**circle the wagons** For a weak defensive player to be uncertain or tentative when fielding a pop fly. **Etymology.** From the practice in the early West to form the wagons of a covered-wagon train into a circle for defense against an Indian attack.

**circuit 1.** *n.* The four bases, collectively, such as those touched after hitting a home run. **2.** *n.* A league; e.g., the National League is called the *senior circuit* and the American League is called the *junior circuit.* **1st Use.** 1880. (*Brooklyn Daily Eagle,* July 22; Edward J. Nichols). **Etymology.** Although the first meaning follows the standard definition of a "circuit" as a circular journey, the second meaning may stem from the theatrical use of the term for a group of theaters visited on a regular basis. **3.** *n.* A term used to modify other terms signifying a home run; e.g., "circuit belt," "circuit blow," "circuit clout," "circuit drive," "circuit smash," "circuit tripper," and "circuit wallop." **Usage Note.** Today these are terms of exaggeration and intended archaism used sparingly and for emphasis. "It is really remarkable that so few of the actual terms used in baseballese ever see the light of a printed page. Now and then they make the newspaper sporting pages, but the commendable modern journalistic trend away from the silly jabber of twenty years ago, when every strikeout was a 'breeze' and every homer a 'circuit clout,' has also militated against the popularization of dozens of words that have become full-standing baseballese by the prime standard of word-legitimization." (*Baseball Digest,* Oct. 1932). **1st Use.** 1908 for "circuit clout." (*New York Evening Journal,* May 14; Edward J. Nichols). 1934 for "circuit drive." (*Journalism Quarterly;* David Shulman).

**circuit slugger** A player who hits many home runs.

**circus catch** A spectacular catch, suggesting the moves of a circus acrobat. Such a catch may involve a jump, dive, flip, roll, or combination thereof. "Circus Solly" Hofman (Chicago Cubs outfielder, 1904–12) was given his nickname because he was known for making acrobatic catches of fly balls. Thomas W. Lawson (*The Krank: His Language and What It Means,* 1888) defined the term as "catching the ball between the upper and under eyelid." See also *Jawn Titus.* Syn. *showboat catch.* **1st Use.** 1886. "Steve Brady made a circus catch and Hardie Henderson tried to get [Ed] Greer to swear out a warrant for him" (*Sporting Life,* Apr. 28; Barry Popik). **Extended Use.** The term has been applied to spectacular football catches for some time and is used metaphorically for any melodramatic feat.

**circus play** A spectacular play. **1st Use.** 1885. (Chicago *Inter-Ocean,* July 15; Edward J. Nichols). By extension, there is also the "circus stop" and the "circus throw"; e.g., "He made circus catches, cir-

cus stops, circus throws" (Zane Grey, *The Red-headed Outfield and Other Baseball Stories,* 1915; David Shulman).

**city series** A series of games between two teams in the same city; esp. the series of postseason games between the White Sox and the Cubs in Chicago in the early part of the 20th century. See also *cross-town series.*

**clamshell catch** A style of catching in which a player puts his wrists flat together and traps the ball between his glove and bare hand. This two-handed method is surer than trying to catch the ball in one hand.

**clang** A bad fielder, presumably from the metaphoric noise made by his glove and skillet-hard hands. Syn. *clank.*

**clank** Syn. of *clang.* Outfielder/first baseman/catcher Curt Blefary was sometimes known as "Clank."

**class** One of the several levels at which professional baseball is played, with the major leagues at the top followed by the various rankings of the minor leagues. The class ranking system was originally set up on the basis of the population of the city or town in which the team played and was used to fix the salaries and prices of players.

**Class A** The next to the lowest level of minor-league baseball, above *rookie league.* Syn. *Single A.*

**Class AA** The middle level of minor-league baseball. Syn. *Double A.*

**Class AAA** The highest level of minor-league baseball. Syn. *Triple A.*

**Class B** Formerly a level of minor-league baseball, below Class A.

**Class C** Formerly a level of minor-league baseball, below Class B.

**Class D** Formerly the lowest level of minor-league baseball, below Class C (and above Class E before it was eliminated).

**Class E** The lowest level of minor-league baseball in 1943, below Class D.

**class F** *arch.* "A term of contempt used among players toward weak players, insinuating that they rank below all organized clubs" (Hugh S. Fullerton, *American Magazine,* June 1912); at that time the minor leagues ranged from class AA down to class D. **1st Use.** 1912. (Hugh S. Fullerton, *American Magazine,* June).

**classic 1.** The World Series; more commonly, *fall classic.* **2.** The All-Star Game; more commonly, *summer classic.*

**Class of . . . 1.** A term used to identify future Hall of Famers who are certain to make it during their first year of eligibility. As early as 1993 the Cooperstown Class of 1999 included Nolan Ryan, George Brett, Robin Yount, Carlton Fisk, and possibly Dale Murphy. **2.** A term used to identify any remarkable group of players, such as the "Class of '25" consisting of the rookies who came into the major leagues in 1925: Jimmie Foxx, Mickey Cochrane, Charlie Gehringer, Freddie Fitzsimmons, Charles "Red" Ruffing, Moses "Lefty" Grove, Chick Hafey, and Lou Gehrig.

**claw** Pine-tar stick used to rub on bats to improve the batter's grip.

**clean 1.** *adj.* Said of a period in which a pitcher gives up no hits or errors; e.g., a "clean inning" or a "clean outing." **2.** *v.* See *clean the bases.*

**clean hit** A safely batted ball that at no point looked as if it would be fielded for an out; a solid hit. **1st Use.** 1880. (Chicago *Inter-Ocean,* June 29; Edward J. Nichols).

**clean house** *v.* To trade or release many players on a team, esp. when a new general manager or manager takes over.

**clean swing** A simple, easy swing with a good follow-through; a good "stroke."

**clean the bases** To get a hit, usually a home run, on which all baserunners score. Syn. *clear the bases.* **1st Use.** 1910. (*New York Tribune,* July 3; Edward J. Nichols).

**clean their clocks** To defeat a team decisively.

**cleanup 1.** Syn. of *cleanup position.* **2.** Syn. of *cleanup hitter.* **1st Use.** 1907. (*New York Evening Journal,* Apr. 15; Edward J. Nichols). **Usage Note.** In the wake of the strike that canceled the 1994 World Series, this term (in its verb form, to "clean up") was defined by one wag as "what baseball now has to do with the mess it has made."

**cleanup hitter** The player who bats in the fourth position in the batting order, usually reserved for a player with a high batting average and the ability to drive in runs with extra-base hits. The assumption is that he is most likely to get a hit that will score any or all of the preceding players who have reached base, thus "cleaning" or "clearing" the bases of baserunners. Sometimes spelled "clean-up hitter." Syn. *cleanup,* 2; *cleanup man; Big Bertha,* 1; *number-four hitter.* **Extended Use. 1.** The most dependable or most skillful person in any group, such as in a team of lawyers. **2.** A political candidate who can help effect reform or a sweeping change in policy. In supporting congressional candidate William S. Mailliard in 1952, an editorial in the *San Francisco Examiner* termed him a "clean-up hitter" who would help get rid of "the New Deal, the Square Deal, the Fair Deal and all the rotten deals we've had for the 20 long years." (Peter Tamony)

**cleanup man** Syn. of *cleanup hitter.*

**cleanup position** The fourth position in the batting order. Sometimes spelled "clean-up position." Syn. *cleanup,* 1. **1st Use.** 1920. "Considering the fact that Olsen, although he held the clean-up position, had not obtained anything like a safe hit from Locke thus far, this looked like poor judgment" (Burt L. Standish, *The Man on First;* David Shulman).

**clear the bases** Syn. of *clean the bases.* **1st Use.** 1870. (*New York Herald,* May 8; Edward J. Nichols).

**clear the bench 1.** For an umpire to order all the substitute players from the dugout to the clubhouse for objectionable conduct (notably the "violent disapproval" of a call) when the offender(s) cannot be identified. A warning must first be given, but if the bench is cleared, all substitutes depart. Players can be recalled by the manager but only as needed for substitution in the game. "The base ump threatened 'to clear the bench' if Anderson Valley had the temerity to question calls following a chorus of groans at one of his calls" (*Anderson Valley Advertiser,* Apr. 10, 1985). Although a rarity in major-league baseball, umpire Frank Dascoli ejected 15 Brooklyn Dodgers on Sept. 27, 1951. **1st Use.** 1914. (*New York Tribune,* Oct. 2; Edward J. Nichols). **2.** For a manager to send into the game all the substitute players when a team is leading or losing by a seemingly insurmountable margin.

**clear the fences** To hit a home run that goes out of the ballpark.

**cleats 1.** The projections on the bottoms of shoes, used to achieve greater traction on the field. They are made of rubber, plastic, or metal. See also *spikes,* 1. **2.** Syn. of *baseball shoe.* **1st Use.** 1935. (Ralph H. Barbour, *How to Play Better Baseball;* David Shulman).

**Cleveland Indians** The name of the American League Central Division franchise since 1901 in Cleveland, Ohio. The team mascot is a cartoon

**Cleveland Indians.** *A pin celebrating a pennant for the Indians.*

Indian named "Chief Wahoo." The team went through a series of name changes before becoming the Indians. Originally known as the Blues for the color of their uniforms, the players themselves voted for a more powerful nickname and settled on Bronchos. In 1903, a local newspaper asked its readers to rename the team; as a result of the contest, they became the Naps in honor of Napoleon Lajoie, their star second baseman. In 1915, after Lajoie left the team, there was another newspaper contest in which the winning entry came from a fan who suggested Indians in honor of Louis Sockalexis, a member (1897–99) of the Cleveland Spiders of the National League, who died in 1913. Sockalexis, a Penobscot from Old Town, Maine, played at Holy Cross and then at Notre Dame where he was spotted and signed by a Cleveland scout, and became the first American Indian to play in the major leagues. In 1897, his rookie year, he batted .338 and captured the imagination of the fans who saluted him with loud war whoops when he took to the field. But two seasons later it all came to a quick halt. Herbert Adams (*Maine Sunday Telegram,* Aug. 10, 1986) reported: "A man of pride and intelligence, Sockalexis' Catholic education and trusting nature left him unprepared for the pressure and exploitation of a big-business game. Alcohol and high living took their toll, and in 1899 he played only seven error-riddled games 'before being booted from the big leagues forever,' says one blunt account, 'due to drunkenness.'"

**clicker** Syn. of *indicator,* 1.

**click on all nine** To possess good teamwork.

**cliff-hanger** A close, hotly contended game whose outcome is decided late in the game.

**climb the ladder** To throw consecutively higher and higher pitches to induce the batter to swing at a pitch out of the strike zone. See also *stair step; up the ladder,* 1.

**clinch 1.** To assure a particular position in the final standings based on an exact number of wins and losses. **2.** For a player to establish a spot on a team's roster or in its starting lineup.

**Clincher.** *The stitching is on the inside of this classic street softball. The 16-inch version dominates the Chicago game.*

**clincher 1.** A game in which a title championship is, or is likely to be, won. "[Bobby] Ojeda Gets Call for Clincher" (*New York Times* headline, Sept. 4, 1986). **2.** Softball invented by Frederick deBeer and made of horsehide and kapok with a hidden seam. Especially suited for the streets and sidewalks of New York City and Chicago, where they are a major factor in the market.

**clinic 1.** An instructional session in which players and/or coaches teach others (usually children) the finer points of baseball. Clearly implied by the term is that problems are brought to the clinic where solutions will be sought. **2.** Magnificent play by a player or team; "[Alvaro] Espinoza Sparks Twins with Clinic on Fundamentals" (*Orlando Sentinel* headline, Mar. 22, 1987) or "The Orioles held a clinic by their superb fielding." **Etymology.** The term, originally indicating a medical facility, appears to have made the leap to other realms in the 1930s and 1940s when, as H. L. Mencken (*The American Language, Suppl. II,* 1948) noted, "clinic" was being used for a beauty parlor. A letter from Atcheson L. Hench (Univ. of Virginia) (*American Speech,* Oct. 1949) notes 13 other nonmedical clinics dating as far back as a 1933 "Clothing Clinic." Hench notes several baseball clinics, starting with an announcement in the *Baltimore Sun* (Jan. 21, 1944): "The second meeting of the baseball clinic sponsored jointly . . . is scheduled for tonight." Another early baseball clinic noted by Hench appeared in a dispatch from Mobile, Ala., which also appeared in the *Sun* (Jan. 7, 1946): "Little Eddie Stanky . . . announced he would open his second annual free baseball clinic for youngsters and oldsters here."

**clinker** An error. **1st Use.** 1937. (*The Sporting News Record Book;* Edward J. Nichols).

**clip 1.** To hit a ball sharply. **1st Use.** 1905. (*Sporting Life,* Oct. 7; Edward J. Nichols). **2.** To pitch a ball that just passes inside one of the four corners of the strike zone; e.g., "to clip the corner."

**clobber 1.** To hit a ball hard. **2.** To hit very well against a specific pitcher; to *pin his ears back.*

**clock** *v.* To hit a ball hard; e.g., "Smith clocked one over the wall." The term is used in reference to the precise timing required to be a successful hitter. **1st Use.** 1932. (*Baseball Magazine,* Oct.; Edward J. Nichols).

**close 1.** *adv.* Said of a runner kept near to his base (usually first base) when the pitcher throws over to the base; e.g., "Smith held the runner close with his throws to first." **2.** *v.* For a pitcher to end a game by retiring the last batter. **3.** *v.* To move the front foot closer to the plate in a batting stance.

**close and late** Said of a game situation in the seventh inning or later and the batting team is leading by one run, tied, or has the tying run on base, at bat, or on deck. The term is used by STATS, Inc., for statistical purposes.

**close call** An umpire's ruling on a split-second or bang-bang play. Because the distances between the bases seem so perfectly set, such calls are common. See also *close play.*

**closed shoulder** A batter's shoulder that has not yet turned out at the instant the bat meets the ball.

**closed stance** A batting position in which the front foot is closer to home plate than the rear foot. Compare *open stance.*

**close out** For a pitcher to retire a batter.

**close play** A play in which a baserunner reaches

a base a split second before or after the ball. He is either just safe or just out. See also *close call*. Syn. *close shave*, 2.

**closer 1.** A starting pitcher who often pitches complete games. **2.** A relief pitcher who tries to get the final out or outs in a game. A closer is the team's most reliable pitcher; he almost never pitches without a lead or for more than one inning. Closers generally are veteran pitchers: "No one is a closer until they've got 40 or 50 saves behind them" (Orioles manager and former pitching coach Ray Miller, quoted in *Baltimore Sun*, Feb. 15, 1998). "The closer has become identified with certain traits. He has an oversized body. Or an outsized personality. Or, at the very least, the sinister face [i.e., with facial hair] of a 19th-century outlaw" (Michael Bamberger, *Sports Illustrated*, Mar. 24, 1997). Syn. *closing reliever; stopper*, 2; *game-ender; finisher*.

**close shave 1.** Any ball that is pitched close to a batter's head, as if it were close enough to shave the whiskers on his face; a knockdown pitch. See also *barber*, 2. **2.** Syn. of *close play*.

**close the door** To pitch the final three outs of a game. See also *shut the door*.

**closing reliever** Syn. of *closer*, 2. "The Atlanta Braves' closing reliever appeared to be his old dominating self in one perfect inning" (profile of Bruce Sutter, *USA Today*, Mar. 12, 1986).

**clothesline** A low line drive whose flight to the outfield resembles a taut clothesline. It is rarely stopped by an infielder because it is normally too far (10–15 feet) off the ground. See also *hemp; frozen rope*. Syn. "clothesliner." **1st Use.** 1937. (*Philadelphia Record*, Oct. 11; Edward J. Nichols).

**cloud buster** A very high fly ball.

**cloud-hunter** *arch.* A ball batted high in the air.

**cloud-scraper** *arch.* A ball batted high in the air.

**cloud-searcher** *arch.* A ball batted high in the air.

**clout 1.** *v.* To hit the ball with power. **1st Use.** 1908. (*New York Evening Journal*, Feb. 24; Edward J. Nichols). **2.** *n.* A ball hit for a long distance, usually a home run. **1st Use.** 1908. (*New York Evening Journal*, May 14; Edward J. Nichols).

**clouter** A power hitter; esp. one who is known for hitting long home runs. **1st Use.** 1908. (*Spalding's Official Base Ball Guide;* Edward J. Nichols).

**clouting spree** An impressive display of hitting by a team.

**clout king** A powerful and outstanding hitter regarded as tops in his league.

**clown** An individual who performs comically on the field before or after a game, or between innings. Clowns range from professionals who have clowned for a few to the antics of catcher Rick Dempsey who occasionally put on his own one-man show during rain delays at Memorial Stadium in Baltimore.

**clowning** An old baseball tradition in which an entertainer, often a former player, puts on a sideshow to go with the game. The clowning takes place before the game, between innings, or during the break between two games of a doubleheader.

**Clown Prince of Baseball** A title first taken by Al Schacht after his playing days (pitcher for the Washington Senators, 1919–21) were over and he became baseball's most famous clown. The next man to adopt the title was Max Patkin.

**club 1.** *n.* A baseball organization that assembles the players and supporting staff for a *team*, provides a playing field, and represents the team in league affairs and the public in general. The original baseball rules from 1845 were for the Knickerbocker Base Ball Club.

Benjamin G. Rader (*Baseball: A History of America's Game*, 1992) writes: "In contemporary sports, the words 'club' and 'team' are used interchangeably. The main, if not the exclusive, purpose of such organizations is to play games against other teams and sometimes to make money. To the Knickerbockers, however, the term 'club' meant far more than simply a team of baseball players bent on victory or monetary remuneration. The Knickerbocker club, like many of the other pioneering baseball clubs, was both an athletic and a social association. While providing opportunities for playing baseball, it also scheduled suppers, formal balls, and other festive occasions in the off-season. Individuals could acquire membership only by election;

the club conscientiously tried to keep out those who had a 'quarrelsome disposition' or who did not fit well into the group for other reasons. The Knickerbockers drew up bylaws, elected officers, and even fined members who breached the organization's code of dress and behavior."

Peter Morris notes that there was once an important distinction implied in the terms "club" and "team"; he cites Albert G. Spalding (*America's National Game*, 1911) who wrote that the founders of the National League (1876) proposed "a sharp line of distinction" between the two terms: "Heretofore Base Ball *Clubs* had won and lost games, matches, tournaments, trophies. Henceforth this would be changed. The function of Base Ball *Clubs* in the future would be to manage Base Ball *Teams*. Clubs would form leagues, secure grounds, erect grandstands, lease and own property, make schedules, fix dates, pay salaries, assess fines, discipline players, make contracts, [and] control the sport in all its relations to the public." **2.** *n.* A baseball *team.* **3.** *n.* A baseball bat. **4.** *v.* To hit a baseball.

**club ball** A generic name for an early English ball game played with some form of a club. According to Robert W. Henderson (*Ball, Bat and Bishop*, 1947), the term was invented by J. Strutt (*The Sports and Pastimes of the People of England*, 1801) and his use of it has "misguided historians with the belief that at one time there was an English ball game called 'Club ball.' So far there is no evidence that there was such a nomenclature in English for a ball game." The term is used in an exhibit at the National Baseball Hall of Fame and Museum to describe an English game around 1200 using a heavy bludgeon and a large ball.

**clubbie** A person who performs many of the menial tasks around the clubhouse, including packing and unpacking players' equipment and personal property, and laundering uniforms.

**clubhouse** The area at a ballpark comprising a team's locker room, showers, lounge, and the manager's office. Every park has two clubhouses: one for the home team and one for the visiting team. "Many ballplayers seem caught in adolescence, their development perhaps arrested by long enclosure, early wealth, and their teammates' high spir-

its and scrutiny. They call their locker rooms 'the clubhouse'" (*New York Times,* Sept. 11, 1983). Compare *dressing room.* **1st Use.** 1869. "Gould's light foul was taken by Foran, up by the clubhouse" (Chadwick Scrapbooks; David Shulman).

**clubhouse lawyer** A player given to complaining and talking of reform and "rights"; "a player who airs bolshevik views in the clubhouse" (*The Sporting News Record Book,* 1937). With the unionization of players through the Major League Baseball Players Association, clubhouse lawyers are less common than they once were. "Bob Farley . . . denied today that he is hard to manage or a clubhouse lawyer, as tagged by Chicago White Sox pilot Al Lopez when traded to Detroit the other day" (*San Francisco News Call Bulletin,* June 28, 1962; Peter Tamony).

Joe Garagiola (*Sport,* Apr. 1992) commented: "A clubhouse lawyer is a .210 hitter who isn't playing. He gripes about everything. His locker is too near the dryer. His shoes aren't ever shined right. His undershirt isn't dry. His bats don't have the good knots in them that the stars' bats have. He's not playing because the manager is dumb. When he does play he says, 'Well, what do you expect? I ain't played in two weeks.' And he's a perpetual second guesser." **1st Use.** 1937. (*The Sporting News Record Book*).

**clubhouse meeting** A gathering of team members, either before or after a game, to receive important messages from the team's management.

**cluster** For a team to get a series of hits or runs in quick succession.

**clutch 1.** Any difficult or critical situation, often one in which the outcome of a game hinges on the success or failure of a team or individual player. See also *pinch,* 1. **2.** That situation in a game, from the seventh inning on, when the lead is three runs or less. The term is used for statistical purposes, such as determining top clutch hitters. **1st Use.** 1937. "But Gabby [Hartnett] has always had the knack of inserting base hits in what the ballplayers call 'the clutch.' When the score is tied and there's a man on, those Chicago players love to see Gab walk up there with his heavy stick" (Quentin Reynolds, *Collier's,* Aug. 21; Peter Tamony). **Etymology.** The origin of the term is suggested in the 1954 *Gillette World Series Record Book* (edited by Hy Turkin): "When a clutch is engaged in any machinery, parts are made to move, and any defect in the clutch will cause faulty operation or danger." (Peter Tamony) **Extended Use.** A key situation in any endeavor.

**clutch hitter 1.** A player known for his ability to get a hit in key situations and/or with runners in scoring position. Players with reputations as clutch hitters included Tommy "Old Reliable" Henrich, Hank Aaron, and Pete Rose. At least one player, Clyde "Dutch the Clutch" Vollmer, had his role acknowledged in a nickname. Syn. *gamer,* 2. **2.** A statistical term for a player with the highest batting average with runners in scoring position. **Extended Use.** Anyone who can come through when it counts the most.

**clutch series** A series of games played between two contending teams when the outcome will have a bearing on team standings.

**coach 1.** *n.* An assistant to the manager in professional baseball. A coach is a team member in uniform and performs several jobs before, during, and between games. A major-league club usually has a pitching coach, a hitting coach, a bullpen coach, a first base coach, a third base coach, and a bench coach. **2.** *n.* A person in charge of a collegiate or scholastic baseball team, similar to a manager in professional baseball; an individual who oversees and teaches playing techniques and practices. **1st Use.** 1882. In a description of an exhibition game between the Detroit Wolverines of the National League and the Univ. of Michigan, which the professionals won easily, it was said of the collegiates: "Their great lack is a 'coach.' It is entirely unnecessary for the pitcher, second baseman or short stop to all back up first base, leaving the second wholly uncovered" (*Detroit Free Press,* Apr. 29; Peter Morris). **3.** *v.* To serve as a coach.

**coacher** An early term for the first base coach or the third base coach. Hugh S. Fullerton (*American Magazine,* June 1912) commented: "The duties of the coachers were to play clown, make noise and strive to excite or anger opposing players. The coacher in the modern game usually is quiet, study-

ing the movements of the opposing pitcher and catcher and assisting base runners." **1st Use.** 1891. (*Chicago Herald,* May 4; Edward J. Nichols).

**coacher's box** Syn. of *coach's box.*

**coaching lines** The outlines of the coach's box. **1st Use.** 1897. (*New York Tribune,* Apr. 26; Edward J. Nichols).

**coach's box** One of two designated areas on a baseball field where the first base coach and the third base coach must remain while the ball is in play. The rectangular box is 5 feet by 20 feet, marked off with chalk or lime and situated 8 feet in foul territory along the baseline. In softball, the rectangle is 6 feet from the baseline and only 15 feet long. Syn. *coacher's box.* **1st Use.** 1896. (Richard G. Knowles & Richard Morton, *Base Ball;* Edward J. Nichols).

**coach's interference** A call by an umpire when a coach touches, grabs, or gets in the way of a baserunner in an attempt to stop the runner. In such cases the runner is called out.

**coat-and-tie decision** A policy decision made by the owner and/or executives of a baseball organization.

**coax a pass** For a batter to earn a base on balls by being patient, fouling off pitches, not swinging at pitches out of the strike zone, making the pitcher throw many pitches, or coming back after being behind in the count. See also *work the count.* Syn. *work a pitcher for a pass.* **1st Use.** 1910. (*New York Tribune,* July 18; Edward J. Nichols).

**Cobb's Lake** The area of dirt in front of home plate at Bennett Park/Navin Field in Detroit, which the groundskeepers kept wet, to slow down Ty Cobb's bunts and cause infielders to slip as they tried to field them.

**Cobb-Wagner grip** A batting grip characterized by space between the hands along the bat, as used by Ty Cobb and Honus Wagner.

**cob-fence route** *arch.* The circuit of small, rural towns visited by teams in the low minor leagues. "The regulars followed the cob-fence route, playing exhibition games each afternoon with minor-league clubs" (Burt L. Standish, *Courtney of the Center Garden*, 1915; David Shulman).

**cock** 1. *n.* The preparatory action of the arm and wrist prior to the forward movement of a throw. 2. *n.* The slant or cant of a hitter's bat. 3. *v.* To position the hitter's bat and arms, slightly tensed and pulled back, in preparation to swing at a pitch; e.g., "Smith cocks his bat toward the pitcher."

**cocked arm** A player's arm pulled back in preparation to throw the ball.

**cockeye** *arch.* A left-handed baseball player, esp. a pitcher. **1st Use.** 1937. (*The Sporting News Record Book;* Edward J. Nichols).

**coed softball** [softball term] An official form of softball played by two teams, each composed of five men and five women who are positioned so that two men and two women are in the outfield, two men and two women are in the infield, and one man and one woman pitch and catch.

**coffee and cake** Syn. of *cake and coffee.* **Extended Use.** Peter Tamony found the term used in jazz circles as early as 1936 for a very poor paying job, one that might only pay carfare, and in boxing, where coffee-and-cakes fighters were willing to enter the ring for little pay.

**coffin corner** Syn. of *third base,* 1, because a ball batted to the third baseman usually results in an out.

**coked up** Said of a player on fire, ready for anything. **Etymology.** The term was used by Casey Stengel in an allusion to the heat and fire of the carbon fuel as opposed to cocaine or Coca-Cola.

**cold bat** 1. The bat of a hitter in a hitting slump. Compare *hot bat,* 1. 2. A player who is wielding a cold bat.

**collar** 1. *n.* A figurative term for the cause or result of a player going hitless during a game; e.g., "he's got a collar" (announcer Brooks Robinson describing Juan Bonilla at the end of a telecast, July 29, 1986) or "he wears the collar" or "he took the collar." See also *horse collar,* 1, *Van Heusen.* **1st Use.** 1932. (*Baseball Magazine,* Oct.; Edward J. Nichols). **Etymology.** A literal "zero" from the round shape of a collar (Harwell E. West, *The Baseball Scrap*

*Book,* 1938). 2. *v.* To have failed to get a hit during a game; e.g., "[Nomar] Garciaparra is Collared" (*Boston Globe* headline, at the end of Garciaparra's 30-game hitting streak, Aug. 31, 1997).

**Collective Bargaining Agreement** A generic term for *Basic Agreement.* Abbrev. *CBA.*

**college try** See *old college try.*

**College World Series** An elimination series of games to determine the best Division I college baseball team. It is sponsored by the National Collegiate Association of America and held each June in Omaha, Neb. Abbrev. *CWS.*

**collision** A player fresh from college. The term is perhaps a Dizzy Dean–like interpretation of "collegian." **1st Use.** 1937. (*The Sporting News Record Book;* Edward J. Nichols).

**collusion** A secret agreement or arrangement; specif., the real or imagined agreement among team owners to forgo the purchase of high-priced free-agent players in 1986–88. The owners settled collusion claims for $280 million in 1990 and agreed to treble damages for future collusion.

**Colorado Rockies** The National League West Division expansion team that began playing in Denver in 1993. Its early years were typified by record ticket sales: six months before its first game, the Rockies ranked behind only the Los Angeles Dodgers and the Toronto Blue Jays in season-ticket sales.

**color bar** The unwritten rule that prohibited black players from playing in the major leagues. It was broken on April 15, 1947, when Jackie Robinson donned a Brooklyn Dodgers uniform. Syn. *color barrier; color line.* **Usage Note.** For reasons difficult to fathom, the term and its synonyms were particular to baseball. Other sports and endeavors had to deal with segregation or discrimination, but only baseball had to deal with the color bar.

**color barrier** Syn. of *color bar.*

**color line** Syn. of *color bar.*

**color man** A radio or television broadcaster, often a former player or manager, who delivers

J.H.Bloomer

**Color bar.** *The* USS Maine *baseball team. All of the members of the team except one were killed when the ship was blown up in Havana harbor in 1898. This is a fascinating image because it depicts an African-American player on an otherwise white team, a rarity then and for the next 50 years.*

background information, anecdotes, and sidelights and/or his own thoughts and analysis of the game to supplement the talk of the play-by-play announcer. Pittsburgh sportscaster Bill Currie once described a color man as "a guy paid to talk while everybody goes to the bathroom."

**colors** A colored uniform that distinguishes one as a member of a team; specif., two or more colors by which a team is identified and known. When Charles O. Finley owned the Oakland A's, he insisted that his team's colors were Kelly Green, Fort Knox Gold, and Wedding Gown White.

**colt** A young player in the 19th century. John

Montgomery Ward wrote in *Baseball and How to Become a Player* (1888): "A great fault with many batters is that they try to hit the ball too hard. This is especially true of the younger players, the 'colts' as they are called."

**comb 1.** To hit the ball straight up the middle of the field, usually coming close to hitting the pitcher; e.g., "Smith's hit back through the box combed the pitcher's hair." **1st Use.** 1912. (*New York Tribune*, Sept. 7; Edward J. Nichols). **2.** To hit the ball; e.g., "Jones combed the pitcher's curves."

**combination ball** *arch.* A pitch that combines elements of two or more pitches, such as a sinking fastball or a knuckle curve. **1st Use.** 1907. "The head of the batting-list came up again, and now by using his combination ball Merriwell succeeded in fanning Strothers" (Burt L. Standish, *Dick Merriwell's Salvation;* David Shulman).

**combination card** A baseball card that contains the images of two or more players.

**combine** To join with one or more other pitchers in establishing a win or loss, such as four pitchers combining on a three-hitter.

**combined no-hitter** A game in which neither the starting pitcher nor one or more relief pitchers yield a base hit; e.g., the Baltimore Orioles defeated the Oakland A's 2–0 on July 13, 1991, when starter Bob Milacki and relievers Mike Flanagan, Mark Williamson, and Gregg Olson yielded no hits.

**come around 1.** To score a run; e.g., "Smith walked and came around to score on the catcher's error." **2.** To perform better; e.g., "Obviously, this team doesn't think I'm coming around" (Sid Fernandez, quoted in *Baltimore Sun,* July 4, 1995).

**come back** *v.* For the hitter to wait until the pitcher throws the ball where the hitter wants it to be.

**comeback** *n.* **1.** A rally by a team behind in the score or the standings. The term can be applied to an individual game or several games over the course of a season or to postseason play. Teams that have rebounded from two-game deficits (2–0, 3–1) to win the World Series are considered comebacks. **2.** A ball that is hit back to the pitcher; a *comebacker,* 1. **3.** A good season by a team, manager, or player, following a poor or mediocre one.

**comebacker 1.** A ball that is hit right back to the pitcher; e.g., "Smith is out on a comebacker to the mound." Syn. *comeback,* 2. **2.** A game in which a team, losing at one point, scores enough runs to tie or take the lead.

**"Come back, little Sheba"** A hallmark phrase used by sportscaster Red Barber for a batted ball that bounced back to the mound. **Etymology.** The term is the name of a William Inge play that was made into a motion picture, a popular 1952 film that won an Oscar for actress Shirley Booth. It is an apparent play on the term "comebacker."

**Comeback Player of the Year** An annual title conferred by a United Press International poll of sportswriters on one player in each major league who made a dramatic reversal from a season or more of decline and poor play. Versions of the award also have been given by *The Sporting News* and the Associated Press.

**come from ahead 1.** To win or be winning in a game after losing a lead and reclaiming it. **2.** To lose or be losing in a game after having a lead; e.g., "The Cubs came from ahead [3–1] to suffer a 4–3, extra-inning loss to the Astros" (*Baltimore Sun,* Sept. 28, 1998).

**come from behind** To be losing in a game before scoring enough runs to tie or take the lead.

**come home** To score.

**come home dry** To fail to take advantage of a scoring opportunity.

**come in 1.** To pitch the ball so it crosses over home plate toward the batter. **2.** To throw a strike after falling behind in the count. **3.** For a fielder to run rapidly toward an advancing ground ball.

**come off** To have played a particular kind of game or series or finished a particular kind of season; e.g., it is sometimes said that a player is "coming off" a good (or bad) spring training season.

**comer 1.** A promising player. **1st Use.** 1902. (*Sporting Life,* July 12; Edward J. Nichols). **2.** A team that is a contender in waiting. **1st Use.** 1889. "The AEtnas considered the Cass club hardly in their class, but a long tie game between the two changed matters, and they recognized that the Cass were comers" (*Detroit Free Press,* Feb. 24; Peter Morris).

**come through** To win.

**come to eat** Said of a fastball that moves in on the batter; one that is likely to take a "bite" out of the batter.

**come up 1.** To join a major-league team from the minor leagues. See also *call up.* **2.** To step up to the plate to hit.

**come up throwing** To field a ball off the ground and get it to the appropriate base with immediacy; e.g., shortstops need to be able to "come up throwing" on balls hit into the hole.

**comfortable** Describing a pitching success that does not involve making the batter look bad or being intimidated. Randy Johnson's three strikeouts of Frank Thomas occasioned this remark from Thomas: "It was a real comfortable 0-fer tonight" (Associated Press dispatch, Aug. 9, 1997).

**comfort zone** That part of the strike zone best adapted to a player's ability to get a hit; e.g., Warren Spahn was a master at keeping the ball away from the hitter's "comfort zone."

**"coming down"** The traditional call made by the catcher to alert the second baseman or shortstop that he is about to throw the ball to second base at the end of the pitcher's warmup between innings.

**Comiskey Park** The home field of the Chicago White Sox since 1910 and named for long-time (1901–31) team owner Charles A. Comiskey. It was the site of the first All-Star Game (1933) and

**Charles A. Comiskey.** *The ballpark he built for his White Sox in 1910 still bears his name, despite a move to new quarters.*

the first exploding scoreboard. After the 1990 season, it moved to a new Comiskey Park across the street from the original.

**command 1.** *n.* The ability of a pitcher to take charge in a game, using an assortment of pitches, esp. the ability to throw a pitch for a strike to get ahead in the count or keep from walking the hitter; e.g., "Smith had command of his pitches by spotting his breaking ball for strikes early in the count." The term does not necessarily mean "control." The confidence of a pitcher to throw a pitched ball or series of balls that arrive at precisely the spot and exactly the velocity he desires while making the ball go in any direction, such as up, down, in, or out, constitutes "command." One of the worst things that can be said of a pitcher is that he has "no command." See also *control.* **1st Use.** 1888. "The more marked the control of the ball the greater will be the success, for no matter how many wonderful curves he may be able to get, unless he has perfect command he will never be a winning pitcher" (John Montgomery Ward, *Base-Ball: How to Become a Player;* Skip McAfee). **2.** *v.* For a pitcher to exert control; e.g., "Smith was commanding the inside corner."

**commando** A livelier type of baseball used in the Mexican League beginning in 1984.

**Commission** See *National Commission.*

**commissioner** The individual selected by major-league owners for a four-year term to formulate and administer the overall policies of the game and to exercise executive supervision of all the activities of major- and minor-league baseball. A commissioner was in place from 1920 (when Judge Kenesaw Mountain Landis was selected in the wake of the Black Sox scandal in an effort to restore public confidence in the game) to 1992 (when Fay Vincent, who was selected to fill out the remainder of the term of A. Bartlett Giamatti, was dismissed). From 1992 until summer 1998, the position was held by a temporary or acting commissioner, Bud Selig.

The duties of the commissioner are varied: a) run the World Series; b) settle grievances of players, teams, or leagues that cannot be settled at lower levels; c) be the final judicial authority on all matters of appeal; and d) investigate and resolve acts that may be detrimental to the game.

**Commissioner's Games** The *World Series,* so-called because the commissioner has supreme authority over these games. Critics say that the commissioner has relinquished some of that authority to the television networks who have a lot to say about the hour at which the games begin.

**Commissioner's Trophy** The official name for the trophy presented to the winner of the World Series.

**commission scout** A *bird dog* who receives a small stipend when a prospect he has found is signed.

**commit oneself** To make a half swing in which the wrists break. If the umpire determines that the batter has "committed himself," a strike is called.

**common card** One of the vast majority of baseball cards that is not rare and that depicts an average player who is not a star or particularly notable for any reason. Having no premium value, all common cards from a given year may bring a standard price. Syn. "common."

**commuter** A baseball player who is being shifted between major-league and minor-league teams.

**comp** A free ticket to a baseball game. Short for "complimentary ticket." **1st Use.** 1902. (*Sporting Life,* Oct. 4; Edward J. Nichols). **Extended Use.** A free ticket to any event for which there is a paid admission charge.

**compensation free-agent draft** The selection of players as compensation for teams that lost Type A free agents in the reentry draft.

**compensation pool** Players up for consideration in the compensation free-agent draft.

**complete game 1.** An official statistic credited to a pitcher who pitches an entire game without relief. The all-time single season record for complete games (50 in 1893) belongs to New York Giants pitcher Amos Rusie; the lifetime record (750) belongs to Cy Young (1890–1911). A fascinating complete-game record belongs to Walter Johnson who pitched 38 complete-game 1–0 victories dur-

ing his career with the Washington Senators (1907–27). Since 1900, the average number of complete games has gone from almost 117 a team to fewer than 25 in the 1980s. In 1991 the New York Yankees set a record of only three complete games. Abbrev. *CG.* **2.** A baseball game that is not postponed, called, or otherwise delayed.

**complete player** A player who has speed and a strong arm, excels in fielding, is a consistent hitter, and hits for power. Such players are few and far between: Hank Aaron was certainly one of them.

**complimentary runner** [softball term] A substitute baserunner who by the mutual consent of the opposing managers does not prevent the original runner from staying in the game.

**computer baseball** A system whereby a manager feeds his own and the opposing team's statistics into a computer and, from the results obtained, forms decisions on how to use his players and manage his team.

**concentration** The edge or advantage a pitcher must possess to succeed. It was once known as *rhythm.* **1st Use.** 1974. "When a veteran pitcher recently explained an early KO by saying, 'I lost my concentration,' my first thought was, 'What the hell does he have to concentrate on for 2½ hours?' Then it occurred to me that this was just another change in the jargon of ballplayers" (*The Sporting News,* July 7). **Usage Note.** This is a tricky term because it does not relate to "concentration" in the traditional sense as much as to the concept of effectiveness on the mound. In fact, a seemingly distracted pitcher throwing a no-hitter might be described as having "concentration."

**Concepcion play** A method of playing on artificial turf, named for Cincinnati Reds shortstop Davey Concepcion, who quickly discovered that sharply hit balls did not slow down when hit through the infield. Concepcion started playing much deeper, almost in shallow left field. Since his throws were longer, he began making them lower so they would reach the first baseman on one true hop.

**concrete ashtray** Syn. of *cookie-cutter.*

**conditioning assignment** Sending a major-league player to a minor-league team for physical and playing conditioning prior to returning to the major-league team. Compare *rehabilitation assignment.*

**confederate soldier** A visiting player in his gray uniform, as opposed to a home-team player in his traditional white uniform.

**conference 1.** *n.* See *mound conference.* **2.** *v.* To meet on the pitcher's mound. "The Orioles conference on the mound" (announcer Jon Miller, radio broadcast, May 10, 1987).

**connect 1.** To hit the ball successfully, squarely, and solidly. **1st Use.** 1905. (*Sporting Life,* Sept. 2; Edward J. Nichols). **2.** To hit a home run.

**consecutive-game hitting streak** A series of successive games in which a player has produced at least one hit per game. The streak is not terminated if all the player's plate appearances (one or more) result in a base on balls, hit batter, defensive interference, or as sacrifice bunt; however, a sacrifice fly and no hit will terminate the streak. The streak is determined by the consecutive games in which the player appears, not by his team's games. Joe DiMaggio of the New York Yankees holds the major-league record: 56 games in 1941. [*Official Baseball Rules,* rule 10.24(b)]

**consecutive-game playing streak** A series of successive games in which a player has appeared in his team's games. *Official Baseball Rules,* rule 10.24(c) states: "[The] streak shall be extended if the player plays one half-inning on defense, or if he completes a time at bat by reaching base or being put out. A pinch-running appearance only shall not extend the streak. If a player is ejected from a game by an umpire before he can comply with the requirements of this rule, his streak shall continue." Cal Ripken Jr. of the Baltimore Orioles holds the major-league record: 2,632 games, from 1982 to 1998. Syn. "consecutive game streak."

**consecutive hitting streak** A series of successive base hits produced by a hitter. The streak is not terminated if the plate appearance results in a base on balls, hit batter, defensive interference, or a sacrifice bunt; however, a sacrifice fly will terminate the streak. [*Official Baseball Rules,* rule 10.24(a)]

**contact** The point at which the bat meets the baseball; e.g., "Smith makes contact" or "Jones has good contact."

**"contact down, we're going"** A coach's instruction to a runner on third base that if the ball is on the ground anywhere he is to go home.

**contact hitter** A hitter known for his ability to get hits by squarely meeting the ball with the bat; a hitter that rarely strikes out. Contact hitters are more likely to hit singles than extra-base hits. "When you talk about contact hitters the discussion must begin and end with Joe Sewell" (*Sports Collectors Digest,* Apr. 15, 1983). The *Baltimore Sun* (Oct. 8, 1996) called Wade Boggs "one of the greatest contact hitters in the history of the game." Compare *power hitter.* **Usage Note.** The term is not universally loved. In a column on overworked sports terminology, sportswriter Jim Murray (*Los Angeles Times,* undated clipping) put "contact hitter" at the top of his list with this comment: "If a guy isn't a good 'contact' hitter, what kind of 'hitter' is he? There's no such thing as a 'non-contact' hitter. Every hit is 'contact,' isn't it?"

**contact play** An offensive play in which the baserunner advances on any contact made by the batter; e.g., a play in which the runner on third base advances to the plate when the batter hits the ball.

**contend** To be in the race for the championship. "Weaver Confident that O's Will Contend" (*Baltimore Sun* headline, Apr. 2, 1982).

**contender** Any baseball team that is capable of winning a championship. Syn. "contending club."

**Continental League** A major league proposed in 1959 after the New York Giants and the Brooklyn Dodgers fled west. It was to include New York, Houston, Toronto, Denver, Minneapolis–St. Paul, Atlanta, Dallas–Fort Worth, and Buffalo. It was a threat to the existing order and the cities were promised teams in the existing leagues if the Continental League did not become a reality. The Continental League was not to be, but the New York Mets resulted from the promise and eventually all of the other cities, except for Buffalo, were given teams.

**contract** A written agreement between a player and his club, in which the terms of employment are set forth.

**contract-jumper** A player who breaks his contract with one team to play with another team. The term got much play when members of the union known as the Brotherhood formed their own Players League in 1890 and several players quit their existing teams and joined new ones. When the new league folded the contract-jumpers were allowed to rejoin their old teams without penalty. There have been other cases of contract-jumping in the 20th century, including the handful of players who joined the "outlaw" Mexican League in 1946. See also *jump, 7; jumper.* **1st Use.** 1891. "Barnie and Mike McDonald raised their holy hands in horror at the thought of employing any so-called contract-jumper" (*Sporting Times,* Oct. 31, 1891; David Shulman).

**contractor's back yard** The bumpy or uneven surface of a poorly kept infield, used before the advent of modern groundskeeping techniques. See also *ash heap; Hogan's brickyard.*

**control** A pitcher's ability to vary the speed, trajectory, and placement of the ball within the strike zone; the pitcher's accuracy. The term also refers to a pitcher's ability to throw enough strikes to get hitters to swing at balls out of the strike zone. Good control is "the pitcher's principal stock in trade" (Hugh S. Fullerton, *American Magazine,* June 1912). New York Yankees outfielder Tim Raines, after facing Greg Maddux of the Atlanta Braves in the 1996 World Series, commented (Associated Press, Oct. 24, 1996): "He's got great control. He pitches in and out." See also *command, 1; location.* **1st Use.** 1887. (*Base Ball Tribune,* June 9; Edward J. Nichols).

**control artist** Syn. of *control pitcher.*

**control pitcher** A pitcher known for his ability to pitch the ball to a precise desired location, both inside and outside the strike zone. Johnny Vander Meer was one of the first to carry this title. Syn. *control artist; Picasso.*

**controman** A modern name for an individual in baseball who always seems to get in trouble when talking to the press; a player who "creates controversy with his quotes" (*The Sporting News,* Mar. 6, 1982).

**conversion** The process by which starting pitchers become relief pitchers.

**Coogan's Bluff** The name of the hill behind the Polo Grounds in New York City. Once synonymous with the name of the ballpark, it was sometimes also known as "Coogan's Hollow."

**cookie 1.** A pitch that is easy to hit; one that is easy to "get your teeth into." **2.** A 1990s syn. used by players for *ribbie* (*Sports Illustrated,* June 15, 1998).

**cookie-cutter** A generic term for a circular, symmetrical, concrete, and bland ballpark characterized by artificial surface, massive parking lots, a large capacity, and multipurpose functions, such as Atlanta-Fulton County Stadium (Atlanta), Busch Stadium (St. Louis), Riverfront Stadium (Cincinnati), Three Rivers Stadium (Pittsburgh), and Veterans Stadium (Philadelphia). Syn. *concrete ashtray; donut, 3.*

**cookie jar** The location of the bat after a check swing that is called a strike; e.g., "Smith's bat was in the cookie jar."

**coop** Syn. of *dugout.* **1st Use.** 1909. (*American Magazine,* May; Edward J. Nichols).

**co-op club** A minor-league club that agrees to develop players from several different major-league organizations rather than to serve as a farm club for a single major-league team. "As a co-op club, they're dependent on last-minute deals with major league teams who don't have room for all their signees on their Class A squads" (*USA Today,* June 17, 1986).

**Cooperstown 1.** The town in New York State that is the traditional home of baseball and the location of the National Baseball Hall of Fame and Museum and of the National Baseball Library and Archives. Syn. *Baseball's Valhalla.* **2.** A synonym for the *Hall of Fame* itself; e.g., "If he stays healthy, Dwight's [Gooden] on his way to Cooperstown" (Gary Carter, quoted in *Newsweek,* Sept. 2, 1985) and "[Mike Piazza's] career statistics . . . put him on a path to Cooperstown" (*Baltimore Sun,* May 23, 1998).

**Cooperstown stuff** Outstanding baseball-playing ability and statistics that are needed to be considered for election to the Baseball Hall of Fame.

**cop** *v.* To win. **1st Use.** 1907. (*Lajoie's Official Baseball Guide;* Edward J. Nichols).

**cork** 1. *n.* A team's most effective relief pitcher; a stopper. "The expression became popular with Ted Wilks, who choked off many rallies as a relief pitcher for the St. Louis Cardinals in the 1940s" (Zander Hollander, *Baseball Lingo,* 1967). 2. *v.* To doctor a bat. See also *corking.* 3. *v.* To hit a ball hard; e.g., "Smith really corked one." **1st Use.** 1876. (Chicago *Inter-Ocean,* May 1; Edward J. Nichols).

**corkball** A variation of baseball that has been played in the St. Louis, Mo., area since the early 1900s. A brochure on the subject published by the Markwort Sporting Goods Co. of St. Louis describes it as a game that has many of the features of baseball yet can be played in a very small area: "It is a good summertime game because no exhausting action is required—the action is centered around the pitcher, the catcher and the batter; there is no baserunning. Corkball is also played in winter in netted areas in gymnasiums." The ball is cork-centered, weighs 1¼ ounces, and is 6¼ inches in circumference. The bat cannot be any longer than 38 inches and cannot be thicker in diameter than that of the ball. It is normally played inside a cage that is about 75 feet long and about 20 feet wide. Teams usually have five players, but can have as few as two—a pitcher and a catcher.

Two strikes constitute an out and five balls a walk and a hit is any ball landing in fair territory. Four walks, four hits, or a combination thereof constitute a run. Each additional walk or hit in the same inning adds a run. There are five innings in a game and three outs to an inning. A batter is out if he hits a foul ball, or hits a fair ball that is caught before hitting the ground or the cage.

There are several corkball leagues in and around St. Louis and Memphis. Announcer Tim McCarver, a former major-league catcher, noted that when he was a youngster in Memphis, "I got an early start on my announcing career while playing corkball, imitating Harry Caray on the play-by-play" (*Oh, Baby, I Love It!,* 1987).

**cork center** The distinguishing feature of the baseball introduced in 1910 to replace the rubber-centered ball. The credit for inventing the cork-centered ball was given to George A. Reach of the sporting goods company that carried his name. "Reach Dies at 86, Pioneered Cork Center in BB" (*New York Mirror* headline above his obituary, Dec. 8, 1954; Peter Tamony).

**corked bat** A *doctored bat* that has been partially drilled out at the barrel end to create a hole with a depth of up to about 12 inches that is filled with cork, rubber, or any of several other substances for the purpose of giving the batter an added advantage over the pitcher. Norm Cash, who won the 1961 American League batting title (.361 average), later admitted he used such a bat.

**corker** *arch.* A good player. **1st Use.** 1867. (*New York Herald,* Aug. 27; Edward J. Nichols).

**corking** Tampering a bat with cork to make the bat lighter and to increase bat speed. There are two theories as to the benefits of corking a bat: 1) the nature of the cork acts as a springboard, allowing the batter to hit the ball farther; and 2) the reduction in weight (about 2 ounces) in the barrel of the bat allows the batter the advantage of a faster swing. As with ball doctoring, any such bat tampering is expressly illegal, but not uncommon. See also *doctor the bat.*

**cork popper** Syn. of *Opening Day.* "Yesterday's cork popper witnessed nine full innings of errorless ball" (undated clipping from a Jack McDonald column, *San Francisco Call-Bulletin;* Peter Tamony).

**corkscrew** An early name for *screwball,* 1.

**corkscrew arm** A left-handed baseball player.

**corkscrew-er** *arch.* A tricky curveball. **1st Use.** 1909. "And how did you like that corkscrew-er?" (Arthur E. McFarlane, *Redney McGaw;* Peter Tamony).

**corkscrew twist** A curveball that takes more than one change in direction. **1st Use.** 1891. (*Chicago Herald,* May 8; Edward J. Nichols).

**corner** 1. One of the two parallel sides of home plate that provides the umpire with a visual basis for determining the inside and outside edges of the strike zone. To be successful, a pitcher must keep his pitches "on the corner" where they are more difficult for the batter to hit. Syn. *edge*, 4. **2.** The point where a foul line meets the outfield fence or wall. **3.** Left field or right field. **4.** First base or third base. **1st Use.** 1891. (*Chicago Herald,* May 5; Edward J. Nichols).

**corner clipper** A pitch that crosses over the edge of the plate. Syn. "corner cutter." **1st Use.** 1913. (*Harpers Weekly,* Sept. 6; Edward J. Nichols).

**cornerman** The first baseman or the third baseman.

**corner outfielder** The right fielder or the left fielder.

**corps** See *mound corps.* **1st Use.** 1902. (*Sporting Life,* Apr. 26; Edward J. Nichols).

**corral 1.** To catch or field a ball. **1st Use.** 1902. (*Spalding's Official Base Ball Guide;* Edward J. Nichols). **2.** To collect accomplishments; e.g., "Smith corralled four assists."

**correction** A term used by baseball executives for the fall of attendance and general interest in the game following a strike or work stoppage. A Milwaukee Brewers official actually termed the strike that ended in 1995 "our industry correction" (*Milwaukee Journal Sentinel,* Sept. 19, 1997).

**couldn't hit . . .** The beginning of any of several highly exaggerated phrases to typify a player who does not do well at the plate; e.g., "he couldn't hit the inside of a barn" or "he couldn't hit a bull in the ass with a shovel." On an Oct. 9, 1982, telecast, Tommy Lasorda said Willie Miranda "couldn't hit water if he fell out of a boat." A variation is "he couldn't knock skin off rice pudding." Similar taunts and insults are used in other realms, from marksmanship ("couldn't hit the inside of a barn") to prizefighting ("couldn't punch his way out of a paper bag") to selling ("couldn't sell ice water in hell") and are not a baseball exclusive.

**count 1.** At any given moment, the tally of *balls and strikes* charged to a batter. It is always given with the number of balls followed by the number of strikes; e.g., "three balls and two strikes." The count is determined and kept track of by the home plate umpire. **1st Use.** 1915. (Ring W. Lardner, short story "Horseshoes," later published in *Round Up: The Stories of Ring W. Lardner,* 1929; Edward J. Nichols). **2.** The paid attendance at the ballpark. **3.** *obs.* Syn. of *ace,* 1.

**counter 1.** *arch.* A run. **2.** Syn. of *indicator,* 1. **3.** [softball term] A scored run; one that counts. Because home runs over a certain limit are now counted in some forms of softball, this term has relevance.

**counting house** Home plate. **1st Use.** 1910. (*Baseball Magazine,* Apr.; Edward J. Nichols).

**"counting your money?"** Once a common belittling remark hollered at a runner picked off base.

**country** Solid or powerful; e.g., Hank Greenberg is "a good country hitter" (*Time* magazine, Nov. 20, 1950; Peter Tamony).

**country club** A derogatory term for a team that has little discipline or has members playing for themselves rather than the team. The Boston Red Sox prior to the "impossible dream" year in 1967 was regarded as a country-club team.

**country-fair hitter** An exceptionally good hitter. The term refers to the big, tough farmers who showed up to play baseball at country fairs.

**country-fair player** A grandstand player; a show-off; a busher. **1st Use.** 1937. (*The Sporting News Record Book;* Edward J. Nichols).

**country mile** The long distance traveled by a batted ball. "He is the answer to a scout's prayer. He can throw a baseball into a barrel at 100 yards, is a ten-second sprint man and can hit a ball a country mile" (*Saturday Evening Post,* Mar. 9, 1935; Peter Tamony). **Extended Use.** A good distance for anything, from a golf ball to a thrown football.

**country sinker** A *spitball.* "That new-old pitch, the 'country sinker,' which you and I know as the spitball" (Arnold Hano, *Roberto Clemente: Batting King,* 1968).

**count the stitches 1.** To look at a slowly pitched ball as it drifts to the plate. **1st Use.** 1937. (National League Service Bureau clipping; Edward J. Nichols). **Etymology.** The term is, of course, based on an exaggerated notion because it would be impossible to see the individual stitches on any pitched ball, no matter how slow. As a matter of fact, there are 216 stitches on a regulation baseball. **2.** To pitch slowly.

**courtesy runner** A substitute in amateur play who is allowed to run for a player without removing that player from the game.

**cousin 1.** A particular pitcher whom a hitter consistently finds easy to hit; a hitter's favorite pitcher. "To [Fred] Lynn, [Jim] Slaton is like a favorite cousin who just doesn't get to town often enough" (Tom Marr, WFBR broadcast, May 22, 1986, following a Lynn home run off Slaton). See also *coz; lamb,* 2. **1st Use.** 1928. "Yeah—they was all callin' him 'Cousin Dick'" (Said of a pitcher who has just been yanked in T. A. Dorgan's column "Outdoor Sports," *San Francisco Call & Post,* Aug. 23; Peter Tamony). The term also appears in *Babe Ruth's Own Book of Baseball* (1928) in which Ruth states that pitcher Paul Zahniser "was a 'cousin' of mine . . . every time he pitched against us I knew I would get two or three hits—and so did he." **Etymology.** The term has been widely attributed to New York Yankees pitcher Waite Hoyt who likened certain batters who faced him to cooperative family members. It was apparently a term more commonly used by players than writers in its early days. William G. Brandt (*Baseball Magazine,* Oct. 1932) lists it as one of the terms "unfamiliar to the public"; in making it "public" Brandt wrote: "Every batter has a list of 'cousins,' pitchers whose deliveries he finds comparatively easy to slap upon the nostrils." **2.** *rare* A hitter whom a pitcher finds easy to strike out. **3.** A team that another team consistently defeats, such as the Kansas City Royals who were cousins to the Baltimore Orioles in a period between May 1969 and Aug. 1970 when the Royals were beaten 23 times in a row. "A's Take 'Tiger' Cousins into Camp for 6th Time" (*San Francisco Examiner* headline, May 27, 1957; Peter Tamony). **Extended Use.** An easy opponent in other sports. An article on how basketball player Bob Lanier commonly scored many points when he played against the Portland Trail Blazers was headlined: "Piston Center Finds Cousins" (*San Francisco Examiner,* Nov. 29, 1972; Peter Tamony).

**cover 1.** To protect a base from an advancing runner by positioning oneself on or near it. **1st Use.** 1861. (*New York Sunday Mercury,* Aug. 10; Edward J. Nichols). **2.** To protect efficiently a section of the playing area; e.g., great outfielders are known for their ability to "cover" a large part of the outfield. The ultimate compliment of this nature may have been issued by Ralph Kiner who once said: "The earth is two-thirds covered by water, and the other one-third is covered by Garry Maddox." See also *cover ground.* **3.** For a pitcher to hide a ball that is about to be pitched so that the grip cannot be spotted and interpreted by the opposition. Some gloves have a tightly woven, basket-style webbing to help hide the ball.

**cover ground** To run across a large amount of the field. See also *cover,* 2. **1st Use.** 1905. (*Sporting Life,* Sept. 2; Edward J. Nichols).

**cowhide 1.** The baseball. **2.** The covering of the baseball. Horsehide was the official cover material for generations until baseball commissioner Bowie Kuhn authorized the use of cowhide in 1974 for the 1975 season. See also *horsehide,* 2.

**cow pasture** A derogatory term for a field that is in poor playing condition.

**cowtail** *v.* To take a long swing of the bat, with the bat held at the very end of the handle. **1st Use.** 1937. (Red Barber, World Series radio broadcast, Oct. 6; Edward J. Nichols).

**cowtail swing** A long swing of the bat held at the very end of the handle. **Usage Note.** Edward J. Nichols likened the long swing to the motion of a cow's tail swishing.

**coz** Short for *cousin,* 1. See also *"hello, Coz."*

**cozy roller** *arch.* A slowly batted ground ball. **1st Use.** 1907. (*New York Evening Journal,* June 5; Edward J. Nichols).

**cp and nc** Scouting report shorthand for "can't play and no chance." "Bad even in wartime baseball . . . cp and nc" (Frank Cashen, of his mid-'40s run as the pepper-pot second baseman for Loyola College in his native Baltimore, *Washington Post,* Oct. 7, 1986).

**crab 1.** *n.* A player who finds fault with others; a grouch. **2.** *v.* To complain; to show a quarrelsome nature. **Usage Note.** Although this slang meaning of "crab" predates baseball, it was so commonly used in baseball circles in the early 20th century that it was considered to be a baseball term. "Many of the worst 'crabs' in baseball are the pleasantest and most genial when off the field, their crabbedness evidently being the result of the nervous strain of playing" (Hugh S. Fullerton, *American Magazine,* June 1912). **1st Use.** 1909. (*New York Evening Journal,* July 8; Edward J. Nichols).

**crack 1.** *n.* The sound made when the bat contacts a pitched ball; e.g., "The outfielder took off at the crack of the bat." **2.** *n.* A baseball bat that has a crack in it. **3.** *n.* An attempt; e.g., "Smith took a crack at stealing a base." **4.** *v.* To hit a pitched ball; e.g., "Smith cracked the pitch for a double."

**crackerbox** A small, old ballpark. Writer Charles Einstein compares (letter, Mar. 5, 1990) "crackerbox" to *bandbox:* "It connotes the same small area that you describe for bandbox, but where bandbox also has the feel of the neat and immaculate, 'crackerbox' denotes the exact opposite—the dilapidated, crumbling state, often beyond repair, that so often characterized the small-town or old-time stadium and led to its eventual replacement."

**crackerjack** A first-rate or spectacular player or team. **Usage Note.** Sometimes spelled "crack-a-jack" in early applications. **1st Use.** 1886. "Tom Stevens brings two cracker-jack two-year-olds from Mobile, so the touts say, in Wary and Poteen" (*Spirit of the Times,* May 1; Peter Tamony). The first use in baseball came five years later: "Shannon is putting up a beautiful game at second base. He is the cracker-jack of the Association, all points considered" (*Sporting Times,* July 11, 1891; Barry Popik). **Etymology.** The term was in use for many years as slang for a sailor's biscuit using salted meat or anything first-rate or excellent. The term did not come into its own until 1896 when the firm of F. W. Rueckheim and Brother of Chicago started selling a confection of popcorn, peanuts, and molasses under the name and trademark "Cracker Jack." (It had been sold as early as the Columbian Exposition in 1893 but without the name.) Before long, it was a baseball park staple (along with peanuts and popcorn) and even shows up in the words to the song "Take Me Out to the Ball Game." In *Mr. Dooley's Opinions* (1910) by Finley Peter Dunne, we read: "A good seat on th' bleachers, a bottle hand f'r a neefaryous decision at first base an' a bag iv' crackerjack was a far as iver I got tow're bein' a sportin' character an' look at me now!"

Some have come to the conclusion that the specific use of the term for baseball players follows its use for the popcorn confection popular at ballparks. Edward J. Nichols traces it back to 1908 and the short story "Dick Merriwell's Magnetism," while Peter Tamony was unable to find anything before 1910, when he finds three citations. An early example: "Good players of all kinds are wanted by every manager, but a 'cracker-jack' third baseman has a strangle hold on his job as long as he bats .200 or better" (S. DeWitt Clough, *Letters from a Baseball Fan to His Son,* 1910).

Research by Gerald Cohen, however, puts the term back to 1888 in a baseball context before the introduction of the confection: "Gov. Hill will be among those who will attend the opening game at the Polo Grounds to-morrow ... The Governor thinks Danny Richardson is a 'Cracker Jack' and Dan thinks the Governor is the greatest man in the country" (*The World* [New York], Apr. 24).

**cradle 1.** *n.* A training device built of long wooden slats used to sharpen the reflexes of infielders. Shaped like a large cradle, balls are thrown into it so they will carom off at odd and unpredictable angles. **2.** *v.* To use the arms and chest to field a ball, as a mother cradles a baby in her arms. "You'll see him [Cal Ripken Jr.] cradle the ball a lot. The last person I saw do that was Brooksie [Brooks Robinson]" (Mark Belanger, quoted in *Baseball Digest,* Dec. 1982).

**cradle-snatcher** A scout or bird dog who trails extremely young prospects.

**crafty** Said of certain skillful and cunning left-handed pitchers, of small stature, such as Whitey Ford and Bobby Shantz. Going against tradition, Wade Boggs called Greg Maddux a "crafty righthander," but acknowledged that "crafty is usually reserved for a lefty" (Associated Press, Oct., 24, 1996).

**crank 1.** *n./obs.* A baseball fan. In his work on baseball slang used in *The World* (New York) in the 1880s, Gerald Cohen (*Comments on Etymology,* Apr. 1986) reports: "At least from 1888 through 1890 the standard term for a baseball fan was a 'crank,' short for 'baseball crank.' I don't recall seeing the term 'fan' used at all in this time span." **1st Use.** 1882. Cohen reports others finding the term in use from 1882 to 1910 and gives 13 examples of it in use, including this from *The World* (May 23, 1889): "The arrival of Father Adrian Clapdoodle Anson and his lavender conspirators in the metropolis is always a signal for a general uprising of the cranks." See also *crankess; crankism; krank.* **2.** *v.* To pitch. "Max Surkont cranked his sixteenth victory of the . . . season tonight" (*San Francisco News,* Aug. 5, 1950; Peter Tamony). **3.** *v.* To hit the ball for a long distance; e.g., "Smith cranked the first pitch over the sign in right field."

**crankess** *obs.* A female *crank.* Gerald Cohen (*Comments on Etymology,* Apr. 1986) labels the term a "humorous and artificial creation" and gives this example from *The World* (New York) (May 24, 1890): "It was 'ladies day' at the grounds, and . . . about five hundred crankesses took advantage of the Giants' invitation to see the game." See also *crankette.*

**crankette** A female fan in the 19th century (Ken Burns, *Baseball,* inning 1). See also *crankess.*

**crankism** *obs.* "Oddball pessimism" in the late 19th century, according to Gerald Cohen (*Comments on Etymology,* Apr. 1986), who relates an example from *The World* (New York) (Aug. 5, 1888): "The surprisingly good work by the New York team has finally put to rest all adverse criticism, and even those persons who are soaked and sodden with crankism are at last losing sight of their *ignis fatuus* in the broad glow of hope which the Giants are shedding."

**crank up 1.** To wind up to deliver a pitch. **2.** To hit the ball. "If [knuckleball] just floats up to batter, big and fat, batters crank up on pitcher" (San

Francisco Giants pitcher Billy Muffett, pregame radio interview, June 17, 1959; Peter Tamony).

**crash 1.** *v./arch.* For a team to make successive hits. Hugh S. Fullerton (*American Magazine,* June 1912) wrote: "Verb used in baseball, not to signify a single sound, but a series of hard hits. A team 'starts crashing,' when three or four batters in succession make hits." Today, the term would suggest a team that was falling apart. **2.** *n./arch.* A hard batted ball. **1st Use.** 1912. (*Outing Magazine,* June; Edward J. Nichols). **3.** *v.* To hit a ball very hard; e.g., "Smith crashed the ball into the stands for a homer."

**cream** To hit a ball hard.

**cream puff** An easy ball to hit, such as one thrown by a batting-practice pitcher; e.g., Joseph "Stretch" Suba, a batting-practice pitcher, served up "big, fat, medium fast cream puffs for the All-Star hitters to feast on" (Mickey Herskowitz, *Houston Post,* July 15, 1986; Charles D. Poe). See also *Cuban sandwich.*

**cream-puff hitter** A weak hitter, one who is not a power hitter.

**crew 1.** The group of umpires working a particular game. **2.** See *ground crew.*

**crew chief** The umpire in charge of an umpiring crew. He becomes the *umpire-in-chief* when he works behind the plate.

**cricket** An English game, similar to baseball in some respects, popular in certain U.S. cities between 1800 and 1860, frequently requiring two to three days to complete. Traced back to 1598, the game is played with a ball and bat by two teams of usually 11 players each on a large field having two wickets 22 yards (20 meters) apart, each defended by a batsman, the object being to score runs by batting the ball far enough so that one can exchange wickets with the batsman defending the opposite wicket before the ball is recovered. There were several organized cricket clubs by 1840 in the United States.

**cripple 1.** *v.* To put the pitcher in a position where he must throw a strike because he is behind in the count; e.g., "The Cubs crippled Smith who

**Cricket.** *The proper sartorial look of the game circa 1925.*

must throw the ball over the plate and cannot use his trickier deliveries." The term generally is reserved for situations where the count is 3-0, 2-0, or 3-1. **2.** *n.* A pitch thrown when the count is against the pitcher (3-0, 2-0, or 3-1) and he must sacrifice speed for accuracy to ensure that the ball is in the strike zone. Ted Williams would "jump on the cripple" (Chicago White Sox pitcher Thornton Lee, quoted in Edwin Howsam, *Baseball Graffiti,* 1995). Syn. *cripple pitch.* **1st Use.** 1914. (*New York Tribune,* Oct. 13; Edward J. Nichols).

**cripple-a league** [softball term] An early facetious name for slow pitch softball when it was still seen, as one writer put it, as "a game reserved for those who don't happen to care for violent exercise and big-time competition."

**cripple hitter 1.** A hitter who does well when the pitcher makes a mistake or is behind in the count; e.g., Frank Howard, Don Kingman, and Ozzie Smith. See also *mistake hitter.* **2.** A hitter who does well when the pitcher is ahead in the count; e.g., Chili Davis.

**cripple pitch** Syn. of *cripple,* 2.

**cripple shooter 1.** A hitter who takes advantage of a crippled pitcher. **2.** A batter who becomes especially dangerous when ahead in the count (3-0, 2-0, or 3-1).

**crockery limb** A pitcher's arm that has stopped functioning. See also *glass arm,* 1.

**crocus sack** An impending victory. The term became part of broadcaster Red Barber's stunning verbal delivery; e.g., he would say that a game was "all tied up in a crocus sack" if it were almost won.

**crook** *arch.* A curveball. **1st Use.** 1908. (*New York Evening Journal,* May 7; Edward J. Nichols).

**crooked arm** An uncomplimentary reference to a left-handed pitcher or any pitcher with an unorthodox delivery. **1st Use.** 1932. (*Baseball Magazine,* Oct.; Edward J. Nichols).

**crooked number** Any number greater than 1 and less than 10, in reference to the lack of straight lines for numerals 2 through 9. A high-scoring game is one with crooked numbers. A 1–0 game is one in which neither team was able to post a crooked number.

**crooked pitch** The curveball. The term was used by Martin Quigley to title his history (1984) of the curveball.

**Crosley Field** The home field of the Cincinnati Reds from 1912 to 1970. It was known as Redland Field until 1933 when it was renamed for team owner Powel Crosley, who built the Crosley automobile.

**cross bats** *obs.* To compete in a baseball game.

**cross-checker** A scout who looks at specific players, verifying previous assessments of other scouts; a scout who is responsible for a large region and is better able to measure a player's abilities versus other top talent in the surrounding area. Compare *special assignment scout.*

**crossfire** A sidearm pitch that appears to cross the strike zone on the diagonal. It is accomplished when the pitcher begins his delivery by stepping toward the baseline rather than taking the usual step toward home plate (e.g., a right-handed pitcher stepping toward third base). Lefty Eddie Plank of the Philadelphia Athletics (1901–14) was known for this pitch and helped make it famous. **1st Use.** 1902. (*Sporting Life,* Sept. 13; Edward J. Nichols).

**cross-firing** Throwing a sequence of pitches; "sending the ball first over one side of the plate then the other and then right over centre" (Lester Chadwick, *Baseball Joe of the Silver Stars,* 1912; David Shulman).

**cross-handed** Said of an "incorrect" grip or hold on the bat in which the batter's hands are crossed; e.g., left hand on top of the right hand for a right-handed batter or right hand on top of the left hand for a left-handed batter. "[Hank] Aaron started as a cross-handed hitting softball player" (United Press International dispatch, Aug. 1, 1982).

**cross-over pivot** The footwork when turning a double play often required of a second baseman who, after receiving the ball from the shortstop, touches second base with his left foot and relays the ball to first base as he swings his right foot over the bag and plants it. Syn. *double-play pivot.*

**cross-seamer** Syn. of four-seam fastball.

**cross-seam fastball** Syn. of four-seam fastball.

**cross the plate** To score a run.

**cross-town series** A series of games between two teams in the same city. See also *city series.*

**cross up** To fool or mislead a player on one's own team. The term is commonly used when a pitcher delivers an unexpected pitch to the catcher, such as a breaking ball when a fastball is anticipated. **1st Use.** 1935. (Ralph H. Barbour, *How to Play Better Baseball;* David Shulman).

**crouch 1.** *n.* The catcher's playing position: balanced on the balls of his feet with weight on his haunches. **2.** *v.* To assume the catcher's crouch. **3.** *v.* To take a low batting stance.

**crowd 1.** *n.* The spectators as a collective body at a baseball game. **2.** *v.* See *crowd the plate.*

**crowd the corners** To fill the bases with runners.

**crowd the plate** To take a batting stance close

to the plate; to hover close to the strike zone; to crouch on the inner edge of the batter's box as close to the plate as possible. **1st Use.** 1901. (Burt L. Standish, *Frank Merriwell's Marvel;* Edward J. Nichols).

**crow hop 1.** An extra little step at the end of a pitcher's motion. **Usage Note.** Is this term an antique? Tristram Potter Coffin (*The Old Ball Game,* 1971) reports: "In the spring of 1969, pitcher Jerry Johnson was interviewed on the radio. He told how he had rid his pitching motion of a little 'crow hop' . . . during winter ball. Two weeks later members of the Houston Astros . . . denied the phrase was still in use." **2.** [softball term] "The act of a pitcher [in fast pitch softball] who steps, hops, or drags off the front of the pitcher's plate, replants the pivot foot, establishing a second impetus (or starting point), pushes off from the newly established starting point and completes the delivery" (Amateur Softball Association of America, *Official Rules of Softball,* 1998).

**crow hopping** [softball term] Jumping off the mound before the ball has been released. It is an illegal pitch that is often associated with the windmill windup. Compare *leaping.*

**crown** An honor figuratively worn by a player or team that comes in first place, either in the standings or in the statistical accounting of some aspect of performance; e.g., the "batting crown" goes to the player who has the highest batting average in his league.

**cruise** To win a game easily; e.g., "The Mariners cruised past the Twins, 8–2."

**crunch** A difficult position; a *jam,* 1.

**crush 1.** To hit a pitched ball with great strength. **2.** To defeat a team overwhelmingly.

**crush zone** The point or area where the batter is most likely to hit the ball; the batter's *wheelhouse.* "A pitch thrown right in the crush zone, I mean, when it leaves the pitcher's hand the ball is right in a place where the batter was swinging—and he got all of it" (Keith Moreland, *Vineline,* Aug. 1987).

**crybaby** A derogatory name for a player with a reputation for arguing with umpires.

**CS** Standard box score and scorecard abbrev. for *caught stealing.*

**cub** *arch.* A recruit or rookie. The term was popular at the beginning of the 20th century, which probably influenced the naming of the youthful Chicago Cubs. **1st Use.** 1906. (*Sporting Life,* Mar. 10; Edward J. Nichols).

**Cuban** A name for a black American ballplayer in the days before many Latin Americans were in the major leagues and well before the color bar was broken. Franklin P. Huddle (*American Speech,* Apr. 1943) noted: "Since Negroes have, by devious means, been kept out of major league baseball, their evasion is to sometimes call themselves Cubans. Thus, Cuban All-Stars is a frequent name of a Negro team."

**Cuban forkball** A *spitball.* The term received a boost through an often-repeated comment by relief pitcher John Wyatt who played during the 1960s: "I use a Cuban forkball. I learned to use it while I was swimming in the Mediterranean Sea." The term also was used by Orlando Peña when he staged a comeback and returned to the major leagues in 1973 and, according to Gaylord Perry (*Me and the Spitter,* 1974; Charles D. Poe), "it is not a dry pitch."

**Cuban palmball** A *spitball.* "A prime suspect in those days was Pedro Ramos, who resembled [Gaylord] Perry by touching his cap and shirt frequently before pitching his 'Cuban palmball.' The ball did so many tricks en route to the plate that the umpire once made Ramos go into the clubhouse and change his shirt three times" (Joseph Durso, *New York Times,* Aug. 31, 1982).

**Cuban sandwich** An especially tantalizing pitch thrown by a batting-practice pitcher, such as those thrown by Minnesota Twins hitting instructor Tony Oliva, who said: "The Cuban sandwich is a confidence builder. If you cannot hit a long ball off a Cuban sandwich, you are in trouble" (Patrick Reusse, *The Sporting News,* 1986). See also *cream puff.*

**Cubbies** An affectionate nickname for the Chicago Cubs, making it a nickname for a nickname. Joey Johnston (*Tampa Tribune,* Oct. 6, 1984) wrote: "The Cubbies? Other teams aren't called the Metsies or the Soxies. But the Chicago Cubs are different. They are not just a team, but a shared experience that has been passed through the generations."

**Cubs factor theory** See *ex-Cubs factor theory.*

**cudgel** A baseball bat. **1st Use.** 1908. (*Baseball Magazine,* June; Edward J. Nichols).

**cue ball shot** A fluke base hit when the ball hits off the top of the bat, suggesting a cue stick striking a billiard ball. Such a hit is sometimes said to have been "cued up." Syn. "cue shot."

**cunny-thumb** Said of a pitcher who throws slow balls. "It's a crime to get beat by the cunny-thumb pitching they have. Brother, I'd like to be playing them during the regular season" (Marty Marion, manager of the St. Louis Browns, quoted in *San Francisco Examiner,* Apr. 4, 1953; Peter Tamony). See also *cutty-thumb.* Syn. "cunning thumb." **1st Use.** 1937. (*New York Daily News,* Jan. 17; Edward J. Nichols).

**cunny thumber** A player with a poor throwing arm; a player who throws "like a woman." Syn. "cunning thumber." **Etymology.** This is an old term used in marbles played by children on both sides of the Atlantic Ocean. In marbles it refers to a shooter using the "female manner"; i.e., from a closed fist with the thumb tucked under the first three fingers. Eric Partridge (*Dictionary of Slang and Unconventional English,* 1984) notes that "cunny" is a reference to female genitalia (*pudendum muliebre*) dating back to the 17th century. Despite this clearly sexual reference, there seems to have been no taboo about its use in baseball (or in marbles for that matter) as it shows up in such places as the *New York Daily News* (Jan. 17, 1937) and Dizzy Dean's various glossaries. Its decline in use as a baseball term has paralleled the decline in marbles as a childhood pastime.

**cup** A small, hard, metal or plastic device commonly worn by players to protect their genitals. Jim Bouton (*Ball Four,* 1970; Charles D. Poe) writes: "What baseball players do to each other is punch each other in the groin and say 'cup check.'"

**cup of coffee** A brief trial with the parent club by a minor-league player; e.g., "Billy Williams' cup of major league coffee cooled in just 10 days" (United Press International story, *San Francisco Chronicle,* Aug. 29, 1969; Peter Tamony). These trials often take place during the month of September, when teams are allowed to expand their rosters to 40 players. It allows the brass of the major-league team to get a glimpse at its new talent. **1st Use.** 1908. "It isn't often that Hank O'Day is caught napping, but a young player just getting his 'cup of coffee' in the league put one over on Hank and Mr. Klem yesterday" (*New York Globe,* June 11; Peter Morris). **Etymology.** The phrase seems to have derived from the observation that a young player's first taste of the major leagues is usually quite short, figuratively just long enough to drink a cup of coffee. **Extended Use.** The term has been applied to quick trial periods in other sports. An example from pro football: "[Henry] Schichtle had a cup of coffee last season with the New York Giants and was picked up by the new Atlanta Falcons and put on waivers there before the 49ers took a look at him" (*San Francisco Chronicle,* Aug. 2, 1966; Peter Tamony).

**cupped barrel** The barrel of a cupped bat with a teacup end.

**cupped bat** A baseball bat whose top end has been scooped out to form a *teacup end.* A Japanese innovation, cupped bats have been legal in the major leagues since 1971. The indentation in the end of the bat must be curved with no foreign substance added and may be no deeper than one inch, no wider than two inches, and no less than one inch in diameter [*Official Baseball Rules,* rule 1.10(b)]. The concave shape allows the bat weight to be shaved by an ounce or so over the same bat with a convex (rounded) end. Some believe that the cup creates a vacuum, which allows the batter to obtain extra speed in his swing; but the Official Playing Rules Committee disputed this notion when it legalized the bat with the conclusion that "the driving power is not accentuated, and batter does not have an advantage."

**curfew** **1.** The time of the day that players must be in quarters according to rules established by the manager. **2.** The hour that a game must end in accordance with a league curfew rule or local regu-

lations. "Suspension of Saturday's game after eight innings because of the league's 1 A.M. curfew was the first at Memorial Stadium since July 31, 1978" (*USA Today,* June 22, 1987).

**curfew rule** A municipal or league regulation stipulating the hour at which a game must be terminated or suspended; e.g., in the American League all night games must be called at 1 A.M. local time, but if an inning is started prior to that time, the game can be completed.

**curse of the Bambino** A term created by *Boston Globe* writer Dan Shaughnessy to emphasize the fact that the Boston Red Sox last won a World Series in 1918 and have not been able to repeat that feat because the team sold Babe Ruth to the New York Yankees after the 1919 season. The term is

**Curse of the Bambino.** *Invoked up to and beyond the Red Sox' lackluster showing in the 1998 American League playoffs against the Cleveland Indians.*

also the title of a 1990 book by Shaughnessy. Stephen King (*Boston Globe,* Oct. 2, 1995) wrote: "There is no Curse of the Bambino. I, who was writing about curses and supernatural vengeance when Mr. Shaughnessy was still learning not to eat the ends of his Crayolas, tell you that it's so. . . . The Red Sox have been victims of an extraordinary run of ill luck, that's all." See also *Babe Ruth curse.*

**curtain call** The practice of a player coming out of the dugout to acknowledge the fans. The call usually starts in the form of a chant of the player's name ("Rusty-Rusty-Rusty" or "Ed-die-Ed-die-Ed-die") to honor the player for a home run, personal milestone, crucial hit, or, in the case of a pitcher, a number of strikeouts.

No clear idea exists as to when the practice began, but its widespread use certainly dates back no further than the late 1970s, when the Chicago White Sox started the practice. Roger Maris, upon hitting his 61st home run on Oct. 1, 1961, was forced/pushed out of the dugout by his teammates. George Vecsey (*New York Times,* Aug. 15, 1982) asked: "Can you imagine what Early Wynn would have done to the next batter after somebody took a bow for hitting a home run? There is reason to believe the current practice of curtain calls did not begin until Bob Gibson was safely retired after 1975."

During his last at-bat in Fenway Park in 1960, Ted Williams hit a home run that John Updike (*The New Yorker,* Oct. 22, 1960) recalled: "Though we thumped, wept, and chanted 'We want Ted' for minutes after he hid in the dugout, he did not come back." Updike later learned that both the players and the umpires had begged Williams to come out and acknowledge the crowd.

Compare this to Carl Yastrzemski's final at-bat in Fenway Park in 1983. He popped out to the second baseman, and then, as described by Stephen Williams (*Inside Sports,* Jan. 1984): "The fans clamored for Yaz and he came out and lifted his hat, and then he came out again, and later that night, when he was supposed to be attending a cocktail party in his honor, he stood on a street in the Back Bay and signed autographs for an hour."

**curtain-raiser** The first game of the season, a series, or a doubleheader. **1st Use.** 1912. (*New York Tribune,* Sept. 9; Edward J. Nichols).

**curve** Syn. of *curveball.*

**curveball** A pitch that is thrown with a forceful, downward spin and snap of the wrist, causing it to drop or break and veer to the side as it nears home plate. A right-handed pitcher's curveball tends to veer to the left while that thrown by a left-handed pitcher veers to the right. Although few now doubt the fact that the ball actually curves, there have been those who maintained that it was an illusion. Several experiments determined that it was real; e.g., in a well-publicized 1959 experiment, physicist Lyman J. Briggs (with the aid of former Brooklyn Dodger infielder Cookie Lavagetto) determined that a curveball does in fact curve and that the absolute maximum curve (or break) from the line of trajectory was 17.5 inches over the distance of 60.5 feet from the mound to the plate. There are many synonyms for "curveball," including: *curve; Uncle Charlie; yellow hammer.* Also spelled "curve ball." **1st Use.** 1874. (*New York Herald,* July 7; Edward J. Nichols). **Etymology.** The pitch has been credited to Candy Cummings of Brooklyn, who first began working on it in 1864 at boarding school. He later said he came on the idea in 1863 while throwing clamshells, which naturally curved. In 1867, he first applied it in a game while playing for the Brooklyn Excelsiors. But there are many other claims. In 1973, the National Baseball Library and Archives collected the various claims made by or on behalf of five other men. See Martin Quigley (*The Crooked Pitch,* 1984) for a history of the curveball in American baseball. **Extended Use. 1.** *n.* A surprise; e.g., "Russians Throw Curve Into Suez Parley" (*San Francisco News* headline, Aug. 10, 1956; Peter Tamony). **2.** *n.* A tough, tricky question, such as one that shows up in an examination. A character in a Steve Canyon comic strip says: "That's an unfair curve to throw at a newspaperman" (*San Francisco Examiner,* July 17, 1956; Peter Tamony). **3.** *adj.* By extension, "curvy" has come to mean dishonest or full of surprises. "Some of these make-money-at-home outfits are curvy" (Ann Landers column, June 13, 1964; Peter Tamony).

*Curveball.*

**curveballer** A pitcher who relies chiefly on his curveball. **Extended Use.** A person with questionable ethics. "In a business [prizefighting] full of curve ballers, Fran threw right down the middle" (*San Francisco Chronicle,* Mar. 2, 1968; Peter Tamony).

**cushion 1.** Syn. of *base,* 2. **1st Use.** 1891. (*Chicago Herald,* May 5; Edward J. Nichols). **2.** A comfortable lead in a game, a series of games, or the overall standings.

**cushion night** A promotion at a night baseball game in which seat cushions are given away to fans. More often than not, it seems, many fans forgo sitting on the cushions for throwing them on the field. "For the second straight year, the Chicago White Sox 'Cushion Night' resulted in a delay of play Friday night" (*Des Moines Register,* May 31, 1987).

**cuspidor curve** *arch.* A *spitball.*

**cut 1.** *n.* A batter's swing. "Lord, he has a wicked cut" (Dennis "Oil Can" Boyd, on first pitching to Jose Canseco, quoted in *USA Today,* May 16, 1986). **1st Use.** 1932. (*Baseball Magazine;* Edward J. Nichols). **2.** *n.* An opportunity to swing the bat, either in a game or in batting practice. Often used in the plural; e.g., "I need to get my cuts." **3.** *n.* The release of a player from the team; e.g., "Smith could not survive the cut and was returned to the farm." **4.** *v.* To release a player. **5.** *v.* See *cut base.* **6.** *v.* See *cut the corner.* **7.** *v.* To hit, drive, or throw a baseball so that it spins or is deflected. **8.** *n.* A *cut fastball,* 1; e.g., "Jones is developing a nice cut." **9.** *v.* Syn. of *cut off.*

**cut ball** A ball that is cut, slit, or deeply scratched so that when thrown it will create an irregular airflow, which will cause it to break unnaturally. "Mike Scott throws the best one. It's scraped on one side of the ball. If you hold it in the middle to throw it the ball will break in the opposite direction of where you cut it" (Keith Moreland, *Vineline,* Aug. 1987).

**Cut base.** *Postcard alluding to Fred Merkle's failure to touch second base, which cost the 1908 New York Giants the National League pennant.*

**cut base** To fail to touch a base while running or advancing.

**cut down** To throw out a runner, especially when an extra base or stolen base is being attempted. **1st Use.** 1912. (*New York Tribune,* Sept. 5; Edward J. Nichols).

**cut-down day** The date on which a major-league team must reduce its roster to the maximum number of players allowed (currently 25). The surplus players must be traded, sold, or sent to minor-league teams by the deadline. Jim Brosnan (*Pennant Race,* 1962) remarked: "Cut-down day is a time of man-sized tears and tribulations."

**cutey** A pitcher who specializes in throwing curveballs and slow stuff on the corners.

**cut fastball 1.** A variation of the slider, thrown with one's top two fingers slightly offside and a flick of the wrist (as if cutting cheese) instead of a complete turn; a semislider that moves from the middle of the plate to the corner because the pitcher "cuts" his delivery, turning his wrist a bit to pull down through the ball when releasing it. When thrown by a right-handed pitcher, a cut fastball tails away from a right-handed batter but moves in on a left-handed batter; for a southpaw, the movements are opposite. The cut fastball has been described as a flat, hard slider with a smaller, sharper break and as a cross between a slider and a fastball. Keith Hernandez (*Pure Baseball,* 1994) writes: "The cut fastball breaks the least of all the pitches that break at all, but that little bit is enough to be effective if located properly." In 1988, Joe Garagiola insisted that a "bad slider" becomes a cut fastball: "it also becomes a triple." See also *little cutter.* Syn. *cut,* 8; *cutter.* **2.** A fastball that breaks in a direction opposite to that which the batter expects; one that breaks late and sails.

**cut loose** To pitch hard and with authority after warming up.

**cut off** *v.* To intercept a throw coming in from the outfield on its way to home plate or another base. Syn. *cut,* 9. **1st Use.** 1863. (Chadwick Scrapbooks; Edward J. Nichols).

**cutoff** *n.* The interception of a throw coming in from the outfield on its way to home plate or another base.

**cutoff man** The player (usually an infielder and sometimes the pitcher) who intercepts or intends to intercept a throw from the outfield and then decides whether to relay the ball to the plate or another base or to hold the ball. "With a runner on second and a hit to center field, it is vital to hit the cutoff man. That can be one of the toughest plays in baseball." (Toronto Blue Jay outfielder Lloyd Moseby, quoted in *USA Today,* Apr. 6, 1987). Syn. *bounce target.*

**cutoff play** A play in which the ball, hit to the outfield with one or more runners on base, is thrown in and intercepted by another player (usually an infielder) who then must decide to try to retire the lead runner, who may be attempting to score, or to throw the ball to another base in an effort to prevent another runner from advancing, or to hold the ball. The unpredictable outcome of the cutoff play based on the fielder's split-second decision makes it an exciting play for the spectator.

**cutoff position** The point on the field where a throw from the outfield can be intercepted.

**cutouts** The heel and toe areas of a player's outer or team socks that have been left out of the socks to create a stirrup and allow some of the white sanitary socks to show. Roger Angell (*The Summer Game,* 1972) noted that Frank Robinson "wears the highest cutouts in the American League."

**cutter** 1. A batter who swings at many pitches outside the strike zone. **2.** Syn. of *cut fastball,* 1. **3.** See *grass cutter* and *daisy cutter.*

**cut the corner** To pitch a ball across the inside or outside edge of the plate; e.g., "Smith's fastball cut the inside corner of the plate for a called strike." **1st Use.** 1908. (*Spalding's Official Base Ball Guide;* Edward J. Nichols).

**cut the plate** To pitch a ball over the center of home plate, as if to cut it in half.

**cutty-thumb** Said of a slow-ball or junk-ball pitcher. David Halberstam (*Summer of '49,* 1989) quotes Joe Page referring pejoratively to Eddie Lopat as a "cutty-thumb" pitcher. See also *cunny-thumb.*

**cut way to bases** *arch.* To slide into a base feet first with one's spikes up. **1st Use.** 1911. (*American Magazine,* May; Edward J. Nichols).

**CWS** Abbrev. for *College World Series.*

**cycle** A single, double, triple, and home run (not necessarily in that order) hit by a player in the same game. See also *hit for the cycle.* **1st Use.** 1954. (Hy Turkin, *Gillette World Series Record Book*).

**cyclone pitcher** A pitcher who delivers the ball with great speed. It is from this that Denton True Young became known as "Cy." The names "Cyclone" or "Cy Clone" have been used to describe some young pitchers of the modern era because of their resemblance to previous winners of the Cy Young Award. A story on the resemblance of pitcher Storm Davis to his Oriole teammate Jim Palmer received this headline (*Washington Post,* June 12, 1983): "Storm Davis: A 'Cy Clone' Composite." **1st Use.** 1891. (*Chicago Herald,* July 1; Edward J. Nichols).

**cyclops** *arch.* A player who wears glasses.

**Cy Young Award** An annual award presented by the Baseball Writers Association of America to the outstanding pitcher in the major leagues from 1956 to 1966 and to the outstanding pitcher in each major league since 1967. Selections are made by two writers from each league city. Since 1970, writers name three pitchers, with 5 points allotted for each first-place vote, 3 points for each second-place vote, and 1 point for each third-place vote. The award is named for Denton True "Cy" Young, who won 511 games from 1890 to 1911. Officially known as "Cy Young Memorial Award."

**Cy Younger** A recipient of the Cy Young Award.

**Cy Young Jinx** Apparent bad luck that afflicts a Cy Young Award winner the following year. The idea took root in the 1980s when Steve Stone, Pete Vuckovich, LaMarr Hoyt, and Guillermo Hernandez won the American League Cy Young Award and then fell on hard times. Jerry Howarth (*Baseball Lite,* 1986) defines the Cy Young Award as "the kiss of death, often followed by an arm injury, surgery or simply an off year."

**Czar** A name associated with the commissioner of baseball because of his great personal power when dealing with issues having to do with the best interests of the game. Before there was a commissioner, the term was applied to the presidents of the two major leagues (esp. Ban Johnson of the American League). It is hardly a misnomer, as the commissioner has absolute power in a few critical areas. When, in the wake of the 1919 Black Sox scandal, Judge Kenesaw Mountain Landis was appointed the commissioner, he was often referred to as "Czar" Landis in the newspapers. Besides the other commissioners following Landis, the title has been bestowed on other powerful baseball figures; e.g., a United Press International story on Los Angeles Dodgers owner Walter O'Malley is titled "Baseball Czar" (*San Francisco Chronicle,* Jan. 29, 1969; Peter Tamony). **1st Use.** 1912. (*Hampton Magazine,* May; Edward J. Nichols). **Etymology.** Originally the title of the powerful Russian emperors, the term was applied to railroad magnates and political bosses, among others, before it came to baseball. "Czar is what they call me in the papers when they do not call me 'rogue'" (Alfred Henry Lewis, *The Boss, and How He Came to New York,* 1902). It was also used as a nickname for

**Czar.** *Commissioner Kenesaw Mountain Landis throwing out the first ball to start the second game of the 1922 World Series.*

T. B. Rein during the years (late 19th century) he was speaker of the House of Representatives and ran that body with rigid, rigorous adherence to the parliamentary rules. Since the title was pinned on Landis it has been used liberally for people given extraordinary powers.

# D

**D 1.** See *Class D.* **2.** Syn. of *defense.* **3.** Abbrev. for *double,* 1.

**Da Bums** Syn. of *Dem Bums.*

**daffiness boys 1.** A nickname for a team with a madcap or clownishly inept reputation. "No manager ever had more woes than [Casey] Stengel in the days when he piloted the 'daffiness boys' of the Brooklyn Dodgers and later the equally inept Boston Braves" (*San Francisco News,* June 21, 1956; Peter Tamony). The daffiness label seems to have a special place in baseball, where it can stick with a team or player for years; e.g., "Floyd Caves (Babe) Herman, 84, one of baseball's top batters who was probably best known for his part in bringing the Brooklyn Dodgers and Brooklyn itself a national reputation for irrepressible daffiness, died yesterday" (*Washington Post,* Nov. 30, 1987). **2.** A collective nickname for Jay Hanna "Dizzy" Dean and Paul Dee "Daffy" Dean, brothers from Arkansas who were first-rate pitchers in the 1930s for the St. Louis Cardinals, a team that captured the public fancy as cutups and pranksters. "Me and Paul can do it all" was Dizzy's famous line on the combo.

**daily win** A team meeting held before the game.

**daisies** The outfield; e.g., "Jones patrols the daisies."

**daisy clipper** Syn. of *daisy cutter.* **1st Use.** 1888. A ball bouncing through a meadow as "the sphere in the act of parting a Kranklet from her bonnet" (Thomas W. Lawson, *The Krank: His Language and What It Means*).

**daisy cutter** A hard-hit ground ball that skims the grass without rebounding, presumably removing any daisies in its path. Henry Chadwick wrote of the daisy cutter: "It is a hit ball very difficult to field, and, consequently, shows good batting." See also *grass clipper; skimmer.* Syn. *daisy clipper; daisy*

**Daffiness boys.** *Jay Hanna "Dizzy" Dean on the left and Paul Dee "Daffy" Dean on the right.*

*dipper; daisy scorcher; timothy trimmer.* **1st Use.** 1866. (*New York Herald;* Edward J. Nichols). **Extended Use.** The term shows up in the 1881 glossary in the turf section of the *New York Clipper Almanac* (Peter Tamony): "A horse that keeps his feet near the ground in trotting or running." Much later the term became a name for small World War II rockets (*Time* magazine, Feb. 7, 1944): "Marines promptly nicknamed the skipping, hell-raising rocket shells 'Daisy Cutters.'" It was also the official nickname for a bomb in the Vietnam War.

**daisy dipper** Syn. of *daisy cutter.*

**daisy hit** A line drive just over the shortstop's head (Maurice Thompson, *The Boys' Book of Sports,* 1886; David Shulman).

**daisy scorcher** Syn. of *daisy cutter.* **1st Use.** 1910. "Hagner bumped a daisy scorcher to Joe" (Christy Mathewson, *Won in the Ninth;* David Shulman).

**damp sling** A *spitball,* 1.

**D&M model glove** The type of glove presumably worn by a fielder who has committed an error. Such a player was once taunted by his teammates: "What are you using, the D&M ['dropping and moaning'] model?" The initials stand for Draper & Maynard, a legitimate brand name.

**dancer** A *knuckleball.*

**Daniel Webster** A player who is good at taunting umpires and possesses other verbal skills; a player who looks or acts wise. The term refers to the oratorical skills of the 19th-century statesman Daniel Webster.

**Danny Thompson (Memorial) Award** An annual award given by Baseball Chapel for "exemplary Christian spirit in baseball." It honors Thompson, an infielder for the Minnesota Twins in the 1970s, who died of leukemia in 1976.

**dart** A fastball.

**darter** A line drive. See also *blue darter.*

**darting hummer** A fastball with an erratic flight.

**dash off with the pennant** To win the league championship.

**Dauvray Cup** A trophy made by Tiffany's and awarded to the world champions between 1887 and 1893. It was commissioned by the famous actress Helen Dauvray in 1887, shortly before her marriage to John Montgomery Ward. It carried, at Dauvray's behest, the unique stipulation that the first team to win it three straight years would get to keep it. Boston claimed it after winning in 1891, 1892, and 1893, and it was succeeded by the *Temple Cup.*

**day 1.** A ceremony or celebration to commemorate a player, manager, coach, or other baseball individual, given before or after a game or between games of a doubleheader. Gifts often are given to the person being honored. Days can be set for players about to retire, retiring, or after retirement. "[Ron] Guidry was a classy member of the Yankees for 11 years. His exit should have been marked by a 'day' at Yankee Stadium at the end of his career, not by a meaningless midnight telephone call to Lafayette, La." (Murray Chass, at a moment when it looked like Guidry would retire, *New York Times,* Jan. 11, 1987). **2.** A promotional event at a baseball game. Charles D. Poe jotted down some of the special days that he encountered while reading baseball books: Cap Day, Bat Day, Poster Day, Hot Pants Day, Senior Citizen's Day, and Fan Appreciation Day. If the event is held after sundown, it is sometimes called a "night."

**day at the beach** A derogatory term for a poor hitter, one considered an "easy out." Compare *no day at the beach.*

**day ball** Baseball played during the daylight hours, as opposed to *night ball;* specif., baseball as played at Wrigley Field in Chicago, where there were no lights for night games until 1988. "Everybody wants to say we [the Cubs] lost in '69 because of day ball" (catcher Randy Hundley, quoted in *Sport,* Oct. 1984). Syn. *day baseball.*

**day baseball** Syn. of *day ball.*

**day game** A game played in natural light. It is a distinction that came about with the advent of artificial lights and the *night game.*

**daylight play** A defensive maneuver performed by an infielder and the pitcher in an effort to pick

**Day.** *Cy Young (left) and catcher Lou Criger on Cy Young Day, August 13, 1908, in Boston. The caption on the back of the original photograph says, in part, "Crowd of 28,000 attended. Young received $8,500."*

off a baserunner. While the runner takes his lead, the infielder quietly slips back to the base; simultaneously the pitcher steps off the rubber and spins around toward that base. If the pitcher feels there is a chance to pick off the runner (if he sees "daylight" between the runner and the base), he throws the ball to the infielder for the attempted pickoff. If the pitcher does not see daylight, he simply holds the ball, having at least moved the runner back to the base.

**day-night doubleheader** A doubleheader wherein the second (night) game starts several hours later and in which there are separate admissions.

**dead** *adj./arch.* Syn. of *out,* 1; e.g., "three hands dead" in the 1845 Knickerbocker Rules meant the side was retired.

**dead arm** The fatigued arm of a pitcher. Mike Mussina told the *Baltimore Sun* (Sept. 21, 1996) that he was going through a "dead-arm period." Colorado Rockies pitching coach Frank Funk referred to dead arm as "a case of asking your arm to do more than it has ever done before, and it goes through a stage where it gets fatigued, but it's not sore. It just feels weak. You try to throw the ball just as hard as you ever did. It just doesn't go that hard" (*Sports Illustrated,* Aug. 24, 1998).

**dead ball 1.** A ball that is not in play because of a legally created, temporary suspension of play. The ball may be deemed "dead" if it has hit a batter, been handled by a spectator, come in contact with an umpire or baserunner, been thrown out of play. Other dead-ball situations include a pitcher's balk,

*Dead Ball.*

interference by a baserunner, an uncaught foul ball, and time out called by an umpire. If an area of the field is ruled dangerous for play, a ball hit to that area is ruled dead. The ball becomes live again when the umpire allows the pitcher to take the ball and step on the pitching rubber. Compare *live ball,* 1. See also *delayed dead ball.* **1st Use.** 1869. (*New York Herald,* Aug. 1; Edward J. Nichols). **2.** A baseball that, due to certain properties of its component materials, deadens the impact when hit with a bat; specif., a baseball used before 1920 without a resilient core. Compare *lively ball,* 1.

**dead-ball era** The period, which ended with the 1919 season, when the game was played with a much less lively baseball. The dead ball was phased out by organized baseball to give Babe Ruth a better opportunity to show off his home run hitting ability. The term is still used today in lines like this: "Since the deadball era, only nine teams have made it to the World Series batting less than .250" (*Baltimore Sun,* Aug. 13, 1995). Compare *lively ball era.* Also spelled "deadball era."

**dead batter** A batter who approaches the plate without a bat. Bert Dunne (*Folger's Dictionary of Baseball,* 1958) adds: "Dugout legalists claim there is no rule in book that forces batter to use a bat at the plate, and that umpire must proceed in normal fashion, calling balls and strikes."

**dead body** A bench jockey's description of a nonchalant or low-key player.

**deaden** To bunt the ball in such a manner that it slows quickly after it hits the ground; e.g., "to deaden the ball" is to bunt effectively.

**dead fish 1.** A slowly pitched ball; a *nothing ball.* Syn. *dead mackerel.* **2.** An unorthodox pitch of any kind. "Ron Guidry calls his new pitch the 'dead fish.' It's a little like a screwball, and it has him off to a 2-0 start for the New York Yankees in 1986" (*Washington Post,* Apr. 14, 1986). **3.** A bunted ball that scurries a short distance and then stops ("dies") in the grass. Such a hit rarely occurs on artificial turf. Nellie Fox mastered this type of bunt.

**dead hands** The hands of a batter who keeps them locked in a rigid position while swinging, rather than rolls his wrists.

**deadhead 1.** *v./arch.* To get a base on balls; to get a "free ride." **1st Use.** 1912. (*New York Tribune*, Oct. 6; Edward J. Nichols). **2.** *n.* A spectator admitted to a baseball game on a complimentary ticket. **Etymology.** The term appears to have been in use in the theater (for a patron admitted free) and in the railroad industry (for a person who takes a free ride) before its baseball application.

**dead mackerel** Syn. of *dead fish,* 1. "He kept feeding me the dead mackerel and what could I do?" (*Baseball Digest,* Aug. 1945).

**dead-pull hitter** A hitter who always pulls the ball to his field of maximum power.

**dead-red** A fastball. To "sit dead-red" is to wait for a fastball, or to "look dead-red" is to anticipate the fastball.

**Dead Sox** A derogatory nickname for the Boston Red Sox. In Stephen King's *Different Seasons* (1982), a character's mood is elevated when the 1967 Red Sox win the pennant: "There was a goofy sort of feeling that if the Dead Sox could come to life, then maybe *anybody* could." (Charles D. Poe)

**dead spot** A period of ineffective pitching. "Pitchers go through a dead spot in the spring where they try to throw something good and nothing comes out. Your arm feels good and your delivery is good but it's just not there. I think some of our guys are going through that now." (Toronto Blue Jays manager Jimy Williams, quoted in *St. Petersburg Times,* Mar. 26, 1986).

**deal 1.** *v.* To trade a player or players. To say that a team will not "deal" a certain player is to say he will not be traded. **2.** *n.* A trade. **3.** *v.* To defeat a team; e.g., "Pirates deal Braves fourth straight loss."

**deal from the bottom** To pitch underhand. Syn. "deal off the bottom"; "deal from the bottom of the deck." **1st Use.** 1937. (*The Sporting News Record Book;* Edward J. Nichols). **Etymology.** From the poker term indicating an unfair or "underhand" passing out of cards. (Edward J. Nichols)

**Deanism** Any one of scores of words, phrases, and statements coined by pitcher and announcer

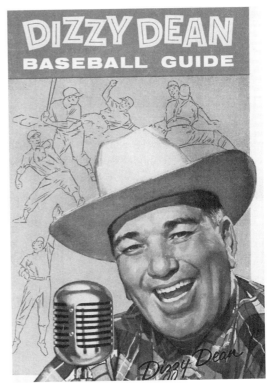

*Deanism.*

Jay Hanna "Dizzy" Dean. Though many were grammatically incorrect, they often were quite inventive and descriptive. In his own vernacular, for instance, players always "slud" into a base or players returned to their "respectable bases," or "the doctors X-rayed my head and found nothing" (after being hit in the head by a thrown ball in the 1934 World Series). Jerry Howarth (*Baseball Lite,* 1986) insists that Dean helped to establish the popularity of the live television "Game of the Week" when, on the air, he referred to an act of courage as "testicle fortitude."

**death march** A series of losses. "It's a death march" is the comment that manager Phil Garner made about the Milwaukee Brewers's fourth straight loss (*Milwaukee Journal Sentinel,* Aug. 11, 1997).

**death valley 1.** A particularly deep outfield area in a given ballpark. Because of the deep dimensions, it is more difficult to hit home runs, and fly balls are almost certain outs. Well-known "death valleys" are left-center field in Yankee Stadium and center field in Tiger Stadium. **2.** The central swath of home plate, excluding the inside and outside portions, where a batter can easily drive the ball. (Thomas P. McDonald)

**decent wood** Syn. of *good wood.*

**decision 1.** The scoring outcome of a game; e.g., "The Cubs won by a 3–2 decision." **2.** A win or a loss by a pitcher or a team. **3.** A ruling by an umpire.

**decision pitch** The pitch delivered on the count of three balls and two strikes.

**deck 1.** *n.* The location or position of the player next in line to hit after the present batter. See also *on deck; on-deck circle.* **2.** *n.* A layer or tier of seats in a ballpark. **3.** *v.* Syn. of *knock down.*

**decking** The act of knocking down a batter, or being knocked down, by a pitch.

**decoy 1.** To run in such a manner as to deceive a defensive player; e.g., a batter singles and acts as if he will stop at first base to trick the fielder into thinking the play is ending, at which point he breaks for second base. **2.** To lure a baserunner off his base; e.g., using the hidden-ball trick or fielding a ball as though it will be misplayed. A rarer example would be for the second baseman to act in such a way as to entice the runner on first to try and steal. Syn. *deek; deke.* **3.** To lead a batter to guess incorrectly the type or location of the next pitch.

**deek** Short for *decoy,* 2.

**deep 1.** *adv.* Far from home plate; e.g., both infielders and outfielders may "play deep," while the batter may hope to hit the ball "deep" or "go deep." A batter planning to touch up a pitcher might say "I'm going to take him deep." Compare *shallow,* 2. **2.** *adj.* Said of that part of the field that is the greatest distance from home plate; e.g., "deep center" or "deep left." Compare *shallow,* 1. **3.** *adj.* Rich in talent; e.g., a "deep bench" or a "deep bullpen." Earl Weaver's term for a team with much talent in reserve was "deep depth." **4.** *adj.* With a high ball-strike count; e.g., "Smith went deep in the count when the 3-2 pitch was thrown." **5.** *adj.* [softball term] Said of a pitch

that falls past the batter in slow pitch softball, analogous to "high" in baseball or fast pitch softball. Compare *short,* 4.

**deep count** A tally against the batter of either two balls and two strikes (2 and 2) or three balls and two strikes (3 and 2).

**deep in the hole** Said of the area toward the outfield between the shortstop and third base.

**deep-pocketed club** A baseball organization with much money to spend on players.

**deep short** The area in shallow outfield that is some distance further back than the shortstop's normal playing position.

**deer** A fast runner; a player who can "hightail it."

**deface** To mar the surface of the ball so that it moves erratically when pitched.

**defense 1.** The team, or any player on that team, in the field. **2.** The total strategy of the team in the field, involving such variables as the positioning of fielders, pickoff plays, and pitchouts. The purpose of the defense is to get three outs per inning without allowing the offense to score a run. Syn. *D.*

**defensive indifference** See *indifference.*

**defensive replacement** A player sent late into a game by the team in the lead to replace a player who can hit better than he can field.

**defo** [softball term] A player in fast pitch softball who can take the 10th place in the batting order but only plays defense. See also *designated player.*

**deke** Short for *decoy,* 2. **Etymology.** The term is long established in hockey for pulling the goaltender out of position. It also has a long football application. It began to find wide baseball application about 1990.

**delay** An official suspension of play before or during a game. "After a 36-minute pre-game sun delay, an 86-minute delay due to power failure, and 10 innings of baseball, the [Pittsfield] Cubs and [Albany-Colonie] Yankees finished in a 4–4 tie in a game suspended by an Eastern League curfew rule" (*Berkshire Eagle,* July 5, 1985).

**delayed dead ball** A *dead ball* when an infraction occurs before a play is completed, at which time the ball is declared "dead" by the umpire; e.g., interference by a batter during an attempted putout on a runner, obstruction with the batter by the catcher, obstruction of a baserunner by a fielder, interference by an umpire with the catcher attempting to throw, and intentionally throwing a fielder's glove at a batted or thrown ball.

**delayed double steal** A *double steal* attempted when there are baserunners at first base and third base. The play begins when the runner at first moves toward second on an apparent steal attempt. Before the catcher, who has the ball, makes the throw to second, the runner stops as if to return to first. If the catcher relaxes, the runner then starts again for second at top speed to induce the catcher's throw. As the ball is thrown, the runner on third breaks for home.

**delayed steal** A baserunning maneuver in which the runner advances to the next base after the ball has been returned to the pitcher or after the defensive team has started another play. The success of the maneuver hinges on the extent to which the element of surprise has caught a fielder unaware or out of proper defensive position. **1st Use.** 1908. (*American Magazine,* May; Edward J. Nichols). Lee Allen (*The Hot Stove League,* 1955) notes that the maneuver was "apparently first employed by Miller Huggins . . . in 1903."

**deliver 1.** To pitch; to complete one's delivery. **1st Use.** 1866. (Constitution and By-Laws of the Olympic Baseball Club of Philadelphia; Edward J. Nichols). **2.** To come through in a pinch; to get a hit in a clutch situation. **3.** To bat in a runner; e.g., "Jones delivered Smith with a double."

**delivery 1.** The complete combination of pitcher movements in executing a pitch, from windup to the release of the ball. **2.** The manner and quality by which a pitch is executed. **1st Use.** 1876. (*New York Tribune,* July 26; Edward J. Nichols). **3.** A pitched ball.

**Dem Bums** Traditional affectionate nickname for the Brooklyn Dodgers, established and characterized by a cartoon tramp drawn by Willard Mullin. See also *Bums.* Syn. *Da Bums.* **1st Use.** 1940.

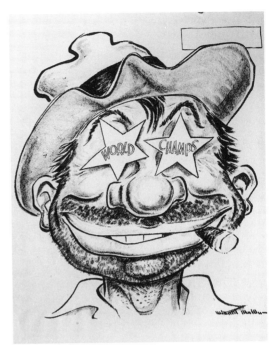

**Dem Bums.** *Willard Mullin's Bum in 1955, after the Brooklyn Dodgers defeated the New York Yankees in the World Series four games to three.*

Mullin's cartoon in the *New York World-Telegram* (Apr. 20) is titled "Dem Bums": it shows the Brooklyn caricature dressed as a drum major leading the National League. (Barry Popik) **Etymology.** Willard Mullin (*The Sporting News,* Dec. 3, 1958) revealed that the character of the bum was inspired by his taxicab driver who asked him "How did our Bums come out?" after the Dodgers won the first game of a doubleheader, thereby putting them in fourth place, then losing the second game, sending them back into the second division.

**demolition derby** A *grand slam* home run.

**dent the ball** To hit the ball hard.

**dent the garden wall** To hit a ball off the outfield fence.

**dent the plate** To score a run.

**department** A position on a club; e.g., the "catching department."

**deposit the pill** To hit the ball a long distance;

e.g., to hit a home run is often stated as "to deposit the pill in the seats."

**depth** The situation in which a team has two or more qualified players who can fit in at any playing position (except pitcher); the bench strength of a baseball team. Earl Weaver referred to a superior bench as "deep depth."

**derrick** To remove or *yank* a pitcher from a game; to "lift" a pitcher from a game. See also *hook*, 8.

**designated for assignment** Said of a player whose team must trade or release him within ten days or reassign him (if he accepts) to a minor-league team within seven days.

**designated hitter** A hitter in the American League, listed in the starting lineup and assigned to bat for the starting pitcher and all subsequent pitchers in the game. The designated hitter may be used defensively, continuing to bat in the same position in the batting order, but the pitcher must then bat in the place of the substituted defensive player. The designated hitter has been in effect since the beginning of the 1973 season and is used throughout baseball in the minor leagues, colleges, and elsewhere, except in the National League. During the World Series, both teams can use a designated hitter in games played in the American League ballpark, but neither team can use it in the National League ballpark. Between 1976 and 1986, before this World Series plan went into effect, the rule had been to use the designated hitter in alternating years. See also *designated pinch hitter; option batter*. Abbrev. and syn. *DH*. Syn. *tenth man*, 3. **1st Use.** 1973. "In the baseball box scores this summer, he will be listed as the 'dh,' the designated hitter for the pitcher" (Joe Durso, *New York Times*, Feb. 4). The first designated hitter was Ron Blomberg of the New York Yankees; he drew a walk against Luis Tiant of the Boston Red Sox on Apr. 6, 1973. **Etymology.** The idea was not a new one when it was adopted by the American League. It was suggested by National League president John H. Heydler in 1928, and by others decades before that; e.g., Philadelphia Athletics manager Connie Mack suggested in 1906 that the pitcher be denied a chance to bat, and a substitute player sent up for him every time: "He argues that a pitcher is such a poor hitter that his time at bat is a farce, and the game would be helped by eliminating him in favor of a better hitter" (*Philadelphia North American*, Feb. 3, 1906; Bill Deane). **Extended Use.** "Designated hitter" and "DH" are beginning to show up as terms for an announcer who steps in and helps out. "Nice DH job turned in by Brent Musburger for the ailing Harry Caray . . . Tuesday, during the Cubs' opening 9–3 loss to the St. Louis Cardinals." (*USA Today*, Apr. 8, 1987).

**designated pinch hitter** An early term for *designated hitter*, but seldom used since its adoption by the American League in 1973.

**designated player** [softball term] A player in fast pitch softball who may be substituted for any player in a game but who must stay in the same position in the batting order while remaining in the game. The player is designated before the game and may reenter once only if the reentry is into the same position in the batting order. The designated player can play defense, or the player whose bat has been taken over by the designated player can stay in the game defensively. The defense-only player is known as *defo*. Compare *extra player*. Abbrev. *DP*.

**designated runner** A player whose only role is to enter the game as a substitute baserunner. The term was created for Herb Washington, a track star hired in 1974–75 to pinch run for the Oakland A's. Washington scored 33 runs without ever once appearing at the plate.

**designated sitter** A designated hitter during a World Series when the designated hitter was not used; specif., Don Baylor of the Boston Red Sox during the 1986 World Series.

**Detroit Tigers** The name of the American League Central Division franchise in Detroit, Mich., a charter member of the league since 1901. George Stallings, the team's first manager, claimed he was the first one to use the nickname "Tigers" after having the players don black-and-yellow striped socks when he was managing Detroit's entry in the minor Western League in 1896. Other sources attribute the nickname to *Detroit Free Press*

**Detroit Tigers.** *A charter member of the American League, the source of the team's name is still in dispute.*

sports editor Philip J. Reid who noted that the socks' colors were similar to those of the athletic uniforms of Princeton Univ., whose mascot was the tiger. The team also has been referred to as the Bengals and, during Ty Cobb's reign (1905–26), the Tygers.

**deuce 1.** The curveball. Baltimore Orioles pitcher Rick Krivda had "I believe in the deuce" inscribed on the bill of his cap (*Orioles' Gazette,* Aug. 6, 1992). **Etymology.** A borrowing from the most basic level of sandlot baseball where the catcher has two signals: one finger for the fastball and two for the curveball. (David Shulman) **2.** A double play. "They're going to turn the deuce— [Eddie] Murray to [Cal] Ripken and back to Murray" (Tom Marr, broadcast of Baltimore Orioles vs. Milwaukee Brewers game, June 30, 1986).

**deuces wild** A situation in a baseball game in which there are two outs, the count is two balls and two strikes on the batter, and, perhaps, two runners are on base and/or two runs have been scored. Popularized by broadcasters Vin Scully and Joe Garagiola on NBC-TV's "Game of the Week," this term is occasionally used to describe such situations by radio and television announcers.

**development contract** The name of the legal arrangement made by a major-league team and a minor-league club under which the latter will develop the skills of a specific player. A recent estimate is that a third of the cost of running a minor-league club can be offset with the money from such contracts.

**DH 1.** Abbrev. for *doubleheader.* **2.** Abbrev. for *designated hitter.* Also "dh." **3.** *n.* Syn. of *designated hitter.* **4.** *v.* To perform as a designated hitter; e.g., "[Cal] Ripken Will Rest, Won't DH" (*Washington Post* headline, Sept. 26, 1997).

**DH-ing** Acting as the designated hitter; batting but not fielding. "'I'd rather be DH-ing, and that's God's truth,' said [Reggie] Jackson, whose two forays into right field this season were, to be kind, an adventure" (Doug Cress, *Washington Post,* May 18, 1986).

**dial 8** To hit a home run or a long ball. The term is a reference to dialing the number 8 on a hotel phone to get long distance.

**diamond 1.** *n.* The entire playing surface on which the game of baseball is played. "You looked down, and there was the diamond. It glistened. The grass was green. I've been to Ireland, and they have the greenest grass I've ever seen since, and still it wasn't as green as the grass at Ebbets Field." (Bill Reddy, quoted in Peter Golenback, *Bums,* 1984). **2.** *n.* The enclosed square, resembling a diamond-shaped figure, formed by home plate, first base, second base, and third base; the infield of a baseball field. **3.** *adj.* Pertaining to the game of baseball; e.g., "The Diamond Sport's Flaw" (*Christian Science Monitor* editorial title, Apr. 3, 1987). **1st Use.** 1858. (Chadwick Scrapbooks; Edward J. Nichols). **Etymology.** Immediately after Alexander Cartwright laid out the first regulation playing field in 1845, the term "diamond" came into play. Dan Schlossberg (*The Baseball Catalog,* 1980) notes that baseball's infield is actually not a diamond at all: "A true diamond has two acute and two obtuse angles, but the infield has four 90-degree angles. Since the diamond is best viewed from the catcher's perspective, however, the diamond reference is apparent." Originally, the term referred only to the infield but it has long since become a term for the total playing

**Diamond.** *Alexander Cartwright, who codified 90 feet between the bases and divided the field into fair and foul territories.*

area as well. However, it is clear that the distinction was blurred before the beginning of the 20th century. Richard G. Knowles & Richard Morton (*Baseball,* 1896) explain: "The ground is called a diamond by reason of its appearance when viewed from the grand stand."

**diamond artist** *arch.* A term used during the 1930s for a ballplayer.

**diamond ball** [softball term] A forerunner of modern softball. The term came into use as a replacement for *kitten ball* in 1922 by the Minneapolis Park Board. The first group that tried to organize softball on a national scale was the National Diamond Ball Association, which was founded in 1925 and continued until the formation of the Amateur Softball Association of America in 1933.

**diamond bug** *n./arch.* A term used during the 1930s for a baseball fan.

**diamondeer** *arch.* A term used during the 1930s for a ballplayer.

**dick 1.** See *house dick.* **2.** See *Dick Smith.*

**Dick Howser Trophy** A trophy given annually to the best college baseball player in the United States. Howser was a popular shortstop and manager who died of cancer in 1987.

**Dick Smith** A loner; a sponger or freeloader; a player who won't be one of the boys, who travels and eats alone, and, according to Dizzy Dean, "seldom ever treats."

Tom Laird (*Collier's,* Mar. 22, 1940; Peter Tamony), writing about Joe and Dom DiMaggio, asked Joe if his younger brother will be "a Dick Smith"; Joe replied: "Not if I can help it. That was one of my big mistakes—being a lone wolf. I was afraid to talk about anything, not only to the newspapermen but to my teammates as well, and I got to be known as a Dick Smith."

Peter Tamony (*Newsletter and Wasp,* Sept. 15, 1939) noted that the term was virtually unknown to fans, but common among players. "He [the generalized "Dick Smith"] is the man who has never been known to say 'Here's how' to anyone. If he is treated he does not return the favor, and if in company he is the chap who never picks up the check."

**Etymology/1st Use.** 1876. Dick Smith clearly does not appear to be the name of an old ballplayer, as has often been asserted. Tamony notes that Dick Smith "must have been a well known character before baseball became the national pastime" for he is mentioned in the *Congressional Record* (June 29, 1876) and his name is there used as a synonym for "sponging." The term came up in the context of the custom of the House of Representatives to provide lemonade and iced tea for its members in the warm months. The drinks were paid for out of the House contingency fund until the practice was halted by Rep. "Blue-Jean" Smith (Ind.). Members then had the choice of running to the Senate for drinks or drinking "iced Potomac" (river water, which apparently caused its share of illness and intestinal distress). In supporting a bill to rectify this, Rep. Conger (Mich.) proposed that the House enable itself "to supply the necessary wants of its members, without either playing 'Dick Smith' on the Senate or leaving so many of its members confined to their rooms by sickness resulting from drinking iced Potomac."

Tamony examined the *Dictionary of American Biography* and found that there was, in fact, a well-known person whose reputation was such that it could have become an eponym for sponging. Richard Penn Smith (1799–1854) fit the bill. Tamony wrote: "In 1821 he published a series of moral and literary essays under the title of 'The Plagiary.' Between 1825 and 1833 he wrote twenty plays, of which fifteen were performed. Some of these plays were of extreme and lasting popularity, and Smith is given much space in the histories of the drama in America. But Smith was a practical playwright. For his dramas he depended mainly on foreign writers for his inspiration. Did this plagiarism, this dependence on others for ideas and inspiration, make Smith's name a synonym for sponging? It is very likely that it did."

**Extended Use.** H. L. Mencken (*The American Language, Suppl. II,* 1948) notes that the term is also used on the racetrack. Tamony finds it as a logger's term for a drink of liquor consumed privately and a bar term for a lone drinker. Columnists from Damon Runyon to Charles McCabe have used the term in the context of bar culture. "One proprietor I know has a great fancy for Irish bartenders, and for a peculiar reason. He knows they are addicted to Dick Smithing and other weaknesses." (Charles McCabe, *San Francisco Chronicle,* Dec. 17, 1974; Peter Tamony).

**die 1.** To be left on base at the end of an inning. **2.** To be put out; to be "retired." **1st Use.** 1880. (Chicago *Inter-Ocean,* June 29; Edward J. Nichols). **3.** To have failed; to have had a bad day at the ballpark. **4.** To be released from the team; e.g., players refer to a player who has just been released as having "died" (Rick Wolff, *New York Times,* Apr. 23, 1989).

**die-hard** [softball term] A softball player who plays in six or more competitive tournaments in a year. There are approximately four million die-hards in the United States.

**differentials** Dizzy Dean's term for "credentials" when he was in broadcasting.

**dig 1.** *n.* The movement on a breaking ball. A press release from the Univ. of Denver on Mile High Stadium noted: "Knuckleballs and curveballs will have less 'dig' in Denver: A 14-inch curveball at sea level will curve only 11 inches in Denver." **2.** *v.* An exhortation to the batter-runner to run fast.

**dig in 1.** To twist one's spikes into the dirt of the batter's box; esp. with the back foot, to gain better traction for swinging the bat; to anchor one's self in the batter's box. **2.** To focus one's concentration on a key play or situation.

**dig out** To field successfully a poorly thrown ball or one that bounces in the dirt; e.g., a first baseman must learn how to "dig out of the dirt" a wild throw from the shortstop. **1st Use.** 1909. (Burt L. Standish, *Frank Merriwell's Schooldays;* Edward J. Nichols).

**dilly 1.** *arch.* A spectacular hit. **2.** A great player. "Pittsburgh may be a one-man team, but that man [Honus Wagner] is a 'dilly'" (New York Giants pitcher Hooks Wiltse, quoted in *New York American,* Aug. 9, 1908; Peter Morris).

**dime** A tight spinning slider. Compare *quarter.*

**dime hit** Syn. of *scratch hit.* **1st Use.** 1907. (*New York Evening Journal,* May 8; Edward J. Nichols).

**dimensions** The particular measurements of a given ballpark, both in terms of overall size and of the playing field itself. By extension, the term also serves to underscore the differences among ballparks.

**dime player** An infielder who lacks hustle and spirit; one who cannot or will not "get off the dime."

**dime 'ya** For a pitcher to display exceptional control. When speaking of a particularly capable pitcher, Casey Stengel was known to say: "He can dime 'ya."

**ding** To get a base hit or score a run; e.g., "The Expos dinged Smith for single runs in the second and third innings."

**ding-dong** A cry yelled from the dugout when the catcher takes a foul tip off his protective cup.

**dinger** A *home run.* "Bang, there goes another one. It seems every day in baseball is dinger day" (*USA Today,* June 30, 1987).

**dink 1.** To hit a slow ground ball; e.g., "Smith dinked a grounder to the pitcher." **2.** To pitch a slow ball; e.g., "Jones dinked up a junk pitch." **1st Use.** 1916. (*American Magazine,* Aug.; Edward J. Nichols).

**dinky-doo** Syn. of *dipsy-doodle.*

**dinky fly** A batted ball that goes neither high nor far and is easily caught.

**dinner tongs** *arch.* A player's hands. "'Blondy' Moeller . . . allowed the ball to ooze through his dinner tongs" (Edward M. Thierry, *Baseball Magazine,* Sept. 1909). Syn. *lunch hooks.*

**dip** To go downward when a forkball is thrown.

**dipsy-doodle 1.** A slow, tantalizing curveball. **2.** Any odd-breaking pitch, such as a sharp curveball or a suspected spitter. "Say, that's a regular dipsy-doodle you got there! . . . How do you do it, Professor?" (Valentine Davies, *It Happens Every Spring,* 1949; Charles D. Poe). **1st Use.** 1932. (*Baseball Magazine,* Oct.; Edward J. Nichols). **3.** A swinging strikeout. Pioneer sportscaster Rosey Rowswell in Pittsburgh called such an out "the old dipsey-doodle." **Usage Note.** Variations of the term include "dipsey-doodle," "dipsey-dow," "dipso-do," "dipsy-dew," "dipsy-do," "dipsy-doo," *"dypsydo,"* and *"dinky-doo."* Edward J. Nichols comments: "This uncertainty as to spelling is typical of terms invented by the players rather than the sports reporters." A dipsy-doodle is a quick, sliding motion of the body, such as that made by a ballcarrier to evade tacklers in football.

**dipsy-doodler** A pitcher who throws a dipsy-doodle. Gayle Talbot (Associated Press dispatch, Oct. 3, 1952) characterized Ed Lopat as "the greatest of the dipsy-doodlers."

**dirt** The ground around home plate and the basepaths; e.g., the "ball is in the dirt" indicates a low pitch. See also *hit the dirt.*

**dirt ball** A pitched ball that lands in the dirt, usually just in front of or alongside the plate, that is difficult to handle. Also spelled "dirtball."

**dirter** A term used by Casey Stengel for a ground ball.

**dirt save** A save credited to a catcher when he deflects a legally pitched ball that goes in the dirt which, in the official scorer's judgment, prohibited any and all baserunners from advancing. The term was introduced in 1988 and included on the scorecard of Memphis State Univ.'s baseball games for three seasons.

**dirty ball** Dishonest or unsportsmanlike play. **1st Use.** 1902. (*Sporting Life,* July 12; Edward J. Nichols).

**disabled list** A list of players who have been removed from the team for a specified period because of illness or injury. The period of inactivity has varied over the years, including 15, 21, 30, and 60 days. It was originally one month for severely injured players; later three weeks in 1966 and two weeks in 1970. A player on the disabled list remains on the roster, but the team is permitted to add a substitute player during the time the disabled player is out of action. See also *injury list.* Abbrev. and syn. *DL.*

**discernible stop** The pause at the belt by a pitcher in the set position following his stretch and before releasing the ball toward the plate or throwing it to a base. Failure to come to such a stop results in a balk. See also *stop position.*

**Disco Demolition Night** A promotional event held on July 12, 1979, by the Chicago White Sox at Comiskey Park in which there would be a gigantic bonfire between games, during which thousands of disco records would be burned; it resulted in the White Sox forfeiting the second game of a doubleheader to the Detroit Tigers as about 6,000 fans poured onto the field, drinking beer, ripping up the turf, and improvising fires. Thirty-seven fans were arrested.

**dish** Syn. of *home plate,* an obvious play on the word "plate." See also *platter.* **1st Use.** 1907. (*New York Evening Journal,* Apr. 17; Edward J. Nichols).

**dislodged base** [softball term] A base that is displaced from its proper position. A baserunner is not penalized for a dislodged base, nor is the runner expected to tag a base that is far out of its proper position.

**disputed** Applied to an umpire's call or to an entire game whose outcome is being questioned by one of the teams.

**distance** See *go the distance.*

**dive 1.** To slide into a base headfirst. **2.** To reach over the plate to hit an outside pitch.

**divide a pair** To split a doubleheader.

**diving catch** An acrobatic catch in which a fielder throws himself headfirst to the ground to reach the ball. It is one of the more dramatic ways a player shows off his fielding skills. Dan Sperling (*A Spectator's Guide to Baseball,* 1983) notes: "Diving catches made at the 'hot corner' are perhaps the most remarkable of all, because third basemen usually have only a split-second in which to react."

**Division** One of the three classifications (East, Central, and West) of the teams in the American League and in the National League that has its own standings throughout the regular season.

**division** One of two informal classifications determined by the standings of the eight teams in the American League (1901–60) and in the National League (1900–61) and of the ten teams in the American League (1961–68) and in the National League (1962–68). A team that finished among the top four (later, five) was in the first division and one that finished among the bottom four (later, five) was in the second division.

**Division Series** One of two sets of playoff games (best three of five) among the three Division winners and a wild card in each of the major leagues (National League and American League) to determine the two teams in each league to play in the *Championship Series.* The series began in 1995 when the third Division and the wild card were first introduced. Many argue that a best-of-seven format is a better way to test the clubs involved.

**DL 1.** Abbrev. for *disabled list.* **2.** *n.* Syn. of *disabled list;* e.g., "Smith went on the DL for the second time." **3.** *v.* To put on the disabled list. "If he can play in a week, we don't DL him [B. J. Surhoff]." (Davey Johnson, quoted in *Boston Globe,* April 24, 1997).

**do a Casey** To fail in the manner of *Casey,* the figure in Ernest L. Thayer's 1888 poem, "Casey at the Bat"; specif., to strike out. Syn. *pull a Casey.* **1st Use.** 1926. "To fan out, to fail to make a hit" (Clement Wood, *A Dictionary of American Slang;* David Shulman).

**do a Sammy Vick** To overeat. Sammy Vick (a New York Yankees outfielder from 1917 to 1920) was "noted for possessing one of the most voracious appetites in the big leagues" (Babe Ruth, *Babe Ruth's Own Book of Baseball,* 1928).

**doctor 1.** *v.* To gain an edge, by secretly tampering with the bat, ball, or home field. Most doctoring is both difficult to detect and illegal. Real or imagined doctoring has led to some of the most heated and prolonged debates in baseball. See also *doctor the ball; doctor the bat; doctor the grounds.* **2.** *n.* A temporary nickname for someone caught or suspected of the act of doctoring. **Etymology.** The term was applied to baseball high jinks long after establishing itself elsewhere as a term for secret product adulteration. "There is very little beer that is not 'doctored' and made even worse than in its original state by deleterious drugs" (John B. Gough, *Sunlight and Shadow, At Home and Abroad,* 1881; Peter Tamony).

**doctored ball** A baseball that has been altered purposely to affect its flight when pitched. See also *marked ball.*

**doctored bat** A baseball bat that has been altered illegally. In 1994, Albert Belle was given a 10-day suspension for using a doctored bat. Compare *altered bat.* See also *corked bat; hollow bat.*

**doctored grounds** A playing area that has been modified to improve the performance of the home team.

**Dr. Longball** A home run; e.g., "Dr. Longball made a house call at Fenway Park today." Baltimore Orioles manager Earl Weaver created the term: he often described hitting a home run as a "call to Dr. Longball." See also *long ball*, 1.

**doctor the ball** To do something illegal to the ball to make it move erratically after it has been pitched. This may involve the use of a substance or damage to the ball. Any list of agents that have been used to doctor balls would include: BB shot, bottle cap, dirt, emery paper, licorice, nutmeg grater, oil, paraffin, phonograph needle, pine tar, resin, slippery elm, spikes, spit, talcum powder, K-Y jelly, and Vaseline.

**doctor the bat** To modify a baseball bat for the advantage of the batter, usually to make the bat lighter and livelier while maintaining the mass of a heavier bat. This feat is accomplished by drilling out a hole in the heavy end of the bat and leaving a hollow spot or filling it with a light material such as cork. The hole is hidden with a plug of wood shavings and glue. See also *corking*.

**doctor the grounds** To modify the home field or its boundaries to give the home team the advantage; e.g., to keep a spot near first base wet or soft to deter an especially good base stealer or to raise, lower, or tilt the pitching mound in the visitors' bullpen to confuse pitchers who warm up on an unconventional mound but then perform on a conventional one. "I'm not accusing the Yankees of doctoring the infield but it's very thick-sodded and that's certainly a great help to their infield" (Detroit Tigers manager Jack Tighe, quoted in an Associated Press dispatch, May 1, 1958; Peter Tamony). See also *Cobb's Lake*.

**do damage** To score one or more runs.

**Dodger blue** The color of the Los Angeles Dodgers. The term is used in reference to the uniform or the team; e.g., manager Tommy Lasorda is so loyal that he "bleeds Dodger blue."

**Dodger Stadium** Home field of the Los Angeles Dodgers from 1962 to the present. It is located in Chavez Ravine on a hill overlooking downtown Los Angeles, Calif. The Dodgers moved there from the Los Angeles Memorial Coliseum where

they had been since 1958. Between 1962 and 1965, it was also the home field of the American League California Angels, who chose to call the park Chavez Ravine instead of Dodger Stadium.

**Dodgertown** A 450-acre complex in Vero Beach, Fla., where the Los Angeles Dodgers hold spring training. Dreamed up in 1949 by Branch Rickey when he was president of the Brooklyn Dodgers, it soon got the reputation as the most progressive and well-equipped of the spring camps. Arthur Daley (*New York Times,* March 18, 1956) described Dodgertown: "It is a factory that rolls ball players off an assembly line with the steady surge of Fords popping out of the River Rouge plant." Today it features two golf courses, a conference center, and villas for the players. Streets are named for Dodger greats.

**dodge the bullet** To get out of a threatening situation, esp. appropriate to pitchers. **Etymology.** Bert Dunne (*Folger's Dictionary of Baseball,* 1958) suggests that the term is a literal and graphic reference to the infielder who "lifts his leg" to get out of the way of a hard-hit ground ball.

**do-fer pitch** A term used by pitcher Tommy John for a pitch that will work ("do-fer awhile") until the pitcher gets something else working (*Tampa Tribune,* July 21, 1987).

**doghouse** A figurative place of exile for a player who has displeased the manager; e.g., a player who is in a lot of trouble is "deep in the doghouse." Boston Red Sox manager John McNamara was known as "a manager without a doghouse" (*New York Times,* Oct. 23, 1986).

**dog it 1.** To malinger; to slow down for a minor ache or pain. "[Houston Astros pitcher J. R.] Richard had been complaining of injuries all season, and his teammates had thought he was 'dogging' it. . . . When the true seriousness of Richard's injuries became known, the team pulled together and became a winning unit." (Edwin Silberstang, *Playboy's Guide to Baseball Betting,* 1982; Charles D. Poe). **2.** To not play one's best; to play lazily. The term is often applied to a batter-runner who does not try to beat the ball to first base or to a fielder who backs away from a sharply hit ball. **1st**

**Use.** 1911. "I've seen plenty of his kind before; he'll dog it, I tell you" (Charles Van Loan, *The Big League;* David Shulman).

**dog meat** A utility player.

**dog robber** A derisive name for an umpire.

**dollar 1.** A .100 batting average. See also *buck.* **2.** One hundred points of batting average; e.g., "Smith is still batting below the two-dollar [.200] mark."

**dome** One of several enclosed ballparks used for baseball and other sports, all of which (to date) have "dome" in their names; e.g., Metrodome (Minneapolis), Skydome (Toronto), Kingdome (Seattle), and Astrodome (Houston), the original enclosed ballpark.

**domeball** Baseball played in a domed ballpark. The term is used to emphasize the differences between indoor and outdoor baseball; e.g., the type of baseball played on artificial turf under a dome. ("Inside Information: The Mysteries of Domeball," *Sport* magazine, Apr. 1984).

**dome dong** Syn. of *domerun.*

**dome-field advantage** The real or imagined edge held by a team playing in a domed ballpark, due to fan support and familiarity with the dimensions and physical features under the dome. The term is a play on the concept of *home-field advantage.*

**Dome Head** A Houston Astros fan in the Astrodome. "The Astrodome, which Larry McMurtry first likened to the 'working end of a gigantic roll-on deodorant,' rocks with standing-room-only crowds of Dome Heads as the Astros challenge the Mets in a best-of-seven series for the National League pennant" (David Maraniss, *Washington Post,* Oct. 9, 1986).

**domerun** A home run hit in a domed ballpark, such as the "cheap" home runs that can be hit in Seattle's Kingdome, whose configuration and controlled atmosphere can be kind to powerful hitters who find it easier to hit home runs under a dome. Clearly implied is that the domerun would not have been a home run if hit in a traditional open-air ballpark.

**dong** A home run. "He's [Brady Anderson] got 15 dongs and leading the league" (Billy Ripken, quoted in *Boston Globe,* Apr. 6, 1996).

**donkey** A rookie or a minor-league player up for a tryout with a major-league team.

**donkey baseball** A baseball game played for laughs by players mounted on donkeys. Although still staged, such intentional fiascos are not as popular as they once were.

**donnybrook 1.** A high-scoring game. **2.** An inordinately wild fight among baseball players.

**don the spikes** To take part in a baseball game.

**"don't lose the glove"** A traditional barb yelled by the opposition to a player who is a good fielder but not much of a hitter.

**donut 1.** Syn. of *doughnut.* **2.** A rubber circle that some batters wear on their thumbs while batting to cut down on the painful reverberation of the bat. **3.** Syn. of *cookie-cutter.*

**do one's chores** To perform well in a game.

**doorkeeper** The first baseman. Harry Grayson (*They Played the Game,* 1944) on Hal Chase: "No doorkeeper played as deep and far from the bag."

**doozy marooney** An extra-base hit. The term was coined by pioneer Pittsburgh Pirates broadcaster Rosey Rowswell and often stated as "the ol' doozy marooney."

**dope 1.** Inside information or opinion. "The dope will prove that a care-free player will do better than one who carries his troubles on the diamond" (S. DeWitt Clough, *Letters from a Baseball Fan to His Son,* 1910). **1st Use.** 1902. (*Sporting Life,* Sept. 20; Edward J. Nichols). **2.** *arch.* The curve and speed of a pitched ball; a pitcher's *stuff,* 1. **3.** [softball term] A substance other than rosin that a pitcher puts on his hands. **Etymology.** Alfred H. Holt (*Phrase Origins,* 1936) wrote: "Though cursed with a multiplicity of uses in American slang, the little word seems to be traceable in almost every sense to the Dutch 'doop' (pronounced 'dope'), a thick liquid or sauce." Holt notes that one form of dope is any drug used to stimulate a horse in a race. To have knowledge of this may have lead to the idea of inside or secret information as "dope."

**dope book** A reference book that contains baseball records and statistics. **Etymology.** Peter Tamony noted that a "dope-book" in the earlier context of horse racing is a book containing a chart of previous performances of racehorses. The slang verb "dope," for "to figure out," is at play here.

**dopester** One who compiles baseball statistics and other information. **1st Use.** 1915. (*Baseball Magazine,* Dec.; Edward J. Nichols).

**"do they show movies on a flight like that?"** A colorful quip about a long, high home run. Similar aviation reference to a home run is the line: "That ball traveled so far that it should have a stewardess on it."

**double 1.** *n.* A hit on which the batter reaches second base safely. Abbrev. *D,* 3; *2B,* 3. Syn. *two-baser; two-base hit; two-sacker; two-bagger; two-cushion shot; double bagger; keystone hit.* **1st Use.** 1880. (*Brooklyn Daily Eagle,* Aug. 27; Edward J. Nichols). **2.** *n.* A double play. **3.** *v.* To hit a double; e.g., "Smith doubled twice in the same game." **4.** *v.* To complete a double play; e.g., "White doubled Brown at first."

**Double A** Syn. of *Class AA.*

**double bagger** Syn. of *double,* 1.

**double bill** Syn. of *doubleheader.*

**double clutch** A motion made by a fielder in which he pumps his arm once before throwing the ball. It gives extra velocity to the throw. Syn. *double pump,* 2.

**double curve** The fanciful pitch that breaks twice on its way to the plate, as thrown by the fictional Dan Manly (George C. Jenks, *Double Curve Dan, the Pitcher Detective,* 1888). See also *double shoot.*

**Doubleday myth** The controversial claim that General Abner Doubleday invented baseball in 1839 in Cooperstown, N.Y. Though Doubleday never claimed to have invented the game, credit was given to him after his death by Albert G. Spalding and a commission formed to prove that

MAJOR ABNER DOUBLEDAY,

**Doubleday myth.** *A Union officer stationed at Fort Sumter, S.C., Doubleday's involvement with baseball has long been debunked.*

baseball was a purely American creation. Since then, its debunkers have become legion. "The Doubleday myth, however, is as much a part of our culture as George Washington's chopped-down cherry tree" (Bill Tammeus, *Kansas City Star,* Aug. 21, 1986).

The debunkers have had a field day creating lines on the subject. "Abner Doubleday didn't invent baseball," wrote Harold Peterson (*The Man Who Invented Baseball,* 1973). "Baseball invented Abner Doubleday." Sportswriter Bob Allison once said: "Columbus didn't discover America either, but he was the one who made it pay." See also *Cartwright myth.* **1st Use.** 1936. "The Myth of Doubleday," headline for column by Joe Williams (*New York World-Telegram,* June 13; Barry Popik).

**double duty pitcher** A pitcher who, within a single season or over the course of a career, is used both as a starting pitcher and as a relief pitcher. Few pitchers have matched the combined effort in this regard of Woodie Fryman who had 322 starts and 303 relief appearances over the course of his career (1966–83).

**double elimination 1.** [softball term] A tournament format by which a team must be defeated twice before it is eliminated from play. It is the dominant format in the higher levels of the game as it ensures that a top team will not be eliminated too early in the tournament and that the weaker teams have two chances. See also *round-robin; single elimination.* **2.** A tournament format used until 1987 in the College World Series for its eight finalists by which a team must be defeated twice before it is eliminated from play. The National Collegiate Association of America switched to a final-four format for the 1988 season.

**double figures** Any baseball statistic (runs, hits, steals, etc.) between 10 and 99.

**doubleheader** *n.* A set of two games played in succession on the same day between the same two teams and to which spectators are admitted for the price of a single game. Traditionally, there is a 20-minute break between games. Some doubleheaders (such as the *day-night doubleheader*) have separate admissions. Historically, there have been two reasons for doubleheaders: postponements of previously scheduled games and games scheduled in advance as a means of attracting fans. The first major-league doubleheader took place on Sept. 25, 1882, between Worcester and Providence of the National League. Doubleheaders are becoming rarer in the major leagues: "Like the movie double features, the baseball doubleheader is on the verge of extinction" (*Forbes,* Mar. 9, 1987). See also *twinight doubleheader.* Abbrev. *DH.* Formerly spelled "double header"; "double-header." Syn. *double bill; twin bill; bargain bill.* **1st Use.** 1896. "In case rain should stop to-day's or tomorrow's games double headers will have to be played the next day as there is no open time in the new Pittsburgh series to play off any postponed games" (*Cincinnati Enquirer,*

July 20; Mitford Mathews, *A Dictionary of Americanisms,* 1951). **Etymology.** Dating back to the 1870s, the term was used in railroad circles to describe a railway train having two engines or two trains traveling so close together that they move as one. "The two extras were bowling along merrily when they struck this grade; and although there is a time card rule that says that trains will be kept ten minutes apart, they were right together, helping each other over the grade. In fact, it was one train with two engines, something of a double header with the second engine in the middle." (Jasper Ewing Brady, *Tales of the Telegraph: The Story of a Telegrapher's Life and Adventures in Railroad, Commercial and Military Work,* 1900). Because railroad doubleheaders could be used to economize on labor they became an issue in the railroad strikes of 1877. **Extended Use.** Two paired or consecutive events; e.g., "A doubleheader at the big prison is the simultaneous execution of two inmates in the state's pale green gas chamber" (*San Francisco Examiner,* July 4, 1967; Peter Tamony). In his book *The Scotch* (1964) John Kenneth Galbraith talks of two back-to-back one-hour sermons which he terms "a devotional doubleheader."

**double hit** The rare situation in which the batter's bat actually hits the ball twice. It usually occurs on a lightly hit ball when a batter accidentally lets go of the bat. Moving faster than the rolling ball, the bat catches up to it and hits it again. The batter who accomplishes this feat is summarily called out by the plate umpire.

**double killing** Syn. of *double play.*

**double-name job** The locker of a rookie in an overcrowded spring-training camp. "This is rookie talk. When spring training camps are crowded with players from all over the system there aren't enough individual lockers to go around. The rookies are asked to double up. That means there are two names hung over the locker, both with astronomically high uniform numbers, like 73 and 94. That's the kind of number you get when you're in one of those double-name jobs." (Leonard Shecter, *Baseball Digest,* June 1963).

**double off** To be caught off base and put out

before tagging up after the batter has flied or lined out, resulting in a double play; e.g., "Smith was doubled off when Jones caught Brown's line drive at first base."

**double play** A defensive play in which two players are put out as a result of continuous action, providing that no error is committed between putouts. Both outs must occur between the time the ball leaves the pitcher's hand and is returned to him on the pitcher's mound. Speaking for many fans, reporter Alistair Cooke once said: "Next to a triple play, baseball's double play is the most exciting and graceful thing in sports." Abbrev. *DP.* Syn. *double killing; twin killing; two-ply killing.* **1st Use.** 1858. (Chadwick Scrapbooks; Edward J. Nichols). **Etymology.** Shortstop George Wright has been credited with having made the first double play while playing for the Cincinnati Red Stockings. Wright supposedly used the hidden-ball trick. However, Edward J. Nichols revealed a published reference to the double play before the Red Stockings came into being in 1866. **Extended Use.** Two accomplishments made at the same time.

**double-play ball** A ground ball hit to a fielder at a speed and location ideal for turning an easy double play.

**double-play combination** The shortstop and the second baseman collectively, because the most common double play involves a precisely timed maneuver between these two players. The shortstop or second baseman fields the ball and tosses it to his teammate who steps on second base to force the runner coming from first and then throws on to that base to retire the batter. "But the day when he [second baseman Billy Ripken] forms a double-play combination with his brother Cal may not be that far away" (*Washington Times,* Feb. 26, 1987).

**double-play depth** The positions taken by the shortstop and second baseman to enhance the possibility of turning a double play. The positions are taken when there are fewer than two outs and first base is occupied.

**double-play pivot** Syn. of *cross-over pivot.*

**double pump 1.** The part of a pitcher's windup when he throws his arms back over his head twice

before delivering the ball. See also *pump,* 1. **2.** Syn. of *double clutch.*

**double shoot** The fanciful curveball that veers in two different directions on its way to the plate, as thrown by the fictional Frank Merriwell (Burt L. Standish, *Frank Merriwell's Danger,* 1897). See also *double curve.*

**double steal** A strategic baserunning maneuver in which two baserunners advance to the next base without the aid of a hit, error, balk, base on balls, or hit batter. Usually employed when first base and second base are occupied, it is a risky play that is not easy to execute, hence it is something of a rarity. See also *delayed double steal.* **1st Use.** 1897. (*New York Tribune,* July 6; Edward J. Nichols).

**double switch** A lineup shuffle used to get a good batter into the pitcher's place in the batting

Double steal.

order while bringing in a relief pitcher. It usually comes in the late innings of a close game in the National League or at any other level of the game where there is no designated hitter. It occurs on defense as the manager removes the pitcher for a reliever. Knowing that the pitcher's turn in the batting order is coming up in the next offensive inning, the manager brings in the reliever as well as a second new defensive player. The new player who is not the pitcher (and presumably a good hitter) is inserted into the pitcher's spot and the new pitcher is put in the spot from which the original player has been removed.

**double up** To retire or be retired by a double play. The term is usually applied to the second player to be put out; e.g., "Jones is out, Smith is doubled up" or "The shortstop tagged Jones and doubled up Smith by throwing to first." **1st Use.** 1880. (Chicago *Inter-Ocean,* Aug. 2; Edward J. Nichols).

**doughnut** A common name for the heavy, circular *bat weight* used by batters warming up in the on-deck circle. It is a modern alternative to the earlier practice of warming up by swinging two bats at once. It was introduced by New York Yankees catcher Elston Howard in the early 1960s and, according to the *The Sporting News,* was in use in most spring-training camps by 1968. Marketed originally as "Elston Howard's On-Deck Bat-Weight," it was immediately dubbed the "doughnut" or "iron doughnut" by those who used it. "The purpose of the weight is to help a batter in such areas as speeding up his swing and developing stronger wrists and forearms," said Howard (*The Sporting News,* Apr. 27, 1968), who added that it also loosened shoulders, would fit over the bat actually used during a game, and could be removed by simply tapping the bat handle against the ground. Syn. *donut,* 1.

**down 1.** *adj.* Syn. of *out,* 1; e.g., "two down" is two out. **1st Use.** 1888. (Chicago *Inter-Ocean,* July 12; Edward J. Nichols). **Extended Use.** Tim Considine (*The Language of Sport,* 1982) states that when one says "two down, one to go," it is a borrowing from baseball. **2.** *adj.* Defeated or trailing the opposing team. **3.** *adv.* Toward second base from home plate. An item in *American Speech* (Dec.

1956) comments on the confusing terminology of directional words: "The pitcher who stands on a mound to deliver the ball, throws his pitches up to the plate; whereas the catcher . . . pegs the ball down to second. Oddly enough, the same pitcher while in the process of warming up is described as throwing down to his receiver, and none of the fielders is said to throw up to the plate." **4.** *adv.* Toward home plate from the mound. **5.** *adj.* Said of a low pitched ball; e.g., "Smith threw the pitch down and away." **6.** *v.* To defeat in a baseball game; e.g., "The Giants downed the Dodgers last night."

**down and away** Syn. of *low and outside.*

**down-and-up** *arch.* Syn. of *pop-up slide.* **1st Use.** 1935. "There are several variations on the feetfirst slide, as the hook, fall-away, down-and-up, etc." (Ralph H. Barbour, *How to Play Better Baseball;* David Shulman).

**downer** An overhand curveball that drops close to the batter's ankles. Syn. *dropball; sinker,* 2.

**down shoot** *arch.* A pitched ball that drops precipitously as it nears home plate. Compare *upshoot,* 1.

**downstairs** The location of a ball that is pitched low. Compare *upstairs,* 2.

**down the chute** Syn. of *down the middle,* 2.

**down the cock** Syn. of *down the middle,* 2.

**down the line 1.** *adj.* Said of a batted ball that closely follows a foul line, esp. a base hit along the side of either foul line. **2.** *n.* A home run hit at Yankee Stadium because of a shorter-than-most distance for the ball to travel.

**down the middle 1.** Said of the four defensive players positioned along the imaginary center line of the field from home plate to center field and who are said to anchor the defense: catcher, second baseman, shortstop, and center fielder. "But we've got to be solid down the middle or none of us will look good to anyone" (Brooks Robinson, *Third Base is My Home,* 1974; Charles D. Poe). **Usage Note.** In what seems contradictory, in baseball parlance, a synonym for "down the middle" is *up the middle,* 2. **2.** Said of a pitch, usually a fastball, that is delivered straight through or splits the center or middle of the strike zone, thereby becoming an inviting pitch to hit. Such a pitch, if taken by the batter, is said to be an "automatic" strike. "But all Jones wanted was an out and the first ball was down the middle for a strike" (Dick Friendlich, *Relief Pitcher,* 1964; Charles D. Poe). Syn. *down the chute; down the cock; down the pike; down the pipe;* "down the alley"; *right down Broadway.*

**down the pike** Syn. of *down the middle,* 2.

**down the pipe** Syn. of *down the middle,* 2.

**down the river** Said of a trade or sale that sends a player to the minor leagues or a team that is lower in the standings.

**down the slot** Across the plate. "However, a third fast ball down the slot seemed to find him unprepared for again he was late swinging and got underneath the pitch, raising a pop fly that climbed in front of the plate" (Dick Friendlich, *Relief Pitcher,* 1964; Charles D. Poe).

**down the stretch** Said of the last four to five weeks of the regular season.

**down to the wire** Said of a game or season whose final outcome is not known until the last play or game, respectively.

**downtown 1.** *n.* The figurative landing site of a deep home run ball. Hitting a home run is often referred to as "going downtown." Compare *suburbs,* 1. **2.** *v.* To hit a long home run. "Come on, Lefty, downtown one and gag those bench jockeys" (Edward R. Walsh, USAir in-flight magazine, Sept.

**Downtown.** *Ted Williams drives one out of Fenway Park, circa 1948.*

1982). **Etymology.** Peter Tamony suggested that the term had an early association with outfielder Ollie Lee Brown. It started in 1964 when he was a member of the minor-league team in Fresno that played on the outskirts of town. According to Tamony's notes, the fans came up with the cheer, "Hit it downtown, Ollie." Writer Charles Einstein adds and predates Tamony (letter, Mar. 5, 1990): "When he [Brown] later came up to the San Francisco Giants, he did pick up the nickname 'Downtown' Brown, at least partially for the euphony, and he may have had it at Fresno. But the term was in use before that. I myself was using it in 1961 while covering the Giants at spring training, as a generic to describe balls disappearing far over the left field wall—with inordinate frequency, in that dry, thin air—in the direction of downtown Phoenix, which was only a few blocks north of the crackerbox old park at Central and Mohave, where the club trained in those days."

**downtowner** A home run. "[Reggie Jackson's] startling production of downtowners (forty to date) may bring him within range of Roger Maris' record by mid-September" (Roger Angell, *The Summer Game,* 1972; Charles D. Poe).

**DP 1.** Box score and scorecard abbrev. for *double play.* **2.** [softball term] Abbrev. for *designated player.*

**draft 1.** *n.* One of several established procedures by which teams acquire players from a choice group so that each team receives some of the most promising players. See also *free-agent draft; free-agent reentry draft; minor-league draft.* **1st Use.** 1905. (*Sporting Life,* Sept. 2; Edward J. Nichols). **2.** *n.* A special selection of players when an expansion team is created; see *expansion draft.* **3.** *v.* To acquire a player in the draft.

**draft pick** A player selected by virtue of the draft.

**drag 1.** To execute a drag bunt. **1st Use.** 1927. (*New York Sun,* July 18; Edward J. Nichols). **2.** To pull a leveling device over the dirt surface of the infield to smooth the surface irregularities caused by the players' spiked shoes.

**drag a piano** To run slowly. A plodding baserunner is one who is "dragging a piano."

**drag bunt** A bunt purposely hit away from the pitcher down the first base line. A properly executed drag bunt is nearly impossible to defense. Seeing the batter setting to bunt, the infielders charge to the spot directly in front of home plate, the most common location of a bunted ball. Meanwhile, the ball trickles along so slowly down the line that the batter is able to beat it to first base. The bunt gets its name because the ball appears as if it is being dragged by the batter on his way to first. With the drag bunt, the batter is bunting for a base hit as opposed to a *sacrifice bunt,* where the batter's primary goal is to advance a runner already on base. Proficient drag bunters included Mickey Mantle, Rod Carew, and Maury Wills. **1st Use.** 1934. "He put everything he had into every pitch after [Goose] Goslin had opened with a double and [Billy] Rogell had beaten out a drag bunt to [Ripper] Collins" (*New York American,* Oct. 8; David Shulman).

**drain** To be exhausted as a starting pitcher; e.g., "Smith was drained by the ninth inning."

**draw 1.** *v.* See *draw a throw.* **2.** *v.* See *draw a walk.* **3.** *n.* The number of people in attendance at a game.

**draw a blank** To fail to score. **1st Use.** 1865. (*New York Herald,* July 25; Edward J. Nichols).

**draw a throw** To make a fielder throw to a base; e.g., a runner at first base takes a large lead to "draw a throw" from the pitcher. Forcing a pitcher or catcher to throw can benefit the offensive team if it causes a wild throw or helps another runner steal. The gist of this strategy is to give the fielder the impression that he can get the runner out. **1st Use.** 1896. (Burt L. Standish, *Frank Merriwell's Schooldays;* Edward J. Nichols).

**draw a walk** To be issued a base on balls.

**draw in** To bring the infielders in closer to the plate in anticipation of a bunt or a play at the plate.

**drawing card** A player who attracts paying customers. Babe Ruth's Hall of Fame plaque states that he was the "greatest drawing card in history of

*Drawing card.*

baseball." **1st Use.** 1895. (*Spalding's Official Base Ball Guide;* Edward J. Nichols).

**drawn game** *obs.* A game that ends with each team having the same number of runs after each has come to bat in the same number of innings. **1st Use.** 1867. (*New York Herald,* July 4; Edward J. Nichols).

**drawn-in infield** A defense in which the infielders are positioned closer to home plate to give them a better chance to throw out a runner at the plate if the batter hits a ground ball. Syn. *drawn-up infield.*

**drawn-in outfield** A defense in which the outfielders are positioned closer than normal to the infield when the potential winning run is at third base with less than two outs.

**drawn-up infield** Syn. of *drawn-in infield.*

**dreamer** A player who is not paying attention to the game.

**dreamer's month** The month of March, because the regular season usually does not get under way until early April and the only games being played are spring-training exhibition games. At this point in the baseball year, anything seems possible for any team. "They call it Dreamer's Month. In March, on paper, every team looks stronger than it did a year ago, and they are counting heavily on a player they got in a trade with a team that no longer wanted him." (Bob Uecker, *Catcher in the Wry,* 1982; Charles D. Poe).

**dream game** The *All-Star Game.* The term used by the press when the Game was first being planned as an event for the Century of Progress Exposition in Chicago in 1933. Although the first game was successful and exciting (Babe Ruth won it with a two-run homer), it was not until the second All-Star Game in 1934 that the "dream game" description seemed to fit. An article by Kenneth B. Byrd (*Baseball Magazine,* Sept. 1934), entitled "Carl Hubbell and the Dream Game," ends: "But we will wager that twenty or thirty years from now the score will be forgotten. All that will be remembered of the classic is the phenomenal pitching performance of Carl Hubbell. He has assured the permanency of the 'dream game' by making it—for Ruth, Gehrig, Foxx, Simmons, and Cronin—a nightmare."

**dream week** A session of a *fantasy baseball camp* in which adults pay to train, work out, and play baseball with ex-players.

**dream weeker** An attendee of dream week.

**dress** Syn. of *suit up.*

**dressing room** An area at a ballpark where the umpires don and doff their clothing and equipment. Compare *clubhouse.* Syn. *locker room.*

**dribble** To hit a ball weakly. "Pinch hitter Mark Jones broke up the no-hitter in the eighth, dribbling a 1-2 inside fastball past the mound" (*Tampa Tribune,* July 26, 1989).

**dribbler** A slow-rolling ground ball or one that bounces in short hops, often hit off the end of the bat or close to the handle. See also *squibber.* **1st Use.** 1915. "The batter hit the next one for a dribbler, and just managed to reach first" (Lester Chadwick, *Baseball Joe in the Big League*).

**drill 1.** *v.* To hit a ball hard, on a straight line and well-placed; to hit a line drive; e.g., "Smith drilled a double to right field." **2.** *v.* To be hit hard or hurt. The term is applied when a player is hit by a thrown, pitched, or batted ball, by a bat, or by collision with another player. "One of the worst feelings in baseball is seeing someone get drilled like that" (Alan Ashby, on Dickie Thon's severe beaning, quoted in *Washington Post,* Oct. 14, 1986). **3.** *v.* To hit a batter with a pitched ball or a runner with a thrown ball. When Bob Sebra hit Tracy Jones with a ball in 1990, he bragged: "I drilled him, I hit him on purpose" (*Tampa Tribune,* July 2, 1990). **4.** *v.* To train players in the basics of baseball. **5.** *n.* A physical conditioning exercise or routine.

**drive 1.** *n.* A hard-hit ball. See also *line drive.* **1st Use.** 1881. (*New York Herald,* July 23; Edward J. Nichols). **2.** *n.* A base hit. **3.** *v.* To hit the ball hard; specif., to hit a ball with strength and quickness to a deep part of the outfield or between the outfielders; e.g., "Smith wants to drive the ball to the alleys." **1st Use.** 1861. (Chadwick Scrapbooks; Edward J. Nichols). **4.** *n.* A campaign; e.g., a "pennant drive."

**drive from the hill** To force a pitcher from the game by getting base hits.

**drive in** To score a baserunner by way of a hit, sacrifice, sacrifice fly, groundout, walk, or other means.

**drive the yellow bus** To pitch with great effectiveness. The term is applied to pitchers of the magnitude of Randy Johnson, who takes large numbers of batters "to school" or "schools" them. The yellow bus refers to the traditional American school bus.

**drive to the showers** To get so many hits off a pitcher that his manager removes him from the game.

**driveway** The path of a pitched baseball; e.g., "Smith watched the curve come down the driveway."

**drizzler** A weakly hit ground ball. **1st Use.** 1912. "[He] pounded out a little drizzler that Sam quickly gathered in and threw to first" (Lester Chadwick, *Baseball Joe of the Silver Stars;* David Shulman).

**drooler** A *spitball,* 1.

**drooper** Syn. of *Texas Leaguer.* **1st Use.** 1932. (*Baseball Magazine,* Oct.; Edward J. Nichols).

**drop 1.** *n.* A pitch that suddenly sinks as it nears the plate. Although the term is still in use, it is now more likely to be called a *sinker.* Syn. *dropball,* 1. **1st Use.** 1890. (*New York Press,* July 16; Edward J. Nichols). **2.** *n.* The sudden downward path of a curveball. **3.** *v.* To mishandle a ball in play, usually resulting in an error. **4.** *v.* To lose a baseball game; e.g., "The Braves dropped the next five games to go into fourth place."

**drop a bunt** To lay down a bunt. Syn. *drop one.*

**dropball 1.** Syn. of *drop,* 1. **1st Use.** 1886. "They have the straight delivery . . . and dropball" (*The Sporting News,* May 24; David Shulman). **2.** Syn. of *downer.* **3.** [softball term] A ball thrown in fast pitch softball with a straight downward spin,

*Dropball.*

with the ball dropping as it comes to the plate, forcing the batter to take a golflike swing. Pitchers use it when they want the batter to hit a ground ball and top pitchers use it to get a strike. It has been likened to the "sinker" in baseball but drops more abruptly and graphically. Syn. *drop pitch,* 2.

**drop down** To pitch sidearm. "Rusty Staub's the last left-handed batter I ever dropped down on . . . and he ripped a pea. . . . I've never dropped down since and won't." (Bob Ojeda, quoted in *USA Today,* June 6, 1986).

**drop off the table** See *off the table.*

**drop one** Syn. of *drop a bunt.*

**dropped ball** A batted ball that is handled by a fielder but not held long enough to constitute a catch.

**dropped third strike** An error charged to the catcher when the third strike on a batter is not caught, providing first base is unoccupied or first base is occupied with two out, and that allows the batter to advance safely to first base. The pitcher is credited with a strikeout even if the batter reaches first base on a dropped third strike.

**dropper** A fly ball that falls in for a hit. **1st Use.** 1876. "[Deacon] White's contribution was a dropper into left field, on which he reached second, while [Cal] McVey scored" (Spalding Scrapbooks, vol. 3; David Shulman).

**drop pitch 1.** A breaking ball that drops sharply as it nears the plate. **2.** [softball term] Syn. of *dropball,* 3.

**drop step** [softball term] A defensive technique that allows the fielder to approach a grounder or fly in the most efficient manner and gain depth on those balls hit away from the fielder.

**drop-the-bat** *obs.* A now-illegal ploy in which the batter would drop his bat during the pitcher's windup to cause a halt in the delivery and a balk. It was once practiced on unexperienced pitchers with runners on second or third.

**drought** An extended period of futility for a hitter, pitcher, or the whole team. "Overdue Bill: Drought Ends for [Bill] Dawley" (*St. Louis Post-Dispatch*

headline, May 29, 1987). Baseball's longest drought is being experienced by the Chicago Cubs, who last won the World Series in 1908. See also *slump,* 1; *dry spell.*

**drub** To defeat decisively. **1st Use.** 1883. (Chicago *Inter-Ocean,* May 24; Edward J. Nichols).

**drunk** Said of the bases when each is occupied by a runner. *Newsweek* (May 15, 1987) commented that the term "sacks are drunk" is baseball slang for the bases are loaded, and noted the old barroom boast: "The bases were loaded and so was I."

**dry-dock** To bench a player; e.g., "The manager intentionally dry-docked Smith with a sore elbow." **Etymology.** A clear borrowing from the dry-docking of ships which are brought out of the sea into an enclosed and drained dock so that repairs can be made below the water line.

**dry spell 1.** A period of no specific duration during which a player remains hitless, does not get on base, drive in any runs, or does anything productive for the team. See also *slump,* 1; *drought.* **2.** A period of time when a starting pitcher is not able to pitch complete games nor win any. See also *drought.* **3.** A period during which a team does not win a pennant or a World Series. See also *drought.*

**dry spitter 1.** A slider that behaves like a spitball and that the batter insists is a spitball (but which, of course, when examined by the umpire, is dry). **2.** *arch.* A term used by pitcher Eddie Cicotte for his *emery ball.* **3.** A baseball that has been unintentionally doctored by the dust on the pitcher's hand.

**dry ups 1.** Dry heaves suffered by a pitcher who gets too nervous before a game. **2.** The times that a relief pitcher warms up without getting into a game.

**dub** *arch.* An inexperienced or poor player.

**ducksnort** Syn. of *dying quail.* The term was used by announcer Ken Harrelson.

**ducks on the pond** The situation when there are runners on the bases (as if they are bobbing about) waiting for a hit to send them home. **1st Use.** 1939. "DiMaggio's runs batted in record would indicate he doesn't hit when there's 'ducks on the pond'" (*San Francisco News,* Aug. 5, 1939;

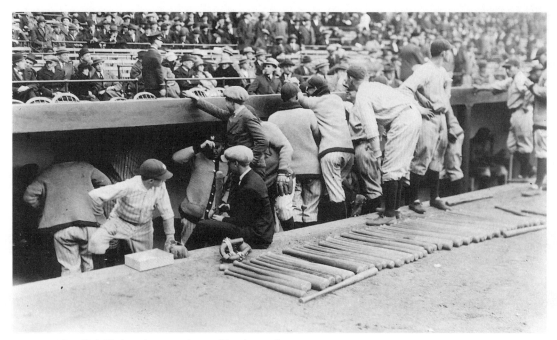

**Dugout.** *New York Yankees dugout replete with* lumberyard.

Peter Tamony). **Etymology.** Coined, or at least brought to baseball, by Washington Senators broadcaster Arch McDonald.

**dues collector** A baseball bat, in the candid vernacular of Reggie Jackson, who, in 1974, "actually took a felt-tip pen and wrote 'Dues Collector' on the sweet spot of his lumber" (Scott Ostler, *Los Angeles Times,* 1986).

**Duffy's cliff** A 10-foot-high mound that formed a steep incline in front of the left field wall in Fenway Park, Boston, from the opening of the park in 1912 until 1933, when it was greatly reduced, but not eliminated. It got its name from Red Sox left fielder Duffy Lewis, who excelled at playing on and around the incline from 1912 to 1917. The original purpose of the mound was as a picnic area for fans who preferred lawn seats.

**dugout** An enclosure for the seating facilities reserved for players and other team members in uniform when they are not in the field. Major-league rules state that the dugout must be roofed and closed at the back and at either end. It gets its name because it is traditionally dug into the ground, with the bench below the playing field. Despite the name, many dugouts are built on top of the ground, especially in parks where amateurs play. Syn. *coop; bench,* 2; *hole,* 4; *pit,* 2. **1st Use.** 1908. "The dugouts of the new-fangled players' benches have been put into good shame" (*Brooklyn Eagle,* Apr. 13; Peter Morris). **Extended Use.** Realm of nonparticipation. When California passed on the first ballot at the 1960 Democratic Convention in which John F. Kennedy was nominated, the *San Francisco Examiner* (July 14, 1960) ran the headline: "State Stayed in the Dugout" (Peter Tamony).

**dugoutese** The inside slang of ballplayers. **1st Use.** 1943. "In fact, even many of the accepted terms usually are sidestepped by most writers . . . everyday dugoutese" (*Baseball Magazine,* Jan.; David Shulman).

**dummy signal** A sign or signal from the catcher, dugout, or coach's box that is meaningless and meant only to mislead and confuse those trying to steal the signal.

**dump 1.** To remove a pitcher from the game; e.g.,

"The manager dumped Smith for Jones in the fourth inning." **2.** See *dump one.* **3.** To hit a baseball; e.g., "Smith dumped a single to left." **4.** To win a baseball game; e.g., "The Giants dumped the Dodgers, 7–3." **5.** To throw or lose a game deliberately. **6.** For an umpire to eject a participant from the game.

**dumper** A player who works to throw or lose a game; a traitor. In discussing the barring of Louisville players in 1877, Leonard Shecter (*The Jocks,* 1969) wrote: "[Louisville] collapsed because in its second season, it collected the dumbest group of dumpers the baseball world has ever known."

**dump list** A list of players who are available for trading or releasing, or who are not protected in an expansion draft.

**dump one** To bunt the ball. **1st Use.** 1922. (*New York Times,* June 4; Edward J. Nichols).

**dungeon** The last place in the standings.

**dunk** To hit a ball that drops quickly.

**dunker** A batted ball that pops up over the infield; a *Texas Leaguer.* **1st Use.** 1937. (*The Sporting News Record Book;* Edward J. Nichols).

**Dunlap** *arch.* A spectacular catch. **1st Use.** 1893. "A volley of cheers followed the drive and doubled in volume when Long was seen to make what the players called a 'Dunlap' or grand-stand catch" (*Donahoe's Magazine,* Aug. 27; David Shulman).

**duro seam** [softball term] A softball that has concealed stitches.

**dust** To pitch a ball deliberately close to the batter. See also *dust off.*

**dust bowl** A particularly dusty field; one that has not been watered down before play begins.

**duster** A pitch thrown so far inside that the batter has to drop to the ground (in the dust) to keep from being hit. Although the distinction is often lost on the batter when one comes his way, a duster is not a beanball because it is not aimed at his head. "Danger in Dusters" (*The Sporting News* headline, June 20, 1970). See also *ear duster.* Syn. *dust-off pitch.* **1st Use.** 1932. (*Baseball Magazine,* Oct.; Edward J. Nichols).

**dusting bee** A game characterized by dusters; a pitching "war" fought with dusters.

**dust off** To pitch a duster. See also *dust.* **1st Use.** 1928. Babe Ruth (*Babe Ruth's Own Book of Baseball*) defined "dusting off" as "making the hitter drop to the ground by pitching at him" (David Shulman).

**dust-off pitch** Syn. of *duster.*

**dust sprayer** A player who slides frequently.

**dustup** Syn. of *rhubarb.*

**dyed-in-the-wool fan** An extremely enthusiastic and loyal fan. **1st Use.** 1902. (*Sporting Life,* Sept. 27; Edward J. Nichols).

**dying quail** A pop fly that drops suddenly and unexpectedly, like a bird that has been shot on the wing. It often falls between fielders for a base hit. A wind blowing in from the outfield may be an important factor. "That was a dying quail single that will look like a line drive in the paper tomorrow" (Brooks Robinson, WMAR telecast, May 29, 1986). Syn. *ducksnort; quail shot; dying seagull; dying swan; wounded duck.*

**dying seagull** A *dying quail* when close to either coast. Peter Tamony notes in his file on the term: "This figure of speech would probably not be familiar to inlanders."

**dying swan** Syn. of *dying quail.* "Then Gil McDougald pumped a dying swan over second base that no one could reach" (Mickey Mantle, *The Mick,* 1985; Charles D. Poe).

**dynamite bat** A bat wielded by a strong, powerful hitter.

**dynasty** A team able to come up with a cluster of championship seasons. The team generally acknowledged to have established the most dynasties is the New York Yankees, who have eight of them, starting with the 1921–23 dynasty. **Usage Note.** For reasons unclear, baseball never has empires or eras but only dynasties. **Etymology.** From the dynasty established by a string of rulers from the same family or group; e.g., the Ming Dynasty in China.

**dypsydo** Syn. of *dipsy-doodle.*

# E

**E 1.** Common box score and scorecard abbrev. for *error*. "[Graig Nettles] still stencils 'E-5' (the score-keeper's shorthand for 'error-third baseman') on his glove to remind him 'to be humble'" (*New York Times,* Aug. 29, 1982). In the ballpark, "E" takes on special meaning as it is flashed on the scoreboard when the official scorer decides that a player has committed an error. (If the official scorer rules a tough chance by a fielder to be a base hit, "H" is flashed on the scoreboard.) One of the more ingenious, if commercial, systems for showing "E" and "H" appeared in Ebbets Field after World War II: it was a huge sign for Schaefer Beer, whose "H" or one "E" lit up when the scorer made his ruling. **2.** Syn. of *error*. **3.** See *Class E.*

**eagle claw** *arch.* A term used in the 1930s for a baseball glove.

**eagle eye** Unusually sharp visual power for judging pitched balls.

**ear bender** A stranger who talks with players in hotels.

**ear duster** A *duster* thrown at or close to the batter's head.

**ear flap** An enlargement of the standard batting helmet that covers the batter's ear on the side facing the pitcher. It began as a Little League safety precaution and, according to Frederic Kelly (*Baltimore Sun,* Apr. 5, 1981) "worked its way into the big leagues when Baltimore's Brooks Robinson adopted it."

**early bloomer** A rookie who looks particularly good in spring training or the early days of the regular season, but who fades quickly and must be dropped from the team. See also *bloomer,* 1.

**early man** A player who takes his batting practice before the players who are in the starting lineup that day. "The 'early men' were those not in the day's lineup, or who needed extra batting practice. The starters monopolized the batting cage once the formal practice began." (Dick Friendlich, *Relief Pitcher,* 1964; Charles D. Poe).

**early reliever** A relief pitcher who is brought into the game in the early innings, usually before the third.

**early shower** The figurative destination of a player ejected from the game by an umpire.

**early swing** A swing at a pitch that is far out in front of the plate. The ball is usually missed altogether or, at best, hit into foul territory.

**earned run** A run that is scored without the aid of an error, passed ball, obstruction, or catcher's interference and that is charged to the pitcher. Compare *unearned run.* Abbrev. *ER.* Syn. *earnie.* **1st Use.** 1871. (*New York Herald,* Sept. 5; Edward J. Nichols).

**earned run average** A pitcher's statistic representing the average number of runs legitimately scored from his deliveries for a full nine-inning game (27 outs). The figure is usually carried to two decimal points. It is computed by multiplying the number of earned runs times 9, which is then divided by the number of innings pitched (9ER/IP); e.g., if a pitcher has worked 20 innings and has given up seven earned runs, his earned run average is 9 times 7 = 63 divided by 20 = 3.15. Along with the won-lost record, this statistic is the mark of a pitcher's efficiency over the course of a season. Generally, an earned run average of less than 3.00 is considered excellent. Abbrev. *ERA.* Syn. *big E.*

**earned runs prevented** A pitcher's statistic that accounts for the number of earned runs below the league average collected by a given pitcher.

**earnie** Short for *earned run.*

**ear syphilis** A condition in which an umpire is overly sensitive to comments from players and fans and thereby affecting his performance. Bill McKinley (quoted in Larry R. Gerlach, *The Men in Blue,* 1980): "That happened to [Nicholas] Red Jones. Red was a good umpire, but he had what we called ear syphilis. He heard everything. It took his concentration off the game. It bothered him so much that they finally had to fire him after six years."

**East Division 1.** See *American League East.* **2.** See *National League East.*

**Eastern Colored League** A *Negro league* formed in 1923 by Ed Bolden, owner of the Philadelphia Hilldales. Other teams included the Bacharach Giants (Atlantic City), Brooklyn Royal Giants, New York Lincoln Giants, Baltimore Black Sox, and eastern Cuban Stars. The league met the western Negro National League in a world series from 1924 to 1927, the west winning three of them. The league disbanded in 1928. (John Holway)

**Eastern Shuttle Series** A nickname for the 1986 World Series between the New York Mets and the Boston Red Sox. Despite the best efforts of Pan American, which had just initiated a shuttle service between the two cities, the name of the long-established but now defunct Eastern Air Lines air bus between the two cities is the one that stuck.

**easy** Vulnerable; quickly dispatched. Neither a batter nor a pitcher would like to be known as "easy." **1st Use.** 1897. (*New York Tribune,* July 14; Edward J. Nichols).

**easy money** *arch.* An opponent who is weak. **1st Use.** 1907. (*New York Evening Journal,* Apr. 17; Edward J. Nichols).

**easy out 1.** A hitter who poses no substantial threat. The term is often applied to a pitcher when he comes to bat. A pitcher will often complain that there are no "easy outs" in an opponent's lineup. See also *sure out,* 2. **2.** A common cliché chanted at the amateur level of the game, used to rattle the batter who may, in fact, be a good hitter. **Extended Use.** Anyone or anything that can be dealt with easily.

**eat the ball** To hold on to a safely hit ball without getting rid of it quickly. Phil Rizzuto (quoted in Roger Kahn & Al Helfer, *Mutual Baseball Almanac,* 1954) advises: "The only way to avoid eating it is to reach into your glove and grab it in a hurry. That's just a matter of reflexes, but you have to have the reflexes."

**eat up** To field a ground ball quickly and skillfully. **1st Use.** 1907. (*New York Evening Journal,* Apr. 18; Edward J. Nichols).

**Ebbets Field** Home field of the Brooklyn Dodgers in Brooklyn, N.Y., from 1913 to 1957. Named for Charlie Ebbets, the man who had it built, the park was demolished in 1960, and a housing development is now located on its former site. "But more than the scenery has changed—a sign on the apartment building says: 'No Ball Playing'" (*USA Today,* June 24, 1993). Nickname: *Wacks Museum.*

**E-card** A candy or gum baseball card (as opposed to one given out with tobacco) issued before 1930.

**Eck-ese** Baseball slang dispensed by pitcher Dennis Eckersley; e.g., a home run is a "bridge," off-speed stuff is a "salad," and a slider is a "slide piece."

**ecology pitch** A 55-miles-per-hour pitch. **Etymology.** Attributed to pitcher Allen Ripley of the Chicago Cubs by Joe Goddard (*The Sporting News,* Mar. 6, 1982). It was inspired by the 55-miles-per-hour speed limit in effect after the oil embargo imposed in the 1970s by the Organization of Petroleum Exporting Countries (OPEC).

**edge 1.** *v.* To win or lose a game by one run; e.g., "The Giants edged out the Dodgers, 4–3." **2.** *n.*

**Ebbets Field.** *Players hauling the flag into place for Opening Day, April 14, 1914.*

The balance in favor of one team over another; e.g., "The Dodgers have an edge over the Giants because of their pitching." **3.** *n.* The bite on a pitched ball. **4.** *n.* A *corner* of the plate.

**edge off** To take a lead from a base; e.g., "The potential tying run was edging off third."

**Edison** *arch.* A pitcher who is always experimenting with new pitches. The term refers to Thomas Edison, the great American inventor. Syn. *Thomas Edison.* **1st Use.** 1943. "An 'Edison' is a pitcher who is experimenting all the time" (*Baseball Magazine*, Jan.).

**Edna** *arch.* A generic name for the wife of a baseball player (ca. 1958) who, according to Bert Dunne (*Folger's Dictionary of Baseball*, 1958), is "married to a genius," namely the player in question.

**eephus** A high-arcing pitch likely to reach an apex of 25 feet above the ground between the mound and the plate. The ball is thrown overhand and aimed upwards in the hope that it will, at its most effective, drop from the top to the bottom of the strike zone as it crosses the plate. The pitch will always be associated with pitcher Truett "Rip" Sewell. In the 1946 All-Star Game at Fenway Park, Sewell threw three straight eephus pitches to Ted Williams. Anticipating the third one after tak-ing the first and fouling off the second, Williams ran up a few feet toward the mound and drove the ball over the right-field fence.

"Eephus" is one of several names for this un-orthodox pitch, which is also known as *blooper ball, gondola, parachute, balloon ball,* and *La Lob.* However, "eephus" seems to be reserved for the bloopers of the most outlandish trajectory. Pron. "ee-fuss." Syn. "eephus pitch."

**Etymology/1st Use.** 1942. The pitch was first thrown by Sewell of the Pittsburgh Pirates in a 1942 exhibition game against the Detroit Tigers in Muncie, Ind. Catcher Al Lopez called for a changeup with a 3-2 count on Dick Wakefield, and Sewell threw the blooper. Sewell (quoted by Ray Fitzgerald, *Boston Globe,* July 12, 1981) de-scribed what happened next:

"Wakefield started to swing, then he stopped, and then he swung again and almost fell down when he missed. After the game, when everybody stopped laughing, [Pirates manager Frankie] Frisch wanted to know what I called the pitch, and Mau-rice Van Robays, an outfielder, said 'that's an eephus ball.' 'What's an eephus?' I asked him. 'Eephus ain't nuthin.' So it was always eephus after that."

Sewell also told Fitzgerald that he had devel-oped the pitch as a result of a hunting accident that left 14 pieces of buckshot in his foot. After the accident, he was unable to pivot as before and adopted a straight, overhand motion, "something like an Australian crawl." The eephus came out of this and was thrown "by holding the ball in the palm of his hand with the fingers on top and delivered much in the manner of a shotputter."

Before the term was used by Sewell, "ephus," "e-phus," or "ephus ophus" were used as slang for dependable information, the lowdown, or the right "dope." Peter Tamony notes its use in both underworld and political contexts before and after Sewell's time in the major leagues; e.g., "The ephus is that by delaying things this long, Governor Olson has quietly knocked the election into a cocked-ballot" (*San Francisco News,* June 19, 1939). **Usage Note.** Since Sewell's retirement the term has held on, but seems to be used humorously. For instance, in a Grapefruit League contest between the Toronto Blue Jays and the Philadelphia Phillies on Mar. 6, 1988, Blue Jays pitcher Jose Nuñez, unaccustomed to hitting because of the designated hitter rule, came to the plate and stood on the first base side of the batter's box even though he is right-handed and was wearing a right-handed batter's helmet. After getting a laugh from the crowd he went to the other side of the plate. According to the account of the game in the *St. Petersburg Times,* the Phillies thought Nunez was making a joke out of appearing at the plate and Mike Schmidt was heard yelling to Phillies pitcher Kevin Gross, "Throw him the eephus, eephus." Gross threw one and Nunez got enough of it to ground out to second.

**"Ee-yah"** The ear-splitting call or shout made famous by coach Hughie Jennings before World War I. It unnerved other teams and became so well known that American soldiers, going "over the top" of trenches in World War I assaults, let out the trademark Jennings cry. Research reported by Peter Morris notes that *Detroit Free Press* (Apr. 3, 1908) gives a lengthy history of the term's evolution. When Jennings was a youth, he worked as a mule driver and, to speed the mules on their way so he could get to the baseball field, he would yell "Wee-up now!" The phrase gradually evolved to "Wee-Yah," "Swee-Yah," and finally "Ee-yah."

**"Ee-yah."** *Coach Hughie Jennings in full shout, circa 1910.*

**egg** A baseball.

**egg feast** A low-scoring game; one with many "goose eggs" on the scoreboard. **1st Use.** 1891. (*Chicago Herald,* June 8; Edward J. Nichols).

**8** The scorekeeper's designation for the center fielder.

**800 club** A mythical group of select pitchers who have worked in 800 or more major-league games. Members include Hoyt Wilhelm (1,070), Cy Young (906), and Walter Johnson (801).

**eighth 1.** *n.* The eighth inning. **2.** *adv.* Said of the eighth position in the batting order; e.g., "Smith is batting eighth."

**Eighth Wonder of the World** The *Astrodome* in Houston, so-called by Houston Astros president Roy Hofheinz when it opened in 1965.

**eject** For an umpire to remove a participant from the playing area.

**ejection** The banishment from a game of a player, coach, manager, or spectator who, in an umpire's judgment, has violated a given rule or behaved in an unsportsmanlike manner. Several managers have been so contentious that they normally get ejected more than once during a season. The most notable ejectee of the modern era was Baltimore Orioles manager Earl Weaver, whose personal record for ejections in a season was 10 in 1975. On May 4, 1995, a fan was ejected from Wrigley Field for heeding his father's last request by dumping his father's ashes over the left-field wall from the bleachers during the seventh-inning stretch of a Cubs game.

**elbow bender** A pitcher. **1st Use.** 1937. (*Philadelphia Record,* Aug. 22; Edward J. Nichols).

**elbowing** Pitching.

**electronic pitcher** A pitcher outfitted with a transistorized radio device, which is used to receive instructions from the dugout. This idea has been experimented with in the minor leagues (e.g., Atlanta of the International League in 1964). However, the bench-to-mound radio has never gathered much long-term interest.

**elevator shaft** The figurative destination of a high pop-up hit directly over the batter in the batter's box. **Usage Note.** The term is a play on the notion that the ball is shot up into an elevator shaft.

**eleven immortals** The select group of living inductees who were present at the Baseball Hall of Fame when it was dedicated in 1939: Babe Ruth, Ty Cobb, Walter Johnson, George Sisler,

**Eleven immortals.** *Only Ty Cobb is absent from this photo taken at the Hall of Fame dedication (1939). L. to r., front: Eddie Collins, Babe Ruth, Connie Mack, Cy Young; back: Honus Wagner, Grover Cleveland Alexander, Tris Speaker, Nap Lajoie, George Sisler, Walter Johnson.*

Nap Lajoie, Connie Mack, Cy Young, Honus Wagner, Grover Cleveland Alexander, Eddie Collins, and Tris Speaker. See also *immortal; baseball immortal.*

**El Foldo** A collapse or failure. **1st Use.** 1938. "Getting back to the class of the National League's favored clubs, there has been a lot of comments on the 'El Foldo' acts being staged by the Pirates, Giants, Cubs, and Reds" (Charles J. Doyle, *The Sporting News,* Sept. 1; Barry Popik).

**Elias scale** A set of statistics compiled by the Elias Sports Bureau to rank, by playing position, all major-league players who are eligible to be free agents. Under the terms of baseball's Basic Agreement, this ranking determines if a team will be compensated when a player signs with a new team. First compiled in 1981, the first player to be given a perfect ranking score of 1.000 was New York Yankees first baseman Don Mattingly in 1987.

**emergency swing** A defensive swing taken when the pitch is coming at the batter.

**emery ball** A pitched ball that has been roughed up with emery cloth, sandpaper, or other abrasive agent. When such a ball is pitched, the scuffed side is more resistant to the force of air, causing it to move erratically as it nears the plate. Syn. *dry spitter,* 2. **Etymology/1st Use.** 1914. (*New York Tribune,* Sept. 20; Edward J. Nichols).

Lenny Anderson (*Seattle Post-Intelligencer,* Sept. 29, 1971) asserts that the emery ball was discovered "by accident" before World War I by right-handed pitcher Russell Ford. The source of this information was an octogenarian, William L. "Doc" Green (Mercer Island, Wash.), who knew Ford. According to Ford, he came on the trick pitch in Spring 1908 while with Atlanta of the Southern Association. On a rainy day, while working under a grandstand, he accidentally threw a ball into a wooden upright, marring the ball's surface. He used the ball again and was surprised by the "amazing curve" that it made. He noted the scuff and went back to his customary technique (a then-legal spitball using tobacco and

**Emery ball.** *A dapper Russell Ford at spring training camp in Gray, Georgia, circa 1909.*

slippery elm). He applied what he had learned, winning 26 games for the New York Yankees in 1910.

As for the emery ball, Green recalled: "He worked out a very careful way of scuffing up the ball with emery cloth. He had the emery cloth on his middle finger and when he got the ball, he slid his finger out through a hole in the pocket of the glove—a lot of players used to cut out the middle of the glove—and scuff up the ball."

Ford gave up the emery ball after 1910, choosing instead to rough up the ball with his fingernails. The emery secret got out in 1914 and everybody wanted to use it. This is also the year that the term began to appear in print. As Ford later recalled: "Some pitchers even used files to rough the ball. Others used potato graters." The emery ball was declared illegal in Winter 1914–15 at the meeting of the baseball rules committee.

In 1987, when knuckleballer Joe Niekro was caught with a verboten emery board in his pocket, he explained that he just liked to work on his nails between innings.

**emigre** A player who moves from one team to another.

**empty base 1.** A base that is not occupied by a baserunner. **2.** A base that is not covered by a defensive player. Fielders fear the empty-base throw. "[Cleveland] Indians third baseman Travis Fryman must have felt silly when he charged a bunt . . . threw to first base—and nobody was there. The fans gasped and the press box filled with laughter." (*St. Petersburg Times,* April 12, 1998).

**endorsement** A practice pioneered by baseball players as they found they could earn a few extra dollars by lending their names and faces to a product or service. Modern players sometimes make hundreds of thousands of dollars through endorsements.

**English 1.** *n.* A spinning motion or rotation of a batted or pitched ball with just enough spin to cause it to veer from its natural course. **1st Use.** 1910. (*American Magazine,* June; Edward J. Nichols). **2.** *v.* To bunt or bat a ball that acts oddly due to a spinning motion. Ted Shane (*Saturday Evening Post,* July 27, 1940; Peter Tamony) wrote: "Some [Negro league players] are positive magicians at bunting, being able to English it so that it either stops dead as a fielder reaches for it, or corkscrews back around a catcher as he tries to pounce on it." **Etymology.** From the spin of a billiard or pool ball, which is accomplished by hitting the cue ball off-center.

**enshrine** To be inducted into the Baseball Hall of Fame.

**entrepreneurial player** A player who takes the assets he has and puts them to especially good use; it is a compliment of the first order. Carl Yastrzemski was once called the "best and last great entrepreneurial player" (*Boston Globe,* June 1, 1986).

**EP** [softball term] Abbrev. for *extra player.*

**Epworth League** *arch.* A figurative repository for players outside the game. To be sent to the Epworth League is "to be dropped outside of organized baseball" (Franklin P. Huddle, *American Speech,* Apr. 1943).

**equalizer 1.** The curveball. **2.** A run that ties a game, esp. late in the game.

**equipment 1.** A team's game paraphernalia, including such items as bats, gloves, and the catcher's protective gear. **2.** A pitcher's *stuff,* 1.

**equipment manager** The club official responsible for obtaining, maintaining, and transporting the team's equipment.

**ER** Abbrev. for *earned run.*

**ERA** Abbrev. for *earned run average.*

**erase 1.** To put out a baserunner. **2.** To retire a batter, esp. to strike out a batter; e.g., "Smith erased Jones on three pitches."

**eraser rate** A statistic marking a team's success at catching opposing base stealers. Listed as a percentage, it is computed by dividing the number of opponents caught stealing by the number of their attempted steals. For a period in the early 1980s, Eraser Rate Awards were presented to the team with the best record in each league. The awards were sponsored by Major League Baseball and Eraser Mate, a pen produced by Paper Mate.

**Ernie Banks' dictum** See *Banks' dictum.*

**error** A misplay on the part of the defensive team that helps the offensive team. An error occurs when a batted ball is missed or dropped, when a wild throw is made, or when a putout is missed because the ball is mishandled. Errors are determined by the subjective judgment of the official scorer and are given to a specific player and his team. They are recorded in the most basic accounting of a game, which calls for giving each team's tally in terms of "hits, runs, and errors."

*Error.*

Syn. and abbrev. *E.* **1st Use.** 1858. (Chadwick Scrapbooks; Edward J. Nichols).

**errorless** Having completed a game, a series of games, or a string of consecutive innings without committing an error. The term is applied to individuals, parts of a team (such as a collective infield), and teams as a whole.

**ethyl chloride** A chemical spray that is used as a local anesthetic to "freeze" a painful area so that a player may stay in the game. It is often used after a batter has been hit by a pitch.

**even** Said of a 1-1 or 2-2 ball-and-strike count.

**even the count** To make the ball-and-strike count even (the same number of balls and strikes) by the batter or by the pitcher.

**every-day eight** A lineup that seldom changes. The term is applied to a team that sees strategic value in using the same players (except the pitcher) day after day, as opposed to platooning players at one or more positions. "Yankee Strategy for Pennant Drive: Every-day Eight" (*USA Today* headline, Aug. 14, 1986).

**everyday player** A player who appears regularly in the starting lineup.

**ex-** A prefix indicating "former"; e.g., "ex-player," the last (and 18th) stage in the life cycle of a player, according to Frank Deford (*Sports Illustrated,* July 27, 1981).

**ex-Cub factor theory** A theory created by columnist Mike Royko which held that a) the greater the number of former Chicago Cubs players on a team, the worse that team will be, and b) no team with more than three ex-Cubs on it can win the World Series or the team with the most ex-Cubs on it will lose the World Series. Andy Knobel (*Baltimore Sun,* Apr. 1, 1995) figured that 14 teams with three or more former Cubs have played in a World Series since 1945 and that the ex-Cub teams have gone 1-13 with the lone winner being the 1960 Pittsburgh Pirates. *USA Today* (Oct. 30, 1986) concluded: "Since 1970, a dozen ex-Cubs have played for world championship teams and 23 have played for losing teams." In the 1986 World Series, the New York Mets, with no former Cubs on its roster, defeated the Boston Red Sox, whose first baseman, ex-Cub Bill Buckner, committed a critical error in Game 6. **Usage Note.** The basis for the theory is the fact that the Cubs is the team that has gone the longest without winning a World Series. The last year the Cubs won the World Series is 1908.

**excuse-me hit** A base hit, most commonly a single, resulting from an excuse-me swing. The hit is such a fluke that the batter is expected to "excuse" himself.

**excuse-me swing** A check swing in which the batter, unintentionally making contact with the pitch, gets a base hit.

**execute** To make a play or carry out a specific action dictated by a situation in the game. **1st Use.** 1912. (*New York Tribune,* Sept. 5; Edward J. Nichols).

**Executive Council** The 13-member governing body that operated Major League Baseball in the absence of a commissioner (1992 to 1998). It consisted of ten owners (five from each major league, chosen by their peers), the president of each league, and the acting commissioner, who also served as chairman.

**exhibit card** A baseball card sold from vending machines in amusement park arcades. According to Beckett's *The Baseball Card Price Guide,* the name comes from the Exhibit Supply Co. of Chicago, which was the principal manufacturer of these cards. Syn. *arcade card.*

**exhibition game** An unofficial game that does not count in the standings; esp., a spring-training game. Exhibition games often are scheduled between teams that do not meet during the regular season or between a major-league team and one of its farm clubs. The annual All-Star Game is a special example of an exhibition game, as is the one staged every year at Doubleday Field in Cooperstown, N.Y., at the time when new members are inducted into the Baseball Hall of Fame. **1st Use.** 1874. (Chicago *Inter-Ocean,* July 25; Edward J. Nichols).

**expand the strike zone** For an umpire to allow a pitcher to throw successive strikes further outside the strike zone.

**expansion** The addition of one or more new franchises to the major leagues. A special draft is held at such times to enable the new teams to select players from existing teams. Between 1901 and 1960 there was no expansion, but new teams have since been added in 1961 (Los Angeles Angels and expansion Washington Senators, now Texas Rangers), 1962 (Houston Colt .45s and New York Mets), 1969 (Seattle Pilots, now Milwaukee Brewers, and Montreal Expos, San Diego Padres, and Kansas City Royals), 1977 (Seattle Mariners and Toronto Blue Jays), 1993 (Florida Marlins and Colorado Rockies), and 1998 (Tampa Bay Devil Rays and Arizona Diamondbacks). Because of expansion, the regular-season schedule was increased from 154 to 162 games in 1961 (American League) and 1962 (National League).

**expansion draft** A special selection of players when an expansion team is created in which existing teams are required to make available a group of players from which the new team builds its roster. The existing teams are allowed to exclude (protect) a specified number of players. In the Nov. 1997 draft, teams were allowed to protect 15 players and Arizona and Tampa Bay were allowed to select 70 nonprotected players.

**expansion team** A team that has been created through expansion and often referred to as such for many years after its entry into a league; e.g., the Florida Marlins, a Cinderella story in expansion having gone from a 1993 inaugural season to World Series victors in 1997.

**expectoration exhibitor** *arch.* A flamboyant name for a spitball pitcher. **1st Use.** 1907. (*New York Evening Journal,* June 7; Edward J. Nichols).

**explode** 1. To get maximum energy behind a hit, throw, or pitch; e.g., a ball pitched so fast that the batter's eye cannot follow its approach is said to "explode" rather than grow larger upon arriving so quickly. One criticism of Michael Jordan as a baseball player was that he had no "explosiveness" in his hands. **2.** For a fastball to appear to jump during the last six or eight feet of its trajectory to the plate. **3.** To unleash a barrage of hits or score many runs. The term is usually applied to a team; e.g., "The Twins exploded for 10 runs in the fifth."

**exploding scoreboard** A scoreboard configured to make a flashy and noisy display when the home team hits a home run or accomplishes some other feat. **Etymology.** The term and the concept came from the fertile mind of Bill Veeck who introduced the first exploding scoreboard in the original Comiskey Park in Chicago in 1960. Replete with mortars for Roman candles, smoke, and strobe lights, Veeck later reported in his autobiography (*Veeck...as in Wreck,* 1962) that the exploding scoreboard was inspired by a pinball machine that hits the jackpot at the finale of William Saroyan's play, *The Time of Your Life* (1939).

**extended spring training** A period during which a player or players remain in spring-training camp for a few extra weeks to report to a minor-league club, to recover from an injury, or to remedy some other specific problem.

**extension 1.** The ability of a pitcher to stretch his body and be relaxed; e.g., the more "extension" a pitcher has, the better he is able to deliver pitches with a lot of stuff. **2.** The practice whereby a batter puts his arms over the plate so that his swing will give maximum velocity to the bat.

**extra base** An additional base gained on a base hit, such as when a hitter stretches a single into a double. See also *take the extra base.*

**extra-base hit** A double, triple, or home run; a hit on which the batter advances safely past first base. Syn. *long hit.*

**extra bases** The bases taken by doubles, triples, and home runs.

**extra inning** Any additional inning of play beyond a game's regulation nine-inning length.

**extra innings game** Any game that goes beyond the regular nine innings. In the event of a tie after nine innings of play, play continues until one team has scored more runs than the other at the end of a complete inning or when the home team scores the tie-breaking run. **1st Use.** 1885. (*Spalding's Official Base Ball Guide;* Edward J. Nichols).

**extra pitch** A pitch that pitchers are encouraged to develop when they are not successful with their particular repertoire of pitches.

**extra player** [softball term] An optional 11th player in slow pitch softball or the 11th and 12th in co-recreational slow pitch softball. The extra player remains in the same position in the batting order for the entire game and does not play defense (equivalent to the designated hitter in baseball). Compare *designated player.* Abbrev. *EP.*

**eye** A batter's ability to determine the location of an oncoming pitch in relation to the strike zone. **1st Use.** 1901. (Burt L. Standish, *Frank Merriwell's Marvel;* Edward J. Nichols).

**eyeballing** A situation in which an umpire and a manager or player disagree vociferously, their noses almost touching and their eyes glaring at each other.

**eye-in-the-sky** A strategic observer, such as a coach positioning the defense, a scout, or other individual, in a press box or other elevated position who communicates with the dugout. "[Houston Astros general manager] Dick Wagner does not permit opposing teams to use an eye-in-the-sky" (*San Francisco Chronicle,* June 6, 1987). **Usage Note.** This may amount to a term for coaching in Siberia. Reporting on Billy Martin's fifth return as New York Yankees manager, *The Sporting News* (Nov. 9, 1987) described the prospects for coach Jeff Torborg on the 1988 Yankees: "Torborg, never a Martin favorite, has one year remaining on his contract and is expected to be the club's 'eye-in-the-sky' coach."

**eyes on it** Said of a batted ball that seems to find its way past fielders. See also *ball with eyes on it.*

# F

**F 1.** Abbrev. for *fly,* 1. **2.** Abbrev. for *flyout.* **3.** Abbrev. for *foul fly.*

**face 1.** To come to bat; e.g., "Smith always struck out when he faced a fireballer." **1st Use.** 1874. (*New York Sun,* July 31; Edward J. Nichols). **2.** To pitch to a batter; e.g., "Jones faced only 29 batters."

**face ball 1.** Syn. of *brushback pitch.* **2.** Syn. of *knockdown pitch.*

**face mask** A protective head device, worn by the catcher and plate umpire, that covers the face with a wire cage. See also *catcher's mask.*

**factory set** A complete set of baseball cards assembled and collated at the printing company rather than one assembled and collated by a dealer or collector.

**fadeaway** *arch.* **1.** A *screwball,* 1. Syn. *fader.* **1st Use.** 1908. (*New York Evening Journal,* Mar. 5; Edward J. Nichols). **Etymology.** First attributed to Christy Mathewson (active 1900–16), who is credited with its invention and naming around 1908. The term apparently derives either from the fact that the pitcher seems to fall off the mound after he has delivered the ball or that the ball loses speed suddenly as it approaches the batter and falls, or "fades" away at an unnatural angle. Douglass Wallop (*Baseball: An Informal History,* 1969) writes: "Big Six, he [Mathewson] was called, the man who gave the nation a new word—'the fadeaway,' a perverse curve never before mastered by a right-handed pitcher, one that broke down and toward a right-handed batter." **2.** A slide in which

**Fadeaway.** *Christy Mathewson as he looked in 1916, the final year of his playing career.*

the baserunner throws his body sideways to avoid being tagged.

**fader** Syn. of *fadeaway,* 1.

**fagot** *arch.* A 19th-century nickname for a baseball bat. **1st Use.** 1891. (*Chicago Herald,* May 21; Edward J. Nichols). **Etymology.** From the word for a bundle of sticks.

**fair** In fair territory, and therefore playable.

**Fall classic.** *Fans line up outside the Polo Grounds for World Series tickets.*

**fair ball** A ball in play; a batted ball that lands in fair territory (between the foul lines), or remains in fair territory until it passes first or third base, or remains between the foul lines until it clears the outfield fence or wall. **1st Use.** 1854. (Knickerbocker Rules; Edward J. Nichols).

**fair-foul hit** A base hit, allowable under early rules, in which the batter deliberately hits the ball with tremendous backspin so that after hitting in fair territory, the ball immediately spun into foul territory. The technique was mastered by several hitters, esp. Roscoe Barnes, but was banned after the 1876 season.

**fair ground** Syn. of *fair territory.*

**fair side** The infield edge of first base and of third base.

**fair territory** The playing area within and including the foul lines, from home plate to the bottom of the playing field fence and perpendicularly upward. Syn. *fair ground.*

**fair-weather fan** A fan who roots for or supports a team only when it is doing well or challenging for the pennant.

**faithful, the** Baseball fans. **1st Use.** 1902. (*Sporting Life,* Sept. 13; Edward J. Nichols).

**fake bunt** A bluff, in which the batter assumes the bunting stance without attempting to bunt the ball. It is used to draw the infielders in close and away from their bases.

**fake grass** *Artificial turf,* without affection; e.g., "So far this season, the Brewers have a 7-12 record on fake grass."

**fake tag** A form of obstruction (in softball and high school baseball) by a fielder who neither has the ball nor is about to receive the ball, and which impedes the progress of a runner (such as slowing down or being forced to slide) either advancing or returning to a base. The umpire shall award the obstructed runner and each other runner affected by the obstruction the bases they would have, in his opinion, reached had there been no fake tag.

**fall away** *arch.* A curveball that drops slowly toward the ground as it nears the plate.

**fallaway slide** A slide into a base featuring a sudden, evasive drop to the ground just before reaching the base. See also *hook slide*. Also spelled "fall-away slide." **1st Use.** 1910. (*Baseball Magazine*, May; Edward J. Nichols).

**fall classic** Syn. of *World Series*. The term is one of baseball's oldest clichés, fully expressed in the large cliché of "titans clashing in the fall classic." Sometimes spelled Fall Classic.

**fall in** *v.* For a ball to land in the outfield without being caught; e.g., "Smith's pop fly fell in for a single."

**fall-in** *n.* A fly ball that falls in; e.g., "Too many fall-ins lead to too many runs."

**fall on a pitcher** To get many hits off a pitcher during an inning or over the course of a game.

**falsie** An extra-thick sliding pad.

**family day** A promotional event at a ball game in which a) families get a special rate on tickets or b) the players are brought onto the field before the game with their families. Such an event held in conjunction with a night game is a "family night."

**fan 1.** *v.* To *strike out* a batter; to be put out on strikes; to whiff. **2.** *v.* To swing and miss. Edward J. Nichols collected several constructions based on this meaning including, "fan the air," "fan the climate," "fan ether," and "fan ozone." **1st Use.** 1884. "In Chicago a man who strikes out is said to have 'fanned the air with his crutch'" (*Sporting Life*, May 28; Barry Popik). **3.** *n.* A strikeout. **4.** *n.* An enthusiastic follower of the game of baseball; a devotee. **5.** *n.* Any spectator at a baseball game. **1st Use.** 1889. "Their work on the diamond is a revelation to local 'fans'" (*Breeder and Sportsman*, Dec. 7; Peter Tamony). Also: "Kansas City baseball fans are glad they're through with Dave Rowe as a ball club manager" (*Kansas City Star & Times*,

A fan out.

FAN SERIES, COPYRIGHTED 1906, BY F. DERBES, PUBLISHED BY A.M.

*Fan.*

Mar. 26; Peter Tamony). In his studies of *The World* (New York), Gerald Cohen found the first use on July 12, 1890: "'Give us more batting in professional games' has been the cry of 'fans' for years." Cohen added: "This attestation of fan(s) is the only unambiguous one I have noticed in the 1887–1890 columns of *The World* and significantly, it was not written by a New York sportswriter but is reprinted from another city's newspaper. In New York City, the only word for 'fan' at that time was 'crank.'" **Etymology.** While it is commonly assumed and quite often stated that the term is a back formation or clipping of "fanatic," other evidence has been presented. William Henry Nugent (*American Mercury*, Mar. 1929) shows how many common sports terms used in North America are not Americanisms but rather much older transplants from the British Isles. Nugent traces several terms back to the writings of Pierce Egan, whom he calls "the father of newspaper sports slang." Egan, who published many books and articles on sports in the 1820s, used much of the "flash and cant" of the boxing ring and racetrack in his account of events, while others writing on the same subjects left them out. This was not just the slang of the sportsman but, as Nugent points out, "words that he had picked up from the speech of vagabonds, jail birds, bartenders, soldiers and actors." Among others, Nugent traced these terms to Egan's era and his writings: "palooka" (for a fifth-rate boxer, from a pure Gaelic word); "ham" (for a poor performer, from a Cockney abbreviation of "amateur" to "am," which was pronounced "h'am"); and "Chinaman's chance" (which has nothing to do with Asiatics, but came from a light-hitting boxer of the 1820s named Tom Spring who was likely to break during a long fight—a "china man" meaning a fragile individual, one made out of porcelain). (Other terms with a familiar ring that Nugent found in Egan's dictionary: "to kid," "to fake," "to crab," "to sting," "to pony up," "sucker," "lame duck," "faker," "lucky break," "pink of condition," "racket," and "scab").

Nugent's evidence on "fan" comes in part from a lexicon that Egan compiled in 1823, and that was published in the third edition of a book first issued in 1785 by Francis Grose, titled *Francis Grose's Dictionary of the Vulgar Tongue as Revised and Corrected by Pierce Egan*. The book contains the following entry:

"The Fancy: one of the fancy is a sporting character that is either attached to pigeons, dog-fighting, boxing, etc. Also, any particular article universally admired for its beauty; or which the owners set particular store by, is termed a fancy article, as a fancy clout, a favorite handkerchief, etc; also, a woman, who is the particular favourite of any man, is termed his fancy woman and vice versa."

Nugent concludes: "The 'fancy' was long a class name in England and America for followers of boxing. Baseball borrowed it and shortened it to 'the fance,' 'fans,' and 'fan.'"

An even earlier use of "fancy" can, in fact, be found in Egan's *Boxiana* (1818): "The various gradations of the fancy hither resort to discuss matters incidental to pugilism." The term was firmly established and, for example, shows up in J. S. Farmer & W. E. Henley's monumental *Slang and its Analogues* (published in several volumes between 1890 and 1904) where it is defined as: "The fraternity of pugilists: prize-fighting being once regarded as THE FANCY *par excellence*. Hence by implication people who cultivate a special hobby or taste." Farmer & Henley also point to "fancy-bloke," a sporting man, as a variation.

Despite all of this evidence, the word "fan" is still regularly asserted to be a clipped form of "fanatic." According to Gerald Secor Couzens (*A Baseball Album*, 1980), the supposed clipper of the word was Timothy P. "Ted" Sullivan, manager and scout in the early 1880s. Others claim it was clipped by Chris Von der Ahe, owner of the St. Louis Browns in the 1880s, who supposedly had trouble pronouncing the word "fanatic" with his thick German accent.

Peter Tamony did much research on the term and sided with the Sullivan theory, which he spelled out in a letter to Jim Brosnan (Dec. 9, 1963). The crucial paragraph: "A much better claim to origination is made by . . . Sullivan, one of the real founders of the modern game, in his book, *Humorous Stories of the Ball Field: A Complete History of the Game and Its Exponents* (1903). Sullivan writes that Charles Comiskey called an enthusiast who visited the clubhouse in St. Louis a 'fanatic' and that he [Sullivan] clipped the word to 'fan.' He sets the date as 1883: he was then building the St. Louis team which was later to be taken over by Comiskey to win the league championship four times, and the world championship in 1885–1886; Von der Ahe was owner of the Club."

While these are the two major theories, there are several lesser ones as well. Occasionally, one runs into a restatement of the claim made by Connie Mack that "fan" was first created to describe spectators who fanned themselves to keep cool. Peter Morris fans the embers of this theory: "It certainly doesn't prove anything, but I found a very suggestive note from 1879 indicating that scorecards now had handles attached so they could be used as fans. The avid fans would have been the ones who purchased scorecards, so their association with the word 'fans' would make sense."

However, the final word may in fact be at hand. Barry Popik and Gerald Cohen (*Comments on Ety-*

**Fan.** *Jolly crew at the Polo Grounds in New York April, 1911.*

*mology,* Oct. 1996) have concluded: "It is already recognized that 'fan' probably derives from 'fanatic' and is attested at least by 1889." Here is their overview as it appeared in the article, quoted directly:

"1) Sports 'fan' very probably arose in St. Louis, ca. 1883, and its origin most likely involves baseball maven Ted Sullivan. In a January 18, 1896 account in *The Sporting News* Sullivan credits Chris Von der Ahe with coining the term in conversation with him, and Sullivan immediately picked up the term and spread it ('The expression was a hit with me. Comiskey and the players took it up, and then the newspapers'). In 1898 Sullivan claimed sole credit for originating the term, but there seems no reason to remove credence from the earlier version involving both Von der Ahe and Sullivan.

"2) Barry Popik has spotted two attestations from 1887—two years earlier than the previously noticed first attestation—and, most importantly, with the first one in a St. Louis publication (*The Sporting News*). From Missouri, sports 'fan' spread first to Philadelphia, and the second 1887 quote appears in a Philadelphia publication (*Sporting Life*).

"3) The third attestation thus far noticed . . . is from March 26, 1889 in the *Kansas City Star & Times,* a Missouri publication. This attestation, together with the first 1887 one, help point to Missouri as the birthplace of sports 'fan.'

"4) The Missouri newspapers from 1883–1887 should now be zeroed in on as the most promising source of additional information on the term.

"5) 'Fan,' of course, won out over the previously standard term, 'crank,' with acceptance coming first in the Midwest and Philadelphia, only slowly in New York.

"6) The emergence of 'fan' in 1889 outside of St. Louis was probably aided by the presence of the St. Louis team in the 1887 and 1888 baseball championships."

**fancy Dan** *arch.* A player who works to make every play seem spectacular; an excellent fielder. **1st Use.** 1927. (*The Sporting News Record Book;* Edward J. Nichols).

**fandango** A strikeout.

**fandom** *arch.* Baseball fans collectively; the realm of the fan. "Fandom also means agony, and one agony in being an Orioles fan is that the only seats they'll sell you for games with the Red Sox, Yankees, Indians, Blue Jays, Tigers and Brewers are so high above the field that acrophobia can make you hysterical" (Russell Baker, *New York Times Magazine,* 1980).

**fan interference** Syn. of *spectator interference.*

**fanning bee 1.** An artful display of pitching in which swinging strikes are plentiful. **1st Use.** 1910. "On this occasion there was always a 'fanning bee,' as the boys call it" (Christy Mathewson, *Won in the Ninth;* David Shulman). **2.** A tryout, or practice baseball game (Martin Gardner, *Annotated Casey at the Bat,* 1967). **3.** A gathering of fans, as at a soda fountain or general store, to discuss baseball (Donald Gropman, *Say It Ain't So, Joe!,* 1979). See also *hot stove league.*

**fantasy baseball camp** A mock training camp in which ordinary fans can, for a hefty fee, practice and play baseball with retired major leaguers and get a feel for the life of a professional ballplayer. An ad for "The Mickey Mantle–Whitey Ford Fantasy Baseball Camp" carried the line, "Play ball with your Yankee Heroes" (*Wall Street Journal,* Aug. 1986). Not to be confused with *baseball camp.* See also *dream week.* Syn. "fantasy camp." **Etymology/1st Use.** 1983. The first of these camps took place in 1983 featuring ex-Cubs and ex-Dodgers. The word "fantasy" was quickly attached to them. "Baseball fantasy to be fulfilled" (Associated Press story on the Dodgers camp, *Oneonta Star,* Feb. 3, 1983). "Fantasy Island in the desert" (story on the Cubs camp, *Washington Post,* Jan. 23, 1983).

**fantasy baseball league** A simulated baseball game, such as *Rotisserie League Baseball,* in which the statistical performances of real major-league players determine the outcome. **1st Use.** 1991.

"I'm involved, romantically or not, in a fantasy baseball league" (*USA Today,* July 16).

**fantasy-camper** One who pays to come to a fantasy baseball camp. "Luis Tiant hurls a pitch to a fantasy-camper Sunday afternoon in Winter Haven" (*St. Petersburg Times* photo caption, Feb. 8, 1988).

**fantasy game** A game in which two teams clash on paper, in a computer, or by some other artificial means. Fantasy games were popular during the baseball strike of 1981 when some radio stations took to broadcasting them.

**far corner** *arch.* Syn. of *third base,* 1. **1st Use.** 1913. (*Harper's Weekly,* Sept. 13; Edward J. Nichols).

**farm 1.** *n.* A *farm club.* "Phils Plan Harvest of Farm Products" (*Philadelphia Daily News* headline, June 25, 1987). See also *baseball farm.* **2.** *v.* To send a player to a lower-level team for development. See also *farm out.* **1st Use.** 1898. "On Monday last, too, the Eastern and Western Leagues got together in a sort of offensive and defensive alliance on the subject of drafting and sale of players, so far as the scheme was to be used by the National League to facilitate the practice of 'farming'" (*Detroit Free Press,* Jan. 30; Peter Morris).

**farm club** A minor-league baseball club owned by or having an agreement with a major-league team for the purpose of developing young or inexperienced players. Syn. *farm,* 1; *farm team.*

**farm hand** A minor-league player assigned to a farm club; a player who labors in the farm system. "Pirate Farm Hand Fans 27 in Hurling No-Hit Victory" (*San Francisco News* headline, describing Ron Necciai's Class D-league baseball feat, May 14, 1952). Also spelled "farmhand." **Etymology.** From the name for a hired man in agriculture (farm hand, hired hand, ranch hand).

**farm out** To assign a player to a minor-league club; to return a player to the minor leagues for further training and experience; to send a player back to the farm. "In 1908, Pittsburgh 'farmed him out' to Louisville" (William Patten & J. W. McSpadden, *The Book of Baseball,* 1911; Peter Tamony). Before there was a farm system as such, teams would place players on minor-league teams to let them gain experience. It was regarded by some as an abuse by which the richer teams were able to reserve younger players and recall them at will. See also *farm,* 2. **1st Use.** 1902. (*Sporting Life,* July 12; Edward J. Nichols). **Extended Use.** To reassign; e.g., "I'd like to farm out some of this work."

**farm system** A major-league team's network of affiliated minor-league teams. A club in the farm system may be owned by the parent club or may be independently owned and operated. In the case of independent ownership, the minor-league club contracts with the major-league team on an exclusive basis to manage and develop players. See also *chain-store baseball.* **Etymology.** The first modern farm system was the brainchild of Branch Rickey, who developed it for the St. Louis Cardinals and later the Brooklyn Dodgers. He came up with the idea "by necessity" after the 1918 season when the

*Farm system.*

Cardinals finished in last place. As he later told a congressional subcommittee on monopoly power, which was looking into organized baseball in 1952, he needed a way to compete with the richer clubs by ensuring himself a steady supply of players. He started by buying a half-interest in a Class D team in Arkansas for "a pittance." Using borrowed money, he bought half-interests in the Houston and Syracuse teams in the Texas and International leagues, respectively. Thus, the Cardinals cultivated their own talent. Previously, players had been optioned to minor-league teams on an individual basis.

**farm team** Syn. of *farm club.* **Etymology/1st Use.** 1898. The term and concept date back into the 19th century. Edward J. Nichols found reference to a farm team in the *New York Herald Tribune* (June 17).

**far turn** *arch.* Syn. of *third base,* 1. **1st Use.** 1912. (*New York Tribune,* Sept. 8; Edward J. Nichols).

**fashion a hit** To hit safely. **1st Use.** 1928. (*New York Times,* Oct. 7; Edward J. Nichols).

**fastback** The hole for one's forefinger in a baseball glove.

**fastball** **1.** A pitch thrown at top speed and with great power. It has a relatively even trajectory but usually has a backward spin, which can cause it to hop when it reaches the plate. When thrown by a right-handed pitcher, a fastball tails off to a left-handed batter. It is the most common pitch in baseball. Also spelled "fast ball." **1st Use.** 1905. (*Sporting Life,* Sept. 2; Edward J. Nichols). **Etymology.** Because overhand pitching was not allowed until 1884, the fastball as we know it did not come along until then. Before then fastballs existed, but came from the waist or below. **Extended Use.** Energy, spirit. To "lose something off one's fastball" is to slow down. **2.** [softball term] The game of fast pitch softball in Canada. **3.** [softball term] A pitch that comes off the fingers with a straight but slightly downward spin in fast pitch softball. It drops slightly as it comes to the plate and is most effective when thrown to the corners of the strike zone.

**fastballer** A pitcher who relies chiefly on his fastball; e.g., Nolan Ryan, whose pitch has been clocked at 100.9 miles per hour.

**fastball motion** The pitcher's motion designed to simulate a fastball but delivering an off-speed pitch.

**fast-breaking curve** A pitch that early in its flight breaks into a curveball.

**fast company** *arch.* The major leagues. **1st Use.** 1902. (*Sporting Life,* Apr. 26; Edward J. Nichols).

**Fast Food Fall Classic** The 1984 World Series, which pitted the Detroit Tigers (owned by Tom Monaghan of Domino's Pizza) and the San Diego Padres (owned by the heirs to McDonald's).

**fast hook** The removal of a pitcher at the first sign of trouble.

**fast pellet** A nickname for the livelier ball introduced in 1920.

**fast pitch softball** [softball term] An official and once dominant form of softball played by teams of nine players, in which the underhand pitch is delivered to the batter with great speed and, depending on the skill of the pitcher, a varying element of deception. Compare *slow pitch softball.* Also called "fast pitch." Syn. *original softball.*

**fat 1.** *n.* The part of the bat where the ball is best hit; e.g., "He hit it right on the fat of the bat." See also *fat part of the bat.* **2.** *adj.* Said of a high earned run average.

**Fatal Fenway** A pitcher's name for the home field of the Boston Red Sox (Bob Feller, *Strikeout Story,* 1947).

**fat bat** Syn. of *bottle bat.*

**fat cat syndrome** The pattern of a team that falls apart the season after winning a championship. It implies a certain level of collective self-satisfaction seasoned with a dash of winter dissipation.

**Father of Baseball 1.** Patronym assigned to writer Henry Chadwick (1824–1908). "A cloud was cast upon the opening of the season by the death on April 20 of Henry Chadwick, 'the Father of Baseball.' 'Father Chadwick' . . . had been a baseball enthusiast for more than half a century." (*Collier's,* May 2, 1908). Chadwick, who was born in England, advanced the theory that baseball had evolved from the British game of rounders. This led to the appointment of a national commission of "fans" to determine the origin of the game. A short time before Chadwick's death, the commission concluded that baseball was a purely American invention. Chadwick expanded the box score, developed a scoring system, prepared baseball's first guide, and served on early rules committees. **2.** Patronym sometimes applied to baseball missionary Alexander Cartwright (1820–92), a New York bank teller who helped organize the Knickerbocker Base Ball Club in 1845, transforming a children's game into an adult sport by formalizing a game already growing in popularity and codifying three innovations: 1) 90 feet between the bases; 2) dividing the field into fair and foul territories; and 3) forbidding the practice of putting out baserunners by throwing the ball at them, thereby introducing a harder ball which led to faster and sharper play.

**fat one** A home run pitch; a pitch that is delivered down the middle of the strike zone and easy to hit. "Mariners Go Far, 5–1, On [Ken] Dixon's Fat Ones" (*Washington Post* headline, June 5, 1986).

**fat part of the bat** The barrel end of the bat. See also *fat, 1.*

**fat pitch** A pitch that is slow and easy to hit; a pitch that is so hittable, it appears larger to the batter. "[He] wasn't the first baseball player haunted by one terrible game, one fat pitch, one bobbled ball" (*Tampa Tribune,* July 23, 1989).

**fatted calf** *arch.* A player who is not in good physical condition. **1st Use.** 1937. (*New York Daily News,* Sept. 5; Edward J. Nichols).

**fatten the average** To hit safely, thereby increasing a player's or a team's batting average. **1st Use.** 1897. (*New York Tribune,* June 2; Edward J. Nichols).

**FC** Scorecard abbrev. for *fielder's choice.*

**FDR pitch** Lew Burdette's term for a wild pitch: *f*ire, *d*uck, and *r*un.

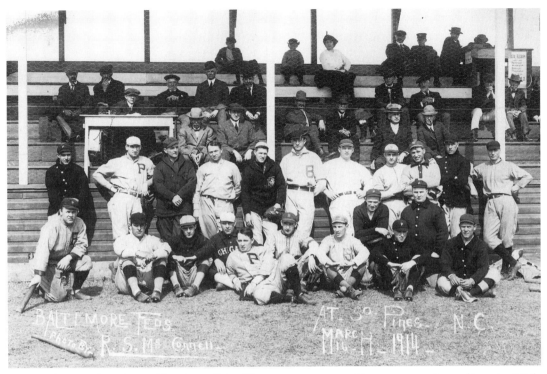

**Federal League.** *The Baltimore Terrapins, a Federal League team as presented in a rare postcard created in spring 1914. The picture was taken before the team's new uniforms arrived.*

**Federal League 1.** An outlaw professional baseball league formed in 1913 with teams in six cities (Chicago, Cleveland, Indianapolis, Pittsburgh, St. Louis, and Covington, Ky., which later was transferred to Kansas City, Mo.) using highly touted semiprofessionals from local leagues, marginal minor leaguers, and former major-league players. **2.** An outlaw major league that fielded eight teams in 1914 and 1915 (Indianapolis Hoosiers [1914 only], Newark Peppers [1915 only], Chicago Whales, Baltimore Terrapins, Buffalo Blues, Brooklyn Tip-Tops, Kansas City Packers, Pittsburgh Rebels, and St. Louis Terriers) using many players that jumped from the American League and the National League. The league challenged the antitrust nature of organized baseball's reserve clause, but presiding judge Kenesaw Mountain Landis's reluctance to hand down an immediate decision clouded the league's future. The league foundered due to generous player contracts, legal fees for injunctions and court rulings over player contracts, and capital investments in new ballparks. The Federal League was the last serious attempt to establish a third league of professional baseball at a major-league level. See: Marc Okkonen, *The Federal League of 1914–1915* (1989). Syn. *Feds.*

**Feds** Short for *Federal League,* 2.

**feeder 1.** A forerunner of baseball, played as a variation of rounders on a diamond-shaped field in Engilsh metropolises and in New England in the early 1800s (*The Boy's Own Book,* 1829). When the batter strikes the ball, he "drops the bat, and runs," but in a clockwise direction. The batter is out "if he misses three times," if the ball is caught, or if he is struck by a thrown ball while running between bases. **2.** The pitcher in the game of feeder. Syn. *pecker.* **3.** A player or coach who stands behind the mound during batting practice and supplies the pitcher with balls.

**feel the apple** To choke up. The term is a reference to one's Adam's apple. See also *apple comes up.* Var. "feel the apple in his throat."

**fence 1.** Any boundary surrounding the field of play. "When you go into the fence, you use the fence to come back throwing. Don't let the fence use you." (Willie Mays, quoted in *New York Times,* Mar. 3, 1986). **2.** That portion of the field's boundary over which home runs are hit. **1st Use.** 1861. "He sent a whizzer away 'over the fence'" (*New York Mercury,* Oct. 16; David Shulman).

**fence-buster** A long-ball hitter. "Fence-busters [Willard] Marshall, [Johnny] Mize, [Walker] Cooper" (*Time* magazine photo caption, Aug. 25, 1947). Also spelled "fence buster." **1st Use.** 1907. (*New York Evening Journal,* Apr. 8; Edward J. Nichols).

**Fenway Park** Home field of the Boston Red Sox since 1912. Located in Boston, Mass., it is one of the last of the old-time ballparks and is much admired for its cozy atmosphere and odd dimensions, which were dictated by the path of railroad tracks rather than the ingenuity of architects. It is the smallest ballpark in the major leagues and is dominated by a gigantic left-field wall known as the Green Monster. The park was named by former owner John I. Taylor for the fact that it was in the Fenway section of Boston. "I love this park. I think Fenway is the essence of baseball." (Tom Seaver, quoted in *Boston Globe,* July 1, 1986). **Etymology.** A fen is an area of low marshland, which described the Back Bay section of Boston until it was filled in during the late 1800s. However, part of the area was maintained in its original state as a park and the road between downtown Boston and the Back Bay fen was named "The Fenway." The name attached itself to the neighborhood surrounding the site of the ballpark.

**fernalia** Syn. of *catcher's equipment.* **Etymology.** "Obviously, a corruption of the word 'paraphernalia.' Some catcher couldn't pronounce it and gave up." (Frank Gibbons, *Baseball Digest,* May 1959).

**Fernandomania** Wild enthusiasm for Mexican pitcher Fernando Valenzuela, who had a sensational season for the Los Angeles Dodgers in 1981, leading the National League in strikeouts, innings pitched, and complete games.

**fiddle hitcher** A pitcher who uses delaying tactics. Dizzy Dean explained: "Usually a pitcher who's been up there a long time and has lost his stuff, so he takes to fiddle hitchin' to get them batters out. He's a guy what fiddles around—hitchin' his trousers, fixin' his cap, kicken' around in the dirt—so's the opposin' batter will get riled up and blew up."

**field 1.** *n.* The playing area; the baseball field itself. **1st Use.** 1845. (Knickerbocker Rules). **2.** *n.* A ballpark; e.g., Ebbets Field and Wrigley Field. **3.** *n.* The outfield of a baseball park. **4.** *n.* The active players on a baseball team. **5.** *n.* The defensive team; the players who are in the field. **6.** *v.* To stop, catch, or throw a baseball in play. **1st Use.** 1870. (*New York Herald,* May 15; Edward J. Nichols). **7.** *v.* To play as a fielder; to have players on the field; to deploy defensively, as in "to field" an infield.

**fielder** A player in any defensive position (although the term is seldom applied to the pitcher or catcher). See also *infielder; outfielder.*

**fielder's choice 1.** The act of a defensive player who fields a batted ball and attempts to put out a baserunner rather than retire the batter-runner; i.e., the fielder has chosen to allow the batter-runner to take first base so that a preceding runner can be put out. Whether there has been a fielder's choice is determined by the official scorekeeper. When one is ruled, the batter is charged with a turn at bat, but he is not credited with a base hit, even though he reached base. Syn. *fielder's option.* **1st Use.** 1898. (*New York Tribune,* May 1; Edward J. Nichols). **2.** A term used by the official scorer to account for a) a batter who reaches base safely when the defense attempts to put out a runner farther along the basepath, b) a baserunner who advances a base while the attempt is made to put out another runner, and c) a baserunner who makes an undefended steal of a base. Abbrev. *FC.*

**fielder's option** Syn. of *fielder's choice,* 1. **1st Use.** 1912. (*New York Tribune,* Sept. 29; Edward J. Nichols).

**field general** A team's manager as opposed to the general manager.

**field goal** Kicking the ball, similar to a football player kicking a field goal. During the fifth inning of the third game of the 1951 World Series, New York Giants second baseman Eddie Stanky kicked the ball out of the hands of New York Yankees shortstop Phil Rizzuto while sliding into second base on an attempted steal. The ball went into center field as Stanky reached third base. The play led to a five-run inning that enabled the Giants to win, 6–2. The play became known as "Stanky's field goal."

**field hand** A baseball player.

**fielding** The defensive act of catching, stopping, controlling, and throwing batted and thrown balls.

**fielding average** A statistic that is used to evaluate a player's fielding ability. It is computed by dividing a player's total number of putouts and assists by the sum of his chances (putouts, assists, and errors). A player with 670 putouts and assists in 687 chances has a fielding average of .975. See also *fielding percentage.* **1st Use.** 1902. (*Sporting Life,* Sept. 20; Edward J. Nichols).

**fielding glove** See *glove,* 1.

**fielding percentage** A *fielding average* expressed as a percentage; e.g., 97.5% as opposed to .975. Abbrev. *FP.*

**fielding practice** Pregame warmup, which usually involves a coach hitting balls with a fungo bat. **1st Use.** 1908. (*Baseball Magazine,* June; Edward J. Nichols).

**field manager** The individual who oversees the actual playing activities of a baseball team.

**field of dreams** Baseball as a metaphor of hopes and mythology. The term came into general use after the movie *Field of Dreams,* based on W. P. Kinsella's *Shoeless Joe* (1982), appeared in 1989.

**field umpire** An *umpire* stationed anywhere but behind home plate. The field umpire may take any position on the playing field that he thinks is best suited to make impending decisions on the bases. See also *base umpire.*

**fifth 1.** *n.* The fifth inning. **2.** *adv.* Said of the fifth position in the batting order; e.g., "Smith is batting fifth."

**fifth infielder** A role that belongs to—but is not always assumed by—the pitcher. The term is used by coaches and managers to emphasize the importance of a pitcher being ready to field a ball after it has been delivered. "Most balls hit through the box go for base hits, which is why the pitcher should be the fifth infielder" (New York Yankees pitcher Vic Raschi, quoted in *San Francisco News,* July 6, 1949; Peter Tamony).

**50-50 club** A mythical group of players who have hit 50 home runs and stolen 50 bases in a single season. New York Mets outfielder Darryl Strawberry aspired publicly to becoming a member in 1989 (he failed: 29 home runs and 11 stolen bases). Compare *30-30 club; 40-40 club.*

**55-footer** A bad pitch that bounces in the dirt before reaching home plate. The term is facetious because the actual distance from the pitcher's rubber to the plate is 60 feet, 6 inches. Var. "55-foot breaking ball"; "55-foot fastball."

**figger filbert** Var. of *figure filbert.* **1st Use.** 1842. "Figger Filbert" (*Baseball Magazine* caption, Aug. David Shulman).

**fight off 1.** To be a persistent batter who fouls off pitches until he gets the pitch he wants; e.g., "Smith fought off the well-placed pitches by getting a piece of the ball." Typically, a batter with a two-strike count will foul off a pitch that would be difficult to hit but would be a called third strike if he did not attempt to hit it. **2.** To hit an inside pitch, such as one near the batter's fists.

**fight the ball** For a defensive player to have a difficult time fielding a batted ball. "[Buck Weaver's] tendency to make every play as fast as possible has kept him 'fighting the ball' thereby making for himself a lot of hard chances which he could handle easier" (Irving Sanborn, *Chicago Tribune,* Apr. 1914). **1st Use.** 1910. (*New York Evening Journal,* Mar. 10; Edward J. Nichols).

**figure eight** [softball term] A delivery in fast pitch softball in which the arm is swung in a figure eight, combining some of each of the *slingshot* and *windmill* deliveries. The ball is moved back quickly, but not shot forward as in the slingshot; rather, it describes a figure-eight pattern as it heads toward the batter. It is more difficult to master than the other two deliveries.

**figure filbert** One who loves numbers; a statistics nut. A filbert is a type of nut. Syn. *figger filbert.* **1st Use.** 1943. "With the Figure Filberts" (*Baseball Magazine* article title, Apr.; David Shulman).

**fill in** To substitute for a regular player on a short-term basis.

**fill the bases** To put runners at first base, second base, and third base. **1st Use.** 1884. (*DeWitt's Base Ball Guide;* Edward J. Nichols).

**find a pitcher** To get hits off a pitcher, as if one has "found" his secret or weakness. **1st Use.** 1888. (Chicago *Inter-Ocean,* July 7; Edward J. Nichols).

**find the handle 1.** For a fielder to control or keep a firm grip on a batted or thrown ball; e.g., "Smith failed to throw to third as he could not find the handle on the ball." **2.** A command shouted to a fielder who has just made a glaring error.

**find his pots and pans** To pitch a jamball; to get into a batter's "kitchen."

**fine 1.** *n.* A monetary penalty imposed on an individual for behavior deemed detrimental to the club, the league, baseball in general. Fines can be imposed by the manager, the owner, the league president, or the commissioner. **2.** *adv.* Precise or exacting; e.g., "That's when I stopped trying to be so fine with every pitch and just threw the ball" (Baltimore Orioles pitcher Eric Bell, quoted in *Washington Post,* July 24, 1987).

**finesse pitcher** A pitcher who relies on placement, deception, change of speed, and guile rather than velocity and power. "I know that there will come a day when I'll have to make a transition from a power pitcher to a finesse pitcher, but by that time I'll have 11 years in the game" (New York Yankees pitcher Ron Guidry, quoted in *Baltimore Sun,* June 13, 1982). Compare *power pitcher.* Syn. "finesser."

**fingering** The "mysterious science" used by pitchers to obtain the proper grip on the ball, depending on the desired pitch. It is accomplished by employing a combination of finger position and pressure on the ball. An important element of fingering is how the pitcher's fingers are positioned in regard to the seams of the ball.

**fingernail ball** Syn. of *fingertip ball.*

**finger system** The system of communication by which the catcher signals a suggested pitch to the pitcher by flashing the fingers on his bare hand. From the crouched position, the catcher gives the finger signals between his legs to keep the batter from seeing them. Traditionally, one finger is given for a fastball and two for a curveball. Many catchers put white adhesive tape on their fingers so they can be seen from the mound.

**fingertip ball** A *knuckleball* thrown by gripping the ball with one's fingertips. It appears to have been first delivered by Detroit Tigers pitcher Ed Summers in 1908. Syn. *fingernail ball.*

**fingertip pitch** A knuckleball.

**finisher** Syn. of *closer,* 2.

**finish off** For a pitcher to get a batter out.

**Finleyites** A nickname for the Kansas City A's and Oakland A's when the team was owned (1961–80) by Charles O. Finley.

**fire 1.** *v.* To throw the ball with power and force, such as a pitcher throwing a fastball or an infielder throwing to first base to retire a speedy hitter. **2.** *n.* A rally or threat to score. Relief pitchers are brought in to "put out fires." **3.** *n.* An exceptional fastball.

**fire and fall back** To swing the bat with such force that one falls backward. The term is a play on the recoil that results from firing a powerful firearm.

**fireball** A fastball. **1st Use.** 1931. (*The World* [New York], Feb. 26; Edward J. Nichols).

**fireballer** A pitcher whose primary pitch is the fastball.

**fire brigade** That part of a pitching staff consisting of relief pitchers. "Orioles Owe Medals to Their Fire Brigade" (*Washington Post* headline, June 22, 1989).

**fireman 1.** A relief pitcher, one who comes in "to put out a fire" (a rally by the opposition). Syn. *hoser.* **Etymology/1st Use.** 1939. "Johnny Murphy, grand old fireman of the Yankees, today had his first defeat of 1939 tagged onto his entry in the pitching records of the American League" (*New*

*York World-Telegram,* June 15; Barry Popik). In a letter (June 12, 1960) to Jack McDonald of the *San Francisco News-Call Bulletin,* Peter Tamony pointed out that the term had been in use colloquially in the 1920s (based on his interviews with players of the period), that it was showing up in print by 1940, and by the end of the 1950s it was "the name . . . of a new era in baseball." The first player whose name was broadly associated with the term was New York Yankees relief pitcher Johnny Murphy, who was nicknamed "Fireman." "As he doused rallies, Johnny Murphy . . . evoked the term 'fireman'" (Peter Tamony, letter to *San Francisco Chronicle,* Feb. 26, 1979). In the late 1940s, New York Yankees relief pitcher Joe Page was nicknamed "Fireman" and, in fact, posed for publicity photographs in a fire chief's hat. **2.** *arch.* A player who showers and dresses quickly after a game, in the manner of a fireman preparing to go out and fight a fire. **Usage Note.** An interesting distinction was made when both meanings of the term coexisted in Herbert Simons's (*Baseball Magazine,* Jan. 1943) article on baseball language: "A 'fireman' in baseball writers' parlance, usually is a relief pitcher who rushes in to quench the conflagration, but to the player, he's the teammate who showers and dresses the fastest after a game."

**Fireman of the Year Award** An annual award presented by *The Sporting News* since 1960 to the relief pitchers in each major league with the highest combined totals of wins plus saves. See also *Rolaids Relief Man Award.*

**fireplug** A short, stocky player.

**firepower** The offense of a baseball team.

**fire sale** Large-scale sale or trading of players to reduce costs while making money; e.g., "the Great San Diego Fire Sale" of 1993 when the Padres traded Gary Sheffield and Fred McGriff. "The world champion [Florida] Marlins' fire sale [1997–98] is nothing new to baseball" (Keith Olbermann, *Sports Illustrated,* May 25, 1998).

**Firestone** A zero on the scoreboard. During a telecast of a Minnesota Twins game on Aug. 25, 1989, broadcaster Jim Kaat uttered "keep hanging up those Firestones." At that time Kaat, a former

player, explained the term was "an old one" that was often heard in dugouts. The allusion is to Firestone tires, which resemble zeros.

**fireworks** An impressive offensive display, usually including a rapid succession of extra-base hits.

**firing line** Syn. of *mound,* 1. The term jibes nicely with "battery." **1st Use.** 1902. (*Sporting Life,* Apr. 26; Edward J. Nichols).

**first 1.** *n.* Short for *first base.* **2.** *n.* The first inning. **3.** *adv.* Said of the first position in the batting order; e.g., "Smith is batting first." **4.** *n.* That which is new to the game. Baseball is usually fascinated by "firsts." An exception was pointed out in a *Life* magazine editorial (Aug. 13, 1971) on the 1971 All-Star Game: "They [the announcers] didn't allude to an All-Star 'first'—for the first time both starting pitchers were black."

To underscore the game's infatuation with firsts, here are a few examples from the file marked "firsts" in the National Baseball Library and Archives in Cooperstown, N.Y.:

The first woman to receive a World Series share: Edna Jameson, who worked for the Cleveland Indians, was given a slice of the Series proceeds in 1920.

The first time two black managers faced each other in a game: June 27, 1989, when the Toronto Blue Jays (managed by Cito Gaston) played the Baltimore Orioles (managed by Frank Robinson).

The first player in baseball history to be still active while eligible for a pension: Hoyt Wilhelm (according to *The Sporting News,* May 3, 1969).

The first professional player to hit a home run from opposite sides of the plate in the same inning: Gary Pellant of the Carolina League Alexandria Mariners on Apr. 30, 1979.

The first game in which two triple plays were accomplished: The July 17, 1990, game between the Minnesota Twins and the Boston Red Sox when the Twins executed two 5-4-3 triple plays.

The first wedding at home plate: League Park in Cincinnati on Sept. 18, 1893.

The first team to wear shorts: The Hollywood Stars on Apr. 1, 1950.

The first major-league club to travel by airplane: The Boston Red Sox, which flew from St. Louis to Chicago on July 30, 1936.

The first written reference to the existence of a ball: The Bible, Isaiah 22:18—"[He will seize firm hold on you,] and whirl you round and round, and throw you like a ball into a wide land; there you shall die . . ."

**first and fifteenth player** A player who thinks only of paydays, such as the first and fifteenth days of the month.

**first bagger** Syn. of *first baseman.*

**first ball** **1.** A ceremonial ball that is tossed before the beginning of the game, most commonly associated with the opening day of the season, but which increasingly has been used at other games, such as the All-Star Game and World Series games. At its most spectacular, the President of the United States throws out the first ball on Opening Day to signal the beginning of another season. Sometimes the symbolism is even greater than the actual event.

When President Harry Truman threw out the first ball in 1946 at Griffith Stadium, he was showing the nation that the war years were indeed over and that the President once again had time for such trivial pursuits as throwing out the first ball. At a lower level, various people are asked to throw out balls as an honor, for reasons as simple as being the president of the company sponsoring Seat Cushion Night. See also *throw out the first ball.* **2.** The first pitch thrown to a batter.

**first-ball hitter** A hitter who routinely swings at the first pitch; e.g., Chicago White Sox shortstop Ozzie Guillen.

**first-ball itch** A compulsion to swing at the first pitch.

**first base** **1.** The base located to the right side of and 90 feet from home plate, which is one quarter of the way around the bases on the way to scoring

**First ball.** *President Franklin D. Roosevelt throwing out the first ball before the U.S. entered World War II. For reasons of security and propriety, F.D.R. did not involve himself in this ceremony while there was a war on.*

a run; the base to be touched first by a baserunner. "The first in order of the fair stations comprising the diamond," according to Edward J. Nichols. Abbrev. *1B.* Syn. *first,* 1. **2.** The position played by the first baseman. Abbrev. *1B.* Syn. *first,* 1. **1st Use.** 1845. (Knickerbocker Rules). **Extended Use. 1.** Initial success, often phrased in the negative: "I never got to first base." **2.** In teenage slang, at various times since the 1930s, first base has meant kissing. In this context each base represents a further level of sexual involvement up to the ultimate home run.

**first base coach** A member of the managerial staff who stands in the coach's box adjacent to first base. His primary job is to instruct the baserunner on first base on whether it is safe to advance. He may also relay signals from the manager to the batter or to a runner on second base. Syn. *barker.*

**first base line** The line extending from home plate to first base. See also *right field line.*

**first baseman** The defensive player stationed at first base. Abbrev. *1B.* Syn. *first bagger; first sacker.*

**first baseman's mitt** A special, scooplike, thinly padded glove that enables the first baseman to more easily catch thrown balls.

**first division** *obs.* The top half of a league's standings (the first four teams in an eight-team league or the first five teams in a ten-team league) before 1969, when each of the two major leagues was broken into two Divisions. Compare *second division.* **1st Use.** 1892. (*Chicago Herald,* June 30; Edward J. Nichols).

**first half 1.** That part of the baseball season before the All-Star break in mid-July. Compare *second half,* 1. **2.** That part of the inning when the visiting team gets its turn at bat. Compare *second half,* 2. Syn. *top,* 1; *top half; upper half,* 1.

**first pitch** The first ball pitched to a batter in a game or starting an inning.

**first sacker** Syn. of *first baseman.*

**first string** *n.* The collection of players on a team who are best at their positions and who are chosen for regular play. Compare *second string.* **1st**

**Use.** 1912. (*New York Tribune,* Apr. 15; Edward J. Nichols).

**first-string** *adj.* Said of a player who is given a regular playing assignment; e.g., starting lineups are composed of "first-string" players. **Etymology.** See *second-string.*

**first stringer** A player in the starting lineup. **1st Use.** 1920. "Cady was a young pitcher . . . even though he had not been accepted as a first stringer" (Burt L. Standish, *The Man on First;* David Shulman).

**first ups** The team to come to the plate at the very beginning of the game. In organized baseball, the visiting team always has first ups. "We used to choose up sides by palming our hands on a bat and the guy whose fist last closed around it got 'first ups'" (Jim Murray, *The Best of Jim Murray,* 1965).

**fish 1.** *v.* To swing at a pitch outside the strike zone; e.g., "The pitcher tried to make me fish." See also *go fishing.* **2.** *n.* A batter who refuses the lure of swinging at pitches outside the strike zone; e.g., "The fish ain't biting."

**fish cakes** *arch.* Low pay, particularly that which is paid in the minor leagues. The term appears to have been popular in the 1930s. **1st Use.** 1943. (*Baseball Magazine,* Jan.; David Shulman).

**fisherman** A batter who chases ("casts for") pitches out of the strike zone.

**fish hook** A curveball.

**fishing trip** A swing at a bad pitch. "A player who goes on 'a fishing trip' hasn't been away on a vacation. He merely took a swing at a bad ball." (*Baseball Magazine,* Jan. 1943; David Shulman). **1st Use.** 1937. (*Pittsburgh Press,* May 2; Edward J. Nichols).

**fist 1.** To jam the batter; to throw the ball in at his fists; e.g., "The pitcher fisted him with a slider inside." **2.** To hit a pitch with the part of the bat just above the batter's hands; e.g., "Smith fisted a single into left."

**fitness of the ground** Field conditions as they are affected by the weather, groundskeeping, and other uses (such as a football game) of the playing surface.

**5** The scorekeeper's designation for the third baseman.

**five-and-ten player** Syn. of *ten-and-five player.*

**five-cent curve** Syn. of *nickel curve.*

**five-dollar ride in a Yellow Cab** A long home run.

**5-4-3** A scorekeeper's notation for a double play in which the ball went from the third baseman (5) to the second baseman (4) to the first baseman (3).

**.500 baseball** The performance of a team that wins as often as it loses. Syn. ".500 ball."

**500 homer club** A mythical club for those with 500 career home runs. Eddie Murray became the 15th member in 1996, the first since Mike Schmidt joined in 1987.

**five-man rotation** A rotation of five starting pitchers in which each works every fifth day. See also *four-man rotation.*

**five-o'clock hitter** A great batting-practice slugger "who turns meek once the game starts"; e.g., "Billy Ashley, Mark Parent and Jeff Manto . . . put on shows that prompt teammates to wonder aloud, 'What time is it?' " (*Sports Illustrated,* May 11, 1998). See also: *ten-o'clock hitter; one-o'clock hitter; two-o'clock hitter; six-o'clock hitter; seven-o'clock hitter.*

**five-o'clock lightning** *arch.* The scoring of runs late in the game. The term was used when baseball was played exclusively during the day, with most games beginning around three o'clock. Phil Rizzuto has said the ability to strike five-o'clock lightning was characteristic of some of the New York Yankees teams on which he played in the 1950s.

**flag 1.** *n.* The *pennant,* 1. **1st Use.** 1883. (*Sporting Life,* Aug. 13; Edward J. Nichols). **2.** *v.* To signal a runner as he approaches a base. **1st Use.** 1935. (Ralph H. Barbour, *How to Play Better Baseball;* David Shulman). **3.** *v.* To catch or stop a batted ball; e.g., "Jones flagged Smith's line drive." The term probably was derived from the railroad term for stopping a train with a red flag. **1st Use.** 1920. (*New York Times,* Oct. 10; Edward J. Nichols).

**flag chase** Syn. of *pennant race.*

**flag down** To catch a pitched baseball; e.g., "The catcher could not flag down Smith's knuckleball."

**flake** An odd or eccentric player; a kidder or comic. "Reporters, for reasons no one can really understand, want to be kind to them. A flake can literally go berserk in the clubhouse and the news never gets out." (Wells Twombly, *San Francisco Examiner,* Dec. 1, 1970; Peter Tamony). **Usage Note.** The term carries a certain element of endearment and tends to be applied to likable, but not always reliable, kooks. **Etymology.** Tim Considine (*New York Times Magazine,* 1982) reports that the term "was first applied in the 1950s by baseball Giants teammates . . . to the offbeat San Francisco outfielder Jackie Brandt, from whose mind, it was said, things seemed to flake off and disappear." Maury Allen (*Bo: Pitching and Wooing,* 1973) says that Brandt's St. Louis Cardinals teammate Wally Moon created the term in 1956: "Moon suggested that Brandt was so wild his brains were falling out of his head, flaking off his body, hence, a flake." Other famous baseball flakes include Phil Linz, Denny McLain, Bill Lee, Doug Radar, Ross Grimsley, and Jay Johnstone.

The term, however, had earlier slang meanings. It has referred to a small packet of cocaine since the 1920s. In another earlier incarnation, Walter Winchell (*San Francisco Call-Bulletin,* Feb. 8, 1935; Peter Tamony) noted in an article on Harlem slang that it was one of several nicknames (along with "ofay," "pink," and "keltch") for a white person.

**flaky** Strange, eccentric, a bit off; said of a player who behaves oddly. "I found it's much easier to have a flaky front and do as you wish underneath, rather than present a straight intellectual front. Then when you do something flaky, they say, 'Oh, my gosh, look at this one.' Now they come to expect it and you do something weird and they say, 'Yeah, that's him.' " (Texas Rangers relief pitcher Jim Kern, on the subject of "floating with life," *San Francisco Examiner,* Nov. 30, 1979; Peter Tamony). Also spelled "flakey." **Etymology.** See *flake.* Eric Partridge (*Dictionary of the Underworld,*

1949) noted that "flaky" has been a term for co-caine addiction since the 1920s. **Extended Use.** The term is used widely in other realms, such as when President Reagan said that Col. Mu'ammar al-Gadhafi of Libya was "flakey." Ann Landers said in a 1962 column: "This man is as flakey as mother's apple-pie crust."

**flameball** A high-velocity fastball.

**flamethrower** A fastball pitcher; e.g., Nolan Ryan and Roger Clemens.

**flame-throwing** Possessing a superior fastball.

**flare 1.** *n.* A looping fly ball likely to fall in between the infield and outfield and usually hit to the opposite field. Since the 1970s, the term has been another synonym for *Texas Leaguer* or *blooper,* 1. "Against a right-hander like [Mike] Boddicker the left-handers have to get on [base]. You can't expect a right-hander to hit defensively against him and get a flare to right." (Mike Schmidt, quoted in *New York Post,* Oct. 13, 1983). **Usage Note.** Announcer Vin Scully said during World Series broadcast (Oct. 21, 1986) that the modern player preferred "flare" to "Texas Leaguer." **2.** *v.* To hit a flare; e.g., "I flared a single" (Jeff Reboulet, quoted in *Baltimore Sun,* Apr. 27, 1998).

**flash 1.** *v.* To give signals quickly in the hope that one's opponents cannot steal them. **2.** *n.* A signal given only once and quickly, such as a tug of the belt.

**flat** Said of a pitch that has a straight trajectory and no deceptive movements and is usually easy to hit. Compare *live,* first entry.

**flat-footed 1.** Unprepared, asleep, not on one's toes; said of a player caught napping. **2.** Said of a baserunner who runs on his heels rather than the balls of his feet. **3.** Said of batting stance with both feet flat on the ground as opposed to a stance in which the batter rests on the balls of his feet; said of a batter who does not stride. The flat-footed position is considered to be the optimum one for hitting a sacrifice fly.

**flea-box** A very small ballpark.

**flew 1.** See *fly,* 2. **2.** See *fly out,* 1.

**fling** To pitch a baseball.

**flinger** A pitcher. **Usage Note.** The term is often used in a context with a clear derogatory edge, long paired with "alleged," which makes it an outright insult. **1st Use.** 1908. (*New York Press,* May 6; Peter Morris).

**flip 1.** *n.* A pitch thrown in the direction of the batter's body. "A good flip may require that the pitcher throw the ball at a spot where the batter would be if he knew the pitch was meant just for him, and duck" (Jim Brosnan, *The Long Season,* 1960). **2.** *v.* To throw a pitch in the direction of a batter's body; to cause a batter to hit the dirt. **3.** *n./arch.* Syn. of *flipper,* 2. **4.** *n.* A light, underhand toss that goes only a short distance. **5.** *v.* To toss the ball underhand without much velocity; e.g., the second baseman "flips" the ball to the first baseman. **6.** *v.* To propel a fielded ball with a snap of the wrist.

**flip game** A game played by baseball players in which a ball is batted gently to a line of players who flip it back and forth until the ball touches the ground. "It's a good game, passes the time, and probably adds to your manual dexterity" (Jim Bouton, *I'm Glad You Didn't Take It Personally,* 1971).

**flipper 1.** A pitcher. **2.** A player's throwing arm. Syn. *flip,* 3.

**flipping** A game played with baseball cards. Cullen P. Vane (San Jose, Calif.) describes the version he played as a child: "The game involved two players who would turn over a stack of cards and start 'flipping' them over with each player alternating. If I flipped over a Yankee and my opponent flipped a Yankee on top of it, then he would get the whole pile of cards that had built up. This is similar to War, which is played with a regular deck of cards. I can remember playing this game for hours during recess with hundreds of cards being exchanged. Of course it was always important to take out your favorite player's cards before starting."

**flip-ups** Pull-down sunglasses.

**flivver** *arch.* A player who fails to use or show his ability. **1st Use.** 1915. (*Baseball Magazine,* Dec.; Edward J. Nichols).

**floater** A slowly pitched ball with very little spin or twist, intended to catch the batter off balance; a pitch that seems as if it "floats" its way toward home plate. According to the National Baseball Library and Archives, the pitch was first made popular by Bill Phillips at Indianapolis around 1906. See also *folly floater; freaky floater.* **1st Use.** 1906. (*Sporting Life,* Mar. 3; Edward J. Nichols).

**Flock** A nickname for the Brooklyn Dodgers.

**flock hits** Syn. of *bunched hits.*

**floop** To hit weakly, but safely; to bat poorly, but successfully. The term is perhaps a blend of "flub" plus "bloop," or "fluke" plus "bloop." **1st Use.** 1937. (*New York Times,* Oct. 10; Edward J. Nichols).

**floper** A spectator to those on the field and in the front office.

**Florida Marlins** A National League East Division expansion team in Miami that came into being in 1993 and were world champions by 1997.

**fluffy duff** A player who is easily hurt. The term was used by Dizzy Dean and may have been coined by him.

**fluid hitter** A hitter whose swing is smooth and easy, not intermittent.

**fluke** A play or score made by chance or accident.

**fluke hit** A hit that should have resulted in an out but by a fluke, the batter reached base safely. See also *Chinese blow.*

**flutterball** A pitch that wobbles and travels slowly. It is a variation of a knuckleball delivered with a snap of the wrist. Also spelled "flutter ball."

**fluttering cuff** The loose, ragged sleeve of pitcher Dazzy Vance, which so distracted batters that a rule was established that prohibited pitching with ragged or slit sleeves.

**fly** 1. *n.* Short for *fly ball.* Abbrev. *F,* 1. **1st Use.** 1860. Edward J. Nichols found two references for this year: the minutes of the Knickerbocker Base Ball Club and *Beadle's Dime Base-Ball Player.* **2.** *v.* To bat a ball high into the air that is caught by a fielder before touching the ground. Past tense: "flied" or sometimes "flew." **1st Use.** 1908. (*Brook-lyn Daily Eagle,* May 28; Edward J. Nichols). **3.** *n.* A pest; a persistent fan who will not leave a player alone. See also *green fly.*

**fly away** To be put out by hitting a fly ball that is fielded before hitting the ground; e.g., "Smith flied away to the center fielder."

**fly ball** A batted ball that rises high into the air before it drops, as opposed to one batted on the ground. A traditional rule of thumb is that to be called a fly ball, the ball should reach a height of around 15 feet before dropping. A fly ball that is caught before touching the ground is an out. Such a fly ball was not part of the original rules of the Knickerbocker Base Ball Club, but one member of the club, J. W. Davis, waged a long campaign to have it adopted. The Knickerbockers adopted it in 1865. Sometimes spelled "flyball." Syn. *fly,* 1; *air ball; palomita.* **1st Use.** 1865. (*New York Herald,* Aug. 25; Edward J. Nichols). **Extended Use.** Someone who is goofy, semi-nutty, or an oddball.

**fly-ball pitcher** A pitcher who entices batters to hit fly balls rather than ground balls.

**fly catch** *arch.* The fielding of a fly ball before it touches the ground. **1st Use.** 1862. (Chadwick Scrapbooks; Edward J. Nichols).

**flycatcher** An outfielder. Arnold Hano (*A Day in the Bleachers,* 1955) writes: "I have been a Giant fan for years . . . and I have seen balls hit with violence to extreme center field which were caught easily by Mays, or Thomson before him, or Lockman or Ripple or Hank Leiber or George 'Kiddo' Davis, that most marvelous flycatcher." **Etymology.** From the name of a class of birds that all contain the word "flycatcher" in their names; e.g., the least flycatcher, the scissor-tailed flycatcher, and the great crested flycatcher, the latter being known for its prodigious appetite for weevils, beetles, and other insects that feed on crops.

**fly chaser** An outfielder.

**flyer** A fast runner.

**fly game** A mid-19th century baseball game in which the participants agreed that a batter can be retired if a fielder catches a batted ball "on the fly" rather than "on the bound."

**flyhawk** An outfielder. See also *hawk; ball hawk,* 1.

**fly open 1.** To allow the pitcher's shoulder to turn too far. For a right-hander, the left shoulder is turned too far too soon, the torso is out in front of the arm, leaving the arm to do too much of the work, unassisted by the position of his frame, thereby causing everything the pitcher throws to be harder and thus flatter than it should be. Catcher to pitcher Mike Mussina: "Watch your front side flying open" (*Baltimore Sun,* Feb. 25, 1996). See also *open up,* 2. **2.** Syn. of *open up,* 1.

**fly out 1.** *v.* To hit a fly ball that is caught for an out before it hits the ground. **Usage Note.** Although the past tense of this verb is sometimes stated as "flew out," it is now customary to say or write "flied out." As William Safire (*On Language,* 1980) notes: "When a batter has hit a fly ball which is then caught, the past tense of his action is 'flied out.' The only time 'flew out' would be correct is if the batter dropped his bat, flapped his arms, and soared out of the stadium, thereby earning himself the frothiest head in the *Guinness Book of World Records.*" It has not always been so. Peter Morris discovered that every instance of this tense in the *Detroit Free Press* during the 1881 season (several hundred such) is either "flew out to" or, more commonly, "flew to." "This raises the interesting questions of when and how 'flied out' evolved, but clearly it, and not 'flew out,' is the traditional form." **1st Use.** 1870. (*New York Herald,* May 8; Edward J. Nichols). **2.** *n.* Syn. of *flyout.*

**flyout** *n.* A ball batted in either fair or foul territory that is caught before it touches the ground; a fly-ball out. With the exception of the foul tip, it counts as an out; e.g., "He got two flyouts in the ninth inning." Sometimes spelled *fly out;* "fly-out." Abbrev. *F,* 2.

**fly the flag** To win the league championship; to win the pennant.

**FO** Abbrev. for *force out,* 1.

**FOBs 1.** *arch.* An initialism from the days of the Brooklyn Dodgers for bases that were "full of Brooklyns" or "full of Bums." **2.** An initialism used in Pittsburgh for "full of Bucs." **3.** An initialism used by Baltimore Orioles announcers for "full of Birds."

**fog 1.** *v.* To throw a baseball with great force; e.g., "the center fielder fogged the ball to third" or "the pitcher fogged it in." See also *fog it through.* **2.** *n.* A fastball. **1st Use.** 1937. (*New York Daily News,* Sept. 5; Edward J. Nichols).

**fogger 1.** A fastball pitcher. **1st Use.** 1940. "He's a fogger with a fast one that's fast, a curve that breaks, and he pitches with his noodle" (John R. Tunis, *The Kid from Tomkinsville*). **2.** A baseball thrown with great force. **1st Use.** 1937. (*New York Daily News,* Jan. 31; Edward J. Nichols).

**fog it through** To throw a fastball past a batter. The phrase was created by Dizzy Dean and associated with his delivery, but applied to others as well. See also *fog,* 1. **Etymology.** Dean explained that when he reached back for that something extra for his fastball, it appeared so quickly that it seemed to be coming out of a fog.

**fold 1.** *v.* To fall from a strong position in a game or in the standings. **2.** *n.* The point at which a team fails. Dwight Evans, on the Boston Red Sox team that blew a 14-game lead: "I don't look at 1978 as a fold" (*USA Today,* July 28, 1986). A *Washington Post* headline (Oct. 10, 1988), after the Oakland Athletics won the American League Championship, simply read: "Red Sox 'Outplayed' in '88 Version of Fold."

**follow-through 1.** The continuation of the arm and body in the direction of a pitch or throw; the final stage of a pitcher's motion. **1st Use.** 1909. (*American Magazine,* May; Edward J. Nichols). **2.** The continuation of the swing by the batter after the ball has been hit or missed, bringing the bat all the way around for maximum power. Rogers Hornsby (*My Kind of Baseball,* 1953) discussed a "free follow-through so essential to good hitting."

**folly floater** A *blooper ball* thrown from a hesitation motion by New York Yankees pitcher Steve Hamilton. Although Hamilton described the pitch as a "gag" or novelty, he actually did use it in games. See also *floater.*

**foot in the bucket 1.** The position of a batter who pulls away from the plate as he swings at the ball. It may come as a result of fear of being hit by the ball. It is an awkward move that suggests that the batter's back foot is stuck in an imaginary bucket. More commonly, however, it seems to result from the batter being fooled by the speed or delivery of a pitch, causing a premature swing and shift of weight. This causes the front foot to come forward. John McGraw (*My Thirty Years in Baseball*, 1923): "He [Hughie Jennings] had the bad habit of pulling away with his forward foot when swinging at the ball. In baseball we call that putting one's foot in the water bucket, the idea being that a player will pull so far away as to step to the bench." See also *step in the bucket.* **2.** An unorthodox batting stance in which the batter's front foot is pulled back toward the foul line rather than pointed out toward the pitcher. Dizzy Dean's description: "Sort of a sprattle-legged stance at the plate. The batter looks like he has got a pain in the hip and he sticks his left foot out toward third base." Although such a stance might be interpreted as a sign of timidity in a batter, it is actually an effective, respected stance, used by such successful hitters as Arky Vaughan, Roy Campanella, Al Simmons, and Vern Stephens. So closely was Simmons associated with this stance that when he died on May 26, 1956, the first line of his Associated Press obituary read: "Al Simmons, whose batting feats with an odd 'foot in the bucket' stance earned him a niche in baseball's Hall of Fame, died here early today four days after his 54th birthday." Syn. *foot in the dugout.* **Etymology/1st Use.** 1913. "Take your foot out of the water-bucket, Mister Conley, says Buzz" (C. E. Van Loan, *Score by Innings,* 1919, copyrighted 1913; David Shulman). Phil Pepe (*The Encyclopedia of Sports Talk,* 1976) states that the stance took its name from the front foot, which is withdrawn toward the foul line, "toward the old water bucket in the dugout." Evidence from the first use of "water bucket" used metaphorically, discovered by Peter Morris, suggests it derives from another then-common term as illustrated in this quotation from the *New York American* (Oct. 3, 1908): "[Pitcher George McQuillan] has sent many a Giant back hitless to the water bucket in days gone by." Thus, Morris concludes the term "foot in the bucket" implied that the batter would soon be headed back to the bench. **Extended Use.** To have one's "foot in the bucket" is to act timidly. "Secretary-General Thant of the United Nations shows signs of having his foot in the bucket in getting ready to duck a formal request by the South Vietnamese Government for U.N. observers at the September elections" (*San Francisco Examiner,* June 7, 1966; Peter Tamony).

**foot in the dugout** Syn. of *foot in the bucket,* 2.

**foozle** A bungled play. "Goldblatt . . . scored on Shaneman's foozle of Sullivan's fly" (*Dartmouth Alumni Magazine,* Feb. 1922; David Shulman). **1st Use.** 1905. (*Sporting Life,* Sept. 9; Edward J. Nichols).

**Forbes Field** The home field of the Pittsburgh Pirates from 1909 to 1970. When the Pirates moved into their current park, Three Rivers Stadium, in 1971, Forbes Field was closed and demolished. The original site is now part of the Univ. of Pittsburgh. According to Philip J. Lowry (*Green Cathedrals,* 1992): "Home plate remains in almost its exact original location; only now, it is encased in glass on the first floor walkway of the University of Pittsburgh's Forbes Quadrangle near the exact original location, which is now in a ladies bathroom." The ballpark was named for British General John Forbes who captured Fort Duquesne and renamed it Fort Pitt during the French and Indian War. The fact that there was never a no-hitter thrown in Forbes Field is just one of several odd facts about the park. See also *Greenberg Gardens; Kiner's Korner.*

**force 1.** *n.* Syn. of *force play.* **1st Use.** 1869. (*DeWitt's Official Base Ball Guide;* Edward J. Nichols). **2.** *v.* To cause a baserunner to be put out in a force play. **3.** *v.* To cause a baserunner to advance a base without liability to be put out when the batter or another runner is awarded a base; e.g., preceding runners are "forced" to advance by the award of bases as the penalty for obstruction, or a runner on first base is "forced" to advance to second base upon the batter being hit by the pitch. See also *force in.* **4.** *v.* For a tired pitcher to throw the ball with difficulty; e.g., "Smith forced the ball to the plate."

**force double play** A fielding play in which two putouts are made on a force play. Typically, with a runner on first base, the batter hits a ground ball, which is thrown to the fielder covering second base, who touches the bag for a force out, and then throws the ball to first base to retire the batter. The fielder at second base is the key to this play because he must touch the base and throw the ball to first base while avoiding the sliding runner. Dan Sperling (*Spectator's Guide to Baseball,* 1983) writes: "Although it's a fairly common baseball occurrence, a force double play involving the batter, a baserunner and three fielders is a thing of beauty to behold because of the clockwork precision with which it is executed." Compare *reverse force double play.*

**force in** To cause the baserunner on third base to score a run by walking the batter with the bases loaded.

**force off** *n.* A term frequently used in written rules of the early 1880s to designate any play that forces a runner to leave a base. According to research conducted by Peter Morris, a runner on first base would be "forced off" by a ground ball or a dropped fly ball. The term was frequently used to signify instances when a fielder deliberately dropped the ball. This could be done not only by dropping infield flies, but also by taking advantage of a rule forcing off runners on a dropped strikeout: a catcher could deliberately drop a third strike with the bases loaded and turn it into a triple play. *Spalding's Official Base Ball Guide* (1885): "There is comparatively but little doubt as to the character of a catch, or of the nature of a failure to hold the ball sufficiently as to constitute a legal catch under the rule, under the varying circumstances of a game, except in the case of a 'force off,' that is, when it becomes a point of skillful play to purposely drop a fly ball or miss a catch in order to force a base runner to leave a base." It is easy to see how efforts to discourage deliberate "force offs" eventually gave way to the infield fly rule and no dropped third strikes with first base occupied and less than two outs.

**force out 1.** *n.* The putout of an advancing baserunner who is forced to move to the next base. Abbrev. *FO.* Also spelled "force-out"; "forceout." **1st Use.** 1870. (*New York Herald,* May 8; Edward

J. Nichols). **2.** *v.* To put a runner out by touching the base in a force play.

**force play** A play in which a baserunner legally loses his right to occupy a base when the batter becomes a runner. The defensive action results in the retiring of a baserunner by touching the base to which he is headed and must (is "forced" to) occupy because there is an advancing runner behind him. In such plays, a fair ball (other than one caught on the fly) with a runner on first base forces the runner to advance to second base. In a force play, the runner does not have to be tagged. Syn. *force,* 1.

**Ford C. Frick Award** An award established in 1978 to honor members of the broadcasting profession who have made major contributions to baseball. The award is often erroneously referred to as induction into the "broadcasting section" of the Baseball Hall of Fame. It is named in honor of the former sportswriter, radio broadcaster, National League president, and commissioner of baseball.

**foreign substance** A generic term used in the rules of baseball for illegal materials, such as pine tar, petroleum jelly, and hair dressing, applied to the ball to give the pitcher an advantage. The one substance that is officially allowed is rosin.

**forfeit 1.** *v.* To lose a *forfeited game.* **2.** *n.* Syn. of *forfeited game.*

**forfeited game** A game in which a victory is awarded to a team by the umpire-in-chief because the opposition acts in violation of the rules of baseball. A team can be forced to forfeit a game if it refuses to play, delays the game, fails to remove an ejected player, or fails to place nine players on the field. A game may also be forfeited to the visiting team in the case of unruly behavior on the part of the hometown fans. The official score of a forfeited game is 9–0 because many early forfeited games occurred when one team could not field nine players. See also *Beer Night; Disco Demolition Night.* Syn. *forfeit,* 2.

**"forget it!"** An exclamation used by some sportscasters to describe a long, powerful hit that is obviously a home run. The term is uttered after the outcome of such a hit is never in doubt. Also stated as "you can forget about that one."

**forkball  1.** A pitch gripped between the thumb and the first and middle fingers, which are spread apart, suggesting a two-pronged fork, that breaks on a downward path as it approaches the plate. The grip limits the spin of the ball and causes it to drop or sink sharply as it reaches the plate. See also *split-fingered fastball.* Sometimes spelled "fork ball." Syn. *forked-ball pitch.* The first pitcher to become known for his forkball was Joe Bush. It is associated with Ernie Bonham and was popularized by Elroy Face during his years (1953, 1955–68) with the Pittsburgh Pirates. Face held the ball between his index finger and middle finger on the "smooth" part of the ball. "Jack Morris . . . holds the ball deeper between the second and third fingers, which gives him a more dramatic break but without as much velocity . . . The action on Morris' forkball is classic, too: straight down and violent." (Bob Klapisch, et al., *Inside Sports,* Feb. 1992). **1st Use.** 1916. "[Grover Cleveland] Alexander uses . . . the 'fork ball,' which was talked about so much last year" (*National Police Gazette,* Jan. 29; David Shulman). **2.** Euphemistic name for a "spitball." A profile of pitcher Gaylord Perry (*American Way,* Sept. 1962) noted: "He also acquired another pitch for his repertoire, a pitch he sometimes calls a 'spitter' but most frequently refers to as a 'forkball.'" **3.** A ball pitched by a forkhander.

**forked-ball pitch**  Syn. of *forkball,* 1.

**forkhander**  A left-handed pitcher.

**forkle**  A term used by pitcher Rod Nichols for a pitch which is held like a forkball but is said to react like a knuckleball (*Baltimore Sun,* July 21, 1991).

**for the first time in history**  A phrase that, when written or spoken, indicates the occurrence of an event in baseball that has never happened before. Because such events are rare, the words have taken on a special significance. "For the first time in history, three grand slams were hit in a major league game—a phenomenally bizarre 13-11 Texas Rangers victory over the Baltimore Orioles tonight in Memorial Stadium" (Thomas Boswell, *Washington Post,* Aug. 6, 1986).

**45-foot lane**  A designated area that the batter-runner must stay within when running to first base. Three feet wide, the lane begins halfway down the baseline from home plate and extends 45 feet to first base. The lane is designed to keep the batter-runner from going inside the diamond and interfering with the throw to first. A batter-runner ruled to have left the lane in a deliberate attempt to interfere with the defensive play is called out by the umpire. The batter-runner must stay within the double lines except when getting into position to round first base on his way to second base. See also *three-foot line.*

**40-40 club**  A mythical group of players who have hit 40 or more home runs and stolen 40 or more bases in a single season. It came into prominence at the end of the 1988 season as explained by Eric Brady (*USA Today,* Oct. 4, 1988): "[Jose] Canseco hit 42 home runs and stole 40 bases. Baseball records go back 112 years, but you can count the 40-40 club members on one finger. Canseco. Period. End of list." However, Barry Bonds joined the 40-40 club in 1996 and Alex Rodriguez joined in 1998. Compare *30-30 club; 50-50 club.*

**foshball**  A pitch attributed to Mike Boddicker, David Nied, and a few others that combines the properties of a changeup and split-fingered fastball. "It breaks away from left-handers and is the pitch [Rod] Carew, George Brett and other lefties have found so frustrating" (*USA Today,* Sept. 8, 1983). See also *fush ball.* **Etymology.** "'Fosh' sounded like the perfect word for the movement of the pitch" (David Nied, quoted in *USA Today Baseball Weekly,* Dec. 30, 1992).

**foul  1.** *n.* Syn. of *foul ball.* **1st Use.** 1845. (Knickerbocker Rules). **2.** *v.* To hit a ball into foul territory. **3.** *n.* Syn. of *foul territory.* **4.** *adj.* In foul territory.

**foul away**  Syn. of *foul out.*

**foul back**  To hit a ball backward into foul territory; e.g., "Smith fouled one back to the screen."

**foul balk** *arch.* A term used in early rule books that evolved simply into *balk.*

**foul ball** A legally batted ball that settles in foul territory before reaching first base or third base, or first touches the ground in foul territory beyond first base or third base, or while in or over foul territory, touches an umpire, player, or any foreign object. A batted ball that hits the pitcher's rubber and rebounds into foul territory between home plate and either first base or third base is a foul ball. A foul ball counts against the batter as a strike, unless it is caught on the fly, which then counts as an out. A batter cannot strike out on a foul ball, however, unless he bunts the ball foul with two strikes. Syn. *foul,* 1. **1st Use.** 1860. (*Beadle's Dime Base-Ball Player;* Edward J. Nichols). **Extended Use.** A bad or ignorant person. There is much evidence to suggest that cartoonist/writer T. A. Dorgan was the first to apply the term to an individual. Peter Tamony collected several examples from Dorgan's work, including one in which one of his characters says in reference to a boasting athlete: "Oh, he's just a foul ball" (*San Francisco Call & Post,* July 1, 1925).

**foul ball indicator** A device that determines if a long ball has passed the foul pole in fair or foul territory. Several such devices have been developed over the years, but none has yet to establish itself in the game. One system that received much press attention in 1949 was based on a foul pole with free-swinging rods attached: if the ball touched one of the rods on the foul side a red light went on, while a green light was lit if it passed on the fair side. It was granted U.S. patent 2,461,936.

**foul bound** *obs.* A foul ball caught after taking one bounce. Under early rules of the game, a foul bound was an out. **1st Use.** 1874. (*New York Sun,* June 24; Edward J. Nichols).

**foul bunt** A bunt that lands in foul territory. If a player bunts foul after two strikes, it is counted as a third strike.

**foul fly** A foul ball that rises high into the air. Abbrev. *F,* 3.

**foul ground** Syn. of *foul territory.*

**foul line** One of the two white boundary markings that extend from home plate to the left-field foul pole and from home plate to the right-field foul pole, forming a 90° angle at home plate. **1st Use.** 1875. (*DeWitt's Base Ball Umpire's Guide;* Edward J. Nichols).

**foul off** To hit a pitched ball foul. **Extended Use.** *adj.* Screwed up. "I have seen a buffoon platoon become the company pride in eight weeks, and I have seen a foul-off gun crew develop into a crack outfit in three weeks" (Robert C. Ruark, on the new draft, *San Francisco News,* Aug. 6, 1948; Peter Tamony).

**foul out** *v.* To hit a fly ball that is caught for an out in foul territory. Syn. *foul away.* **1st Use.** 1876. "Hoffman who fouled out" (*Detroit Free Press,* July 27; Peter Morris).

**foul-out** *n.* A fly ball that is caught for an out in foul territory.

"FOUL!"

*Foul.*

**foul pole** Either of two vertical posts erected at the intersection of the outfield fence and the foul line. It aids the umpires to determine if a ball that is hit over the fence is fair or foul. A batted ball that hits the foul pole on the fly is a home run. The foul poles in major-league ballparks must be at least 10 feet tall.

**foul screecher** An untutored spectator who cheers foul balls not knowing that they are not hits. According to Dizzy Dean: "A ladies' day fan who screams on every pop foul."

**foul strike** The proper term for a foul ball, batted with fewer than two strikes, that is not caught on the fly. Originally, a ball batted foul was not counted as a strike, but the rule was changed in 1901, counting fouls as strikes unless there were already two strikes on the batter. **1st Use.** 1845. (Knickerbocker Rules; Edward J. Nichols).

**foul territory** That part of the playing field outside the lines of the 90° angle formed by the foul lines, extended to the fence and perpendicularly upward. A fly ball is playable within foul territory unless it is in an area that has been deemed to be out of play. Charles F. Dery, who collects baseball broadcast slang and phraseology, prizes this brilliant but probably unintentional pun: "The ball landed in foul territory, in the midst of a flock of seagulls." Syn. *foul, 3*; *foul ground*. **1st Use.** 1908. (*Brooklyn Daily Eagle,* May 21; Edward J. Nichols).

**foul tick** A foul ball, not considered a strike, per 1845 Knickerbocker rules.

**foul tip** *n.* A ball that glances off the bat directly into the catcher's hands and legally caught. It counts as a regular swinging strike rather than as a foul ball; thus the batter is out if he foul tips a ball with two strikes against him and the ball is in play. A tipped ball is not counted as a foul tip if it hits any part of the catcher's body before landing in his hands. Syn. *tip-foul.* **1st Use.** 1861. (*Beadle's Dime Base-Ball Player;* Edward J. Nichols).

**foul-tip** *v.* To hit a foul tip.

**4** The scorekeeper's designation for the second baseman.

**four aces** *arch.* A grand slam home run. **1st**

**Use.** 1845. (*New York Morning News,* Oct. 21). An account of a game in Hoboken, N.J., at the Elysian Fields describes a game in which "four aces" were scored off a single hit (Fox Butterfield, *New York Times,* Oct. 4, 1990).

**4-A player** A player who is too good for Class AAA minor leagues but not quite good enough for the major leagues (*USA Today,* May 19, 1998).

**four-bagger** Syn. of *home run.* **1st Use.** 1883. (Chicago *Inter-Ocean,* June 25; Edward J. Nichols).

**.400 hitter** A hitter who has achieved a benchmark season's batting average of .400 or higher. The feat was last accomplished by Ted Williams when he batted .406 in 1941. Ever since Williams's achievement, a perennial question is asked: Will there ever be another .400 hitter? Rod Carew, George Brett, and Wade Boggs have flirted with the number for parts of seasons but all have come up short. Should another one come along, his manager would do well to listen to manager Joe McCarthy's decades-old comment on the subject (*The Sporting News,* 1948): "A manager who cannot get along with a .400 hitter ought to have his head examined." **Extended Use.** A heavy hitter in any realm. A headline (*Bangor* [Maine] *Daily News,* July 18, 1987) on the performance of Maine's senators in the Iran-Contra hearings: ".400 Hitters on a Mediocre Team."

**400-400 club** A mythical club created in 1998 when Barry Bonds became the first player to hit 400 home runs and steal 400 bases in a career.

**four-man rotation** A rotation of four starting pitchers in which each work every fourth day. In the present era, teams with such a rotation are often looking for a fifth starter. See also *five-man rotation.*

**four-master** *arch.* A home run.

**four o'cat** Syn. of *four old cat.*

**four old cat** A variant of *one old cat,* using eight players. Syn. *four o'cat.*

**four-ply wallop** A home run. Syn. "four-ply blow."

**four-seam changeup** A changeup thrown with the middle and ring fingers held across two seams. See also *two-seam changeup.*

**four-seamer 1.** A home run hit on a fat pitch, as described by Joe Goddard (*The Sporting News,* Mar. 6, 1982): "The ball doesn't move at all. It goes straight down the middle, about thigh-high, and the hitter gets all four seams. The result makes the fans go 'ooh-ah.'" Compare *two-seamer,* 1. **2.** Syn. of *four-seam fastball.*

**four-seam fastball** A fastball in which the ball is gripped across (not with) the four seams so that as it comes rotating out of the hand the four seams (instead of just two) are spinning into the air, giving maximum motion to the ball, which will rise with a hop to it. The pitch is thrown by Roger Clemens, among others. Compare *two-seam fastball.* Syn. *four-seamer,* 2; *cross-seamer; cross-seam.*

**4-6-3** A scorekeeper's notation for a double play in which the ball went from the second baseman (4) to the shortstop (6) covering second base to the first baseman (3). Compare *6-4-3.*

**fourth 1.** *n.* The fourth inning. **2.** *adv.* Said of the fourth position in the batting order; e.g., "Smith is batting fourth."

**Fourth of July** The date, roughly halfway through the regular season, that is a standard landmark for measuring a team's success. It is often said that the teams in first place on the Fourth of July will win their divisions, but this actually happens less than half the time.

**four wide ones** Syn. of *base on balls.*

**FP** Abbrev. for *fielding percentage.*

**fracas** Syn. of *rhubarb.*

**frame** Syn. of *inning,* 1. **1st Use.** 1910. (*New York Tribune,* July 13; Edward J. Nichols). **Etymology.** Edward J. Nichols concluded that the term was taken from bowling as "both 'inning' and 'frame' [constituted] divisions of play in their respective games."

**frame the pitch** For a catcher to keep his glove in the strike zone, or as close to it as possible, when receiving the pitch, thereby giving the plate umpire the impression that the pitch is in the strike zone, even if it is not. Keith Hernandez (*Pure Baseball,* 1994) comments: "Gary Carter was ter-rific at framing the pitch for his pitchers and getting more than his share of strike calls on the close ones. If a pitch was called a ball and Gary agreed, he tossed it right back to the pitcher. But if he thought it was a strike, he'd hold the ball perfectly still for a couple of seconds, a polite way to say to the ump, 'Look again. I think you missed that one.'" See also *pull a pitch.*

**franchise 1.** The formal agreement or grant that establishes the existence and ownership of a baseball club. It amounts to a license, which can only be legally granted by Major League Baseball and either the American League or National League. When a club moves from one city to another, the franchise or license remains in force but has been relocated. **1st Use.** 1913. "Besides the legitimate expenditure charges . . . or the 'franchise,' as it is usually called, the depreciation charges, the interest on money invested in players, and a 'charge off' for the depreciation in the value of human flesh and blood, must be considered before profits can be reckoned" (*Technical World,* Jan.; David Shulman). **2.** Syn. of *franchise player.* **1st Use.** According to Peter Tamony, the term was not used in the sense of its application to a player until after World War II, and it may not have come into its own until it began to be attached to Willie Mays. Curley Grieve (*San Francisco Examiner,* Sept. 29, 1957) pointed out that Mays was "the franchise" just as Carl Hubbell was "the meal ticket." Grieve added that the Mays's partisans emphasized: "Hubbell showed once every four days. Willie you can see every day. That's why he's the franchise and not merely a meal ticket" (Peter Tamony). *Time* magazine (June 27, 1977) headlined its article on Tom Seaver's trade from the Mets to the Cincinnati Reds: "How the Franchise Went West." (Peter Tamony).

**franchise player** A superior player around whom a successful team can be built; a player who gives significant added value to the franchise. "He [Cal Ripken Jr.] is what baseball men covet beyond all else, a franchise player. The pilings on which pennant-winners rest, a neophyte Mike Schmidt or Johnny Bench." (Phil Musick, *USA Today,* Mar. 16, 1983). Franchise players included Lou Brock (St. Louis Cardinals), Mickey Mantle (New York Yankees), Willie Mays (New York/San

***Franchise player.*** *Before Mantle, Mays, Musial, Ripken, and McGwire, there was Nap Lajoie. Here he is shown being presented with a horseshoe embedded with 1,009 silver dollars. The money was given to him to celebrate his 10th anniversary in a Cleveland uniform.*

Francisco Giants), and Tom Seaver (New York Mets). Syn. *franchise*, 2.

**frank** *arch.* To be given a base on balls. **1st Use.** 1922. (Ernest J. Lanigan, *Baseball Cyclopedia;* Edward J. Nichols). **Etymology.** Since the early 19th century, the verb has been used to allow a person or thing free passage. The most common use then and now is to mark a piece of mail with an official mark permitting the sender free mailing. Members of Congress and federal agencies retain the privilege.

**Fraternity of Professional Baseball Players of America** Formal name for *Players Fraternity.*

**fraternization** Conversation between players of opposing teams on the field of play. Such behavior is prohibited: "Players of opposing teams shall not fraternize at any time while in uniform" (*Official Baseball Rules,* rule 3.09). But the prohibition is seldom enforced. The term was used frequently during the 1950s when it was argued that the practice would somehow reduce the intensity of performance. Steve Fiffer (*How to Watch Baseball,* 1987) points out that different managers have different policies on fraternization; e.g., New York Mets manager Davey Johnson is quoted: "I don't believe in fraternization. I frown on my players talking to guys on the other team, but I don't have a rule." Rich Marazzi (*The Rules and Lore of Baseball,* 1980) points out that first baseman Willie Stargell of the Pittsburgh Pirates was so given to chatting with runners who stopped at his station that some players and writers ironically referred to the rule as "the Stargell Rule."

**freak delivery** An unconventional pitching delivery, designed to fool the batter. Babe Ruth (*Babe Ruth's Own Book of Baseball,* 1928) wrote: "Most of the 'freak' deliveries have been developed because of some hunch on the part of the pitcher. For instance, in my pitching days, the balls we used had printed on them the trade mark and the name of the league president. It was my hunch that this ink on the side of the ball gave just an added atom of weight to the printed side. Consequently in pitching a curve ball I was careful to hold the inked side of the ball on the side that I wanted the curve to break. A foolish notion, perhaps, but one that I always followed."

**freak pitching** An unconventional method of pitching, usually designed to throw off or fool the batter. It is sometimes applied to illegal pitches, such as emery balls and mud balls, but also to a pitch that is legal but idiosyncratic. **1st Use.** 1922. "Passing of 'Freak' Pitching" (J. E. Wray, *How to Pitch,* caption; David Shulman).

**freaky floater** A *blooper ball.* Wayne Minshew, describing a Phil Niekro pitch (*The Sporting News,* Aug. 28, 1971): "The pitch is off-speed but slower than the normal change-up. It floats to a height of about 10 to 15 feet, but not as high as the blooper [eephus] Rip Sewell threw a few years ago."

**Fred Hutchinson Award** An annual award given to a player for dedication to team, community, and family, for competitive spirit, and for overcoming adversity with courage, honor, and dignity. It honors the memory of Fred Hutchinson, Detroit

Tigers pitcher and manager of three teams, who died of cancer in 1964. Syn. *Hutch Award.*

**free agency 1.** The state of being a free agent. **2.** The system under which free agents operate. It allows players with at least six years of major-league experience to sign with the clubs of their choice after their current contracts expire (players with fewer than six years of experience are bound to their clubs by the reserve clause). Modern free agency came to Major League Baseball as a result of a dispute involving pitchers Andy Messersmith and Dave McNally, who after the 1975 season, persuaded arbitrator Peter Seitz that the standard major-league players' contract gave clubs only a one-year option on their players' services, not the perpetual option claimed by the clubs. Rules governing free agency were first formalized in the 1976 Basic Agreement. Ten years later, Murray Chass (*New York Times,* Dec. 22, 1985) wrote: "After Seitz created free agency, free agency created millionaires, agents and unhappiness among owners, but it also produced unprecedented popularity for baseball." "In moves that may signal the re-birth of free agency in major-league baseball, two significant players switched teams yesterday" (Richard Justice, *Washington Post,* Dec. 2, 1987).

**free agent 1.** A professional baseball player who has no contractual obligation to play for one team and is free to negotiate directly with any team, including the one he was playing for when the contract expired. One can also become a free agent when released by a club. **1st Use.** 1908. (*Brooklyn Daily Eagle,* May 23; Edward J. Nichols). **2.** A player with six or more full seasons of major-league experience who is without a contract for the following season. He may play for any team that meets his salary demands. If a free agent is not signed by Jan. 8, his former team cannot re-sign him until May 1. See also *Type A free agent; Type B free agent; Type C free agent.* **3.** A player who has been discharged or is unemployed. This euphemistic application of the term is significantly different from its true meaning.

**free-agent draft** A *draft* in which eligible high school and college players are selected by teams in reverse order of their positions in the final standings of the previous season. Syn. *amateur draft.*

**free-agent reentry draft** A *draft* in which veteran players who played out their options and chose to be free agents were selected. The draft, used in the 1970s and 1980s, was eliminated in 1985.

**free check** *arch.* Syn. of *base on balls.* **1st Use.** 1902. (*Sporting Life,* July 12; Edward J. Nichols).

**free-look free agency** Syn. of *new-look free agency.*

**free pass** Syn. of *base on balls.*

**free passage** Syn. of *base on balls.* **1st Use.** 1917. (*New York Times,* Oct. 8; Edward J. Nichols).

**free ride** Syn. of *base on balls.*

**free spirit** A player who lacks inhibition; a nonconformist. "Reliever Randy Niemann is the New York Mets comic relief specialist who is gaining recognition as one of baseball's funniest free spirits" (Gannett Westchester [N.Y.] Newspapers, June 28, 1986).

**free swinger 1.** A batter who tends to swing at pitches out of the strike zone; one who will swing at almost any ball pitched to him. Free swingers seldom walk. "[Benito Santiago] is renowned for his ability to swing at any pitch within a time zone at home plate, a living definition of the term 'free swinger'" (Buster Olney, *Baltimore Sun,* Oct. 12, 1995). **1st Use.** 1909. (*Baseball Magazine,* Nov.; Edward J. Nichols). **2.** A power hitter.

**free ticket** Syn. of *base on balls.* **Usage Note.** A free ticket is seldom simply thrown or delivered but issued: "[Wade] Boggs was issued a free ticket in the second inning Friday night" (*Boston Globe,* Aug. 10, 1986). **1st Use.** 1917. (*New York Times,* Oct. 7; Edward J. Nichols).

**free transit** Syn. of *base on balls.*

**free transportation 1.** Syn. of *base on balls.* **2.** An awarded base given to a batter who has been hit by a pitched ball.

**free trip** Syn. of *base on balls.*

**freeze 1.** For a pitcher to intimidate a hitter; e.g., "Smith can freeze a hitter with his fastball and curve." **2.** For a pitcher to throw a strike on a pitch the batter did not expect; e.g., "He froze him with a looping curveball on the outside corner of the plate" (*Tampa Tribune*, Nov. 2, 1989). **3.** To cause a baserunner to hold his lead; e.g., "Jones froze the runner with his quick move to first."

**freeze a ball 1.** To catch a fly ball or field a ground ball gracefully. **1st Use.** 1868. (*New York Herald*, Aug. 14; Edward J. Nichols). **2.** To dampen a ball's life by keeping it in a freezer or refrigerator in an attempt to help a pitcher. The practice and the belief that a warm ball goes farther than a cold one goes back many years. Frederick G. Lieb (*The Pittsburgh Pirates*, 1948; Charles D. Poe) wrote: "There used to be an icebox in the Pittsburgh Club's offices, and Connie [Mack] conceived the idea of stuffing boxes of baseballs into the icebox, and freezing them overnight. The practice supposedly froze the life out of baseballs." Roy Campanella (*It's Good to Be Alive*, 1959; Charles D. Poe) wrote: "Freezing the balls was supposed to deaden them and help to keep those heavy-hitting Homestead Grays down to size. It never stopped Josh [Gibson]."

**freight delivery** *arch.* Slow pitching. **1st Use.** 1892. (*Chicago Herald*, May 4; Edward J. Nichols).

**fresh leaguer** *arch.* Syn. of *rookie,* 1. **1st Use.** 1885. "The new-comers to the American Association arena were known as 'fresh leaguers' to distinguish them from vets or 'old leaguers'" (*Sporting Life,* Jan. 14; Barry Popik).

**friendly confines** A home ballpark; specif., the particularly cozy quarters of Wrigley Field, the home ballpark of the Chicago Cubs.

**fringe player** A player who makes just enough effort to get by; a mediocre player who soon will be returned to the minor leagues.

**front 1.** See *out in front.* **2.** *arch.* Syn. of *mound,* 1. **1st Use.** 1915. (*Baseball Magazine*, Dec.; Edward J. Nichols). **Etymology.** Edward J. Nichols noted in his 1939 Ph.D. dissertation, An Historical Dictionary of Baseball Terminology: "The influence of the World War added this synonym to one already in use . . . 'firing line.'"

**front-and-backer** *arch.* A "perfect strike through the plate, which was one of Kid Gleason's favorite

expressions" (Herbert Simons, *Baseball Magazine,* 1943).

**front foot** The batter's foot nearest the pitcher. Compare *back foot.*

**front-foot hitter** A hitter who swings with his weight on his front foot.

**front-line** Said of a strong defensive starter; e.g., "Smith is a front-line catcher."

**front office** The business and financial side of a baseball club; the realm of a club's general manager and his staff. The front office is responsible for obtaining, contracting for, and trading players. **Etymology/1st Use.** 1948. The term has a long history as an underworld term for police headquarters, an interrogation room, or the warden's office in a prison. Peter Tamony first found it applied to baseball in two 1948 newspaper articles, including this from the *San Francisco Call-Bulletin* (Jan. 19): "More than 250 baseball executives gathered here today for a unique five day 'school' on front office matters."

**front runner 1.** An individual who only favors a successful team. "He's no front runner; he was here when they were struggling," said broadcaster John Lowenstein on Boston Red Sox fan and once Speaker of the House Thomas P. "Tip" O'Neill (Home Team Sports telecast, Sept. 10, 1986). "I hate front-runners," wrote Ted Williams (*My Turn at Bat,* 1969), who defines them as "people who are with you when you're up and against you when you're down." **2.** A player who only performs well when his team is winning.

**frostie** [softball term] A pitch in slow pitch softball that is above 12 feet in arc. It alludes facetiously to the frost that appears at higher altitudes.

**frozen 1.** Said of a minor-league player whose playing ability is such that there is very little hope he will ever be called up to the major leagues. **2.** Said of a major-league player whose playing ability is such that he can play only one position; e.g., "Smith was frozen at first base by his lack of throwing ability."

**frozen rope** A hard-hit line drive, so-called because of the rigid, low, and straight path it takes.

"You can almost see the icicles dripping off it," wrote Leonard Shecter in defining the term (*Baseball Digest,* June 1963). Because it is so much hyperbole, the image is often embellished with something on the order of broadcaster Red Rush's "you could hang a week's wash on it and not have to worry." See also *rope,* 1; *hemp; clothesline.* **Extended Use.** A term used in military intelligence for a very important message that has been intercepted by a third party.

**fudge** An informal pickup game played by a few players who periodically switch positions. "Sometimes enough boys were present to permit a game of what they called 'fudge,' each taking his turn at fielding, playing first base, pitching, catching and batting" (Christy Mathewson, *Pitcher Pollock,* 1914; David Shulman).

**full count** Three balls and two strikes on a batter. Syn. *long count; three-two count.* **1st Use.** 1937. (Tom Manning, NBC radio World Series broadcast, Oct. 6; Edward J. Nichols).

**full house** Syn. of *bases loaded.* **1st Use.** 1922. (Ernest J. Lanigan, *Baseball Cyclopedia;* Edward J. Nichols). **Etymology.** A clear borrowing from the game of poker.

**full route** All of the game; nine innings (or more in the event of an extra-inning game); e.g., a pitcher who has gone the "full route" has pitched a complete game.

**full swing** A swing at a pitch with the full reach or extension of the batter's arms.

**full windup** A complete, legal delivery that begins with the pitcher swinging his arms above his head as he steps back with one foot. It is usually taken when the bases are empty. A full windup takes more time and allows baserunners to take longer leads.

**fumble 1.** *v.* To make an error. **2.** *n.* An error. **1st Use.** 1876. "Gilliam went to bat and got first by a fumble from Gillespie" (*Jackson Weekly Citizen,* June 27; Peter Morris).

**fundamentals** The basic elements of winning baseball, such as throwing to the right base, moving runners up, and executing rundowns, cutoff

**Full count.** *Displayed on a 19th-century umpire's indicator.*

plays, and pickoff plays. Fundamentals may be boring, but they win games. Bill Starr (*Clearing the Bases,* 1989) amplifies: "When a manager talks about fundamentals, he is generally talking about three aspects of baseball: the hit and run; hitting a ground ball behind a runner on second base with no one out, so as to advance the runner to third; and for outfielders, to hit the cutoff man on throws to the plate or third base." A baseball fundamental is "any baseball act that is so simple that the man in the stands thinks, 'I could do that. Why can't those big leaguers?'" (Ken Singleton, quoted in Thomas Boswell, *How Life Imitates the World Series,* 1982). Compare *tools,* 1.

**fungo 1.** *n.* A fly ball hit to a player during practice. "Then him and Carey was together in left field, catchin' fungoe." (Ring W. Lardner, *Round Up,* 1929). Plural "fungoes" **2.** *v.* To hit a fungo to a player during practice. The ball is usually thrown up in the air by the batter (often a coach) who hits it as it descends. The primary purpose is to give fielders practice in catching fly balls. See also *fungo bat,* 2. **3.** *n.* A very long, light bat used in practice to hit flies to the outfield. Its design gives the batter the ability to place his hits with greater accuracy. See also *fungo bat,* 1. **4.** *n.* A scratch hit.

**1st Use.** 1867. According to *Joe Reichler's Great Book of Baseball Records,* a 1957 newsstand publication, the term first appeared in *Haney's Book of Reference,* which was published by Henry Chadwick. In it, "fungo" is defined as: "A preliminary practice game in which one player takes the bat and, tossing the ball up, hits it as it falls, and if the ball is caught in the field on the fly, the player catching it takes the bat. It is useless as practice in batting, but good for taking fly balls." David Shulman was able to date the use of "fungo" back to *Sporting Life* (Mar. 3, 1886): "While watching some of our freshmen practicing 'fungo' batting the other afternoon it occurred to me that it was about the worst kind of practice a batsman could imagine in training his eye in batting." Edward J. Nichols was able to find "fungo" used as a verb as early as 1892 (*Brooklyn Daily Eagle,* July 17).

**Etymology.** The etymology of "fungo" is uncertain, which allows for plenty of good theories, and a certain amount of linguistic frustration. John Ciardi (*Good Words to You,* 1987) wrote: "Fungo in baseball has never been explained. I have seen efforts to derive it from L.[atin] 'fungo,' I do, I understand to discharge an obligation." He then adds with clear disdain: "Having noted the suggestion, I understand to believe the form remains unexplained."

There are five theories, summarized below:

1) "The 'Fun/Go' Theory." David Shulman (*American Speech,* Feb. 1937) guessed that "fungo" may be explained through the elements of a compound word, "fun" and "go." Bill Bryson (quoted in *The Sporting News,* May 23, 1981) reports that the chant, "One goes, two goes" etc., comes from a street game in which a player catching a certain number of fly balls was qualified to replace the batter. A variation on this theory is discussed by Patrick Ercolano (*Fungoes, Floaters and Fork Balls,* 1987): "Still others believe that the word has its derivation in rhyme recited during early versions of fungo, a rhyme consisting of the words 'run and go.'" Hy Turkin (*Baseball Almanac,* 1956) suggests "an old game in which the man using this style of hitting would yell, 'One go, two goes, fun goes.'" Still another variation on this theory is discussed by William Safire (*What's the Good Word,* 1982), who noted no less than 13 theories (genuine and tongue-in-cheek) that were originally sent to him in response to a query in his *New York Times* language column. A letter from Frederick L. Smith (Short Hills, N.J.) says: "In a substantial amount of this century's earlier English literature, especially some humorous things by P. G. Wodehouse, there is reference to the warm-up for cricket

matches involving 'fun goes'; i.e., practice strokes before the game began in earnest. I have always taken it as a fact of life that 'fungo' represents a shortening of this English usage."

2) "The Fungible Theory." As stated by Zander Hollander (*Baseball Lingo,* 1967): "The word 'fungible' means something that can be substituted for another and it is thought that in baseball the thin fungo stick got its name because it replaces the conventional bat."

3) "The Fungus Theory." According to a note made by Peter Tamony, the matter was discussed on KLX radio in San Francisco on Apr. 10, 1956. Bert Dunne, radio-TV director of the San Francisco Seals and a student of baseball terminology, attributed the term to an unnamed Princeton professor who claimed the bat hitting the ball sounded like fungus wood. Dunne added that the early fungo bats were regular bats that had been split in two and then bound with tape. Tamony himself had written (*American Speech,* Oct. 1937) that the word "refers to the lightness of the instrument." Several others believe the term came from the feel rather than the sound of fungus; e.g., Joseph McBride (*High and Inside,* 1980) explained that "the bats, with very narrow handles and extra thick heads, were so soft that they seemed to be made of fungus." Another fungus variation appears in the Safire collection of letters (see above). Stephen V. Fulkerson (Santa Paula, Calif.) wrote that he first heard the term in the early 1930s as a synonym for "nongenuine" or "not bona fide," such as a fungo that is not a real fly ball. He relates this to fungus in the sense that rural people regard a fungus as lacking the character of a real plant, which puts its roots in the ground.

4) "The Fang-en Theory." Gerald Cohen (*Comments on Etymology,* Feb. 1, 1987) of the Univ. of Missouri–Rolla wrote: "Perhaps its origin is to be sought in German 'fang-en,' 'to catch'; we now think of fungoing a ball as hitting it, but the early quotes . . . show clearly that the emphasis of a fungo game was on the ball's being caught." One of Cohen's citations is this explanation of a fungo game from *American Folk-Lore IV* (1891): "The game is played on a vacant lot, or in the middle of a wide street. One boy is chosen for batsman, and the

others stand around at some distance from him. A base ball is used, and the batsman throws it in the air, and then bats it out to the fielders, who endeavor to catch the ball 'on the fly.' The one who first catches the ball a certain number of times that has been agreed upon, takes the batsman's place for another game." Cohen also provides some instances of fungo as it was used in *The World* (New York) in the 1889–90 period, including this one: "Ward's fungo was simply pousse-café for Corkhill, and he swallowed it smoothly" (Oct. 26, 1889).

5) "The Fung Theory." Another letter in the Safire collection (see above) is from Joan H. Hall, associate editor for the *Dictionary of American Regional English.* She asserts that it is from a Scottish verb, "fung." Her letter reads in part: "According to *The Scottish National Dictionary,* the verb 'fung,' meaning 'to pitch, toss, fling,' was in use in Aberdeen as early as 1804: 'Ye witches, warlocks, fairies, fien's! Daft fungin' fiery pears an' stanes.'" She says that the connection with ball playing is that the ball is flung into the air before it is hit and that the "-o" ending is common in other games (bingo, beano, bunco, and keno).

**Extended Use.** The act of striking or clubbing with a bat or stick. "I'm sure that if most Americans should walk through the crowded wards [of wounded] they would grab baseball bats and hit a few fungoes the next time the Communists assemble in Union Square" (Jimmy Cannon, on a Communist rally in New York, quoted in *Time* magazine, Aug. 28, 1950; Peter Tamony).

**fungo bat 1.** *n.* A bat used for pregame hitting practice. It is usually longer, lighter in weight, and thinner than a regular bat. See also *fungo,* 3. Syn. *fungo stick.* **2.** *v.* To hit a fly ball to a player during practice. See also *fungo,* 2. **1st Use.** 1915. "He used to come out sometimes on Saturdays and fungo bat for the players" (Burt L. Standish, *Covering the Look-In Corner;* David Shulman).

**fungo bazooka** A mechanical device that uses air pressure to fire balls into the air for fielding practice.

**fungo circle** One of two circular patches of dirt located on either side of home plate in foul territory. They are used by fungo batters and average about seven feet in diameter.

**fungo hit** *arch.* A high fly ball or pop fly; a ball that appears to have been hit with a fungo bat. **1st Use.** 1889. "In the sixth inning fungo hits to the outfield disposed of the first two batters" (*Brooklyn Eagle,* Sept. 8; Peter Morris).

**fungo hitter** *arch.* A hitter with a reputation for fungo hits.

**fungo stick** Syn. of *fungo bat,* 1.

**furlough** *arch.* Syn. of *base on balls.* **Etymology.** The term apparently was brought back from World War II by players who had been in the armed forces. Chester L. Smith (*Baseball Digest,* May 1946) included the term in his article entitled "Diamond Slang Goes G.I." The term stuck as a lesser synonym for "base on balls," but most of the other terms cited by Smith, who had obviously been listening to the Pittsburgh Pirates, did not.

**fush ball** A pitch that combines the properties of a changeup and forkball. The pitch is delivered by pushing the ball from between the pitcher's spread-out index and middle fingers. The term appears to have been quickly turned into *foshball.* **1st Use.** 1983. "[Mike] Boddicker calls it a fork ball, but since he pushes it from between his fingers with a sidespin that produces a screwball, his pitching coach, Ray Miller, has named it the 'fush ball'" (Thomas Boswell, *Washington Post,* July 17, 1983). **Etymology.** A blend of "fork" plus "push."

**future Hall of Famer** An active player whose career statistics and accomplishments in the game all but assure his being voted into the Hall of Fame. "Future Hall of Famer Nolan Ryan is hardly on future Hall of Famer Mike Schmidt's 'loves to face' list" (*USA Today,* May 2, 1986).

**fuzzy concrete** Astroturf and other artificial surfaces to players who prefer real grass.

# G

**G** Abbrev. for *game,* 3.

**gab-circuit** Off-season baseball talk (chatter, conjecture, speechifying, etc.) beloved of fans. See also *hot stove league.*

**gaijin** Japanese for "outsiders." The term has a specific meaning and application in the context of baseball as it is used to describe American players who are contracted to play for teams in Japan. "Even if none of this year's gaijin measure up, the 'cash-flapping rush' for new [Bob] Horners, as one magazine called it, will continue" (*Washington Post,* Feb. 4, 1988). The "gaijin waku," or outsider quota, for each team previously was two, but was increased to three in 1994.

**game** **1.** A contest between two teams that is the basic unit of baseball competition. A game usually consists of either eight-and-a-half or nine innings (when the home team is ahead after eight-and-a-half innings have been played, the last half inning is not played). Games are also deemed complete if play is suspended for rain or other reason after the team that is losing has been at bat at least five times. A game is won by the team with the most runs, which means that extra innings must be played if the two teams are tied at the end of the ninth inning. **Usage Note.** In recent years it has become customary in both the electronic and print media to refer to games in the Division Series, the League Championship Series, and the World Series as Game 1, Game 2, etc. When used in this context, the word "game" is always capitalized. **2.** A unit of measurement used to determine a team's exact position in the standings. This unit is expressed in terms of full and half games out of first place or *games behind.* See also *length.* **3.** A unit of measurement used to determine the extent of participation by a player or a team; e.g., Pete Rose played in 3,562 games, more than any other player in major-league history. Abbrev. *G.* **4.** The call made by the umpire to signify the end of a contest. **5.** The sport and business of baseball itself. "I see great things in baseball; it's our game—the American game" (Walt Whitman, *Brooklyn Daily Eagle*). **6.** The overall baseball ability of an individual player; e.g., "People would . . . ask me about trades more than about my game" (Jeffrey Hammonds, quoted in *Baltimore Sun,* Feb. 25, 1998).

**game ball** **1.** A ball that has actually been in play as opposed to a souvenir ball; specif., the first ball used in a game. **2.** The ball in play at the end of a game, given to the most deserving player, often the pitcher.

**game-ender** A late-inning relief pitcher; the *closer.*

**game face** The laserlike glare that indicates the high level of concentration of an athlete. Pitcher Dave Stewart used his game face to intimidate batters: "He stares at batters with a glare that just dares them to hit his pitch" (Hal Bodley, *USA Today,* Oct. 17, 1990).

**game of inches** A euphemism for the game of baseball because there are so many close plays decided by inches or fractions thereof. This time-honored phrase encompasses several givens about the game. For instance, by a matter of inches, it is often seen that a batter-runner is safe or out at first base, a batted ball is either fair or foul, a pitch is either a ball or a strike, and a player stealing a base is safe or out. "Baseball is, after all, a game of inches and even fractions" (Shirley Povich, *Washington Post*, Oct. 21, 1986).

**Game of the Week** A baseball game esp. selected to be televised each week, beginning in 1953 by ABC, later by CBS, and from 1966 to 1989 by NBC. "The other morning, I was telling some of our young players here how I used to wait all week for Saturday when I was a kid, to watch the old 'Game of the Week' on television. They couldn't get over that: '*One* game—get out of here!' They couldn't believe it." (Oakland A's pitcher Ron Darling, quoted by Roger Angell, *The New Yorker*, May 3, 1993).

**gamer 1.** A player who approaches the game with a tenacious, spirited attack and continues to play even when hurt; a competitor; a player who doesn't make excuses. The term is a compliment, most esp. when it comes from another player. "He's a gamer" (Cincinnati Reds manager Jack McKeon said of outfielder Chris Stynes, *Sports Illustrated*, May 4, 1998). "His ever protective teammates counter that [Baltimore Orioles first baseman Eddie] Murray is a 'gamer,' that he is playing in pain" (*Washington Times*, Aug. 28, 1986). **Etymology.** From the idea of a player who is "game." **Extended Use.** Anyone who is willing to carry on in the face of adversity. **2.** A player who delivers in big games; a *clutch hitter*, 1. **3.** *arch.* Any player in a game. **4.** The winning run. **1st Use.** 1980. "Reggie Jackson singled home the gamer" (*New York Post*, Oct. 21; David Shulman). **5.** A favorite glove, or a glove reserved for use in a game. "San Diego infielder Tim Flannery . . . had four gloves . . . [including] his 'gamer,' an old third baseman's glove he picked up . . . from California manager Doug Rader" (J. E. Vader, *Sports Illustrated*, June 5, 1989). **6.** A favorite bat.

**games back** Syn. of *games behind*.

**games behind** The number of games by which a team in a division or league is out of first place. It is expressed as a combination of whole and half numbers, with each victory or loss counting as a half of a game. To compute the number of games a team is ahead or behind, add the difference in the number of wins and the difference in the number of losses and divide by 2. The term is usually used in comparison to the first-place team, but can be used to compare any two teams in the same division. Abbrev. *GB.* Syn. *games back.*

**Game 7** The last and deciding game of a best-of-seven League Championship Series or World Series.

**games finished** The number of games in which a relief pitcher was the last pitcher. Abbrev. *GF.*

**game situation** The "turning point" in a game (Keith Hernandez, *Pure Baseball*, 1994).

**Game 6** The sixth game of a best-of-seven League Championship Series or World Series. The term is often associated with the Boston Red Sox, who have been involved in two classic Game 6s: 1) Carlton Fisk's dramatic 12th-inning home run to defeat the Cincinnati Reds 7–6 in the 1975 World Series; and 2) the New York Mets 6–5 victory when a wild pitch by Bob Stanley and an error by Bill Buckner spelled the difference in the 1986 World Series. **Extended Use.** Esp. in New England, a mention of Game 6 (e.g., "It's Game 6 all over again") is to talk about a run of bad luck.

**games started** The number of games in which a given pitcher was the starter. Abbrev. *GS.*

**game winner 1.** The pitcher credited with winning a game. **2.** The run that results in a victory.

**game-winning RBI** The run batted in that gives the winning team the lead it never relinquishes. The game-winning RBI was an officially kept statistic from 1980 to 1988 and it appeared in the box scores of games. Although no longer kept as an official statistic beginning in 1989, broadcasters and fans still allude to it. It was dropped because it proved to be meaningless in lopsided games, particularly when the winning run scored in the first inning of an 11–1 laugher. Abbrev. *GWRBI.*

**gap** The space between outfielders. Because only three players cover the entire outfield, wide stretches of uncovered field exist. The size of the gaps (between the center fielder and the left fielder and between the center fielder and the right fielder) is determined by the defensive position of the outfielders. In ballparks where advertising is allowed on the outfield wall, ads for The Gap clothing chain began to appear in the spaces between outfielders in the late 1990s. Compare *hole*, 1.

**gap hitter** A hitter (such as Tony Gwynn) who hits the ball between the outfielders.

**gapper** A batted ball that goes into the gap. If such a ball falls safely, it usually rolls to the wall and goes for an extra-base hit; "[Cal Ripken's] fifth-inning gapper . . . drove in two runs" (*Baltimore Sun,* Mar. 18, 1996). Syn. *gap shot.*

**gap power** The strength and ability to drive balls between outfielders.

**gap shot** Syn. of *gapper.*

**garden** *arch.* The outfield, short for *outer garden.* See also *inner garden.* **1st Use.** 1869. (*New York Herald,* Sept. 14; Edward J. Nichols).

**gardener** *arch.* Syn. of *outfielder.* **1st Use.** 1902. (*Sporting Life,* July 12; Edward J. Nichols).

**gardening** Smoothing the dirt on a baseball field, such as by a pitcher around the mound or by a batter preparing the batter's box before stepping in to bat.

**garner** To hit safely; e.g., "Smith garnered four hits today." **1st Use.** 1892. (*Chicago Herald,* June 13; Edward J. Nichols).

**Garrison finish** A game whereby a team, which initially seems hopelessly behind, comes through to win the game. It has been said that a true Garrison finish requires the winning team to have been down by five runs with two outs in its last at-bat. **Etymology.** From the legendary ability of the 19th-century jockey Snapper Garrison to win horse races at the wire.

**gas 1.** *n.* A very good fastball. **2.** *n.* Fastball pitching. "He [Roger Clemens] just came in throwing gas" (Marty Barrett, quoted in *Boston Globe,* Aug. 4, 1986). **3.** *v.* To fire or discharge. "Blue Jays Gas Gaston" (*Milwaukee Journal Sentinel* headline, Sept. 25, 1997).

**Gashouse Gang** A nickname given to the St. Louis Cardinals of the mid-1930s, but most strongly associated with the 1934 world champions. They were a rowdy, passionate crew that included Dizzy Dean, Pepper Martin, Ducky Medwick, Leo Durocher, and manager Frank Frisch. Also spelled "Gas House Gang." **Etymology.** Originally, the Gashouse District was an area on the lower East Side of Manhattan that once housed several large gas tanks. It was a rough neighborhood described in part by Frank Moss (*The American Metropolis,* 1897): "Perhaps the most unique of all vicious drinking places is a 'dead house' on 18th Street in what is called the 'gas-house district,' a 'Mecca' for vagrants and 'bums' of New York, Brooklyn and New Jersey." The neighborhood, however, was best known for a vicious band of thugs known as the Gashouse Gang.

There are several versions of how the cognomen was applied to the Cardinals. One version has the St. Louis team coming into New York from Boston where they had just played in the rain. Their uniforms were particularly dirty because they were a "sliding" team, and the equipment man did not have time to have them cleaned. When they appeared on the field at the Polo Grounds, one shocked reporter commented that they looked like "the gang from around the gas house." This version was given by Frisch in a radio interview (May 11, 1963) in which he acknowledged that his was not the only version of the story. Frisch added that he thought the reporter was Frank Lamb of the *New York Evening Journal.* (Peter Tamony)

In his biography of Dizzy Dean (*Ol' Diz,* 1992), Vince Staten questions this version. "If that were true, the date would have been either May 20 or July 23. Those were the only two days during the '34 season that the Cardinals played in New York a day after a game in Boston. The problem is both those contests in Boston were played under clear skies, with not even a trace of rain, according to weather information published in the *Boston Globe.* In fact the second occasion, July 22, was so hot and dry across the country that the *New York Times* published a story about the heat wave on its front page, sandwiched between stories about a bus crash and the police slaying of mobster John Dillinger."

More commonly heard is the story of a conversation between Frank Graham of the old *New York Sun* and Durocher. Graham said that the Cards were so good that they could play in the American League, then regarded as superior to the National League. Durocher replied: "They wouldn't let us play in the American League. They'd say we were just a lot of gashouse players." From then on Graham called the team the Gashouse Gang. The very same story has been told and published with Pepper Martin in Durocher's place.

Then, one must consider what Durocher himself wrote in his autobiography (*Nice Guys Finish Last*, 1975). He tells of the team arriving dirty and unkempt for the confrontation with the Giants. "The next day I saw a cartoon in the *World-Telegram* by Willard Mullin. It showed two big gas tanks on the wrong side of the railroad track, and some ballplayers crossing over to the good part of town carrying clubs over their shoulders instead of bats. And the title read: 'The Gas House Gang.'"

Finally, Staten points to the autobiography, as told to J. Roy Stockton, of Frankie Frisch (*Frank Frisch, the Fordham Flash*, 1962), the manager and second baseman on the Gashouse Gang, who credits Warren Brown of the *Chicago Herald-Examiner* with using the phrase in print in July 1935. Frisch writes: "[Brown] climbed aboard the Cubs' train, New York bound. Curtains were drawn. All the little and big Cubs apparently had turned in for the night. 'What's the matter?' Brown wanted to know in a loud voice. 'Are you boys afraid that Pepper Martin is on the train? You had all better stay on your side of the tracks, or the Gas House Gang will get you.'"

**gate** 1. Total paid attendance. **1st Use.** 1888. "There is a 'big gate' awaiting the championship should they decide on making the trip" (*Sporting Life*, Nov. 21; David Shulman). 2. Short for *gate receipts*. 3. A strikeout; e.g., "Jones gave Smith the gate." 4. An ejection. **1st Use.** 1918. "Umpire [Billy] Evans thought Harry got too abusive, however, and gave him the gate" (*Detroit Free Press*, July 5; Barry Popik).

**gate crasher** An individual who gains admission to an important event, such as the World Series, without paying admission. The practice became something of a fad in the 1920s when the newspapers covered several daring gate crashers who seemed able to get in everywhere.

**gate money** The money that is collected at the turnstiles. According to the National Baseball Library and Archives, the first baseball game where gate money was collected was between the Knickerbockers and Brooklyn on July 20, 1858. See also *gate receipts*. **1st Use.** 1869. (*DeWitt's Official Base Ball Guide;* Edward J. Nichols).

**gate receipts** The total amount of money received in admission prices to a baseball game. See also *gate money*. Syn. *gate*, 2. **1st Use.** 1870. "In 1867 the Red Stockings . . . became so famous that their gate-receipts were very large" (*Lakeside Monthly* [Chicago]; David Shulman).

**gateway** First base; the threshold to the other bases and the opportunity of scoring. The term is flamboyant baseballese.

**gather in** To field a batted ball. **1st Use.** 1874. (Chicago *Inter-Ocean*, July 30; Edward J. Nichols).

**gazoonie** *arch.* A *rookie*, 1. **1st Use.** 1943. "'Gazoonies' is probably the most modern nickname for recruits, who through the years have come to be known as 'rookies'" (Herbert Simons, *Baseball Magazine*, Jan.).

**GB** Abbrev. for *games behind*.

**GDP** Abbrev. for *grounded into a double play*.

**Gehrig Award** Short for *Lou Gehrig Memorial Award*.

**Gehrig's disease** See *Lou Gehrig's disease*.

**general admission** 1. A catchall term that refers to the areas of the ballpark where seats are not reserved and are filled on a first-come, first-served basis. The term commonly applies to seating in the bleachers in portions of the upper deck. General admission tickets carry a common price although there are sometimes special prices for children and/or senior citizens. 2. The price for an unreserved seat in the grandstand.

**general manager** The director of a club's baseball matters and personnel, who, among other things, is responsible for signing and trading players. According to Lou Piniella (*Sweet Lou,* 1986): "The definition of a good general manager is a guy who can call up another GM at three o'clock in the morning and have the guy help him out with a player, instead of screaming at him for the early wake-up call." Abbrev. *GM.* **1st Use.** 1927. "The term 'General Manager' was first applied to William Evans, a former American League umpire who became General Manager of the Cleveland Indians in 1927" (Bill James, *The Bill James Historical Baseball Abstract,* 1986).

**gentleman's agreement** The 60-year-old unwritten rule on racial exclusion in organized baseball that was broken in 1946 when Jackie Robinson played for Montreal of the International League in preparation for a career with the Brooklyn Dodgers.

**George Brett numbers** A shorthand term used in the 1980s for a player posting batting statistics in the vicinity of those collected by Kansas City Royals slugger George Brett, an excellent hitter whose numbers have constituted a standard of excellence: .305 batting average, 3,154 hits, 665 doubles, 317 home runs, 1,583 runs, and 1,595 runs batted in.

**George factor** The real or imagined influence of principal owner George Steinbrenner on his New York Yankees. "One thing we don't have is the George factor. That's good for two or three losses down the road." (Toronto Blue Jays outfielder Joe Carter, quoted in *USA Today Baseball Weekly,* May 25, 1994).

**George Stallings pitcher** "A 3-and-2 pitcher; one who gets behind every batter; a 'wild hurler'" (Gordon S. "Mickey" Cochrane, *Baseball: The Fan's Game,* 1939). **Etymology.** Named for 1914 Miracle Braves manager George Stallings, whose presumably last words as he emerged from a coma to address his doctor, who asked about the cause of his sickness: "Bases on balls, you fathead, was the cause of it all" (Rabbit Maranville, *Run, Rabbit, Run,* 1991).

**get 1.** To retire an opposing player; to put out; e.g., "Smith got Jones by catching his pop fly." **2.**

**George Stallings pitcher.** *The eponymous Stallings as Yankee manager (1909–1910) at spring training in Gray, Georgia.*

To deceive another player; to trick an opponent. Walter Camp (*Century,* Apr. 1910) gives several examples, including one in which Boston Red Sox catcher Lou Criger "got" Cleveland's Nap Lajoie: "There were two strikes and three balls on Lajoie. Criger had returned the ball to the pitcher, but had his mask off and was pretending to fasten a buckle on it, saying to Lajoie, 'We'll get you this time.' Lajoie turned slightly, and, seeing Criger with his mask off, said, 'You will, will you?' when the pitcher shot the ball over the plate, catching Lajoie entirely unprepared as he heard the umpire say, 'Strike three, and out!'"

**get across** To score a run; e.g., "The Giants got four runs across in the sixth."

**get a jump 1.** For a baserunner to make a quick break toward the next base as the pitcher begins his motion toward the plate. **2.** For a fielder to begin to move before, or just as, the ball is hit toward the point on the field where the ball can be caught or fielded.

**get all of the ball** To hit the ball solidly and with power, usually for a home run, but at least extra bases. Syn. *get it all;* "get all of it."

**get a piece of the ball** For a batter to make contact with the ball, even if it's a foul ball. Batting with two strikes, a player will try to "get a piece of the ball" to keep from striking out. Syn. "get a piece of it."

**get around** To swing the bat fast enough to hit the pitch; e.g., "Smith got around on the fastball and pulled it down the line."

**get a ticket** To receive a base on balls.

**getaway** The frequency with which baseball games are won at the beginning of the season; e.g., "Baltimore's sluggish getaway was the big mystery of the new season."

**getaway bag** *arch.* First base. **1st Use.** 1907. (*Lajoie's Official Base Ball Guide;* Edward J. Nichols).

**getaway day 1.** The last day of a long home stand for a team; the day the club gets away for a road trip. **2.** The last day of a series between two teams, on which one or both of the teams leaves for another city. Both teams have a getaway day when the visitors leave and the home team ends its home stand.

**get down** To slide; e.g., "I got down so I wouldn't be hit."

**get healthy** To hit successfully, individually or as a team, against a pitcher or group of pitchers, esp. for an individual or team that has not been hitting well. In a game in which the Boston Red Sox defeated the Baltimore Orioles 15 to 4, Jack Wiers (WTOP radio, June 10, 1987) said: "A lot of Red Sox got healthy tonight."

**get him over** To advance a baserunner with a bunt or sacrifice.

**get hold of it** For a batter to connect solidly with the pitch. Syn. "get hold of one"; "get hold of the ball." **1st Use.** 1914. (*New York Tribune,* Oct. 12; Edward J. Nichols).

**get in one's kitchen** See *kitchen.*

**get into the bullpen** To cause an opposing team to use its relief pitchers.

**get it all** Syn. of *get all of the ball.*

**get it started** For a batter to begin his swing. "It's the lightest bat I've ever used. When I was with the Giants I swung at least 35 ounces and used a bat with a thicker barrel. This bat feels like a toothpick in comparison, but I can get it started quicker" (Jack Clark, quoted in *Philadelphia Daily News,* June 25, 1987).

**get loose** For a relief pitcher to warm up and get ready in the bullpen.

**get naked** For a pitcher to *bear down.* "A coach might yell to a pitcher who seems to be losing his concentration: 'Hey, get naked out there'" (Leonard Shecter, *Baseball Digest,* June 1963).

**get on** To advance to one of the bases; specif., to get to first base. **1st Use.** 1909. (*Baseball Magazine,* July; Edward J. Nichols).

**get one's innings** Syn. of *have one's innings,* 2.

**get-small-quick ball** A home run, so-named because of the way the ball appears to get smaller and smaller as it travels into the stands or out of the ballpark. Shirley Povich quoted Washington Senators pitcher Walter Johnson: "The balls [Babe] Ruth hit got smaller quicker than anyone's" (Gordon Beard, *Orioles Gazette,* Aug. 13, 1993).

**get the bats going** To increase offensive production; e.g., "The White Sox got the bats going and won six games."

**get the bounce** To be lucky; e.g., a hard-to-field ball is either fielded or goes for a hit, depending on which team "gets the bounce."

**get the call 1.** To be chosen to play, often applied to a relief pitcher when he gets the signal to come into the game. **1st Use.** 1920. (*New York Times,* Oct. 4; Edward J. Nichols). **2.** To receive the umpire's benefit of doubt on a close play or a pitch on the border of the strike zone.

**get the gate** To be thrown out of the game by the umpire.

**get the leading lady** To force out the baserunner farthest along the basepath.

**"get the spring out"** A comment said to a fielder who looks in his glove after committing an error.

**get the thumb** To be ejected from the game.

**get to** To hit successfully, individually or as a team, against a particular pitcher; e.g., "The Cubs got to Smith with five consecutive doubles." **1st Use.** 1905. (*Sporting Life*, Sept. 2; Edward J. Nichols).

**get to first base** To make an offensive start by putting a runner on first base by means of a hit, base on balls, or hit batsman. **Extended Use.** To achieve the first step in a procedure or activity. See also *base, 2.*

**"get two"** 1. To turn a double play. 2. A cry of encouragement to the infielders when there is a runner at first base with less than two outs.

**get under** 1. To swing a bat and hit the bottom part of the ball, resulting in a pop-up or a long fly ball; e.g., "Smith got under it with his uppercut swing." 2. To position oneself in preparation to catch a ball hit high in the air; e.g., "Jones moved several paces to his left to get under the ball." **1st Use.** 1905. (*Sporting Life*, Oct. 7; Edward J. Nichols).

**get-up-off-the-bench hitter** A pinch hitter who comes in cold and is often successful.

**get up with the pitch** For a runner on first base to face the catcher, begin to glide sideways toward second base, and then turn smoothly and sprint off the glide as the ball is put in play (George F. Will, *Men at Work*, 1990).

**GF** Abbrev. for *games finished*.

**ghost runner** An imaginary runner. According to Cullen P. Vane (San Jose, Calif.), in a letter to the compiler of this dictionary: "The term was used in [childhood] games in which we didn't or couldn't field full teams. If we were playing three on three and I led off our inning with a double and the following two batters made outs then I would declare, 'ghost runner,' and then take my turn at bat, thus having [an imaginary] runner occupy my base. There was a standard rule that the ghost runner could only advance as many bases as the batter; that is, with a ghost runner on second and the batter singled, then the ghost runner advanced just the one base. Even if the runner whom the ghost runner had replaced was fast enough to have scored on the single, 'he' was allowed but one base." See also *invisible man, 2.*

**GIDP** An acronym for *grounded into a double play.* The term is used in referring to the statistic that accounts for "times grounded into double plays." Pron. "gidap."

**gift** 1. Syn. of *base on balls.* **1st Use.** 1895 (*New York Press*, July 3; Edward J. Nichols). 2. Anything given up by the defense because of bad play or inattention; e.g., a single that went for a "double" because of an error. 3. An error or misplay that puts a batter on base or allowed a baserunner to advance. **1st Use.** 1879. (*Spirit of the Times*, Aug. 28; Edward J. Nichols).

**Gillette** A pitch thrown in the direction of a batter's head; a brushback pitch that is likely to come close to (in the manner of a Gillette razor) but not hit the batter. The term is an obvious play on the idea of a "close shave." **1st Use.** 1937. (*The Sporting News Record Book;* Edward J. Nichols).

**gilt-edge ball** *obs.* Good playing. "This phrase was in constant use throughout 1880s and '90s, but appears to have dropped out of baseball writing shortly after 1900" (Edward J. Nichols, *An Historical Dictionary of Baseball Terminology,* 1939 Ph.D. dissertation).

**gimme** An easy pitch to hit, such as a belt-high fastball. **Etymology.** From "give me"; e.g., "Give me an easy ball to clobber."

**ginger** The zest and vigor of a player; e.g., Chicago White Sox infielder Buck Weaver was called "The Ginger Kid" because of his enthusiastic play. **1st Use.** 1890. (*New York Press*, July 10; Edward J. Nichols).

**give him the player** To direct the first baseman and the third baseman to play away from the foul lines. Syn. *give up the line.*

**give in** For a pitcher to capitulate to the batter by throwing him a pitch that he likes to hit. The term is usually stated in the negative; e.g., "Smith refused to give in to the batter." Compare *go after*.

**give oneself up** To hit the ball behind a teammate on base in an effort to bring him home or advance him to scoring position.

**giver** *obs.* The pitcher.

**give the nod** **1.** For a manager to indicate that a player, usually a starting or relief pitcher, has been selected to play. The term commonly is used to indicate which pitcher has been chosen to come in from the bullpen. **2.** To get a favorable decision from the umpire. **Etymology.** From the nod of approval. Harold Wentworth & Stuart Berg Flexner (*Dictionary of American Slang*, 1960) state that the term has been a common sports expression since about 1920 and was first used to describe a boxer who won a prizefight ("got the nod") because of the referee's or judge's decision rather than a knockout.

**give up** To allow the opposition an advantage whether it be a walk, hit, or run; e.g., "Smith gave up six hits and three runs in four innings."

**give up the line** Syn. of *give him the player*.

**glancing blow** A slight impact when the ball strikes a batter or fielder and bounces away, usually with no injury to the player.

**glass arm** **1.** A sore throwing or pitching arm. See also *crockery limb*. **2.** A player with a chronically weak or sore arm. "The Glass Arm Pitcher Is No Worse Off Than the Slugger With a Hole in His Bat" (*San Francisco Call* headline, Sept. 27, 1913; Peter Tamony). **1st Use.** 1891. "For a back number with a 'glass' arm, George Hanley seems to be holding up his own end in [keeping] the San Jose team in great shape" (*Sporting Times,* June 13; David Shulman). Shulman also noted that the following issue of the same sports weekly reported that the term "glass arm" was becoming obsolete and replaced by "crockery limb." Peter Tamony noted that the glass metaphor is not limited to baseball, as it was a reference to fragility in other sports, such as the boxer's "glass jaw." **Etymology.** H. L . Mencken (*The American Language; Suppl. II,*

1948) thanks Adm. C. S. Butler (letter, Nov. 30, 1943), who noted that a "glass arm" was usually myositis (inflammation) of the long tendon of the biceps muscle: "Its action is three- or four-fold and its relations to synovial sheaths, bursas and joints complicated. Damage of these structures often produces a stiffness and rigidity accompanied by loss of the power to supinate the forearm . . . The arm feels rigid, and as if likely to break like glass." **Extended Use.** The term has been applied to stiff or weak arms in other realms. An article on short-wave radio (*American Speech,* Oct. 1929) reports its use as a synonym for "telegrapher's cramp."

**gliding** A flaw in a pitcher's delivery when, instead of pushing toward home plate with the pitch, the pitcher drifts away and throws across his body.

**globe** *arch.* The baseball. **1st Use.** 1891. (*Chicago Herald,* May 7; Edward J. Nichols).

**globule** The baseball.

**glory circle** *arch.* Baseball's elite; its unofficial hall of fame before there was a Baseball Hall of Fame. **1st Use.** 1908. (*Spalding's Official Base Ball Guide;* Edward J. Nichols).

**glory time** A period late in a game during which a relief pitcher earns a save.

**glove** **1.** *n.* A covering of padded leather worn on a fielder's hand used to protect the hand and help catch and retain a batted or thrown ball. A glove originally was intended solely as a means of protecting a player's hand by softening the impact when handling balls, but it soon began to evolve as a means to better fielding. In the major leagues, a glove shall not measure more than 12 inches in length and 7¾ inches in width. Compare *mitt,* 1 and 2. **2.** *n.* Fielding ability. An exceptional defensive player is said to have a "good glove." Wil Cordero "can't hide glove: former infielder tries the outfield" (*Sports Illustrated,* Mar. 31, 1997). **Usage Note.** The term "glove" alone means the same as "good glove." Tim Horgan (*Baseball Digest,* June 1964) wrote: "If you chance to overhear Player A say to Player B, 'Don't lose your glove,' it doesn't mean there's a sneak thief in the house. It

**Glove.** *Player with two gloves. It is not known whether he played with both or simply used them when posing for photographs.*

means Player B can't hit his weight and the only thing that keeps him in the lineup is his fielding prowess." **3.** *n.* A fielder, usually a skilled one. **4.** *v.* To catch and control a ball; to field a ball with a glove. **1st Use.** 1887. (*Harper's Weekly,* Sept. 10; Edward J. Nichols). **5.** See *batting glove.*

**glove action** The fielding skill of a player. "[Cal Ripken Jr.] has the best glove action I've seen" (Mark Belanger, quoted in *Baseball Digest,* Dec. 1983).

**glove and a prayer** The assets of a poor pitcher. See also *prayer ball.* **1st Use.** 1912. "All he has when he goes to the box is a glove and a prayer" (*Sporting Life,* May 18).

**glove-and-throw** Said of a fielding play in which the ball was fielded and quickly thrown to the appropriate teammate; e.g., "It was a fine glove-and-throw assist."

**glove doctor** An individual (sometimes a trainer) who helps players customize their gloves.

**glove hand** The catching hand on which the glove is worn. A fielder who throws with his right hand wears the glove on his left hand.

**glove man** **1.** A good defensive player. The term is applied sparingly to identify excellent fielders such as Marty Marion, Brooks Robinson, and Ozzie Smith. Also spelled "gloveman." **2.** A weak hitter whose defensive ability keeps him on the team. Joseph McBride (*High and Inside,* 1980) noted that the term is used as a "back-handed insult."

**glove work** Defensive ability; the art of fielding baseballs. "Indians manager Mike Hargrove must've been jealous watching the Orioles' glove work" (*Baltimore Sun,* Apr. 14, 1996). Sometimes spelled "glovework."

**glue to the bag** To keep a baserunner close to the base. **1st Use.** 1910. (*New York Tribune,* July 12; Edward J. Nichols).

**GM** Abbrev. for *general manager.*

**go** **1.** To pitch. **2.** To try to advance to the next base.

**go after** For a pitcher determined to retire the batter and not to capitulate to him; to pitch a batter tough; to *challenge* a batter; e.g., "Smith will go after Jones with intimidating pitches inside." Compare *give in.* Syn. *go at; attack.*

**go against the book** To violate the conventional wisdom of baseball strategy.

**go-ahead inning** The inning in which the team that is losing scores enough runs to take the lead.

**go-ahead run** The run that would put a team in the lead. The term is often used to describe a man on base; e.g., "The tying run is at second, the go-ahead run is on first." It is sometimes but not always the game-winning run.

**goal ball** Syn. of *rounders,* in which the bases were known as "goals."

**go all the way 1.** To pitch a complete game. **2.** To win a division or league title.

**goal tender** A batter who patiently waits for good pitches at which to swing. **1st Use.** 1937. (*New York Daily News*, Sept. 5; Edward J. Nichols).

**go around** To swing through a pitch; e.g., "Smith went around for strike three on a pitch in the dirt."

**go at** Syn. of *go after*.

**goat** A derisive name for a player who is singled out for a serious lapse in performance; one who loses (or appears to lose) a game for his team. Because of the severity of the term, it is more likely to come into play after the loss of an important regular season game or during the playoffs or World Series. It is correctly known as a "postgame sobriquet." "Mickey 'Goat' as Sox Win" was the headline for an article on a game in which Mickey Mantle allowed a run to score because he had collided with another player (*San Francisco Call-Bulletin*, May 22, 1957; Peter Tamony). The term and the concept are regarded with some seriousness. As Doug DeCinces put it when talking about playing in the World Series: "In the back of every player's mind is the hope not to be the goat." On occasion the term is applied to a manager or an umpire. "Often the player seeks to cover up his own blunder by making the umpire the 'goat'" (Billy Evans, *Pearson's Magazine*, Sept. 1912).

   **1st Use.** 1910. "No more for me, I've quit being the goat" (T. A. Dorgan's comic strip, *San Francisco Examiner*, Jan. 5; Peter Tamony). **Etymology.** Most references to this term note that it is a derivative or "clipped" form of "scapegoat" and applied to a player whose error is being blamed for a team's defeat. Gerald Cohen (*Comments on Etymology*, Dec. 1, 1985) insists that there is a major "discrepancy" in this theory: "A scapegoat is innocent, whereas the goat is not; he has blundered, usually at a crucial moment. And the standard etymology of goat as a shortening of scapegoat is therefore almost certainly in error." Cohen cites the 1889 sports pages of *The World* (New York), where an article on the New York Giants noted "the meek and lowly goat, whose job it is to haul the peanut wagon up and down the board walk." Cohen's theory is that "the original 'goats' were players severely humbled by their errant play."

**goatland** The mythic resting place for baseball's famous goats. **1st Use.** 1920. (*Spalding's Official Base Ball Guide;* Edward J. Nichols).

**goat's beard** The dangling flap hanging down from a catcher's or umpire's mask as a means of protecting the throat.

**gobble** To field a thrown or batted ball, often stated as "gobble the ball" or "gobble up." **1st Use.** 1873. (*New York Herald*, Aug. 10; Edward J. Nichols).

**go deep 1.** To hit a home run; "[Javy] Lopez became the 11th player to go deep in his first All-Star at-bat" (*Milwaukee Journal Sentinel*, 1997). See also *take deep*. **2.** To hit a ball for a long distance, resulting in an out or a hit. **3.** For a pitcher to go to a 2-2 or 3-2 count.

**go down and get it** For a batter to hit a pitch that is down and in.

**go down looking** Syn. of *strike out looking*.

**go down swinging** Syn. of *strike out swinging*.

**go downtown** To hit a home run.

**go fishing** To be lured into swinging at a ball thrown (usually low) just outside the strike zone. See also *fish, 1*.

**go for a bagel** To go hitless at the plate. "Reggie Jefferson went for a bagel in five at-bats" (*Boston Globe*, Aug. 11, 1997).

**go for the downs** To try to hit a home run.

**go for the fences** To consciously swing for a home run.

**go for the pump** To try to hit a home run. **Etymology.** Surmise points to the celebratory pumping arm motion—clenched fist, quick pullback of the arm into the body—that so many home run hitters of the 1990s seem to favor.

**Go-Go Sox** Popular nickname for the Chicago White Sox in the 1950s (esp. 1959) when they were stealing many bases.

**"going, going, gone" 1.** A popular and dramatic description of a home run ball in flight. **Etymology.** The phrase was made popular by

New York Yankees announcer Mel Allen who used it to describe balls heading into the outer reaches of Yankee Stadium. Sometimes the "gone" was omitted from the phrase if the ball was caught at the wall. This serves to heighten the drama for those moments when the announcer pauses after saying "going, going . . ."

Allen did not invent the phrase and probably was not the first to apply it to baseball. Patrick Ercolano (*Floaters, Fungoes and Fork Balls,* 1987) claims it was coined by Cincinnati Reds announcer Harry Hartman in 1929. It is, after all, an echo from the auction house where the same words are used to signal a sale. It was also an advertising slogan used for a bottled hair-remover known as Newbro's Herpicide. **2.** Description for anything that is departed. "GOING, GOING, GONE: Payroll Purge, Marlins to Dump Stars, Salaries" (*Miami Herald* headline, May 16, 1998).

**gold coast** *arch.* The group of clubhouse lockers reserved for bonus babies.

**golden age** A period when baseball seems to have been played to near perfection; specif., the 1950s. The term was given a special baseball context and perspective by Lawrence Ritter (*Glory of Their Times,* 1966): "From an emotional standpoint, I think each individual fan has his own 'Golden Age.' It's the period when that fan was between 8 and 16 years old. That's when baseball first captured the imagination; when players had appeal beyond human bounds." Syn. *golden era.*

**golden era** Syn. of *golden age.*

**Golden Shoe Award** An annual award presented by *The Sporting News* to the major-league player who stole the most bases during the regular season.

**golden sombrero** A mythical award given to a batter who strikes out four times in a game. See also *hat trick,* 2; *Olympic rings; Horn.* Syn. *silver sombrero.* **1st Use.** 1989. "I . . . struck out 4 of the next 5 at-bats, my first-ever 'golden sombrero'" (Don Baylor, *Don Baylor*).

**Golden Spikes Award** An annual award presented by the United States Baseball Federation to the top amateur baseball player in the United States.

**golden spine** High-paid players comprising the "spine" of the defense: catcher, second baseman, shortstop, and center fielder.

**Gold Glove Award** An annual award for fielding excellence, cosponsored by *The Sporting News* and Rawlings beginning in 1957, given to a player at each position in the American League and the National League, as chosen in vote by major-league managers and coaches late in the regular season. Defensive excellence includes such factors as range, general glove work, ability to make tough plays, and minimum errors.

**golf** *v.* To bat a low pitched ball, lifting it up as if it were a golf shot. "He golfed the ball into right field for a home run" (*USA Today,* Oct. 16, 1986). **1st Use.** 1917. (*New York Times,* Oct. 9; Edward J. Nichols).

**golf ball** A very low pitch that is batted in an upward fashion in the manner of a golf swing. Golf balls usually result in fly balls.

**golf hitter** A hitter given to swinging at low pitches.

**GOM** An initialism for "grand old man," applied to Connie Mack, manager of the Philadelphia Athletics for 50 years (1901–50). Jim Bouton (*"I Managed Good, But Boy Did They Play Bad,"* 1973) insisted that Mack was the "GOM of the GOG" ("great old game"). William Safire (*Political Dictionary,* 1978) noted that British statesman William Gladstone was also known as "the GOM." See also *Grand Old Man.*

**gondola** Syn. of *eephus.*

**gone 1.** Syn. of *out,* 1; e.g., "Two gone in the bottom of the fifth" means there are two outs. **1st Use.** 1899. (Burt L. Standish, *Frank Merriwell's Double Shot;* Edward J. Nichols). **2.** Ejected from a game. **3.** Said of a ball hit for a home run. See also *"going, going, gone."*

**gonfalon** Syn. of *pennant,* 2. The Italian word for "flag" is "gonfalone." **1st Use.** 1910. (*Baseball Magazine,* Sept.; Edward J. Nichols).

**gonfalonia interruptus** A facetious, pseudo-medical term for the struggles of a team bogged down in its quest for the pennant (gonfalon). "The type of pitcher he is [Tom Seaver] and the type of person he is may cure that ancient regional affliction of gonfalonia interruptus" (*Boston Globe,* July 1, 1986).

**go nine** To pitch a complete game.

**good** Excellent, in the context of baseball. This understatement is present in many baseball terms, from "good arm" to "good wood."

**good arm** **1.** A fielder with the ability to throw the ball accurately and for distance. **2.** A pitcher with a strong delivery and a good fastball.

**good ball** A pitch in the strike zone.

**good camp** A successful spring training. Regarding the 1962 New York Mets: "Despite a 'good camp' in St. Petersburg, the Mets finished 40-120" (*St. Peterburg Times,* Mar. 1987).

**good cheese** A blurring fastball. See also *cheese.* Syn. *good express.*

**"good cut!"** An exclamation said to a batter who takes a mighty swing at the ball and misses. Marian Edelman Borden (*New York Times,* undated) points out that in Little League the phrase is "yelled to the batter who has swung with a great deal of force at the ball over the umpire's head."

**good express** Syn. of *good cheese.*

**"good eye!"** An exclamation said to a batter who does not swing at a pitch out of the strike zone.

**good field, no hit** The classic description of the exceptional defensive player who is not a good hitter. "Fittingly, it was good-field-no-hit Marty Castillo who got one of the night's few fat pitches—a high fastball that he returned to the upper deck for a two-run second-inning homer" (*Newsweek,* Oct. 22, 1984). **Etymology.** All accounts trace the phrase back to Cuban-born Miguel "Mike" Gonzalez, whose command of English was less than perfect. Writing in *P.M.* on the retirement of Moe Berg in 1941 a week after the Japanese attack on Pearl Harbor (Berg was retiring to become a spy for the U.S. Government), Tom Meany wrote: "It is ironic that the suave and polished Berg should have been the subject of base-

***Good field, no hit.*** *Author of the immortal line Miguel "Mike" Gonzalez.*

ball's most illiterate message: 'Good field, no hit.' But it was so." In 1924, Berg was a young shortstop with the Brooklyn Dodgers at its Clearwater, Fla., spring training site. Mike Kelley of Minneapolis wanted to purchase Berg's contract and wired Gonzalez, a catcher for the St. Louis Cardinals, for his opinion, which resulted in Gonzalez' famous four-word telegraphic message. Berg batted .186 in 49 games with Brooklyn in 1923.

**good pair of hands** The asset of a good defensive player.

**good stuff** The repertoire of a pitcher who has command of his pitches and uses them effectively. **Usage Note.** To be told that one has "good stuff" is to be paid a major compliment. The term can be applied to a particular pitching performance or to a pitcher's overall ability.

**good town** A player's term for an enjoyable city to visit on a road trip. "'Good town' is as much a part of the baseball vernacular as 'line drive.' Montreal is perhaps the best, but San Diego and

Chicago are not far behind in the opinion of the Braves, who were asked to rate National League cities" (*The Sporting News,* July 1, 1978).

**good wood** The barrel, or thickest part, of the bat, where the ball is hit with the greatest power. To hit with "good wood on the ball" is to hit the ball solidly. See also *wood.* Syn. *decent wood.*

**go on the pitch** To try to steal a base at the moment the pitcher goes into his motion.

**goose egg** A zero on the scoreboard, in allusion to the shared oval shape of a goose egg. "Goose-Egg Diet Plunges Seals into Basement" (*San Francisco News* headline, June 27, 1952; Peter Tamony); in the story that followed it was claimed that the "Seals recently have accumulated enough goose-eggs to open a market." Syn. *hen fruit.* **1st Use.** 1867. "The Buckeyes in this inning were treated to a goose egg" (Chadwick Scrapbooks, October; David Shulman). **Etymology.** Charles Earle Funk (*A Hog on Ice and Other Curious Expressions,* 1948) points out that the egg in the expression, "to lay an egg," is derived from the goose egg of the scoreboard and "has no bearing whatsoever on the output of a hen." **Extended Use.** The egg stands for the zero cipher in other sports. To "crack" or "break an egg" is to begin to score in cricket (just as not scoring is to "lay an egg") and the zero-term in tennis, "love," derives from *l'oeuf,* which is French for egg. Both "goose egg" and "lay an egg" have generalized to any realm in which one fails to score.

**go out** To get credited with an out; e.g., "Smith went out [flied out] to center." **1st Use.** 1863. (Chadwick Scrapbooks; Edward J. Nichols).

**go out and get it** To swing at an outside pitch and hit it solidly.

**gopher ball 1.** A pitch that is destined to be hit for a home run; one that will "go for" extra bases. Jim Brosnan (*The Long Season,* 1960) defined the term: "Similar to the ordinary, legal-size baseball, but dangerous for pitchers to handle . . . should be avoided." In some earlier explanations of the term it is said that it is a contraction of "go far," but usage suggests it is the "go fer" as in "go for a double, triple, or home run." Syn. *gopher.* **2.** A

home run given up by a pitcher. **Usage Note.** The term is now used without a hint of its punnish origin: "Any informed student of the game knows that no pitcher wants to go down in the record books as having been the pitcher who served up a record-breaking gopher ball; thus careful pitching is the order of the day" (Tom Mitchel, letter to *International Herald Tribune,* Sept. 22, 1986). **1st Use.** 1932. (*Baseball Magazine,* Oct.; Edward J. Nichols). **Etymology.** Hy Turkin (*Baseball Almanac,* 1955) reports that the term was coined by Lefty Gomez when he pitched for the New York Yankees (1930–42); he used it in lines such as: "When they hit that pitch, it will go fer (gopher) a homer." Although there have been many published explanations of this term being a play on "go fer," opinion is not unanimous. Parke Cummings (*Dictionary of Baseball,* 1950) reports: "Like the gopher, which vanishes into its hole, the ball quickly vanishes into the stands or out of the park." Along those same lines, Ray Corio (*New York Times,* Feb. 8, 1988) adds: "But there's also the line of thought that the expression reflects how a pitcher feels as he watches his pitch soar over a fence: like digging a hole and crawling into it, gopher style."

**gophergate** A term created by Thomas Boswell to describe the scandal surrounding the huge increase in the number of home runs hit in 1987. **Etymology.** The term is one of several that were created after the Watergate scandal to indicate irregularity by using the suffix "-gate."

**gopher hunter** *arch.* A sharply batted ground ball.

**gorker** A term used by Baltimore Orioles manager Earl Weaver for a cheap hit. "In the ninth, Tippy Martinez . . . gave up two cheap singles. 'You hate to take a guy out after two gorkers,' manager Earl Weaver said" (*Washington Post,* June 12, 1983).

**go sign** A sign given by a base coach to a baserunner to attempt to steal or to advance to the next base. See also *green light,* 2. Syn. "go signal."

**go south 1.** To depart for spring training. **1st Use.** 1906. (*Sporting Life,* Feb. 10; Edward J.

Nichols). **2.** To lose a game. **1st Use.** 1915. (*Baseball Magazine,* Dec.; Edward J. Nichols).

**got a big one left** Said of a batter with two strikes against him.

**go the distance** To pitch a complete game. Syn. *go the route.*

**go the other way** To hit to the opposite field; i.e., for a right-handed batter to hit the ball to right field or for a left-handed batter to hit the ball to left field.

**go the route** Syn. of *go the distance.*

**"got him!"** A broadcaster's terse comment that a batter has been struck out; "a simple salute to the strikeout," said one critic after hearing Vin Scully use the term.

**got too much** Said when a pitcher has an excess of deceitful motion (curve, slide, etc.) on the ball and therefore cannot control his delivery.

**go to school** To learn from another player through experience.

**go to the hat** For a pitcher to touch, tug, or otherwise fuss with his cap while on the mound. It is an affectation that can come in handy if one has hidden an illegal substance on the cap and is "loading up" for an illegal pitch, or, as Gaylord Perry has been known to do, touch a clean cap to encourage the batter to think that he is fueling up for an illegal pitch.

**go to the mouth** To touch the lips or mouth. This action is illegal if it is made by a pitcher while on the mound and can cause his ejection from the game. The move is illegal because it suggests that the pitcher may be preparing to throw a spitball. If a pitcher needs to touch his mouth, he must step down from the mound. On a particularly cold day, a pitcher can ask for and receive from the plate umpire permission to blow on his hand without stepping off the mound.

**go to the wire** To be decided at the end of a game or season; e.g., to characterize a game whose outcome is not known until the ninth inning or a team's season whose final standing is not known until the final day. **Etymology.** The term originated in horse racing for a close race. "Wire" is long-established track slang for the finish line.

**go up** For a player to move to a higher level of minor-league play or to break into the major leagues. **1st Use.** 1909. (*Baseball Magazine,* Oct.; Edward J. Nichols).

**go with the pitch** To hit the ball to the side of the plate where it is pitched rather than to try to pull or "overpower" it; e.g., a right-handed batter would hit an outside pitch to right field and an inside pitch to left field whereas a left-handed batter would hit an outside pitch to left field and an inside pitch to right field.

**go yard** To hit a ball over the fence; e.g., hitting a home run is "going yard." "[Mark McGwire] went yard for the 16th time" (*Sports Illustrated,* June 1, 1998).

**grandmother** A woman whose fictional funeral traditionally figures into excuses for people to get out of work for an afternoon at the ballpark. The death rate among grandmothers has decreased in direct proportion to the decrease in day games played during the workweek.

R. E. Sherwood (*Baseball Magazine,* Sept. 1913) defined the term: "An elderly female in high favor with office boys in general. Her death often forms an excuse among them for leave of absence. If the home team is on the road, the excuse goes; if at home the office boy GOES—to look for another job."

An earlier and more disarming reference appears in the *Atlantic* (Aug. 1908) in the form of this immortal stanza: "Lives there a man with soul so dead/But he unto himself has said,/'My grandmother shall die to-day/And I'll go see the Giants play'?" In the next paragraph, an expert fixed "the average daily baseball mortality among grandmothers at seven thousand."

**Grand Old Man** Honorific term for a baseball man with great experience and respect. Connie Mack won the honor, as did Cy Young, "the 'Grand Old Man' among pitchers" (*The Sporting News,*

June 3, 1905). See also *GOM*. **1st Use.** 1886. "I don't believe the 'grand old man' [Henry] Chadwick would join in such a combination" (*Sporting Life,* May 26; Barry Popik).

**Grand Ol' Game** The game of baseball.

**grand salami** A punning play on *grand slam* home run.

**grand slam 1.** A home run hit with the bases loaded. Abbrev. *GS.* Syn. *grand slammer; grand salami; salami; grannie; slam,* 3; *slammer; jackpot; bases-loaded home run; demolition derby.* **1st Use.** 1940. See *grand slammer.* **Etymology.** The term, which is now used in many other sports, was first used in the game of contract bridge where it applies to the taking of all 13 tricks. It would appear that it first moved to golf in 1930 when it was widely applied to Bobby Jones's feat of winning all of golf's four major championships (the British and U.S. opens and the British and U.S. amateurs). It has since been applied to the four major tennis tournaments (Wimbledon and the French, Australian, and U.S. opens). **Extended Use.** Anything extraordinary and/or powerful. The term has been applied to a diversity of things and events outside sports. Peter Tamony collected several, including these two headlines: "A Grand Slam for Culture" (when two new theaters opened in Los Angeles) and "Grand Slam Driver Held" (he ran into four other cars). The term was also the name of a powerful British bomb used during World War II; in fact, when the first atomic bomb was dropped on Japan in 1945, it was said to have 2,000 times the power of the British "grand slam" bomb, the largest previously used. The term is also the name of a cocktail (made by mixing ½ jigger of blended whiskey, ¼ jigger of vermouth, ⅛ jigger of curaçao, and ⅛ jigger of lime juice). **2.** A *sweep,* 3. Barry Popik reports that the first baseball "grand slam" was not a home run! The term was used when a team swept all four games of a series; e.g., "Grand Slam Gives Yankees 24 Wins in 27 Series Games" (*The Sporting News* headline, Oct. 13, 1938) after the New York Yankees defeated the Chicago Cubs in the World Series, four games to none. Popik concludes: "The path from 'grand slam' in bridge to 'grand slam' series sweep to 'grand slam' home run with bases loaded is simple and clear." Syn. *slam,* 4.

**grand slammer** Syn. of *grand slam,* 1. **1st Use.** 1940. "Jim Tabor smashed out a 'grand slammer' against Johnny Humphries in the fourth inning" (*San Francisco News,* Aug. 20, 1940; Peter Tamony). Evidence that the term did not come into use until 1940 can be found in the fact that it was not mentioned by Edward J. Nichols (*An Historical Dictionary of Baseball Terminology,* Ph.D. dissertation, 1939).

**grandstand 1.** *n.* The location of the main seating area at a ballpark, traditionally behind the box seats. The grandstand is usually covered and contains reserved seats, which are priced between the cheap (bleachers) and the expensive (box) seats. See also *stands.* **1st Use.** 1870. "The immense audience disposed for the most part, on the seats of the 'grand stand'" (*Lakeside Monthly,* 4; David Shulman). **2.** *v.* To play for the admiration and applause of the crowd; to show off. R. E. Sherwood (*Baseball Magazine,* Sept. 1913) noted "the custom prevalent among players of taking a drink of water in front of the grandstand after making a home run." See also *play to the grandstand.* **1st Use.** 1889. "On the New York team there is always a temptation to individual 'grand-stand' or theatrical play" (Chadwick Scrapbooks; David Shulman). **Extended Use.** To show off in other realms.

**grandstander 1.** Syn. of *grandstand player.* **2.** A person sitting in the grandstand. Also spelled "grand-stander." **1st Use.** 1891. "During the four New York games there were never less than 2,200 people at a game, and 50 per cent of the patrons here were 'grand-standers'" (*Sporting Times,* May 23; David Shulman).

**grandstand manager** A spectator who second-guesses the manager and tends to be quite vocal about it. "Grandstand managers, some of them with horns, have sprouted up all over since Lefty O'Doul sent outfielder Joe Brovia to Portland" (*San Francisco Call-Bulletin,* Mar. 4, 1949; Peter Tamony).

his side (each move a picture), and the spectators would applaud. Hunter is a good back stop, and grand stand worker, but his throwing and batting is [sic] deficient." (*Grand Rapids Eagle,* Aug. 10, 1883; Peter Morris). Three days earlier, the *Grand Rapids Daily Democrat* had written that Hunter worked "the grand stand racket too much." **Extended Use. 1.** A showy move or style that is usually both spectacular and ineffective. "They spent so much time in arguin' and makin' grand-stand play, that the interests of the city were forgotten" (William L. Riordan, *Plunkitt of Tammany Hall,* 1905; Peter Tamony). **2.** An unexpected and dramatic move in the courtroom. "Defense attorneys in the Nick De John murder trial demanded perjury charges yesterday against Mrs. Anita Rocchia Venza, and were met by snorts from the prosecution of 'grandstand play'" (*San Francisco Examiner,* Feb. 26, 1949; Peter Tamony).

**grandstand player** A player who seeks the adulation of the crowd by routinely making easy plays look hard. "It's little things of this sort which makes the 'grand stand player.' They make impossible catches, and when they get the ball they roll all over the field." (Mike J. Kelly, *"Play Ball,"* 1888; David Shulman). Syn. *grandstander; Hollywood player; jumping jack.* **Usage Note.** Although a grandstand play here and there is tolerated and even appreciated, a player does not want to become known as a grandstand player. Alfred H. Spink wrote of Charles Comiskey (*The National Game,* 1910): "He had no use for the grandstand player who could hit the ball over the fence when the bases were clear and his side a mile ahead, but he loved the man who could hit the ball right on the nose when a run was needed and a good clout meant the game." **1st Use.** 1886. "'Kid' Baldwin of the Cincinnati's, has the credit of being the greatest grandstand player" (*The Sporting News,* May 24; David Shulman).

**grand tour** Syn. of *home run trot.* **1st Use.** 1912. (*New York Tribune,* Oct. 7; Edward J. Nichols).

**grannie** Syn. of *grand slam,* 1. The term began to be heard during the 1997 season. Also spelled "granny."

"A GRAND-STAND PLAY"

*Grandstand play.*

**grandstand play** Any play that is staged to elicit applause. The play may be a simple one but it is embellished and made to look difficult and even heroic. "When necessary, bench a man for each attempt at grandstand play. Most coaches need a little courage in this respect." (Coleman R. Griffith, *The Psychology of Coaching,* 1926). See also *play to the grandstand.* **1st Use.** 1883. "Little [William] Hunter of Saginaw worked the grand stand almost to death yesterday, and several others were guilty of the same piece of foolishness! Grand stand plays are monotonous and since Umpire Burnham's demise this city has been free from it [sic]. Every other ball pitched Hunter would execute a combined acrobatic song and dance, fall on

**grapefruit** The baseball as viewed by a batter who is hitting well or by the catcher when the pitcher has nothing on the ball. "[The manager] asked why his staff continued to serve up grapefruits to the opposition" (*Milwaukee Journal Sentinel,* May 1994). **1st Use.** 1943. (*Baseball Magazine,* Jan.; David Shulman).

**grapefruit circuit** Syn. of *Grapefruit League.* **1st Use.** 1946. "News from the Grapefruit Circuit" (*Time* magazine headline, Mar. 25).

**grapefruit game** A spring exhibition game played in Florida. **1st Use.** 1961. "Last year 306,000 attended 143 grapefruit games in Florida" (*New York Times,* Feb. 19; David Shulman).

**Grapefruit League** The name for the major-league teams that conduct spring training and play exhibition games against each other in Florida. Although the first team to make a southern spring training trip was the Chicago White Stockings who went to New Orleans in 1870, the first to train in Florida was the 1888 Washington Nationals, who went to Jacksonville. Compare *Cactus League.* Syn. *grapefruit circuit; grapefruit loop.* **Etymology/1st Use.** 1929. "Clubs of the 'Grapefruit League,' that mythical circuit which springs up annually along the banks of the Suwannee and Florida Gulf" (Horace C. Renegar, *Arizona Republic,* Jan. 14). The first use of the term in Peter Tamony's collection was this quote from Neill Sheridan of the Boston Red Sox, who struck out in the only at-bat of his major-league career: "I wound up hitting over .300 in the Grapefruit League. But once the season started I only rode the bench." (*San Francisco Call-Bulletin,* May 10, 1948).

**grapefruit loop** Syn. of *Grapefruit League.* **1st Use.** 1937. (*Philadelphia Record,* Mar. 31; Edward J. Nichols).

**graphite bat** A baseball bat made from a lightweight, virtually unbreakable combination of graphite, fiberglass, and polyester resin. Although graphite bats are in use in softball and at various levels of baseball, their only plate appearance in major-league baseball has been in spring-training experiments. Unlike *aluminum bats,* which give off a "ping" sound, graphite sounds more like wood when the ball is hit.

**grass 1.** Traditional vegetation that is grown as the surface for a baseball field and that covers everything except the pitcher's mound, basepaths, and other specific areas, which are covered with dirt. Syn. *greensward.* **2.** A specific grassy area of the playing field, esp. the infield; e.g., "Jones is in the grass" indicates an infielder who, for defensive reasons, has come in close to the plate and out of the basepath.

**grass burner** Syn. of *grass clipper.*

**grass clipper** A sharply hit grounder that skims along the grass or hugs the ground and does not hop. See also *lawn mower; skimmer; daisy cutter.* Syn. *grass burner; grass cutter.* **1st Use.** 1868. "Wright goes to first on his short grass clipper to center field" (Chadwick Scrapbooks; David Shulman).

**grass cutter** Syn. of *grass clipper.* **1st Use.** 1910. "Jones . . . pushed a grass cutter to Hagner" (Christy Mathewson, *Won in the Ninth;* David Shulman).

**grasser** A ground ball. **1st Use.** 1906. "And the average fan, watching the speed and certainty with which Hans [Wagner] goes after the grassers and yanks down the soarers, forgets the shortstop's seeming clumsiness and thinks of him rather as the 'Flying Dutchman'" (*The Sporting News,* Mar. 3).

**grass puller** A coach, so-called because some signs literally involve pulling grass. **1st Use.** 1908. (*Baseball Magazine,* July; Edward J. Nichols).

**gravy hop** A high, easy-to-field bounce of a ground ball. "Hit sharply towards third, takes a gravy hop" (Tom Marr, WFBR radio, June 11, 1983).

**grays** See *road grays.*

**grazer** An outfielder.

**grease ball** An illegal pitch that has been doctored with a secret dollop of hair dressing, petroleum jelly, lard, or similar sticky substance to give the ball an unpredictable trajectory. "Today, people still talk about the spitter, but the spitter is dead. Nowadays, it's a grease ball the pitchers are throwing." (Gaylord Perry, *Me and the Spitter,*

1974; Charles D. Poe). Also spelled "greaseball." Syn. *jellyball.*

**great** *n.* A baseball player whose feats have become legendary; e.g., "Babe Ruth is among the greats of baseball."

**Greatest Week in Baseball History** Oct. 7–15, 1986. The term was used widely during the League Championship Series in both the American League and the National League in which the New York Mets and the Boston Red Sox emerged with their respective pennants after particularly exciting and suspenseful wins over the Houston Astros and California Angels, respectively. "The greatest week in baseball history is over. The World Series begins tomorrow night at Shea Stadium." (Bill Livingston, *Cleveland Plain Dealer,* Oct. 17, 1986). Livingston was one of many to deem it the greatest week yet beheld in the history of baseball.

**Greenberg Gardens** The 30-foot area between the former and new left-field fences of Forbes Field when Hank Greenberg joined the Pittsburgh Pirates in 1947. To encourage more home runs from the slugger, the fence was moved in from 365 feet to 335 feet. From 1948 to 1953, after Greenberg retired, when Ralph Kiner remained the team's great slugger, the same happy hunting ground became known as *Kiner's Korner.* **1st Use.** 1947. "The 'Greenberg Gardens' plot in the Forbes Field . . . has sprouted a flourishing crop of home runs—nine in four games" (*San Francisco Examiner,* Apr. 21; Peter Tamony).

**green cathedral** A baseball park, field, or stadium. The term was first used by Philip J. Lowry for the title of his book *Green Cathedrals* (1986) and is now often used to refer to a baseball park. In the introduction to the revised edition (1992) of *Green Cathedrals,* Lowry hoped the title of the book would a) convey the "quiet spiritual reverence" for the ballpark, which "holds treasured memories and serves as a sanctuary for the spirit, a haven where the ghosts of . . . greats from the past can continue to roam among their modern-day counterparts" and b) celebrate "the mystical appeal of the hundreds of ballparks, past and present, where the soul of the game of baseball resides."

**green fly** A derisive modern name for a female who is constantly working to be in the company of professional players; the baseball equivalent of the rock groupie. "When a green fly comes around, you may hear someone yell, 'Get the swatter'" (Mike Gonring, *Baseball Digest,* June 1979). A quote from the *Boston Globe,* which was reprinted in the *Atlantic* (July 1987), noted that "[players] speak disparagingly of this pesky breed as 'greenflies' referring to the species that is soft-bodied, pear-shaped, and gathers in colonies." See also *fly,* 3. Also spelled "greenfly." **Etymology.** Named for the most persistent and obnoxious kind of insect. The greenfly (*Coloradoa rufomaculata*), an aphid, is an important pest of chrysanthemums. The green peach aphid, bluebottle fly, and blowfly have all attracted this name.

**green light 1.** A coach's sign flashed to a batter allowing him to swing. It is most commonly given on a 3-0 count. See also *hit sign.* **2.** A *go sign* given to a baserunner to take an extra base or attempt to steal at the discretion of the baserunner. Keith Hernandez (*Pure Baseball,* 1994) writes: "Speed has changed all the old thinking about base stealing. The quick guys have a permanent green light. When they get a jump, they can go." Compare *stop sign; red light.* **3.** President Franklin D. Roosevelt's letter of Jan. 15, 1942, to commissioner Kenesaw Mountain Landis to continue playing baseball during World War II. The President wrote in response to Landis's offer to cancel baseball: "If 300 teams use 5,000 or 6,000 players, these players are a definite recreational asset to at least 20,000,000 of their fellow citizens—and that in my judgment is thoroughly worthwhile." **Etymology.** An obvious borrowing from the green light of traffic control.

**Green Monster** The imposing 37.17-foot-tall left-field wall at Fenway Park in Boston, marked as 315 feet from home plate. "Myth-killer [Bruce] Hurst Doesn't Fear the 'Green Monster'" (*USA Today* headline, Oct. 23, 1986). Before it was painted green in 1947, it was covered with advertisements. It has been blamed and credited for things ranging from turning line-drive home runs into sliding doubles as they bounce off the wall and converting high fly balls into home runs when

**Green monster.** *A youthful Ted Williams, right, and collegue jogging past the Green Monster and the ever-popular Fenway Park hand-operated scoreboard.*

such balls are lofted over it. Atop the Green Monster is a 23.3-foot screen, the last barrier between home runs and the windows on Lansdowne Street and/or the Massachusetts Turnpike. Although the wall is marked at 315 feet, Dan Shaughnessy (*Boston Globe,* Apr. 25, 1995) insisted it's not 315 feet: "It's 309 feet, 3 inches. I know. I measured it myself." Syn. *Wall, The.*

**green pea** A *rookie,* esp. one with little experience; a real novice. **1st Use.** 1912. This was Casey Stengel's favorite term for a young and inexperienced player and one that was eventually regarded as an element of Stengelese. The term shows up in a 1912 *Sporting Life* article on player slang: "You're the green pea of the American League." By the 1920s, it appears to have been common slang. **Extended Use.** A novice in other areas. "The delegation which arrived here [at the Democratic National Convention] last Saturday, for the most part 'green peas' in national convention work, are now veterans" (*San Francisco News,* July 26, 1952).

**greensward** Syn. of *grass,* 1. The term was commonly used during the first decade of the 20th century.

**green weenie 1.** A plastic, gag-store hot dog painted green, which was first brought into play by the Pittsburgh Pirates in 1960 when a trainer noted that when it was pointed at an opposing pitcher—when he was given "the green weenie"—the Pirates started hitting. They went into mass production and were sold as souvenirs in 1966. One was wielded by sportscaster Bob Prince in the booth to put hexes and jinxes on opponents of the Pirates on its way to the 1971 National League pennant. **2.** A pitch that a batter does not like.

**Griffith Stadium.** *A rare aerial view of a classic ballpark.*

Jim Brosnan (*The Long Season,* 1960) referred to "slipping the green weenie past" Ernie Banks.

**grenade** A bloop hit. "I knew I could just drop a little grenade down the leftfield line." (Tony Gwynn, quoted in *Sports Illustrated,* June 15, 1998). See also *hand grenade,* 2.

**Greyhound squad** The daily list of players cut from a major-league club's spring-training roster, who then presumably left for their minor-league assignments on Greyhound buses (Bob Uecker, *Catcher in the Wry,* 1983; Charles D. Poe).

**Griffith Stadium** The home field of the Washington Senators from 1911 until the end of the 1961 season. It was a quirky, classic stadium whose center-field wall detoured around five houses and a large tree. It was named for Senators owner Clark C. Griffith.

**Griffmen** *arch.* A nickname for the *Washington Senators,* 2, under the stewardship (1920–60) of owner Clark C. Griffith. Syn. "Griffs."

**grinder** A reliable workhorse pitcher; one who "grinds" out victories. "Grinder Sutton Polishes off No. 300" (*The Sporting News* headline on Don Sutton's 300th win, June 30, 1986).

**grip 1.** The exact manner in which a batter holds the bat at the plate. The grip will vary considerably depending on whether a batter is swinging away or bunting. Batters use batting gloves and pine tar to keep their grips from slipping. **2.** The exact manner in which a pitcher holds the ball as

**Grip.** *A photo of what is believed to be Lou Gehrig's grip.*

he prepares to deliver it. The grip taken for a given pitch usually determines the type of pitch to be thrown.

**grooming** The preparation and maintenance of the playing field by the ground crew.

**groove 1.** *n.* The path a pitch takes down the middle of the strike zone, where a batter would most easily hit the pitch. **1st Use.** 1912. (*New York Tribune,* Oct. 6; Edward J. Nichols). **2.** *v.* To throw a nonbreaking pitch down the middle of the strike zone where it is most hittable for the batter. **1st Use.** 1911. (*Spalding's Official Base Ball Guide;* Edward J. Nichols). **3.** *n.* A period when one performs at one's absolute best or in a consistently high form; e.g., when a batter is hitting well over a period of games, he is said to be "in a groove," where everything feels right, and the ball appears to be as large as a beach ball.

**groover** A nonbreaking pitch delivered to the heart of the strike zone. **1st Use.** 1911. "The big

left-hander set himself and whipped in a 'groover' " (Charles Van Loan, *The Big League*).

**ground 1.** *v.* To be thrown out as a result of hitting a ground ball; e.g., "Smith grounded to third." Syn. *ground out.* **2.** *v.* To win by a shutout; e.g., "The Yanks grounded the Royals, 4–0."

**ground ball** A batted ball that hits the ground as it comes off the bat and then rolls or bounces along the ground. Syn. *grounder.* **1st Use.** 1860. (*Beadle's Dime Base-Ball Player;* Edward J. Nichols).

**ground-ball pitcher** A pitcher who entices batters to hit ground balls rather than fly balls; e.g., sinkerballer Scott Erickson.

**ground coverer** A defensive player who is able to field successfully balls that are hit to a wide range of the field. **1st Use.** 1902. (*Sporting Life,* July 12; Edward J. Nichols).

**ground crew** A group of workers who, under direction of the groundskeeper, prepares and maintains the condition of the playing field. The crew's duties include protecting the field from rain, sweeping the basepaths, and chalking the various lines and boxes on the field. Syn. *grounds crew.*

**grounded into a double play** A statistic for the number of times a player grounded into a double play. Abbrev. *GDP.* Acronym *GIDP.*

**grounder** Syn. of *ground ball.* **1st Use.** 1860. "Tomes then took the bat on the part of the Exercise [Ball Club] nine, and by a good 'grounder' to left field, made his first base" (*New York Clipper,* July 21). Despite early use, the term was on the road to obscurity when Casey Stengel began to use it constantly. **Extended Use.** A case that is handled easily, like a soft ground ball (William J. Caunitz, *One Police Plaza,* 1984).

**ground hog** *arch.* **1.** A member of the ground crew. **2.** Syn. of *groundskeeper.*

**ground out** *v.* To be thrown out as the result of hitting a ground ball; e.g., "Smith grounded out to third." See also *ground,* 1.

**groundout** *n.* An out resulting from a ball being hit on the ground.

**ground-rule double** *n.* A two-base hit awarded by the umpire that results from hitting into a special situation outlined in the ground rules, esp. when a batted ball bounces in fair territory and goes over the fence or into the stands. Previous to 1930 in the American League and 1931 in the National League, a ball that bounced over the fence was considered a home run. See also *roof-rule double.* **Etymology.** Gerald Cohen (*Comments on Etymology,* Apr. 1, 1986) noted that an article titled "Stopped by the Police" (*The World* [New York], Aug. 26, 1889) contained "what seems to be an account of the first ground-rule double in baseball history, although the term was yet to be coined." The article tells of a game in Hamilton, Ohio, between teams from Brooklyn and Cincinnati, which drew such an immense crowd that the game had to be halted. At one point in the account of the shortened game, we hear: "The entire outfield was lined with people, and the fences were black with humanity. The crowd within so completely filled the grounds that hundreds refused to

go in when they found that there were no accommodations. . . . The crowd encroached so on the fielders that a ground rule allowing but two bases on a ball batted into the crowd was made."

**ground rules** A set of special rules unique to the specific conditions and dimensions of a given ballpark. The rules are made by the home team and must be understood by both teams before play begins. Many of the rules address whether a ball is in play if it hits an obstacle, such as a rolled tarp; e.g., a ball that reaches the catwalk 300 feet from the plate at Tropicana Field (home field for the Tampa Devil Rays) is ruled a home run. One of the odder ground rules ever established was during the first game of the 1965 World Series, which was attended by then Vice President Hubert H. Humphrey. It was decided that even if a ball hit the Secret Service man sitting on the field in front of Humphrey, the ball would remain in play. **Extended Use.** A basic set of rules and procedures that is set out in advance, whether it be for an election debate or a pie-eating contest.

**grounds** **1.** The area in which baseball is played, including both the field and the stands. **1st Use.** 1845. (*Brooklyn Daily Star,* Oct. 23; Edward J. Nichols). **2.** A ballpark; e.g., the Polo Grounds in New York City.

**grounds crew** Syn. of *ground crew.*

**groundskeep** To serve as a groundskeeper; to prepare and maintain the condition of the playing field.

**groundskeeper** The chief of the ground crew. Because the way in which the grounds are kept can give the home team small advantages, the position can have a certain strategic importance; or, as Bill Veeck once put it: "A good groundskeeper can be as valuable as a .300 hitter." For instance, such factors as the length of the infield grass, the moistness of the basepaths, and the subtle slope of the ground around the foul lines are variables in the hands of the groundskeeper. Milt Richman (*Baseball Digest,* May 1947) identified the groundskeeper as "the guy who smoothens every position except your own." Sometimes spelled "groundkeeper." Syn. *ground hog,* 2; *manicurist.* **1st Use.** 1942. "Cy

Slapnicka . . . groundkeeper" (*Baseball Magazine,* June; David Shulman).

**groundskeeper single** A single that occurs when the batted ball strikes a pebble (*San Francisco News,* Dec. 8, 1953).

**GS 1.** Abbrev. for *games started.* **2.** Abbrev. for *grand slam,* 1 (a home run). It tends to be used in headlines; e.g., "[Mike] Greenwell GS Powers Red Sox Past Rangers" (*Bangor Daily News,* Aug. 3, 1988).

**guardian angel** Syn. of *angel,* 1.

**guard the bag** For a fielder to play close to a base.

**guard the line** To position the first baseman close to the first base line or the third baseman close to the third base line to prevent extra-base hits down the line. It is a defensive strategy that is usually taken in the late innings of a close game.

**guard the plate** For a batter with two strikes to swing at any pitch close to the strike zone.

**guesser** *arch.* An umpire. **1st Use.** 1937. (*The Sporting News Record Book;* Edward J. Nichols).

**guess hitter 1.** A hitter who tries to anticipate a pitch or outguess the pitcher based on the situation at hand (bases loaded, 3-2 count, etc.). "As with all big sluggers, . . . [Hank] Greenberg was sometimes labeled 'guess hitter.' He resented it. 'Guess hitter, bull,' he said. 'We're all guess hitters, if everybody would only tell the truth.'" (Shirley Povich, *Washington Post,* Sept. 9, 1986). **2.** An indecisive hitter who often swings at any pitch.

**guide 1.** For a pitcher to pinpoint a pitch; e.g., "Smith guides the ball to the outside part of the plate." **2.** For a hitter to place the ball where he wants it to go; e.g., "Smith guided the ball to left."

**gum the bases** To run slowly along the basepath. **1st Use.** 1913. "In spite of his fielding delinquencies and his habit of gumming the bases when in transit, the cap was the most popular player" (Charles Van Loan, *The Lucky Seventh;* David Shulman).

**gun 1.** *n.* A strong throwing arm. See also *rifle,* 1; *shotgun.* **2.** *n.* A pitcher's arm. **3.** *v.* To throw hard and accurately; e.g., "Smith gunned the ball to first base." See also *rifle,* 2; *shoot,* 1. **4.** *n.* Syn. of *radar gun.*

**gun down** To throw out a baserunner with a strong throw.

**gun pitcher** A pitcher whose fastball is better on radar than it is to the batter; e.g., Kevin Tapani (*Sports Illustrated,* Aug. 7, 1989).

**gun-shy** Said of a player who is afraid of the ball, esp. after having been hit by a pitched or batted ball.

**guy** *n./obs.* To jeer at; to rib. Gerald Cohen (*Comments on Etymology,* 1986–1987) concluded: "It is now clear from *The World* (New York) that the term was entrenched in baseball speech of the late 19th century, and the only question is why it later died out." An example from *The World* (Aug. 4, 1888) in which "black" refers to the New York Giants: "They guyed the red stockings and cheered black."

**GWRBI** Scorecard and box score abbrev. for *game-winning RBI.*

# H

**H 1.** Scorecard and box score abbrev. for *hit*, 1. **2.** Box score abbrev. for *hold*, 4.

**hack 1.** *n.* An opportunity to bat; e.g., "I need to get a couple of hacks." **2.** *v.* To swing at a pitched ball. Chuckie Carr rejected a 2-0 take sign and later explained: "Chuckie don't play that game. Chuckie hacks on 2-0." (*Milwaukee Journal Sentinel*, Sept. 2, 1997). **3.** *v.* To swing without form or grace. **4.** *n.* A poor or clumsy swing at a pitch out of the strike zone. **5.** *n.* An aggressive or hard swing at a pitched ball. **6.** *n.* An attempted place hit; e.g., "Smith took a hack at right field, but fouled it off."

**hacker** A batter with poor form at the plate or one who regularly takes reckless or undisciplined swings at pitches outside the strike zone.

**hair** Velocity as applied to a moving ball, whether it be a pitch or a line drive. San Diego Padres announcer Jerry Coleman described a fastball that "had a little hair on it" (*Baseball Digest*, Dec. 1983).

**Hairs vs. Squares** A nickname for the 1972 World Series that pitted the hirsute Oakland A's ("The Mustache Gang") versus the clean-shaven Cincinnati Reds.

**half 1.** Syn. of *half inning*. **2.** One game of a doubleheader. **3.** One of two parts of a baseball season, before or after the All-Star break in July.

**half gainer 1.** A headfirst dive for a catch. **2.** Syn. of *headfirst slide*. **Etymology.** From the name of a common dive in aquatic sports.

**half inning** One of two equal portions of a full inning, when one team is at bat and the other team is in the field. The visiting team bats during the first (top) half and the home team bats during the second (bottom) half. When the fielding team records three outs, the teams switch positions and begin a new half inning. Syn. *half*, 1.

**half-rubber** A schoolyard variation of baseball played with a sponge-rubber ball that has been cut in half and a thin bat, which is likely to have been fashioned from a broomstick. Its appeal comes from the fact that it allows for several, odd sidearm breaking pitches and is difficult to get hits. There are two players on each team and there is no baserunning; rather, bases are reached by imaginary men and earned when the ball is hit beyond a designated line. The game is discussed in detail by Hugh M. Thomason (*Western Folklore*, Jan. 1975) who describes the game as he played it in rural southeastern Georgia in the mid-1930s. Lowry Axley (*American Speech*, Aug. 1927) claims that the game and its name were invented in Savannah, Ga., where, according to one player, it was originated "some eight or ten years ago by two boys who got the idea when they were hitting pop-bottle caps with broom handles." Also spelled "halfrubber."

**half swing** A swing that is stopped before going past the front of the batter's body, usually resulting in a called strike. See also *check swing*.

**halfway 1.** Said of the position taken by a baserunner between bases when a fly ball is hit so that he will have time to retreat to the original base if the ball is caught. **2.** Said of the defensive position often taken by the infield when there is a slow runner on third base and fewer than two outs. The position puts the fielder in a spot midway between regular depth and the "in" position. It sets up an opportunity for a play at the plate without fully compromising the defensive positioning.

**Hall of Fame 1.** The pantheon of the game's greatest players in the form of a list of those players. Syn. *Cooperstown,* 2. **2.** The shortened name of the *National Baseball Hall of Fame and Museum* in Cooperstown, N.Y., and the place within that museum reserved for bronze plaques depicting and honoring the great players who have been elected and inducted into the Hall of Fame. Both the mu-

**Hall of Fame.** *An early postcard with the notion of a baseball hall of fame many years before one was actually created.*

seum and the Hall itself were established in a building (baseball's "shrine") in 1939; however, the first players were elected to the Hall of Fame in 1936. The first group of inductees, selected by the Baseball Writers Association of America, were Ty Cobb, Walter Johnson, Christy Mathewson, Babe Ruth, and Honus Wagner. In addition to the great players, eligible candidates include managers, umpires, pioneers, and executives who have contributed to the game. The rules governing election to the Hall of Fame require that players be retired for five years and that the election is conducted by polling baseball writers by secret ballot. A candidate must receive a vote from 75% of those voting to be elected. Sportswriter Jimmy Cannon's candid definition of the Hall of Fame was: "Where baseball writers send their friends." Abbrev. *HOF.* **1st Use.** 1908. The term predated the establishment of the Cooperstown shrine by many years. In his Ph.D. dissertation, submitted in 1939 when the Hall of Fame was created, Edward J. Nichols noted that "Hall of Fame" originally meant "an honor roll of pitchers who have pitched full games without allowing opposing teams to hit safely" (*Baseball Magazine,* Nov. 1908). **Etymology.** The idea for the Hall of Fame was proposed by Ford C. Frick in 1935 soon after he became president of the National League. Many other halls of Fame have followed the one in Cooperstown, which, though the most famous, was not the first American example. The prototype American institution is the Hall of Fame at New York Univ., a national shrine that commemorates the names of outstanding Americans. In sports alone, there are now dozens of halls of fame, including the National Jockeys Hall of Fame, the Lacrosse Hall of Fame and Museum, and the U.S. Croquet Hall of Fame.

**Hall of Fame Game** A special exhibition game played at Abner Doubleday Field in Cooperstown, N.Y., between two major-league teams and in conjunction with the annual Hall of Fame induction ceremonies. The game is usually played on the first Monday in August.

**Hall of Famer** An individual inducted into the Hall of Fame; a *baseball immortal.*

**hall of shame** A list, book, article, or other place

where poor performances, error rates, and other negatives are collected. The term is, of course, a play on "Hall of Fame." Authors Bruce Nash and Allan Zullo have turned the idea into a series of books, but they seem to be running out of material. Does Mike Schmidt really belong in *The Baseball Hall of Shame* because he once forgot to buckle his pants and walked onto the playing field?

**Halos** A nickname for the Anaheim Angels.

**ham-and-cheese** A desirable pitch from the batter's standpoint. "Tonight, he just threw me a ham-and-cheese over the plate, and I hit it for a three-run triple" (Henry Rodriguez, quoted in *Milwaukee Journal Sentinel,* June 10, 1997).

**ham-and-egg reliever** A relief pitcher who is usually brought in after the game has been decided. "He is reliable but nondescript, like a meal of ham and eggs" (Patrick Ercolano, *Fungoes, Floaters and Fork Balls,* 1987).

**ham hitter** *arch.* An inferior hitter.

**hammer** **1.** *v.* To hit the ball with great power. Dick Allen said on more than one occasion: "I don't use the strike zone much. I'm looking for something to hammer." **1st Use.** 1895. (*New York Press,* Aug. 7; Edward J. Nichols). **2.** *v.* To hit well against a pitcher in a particular game. **1st Use.** 1869. (*New York Herald,* Sept. 7; Edward J. Nichols). **3.** *n.* A player who hits pitches with hammerlike blows; e.g., Henry Aaron was known as "Hammerin' Hank" and his autobiography is entitled *I Had a Hammer* (1991). **4.** *n.* An effective pitcher. **5.** *n.* Syn. of *breaking ball.*

**hand** *obs.* A turn at bat during the earliest days of baseball. Robert Smith (*Baseball,* 1947) observed that the early game of baseball was a gambling vehicle and made this point: "The very language of early baseball, as evolved by the Knickerbockers, was that of the gaming table: a turn at bat was a 'hand' and a run was an 'ace.'"

**handcuff** **1.** *v.* To defy easy handling when a ball is batted into the field; e.g., "A bullet handcuffed the third baseman" (Keith Jackson, ABC-TV broadcast, Oct. 14, 1986). **1st Use.** 1935. "An infielder is said to be 'hand-cuffed' when unsuccessfully attempting to catch a hard drive" (Ralph H.

Barbour, *How to Play Better Baseball;* David Shulman). **2.** *n.* The glove hand of a fielder when he cannot get it on a batted ball (as if he were wearing handcuffs). The situation is more likely to occur with hard-hit balls. **3.** *v.* For a pitcher to hold the opposition to very few hits (as if the batters were handcuffed). See also *shackle.* **1st Use.** 1939. "Morris Handcuffs Seals" (*San Francisco News,* Apr. 10; Peter Tamony). **Etymology.** The term may have had its first sports application in boxing, where it referred to a fighter who was not using his hands to full advantage. When writer Stuart Bell of the *Cleveland Press* discovered a fight to be a fake, the *San Francisco News* (May 4, 1933; Peter Tamony) reported: "Bell had every reason to believe that one of the fighters was wearing handcuffs. Not only did the referee toss the middleweights from the ring, but the fans did some rioting."

**hand grenade** **1.** The baseball. **2.** A hit lobbed over the infield. "It was a hand grenade—a hit lobbed over the infield—but as far as [Kevin] Higgins was concerned, it could have been a rocket off the center-field wall" (Kevin Kernan, *San Diego Union-Tribune,* May 30, 1993). See also *grenades.*

**hand grenader** *arch.* A pitcher.

**handle** **1.** *n.* The narrow end of the baseball bat. **2.** *v.* To field successfully a batted or thrown ball. **1st Use.** 1862. (Chadwick Scrapbooks; Edward J. Nichols). **3.** *n.* The nonexistent part of a batted or thrown ball that must be grasped to field it successfully; e.g., "Smith couldn't find the handle on the ball as Jones reached second on the error." **4.** *n.* A ground ball that takes a high, easy hop for the fielder. **5.** *v.* See *handle a pitcher.* **6.** *v.* See *handle the stick; handle the bat.*

**handle a pitcher** To play effectively the role of a catcher for a particular pitcher. Edward J. Nichols notes that the term "usually refers to the ability of the catcher to obtain effective cooperation from a pitcher." To handle a pitcher also involves giving him good direction in the form of signals and being able to keep the pitcher calm when he is having difficulties. **1st Use.** 1894. (*Spalding's Official Base Ball Guide;* Edward J. Nichols).

**handle hit** A hit made off the handle of the bat, often a ground ball that dribbles down the line.

**handle the bat** To bat well. "I've got to show them I can handle the bat at the major-league level" (Charlie Greene, quoted in *Baltimore Sun,* Feb. 23, 1998).

**handle the stick** To bat well. "A guy who handles the stick the way you did isn't forgotten so easily" (Paul Benjamin, *Squeeze Play,* 1984).

**hand out** *n.* An out when a ball is caught, under the Knickerbocker Rules (rules 11, 12, 14) of 1845.

**handout** Syn. of *base on balls.*

**hands 1.** Fielding ability. A capable defensive player is said to have "good hands." "Dave Kingman has feet for hands" (Glen Waggoner & Robert Sklars, *Rotisserie League Baseball,* 1987). **2.** Hitting ability. A capable hitter is said to have "good hands." "A player who hits singles has baby hands. A player in a slump, well, his hands went on vacation." (Glen Waggoner & Robert Sklars, *Rotisserie League Baseball,* 1987).

**hands lost** *obs.* "The old way of recording the outs in a match. Whenever a player is put out, a 'hand is lost,' and an 'out' is recorded in the score books." (Henry Chadwick)

**hands made of stone** The hands of an inept fielder.

**hands out** *obs.* Players declared out. Edward J. Nichols noted: "The term was carried over from cricket but dropped before the Civil War." **1st Use.** 1845. (Knickerbocker Rules).

**handyman** A player who can play several positions as well as bat; a "handy" man to have around. An article on Rick Cerone (*Boston Globe,* May 22, 1988) is headlined "Designated Handyman" alluding to the fact that he had been used for short periods at more than one position, including an inning each in two different games as a pitcher for the 1987 New York Yankees.

**hang 1.** To throw a pitch (such as a curveball) that does not break, or breaks slowly and slightly; e.g., a pitch that "hangs" over the plate, usually up and in the middle of the strike zone. "For a pitcher, a mortal sin. He who hangs too many curves, soon hangs up his glove forever." (Jim Brosnan, *The Long Season,* 1960). **1st Use.** 1937. Edward J.

Nichols traces the term to an interview he conducted with Boston Braves pitcher William "Roy" Weir. **2.** Syn. of *strand,* 2.

**hang a clothesline** To hit a line drive, which, in flight, resembles a white clothesline. Syn. *hang out the clothes; hang out the hemp; hang out the wash.* **1st Use.** 1932. (*Baseball Magazine,* Oct.; Edward J. Nichols).

**hanger** Syn. of *hanging curve.*

**hang in** Syn. of *hang tough.*

**hanging curve** A high curveball that only breaks slightly, thereby giving the batter an easy target. It is the bane of pitchers and the delight of batters. Syn. *hanger.*

**hang out the clothes** Syn. of *hang a clothesline.*

**hang out the hemp** Syn. of *hang a clothesline.*

**hang out the wash** Syn. of *hang a clothesline.*

**hang out to dry** To pick off a baserunner.

**hang them up** Syn. of *hang up one's spikes.*

**hang time** The length of time it takes a fly ball to descend from its peak in flight to being fielded.

**hang tough** For a batter to foul off pitches, working the count to his favor, and not capitulating to the pitcher. Syn. *hang in.*

**hang up 1.** To catch a runner between bases. **2.** To be caught in a rundown.

**hang up one's spikes** To retire from playing professional baseball. Syn. *hang them up.*

**Hank Aaron Trophy** The proper name for *Arby's RBI Award.* It is named for the all-time major-league leader in runs batted in (2,297).

**happy zone** The middle of the strike zone where batters most enjoy seeing a pitch; the area "where a hitter's average jumps by 100 points" (*Baltimore Sun,* May 2, 1994).

**hard** With velocity and power; e.g., a "hard" line drive or a "hard" slider. Compare *soft,* 1.

**hardball** A term that seemingly refers to baseball—the game as well as the ball. When the term is used in the context of baseball it refers to a tough style of play. Headline (*San Francisco Examiner,* Mar. 25,

1981; Peter Tamony) for story on Oakland A's manager Billy Martin and the efforts of the A's front office to promote his style of management at the gate: "'Billy' Campaign Adds Major Hard Sell to A's Hard-Ball Style." **Usage Note.** The term does not sit well with baseball purists who see it as a misnomer. Red Smith (*New York Times,* July 1, 1981) commented that it is a "misbegotten term" that has been given "an unappetizing usage, signifying nothing"; Smith was quick to point out: "There is a game called softball; in fact, there are two—slow pitch and fast pitch softball. There is no game called hardball. Nobody plays hardball." **1st Use.** 1944. In a discussion of the highly competitive newspaper business in Chicago, it was stated (*Time* magazine, Oct. 30; Peter Tamony): "Last week a man with a winning streak stepped into what he called this 'hard-ball league.'" **Etymology.** It is commonly assumed that "hardball" came into being as a way to distinguish baseball from softball; e.g., "What shall we play Sunday? Softball or hardball?" However, Peter Tamony discovered an item in a club newsletter (Olympic Club's *Olympian,* Mar.–Apr. 1945) that discusses the club's changeover from a "soft ball" (a tennis ball) to a "hard ball" (black-rubber Irish handball). **Extended Use.** Currently, the term seems to be used most commonly to refer to a tough, relentless adversary or adversarial situation. Presumably, no soft balls are thrown when hardball is being played. "More Hardball Over Big Government" (*Washington Post* headline, Jan. 6, 1987). An article on Jim Bunning, a new Congressman and a former major-league pitcher, was headlined: "Bunning Ready to Play Some Hardball in D.C." (*USA Today,* Oct. 6, 1986). The term has a specific use among drug addicts: "Mixing cocaine with heroin is called speedballing or hardballing" (*San Francisco Examiner,* on the death of John Belushi, Mar. 12, 1982; Peter Tamony).

**hard cheese** A fastball. "[Nolan Ryan] threw some good hard cheese up there" (Wally Backman, quoted in *St. Petersburg Times,* Mar. 5, 1987).

**hard-nosed** Said of player (such as Ty Cobb, Pete Rose, and Lenny Dykstra) whose style of play is tough and tenacious.

**hard one** A fastball.

**hard out** A player who is difficult to retire; a batter with a good eye for balls outside the strike zone.

**harness** *arch.* The uniform and equipment of a player, esp. those of a catcher. **1st Use.** 1902. (*Sporting Life,* July 5; Edward J. Nichols).

**Harvey's Wallbangers** A nickname given to the hard-hitting 1982 Milwaukee Brewers after Harvey Kuenn became manager in June. According to *Newsweek,* Kuenn told his players: "Look, you guys can flat-out hit. So just go out there and have some fun." The name was a play on the name of a mixed drink called a Harvey Wallbanger.

**hassock** *arch.* Syn. of *base,* 2. See also *hazzard.* **1st Use.** 1907. (Burt L. Standish, *Dick Merriwell's Magnetism;* Edward J. Nichols).

**hat trick** **1.** The achievement of a batter who has *hit for the cycle,* 1. The term, only occasionally used in baseball, is much more commonly used in hockey or soccer for a player who has scored three goals in one game, or in horse racing for a jockey who wins three races in a row. **2.** A mythical award given to a player who strikes out three times in a game. See also *golden sombrero; Olympic rings; Horn.* **Etymology.** The term comes from cricket where it was created in the 19th century for the practice of presenting a bowler a new hat when he took—or knocked down—three wickets on three consecutive balls. The *Oxford English Dictionary* lists the term in use as early as 1882 in this context. "He thus accomplished the feat known as the 'hat trick,' and was warmly applauded" (*Daily Telegraph,* May 19). It has also been stated that the term is Canadian and that it was created to describe spectators collecting money in a hat for a hockey player who had just scored three goals. This practice may well have been common, but the application of the term to hockey clearly postdates its appearance in cricket by many years.

**haul it in** To catch a batted or thrown ball.

**have bells on** Said of a ball that has been hit hard. **1st Use.** 1908. (*New York Evening Journal,* June 19; Edward J. Nichols).

**have one's innings** **1.** To have one's proper turns at bat. **2.** To accumulate sufficient playing time. Syn. *get one's innings.* **Extended Use.** To have had a chance; e.g., "Jones had his innings when he was given the opportunity to present his proposal."

**hawk** An outfielder who covers his territory with speed and skill. See also *ball hawk,* 1; *flyhawk.*

**hazzard** A base, in the parlance of Dizzy Dean, who was giving his own twist to *hassock.*

**HB** Abbrev. for *hit batter.*

**HBP** **1.** Scorecard and box score abbrev. for *hit by pitch.* **2.** Abbrev. for *hit by pitcher.*

**head** **1.** The thick end of a baseball bat. **2.** One's physical appearance, usually used in a negative context. "Men who are considered to have 'the bad head' include Rocky Bridges, Don Mossi, and Yogi Berra" (Leonard Shecter, *Baseball Digest,* June 1963).

**head case** A temperamental player.

**head fake** A deceptive tactic by which the player with the ball looks at a baserunner in the hope that the glance will be enough to get the runner to stop or return to a base, allowing the player with the ball to throw to another base. Compare *arm fake.*

**headfirst slide** A slide characterized by a dive with arms outstretched to reach or return to base. It is a risky move, hence it is used as a measure of a player's mettle. See also *belly whopper.* Syn. *belly slide; half gainer.*

**headhunter** A pitcher who throws beanballs; one who aims for the head. "There are certain pitchers who are known as headhunters, there are other pitchers who won't throw at anybody, like Catfish [Hunter], and then there are pitchers who can't throw at anybody, like Wilbur Wood" (Ron Luciano, *The Umpire Strikes Back,* 1982; Charles D. Poe). *USA Today* headline (May 27, 1994): "NL's [Leonard] Coleman Vows Crackdown on 'Headhunters.'" Also spelled "head hunter."

**head in the locker** The figurative condition of a player with little or nothing to say to anyone, including his teammates.

**"heads up"** *interject.* A command to stay alert.

**heads-up** *adj.* Alert and quick-thinking; e.g., "heads-up play" or "heads-up ball."

***Headfirst slide.*** *Pepper Martin launches one of his famous headfirst slides.*

**head-to-head** In direct personal opposition; e.g., "Pitchers Smith and Jones are going head-to-head."

**head-work** *arch.* The thinking of a player using good judgment in his work. This term was common in the late 19th century. Henry Chadwick (*The Game of Base Ball,* 1868) commented: "This is a term specially applied to the pitcher who is noted for his tact and judgment in bothering his batting opponents by his pitching. A pitcher who simply trusts to pace, in his delivery, for effect will never succeed with skillful batsmen opposed to him. A pitcher, however, who uses head-work in pitching tries to discover his adversary's weak points, and to tempt him to hit at balls, either out of his reach or pitched purposely for him to hit to a particular part of the field. Pitchers, in general, have greatly improved in this respect within the past few years."

**healthy** *arch.* A batter's swing at a pitched ball. Edward J. Nichols gives this example: "He walked to the plate and took his 'healthy.'" **1st Use.** 1915. (Ring W. Lardner, "My Roomy"; Edward J. Nichols).

**healthy average** A good percentage, usually applied to a batting average.

**hear the bell ringing** To open the season. "Maybe the Cincinnati Reds hear the bell ringing. That's old baseball talk meaning the start of the season." (*Tampa Tribune*, Apr. 4, 1986).

**hearth stone** Syn. of *home plate*.

**heart of the game** Pitching, so called by those who see it as the key to the sport.

**heart of the order** That part of the batting order with the best hitters, commonly the third, fourth, and fifth positions. Pitchers test their mettle going through the "heart of the order."

**heat 1.** *arch.* Syn. of *inning*, 1. The term was borrowed from horse racing. **2.** A fastball of high quality. **3.** The ability to throw the fastball. "Baseball can bring you to your knees . . . I never thought this could happen when I was on top and I had my heat, but now I know . . . baseball can knock you right down to your knees." (Dennis Eckersley, quoted by Michael Madden, *Boston Globe*, July 10, 1983). Syn. *heater.*

**heater** Syn. of *heat*, 2.

**heave 1.** *v.* To pitch or throw. **2.** *n.* A thrown or pitched ball. **1st Use.** 1907. (*Harper's Weekly*, Dec. 14; Edward J. Nichols). **3.** *v.* To throw a game. An article in the *New York Clipper* (Nov. 11, 1865), unearthed by Peter Morris, entitled "How to Heave a Game," included the following: "Charges made against William Wansley—the catcher of the Mutual club—of 'selling' or 'heaving' the game, as it is technically termed." The article also quoted a letter (Oct. 25, 1865) from Mutuals shortstop Thomas Devyr: "We are going to 'heave' this game."

**heave-ho** Ejection of a player from the game; e.g., "Smith got the old heave-ho for arguing too strenuously."

**heaver** A pitcher. **1st Use.** 1914. (*Harper's Weekly*, May 2; Edward J. Nichols).

**heavy** Said of an exceptionally good baseball player; e.g., "Smith was heavy at shortstop."

**heavy ball 1.** A ball that feels weighty or hard to the catcher because of the way it was thrown. An odd or eccentric spin on the ball is often the cause. It brings an extra sting to the hands of the catcher. **2.** A ball that, when hit by the batter, causes the batter's hands to sting, as if he had hit a rock. **3.** A sinking pitch that drops sharply as it nears the plate, causing the batter to hit ground balls. In 1997, Scott Erickson was credited as having the "heaviest ball" in the American League. Syn. *heavy pitch.* **4.** A ball saturated with water.

**heavy hitter** A hitter who hits the ball hard; a hitter who hits home runs and extra-base hits. **1st Use.** 1870. (*Cleveland Leader*, July 30; Peter Morris). **Extended Use.** An individual to be reckoned with; someone important. "Stephen King's apparent desire to be a literary heavy hitter weighs down his already elephantine new novel" (*Newsweek*, Sept. 1, 1986).

**heavy pitch** Syn. of *heavy ball*, 3.

**he can throw a lamb chop past a wolf** A phrase created by Arthur "Bugs" Baer to describe the speed of Walter Johnson's fastball (*San Francisco Examiner*, Mar. 27, 1956; Peter Tamony).

**he can't spit** To show fear. "[S]cout's comment on a pitcher who is inclined to go into a panic in a tight situation. It derives from the fact that fear or excitement usually stops the flow of saliva." (Herbert Simons, *Baseball Magazine*, Jan. 1943).

**Hefty bag** Syn. of *trash bag*.

**heifer step** A unit of measurement used by broadcaster Dizzy Dean to describe the distance a runner was short of a base. The term lacked a certain precision, however, because he defined it as 2½ feet in "Dizzy Daisies" and "about 36 inches" in *Dizzy's Definitions*.

**helicopter 1.** A high, breaking pitch. **1st Use.** 1987. "Look out for that helicopter" (*St. Petersburg Times*, Mar. 5). **2.** The bat as it turns like the rotor blades of a helicopter when accidentally thrown by a batter upon swinging and missing.

**"hello, Coz"** An occasional (and provocative) greeting from a batter to his favorite pitcher or *coz*.

**helmet** See *batting helmet*.

**help out** For a batter to try to obstruct or hinder the throw of the catcher who is trying to stop an advancing runner. **1st Use.** 1911. (*American Magazine,* May; Edward J. Nichols).

**hemp** A hard-hit line drive. "[Larry] Hisle was laying out some hemp" (*Baseball Digest,* June 1979). The term is a play off other terms with the same meaning: *clothesline* and *frozen rope.*

**hen fruit** Syn. of *goose egg.* **1st Use.** 1891. (*Chicago Herald,* June 24; Edward J. Nichols).

**hen house hoist** A foul ball.

**hen on** *arch.* Something important in preparation. "From what [Buck] Ewing says there is no longer any doubt that there is a very large National League hen on" (*The World* [New York], July 1, 1890; Gerald Cohen). **Etymology.** From the image of a hen sitting on her eggs, which will soon hatch.

**"here comes Charley"** *arch.* A greeting for a limping player presumed to be suffering from a *charley horse.*

**herky jerky** Said of the motion of a pitcher with an esp. awkward delivery.

**hesitation** [softball term] A false or deceptive move or bluff legally allowed in 16-inch slow pitch softball to throw off the timing of the batter. Each real pitch of the ball can be accompanied by two hesitations.

**hesitation pitch** A pitch that is delivered with a pause, or hitch, between the windup and the throw. Such an abnormality can cause the batter problems in timing his swing. The pitch was developed by Satchel Paige before he came to the major leagues from the Negro leagues in 1948.

**H glove** A glove that allows the fielder to look through the webbing as he shields his eyes when trying to catch a fly ball.

**hiccup** A small difficulty or minor setback; e.g., a relief pitcher who earns a save after giving up one or more runs is sometimes accused of a "momentary hiccup."

**hickory** *arch.* A baseball bat, despite the fact that most bats are made of ash. **1st Use.** 1892. (*Chicago Herald,* May 31; Edward J. Nichols).

**hidden-ball trick 1.** A time-honored legal ruse in which a baseman conceals the ball and hopes that the baserunner believes it has been returned to the pitcher. When the runner steps off the base, he is summarily tagged out with the hidden ball. One of the oddest versions of the hidden-ball trick came in 1958 when Chicago White Sox second baseman Nellie Fox asked Billy Gardner of the Baltimore Orioles to step off the bag for a moment while he cleaned it off. Gardner obliged and got tagged out by Fox. Those who think that this is part of the game's storied past should be reminded that Cleveland Indians third baseman Matt Williams pulled the trick on a rookie on Sept. 19, 1997. **1st Use.** 1908. (*Spalding's Official Base Ball Guide;* Edward J. Nichols). **2.** An illegal play in which a hidden second ball is brought into play. If the trick is still occasionally performed, it is rarely detected. However, cases come to light from time to time. Here, for example, is the beginning of an Associated Press story (June 26, 1964) of a Class A New York–Pennsylvania League at Binghamton, N.Y.:

"As a high fly hit by Dan Napoleon soared toward the fence last night, evidently bound for home

**Hesitation pitch.** *Leroy "Satchel" Page in the uniform of the Kansas City Monarchs.*

run territory, it was suddenly snared from the air in a spectacular catch—or so it appeared. But later, [Binghamton outfielder] John May . . . admitted he didn't catch the ball after all. He said he went through the gestures, but actually substituted a ball from his pocket for the one that was hit out of the park." The story goes on to say that Napoleon was credited with a home run and the Binghamton team lost the game. **3.** A pitcher's ability to keep the ball hidden from the batter's view until it is delivered. Because the pitcher's grip on the ball determines the type of delivery, a pitcher will try to hide the ball until the last moment. "'Hidden Ball Trick' Gave Cardwell $2,000 'Bonus'" (United Press International dispatch, May 17, 1960; Peter Tamony) on how Chicago Cubs pitcher Don Cardwell credited his no-hitter to his ability to hide the ball. **Etymology.** There is a hidden-ball trick in football, which dates back to the 19th century and was first employed by Vanderbilt in a game with Auburn in 1895. (Peter Tamony) **Extended Use.** Variations of the term are used for deceptive moves in other areas, esp. politics. In a comment on the House of Representatives' "quick fixes" for problems, Thomas L. Stokes wrote: "Those are 'hidden ball' plays—now you see it, now you don't" (*San Francisco News,* Aug. 9, 1948; Peter Tamony).

**hide 1.** *obs.* See *horsehide.* **2.** See *cowhide.*

**high** Above the strike zone.

**high and inside** Said of a pitch that is high and close to the batter and that may or may not be in the strike zone. Syn. *high and tight; up and in.* **Extended Use.** Describing something that is difficult to handle; thorny. "Mayor Elmer Robinson wound up and pitched a fast one high and inside today to Supervisor Edward T. Mancuso" (*San Francisco Call-Bulletin,* Sept. 8, 1953; Peter Tamony).

**high and outside** Said of a pitch that is high and far from the batter and that may or may not be in the strike zone.

**high and tight** Syn. of *high and inside.*

**high ball** Syn. of *high pitch.*

**high-ball hitter** A hitter with a reputation for swinging at balls that come in above his belt. Compare *low-ball hitter.*

**high cheese** A fastball delivered high in the strike zone. A Dwight Gooden pitch was described as "high cheese for strike two" (WOR-TV, Apr. 8, 1986). Syn. *alto queso.*

**high chopper** A batted ball that bounces high. The cliché is that infielders wait "an eternity" for high choppers to come down. See also *chopper,* 1.

**high-drop mound** A pitcher's mound that appears to be higher than normal. Compare *low-drop mound.*

**high five** Celebratory hand-slapping that takes place with one's arms extended high over one's head. It began to show up in baseball in 1980 as a way of welcoming a player at the plate after hitting a home run. It is one of several slaps, clasps, and other congratulatory gestures that have been popular. Compare *bone,* 3. **Etymology.** The origin of the gesture and the term were claimed by Derek Smith of the Univ. of Louisville basketball team, which won the NCAA championship for the 1979–80 season. Smith was quoted in *The Sporting News, New York Times,* and elsewhere to the effect that he and two fellow Georgians (Wiley Brown and Daryl Cleveland) on the Louisville squad decided to come up with something "a little odd." The high five was created during preseason practice and introduced to the nation in 1979 as the team made numerous TV appearances.

**high-flier** *arch.* Syn. of *high fly.* **1st Use.** 1867. "Smith sent a high-flier toward the right field, but King took it in nicely" (Chadwick Scrapbooks, Oct.; David Shulman).

**high fly** A batted ball that is hit high in the air. Syn. *high-flier.* **1st Use.** 1881. "Another part of a shortfielder's work is his attending to the class of high fly-balls hit over the heads of the third or second baseman" (Chadwick Scrapbooks; David Shulman).

**high, hard one** A powerful fastball that comes in high in the strike zone. The term is the title of a 1967 book by former pitcher Kirby Higbe and Martin Quigley. **1st Use.** 1928. (*New York Times,* Oct. 7; Edward J. Nichols).

**high-low** A warm-up drill for fielders in which the ball is deliberately thrown high and low for added difficulty. See also *pepper*, 2. **1st Use.** 1910. (*American Magazine*, Apr.; Edward J. Nichols).

**high mass** *arch.* A Sunday doubleheader.

**high pitch** A pitch that is above the strike zone. Unless swung at by the batter, a high pitch should be called a ball by the plate umpire. Syn. *high ball*.

**highpockets** A name for a skinny player with long legs; e.g., 1920s New York Giants first baseman George "Highpockets" Kelly, who was 6′4″ and weighed only 190 lb.

**high pop** A pop fly that rises high in the air.

**high school** *adj.* Said of an amateur or bush-league player.

**high school hop** A batted ball that takes a big bounce that is easy to field.

**high school rule** A rule adopted by Major League Baseball in the early 1950s prohibiting a team from even discussing a professional career with a promising player who still had high school eligibility remaining. The rule came about because teams had signed and sent high school players to the minor leagues before they graduated and thus completed their eligibility.

**high sky** A cloudless, bright blue sky under which it is difficult to judge fly balls.

**high strike** A pitch thrown high in the strike zone that umpires sometimes call a ball.

**hightail it** To move quickly. **1st Use.** 1939. "On throws from right or center field, with no play at the plate suggested, the pitcher should hightail it over behind the third baseman" (Gordon S. "Mickey" Cochrane, *Baseball: The Fan's Game*; David Shulman).

**hill** The pitcher's mound. "I was interested to see you out there on the hill in the ninth" (Dick Friendlich, *Relief Pitcher*, 1964; Charles D. Poe). Syn. *hillock; hilltop*. **1st Use.** 1908. (*New York Evening Journal*, Mar. 11; Edward J. Nichols).

**hillock** Syn. of *hill*.

**hill staff** The pitching staff of a team.

**hilltop** Syn. of *hill*. **1st Use.** 1920. "They continued to play well, but not well enough to beat a team like the Hawks—not with Powder Hurley on the hilltop" (Burt L. Standish, *The Man on First;* David Shulman).

**hind snatcher** *arch.* The catcher.

**Hindu** Doing a play over again; a "do-over."

**hipper-dipper** *arch.* A curveball with a sharp break in its trajectory.

**hippodroming** *arch.* The practice of promoting baseball with stunts, such as using prizefighters John L. Sullivan and Jim Jeffries as umpires. "When he got to the big leagues . . . [Ed] Barrow eschewed all such hippodroming for he felt baseball by itself was all the entertainment a man needed" (Robert Smith, *Baseball's Hall of Fame*, 1965; Charles D. Poe). **Etymology.** From the name of ancient structures and arenas used for equestrian shows and other spectacles, including chariot races held in ancient Greek and Rome. More to the point was the Hippodrome in New York City, an immense showcase for vaudeville acts and spectaculars.

**historic baseball** Syn. of *vintage base ball*.

**his umps** *arch.* An umpire's title, a play on "his honor" or "his highness." **1st Use.** 1908. (*Baseball Magazine*, July; Edward J. Nichols).

**hit 1.** *n.* A batted ball that moves in fair territory and allows the batter to reach a base safely before the ball and without the help of an error and without the ball being caught on the fly. Although most are obvious and automatic, the official scorer may have to decide whether a given batted ball is to be credited as a hit or an error. The ability to get 200 hits in a season is regarded as an exceptional feat. Pete Rose had 10 such seasons, a record. See also *base hit*, 2. Abbrev. *H*, 1. **1st Use.** 1862. (*New York Sunday Mercury*, July 13; Edward J. Nichols). **2.** *n.* Any batted ball. **3.** *v.* To bat a ball; e.g., "Smith hit a ground ball to third." **1st Use.** 1866. (*New York Sunday Mercury*, Sept. 16; Edward J. Nichols). **4.** *v.* To bat a ball and get on base safely; e.g., "Jones hit a double." **5.** *v.* To take a turn at the plate. **6.** *v.*

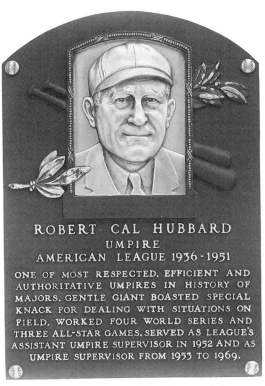

ROBERT CAL HUBBARD
UMPIRE
AMERICAN LEAGUE 1936-1951
ONE OF MOST RESPECTED, EFFICIENT AND
AUTHORITATIVE UMPIRES IN HISTORY OF
MAJORS. GENTLE GIANT BOASTED SPECIAL
KNACK FOR DEALING WITH SITUATIONS ON
FIELD. WORKED FOUR WORLD SERIES AND
THREE ALL-STAR GAMES. SERVED AS LEAGUE'S
ASSISTANT UMPIRE SUPERVISOR IN 1952 AND AS
UMPIRE SUPERVISOR FROM 1953 TO 1969.

**His umps.** *One of the men in blue who earned the honorific.*

For a pitcher to strike a batter with a pitched ball; e.g., "Brown walked four batters and hit two."

**hit air** To swing and miss. **1st Use.** 1908. (*Baseball Magazine*, July; Edward J. Nichols).

**hit an air pocket** To hit a fly ball that caused the fielder to drop it.

**hit and run 1.** *n.* Syn. of *hit-and-run play.* Sometimes spelled "hit-and-run." **2.** *v.* To attempt or execute the hit-and-run play. **Extended Use. 1.** The term "hit and run" began showing up as a description for automobile accidents in which injury is done and the driver of the car leaves the scene. Edward J. Nichols gives several examples, including this *New York Herald Tribune* headline (Dec. 6, 1936): "Mother Jailed in Hit-and-Run Injury of Boys." Peter Tamony found examples dating as far back as 1929. **2.** Generally, the term "hit and run" refers to anything that strikes quickly. A letter to "Dear Abby" opens: "There is a cheap little flirt

who is a freshman at school and she is the hit and run type. She likes to go after a boy who is going with another girl just to see if she can get him. After she breaks them up, she drops the boy and finds somebody else to break up." (*San Francisco Chronicle,* Oct. 18, 1968; Peter Tamony). *Time* magazine (Nov. 20, 1950) describes certain strike techniques used against American Telephone and Telegraph as "'hit and run' picketing": to create maximum effect, the pickets would show at one locale, where fellow workers would refuse to cross picket lines, and then abruptly move to another site.

**hit-and-run game** Use of the *hit-and-run play* as part of one's offense. The *Detroit Tribune* (Mar. 16, 1905) contains an interesting insight into its history, quoting Philadelphia Athletics third baseman Lave Cross: "Pete Browning was the originator of the hit-and-run game. He was hard of hearing, and one day he couldn't hear the coacher after getting to first on a hit, and started for second on the first ball pitched. He ran like a wildcat and got to third on a single. Pete would not have gotten past second had he not misunderstood the signals, or if he could have heard the coacher. As it was, when he started off on his mad run he got to third safely, and would have been on the way home if he hadn't been held by the man coaching on third. Hughey [sic] Jennings heard of it, and the system was introduced in Baltimore and worked with great success."

**hit-and-run play** A prearranged offensive play in which, to get a head start, a baserunner starts to run to the next base as soon as the pitcher delivers the ball to the batter, who must try to hit it to protect the runner. The play is usually undertaken with a runner on first base only: as he heads to second base, either the shortstop or the second baseman moves to cover the bag, giving the batter a gap in the infield defense through which to hit the ball. If the batter gets a hit, the baserunner usually is able to advance to third base. If the ball is hit to an infielder, the baserunner's head start reduces the defense's chance of turning a double play. However, if the batter swings and misses, the runner may be thrown out, and if the ball is hit for a pop fly or line drive, the runner is likely to become part of a double play. Broadcaster Ralph Kiner and others have observed that "hit-and-run play" should

*Hit-and-run play. The two men standing in this picture—Willie Keeler (l.) and John McGraw (r.)—are given credit for inventing the hit-and-run play. Along with Joe Kelley (sitting, l.) and Hughie Jennings (r.), these four Baltimore Orioles were known as baseball's "Big Four" in the mid-1890s.*

really be "run-and-hit play" because the runner runs before the ball is hit. Compare *run-and-hit play*. See also *steal and slam*. Syn. *hit and run*, 1. **1st Use.** 1902. (*Sporting Life*, Oct. 4; Edward J. Nichols). **Etymology.** The hit-and-run play was, by all accounts, created by the Baltimore Orioles of the mid-1890s, specif. John McGraw and Willie Keeler. According to Frank Graham (*McGraw of the Giants*, 1944): "They trained in New Orleans in that spring of 1894. With the enthusiastic encouragement of [Ned] Hanlon, McGraw began to devise plays calculated to upset the enemy. He and Keeler originated the hit-and-run play. They all polished their bunting game. They invented so many tricks, that, in order to curb them, the owners of the other clubs had to draft new rules or change some of the old ones."

**hit around** For a team to rough up ("push around") a pitcher.

**hit a ton** 1. To be on a hitting streak. 2. To hit a baseball with great force.

**hit away** To take a full swing at the pitch. The term is normally used to describe a situation where one might assume that the batter would not take a full cut at the ball; e.g., when the count on the batter is 3-0 or when a bunt seems appropriate. See also *swing away*.

**hit back to the box** To hit the ball back to the pitcher.

**hit batsman** Syn. of *hit batter*.

**hit batter** A batter hit by a pitched ball. If the batter makes a reasonable effort to get out of the way of the pitch and does not swing at the ball, he is awarded first base. Abbrev. *HB*. Syn. *hit batsman*. **Etymology.** The rule first came into play in 1884 in response to a minor-league pitcher named Will White who made a practice of hitting batters to keep them away from the plate.

**hit-batter pitch** A pitch intended to hit a batter's body but not to hit him in the head. Explaining his hit-batter pitch in the *New York Times* (July 13, 1986), Bob Gibson commented: "Note that I didn't say 'beanball' pitch. Nobody in his right mind throws a rock 90-plus miles an hour at a guy's head."

**hit behind the runner** To hit the ball down the first base side of the field to help a baserunner advance to the next base. This is a common element in successful hit-and-run plays in which the ball is hit into right field. One of the earliest and strongest advocates of hitting behind the runner was John McGraw, who once said: "You see, the fact that a baseball diamond is so laid out that the runners advance by turning to the left and away from right field puts a premium on hits in that direction when the bases are occupied." In the 1980s, Dwight Evans of the Boston Red Sox excelled at hitting behind the runner. **Usage Note.** It would be difficult to underemphasize the degree to which this phrase—and the advice behind it—has become an element of the game. Arthur Mann once wrote down the conventional wisdom on this matter: "But the biggest problem found among young players is presented by the chronic left-field hitter. No matter how good a young batter may be, he must be taught to 'hit behind the runner,' or into right field when a man is on base, for this placement facilitates the runner's trip around the base paths." (*American Mercury*, Mar. 1933; Peter Tamony).

**hit by pitch 1.** *v.* To be struck by a pitched ball while in the batter's box. Unless the batter leans in or is clearly at fault in not getting out of the way, the batter is awarded first base. If the umpire deems that a pitcher has intentionally hit a batter, the pitcher will be ejected from the game. Abbrev. *HBP.* Syn. *hit by pitcher.* **1st Use.** 1905. (*Sporting Life*, Sept. 2; Edward J. Nichols). **2.** *n.* Awarding first base to a batter who has been hit by a pitch.

**hit by pitcher** Syn. of *hit by pitch,* 1. Abbrev. *HBP; HP.*

**hitch 1.** A hesitation, extra motion, or other abnormality in a batter's swing that usually affects his timing and prevents a "smooth swing." Two common hitches occur when the batter drops his hands just before the pitch is delivered and when he draws the bat backward just before starting his swing. Depending on the context in which it appears, the term can be used to refer to a flaw or a strength, but it tends to be used more often in pointing to a defect. Here it is used in a positive way: "One of the things the Orioles liked about [Jim] Traber this spring is that he has enough of a hitch in his swing to spray the ball to all parts of the field" (*Washington Post*, July 23, 1986). Babe Ruth, Walker Cooper, Jimmie Foxx, Rudy York, and Willie Mays were noted for the hitch in their swings. And as Joe Garagiola put it during a telecast: "Nobody complained about Hank Aaron's hitch." **2.** A pause in a pitcher's windup intended to throw off the batter's timing; the key element in a hesitation pitch. **Extended Use.** The term may be nautical in origin, coming from a hitch in a rope, a jam that prevents it from running smoothly through a block.

**hitchy-koo** *arch.* Fidgeting at the plate; e.g., "Some rookies and nervous batters are hitchy-koo when first playing in the majors."

**"hit 'em where they ain't"** The rallying cry for

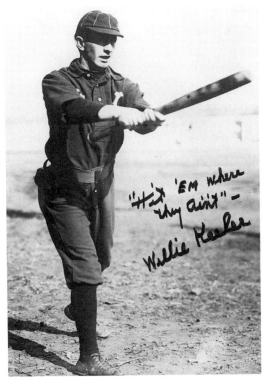

**"Hit 'em where they ain't."** *Lest there be any question as to Keeler being aware of his famous line, note how he autographed this photograph.*

batters through the decades since 1897 when William "Wee Willie" Keeler hit .432. He was asked by a reporter how a man of his size (5′4½″, 140 lb.) could put together such an average. "Simple. I keep my eyes clear and I hit 'em where they ain't." Although the line was undisputedly Keeler's, the idea behind it was hardly new. "For the Mutuals, Hunt sent a very safe one to center, where 'nobody was,' and Bearman sent him home" (*New York Clipper*, Sept. 7, 1867; Peter Tamony). The phrase is one of baseball's hoariest axioms and shows up in various contexts. In the 1920s, Arthur "Bugs" Baer wrote: "Willie Keeler hits them where they ain't. Babe Ruth hits 'em where they're never going to be." J. G. Taylor Spink (*Judge Landis and Twenty-Five Years of Baseball*, 1947) even tried to turn the phrase into a nickname for Keeler: "Hit 'em Where They Ain't Willie Keeler."

**hit famine** A hitting slump for a team or individual.

**hitfest** A game in which many hits are made and hence many runs are scored.

**hit for average** To get a hit that will improve or maintain a player's batting average; specif., to concentrate on hitting safely rather than hitting the long ball.

**hit for distance** To hit the long ball.

**hit for the circuit 1.** To hit a home run. **2.** Uncommon syn. of *hit for the cycle,* 2.

**hit for the cycle 1.** To hit a single, double, triple, and home run (not necessarily in that order) within the course of a single game. It is a rarity that many top hitters (such as Willie Keeler, Ty Cobb, Babe Ruth, and Willie Mays) never accomplished in a career. Only two players have done it three times: Babe Herman and Bob Meusel. Compare *throw for the cycle.* See also *hat trick,* 1. **Usage Note.** The emphasis on this feat has increased in recent years and, as Brooks Robinson has noted, many old-timers may never have heard of it during their playing years. Dave Kingman drove this home when he hit for the cycle as a rookie in 1972: "When Chris Speier mentioned it to me in the dugout, I didn't know what it meant. I had never done it, and I had never even heard of it." (*San Francisco Examiner,* Apr. 17, 1972; Peter Tamony). Charles D. Poe notes an odd variation of the term in Ron Luciano's *The Umpire Strikes Back* (1982). After asserting that Lou Piniella was the worst baserunner of all time, Luciano noted that Piniella did something unequaled in baseball history: "He ran for the cycle. In a single game he managed to get himself thrown out at every base." Odder still is the variation that appears in Robert Whiting's *Chrysanthemum and the Bat* (1977) when he discusses the effect of American Daryl Spencer on Japanese baseball. In the course of the 1967 season, Spencer takes out a man at first, decommissions a second baseman "with a vicious slide," slides into a third baseman who needs stitches, and removes a catcher from "both the play and the game." **2.** To hit at least one home run in every city in the league during a season. The first player to accomplish this feat was Babe Ruth when he hit 29 home runs in 1919. Syn. *hit for the circuit,* 2.

**hit in a pinch** To pinch hit.

**hit in the slats** To be hit by a pitched ball in the upper torso. "Slats" were defined as "ribs" in the early 1900s (Robert L. Chapman, *New Dictionary of American Slang,* 1986).

**hitless 1.** Said of a team or player without a base hit during a given number of at-bats or games. **2.** Having given up no hits; e.g., "Smith pitched five hitless innings." **3.** Said of a team with a poor batting average; specif., the *Hitless Wonders.*

**Hitless Wonders** The nickname given to the early 20th-century Chicago White Sox for their ability to win games with light hitting. The name got special play in 1906 when the team won the American League pennant with a team batting average of .230, the lowest in the league. The White Sox won the World Series with an average of only .198. The key was the team's pitching staff, which, among other accomplishments, recorded 32 shutouts during the season. Gustav W. Axelson (*"Commy": The Life of Charles A. Comiskey,* 1919) wrote: "In hitting the [White Sox] had, year after year, gradually dropped from .275 [actually .276] in 1901 to .237 in 1905. They had already acquired the title of 'hitless wonders,' but they were rapidly becoming more hitless without being wonders." **1st Use.** 1905. (*Sporting Life,* Oct. 7; Edward J. Nichols).

**hit metal** To hit a ball that is misplayed by a fielder who presumably is playing with an iron glove.

**hit off the fists** To hit an inside pitch off the handle of the bat near the fists. The hands will sting and the ball, most likely, will be a bloop hit.

**hit one's weight** To hit poorly; to have a low batting average. The phrase is usually used negatively, as in "he's not even hitting his weight." The phrase links a player's three-digit weight with a three-digit batting average and, because most players weigh less than 225 lb., a player not hitting his weight would not have a very good average.

CHICAGO
WHITE SOX

1. ALTROCK
2. DAVIS
3. DOUGHERTY
4. DONAHUE
5. DUNDON
6. JONES
7. ISBELL
8. HAHN
9. McFARLAND

WORLDS
CHAMPIONS
═1906═

10. O'NEIL
11. OWEN
12. PATTERSON
13. ROHE
14. SULLIVAN
15. TANNEHILL
16. TOWNE
17. WALSH
18. WHITE

*Hitless Wonders. The 1906 Chicago White Sox hit only seven home runs and batted a mere .230 as a team.*

**hit on the screws** To hit a pitch solidly and squarely. The term is used by broadcaster Bob Uecker.

**hit over one's head** To hit better than expected; to hit greater than one's average for an earlier period, such as the previous season.

**hit safely** To hit the ball so that it cannot be fielded for an out.

**hit sign** A sign given to the batter by the manager or a coach to swing at the next pitch or series of pitches. See also *green light,* 1.

**"Hit Sign, Win Suit"** The words on a sign installed on the right-center field wall in Ebbets Field in 1931 by clothier, politician, and Brooklyn Dodgers fan Abe Stark. The sign advertised Stark's

family clothing store and was a pledge that any player hitting the sign on the fly would be given a free suit from the store. The sign stayed in place until 1958 when the Dodgers moved to Los Angeles. The first two balls to hit the sign were hit by Mel Ott of the rival New York Giants.

**hitsman** *arch.* Syn. of *hitter,* 1.

**hitsmith** A term used in the early 1900s for a good hitter. **1st Use.** 1907. (*New York Evening Journal,* Apr. 5; Edward J. Nichols).

**hits, runs, and errors** The scoreboard line that records a team's offensive prowess and defensive shortcomings. **Extended Use.** A method of tallying one's success in almost any endeavor, including war. "I have had to lay off tellin' about the battle till my next, Joe, because they ain't added up the hits, runs, and errors yet" (H. C. Witwer, *A Smile a Minute,* 1919; David Shulman).

**hit straightaway** To hit the pitch up the middle or to the opposite field rather than pulling it.

**hittable** 1. Said of a pitcher who is relatively easy to hit against. 2. Said of a pitch that is relatively easy to hit.

**hitter** 1. A *batter;* esp., one who hits the ball. Syn. *hitsman.* 1st Use. 1883. (*Sporting Life,* Apr. 15; Edward J. Nichols). 2. A batter who gets many hits; e.g., "Smith is quite the hitter."

**-hitter** A suffix to describe a pitching performance or game in terms of the number of hits allowed; e.g., "no-hitter," "one-hitter," "two-hitter," and "12-hitter."

**hitterish** Said of a player or team in the midst of a hitting streak. The term was used by broadcaster Dizzy Dean.

**hitter's park** A ballpark with relatively small dimensions that appeals to hitters; e.g., Wrigley Field with the wind blowing out, Ebbets Field, Crosley Field, Fenway Park, and Oriole Park at Camden Yards.

**hit the black** To throw a pitch that crosses the inside or outside edges of the plate for a strike.

**"hit the bull"** A frequent exhortation in the days when Bull Durham signs were on outfield fences. The phrase was associated with a scheme, hatched by the makers of Bull Durham tobacco prior to World War I, that awarded a player $50 for hitting their sign. The signs were cut out in the shape of a bull and placed on the outfield fences of as many as 150 major-league and minor-league parks. See also *bullpen.* 1st Use. 1909. (*Baseball Magazine,* June; Edward J. Nichols).

**hit the corners** To throw pitches that pass just inside or outside the edges of the strike zone.

**hit the dirt** 1. For a batter to drop to the ground to avoid getting hit by a pitched ball. 2. For a baserunner to begin his slide into a base. 1st Use. 1908. (*New York Evening Journal,* Apr. 18; Edward J. Nichols). 3. For a baserunner to dive back to-

ward the base he occupied to avoid being picked off.

**hit the Dixie Highway** To have been released or fired from the team.

**hitting coach** An offensive team coach responsible for the welfare and success of the team's hitters. Syn. *batting coach.*

**hitting shoes** The figurative shoes of the hitters on a team that is batting around.

**hitting slump** A period of poor performance by a hitter, such as two hits in 27 at-bats. See also *batting slump.*

**hitting streak** 1. See *consecutive hitting streak.* 2. See *consecutive-game hitting streak.*

**hitting zone** The most comfortable position for a hitter in making his swing; e.g., "Today's hitters wait for the pitch in their hitting zone."

**"hiya, Kid"** Babe Ruth's traditional greeting, used often because of his legendary inability to recall names. Those who heard Ruth attested to the fact that he did not say "kid," but "keed." There

**"Hiya, Kid."** *Babe Ruth poses with the local sheriff and kids in the bleachers at Brooks Field, Scranton, Pennsylvania, in 1926. The picture was taken after the World Series when the Babe was on a barnstorming tour.*

were a few variations: older men were "Doc" and teammates were "Stud."

**"hoe her down"** *arch.* An encouragement yelled to a baserunner to run fast. **Etymology.** A clear derivation from "hoedown." "[Buck] Ewing stood on the coaching lines with his hat in his hand and his hair standing straight on end. 'Go it, John,' he yelled. 'Hoe her down.' John was 'hoeing her down' for all he was worth." (*The World* [New York], Aug. 13, 1889; Gerald Cohen).

**HOF** Abbrev. for *Hall of Fame,* 2.

**Hogan's brickyard** *arch.* A rough or stony baseball field; a vacant lot used as a baseball field. The term may have derived from an early (ca. 1905) comic strip called "Hogan's Alley." See also *ash heap; contractor's back yard.*

**hog tie** To keep the opposition from scoring.

**hold** 1. *v.* See *hold a runner.* 2. *v.* For a runner to remain at a base when the ball is pitched or hit. 3. *v.* To prevent a hitter from taking an extra base; e.g., "The outfielder cut the ball off and held the hitter to a single." 4. *n.* A *save opportunity* credited to a relief pitcher who preserves the lead and passes it on to another pitcher. The relief pitcher must not give up any runs (earned or unearned), pitch a minimum of one inning, and not receive a win, loss, or save. The term and statistic were created by *USA Today.* Compare *squander,* 2. See also *Miller-Brown System; attaboy.* Abbrev. *H,* 2.

**hold a runner** 1. To keep a runner on base from taking a large lead. Infielders do their part by staying close to the base awaiting a possible pickoff throw from the pitcher. The pitcher keeps his eye on the runner and occasionally throws to the base in question. Syn. *hold on; hold up a runner,* 2. 2. *v.* To prevent a baserunner, who is not forced to run, from advancing to the next base during a play. This is usually accomplished by the fielder with the ball either faking a throw toward the runner being held or just looking in his direction.

**holder** A relief pitcher credited with a hold. The term was proposed by Buster Olney of the *Baltimore Sun.*

**hold on** Syn. of *hold a runner,* 1; e.g., "The first baseman was holding the runner on by standing at the bag waiting for a possible pickoff throw from the pitcher."

**hold out** *v.* To decline to accept and sign a tendered player's contract, usually for more money or better terms.

**holdout** *n.* 1. An act or instance of holding out. *Washington Post* headline (Apr. 5, 1987): "[Roger] Clemens Ends 29-Day Holdout." 2. A player who has not come to terms with his team and misses part or all of spring training and, in a few cases, some of the regular season. In an extreme case, Edd Roush of the New York Giants sat out the entire 1930 season because his team wanted him to take a pay cut after coming off a .324 season. Traditionally, a player becomes a holdout when he returns his unsigned contract to the team's front office. Babe Ruth was a holdout on several occasions. **Etymology/1st Use.** 1888. "First used by the *New York Press* to describe a player who delayed in accepting salary terms (Dan Schlossberg, *The Baseball Catalog,* 1989). The practice may have predated the term. Gerald Secor Couzens (*A Baseball Album,* 1980) suggests that the first holdout was Cincinnati Red Stockings second baseman Charles Sweeney: "In the 1869 season he was paid $800 which he thought was insufficient. The following year he held out for $1,000 and didn't report until he was paid that sum."

**hold up a runner** 1. For a third base coach to signal (usually by holding his arms up) a baserunner not to advance to the next base. 2. Syn. of *hold a runner,* 1. **1st Use.** 1912. (*American Magazine,* June; Edward J. Nichols).

**hole** 1. The space between any two infielders; commonly, the area between the third baseman and the shortstop, near the outfield grass. "But with two men out and runners on second and third, he'd go into the hole, backhand the ball, and throw the runner out by a step and a half" (Bill Lee, *The Wrong Stuff,* 1984). Compare *gap,* which is the space between outfielders; tradition dictates this distinction, although "hole" is occasionally applied to the space between outfielders. Syn. *third base hole.* 2. A position in the batting order; e.g., "[Roberto] Alomar Returns to 2-hole" (*Baltimore Sun* headline, June 26, 1996). **3.** The position of the batter in the dugout following the hitter in the on-deck circle; the position of the third batter in the batting order at any given point in a game. See also *at bat, on deck, in the hold.* **1st Use.** 1937. (Red Barber, NBC World Series broadcast, Oct. 10; Edward J. Nichols). **Etymology.** From the nautical "hold," which, according to Joanna Carver Colcord (*Sea Language Comes Ashore,* 1945), was originally "hole" and became "hold" through what she terms "a mistaken etymology." Baseball turned it back to "hole," although the common nautical pronunciation of "hold" is "hole." **4.** Syn. of *dugout.* **5.** A difficult position during a game, such as for a pitcher with runners on base and heavy hitters coming to bat, or for a pitcher whose team is behind by two or more runs, or for a batter or pitcher behind in the count; a distinct disadvantage during a game, such as trailing by five runs in the sixth inning. **1st Use.** 1922. "Avoid 'getting in the hole' to the batter" (John E. Wray, *How to Pitch;* David Shulman). **6.** A losing position; e.g., "The Yankees dropped the next two games and went in the hole by seven games." **7.** See *hole in his swing.*

**hole in his swing** A batter's weakness. "They say that every great slugger has a hole in his swing, a vulnerable place in the arc of presumed contact" (Jane Leavy, *Squeeze Play,* 1990).

**hole in the bat** A humorous excuse for a missed swing, as if the ball went right through the bat. **1st Use.** 1908. (*New York Evening Journal,* May 20; Edward J. Nichols).

**hole in the glove** A humorous excuse for a ball that is totally missed by a fielder, as if it went right through a hole in the glove. **1st Use.** 1903. (*Hackensack* [N.J.] *Weekly,* scrapbook clippings; Edward J. Nichols).

**holiday** *arch.* A doubleheader.

**holler guy** A coach or player known for his constant chatter and shouts of encouragement. The cliché is that every good team needs a holler guy.

**hollow bat** A *doctored bat;* one that has been made lighter by drilling a hole in the thick end,

which is then filled with a light material such as cork or sawdust and capped to avoid detection.

**Hollywood hop** A batted ball that takes an easy bounce into a fielder's glove, which presumably makes him look good enough for the movies.

**Hollywood player** Syn. of *grandstand player.*

**"holy cow!"** Signature phrase of broadcasters Harry Caray and Phil Rizzuto. Caray developed the phrase during a semipro basketball tournament in Battle Creek, Mich. (Harry Caray, *Holy Cow!,* 1989). When Lisa Winston (*USA Today,* Dec. 25, 1994) looked into the origin of the phrase, she concluded that it was heard on the radio as early as the 1930s when Jack Holiday of WTPS in New Orleans used it frequently during broadcasts of games of the New Orleans Pelicans of the Southern Association. The phrase achieved a certain notoriety when Rizzuto repeated it several times on Oct. 2, 1978, after New York Yankees shortstop Bucky Dent hit the game-winning home run in the division playoff against the Boston Red Sox. During Phil Rizzuto Day at Yankee Stadium, the venerable Yankee shortstop and announcer was presented with a live cow furnished with a gleaming halo!

**home 1.** *n.* Short for *home plate.* **1st Use.** 1854. (Knickerbocker Rules). **2.** *adv.* To, at, or toward home plate; e.g. "A hit may bring Smith home." **3.** Short for *home field.* **4.** *n.* Short for *home team.* **5.** *adj.* Said of a game played on one's home field.

**home bagger** A home run.

**home base** Syn. of *home plate.* The term is seldom used today.

**home-brew field** A rough, pebble-strewn playing surface; one on which a ground ball takes many unexpected hops. This is a play on "hops" as an ingredient of beer. **1st Use.** 1937. (*The Sporting News Record Book;* Edward J. Nichols).

**home field** The ballpark where the home team plays. Syn. *home, 3; home grounds; home orchard; home pasture.*

**home-field advantage** The combination of factors that gives the home team presumed extra help, ranging from knowledge of the grounds to the enthusiasm of the fans. See also *dome-field advantage*. Syn. *home-field edge*.

**home-field edge** Syn. of *home-field advantage*. San Francisco Giants manager Roger Craig wondered: "I don't know why we can't turn playing in Candlestick into the biggest home-field edge in baseball" (*USA Today*, Mar. 4, 1986).

**home free** Said of a team that has a large lead and certain to win the game; e.g., "A 10-run lead in the last of the eighth assured the Brewers they would be home free." Syn. *on ice*.

**home game** A contest that a team plays at its own ballpark. Compare *away game*.

**home grounds** Syn. of *home field*. **1st Use.** 1898. (*New York Tribune*, May 26; Edward J. Nichols).

**home half** The *second half* of an inning when the home team gets its turn at bat.

**home orchard** *arch.* Syn. of *home field*.

**home pasture** *arch.* Syn. of *home field*.

**home plate** The base from which one bats and which the baserunner must touch to score a run; the focal point of the game. It is a five-sided slab of white rubber, 17 inches wide at the end facing the pitcher and 17 inches deep, that is securely anchored and flush with the ground at the intersection of the foul lines, its rear end forming a right angle, which determines the direction of the foul lines. The width of home plate determines the

*Home plate.*

horizontal extent of the strike zone. Syn. *home, 1; home base; home turkey; turkey; dish; platter; plate, 1; pan; pay station; registry station; rubber, 2; slab, 2; hearth stone.* **1st Use.** 1867. (*New York Herald*, Sept. 26; Edward J. Nichols). **Extended Use.** In U.S. Navy jargon, "homeplate" is the nickname for a carrier.

**home plate is jumping around** The condition that describes a pitcher's location when he constantly misses the strike zone with pitches on the corners; e.g., the outside corner pitch is too far outside and the inside corner pitch is too far inside. See also *plate jumping*.

**home plate umpire** Syn. of *plate umpire*.

**homer 1.** *n.* A *home run*. **1st Use.** 1891. (*Chicago Herald*, May 5; Edward J. Nichols). **2.** *v.* To hit a home run. **3.** *n.* A broadcaster or sportswriter who shows obvious bias for the home team. "He was loud. He was obnoxious. He was the worst homer in the history of baseball broadcasting." (Ken Fuson on Harry Caray, *Baltimore Sun*, Feb. 20, 1998). **4.** *n.* An umpire whose decisions seem consistently to favor the home team. Larry R. Gerlach (*Men in Blue*, 1980) quotes umpire Ernie Stewart who said that a homer is a "gutless umpire" and proudly proclaimed: "I never was called a homer." Syn. *home umpire*. **1st Use.** 1888. (*New York Press*, June 3; Edward J. Nichols). **Extended Use.** The term is used for officials in all major sports and is just as likely to show up in football where it may have come into use earlier. For instance, Peter Tamony found this quote from a football coach (*San Francisco News*, Nov. 13, 1932): "Referee Arthur Badenock is an out and out 'homer.' He cost Stanford a game and did his best to take the UCLA game away from the Gaels."

**homer ball** Syn. of *home run ball*.

**Homerdome** A nickname for the *Hubert H. Humphrey Metrodome* because it is easy to hit home runs in it.

**homer hankie** An imprinted souvenir handkerchief-sized square of white cloth held and waved by Minnesota Twins fans in 1987 during the American League pennant drive and World Series, during which it achieved visual prominence. Homer

*A "Home Run," when needed, is almost as rare as a $5⁰⁰ bill the day after Christmas.*

**Home run.**

hankies were sold as a promotional stunt by the local newspaper, the *Star Tribune,* whose name was on each hankie, along with the words "Twins 1987" inscribed above a red baseball and "Championship Drive" inscribed below the ball.

**homer in the gloamin'** A dramatic home run hit on Sept. 28, 1938, under darkening skies at lightless Wrigley Field by Chicago Cubs player-manager Gabby Hartnett off Pittsburgh Pirates pitcher Mace Brown in the bottom of the ninth inning to win the game, 6–5, and propel the Cubs into first place ahead of the Pirates and eventually to the National League pennant.

**homer ratio** Syn. of *home run percentage.*

**home run** A four-base hit on which the batter scores. It is usually accomplished by driving the ball out of the playing area but into fair territory. The batter and his team are awarded a run when he has touched all four bases. A ball that does not leave the park but allows the batter to score with-

out the help of an error is an *inside-the-park home run.* A home run causes all the runners on base to score. The home run provides baseball with much of its excitement and drama. Home runs routinely change the course of a game and are instrumental in putting fans in the seats. The ability to hit the home run has been at the core of the star quality of many greats, including Babe Ruth, Mickey Mantle, Willie Mays, and Hank Aaron. There are many slang synonyms for the home run, including: *homer,* 1; *bomb,* 3; "circuit; clout"; *dinger; four-bagger; four-ply wallop; moon shot; rainbow drop; round-tripper; seat-boomer; tater.* Abbrev. *HR.* **1st Use.** 1861. (*Beadle's Dime Base-Ball Player;* Edward J. Nichols). **Etymology.** The term predates baseball in cricket, where it refers to a ball outside the boundaries of the game scoring multiple runs.

**Extended Use. 1.** The term is applied to big scoring plays in other sports. A spectacular touchdown in football or a three-point play in basketball may be called a "home run." It may even apply to a boxing punch: "He [Ingemar Johansson] earned it the way a real champ should by blasting home runs with a lethal right that caused many to compare it with the blockbusters Rocky Marciano used to fell challengers" (*San Francisco Examiner,* June 30, 1959). **2.** A common metaphor for an action that has been a clear success. An article that questions the ability of a major corporation to come up with a dramatically new product is headlined: "Does Kodak Have Any Home-Run Hitters?" (*Washington Post,* Sept. 11, 1986). When Dan Rather defended in court an investigative report on insurance fraud, which had appeared on *60 Minutes,* he declared the segment "a home run" (Associated Press, May 31, 1983). "[President] Clinton Tells Aides to Keep Hunting for a 'Home Run' Court Nominee" (*Washington Post* headline, May 6, 1993). **3.** A large capital gain in a stock in a short period of time, according to the *Equity Trading Glossary* produced by Goldman Sachs. **4.** Intermittent teenage slang for sexual intercourse, on a scale of physical involvement that starts at first base. A letter from a teenage girl to "Dear Abby" (published in her column on Dec. 31, 1967) concluded: "So far I've gone only to 'second and third base.' I'm afraid I can't stop myself. Is something wrong?" Abby's answer in part: "If, at age 14, you've gone to 'second and third base' you had better get out of that league or you'll be known as the 'Home-Run Queen' by the time you're 16."

**home run ball** A pitch that is hit for a home run. Syn. *homer ball; home run pitch.* **1st Use.** 1937. (*Philadelphia Record;* Sept. 28; Edward J. Nichols).

**home run cut** Syn. of *home run swing.*

**home run derby 1.** A game in which many home runs are hit by one or both teams. **2.** An exhibition in which a few sluggers compete to see how many home runs they can hit. In such contests, anything short of a home run is considered an out. **3.** A race to determine who will hit the most home runs; e.g., on the occasion when Mark McGwire and Sammy Sosa each hit his 66th home run on Sept. 25, 1998, the *Baltimore Sun* (Sept. 26, 1998) began its article: "Two games to go in the Great Home Run derby, and Mark McGwire is determined to enjoy the last ride while Sammy Sosa hopes any homers that he hits can help the Cubs make the National League playoffs.

**home run in an elevator shaft** A ball that is hit straight up and esp. high and that is usually caught on the fly near home plate.

**home run king 1.** An unofficial title for the player who has hit the most home runs in the league by the end of the season. **2.** (usually capitalized) The player with the most home runs in the history of the game; i.e., Hank Aaron.

**home run percentage** A statistic that accounts for the number of home runs hit per 100 times at bat. It is computed by dividing the number of home runs by the number of at-bats and multiplying by 100. Babe Ruth's home run percentage of 8.5 is the best in major-league history. Hank Aaron and Willie Mays both had career home run percentages of 6.1. Syn. *homer ratio.*

**home run pitch** Syn. of *home run ball.*

**home run rule** [softball term] A restriction on the number of home runs allowed in a slow pitch softball game. Excess home runs are counted as fouls or outs.

**home run swing** A very powerful swing in which the batter is obviously trying to hit a home run. It is often cautioned against by managers and batting instructors who see it as an ineffective way to get a home run and an effective way to increase strikeouts. Syn. *home run cut.*

**Home run king.** *A button commemorating Hank Aaron's record.*

**home run trot** The jog of a batter touching the bases after hitting a home run; "one of the last truly American joys" (Rick Reilly, *Sports Illustrated,* May 11, 1998). Home run trots have included Babe Ruth's little mincing steps, Mickey Mantle running head down as if in shame, Jimmy Piersall going around backward on his 100th home run, and Jeffrey Leonard's "one flap down" (left arm hanging limp while leaning toward the pitcher as he ran). See also *Cadillac trot.* Syn. *grand tour.*

**homestand** A series of two or more consecutive games played at home against one or more visiting teams. "They . . . recently finished the franchise's worst homestand in history (0-7)" (Richard Justice, *Washington Post,* May 16, 1987). Also spelled "home stand." **1st Use.** 1902. (*Sporting Life,* July 5; Edward J. Nichols).

**homestretch 1.** Approximately the last month of the regular season when teams vie for their places in the final standings. Sometimes spelled "home stretch." Syn. *stretch,* 5. **Etymology.** The term is an obvious borrowing from horse racing, where the homestretch is the straight part of the racetrack from the last turn to the finish line. **2.** The ninth inning of a given game. **1st Use.** 1881. (*New York Herald,* Aug. 10; Edward J. Nichols). **3.** The path between third base and home plate.

**home sweet home team** *arch.* A team that plays well at home but badly on the road.

**home team** The team that hosts a visiting team on its own field. By tradition (and since 1950 by the rules) the home team always bats in the bottom, or second, half of each inning, which gives it the final chance to score. If a game is played on neutral grounds, the home team is designated by mutual agreement. Syn. *home,* 4; *host team.* **1st Use.** 1880. (*Brooklyn Daily Eagle,* July 7; Edward J. Nichols).

**hometown series** A World Series played by two teams from the same metropolitan area; e.g., the 1941, 1947, 1949, 1952, 1953, 1955, and 1956 World Series between the New York Yankees and the Brooklyn Dodgers.

**home turkey** Syn. of *home plate.* Gerald Cohen speculates that the 19th-century home plate was likened in shape to a turkey plate; thus, a blend of "home plate" and "turkey."

**home umpire** *arch.* Syn. of *homer,* 4. "They [the players] at once seek to discover if he is a home umpire. Woe unto him if the players see he has a penchant for favoring the home team." (Billy Evans, *Pearson's Magazine,* Sept. 1912; Peter Tamony).

**home whites** The traditional uniform worn by a team on its home field. Compare *road grays.*

**hoodoo 1.** *n.* An unlucky object, sign, player, or anything else about which a player, coach, or manager is superstitious. "[Mike] Cuellar Authority on Whammies and Hoodoos" (*The Sporting News* headline, Aug. 5, 1972). Dizzy Dean defined the term as "what ol' Diz used to have on all them batters in the National League when I was the world champion player." See also *whammy.* **1st Use.** 1883. (Chicago *Inter-Ocean,* June 26; Edward J. Nichols). **Usage Note.** Although synonymous with *jinx,* "hoodoo" seems to have a closer association with the game of baseball, and one is much less likely to hear it applied in other areas. Under the heading "Jinxes and Hoodoos," *The SABR Bulletin* (Oct. 1986) gives a sampling that includes spilling coffee, cutting oneself while shaving, picking up the wrong bat, stepping on a baseline, seeing a dog on the diamond, having the entire team on the bench at once, and chewing gum in the outfield. **Etymology.** Although direct links are hard to find, it seems quite likely that "hoodoo" is a play on the word "voodoo." One link of sorts appears in an article on superstition (*The Sporting News,* Dec. 26, 1929) that discusses the players and their "versions of voodoo medicine." **2.** *v.* To create bad luck. "Most of them think a change in hotels would surely 'jinx' or hoodoo them" (*Literary Digest,* May 9, 1914).

**hook 1.** *n.* Any curveball, because of its hooklike trajectory. **1st Use.** 1910. (*American Magazine,* June; Edward J. Nichols). **2.** *v.* To throw a curveball; e.g., "Smith usually hooks Jones a lot." **1st Use.** 1908. (*New York Evening Journal,* Mar. 5; Edward J. Nichols). **3.** *n.* The tendency of a manager to remove a pitcher from the game. A manager may have a "quick hook" (removal of a pitcher at the first sign of trouble) or, if he does it enough, may be called "Captain Hook" (e.g., Sparky Anderson when he managed the Cincinnati Reds) or "Dr.

Hook." **Etymology.** From the theatrical image of an actor or performer who is so bad that he or she is pulled off the stage by a theater manager wielding a long pole with a hook on its end. This was reportedly a custom practiced on amateur nights during the age of vaudeville and became a staple sight gag in movie cartoons. **4.** *n.* The removal of a pitcher who is getting into trouble, usually used in the phrase "to get the hook." "In case the Mets get hot, they'll go for the hook" (broadcaster Vin Scully, Game 2 of the 1986 World Series, Oct. 19). See also *slow hook; quick hook,* 2. **5.** *n.* A batted ball that curves away to the left when hit by a right-handed batter or to the right when hit by a left-handed batter; e.g., "Smith's hook went down the left-field line." **6.** *n.* The path of a batted ball that curves away to the left when hit by a right-handed batter or to the right when hit by a left-handed batter; e.g., "That ball had a lot of hook on it." **7.** *v.* To hit a ball that veers off in one direction; e.g., "Jones hooked the ball foul into the seats." **8.** *v.* To replace or be replaced by a relief pitcher. See also *derrick.* **9.** *n.* Syn. of *jam,* 1. See also *off the hook.* **10.** *n.* See *hooks.*

**hook arm 1.** A left-handed pitcher. **2.** The pitching arm of a pitcher.

**hooks 1.** The hands of an adept fielder; e.g., "Smith has a good pair of hooks." **2.** The clumsy hands of a fielder, in allusion to the hook of Captain Hook. Clifford Jordan (letter, Aug. 5, 1989) recalls how the term was used in his younger days: "We would gleefully call out 'hooks' when an opposing player made a noticeably clumsy error. That is, rather than 'hooks' meaning he could hook into anything, 'hooks' meant he owned awkward metal prongs, not soft, capable hands."

**hook slide** A feet-first slide during which the runner tucks one leg under his body and uses the other to catch, or hook, the side or one corner of the bag as he passes it. The hook slide is used to avoid being tagged by giving the defensive player a smaller target. See also *fallaway slide.* Syn. *Chicago slide.* **1st Use.** 1906. (*The Independent;* Edward J. Nichols). **Etymology.** It is generally agreed that the hook slide was first perfected by Mike Kelly of the Chicago White Stockings, who taught it to other members of his team; thus, it became known as the "Chicago slide." However, Lee Allen (*The Hot Stove League,* 1955) noted that it was first used by William S. Gummere (later to become Chief Justice of the Supreme Court of New Jersey) while playing for Princeton in a game against the Philadelphia Athletics in the 1860s: "He slid and buried his face in his right arm, the style later adopted by Ty Cobb."

**hookworm league** *obs.* A derisive nickname for spring training played in the southeastern United States, a region with a prevalence for the hookworm parasite. **1st Use.** 1917. (*American Magazine,* July; Edward J. Nichols).

**hoopdy-scoop** A curveball.

**hootenanny throw** An overthrown ball that sails over the head of the intended fielder and out of play; e.g., "Smith leaped at first base but he couldn't reach that hootenanny throw, straight into the dugout on the fly."

**hooter** A particularly noisy fan. "Winning baseball isn't all that's missing at Comiskey Park this season. Each night, Chicago broadcaster Don Drysdale has his camera scan the stadium looking for 'The Hooter,' the rumpled old man whose howl could be heard all over Comiskey when the White Sox were hitting." (*USA Today,* May 13, 1986).

**Hoover 1.** A highly adept infielder who appears to sweep or suck up batted balls in the manner of a Hoover *vacuum cleaner.* Sometimes spelled "hoover." Pittsburgh Pirates broadcaster Bob Prince would often use the expression "we need a Hoover" when the opposition got men on the bases. Mel Durslag (*TV Guide,* May 17, 1975) reported: "The station Prince works for was unhappy. They figured this was a commercial reference Hoover wasn't paying for. Prince started observing, instead, 'We need a J. Edgar.'" **2.** A batter adept at hitting successfully with men on base; one who cleans the bases.

**hop 1.** A bounce of a thrown or batted ball. A ball that bounces erratically takes what is commonly called a *bad hop,* while a bounce that makes it easy for a fielder is called a "good hop." **1st Use.** 1908. (*New York Evening Journal,* Mar. 19; Edward J. Nichols). **2.** The apparent jumping motion of an extremely fast pitch; the slight, sudden change in elevation of a fastball. **1st Use.** 1914. (*New York Tribune,* Oct. 10; Edward J. Nichols).

**hop ball** The fictional pitch in the book by Shirley W. Smith & Valentine Davies and 1949 movie *It Happens Every Spring,* in which a chemistry professor discovers a mixture that makes baseballs repellent to wood (i.e., baseball bats). The ball hopped like "Barnum's flea."

**hopper 1.** A batted ball that bounces on the ground, often modified as a "high hopper," "lazy hopper," "two-hopper," etc. Syn. *rabbit ball,* 3. **2.** A fastball that has a hop on it. **1st Use.** 1915. "Courtney missed a hopper, though he almost fancied his bat lightly touched the whistling ball as it sped past" (Burt L. Standish, *Courtney of the Center Garden;* David Shulman).

**hopping** Said of a fastball with such velocity that it appears to jump slightly before it reaches the plate.

**Horn** An eponymous term coined by Mike Flanagan (*Sports Illustrated,* July 29, 1991) for a batter who strikes out six times in a game. This feat was first done by a nonpitcher by Sam Horn of the Baltimore Orioles in a game against the Milwaukee Brewers on July 17, 1991. See also *hat trick,* 2; *golden sombrero; Olympic rings.*

**horse 1.** A reliable, durable, or tireless player, esp. a pitcher. Baltimore Orioles pitcher Scott Erickson has been described as a "horse" because he can be depended on to pitch more than 200 innings in a season. "If [Atlee] Hammaker were a horse, they probably would have shot him. But because he is a horse, at least in the baseball slang that means a top player, the Giants stuck with him." (Sam Smith, *Chicago Tribune,* June 30, 1987). **Etymology.** Probably a clipped form of *workhorse.* **2.** See *on his horse.*

**horse-and-buggy league** A minor league in which the teams travel by bus rather than by air or, when the phrase first came into use, by rail. **1st Use.** 1937. (*New York Daily News,* Sept. 5; Edward J. Nichols).

**horse collar 1.** *n.* A score of zero. Babe Ruth (*Babe Ruth's Own Book of Baseball,* 1928) defined

the term as "a zero in the box score hit column." "The Yankees won yesterday, but Joe DiMaggio didn't get a hit. It was his first 'horse collar' in six games." (*San Francisco News,* June 6, 1940). See also *collar,* 1. Sometimes spelled "horsecollar." **1st Use.** 1907. (*New York Evening Journal,* Apr. 25; Edward J. Nichols). **Etymology.** The term derives from the shape of the box-score cipher (0), which resembles the horse collar of a workhorse. **2.** *v.* For a pitcher to prevent the opposing team or batter from scoring or making a base hit, respectively.

**horsehide 1.** The baseball. **2.** The covering of the baseball. Horsehide had been the traditional cover for baseballs since the 19th century, but a shortage of quality horsehide in the early 1970s prompted the rules committee to allow cowhide covers along with horsehide. Cowhide balls began showing up in the major leagues in 1974 and the horsehide balls were dropped in 1995 by manufacturers. See also *cowhide,* 2. **1st Use.** 1895. (*New York Press,* July 20; Edward J. Nichols).

**horsehider** A baseball player during the time the horsehide ball was still in use.

**horseshoes 1.** *arch.* A lucky catch or stop. **2.** A lucky player. **1st Use.** 1915. (Ring W. Lardner, short story "Horseshoes"; Edward J. Nichols). **Etymology.** Both definitions relate to the long-established superstition that horseshoes bring good luck.

**hose 1.** A player's throwing arm. **2.** Socks; e.g., the Chicago White Sox are nicknamed the "Pale Hose" and the Boston Red Sox are nicknamed the "Carmine Hose." Roger Angell (*The Summer Game,* 1972) used the term "Hose" as a synonym for the Red Sox.

**hoser** A relief pitcher. See also *fireman.*

**hospital throw** A throw by an infielder to another that leaves the latter exposed to injury by a sliding or charging baserunner.

**hostilities** Play; competition. The term is likely to be used during a particularly hard-fought series of games.

**host team** Syn. of *home team.*

**hot 1.** Said of a baseball that is thrown or batted with great speed; hard-hit, as in a "hot ground ball" or a "hot ball," defined by Mrs. John A. Logan (*Home Manual,* 1889) as a "lightning-like shot thrown or hit to the infielders." **1st Use.** 1867. "Millholland taking lots of 'hot' balls from the bat" (*Detroit Advertiser and Tribune,* July 3; Peter Morris). **2.** Said of a player or team performing effectively or at one's (its) best; e.g., "He's [Will Clark] so hot he could fire a gun up into the air and kill a fish" (San Francisco Giants outfielder Candy Maldonado, Aug. 10, 1987; heard by Tom Gill on a Giants' broadcast). **1st Use.** 1899. (Burt L. Standish, *Frank Merriwell's Double Shot;* Edward J. Nichols).

**hot bat 1.** The bat of a player who is hitting well or is on a hitting streak; e.g., "Smith is wielding a hot bat" or "Jones's hot bat made five hits in five at-bats." Compare *cold bat,* 1. See also *live bat.* **2.** A player who is wielding a hot bat.

**hot box 1.** The location of a runner caught between two bases and two infielders who are trying to tag him out. **2.** An infielding or baserunning drill in which a runner travels back and forth between two bases trying to beat the tag.

**hot-bread belt** The Southern spring-training area, so named from the "association of southern training regions with hot bread" (Edward J. Nichols). **1st Use.** 1910. (*American Magazine,* Apr.; Edward J. Nichols).

**hot corner** Syn. of *third base,* 1. "I liked the whiplash grace of a third baseman's throw from the 'hot corner'" (Ted Berkman, *Christian Science Monitor,* Mar. 10, 1983). **Etymology/1st Use.** 1889. It is commonly assumed that the term came about because of the hot shots aimed at the third baseman, but the explanation is not universally accepted. "Third base was so named about 40 years ago when most of the star sluggers were right-handed. Nowadays, however, with so many hardhitting left-handers, first base is equally 'hot.'" (*Fan and Family,* Oct. 1935). Hy Turkin (*Baseball Almanac,* 1955) traces the term to Cincinnati writer Ren Mulford who created it during a certain game in 1889 during which Cincinnati third baseman Hick Carpenter "fielded seven sharp drives that almost tore him apart." Mulford wrote: "The Brooklyns had Old Hick on the hot corner all afternoon and it's a miracle he wasn't murdered." **Extended Use.** Any particularly tough or tight spot.

**hot dog 1.** A player who calls attention to himself with theatrics or plays to the crowd and/or the TV camera; a player who grandstands or "exaggerates

**Hot dog.** *Fans load up on hot dogs while waiting for the gates to open at Ebbets Field, Brooklyn, for the second game of the World Series, Oct. 6, 1920.*

his place in the mortal scheme of things" (Jim Brosnan, *The Long Season,* 1960). Defenders of hot dog players have puckishly suggested the term came from the fact that these guys play the game "with relish." Syn. *Mr. Mustard; mustard man.* **2.** A traditional food of ballpark denizens. See also *ballpark frank.* **Etymology/1st Use.** 1906. Reportedly, hot dogs were introduced to baseball in 1901 at the Polo Grounds, home of the New York Giants. It seems, according to an oft-told version, that concessionaire Harry Stevens was having a difficult time selling ice cream and soda in April and so he decided to offer small wursts, which were commonly known as "dachshund" sausages. He had them loaded into tanks and sent his vendors out into the stands chanting: "They're red hot! Get your red hots here!"

But an interview conducted by Fred Lieb with Stevens (*The Sporting News,* Nov. 11, 1918) carried this version: "I have been given credit for introducing the hot dog in America. Well, I don't deserve it. In fact, at first I couldn't see the idea. It was my son, Frank, who first got the idea, and wanted to try it on one of the early six-day bicycle crowds at Madison Square Garden. 'Pop, we can sell those people frankfurters and they'll welcome them for a change,' Frank told me. At the time we had been selling mostly beer and sandwiches, and I told Frank that the bike fans preferred ham and cheese. He insisted that we try it out for a few days, and at last I consented. His insistence has all America eating hot dogs."

Research conducted by Peter Tamony suggests that they were first called "hot dogs" in print and in a humorous context by sports cartoonist T. A. "Tad" Dorgan in 1915. According to Tamony, the earliest appearance in print was in an article in the *New York Sun* (Aug. 12, 1906) about Coney Island, where they were called "hot dog sandwiches."

**hot dogging** Playing the game in the manner of a hot dog. When asked about his antics on the mound by Richard Justice (*Washington Post,* July 23, 1986), Dennis "Oil Can" Boyd replied: "That ain't hot doggin'. That's the way we pitch back home." Sometimes spelled "hot-dogging"; "hotdogging." **Etymology.** The term is used in other sports and activities and may first have been applied to acrobatic skiing. John Ciardi (*Second Browser's Dictionary,* 1983) defined the term as "a recently popular form of suicide on skis"; he added that it was "perhaps so called by association with festive exuberance; perhaps because the skier is likely enough to end up as dog meat."

**hot grounder** A ground ball hit with great speed.

**hot-handed** Said of a pitcher who has lots of stuff.

**hot rock** A fastball.

**hot shot 1.** A hard-hit ball. **1st Use.** 1884. "The season is but a month old and yet there is not a club which is not more or less handicapped by crippled players. Base ball contests nowadays seem more like battles and often the phraseology of the game assumes a war-like aspect, when we speak of 'batteries,' 'firing the ball in,' 'hot shots,' etc." (*Sporting Life,* June 4; Barry Popik). **2.** A cocky player.

**hot stove league** The gab, gossip, and debate that take place during the winter months when baseball is not being played. These discussions—replaying the past season and anticipating the next—occurred at such gathering places as saloons, poolrooms, general stores, barbershops, and drugstores where there was a coal- or wood-burning, potbellied stove at the center of the conversational group. The term was given added popularity with the publication of Lee Allen's book, *The Hot Stove League* (1955). See also *fanning bee,* 3; *gab-circuit.* Syn. *stove league.* **1st Use.** 1912. "O'Day decided to try some of his new material which will win the pennant sometime in February in the Hot Stove League" (*New York Tribune,* Sept. 13; David Shulman). **Etymology.** Quoting from Allen's book: "No one knows when baseball followers first began to gather in winter around the hot stove of a barber shop or country store. Obviously, there has been talk about baseball as long as the game has existed. The phrase, 'hot stove league,' is of uncertain origin. Ernest J. Lanigan . . . thinks it was almost certainly coined by a sports writer around the turn of the century, perhaps by Ren Mulford, who covered baseball in Cincinnati and wrote long winter columns about the sport. A glossary of baseball terms published in 1897 does not include it."

However, Peter Tamony assembled information showing that the term predates 1900 when it was used to describe the off-season in horse racing. A dispatch from Knoxboro, N.Y. (*Spirit of the Times,* Mar. 20, 1886), contained this line: "The sleighing has gone, and most of the trotting is done around the hot stove at present." An even earlier report (*Spirit of the Times,* Mar. 17, 1877) contained a reference to "stove speed" ascribed to a trotter: it would seem to be a clear reference to a speed imagined during a gathering of the hot stove league.

The general idea is even older. Tamony discovered this quotation from P. T. Barnum's *Struggles and Triumphs* (1927) under "hot stove league": "In nearly every New England village, at the time of which I write [in the 1820s], there could be found from six to twenty social, jolly, story-telling, joke-playing wags and wits, regular originals, who would get together at the tavern or store, and spend their evenings and stormy afternoons in relating anecdotes, describing their various adventures, playing of practical jokes upon each other, and engaging in every project out of which a little fun could be extracted by village wits whose ideas were usually sharpened at brief intervals by a 'treat,' otherwise known as a glass of Santa Cruz rum, old Holland gin or Jamaica spirits."

Barry Popik offers the following from *The Sporting News* (Dec. 29, 1939), putting the idea in a baseball context back into the 19th century: "In Selma [Ohio] . . . exists one of the oldest Hot Stove leagues in the country. It was founded 45 years ago in Clark's general store and post-office, where it still holds its sessions, and while some of the original members have passed on, the same old stove still crackles and the surroundings generally are much the same as they were in the mid-nineties."

**hot-stover** A follower of the game who is given to off-season talk of baseball. "Metropolitan hot-stovers believe that Sergeant Joe DiMaggio was on the verge of getting a medical discharge from the Army Air Force because of threatened stomach ulcers, just when the European war situation became grave" (*San Francisco News,* Dec. 25, 1944; Peter Tamony).

**hot-stove season** The winter to those who play or are fans of the game. **1st Use.** 1937. "The best time to sell a baseball serial used to be during the winter months, called the Hot-Stove season" (Christy Walsh, *Adios to Ghosts!;* David Shulman).

**hot stoving** Rehashing plays, decisions, calls, trades, etc. The term is analogous to "Monday morning quarterbacking" in professional football.

**Houdini** A pitcher with a repertoire of trick pitches and deceptive deliveries, who, like the famous escape artist, is able to get out of tight spots.

**house dick** A player "who spends most of his off-the-field time sitting around the hotel lobby" (*Baseball Magazine,* Jan. 1943; David Shulman). **Etymology.** This is a clear allusion to the hotel detective, who has long been known as a "house dick" in American slang and who also hangs around the hotel. The presumption at work here is that the hotel-bound player might be mistaken for the hotel's detective.

**house man** A sportscaster who is unequivocally and relentlessly loyal to the home team. After losing his job as a pregame/postgame show host on a Chicago White Sox cable television program, Jimmy Piersall was quoted: "I called it the way I saw it and that's the reason I'm losing my job. I wouldn't be able to get up and shave my face in the morning without cutting my throat if I became a house man." (*Washington Post,* Apr. 7, 1983).

**House of . . .** A term used to give a ballpark an apt nickname. Joe Henderson (*Tampa Tribune,* Dec. 11, 1988) called San Diego's Jack Murphy (now Qualcomm) Stadium the "House of Chablis" because: "Boxseats there should come equipped with hot tubs. They lose there you know, but they just don't worry much about it."

**House of David** A nickname given to several barnstorming teams whose distinguishing characteristic was that all the players wore long beards. Franklin P. Huddle (*American Speech,* Apr. 1943) noted that because such teams were likely to have members who had been thrown out of organized baseball, "the beards serve the twin purpose of advertising and disguise"; the teams were also known as the *Bearded Wonders.* A character in William Brashler's *The Bingo Long Traveling All-Stars and Motor Kings* (1973) says: "You got to watch out for the other barnstormers like Max Helverton's Hooley Speedballers and them white teams from Michigan, them House of David boys with the beards." **Etymology.** The term is derived from a religious organization founded in 1903.

**house pet** A management favorite; a "player who sits in manager's lap" (Bert Dunne, *Folger's Dictionary of Baseball,* 1958).

**House That Ruth Built, The** A syn. of *Yankee Stadium,* so-called, in most accounts, because of the fame Babe Ruth brought to the New York Yankees and its ballpark. The term is a play on the nursery rhyme title, "The House That Jack Built."

Donald Dewey (letter, Mar. 31, 1990) reported: "The phrase was actually born before construction on Yankee Stadium was completed [1923] and refers more properly to the fact that the Stadium had to be built because the Giants booted the Yankees out of the Polo Grounds (no, your lease will not be renewed). The reason the Yankees were shown the gate was because Yankee attendance was beginning to leave Giants attendance in the dust, mainly because of Ruth, and the Giants were beginning to feel like guests in their own home. Thus 'The House That Ruth Built' was originally meant a little more literally than most people today realize." Bill Deane (letter, Jan. 1998) notes: "My understanding is that Ruth's exploits of 1920–1922, leading the Yankees to their first two pennants and doubling attendance, enabled the team to build its own stadium rather than continuing to share the Polo Grounds with the Giants."

**Houston Astrodome** See *Astrodome.*

**Houston Astros** The name of the National League Central Division franchise in Houston, Tex. At its inception in 1962, the team was named the Colt .45s, but the Colt Arms Company complained and others were bothered by the violent notion of a team named for a handgun. When the team moved into the brand-new Astrodome in 1965, it sported a new name, the Astronauts, but this was quickly shortened to the Astros.

**Houston Colt .45s** The first name of the Houston Astros from the time of their first season in 1962 to 1964, when they became the Astros. Despite their firearms name, almost everybody referred to the team as the Colts.

**"How about that!"** A comment that followed a home run, or other exciting or unusual occurrence, when Mel Allen was in the broadcast booth.

**HP** Abbrev. for *hit by pitcher.*

**HR** Abbrev. for *home run.*

**Hubert H. Humphrey Metrodome** The domed home field since 1982 of the Minnesota Twins in Minneapolis. The name honors the late senator and Vice President from Minnesota. Syn. *Metrodome; Homerdome.*

**huckleberry** Syn. of *rookie,* 1.

**hug** **1.** For a first baseman or third baseman to position himself close to a foul line. **2.** For a baserunner to stay close to a base. **1st Use.** 1869. (*DeWitt's Official Base Ball Guide;* Edward J. Nichols). **3.** For a batter to stand close to the plate.

**human rain delay** A batter who takes considerable time preparing to receive each pitch by warming up, swinging the bat, moving in and out of the batter's box, adjusting his helmet or batting gloves, calling time, etc. The term was applied specif. to Mike Hargrove and Carlton Fisk.

**human whiff machine** A hitter with a very low batting average.

**humidity dispenser** *arch.* A particularly waggish synonym for *spitball.* **1st Use.** 1912. (*New York Tribune,* Sept. 22; Edward J. Nichols).

**"humm-babe"** A unit of chatter that permeates every level of the game from the school yard to the major leagues. Roger Craig of the San Francisco Giants used it so much that during the 1987 season *Sports Illustrated* termed it "a cult phrase in San Francisco." **Etymology.** The phrase probably evolved from more articulate chatter along the lines of encouraging the pitcher to "hum that ball," or "throw the hummer," or "come on babe."

**hummer** **1.** The fastball, named for the whizzing

sound it seems to make as it comes across the plate. "At age 59, if that's what he was, Satch [Paige] had lost the hummer" (Jack Mann, *Washington Times,* June 10, 1982). See also *buzzer.* **2.** *obs.* A hard-batted ball.

**humpbacked liner** A batted ball that soars like a line drive, then sinks precipitously: metaphorically, a cross between a frozen rope and a parachute. According to Harwell West (*The Baseball Scrap Book,* 1933), the term got its start in the Southern Association. Also spelled "humped-back liner"; "humpback liner"; "hump-backed liner."

**humpty-dump** A type of music played by ball-park organists at odd times during a game, which many fans find disconcerting and annoying.

**humpty-dumpty 1.** A player, often unskilled, who is unpopular or unproven with his teammates. **2.** A substitute player. Leo Durocher (*Nice Guys Finish Last,* 1975) states: "The way it has always been in baseball, the humpty-dumpties, the substitutes, come out early to take their batting and fielding practice, and then the bell rings and the hitting cage belongs to the regulars."

**Hundred Thousand Dollar Infield** See *One Hundred Thousand Dollar Infield.*

**hungry** Said of a player or team wanting to do well because of previous failures; said of a player eager to make a name for himself.

**hunt leather** *arch.* To try to hit the ball. **1st Use.** 1885. (Chicago *Inter-Ocean,* May 3; Edward J. Nichols).

**hurl 1.** To deliver the ball from the pitcher's mound; to pitch. **2.** To throw a baseball.

**hurler** Syn. of *pitcher,* 1. **1st Use.** 1908. (*Baseball Magazine,* Nov.; Edward J. Nichols).

**hurry the throw** For an infielder to get rid of the ball as quickly as possible, esp. when trying to turn a slow roller, bunt, or bobbled ball into an out.

**hurt** To destroy an opponent's chances of winning by being effective at the plate or on the mound.

**hustle 1.** *v.* To play aggressively, quickly, and alertly. **2.** *n.* Playing baseball in an alert and aggressive manner. **Usage Note.** A noted modern player who performed in an aggressive manner was Pete Rose, who attracted the nickname "Charlie Hustle." Ira Berkow (*New York Times*) has written that it was a derisive nickname at first, but Rose wore it as a "badge of distinction." **Etymology.** Although the term has often been described as an Americanism, Peter Tamony showed that it was, in fact, "employed by English pickpockets from about 1750 on." In a paper he delivered (Oct. 19, 1962) to the International Society for General Semantics, he summarized his findings: "'Hustle,' the English word, has cognates in Dutch and Low and High German, and the import in these languages is 'to shake together, to toss.' In the early 19th century, these older terms came to mean 'to push forward, to impel, to urge, to move hastily, to hurry, to bustle . . . to work busily.' As hustle and bustle characterized American life and seemed so characteristic of Americans, hustle was upgraded or ameliorated, and became an admired American trait. . . . The meaning has persisted in criminal slang, and indicates almost anyone who seems to be getting by without visible means of support— someone with a racket. It has been closely connected with prostitution and pimps and, of course, all kinds of gambling and games of chance."

**hustle blister** Syn. of *strawberry.*

**hustle bump** One of the "marks and bruises on a player's body" according to Fresco Thompson (*Every Diamond Doesn't Sparkle,* 1964).

**hustlersville** *arch.* The figurative breeding ground of hustlers. Syn. *hustletown.* **1st Use.** 1891. "[Tim] Murnane is a hustler from Hustlersville and when there is anything on writing a baseball war, his sensational and newsy stories are looked for and read by all" (*Sporting Times,* Nov. 14; David Shulman).

**hustletown** Syn. of *hustlerville.* **1st Use.** 1889. "Latham's Song . . . I'm a hustler from Hustletown" (Chadwick Scrapbooks; David Shulman).

**Hutch Award** Short for *Fred Hutchinson Award.*

# I

**I** Abbrev. for *interference,* 1.

**IBA** Abbrev. for *International Baseball Association.*

**IBB** Abbrev. for *intentional base on balls.*

**ice** To all but assure the final outcome of a game through a hit or defensive play; e.g., "Smith's grand slam iced the game."

**ice box** The bullpen.

**ice-cream cone 1.** A ball that is caught in the top of the webbing of a fielder's glove, so-called because the ball sticks up out of the glove like a scoop of ice cream. **2.** A catch in which the ball is lodged in the top of the webbing of a fielder's glove. See also *snow cone.*

**ice down** To use ice or some other cooling agent to soothe and reduce swelling or inflammation; e.g., to "ice down" a pitcher's throwing arm after the game. When asked if he did this during his years as a major-league pitcher, Warren Spahn answered: "Ice is for mixed drinks" (*Boston Globe,* May 21, 1988).

**ice man** A relief pitcher; one who is able to "freeze" an opposing team's rally. Interestingly, this term and "fireman" are synonyms.

**ice wagon** *arch.* A player who runs slowly, resembling the labored movement of an ice wagon. **1st Use.** 1908. (*New York American,* Apr. 30; Peter Morris).

**IF 1.** Abbrev. for *infield,* 2. **2.** Abbrev. for *infielder.* **3.** Abbrev. for *infield fly,* 1.

**"if you're waving at me, howdy"** An expression said to a player who has just struck out swinging (*Sports Illustrated,* Sept. 13, 1982).

**ignite** To start a rally.

**igniter** The player who starts a rally. See also *spark.*

**IL** Abbrev. for *International League.*

**"I'll be there" play** A play in which a fielder throws the ball to a place where a teammate will be when the ball arrives, such as a catcher throwing to second base with the knowledge that the second baseman or shortstop is on his way to cover the bag. "[Rich] Gedman pulls off an 'I'll be there' play" (broadcaster Joe Garagiola, Oct. 27, 1986). Syn. *be-there play.*

**illegal** Contrary to the rules of baseball.

**illegal bat** [softball term] A bat that does not meet the requirements stated in the rules of the Amateur Softball Association of America or other body and is not marked by the words "OFFICIAL SOFTBALL" by the manufacturer; e.g., a baseball bat honed down to softball size. Compare *altered bat.*

**illegally batted ball** A ball hit with either of the batter's feet outside the batter's box. In such cases, the ball is dead and the batter is out. The same is true for a ball that is hit twice, such as one that is popped up in front of the batter and hit again as it comes down. A ball hit with a bat that has been doctored is also deemed to be illegally batted.

**illegally caught ball** A ball stopped or caught with a cap, glove, or any other part of the player's uniform or equipment that is detached from its proper place, such as by throwing the glove to stop the progress of a batted ball. Such action results in an automatic triple being awarded the batter.

**illegal pitch** A pitch that violates the rules; specif., a) a pitch delivered to the batter when the pitcher's pivot foot is not in contact with the rubber and b) a *quick return pitch,* 1. When ruled, an illegal pitch is a balk with runner(s) on base and a ball if there are no runners on base, provided that the batter does not swing at the pitch. If a batter reaches first base on an illegal pitch, the play counts.

**illegal pitcher** [softball term] A player legally in the game but who may not pitch as a result of being removed from the pitching position by the umpire because of two charged conferences in one inning or pitching with excessive speed (in slow pitch softball) after a warning.

**illegal player** [softball term] A player who has entered the game without reporting. When brought to the plate umpire's attention by the offended team after the first legal or illegal pitch and before the team in violation informs the umpire, the player is ejected from the game.

**imaginary line** A painted line marking off areas of a ballpark in fair territory in which no plays can be made. Balls hit or bouncing into such areas are considered ground-rule doubles or home runs.

**immortal** A player or other individual elected to the Baseball Hall of Fame. Election has invoked the notion of baseball immortality. A modicum of reality was imposed at the moment Dizzy Dean was told that he had been elected and he responded: "Well, I guess now I'm 'mongst them mortals." See also *eleven immortals; baseball immortal.*

**impact player** A player who has an effect on the team's ability to win ball games.

**import** A player's wife or girlfriend brought on a road trip.

**improved bat** An improvement in a player's ability to get timely hits.

**in 1.** *adv.* Toward home plate, such as an infield that is playing close in anticipation of a bunt or a play at the plate. Syn. *up,* 4. **2.** *adv.* Toward the batter, such as a pitch thrown inside or close to the batter; e.g., "Smith's pitch was up and in." **3.** *adv.* Said of a pitch that is in the strike zone; e.g., "The pitch was in there for strike three." **4.** *adv.* Across home plate; e.g., "The run is in to tie the score." **5.** *adv.* Participating in a game; e.g., "Jones is in, replacing Brown." Compare *out,* 5. **6.** *n.* The side at bat.

**in a breeze** See *breeze,* 3.

**in a hole** See *hole.*

**in and out play** A game or sequence of innings characterized by a quick succession of outs.

**in-between** Said of a ball fielded on the short hop.

**in-betweener** A base hit that falls between an infielder and an outfielder. Conventional baseball practice assigns in-betweeners to the outfield. See also *tweener.*

**incentive clause** That part of a player's contract that promises a bonus for achieving certain goals and/or honors during the season. A common incentive stipulates that a player will be given a cash bonus if he makes the All-Star team. "Once upon a time, general managers tossed incentive clauses into contracts because a) they wanted to get an obnoxious agent out of their office, b) they thought giving incentives instead of higher base salaries would keep payrolls lower, or c) they figured the incentives wouldn't be met" (Richard Justice, *Washington Post,* Aug. 24, 1986).

Incentives can be many and varied. According to Murray Chass in the *New York Times* (Jan. 11, 1987), in his 1987 contract with the Oakland A's, Reggie Jackson was given the following: a) $1,000 per plate appearance from his 476th through the 600th; b) 15 cents for each home admission from 1.6 to 1.7 million, 20 cents for each home admission from 1.7 to 1.8 million, and 30 cents for each admission greater than 1.8 million; and c) $250,000 if he is named the league's Most Valuable Player, $125,000 for second through fifth in voting, and $50,000 for sixth through tenth.

**incomplete game** A game of less than five complete innings.

**in contention** Said of a team that is competing for a division title.

**incurve** *arch.* A pitch thrown by a right-handed pitcher that curves in toward a right-handed batter or one thrown by a left-handed pitcher that curves in toward a left-handed batter. The pitch is now known as a *screwball.* See also *inshoot.* Compare *outcurve.* Also spelled "in-curve." **1st Use.** 1901. (Burt L. Standish, *Frank Merriwell's Marvel;* Edward J. Nichols).

**independent league** A minor league that is formed and developed without the sanction of Major League Baseball e.g., the Carolina League (1936–38). The Northern League (1993) and the Texas-Louisiana League (1994) were the first of the modern independent leagues.

**independent team** A minor-league team not affiliated with a major-league team.

**Indian ball** Syn. of *rounders.*

**Indian sign** A jinx or hoodoo. **1st Use.** 1908. (*Baseball Magazine,* June; Edward J. Nichols).

**indicator 1.** A card or a small handheld mechanical device used by an umpire to keep track of balls, strikes, outs, and innings. Some modern indicators have the capacity to display runs scored as well. "Steve Zabriskie and Ralph Kiner are second-guessing umpires so much, I am going to give them indicators" (Tom Gorman, supervisor of National League umpires, quoted in *Newsday,* June 30, 1986). Syn. *clicker; counter,* 2; *ouija board.* **1st Use.** 1905. (*Sporting Life,* Oct. 7; Edward J. Nichols). **2.** A sign, given by the manager or a coach, that is embedded in a sea of meaningless gestures and precedes the real sign; e.g., an indicator might be going to the bill of the cap with the left hand after which the next sign is the operative one. Compare *wipe-off sign.*

**indifference** Allowing a runner to advance a base without attempting to stop him. No stolen base is awarded when a runner advances solely because of the defensive team's indifference to his advance; it is scored as a fielder's choice. Syn. *defensive indifference.*

**individual offensive bunt** A bunt to get the batter on base rather than one whose purpose is to advance runner(s) already on base.

**indoor baseball 1.** [softball term] The original name for the game from which modern *softball* derived. Its rules were written by George W. Hancock of Chicago who was one of the group of young men who created the game, using a boxing glove for a ball and a broomstick for a bat, while waiting at the Farragut Boat Club for the telegraphed results of the Army-Navy football game on Thanksgiving Day, 1887. Thus, softball in its first incarnation was baseball played inside a gymnasium. See also *indoor-outdoor; playground baseball.* **2.** A facetious term for baseball played in domed ballparks. **3.** Baseball adapted for playing indoors.

**indoor cage** An indoor *batting cage* that uses a tee.

**indoor-outdoor** [softball term] *Indoor baseball* adapted for playing outdoors. Less than a year after indoor baseball was invented, it had caught on to such an extent that by Summer 1888 it was being played outdoors and some preferred to call it "indoor-outdoor."

**indoor team** Any team that plays its home games in a domed or enclosed ballpark.

**industrial league** A generic name for a baseball or softball league that is sponsored by and named after an industrial or commercial enterprise.

**industrial softball** [softball term] Softball in which the teams are sponsored by industrial or commercial enterprises for their employees. For many years softball has been a popular sport for both sexes in the recreation programs sponsored by industrial and commercial firms. One company (Avco Lycoming) spoke for many when it stated that its reasons for an active softball program were that interdepartmental softball competition: a) promotes job efficiency, morale, and a strong sense of

CHICAGO in door Base Ball Team copyright By X.O. Howe 97

**Indoor baseball.** *Taken in 1897, this may be the earliest known photograph from the game that became softball.*

company loyalty; b) functions as a social "leveler" by affording friendly contact among employees at all personnel levels; c) promotes the physical and mental well-being of employees; and d) promotes an excellent medium for observing the potential leadership abilities of employees (*Balls and Strikes*, April 1967).

**industrial team** A baseball or softball team in an industrial league.

**infield 1.** The area on the playing field bounded by the four baselines; the diamond. **1st Use.** 1858. (Chadwick Scrapbooks; Edward J. Nichols). **2.** The area on the playing field bounded by the "outside edges" of the basepaths. This definition applies because there is no official definition of where the infield actually ends and the outfield begins. Abbrev. *IF,* 1. **3.** The defensive positions comprising first base, second base, third base, and shortstop, taken collectively. **4.** The infielders (first baseman, second baseman, third baseman, and shortstop) considered as a group. Technically, the pitcher and catcher are infielders but generally are not being referred to when a team's infield is being discussed. **1st Use.** 1883. (*Sporting Life*, May 27; Edward J. Nichols). **5.** Short for *infield practice;* e.g., "Let's take a little infield."

**infield back** Said of the infield playing at its normal depth. Compare *infield in.*

**infield chatter** The rhythmic talk of infielders intended to bolster spirit and encourage the pitcher.

**infielder** A defensive player positioned in the infield; specif., the first baseman, second baseman, third baseman, or shortstop. Abbrev. *IF,* 2. **1st Use.** 1865. (*New York Herald,* July 1; Edward J. Nichols).

**infield fly** **1.** A batted ball popped up over the infield. Abbrev. *IF,* 3. **2.** A declaration by the umpire that the infield fly rule is in effect. **3.** Short for *infield fly rule.*

**infield fly rule** A special rule to protect the baserunners, in which the batter is declared automatically out by the umpire when, in his judgment, a fair fly ball (not including a line drive nor an attempted bunt) can be caught with ordinary effort by an infielder (and the pitcher, the catcher, or an outfielder who stations himself in or near the infield) facing the infield, when first and second bases are occupied or when the bases are loaded, and there is less than two out. The fielder does not need to catch the ball.

The umpire declares the rule is in effect by saying "infield fly" and signals it by raising a clenched fist straight overhead. If the ball is near the baselines, the umpire yells "infield fly, if fair." If the fly becomes a foul ball, it is treated the same as any foul. The umpire's judgment governs the rule: in no sense is it considered an appeal play.

The rationale for the infield fly rule is to prevent the fielder from intentionally dropping the ball, picking it up quickly, and forcing the offensive team into a double play; i.e., the rule removes the force situation which would cause two runners to be doubled up after an intentional drop. The ball is live and all baserunners may advance at the risk of the ball being caught, or retouch and advance after the ball is touched by the fielder. If a runner is off base and hit by the ball, both the runner and the batter are out; however, if the runner is on the base and is hit by the ball, only the batter is out. In either case, the ball is dead. Syn. *infield fly,* 3. **1st Use.** 1909. (*American Magazine,* May; Edward J. Nichols).

**infield hit** Any hit that does not escape the infield but allows the batter time to reach first base safely. Such hits must be either hit slowly enough or placed well enough to allow the batter to outrun a throw to first base. **1st Use.** 1895. (*New York Press,* Aug. 3; Edward J. Nichols).

**infield in** Said of an infield playing closer to home in anticipation of a bunt or a play at the plate. The infield often plays in when there is a runner on third base and less than two out. "[Col-orado] Rockies manager Don Baylor always plays his infield in at Coors whether Colorado is leading or not. 'It's automatic if you're standing there [in the dugout] thinking about it,' Baylor says." (*Sports Illustrated,* May 13, 1996). Compare *infield back.* Syn. *infield up.*

**infielding** Infield defensive play.

**infield out** An out made on a ball hit within the infield.

**infield practice** That period of pregame set aside for infielders to improve their fielding (catching and throwing) skills. Syn. *infield,* 5.

**infield roller** A slow ground ball that is batted onto the infield.

**infield rule** See *infield fly rule.*

**infield up** Syn. of *infield in.*

**infinite regression** A situation in a ball game in which managers try to outthink each other; e.g., Atlanta Braves manager Bobby Cox "is standing in his dugout thinking that [Philadelphia Phillies manager Jim] Fregosi knows that I know that he knows . . . what we ballplayers call an infinite regression" (Keith Hernandez, *Pure Baseball,* 1994).

**in flight** Said of a batted, thrown, or pitched ball that has not yet hit the ground or been touched by a fielder or other object.

**inherited runner** A baserunner at the time a relief pitcher enters the game. In 1992, box scores began to note the number of inherited runners and how many of them scored off each reliever.

**in his kitchen** See *kitchen.*

**I-95** A batting average of .195, a play on the north-south Interstate Highway 95. A player who cannot get his average off I-95 is one who cannot break .200.

**I-95 Series** A nickname for the 1983 World Series between the Philadelphia Phillies and the Baltimore Orioles, their two cities linked by Interstate Highway 95.

**initial** Describing first base. Terms popular from the late 1880s until about 1910 included "initial bag," "initial corner," "initial cushion," "initial hassock," and "initial sack."

**in jeopardy** Said of the state of an offensive player who, while the ball is in play, is in a position to be put out.

**injured reserve** The status of a player who, not playing because of an injury or illness, can return to the team at any point because he has not been permanently replaced on the roster.

**injured reserve list** A list of players not capable of playing because of injury or sickness. A player is usually placed on the list for a specified number of days, during which his place on the roster can be filled temporarily.

**injury list** A list of players temporarily unable to play because of injuries. See also *disabled list.*

**injury rehabilitation assignment** A *rehabilitation assignment* in which the player is recovering from an injury.

**ink 1.** *v.* To put one's signature to, as on a contract or other legal document. "One might be tempted to wonder, given this mythic rise, if [Cal, Jr.] Ripken hasn't also inked a contract with the devil: Shoeless Joe Hardy in a Baltimore reprise of *Damn Yankees*" (Paul Hendrickson, *Washington Post,* April 1, 1984). **2.** *n.* Media recognition (formerly printed media only, but now all media). Jim Brosnan (*Pennant Race,* 1962) called pitchers who solicit media attention "ink hounds." **Usage Note.** The term is self-conscious sports talk, beloved of sportswriters, just as "hoop tilt" is for a basketball game.

**in motion** Said of a baserunner who begins a movement toward a steal of the next base.

**inner game** The strategy and tactics of baseball as it relates to such matters as batting order, defensive positioning, and the use of pinch hitters. See also *inside baseball.*

**inner garden** *arch.* The infield. Compare *outer garden.* **1st Use.** 1907. (*New York Evening Journal,* May 24; Edward J. Nichols).

**inner-outer** A fictional pitch thrown by Burt L. Standish's Frank Merriwell, which curved twice on its flight to the plate. Compare *upper-downer.*

**inner works 1.** *arch.* The area in which the infielders play. Compare *outer works.* **2.** *arch.* The infielders as a working unit. **1st Use.** 1908. "The inner works held together well" (John B. Foster, *Collier's New Dictionary of the English Language*).

**inning 1.** That part of a game within which the two teams alternate on defense and offense and during which there are three putouts for each team. Syn. *canto; chapter; chucker,* 2; *stanza; frame; heat,* 1; *verse; loop,* 4; *round; session; spasm.* **2.** One unit of a pitcher's statistic referring to the opposition's times at bat. See also *innings pitched.* **1st Use.** 1845. "[Brooklyn] decided in favor of giving their antagonists the first innings" (*New York Morning News,* Oct. 22). **Etymology.** The term was used in its modern sense in the rules of the original Knickerbocker Club in 1854, but not in the first 1845 set of rules. "Inning" was borrowed directly from cricket, a sport in which the team at bat is "in" and the one on the field is "out": a time at bat (an at-bat) is an "innings." British writers taking a crack at writing about baseball will initially refer to an "inning" as "innings." **Extended Use.** A period of play in other sports and games; e.g., a bowling frame (one bowler's turn) is called an "inning." Peter Morris discovered that when the Univ. of Michigan played its first intercollegiate football game against Racine College in 1879, the two halves were referred to as "innings."

**innings 1.** The work of a pitcher in preparing for a game; e.g., "Smith got his innings in today for the game on Tuesday." **2.** The work of a player during a game; e.g., "Jones will see some innings at shortstop tomorrow." "If he [Doug Drabek] keeps the ball down, he's going to give you innings" (Ray Miller, quoted in *Baltimore Sun,* Feb. 26, 1998). **3.** A unit of play in cricket in which each team, or individual player, has a turn at bat. **Extended Use.** An opportunity or chances; e.g., "Smith had his innings." It is difficult to tell whether the American use of the word "innings" outside baseball is a product of baseball or cricket. It may well be cricket. Logan Pearsall Smith (*Words and Idioms,* 1925) listed "to have one's innings" as a borrowing from cricket.

**innings pitched** A pitcher's statistic referring to the opposition's times at bat, expressed in fractions, with each out counting as one-third of an inning; e.g., a starting pitcher removed with one out in the seventh inning is credited with 6⅓ "innings pitched." Abbrev. *IP.*

**in order 1.** Referring to the retirement of the first three batters in an inning; e.g., "The team goes down in order." **2.** Referring to three consecutive outs in one inning without a hit or a runner reaching first base; e.g., "Smith retired the next three batters in order."

**in play 1.** Regarding that period when the game is being played as opposed to a period when plays cannot begin or continue. Compare *out of play,* 1. **2.** Describing a ball that is live, when runners can advance or be put out and runs can score. The ball is in play until it is ruled dead by the umpire or a third out is made. A ball is put back in play only after it is in the hands of the pitcher in position and the plate umpire has called "Play!" Compare *out of play,* 2. **3.** Said of a fair ball hit by a batter who is able to make contact; e.g., "Smith put the ball in play with the nubber." See also *put the ball in play.*

**in relief** Said of a relief pitcher in a game; e.g., "Smith was in relief for three innings."

**inshoot 1.** A pitch that curves toward the batter. Compare *offshoot.* See also *incurve.* Also spelled *in-shoot,* 1.

**in-shoot 1.** Alternate spelling of *inshoot.* **1st Use.** 1881. (*New York Herald,* July 29; Edward J. Nichols). **2.** [softball term] An underhand pitch in fast pitch softball that curves toward the batter.

**inside** Said of a pitch that comes between the batter and the strike zone. During the 1986 World Series, broadcaster Vin Scully said that the best story to come out of that year's spring training involved a pitching coach telling a rookie pitcher that he would have to learn "to pitch inside." The pitcher's response: "Have I been traded to Houston?" Compare *outside.*

**inside ball** Syn. of *inside baseball.* **1st Use.** 1902. (*Sporting Life,* Apr. 26; Edward J. Nichols).

**inside baseball** Smart, strategic baseball involving teamwork and techniques such as stealing, sacrificing, and the hit-and-run play. John B. Foster (*Collier's New Dictionary of the English Language,* 1908) noted the term is "a much abused expression to denote clever team work much of which is the result of a vivid imagination." It was the gospel of managers Ned Hanlon and John McGraw. Compare *outside baseball.* See also *inner game; scientific baseball.* Syn. *inside ball; inside game; inside work.* **Extended Use.** William Safire (*New York Times,* June 19, 1988) explored the term's new "political or professional denotation," which he defined as "minutiae savored by the cognoscenti, delicious details, nuances discussed and dissected by aficionados." Safire gave several examples of the term in use outside of baseball, including this line from Richard Weiner, chairman of the Michigan Democratic Party: "The people in my state are interested in jobs, the economy and education. The rest is inside baseball." The earliest example mentioned by Safire was in 1978 by Sen. Edward M. Kennedy (D.-Mass.) in a letter quoted by Myra MacPherson of the *Washington Post,* in which Kennedy speaks of a legislator who "chairs endlessly boring hearings . . . then cuts through testimony with inside baseball jokes that no visitors understand but laugh at anyway."

**inside corner** The side corner of home plate that is closest to the batter. Compare *outside corner.* **1st Use.** 1896. (Burt L. Standish, *Frank Merriwell's School Days;* Edward J. Nichols).

**inside game** Syn. of *inside baseball.* **1st Use.** 1906. (*Lajoie's Official Base Ball Guide;* Edward J. Nichols).

**inside hitter** A hitter who is adept at hitting pitches thrown close to him. **1st Use.** 1932. (*Baseball Magazine,* Oct.; Edward J. Nichols).

**inside out** *v.* To sweep the bat through the strike zone at a slight angle, from the back inside portion of the plate toward the outside front portion, resulting in the ball being hit to the opposite field; e.g., "Smith, a left-handed hitter, inside outed the pitch to left field."

**inside-out swing** A swing in which the batter's hands move ahead of the barrel of the bat so that when contact is made the ball tends to head toward the opposite field. Wade Boggs and Tony

Gwynn are modern hitters known for their prowess with this swing.

**inside pivot** A *pivot* in which the shortstop or second baseman receives the ball and then tags second base before throwing to first base in an attempt to turn a double play. Compare *outside pivot*.

**inside-the-park home run** A home run in which the ball does not leave the field of play. It usually occurs when a fleet-footed batter hits a ball that bounces away from an outfielder. Baltimore Orioles slugger Boog Powell holds the distinction of being the heaviest (250 lb.) batter to hit an inside-the-park home run in the ninth inning of a game against Seattle on Aug. 16, 1969.

**inside work** Syn. of *inside baseball.* **1st Use.** 1908. (*Baseball Magazine,* July; Edward J. Nichols).

**inspect the ball** For an umpire to examine the ball to determine that it is fit for continued play. The inspection commonly is done after a batted ball is returned to the pitcher or if a ball is thrown in the dirt. If the ball is nicked or badly scuffed or has pulled stitches, it is removed from play. A ball may also be inspected if there is suspicion that it has been doctored.

**instructional league** A special league sponsored by major-league teams to give the youngest and least-experienced professional players further instruction. See also *winter instructional league; Arizona Fall League.*

**insurance** **1.** The addition of runs to an existing lead which the opposition will not likely to surmount. **2.** The availability of a nonstarting player who can be called on to do a capable job of filling in for a regular; e.g., "Manager Smith kept Jones for insurance." **3.** A nonstarting player who can be called on to do a capable job of filling in for a regular; e.g., "Jones is insurance in the event Brown cannot play." **4.** A pool of capable reserve players.

**insurance man** A relief pitcher who can put down a rally and turn around what seems to be a losing game.

**insurance policy** **1.** A player who can play more than one position effectively. **2.** A backup player at a given position.

**insurance run** Any run that is made by a team already ahead in a game; specif., the run that adds to a team's one-run lead.

**intensity** Concentration and/or determination possessed by a player or a team. "This year, I'm feeling good. I have that intensity again and that hunger." (Tom Herr, quoted in *St. Petersburg Times,* Mar. 27, 1987).

**intentional base on balls** Syn. of *intentional walk.* Abbrev. *IBB.*

**intentional pass** Syn. of *intentional walk.* **1st Use.** 1898. (*New York Tribune,* Apr. 24; Edward J. Nichols).

**intentional walk** A base on balls in which the pitcher deliberately throws the fourth ball outside the strike zone. This action, almost always a decision made by the manager, is usually taken to a) avoid pitching to a particularly good or hot hitter, b) get to a right-handed batter if the pitcher is right-handed or get to a left-handed batter if the pitcher is left-handed, and c) fill first base if it is unoccupied, with runners on second base and/or third base, thereby setting up a force situation to enhance the chance for a double play. The catcher must remain in the catcher's box until the pitch is delivered.

A batter cannot legally hit a ball if he is outside the batter's box, so there is no chance of one of these pitches being hit unless the pitcher accidentally throws it in or close to the strike zone. Dizzy Dean opined: "I never did like to give an intentional pass. I always figgered that I was just about as good as the hitter comin' up there and I figgered that I could get anybody out and I hated to put those men on base because when you put them on there, they are not in the dugout and that's where I would rather have them settin'." Compare this to the bewildering definition given by a British fan after first seeing the 1986 World Series, which was telecast on Britain's Channel 4: "That means he's deliberately given unplayable to force him to settle for a first-base advance" (*New York Times,* Oct. 27, 1986).

The first intentional walk occurred in 1896 when William "Kid" Gleason, captain of the New

York Giants, told pitcher Jouett Meekin to walk Chicago Colts slugger Jimmy Ryan to get to weak hitter George Decker, who struck out to end the game (Richard Cahan & Mark Jacob, *The Game That Was,* 1996). Abbrev. *IW.* Syn. *intentional base on balls; intentional pass.*

**intercept** To cut off a throw coming in from the outfield on its way to home plate.

**interference** **1.** An act by the team at bat that impedes, hinders, or confuses any fielder attempting to make a play. Examples include: intentionally deflecting the course of a batted or thrown ball; leaving the baseline for the obvious purpose of crashing into the pivot man on a double play; stepping out of the batter's box to hinder a catcher's throw; and failing to avoid a fielder who is attempting to field a batted ball. See also *runner's interference.* Compare *obstruction.* Abbrev. *I.* **2.** An act by a fielder that hinders or prevents a batter from hitting a pitch; e.g., *catcher's interference.* **3.** See *umpire's interference.* **4.** See *fan interference; spectator interference.*

**interference at first base** A specific case of interference in which the batter-runner collides with the first baseman. If it occurs with the first baseman receiving the throw in fair territory, the runner is out. If the collision occurs in foul territory, however, the runner is given first base.

**interim manager** An individual picked to fill a team's managerial position on a short-term basis while a long-term, permanent manager is being sought. An interim manager is usually hired from the ranks of a team's coaching staff when the manager is fired during the course of a season.

**interleague play** Games between teams in different leagues. For generations, interleague play at the major-league level was restricted to exhibition games, the All-Star Game, and the World Series, but this came to an end on June 12, 1997, when the San Francisco Giants and Texas Rangers began the first regular-season interleague game at The Ballpark in Arlington, Arlington, Tex. In 1997, 214 interleague games were played during the regular season, during which home-team rules applied (use of the designated hitter in American League ballparks; pitchers batting in the National League ballparks).

**intermission** The period (usually 20 minutes) between games of a doubleheader.

**International Baseball Association** A worldwide organization, based in Indianapolis, Ind., and represented by 76 nations, dedicated to the advancement of amateur baseball. It succeeded in getting baseball adopted as an Olympic medal sport beginning in 1992 in Barcelona, but rejected a proposal to allow professional baseball players to play in the Olympic Games. Abbrev. *IBA.*

**International League** A minor league (Class AA from 1912 to 1945 and Class AAA since 1946) with franchises primarily in the eastern parts of the United States and Canada. Abbrev. *IL.*

**International Softball Congress** [softball term] A federation of men's fast pitch softball teams, based in Anaheim Hills, Calif. It was founded in 1946 when the International Softball League merged with the National Softball Congress.

**Interstate** A batting average below .200 (or a "*buck* and change"), so called in reference to the U.S. Interstate Highway system with numbers less than 100; e.g., I-95 = .195. "It feels good to get off that Interstate" (New York Yankees outfielder Jesse Barfield, who was batting .238, quoted in *New York Times,* June 18, 1989). Sometimes spelled "interstate."

**intestinal fortitude** Courage. The term was created around 1937 as a gentle way of saying "guts." This euphemism may not have started in baseball, but it commonly has been used to describe individual action in baseball.

**in the bag** Safely won.

**in the dirt** Said of a pitch that hits the ground.

**in the field** Said of a team playing on the defense. **1st Use.** 1860. (Constitution and By-Laws of the Excelsior Base Ball Club; Edward J. Nichols).

**in the groove** **1.** Said of a pitch through the center of the strike zone or that is easy to hit. **1st Use.** 1912. (*New York Tribune,* Oct. 6; Edward J. Nichols). **2.** Describing a player who is consistently performing well. **3.** Describing a team that is winning a high percentage of its games.

**in the hole** See *hole.*

**in the neighborhood** Said of a fielder who is close enough to touch a base in a *neighborhood play.* "A shortstop or second baseman is 'in the neighborhood'—but doesn't touch—second base, because he's avoiding an incoming slide. An out, at umpire's discretion." (Rudy Martzke, *USA Today,* Oct. 15, 1986).

**in there 1.** Said of a pitch in the strike zone; e.g., "The pitch was in there for a called strike." **2.** Said of a fly ball that falls in for a hit.

**in the slot 1.** Syn. of *on deck.* **2.** Said of the position of the plate umpire looking over the catcher's shoulder nearest the batter.

**in the soup** In trouble; at a disadvantage.

**in the tank** Said of a contending team that goes into a losing streak.

**in-the-vicinity play** Syn. of *neighborhood play.*

**in the well** Said of a fly ball hit to an adept outfielder.

**into the stands** Said of a ball hit into the spectators' seating area and, depending on where it falls, is either a foul ball or a home run.

**intra-squad game** A game played between members of the same team, commonly during the early days of spring training.

**invisible man** *arch.* **1.** A sportswriter when things are going well for the home team and nothing negative is being written. **2.** An imaginary runner, employed in playground baseball and variations of softball, with fewer than four players on a side when it is a baserunner's turn to bat again. See also *ghost runner.*

**IP** Abbrev. for *innings pitched.*

**iron arm** The arm of a pitcher who is able to pitch effectively for long periods of time.

**iron-armed pitcher** Syn. of *iron mike.*

**iron bat** The bat of a player who is able to hit the ball consistently for distance.

**iron doughnut** See *doughnut.*

**iron glove 1.** A sloppy fielder, one who is prone to making errors. "All-Iron Glove Team" (*USA Today* headline for list of leading error-makers, June 6, 1986). **2.** The glove of a player who is not a good fielder. Charlie Hough has been widely quoted on Texas Ranger teammate Pete Incaviglia: "He has a glove contract with U.S. Steel."

**iron hand** A fielder who plays as though his hands were made of iron. See also *metal.*

**iron man 1.** A pitcher who works without seeming to tire or lose concentration. The "iron" in this case refers to the durability of a pitcher who can pitch as often as the needs of the rotation dictate. Jim Bouton (*Ball Four,* 1970) says that the proper form of address for a player so gifted is: "Give me some steel, baby." **1st Use.** 1901. "Unless it is Joe McGinnity, is there any twirler with as strong an arm as Tony Mullane had when he worked for Louisville, St. Louis, and Cincinnati? The Count was the original Iron Man." (*The Sporting News,* Feb. 16; Barry Popik). **2.** *obs.* A pitcher who pitches two complete games back to back. New York Giants pitcher Joe "Iron Man" McGinnity was one of the first pitchers to earn the nickname. On three occasions in one month during the 1903 season he won both games of a doubleheader. McGinnity wore the title well as evidenced by a headline from the *Police Gazette* in the mid-1920s: " 'Iron Man' McGinnity Still Pitching at Fifty-Four" (for Dubuque of the Class D Mississippi Valley League). **1st Use.** 1900. "Had it not been for McGinnity, who has truly proven his title to be called the 'Iron Man' there would have been a worse tale to tell. But he went in on consecutive days and pulled out a draw and a victory." (*The Sporting News,* Sept. 15; Barry Popik). But Noel Hynd (*The Giants of the Polo Grounds,* 1988) points out: "Contrary to present-day legend McGinnity did not obtain his nickname of 'Iron Man' through the durability of his arm. Rather when he first came to pitch in New York he already had the nickname. It was a relic of his minor league days with Kansas City, where a sportswriter had asked him what he did in the offseason. 'I work in a foundry,' McGinnity had replied, 'I'm an iron

**Iron man.** *Joseph McGinnity.*

man.'" **3.** Any player who is tough, not easily injured, and seldom, if ever, misses a game. "The Iron Man" and "The Iron Horse" were two of Lou Gehrig's nicknames earned while playing 2,130 consecutive games (1925–39). The most recent "Iron Man" is Cal Ripken Jr. who earned the title by playing in 2,632 consecutive games (1982–98). **4.** *arch.* The price of admission to a ball game. **Etymology.** Joseph McBride (*High and Inside,* 1980) noted: "Silver dollars were once called 'iron men,' and $1 was formerly a common price for a general-admission ticket." The term showed up often in T. A. Dorgan's cartoons: "You know papa left me two million iron men and I must spend it

some way" (*San Francisco Examiner,* Aug. 22, 1911; Peter Tamony).

**iron mike** A generic name for any mechanized pitching device used in batting practice. Although mechanical *pitching machines* have been in existence since the late 19th century, it was not until the Brooklyn Dodgers used one in their spring-training camp just after World War II that they became accepted. They are as fast as their warm-blooded counterparts and have improved over the years, but they still lack the cleverness and deceptive ability of humans. Syn. *iron-armed pitcher; mechanical pitching machine.* **Etymology/1st Use.** 1950. *Time* magazine (Apr. 17) contained an article entitled "Iron Mike" about a highly publicized game between Wake Forest and North Carolina. In the game both teams batted against the machine. "Wake Forest College, which calls its apparatus 'Iron Mike,' got eleven hits (three of them homers), and waited out Iron Mike for two walks."

**irregular 1.** A player for a ragtag team of amateur baseball or softball players put together to face a team that regularly plays together. Irregulars are often given special compensatory opportunities to score. An item in the company newsletter (Sept. 1972) of the Foster Manufacturing Co., Wilton, Maine, tells of a formula for irregular scoring that "allows 7 runs for each run scored by a player over 35 years of age, and 7½ runs for each run scored by a player 35 years old who is also overweight 35 or more pounds." **2.** A player who is normally found on the bench; one who is not a regular starter.

**irregular regular** An off-and-on type of player.

**irrevocable waivers** A form of *waivers* in which the player, by clearing waivers without being claimed, is released.

**I-70 Series** A nickname for the 1985 all-Missouri World Series between the St. Louis Cardinals and the Kansas City Royals, whose cities are linked by Interstate Highway 70. See also *Show-Me Series.*

**issue a pass** To walk a batter.

**"it ain't over, 'til it's over"** An aphorism that summarizes baseball's ability to go down to the last moment of play. It is also Yogi Berra's most famous line, which has become a baseball axiom. "Yogi's line gets better and better," was the reaction of John McNamara to the late-inning heroics on display during the 1986 American League Championship Series (*Cleveland Plain Dealer,* Oct. 16, 1986). **Extended Use.** Widely applied to the world at large.

**"it's only a game"** The ritualized reassurance given to those (esp. youngsters) who have lost a game that it is, in fact, not the end of the world. It is deemed a "famous speech by [Little League] parents in a station wagon on the way home" (Marian Edelman Borden, *New York Times,* undated).

**ivory 1.** One or more skilled ballplayers who are considered a valuable commodity. "Cuba, which long has developed 'ivory' for the American market, has splendid representatives in Conrado Marrero, Sandy Consuegra, and Minnie Minoso" (Fred G. Lieb, *Baseball Magazine,* Aug. 1953). **1st Use.** 1913. "[Ivory is] a natural growth found in the bush league jungle, and polished up in the major league" (J. E. Sherwood, *Baseball Magazine,* Sept.). **2.** A high-priced rookie. **Usage Note.** The link between the hard, white matter (a variety of dentine) and baseball players is that both are valuable commodities.

**ivory-headed** Dumb. Martin Rothan (*New Baseball Rules and Decisions,* 1947) explained that an ivory-headed player is one "who doesn't act quick, makes the wrong play, does not use his brains." **Usage Note.** Thomas P. McDonald (letter, Apr. 13, 1991) noted that "bone-headed" is a common expression for dumbness: "Perhaps 'ivory-headed' derives in some convoluted way from the common misconception that ivory is bone, although as far as I know, either term could have been derived from the other. But there are certainly instances in which ivory and bone are used in synonymous fashion (e.g., piano keys, which are called both bones and ivories)." Tris Speaker was quoted by Donald Gropman (*Say It Ain't So, Joe!,* 1979): "I pulled an ivory play, a boner pure and simple." Note the contrary use of "ivory" as signifying both a dumb player and a skillful player (see *ivory*).

**ivory hunter** A scout who searches for young, talented players. "The baseball scouts, who call themselves ivory hunters, met the other night . . . to honor John J. 'Patty' Cottrell, voted Pro Scout of the Year" (Art Rosenbaum, *San Francisco Chronicle,* Feb. 15, 1974; Peter Tamony). **1st Use.** 1915. "You'll pick up diamond tiaras just about as often as you will pitchers who are undiscovered wonders. Any ivory hunter will tell you that." (Burt L. Standish, *Covering the Look-in Corner;* David Shulman). **Extended Use.** Arch. student slang for a corporate recruiter who visits college campuses.

**ivory tip** *arch.* A dumb player or person. "To be dubbed a bonehead in a fashionable New York Club, one has to have an ivory-tip of surpassing solidity" (*Munsey's Magazine,* July 1913; Peter Tamony). Syn. "ivory top."

**IW** Scorecard abbrev. for *intentional walk.*

# J

**jab** To hit the ball for a short distance. **1st Use.** 1920. (*Spalding's Official Base Ball Guide;* Edward J. Nichols).

**jack 1.** *n.* A home run. "Dude, I'm a 20-jack guy" (Brady Anderson, quoted in *Baltimore Sun,* Apr. 27, 1996). **2.** *v.* To hit a ball a great distance; e.g., "Smith jacked a three-run homer in the ninth." **3.** To remove a pitcher from the game. Syn. *jerk,* 2. **1st Use.** 1931. (*The World* [New York], Feb. 25; Edward J. Nichols).

**Jackie Robinson Award** Since 1987, the official name for the *Rookie of the Year Award,* named for the player who was the first Rookie of the Year in 1947.

**jackpot** Syn. of *grand slam,* 1.

**jackrabbit 1.** A baseball that seems to carry farther than most regular balls. The term comes back into use every time the number of home runs hit rises dramatically, prompting calls of a "lively" ball: "Rumors go the rounds that the manufacturers are still experimenting with the ball in hope of eliminating much of the jackrabbit" (*New York Press,* Jan. 28, 1931). See also *juiced ball.* Syn. "jackrabbit ball." **1st Use.** 1912. (*New York Tribune,* Sept. 11; Edward J. Nichols). **2.** A speedy ballplayer. "I was watching the game on TV the other day and it was amazing the way the Cardinal outfielders were running around out there. Jackrabbits. Jackrabbits all over the place." (Atlanta Braves general manager Bobby Cox, quoted in *New York Post,* June 29, 1987).

**jake 1.** *n.* A player who is often out of the lineup because of a real or imagined ailment; a player who will not exert himself or is given to loafing or stalling. Syn. *jaker.* **2.** *v.* To loaf or to stall. Press reports had New York Yankees owner George Steinbrenner saying that Lou Piniella had accused Rickey Henderson of "jaking it" and asked to have him traded (*Tampa Tribune,* Aug. 12, 1987). **Usage Note.** A serious charge. "Do you want to know what they were saying about [Houston Astros pitcher] J. R. Richard even three days ago?" wrote Art Spander (*San Francisco Examiner,* Aug. 1, 1980; Peter Tamony) after Richard was found to have a potentially fatal blood clot. "They were saying that he was 'jaking,' that he could have played but didn't want to, that he was letting down his teammates." **1st Use.** 1927. According to Frank Graham (*New York Sun,* July 18), the term "jake," meaning one who stalls, was applied by Earle Combs to New York Yankees teammate Tony Lazzeri. Graham recorded their conversation: "'I never thought you'd be a jake,' remarked Combs. 'I'm not a jake,' replied Lazzeri. 'Hug [Yankee manager Miller Huggins] just told me [Mark] Koenig was going to play shortstop and [Ray] Morehart second base. What could I do?'" Graham also noted that the term derived from American League manager and first baseman Garland "Jake" Stahl (1903–19). **Etymology.** There is universal agreement that the term derived from Stahl; however, there is some dispute as to why. One theory, favored by *The Sporting News,* Hy Turkin, and others, says that Stahl was an aggressive player with a

**Jake.** *Managers Garland "Jake" Stahl of the Red Sox (l.) and John McGraw of the Giants pose for the traditional handshake before the 1912 World Series.*

lot of hustle whose trip to eponymity came about because his name was pronounced "stall." Thomas P. Shea (*Baseball Nicknames,* 1946) insists that when Stahl played for the Boston Red Sox he refused to play first base because of a bad foot and that is where the loafing connection was made.

**jaker** Syn. of *jake,* 1.

**jam 1.** *n.* A difficult situation during a game. Usually it is said that a pitcher is in a "jam" when the opposing team is in a position to score, such as when the bases are loaded with no outs. See also *crunch.* Syn. *hook,* 9. **2.** *v.* See *jam the batter.* **3.** *v.* To load the bases; e.g., "Smith jammed the bases after issuing his third consecutive walk." **4.** *arch.* A rally. "When the 'jam is on,' a rally is under way" (*Giant Book of Sports,* 1948).

**jamball** A ball pitched inside in such a way that it is difficult for a batter to hit it solidly or get good wood on it.

**jammer** A fastball on the fists; a fastball or slider that moves in on the batter.

**jam sandwich** "A term used when a batter gets hit on the fists by a pitcher with some good cheese" (John Maffei, *Padres Magazine,* 1993).

**jam shot 1.** A brushback pitch. **2.** A knockdown pitch.

**jam the batter** To throw the ball close to the batter, making it difficult for him to hit successfully and keeping him off balance; to throw inside. The intention is not to hit the batter, but rather make him a lot less effective by forcing him to hit with the lower end of his bat.

**Japanese liner** *arch.* A *Texas Leaguer* in the Pacific Coast League.

**jar** To bat a ball hard; e.g., "Smith jarred the pitcher with a line drive to left." **1st Use.** 1908. (*Baseball Magazine,* Dec.; Edward J. Nichols).

**jaw** To argue; e.g., "Smith jawed the umpire over a call." **1st Use.** 1898. (*New York Tribune,* June 16; Edward J. Nichols).

**Jawn Titus** *arch.* A spectacular catch; a *circus catch.* **1st Use.** 1917. (*American Magazine,* July; Edward J. Nichols). **Etymology.** Nichols noted: "Derivation uncertain, but may refer to a player named [John] Titus [Philadelphia Phillies outfielder, 1903–12] . . . who may have been known for making sensational catches."

**jay** *arch.* A derogatory term for an amateur player.

**jeep** *arch.* A small, fast player in the immediate post–World War II era.

**jellyball** Syn. of *grease ball.*

**jelly bean** *arch.* A new, inexperienced player; a *rookie,* 1.

**jerk 1.** To hit an inside pitch out of the park. **2.** Syn. of *jack,* 3. **1st Use.** 1912. (*New York Tribune,* Apr. 21; Edward J. Nichols).

**jersey** A long-sleeved pullover that may be worn under a player's uniform shirt.

**Jesse James** A players' term for *umpire* because of what he "robs" from them. Before there were three umpires for each game, it was common to refer to the two umps as "Jesse and Frank" or "the James Brothers."

**Jesse James single** A base hit that is allowed when a batted ball strikes an umpire.

**J. G. Taylor Spink Award** An annual award presented by the Baseball Writers Association of America for "major contributions" to baseball writing. The award is presented during the annual Hall of Fame induction ceremonies at Cooperstown, N.Y., and winners are often erroneously referred to as inductees into the Hall's "writers wing." Named for the late editor of *The Sporting News.*

**Jim Dandy** An admirable person, thing, or feat; a prime example; something of superior quality. **1st Use.** 1887. The term, which the *Oxford English Dictionary* traces in a nonbaseball context to 1887, shows up quickly in baseball writing. In fact, Gerald Cohen has written that his work on the baseball columns of *The World* (New York) "provides the startling indication that 'jim-dandy' either arose in baseball speech or was spread into standard English by it." His earliest published example from *The World* (June 19, 1887): "The Giants gave the local patrons of the game a couple of surprises during the past week, and whereas on Wednesday night they were proclaimed 'Jim Dandy' players, they were on Thursday declared to be 'no good.'"

**jineger** *arch.* Vigor or energy. The term may have derived from "ginger," "vinegar," or a combination of the two. Also spelled "jinnegar."

**Jints** A colloquialism for the Giants when they were in New York City. To call the Giants "the Jints" was to use a friendly nickname, akin to calling the Brooklyn Dodgers "Dem Bums."

**jinx 1.** *n.* A run of bad luck. See also *hoodoo; whammy.* **2.** *v.* To create bad luck. "Most of them think a change in hotels would surely 'jinx' or hoodoo them" (*Literary Digest,* May 9, 1914; Peter Tamony). **Usage Note.** "Jinx" is a 20th-century word that was so strongly associated with the game of baseball that it appears as baseball slang—rather than general slang—as late as 1927 (so identified

by V. Samuels, *American Speech,* Feb.). John B. Foster (*Collier's New Dictionary of the English Language,* 1908) defined it as "another name for a ball player's superstitious ideas." Lest anyone suggest that this is an idea of the past, the late 1980s and early 1990s have seen the emergence of the Toronto Blue Jays jinx, to join established curses and jinxes belonging to the Boston Red Sox, Chicago Cubs, and those hapless souls who appear on the covers of *Sports Illustrated.* **Etymology/1st Use.** 1912. Alfred H. Holt (*Phrase and Word Origins,* 1936) linked the use of the term in baseball (the *Oxford English Dictionary* cites a 1912 usage by Christy Mathewson) for "a hoodoo of some sort" and the wrynecked woodpecker or "jynx," which was associated with charms and spells; according to Holt, "that particular bird was sometimes used to cast charms." Webb Garrison (*Why You Say It,* 1954) tells more of the bird: "Medieval scholars considered it to have special links with occult forces. So jynx feathers were widely used in making 'philtres, allurements, baits and enticements' for the lovelorn. Jumping the Atlantic, the name of the wizard's bird [of preference] became linked with voodoo and other forms of black magic—hence, any symbol of bad luck is known as a jinx." **Extended Use.** Bad luck in all realms.

**jock 1.** *n.* An athlete. **2.** *n.* Short for *jockstrap.* **3.** *v.* To be overpowered. "We were getting jocked, and by the sixth inning, I realized that we were going through an awful lot of pitchers" (Bill Lee, *The Wrong Stuff,* 1984; Charles D. Poe).

**jockey 1.** *n.* A player who bedevils or "rides" the opposition. Sometimes called a *bench jockey* because the heckler often comes from the dugout where he also "rides" the bench or the pine. Defined by William Morris (*It's Easy to Increase Your Vocabulary,* 1957) as: "A loud voiced, often sharp-witted player who continuously ridicules the opposing players with well-timed references to their real or supposed inadequacies of antecedents." **1st Use.** 1927. (*New York Sun,* July 18; Edward J. Nichols). **Etymology.** An obvious and neat play on the word "ride," a point that is made in explanations of the term when it was still new; e.g., Frankie Frisch, writing about the Gashouse Gang: "It was bitterly fought and there was much jockeying between the benches. A jockey is a player who verbally rides the opposition from the dugout, and we had some great ones on our side." (*Saturday Evening Post,* June 4, 1936). **2.** *v.* To heckle the opposition and/or the umpires; "to reveal an opponent's private life—but loudly, and sarcastically when possible" (Gordon S. "Mickey" Cochrane, *Baseball: The Fan's Game,* 1939).

**jockeying** Yelling derisive comments at opposing players and umpires. A report on an amateur game that ended in a brawl contained this telling line: "But wildness occasioned by constant jockeying from the Portola bench, provided Gentile's downfall" (*San Francisco Examiner,* Jan. 20, 1951; Peter Tamony).

**jockey silks** A derisive name for the bright uniform colors worn by American Association (1882–91) players. (Jonathan Fraser Light, *The Cultural Encyclopedia of Baseball,* 1997).

**jockstrap** An *athletic supporter.* Syn. *jock,* 2. **1st Use.** 1919. "You can enjoy perfect comfort and freedom. Schnoter's Suspensories and Jock Straps have gained their widespread popularity by quality, wear, fit and low price." (*The Billboard* [Cincinnati], Dec. 20; Peter Tamony).

**jockstrap sniffing** A derogatory term for a sportswriter's quest for a story or good quote on an otherwise slow day. Leonard Shecter (*The Jocks,* 1969; Charles D. Poe) writes that the term refers to the fact that some sportswriters "must go to the clubhouse and elicit clever quotes from dull men."

**Joe Bush** A college ballplayer, esp. one who shows his lack of experience. See also *bush,* 3.

**Joe College** An individual who typifies the enthusiasm of collegiate athletics. **Etymology.** J. L. Kuethe (*American Speech,* June 1932), writing on college slang, reported that "Joe" was a "term used to designate anyone whose real name is unknown. When used with a place or profession 'Joe' indicates a perfect example of the type connected with that place or profession. Thus 'Joe College' is the perfect specimen of the college man."

**Joe Cronin Award** An annual award given for "distinguished achievement" by an American

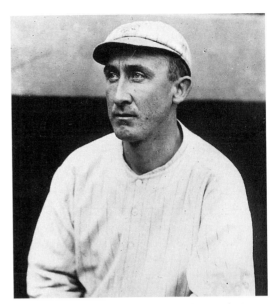

**John Anderson.** *Nicknamed "The Terrible Swede," Anderson failed to notice that the bases were loaded when he tried to steal.*

League player. It is named for the former American League president and Hall of Fame shortstop.

**Joe Quote** A player who talks a lot, esp. to the press; a *motormouth.*

**John Anderson** The particular boner committed when a runner attempts to steal an occupied base. The term is named for the outfielder/first baseman who, while playing for the New York Highlanders in 1904, tried to steal with the bases loaded. Sometimes spelled "john anderson," as in "pulling a john anderson."

**John fan** *arch.* A typical male enthusiast.

**Johnson & Johnson 1.** A player who commonly has adhesive tape showing. **2.** A player who is accident prone or easily hurt. **1st Use.** 1937. (*New York Daily News,* Sept. 5; Edward J. Nichols). **Etymology.** Named for the manufacturer of bandages and surgical dressings.

**John T. Brush Rules** See *Brush Rules.*

**Jonah 1.** *v./arch.* To bring bad luck. "It is a well-known fact that a cross-eyed man will Jonah the squarest ballgame that was ever played" (*The*

Drawn by E. W. Kemble

"JUDGMENT!"—A PROBLEM FOR THE UMPIRE

**Judgment call.**

*World* [New York], Aug. 28, 1888). **2.** *n./arch.* A person or thing that brings bad luck; e.g., a beautiful woman who rattles the players on the field. **1st Use.** 1886. "The new hats have certainly been a dead Jonah to Gus and his men as they have lost five to the Browns" (*Sporting Life,* Apr. 21; Barry Popik). **3.** *n./arch.* One who suffers bad luck. **Usage Note.** According to Gerald Cohen (*Comments on Etymology,* Apr. 1, 1986), the term had great significance in the baseball world of the 1880s and 1890s, as indicated by the three variations given above. **Etymology.** The term is a reference to the Jonah of the Bible who, before he was thrown to the whale that devoured him, had brought the wrath of God down on his ship. The term has had a long history in nautical talk. Robert Hendrickson (*Salty Words,* 1984) noted: "A 'Jonah' still means a bringer of bad luck who spoils the plans of others. The phrase is so popular that it has even become a verb, 'Don't jonah me!'"

**jonrun** A Spanish (pochismo) term for home run.

**journey** A baseball game.

**journeyman** A veteran ballplayer who is reliable but not a star; esp. one who has played for several teams.

**joy spot** Syn. of *sweet spot.*

**joy zone** Syn. of *sweet spot.*

**J. Pluvius** Syn. of *Jupe Pluvius.*

**judgment call** A ruling by an umpire for a situation that is not specifically covered in the rule book; e.g., when Dave Kingman sent a towering fly through the Metrodome roof, the umpire ruled it a ground-rule double.

**judy** Syn. of *Punch-and-Judy hitter.*

**Judy hitter** Syn. of *Punch-and-Judy hitter.*

**jughandle** A curveball with a sharp break or broad arc that bends like the handle of a jug. See also *rainbow,* 1; *roundhouse curve.* Also spelled "jug handle"; "jug-handle." Syn. "jughandle curve." **Etymology/1st Use.** 1920. Edward J. Nichols (*An Historical Dictionary of Baseball Terminology,* Ph.D. dissertation, 1939) reported that the term was a nickname for Pittsburgh Pirates pitcher John Morrison in the 1920s "because of his sharp-breaking curve."

**juggle** To mishandle a batted or thrown ball. While a fielder may juggle a ball without dropping it, the act may consume enough time to allow a runner to be safe who otherwise would have been put out. See also *bobble,* 1. **1st Use.** 1873. (*New York Herald,* Sept. 13; Edward J. Nichols).

**Jugs gun** A *radar gun* used to measure the velocity of a pitched ball between 3 to 5 feet after it leaves the pitcher's hand. The early reading eliminates variables, ensuring consistency, and is generally considered to be three or four miles per hour faster than the *Ra-gun*. The average major-league fastball registers 90 mph on the Jugs gun. It is manufactured by Jugs Pitching Machines or by Jugs Co., Portland, Ore. Sometimes spelled "jugs gun"; "JUGS gun." Syn. "Jugs."

**juice 1.** To hit the ball with great power for distance; to crush the ball. **2.** To make the baseball more lively. **3.** To alter a baseball so that its flight pattern will not be normal; e.g., "Smith juiced up the ball so that it would swerve."

**juiced ball** A baseball with extra carrying power. The 1993 and 1994 baseballs were believed by some to have been juiced. Others did not agree: "It ain't juiced for me, that's for sure" (Texas Rangers third baseman Dean Palmer, quoted in *USA Today,* May 10, 1994). See also *jackrabbit,* 1. Syn. "juice ball."

**jump 1.** *n.* The first step of a baserunner to leave a base quickly when the ball is pitched. A good jump involves the distance taken by the runner and his timing of the pitcher's motion. **2.** *n.* The move that a fielder makes toward the ball as soon as it is hit; e.g., "Smith got a good jump on the ball on the crack of the bat." **3.** *v.* For a baserunner or fielder to move quickly on the sound of the ball making contact with the bat; e.g., "Outfielder Smith jumped on the ball when he heard the crack of the bat." **4.** *v.* For a batted ball to take off with an extra spurt. "I know the way the ball can jump off my bat. Seems like one at-bat I'll have it, and the next two or three it might be gone." (Jack Clark, quoted in *St. Louis Post-Dispatch,* May 29, 1987). **5.** *n.* The hopping motion on a good fastball as it crosses the plate. Hugh S. Fullerton (*American Magazine,* June 1912) explained: "Sometimes pitchers throw much faster than at others, and on such days they 'have the jump on the fast one' which means that the ball, revolving rapidly, piles up a mound of compressed air and actually jumps over it, rising sometimes, it seems, an inch or two during its sudden leap before resuming its way to

the plate." **6.** *v.* To leave a baseball team without permission. **1st Use.** 1888. "Not a word has been heard from Smith, and it is presumed he will jump his contract" (*The Sporting News,* Mar. 29; David Shulman). **7.** *v./arch.* To break one's contract. See also *contract-jumper.* **1st Use.** 1886. "There was a time when [he] was ripping Jack up the back for jumping the Clevelands" (*The Sporting News,* May 24; David Shulman). **8.** *n.* An early lead in a game; e.g., "The Yankees got the jump on the Orioles by scoring three runs in the first inning." **9.** *v.* To lunge at a pitch, as though swinging for the fences or anticipating a different type of pitch. **10.** *n.* A promotion from the minor leagues to the major leagues; e.g., "Jones made the jump to Cincinnati yesterday."

**jump around** See *home plate is jumping around.*

**jumper** A player who has left a team, without permission, to play elsewhere or engage in another line of work; a player who has broken his contract with a team. After Sal Maglie left the New York Giants to play in the outlaw Mexican League, he returned to the Giants; commenting on Maglie's return, Giants manager Leo Durocher wrote: "I'll play an elephant if he can do the job, so why shouldn't I play a jumper" (*Nice Guys Finish Last,* 1975; Charles D. Poe). See also *contract-jumper.*

**jumping jack** A player who shows off; a *grandstand player.*

**jump on 1.** To hit the ball hard; e.g., "Smith jumped on Jones's fastball and lined it to center." **2.** To take control of a baseball game; e.g., "The Giants jumped on the Dodgers with eight runs in the first inning."

**June bug** A rookie who is sent back down to the minor leagues by early summer. **1st Use.** 1950. "June Bug [is a] recruit who is on his way back to the minor leagues by June" (Sam Nisenson, *A Handy Illustrated Guide to Baseball;* David Shulman).

**June swoon** The falling apart after Memorial Day of a team that got off to a good start in Apr. and May. The term has been applied to several teams, but it has been most closely associated with the San Francisco Giants since the franchise moved there from New York in 1958. Tom Weir (*USA Today,* May 29, 1986) noted that since moving to San Francisco the team had a composite record of 373–405 in the month of June (not good, not awful); he added: "If the Giants of the Mays-McCovey-Marichal era hadn't always been so hot in April and May—387–256 from 1958–71—the supposed swoon never would have been coined." **Etymology.** Sportswriter Art Rosenbaum, who popularized the phrase in the late 1950s and early 1960s, when the Giants seemed destined for an annual fall from the top of the National League standings after quick starts, wrote (*San Francisco Chronicle,* June 22, 1989): "It just slipped into my typewriter, and it became an annual story. The songs of those days rhymed with June as in swoon, moon, tune—and the Giants were accommodating to the phrase. They would fall dead in that month every year. It's one of those things you write about and not think about until later."

Rosenbaum first used "June Swoon" in Summer 1959, but according to researchers at the Tamony Collection at the Univ. of Missouri, the first printed use of the term came in *Time* magazine (June 17, 1957). A nonbyline story on Nellie Fox and the Chicago White Sox made just a passing reference: "The White Sox get off to a fast start, then fall into a 'June Swoon.'"

Over the years Rosenbaum has written several articles claiming to have started the Swoon craze, although he acknowledged that Bob Stevens, the *Chronicle*'s baseball writer at the time, may have actually coined the term. But Rosenbaum didn't seem too disappointed to find the phrase had preceded his usage. "I knew Peter Tamony, and if he said that's where it began, that's good enough for me. He would take a phrase, any phrase or jargon, and go back and research it until he found the very origin of it and what it meant."

**junior circuit** The *American League,* because it came into being when the National League was 25 years old. The term is still used but much less commonly than it was before World War II. Compare *senior circuit.*

**Junior World Series** Syn. of *Little World Series.*

**junk** The assortment of slower and softer pitches characterized by erratic and deceptive movement, as opposed to the standard fastballs and curveballs. Bert Dunne (*The Folger Dictionary of Baseball,* 1958) defined the term as "slowly-thrown balls for which hitter must supply his own power." Something of a misnomer, junk can be as effective as the faster stuff. "An old Cuban named Conrado Marrero has buried American League under a load of 'junk'" (*Life* magazine, June 11, 1951; Peter Tamony). **1st Use.** 1949. "[Mickey] Haefner, noted for his knuckle ball, said he didn't use much 'junk'" (Associated Press dispatch on a one-hitter thrown by Washington Senators pitcher Haefner, May 11; Peter Tamony).

**junk ball** An unorthodox, tricky, or abnormal pitch. **1st Use.** 1944. "His variety of pitches, and his frequent reliance on 'junk balls' serves to set up his pitches" (*Baseball Magazine,* Dec.; David Shulman).

**junkballer** A pitcher who relies on off-speed pitches and trickery rather than the fastball. Also spelled "junk baller." Syn. *junk man;* "junk pitcher." **Usage Note.** Despite how it sounds, the term carries with it a certain admiration. Hoyt Wilhelm, Eddie Lopat, Doyle Alexander, and Stu Miller have been noted as junkballers. It was said of Miller that he had three speeds: slow, slower, and slowest.

**junk man** Syn of *junkballer.*

**Jupe Pluvius** *arch.* Rain that interrupts or mars a game. Syn. *J. Pluvius; Old Pluvy.* **1st Use.** 1868. (*New York Herald,* Aug. 13; Edward J. Nichols). **Etymology.** From the ancient incantation to Jupiter Pluvius, with "Pluvius" being an ancient epithet for Jupiter as rainmaker.

# K

**K 1.** The symbol for *strikeout,* 2. The "K" has long been a staple of headlines for the simple reason that it takes up much less space than the word "strikeout"; e.g., "[Bob] Feller Setting 'K' Record" (*San Francisco Call-Bulletin,* June 5, 1946; Peter Tamony). Fans sometimes keep track of the number of strikeouts a pitcher has thrown by hanging signs that read "K" over the ballpark railings. "It's undeniable that Dr. K is a great moniker for Dwight Gooden, and so are the K banners that unfurl from the cheap seats in Shea Stadium every time he puts the Kibosh on an opposing batter" (Michael Olmert, *Washington Post,* May 4, 1986). **Etymology.** There are two theories as to how "K" came to stand for strikeout. When Henry Chadwick invented a scoring system in 1861, he developed a series of letter symbols. He selected "K" for "struck out" and later (1883) explained the decision: "It was the prominent letter of the word 'strike,' as far as remembering the word was concerned." The second version is similar except that the symbol was created by M. J. Kelly of the *New York Herald* and not by Chadwick. The symbol was given new prominence with the nicknaming of strikeout pitcher Dwight Gooden as "Dr. K." **2.** *n.* Syn. of *strikeout,* 2; e.g., "The K Factor" (title of article in *Sports Illustrated*). Plural is "K's." **3.** *v.* To *strike out,* 2; e.g., "Smith K'd Jones with fastballs."

**ꓘ** (backwards K) Scorecard symbol for a strikeout on a called third strike. Syn. *KC.*

**kalsomine** *arch.* To hold scoreless; to whitewash. **Etymology.** Patrick Ercolano (*Fungoes, Floaters and Fork Balls,* 1987) explained that the term was so called "because calcimine—which some creative misspeller long ago turned into 'kalsomine'—is a type of whitewash, and 'whitewash' is a synonym for 'shut out.'"

**kangaroo** *n.* 1. A runner who leaps or takes high strides. **2.** *v.* To bounce over. "That ball almost kangarooed over Davis's head" (Vin Scully, All-Star Game broadcast, July 11, 1989).

**kangaroo ball** A lively baseball. "Salt Lake was using a kangaroo ball and the theory was soberly propounded that singles went for homers because the air was thin" (Westbrook Pegler, *San Francisco Call-Bulletin,* May 14, 1958; Peter Tamony). See also *rabbit ball,* 1.

**kangaroo cave** *arch.* A section of the grandstand reserved for sportswriters. **1st Use.** 1908. (*New York Evening Journal,* Aug. 21; Edward J. Nichols).

**kangaroo court** A clubhouse session during which a senior player assesses guilt and small fines for errors and omissions on the field. "For the chief justice of the Red Sox Kangaroo Kourt, nothing else would do" (Paul Hoynes, on Don Baylor, *Cleveland Plain Dealer,* Oct. 17, 1986). Frank Robinson was the self-appointed judge of the Baltimore Orioles Kangaroo Court of the late 1960s: he would don a mop as a headdress before games to conduct trials and impose fines, which were put aside for postseason parties. Teams establish kangaroo courts to create team unity. **Etymology.** The term has a long history as an irregular or mock court, such as one convened by prisoners in a jail. They are characterized by a disregard of normal court procedures. Darryl Lyman (*The Animal Things We Say,* 1983) states that the expression apparently stems from the jumping of the kangaroo and the fact that "the principles of law and justice are disregarded or perverted (that is, 'jumped' over)" in such a court. Charles Earle Funk (*A Hog on Ice,* 1948) guesses that the term may refer to the idea that the earliest kangaroo courts (about the time of the 1849 Gold Rush) were convened to try "jumpers" (those who stole the mining claims of others).

**kangaroo hop** An Australian term for a leadoff first base (*Sports Illustrated,* July 27, 1981). Syn. *'roo hop.*

**Kansas City Athletics** The name of the American League franchise in Kansas City, Mo., from 1955 through the 1967 season. It had come from Philadelphia and moved on to Oakland, Calif.

**Kansas City Royals** The name of the American League Central Division franchise located in Kansas City, Mo. A 1969 expansion club, the "royal" in the team's name is an allusion to American Royal Parade, a major event in the livestock world. The name was selected from entries submitted in a contest held among the fans.

**KC** Scorecard symbol for a strikeout on a called third strike. Syn. ꓘ.

**K corner** The left-field corner of the upper deck at Shea Stadium where fans hung cardboard K's over the railing every time New York Mets pitcher Dwight Gooden got a strikeout. The custom of counting K's started in the 1985 season.

**keep alive** To prolong a rally; e.g., "Smith and Jones kept the inning alive by hitting back-to-back doubles."

**"keep both hands on the ball"** [softball term] An instruction given to softball pitchers who legally must have both hands in front of the body and on the ball before delivering it.

**"keep him honest"** An instruction given to the pitcher to throw strikes, the idea being that if the batter is to reach base, he should earn it with a hit rather than a walk.

**keep one's head in the locker** To have little or nothing to say; to lack the ability to communicate.

**keep the team in the game** For a starting pitcher to keep the score close even though his team may not be leading. Typically, a pitcher leaving the game in the sixth inning with a 1–0 deficit would be congratulated for "keeping the team in the game."

**"keep your eye on the ball"** An instruction or reminder given to a batter to watch the pitch carefully as it is delivered.

**keep your skirt down** To stay close to the ground to field a ground ball. Kenneth Forehand (letter, Apr. 29, 1994) explains its significance: "This may be one of the most used terms in baseball instruction in reference to a fielder (usually an infielder) who raises up on a ground ball and allows it to go between his legs."

**Kentucky wonder** *arch.* A pitch thrown close to the batter. **1st Use.** 1943. "Such a pitch is known as a 'bean ball,' 'Kentucky wonder,' or 'duster'" (Franklin P. Huddle, *American Speech,* Apr.).

**key 1.** *n.* A sign given to a player that reveals the pattern of a subsequent sign. **2.** *v.* To be instrumental in starting or ending a rally. "Frank Thomas keyed a seventh-inning comeback with a two-run single" (*Tampa Tribune,* Sept. 30, 1990).

**key hit** A timely hit that turns the game around or determines its outcome; e.g., "Smith's key hit in the ninth brought in the winning run."

**keyhole fastball** A fastball thrown with great precision, as if it could be thrown through a keyhole.

**keystone 1.** *n.* Syn. of *second base,* 1. **1st Use.** 1935. (Ralph H. Barbour, *How to Play Better Baseball;* David Shulman). **Etymology.** It is often claimed that the term is a play on the fact that many important, or "key," defensive plays involve second base. Hy Turkin (*Baseball Almanac,* 1955) posits a minority opinion: "Viewed from the plate, second base seems to be the middle of the arch formed by the basepaths. In architecture, a keystone is the tapering stone at the crown of an arch." Since these two explanations are complementary, they may both have been a factor in the creation of the term. **2.** *adj.* Describing defense or fielding up the middle of the infield. "Yeah, kid—you're the keystone tenant. But holding onto it depends on how well you do" (Ed Conrow, *Ellery Queen's Mystery Magazine,* Oct. 1986).

**keystone bag** Syn. of *second base,* 1. **1st Use.** 1910. "Everson dropped one in front of the rubber, Gibbie annexing [getting to] the keystone bag" (Christy Mathewson, *Won in the Ninth;* David Shulman).

**keystone combination** The shortstop and the second baseman, collectively.

**keystone hit** Syn. of *double,* 1.

**keystoner** *arch.* Syn. of *second baseman.*

**keystone sack** Syn. of *second base,* 1. **Usage Note.** Long regarded as a synonym by sportswriters tired of repeating the term "second base"; e.g., "A term used by baseball writers who are paid by the word, to designate second base. Generally believed to be stone from the number of runners who limp after sliding into it." (R. E. Sherwood, *Baseball Magazine,* Sept. 1913). **1st Use.** 1907. (*New York Evening Journal,* Apr. 8; Edward J. Nichols).

**kick 1.** *n.* An element of the pitcher's windup that occurs when he lowers his arms, raises his nonpivot leg, and strides toward home plate. Runners know that they have a better chance of stealing a base from a pitcher with a big kick. See also *leg kick.* **2.** *v.* To protest the decision of the umpire; to complain. In 1896, there was a ban on "kicking" or arguing with umpires. Baltimore Orioles manager Ned Hanlon argued vehemently against the ban (*Baltimore Sun,* July 8, 1996): "Had the Orioles had less of that aggressiveness, we would never have won any pennants. Players are only human, and when they are compelled to suppress all noise and excitement, their hearts will go down in their boots, they will become indifferent, the game will go glimmering and the public will leave in disgust." **1st Use.** 1883. "Ungentlemanly

language and conduct, 'kicking' against decisions by the umpire, and disgraceful conduct on the part of the players when off the field have kept an odor about the noble pastime that it does not deserve" (*Detroit Free Press,* Apr. 8; Peter Morris). **3.** *v.* To mishandle a ground ball; to commit an error; e.g., "Smith kicked one." See also *boot,* 2. **1st Use.** 1914. (Ring W. Lardner, *You Know Me Al;* Edward J. Nichols). **Etymology.** A play on the error that occurs when the fielder boots the ball as he tries to field it. **4.** *v.* For an umpire to make a bad or wrong decision; to blow a call or play. "If you kick it [a play], you just handle whatever arises from your error of judgment and go on with the game" (umpire Shag Crawford, quoted in Larry R. Gerlach, *The Men in Blue,* 1980).

**kick at the can** A chance to win. A team that is behind by a few runs has a last "kick at the can" in the ninth inning. The term probably derives from the childhood game of kick the can.

**kick away** *arch.* To lose a game through ineptitude and blundering. **1st Use.** 1918. (*Spalding's Official Base Ball Guide;* Edward J. Nichols).

**kickball** A variation of baseball, using a large rubber ball (approximately 10 inches in diameter) in which one bats with one's foot and outs are made when a runner is tagged or hit with the ball. John Thorndike (*Country Journal,* Aug. 1984) explained the backyard game: "Five can play on a side, or eight or ten. The pitcher rolls the ball toward the kicker, who may wait through any number of rolls for a good pitch. The rest of the rules are like baseball, save that the runner is out when hit with the ball, as well as when forced at a base." The game is a popular elementary school recess game.

**kick it out** To ensure that a ball rolling on the foul side of the first base line or third base line stays foul and does not become fair by rolling into fair territory by the fielder kicking the ball.

**kicks** Spikes or cleats; a ballplayer's shoes.

**Kid 1.** An affectionate nickname for a young, promising player; specif., Ted Williams, who was known as "The Kid." Boston Red Sox rookie shortstop Nomar Garciaparra assumed the nickname as the *Boston Globe* (Aug. 31, 1997) noted "The Kid kicked at the first base in frustration." **2.** See *"hiya, Kid."*

**kill 1.** *v.* To put out; e.g., "The Cubs killed Smith attempting to score." **2.** *n.* A putout.

**kill the ball** To swing at a pitch with great ferocity. The term is usually used facetiously since "killing" the ball usually leaves the batter off balance and the ball untouched. One of the commonest bits of advice given to youngsters learning the game is: "Don't try to kill the ball." **1st Use.** 1896. (Burt L. Standish, *Frank Merriwell's School Days;* Edward J. Nichols).

**kill the rally** To end a scoring opportunity, such as making the third out with the bases loaded.

**"kill the umpire"** The ritualistic response to a perceived bad call by the umpire. The phrase was first recorded in Ernest L. Thayer's 1888 poem "Casey at the Bat," although the term was in use earlier.

**kindergartner** *arch.* Syn. of *rookie,* 1. **1st Use.** 1917. (*New York Times,* Oct. 4; Edward J. Nichols).

*"Kill the umpire."*

**kindling** A team's bats rendered "useless" by a pitcher recording strikeouts and broken bats. Greg Maddux has been associated with creating splintered wood that is useful only to start fires.

**Kiner's Korner** The name of the left-field area at Forbes Field in Pittsburgh originally named *Greenberg Gardens,* created to increase home run production. By erecting a chicken-wire fence inside the scoreboard as a new wall, home run balls did not have to be hit as far. Greenberg Gardens was renamed in 1948 for Ralph Kiner, Pittsburgh's prodigious home run hitter.

**King and His Court, The** [softball term] A barnstorming softball team of four players led by Eddie Feigner, a pitcher who founded the team in 1946.

**King of Swat** A nickname applied to sluggers; specif., Babe Ruth.

**kiss** To hit a ball hard. Edward J. Nichols (*An Historical Dictionary of Baseball Terminology,* Ph.D. dissertation, 1939) notes the association of the term with "smack." **1st Use.** 1912. (*New York Tribune,* Sept. 5; Edward J. Nichols).

**"kiss it goodbye"** A salutation for a home run made famous by Pittsburgh Pirates announcer Bob Prince and used by Washington Senators broadcaster Shelby Whitfield.

**kitchen** The area of a batter's torso inside or at the edge of the high and inside portion of the strike zone. A fastball coming into this area—"pitchin' in the kitchen," "getting in his kitchen," "cheese for your kitchen," etc.—is esp. tough, if not impossible, to hit. The term is often used in more elaborate metaphors; e.g., "He got in his kitchen and broke a few dishes." The term may also be father to others of a culinary nature, such as "he comes to eat" for a ball that moves in on a batter. See also *pots and pans.*

**kitten ball** [softball term] A historic name for softball. Minneapolis was the second city to embrace the new game created in Chicago in 1887. It was introduced in Minneapolis in 1895 by Lt. Lewis Rober of Fire Company #11 as a form of exercise. The first team took the Kittens as their nickname and set up a small diamond in the vacant lot next to the station. The game soon took off in Minneapolis and, in honor of the first team, was called "kitten ball." The term still has application as 16-inch-softball players talk disparagingly about folks who play with a 12-inch ball. *Windy City Softball* (1976) tells of a "kitten ball" team from Indiana being introduced to Chicago-style ball, and being whomped. See also *diamond ball*. Also spelled "kittenball." Syn. *kitty-ball*.

**kitty-ball** Syn. of *kitten ball*.

**Klem's line** The line drawn in the dirt by umpire Bill Klem during an altercation. Any player or manager who crossed that line was ejected from the game. "Klem's line is a symbol applicable not only to player-umpire relationships, but to player-fan and player-player relationships as well. For an umpire or another player will take a surprising amount of abuse if the proper clichés are used and the matter doesn't drag on too long." (Tristram Potter Coffin, *The Old Ball Game*, 1971).

**Klutz World Series** A nickname for the 1945 World Series between the Detroit Tigers and the Chicago Cubs as played by unseasoned kids and retreads taking the place of regular players serving in the armed forces.

**knee-knocker** A low pitch intended to hit or come extremely close to a batter's legs.

**Knickerbocker Rules** The first codification of a game that could be termed baseball in the modern sense. The present rules of the game evolved from the basic set of 20 rules that was first adopted by Alexander J. Cartwright and a band of New Yorkers on Sept. 23, 1845, the same day on which they gave themselves the name Knickerbocker Base Ball Club, or Knickerbockers. The rules:

1st. Members must strictly observe the time agreed upon for exercise, and be punctual in their attendance.

2nd. When assembled for exercise, the President, or in his absence, the Vice-President shall appoint an Umpire, who shall keep the game in a book provided for that purpose, and note all violations of the By-Laws and Rules during the time of exercise.

3rd. The presiding officer shall designate two members as Captains, who shall retire and make the match to be played, observing at the same time that the players opposite to each other should be as nearly equal as possible, the choice of sides to then be tossed for, and the first in hand to be decided in like manner.

4th. The bases shall be from "home" to second base, forty-two paces; from first to third base, forty-two paces, equidistant.

5th. No stump match shall be played on a regular day of exercise.

6th. If there should not be a sufficient number of members of the Club present at the time agreed upon to commence exercise, gentlemen not members may be chosen in to make up the match, which shall not be broken up to take in members that may afterwards appear; but in all cases, members shall have the preference, when present, at the making of a match.

7th. If members appear after the game is commenced, they may be chosen in if mutually agreed upon.

8th. The game to consist of twenty-one counts, or aces; but at the conclusion an equal number of hands must be played.

9th. The ball must be pitched, not thrown, for the bat.

10th. A ball knocked out of the field, or outside the range of the first and third base, is foul.

11th. Three balls being struck at and missed and the last one caught, is a hand out; if not caught is considered fair, and the striker bound to run.

12th. If a ball be struck, or tipped, and caught, either flying or on the first bound, it is a hand out.

13th. A player running the bases shall be out, if the ball is in the hands of an adversary on the base, or the runner is touched with it before he makes his base; it being understood, however, that in no instance is a ball to be thrown at him.

14th. A player running who shall prevent an adversary from catching or getting the ball before making his base, is a hand out.

15th. Three hands out, all out.

16th. Players must take their strike in regular turn.

*Knock.*

17th. All disputes and differences relative to the game, to be decided by the Umpire, from which there is no appeal.

18th. No ace or base can be made on a foul strike.

19th. A runner cannot be put out in making one base, when a balk is made on the pitcher.

20th. But one base allowed when a ball bounds out of the field when struck.

An additional rule was adopted at the Club's fourth annual meeting (Apr. 1, 1848), which stated that the player running to first base is out without being touched with the ball if the fielder on first is holding the ball.

The rules were amended and expanded in 1854.

**knight of the keyboard** A term used by Ted Williams for a sportswriter. The term is usually used in the plural.

**knob** The rounded projection at the end of the bat handle that helps keep the bat from slipping out of the batter's hands.

**knock 1.** *v.* To hit the ball. **1st Use.** 1866. (Constitution and By-Laws of the Olympic Base Ball Club, Philadelphia; Edward J. Nichols). **2.** *n.* A batted ball, usually a base hit; specif., a *base knock.* "Get yourself a knock" is a suggestion a teammate will make to the next batter. **1st Use.** 1885. (Chicago *Inter-Ocean,* May 13; Edward J. Nichols). **3.** *v.* To be removed from a game; e.g., "Smith was knocked for baiting the umpire" or "Jones was knocked for a pinch hitter."

**knock down** *v.* To force a batter to drop to the ground with a pitch that either intimidates or directly hits the batter. Syn. *deck,* 3.

**knockdown** *n.* Syn. of *knockdown pitch.*

**knockdown pitch** A vicious pitch that forces the batter to drop to the ground to avoid getting hit. Bill Starr (*Clearing the Bases,* 1989) writes: "Brushback pitches do no harm. It's the knockdown pitch, a pitch at the batter's shoulders, that is dangerous. It's the rare pitcher who will use the batter's shoulders for a target." Compare *beanball; brushback pitch.* Syn. *knockdown; face ball,* 2; *throat cut-*

KNOCKED OUT OF THE BOX

*Knock out of the box.*

*ter.* **1st Use.** 1962. "There's the brushback, and there's the knockdown pitch" (*Saturday Evening Post,* June 30; David Shulman).

**knockdown rule** A rule stipulating that if in the umpire's judgment a pitch was thrown intentionally at a batter, the umpire may: a) expel the pitcher, or the pitcher and the manager, from the game; or b) warn the pitcher and managers of both teams that another such pitch will result in the immediate expulsion of that pitcher (or his replacement) and the manager [*Official Baseball Rules,* rule 8.02(d)]. The rule effectively has reduced knockdown pitches back to one per game.

**knock in** To bat in a run.

**knock on the door** For a minor leaguer to perform in such a manner that he is ready to join a major-league team.

**knockout comer** A young player who has the potential to be an outstanding player.

**knock out of the box** To cause a pitcher to be removed from the game, usually because of timely hitting. Syn. *send to the showers,* 2. **1st Use.** 1890. (*New York Press,* July 15; Edward J. Nichols). **Etymology.** "Knock out" has an obvious antecedent in prizefighting. **Extended Use.** To defeat or diminish.

**knock the ball over the fence** To hit a home run. **Extended Use.** The phrase is used as a metaphor for success in other fields. In 1967, President Lyndon B. Johnson said: "They booed Ted Williams, too, remember? They'll say about me I knocked the ball over the fence—but they don't like the way that he stands at the plate." (*New York Times,* May 30, 1968).

**knock the cover off the ball** To hit the ball with such great force that the ball, figuratively, unravels. Other "knock" phrases include: "knock the blood out of it," "knock the juice out of it," and "knock the cover loose." **1st Use.** 1873. (*New York Herald,* Aug. 10; Edward J. Nichols).

**knot** To even the score or a count; e.g., "An RBI single that knotted it again at 5 in the eighth" (*Baltimore Sun,* June 15, 1997) or "Smith took a strike to knot the count at 2 and 2." **1st Use.** 1915. (*Baseball Magazine,* Dec.; Edward J. Nichols).

**knothole club 1.** *arch.* A group of young fans who try to see a baseball game without paying admission. **2.** A group of young fans formed by a major-league team as a promotional effort. Typically, youngsters would get a card that would enable them to receive discounted or free tickets to games and the right to attend special clinics. It is generally agreed that the St. Louis Cardinals under Branch Rickey in 1917 was the first team to organize a knothole club. The Brooklyn Dodgers shepherded 2,256,000 youngsters into Ebbets Field on free Knothole Club passes between 1940 and 1957, the year the Dodgers left Brooklyn. See also *knothole gang.* **Etymology.** From the image, favored by cartoonists and illustrators, of youngsters watching the game through knotholes in the tight wooden outfield fence.

**knothole customer** A spectator who found a way to see a baseball game without paying admission. Under the heading, "Curing a Knot-Hole Customer," *The Sporting News* (Aug. 1, 1929) tells of an adult, watching a Laurel (Miss.) game through a knothole, who gets a broken nose when an outfielder slams into the fence.

**knothole day** A day, usually a Saturday, when the knothole club was able to get into the ballpark free or at a reduced rate.

**knothole gang** Syn. of *knothole club.* Marshall K. McClelland (*Pacific Stars and Stripes,* undated) reported that early in 1889, Abner Powell, the innovative owner of the New Orleans Pelicans, gathered together the youngsters of New Orleans and organized the first "Knot Hole Gang." "As long as the kids observed strict rules of personal behavior both inside and outside the park, Abner permitted them to see a free game or two each week the Pelicans were at home."

In the 1930s, the Boston Braves had a Knothole

*Knothole gang. Commissioner Kenesaw Mountain Landis at the knothole with two young fans.*

Gang, which was described by 71-year-old Gaspar Fabiano (*Boston Globe,* June 26, 1973): "Gang members were children who bought knotted wood pieces for 50 cents: the wood served as a season-long ticket to the left field seats."

When the Dodgers were still in Brooklyn, there was a television show before each game hosted by Happy Felton called "The Knot Hole Gang" on which three sandlot players appeared. As Mel Allen & Frank Graham Jr. (*It Takes Heart,* 1959; Charles D. Poe) explained: "The boys were asked to pitch or field grounders and fly balls, and the one judged best was allowed to return to the show on the following day and interview the Brooklyn player of his choice."

**knubber** A lucky hit that squirts through the infield; a scratch hit. See also *nubber.* **1st Use.** 1937. (*New York Daily News,* Jan. 17; Edward J. Nichols).

**knuckle 1.** *n./arch.* Abbreviated version of *knuckleball,* 1. **1st Use.** 1913. "There was 'the hook,' 'the knuckle' . . . and so many others that there seemed to be no end to them" (J. W. Duffield, *Bert Wilson's Fadeaway Ball;* David Shulman). **2.** *v.* To show the various movements of the knuckleball. Jim Bouton (*I'm Glad You Didn't Take It Personally,* 1971) wrote: "When a knuckleball doesn't knuckle it's not a knuckleball, its a piece of cake, pound cake."

**knuckleball 1.** A slowly pitched ball that is gripped with the fingertips, fingernails, or knuckles of the middle two or three fingers pressed against the ball and thrown with little or no spin so that it will dance, float, flutter, dart, bob, wobble, or dip in a totally unpredictable manner; "a curveball that doesn't give a damn" (Jimmy Cannon). Because the ball does not rotate and is moving slowly, it is more directly affected by air currents and breezes. It is thrown without twisting the hand or wrist. The pitch can be devilishly difficult to hit and not at all easy to catch (hence, not a great pitch to use when runners are in scoring position). Bob Uecker once said that the best way

**Knuckleball.** *Eddie Fisher demonstrates the traditional grip, 1968.*

for a catcher to handle the pitch was to wait for it to stop rolling and then pick it up. Chicago White Sox pitcher Eddie Cicotte is thought to have been the first major-league player (around 1908) to specialize in throwing the knuckleball. Other pitchers include Emil "Dutch" Leonard, Hoyt Wilhelm, and Phil Niekro. When Cleveland Indians manager Mike Hargrove was asked how to hit a knuckleball, he answered: "Stick your tongue out the left side of your mouth in the even innings and out the right side in the odd innings. I don't know. You just hope he throws one that hits your bat." See also *fingertip ball.* Also spelled "knuckle ball." Syn. *knuckle,* 1; *knuckler,* 1; *bob-and-weave; butterfly; dancer; mariposa.* **1st Use.** 1906. (*Baseball Magazine,* July; Edward J. Nichols). **2.** [softball term] A ball that breaks suddenly with little rotation in fast pitch softball. The ball is pushed out of the hand rather than rolling off the fingers.

**knuckleballer** A pitcher whose main pitch is a knuckleball. "They say you don't want to have a knuckleballer pitching for you or against you" (Los Angeles Dodgers manager Tommy Lasorda, quoted in *Milwaukee Journal Sentinel,* Aug. 4, 1987). Syn. *knuckles.*

**knuckle curve** A curveball thrown from a knuckleball grip, which causes the ball to drop sharply just before it reaches the batter. A blend of knuckleball and curveball, it seems to cause the ball to drop into the catcher's mitt, like a coin into a slot machine. The pitch is thrown by Baltimore Orioles pitcher Mike Mussina.

**knuckle duster** A pitch thrown close to the batter's knuckles.

**knuckler 1.** Syn. of *knuckleball,* 1. **2.** A pitcher who throws knuckleballs.

**knuckles** Syn. of *knuckleballer.*

**Koufaxian** In the manner of Brooklyn/Los Angeles Dodgers left-handed pitcher Sandy Koufax (1955–66); said of masterful pitching technique. "Ken Dixon, who might need a Koufaxian final three weeks to oust any of the top four starters, has looked sharp" (*Baltimore Sun,* Mar. 16, 1986).

**THE BASE BALL CRANK**

He's a howling megaphone, a human idiot,
When will he cease to talk unmitigated rot,
When will he stop his senseless howl
Of strike and base and home and foul.
He talks of nothing else but ball,
That is he does not talk, he can only bawl.

**Krank.** *Early postcard using an alternative spelling.*

**KP duty** Assignment to the bullpen. **Etymology.** A term brought back from World War II by players who had been in the armed forces.

**krank** *arch.* A baseball fan. See also *crank,* 1. The term appears in the title of Thomas W. Lawson's 1888 book on baseball slang: *The Krank: His Language and What It Means.*

**kranklet** A female krank.

**KS 1.** Scorecard symbol for a strikeout when the third strike is a swing and a miss. **2.** A cheer, chanted "kay ess, kay ess," when a pitcher strikes out a batter.

**K 2-3** Scorecard notation for a strikeout in which the catcher drops the third strike and must throw the ball to first base to retire the batter.

**kudo** A term used by pitcher Dennis Eckersley for the bow a batter takes when he bails out or falls away from a pitch (*Sports Illustrated,* Dec. 12, 1988).

**KY** A strikeout attributed to pitches with balls doctored with K-Y lubricant. "Gaylord Perry, a nonentity at twenty-seven, discovered Vaseline, K-Y vaginal jelly, and hitter hydrophobia (spitter on the brain), and has won 296 games (so far)" (Thomas Boswell, *How Life Imitates the World Series,* 1982).

# L

**L 1.** Abbrev. for *loss*. **2.** Box score abbrev. for *losing pitcher*. **3.** Abbrev. for *line drive*.

**label 1.** *n.* The printed or branded portion of the head of a baseball bat that contains the manufacturer's name. **2.** *v./arch.* To bat a ball; to "mark" the ball for a base hit.

**label for four** To hit a home run.

**lace** To hit the ball hard; e.g., "Smith laced one to left." **1st Use.** 1888. "Lace it out" (a caption; Thomas W. Lawson, *The Krank: His Language and What It Means;* David Shulman).

**ladder 1.** See *climb the ladder.* **2.** See *up the ladder.* **3.** See *up-and-down the ladder.*

**ladies day** A promotional event offering women free or reduced admission to the ballpark on certain days. **Etymology/1st Use.** 1883. In an attempt to lure more women to the ballpark, various clubs experimented with the idea as early as 1883. "Thursday is 'ladies day' at Columbus. On other days they must pay." (*Sporting Life,* Apr. 29, 1883; David Shulman). "At the baseball game between the Portlands and the Lewistons on the afternoon of the 4th, ladies will be admitted to the grounds free" (*Portland* [Maine] *Daily Advertiser,* July 3, 1884; Peter Tamony). Barry Popik found a line from *Sporting Life* (Aug. 25, 1886) stating "'Ladies' Day' is now six years of age." But the custom is said to have first taken hold with the Cincinnati Red Stockings in the latter part of the 1880s. Club owner Aaron Stern noted that the number of women in the stands increased significantly when a handsome pitcher named Tony "Count" Mullane was on the mound. Early in 1889, Stern announced that Mullane would pitch each Monday and all women would be admitted free providing they were accompanied by a paying male escort. This became a regular attraction and soon spread to other clubs. Some early promotions of this nature required that the women have a male escort. This resulted in crowds of women waiting outside the ballpark for men to take them through the turnstiles. The custom was given a boost in the days after World War II when owners used ladies days to attract customers to their ballparks. The practice was stopped as too many ladies were getting their escorts at the box office. **Extended Use.** Stuart Berg Flexner (*Listening to America,* 1982) notes that the term predated baseball and was used to designate a day when men could bring women to their clubs. He finds it used as early as 1787: "George Washington recorded the term in his diary that year, noting that a club at which he dined had a 'ladies' day' every other Saturday."

**ladle** To hit a ball hard.

**Lady Godiva pitch** A pitch with nothing on it. Syn. *nudist pitch.*

**La Lob** A trick pitch, invented and named by New York Yankees (1981–83) pitcher Dave LaRoche, that slowly floats toward home plate with a high-arching trajectory. Frederick C. Klein (*Wall Street Journal,* Oct. 5, 1982) described it as "the sort of pitch you throw to your seven-year-old son in your backyard." Klein was recalling two "La Lob" confrontations between LaRoche and Milwaukee Brewers slugger Gorman Thomas. Late in the 1981 season, Thomas struck out swinging at the pitch. They met again on June 30, 1982, and LaRoche threw seven consecutive La Lobs. Five were fouled off, one was taken for a ball, and the last one was lashed into left field for a hit. When Thomas reached first base, he raised his fists over his head, Rocky style. See also *eephus*.

**lam** To bat a ball hard.

**lamb 1.** A youngster; an innocent victim. According to Herbert Simons (*Baseball Magazine,* Apr. 1943), Ted Williams used the term so frequently that he became known as "The Lamb." **2.** A pitcher who is easy to hit; a *cousin,* 1.

**lambaste** To bat a ball hard. **1st Use.** 1908. (*New York Evening Journal,* Aug. 21; Edward J. Nichols).

**laminate** To hit the ball extremely hard. **1st Use.** 1914. "Murder it, Ted, old man! Laminate it!" (Burt L. Standish, *Lefty O' the Blue Stockings;* David Shulman).

**lamp** To look at. "Lamp the girl in row 22" (John Hall, *Baseball Digest,* Dec. 1973).

**lamps** Eyes. "[Bill Klem] said he didn't miss any [calls] in his heart, but he didn't say anything about his lamps" (Shag Crawford, quoted in Larry R. Gerlach, *The Men in Blue,* 1980).

**landing gear** The arms and front of the body as applied to a player sliding into a base. Broadcaster Vin Scully used the term to describe Bo Jackson dropping down to slide in the All-Star Game, July 11, 1989.

**land on** To bat a ball hard; e.g., "Smith landed on that pitch." **1st Use.** 1905. (*Sporting Life,* Oct. 7; Edward J. Nichols).

**larceny** Syn. of *base stealing.*

**Laredo** See *throw Laredo.*

**large market club** Historically, a major-league club in a heavily populated metropolitan area, such as New York or Los Angeles, which tended to have higher attendance and received more money than other clubs for the television and radio rights to their games. The term now more properly refers to high-revenue clubs (thanks in part to income from luxury boxes in their new ballparks), regardless of their market size. Large market clubs include the New York Yankees, New York Mets, Los Angeles Dodgers, Cleveland Indians, Baltimore Orioles, Colorado Rockies, Atlanta Braves, and Chicago Cubs. Compare *small market club.*

**larrup** To hit a baseball with force. One of Lou Gehrig's many nicknames was "Larrupin' Lou." **1st Use.** 1887. (Chicago *Inter-Ocean,* May 10; Edward J. Nichols). **Etymology.** A colloquialism among the Irish dating back to at least the early 19th century. It means "to beat, thrash, or flog" and is said to be a corruption of the nautical term "lee rope." The earliest example listed in the *Oxford English Dictionary* dates to 1823.

**larruper** A powerful hitter. **1st Use.** 1908. (*New York Evening Journal,* Aug. 26; Edward J. Nichols).

**lash** To hit a ball hard; e.g., "Smith lashed a grounder that moved quickly past the shortstop." **1st Use.** 1917. (*New York Times,* Oct. 8; Edward J. Nichols).

**last** For a pitcher to remain in the game; e.g., "Smith lasted for six innings." **1st Use.** 1902. (*Sporting Life,* July 5; Edward J. Nichols).

**last bullet** [softball term] The upcoming third out in the last inning for the losing team.

**last half** The *second half,* 2, of an inning.

**late foot** A winning or hitting streak toward the end of the season; e.g., "The White Sox are showing late foot."

**late-inning** *adj.* Toward the end of the game. **Extended Use.** Late in any realm. "Late-Inning Hardball in the House" (*Washington Post* headline, Dec. 28, 1987).

**late-inning defensive replacement** A good defensive player inserted into the lineup toward the end of the game, generally to help protect a lead.

**late-inning pressure situation** A statistic coined by the Elias Sports Bureau for an at-bat in the seventh inning or later with the hitter's team tied or trailing by three or fewer runs, or by four runs with the bases loaded (*Sports Illustrated,* June 11, 1990). Abbreviation *LIPS.*

**late innings** The seventh, eighth, and ninth innings of a baseball game.

**late reliever** A relief pitcher brought into a game in the late innings.

**late-season pickup** A player signed or acquired after the All-Star break, often seen as valuable to a pennant drive. Syn. "late-season acquisition."

**latest line** A gambling tool featuring a list of odds favoring or disfavoring teams before a given day's games. Latest lines are published in many newspapers and their prime function is to aid betting.

**lather** To hit. **1st Use.** 1934. (*Journalism Quarterly;* David Shulman).

**laugher** A game with a lopsided score; an easy win. "When Lee Lacy hits three home runs and drives in six runs, you figure the game is going to be a laugher. But at one point, it sure wasn't." (Baltimore Orioles manager Earl Weaver, quoted in *USA Today,* June 9, 1986). See also *blowout,* 2; *romp.*

**launching pad 1.** A ballpark from which many home runs emanate. After the Baltimore Orioles set a single-month home run hitting record in May 1987, coach Frank Robinson said of Memorial Stadium: "It's a launching pad" (UPI dispatch, June 2, 1987). Atlanta-Fulton County Stadium long enjoyed the nickname "The Launching Pad." The term has also been applied to Wrigley Field in Chicago and Coors Field in Denver. **2.** The pitcher's *mound,* 1.

**lawn mower** A hard-hit ground ball. See also *grass clipper.* **1st Use.** 1876. "Gifford led off with a 'lawn mower'" (*Detroit Free Press,* Aug. 13; Peter Morris).

**law of retaliation** An unwritten understanding among players that if a pitcher on team A throws at a batter on team B, the pitcher on team B will throw at a batter on team A. This thinking has resulted in many bench-clearing incidents that have been detrimental to baseball in general.

**lawyer 1.** A player who talks or complains a lot. See also *clubhouse lawyer.* **2.** A player, coach, or manager who tends to contest the decisions of umpires.

**lay an egg** To fail to score. See also *goose egg.*

**lay back** To play baseball in a nonaggressive manner.

**lay down** See *lay one down.*

**"lay it in there"** An encouragement to a pitcher to throw a strike or to give the batter something easy to hit.

**lay off** *v.* To refrain from swinging at a borderline pitch or a pitch out of the strike zone; e.g., many hitters cannot "lay off" swinging at a rising fastball at the top edge of the strike zone. Compare *chase,* 4.

**layoff** *n.* A period of inactivity for either a player or a team. Sometimes spelled "lay-off." **1st Use.** 1912. (*New York Tribune,* Oct. 7; Edward J. Nichols).

**lay one down** To execute a bunt; e.g., "Smith laid one down the third base line." **1st Use.** 1908. (*New York Evening Journal,* June 17; Edward J. Nichols).

**lay the bat on the ball** For a batter to make contact. "[Gorman] Thomas spread his stance and cut down his swing, just looking to lay his bat on the ball" (*Sports Illustrated,* Oct. 25, 1982).

**lay the wood** *v.* To hit the ball; e.g., "Smith laid the wood to the ball" or "Jones laid the wood on the ball." **1st Use.** 1908. (*Baseball Magazine,* June; Edward J. Nichols).

**lazy 1.** *adj.* Describing a ball without great velocity; e.g., "Smith hit a lazy pop-up to short." **2.** *n./ arch.* Syn. of *Texas Leaguer.*

**LCS** Abbrev. for *League Championship Series.*

**lead** [Pron. "leed"] **1.** *n.* The distance a baserunner stands from the base he occupies in the direction of the next base when the ball is pitched. The runner tries to take a lead that gives him an advantage for reaching the next base safely while still allowing him the option of getting back to the original base before the pitcher or catcher can pick him off. **1st Use.** 1896. (Burt L. Standish, *Frank Merriwell's School Days;* Edward J. Nichols). **2.** *n.* The advantage in runs scored by one team over another. **3.** *v.* To have scored more runs than the opposing team at any given time during a game. **4.** *v.* To be ahead in a particular statistical category; e.g., a team in first place "leads" other teams in the standings or the player with the most home runs leads in the chase for the home run crown.

**lead bat** A bat that has been weighted down with lead or other metal. It is swung in the on-deck circle to make one's regular bat seem lighter and easier to swing.

**leader card** A baseball card that depicts a player who leads his respective league or division in a particular statistical category during the previous season.

**lead glove** The figurative glove employed by an inept fielder or one with "hands made of stone."

**leading lady 1.** Syn. of *lead runner.* **2.** The first batter up in an inning.

**lead off** *v.* To be the first batter in the batting order or in an inning. **1st Use.** 1874. (*New York Sun,* July 3; Edward J. Nichols).

**leadoff 1.** *adj.* Said of the first in an inning or game; e.g., "leadoff double," "leadoff run," or "leadoff walk." "[Brady] Anderson had batted leadoff in all 15 of his starts" (*Baltimore Sun,* May 12, 1998). Also spelled "lead-off." **2.** *n.* Syn. of *leadoff batter.* Also spelled "lead-off." **1st Use.** 1935. "Lead-off—First batsman at bat at the beginning of an inning" (Ralph H. Barbour, *How to Play Better Baseball;* David Shulman).

**leadoff batter 1.** The player who is first in the batting order. Because this batter comes to bat more than any other player on the team, the position is normally reserved for a player with a high on-base percentage, good speed, and the ability to steal bases. Exceptional leadoff batters include Tim Raines, Maury Wills, Lou Brock, and Rickey

Henderson. Also spelled "lead-off batter." Syn. *leadoff,* 2; *leadoff hitter; leadoff man; anchor man.* **2.** The player who is the first to bat for a team in an inning.

**leadoff hitter** Syn. of *leadoff batter.*

**leadoff man** Syn. of *leadoff batter.* **1st Use.** 1910. (*Baseball Magazine,* Apr.; Edward J. Nichols).

**leadoff runner** The first player to get on base in an inning or a game.

**lead runner** The baserunner farthest along the basepath. Syn. *leading lady,* 1.

**league** A group of teams or clubs who play each other in a prearranged schedule to decide on a championship from among its members and who are governed by a common set of rules and regulations.

**League Award** The forerunner (1922–29) of the present Most Valuable Player Award.

**League Championship Series** The *Championship Series* in either the National League or the American League; specif., the *American League Championship Series* and the *National League Championship Series.* Abbrev. *LCS.*

**league play** [softball term] Syn. of *round-robin.*

**league president** The official charged with the responsibility for the day-to-day activities of the teams in a given league. The *Official Baseball Rules* specify that the league president enforces the rules of the game, resolves rules disputes, determines the resolution of any protested games, and at his discretion imposes fines and suspends players, coaches, managers, and umpires for violations of the rules.

**leaguer** An individual identified with a particular league; e.g., "major leaguer," "Negro leaguer," and "Little Leaguer." **1st Use.** 1908. (*Baseball Magazine,* Sept.; Edward J. Nichols).

**lean** To take a lead toward the next base; "to take an exceptionally long lead, preparatory to a steal" (Babe Ruth, *Babe Ruth's Own Book of Baseball,* 1928). To be picked off while taking such a lead is to be caught "leaning the wrong way."

**lean against it** To bat a ball hard. Syn. "lean on it." **1st Use.** 1907. (*New York Evening Journal,* Apr. 25; Edward J. Nichols).

**leaping** [softball term] An act by the pitcher in fast pitch softball that causes him to be airborne on his initial move and push from the rubber. The momentum built by his forward movement causes his entire body, including both the pivot foot and the nonpivot foot, to be in the air and move toward home plate as the delivery is completed. With this style of pitching, the pitcher will release the ball prior to or simultaneously with his return to the ground. The pivot foot will then slide to the side and drag as the pitcher follows through or completes the delivery. At the completion of the leap, the nonpivot foot is planted but will not allow the pitcher to gain further distance toward the plate; therefore, the slide and drag of the pivot foot is a legal act. Compare *crow hopping.*

**leaping Lena** Syn. of *Texas Leaguer.*

**learn a hitter** To study the habits of a hitter to understand the pitches he will hit and the direction in which such hits will go.

**learn the pitcher** To study the habits of a pitcher to better understand the giveaway motions that will indicate the type of ball he intends to deliver.

**leather 1.** *n.* A fielder's glove or gloves. "We told [Tim] Teufel, 'Way to get leather on it.' He just got the wrong leather." (New York Mets manager Davey Johnson, on Teufel's error during the 1986 World Series, quoted in *Washington Post,* Oct. 25, 1986). **2.** *n.* A general expression for fielding; e.g., "Smith always showed good leather." A game with several stellar defensive plays is said to be "full of leather." **3.** *v.* To play flawless defense. "They [Baltimore Orioles] just leathered everything. We put the ball in play, but they caught everything. It was really unbelievable." (Seattle Mariners outfielder Jay Buhner, quoted in *Milwaukee Journal Sentinel,* Oct. 7, 1997). **4.** *v./arch.* To hit the ball; e.g., "Smith leathered one to center." **5.** *n./arch.* The baseball, a reference to its cowhide cover. From this meaning has come such outdated slang

as "leather-hunting" for attempting to get a hit. **1st Use.** 1883. (Chicago *Inter-Ocean,* June 6; Edward J. Nichols).

**leather lungs** A loud, critical fan who can be heard throughout the ballpark.

**leather player** A good defensive player; one who is likely to be known for his fielding rather than hitting prowess. Compare *wood player.* Syn. "leather man." **1st Use.** 1937. (*New York Daily News,* Jan. 21; Edward J. Nichols).

**leatherslapper** A good fielder.

**leave on base** To end an inning with one or more baserunners unable to score.

**leave the yard** To hit a home run. Hitting a home run is called "leaving the yard" (*Sports Illustrated,* Nov. 1, 1993). "Hitting in the upper part of the strike zone, where fastballs that leave the yard are often thrown" (*Sports Illustrated,* Apr. 13, 1998).

**Leephus ball** Pitcher Bill Lee's blooper pitch, a play on Rip Sewell's *eephus.*

**left** Short for *left field.*

**left center** The area of the playing field between center field and left field. Syn. "left-center field."

**left field 1.** The left side of the outfield as viewed from home plate. Syn. *left.* **2.** The position of the player who defends left field. Abbrev. *LF* or *lf.* Syn. *left.* **1st Use.** 1854. (Knickerbocker Rules; Edward J. Nichols). **Extended Use. 1.** Things that are unusual, unexpected, or irrational are deemed to have come out of, or from, left field. "You think things are starting to look like they've got a pattern, and all of a sudden there's something that comes . . . from left field" (An investigator working on efforts to determine the cause of the explosion of TWA Flight 800, quoted in *Baltimore Sun,* Aug. 17, 1996). **2.** The political left. "Canadian businessmen last week were playing host to two more trade missions out of far left field. In Canada searching for business were one team of sales-minded Russians and another of inscrutable Hong Kong traders acting as agents for their neighbors, the Communist Chinese." (*Time* magazine, Jan. 20, 1961). **3.** A bad seat in a restaurant or arena. **1st Use.** 1948. "Unless a name is in the register, he is given a seat in left field" (Jack Lait & Lee Mortimer, *New York Confidential*) .

**left fielder** The defensive player who is positioned in left field. Abbrev. *LF* or *lf.* Sometimes spelled "leftfielder." **1st Use.** 1883. (*Sporting Life,* May 20; Edward J. Nichols).

**left field foul line** The line extending from home plate to the fence in deep left field that delineates foul from fair playing areas. Syn. *left field line.*

**left field line** The *third base line* extended beyond the infield; the *left field foul line.*

**left-handed** Said of a player who favors the left hand or the left side of the body. Compare *right-handed.* Also spelled "lefthanded."

**left-handed batter** A batter who swings from the left and faces the pitcher with the right side of his body as he stands on the right (first base) side of home plate. A left-handed batter has a natural, one-step headstart on the basepath when he completes his swing. Since batters tend to have an advantage over pitchers throwing from the opposite side of the body, left-handed batters tend to have an advantage because there are many more right-handed pitchers. Because of these advantages, many batters have learned to bat left-handed while still throwing with their right hand. Abbrev. *LHB.*

**left-handed pitcher** A pitcher who throws with his left arm. Abbrev. *LHP.* Syn. *southpaw,* 1.

**left-hander** A left-handed player; esp., a pitcher who throws with his left arm. There are many left-handed pitchers, but second basemen, third basemen, shortstops, and catchers typically do not throw left-handed. After New York Yankees first baseman Don Mattingly played five innings of a game at third base in 1986, the *Washington Post* said of him: "[He] is believed to be just the 11th left-hander to play third base in the major leagues since 1900." Traditionally, the left-handed player has had to overcome a certain amount of prejudice. E. V. Durling (*San Francisco Examiner,* Sept. 17, 1956; Peter Tamony) actually wrote: "Right handers are steadier than left handers. They steady

an infield. The southpaws are usually temperamental and easily rattled. They are also inclined to fancy 'show off' playing such as overdoing the one hand catch." The term is also used for a left-handed batter. Compare *right-hander.* Also spelled "left hander"; "lefthander." **1st Use.** 1879. (*Spirit of the Times,* Aug. 23; Edward J. Nichols).

**leftie** Var. of *lefty.*

**left on** Describing a runner remaining on base when the third out is made. Abbrev. *LO.*

**left on base 1.** *adj.* Said of the situation in which one or more runners are on base when the third out is made in a half inning. Syn. *stranded.* **2.** *n.* The number of runners remaining on base at the end of a half inning. As a statistic, the collective number of runners left on base during a game or a number of games is a barometer of a team's overall inability to score. Abbrev. *LOB.* **1st Use.** 1858. (Chadwick Scrapbooks; Edward J. Nichols).

**left out** A common nickname for the left fielder at the amateur level. It refers to the fact that the ball is seldom hit to left field at the non-professional level where batters tend to push the ball to the right.

**left patrol** The left fielder.

**lefty** A left-handed player; one who throws with the left arm or bats from the right side of home plate as he faces the pitcher. Var. *leftie.* Syn. *zurdo.* **1st Use.** 1886. "In last Wednesday's game Nashville presented her left-handed battery . . . to offset our 'lefty' battery" (*Sporting Life,* Apr. 7, 1886; David Shulman). **Extended Use.** Slang for a leftist, especially during the 1950s. "In your June 2 editorial re the Oppenheimer case, you describe Dr. Albert Einstein as a 'dedicated international lefty'" (*San Francisco News* letter to the editors, June 7, 1954; Peter Tamony).

**legal** That which is in accord with the official rules of the game.

**legal game** A game that lasts five innings (or 4½ innings with the home team in the lead) before being officially called by the umpire because of rain, darkness, or other condition that warrants the halt of play.

**legger** Syn. of *leg hitter.*

**leg hit** An infield single accomplished by the speed of the batter-runner. A key ingredient of a leg hit is that, while the ball has been properly fielded without error, the batter-runner outruns the ball to the base. Pittsburgh Pirates outfielder Lloyd "Little Poison" Waner set a record for singles (198 in 1927) because of many leg hits.

**leg hitter** A fast player who is adept at beating out infield hits and bunts. The player's speed can, to some degree, compensate for being a weak hitter. "The National League decided to make official the practice of rolling infields after five innings. . . . It brought no joy to leg hitters who sometimes beat out . . . balls which strike errant pebbles." (*San*

**Leg hitter.** *Lloyd "Little Poison" Waner, who was a terror when it came to getting to first base on* slap hits.

*Francisco News,* Dec. 8, 1953). Syn. *legger.* **1st Use.** 1937. (*The Sporting News Record Book;* Edward J. Nichols).

**leg-in-the-face** Said of a pitcher's high leg kick.

**"leg it!"** *obs.* A common 19th-century call from the grandstand, urging a player to "run!"

**leg it out** See *leg out.*

**leg kick** The element in a pitcher's delivery when he raises his nonpivot leg. Base stealers take advantage of a pitcher with a high leg kick: "Jesse Orosco, with his high leg kick, was responsible for two [steals] in the eighth inning" (*Baltimore Sun,* Apr. 24, 1996). See also *kick,* 1.

**leg out 1.** For a batter or runner to arrive safely at a base ahead of the ball; e.g., "Ken Griffey Jr. legged out the second inside-the-park home run of his career" (*Tampa Tribune,* June 21, 1990). See also *beat out.* **2.** To chase down a ground-ball hit; e.g., "Smith legged it out to reach the ball in the gap."

**legs cut out from under it** Description of a well-hit ball that falls short of its destination because it has been hampered by the wind.

**lemon 1.** *n./arch.* A player of poor ability, esp. one of whom much was expected. **1st Use.** 1908. "When Manager John McGraw strayed out to Springfield, Ill., to pick a peach from the Three-Eye baseball orchard, he evidently took a bridle path instead of the highway, and wound up in a lemon grove. He is reported to have paid something like $4,000 for the privilege of plucking a particular fruit named [Larry] Doyle." (*St. Louis Post-Dispatch,* May 21; Peter Morris). **2.** The baseball; e.g., "[Lou Gehrig] would come up and bust the lemon out of the country" (Paul Gallico, *Lou Gehrig, Pride of the Yankees,* 1942).

**Lena Blackburne Rubbing Mud** See *rubbing mud.*

**length** A unit of measurement (number of games) used to determine a team's exact position in the standings; e.g., "The Tigers were 15 lengths ahead of the Orioles." The expression is borrowed from horse racing. See also *game,* 2.

**"let him know you're out there"** An exhortation to the pitcher to throw close to a batter's body.

**"let's play two"** The exuberant exhortation of Ernie Banks, former Chicago Cubs infielder (1953–71), who professed an infectious enthusiasm for the game of baseball. See also *Banks' dictum*.

**letter-high** Said of a pitched ball that comes in across the chest at the level of the letters on the batter's jersey spelling out the name or initials of his team. **1st Use.** 1927. (Hal Totten, WMAQ-Chicago broadcast, June 17; Edward J. Nichols).

**letter mailer** A term used by Casey Stengel for a player who stayed out late at night. The term presumably stems from the time-honored excuse of curfew breakers who have been caught returning at a later hour: "Gee, I only went out to mail a letter."

**letter of intent** A document signed by a prospective player indicating he will play for a specified club.

**letters** The name of the team as written across the batter's jersey, indicating the approximate top of the strike zone. See also *numbers, 3*.

**let the ball play him** For a fielder to wait on a ground ball without moving, instead of taking a step either forward or back, thereby presenting an awkward hop that could result in a bobbled catch or wild throw.

**lettuce ball** Syn. of *rabbit ball, 1*. The term is so called because it "eats lettuce for breakfast" (*The Sporting News*, May 17, 1969).

**let up** *v.* To throw a slow ball after a fast one, using the same motion.

**letup** *n.* Syn. of *letup pitch*.

**letup ball** Syn. of *letup pitch*. "Then he fed me a high change of pace, a let-up ball you might call it. I swung as hard as I had the day before. But this time I missed." (Harry "Cookie" Lavagetto, quoted in *San Francisco Examiner*, Jan. 18, 1948; Peter Tamony).

**letup pitch** A pitch that is used to confuse the batter because it comes after a fastball and has less speed. See also *changeup*. Syn. *letup; letup ball*.

**level** To even up a ball-and-strike count; e.g., "The count levels at 2 and 2."

**level swing** A swing that cuts across a flat plane as opposed to one in which the batter chops or uppercuts at the ball.

**LF 1.** Abbrev. for *left field*. **2.** Sometimes *lf*. **2.** Abbrev. for *left fielder*. Sometimes *lf*.

**LHB** Abbrev. for *left-handed batter*.

**LHP** Abbrev. for *left-handed pitcher*.

**lick 1.** *n.* A time at bat; e.g., "The Giants are getting their last licks in the bottom of the ninth." **2.** *n./arch.* A safe hit. "In the sixth and last inning, the Mutuals got off some of their 'biggest licks'" (*New York Sunday Mercury*, Oct. 16, 1861; David Shulman). **1st Use.** 1860. (Chadwick Scrapbooks; Edward J. Nichols). **3.** *v.* To beat decisively.

**licorice** *arch.* Vigor or energy. **1st Use.** 1907. (*New York Evening Journal*, Apr. 12; Edward J. Nichols).

**licorice ball** A pitched ball that has been doctored with licorice. Edward J. Nichols (*An Historical Dictionary of Baseball Terminology*, Ph.D. dissertation, 1939) noted that pitchers once used licorice to get a better grip on the ball (*Sporting Life*, Sept. 2, 1905).

**lid is off** The beginning of a baseball season.

**lidlifter 1.** An Opening Day game. **2.** The first game of a doubleheader.

**life 1.** Another chance for the batter or the batting team, such as when a catchable foul fly ball is dropped. **1st Use.** 1868. "Howe had a life given him by Schaffer muffing his fly in right field" (Chadwick Scrapbooks; David Shulman). **2.** Syn. of *base on balls*. **1st Use.** 1874. (Chicago *Inter-Ocean*, July 6; Edward J. Nichols).

**lifer** An individual whose lifetime income is derived solely from participating in professional baseball; one who begins his career as a player and spends the rest of his working life as a manager, coach, scout, or executive; e.g., Casey Stengel, Don Zimmer, John McGraw, Connie Mack, and Earl Weaver.

**Lifer.** *Manager John J. McGraw (l.) with Christy Mathewson. McGraw has been typified as the quintessential baseball lifer.*

**lift 1.** To remove a pitcher from the game. **1st Use.** 1914. (*New York Tribune*, Oct. 1; Edward J. Nichols). **2.** To hit a ball high and far; e.g., "Smith lifted the next pitch out of the park." **1st Use.** 1868. (Chadwick Scrapbooks; Edward J. Nichols). **3.** To win a baseball game; e.g., "[Kirby] Puckett's HR in 10th Lifts Twins" (*Tampa Tribune* headline, June 27, 1989).

**light ball** A ball that is thrown with such a slow spin that it feels light in weight to the catcher.

**light bat** A player who is not a power hitter.

**lighted frolic** *arch.* A night game under the lights in the 1930s and 1940s, when such games were still a novelty.

**light-hitting 1.** Said of a team that lacks power hitters. **2.** Said of a player who is not a power hitter.

**lightning ball** [softball term] An early name for softball.

**lights** Artificial illumination provided for night games.

**light up** To get several hits off a pitcher; e.g., "The Orioles lit up Smith for ten hits in two innings." John Maffei (*Padres Magazine*, 1993) defined the term as "what happens to a pitcher when he doesn't have a good yakker, isn't throwing hard, and can't pull the string."

**limber up** To flex and bend the body before a game. See also *warm up.*

**limit** See *player limit.*

**Linda Ronstadt** A fastball. Dave Scheiber (*St. Petersburg Times,* Mar. 5, 1987) reported: "Good fastballs enjoy an updated alias as well. They're called a Linda Ronstadt. No, the sultry singer was never known for her pitching prowess, but she did record the tune 'Blue Bayou.' And baseball linguists soon turned that into 'blew by you'—as in what that sizzling fastball just did." See also *Louisiana.*

**line 1.** *v.* To hit a ball along a straight path; to hit a line drive. **1st Use.** 1892. (*Brooklyn Daily Eagle*, Aug. 1; Edward J. Nichols). **2.** *v.* Syn. of *line out.* **3.** *v.* To mark the foul lines on the field. **4.** *n.* One of the various boundary marks on and around the playing field; e.g., a foul line or a baseline. **1st Use.** 1866. (Constitution and By-Laws of the Olympic Ball Club of Philadelphia; Edward J. Nichols).

**linea** Spanish for *line drive.*

**linear weights system** A formula, developed by baseball analyst Pete Palmer, that incorporates a player's hitting, baserunning, fielding, and pitching contributions. Normalized for such variables as the ballpark in which the player performs, it expresses a player's effectiveness in terms of "wins" that he contributes to (or costs) his team in comparison with an average player at his position.

**line ball** *arch.* A ball that travels a straight line; a line drive. **1st Use.** 1866. (*New York Herald,* July 7; Edward J. Nichols).

**line drive** A solidly batted ball, usually a base hit, that approximately parallels, and moves close to, the ground during its flight rather than arcing in the manner of a fly ball. See also *blue dart; blue darter; bee liner; rifle shot,* 2; *linea.* Abbrev. *L,* 3. Syn. *bolt; liner; line shot; line-hit.* **1st Use.** 1895. (*New York Press,* July 4; Edward J. Nichols).

**line drive to the catcher** A swinging strikeout. "He'll relate later that he hit a 'line drive to the catcher' for his missed third strike" (*Baseball Magazine,* Jan. 1943).

**line-hit** Syn. of *line drive.* "Jack Strobe cleaned the bases with a long line-hit" (Christy Mathewson, *First Base Faulkner,* 1916; David Shulman). **1st Use.** 1880. (*New York Herald,* Aug. 20; Edward J. Nichols).

**line hitter** A hitter who hits line drives. **1st Use.** 1932. (*Baseball Magazine,* Oct.; Edward J. Nichols).

**line-hugger** A batted ball that follows the first base line or the third base line.

**line out** *v.* To hit a line drive that is caught for an out. Syn. *line, 2.*

**line-out** *n.* A line drive that is caught for an out. Sometimes spelled "lineout."

**liner** **1.** Syn. of *line drive.* **1st Use.** 1872. (*Beadle's Dime Base-Ball Player*). **2.** A warmup exercise in which a player runs on the warning track from one foul line to the other.

**lines** **1.** See *between the lines.* **2.** See *white lines.*

**line score** An inning-by-inning account of the runs scored in a game, commonly displayed on scoreboards in the ballpark; also, game statistics that include total runs, hits, and errors. An example:

|          |     |     |     | R | H | E |
|----------|-----|-----|-----|---|---|---|
| New York | 001 | 201 | 000 | 4 | 6 | 0 |
| Atlanta  | 000 | 100 | 100 | 2 | 5 | 1 |

**line shot** Syn. of *line drive.*

**lineup** The players composing the batting order and the defense at any given moment during a game. It is always presented at the beginning of the game and updated with substitutions during the game. Sometimes spelled "line-up." **1st Use.** 1905. (*Sporting Life,* Oct. 7; Edward J. Nichols). **Extended Use.** Any listing of events or participants.

**lineup card** A card that lists the starting players in their proper batting order and by position and that is presented to the umpire-in-chief by a representative of each team at the beginning of each game. Syn. *batting-list.*

**liniment** *arch.* The worst; anything that is very bad or very poor.

**lip** The part of the playing field where the infield dirt area meets the grass in the infield or the grass behind the infield.

**lipper** A ball that is hit off the edge or lip of the infield.

**LIPS** Abbrev. for *late-inning pressure situation.*

**little ball** **1.** A fastball that is difficult to see as it comes in toward the batter. **2.** Bunting as opposed to swinging away. "Manager Gene Mauch used the squeeze bunt—'little ball' is his expression for it—earlier in the season because the [California] Angels were not scoring many runs" (*New York Times,* Oct. 18, 1982). **3.** Playing for one run per inning, or one run at a time. See also *small ball.*

**little bo-bo** *arch.* A manager's favorite player. See also *bobo.*

**little cutter** A *cut fastball* that is "thrown like a straight fastball but with a little pressure on one side of the ball, which makes it move" (Roger Angell, quoted in *Washington Post,* Oct. 19, 1997).

**Little Eva** A player who performs well even though he is obviously tired and suffering from a hangover. **1st Use.** 1937. (*New York Daily News,* Sept. 5; Edward J. Nichols). **Etymology.** The term comes from the innocent Little Eva of *Uncle Tom's Cabin* who is the exact opposite of the dissipated ballplayer dragging himself onto the field and showing the effects of the previous night's revelry.

**Little League** **1.** An organized international network of baseball for boys and girls up to 12 years in age. It was started in 1939 by Carl E. Stotz of Williamsport, Pa. Although the rules are basically the same as those observed by adult organizations, the physical dimensions of the field are smaller: two-thirds the size of a major-league field and 60 feet (rather than 90 feet) between the bases. Little League is highly structured and provides a path for play right up to and including the Little League

World Series, which is held annually in Williamsport. Although created for boys only, a 1974 court order included girls in the Little League program for the first time. Several major-league players first played in Little League, the first of whom was Joey Jay who pitched for the Milwaukee Braves and the Cincinnati Reds (1953–66). Abbrev. *LL*. **2.** A generic term for baseball at the preteen level.

**Little League elbow** A childhood injury that can result from the stress of continually trying to throw a baseball hard. A similar injury is "Little League shoulder."

**Little Leaguer** An individual who plays on a Little League team.

**Little Miracle of Coogan's Bluff** The miraculous finish to the New York Giants 1954 season in which the team took the pennant and swept the Cleveland Indians in the World Series four games to none. Not to be confused with *Miracle of Coogan's Bluff.*

**Little World Series** The postseason playoff games involving the champions of the three Class AAA minor leagues. Syn. *Junior World Series.*

**live** (Pron. "lyve") *adj.* Said of a pitch that hops, jumps, dances, sails, floats, or otherwise deviates from a straight trajectory. Compare *flat.*

**live** (Pron. "liv") *v.* To have excellent control; e.g., "[Roger] Clemens lived on the outside inch of home plate, coming inside just often enough to keep everybody off balance" (*Baltimore Sun,* May 18, 1994).

**live arm** An attribute of a pitcher with a good fastball. The term often appears in the scouting report on a pitcher with strength. "[Norm Charlton] has a great, live arm. He throws 92, 93 [mph]." (Baltimore Orioles manager Ray Miller, quoted in *Baltimore Sun,* Feb. 25, 1998).

**live ball 1.** A ball that is in play. Compare *dead ball,* 1. **2.** A baseball that is, or is believed to be, inherently livelier and therefore will go farther when hit. "Actually, the terms 'live' and 'dead' have been applied to baseballs for more than 100 years" (a Rawlings executive, quoted in *USA Weekend,* July 10, 1987). **1st Use.** 1914. "At that time 'live'

balls were used, that is, balls which had a good bit of rubber in them" (*Outing Magazine,* Jan.; David Shulman).

**live-ball era** Syn. of *lively ball era.*

**live bat** The bat of a hitter who is in the midst of a hot streak. See also *hot bat,* 1.

**live hitter** A hitter in a real game situation as opposed to a hitter in a simulated game. The term is used in reference to a pitcher getting ready during a rehabilitation assignment or extended spring training.

**live in a mustard jar** To act like a "hot dog" player; to show off.

**lively ball 1.** A baseball that *appears* to have more zip and distance in it than others because of the way it has been manufactured. The lively ball is often described as one that seems to jump right off the bat on its way to a long voyage. Compare *dead ball,* 2. See also *rabbit ball,* 1. **1st Use.** 1870. (*New York Herald,* June 10; Edward J. Nichols). **2.** A baseball used during a specific season when many players, managers, and coaches insisted that the balls had more "life" to them; e.g., in 1920, the ball underwent a change with the use of an improved yarn and tighter winding, resulting in more robust batting averages. Recent lively ball years were 1987 and 1996. Christy Mathewson (*Spalding's Official Base Ball Guide*), addressing the 1922 season when batting averages hit an all-time high, remarked: "All this talk of a lively ball appears to be alibi stuff. The players are using long-handled bats trying for home runs because it is so popular. The bat is changed so that the batter can get a full grip."

**lively ball era** The period beginning with the 1920 season when baseballs were made with resilient cores. Norman L. Macht suggests an earlier date: "I believe the so-called lively ball era really began with the cork center ball in 1910. American League batting averages jumped in 1911; the National League's did so in 1912. But the style of the game did not change, and the prolonged use of dark, discolored, mushy balls did not change. The big change that began in 1920 came from banning the doctoring of the ball, the tighter windings of the yarn, and the use of superior materials, combined with Babe Ruth's swinging for the fences. It would be more appropriate to call it the 'clean ball era.'" Compare *dead-ball era.* Syn. *live-ball era.*

**live pitching** Pitching in a real game situation as opposed to pitching in a simulated game or during batting practice. The term is used in reference to a batter recovering from an injury or layoff.

**LL** Abbrev. for *Little League.*

**LO** Abbrev. for *left on.*

**load 1.** To apply an illegal foreign substance to a baseball; e.g., "Smith loaded the ball with slippery elm." See also *load up.* **2.** See *load the bases.*

**load of coal** A slow, soft pitch; a changeup. Syn. "load of garbage."

**load the bases 1.** For the team at bat to put runners on first base, second base, and third base. **2.** For the team in the field to allow runners to occupy first base, second base, and third base.

**load up** To doctor the baseball by adding a foreign substance such as saliva or hair oil. "Pitchers will load up by putting stuff on their eyebrows, in their hair, on the hair on their chest, on their wrists, all over" (Billy Martin, *Billyball,* 1987). See also *load,* 1.

**lob 1.** *n.* A soft throw or toss between two fielders who are relatively close to each other. **2.** *v.* To throw a ball softly and gently. **1st Use.** 1911. (*Baseball Magazine,* Oct.; Edward J. Nichols). **3.** *v.* To hit a ball into a slow, high arc.

**LOB** Scorecard and box score abbrev. for *left on base.*

**lobby sitter** A player who hangs out in hotel lobbies between games on road trips.

**lobster net** Syn. of *orange crate.*

**lobster trap** Syn. of *orange crate.*

**local World Series** A World Series involving teams from the same city, such as New York Yankees vs. New York Giants (1936 and 1937), St. Louis Browns vs. St. Louis Cardinals (1944), and Chicago White Sox vs. Chicago Cubs (1906).

**locate 1.** For a pitcher to throw the ball where he wants it. "What makes him [Bret Saberhagen] so tough is that he can locate the ball anywhere in the strike zone on any pitch" (Travis Fryman, quoted in *Sports Illustrated,* May 4, 1998). **2.** To get hits off a pitcher.

**location** A pitcher's ability to place the ball where he wants it. Russell Baker (*New York Times,* Oct. 9, 1979) recalled a line he heard on television: "Ryan has good velocity and excellent location." After noting that the line sounded like something that happened in a physics lab, he translated it into traditional baseballese: "Ryan is throwing smoke and nicking the corners." See also *control.* **Usage Note.** Joe Goddard (*The Sporting News,* Mar. 6, 1982) reported that "location" seems to have replaced "control," much as "velocity" has replaced "speed": "It's because some real estate agent became a pitcher," speculated Kansas City Royals relief pitcher Dan Quisenberry. Rick Horowitz (*Chicago Tribune,* June 5, 1986) opined: "'Location' is whether it gets there; you used to call it 'control.'"

**lock 1.** *n.* A certainty; a sure bet. "St. Louis manager Whitey Herzog figures the Cardinals are a lock to steal 200 bases for the seventh year in a row" (*St. Petersburg Times,* Mar. 6, 1988). **1st Use.** 1958. "We haven't had a 20-game winner since [Ewell] Blackwell in '47 and this guy [Bob Purkey] looks like a lock now" (A. Murray, *New York Post,* June 11). **Etymology.** Harold Wentworth & Stuart Berg Flexner (*Dictionary of American Slang,* 1960) trace the term to the wrestling term "mortal lock" for a deadly hold that cannot be broken. **2.** *v.* For a batter to become focused and to concentrate on the pitch to be delivered. "[Leo Gomez is] not getting fooled. He's not swinging at bad pitches. He's hitting everything hard. He's locked, as we like to call it." (Rafael Palmeiro, quoted in *Baltimore Sun,* June 7, 1994). Syn. *lock in.*

**locker room** Syn. of *dressing room.*

**lock in** Syn. of *lock,* 2.

**lock up** To be a sure winner; e.g., "The Yankees have locked up the World Series by winning the first three games."

**locust hitter** A weak hitter, so called because of the poor quality of locust wood; i.e., the hitter is so weak that it seems as if he is using a bat of locust. **1st Use.** 1907. (*Lajoie's Official Base Ball Guide;* Edward J. Nichols).

**loft** To hit a high fly ball; e.g., "Smith lofted one to center." **1st Use.** 1915. (*Baseball Magazine,* Dec.; Edward J. Nichols).

**log** A baseball bat.

**lollipop 1.** A soft pitch or weak throw. The term is usually used to describe a pitch that is extremely easy to hit, like a lollipop held out in front of the batter. "He hasn't got the fastball anymore; he throws lollipops" (Russ Hodges, San Francisco Giants broadcast, Sept. 15, 1963; Peter Tamony). At the annual home run derby staged before the annual All-Star Game, the pitcher's job is to serve lollipops to baseball's leading sluggers. Also spelled "lollypop." **2.** Syn. of *Texas Leaguer.*

**lollipop arm** A weak throwing arm.

**long ball 1.** A home run. See also *Dr. Longball.* **2.** A batted ball that travels a considerable distance, usually deep in the outfield; a ball that will require an extraordinary catch or go for extra bases. Jim Brosnan (*The Long Season,* 1960) wrote that the term is "often used as a nickname for catchers who signal for too many bad pitches." **3.** A style of play characterized by power hitting; e.g., "The Red Sox are playing long ball tonight."

**long-ball hitter** A home run hitter. **Extended Use.** A powerful or dramatic performer. "And the fact that he [boxer Rocky Marciano] is a long-ball hitter gives him extraordinary and exciting appeal" (Joe Williams, *San Francisco News,* Sept. 25, 1952; Peter Tamony).

**long bat** *arch.* A hot streak at the plate.

**long bench** A superior collection of substitute players. The term appears to have started in football and jumped to baseball.

**long catch** An exercise used by pitchers to strengthen their arms in which the ball is thrown a much greater distance than that between the pitcher's mound and home plate. New York Yankees pitcher Ron Guidry "increased his activity of playing long catch in the outfield from 130 to about 150 feet" (*Newsday,* Mar. 27, 1988).

**long count** Syn. of *full count.*

**long distance orator** *arch.* A player who argues from long range.

**long hit** Syn. of *extra-base hit.*

**long man** Syn. of *long reliever.*

**long out** A putout in which the ball comes close to being a home run but is caught on the fly deep in the outfield.

**long potato** A well-hit home run. The term is said to have originated in the Negro leagues. The term was also used in the Class A California League in 1966 (Ron Bergman, *The Moustache Gang,* 1973). See also *long tater.*

**long relief 1.** The replacement of a pitcher early in the game. **2.** A period of relief pitching, usually three innings or more, early in the game.

**long reliever** A relief pitcher who works in long relief. He often enters the game during the first three innings and may either finish the game or be replaced by another relief pitcher; he often pitches in mop-up duty or blowout situations. Compare *middle reliever; short reliever.* Syn. *long man.*

**long shot** A ball hit for a long distance; e.g., "Smith drove a long shot out of the park."

**long side** The left side of the infield (as viewed by the batter) from which throws to first base are the longest.

**long strike** A foul ball that goes a long distance. **1st Use.** 1937. (*The Sporting News Record Book;* Edward J. Nichols).

**long summer** The seemingly never-ending season for a team low in the standings. Typically, a sloppy early-season loss will occasion the line, "This could be a long summer."

**long tater** A well-hit home run. See also *tater; long potato.*

**long toss 1.** A ball thrown for a long distance, as from deep center to shortstop. **2.** A high, arching throw by a player while warming up; esp., such a throw by a pitcher to a point some 20 feet behind home plate. **3.** A high, arching throw by a pitcher who has been ailing and is starting to use his arm again. See also *soft toss*.

**long tossing** Exercise of high, arching tosses by a player, usually a pitcher, recovering from arm problems. "I definitely notice a difference in what I can do now. I've been long tossing every day. I can notice a progression from week to week." (Baltimore Orioles catcher Chris Hoiles, quoted in *Baltimore Sun,* Mar. 13, 1996). See also *soft tossing.* Sometimes spelled "long-tossing."

**long winter** The off-season following a disappointing year. After the Cleveland Indians eliminated the New York Yankees in the 1997 American League division Series, Yankees catcher Joe Girardi said: "As much fun as we had this year, this season is really empty. . . . [It] will be a long winter." (*USA Today,* Oct. 7, 1997).

**look 1.** *v.* For a pitcher to glance or stare at a baserunner before delivering the ball; e.g., "Smith looked the runner back to deter him from taking too long a lead." **2.** *n.* A glance made at a baserunner by the pitcher before delivering the ball. **3.** *v.* For a fielder with the ball to hold a baserunner during a play by glancing in his direction rather than throwing the ball to the base; e.g., "Smith looked Jones back to third after fielding the grounder and before throwing to first." **4.** *v.* For the batter to allow a pitched ball to go by without swinging at it; to take a pitch; e.g., "Smith looked at the curveball just off the outside corner."

**looker 1.** A batter who patiently waits for the right pitch to hit. **2.** A batter who is not aggressive enough at the plate, who prefers to draw a walk rather than expose his batting weakness.

**look for** To come to the plate anticipating a certain pitch or sequence of pitches; e.g., to "look for" a walk is to anticipate called balls.

**looking 1.** Waiting for a pitch that suits the batter. **2.** See *catch looking.* **3.** See *strike out looking.*

**looks like a line drive in the box score** A phrase directed at a batter who has just beaten out a scratch hit to remind him that the box score will not differentiate between such hits and scorching line-drive hits. Var. "looks like a line drive tomorrow."

**look them over 1.** For a batter to wait for a good ball to hit even if it means taking a pitch for a strike. **1st Use.** 1937. (*The Sporting News Record Book;* Edward J. Nichols). **2.** An instruction shouted to the batter to encourage patience.

**loony Joe** A left-handed pitcher.

**"Looooo"** A cheer that commonly accompanied plate appearances by batters named Lou or Lew, such as that accorded Lou Piniella at Yankee Stadium and Lou Whitaker at Tiger Stadium. It is notable because the uninitiated often mistook the cheer as a boo. Similar cheers include "Moooooooookie" (for Mookie Wilson) and "Dewwwwwwwwwey" (for Dwight Evans).

**loop 1.** *n.* A baseball league or conference. **2.** *v.* To hit a high, arching ball. **3.** *n.* A poorly hit pop fly. **4.** *n.* Syn. of *inning,* 1.

**looper** A fly ball that carries just beyond the infield for a hit; a *Texas Leaguer.* In print, one often finds that a looper has been "plopped." **1st Use.** 1937. (*The Sporting News Record Book;* Edward J. Nichols).

**loose 1.** *adj.* Said of a ball that is not under the control of a defensive player or said of an infield characterized by poor fielding. The term underscores a paradox of baseball talk: it is good for hitters to be "loose," but fielders should be "tight." Compare *tight,* 2. **1st Use.** 1861. (*New York Sunday Mercury,* Oct. 2; Edward J. Nichols). **2.** *adj.* Descriptive of a fluid, easy swing of the bat. "One of the loosest—and most productive—swings in the Pacific Coast League belongs to San Diego's swivel-jointed outfielder, Harry Simpson" (*San Francisco Call-Bulletin,* Aug. 17, 1950; Peter Tamony). **3.** *adj.* Descriptive of a generally good attitude and easy approach toward the game. A team that is winning is often described as "loose." A player who remains relaxed or lacks tension before a game or between innings is said to be "staying loose." **4.** *adv.* Said of a pitcher warming up in the bullpen; e.g., "Smith is getting loose and ready to relieve Jones."

**loose-as-a-goose** Said of a player who is completely relaxed on the field, or whose moves are easy, graceful, and seemingly effortless. Var. "loose-as-ashes." Syn. *loosey-goosey.*

**loosener** A pitch thrown to loosen a batter up. **1st Use.** 1932. (*Baseball Magazine,* Oct.; Edward J. Nichols).

**loosen up 1.** To begin hitting freely against a pitcher; e.g., "The Giants began to loosen up Smith." **1st Use.** 1928. (*New York Times,* Oct. 6; Edward J. Nichols). **2.** To throw a brushback pitch or a knockdown pitch to, presumably, move the batter away from the plate; e.g., "Jones loosened the batter up by throwing a pitch close to his head." **1st Use.** 1937. (*Baseball Magazine,* Jan. 11; Edward J. Nichols).

**loosey-goosey** Syn. of *loose-as-a-goose.*

**Lord Charles** An appreciative name for a superb curveball, which elevates *Uncle Charlie* to a regal level. See also *Sir Charles.* **Etymology.** The term was created during the 1985 season to describe Dwight Gooden's majestic curveball, requiring a nickname with more dignity than "Uncle Charlie."

**lords of baseball** The owners of major-league baseball teams. The term, created by the late sportswriter Dick Young, is sometimes capitalized: "The message has gone out to the Lords of Baseball that the game needs to broaden its appeal and take in more youth" (*Baltimore Sun,* Oct. 18, 1995). Two books have given the term added currency: Harold Parrott's *The Lords of Baseball* (1976) and John Helyar's *Lords of the Realm* (1994).

**Los Angeles Angels** An expansion team that joined the American League in 1962. When the team moved from Chavez Ravine in Los Angeles (a.k.a. Dodger Stadium) to Anaheim in 1965, it changed its name to California Angels. After the 1996 season, the team changed its name to Anaheim Angels.

**Los Angeles Dodgers** The name of the National League West Division franchise located in Los Angeles, Calif. The team began as the Brooklyn Dodgers and moved to Los Angeles in 1958. The original reference to trolley-dodging Brooklynites seemed out of place here, but some pointed out that Los Angeles pedestrians had to be adroit automobile dodgers.

**lose 1.** To allow the opponent to score more runs in a baseball game. **2.** For a pitcher to issue a base on balls, usually after being ahead in the count; e.g., "I was ahead of him 0-2, but I lost him." **3.** To allow a weak hitter to hit safely.

**lose a baseball** To hit a home run out of the ballpark. "Pete Rose has just lost a baseball in Philadelphia" (Cleveland Indians broadcaster Herb Score, Sept. 18, 1982). Var. "lose one."

**lose a fly** To misjudge or lose sight of a fly ball, such as a ball that is lost in the sun or in the lights. **1st Use.** 1902. (*Sporting Life,* July 5; Edward J. Nichols).

**lose a step** To slow down; e.g., a player well into his 30s will often be said to have "lost a step or two."

**loser 1.** Syn. of *losing pitcher.* **2.** The team that does not win a game.

**losing pitcher** The pitcher who is charged by the official scorer with the loss of a game because he is responsible for the baserunner who scores the opposition's winning run. No matter how many pitchers are involved in a losing effort, only one pitcher can be charged with responsibility for the other team's winning run. Compare *winning pitcher.* Abbrev *LP.* Box score abbrev. *L,* 2. Syn. *loser,* 1.

**losing spin** Syn. of *losing streak.*

**losing streak** Two or more games lost in succession by either a pitcher or a team. Syn. *losing spin.*

**loss 1.** A defeat. **2.** That which is credited against a losing pitcher and is counted both in his single-season and career records. In giving this statistic, the losses always appear after the number of wins; e.g., a season record of 18-8 means 18 wins and 8 losses. Abbrev. *L*, 1.

**lot 1.** A ballpark. **1st Use.** 1866. (Constitution and By-Laws of the Olympic Base Ball Club of Philadelphia; Edward J. Nichols). **2.** Short for *sandlot*, 1. **1st Use.** 1908. (*Baseball Magazine*, July; Edward J. Nichols). **3.** A baseball diamond, regardless of its size or location.

**loud foul** A foul ball, other than a foul tip; esp., a foul ball hit for a long distance, usually close to the foul pole.

**Lou Gehrig Memorial Award** An award presented to a player who exemplifies the "giving character" of Hall of Famer Lou Gehrig. Syn. *Gehrig Award.*

**Lou Gehrig's disease** The popular name for amyotrophic lateral sclerosis (ALS), the fatal paralytic disease that claimed the life of Hall of Famer Lou Gehrig in 1941 at age 37. The term has long been applied to all sufferers of the disease, and has done much to increase public awareness of the affliction. **Extended Use/1st Use.** 1941. The term "Gehrig's disease" had come into use even before the

player succumbed to it. One of its first uses in print came in an Associated Press story by Harold C. McKinley on the day (June 4, 1941) of Gehrig's funeral. That story, which ran in the *Washington Evening Star* of that date under the headline "Science Helpless Treating It, Is Ignorant Even of Cause of 'Gehrig's Disease,'" said that the disease had already been "popularly" termed "Gehrig's disease."

**Louisiana** A *Linda Ronstadt,* in reference to Ronstadt's remake of Roy Orbison's hit record, "Blue Bayou" (Scott Ostler, *Los Angeles Times,* 1986).

**Louisville** *v.* To hit the ball hard, as with a Louisville Slugger. **1st Use.** 1942. "The good-looking kid . . . Louisville'd for .343 in his first season" (*Baseball Magazine*, Aug.; David Shulman).

**Louisville Slugger** A heavy baseball bat; originally, the trade name of a heavy bat manufactured by the Hillerich and Bradsby Co., originally of Louisville, Ky., but now based in nearby Jeffersonville, Ind. It was named in honor of Pete Browning, a slugger for the Louisville Colonels, whose bat in the 1884 season measured 37 inches and nearly 48 ounces. Syn. *slugger*, 3.

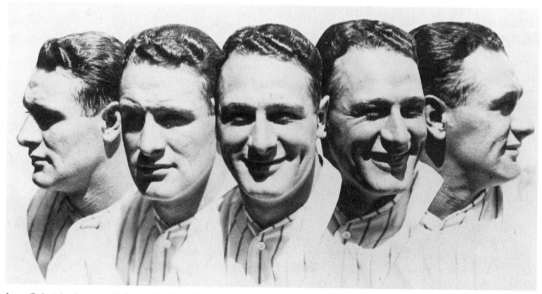

**Lou Gehrig's disease.** *Gehrig as he looked in his prime. These are still photographs from a short film in which he is called "The Crown Prince of Swat."*

**low** Below the strike zone.

**low and away** Syn. of *low and outside*.

**low and inside** Said of a pitch that is low and close to the batter and that may or may not be in the strike zone.

**low and outside** Said of a pitch that is low and far from the batter and that may or may not be in the strike zone. Syn. *down and away; low and away*.

**low ball** Syn. of *low pitch*. **1st Use.** 1867. (*New York Herald*, July 3; Edward J. Nichols).

**low-ball hitter** A hitter with a reputation for swinging at balls that come in below his knees. Compare *high-ball hitter*.

**low bridge 1.** *v.* To brush the batter back from the plate, causing him to bend back as if he were going under a low bridge. "Once in a while they 'low bridge' you, but no real shooting" (Philadelphia Athletics first baseman Ferris Fain, quoted in *San Francisco Examiner*, Aug. 3, 1949; Peter Tamony). **2.** *n.* "The position assumed by a batter who is stooping to avoid being hit by a high or wide pitch" (Edward J. Nichols, *An Historical Dictionary of Baseball Terminology*, Ph.D. dissertation, 1939). **1st Use.** 1937. (Red Barber, NBC World Series broadcast, Oct. 6; Edward J. Nichols). **3.** *v.* To knock a runner down. "Bert Campaneris started a brawl using a relay throw to low bridge the baserunner" (Don Baylor, *Don Baylor*, 1989). **Etymology.** The term originates from the days of the canal boat. "The boat moved so slowly that the passengers had fairly long conversations with people walking along the canal bank. Now and then the boat would pass under a bridge. If it were dangerously low the captain or helmsman would yell 'Low Bridge' and the passengers would duck their heads." (W. E. Woodward, *The Way Our People Lived*, 1944; Peter Tamony). The term is also alluded to in a popular American folk song, "The Erie Canal," refrain: "Low bridge, ev'ry body down!/Low bridge, for we're going through a town,/And you'll always know your neighbor,/You'll always know your pal,/If you ever navigated on the Erie Canal" (Carl Sandburg, *The American Songbag*, 1927).

**Lowdermilk.** *Wild pitcher Grover Cleveland "Slim" Lowdermilk.*

**Lowdermilk** *arch.* Eponymous term for a pitcher given to wildness. From Grover Cleveland Lowdermilk whose lackluster pitching (career record of 23-39 between 1909 and 1920, with 296 strikeouts and 376 bases on balls) was characterized by legendary wildness. Lowdermilk attracted some new attention in the mid-1980s when the value of his 1912 baseball card hit $1,200.

**low-drop mound** A pitcher's mound that appears to be lower than normal. Compare *high-drop mound*.

**lower half 1.** The *second half*, 2, of an inning. **2.** The personal makeup of a baseball player: what he is like inside, how he lives, and what he believes in. A scout uses the term to describe what he looked for in a prospect in Roger Angell's *Five Seasons* (1977). Compare *upper half,* 2.

**low-impact ball** A baseball used in some youth programs that acts like a regular ball but causes less damage if a child is hit with one. The pioneering low-impact ball is the RIF (Reduced Injury Factor) ball created by the Worth Sports Co. of Tullahoma, Tenn.

**low lead** A good fastball.

**low minors** Professional baseball at the entry level; "a world of prospects, suspects and roster fillers playing 140 games in 143 days for $200 a week" (Robert Schmuhl, *Chicago Tribune,* Aug. 19, 1990).

**low pitch** A pitch that is below the strike zone. Unless swung at by the batter, a low pitch should be called a ball by the plate umpire. Syn. *low ball.* **Extended Use.** A crooked deal. "The major sure swings at low pitches! He'll trust a stranger with a face that would set off a bank alarm!" (*Our Boarding House* cartoon, June 13, 1956; Peter Tamony).

**low strike** A pitch thrown low in the strike zone that umpires sometimes call a ball.

**LP** Abbrev. for *losing pitcher.*

**lucky seventh** *arch.* The second (bottom or home) half of the seventh inning, which was once regarded as lucky for the home team. **1st Use.** 1890. (*New York Press,* July 11; Edward J. Nichols). **Etymology.** Nichols suggests that it was probably named from the idea of the lucky 7 as known in the game of dice. However, broadcaster Lindsey Nelson (NBC radio, July 20, 1963) reported that the term can be traced back to pitcher John Clarkson, who created the idea when he noted that his highly successful National League team in Chicago (1884–87) won many games by scoring runs in the seventh inning. So common was the belief that the seventh inning was a time for big scoring that in 1934 Ford Frick, then head of the National League service bureau, did a statistical analysis of 100 games to see if there was anything to it. He determined that the seventh inning ranked as the sixth most prolific inning and that the most runs

were scored in the first inning. (*The Sporting News,* Sept. 13, 1934).

**lug the bunting** To win the pennant.

**lulu** A player of little skill. The term appears in the third stanza of Ernest L. Thayer's 1888 poem, "Casey at the Bat": "And the former [Flynn] was a lulu and the latter [Jimmy Blake] was a cake."

**lumber 1.** A baseball bat or bats. "Ready with their 'lumber' preparatory to opening a big five-game series against the Giants tomorrow . . . are the 'big three' sluggers of the Pittsburgh Pirates" (*San Francisco Call-Bulletin* photo caption, May 3, 1958). **1st Use.** 1943. "On that trip to the plate he merely 'carried lumber' [after missing a third strike]" (*Baseball Magazine,* Jan.; David Shulman). **2.** A lineup or a portion of a lineup filled with good hitters, such as the Pittsburgh Pirates "Lumber Company" of the 1970s, composed of Dave Parker, Willie Stargell, Al Oliver, and Manny Sanguillen.

**lumberjack** A player who can hit reasonably consistent long balls and home runs.

**Lumber.** *Ty Cobb (l.) and Joe Jackson during the 1913 season while Jackson still wore the Cleveland Indians uniform.*

**lumber legs** The legs of a slow-running player; e.g., "Smith's lumber legs seemed to be made of wood."

**lumber man** A player who is primarily a hitter; one who is likely to be known for his hitting rather than fielding prowess. See also *wood player*.

**lumberyard 1.** Syn. of *bat rack.* **2.** Figurative source of talented hitters. "You can shake a tree and a thousand guys who can field will drop out. But it's harder to find guys from the lumber yard. Dave Winfield doesn't make $1.5 million because he's a good defensive outfielder." (Kansas City Royals designated hitter Hal McRae, quoted in *San Francisco Examiner,* May 22, 1981; Peter Tamony). Also spelled "lumber yard."

**lumps** Hard hitting against a pitcher. A pitcher getting back into the rotation after an injury will often remark that he will "take my lumps" until he is in the groove again. **1st Use.** 1937. (*New York Times,* Oct. 8; Edward J. Nichols).

**lunch** Getting hit very hard; e.g., "The pitcher had his lunch handed to him after the barrage of hits."

**lunch hooks** Syn. of *dinner tongs* (Edward M. Thierry, *Baseball Magazine,* Sept. 1909).

**lunge** An erratic move made by a batter trying to get at a ball in front of the plate. It is usually the result of the batter misjudging the speed or trajectory of the pitch.

**luxury tax** An assessment on a major-league club's player payroll (including earned bonuses), designed to limit the rate of increase in player salaries and slow the spending of large market clubs. As implemented in the 1996 Basic Agreement, the luxury tax requires the clubs with the five highest payrolls to pay a 35% tax on the amount of their payrolls that exceeds the midpoint between the fifth and sixth highest payrolls (about $55 million for 1998). The luxury tax falls to 34% in 1999, and will disappear thereafter unless re-adopted in the next Basic Agreement. Under the method of accounting used for the tax, payrolls are based on the average annual values of all contracts for players on the 40-man rosters; each payroll includes funds for benefits, such as pensions and health insurance. Money from the luxury tax goes into a pool that is distributed to financially needy clubs.

# M

**mace** *arch.* A baseball bat. **1st Use.** 1928. (*New York Times,* Oct. 7; Edward J. Nichols).

**machine** A baseball team; specif., one that works smoothly, precisely, and with good teamwork, such as the "Big Red Machine" of the Cincinnati Reds in the 1970s. **1st Use.** 1908. (*Baseball Magazine,* Nov.; Edward J. Nichols).

**machine-gun ticket** A complimentary ticket to a baseball game, esp. in the 1930s. See also *Annie Oakley,* 1.

**mackerel** See *dead mackerel.* **Etymology.** From the old saying "dead as a mackerel," which is how it appears when compared to the fastball.

**Mackmen** A nickname for the Philadelphia Athletics during the years (1901–50) that Connie Mack was manager.

**Macmillan** A baseball encyclopedia, in reference to *The Baseball Encyclopedia* published by Macmillan in 10 editions beginning in 1969 (the 10th edition was published in 1996). Syn. *Big Mac,* 1.

**maestro** *arch.* A baseball manager. The term is usually applied to one who insists on running the team right down to minor details.

**maggot** *arch.* An owner of a baseball club. **Etymology.** H. L. Mencken (*The American Language; Suppl. II,* 1948) lists the term as a piece of baseball slang, an apparent play on the word "magnate."

**magic number** The combination of wins and losses that add up to a championship for a first-place team; specif., the total number of games that the leading team in a division or league must win and/or the second-place team must lose to clinch the championship for the leader. If, for example, the Phillies magic number is six with the Mets in second place, any combination of Phillies wins and Mets losses adding up to six gives the championship to the Phillies. To determine the magic number, combine the second-place team's wins and number of games remaining; from this total, subtract the leading team's number of wins. The difference plus one equals the magic number. The magic number comes into play at the end of a season to dramatize the end of the pennant race and is often featured in headlines. "Red Sox Win, 2–0; Cut Magic Number to One" (*Buffalo News* headline, Sept. 28, 1986). When a team is eliminated, the term is sometimes used facetiously; e.g., "'Magic Number' for S.F. is 1961" (*San Francisco Chronicle* headline, Sept. 13, 1960; Peter Tamony). According to Tamony, the term and the concept are clearly modern, dating back to the 1940s or perhaps a bit earlier. See also *tragic number.*

**magic wand** *arch.* The bat of a player who is getting several lucky hits.

**magic word** A word or phrase that, when uttered to an umpire, almost certainly provokes the speaker's ejection from the game. Jim Bouton (*Ball Four,* 1970) has a detailed discussion of the word itself.

**magnate** An owner or stockholder of a baseball team. The term has been in common use since the late 1880s. **1st Use.** 1887. "In the eyes of the

*Mackmen.*

base-ball 'magnate' the player has become a mere chattel" (John Montgomery Ward, *Lippincott's Magazine,* Aug.; Peter Morris).

**mailbox baseball** An act of vandalism in which rural mailboxes are struck from a moving car by a person swinging a baseball bat. It is a federal offense. A scene in the film *Stand By Me* (1986), in which the game is played from the open window of a 1949 Ford, may have given the practice ill-deserved publicity.

**major company** *arch.* Syn. of *major leagues.* **1st Use.** 1902. (*Sporting Life,* July 12; Edward J. Nichols).

**major league** *n.* **1.** A league at the highest level of organized or professional baseball; specif., one of the two leagues (National League since 1876 and American League since 1901) that currently constitute the *major leagues.* Previous major leagues included the American Association (1882–91), Union Association (1884), Players League (1890), and Federal League (1914–15) The Special Base-

ball Records Committee decided that these six leagues would be considered "major league" for purposes of the official record. Some baseball historians consider the National Association (1871–75) to be the first professional league in the major-league category, but the Committee cited the Association's "erratic schedule and procedures" as reason enough for exclusion. Syn. *big league.* **2.** The highest level of professional baseball in other countries, such as Taiwan and Japan.

**major-league** *adj.* Referring to a level of play, behavior, or scale that is at the level of the major leagues; e.g., a college or minor-league player may be said to have "major-league aspirations." Syn. *big-league.* **Extended Use.** Anything imposing and of the highest level, whether it be a "major-league client" or a "major-league headache."

**Major League Agreement** An agreement between the American League and the National League regarding business affairs, such as waivers and free agency.

**major-league arm** The arm of a pitcher with great potential. "[Bo Belinsky] had what they call in the trade a major-league arm. That is, he could throw hard and his ball moved." (Phil Pepe, *No-Hitter,* 1968).

**Major League Baseball** The organizational entity that comprises the business and sport of the major leagues. Abbrev. *MLB.*

**Major League Baseball Players Alumni Association** An association of former major-league baseball players, headquartered in Lakeland, Fla. It sponsors golf tournaments and other charity events, maintains biographical information on former players, and assists players with drug and alcohol rehabilitation. Abbrev. *MLBPAA.*

**Major League Baseball Players Association** The labor union of major-league baseball players formed in 1956 to represent the players in disputes with the owners. Also known as *Players Association.* Abbrev. *MLBPA.*

**Major League Baseball Properties** The licensing arm of the major leagues that works to actively protect the trademarks of teams. Abbrev. *MLBP.*

**Major League Baseball Umpires Association** An association of major-league umpires formed in 1968 to represent the umpires in disputes with the owners or players. In 1997, the Association advocated a system in which players cannot serve suspensions at their convenience and continue to be paid.

**major leaguer** A major-league baseball player. Syn. *big leaguer.* **1st Use.** 1908. (*Baseball Magazine,* Sept.; Edward J. Nichols).

**major leagues** The highest level of professional baseball, consisting of the National League and the American League. Each of these two leagues is subdivided into East, Central, and West divisions. Abbrev. *ML.* Sometimes spelled "Major Leagues." Syn. *majors; major company; big leagues; big show; big tent; big time; biggies; Bigs, the; Show, the.*

**Major League Scouting Bureau** An independent, freelance organization formed in 1968 to gather, evaluate, and make available (to club owners for a fee) reports on prospective baseball players.

**Major League Scout of the Year Award** An annual award, presented by Coors Beer and Topps chewing gum to honor an outstanding scout, based on the voting of more than 200 baseball scouts.

**major-league waivers** A form of *waivers* that is required if a player is to be included in a deal after the July 31 trading deadline.

**majors** Syn. of *major leagues.* **1st Use.** 1911. (*Baseball Magazine,* Oct.; Edward J. Nichols). **Extended Use.** The top level of competition.

**make a living** For a major-league player, esp. a pitcher, to perform what he does best or what he must do to continue his career. "The only thing I would say is, 'Do not quit pitching inside.' That's where he's going to make his living. As a stopper, he's going to need to do it even more." (Boston Red Sox pitcher Pedro Martinez, advice for Baltimore Orioles relief pitcher Armando Benitez, quoted in *Baltimore Sun,* June 5, 1998).

**make a right turn** Good fielding. The term refers to a retired batter-runner who turns right at first base on his way back to the dugout.

**"make it be good"** *arch.* A once-common instruction to a batter to wait for a good pitch. **1st Use.** 1912. "The war cry of coaches and the order of managers to the batter when the opposing pitcher shows signs of wildness, the meaning being that the batter is not to hit the ball unless it is a perfect strike, whether or not he hits" (Hugh S. Fullerton, *American Magazine,* June; Edward J. Nichols).

**make it look easy** To make a difficult play appear to be simple. The term is usually applied to those of consummate skill.

**make it look harder than it is** To make a routine play look spectacular, sometimes stemming from ineptness.

**make it too good** To throw a pitch that is easy for the batter to hit; e.g., when a pitcher has to throw the ball in the strike zone on a 3-0 count.

**make-or-break season** That baseball season late in a player's career during which he must either produce or retire from active participation in the game.

**make the cut** To be selected to remain on a

team's roster after it is cut to 25 players following spring training.

**make the team** To be put on a team's roster as a regular major-league player; e.g., "Smith was the 25th player to make the team."

**makeup** The attitude and poise of a player; a player's character.

**make-up date** The date set to play a make-up game.

**make-up game** A game that has been rescheduled or a previously scheduled game that has been rained out or postponed. Many make-up games are scheduled as parts of doubleheaders.

**make vitamins** To commit errors. Tom Gill (Davis, Calif.) reported that San Francisco Giants catcher-turned-third baseman Bob Brenly used the term self-assuredly on a broadcast to refer to making errors "one-a-day." On Sept. 14, 1986, several days after explaining the term, Brenly became the first major-league player since 1901 to make four errors in one inning. **Etymology.** From the name of a popular One-A-Day vitamin product.

**man, the** The manager of a baseball team.

**manage** To act as a manager.

**manager** The uniformed individual appointed by the club to run the team on the field. Traditionally, the manager determines the lineup and batting order, makes substitutions, plans the game strategy, and represents the team in communications with the umpires and the opposing team. **1st Use.** 1876. (*Detroit Free Press,* June 22; Peter Morris).

**Manager of the Year** An annual award presented since 1983 by the Baseball Writers Association of America to the best manager in each major league, as voted by sportswriters. Other versions of the award have been given since the 1930s by the likes of *The Sporting News* and the Associated Press.

**M&M Boys** Roger Maris and Mickey Mantle when they were members (1960–66) of the New York Yankees. "Relive . . . the glory days of the

**M&M Boys.** *Sluggers Roger Maris (l.) and Mickey Mantle of the New York Yankees present a bat to former President Harry S Truman at Yankee Stadium.*

New York Yankees: The 'M&M Boys' chasing the Babe's home-run crown" (Mickey Mantle, *The Mick,* 1985). **Etymology.** The term clearly was inspired by the name of the popular M&M chocolate candy.

**man from outer space** A player whose feats are extraordinary.

**manicurist** Syn. of *groundskeeper.*

**man in blue** An umpire.

**man in the middle** A baserunner caught in a rundown on the basepath.

**manliness** The quality or behavior of the grown workingman in mid–19th century America. The term and concept played a critical role in the early history of baseball by separating the "national game" as a legitimate and serious activity requiring "manly" behavior and self-control from its simple and primitive origins in children's or "boyish" games. Baseball "requires the possession of muscular strength, great agility, quickness of eye, readiness of hand, and many other faculties of mind and body that mark a man of nerve. . . . Suffice it to say that it is a recreation that anyone may be proud to excel in, as in order to do so, he must possess the characteristics of true manhood to a considerable degree." (Henry Chadwick, *Beadle's Dime Base-Ball Player,* 1860).

**man on the firing line** The pitcher.

**man overboard** A runner who has run or slid past a base. **Etymology.** A term brought back from World War II by players who had been in the armed forces.

**manufacture** To score runs by stringing together singles, bunts, stolen bases, sacrifices, walks, and hitting behind the runner, without the benefit of extra-base hits; to score runs by employing the basic fundamentals of baseball.

**marathon** A long, extra-inning baseball game.

**marble 1.** *arch.* The baseball. **2.** *obs.* Home plate. Before it was replaced by rubber in 1887, home plate was commonly a marble slab (Patrick Ercolano, *Fungoes, Floaters and Fork Balls,* 1987).

**mariposa** Spanish for *knuckleball,* 1 (literally, "butterfly").

**marked ball** A ball that has been scratched, cut, or scuffed to make it move erratically when pitched. See also *doctored ball.*

**marker** *arch.* A run. **1st Use.** 1922. (Ernest J. Lanigan, *Baseball Cyclopedia;* Edward J. Nichols).

**marquee name** A popular player. When the Oakland A's lost the "Bash Brothers" (Jose Canseco and Mark McGwire), it was said to have lost its "marquee names." **Etymology.** From the large signboards atop theaters where star actors find their "names up in lights."

**mascot 1.** A youngster, often the batboy, who takes care of the equipment, does odd chores, and is commonly felt to bring luck to the team. "Little Nick is the luckiest man in the country and is certainly the Browns' mascot" (*Sporting Life,* Apr. 26,

**Mascot.** *Disarming image of the New York Yankees' and Washington Senators' mascots (circa 1919).*

1886; Barry Popik). Many team photos of the late 19th century show a uniformed boy identified as the mascot (examples on file at the Library of Congress show a mascot as early as the 1888 St. Louis Browns). Ira L. Smith & H. Allen Smith (*Low and Inside,* 1949) explain the traditional linking of mascots and batboys in baseball: "In the game of baseball the mascot has generally been utilitarian—it's all right to have him around for good luck, but the little twerp oughta do some work too." Some mascots were important figures. "Sharing honors with [Connie] Mack in bringing three world's titles to Philadelphia in four years was the little hunchbacked mascot, Louis Van Zelst. A kindly, good-natured boy, he had come to Mack in 1909 and said he was lucky and indeed he was. Nothing but good luck followed in his wake." (Frederick G. Lieb, *Connie Mack: Grand Old Man of Baseball,* 1945; Peter Tamony). **1st Use.** 1884. "Have the Bostons a Mascotte? They have crawled out of some very small holes the past two weeks." (*Sporting Life,* May 28; Barry Popik). **2.** An animal or costumed figure used to characterize and bring luck to a team. Such mascots are almost always given names. It has been written on several occasions that the custom of the animal mascot in America may have started in college football. "The first football mascot, so far as anyone can now recall, was Handsome Dan, a bulldog who belonged to a member of the Yale class of 1892" (*Sports Illustrated,* Nov. 5, 1956). However, Gerald Cohen (*Comments on Etymology,* Feb. 1, 1987) found the following from *The World* (New York) (May 25, 1887): "It was Pittsburg's first victory from the Giants, and the ever-happy [Pud] Galvin's smile increased in magnitude. The Skye-terrier mascot was left at the hotel." **Etymology.** The direct American origin of the term came in 1880 with the importation of the French comic opera, *La Mascotte.* When looking before that date there are two theories for the derivation of the term: 1) from a Provençal word, "masco," for "sorceress" and 2) from "masque," for "one who is covered or concealed," which in provincial France was applied to a child born with a caul, which was believed to bring luck. From whatever source, the notion of the mascot was quickly accepted in some quarters. "Firm believers in both mascots and

hoodoos are to be found among sporting men, and also among theatrical people. 'Getting a hunch' is an alternative expression for 'getting a tip' and it springs from the fact that hunchbacks, if properly approached, are a sure source of luck." (*The Illustrated American,* May 24, 1980; Peter Tamony).

**mask** Protective facial gear worn by the catcher and the home plate umpire. See also *catcher's mask.* **1st Use.** 1887. (*Harper's Weekly,* Sept. 10; Edward J. Nichols).

**mask and mitten** *arch.* The position of catcher. Syn. "mask and mit work." **1st Use.** 1908. (*Baseball Magazine,* Nov.; Edward J. Nichols).

**mask man** The catcher. **1st Use.** 1905. (*Sporting Life,* Oct. 7; Edward J. Nichols).

**mask work** The catcher's duties. **1st Use.** 1915. (*Baseball Magazine,* Dec.; Edward J. Nichols).

**Massachusetts game** An early variation of baseball played in New England from the early 1800s and esp. popular in the Boston area in the 1850s. It employed a box-shaped (rather than a diamond-shaped) field and 4½-feet-high wooden stakes as bases 60 feet apart and allowed for runners to be retired when hit with a ball thrown by a defensive player. Ten original clubs in and around Boston fixed a set of 21 rules on May 13, 1858; one rule stipulated that there be only one out per side. The Massachusetts game used a softer ball. It replaced *town ball* and was replaced by the *New York game* after the Civil War. Syn. *Boston game; Boston ball; New England game.*

**massage** To bat a ball; e.g., "Smith massaged one in the seventh." **1st Use.** 1932. (*Baseball Magazine,* Oct.; Edward J. Nichols).

**mass hits** *arch.* For a team to collect many hits within a short period, usually an inning. **1st Use.** 1915. (*Baseball Magazine,* Dec.; Edward J. Nichols).

**mass migration** The annual shifting of players from one club to another.

**master fly** A home run. **1st Use.** 1987. "Wow, that sure was some master fly" (*St. Petersburg Times,* Mar. 5).

**mastermind** The manager of a baseball team. The term is sometimes applied with a hint of cynicism, such as in this definition: "Manager who wants to do the thinking for the entire team" (Harwell E. West, *The Baseball Scrap Book,* 1938). The term was often applied to longtime New York Giants manager John McGraw. **1st Use.** 1920. (*New York Times,* Oct. 5; Edward J. Nichols).

**matador** A timid infielder; specif., one who positions his body like a bullfighter to avoid being hit by the ball when fielding it.

**match** A baseball game (Knickerbocker Rules, 1845).

**matching** A baseball-card flipping game in which a player drops a card and a second player must match it to keep both cards. If the first player's card lands with the photo side up ("heads"), the second player must flip heads also or lose both cards. The printed back of the card in this game is regarded as "tails."

**matchup** The two starting pitchers in a baseball game; e.g., "Today's matchup is between Smith and Jones." **Usage Note.** Kenneth Miller notes that in other team sports, the term alludes to the contest between two teams.

**material** Players, especially recruits. **1st Use.** 1896. "The Athletics are a junior club and contain some excellent material, which will only require practice to develop first class players" (*Detroit Advertiser and Tribune,* June 6).

**mathematically eliminated** Said of a team that no longer is able to win its division because the magic number is zero.

**matinee** An afternoon baseball game; specif., the afternoon game that was once traditionally played on the same day as a morning game. Such games were once common on holidays such as July 4th and Labor Day. Although there were no hard and fast rules for matinees, such same-day games were not usually regarded as doubleheaders and one had to pay separate admissions to each game. **1st Use.** 1898. (*New York Tribune,* June 19; Edward J. Nichols).

**mattress** Syn. of *chest protector.* **1st Use.** 1908. (*Baseball Magazine,* July; Edward J. Nichols).

**maul 1.** To get many hits off a pitcher. **2.** To successfully hit for a long distance the balls thrown by a pitcher; e.g., "The Phillies mauled the offerings of Smith." **1st Use.** 1910. (*American Magazine,* July; Edward J. Nichols).

**maximum arc** [softball term] The highest point at which a legally pitched ball in slow pitch softball reaches in its trajectory from its release from the pitcher's hand to the plate. It is measured in feet from the ground (12 feet in Amateur Softball Association of America rules and 10 feet in United States Slo-Pitch Softball Association rules). See also *minimum arc; unlimited arc.*

**McGrawism** An action or strategy (such as the hit-and-run play) characterized by rough, anything-goes baseball, suggested by the play and managerial style of New York Giants manager (1902–32) John J. McGraw.

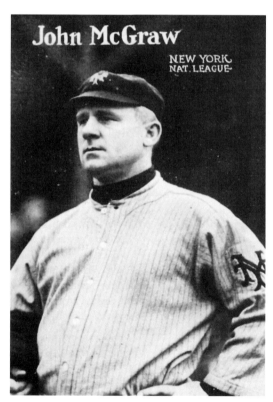

**McGrawism.** *John McGraw in the uniform of the New York Giants.*

**meal ticket** A club's winningest and most effective or dependable pitcher. Dizzy Dean once called Ned Garver of the St. Louis Browns a "meal ticket" because "he keeps 'em eatin' regular." The player most closely tied to the term was New York Giants southpaw Carl Hubbell, who was known as "The Meal Ticket" not only because he kept food on his manager's table, but also because of his reliability between 1933 and 1937, when he won 115 games. Also spelled "mealticket." **1st Use.** 1905. (*Sporting Life,* Oct. 7; Edward J. Nichols). **Etymology.** The term had several slang meanings before it attached itself to Hubbell. However, all of the meanings—ranging from a hobo who carries another hobo's food or food money to a woman supporting a panderer or pimp—refer to a valued asset. Another common application is to a prizefighter who is his manager's meal ticket: "A meal ticket is a valuable asset, but one punch can make it null and void" (*San Francisco Call,* Mar. 14, 1914; Peter Tamony). **Extended Use.** Any person or object that brings success.

**mean** Difficult to cope with; e.g., "Smith threw a mean curve to strike out Jones" or "The Yankees played a mean game of baseball."

**measure bats** *arch.* To meet and play another team. **1st Use.** 1880. (*New York Herald,* July 16; Edward J. Nichols).

**meat 1.** The thickest part of a baseball bat. **2.** The strongest hitters in the middle of the lineup; e.g., "Smith, Jones, and Brown form the meat of the batting order." **3.** The limbs and body of a batter; e.g., to "take one on the meat" is to be hit by a pitched ball. **4.** A baseball player. A familiar greeting among players is "How ya doing, meat?" (John Maffei, *Padres Magazine,* 1993). **5.** *meatball* for short.

**meatball** An easy-to-hit pitch that comes right down the middle of the plate; a pitch that is properly met with the bat for a hit. The term is a clear refashioning of "meet the ball," as in the plaintive cry of the Little League coach: "Just meet the ball."

**meat hand 1.** A fielder's gloveless throwing hand, esp. that of the catcher; the hand with which players are loath to field hard-hit balls, so called because

a ball caught in this hand hits flesh rather than leather. "When I was sixteen, I went to work for the Green & Twichell shoe factory. I remember in that summer we chipped in and bought a glove for two dollars. It was made of buckskin and had no fingers. It was used in turn by one player after another, since it was common property. Up to that time we had played with our 'meat' hands, and the catcher caught the pitcher's offerings on the first bounce." (Connie Mack, *The Saturday Evening Post,* Apr. 4, 1936; Peter Tamony). **1st Use.** 1912. (*American Magazine,* June; Edward J. Nichols). **2.** The hand closest to the knob of the bat when the batter grips the bat.

**mechanical pitching machine** Syn. of *iron mike.*

**mechanics 1.** The technical elements and basic skills required by a pitcher to be effective; specif., the various aspects of a pitcher's stretch, windup, motion, and delivery that maximize the movement, velocity, location, and control of each pitch. Mechanical flaws include: throwing with the pitcher's weight too far forward, forcing him to drag his arm across his body; initiating a delivery by dropping the arm position; twisting the upper body during delivery; failing to get the lower body to drive toward the plate; throwing too much over the top; drifting toward first base or third base rather than moving one's weight forward during delivery; turning one's back to the plate and failing to lift up the front leg; failing to keep the arm angle perpendicular to the ground, thereby causing more stress on the elbow; gliding into the delivery and turning the leg too soon; slumping down when throwing a curve, causing the ball to hit the dirt before it crosses the plate; shortening the stride, thereby causing the pitches to elevate and straighten; and rushing the arm motion to get over the top before the front foot hits the ground. "Mechanics . . . is nothing more than muscle memory, doing the same thing the same way enough times it comes naturally" (Ben McDonald, quoted in *Baltimore Sun,* June 30, 1994). **2.** The technical elements and basic skills required by a hitter to be effective; specif., the various aspects of a batter's stance and swing that maximize his ability to see the ball and meet it solidly on contact. Examples of mechanics include: controlling the leg kick, reducing extra movements in the swing, keeping the front shoulder in and down, bringing the bat through the strike zone, spreading the feet, and flattening the swing to eliminate a loop. "You have to be disciplined in your mechanics because you can't waste any at-bats" (Terry Crowley, quoted in *Baltimore Sun,* June 23, 1994). **3.** The technical elements and basic skills required by a fielder to be effective; specif., the positioning of the hands, feet, and body to maximize a fielder's ability to catch, field, and throw the ball, such as extending the arm through the throwing motion rather than "pushing" the ball. Baltimore Orioles catcher Chris Hoiles "adjusted his mechanics to get his arm in position to throw more quickly" (*Baltimore Sun,* Sept. 30, 1997); Hoiles "is keeping his throwing hand inside his leg instead of below it so he can get to the ball faster, is on the balls of his feet rather than being flat-footed, and has his legs more off-center rather than squared up" (*Baltimore Sun,* Apr. 12, 1998).

**media guide** A highly detailed and richly statistical annual guidebook to a club and its individual players, prepared by the club and released in the spring for the use of the working press during the course of the season. Media guides are also sold to the public. Because they contain so many numbers and statistics, media guides often include minor errors, which are occasionally brought to light. "Media Guide Gaffs Keep Game Light" (*USA Today,* May 13, 1986) was the headline for a story on players who gain 100 pounds or a foot in height with the publication of the guide.

**meet the ball** To swing the bat while the ball is still out in front of the plate so that the two objects meet at a point that is likely to result in a hit; to take less than a full swing. **1st Use.** 1905. (*Sporting Life,* Sept. 9; Edward J. Nichols).

**melee** Syn. of *rhubarb.*

**Mendoza line 1.** The figurative boundary in the batting averages between those batters hitting above and below .215. It is named for shortstop Mario Mendoza whose career (1974–82) batting average for the Pittsburgh Pirates, Seattle Mariners, and Texas Rangers was .215. **2.** The figurative

**Mendoza Line.** *Mario Mendoza as a Pittsburgh Pirate. He also played for Texas and Seattle.*

boundary in the batting averages between those batters hitting above and below .200. "When a struggling hitter pulls his average above .200, he has crossed the Mendoza Line" (*Sports Illustrated,* Sept. 13, 1982). Jim Henneman (*Baltimore Sun,* June 7, 1994) wrote of Brady Anderson: "A few years ago, when he was struggling to stay above the Mendoza (.200) line, Anderson commanded the same defensive strategy." **1st Use.** Coinage of the term has been credited to George Brett, who was quoted: "The first thing I look for in the Sunday papers is who is below the Mendoza line" (Glen Waggoner & Robert Sklars, *Rotisserie League Baseball,* 1987). But according to *Sports Illustrated* (Aug. 20, 1990), the term was coined by Tom Paciorek or Bruce Bochte; broadcaster Mel Proctor (Home Team Sports telecast, Apr. 25, 1996) said Mendoza, while playing for Seattle (1979–80), was hitting above and below .200 and that teammates Paciorek & Bochte commented on that fact in an interview, and later Brett picked up on it and used the term. There have been several claims that it was named for Minnie Mendoza, a .188 hitter for the Minnesota Twins in 1970, but as yet there are no citations to prove this claim. **Usage Note.** This clearly emerging term can have two slightly different meanings (.215 vs. .200), so it is important to specify which Mendoza line is being referred to. However, it seems that the .200 line is used much more commonly than the .215 version; e.g., citations from *Sports Illustrated* and *Baseball Digest* side with the .200 version. **Extended Use.** In an article headlined "My Private Mendoza Line" (*USA Baseball Weekly,* Aug. 25, 1993), Paul White comments that when a certain player retires (in this case, Nolan Ryan), he crosses the line to become "older than every major leaguer."

**men in blue** The umpires. The term was used as the title of a 1980 book by Larry R. Gerlach. See also *boys in blue.*

**mental error** A mistake made when a player was preoccupied, forgetful, or distracted. A classic mental error occurs when, with a runner on first, an infielder throws to first base for a putout when he should have thrown to second base for the force and a possible double play.

**mercy rule** Syn. of *slaughter rule.*

**Merkle** Syn. of *boner,* 1. "His most horrendous boner, a real Merkle, was perpetrated in Boston one night" (Earl Wilson, *Let 'em Eat Cheesecake,* 1949; David Shulman). The term is an eponym for New York Giants first baseman Fred Merkle. Sometimes spelled "merkle."

**Merkle's boner** The baserunning mishap that cost the New York Giants the National League pennant in 1908. See *bonehead* for detailed discussion of the boner.

**merry circle** The trip around the bases.

**merry-go-round** The situation when, with two outs, the bases loaded, and a full count on the batter, all the runners take off on the pitch.

**message pitch** A pitch thrown close to the batter, intended to convey the message: "Don't crowd the plate." See also *purpose pitch,* 1.

**metal** The figurative hand of a fielder who makes an error; e.g., a ball that "hits metal" has been misplayed by a fielder (*Sports Illustrated,* Sept. 13, 1982). The term is an extended metaphor for bad fielding, by which one's hands instead of being soft and pliable are made of iron or become iron skillets off which balls bounce. See also *iron hand.*

**Metness** Fevered fondness for the New York Mets, perhaps a blend of "Mets" and "madness." "Wonder of Metness: Day at Shea" (*New York Times* headline, Apr. 10, 1990).

**Metrodome** Short for *Hubert H. Humphrey Metrodome.*

**Mets theory** A theory that postulates when the New York Mets win, the stock market falls, and when they lose, the stock market goes up. The Mets theory is one of many tongue-in-cheek barometers, including the length of women's hemlines and the winner of the Super Bowl, that tie success or failure of the stock market to events and trends in popular culture. Explained in full in *Forbes* (Sept. 23, 1985), the theory was severely damaged in 1986 when the Mets and the Dow Jones average were both in top form.

**Mexican jumping bean** A major-league player who played in the outlaw Mexican League in 1946–47.

**Mexican League** 1. A Class AA (1955–66) and Class AAA (since 1967) minor league consisting of teams playing in Mexico. 2. An outlaw league organized by multimillionaire liquor distributor Jorge Pasquel and his brothers of Mexico City that flourished briefly (1946–47) in Mexico by luring 18 major-league players (including Max Lanier, Mickey Owen, and Sal Maglie) with lavish salaries. The major leagues blacklisted the players who crossed the border, but threatened by two antitrust suits brought by disgruntled players, settled out of court and rescinded the blacklist and issued amnesties to all fugitive players in 1949.

**Mexican standoff** *n.* A contest or confrontation with no result, but from which one escapes, such as when a pitcher comes out of a game with no decision. **Etymology.** Ramon F. Adams (*Western Words: A Dictionary of the Range, Cow Camp and*

*Trail,* 1948) defines the term: "Getting away alive from any serious difficulty. The Mexican has never had the reputation, among the cowboys, for being a sticker in a fight. They claim that, if he does not win quickly in a gun battle or if he finds much opposition, he leaves in a hurry." **1st Use.** 1891. "'Monk' Cline, who got a Mexican stand-off from Dave Rowe, has signed with Louisville" (*Sporting Times,* Sept. 19, 1891; David Shulman).

**Michelangelo** A superlative pitcher; one who is able to "paint a masterpiece" from the mound. Chicago Cubs pitcher Kerry Wood "hung his 20-strikeout Michelangelo on the Houston Astros" (Rich Reilly, *Sports Illustrated,* June 1, 1998).

**Mickey Finn** *arch.* "A printed schedule of league games for a season; named for a former news reporter who became the first expert modern schedule maker" (Edward J. Nichols, *An Historical Dictionary of Baseball Terminology,* Ph.D. dissertation, 1939). **1st Use.** 1906. (*Sporting Life,* Mar. 10; Edward J. Nichols).

**micro league** Computer-played baseball.

**middle 1.** The center of the plate, as opposed to the corners. **2.** The central part of the playing field; specif., the area between the second baseman and the shortstop. **3.** The collective positions of catcher, pitcher, second base, shortstop, and center field. See also *middle defense.* **4.** That period between the first (top) half and the second (bottom) half of an inning.

**middle bag** Syn. of *second base,* 1.

**middle defense** A team's catcher, shortstop, second baseman, and center fielder, collectively. Syn. of *spine.*

**middle gardener** The center fielder.

**middle infielder** The second baseman or the shortstop.

**middle innings** The fourth, fifth, and sixth innings of a baseball game.

**middle line of knuckles** [softball term] A batting-grip alignment in which the second knuckle of each finger of each hand is in a straight line.

**middle man** Syn. of *middle reliever.*

**middle relief 1.** The replacement of a pitcher in the middle of the game. **2.** A period of relief pitching in the middle of the game, generally the sixth, seventh, and eighth innings.

**middle reliever** A relief pitcher who works in middle relief. A middle reliever usually replaces the starting pitcher and is replaced by the *short reliever,* the setup man, or the closer. Compare *long reliever.* Syn. *middle man.*

**middle station** Syn. of *second base,* 1. **1st Use.** 1910. (*Baseball Magazine,* Apr.; Edward J. Nichols).

**midseason classic** Syn. of *All-Star Game,* 1.

**midsummer classic** Syn. of *All-Star Game,* 1.

**midway** Syn. of *second base,* 1. **1st Use.** 1906. (*Sporting Life,* Mar. 10; Edward J. Nichols).

**Mike Andrews rule** A rule that states that an injured player cannot be replaced on the roster once the World Series begins. The term originated in the 1973 World Series when Oakland A's owner Charles O. Finley tried to replace infielder Andrews under the guise of an injury, when in reality he was upset at Andrews's poor play.

**mile wide** Describing a wild pitch or throw.

**Millennium Plan** A radical plan advanced by Francis C. Richter (*The Sporting Life,* Philadelphia) in 1887 to rid professional baseball of labor unrest, escalating salaries, and other problems and to result in 1,000 years of peace and harmony. The main feature of the plan called for the equalization of the playing strength among the clubs in any professional league by pooling players and distributing them "impartially." It had many other points, including salary caps, reservation of minor-league players by leagues rather than clubs, and a reserve corps of extra players to be used by teams as they were needed during the season. It created much interest at the time and was discussed for several years, but it never seriously interested the players or the club owners.

**Miller-Brown System** A grading system for ranking relief pitchers; specifically a measuring rod for middle relievers. It was devised by Baltimore Orioles pitching coach Ray Miller and Orioles publicist Bob Brown and brought to public attention in an Apr. 1986 article that first appeared in the *Hartford Courant*. Because middle relievers do not usually earn wins, losses, or saves, these statistics are ineffective measures of their abilities. The Miller-Brown System grants one point for a *hold*, 4, two for a victory, and three for a save. One can also get two points for a hold in which three or more scoreless innings are pitched with the score tied or with the team ahead by no more than two runs. One point is subtracted for a *squander* and two for a loss. A special two-point squander can be awarded when the pitcher allows an opponent to tie or go ahead by three or more runs. No more than three points can be accumulated in one game and a reliever can be granted a combination score: hold and victory, hold and loss, hold and squander, squander and save, squander and loss, and squander and victory.

**millionaires club** A group of players whose annual salaries reach seven figures. At the beginning of the 1988 season, the *New York Times* reported that 73 players on Opening Day rosters and disabled lists were in the club, compared to 57 at the beginning of the 1987 season.

**million-ticket year** A milestone in the course of a season that occurs when a club sells its one-millionth ticket. The ability to sell more than a million tickets was once considered a sign of a healthy franchise. Several clubs (e.g., Toronto Blue Jays and Colorado Rockies) have sold more than four million tickets.

**Mills Commission** A group appointed by Albert G. Spalding in 1906 to research the origins of baseball. Rather than conducting research, the commission relied on the evidence provided by old-timers scattered across the nation. The commission's report (Dec. 30, 1907) concluded that "base ball" had its origin in the United States and that the "first scheme for playing it" was devised by Abner Doubleday at Cooperstown, N.Y. in 1839. The commission consisted of Arthur P. Gorman (U.S. Senator from Maryland), former players Alfred J. Reach and George Wright, James E. Sullivan (secretary of the Amateur Athletic Union), and former National League presidents Morgan G. Bulkeley, Nicholas E. Young, and Abraham G. Mills, who chaired the commission.

**Millionaires club.** *Postcard from early in the century suggesting players were overcompensated.*

**Milwaukee Braves** A National League team in Milwaukee, Wis. from the time it ceased being the Boston Braves in 1952 and until it became the Atlanta Braves in 1966.

**Milwaukee Brewers** The name of the National League's Central Division franchise based in Milwaukee, Wis. The Brewers entered the American League in 1970 when the Seattle Pilots, an expansion team in 1969, moved to Milwaukee. The franchise joined the National League beginning with the 1998 season. The nickname is natural for a city that has long regarded itself as America's beer capital. The team is sometimes affectionately referred to as the "Brew Crew."

**mini** A baseball card that is smaller than the traditional 3½ by 2½ inches.

**minicamp** A short training period that is not part of the team's normal spring training.

**minimum arc** [softball term] The lowest apogee at which a legally pitched ball in slow pitch softball reaches in its trajectory from its release from the pitcher's hand to the plate. It is measured in feet from the ground (six feet in Amateur Softball Association of America rules and three feet in United States Slo-Pitch Softball Association rules, which allow the pitcher to release the ball from as low as he or she wants, meaning that a ball released at ground level need only be three feet from the ground). See also *maximum arc; unlimited arc*.

**minimum scale** The lowest salary a league can offer a player.

**Minnesota Twins** The name of the American League Central Division franchise based in Minneapolis, Minn. Named for the twin cities of Minneapolis and St. Paul, the team was the original Washington Senators franchise, which moved to Minnesota in 1960, where it was to begin as the Twin City Twins; but before Opening Day 1961, owner Calvin Griffith decided to name the team for the whole state.

**minnion** A ballplayer who is uglier than a *mullion* (Scott Ostler, *Los Angeles Times*, May 1986).

**minor league** *n.* Any professional North American baseball league other than the two major leagues.

**minor-league** *adj.* Referring to a level of play, behavior, or scale that is below the level of the major leagues; e.g., a "minor-league camp." **Extended Use.** Anything not at the highest level, such as a "minor-league actor."

**minor-league draft** A *draft* in which major-league teams select players from other teams' farm clubs when the players have spent more than a specified period in the minor leagues.

**minor leaguer** A minor-league baseball player.

**minor leagues** The level of professional baseball below that of the major leagues. There are 16 minor leagues today, which are far fewer than in the past when there were as many as 59 such leagues in 1949 (40 million attendance). They are the training ground for the major leagues and are sponsored, controlled, heavily subsidized, and sometimes owned by major-league teams. The minor leagues are classified on the basis of general ability and experience of the players. Since 1963 there are four levels: AAA (highest level), AA, A, and rookie (lowest level). Syn. *minors*.

**minor protest** The efforts of a contending club to move into first place.

**minors** Syn. of *minor leagues*. "I'd rather go to lunch with my ex-wife's attorney than stay in the minors" (Dave Collins on being brought up from the minor leagues, July 1987). **1st Use.** 1898. (*New York Tribune*, June 7; Edward J. Nichols).

**Miracle Braves** The 1914 Boston Braves, so called because it won the National League pennant by 10½ games after falling 15 games behind the New York Giants on July 4 and coming from last place as late as July 19 (winning 68 of their last 87 games). The miracle was complete when the Braves swept the Philadelphia Athletics in the World Series.

**Miracle Game, The** The name given to the no-hit, no-run, 1–0 game pitched by Cleveland Indians hurler Bob Feller against the Chicago White Sox at Comiskey Park on Opening Day (Apr. 16) of the 1940 season.

**miracle man** A manager who achieves success with a reputedly poor team. George Stallings, manager of the 1914 Miracle Braves, who came from last place on July 19 to win the National League pennant and the World Series, was nicknamed "The Miracle Man." **1st Use.** 1914. (*New York Tribune*, Sept. 30; Edward J. Nichols).

**Miracle Mets** The nickname of the 1969 New York Mets who won the National League pennant and the World Series. Previously, the team had never finished higher than ninth place.

**Miracle of Coogan's Bluff** The 1951 New York Giants pennant drive, which ended with Bobby Thomson's pennant-clinching "Shot Heard 'Round the World"—arguably the most famous home run in the history of the game. The home run won a best-of-three playoff series for the National League pennant after the regular season had ended in a tie between the Giants and the Brooklyn Dodgers. Not to be confused with *Little Miracle of Coogan's Bluff*.

**miscue** An error. **1st Use.** 1902. (*Sporting Life,* July 5; Edward J. Nichols). **Etymology.** Edward J. Nichols has traced the term to the game of billiards in which a cue stick and cue ball figure prominently.

**misjudge** For a fielder to end up too far in front, behind, or to the side of a fly ball.

**misplay 1.** *v.* To handle the ball badly. **2.** *n.* An error.

**miss 1.** *v.* To swing at a pitch and fail to hit it; e.g., "Smith swung and missed the ball." **2.** *n.* A failure to hit the ball; e.g., "A swing and a miss." **3.** *v.* For a pitcher to throw a called ball; e.g., "Jones missed the plate with a pitch low and outside." **4.** *v.* For a runner to advance past a base without touching it; e.g., "Brown missed the bag while rounding second."

**mistake** A badly thrown pitch, such as a hanging curve; e.g., "They hit some mistakes, but they also hit some pretty good pitches" (Jeff Tackett, quoted in *Baltimore Sun,* Aug. 13, 1993). See also *mistake pitch.*

**mistake by the lake** A nickname for the immense Cleveland Stadium (formerly known as Municipal Stadium), the home field of the Cleveland Indians (1932–33 and 1947–93). Its capacity reached 78,811 in 1953 and the center-field distance from home plate ranged from 400 feet (1970) to 470 feet (1932). The term also has been applied to the city of Cleveland, Ohio, and to the perennially inept Cleveland Indians of the 1960s through the 1980s.

**mistake hitter** A hitter who takes advantage of a pitcher's mistake; esp. such a hitter who cannot handle the pitcher's best pitch. "[Cecil Fielder] is a good mistake hitter and I just threw him a mistake" (Erik Hanson, quoted in *Baltimore Sun,* Apr. 17, 1996). Other mistake hitters include Steve Balboni and Ryne Sandberg. See also *cripple hitter,* 1.

**mistake pitch** A pitch thrown to a mistake hitter. See also *mistake.*

**Mr. Baseball** A longtime nickname for Connie Mack, manager of the Philadelphia Athletics from 1901 to 1950. In recent years the name has been used in a self-deprecating manner by broadcaster Bob Uecker.

**Mr. Cub** A nickname for Ernie Banks, Chicago Cubs infielder (1953–71) and "franchise player," who had an infectious enthusiasm for the game of baseball.

**Mr. Guess** A nickname for the umpire.

**Mr. Kodak** "A hitter who takes his time getting into the box, allowing photographers time to focus on him" (Joe Goddard, *The Sporting News,* Mar. 6, 1982).

**Mr. March** A spring-training sensation; a player who is great in March and then fails when the season begins.

**Mr. Mustard** Syn. of *hot dog,* 1.

**Mr. October** A nickname for a player who excels in the postseason. It was first applied to Reggie Jackson for his playoff and World Series homer heroics in the 1970s. Jackson hit 18 home runs in 77 postseason games, including three successive home runs in Game 6 (Oct. 18) of the 1977 World Series. In 1997, when John Smoltz's postseason pitching record for the Atlanta Braves reached 10-2, the name was applied to him; after Smoltz defeated the Houston Astros, Paul Newberry (Associated Press, Oct. 4, 1997) opened his story on Smoltz's three-hitter with this line: "Meet the new Mr. October, John Smoltz."

**mit** *arch.* A variant spelling of *mitt* (John B. Foster, *Collier's New Dictionary of the English Language,* 1908).

**mitt 1.** The special *glove* used by a catcher or a first baseman. It has long been said that the term stems from the mittenlike shape of both gloves, which have two sections: one for the thumb and one for the other four fingers. **2.** Any fielder's glove. **Usage Note.** There may be an element of localism involved in calling baseball gloves "mitts." In the author's boyhood neighborhood in Yonkers, N.Y., everything was a mitt while gloves were for boxing and sledding. However, some simply use "mitt" interchangeably with "glove," as this headline and subheadline from the *Miami Herald* (Apr. 5, 1986) would attest: "Mizuno Mitts Make Their Mark: Japanese gloves become popular with major leagues." **3.** A player's hand.

**mix up** To throw an assortment of pitches at various speeds to various locations in and around the strike zone to confuse and deceive the batter; e.g., "Smith mixed up his pitches when facing Jones" or "Brown mixed it up after allowing three successive hits." **1st Use.** 1895. (*New York Press,* July 11; Edward J. Nichols).

**ML** Abbrev. for *major leagues.*

**MLB** Abbrev. for *Major League Baseball.*

**MLBP** Abbrev. for *Major League Baseball Properties.*

**MLBPA** Abbrev. for *Major League Baseball Players Association.*

**MLBPAA** Abbrev. for *Major League Baseball Players Alumni Association.*

**modern** Pertaining to baseball after 1900. The term is used to make a distinction between 19th and 20th centuries; e.g., the "modern era," which excludes anything before 1900.

**modified pitch** [softball term] A form of softball that puts the batter back in the game by prohibiting the fastest and most difficult-to-hit deliveries (the slingshot and the windmill) in fast pitch softball. Syn. "modified."

**moist ball** Syn. of *spitball.* Also spelled "moistball." **1st Use.** 1917. (*New York Times,* Apr. 1; Edward J. Nichols).

**Molly Putz** A name for a player who performs badly on the field. Jim Bouton (*Ball Four,* 1970; Charles D. Poe) wrote that in response to a poor field performance "a lot of managers say their players look like Molly Putz out there."

**momentum** A winning streak; the course of events that keeps a team winning. **Usage Note.** The term is irksome to physicists. Dr. Albert G. Hill, a retired professor of physics at the Massachusetts Institute of Technology, told the *New York Times* (Apr. 6, 1982): "There's a lot of very good physics in baseball. But the use of the word 'momentum' is not one of them. We invent a good word of our own and the sportscasters wreak havoc with it. We mean mass times velocity. They mean hot streak. It's tragic and it gets on my nerves."

**moneybags** Any highly paid player, esp. one who makes more than most of his teammates.

**money ball** A pitch that is hit for a home run.

**money hitter** A hitter with a high batting average.

**money pitch 1.** A pitcher's most effective pitch. See also *out pitch,* 1. **2.** A pitch thrown for a strikeout in a key situation in a game.

**money player 1.** A player who is at his best when the most is at stake, such as one who shines when the team is making a drive for the pennant; a player who delivers in the clutch; one given to winning games. **1st Use.** 1922. (Ernest J. Lanigan, *Baseball Cyclopedia;* Edward J. Nichols). **2.** A player who makes a great deal of money. Joseph McBride (*High and Inside,* 1980) notes: "The term was frequently used in the 1970s to refer to Reggie Jackson and his fellow Yankees, a collection of prima donnas known as 'The Best Team Money Could Buy.'" **3.** A player whose ability attracts many fans.

**money wing** A pitcher's throwing arm. See also *salary arm.* Syn. *pay wing; salary wing.*

**monkey** *obs.* A poor batter, so called because he "makes a monkey" of himself in a futile attempt to get a hit (Edward J. Nichols). **1st Use.** 1888. (*New York Press,* June 3; Edward J. Nichols).

**monkey suit** A baseball uniform. **1st Use.** 1943. "Another animal derivative comes from the standard nickname for uniforms—'monkey suits'" and "Al rushed on to the field as soon as he could don his monkey suit" (*Baseball Magazine,* Jan.).

**monster shot** A home run of major proportions; a tremendous home run, high into the upper stands or out of the ballpark.

**Montreal Expos** The name of the National League East Division franchise in Montreal, Quebec, Canada. An expansion team that came into being with the 1968 season, it was the first major-league team to locate in Canada. The team was named for the popular World's Fair, Expo '67.

**moon shot 1.** A *home run,* esp. one hit for a long distance. A space-age term, it took on new meaning in 1986 when a statistician determined that slugger Mike Schmidt hit best under a full moon. Drew Olsen (*Milwaukee Journal Sentinel*, Sept. 13, 1997) used a more recent example of the term: "Milwaukee Brewers manager Phil Garner and pitching coach Don Rowe have provided their charges with simple advice regarding opponents' home runs. 'If you're going to give them up, make sure they are long moon shots with the bases empty.'" **2.** A home run hit into the left-field stands when the Los Angeles Dodgers played in the Los Angeles Memorial Coliseum (1958–61). It was named for Wally Moon, who hit several home runs over the 42-foot screen erected in short left field. Usually spelled "Moon shot." **Etymology/1st Use.** 1959. Bob Heilman (letter, Jan. 24, 1992) of Myrtle Creek, Ore., wrote: "The term dates back to 1959 when Wally Moon came to the Dodgers from St. Louis. Wally learned to pop the ball over the screen, helping the Dodgers to win the '59 pennant and bringing us the 'Moon shot' with a capital 'M.' It was, of course, the time of Sputnik and the space race, so the happy combination of rocketry and Wally produced the term." Heilman's guess is that it was actually coined by *Los Angeles Times* columnist Jim Murray.

**mop up** To enter the game as a relief pitcher when the game is hopelessly lost. The term is a clear play on the idea of "mopping up" the mess created by the earlier pitcher or pitchers. **1st Use.** 1937. (*Philadelphia Record*, Aug. 28; Edward J. Nichols).

**mop-up duty** Pitching in relief when the game is hopelessly lost; e.g., "[Baltimore Orioles manager Ray] Miller has gradually lost confidence in [Norm] Charlton and now uses him in mop-up duty" (*Baltimore Sun*, May 12, 1998).

**mop-up man** A relief pitcher who commonly enters a game when the outcome is no longer in doubt, usually when the pitcher's team is far behind. A team's top relief pitcher is seldom if ever used as a mop-up man.

**Moriarity** *arch.* A blind or wild swing at a pitch. The term is named for George Moriarity, an infielder (1903–16) who was widely known for swinging without looking at the ball. **1st Use.** 1914. "I tried to slip the fast one over on him and he shut his eyes and took a Moriarity at it—that's all" (*Colliers*, Aug. 1, 1914; David Shulman).

**morning glory** A hitter who shines early in the season but then cools off; a spring hitter. The term is commonly applied to a rookie off to a hot start. **Etymology.** The folk name for a flowering vine that only opens its flowers in the morning. John Ciardi (*Good Words to You*, 1987) notes that the term began showing up in the 19th century as American sports slang for an athlete who begins brilliantly but becomes lackluster when he tires. **Extended Use.** Anyone whose performance lags over time. Ciardi's example: "The official flower for the fiftieth wedding anniversary should be the morning glory."

**morning journal** A baseball bat made of inferior wood, often said to have the effectiveness of a rolled-up newspaper.

**moss** A ballplayer's term for hair.

**Morning glory.** *Cartoon with one of the great morning glory lines featured in a telegram.*

**Most Valuable Player 1.** The player selected by the Baseball Writers Association of America to receive the *Most Valuable Player Award.* From a cynical or jaded perspective, Jimmy Cannon described the Most Valuable Player as "a guy on the club that wins the pennant"; in fact, many Most Valuable Players have come from pennant-winning teams, which is added proof of the value of the player. Abbrev. *MVP.* **2.** An honor voted to an outstanding player at any given time, such as during a specified period (week or month) or in a given venue (e.g., the World Series Most Valuable Player and the All-Star Game Most Valuable Player). **Extended Use.** A key performer in any field.

**Most Valuable Player Award** An annual award presented since 1931 by the Baseball Writers Association of America to the outstanding player in each major league. Selections were made by one writer from each league city (1931–37), three writers from each league city (1938–60), and two writers from each league city (since 1961). Since 1938, each writer votes for 10 players in descending order, with each first-place vote worth 14 points, each second-place vote worth 9 points, and one less point down to 10th place, which is worth one point. The award is a trophy bearing the name of Kenesaw Mountain Landis, baseball's first commissioner.

**motion 1.** The pitcher's movement during his delivery to home plate. Bert Dunne (*Folger's Dictionary of Baseball,* 1958) notes that "hitting at a pitcher's 'motion' means batter was bewildered by arm action and swung at 'motion' instead of ball." **2.** See *in motion.*

**motor 1.** *v.* To run at top speed. **2.** *n.* A player who can run fast.

**motormouth** A player who talks all the time. See also *Joe Quote.*

**mound 1.** *n.* The elevated circle of dirt, 18 feet in diameter, the center of which is 59 feet from the back of home plate toward second base, where the pitcher is situated and from which the ball is delivered to batters. The pitcher's plate or rubber is set in the ground on top of the mound. The mound since 1969 should be no higher than 10 inches at its peak (previously it was 15 inches high). Syn. *pitcher's mound; pitcher's box; firing line; launching pad,* 2; *front,* 2; *turtleback.* **1st Use.** 1907. (*New York Evening Journal,* May 4; Edward J. Nichols). **2.** *adj.* A synonym for "pitching," as in "mound assignment," "mound duel," "mound duty," "mound statesman," "mound mainstay," and, as applied to a relief pitcher in the *Orlando Sentinel* (Feb. 26, 1988), "mound savior." **Usage Note.** The extent to which the word "mound" has become part of the patter of baseballese was driven home in Frank Sullivan's "The Cliché Expert Testifies on Baseball" (*The New Yorker,* Aug. 27, 1949). After explaining "moundsman" and "mound assignment," the expert is asked what the pitcher on the other team is called. He replies: "mound adversary," or "mound opponent," or "mound nominee." The pitchers have a "mound duel"; the winner is the "mound victor" and as a result he is a "mound ace" or an "ace moundsman" of the "mound corps."

**mound conference** A meeting on the mound during a game between the pitcher and the manager or pitching coach, and often including one or more players, esp. the catcher, to discuss pitching strategy, "settle" the pitcher down, or call for a relief pitcher. What actually goes on during these meetings? New York Yankees pitcher Vic Raschi (*San Francisco News,* July 6, 1949; Peter Tamony) noted that most conferences were either held to slow down a pitcher who was working too fast or to relieve tension: "Once in a World Series game, the immortal first baseman, Lou Gehrig, walked over to the great Red Ruffing and asked him what town he was in."

**mound corps** A team's pitchers as a collective group; a team's *pitching staff.*

**moundsman** A pitcher. **1st Use.** 1914. "This information will be received with loud, ringing cheers by that eminent moundsman, Thomas Aloysius Kernohan" (*Colliers,* Aug. 1, 1914; David Shulman).

**mount** To ride an opponent. See also *jockey,* 2.

**move 1.** *n.* The action, speed, and deception of a pitcher when throwing to first base from a set position; e.g., "Smith has a great move to first." **2.** *v.*

To advance a runner; e.g., "Jones moved Brown to second on his ground ball to the right side." **3.** *v.* To advance to the next base; e.g., "Smith moved on the pitch." **4.** *v.* To change a defensive player from one position to another; e.g., "The manager moved Jones from shortstop to center field." **5.** *v.* To trade a player or to send a player to the minor leagues; e.g., "The Orioles moved Jones to Rochester." **6.** *n.* Trading a player or sending a player to the minor leagues. **7.** *v.* See *move the ball around.*

**move-around fielder** A fielder with a wide range, who covers more than the average amount of territory. (H. G. Salsinger, *Baseball Digest,* Apr. 1945).

**move around the box** For a batter to employ several different stances during one plate appearance.

**move in the fences** To reconfigure a ballpark to make it easier for batters to hit home runs.

**move list** A list of players who are available for trading or sale.

**movement** The characteristic of a pitched ball that deviates vertically or horizontally as it approaches and crosses the plate; a measure of deception. *Sports Illustrated* (Aug. 2, 1993) determined that this term was a "new and worse" replacement for the "old and terse" term "stuff"; but then *Sports Illustrated* (Apr. 1, 1995) used the term when it quoted Tony Gwynn on Greg Maddux: "The difference in him the last three years is that everything he throws has great movement."

**move the ball around** To throw a series of pitches to various parts of the strike zone. "I felt like I was throwing the ball well and moving it around today" (Roger Clemens, quoted in *Washington Post,* Aug. 31, 1986).

**move the runner** To cause a baserunner to advance one or more bases by a hit, bunt, sacrifice, walk, hit by pitch, error, fielder's choice, ground-out, or flyout; e.g., "Smith moved the runner along to second with his bunt" or "Jones moved the runner over to third by hitting to the right side."

**move up 1.** *v.* To advance a base; e.g., "Smith moved up to third on Jones's grounder to second." **2.** *v.* To hit a ball that advances a baserunner; e.g.,

"Jones moved Smith up to third on his grounder to second." **3.** *n.* Syn. of *One Eye Jim Bats.*

**mow down** For a pitcher to retire many batters or a series of batters; e.g., "Smith mowed them down for six innings." **1st Use.** 1891. (*Chicago Herald,* May 5; Edward J. Nichols).

**moxie 1.** Nerve and skill used in playing baseball; "a player's guts or know-how shown in a game" (Frank Graham & Dick Hyman, *Baseball Wit and Wisdom,* 1962). The term is usually couched in phrases such as "lots of moxie" or "the old moxie." **2.** General pluck and mettle on or off the field. "Love him or hate him—as club owners did . . . in refusing to renew [commissioner] Bowie Kuhn's contract—but no one can help admiring the moxie of the guy" (*Gloucester County* [N.J.] *Times,* Nov. 3, 1982). **3.** The power that makes a good and hard fastball. A catcher would say to a pitcher: "Put some Moxie on it!" (Edmund A. MacDonald, *Lewiston Daily Sun,* July 12, 1986).

**Etymology/1st Use.** 1908. There is no questioning the fact that the term comes from a drink or tonic that was created and named in 1876 by Dr. Augustin Thompson and marketed as a "nerve tonic" and "nerve food." The link between Moxie and one's nerves led to the obvious "nerve and skill" meaning of the word. William & Mary Morris (*Morris Dictionary of Word and Phrase Origins,* 1977) write: "One theory is that the original 'Moxie' was so bitter that you had to have plenty of courage to drink the stuff." Frank N. Potter (*The Book of Moxie,* 1987) disputed this claim, insisting that it is a simple play on the word "nerve"

**Moxie.** *This advertisement appeared in the first issue of* Baseball Magazine, *May 1908.*

in Moxie Nerve Food: "How do I know that I'm right about the derivation of 'moxie'? Well, before World War I, when I was a kid in Massachusetts, we always said, 'You're full of Moxie'—never 'You've got moxie.' It's as simple as that." But Potter does not dispute the power of the early formula. He has written that the early tonic "got up into your nose like horse radish and made you snort."

The question is how did "moxie" move to baseball? Several possible explanations present themselves. Potter (letter, Dec. 12, 1986) responded: "Moxie's being peddled in ballparks, especially in Boston, could have had something to do with the matter." Q. David Bowers, author of the 760-page *Moxie Encyclopedia* (1985), offered these thoughts (letter, Nov. 25, 1986): "In general, the word 'moxie' in a generic sense apparently began in a big way in the 1920s. The Moxie Co. scrapbooks contain a number of news articles with sports (in particular) references to use of the term at that time. Moxie was used to describe an athlete who had a combination of skill, energy, and enthusiasm—and this is the way it is still used today. The generic word 'moxie' seems to imply a special spirit or quality. Interestingly, the Moxie Co. encouraged the generic use of the name. They issued a number of advertisements and even large metal signs bearing the inscription THE DRINK THAT MADE THE NAME FAMOUS—a reference to Moxie, the beverage, making 'moxie,' the generic word, well known." Significantly, there is an ad for Moxie in the very first issue (May 1908) of *Baseball Magazine*.

As for the origin of the original term as it was applied to the drink, there are several theories. These were mentioned in an article entitled "The Moxie Man" by Ambra Watkins, which appeared in the program for the 5th Annual Moxie Festival held in Lisbon Falls, Maine, on July 8–9, 1988. The article was about Frank "Mr. Moxie" Anicetti, the creator of the festival and a leading collector of Moxiana, and it reported that he had been researching the origin of the term. The possibilities suggested by Anicetti include: 1) it comes from an Indian word meaning "dark water" (the color of the drink is almost black); 2) it was taken from a Moxie Lake north of the Rangeley Mountains in Maine; and 3) it began with a man named Captain Moonsey or a Maine Indian chief named Moxus.

**M's** Short for *Seattle Mariners.*

**muckle** *arch.* Strength or power. The term is a playful corruption of the word "muscle." **1st Use.** 1862. (*New York Sunday Mercury,* July 13; Edward J. Nichols).

**mud 1.** See *rubbing mud.* **2.** See *baseball mud.*

**mud ball 1.** A ball that has been doctored by rubbing mud into its seams so that it will behave unnaturally. (Such a ball is not to be confused with the balls legally rubbed up with mud by the umpires before a game.). **2.** A pitch with an exaggerated break because of a bit of dirt stuck to one side of the ball that has been wetted with saliva. Also spelled "mudball." **Extended Use.** A dirty allegation. A political candidate, after hearing a last-minute charge that he had Ku Klux Klan backing, said: "He has lost his fast ball, he has lost his curve ball. All he's got left is his mud ball." (*Time* magazine, Sept. 2, 1946; Peter Tamony).

**mud field** The playing field after a rain.

**Mudville 1.** The mythical town represented by Casey and his teammates in Ernest L. Thayer's 1888 poem, "Casey at the Bat." By extension, "Mudville" has become the name for any town whose team comes up short. When the 1986 World Series ended, the *Boston Globe* (Oct. 28, 1986) ran this headline: "The Mets Take It, 8–5 . . . and Boston is Mudville Once Again." **2.** The world of baseball, especially professional baseball referred to in a pejorative sense. "Seeking Joy (and Crowds) in Mudville Inc." was the title of a story in the *New York Times* (Apr. 24, 1995), which said in part: "After an eight-month absence, major league baseball returns this week, hoping all is forgiven. But just in case it isn't, the 28 teams are offering mea culpa, cut-rate tickets, free yearbooks, snappy slogans, car giveaways and European vacations."

**muff 1.** *v.* To drop a grounder or fly ball; to miss a catch or bungle a play; to make an error. **1st Use.** 1869. (*DeWitt's Official Base Ball Guide;* Edward J. Nichols). **2.** *n.* Any error. **1st Use.** 1874. (Chicago *Inter-Ocean,* July 1; Edward J. Nichols). **3.** *n.* Short for *muffin.* **Etymology.** J. Louis Kuethe (*American Speech,* Dec. 1937) discusses the baseball glossary that appears in Mrs. John A. Logan's *The Home Manual: Everybody's Guide in Social,*

**Muff.** *A 1907 postcard displays the term.*

*Domestic, and Business Life* (1889) and notes that a "possible explanation of the verb 'to muff' appears from the spelling of the noun form ['muffin'] of the word" as given in Logan's *Manual*, which refers the reader to "drop it like a hot cake." Henry Chadwick's definition: "A fielder is said to 'muff' a ball when he fails to pick it up neatly, or to hold it long enough to make it a fair catch." **Extended Use.** Any kind of error. "Too often cops bring in good cases only to have district attorneys muff them in court" (David Black, *Murder at the Met;* Charles D. Poe). The term also seems to apply in the case of intentional errors or missed shots. In *Wise Guy: Life in a Mafia Family,* by Nicholas Pileggi, a fixer tells how schemes are mounted to make a basketball game pay off: "For instance, if the bookmakers or the Vegas oddsmakers said the line was Boston by ten, our play-

ers had to muff enough shots to make sure they won by less than the bookies' ten points. That way they'd win their games and we'd win the bets" (Charles D. Poe).

**muffed ball** An error. Henry Chadwick noted that muffed balls "are rated as errors of fielding and count against a batsman when he makes bases on them."

**muffer** Syn. of *muffin.* **1st Use.** 1874. (Chicago *Inter-Ocean,* July 25; Edward J. Nichols).

**muffery** Bad or sloppy defensive play. **1st Use.** 1883. "The last inning was commenced and the Athletics got another streak of muffery" (*Sporting Life,* Apr. 15; David Shulman).

**muffin** *arch.* An unskilled or ineffective player; baseball's equivalent of golf's "duffer." Syn. *muff,* 3; *muffer.* **1st Use.** 1859. "Some wild throwing, and otherwise muffin-like play" (*New York Clipper,* July 9; Peter Morris). **Etymology.** Here is how "muffins" were defined by Henry Chadwick: "This is the title of a class of ball players who are both practically and theoretically unacquainted with the game. Some 'muffins,' however, know something about how the game should be played, but cannot practically exemplify their theory. 'Muffins' rank the lowest in the grade of the nines of a club, the list including first and second nine players, amateurs, and, lastly 'muffins.'"

**mug a ball** To make a fielding misplay. **1st Use.** 1874. (Chicago *Inter-Ocean,* July 16; Edward J. Nichols).

**mulligan** A second chance. Making a comeback at age 31 in 1996, pitcher Joe Magrane said: "It's not often a player gets a mulligan in his career" (*Baltimore Sun,* Mar. 31, 1996). **Etymology.** From the golf custom employed by duffers to allow each player one "do over" of a drive per round of golf.

**mullion** An ugly or unattractive person, male or female, but more often than not a player. See also *minnion; scullion.* **Usage Note.** Mike Gonring (*Baseball Digest,* June 1979) termed "mullion" the "most famous" word in baseball, adding that a mullion might also be overweight ("having tonnage") or old ("having mileage"). Scott Ostler (*Los Angeles Times,* May 4, 1986) seemed to concur:

"Ballplayers might sit around the dugout or bullpen and select their major league all-mullion team. . . . One player told me that he once had a teammate named Buckethead, who was also a mullion, and thus was referred to as Muckethead." The term also is used with affection. The legendary Jimmie Reese (California Angels coach, 1973–94), whose career started as a batboy in 1917, called Jim Abbott his "pet mullion," used the term routinely when addressing Bo Jackson, and loved to say to rookies, "Hey, Mullion, who ever said you were a ballplayer?"

**multiple delivery** A pitching style with a variety of pitches.

**murder** *v.* To get the better of an opposing team.

**Murderers' Row 1.** A nickname for the heart of the 1927 New York Yankees batting order, which included Babe Ruth (60 home runs, .356), Lou Gehrig (47 home runs, .373), Earle Combs (.356 and who led the league in hits, singles, and triples), Tony Lazzeri (18 home runs, .309), and Bob Meusel (.337). The team, which won 110 games, did not have one weak hitter. **2.** Any cluster of good hitters on a team who are "murder" on opposing pitchers. The label has been used several times over the years, but it has yet to stick with any team but the 1927 New York Yankees. In 1936, for instance, several New York sportswriters tried to tag the heart of the Yankee order "Murderers' Row #2" or the "Homicide Squad." Also, on the eve of dropping three in a row to the Los Angeles Dodgers in 1963, New York sportswriter Harry Grayson did an article on San Francisco Giants hitters, which he entitled "Giants Make Murderers' Row Look Like Hitless Wonders!" (*San Francisco Call-Bulletin,* May 14, 1963; Peter Tamony). **Etymology/1st Use.** 1858. According to Bill Bryson (*Baseball Digest,* Apr. 1948), the writer who first called the Ruth-Gehrig-Combs-Lazzeri-Meusel combo "Murderers' Row" "probably drew praise from his boss for a fresh, vibrant phrase"; he then notes: "Well, it had been used in a New York newspaper's account of a game a few years before that—about seventy years in fact. The 1858 writer got it from the name given the isolated row of cells containing dangerous criminals in the Tombs

prison in New York." Edward J. Nichols (*An Historical Dictionary of Baseball Terminology,* Ph.D. dissertation, 1939) concurs, noting that there is a clipping in Henry Chadwick's Scrapbooks from 1858 in which the term is applied to a lineup of powerful hitters. Baseball historian L. Robert Davids found that the term was used in describing the 1919 New York Yankees. The earliest application to the Ruth-based Yankees lineup was discovered by Barry Popik (*The Sporting News,* May 6, 1926): "[Manager Miller] Huggins has real 'Murderers' Row' with Ruth doing his part and aiding toward fine team spirit." **Extended Use.** Usually carrying sinister overtones, the term has been applied to "heavy hitters" outside baseball; e.g., during the Presidential campaign of 1952, Adlai Stevenson attacked Dwight Eisenhower for being backed by a "Murderers' Row of reactionaries" (*San Francisco Chronicle,* Oct. 5, 1952; Peter Tamony).

**murder smart stuff** To hit a pitcher's trick pitch; to hit "the one he depends upon to fool the batters" (Samuel Nisenson, *Giant Book of Sport,* 1948).

**Murphy money** Spring-training spending money and/or money given to players for meals while on the road. **Etymology.** Many explanations have been given for this term but it is clear that one is conclusive. When the question of where this term came from was brought up in the sports pages of the *San Francisco Chronicle,* Peter Tamony brought together information that was published in Art Rosenbaum's column (Apr. 12, 1972). In 1946, Boston lawyer Robert Murphy tried to organize a player's union, which was called the American Baseball Guild. He advocated a pension plan for players, minimum salaries, and expense money. Murphy decided to take a stand with the Pittsburgh Pirates, where he said that 95% of the team carried Guild cards. Frederick G. Lieb (*The Baseball Story,* 1950) explained what happened next: "There was considerable feeling when William Benswanger, Pirate president, and his attorney refused to negotiate with Murphy, and a players' strike was voted down before a Pirate-Brooklyn game, June 5. Murphy then called for a strike before a Pittsburgh-New York night game two days later. With the stands full of fans, the players locked manager Frisch, coaches Wagner,

Davis, and Bissonette, and organizer Murphy out of the clubhouse, and took their strike ballot. It was 20 to 16 in favor of the strike, but as two-thirds vote was required, Murphy's strike request was turned down."

The union quickly fell apart, but the owners were eager to block any further efforts by Murphy (and defections by players to the Mexican League) and made several concessions by the time of the 1946 All-Star Game. They included a $5,000 minimum salary, a pension fund, and money for expenses on the road and for the period of spring training, or, as it was then dubbed, "Murphy money."

**muscle 1.** *n.* The strength and playing ability of a baseball team; e.g., "Ruth and Gehrig added muscle to the Yankee lineup." **2.** *v.* To overpower a bad pitch into a hit; e.g., "Smith muscled an inside fastball down the third base line."

**muscle heat** A fastball pitched with great strength and speed.

**mush bag** An old, worn baseball used in batting practice.

**mush ball** [softball term] **1.** The 16-inch softball to distinguish it from the smaller 12-inch version. In some circles before World War II, the softball came to be known as the "mush ball pill." Also spelled "mushball." Syn. *pillow ball*, 1; *mushmelon*, 1. **2.** The game of *softball*, 1, using the 16-inch mush ball. "Swede Pierson Makes Hit With Mushball Moguls" (*San Francisco News* headline, Apr. 19, 1940; Peter Tamony). Also spelled "mushball." Syn. *pillow ball*, 2; *mushmelon*, 2.

**mushmelon 1.** Syn. of *mush ball*, 1. **2.** Syn. of *mush ball*, 2.

**mussy ball** *arch.* A blunder-filled game; a sloppy contest.

**Mustache Gang** A nickname for the Oakland A's of the early 1970s.

**mustard 1.** A fastball. **2.** Velocity; e.g., a good fastball is one with a lot of "mustard."

**mustard man** Syn. of *hot dog*, 1.

**must have hit an air pocket** A common excuse for a misjudged fly ball.

**Mush ball.** *Pitcher Calvin Ammons at a 16-inch tournament in Racine, Wisconsin, 1992.*

**must win** A game that is essential to staying alive in a season or a series, esp. in postseason play. Game 7 of the World Series is a "must win" for both teams.

**MVP** Abbrev. for *Most Valuable Player.* "[Roger] Clemens Is MVP in AL" (*Washington Post* headline, Nov. 19, 1986).

**my pitch** A hitter's favorite pitch; the one he hits most effectively.

**mystifier** A curveball. **1st Use.** 1910. (*Baseball Magazine*, Apr.; Edward J. Nichols).

# N

**nab** To throw or tag a runner out, esp. when he is trying for extra bases.

**NABBP** Abbrev. for *National Association of Base Ball Players.*

**nail 1.** *v.* To throw a runner out, esp. when he is attempting to steal or try for an extra base on a play. **1st Use.** 1888. (*New York Press,* Apr. 19; Edward J. Nichols). **2.** *n.* A good throw; one that "nails" the runner. **3.** *v.* To hit the ball with force. **1st Use.** 1895. "He tried to nail the ball hard, but he only fanned and went back to the bench" (Herbert Bellwood, *The Rivals of Riverwood;* David Shulman). **4.** *n.* A forceful hit. **5.** *n.* A rookie or player with temporary status. Leonard Shecter (*Baseball Digest,* June 1963) explains this usage of the term: "'They gave me a nail' is often the complaint of a rookie who has just joined a team. There aren't enough lockers so he's asked to hang his clothes on a nail. It also means the clubhouse man doesn't expect him to be around long." **6.** *v.* To be hit by a pitched ball; e.g., "Smith was nailed twice by Jones."

**nail-biter** A close, tense game in which both spectators and players are tense and on edge. It has been said of a poor relief pitcher that he can turn seemingly safe leads into nail-biters.

**nails** A team that plays and usually wins tough, close games. "The Seattle Mariners have been nails in the late innings because of a strong bullpen and rallying ability. They have won or tied twelve games in the ninth inning." (*San Francisco Examiner,* June 3, 1982).

**Nails** A generic nickname for a player who is "tough as nails." "At the plate, all twitches and fidgets was . . . Len Dykstra. Nails, the Mets call him." (John Feinstein, *Washington Post,* Oct. 12, 1986).

**"Na, Na, Na, Na"** The fans' victory song, from a 1969 song of farewell titled "Na, Na, Hey, Hey, Kiss Him Goodbye" by the rock group The Steam. It was picked up by Comiskey Park organist Nancy Faust in 1977 and first became popular in Chicago.

**NAL** Abbrev. for *Negro American League.*

**NAPBL** Abbrev. for *National Association of Professional Baseball Leagues.*

**National Agreement 1.** Short for "National Agreement of Professional Base Ball Associations" that came into effect for the 1884 season and succeeded the *Tripartite Agreement.* The name change was necessitated when the Eastern League (a minor league) added itself to the agreement; many provisions were also rewritten, but its purport, mutual recognition of contracts, remained the same. (Peter Morris). **2.** Baseball's constitution. It was defined most directly and given historical perspective by Hugh S. Fullerton (*American Magazine,* June 1912): "The contract entered into by the American and National leagues and later subscribed to by the minor leagues, numbering about forty, to insure peace, protect property rights and assign territory as well as to prevent competitive bidding for the services of players."

**national anthem** The patriotic song that has

been played before all major-league games since World War II.

**National Association** See *National Association of Professional Base Ball Players.*

**National Association of Base Ball Players** An association of amateur baseball players organized by Henry Chadwick in New York City in 1858, and the central administrative body for baseball through 1870. It introduced a uniform code of rules (such as nine-inning games) and ethics. When the Association was unable to control gambling or enforce its rules, and bowed to pressure to include professionals on team rosters, the amateurs walked out, leaving the professionals to develop, in 1871, a new organization, the National Association of Professional Base Ball Players. Abbrev. *NABBP.*

**National Association of Professional Baseball Leagues** The organization of the minor leagues as a unit since 1901. Abbrev. *NAPBL.*

**National Association of Professional Base Ball Players** The first professional baseball league, created in 1871 to govern professional players (rather than clubs). The Association lasted only until 1875 and was marred by drinking, gambling, rowdiness, players switching teams, lack of uniformity in scheduling, and solvency of clubs (there were 25 teams during the Association's five-year history). Only three teams lasted the entire period: Philadelphia Athletics, Boston Red Stockings, and New York Mutuals. A committee on records declined to designate the Association a "major league" because of its haphazard scheduling. Commonly known as *National Association.*

**National Baseball Hall of Fame and Museum** The official museum of baseball located in Cooperstown, N.Y., which was conceived in 1935, opened in 1938, and dedicated in 1939. It includes the *National Baseball Library and Archives.* Syn. *national shrine; Hall of Fame, 2.*

**National Baseball Library and Archives** The baseball research library within the Hall of Fame complex in Cooperstown, N.Y. Syn. *baseball's attic.*

**National Commission** Baseball's governing body, established in 1902 when the National League and the American League came to terms with each other, until Nov. 1920 when Kenesaw Mountain Landis was named the first baseball commissioner. The National Commission consisted of three members: the president of the American League (B. Bancroft Johnson), the president of the National League (various individuals), and the chairman, chosen by the two presidents (August Herrmann, president of the Cincinnati Reds). Hugh S. Fullerton (*American Magazine,* June 1912) described the National Commission's vast scope of major- and minor-league domain as "about 42 leagues, composed of about 338 clubs, and over 10,000 players." Also referred to as *Commission.*

**national game** The name given to baseball at the end of the Civil War when it became the most widely played and popular American game.

*National game.*

Typically it was described in words like these: "The game of base ball has now become beyond question the leading feature of the out-door sports of the United States, and to account for its present truly proud position, there are many and sufficient reasons" (Charles A. Peverelly, *The Book of American Pastimes,* 1866).

George B. Kirsch (*The Creation of American Team Sports,* 1989) suggests that "national game" in America quickly began acquiring an exclusive application to baseball and quotes the *New York Clipper* (Aug. 16, 1856) that baseball "had its origin on this Continent, and is now thoroughly established as an American game, equal, to a certain extent, to the English game of Cricket." Four months later the *Clipper* (Dec. 13, 1856) announced that "the game of Base Ball is generally considered the National game amongst Americans, and right well does it deserve that appellation." By 1859, *Harper's Weekly* (Oct. 15) would claim: "Our people, or that pure and reformed part of them (as one of the old Episcopal collects says) which advocates athletic exercises, excuse the general neglect of cricket in this country by saying that base-ball is our national game." Yet, the term did not always mean "nationwide"; e.g., *Porter's Spirit of the Times* (Nov. 15, 1856) viewed "the continued prevalence of Base Ball as the National game of the region of the Manhattanese." To be sure, baseball continued for a time to be regarded by many writers as but one among numerous actual or potential American "national" sports and games; e.g., a June 1857 editorial in the *New York Times* nominated pilot boat racing.

One of the most fascinating uses of the term "national game" appeared on the editorial page of the *New York Times* in 1881: "There is really reason to believe that baseball is gradually dying out in this country. It has been openly announced by an athletic authority that what was once called the national game is being steadily superseded by cricket. . . . Our experience with the national game of baseball has been sufficiently thorough to convince us that it was in the beginning a sport unworthy of men and that it is now, in its fully developed state, unworthy of gentlemen." (The full version of this premature obituary for baseball appears in Ira L. Smith & H. Allen Smith, *Low and Inside,* 1949.) An equally misdirected claim appeared in *Century*

magazine in 1872: "During these years the quiet and social home game of croquet has been steadily gaining ground, and to-day its devotees, not without justice, claim for it the distinction of the true and only 'National Game' of America."

See also *national pastime.* Sometimes spelled "National Game."

**National League 1.** One of the two major leagues, founded on Feb. 2, 1876, under the leadership of businessman William A. Hulbert of Chicago. The teams that were charter members were Boston, Chicago, Cincinnati, Hartford, Louisville, New York, Philadelphia, and St. Louis. The original league represented four western and four eastern cities and was set up with clear rules and policies, including standard player contracts, a code of conduct, and a prohibition on the sale of intoxicants in parks under the league's jurisdiction. Currently, the National League has 16 teams divided into three divisions: East (Atlanta Braves, Florida Marlins, Montreal Expos, New York Mets, Philadelphia Phillies); Central (Chicago Cubs, Cincinnati Reds, Houston Astros, Milwaukee Brewers, Pittsburgh Pirates, St. Louis Cardinals); and West (Arizona Diamondbacks, Colorado Rockies, Los Angeles Dodgers, San Diego Padres, San Francisco Giants). Abbrev. *NL.* Syn. *senior circuit.* **2.** See *Negro National League.*

**National League Central** The Central Division of the National League, consisting of teams grouped around midwestern cities, created in 1994. The division consisted of five teams from 1994 to 1997 (Chicago Cubs, Cincinnati Reds, Houston Astros, Pittsburgh Pirates, and St. Louis Cardinals) and six teams since 1998 (with the addition of the Milwaukee Brewers).

**National League Championship Series** The *Championship Series* in which the two National League teams that won divisional titles (and since 1995, the Division Series) play for the National League pennant and the right to play the American League champion in the World Series. Abbrev. *NLCS.*

**National League East** The East Division of the National League, consisting of teams grouped around eastern and midwestern cities, created in

1969 when the National League expanded from 10 to 12 teams. The division consisted of six teams from 1969 to 1992 (Chicago Cubs, Montreal Expos, New York Mets, Philadelphia Phillies, Pittsburgh Pirates, and St. Louis Cardinals), seven teams in 1993 (with the addition of the Florida Marlins), and five teams since 1994 (Atlanta Braves, Florida Marlins, Montreal Expos, New York Mets, and Philadelphia Phillies).

**National League style** The real and imagined style of play and officiating in the National League, commonly portrayed as emphasizing the running game and defense. The strike zone is supposedly lower in the National League. Compare *American League style.*

**National League West** The West Division of the National League, consisting of teams grouped primarily around western cities, created in 1969 when the National League expanded from 10 to 12 teams. The division consisted of six teams from 1969 to 1992 (Atlanta Braves, Cincinnati Reds, Houston Astros, Los Angeles Dodgers, San Diego Padres, and San Francisco Giants), seven teams in 1993 (with the addition of the Colorado Rockies), four teams from 1994 to 1997 (Dodgers, Giants, Padres, and Rockies), and five teams since 1998 (with the addition of the Arizona Diamondbacks).

**national pastime** A term commonly applied to baseball in the United States. First used in 1856, it eventually overshadowed other names such as *national game* and "national sport." Geoffrey C. Ward & Ken Burns (*Baseball: An Illustrated History,* 1994) note: "On December 5, 1856, in a fine early example of New York chauvinism, the New York *Mercury* had referred to the game for the first time as 'the National Pastime.'" Fred Ivor-Campbell (Warren, R.I.) cites an article from *Porter's Spirit of the Times* (Nov. 15, 1856) that refers to cricket, "base ball," "foot ball," and "racket" as "sports and pastimes" that "we hope may become national throughout the U.S. of America." Ivor-Campbell also cited a later issue (Jan. 31, 1857) of *Spirit of the Times:* "Base ball has been known in the Northern States as far back as the memory of the oldest inhabitant reacheth, and must be regarded as a national pastime, the same as cricket is by the British."

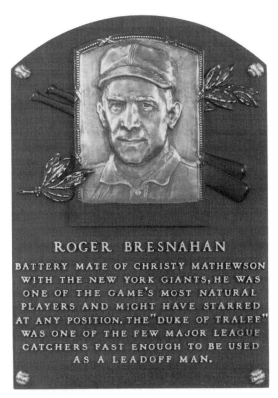

*Natural, the/a.* This man fit the description so well that he is described as such on his Hall-of-Fame plaque.

**Nationals** A nickname for the *Washington Senators,* 2, esp. from 1939 to 1957. See also *Nats.*

**national shrine** Syn. of *National Baseball Hall of Fame and Museum.*

**Nats** A nickname for the expansion *Washington Senators,* 3. See also *Nationals.*

**natural, the/a** A player who seems to have been born with, rather than acquired, the ability to excel effortlessly at the game of baseball. The term has been applied to such players as Roger Bresnahan, Shoeless Joe Jackson, Roy Hobbs (the hero of Bernard Malamud's 1952 novel *The Natural*), and even Jose Canseco; e.g., "Canseco's 'The Natural'" (*Boston Herald* headline, Sept. 3, 1986).

**natural hitter** An easy-swinging and effective hitter with a good eye for the strike zone. **1st Use.** 1910. (*American Magazine,* July; Edward J. Nichols).

**natural stuff** A pitcher's hopping fastball and sharp curveball as opposed to such trick pitches as the screwball and knuckleball.

**Navy Yard home run** *arch.* A strikeout. "The phrase was coined from the fact that at the Navy Yard the men quit work at three strikes of the bell" (*Philadelphia Inquirer,* Sept. 22, 1904).

**near beer pitcher** A pitcher who commonly works himself into a three-ball-and-two-strike (3-2) count. **Etymology.** Patrick Ercolano (*Fungoes, Floaters and Fork Balls,* 1987) notes the term was coined by New York Yankees catcher Aaron Robinson in the 1940s: "The term alludes to near beer, a weakened type of brew that contains only 3.2 percent alcohol and is sometimes also called '3.2 beer.'"

**near no-hitter** The work of a pitcher who has either pitched a one-hitter or taken a no-hitter into the late innings.

**necessities** A word given a special baseball context on Apr. 6, 1987 when it was used to summarize what blacks were accused of lacking and why they were not being given jobs as managers and general managers. It was given this context by Los Angeles Dodger general manager Al Campanis when he was asked by newsman Ted Koppel on ABC-TV's *Nightline* if there was a prejudice against blacks in managerial positions. Campanis's reply: "No, I don't believe it's prejudice. I truly believe that they may not have some of the necessities to be, let's say, a field manager or perhaps a general manager." The word "necessities" became an immediate verbal symbol for prejudice and racism within baseball. Campanis apologized, the Dodgers asked him to resign, and, for a time at least, the issue of blacks in baseball management was brought into focus. At the time, black former pitcher Jim "Mudcat" Grant said, "Maybe Al, in a backward way, did us a favor by bringing this out."

**neck ball** A ball thrown inside in the vicinity of the batter's neck. "It's not necessarily meant as a malicious pitch, but . . . any game I've played in and they've hit back-to-back homers and the next pitch is a neck ball, it's a warning" (Baltimore Orioles manager Davey Johnson, on a pitch thrown at Cal Ripken Jr., quoted in *Baltimore Sun,* Aug. 27, 1996).

**Ned** A name used by Casey Stengel for a dumb player; e.g., "Ned in the third reader" or "Ned standin' up in class" (to describe a dumb player ruining a play).

**need a basket** To field a batted or thrown ball poorly. **1st Use.** 1907. (*New York Evening Journal,* Apr. 27; Edward J. Nichols).

**Negro American League** A *Negro league* formed in 1937 under the leadership of H. G. Hall, with teams located in the Midwest and South, includ-

***Negro leagues.*** *The world record–holding Homestead Grays in action.*

ing Kansas City, Chicago, Birmingham, and St. Louis. The league met the Negro National League in a world series from 1942 to 1948. After the demise of the Negro National League in 1948, the Negro American League absorbed some of the surviving franchises and separated into two divisions in an effort to revive black baseball. It lasted until 1960. Abbrev. *NAL.* (John Holway).

**Negro leagues** A generic term for baseball played by African-Americans and dark-skinned Latin Americans from 1887, when the first professional black team, the Cuban Giants (they were actually North Americans) was formed as a product of the racial segregation established by the major and minor leagues in the 1880s, until 1964, when integration of organized baseball resulted in the disappearance of the last black team, the Kansas City Monarchs.

There were three leagues of black ballplayers, beginning in 1920 when Andrew "Rube" Foster, founder of the Chicago American Giants, formed the first successful black baseball league, the *Negro National League,* which disbanded in 1948. The *Eastern Colored League* existed during the 1920s and the *Negro American League,* formed in 1937, lasted until 1960. Seasons varied from 40 to 90 games, supplemented by barnstorming tours. The Negro leagues played annual all-star games beginning in 1933 and conducted world series (1924–27 and 1942–48). During World War II, the Negro leagues grew into a $2 million-a-year business, probably the single biggest black-dominated enterprise.

The Negro leagues presented an exciting brand of baseball and pioneered night baseball, shin guards, and batting helmets. They also produced some of the greatest players in the country, including 15 who had been enshrined in the Baseball Hall of Fame through 1998: Cool Papa Bell, Oscar Charleston, Ray Dandridge, Leon Day, Martin Dihigo, Big Bill Foster, Andrew "Rube" Foster, Josh Gibson, Monte Irvin, Judy Johnson, Buck Leonard, John Henry "Pop" Lloyd, Satchel Paige, Bullet Joe Rogan, and Willie Wells. Negro leaguers played games against such white stars as Babe Ruth, Ty Cobb, Christy Mathewson, Lefty Grove, and Bob Feller, and won three games for every two they lost. Other Negro league stars included Mule

**Negro leagues.** *The New York Black Yankees were formed in 1931 by dancer Bill "Bojangles" Robinson.*

Suttles, Turkey Stearnes, Smokey Joe Williams, Cristobal Torriente, Dick Lundy, Nip Winters, and Willard Brown.

The breaking of the major league's color bar in 1947 hastened the demise of the Negro leagues. The major leagues began to raid the black teams of their best players. "It's like coming into a man's store and stealing the goods right off the shelves," complained one black owner. Such major-league stars as Paige, Irvin, Jackie Robinson, Roy Campanella, Willie Mays, Larry Doby, Ernie Banks, and Hank Aaron began their professional careers in the Negro leagues.

"The Negro leagues were designed to provide opportunity where opportunity was denied and to offer vibrant proof that there was no legitimate basis for the major leagues' unwritten rule. Their death was their ultimate victory." (Phil Dixon, *The Negro Baseball Leagues,* 1992). (John Holway)

**Negro National League** A *Negro league* formed in 1920 by Andrew "Rube" Foster, founder of the Chicago American Giants, and consisting of eight (later six) teams in the Midwest, including the Indianapolis ABCs, Kansas City Monarchs, Chicago Giants, St. Louis Giants (later Stars), Detroit Stars, Dayton Marcos (later Cleveland Buckeyes), and western (Cincinnati) Cuban Stars. The league died in 1930, a victim of the Great Depression and the death of Foster. An East-West League was formed in 1933, primarily through the efforts of Gus Greenlee, as a six-team league with clubs in Chicago, Philadelphia, Baltimore, Newark, and Pittsburgh (the Crawfords are considered by some to be the best team in black baseball history, with such stars as Satchel Paige, Oscar Charleston, Cool Papa Bell, and Josh Gibson). In 1937, the eastern teams adopted the old Negro National League title with teams in Homestead, Pa. (later Washington, D.C.), Newark, Baltimore, Philadelphia, and New York. The Homestead Grays set a world record of nine straight pennants (1937–45). The league disbanded in 1948. Abbrev. *NNL*. (John Holway).

**neighborhood play** A force play in which the runner is called out because the defensive player with the ball is close enough to touch the base. See also *in the neighborhood; phantom double play*. Syn. *in-the-vicinity play; vicinity play*.

**nervous breakdown** A *screwball*, 2, player. **Etymology.** The term is an obvious play on the neurotic nature of the human screwball.

**new ball game 1.** A situation in which a game turns around quickly; e.g., when one team suddenly overtakes the other by scoring a lot of runs. The term underscores the point that no game can be taken for granted. "It must also be remembered that baseball not only gave to the language the phrase 'it's a new ball game,' but implements it every day" (Shirley Povich, *Washington Post*, Oct. 10, 1986). See also *whole new ball game*. **2.** A tie game, thereby creating the situation as though the game was just starting. **Extended Use.** Any new start. "New Year Is New Ballgame for Cable" (*USA Today* headline, Dec. 29, 1986).

**new breed** *arch*. The name used by *New York Daily News* sportswriter Dick Young to describe the rabid New York Mets fans during the franchise's early years (1960s). Roger Angell (*The Summer Game*, 1972) called them "perversely loyal," adding that their loyalty was in part "engendered by a hatred for the kind of cold-blooded success typified by Mr. O'Malley and by the owners of the New York Yankees."

**New England game** Syn. of *Massachusetts game*.

**new life 1.** An opportunity afforded a player to redeem himself by playing for a different team. See also *change of scenery*. **2.** Another chance afforded a batter after the defense failed to retire him, as, for example, after a dropped foul pop fly.

**new-look free agency** Free agency for players whose efforts to become free agents were thwarted when major-league owners in 1990 were determined to have colluded to depress the free agency market. Due to a $280 million collusion agreement/settlement between the owners and the Major League Baseball Players Association, free agents were given time to sign with new teams or remain with their current clubs. Syn. *free-look free agency; second-look free agency*.

**New York game** The precursor to modern baseball, which most closely resembles it. It was played in and around New York City beginning in the 1840s and codified in the Knickerbocker Rules of 1845. It contrasts with the *Massachusetts game*, which it replaced after the Civil War. The New York game adopted foul lines, three outs per side, a harder ball, and no plugging.

**New York Giants** The National League franchise that began as the Metropolitans in 1883, were next known as the Gothams, and became known as the Giants in 1886. The team was nicknamed by manager Jim Mutrie who called them, "My big fellows! My giants!" within earshot of sportswriters. When the team left for San Francisco in 1958, it kept the name Giants.

**New York Mets** The name of the National League East Division franchise in New York City. An expansion team in 1962, it used a shortened version of Metropolitans, the name of a team that arrived in New York in 1883 and later became known as the Giants. The new team got off to a shaky start, but won the World Series in 1969. This occasioned sportswriter Jack Lang's famous line: "They said man would walk on the moon before the Mets won a championship. Man barely won the race." See also *Amazing Mets; Amazin's*.

**New York Yankees** The name of the American League East Division franchise in New York City and the most successful franchise of the 20th century. Originally known as the Highlanders when the team arrived in 1903 and later the Hilltoppers,

**New York Giants.** *A 1905 scorecard celebrating the team's stars.*

the press started calling them Yankees in 1909, allegedly because it fit the headlines better, and the name stuck. All three names were used until after World War I, when Yankees became the official name of the club. The term "Yankee" originally referred to a New Englander, and later a Northerner during the Civil War. The team is also known by other names, including "Bronx Bombers," "Yanks," and "The Bronx Zoo." Of all the major-league teams, it is the one most commonly associated with big bucks and big egos. Sportswriter Red Smith once pointed out that rooting for the Yankees was like rooting for US Steel. **1st Use.** 1904. Barry Popik reports that "New York Yankees" made its first appearance in 1904 in William Randolph Hearst's *New York Evening Journal,* in a sports section edited by Harry Beecher. Neither the *New York Press* nor the *New York Globe* was using "Yankees" this early.

**next batter's box** Syn. of *on-deck circle* (*Official Baseball Rules,* rule 1.04).

**next stop Peoria** Said of a player who is in a slump, committing several errors, or otherwise on

the skids. It is a reference to a St. Louis Cardinals minor-league team that, under team owner Branch Rickey (1917–19), became baseball's equivalent of Podunk.

**nibbler 1.** A weak ground ball. **2.** A pitcher who consistently hits the corners of the plate; one who paints the black.

**"nice guys finish last"** The famous quote attributed to Leo Durocher during the late 1940s when he was managing the Brooklyn Dodgers. Durocher was proud of the fact that the phrase had gotten him into Bartlett's *Familiar Quotations*—between John Betjeman and Dilys Laing—which cited his 1975 autobiography *Nice Guys Finish Last.* In the book, Durocher states he directed the remark against the Giants in front of several newsmen: "Walker, Cooper, Mize, Marshall, Kerr, Gordon, Thomson. Take a look at them. All nice guys. They'll finish last. Nice Guys. Finish last." Researcher Norman Macht insists that even Durocher had it wrong: "What he did say got twisted, and he used the twisted version, misquoting himself, for his 1975 autobiography. What he really said was: 'Look over

**New York Yankees.** *Fan's button celebrating the most successful franchise of the 20th century.*

there [at the Giants bench]. Do you know a nicer guy than Mel Ott? Or any of the other Giants? Why, they're the nicest guys in the world. And where are they? In last place.' "

**nick 1.** To get hits off a pitcher; e.g., "The Cubs nicked Smith three times in the seventh." **1st Use.** 1912. (*New York Tribune,* Sept. 29; Edward J. Nichols). **2.** To pitch a ball so that it just passes over a corner of the plate yet remains in the strike zone; e.g., "Smith's offering to Jones nicked the corner for a called strike."

**nickel** Syn. of *nickel curve.* **1st Use.** 1932. (*Baseball Magazine,* Oct.; Edward J. Nichols).

**nickelbrick** An extremely cheap baseball of the type once commonly found in five-and-dime stores. Originally, it sold for a nickel (at a time when a regulation ball might cost a dollar or more). Le Pacini (*San Francisco Examiner and Chronicle,* Aug. 20, 1978) wrote: "In my era, however, they went for twenty-five to thirty-five cents, and if you got a rare fifty-center you were kicked out of the neighborhood for showboating." He noted that the ball lacked a certain quality ("it was the only ball ever invented that windows broke") and when hit hard would not unravel, but actually disintegrate. See also *brick,* 1. Syn. *nickel rock.*

**nickel curve** A derogatory term for a slow curveball; a "cheap shot"; an early name for the *slider,* 1. Jim Bouton (*Ball Four,* 1970) said that the nickel curve is what the slider was called by old-time ballplayers "who didn't have to hit against it." Syn. *nickel; five-cent curve.*

**nickel nose** A player or umpire with a large nose. Charles Wilson (letter) attests: "I can recall from hanging around a minor-league ballpark much of my youth during the 1950s: a player or umpire with a hypertrophic proboscis was usually known as Nickel Nose, as in, 'If I had that thing full of nickels, I could buy this ballclub' or something equally complimentary."

**nickel rock** Syn. of *nickelbrick.*

**Nickel Series** A nickname for World Series between New York City teams in the days when it cost a nickel to ride the subway.

**night ball 1.** Baseball played at night. Compare *day ball.* **2.** [softball term] An early name for softball.

**nightcap 1.** The second game of a doubleheader, so called because it is usually played late in the afternoon or early in the evening. **1st Use.** 1917. (*New York Times,* Oct. 5; Edward J. Nichols). **2.** *arch.* An uncommon term for the ninth inning (Maurice H. Weseen, *Dictionary of American Slang,* 1934). **Etymology.** Since the early 19th century, the term is the name for the last drink of the night before retiring.

**night club tan** The pale or washed-out appearance of a ballplayer (*Baseball Digest,* 1959).

**night game** A baseball game played under bright artificial lights in the evening. The night game was once a novelty of the electric age, but now most major-league games are played "under the lights." All major-league ballparks are equipped for night games. An indication of the extent to which baseball has become a nighttime game is the fact that until 1971 all World Series games were played in the daytime. Kansas City and St. Louis engaged in the first all-night World Series in 1985. Between the fifth game of the 1984 Series and the sixth game of the 1987 Series there was not one daylight game. The last major-league ballpark to become equipped for night baseball was Wrigley Field in Chicago, which hosted its first night game against the Philadelphia Phillies on Aug. 9, 1988. Compare *day game*. **Etymology.** Several claims exist as to when the first night game was played. The earliest night game identified by the staff at the National Baseball Library and Archives is a nonprofessional game at Hull, Mass., between two department store teams on Sept. 2, 1880. The lighting was poor and many errors were made.

The first professional night game was a minorleague game on July 3, 1895. According to Gordon Christy, the *Houston Daily Post* (July 4, 1895) reported: "Chattanooga and Little Rock [of the Southern League] played nine innings tonight [July 3] by twenty-four electric arc lights. Chattanooga won, 10-4. Both teams played well, but there was great difficulty hitting. As an exhibition of skill in the National game it would hardly pass, but as an interesting novelty it was a roaring success."

The first major-league night game was played at Crosley Field in Cincinnati on May 24, 1935, when the Reds defeated the Philadelphia Phillies, 2–1.

**Nile Valley league** *n./arch.* A mythical realm where the most spectacular feats in the game of baseball were performed. Hugh S. Fullerton (*American Magazine,* June 1912) noted: "Whenever a player tells some extraordinary yarn concerning a play the other players instantly inquire if it happened in the Nile Valley league." **1st Use.** 1912. (Fullerton, as above).

**nine** A baseball team. The term was coined because there are nine players in the starting lineup. Warren Goldstein (*Playing for Keeps,* 1989) notes that the term was clearly influenced by cricket's eleven. **Usage Note.** Despite the fact that there are actually 10 players on teams using a designated hitter, they are still referred to as nines. **1st Use.** 1860. (minutes of the Knickerbocker Base Ball Club; Edward J. Nichols).

**9** The scorekeeper's designation for the right fielder.

**nine guys named Robinson** A mythical, but remarkable all-star team fielded by players named Robinson: e.g., Don (pitcher), Wilbert (catcher), Eddie (1b), Jackie (2b), Brooks (3b), Craig (ss), Bill (of), Floyd (of), and Frank (of). The phrase

**Nine.** *This tobacco wrapper uses the "First Nine" to refer to the original Cincinnati Red Stockings, the team that went undefeated in 1869.*

originated with Earl Weaver's response to a question about the challenge of managing: "I don't welcome any challenge. I'd rather have nine guys named Robinson."

**nine miles** A dugout exaggeration for the distance traveled by a long ball.

**ninety feet away** Said of a runner on third base, needing 90 feet (the distance between bases) to score a run. The term is commonly used in critical or tight situations when the runner on third represents the lead or tying run.

**ninth 1.** *n.* The ninth inning. **2.** *adv.* Said of the ninth position in the batting order; e.g., "Smith is batting ninth."

**ninth-inning finish** A stirring finale in which one team wins the game in the last inning. **Extended Use.** Anything that is about to be over; the end game. "9th Inning, '2 Outs' for Capital Gains Cut" (*USA Today* headline, July 24, 1989).

**nip** 1. To retire a baserunner on a close play. **1st Use.** 1868. (Chadwick Scrapbooks; Edward J. Nichols). 2. To win a baseball game, usually by one run; e.g., "The Giants nipped the Dodgers, 4–3."

**NL** Abbrev. for *National League*.

**NLCS** Abbrev. for *National League Championship Series*.

**NNL** Abbrev. for *Negro National League*.

**"no batter"** A chant or taunt used to tell the batter that he or she will not get a hit and to encourage the pitcher not to fear the batter.

**no book** Lack of information on the habits and weaknesses of a particular player, manager, or team.

**nod** 1. The manager's decision to start a particular pitcher; e.g., "Smith got the nod for his start of the season." The term implies some deliberation on the part of the manager, such as when it is reported that a particular pitcher "got the nod" for Opening Day. 2. The decision to bring in a particular relief pitcher. **Etymology.** From the head gesture for "yes."

**no day at the beach** A wily hitter. Compare *day at the beach.*

**no-decision** A game in which a starting pitcher is not credited with a win or loss. "When a pitcher [Dave Stewart of the Oakland A's] fails four straight times to win his 20th game—twice throwing complete games and once allowing only one run and six hits over nine innings for a no-decision—he might reasonably be forgiven some overt expression of frustration" (Ron Fimrite, *Sports Illustrated,* 1987).

**no-hit** 1. *adj.* Said of a game or a part of a game during which the pitcher gives up no hits. 2. *v.* To not allow a hit. "Yankees' [Dwight] Gooden No-Hits Seattle" (*Washington Post* headline, May 15, 1996).

**no-hit game** Syn. of *no-hitter.* **1st Use.** 1905. (*Sporting Life,* Sept. 2; Edward J. Nichols).

**no-hit, no-run** Descriptive of a game in which the pitcher allows no hits and no runs scored. It is used to distinguish such a performance from one in which there are no hits but in which one or more runs

score without the benefit of a hit (such as when four batters are walked in an inning). **1st Use.** 1909. (*Baseball Magazine,* Mar.; Edward J. Nichols).

**no hits, no runs, no errors** 1. A description of a perfect game, assuming a strong defense and no walks or hit batters. 2. A common summary of an inning of baseball play. **Extended Use.** John Ciardi (*Good Words to You,* 1987) explains: "Lackluster. Faultless but futile. (And so the once-popular comic epitaph for an old maid: 'Lived a virgin, died a virgin. No hits, no runs, no errors.')."

**no-hitter** 1. A game in which a single pitcher does not yield a single hit to the opposition. See also *perfect game.* Syn. *no-hit game; no-no.* 2. See *combined no-hitter.*

**no-hitter jinx** An old superstition that if one speaks of a no-hit game while it is in progress it will come to an end; i.e., an opposing player will get a hit. It seems that Red Barber was the first to defy the jinx from the broadcast booth. In a profile of Barber, Jack Mann (*Washington Star,* July 31, 1981) wrote: "He did it in Bill Bevens' game against the Dodgers in the 1947 World Series, and again in Don Larsen's perfect game of 1956. But the first time was in . . . Ebbets Field, [on June 15,] 1938, when Johnny Vander Meer was in the midst of his second-straight no-hitter."

**no-man's land** 1. That part of the deep outfield difficult for an outfielder to cover. 2. The area behind third base, because "that's where every bad hop in the world will find you" (Davey Johnson, quoted in *Baltimore Sun,* June 11, 1997). 3. The basepath when a runner is a certain out. "[Pitcher Kenny] Rogers knocked the ball down and found [Jeffrey] Hammonds in no-man's land. After hesitating, Hammonds took off for third base and was easily beaten." (*Baltimore Sun,* May 25, 1998).

**non-affiliated club** A minor-league team that is not tied to a major-league sponsor.

**nonchalant** *v.* 1. To play with indifference. In a 1983 "Game of the Week" telecast, after Pittsburgh Pirates catcher Tony Pena twice fumbled a ball hit in front of the plate, allowing the runner to get to first base, broadcaster Joe Garagiola disgustingly said: "He just nonchalanted that ball." 2. To field with ease or nonchalance. "Capsule comment by Rookie Leo Wells of the White Sox after first glimpse of Dom DiMaggio's fielding smoothness: 'Gosh, he certainly nonchalants them'" (*Baseball Digest,* Oct. 1942).

**nonchalot** *v.* To make a play with great ease or indifference (according to Dizzy Dean). **Etymology.** The term is a creative corruption of the word "nonchalant," recast as a verb.

**nonfan** An individual who does not follow the game of baseball. **1st Use.** 1913. "And if you, a nonfan, ask 'why' . . . you need go no further than a fundamental of American character to understand" (*Technical World,* issue 19, 1913; David Shulman).

**no-no** Slang syn. of *no-hitter.* "Two terrific defensive plays . . . and a diving catch . . . preserved the no-no" (Tim Kurkjian, *Sports Illustrated,* Apr. 18, 1994). **1st Use.** 1969. "Palmer's No-No was Bad Word Only for A's" (Doug Brown, *The Sporting News* headline, Aug. 13).

**non-pitcher** A position player; esp., one who has been given a relief-pitching assignment. Other than running out of pitchers (which is a rare occurrence), the only reason to use a non-pitcher is in a game that is a complete blowout.

**non roster invitee** A player who is invited for a tryout in spring training without being placed on the team's official roster. "One of the most popular trends among major-league clubs in this era of payroll cutbacks is signing veteran players to minor-league contracts and then inviting them to spring training as non-roster invitees" (*USA Baseball Weekly,* Feb. 23, 1994). Abbrev. *NRI.*

**"No Pepper Games"** Common sign prohibiting fast-paced pregame bunting and fielding drills in major- and minor-league ballparks.

**northpaw** A right-handed pitcher, a seldom-used companion term with *southpaw.* Its main use comes in questions such as: "If a left-handed pitcher is a southpaw, is a right-handed pitcher a northpaw?" **1st Use.** 1922. (Ernest J. Lanigan, *Baseball Cyclopedia;* Edward J. Nichols).

**Northside** The Cubs in Chicago. Compare *Southside.* Syn. "Northsiders"; "North Siders."

**nosebleeds** The *cheap seats* high up in the stands.

**nose out** To win a game by one run.

**no sweat** Requiring little effort; accomplished with ease. "No Sweat as [Billy] Pierce Nabs 6–3 Win" (*San Francisco News-Call Bulletin* headline, May 16, 1962; Peter Tamony). **Etymology.** Military slang for a sure or easy task, originating during the Korean War. "Our own Air Force, or flyboys, are credited with 'no sweat,' meaning no trouble at all" (*New York Times Magazine,* June 5, 1955).

**notch 1.** To pitch a winning game; e.g., "Smith notched his tenth win." **2.** To score a run; e.g., "Jones notched his fourth run of the game."

**note-book pitcher** *arch.* A pitcher who keeps records of batters and the most effective pitches to throw against them. **1st Use.** 1922. (Ernest J. Lanigan, *Baseball Cyclopedia;* Edward J. Nichols).

**not get to first base** See *first base.*

**not having a strike zone** The ability of a hitter to either slice a tight pitch or pull it; e.g., a left-handed batter slicing a tight pitch into left field or pulling it down the right-field line.

**nothin' baller** A pitcher on the decline.

**nothing ball** A pitch without speed or anything "on it." See also *nuthin' ball; dead fish,* 1; *salad.* Syn. *nothing pitch.* **1st Use.** 1937. (*New York Herald Tribune,* Oct. 3; Edward J. Nichols).

**nothing but his glove** Descriptive of an ineffective pitcher, unable to throw a curveball or otherwise present a deceptive motion. The term implies that the only advantage the pitcher has is his glove. See also *nothing but the stitches.* **1st Use.** 1911. (*American Magazine,* May; Edward J. Nichols).

**nothing but the stitches** Descriptive of an ineffective pitcher. "Named from the idea that only the stitches on the seams of the ball are in evidence, the pitcher himself applying no skill to this throwing" (Edward J. Nichols, *An Historical Dictionary of Baseball Terminology,* Ph.D. dissertation, 1939). See also *nothing but his glove.* **1st Use.** 1912. (*New York Tribune,* Sept. 5; Edward J. Nichols).

**nothing on the ball 1.** Said of a pitcher who is pitching ineffectively. Compare *on the ball.* See also *not much on the ball.* **1st Use.** 1912. (*New York Tribune,* Oct. 10; Edward J. Nichols). **Extended Use.** Said of a dull or incompetent person, who is not bright or alert. **2.** Said of a pitch with no special "stuff" on it and therefore easy to hit.

**nothing pitch** Syn. of *nothing ball.*

**not in it** Said of a team that is not in contention in the pennant race. **1st Use.** 1891. "Baseball vernacular has invaded the church. The crank who created a sensation in the N.Y. Cathedral last Sunday morning by shouting to Archbishop Corrigan: 'Out of my way, Pontius Pilate! I am the Lord's anointed and you are not in it with me' has evidently been feeding on the slop." (*The Sporting News,* Oct. 3; David Shulman).

**not much on the ball** Said of a pitcher possessing slight effectiveness. See also *nothing on the ball,* 1. **1st Use.** 1912. (*New York Tribune,* Sept. 28; Edward J. Nichols). **Extended Use.** Said of a person who is not very bright.

**no-trade clause** A clause in a player's contract that permits him to be traded only with his consent.

**no windup** An abbreviated delivery by a pitcher in which the *windup* is abandoned. It is done to help prevent a baserunner from stealing.

**no-wood-on-the-ball pitcher** A pitcher (such as Nolan Ryan) with an exceptionally good record for strikeouts.

**NP** Box score abbrev. for *number of pitches* thrown by a pitcher.

**NRI** Abbrev. for *non-roster invitee.*

**nub** 1. *n.* A sore finger from a batted or thrown ball. **1st Use.** 1937. (*The Sporting News Record Book;* Edward J. Nichols). 2. *v.* To hit a slow bouncing ball that stays in the infield.

**nubber** A weak hit that bounces into the infield; a hit that behaves like a bunt, commonly hit back to the mound. See also *knubber.*

**nuclear fission ball** A ball that is hit powerfully and directly at a fielder or the pitcher. It is an exaggerated extension of *atom ball.*

**nudist pitch** Syn. of *Lady Godiva pitch.*

**nugget** The baseball.

**number-four hitter** Syn. of *cleanup hitter.*

**numbering** The system in which numbers are used to identify players. The numbers are put on the backs of the players' uniforms and sometimes on the front. Although not required by the rules, the practice has long been universal among major-league teams. **Etymology.** The first team to number its players permanently was the 1929 New York Yankees. The numbers corresponded to each player's usual spot in the batting order: thus, Babe Ruth wore 3 and Lou Gehrig 4. The 1916 Cleveland Indians and the St. Louis Cardinals of the mid-1920s previously had experimented with numbering.

**numberobabble** Baseball statistics that have gone out of control. A letter to the *New York Times* (Apr. 13, 1991) carries the headline "Some Baseball Numberobabble Has Value" and asks the question: "Does anyone really care who holds the all-time record for consecutive foul tips?"

**number 1** 1. The fastball, so called because the catcher's traditional signal for the pitch is a single finger pointed down. "The name of the game for [Roger] Clemens is good old No. 1, the heater" (*Baltimore Sun,* May 18, 1994). 2. A team's best pitcher; an *ace,* 2.

**numbers** 1. A player's statistical record. "You've got to prove yourself every day you're in uniform. You have to go out and put up some numbers." (Baltimore Orioles manager Ray Miller, quoted in *Baltimore Sun,* Mar. 11, 1998). 2. The presence of several players competing for a position on a team; e.g., "Smith was cut because the numbers were against him." 3. The part of a player's body covered by the jersey with his uniform number; e.g., "The ball hit Smith in the numbers." See also *letters.*

**number 3** The catcher's signal to the pitcher with three fingers pointing down. William G. Brandt (*Baseball Magazine,* Oct. 1932) wrote: "[It] can be almost anything, screwball, fork-ball, knuckleball, slop-ball, squib, dipsy-dew."

**number 2** The curveball, so called because the catcher's traditional signal for the pitch is two fingers pointed down.

**number of pitches** A box score statistic for the number of pitches thrown by each pitcher in a game. Abbrev. *NP.*

**nuthin' ball** A slowly pitched ball that is easy to hit because it does not move deceptively. Dizzy Dean amplified the definition by adding: ". . . like I was throwin' when I hurt my arm." See also *nothing ball.*

# O

**O 1.** The letter "O," which is used in preference to the word "zero" in baseball expressions such as, "Smith was O for four at the plate today" (i.e., he had no hits in four at-bats). **2.** Short for "ovation"; e.g., "The fans gave Smith a standing O."

**oak** A baseball bat. **1st Use.** 1909. (*New York Call,* Aug. 13; Edward J. Nichols).

**Oakland Athletics** The name of the American League West Division franchise in Oakland, Calif. once located in Philadelphia (1901–54), then Kansas City (1955–67), and now in Oakland (since 1968), the team has been known as the A's and Athletics depending on the moment; e.g., in 1987, the Oakland A's officially reverted to the Athletics, a name that was first used for an amateur Philadelphia team in 1860. Syn. "Oakland A's."

**OB** Abbrev. for *organized baseball.* **1st Use.** 1915. (*Baseball Magazine,* Dec.; Edward J. Nichols).

**OBA** Abbrev. for *on-base average,* 1.

**OBP** Abbrev. for *on-base percentage.*

**obs** Abbrev. for *obstruction.*

**obstruction** The act of a defensive player who impedes the progress of a baserunner; specif., such an act when the fielder is not in possession of, or fielding, a thrown or batted ball. If the umpire determines that the runner would have been safe at the next base without the obstruction, the runner is awarded that base. Compare *interference,* 1. Abbrev. *obs.*

**OF 1.** Abbrev. for *outfield,* 1. **2.** Abbrev. for *outfielder.*

**O-fer** Syn. of *oh-fer,* 1.

**ofer** Syn. of *oh-fer,* 1.

**off 1.** Ineffective, or not in good playing form; e.g., "Smith was off his game because he was carousing the previous night." Compare *on,* 2. **1st Use.** 1890. (*New York Evening Post,* May 13; Edward J. Nichols). **2.** At the expense of the pitcher; e.g., "The Red Sox scored two runs off Smith in the third inning."

**off and running** Said of a baserunner who makes a quick getaway for the next base when a hit is made or on a hit-and-run play.

**off base** Said of a baserunner who is taking a lead or is in a position to be put out. **Extended Use.** Out of line; working from the wrong premise. "He [George Meany] doesn't, in his mind's eye, see a union or the labor movement as an impersonal entity or as an institution. He sees it as a bunch of people. And as long as he keeps seeing it that way, he won't get too far off base." (*Saturday Evening Post,* Nov. 20, 1943; Peter Tamony). Not to be confused with *off one's base,* which refers to a person who is mentally unbalanced.

**offense 1.** The team at bat. **2.** The array of tactics used by the team at bat. Such maneuvers as the use of pinch hitters, pinch runners, bunts, and hit-and-run plays are part of the team's offense.

**offer 1.** To swing at a pitched ball; to attempt to bunt a pitch. **1st Use.** 1896. (Burt L. Standish, *Frank Merriwell's School Days;* Edward J. Nichols).

**2.** To pitch a baseball. **3.** To make a player available for trade.

**offering** A pitched ball. **1st Use.** 1910. (*Baseball Magazine,* Dec.; Edward J. Nichols).

**off field** Syn. of *opposite field.*

**official at-bat** An at-bat that is entered in the official record of the game and used as the basis for batting statistics. Four types of plate appearance are not counted as official at-bats: when the batter is a) awarded a base on balls, b) hit by a pitched ball, c) awarded first base because of catcher's interference, and d) hits a sacrifice bunt or sacrifice fly.

**official distance** Any field measurement stipulated by the official rules of the game; e.g., distance between the bases (90 feet) and between the front edge of the pitcher's rubber and the back point of home plate (60 feet, 6 inches).

**official game** Any non-tied game that completes four-and-a-half innings with the home team in the lead or five innings with the visitors leading. The concept comes into play when a game is stopped for rain, darkness, or other reason. If a game is not an official game, it must be played over from the start or, in the case of a curfew or light failure, from the point at which play was suspended.

**official playing rules** The written code of rules that govern the playing of baseball games by professional teams. The ten-member Official Playing Rules Committee reviews and recommends changes to the *Official Baseball Rules.*

**official scorer** An individual whose responsibility is to observe the game, interpret the action taking place, and, using the *Official Baseball Rules,* enter the events and rules of the game into the report of the game. The official scorer also makes judgment calls, including whether a particular play should be recorded as a base hit or an error, and determines official times at bat, assists, passed balls, wild pitches, stolen bases, earned runs, sacrifice hits, the winning and losing pitchers, and who, if anyone, is credited with a save. The rulings of the official scorer have no bearing on the score or outcome of the game. In the major leagues, the official scorer is a local reporter who has been so designated by the league president and observes the game from a position in the press box. It is common for a group of reporters to score on an alternating basis. During the World Series, there are three official scorers. See also *scorer.* Abbrev. *OS.* **1st Use.** 1902. (*Sporting Life,* July 5; Edward J. Nichols).

**off one's base** Said of a baserunner who is taking a lead or is in a position to be put out. **Extended Use.** Said of a person who is mentally unbalanced. While *off base* and "off one's base" are synonymous in the context of the game of baseball, they part company as general metaphors. "Off base" refers to someone who is out of line or incorrect, whereas "off one's base" refers to someone who is mentally unbalanced or crazy. Charles Earle Funk found the latter term in use as far back as 1883 when it appeared in George W. Peck's *His Pa:* "The boy knew the failing, and made up his mind to demonstrate to the old man that he was rapidly getting off his base."

**off one's fists** Said of hitting a ball with the handle of the bat, near the batter's hands.

**off-season** *n.* **1.** The time of year when baseball is not played (from the day after the last day of the World Series in Oct. to the first day of spring training in Feb.); or that time characterized by an "interminable cultural drought" (George F. Will, *Washington Post,* Mar. 29, 1984). **2.** An unsatisfactory season for a player or a team.

**off-season baseball** Professional baseball played outside the continental United States during the winter months. Some major- and minor-league players from the United States play off-season baseball for conditioning and experience.

**offshoot** *arch.* A pitch that curves away from the batter. Compare *outshoot; inshoot.*

**off-side pitcher** A left-handed pitcher. **1st Use.** 1913. (*Harper's Weekly,* Sept. 6; Edward J. Nichols).

**off-speed** Said of pitching characterized by slow pitches; e.g., "I've always had pretty good off-speed stuff" (Roger Clemens, quoted in *Boston Globe,* June 27, 1986).

**off-speed hitter** A hitter who prefers off-speed pitches. "[Jim] Gentile was a good off-speed hitter who would wait well on that slow slop" (Dick Hall, quoted in *Baltimore Sun,* May 25, 1995).

**off-speed pitch** An all-purpose term for any pitch (slider, curveball, knuckleball, forkball, and their many variations) that is thrown at less than full velocity. See also *changeup.*

**off-stride** Said of a batter who steps into the ball before it reaches the plate. An off-stride batter is often overly anxious to swing.

**off the hook** Out of a jam; e.g., a pitcher who gives up five runs in the first inning is said to be "off the hook" when his team scores six runs in the second inning, or a pitcher who has been taken out of the game with his team behind is said to be "off the hook" when his team rallies and saves him from being credited with a loss.

**off the schneid** Said of a team or hitter coming out of a slump. See also *schneid; on the schneid.*

**off the table** Said of a curveball, sinker, or other sharp-breaking pitch that dips precipitously, as though it fell off the end of a table, before reaching the plate.

**off year** An unsatisfactory year for a player or a team.

**O-for** Syn. of *oh-fer,* 1.

**oh-fer** **1.** *adj.* Descriptive of a game or series of games in which a batter fails to collect a hit; e.g., "Smith was oh-fer eight in the series" (i.e., he got no hits in eight at-bats). Sometimes spelled "ohfer." Syn. *oh for; ofer; O-fer; O-for.* **Etymology.** The term is created from "0 [zero] for," as one would say when speaking of an "0 for 3" game. **2.** *n.* A second-rate player. "The players in the pinstripes didn't look like Yankees. They looked like the AAA farm club of the Kansas City Athletics. A bunch of oh-fers." (*San Francisco Examiner,* Aug. 1, 1966; Peter Tamony).

**oh for** Syn. of *oh-fer,* 1.

**"oh, for the long one!"** Broadcaster Harry Caray's pet call when he encouraged a player to hit a home run.

**old** *adj.* For reasons that are unclear, baseball dotes on the adjective "old" in common phrases such as "the old ball game," "the old ballpark," "the old college try," and "the old clutch." This was noted by Frank Graham (*New York Sun,* July 18, 1927): "The fondness for the word 'old' on the part of men who in most cases are so young is as strange as it is pronounced. Invariably, it is the 'old army game,' the 'old life,' the 'old pepper,' and the 'old ball game.'" H. G. Salsinger (*Baseball Magazine,* Aug. 1945) notes that players generally prefix their favorite nickname for the ball ("apple," "pill," etc.) with the adjective "old."

**old army game** A style of play that is straightforward and does not rely on strategy. *The Sporting News* (Aug. 5, 1959) noted that 1959 had revived the old army game: "Many fans have yearned for the 'good old days' when a club fought for one run and won with it. The [Chicago] White Sox are supplying that type of ball." **1st Use.** 1927. (*New York Sun,* July 18; Edward J. Nichols). **Etymology.** The etymology of the term has proven most elusive. It is also confusing because the term has a contrary meaning in slang outside of baseball. Harold Wentworth & Stuart Berg Flexner (*Dictionary of American Slang,* 1960) define the term: "Any swindle; any unfair or crooked gambling game or bet."

**old ball game** A sentimental expression for describing a baseball game or the game of baseball; e.g., Tristram Potter Coffin's *The Old Ball Game* (1971). Var. "ol' ball game."

**old-cat** A pickup game. See *one old cat.*

**old college try** A wild and desperate attempt to make a play. Sometimes the term carries a hint of showboating. Babe Ruth (*Babe Ruth's Own Book of Baseball,* 1928) defined "giving it the old college try" as "playing to the grandstand or making strenuous effort to field a ball that obviously cannot be handled." In a column that appeared in the *Columbus* (Ohio) *Citizen* (Nov. 26, 1927) and was quoted in *American Speech* (Apr. 1930), Billy Evans wrote that "I gave it the old college try" is a term "often used in big league baseball, when some player keeps on going after a fly ball, usually in foul territory, with the odds about ten to one he would never reach it. Teammates of such a player often beat him to it by shouting in unison with the thought of humor uppermost: 'Well, kid, you certainly gave it the old college try,' as he falls short of making the catch." Evans continued: "When some player does something that a professional player might not ordinarily attempt, such as colliding with a fielder who had the ball ready to touch him out, in the hope that he might make him drop the ball, regardless of the danger he was courting, someone is sure to say, often ironically, if the speaker happens to be one of the players in the field: 'That's the old college spirit.'" **Extended Use.** The term was quickly applied to any effort with limited chances of success.

**older game** [softball term] The game of baseball, as contrasted with softball, which is the *younger game.*

**older than baseball** An expression conveying age, on a par with "older than dirt." Correspondent Bob Skole heard a woman comment that the safety deposit boxes in a Portland (Maine) bank were "older than baseball."

**old folks** The traditional nickname for the oldest player on a team.

**old leaguer** *arch.* A veteran or experienced professional ballplayer. **1st Use.** 1885. "The new-comers to the American Association arena were known as 'fresh leaguers' to distinguish them from vets or 'old leaguers'" (*Sporting Life,* Jan. 14; Barry Popik).

**Old Man** The manager of a baseball team. "What hurt most was that he had always looked up to the Old Man, like a son would regard his own father"

(Mickey Mantle on Casey Stengel, *The Mick,* 1985; Charles D. Poe). **1st Use.** 1946. "Manager Frankie Frisch is the 'CO,' the 'Old Man' or 'The Brass,' and he and his coaches have come to be known as 'GHQ'" (*Baseball Digest,* May).

**Oldoriole** *arch.* A player who stays in the game despite injuries. The term derives from the reputation for toughness and relentlessness of the Baltimore Orioles of the 1890s. "If he gets spiked or hit on the head or upset by a base-runner and laughs it off, he's an 'Oldoriole'" (William G. Brandt, *Baseball Magazine,* Oct. 1934). Var. "old Oriole."

**Old Pluvy** Syn. of *Jupe Pluvius.*

**old poison pen** See *poison pen.*

**Old Sal** The name for the underhand, upward curving or "jump" ball thrown by Joe "Iron Man" McGinnity. **1st Use.** 1908. (*New York Evening Journal,* Mar. 5; Edward J. Nichols).

**old styler** *obs.* A term used in the 19th century for *old timer,* 1.

**old timer 1.** A retired ballplayer; a player from a previous baseball generation. See also *old styler.* Sometimes spelled "old-timer." **1st Use.** 1905. (*Sporting Life,* Oct. 7; Edward J. Nichols). **2.** *arch.* A long hit, so named because it became rare after the deadening of the ball in 1870. "Gifford followed with one of his 'old timers'" (*Detroit Free Press,* July 27, 1876; Peter Morris).

**Old-Timers' Day** A promotional ceremony at which retired players are honored and play a short game before the regularly scheduled game.

**Old timers.** *Early convocation of baseball pioneers in Boston, circa 1915.*

**old-timers' game** A game played by retired players on Old-Timers' Day.

**ole** (Pron. "olay") *v.* For a fielder to allow a batted ball to pass, similar to a bullfighter allowing the bull to pass; e.g., "Smith oles the ground ball."

**ole rubber belly** A common nickname for a player with a bulging waistline.

**olive in his throat** Descriptive of a player failing in a crucial situation. See also *choke*, 1.

**Olympic rings** A mythical award given to a batter who strikes out five times in a game. See also *hat trick*, 2; *golden sombrero; Horn.* **Etymology.** The term was coined by pitcher Bill Scherrer and refers to the five interlocking rings that make up the Olympic emblem (*Baltimore Sun,* Apr. 28, 1991).

**on 1.** Occupying a base or bases; e.g., "Smith got on by singling to center." **1st Use.** 1907. (*New York Evening Journal,* Apr. 30; Edward J. Nichols). **2.** Effective, or in good playing form; e.g., "Jones was on his game today." Compare *off,* 1. **3.** Operating or occurring; e.g., "The Cubs have a play on (such as a steal attempt)."

**on base** Said of one or more baserunners who have reached or are occupying one or more bases; e.g., "Smith got on base by singling to center."

**on-base average 1.** Syn. of *on-base percentage.* Abbrev. *OBA.* **2.** The percentage of batters reaching base (via hit, walk, and hit by pitch) against a specific pitcher.

**on-base percentage** A statistic used to illustrate a batter's overall effectiveness at getting on base. It is computed by dividing the number of times the batter reaches base (not including by error) by his number of plate appearances and carrying the quotient to three decimal places. The official formula is hits + walks + hit by pitch, divided by at-bats + walks + hit by pitch + sacrifice flies + sacrifices (H + BB + HBP ÷ AB + BB + HBP + SF + S). The number is particularly important in determining the effectiveness of a leadoff batter, whose job it is (more than any other player) to get on base. See also *RABS.* Abbrev. *OBP.* Syn. *on-base average,* 1.

**on board** Said of a batter who has reached a base; e.g., "Smith was on board with a double."

**on deck** Said of a batter ready to take his turn at bat following the batter at the plate. **1st Use.** 1867. "Well I went on deck and took up a bat" (*Ball Players Chronicle,* Sept. 26; David Shulman). **Etymology.** See *at bat, on deck, in the hold* for full discussion of the etymology of this sequence. **Extended Use.** Said of the next to have a turn; e.g., a barber might say that a customer next in line for a haircut is "on deck." Despite the nautical origin of "deck," the use of "on deck" for "next" originated in baseball. Peter Morris found an interesting extension of the term in 1875 to list upcoming games.

**on-deck circle** One of two circular spaces, each five feet in diameter, set in foul territory in front of each team's dugout where the batter following the player at bat stands or kneels to wait his turn. It provides a space for the on-deck batter to take practice swings. In an effort to speed up the game, the on-deck batter must be in the on-deck circle and not waiting in the dugout. Syn. *next batter's box; batter's circle; batting circle; circle,* 2; *slot,* 6.

**1** The scorekeeper's designation for the pitcher.

**one-armed man** A fielder who makes one-handed catches.

**one away** One out.

**1B 1.** Abbrev. for *first base.* **2.** Abbrev. for *first baseman.* **3.** Abbrev. for *single,* 1.

**one-bagger** Syn. of *single,* 1.

**one-ball hitter** A hitter who is at his best—or, at least not bothered—when there are two strikes against him.

**one base at a time** A style of play, whether intended or not, in which no baserunner is able to gain more than a base on any play. See also *station-to-station.*

**one-base hit** Syn. of *single,* 1. **1st Use.** 1874. (*New York Sun,* July 31; Edward J. Nichols).

**one-cornered cat** Syn. of *one old cat.*

**one cushion shot** A batted ball that caroms off the wall, like a billiard or pool ball. It is often a difficult ball for an outfielder to field.

**one-dimensional player 1.** A player whose talents are limited, usually to slugging. "All I kept hearing was that I was a one-dimensional ballplayer.

I couldn't do this, I couldn't do that." (Jack Clark, quoted in *Tampa Tribune,* Jan. 7, 1988). **2.** A player who consistently hits to the same general area of the ballpark.

**one down** One out.

**one down and two to go** One out with two outs remaining.

**One Eye Jim Bats** A variation of baseball. James S. Hanna (*What Life Was Like When I Was a Kid,* 1973; Charles D. Poe) described how the game was played in his Galveston (Tex.) neighborhood: "As we grew older, baseball consumed much of our time, and if there were not enough to make up two full teams we played a variation called One Eye Jim Bats. This might well have been called progressive baseball, for each prospective player shouted the position he wanted to start at, the number one spot, of course, being 'batter' which was usually won by the biggest and loudest boy, with 'catch,' 'pitch,' 'first,' 'second,' etc. following in rapid order. If the batter succeeded in making a base hit, all players advanced to the next highest position, the catcher now becoming the batter, the pitcher becoming the catcher, and so on. If the batter made a home run he was privileged to bat again; if he were put out, all players advanced and the ex-batter started at the bottom at third base. It was a good game and afforded everyone some experience in playing all positions." Syn. *move up, 3.*

**one for the book** *n.* An odd or freakish play that presumably deserves to be noted in one of baseball's record books. **1st Use.** 1932. (*Baseball Magazine,* Oct.; Edward J. Nichols).

**one game at a time** A cliché applied to the effort of focusing solely on today's game, esp. when a team is trying to catch the leader in a pennant or divisional race.

**one-hand catch** A catch in which the fielder uses one hand only. **1st Use.** 1865. (Chadwick Scrapbooks; Edward J. Nichols).

**one-handed catcher** A catcher who keeps his throwing hand behind his back when receiving the pitch to protect it from foul tips and backswings.

**one-hole cat** Syn. of *one old cat.*

**one-hopper** A batted ball that takes one bounce.

**100 club** A mythical club for pitchers who have won 100 or more games for two different teams. Members include Cy Young (241 for Cleveland Spiders and 192 for Boston Red Sox), Lefty Grove (195 for Philadelphia Athletics and 105 for Boston Red Sox), and Nolan Ryan (138 for California Angels and 106 for Houston Astros).

**100 games** A highly significant count in either the win or loss column. "We could be the first team in history to win 100 games one year and lose 100 the next year" (St. Louis Cardinals manager Whitey Herzog, quoted in *USA Today,* July 11, 1986).

**162-game schedule** The schedule of games each team plays per season in the major leagues; a team's complete schedule of regular season games.

**One Hundred Thousand Dollar Infield** The Philadelphia Athletics infield from 1909 to 1914, consisting of first basemen Harry Davis (1909–10) and Stuffy McInnis (1911–14), second baseman Eddie Collins, shortstop Jack Barry, and third baseman Frank "Home Run" Baker. The infield was named for its alleged value. Also expressed in lower case and as "$100,000 infield." Syn. *Hundred Thousand Dollar Infield.*

**one-name guy** A player who is known by his first name or nickname alone; baseball's equivalent to a household name. Tony Kornheiser (*Washington Post,* Oct. 23, 1987) wrote: "When I think of a World Series, the kind of names that come to my mind are Catfish [Hunter], Yogi [Berra], Brooks [Robinson], and Reggie [Jackson]. One-name guys."

**one o'cat** Syn. of *one old cat.*

**one-o'clock hitter** *arch.* A player who hits well in batting practice and poorly during the game. The term dates back to when games started at two o'clock and batting practice began at one o'clock. See also *ten-o'clock hitter; two-o'clock hitter; five-o'clock hitter; six-o'clock hitter; seven-o'clock hitter.*

**one old cat** A game that predates baseball and is related to *rounders,* but which remained in place as a simple children's game. It is an informal game that is usually played by three children. Rules vary depending on circumstances but a typical game has one base with one player at the plate, one pitching, and one in the field. Outs occur when a ball is caught on the fly or there are three strikes. The batter can score on a hit, which enables him to run to the base and return before being put out. The players rotate and each keeps his own score. Charles Darling's recollection of the game: "A made-up baseball game of three to nine players on each side, played in any suitable open area, using any kind of a stick for a bat and almost anything round for a ball. Sometimes, when there are not enough players to make two teams, the players rotate in having their turn at bat and only one base is used, the batter making a hit must run to the single base and return to home plate before being put out." See also *old-cat; two old cat; three old cat; four old cat.* Syn. *one o'cat; one-cornered cat; one-hole cat.* **1st Use.** 1856. "Just then two of his playmates coming along with a ball, Dick . . . went to join them in a game of 'one-old-cat'" (*The Juvenile Forget Me Not;* David Shulman).

**one-pitch** [softball term] A form of slow pitch softball in which the batter begins his or her at-bat with a count of three balls, two strikes, and one foul. It is a fast game to play.

**one player away** A phrase used by a team when it feels that it can get into postseason play with the addition of one key player. Michael Bauman (*Milwaukee Journal Sentinel,* Aug. 4, 1997) writes: "And the reality is, the Brewers appear to be more than the proverbial 'one player away' from pennant-winning status, anyway."

**one-run game** A contest in which there is a difference of only one run separating the scores of the two teams.

**one-sacker** Syn. of *single,* 1. **1st Use.** 1908. "[It was a] timely one-sacker" (*Atlantic Monthly,* Jan.; David Shulman).

**one-time** Said of a former player; e.g., "Smith was a one-time Dodger."

**one-two-three** *adj.* Said of an inning in which the first three batters are retired in order. "[Mike] Mussina threw 133 pitches, . . . matched a career-high with six walks . . . and had only one one-two-three inning" (*Baltimore Sun,* June 24, 1994). Var. "1-2-3." **1st Use.** 1862. (*New York Sunday Mercury,* Aug. 13; Edward J. Nichols).

**one, two, three** *n.* A practice game in which there are fewer than six fielders on a side. Henry Chadwick (*The Game of Base Ball,* 1868) defined the game as follows: "The field side take their positions and a player takes the bat. When the batsman is put out—unless the ball is caught on the fly, in which case the fielder catching it changes place with the batsman—he takes his position at right field, the catcher takes the bat, the pitcher goes in to catch, and the first baseman takes the pitcher's position, and each of the other fielders advance one step towards the in-field positions. There should be at least four players on the batting side."

**one-way lead** A lead taken when the baserunner has determined that, regardless of the pitcher's move, he will return to the base. As explained by Branch Rickey (*Branch Rickey's Little Blue Book,* 1995): "The reason for a one-way lead, sometimes, is to get acquainted with the pitcher's move; or it could conceivably be used to cause the catcher to call for a pitch-out, thinking that the runner is likely to go. Or it could well be used occasionally to draw a throw and thus break up the pitcher's concentration on his next pitch. No manager recommends it as a part of general practice."

**on his horse** Said of an outfielder sprinting after a fly ball.

**on ice** Syn. of *home free.*

**onion** *n./arch.* The baseball. **1st Use.** 1917. (*American Magazine,* July; Edward J. Nichols).

**on paper** Said of a team that should do well, judging by the names listed on its roster. "On paper, I think we're better, but if it works on paper and doesn't work on the field, that doesn't do you any good" (Cleveland Indians manager

Mike Hargrove, quoted in *Baltimore Sun,* Mar. 26, 1996).

**on schedule to** What will happen if the present ratio is maintained; e.g., "At their present rate, the Angels are on schedule to win 96 games" (Tom Seaver, NBC "Game of the Week," Aug. 12, 1989).

**on the ball** Said of a pitcher who is working well; e.g., a good pitcher with the ability to deceive batters is said to have a lot "on the ball." "Confidence is great stuff but the pitcher must put something else on the ball" (*San Francisco Call,* Oct. 16, 1913; Peter Tamony). **Extended Use. 1.** At one's best; competent. **2.** Bright and alert. The term often appears in the negative; e.g., "He's got nothing on the ball" for someone who is dull.

**on the bench** Inactive, not playing; said of a utility player. **1st Use.** 1905. (*Sporting Life,* Sept. 2; Edward J. Nichols).

**on the black** Said of a pitch thrown over one of the two lateral edges of home plate.

**on the block** Said of a player who is available for sale or trade. **Etymology.** From the notion of being on the auction block.

**on the bound** Fielding a ball as it bounces off the ground. **1st Use.** 1880. (*Brooklyn Daily Eagle,* Aug. 20; Edward J. Nichols).

**on the bubble** Said of a player who is about to be traded or sent back to the minor leagues, or who is either on the verge of being sent down or called up; one whose "bubble" is about "to burst."

**on the fists** Said of an inside pitch that comes close to the batter's hands. Such a pitch is hit off the bat handle, the part of the bat closest to the batter's hands.

**on the fly** Catching a batted ball in the air before it touches the ground. **1st Use.** 1859. (Knickerbocker Base Ball Club correspondence; Edward J. Nichols). **Etymology/Extended Use.** Lowell Edwin Folsom (*Iowa Review,* Spring-Summer 1980) writes: "[Walt Whitman] refers to his own writing techniques in terms of baseball, telling [Horace] Traubel [see Horace Traubel, *With Walt Whitman in Camden,* 1905–1912, 1953, 1964], for example, 'That has mainly been my method: I have caught much on the fly: things as they come and go—on the spur of the moment.' And Traubel uses the same image to evoke some of his more fragmented conversations with Whitman: 'Two or three things I caught from W. on the fly, as I busied about the room.' At that time [1880s], 'on the fly' was an important new baseball term, since the original Knickerbocker rules in 1845 allowed for an out if the ball was caught 'on the first bound.' Only gradually did this rule change; for years, teams would stipulate whether or not the games they played would be 'on the fly' or 'on the bound.' If players chose to play on the fly, they had to be especially awake and alert, awaiting the unexpected. So Whitman probably did not mean to imply, with the figure of speech, casualness about his poetic methods so much as alertness combined with an element of surprise: his method was to be awake for every opportunity that came his way, to 'catch much on the fly.'"

**on the hip** Said of a pitcher who has the opposing batters under control. **1st Use.** 1905. (*Sporting Life,* Sept. 2; Edward J. Nichols).

**on the hook** Said of a pitcher who has left the game with his team losing.

**on the label** Syn. of *on the trademark.*

**on the meat** Said of being hit by a pitched ball; e.g., "Smith took one on the meat."

**on the mound** Said of a pitcher who is currently pitching.

**on the nose** Squarely; directly; e.g., hitting a ball "on the nose" is to connect with it solidly. **1st Use.** 1883. (*Sporting Life,* May 20; Edward J. Nichols).

**on the road** Away from home. "The Tigers fell to 20-57 on the road, the worst mark in the majors" (*Tampa Tribune,* Sept. 20, 1989).

**on the schneid** Said of a hitless period for a hitter or a team. See also *schneid; off the schneid.*

**on the shelf** Said of a player who is temporarily benched because of an injury or other reason.

**1st Use.** 1905. (*Sporting Life,* Sept. 9; Edward J. Nichols).

**on the trademark** Said of the thick part of the baseball bat where the manufacturer's insignia is inscribed. Batters try to hit the ball "on the trademark" for maximum results. Syn. *on the label.* **1st Use.** 1898. (*New York Tribune,* June 14; Edward J. Nichols).

**open base** A base not occupied by a runner. Sometimes, with fewer than two outs and a runner on second base or runners on second base and third base, a batter will be walked intentionally to fill first base to improve the chances of a force out or double play.

**opener** The first game in a season, series, or doubleheader.

**Opening Day** The day on which the regular season begins. Syn. *cork popper.* **1st Use.** 1894. "Opening Day at Eastern Park" (*Brooklyn Daily Eagle Index;* David Shulman). **Usage Note.** The term is usually capitalized; e.g., "They call it Opening Day, but The Day is more like it" (J. Yardley, *Washington Post,* Apr. 8, 1985).

**open market** The availability of free-agent players seeking new connections.

**open spaces** Those parts of a ballpark usually

**Opener.** *A button celebrating a notable opener.*

not defended and where batted balls are difficult to field.

**open stance** A batting position in which the front foot is farther from the plate than the back foot. The front foot is pointed toward third base for a right-handed batter or toward first base for a left-handed batter. Compare *closed stance.*

**open the door** To make an error or otherwise grant the opposition an opportunity to score; e.g., walking two batters with two outs would "open the door" for the team at bat. Syn. "open the floodgates."

**"open the window, Aunt Minnie, here she comes!"** Pittsburgh Pirates radio sportscaster Rosey Rowswell's trademark salutation for a home run by a Pirate at Forbes Field, a small ballpark, situated near a residential area.

**open up 1.** For a batter to turn his front shoulder (closest to the pitcher) and hips ahead of the arrival of the pitch, causing him to be "out in front" (front shoulder turns to right for a left-handed batter, to left for a right-handed batter), often resulting in hooking the ball foul; to turn the front shoulder out too soon. See also *pull off the ball.* Syn. *fly open,* 2. **2.** For a pitcher to turn his shoulder too much toward third base (for a right-hander) or to first base (for a left-hander). See also *fly open,* 1.

**opportunity** A team's turn at bat.

**opposite field** The side of the playing field that is opposite the side of home plate from which a batter bats; e.g., right field is the "opposite field" for a right-handed batter, who bats from the left side of home plate. It is called "opposite" because it is the opposite of the direction in which a batter would naturally pull the ball (a right-handed batter naturally pulls to the left and a left-handed batter naturally pulls to the right). Syn. *off field; wrong field.*

**opposite-field hitter** A hitter who often hits to the side of the field opposite to that from which he bats. An opposite-field hitter takes a shortened swing, swings late, or swings at outside pitches. Syn. *slice hitter.*

**opposite-field home run** A home run hit to the side of the field opposite to that from which a batter hits. Because it is more difficult to hit with power to the opposite field, it is enough of an oddity to merit the lead sentence in a report on a game: "Ernest Riles hit an opposite-field home run to cap a four-run, ninth-inning comeback" (Associated Press dispatch, Mar. 11, 1986).

**opposite-field power** The ability to hit long balls into the opposite field.

**option 1.** *n.* The right of a major-league team to send a player to the minor leagues without putting him on waivers. Under such an arrangement the player is still under contract with the major-league team and can be recalled at any time. **2.** *v.* To return a player (or be returned) to the minor leagues on the condition that the major-league club can reclaim him at any time; e.g., "The Orioles optioned Smith to Rochester" or "Smith was optioned out to Rochester." If returned more than three times, the major-league club loses control of the player's contract. Compare *outright*, 2. **3.** *n.* The right of a player to stay with his present team at the end of his contract or to sign with another. **4.** *n.* A claim on the future services of a player. **5.** *n.* See *fielder's option.* **6.** *v.* To sign a new or prospective player to play with a given team at some future date.

**option batter** *obs.* An early name for the *designated hitter.* The idea had been proposed in the early 1960s and on several other occasions. "Rules Committee Bars Option Batter for PCL" (*Washington Star* headline for an article on a proposal to test the idea in the Pacific Coast League, Apr. 1, 1961). The term became immediately obsolete when the "designated hitter" concept and term were adopted.

**option clause** A provision in a player's contract that allows the club to invoke the terms of an expired contract for an additional season.

**option out** See *option,* 2.

**option year** The year in which a player can become a free agent at the end of the season.

**orange** The baseball.

**orange alert** A description that Oakland A's owner Charles O. Finley used in 1972 for the orange-colored baseball (the color would be "a little brighter than plain orange") that he tried to introduce.

**orange crate** A fielder's glove in which the thumb and forefinger are joined by a deep, wide lacing. "Hank Greenberg . . . may have pioneered the modern orange crate" (Joe Williams, *San Francisco News,* June 4, 1953; Peter Tamony). Syn. *lobster trap; lobster net; basket glove.*

**orchard 1.** The outfield. **2.** A ballpark. **1st Use.** 1922. (Ernest J. Langian, *Baseball Cyclopedia;* Edward J. Nichols).

**orchardman** Syn. of *outfielder.*

**order 1.** See *batting order.* **2.** See *in order.*

**order of the can** A mock honor accorded to someone who has been released ("canned") from a team. **1st Use.** 1908. (*Baseball Magazine,* Aug.; Edward J. Nichols).

**ordinary effort** A criterion used by official scorers in determining whether a play should have been made. If, for example, an infielder allows a batted ball to escape his reach, the scorer will call it a "hit" if it could not be caught with ordinary effort or an "error" if it could have been. It is a subjective term and is at the heart of many scoring controversies.

**organization** A baseball franchise in its entirety; a ball club.

**organized baseball** Professional baseball, including the major leagues, the minor leagues, and the offices that administer them. On May 22, 1922, the U.S. Supreme Court ruled that organized baseball was primarily a sport and not a business and therefore was not subject to antitrust laws and interstate commerce regulations. Abbrev. *OB.*

**oriflamme** *arch.* The *pennant,* 2. **1st Use.** 1915. (*Baseball Magazine,* Dec.; Edward J. Nichols). **Etymology.** The word, borrowed from the French, has become a standard term for a "banner" or "emblem" in English. It refers directly to the red banner of St. Denis used as a military banner for the early kings of France. It undoubtedly entered baseball as part of the quest for new synonyms for "pennant."

**original** *n.* A unique ballplayer, often a flaky one; e.g., Boston Red Sox pitcher Bill "Spaceman" Lee was an "original."

**original softball** [softball term] Syn. of *fast pitch softball.*

**Oriole way** A system of fundamentals, practice, and teaching procedures devised by Baltimore Orioles manager Earl Weaver and coach Cal Ripken Sr. for the proper method of playing baseball throughout the organization, from the lowest minors to the major leagues. The system included a meticulously planned spring training and emphasis on such fundamentals as cutoff plays, relays, throwing to bases, rundowns, baserunning, pitcher's fielding drills, signs, and defending against the bunt and stolen base. The Oriole way also included a tradition of good play, sportsmanship, and dignity (such as not throwing at batters), and a sense of order, moderation, tolerance, and decency. The Oriole way meant that when minor leaguers became Orioles, "they already knew an established method in how they handled game situations" (Frank Cashen, quoted in *Baltimore Sun,* July 12, 1998). Joe Strauss (*Baltimore Sun,* May 31, 1998) noted that the Oriole way is "an organizational Old Testament containing the codified method of character, dress, instruction, and attitude . . . that transcended major and minor leagues."

**OS** Abbrev. for *official scorer.*

**O's** A common nickname for the Baltimore Orioles. Its use is underscored when the national anthem is sung at home and the crowd bellows "Ohhhh!" in the line "Oh say does that star-spangled banner yet wave." The nickname took on a new significance at the beginning of the 1988 season when the "O" became a reference to zero as the club opened with a record-setting losing streak of 21 games.

**Oscar** A player deserving an award for his feats on the field; esp., a player faking something (putting on a act), such as an injury, being hit by a pitched ball, catching a ball that was actually trapped, or decoying a baserunner. The term derives from the nickname for the Motion Picture Academy Awards statuette.

**O'Sullivan sleeper** *arch.* A railroad day coach on which there are no sleeping accommodations. The original version of this term was *Sullivan sleeper* and "O'Sullivan" may be a simple misnomer. "One phrase obsolete in the majors likely will be in vogue again this coming season. That's the 'O'Sullivan sleeper,' the old-timers slang for a day coach." (Herbert Simons, *Baseball Magazine,* Jan. 1943).

**other pitches** Pitches other than fastballs, such as a variety of screwballs and an assortment of changeups.

**other thing** A pitcher's second-best pitch. "Vance's sobriquet 'Dazzy' is said to be derived from his own pet name for his 'other thing' used as a co-weapon with his fast ball" (William G. Brandt, *Baseball Magazine,* Oct. 1932).

**other way** To the opposite field; e.g., "Smith, a right-handed batter, hit the ball the other way to right field."

**OTL** [softball term] Abbrev. for *Over the Line.*

**ouija board** *arch.* The umpire's *indicator.* "Check the batteries in your ouija board" was once a common line from a bench jockey on a bad call. **Etymology.** From the popular Ouija board game.

**out 1.** *adj.* Not successful in getting on base or advancing to the next base; said of a batter or baserunner who has been retired by the defense. Perhaps the best definition of "out" appears in Zander Hollander's *Baseball Lingo* (1967): "What the game is never over until the last man is." Compare *safe,* 1. Syn. *away,* 1; *down,* 1; *gone,* 1; *dead.* **2.** *n.* A putout. **3.** *n.* One of the three required retirements that define the length of the half inning when the offensive team is at bat. **1st Use.** 1845. (*Brooklyn Daily Star,*

**Out.** *A whimsical depiction from 1908.*

Oct. 23; Edward J. Nichols). **4.** *adj.* Away from the batter, such as a pitch thrown outside the strike zone; e.g., "Smith's pitch was down and out." Compare *in,* 2. **5.** *adv.* Not participating in a game; e.g., "Jones is out, replaced by Brown." Compare *in,* 5. **6.** *adj.* Short for *out of play.*

**out by a mile** Exaggerated insistence that a player was out on a close call. When an umpire deems a runner safe at first on a close play, those who disagree are, by baseball tradition, required to say that he was "out by a mile."

**outcurve** *arch.* A curveball. Compare *incurve.* Also spelled "out curve." Syn. *outshoot; out drop.* **1st Use.** 1865. (Chadwick Scrapbooks; Edward J. Nichols).

**out drop** Syn. of *outcurve.* Also spelled "outdrop." **1st Use.** 1893. (*Harper's Weekly,* July 8; Edward J. Nichols).

**outduel** To pitch a better game than the pitcher(s) on the opposing team; to *outpitch.* "[Sid] Fernandez

Outduels Dodgers" (*Washington Post* headline, May 30, 1986).

**outer garden** *arch.* The outfield. Compare *inner garden.* Syn. "outer patch." **1st Use.** 1907. (*New York Evening Journal,* Apr. 11; Edward J. Nichols).

**outer works** The outfield. Compare *inner works,* 1. **1st Use.** 1912. (*New York Tribune,* Oct. 7; Edward J. Nichols).

**outfield 1.** The area of the playing field most distant from home plate; specif., the playing area beyond the infield perimeter or diamond and within the foul lines. Walls or grandstand fences usually set the outside boundaries of the outfield. There is no strictly defined line dividing the infield from the outfield. For any major-league ballpark built after June 1, 1958, the right-field wall and the left-field wall must be at least 325 feet from home plate and the center-field wall must be at least 400 feet from home plate. Abbrev. *OF,* 1. **1st Use.** 1865. (*New York Herald,* July 11; Edward J. Nichols). **2.** The defensive positions comprising left field, center field, and right field, taken collectively. **3.** The outfielders (left fielder, center fielder, and right fielder), considered as a group. **1st Use.** 1888. (*Harper's Weekly,* July 28; Edward J. Nichols).

**outfielder** A defensive player positioned in the outfield; specif., the left fielder, the center fielder, or the right fielder. Abbrev. *OF,* 2. Syn. *gardener; orchardman.* **1st Use.** 1883. (*Sporting Life,* May 20; Edward J. Nichols).

**outfield throw** A ball thrown to an infielder by an outfielder in an attempt to throw out a runner. Dan Sperling (*A Spectator's Guide to Baseball,* 1983) writes: "Among baseball's most thrilling plays and impressive sights is an outfielder's throw to a teammate who tags out a runner sliding into base.... Such a play is baseball theater at its best, as the ball and the runner converge on the base at nearly the same dusty instant, culminating in the umpire's dramatic one-armed gesture signifying 'Out!'"

**outfit** A baseball team. **1st Use.** 1905. (*Sporting Life,* Sept. 2; Edward J. Nichols).

**outhit** To produce more hits than the opposition.

**out in front** Descriptive of a batter who gets a good swing ("he always hits the ball out in front") or swings too early (such as a pull hitter fooled by a changeup).

**outing 1.** A given appearance by a player in a game. The term tends to be applied more often to pitchers rather than players who are in the lineup day after day: "If his last two outings are any indication, [pitcher] Dave Steib is back" (Mike Payne, *St. Petersburg Times,* Mar. 15, 1988). An outing can be long or short: "Gooden pitched two-plus innings—the shortest outing of his career" (*Tampa Tribune,* July 2, 1989). **2.** A given appearance of a team on the field; e.g., "The White Sox and the Red Sox had an outing at Comiskey Field."

**out in left field** Odd; out of it; a bit off. Syn. *out of left field.* **Etymology.** How left field got to be the metaphoric location for oddness has been the subject of no end of speculation. Several have suggested that it comes from the remoteness of left field; but right field is just as remote and, at the lower levels of the game at least, more likely to be populated by an odd player. As Ron Fimrite (*San Francisco Chronicle,* Apr. 28, 1969; Peter Tamony) wrote in an essay on right field: "There was but one position to which the clods, the kids with glasses, the little guys, the sissies, the ones that got good grades, the kids who played with girls, were exiled. That would be right field, the Siberia of my youth. Right field was the back of the bus, the slow-learners class, the children's department, a sideshow.... Anyone directed to play right field would have given anything to 'be out in left field.'"

One major theory postulates that the phrase was an insult heaped on kids who were stupid enough to buy left-field seats in Yankee Stadium, which for many years would have put them far away from a right fielder named Babe Ruth. This theory was suggested by David Shulman in a letter quoted by William Safire (*I Stand Corrected,* 1984): "When I was in my teens, living in the Bronx, we kids were always most anxious to get our seats in the right field where we would be closest to Babe Ruth, so I suppose anybody in the left field was far out."

A second major theory postulates that the phrase was a specific reference to the fact that there was a mental hospital, the Neuropsychiatric Institute, in back of left field in the old West Side Park in Chicago. The most specific description of this theory appears in a letter from physician Gerald M. Eisenberg of Chicago, also quoted in Safire's *I Stand Corrected* (1984): "In Chicago, when someone said that one was 'out in left field,' the implication was that one was behaving like the occupants of the Neuropsychiatric Institute, which was *literally* out in left field." This has been corroborated by researcher Richard Miller of Cincinnati who has been doing research on the Chicago ballparks.

It should also be noted that the phrase "way out in left field without a glove" was used in the 1930s. According to a United Press International dispatch (Apr. 19, 1937; Peter Tamony), which carried George Kirksey's byline, the phrase was not used to describe a player who is out of it, but rather one "as proficient at whipping over a smart crack as a sizzling strike."

**Extended Use.** A phrase applied broadly to describe odd, eccentric, unexpected, or exceptionally misguided people and ideas in all walks of life. See also *left field* (extended use, 1).

**out in order** Said of a situation in which the first three batters coming to the plate in an inning are retired without one of them reaching first base.

**outlaw** *arch.* A player banned from organized baseball. Hugh S. Fullerton (*American Magazine,* June 1912) shows how the term was once used widely: "The club, league or player who offends against baseball law is punished by being 'outlawed' or blacklisted. . . . There are several hundred players on the blacklist at present who cannot play in any clubs belonging to the National Agreement until reinstated by the Commission." **1st Use.** 1906. (*Sporting Life,* Feb. 10; Edward J. Nichols).

**outlaw league** A league that plays outside the rules and control of organized baseball; e.g., the Players League in 1890, the Federal League in 1914–15, and the Carolina League in 1936–38. **1st Use.** 1905. (*Sporting Life,* Sept. 2; Edward J. Nichols).

**out looking** Retired on a called third strike. Compare *out swinging.*

**out man** A weak hitter who is a good bet to make an out; an easy out. Pitchers are often out men.

**out of form** *arch.* Said of a 19th-century pitcher who had lost his effectiveness or a 19th-century batter who was unable to hit the ball.

**out of here** Said of a home run hit out of the ballpark.

**out of his hip pocket** Said of the apparent source of the ball as the pitcher goes into his windup, turns his back to the batter, and delivers the ball.

**out of left field** Syn. of *out in left field.*

**out of line** Outside the baselines.

**out of options** The condition that results when a player has been optioned three times.

**out of order** See *batting out of order.*

**out of play 1.** Regarding that period when the game is not being played as opposed to a period when plays can begin or continue. Compare *in play,* 1. **2.** Describing a ball that is dead, when runners cannot advance or be put out and runs cannot score. Compare *in play,* 2. Syn. *out,* 6.

**out of reach** Practically unwinnable, such as a game in which the score is 9–0 in the eighth inning.

**out of the chute** From the beginning; e.g., teams want to get going right "out of the chute" at the beginning of the season, or at the start of a series.

**out of the inning** Said of a pitcher who has survived a jam, often thanks to a double play that ends the inning.

**out of the park** Said of a ball that is hit hard enough to go out of the ballpark.

**out of turn** See *batting out of order.*

**out of uniform 1.** Said of a player who is not on the roster because of an injury or other reason. **2.** Said of a player who is not suited up at game time; e.g., being "out of uniform" can result in a suspension or fine at the manager's discretion.

**out pitch** *n.* **1.** The pitch that pitchers depend on to get an out; a pitcher's best or special pitch used in a tight spot when an out is required. See also *money pitch,* 1. **2.** A pitch that results in a strikeout.

**outpitch** *v.* To pitch a better game than the opposing pitcher. Syn. *outduel.*

**outpost** The outfield. **1st Use.** 1902. (*Sporting Life,* July 5; Edward J. Nichols).

**outright 1.** *adj.* Said of a transaction between two teams in which a player is obtained for cash alone rather than in a trade or a trade plus cash. **2.** *v.* To send a player to the minors after severing all his contractual ties with the major-league team; to release a player to another club without any conditions; e.g., "The Kansas City Royals outrighted Smith to Omaha." Compare *option,* 2.

**outright waivers** A form of *waivers* in which the player, by clearing waivers, remains with his club.

**outshoot** *arch.* Syn. of *outcurve*. Compare *off-shoot*. **1st Use.** 1881. (*New York Herald,* July 29; Edward J. Nichols).

**outside** Said of a pitch that is delivered away from the batter on the far side of or beyond the strike zone. One of the reasons that pitchers like it when batters stand away from the plate is that they can throw an outside pitch for a strike that the batter cannot reach. Compare *inside.* **1st Use.** 1908. (*Spalding's Official Base Ball Guide;* Edward J. Nichols).

**outside baseball** An offensive strategy that depends on powerful hitting rather than skill on the basepaths. Compare *inside baseball.*

**outside corner** The side of home plate that is away from the batter. Compare *inside corner.* **1st Use.** 1901. (Burt L. Standish, *Frank Merriwell's Marvel;* Edward J. Nichols).

**outside pivot** A *pivot* in which the shortstop brushes second base on the outfield side before throwing to first base in the attempt to turn a double play. Compare *inside pivot.*

**outslug** To get more hits than the opposition in a high-scoring game.

**out swinging** Retired on a swing and a miss for the third strike. Compare *out looking.*

**over** Said of a pitch that is in the strike zone; e.g., "The pitch was over the plate" or "Get the pitch over!"

**overdog** A team that goes from the role of underdog to powerhouse; e.g., the 1969 New York Mets.

**overhand** Said of a pitch or throw delivered with the hand raised above the elbow or the arm raised straight above the shoulder. As *underhand* and *sidearm* pitches are uncommon, most baseball pitches are overhand pitches. **1st Use.** 1911. (William Patten & J. W. McSpadden, *The Book of Base Ball;* Edward J. Nichols).

**overmanage** For a manager to hamper his team by employing more strategy than is called for. The term is commonly used when a team gets into trouble after its manager has called on too many relief pitchers.

**over-pitch** *n./obs.* A pitched ball thrown past the catcher and formerly recorded in the record of a game. **1st Use.** 1862. (*New York Sunday Mercury,* July 13; Edward J. Nichols).

**overplay** To use players at positions where they normally would not play. The practice occurs when there are roster shortages.

**overpower** To swing with excessive force.

**overrun 1.** To touch a base but then run or slide beyond it so that the runner can be tagged out. The batter-runner is allowed to overrun first base "if he returns immediately to the base" [*Official Baseball Rules,* rule 7.08(c)], but if he breaks toward second base, he is liable to be tagged out. **1st Use.** 1880. (*Brooklyn Daily Eagle,* Aug. 20; Edward J. Nichols). **2.** To misjudge the course of a batted ball that falls safely behind an onrushing fielder.

**overshift** A defensive adjustment that is so extreme that it creates vacant spaces, which batters can exploit.

**overslide** To slide into a base with such momentum that the runner loses contact with the base and is liable to be tagged out. **1st Use.** 1908. (*Brooklyn Daily Eagle,* May 29; Edward J. Nichols).

**overstride** To take too large a step toward the pitcher when swinging the bat; to lunge at the ball.

**overswing 1.** To not be selective of the pitches offered a batter; to swing at pitches that normally cannot be hit on the outside chance the batter might get a hit. **2.** To swing when the batter believes the pitcher is throwing harder than he really is.

**over the fence** Said of a ball that is hit out of the ballpark for a home run. **1st Use.** 1861. (*New York Sunday Mercury,* Aug. 10; Edward J. Nichols).

**over-the-fence home run rule** [softball term] One of a series of rules created to limit the number of home runs at various levels of slow pitch softball. A ball hit over the fence in a game by a team in excess of the prescribed limit is ruled an out. When the batter is ruled out because of the rule, the ball is dead and no runners can score.

**Over the Line.** *Pitching and batting are Al Hamilton and Dale Olsen, respectively.*

**Over the Line** [softball term] A variation of softball created on the beaches of San Diego in 1954 by a group killing time waiting for a volleyball court. It is a beach game rather than one intended for traditional softball fields. Each team is composed of three players and each team pitches to its own batters. Kneeling next to the plate, the pitcher gently tosses the ball into the air for the batter to swing at and drive "over the line," which is usually 55 feet away and 60 feet long. Any ball hit short of the line is considered a foul ball. Abbrev. *OTL.*

**over the roof** Said of a home run that is hit over the top of the stands, a feat that is hardly possible in the modern ballparks.

**over the top** Describing an overhand pitching or throwing motion; e.g., "When [Armando] Benitez throws over the top, his control is better, his slider is sharper, and his mechanics are less of a health hazard" (*Baltimore Sun*, Apr. 5, 1995).

**overthrow 1.** *n.* A thrown ball that is too high or too wide of its intended target and that frequently lands out of play. In instances when the ball is thrown out of play, each baserunner is given the base he was heading toward plus one additional base. **1st Use.** 1862. (*New York Sunday Mercury,* July 13; Edward J. Nichols). **2.** *v.* To throw a ball that is too high or wide or cannot be fielded by the intended receiver. **1st Use.** 1891. (*Harper's Weekly,* May 9; Edward J. Nichols). **3.** *v.* For a pitcher to throw too hard or to try to compensate. "There's the classic instance of a pitcher overthrowing, trying to make too good a pitch" (Keith Hernandez, *Pure Baseball,* 1994).

**overtime** Any inning after the ninth. The term is borrowed from those sports whose finale is determined by a clock or timer and in which extra periods are played in the event of a tie at the end of the final period.

**own 1.** For a batter to hit successfully against a

given pitcher over a period of time; e.g., Sam McDowell said Frank Howard "owned" him. Tim McCarver (*Oh, Baby I Love It!,* 1987) noted that Ty Cobb "owned" pitcher Walter Johnson. Cobb knew that Johnson would not use his blazing fastball to intimidate the batter so Cobb would crowd the plate knowing that he would get a good pitch. **2.** For a pitcher to dominate a batter by getting him out on a regular basis.

**owner** One who possesses the title, majority shares, or other form of control over a professional baseball team. **1st Use.** 1943. "And while it is true that your major league clubowner has a lot of other and even more important problems . . . all this presents a very distressing situation to him" (*Baseball Magazine,* Apr.; David Shulman).

**Ozarkism** An aphoristic line attributed to Philadelphia Phillies manager Danny Ozark, who had a particular ability to fracture the English language; e.g., "I have always had a wonderful repertoire with my players," "It is beyond my apprehension," and "Even Napoleon had his Watergate."

**ozone** *v.* To hit the ball hard, high, and long, as if to send it into the ozone layer. **1st Use.** 1905. "When he [the baseball writer] says 'Tinker led off for the Cubs and ozoned,' every legitimate thirty-third degree 'fan' grasps immediately the graphic picture thus painted" (*Sporting Life,* May 20; Barry Popik).

# P

**P** Abbrev. for *pitcher*.

**PA** Abbrev. for *plate appearance*.

**pace 1.** *n.* An illusion of speed in the pitching delivery, as in pitching a slow ball with the same arm movement as a faster pitch. See also *change of pace*. **1st Use.** 1865. (*New York Herald*, June 29; Edward J. Nichols). **2.** *n.* The rate of speed at which a pitcher works. **3.** *v.* To lead; to perform in such a manner that other players want to emulate; e.g., "Smith paced the Yankees to a 6–4 win." **4.** *v.* To field a ball without taking an unnecessary step. **Etymology.** The term is borrowed from horse racing.

**pacesetter 1.** The leading team in a league or division. **2.** The league or division leader in an individual batting or pitching category.

**Pacific Coast League** A Class AAA minor league (1946–51 and since 1958) with teams in the western parts of the United States and Canada. It was formerly a Class A (1904–07) and Class AA (1908–45) minor league. Abbrev. *PCL*.

**package** A trade that involves more than one player or a player and money.

**pack a punch** To hit the ball with power.

**pad 1.** *n.* A padded mitt or glove. See also *pud*. **1st Use.** 1906. (*Sporting Life*, Feb. 10; Edward J. Nichols). **2.** *v.* To score additional runs; e.g., "The Cubs padded their lead with two runs in the eighth."

**paddist** The catcher. A caption in *The Sporting News* (May 31, 1947) refers to Jimmie Wilson as a "top paddist."

**Pads** A nickname for the San Diego Padres; e.g., "Pads Will Pick Pitcher" (*The Sporting News* headline, June 6, 1988).

**Paige's rules for how to keep young** A set of guidelines created by Satchel Paige (*Collier's*, June 13, 1953), baseball's "ageless wonder," to explain his longevity as a pitcher:

1) Avoid fried meats which angry up the blood.

2) If your stomach disputes you, lie down and pacify it with cool thoughts.

3) Keep the juices flowing by jangling around gently as you move.

4) Go very lightly on the vices, such as carrying on in society. The social ramble ain't restful.

5) Avoid running at all times.

6) Don't look back. Something might be gaining on you.

**pain game** A technique for the relief of bullpen boredom: "They pull hairs out of each other's noses and try to see whose eyes water the most" (San Francisco Giants reliever Rod Beck, quoted in *Milwaukee Journal Sentinel*, Aug. 7, 1997).

**paint 1.** *v.* To throw pitches over the black borders (inside or outside corners) of home plate. "[Jack] McDowell painted both edges of the plate with fastballs" (*Baltimore Sun*, Aug. 8, 1995). Syn. *paint the black*. **2.** *n.* The black borders of home plate.

**paint master** A pitcher who "paints the black" or pinpoints his pitches. The term was coined by pitcher Dennis Eckersley.

**paint the black** Syn. of *paint,* 1.

**Pale Hose** A nickname for the Chicago White Sox.

**palm ball** An uncommon off-speed pitch in which the ball is gripped between the pitcher's thumb and palm and is thrown with a pushing motion, making it break in an unpredictable manner with little or no spin on the pitch. "Palm Ball Helps In No-Hitter" (Associated Press dispatch headline on Steve Ridzik's no-hitter, Apr. 5, 1952; Peter Tamony). See also *slip pitch.* Also spelled "palmball."

**pal-ocracy** A vague term for the network of good friends ("pals") who supposedly once ran organized baseball.

**palomita** Spanish for *fly ball.* Literally, the term means "little dove."

**pan** Syn. of *home plate.* **1st Use.** 1891. "These three men make the pitchers put them over the pan day in and day out" (*New York Sporting Times,* May 23; David Shulman).

**pancake 1.** An old, worn, and generally lifeless fielder's glove. **2.** A thinly padded glove preferred by some infielders (mostly shortstops and second basemen) who believe it allows them to handle and release the ball more quickly than would be possible with the more thickly padded *bushel basket.*

**panty waist** [softball term] An early name for softball.

**paper mache** Said of a player who is easily hurt. See also *tissue-paper Tom.* Syn. "paper mashy." **Etymology.** Despite some wild spelling deviation, a clear reference to papier-mâché, a light and moldable pulpy paper.

**paper team** A team whose potential is greater than its actual performance; a team that looks good *on paper* but not in the field. **1st Use.** 1911. (*Baseball Magazine,* Oct.; Edward J. Nichols).

**parachute 1.** A softly hit pop fly that descends slowly between the infield and outfield. See also

*Texas Leaguer.* **2.** A slow pitch; a changeup. "Before [Trevor] Hoffman struck out Ryne Sandberg with a changeup, manager Bruce Bochy stood in the dugout, imploring his closer to 'throw a parachute.' That's the lingo for Hoffman's slow ball. 'Halfway through, pull the rip-cord—it floats in.'" (*San Diego Union-Tribune,* Apr. 4, 1996). **3.** Syn. of *eephus.*

**parachute hitter** A *singles hitter.* The 1952 Pittsburgh Pirates had several such hitters.

**paraffin ball** A ball doctored with wax.

**parallel stance** Syn. of *square stance.*

**parent club 1.** The club that holds a player's basic contract. **2.** A club that owns a minor-league farm club.

**park 1.** *n.* A baseball field; short for *ballpark.* "You know, you take your worries to the park and you leave them there" (Humphrey Bogart, in a 1950s promotional ad for baseball). **2.** *v.* To hit a home run; e.g., to "park" in the bushes, to "park the pill" in the bleachers, and he "parked one" in the street. "They Really Parked 'Em" (*Newsday* headline, May 12, 1987).

**part-time player** A player who does not appear in the lineup on a regular basis.

**pass 1.** *n.* Syn. of *base on balls.* **1st Use.** 1902. (*Sporting Life,* Sept. 20; Edward J. Nichols). **2.** *v.* To walk a batter. **1st Use.** 1910. (*Baseball Magazine,* Dec.; Edward J. Nichols). **3.** *n.* A free admission to a game.

**pass a runner** For a baserunner to illegally pass another runner on the basepath. When this occurs, the runner passing his teammate is ruled out.

**pass ball 1.** Syn. of *passed ball.* **2.** A pitch that does not cross the strike zone.

**passed ball** A legally pitched ball that the catcher fails to hold or control with ordinary effort, thereby allowing one or more baserunners to advance. It differs from a *wild pitch* in that the official scorer rules that the catcher should have stopped it. If a passed ball occurs on the third strike, it is treated as a dropped third strike and the batter may advance to first base. A passed ball is not registered as an error to the catcher and cannot be charged if there are no runners on base. Abbrev. *PB*. Syn. *pass ball,* 1. **1st Use.** 1861. (*New York Sunday Mercury,* Aug. 10; Edward J. Nichols).

**paste** To bat a ball hard; e.g., "Smith pasted one in the sixth." **1st Use.** 1876. (Chicago *Inter-Ocean,* May 6; Edward J. Nichols).

**pasteboard** *arch.* An admission ticket to a baseball game. **1st Use.** 1898. (*New York Tribune,* May 13; Edward J. Nichols).

**pastime** See *national pastime.*

**pasture** 1. The outfield. **1st Use.** 1891. (Chicago *Inter-Ocean,* May 5; Edward J. Nichols). **2.** A ballpark.

**pastureman** An outfielder.

**pastureworker** An outfielder.

**paternal slump** Poor baseball performance linked to impending fatherhood. "[Detroit] Tigers' [Howard] Johnson in 'Paternal' Slump" (*USA Today* headline, August 16, 1984).

**path** See *basepath.*

**patrol** 1. To play a field position; e.g., "Smith patrolled the outfield." **2.** For a base coach to direct baserunners.

**Patsy Flaherty** A pitching delivery without a windup, such as Don Larsen used in the 1956 World Series. **Etymology.** Pete Howe (*San Francisco Examiner,* May 26, 1957; Peter Tamony) wrote: "Patsy Flaherty was an old-time pitcher [early 1900s] in the National League who used the no-windup delivery so much it came to be called the 'Patsy Flaherty.' Casey Stengel batted against him and has described his pitching this way: 'Patsy picked up the ball and umpire hollered strike.'"

**Pawsox** The common name for the Class AAA Pawtucket Red Sox, an International League farm team of the Boston Red Sox, based in Pawtucket, R.I., where the likes of Wade Boggs, Jim Rice, manager Joe Morgan, and Roger Clemens prepped for the major leagues.

**payback pitch** A ball thrown by a pitcher to harm or intimidate a batter in revenge for a real or imagined transgression by the batter's team.

**pay ball** 1. Syn. of *payoff pitch.* **1st Use.** 1937. (*New York Daily News,* May 2; Edward J. Nichols). **2.** A pitch that is easy to hit.

**pay dues** To advance step by step up the ladder of professional baseball by diligent effort without having had any special breaks or treatment.

**payoff pitch** The pitch delivered when the count is full (three balls and two strikes). It is the "payoff" because, barring a foul, the batter must hit the ball, be walked, or strike out. Syn. *pay ball,* 1.

**pay station** Syn. of *home plate.* **1st Use.** 1937. (*New York Daily News,* Jan. 31; Edward J. Nichols).

**pay wing** Syn. of *money wing.*

**PB** Scorecard and box score abbrev. for *passed ball.*

**PCL** Abbrev. for *Pacific Coast League.*

**pea** A pitched or batted ball that is moving so fast that it appears smaller than it actually is. It is said to look like a pea. "Juicier? I know there were a lot of peas out there tonight." (Rocky Colavito on the 1987 model baseball, quoted in *USA Today,* June 30, 1987). **1st Use.** 1910. (*Baseball Magazine,* Apr.; Edward J. Nichols).

**peacherino** *obs.* A sensational play or player. The term is an elaboration of the word "peach." **1st Use.** 1908. (*New York Evening Journal,* Feb. 27; Edward J. Nichols).

**peapatch** A term used by broadcaster Red Barber for a ballpark; e.g., a rallying team or a hitter on a hot streak is "tearin' up the peapatch."

**pebble hit** A base hit made when a rock, pebble, stone, or other field irregularity causes the ball to bounce away from the fielder. "In the old days, that would have been called a 'pebble hit,' but there are no pebbles on infields now" (World Series announcer, Oct. 4, 1952; Peter Tamony).

**pebble hunter** A defensive player, usually an infielder, who picks up real or imaginary pebbles on which to blame his errors. He will allege that a ball took a bad hop because of a pebble. Syn. "pebble picker." **1st Use.** 1912. (Hugh S. Fullerton, *American Magazine,* June; Edward J. Nichols). **Etymology.** Fullerton (see above) wrote: "The term arises from the fact that one old-time player was caught carrying pebbles in his pocket to drop on the ground after he fumbled, and then find, claiming each time that the ball struck a pebble and bounded wrong."

**Pebble Play** An incident, in the 12th inning of the final game of the 1924 World Series between the New York Giants and the Washington Senators, in which Earl McNeely's hit hopped over Giants third baseman Freddie Lindstrom's head leading to a run that gave the championship to the Senators. It was claimed and verified by members of the Giants that the ball did indeed hit a pebble.

**pecker** Syn. of *feeder,* 2.

**pedal music** *arch.* The stamping of enthusiastic fans.

**peddle** To trade a player.

**peddle peruna** *arch.* To be boastful; to advertise oneself. **Etymology.** Peruna was a patent medicine heavily advertised at the turn of the 20th century. Many gave testimonials in its behalf. In Mark Sullivan's *Our Times* (1926–35), a senator from Mississippi gives his testimonial: "For some time I have been a sufferer from catarrh in its most incipient stage. So much so that I became alarmed as to my general health. But hearing of Peruna as a good remedy, I gave it a fair trial, and soon began to improve. I take pleasure in recommending your great natural catarrh cure. Peruna is the best I have ever tried." The medicine was driven from the market by pure-food advocates who faulted it for being loaded with whiskey.

**peeker** 1. A "pitcher who, with men on, can't resist turning head to watch runners as he is in act of delivery, takes eyes off catcher's target and invariably has bad control" (Bert Dunne, *Folger's Dictionary of Baseball,* 1958). **2.** A batter in the batter's box who tries to peek at the catcher's signs.

**peewee** A ball that is smaller than most. "A true peewee is treasured by hurlers, and its departure from the premises, by fair means or foul, is secretly mourned" (Roger Angell, *Five Seasons,* 1972).

**Pee Wee Baseball** A program of play and instruction for boys and girls who are six and seven years old.

**peg** 1. *n.* A long, powerful, esp. accurate throw, traditionally from the outfield to the infield. "He's

had some good pegs from out there. You can't tell him to take it easy." (George Bamberger, on Robin Yount as an outfielder, *Tampa Tribune-Times,* Mar. 30, 1986). **1st Use.** 1908. (*Spalding's Official Base Ball Guide;* Edward J. Nichols). **2.** *v.* To make a peg. **1st Use.** 1862. (*New York Sunday Mercury,* July 13; Edward J. Nichols).

**pegger** The catcher. "All the regulars were in the game, recovered from illnesses and injuries . . . Joe Benz . . . couldn't pitch much, [Ray] Schalk was a bum pegger" (James Crusinberry, *Chicago Tribune,* Aug. 1914).

**Peggy Lee fastball** A fastball that travels more slowly than expected, or has nothing on it. **Etymology.** The term is used in connection with batters who see the pitch and are reminded of Lee's 1969 sad song, "Is That All There Is?" (words by Jenny Leiber and music by Mike Stoller). The move to baseball is attributed widely to pitcher Tug McGraw who specialized in the pitch (his regular fastball minus about 10 miles per hour), but *The Sporting News* cites Dan Quisenberry as father of the term.

**Pekinese poke** Syn. of *Chinese home run.* "16 of First 29 HR's in L.A. Labeled 'Pekinese Pokes'" (*The Sporting News* headline, May 7, 1958; Peter Tamony).

**pellet** The baseball. **1st Use.** 1907. (*New York Evening Journal,* Apr. 25; Edward J. Nichols).

**pelota** Spanish for the baseball.

**pen** 1. *n.* "A row of seats fenced in on all sides in the extreme front of the grandstand" (Thomas W. Lawson, *The Krank: His Language and What It Means,* 1888). **2.** *n.* Short for *bullpen.* "After three days in the pen, [Ed] Whitson's back in the rotation" (Gannett Westchester Newspapers headline, June 13, 1986). Sometimes spelled " 'pen." **3.** *v.* To win a bullpen duel; e.g., "Pirates Pen SD in 15" (*Boston Herald* headline, July 13, 1990). **4.** *n.* Relief pitching. "It really felt good. It was a really good pen, probably the best pen I've thrown since spring training." (Rocky Coppinger, quoted in *Baltimore Sun,* 1997).

**penalty** The application (by the umpire) of the *Official Baseball Rules* following an illegal act; e.g.,

***Pennant.*** *The hapless St. Louis Browns celebrate their sole pennant in 1944. The acute shortage of players because of World War II gave the Browns a singular opportunity. The entire Browns infield had been declared 4-F.*

the umpire will call a ball (the penalty) on the pitcher if his pitching hand comes in contact with his mouth or lips while standing on the mound.

**pencil** A baseball bat; e.g., "Smith wrote out a hit with his pencil."

**pencil in** To enter a player's name in the starting lineup or during the course of a game. "On July 1, 1982, [Baltimore Orioles manager Earl] Weaver made a decision. He penciled [Cal] Ripken in at shortstop." (*Baseball Digest,* Dec. 1983).

**pennant 1.** The title and honorary emblem achieved by the team that wins its division or league championship. Syn. *flag,* 1. **2.** The large triangular commemorative *banner* given to the team that wins the pennant. See also *bunting,* 2; *gonfalon; oriflamme.* **1st Use.** 1879. (*Spirit of the Times,* Sept. 13; Edward J. Nichols).

**pennant fever** The rabid enthusiasm of the fans when it appears the home team might win a division pennant. "It did not take long at all for the bugs in the stands to catch a dose of what they call pennant fever" (Harry Stein, *Hoopla,* 1983).

**pennant insurance** Adding a player (esp. a pitcher) to a pennant-contending team during the late stages of the season.

**pennant porch** The grandstand area created by a short outfield fence for home run hitters; specif., the 296-foot right-field walls in Municipal Stadium in Kansas City in 1965 and in Yankee Stadium.

**pennant race** The competition for the division championship, esp. toward the end of the season when several teams are in contention. Syn. *flag chase.* **1st Use.** 1880. (*Brooklyn Daily Eagle,* July 25; Edward J. Nichols).

**pennant voyage** A baseball season.

**'penner** A relief pitcher; a denizen of the bullpen. "Nothing, [Earl] Weaver fears, is beyond the reach of his 'penners" (*Washington Post,* June 5, 1986).

**pepper 1.** *n.* Vigor and energy. **1st Use.** 1895. (*New York Press,* July 8; Edward J. Nichols). **2.** *n.* A fast-paced pregame bunting and fielding drill played at close range among small clusters of players. One player chops at the ball with a brisk, bunt-like stroke. The batted ball is pitched back to the batter by one of the fielders. The ball is continually thrown, batted, and fielded in rapid succession. Keith Moreland (*Vineline,* 1987) wrote: "Greatest game in the world for a hitter. Short pepper is when a batter tries to hit one-hoppers back to the guy throwing to him in pregame practice." Many ballparks have "No Pepper" or "No Pepper Games" signs stenciled on the dugout walls. Because these prohibitory signs have been visible on television for many years, the term is known to many who have never seen it played. The ban, dating back to the 1950s, apparently stemmed from the fact that the field was sometimes damaged from pepper play and that it constituted a possible danger of injury to fans in the box seats. **1st Use.** 1933. The game was known as *high-low* and perhaps by other names before it became "pepper." "Over at the left of the third-base line pepper games are in progress. Six or eight players, glove in hand, line up a yard apart. Thirty feet away stands a batter. He hits the ball with amazing precision . . . Whoever grabs it returns it to the batter as quickly as he can get it out of his hands, only to have it batted back again double quick. This simple game is very popular among training players" (Arthur Mann, *American Mercury,* Mar. 1933; Peter Tamony). **3.** *n.* The ritual of briskly throwing the ball around the infield after a putout. **4.** *v.* To throw a baseball hard and fast; e.g., "Smith peppered the ball to first." **5.** *v.* To hit a pitch sharply; e.g., "Jones peppered the offering for a clean single." **1st Use.** 1912. (*New York Tribune,* Sept. 8; Edward J. Nichols).

Etymology. The term would appear to derive from "pep" as well as the "peppy" or "peppery" nature of the drill, which in turn appear to be derivatives of "pepper," to give the term a circular etymology. The adjective "peppery" was fairly common in ballpark expressions before World War II; e.g., "peppery grasser" (a hit ball that is low and swift) and "peppery pilot" (a lively, aggressive manager of a team) (Maurice H. Weseen, *Dictionary of American Slang,* 1934).

**pepper practice** A period of pepper play before the game. **1st Use.** 1935. "We can suggest nothing more helpful to the young batter than 'pepper practice' in large doses" (Ralph H. Barbour, *How to Play Better Baseball;* David Shulman).

**percentage baseball** A strategy in which the game is played with the aid of the law of probabilities; e.g., waiting for hits to bring in baserunners rather than taking chances on the basepaths, or walking a batter to create a force situation. **1st Use.** 1932. (*Baseball Magazine,* Oct.; Edward J. Nichols).

**percentage hit** A fluke hit that nevertheless helps one's batting average.

**percentage manager** A manager who makes decisions based on established form, statistics, and odds.

**percentage patsy** A player who plays to enhance his individual statistics rather than for the good of the team as a whole. **1st Use.** 1937. (*The Sporting News Record Book;* Edward J. Nichols).

**percentage point 1.** A unit in a player's batting average, equal to 0.001; e.g., "Smith added 18 percentage points to his batting average (from .282 to .300) in the two weeks following the All-Star Game." **2.** A unit in the won-loss average of a team, equal to 0.001.

**percentage sinker** A *Texas Leaguer.*

**perch** A team's place in the standings.

**perfect game** A *no-hitter* in which no opposing player reaches first base, either by a base hit, base on balls, hit batter, or fielding error; i.e., the pitcher or pitchers retire all 27 opposing batters in order. As of this writing, there have been only 15 perfect games in the major leagues, with the most famous being the one pitched by New York Yankees hurler Don Larsen against the Brooklyn Dodgers in the 1956 World Series. The first perfect game was pitched on

June 12, 1880, by J. Lee Richmond of the Worcester Brown Stockings against the Cleveland Forest Citys. Syn. *perfecto.* **1st Use.** 1922. (Ernest J. Lanigan, *Baseball Cyclopedia;* Edward J. Nichols).

**perfecto** Syn. of *perfect game.* "Sandy Koufax . . . pitches fourth career no-hitter, a perfecto over Chicago Cubs on September 9 [1965]" (*Red Foley's Cartoon History of Baseball,* 1992). "David Wells Perfecto" (*Sports Illustrated* headline, May 25, 1998) regarding the 15th perfect game in major-league history as the New York Yankees pitcher blanked the Minnesota Twins on May 17, 1998.

**period baseball** Syn. of *vintage base ball.*

**person** Any part of the body, clothing, or equipment of a ballplayer or umpire.

**perspiration pellet** *arch.* Syn. of *spitball.* **1st Use.** 1907. (*New York Evening Journal,* June 7; Edward J. Nichols).

**pest** A persistent fan who always wants something, such as an autographed ball. Pests are nothing new, as the following definition from *Baseball Magazine* (Sept. 1913) attests: "A grave-yard comedian as funny as a crutch equipped with a megaphone, a pass, and a .44 caliber voice, who tries to address the players by their maiden names. Generally loses both 'goat' and voice in the first inning."

**Pete Homer** Personification of an umpire who seems to be favoring the home team.

**petit larceny** (Pron. "petty larceny") Syn. of *base stealing.*

**PH** Abbrev. for *pinch hitter.*

**phantom 1.** An item in baseball memorabilia collecting that was created for an event that did not take place, such as playoff tickets for a team that did not make the playoffs. **2.** A player listed in baseball encyclopedias who did not actually play in the major leagues, usually the result of an ancient typographical error.

**phantom double play** A double play in which the out at second base is an illusion because the fielder either crosses the bag without touching it or touches the base without possessing the ball. Despite the fact that the rules state that the bag must be touched with the fielder possessing the ball, many umpires (to keep players from getting hurt in collisions) ignore the violation if the ball beats the runner to second base. See also *neighborhood play.*

**phantom hit** A base on balls. **1st Use.** 1887. "[Tommy] Tucker was given a 'phantom' hit, stole second and scored on [Mike] Griffin's splendid drive to center field" (*The World* [New York], Aug. 11; Gerald Cohen).

**phantom infield** A crowd-pleasing pregame drill in which the infield goes through the rigors of infield practice without the benefit of a ball.

**phantom tag** A missed tag or a tag from a glove without the ball in it, either one of which is mistakenly credited as a legal tag. Some infielders discreetly remove the ball from the glove just before the tag to prevent the ball from being jarred loose as the play is made.

**pheenom** Var. of *phenom.*

**phenom** A highly touted rookie; a rookie who gets off to a spectacular start at the beginning of the season or during spring training; an early bloomer. Var. *pheenom.* **1st Use.** 1881. "[James] Whitney the Boston phenom" (*Detroit Free Press,* July 17; Peter Morris). Morris noted that rookie pitcher Whitney occasioned much comment because of two novelties: his unusual height for the time (6'2") and his having pitched in California the previous season. The *Detroit Free Press* (Apr. 21, 1881) referred to Whitney as the "untamed California 'bonanza,'" but Morris was unable to find any other citations of "bonanza." "Phenom"—at least in its more common form of "phenomenal"—is very common throughout the decade. Morris adds that a song sung at supper by the Knickerbocker Club included the line: "And the infantile 'phenomenon,' who'll play when he gets older."

Although writer Garry Schumacher is widely credited with coining the term for the New York Giants outfielder Clint Hartung in Spring 1947, it regularly shows up in print much earlier. Nor was it an uncommon term at the end of the 19th and the beginning of 20th century. Grantland Rice (*The Tumult and the Shouting,* 1954; Charles D. Poe) recalled a 1904 telegram touting a young "phenom" named Tyrus Raymond Cobb.

A. G. Spalding (*Base Ball: America's National Game,* 1911) tied the term to a rule change: "The removal of the straight-arm pitching restrictions by the amendment of the rules in 1884 was responsible for the evolution of the 'Phenom.' He came into the game from Keokuk, Kankakee, Kokomo and Kalamazoo. He was heralded always as a 'discovery.' His achievements were 'simply phenomenal.' Once in a great while he 'made good.' Usually he proved to be a flat and unmitigated failure."

**Etymology.** Shortened form of "phenomenon" or "phenomenal player." The word "phenomenon" has had a long and distinguished history as a title for a boxer or racehorse. Peter Tamony has found other phenomenons dating back to 1807, when a prizefighter nicknamed the "Israelite Phenomenon" won a 34-round bout in England. In the United States, Tamony found a bay gelding named Awful who had a spectacular season in 1838; his backers nicknamed him "The Phenomenon." Although the shortened form "phenom" has been used for boxers and other athletes, its early use and primary application has been to ballplayers; i.e., it is closely linked to baseball. **Extended Use.** Now used for fast-starters in any field. The title of an article on young CEOs was "Pity the Poor Phenoms" (*Forbes,* Apr. 8, 1985).

**Philadelphia Athletics** The name of three major-league teams: a National League team (1876), an American Association team (1882–91), and an American League team (1901–54), which moved to Kansas City in 1955 and then to Oakland in 1968.

**Philadelphia Phillies** The name of the National League East Division franchise in Philadelphia, Pa., and a member of the league since 1883. The nickname is derived from the name of the city and has been in use since 1883. The team was known as the Blue Jays in 1944 and 1945, although "Phillies" was still declared the official team name.

**Philadelphia triple** *arch.* Three consecutive fly-ball outs in an inning. The term was used in the 1940s.

**Phillips 99 ball** A tightly wound, hopped-up baseball that carried far when hit.

**Phils** A nickname for the Philadelphia Phillies.

**phonographic needle pitch** An illegal pitch given its odd trajectory by the insertion of a 78-rpm stylus in the seam of the ball. It is described in detail by Martin Quigley (*The Crooked Pitch,* 1984), who threw the odd pitch in the 1930s.

**pianola** *arch.* An easy win; a laugher. **Etymology.** Pianola was the trademarked name of a player piano that was easy to play compared to a regular piano.

**Picasso** A *control pitcher;* one who "paints the black."

**pick 1.** *v.* To successfully field a ground ball, esp. one that is hard to handle. The term is often used as part of a compliment by one team member to another for a first-rate defensive play: "way to pick it" or "you really picked 'em." **2.** *n.* A successfully fielded ground ball, esp. one that is hard to handle; e.g., "Smith made a good pick on that sharply hit grounder."

**picked nine** *arch.* Any team that did not play a regular schedule and whose players accordingly were under no obligation to play exclusively for that team. Peter Morris (letter, Dec. 4, 1994) noted that the term frequently was used in the 1880s, but pinning down its meaning is somewhat difficult. The looseness of the definition is implied in the following note from the *Detroit Free Press* (May 1, 1881): "The Buffalos in their practice game have batted heavily and fielded well, but they have played against a 'picked nine,' and that term has a wide range of meaning, anywhere from a lot of muffers to a semi-professional club." Morris found an earlier citation of the term (*Detroit Free Press,* Apr. 21, 1881) "which does nothing to eludicate its meaning." **1st Use.** 1860. (*New York Clipper,* Oct. 6).

**picked off** To be thrown out on a pickoff play.

**picket line** The three outfielders, who are not only arrayed like fence pickets but can presumably "pick it."

**pickle 1.** *v.* To bat a ball hard; e.g., "Smith pickled one." Edward J. Nichols (*An Historical Dictionary of Baseball Terminology,* Ph.D. dissertation, 1939) wrote: "Named from the idea of 'pickling' in the sense of 'to salt away.'" **1st Use.** 1908. (*New York Evening Journal,* Aug. 20; Edward J. Nichols). **2.** *n.* A runner caught in a rundown between bases. Short for "in a pickle." **3.** *n.* A playground drill or game in which two youngsters stand at bases and throw the ball back and forth, trying to put out a runner.

**pickle brine** A salty solution given a role in baseball after pitcher Nolan Ryan started the custom of soaking his hands in it to toughen his skin and prevent blisters.

**pick off** *v.* To throw out a baserunner who has moved too far away from the base he is occupying. **1st Use.** 1888. (*New York Press,* Apr. 21; Edward J. Nichols).

**pickoff** *n.* Syn. of *pickoff play.* **1st Use.** 1939. "Then the danger of a throw to first for the pickoff is that the runner has overrun first not only too far to get back but far enough to make a break for second" (Gordon S. "Mickey" Cochrane, *Baseball: The Fan's Game,* 1939; David Shulman).

**pickoff move** The motion made by a pitcher to pick off a baserunner.

**pickoff play** A play in which either the pitcher or the catcher makes a sudden toss of the ball to an infielder to catch a runner off base by surprise and tag him out. The play requires careful coordination between the players who are setting up the play. Syn. *pickoff.*

**pickoff throw** A throw intended to catch a runner off base; e.g., "The runner scored when the catcher's pickoff throw to second was missed and went into center field."

**pickpocket 1.** One who steals the signs of an opponent. **2.** A quick-handed infielder who "steals" potential base hits and turns them into outs.

**pick up** *v.* **1.** For an outfielder to locate the ball in the air. **2.** For an infielder to field a ground ball. **3.** For a batter to see the ball as it is pitched. **4.** For a batter to drive in one or more baserunners; e.g., "Smith picked up the two runners by doubling to right." **5.** For a player to be successful after another player on the team has not done well; e.g., "Brown's single picked up Jones after he failed to sacrifice" or "We have to pick each other up and do the little things to win" or "Smith kept the ball down and picked us up big time." **6.** To acquire; e.g., "The Cubs picked up Jones to bolster their bullpen."

**pickup** *n.* **1.** The act of fielding a ball immediately after it strikes the ground; e.g., a first baseman often makes "pickups" on low throws in the dirt. "[Brady] Anderson committed an error by not making a clean pickup of a Carlos Baerga single" (*Baltimore Sun,* Mar. 25, 1998). **1st Use.** 1875. (*New York Herald,* Aug. 7; Edward J. Nichols). **2.** An acquisition; e.g., "Jones was a late-season pickup by the Cubs."

**pick-up game** An informal playground or schoolyard game in which players are divided into two teams just before it begins.

**pickup-point** The split second (15/100 of a second according to one estimate) at which the batter can see the pitched ball and decide whether to swing at it. Before reaching this point, the ball is an indistinct blur.

**pie** *adj./arch.* Easy to beat. Gerald Cohen found several examples of this term, apparently derived from "easy as pie." "Those who imagined that the Wolverines would be pie for the pennant-winners yesterday were sadly disappointed" (*The World* [New York], Sept. 19, 1888).

**pie belt** *arch.* A nickname for the major league-clubs and cities of the Middle West. **1st Use.** 1914. (*New York Tribune,* Sept. 19; Edward J. Nichols).

**piece of cake** An easy play by a defensive player, even if the ball is hit hard; an easy out. See also *cake,* 1.

**piece of iron 1.** A baseball bat made of extra-good wood. **2.** *arch.* A baseball bat illegally plugged with nails, screws, or hardware.

**piece of the ball** See *get a piece of the ball.*

**pier six** *adj.* Said of a rough-and-tumble situation, such as a brawl between opposing sides or, to quote one news account, "a pier six free-for-all with the Cubs." **Etymology.** Uncertain, but the use of the term may have been aided by a 1955 movie entitled *Riot on Pier Six.*

**pike** The middle of the strike zone; e.g., "Smith threw the ball down the pike and Brown clobbered it."

**pile into a ball** To hit a ball with great force.

**pilfer** To steal a base. **1st Use.** 1891. (*Chicago Herald,* May 6; Edward J. Nichols).

**pill 1.** The baseball, because it may appear pill-size in approaching the batter. **1st Use.** 1897. The title for a cartoon with the title "Uncle Sam— 'Your Pills Have Saved My Life.'" This was a bad year with a financial depression in full force and the cartoon shows an ailing Uncle Sam consuming a baseball (pill) served on a spoon. (*Sporting Life,* May 15; Barry Popik). **2.** The rubber-covered, cushioned cork center of the baseball.

**pillow** Syn. of *base,* 2. **1st Use.** 1911. "Billie Harrison, whose brilliant playing around the second pillow had startled the natives . . . was elected" (*The Howitzer* [West Point yearbook]; David Shulman).

**pillow ball** [softball term] **1.** Syn. of *mush ball,* 1. **2.** Syn. of *mush ball,* 2.

**pill slinger** *arch.* The pitcher. **1st Use.** 1914. "Of course, he's some pill slinger" (Burt L. Standish, *Brick King, Backstop;* David Shulman).

**pilot 1.** *n.* The manager of a baseball team, so called because he is at the controls. **1st Use.** 1906. (*Sporting Life,* Feb. 10; Edward J. Nichols). **2.** *v.* To manage a baseball team.

**pinball baseball** Baseball as played on artificial turf where balls speed through the infield and take high bounces.

**pinch 1.** *n.* A difficult or crucial situation in a game, such as losing by a run with only one out to go. Christy Mathewson's *Pitching in a Pinch* (1912) gave "pinch" an added boost as a baseball term. See also *clutch,* 1. **1st Use.** 1902. (*Sporting Life,* July 12; Edward J. Nichols). **2.** *adj.* Pertaining to a substitute; e.g., "Smith hit a pinch home run when he batted for Jones." **3.** *v.* For the plate umpire to call pitches that are disputed by the pitcher; e.g., "Jones accused the umpire of pinching him by calling the payoff pitch a ball." See also *squeeze,* 3.

**pinch hit 1.** *v.* To come to the plate and bat in place of the scheduled batter who must then automatically leave the game. **2.** *n.* A hit made by a pinch hitter. **1st Use.** 1907. (*New York Evening Journal,* Apr. 11; Edward J. Nichols). **Etymology.**

Permitting substitutions was added to the rules in 1892, and shortly thereafter the term was created by sportswriter Charley Dryden who saw it as a substitution made in "a pinch." **Extended Use.** To substitute or take over for a regular performer; e.g., "I'll pinch hit for her while she's on vacation."

**pinch hitter** A replacement sent in during the course of a game to bat for the scheduled batter who must then leave the game. Technically, the pinch hitter can only bat once. If he stays in the game, however, he is no longer a pinch hitter but rather a substitute. The idea goes beyond mere substitution: the pinch hitter is put in expressly because he is more likely to get a hit. Abbrev. *PH.* **1st Use.** 1902. (*Sporting Life,* Apr. 26; Edward J. Nichols). There have been claims that the term did not enter the language until 1905 when, according to Bozeman Bulger (*The Saturday Evening Post,* ca. 1930; Peter Tamony), New York Giants manager John McGraw "engaged Sammy Strang as pinch hitter—the first to fill that role in baseball. By that innovation he gave the words 'pinch hitter' to the English language." **Etymology.** The first player to be used as a pinch hitter was Johnny Doyle of the Cleveland Spiders (Joseph McBride, *High and Inside,* 1980). John G. Leyden (*USA Today Baseball Weekly,* Apr. 29, 1992) makes a different claim: "The identity of the first pinch hitter long has been a matter of dispute and probably never will be settled. But the honor of being the first player to actually rap out a hit in the role of substitute batter appears to be a journeyman ballplayer named Charles 'Princeton Charlie' Reilly of the Philadelphia National League team." **Extended Use.** A substitute; an understudy. "Esther Walker went on one night as a 'pinch hitter' at a Winter Garden show in New York and brought down the house" (*Victor Record Catalog,* 1920; Peter Tamony).

**pinch-hitting specialist** A pinch hitter in some minor leagues who is allowed two trips to the plate without the removal of a player from the lineup.

**pinch pitching** The clutch pitching of a relief pitcher who gets his team out of a jam (Gordon S. "Mickey" Cochrane, *Baseball: The Fan's Game,* 1939).

**pinch run** To enter the game as a substitute for a baserunner who must then automatically leave the game.

**pinch runner** A substitute runner sent in for a player who has reached base, usually in a situation requiring a much faster runner or the runner on base was injured during the play. The original runner cannot continue to play in the game. Abbrev. *PR*.

**pine** The bench. To be told to "grab some pine" is to be told to sit on the bench. The legendary Johnny Pesky on Nomar Garciaparra (*Boston Globe*, Aug. 25, 1997): "The best-looking shortstop we've ever had around here. . . . He has good baseball instincts. I'm telling you, if he'd come along in my era, I'd be sitting on the pine."

**pineapple** A minor-league player.

**pine-barren** Said of a team lacking in good hitters.

**pine tar** A thick, sticky, blackish-brown liquid, obtained by destructive distillation of pine wood, that is rubbed on a batter's hands or bat to create a better grip. It is usually applied by means of a cloth or towel that has been saturated with the substance.

**pine tar ball** An illegal pitch in which the ball has been rubbed with pine tar so that it is easier to grip and control. The pine tar is usually placed on the pitcher's glove before transfer to the ball. During the third game of the 1988 National League Championship Series, Los Angeles Dodgers pitcher Jay Howell was ejected from the game and suspended for three days after pine tar was found in his glove.

**pine tar bat** A baseball bat that has been rubbed with a pine tar rag to give the batter a better grip.

**Pine Tar Incident** The infamous July 24, 1983, game at Yankee Stadium in which, with two outs in the ninth inning, Kansas City Royals slugger George Brett hit a home run off Goose Gossage to give the Royals the lead. On protest by Yankees manager Billy Martin, the umpire ruled that the pine tar on Brett's bat extended beyond the legal limit of 18 inches up the bat handle, nullified the home run, and called Brett out to end the game, giving the Yankees the win. The Royals lodged a protest with the American League president, who eventually ruled in Kansas City's favor. The home run was restored and the game was later completed with Kansas City ahead with two outs in the top of the ninth. The Royals won the game 5-4 after it was resumed. Also known as "Pine Tar Game."

**pine tar rag** A pine tar–soaked cloth or towel that batters rub on their bat handles to provide a firmer grip.

**pine tar rule** The rule that stipulates that pine tar may be applied no higher than 18 inches along the handle of a bat. [*Official Baseball Rules*, rule 1.10(c)]

**ping effect** The distinctive sound of the ball hitting an aluminum bat and the (commonly negative) reaction to it. "The sound of a ball struck by an aluminum bat is different to different ears, but no one could confuse it with the distinctive crack of an ash bat. In the bat business, that is called the ping effect." (Phil Patton, *Smithsonian* magazine, Oct. 1984).

**pin his ears back** To amass numerous hits against an opposing pitcher. See also *clobber*, 2.

**pin pointer** A pitcher with precise control.

**pinstripes** A uniform decoration composed of rows of thin vertical stripes. In a baseball context, the term is almost always used to refer to the pinstriped New York Yankees. This is true despite the fact that other teams (including the Detroit Tigers, Philadelphia Phillies, and Chicago Cubs) have worn pinstripes. The first team to wear pinstripes was the Chicago Cubs during the 1907 World Series (Marc Okkonen, *Baseball Uniforms of the 20th Century*, 1991). Pinstripes have come to represent power. They have also created their own mythology. According to *USA Today* (Mar. 12, 1987), the Yankee pinstripes came as a result of Babe Ruth's excessive eating and drinking: "In 1929, Yankees management wanted the slugger to look thinner, so they added pinstripes to the white uniforms to hide his girth." The Yankees, as many photos will attest, had worn pinstripes for many years before 1929, including years before Ruth was on the team. **Extended Use.** A metaphor for active organizational loyalty. A *Baltimore*

*Sun* (Aug. 19, 1996) article on Boutros Boutros-Ghali of the United Nations noted: "The United Nations secretary-general, 73, refuses to hang up his pinstripes."

**Pinstriper** A New York Yankee. A profile of Yankees coach and former player Clete Boyer in the *St. Petersburg Times* (Feb. 16, 1988) was simply titled "Pinstriper."

**pinwheel** For the batter to twirl the bat as he gets ready in the batter's box.

**pipe** Throat. A "hot pipe" is a sore throat.

**Pipp** *v.* To be replaced due to injury or illness and never regain one's position. Bruce Anderson (*Sports Illustrated,* June 29, 1987): "[Wally] Pipp has transcended mere trivia and become a metaphor. His very name conjures up a picture of a player sitting on the bench and watching his replacement sparkle. At the ball yard, nearly everyone knows what it is to be Pipped." See also *Wally Pipp.* Sometimes spelled "pipp."

**pisser and a moaner** One who whines and complains. "[Roger] Maris arrived at the [New York] Yankees with a somewhat seedy but well-earned reputation as a pisser and a moaner, in baseball parlance, a complainer, a griper" (Leonard Shecter, *The Jocks,* 1969; Charles D. Poe).

**pit 1.** The lowest point in the standings; the cellar. **2.** *arch.* Syn. of *dugout.* **1st Use.** 1917. (*American Magazine,* Apr.; Edward J. Nichols). **3.** See *sliding pit.*

**pitch 1.** *n.* The delivery of the ball to the batter by the pitcher. The pitch is only one element of the act of pitching; e.g., "Here's the windup, the stride, the pitch, and the ball nicks the inside corner of the plate." **1st Use.** 1861. (*New York Sunday Mercury,* Aug. 10; Edward J. Nichols). **Extended Use.** A presentation, such as a "sales pitch." **2.** *n.* The ball delivered to the batter by the pitcher; e.g., fastball or curveball. **3.** *v.* To deliver the ball from the pitcher's mound to the batter. **1st Use.** 1845. The 9th rule of the Knickerbocker Rules stated: "The ball must be pitched, not thrown, for the bat." This "pitch" referred to an under-the-hip toss with an unbent arm. The modern unrestricted delivery would be

considered a throw in the original Knickerbocker Rules. **Extended Use.** To become active; to be part of the action; to present. "Some observers opine that Yankee doughboys will be in there pitching for democracy within the next four weeks" (Dispatch from Tokyo, quoting a Japanese newspaper, *San Francisco Examiner,* Sept. 21, 1939; Peter Tamony). Also, in the sense of "to pitch woo" (for "to neck" or "to court" another) or to "pitch" a new product. **4.** *v.* To deliver the ball in a particular way; e.g., "Smith pitched Jones low and inside." **5.** *v.* To play in a game as a pitcher, or to fill the position of pitcher in a game; e.g., "Smith pitched a good game."

**pitch and catch** To throw a baseball back and forth between two or more players.

**pitch around 1.** To risk a base on balls by not throwing good pitches to a good hitter, often when first base is not occupied or when the next batter is a weak hitter. **2.** To try to get a free swinger out on pitches that are out of the strike zone.

**pitch count** A running tabulation of the number of pitches a pitcher has thrown in a game. The manager and pitching coach watch the pitch count to keep a pitcher from exhausting himself or his arm. "[New York Mets manager] Davey Johnson said he would've ended Ron Darling's no-hit bid if his pitch count approached 160" (*New York Post,* June 29, 1987).

**pitcher 1.** The defensive player who starts the game and puts the ball back in play during the game by delivering the ball from the pitcher's mound to the batter. The primary objective of the pitcher is to put out batters. Abbrev. *P.* Syn. *hurler.* **1st Use.** 1854. (Knickerbocker Rules; Edward J. Nichols). **Extended Use.** One who presents ("pitches") ideas and policy. Eugene McCarthy used to call Richard Nixon "the same old pitcher" (*San Francisco Chronicle,* Aug. 28, 1968; Peter Tamony). **2.** A term of distinction for a pitcher with great control, finesse, deceptive moves, and knowledge of the hitters, as opposed to a pitcher who depends solely on speed or power. "Bob Feller, the former great baseball pitcher, has been quoted as saying that the California Angels Nolan Ryan was a thrower, not a pitcher" (*San Francisco Chronicle,* June 28, 1975;

Pitcher.

Peter Tamony). Compare *thrower,* 1. **3.** The position played by the pitcher. Abbrev. *P.*

**pitcher covering first** A common defensive play that occurs when the first baseman moves off the bag to field a batted ball and tosses to the pitcher running to first base for the putout.

**pitcher in the hole** See *hole,* 5.

**pitcher of record** The pitcher who is charged with a win or loss, even if he has been removed from the game. A pitcher who has been removed as the pitcher of record remains so until the score becomes tied or a new lead is established at which point a new pitcher of record is established.

**pitcher reader** A batter who recognizes the upcoming pitch by identifying the pitcher's grip or motion.

**pitcher's battle** Syn. of *pitcher's duel,* 1. **1st Use.** 1880. (*New York Press,* June 2; Edward J. Nichols).

**pitcher's best friend** The double play.

**pitcher's box** Syn. of *mound,* 1. **1st Use.** 1887. (*Harper's Weekly,* Sept. 10; Edward J. Nichols).

**pitcher's duel 1.** A low-scoring game in which the quality of the pitching is quite evidently better than that of the hitting; a game dominated by good pitching. Syn. *pitching duel; pitcher's battle.* **2.** A contest, usually at the sandlot level, in which two pitchers throw to the plate without a batter. The pitcher with the least number of walks wins.

**pitcher's elbow** A generic name for ailments that affect the pitching arm due to stress and strain put on tendons, ligaments, muscles, and nerves.

**pitchers' game** [softball term] A sobriquet since the 1930s for fast pitch softball dominated by the pitcher. The argument has always been stated that this form of the game was not a *team game.*

**pitcher's hand** A putout in sandlot baseball, as explained by researcher Cullen Vane (San Jose, Calif.): "Whenever we didn't have enough players to field two full teams (actually we used to play with just three, four, or five on a team) we would rarely use a first baseman as a fielder and instead the pitcher would serve that position—i.e., if a grounder were hit to shortstop then all he need do was throw to the pitcher on the mound and this would serve as the putout: thus pitcher's hand."

**pitcher's mound** Syn. of *mound,* 1. Early Wynn was once asked if he ever threw the ball at a batter's head and he replied: "The pitcher's mound is my office and I don't like my office messed up with a lot of blood" (George F. Will, syndicated column, Aug. 11, 1986).

**pitcher's paradise** A large ballpark in which it is difficult to hit home runs. The term seems to have been initially applied to Cleveland's Municipal Stadium in the 1940s.

**pitcher's park 1.** A ballpark in which it is difficult to hit home runs. **2.** A ballpark with large outfield dimensions, such as Griffith Stadium in Washington, D.C.

**pitcher's plate** Syn. of *rubber,* 1.

**pitcher's rubber** Syn. of *rubber,* 1.

**pitcher's strike** A pitched ball that gets a pitcher out of a jam. A pitch that results in a pop fly with the bases loaded and two outs is regarded as a pitcher's strike.

**pitching 1.** The art and science of systematically confusing batters. Syn. *box-work.* **2.** The collective pitchers on a team.

**pitching average 1.** The ratio obtained by dividing the number of pitching decisions into the number of games won; e.g., the pitching average of a pitcher with a 10-6 record is 10/16, or .625. **2.** The batting average of a set of players versus a specific pitcher.

**pitching backwards** Pitching opposite of what is expected (Mike Flanagan, TV broadcast, May 24, 1996).

**pitching baseball cards** An adolescent game in which contestants flip or scale baseball cards, with the card coming closest to a wall or step declared the winner. The practice came to a virtual halt with the advent of price guides and the commodification of the cards. See also *flipping.*

**pitching chart** A complete pitch-by-pitch account of a team's pitches in a game, including the type, location, and velocity of the pitches and the results of batted balls. It is used to spot flaws in pitching strategy and technique. Tradition has it that the chart is kept by the pitcher who is scheduled to pitch the next day. See also *chart.*

**pitching coach** A coach who works with the team's pitchers to help them improve their skills and strategy and who advises the manager on pitching changes during a game. See also *bullpen coach.*

**pitching duel** Syn. of *pitcher's duel,* 1.

**pitching in** A standardized version of stickball (Jay Feldman, *Sports Illustrated,* Sept. 11, 1989).

**pitching machine** A mechanical device used to throw balls for batting practice. See also *iron mike; automatic pitcher.*

**pitching rotation** Syn. of *rotation,* 1.

**pitching rubber** Syn. of *rubber,* 1.

*Pitching machine. Cleveland manager Alvin Dark inspects a pitching machine, circa 1969.*

**pitching sequence** The mix of pitches that a pitcher throws. Batters try to determine if there is a set sequence so that they can anticipate the pitches to come.

**pitching staff** The aggregate of starting and relief pitchers on a club's roster. Syn. *arms; mound corps.*

**pitching to the strings** An innovative technique introduced by Branch Rickey whereby pitchers learn to create a visible strike zone in their minds by throwing to a movable structure consisting of two parallel strings (one shoulder high, the other knee high) attached to two six-foot poles 15 feet apart and two vertical strings attached to the top lateral string 17 inches (width of home plate) apart with the strings' bottom extensions wound around the lower lateral string. The strings attached to the poles were moved up and down to simulate the batters' various strike zones. "Pitching to the strings will accelerate the mastery of control, and pitchers, particularly the younger ones, shall be given ample opportunity to use them" (Branch Rickey, *Branch Rickey's Little Blue Book,* 1995).

**pitch of the 1980s** Syn. of *split-fingered fastball.*

**pitch on top** To pitch winning baseball; e.g., "Smith says he will pitch the best he can because he feels like he can pitch on top."

**pitch out** *v.* To throw a pitchout.

**pitchout** *n.* A defensive move made with a runner on base in which the pitcher deliberately throws the ball high and wide of the strike zone so that the catcher can easily catch the ball and throw it to a base that a runner may be attempting to steal. The pitch is thrown wide to keep the batter from swinging at the ball and to give the catcher the best positioning. Used when a steal, squeeze, or a hit-and-run play is expected, it is a play that must be coordinated carefully among the pitcher, catcher, and infielder involved. In most cases, either the catcher or the manager calls for the play. Sometimes spelled "pitch-out." **1st Use.** 1910. (*American Magazine,* July; Edward J. Nichols). **Etymology.** Peter Tamony notes two logical etymologies: a) a pitch "outside" the plate; and b) a pitch calculated to catch the man "out" at second. **Extended Use.** In football, a short lateral pass behind the line of scrimmage, thrown by one back to another. The term may or may not have been adopted from baseball, but it did come many years after the term was common in baseball. Kenneth Versand (*The Polyglot's Lexicon; 1943–1966,* 1973) lists the football meaning as a new one in 1947.

**pitch to spots** To pitch to specific areas of the strike zone, such as the corners; to mix the locations of pitches purposefully in an attempt to deceive the batter.

**Pittsburgh chopper** A batted ball that becomes a hit because it bounces over a fielder's head. Its success depends on a downward-chopping swing and a hard infield. Named by and for the 1960 world champion Pittsburgh Pirates who specialized in such hits. Compare *Baltimore chop.*

**Pittsburgh Pirates** The name of the National League Central Division franchise in Pittsburgh, Pa. First called the Alleghenys in 1886 and then the Innocents, they were dubbed Pirates in 1891 when they raided the American Association, a rival league, for players.

**pivot** The maneuver in which a defensive player (usually the second baseman) touches second base

**Pittsburgh Pirates.** *Composite from 1909 that takes the Pirates nickname to its limit.*

with one foot and whirls about to throw the ball to first base in an attempt to turn a double play. See also *inside pivot; outside pivot.*

**pivot foot** **1.** The foot used by an infielder when touching second base and whirling about to throw to first base in an attempt to turn a double play. **2.** The foot used by the pitcher to push off the rubber as he delivers the ball. The pivot foot must remain in contact with the rubber until the ball is released. The pitcher supports himself with the pivot foot as he strides forward with the *stepping foot.* A pitcher's pivot foot is always on the same side of the body as the arm he pitches with (a right-handed pitcher's pivot foot is always the right one).

**pivot man** The second baseman who serves as the relay player at second base during an attempt to turn a double play. Second baseman Joe Gordon once put this term in perspective: "Without a good pivotman a double play cannot be made. Without double plays a club will win few close games." (*San Francisco News,* June 29, 1949; Peter Tamony). Jackie Robinson (*Mutual Baseball Almanac,* 1954) discussed the role of the pivot man: "If a second baseman doesn't pivot right, he won't pivot often. He'll be belted, spiked and stepped on, and he won't make double plays. On the double play that starts at shortstop, the second baseman can play two roles. He can be the pivot man. He can be the sitting duck. Myself, I preferred being a pivot man." Also spelled "pivotman."

**place** To hit a ball to a predetermined area on the field. Syn. *place hit,* 1. **1st Use.** 1880. (*Brooklyn Daily Eagle,* Aug. 22; Edward J. Nichols).

**place hit** **1.** *v.* Syn. of *place.* **2.** *n.* A base hit in which the ball is batted to a predetermined area on the field. **1st Use.** 1908. (*Baseball Magazine,* July; Edward J. Nichols).

**place hitter** A hitter with the proven ability to hit the ball to a desired location on the field. See also *sharpshooter,* 1. **1st Use.** 1928. "The place hitter is the chap who can take a ball which ordinarily he would hit to right, and hit it to left, or vice versa" (Babe Ruth, *Babe Ruth's Own Book of Baseball,* 1928; David Shulman).

**plank** **1.** To hit the ball hard, as if whacking with a plank. **2.** To drive in a run; e.g., "Smith planked Jones with a double to right."

**plant** **1.** *n.* The placement of the pitcher's front (stepping) foot on the ground before he releases the ball. **2.** *v.* To place the pitcher's front (stepping) foot on the ground before he releases the ball. **3.** *v.* To bat a ball; e.g., "Smith planted one down the line." **1st Use.** 1908. (*Brooklyn Daily Eagle,* May 22; Edward J. Nichols).

**plaster** **1.** To defeat badly. **2.** To hit a ball hard; e.g., "Smith plastered one into center." **1st Use.** 1910. (*Baseball Magazine,* Dec.; Edward J. Nichols).

**plate** **1.** *n.* Short for *home plate.* **1st Use.** 1869. (*DeWitt's Official Base Ball Guide;* Edward J. Nichols). **2.** *adj.* Relating to home plate. **3.** *v.* To score; to drive in a run; e.g., "Smith plated Jones with a double." **4.** *n.* Syn. of *rubber,* 1.

**plate appearance** An official statistic for the batter coming to the batter's box, including those times when the batter walks, sacrifices, is hit by a pitched ball, or is interfered with by the catcher. Compare *at-bat,* 2. Abbrev. *PA.*

**plate blocker** **1.** A catcher who tenaciously holds his position in front of home plate during close plays with a baserunner who is trying to score. See also *blocker,* 1. **2.** A catcher with the ability to prevent potential wild pitches.

**plate coverage** The ability of a batter to stay close enough to the plate to reach all pitches thrown in the strike zone.

**plate jumping** The mock complaint by a wild pitcher that the plate (i.e., the strike zone) will not stand still. See also *home plate is jumping around.*

**plate record** Syn. of *batting average.*

**plate shy** Said of a batter who is afraid to stand close to the plate.

**plate umpire** The *umpire* stationed behind the catcher at home plate. See also *umpire-in-chief; ball-and-strike umpire.* Syn. *home-plate umpire.*

**platoon** To use two or more players, on an alternating basis, for the same defensive position, thereby taking advantage of each player's offensive and defensive strengths. "The [New York] Mets even have a bench this year, at last permitting manager [Gil] Hodges to do some useful platooning" (Roger Angell, *The Summer Game,* 1972; Charles D. Poe).

**platoon player** A player who is alternated with another at one defensive position. Platoon players usually are not among the stars or outstanding players on a team and would like to work themselves out of that role. "[Andy] Van Slyke Making Effort to Shed Platoon Player Label" (*St. Petersburg Times* headline, Mar. 29, 1987).

**platoon system** A management style in which players are moved in and out of the lineup depending on the circumstances. New York Yankees manager Casey Stengel was the first to employ the system on a large scale in 1949: "Where Casey relied heavily on the platoon system, Ralph [Houk] went for the set lineup" (Mickey Mantle, *The Mick,* 1986; Charles D. Poe). Harry Rosenthal (*New York Herald Tribune,* May 1949) noted that the system was just "coming in" in football. Boston Braves pitcher William L. (Seattle Bill) James commented on his manager, George Stallings of the Miracle Braves of 1914: "I believe he was the first major-league manager to use the platoon system. He used to do it with our outfielders and I think it worked pretty well" (*The Sporting News,* 1971).

**platter** Syn. of *home plate.* The term is an obvi-

ous play on the word and image of "plate" as tableware and, without pushing too far, in the serving of a pitch. See also *dish.* **1st Use.** 1910. (*Baseball Magazine,* Dec.; Edward J. Nichols).

**play 1.** *n.* Any specific act, event, maneuver, or point in a baseball game, such as a double play, a pickoff play, or any action (such as errors, putouts, and stolen bases) that occurs between pitches; e.g., "Smith makes all the plays required of a shortstop." **1st Use.** 1858. (*Brooklyn Daily Times,* June 18; Edward J. Nichols). **2.** *v.* To participate in a game. **3.** *v.* To assume the duties of a particular position; e.g., to "play third base." **4.** *v.* To catch or position oneself for catching a ball; e.g., "Smith played the ball off the wall." **5.** *v.* To place oneself on the defense where one's knowledge and experience indicate where the batter most likely will hit the ball; e.g., "Smith knows how to play the hitter." **6.** *v.* To perform, as in "play to the grandstand." **7.** *imper.* See *play ball!*

**playable** Said of any ball that is live or in play.

**play at the plate** Any play involving a fielder (usually the catcher) covering home plate and a baserunner attempting to score. **Usage Note.** Because such plays tend to be exciting ones at key moments of the game, the phrase carries with it an extra amount of emotion.

**"play ball!" 1.** The command issued by the plate umpire to start a game or to resume action follow-

*Play at the plate.*

ing any dead ball. It is sometimes abbreviated to a simple order of *"play!"* **1st Use.** 1901. (Burt L. Standish, *Frank Merriwell's Marvel;* Edward J. Nichols). **2.** Emblematic phrase for the start of any baseball game, from Opening Day to the opener of the World Series. **Extended Use.** To co-operate or participate: e.g., "If the union will play ball with us on this one, I think we can make the deadline." One of the more interesting uses of these words took place in the context of the 1987 Washington summit meeting between Mikhail S. Gorbachev and Ronald Reagan. According to the *New York Times* (Dec. 15, 1987), Joe DiMaggio, who had been a guest at the dinner honoring the Gorbachevs, asked President Reagan if he could get the Soviet leader to autograph a baseball for him. Reagan got the autograph personally and used the occasion "to tell his guest that the two leaders should 'play ball' with each other."

**play-by-play** *n.* A running description of a game, with all the details. The term is usually applied to the commentary on a game on radio and television, although technically it only applies to printed accounts, now rare, in which each play of the game is reported. *Sports Illustrated* once wrote of longtime broadcaster Red Barber: "If Barber didn't invent play-by-play, he came close." **1st Use.** 1912. (*New York Tribune,* Oct. 15; Edward J. Nichols). **Extended Use.** Any detailed verbal account: e.g., "I had to sit there and listen to his play-by-play of the whole argument."

**play by the book** To play baseball in accord with the conventional wisdom of the game. **1st Use.** 1911. (William Patten & J. W. McSpadden, *The Book of Base Ball;* Edward J. Nichols).

**play deep and cut across** To position the out-fielders when the defense anticipates balls being hit deep. "Advice to outfielders from a pitcher who doesn't feel well and expects to be shelled off the mound during the game," according to Jim Brosnan (*The Long Season,* 1960).

**player 1.** One who plays baseball; a ballplayer. **2.** One who is admired by teammates and opponents as a ballplayer.

**player development** Providing experience and instruction for minor-league players. "IBM calls it

R&D [research and development]. The Dodgers call it 'player development.'" (*Forbes,* Apr. 12, 1982).

**player development contract** An agreement between the major leagues and the minor leagues to cover areas subsidized by the majors in their working agreements with minor-league affiliates. It includes expenses for salaries (players, managers, coaches), spring training, medical payments, and travel.

**player limit** The maximum number of players that a team may have on its roster at a given time during the season. In the major leagues the number during most of the season is officially 25 (team owners unofficially reduced the number to 24 in 1986). A team's roster may expand to 40 on Sept. 1 when promising minor leaguers are called up and it can be 40 until Opening Day.

**player-manager** A manager who is also an active player on the team. Those who fill this position (such as Pete Rose with the Cincinnati Reds in 1984) tend to be senior players who concentrate more on managing than playing as they phase

**Player-manager.** *Bucky Harris, functioning in both roles, in the Senators dugout, 1924 World Series.*

themselves out of the regular lineup. Player-managers are no longer as prevalent as they once were in pre–World War II baseball. Other notable player-managers were John McGraw, Connie Mack, Mickey Cochrane, Lou Boudreau, and Frank Robinson. Syn. *playing manager.*

**Player Relations Committee** A committee consisting of representatives of club owners for the purpose of representing management concerns with the Major League Baseball Players Association. Abbrev. *PRC.*

**player representative** The member of a major-league team who has been elected by his teammates as their delegate to the Major League Baseball Players Association and who serves as the liaison for the team on all player-management issues. Syn. *rep,* 2; "player rep."

**player running bases** *arch.* A batter-runner. "The moment the striker has hit a fair ball he ceases to be 'the striker' and becomes 'a player running the bases'" (Henry Chadwick, *The Game of Base Ball,* 1868).

**Players Association** Short for *Major League Baseball Players Association.*

**Players Fraternity** An early union of baseball players, founded in 1912 and led by former player-turned-attorney David L. Fultz and officially recognized by the National Commission in 1914 when the Federal League emerged to challenge the American League and the National League. The owners agreed to pay for uniforms, require green outfield fences (for better visibility and reduced injuries), supply written reasons for player suspensions, and give 10-year veterans the right to unconditional release from their contracts (a provision that would evolve into today's waiver rule); the concessions kept players loyal to their teams (the Federal League disbanded in 1915 in part because it was unable to recruit established players). The Fraternity focused primarily on reforms in the minor leagues, where most of its membership was based. Fultz called a general strike in 1917 over improvements in the minors, but he overestimated the support of the American Federation of Labor and major-league players, as the strike never materialized. The Fraternity could not recover momentum and dissolved late in

1917. Formal name: *Fraternity of Professional Baseball Players of America.*

**Players League** An outlaw major league created by members of the *Brotherhood of Professional Base Ball Players* who were frustrated by salary ceilings, fines, the reserve clause, and other realities of the existing major leagues. It had but one season (1890); lack of money and organization put the league out of business before Opening Day 1891. The league included the Boston Reds, Brooklyn Wonders, New York Giants, Chicago Pirates, Philadelphia Quakers, Pittsburgh Burghers, Cleveland Infants, and Buffalo Bisons. Full name: Players National League of Professional Base Ball Clubs. Also known as *Bolshevik League.*

**player's manager** A team manager who commands special respect from players. Don Baylor (*Don Baylor,* 1989) commented on Billy Martin: "Billy had a reputation for being a player's manager. He was known to be fair, making decisions on ability and not based on skin color."

**player's player** A player with widespread respect and admiration from other players. "In the clubhouse, he [Don Baylor] was a legendary force, the player's player" (*USA Weekend,* Apr. 24, 1993). **Extended Use.** A respected individual in a given profession. Guitar virtuoso Michael Hedges "was a player's player . . . he had an intensity and drive that earned him a lot of respect with rock players" (Chris Gill, *Baltimore Sun,* Dec. 5, 1997).

**Players Protective Association** See *Protective Association.*

**player to be named later** A mutually acceptable player to be delivered at some future date to a team to complete a trade. In a trade on Aug. 8, 1985, that sent catcher Bo Diaz and pitcher Greg Simpson from the Philadelphia Phillies to the Cincinnati Reds for infielder Tom Foley and catcher Alan Knicely, the Phillies also received infielder Fred Toliver as the "player to be named later" on Aug. 27, 1985. Abbrev. *PTBNL; PTNL.* **Extended Use.** Jocular use in (fill-in-the-blank) to be named later; e.g., "I'll bet you dinner in a restaurant to be named later that Smith will defeat Jones."

**player transfer sheet** A daily report that indicates whether players have passed through waivers.

A club can place a maximum of seven players per day on the sheet.

**play for one run** An offensive strategy that argues against swinging for the fences and for moving a runner along a base at a time and staying out of double plays.

**play for the grandstand** Var. of *play to the grandstand.* **1st Use.** 1866. "He plays now for his side rather than for the grandstand" (*The Sporting News,* May 10; David Shulman).

**playground average** A high batting average, such as one that could be achieved in a playground league where a strong hitter can overwhelm young pitchers.

**playground ball** [softball term] An early name for softball.

**playground baseball** [softball term] A name given to an early version of *softball* in 1908 by the National Amateur Playground Ball Association. It was the linear descendent of *indoor baseball,* 1.

**play hard** To do everything physically needed to win a baseball game so long as the rules are not violated.

**play hurt** To play baseball even when one is not feeling well or nursing an injury.

**playing manager** Syn. of *player-manager.*

**playing streak** See *consecutive-game playing streak.*

**play it off the wall** To field a fly ball just before it hits an outfield wall or to field the ball after it bounces off the wall and before it hits the ground.

**playoff** **1.** *n.* A series of games between the leading teams in a league to determine a championship; specif., *Division Series* and *League Championship Series.* **2.** *n.* The playing of an extra game or games to break a tie in the standings at the end of the regular season. The first playoff since 1900 occurred in 1946 when the St. Louis Cardinals defeated the Brooklyn Dodgers in two games to decide the National League championship. The most famous playoff occurred in 1951 when the New York Giants, on Bobby Thomson's dramatic ninth-inning three-run home run, defeated the Dodgers in two of three games to decide the National League championship. **3.** *n./obs.* The replaying of a game

that originally resulted in a tie. Also spelled "play-off." **1st Use.** 1880. (Chicago *Inter-Ocean,* June 7; Edward J. Nichols). **4.** *adj.* Of or pertaining to a playoff game or series; e.g., "playoff hopes."

**play out the string** **1.** For a player to put in his time at the end of his career. **2.** For a team to continue to play although it is not in contention. **1st Use.** 1912. (*New York Tribune,* Sept. 15; Edward J. Nichols).

**play over one's head** To perform better than usual or better than expected.

**play to the grandstand** To show off; to perform. See also *grandstand,* 2; *grandstand play; play for the grandstand.* **1st Use.** 1888. "Playing to the Grand-Stand. To accomplish this it is only necessary to smile, strike an attitude, and strike out." (Thomas W. Lawson, *The Krank: His Language and What It Means;* David Shulman). **Etymology.** Charles Earle Funk (*Heavens to Betsy!,* 1955) asserts that the expression is related to the earlier "play to the gallery." Funk explained: "Originally, it had reference to those actors, especially in an English theater, who, going over the heads of the near-by, and frequently inattentive, occupants of orchestra seats or stalls, deliberately overacted their roles in seeking to gain the approval of the larger populace in the gallery."

**play the percentages** To manage with an eye on previous performance; e.g., if a pitcher is slow to pick off leading runners, the percentages suggest that the runners try to steal against him.

**play under protest** To continue to play a game even though the manager of one team has indicated he intends to file a protest with the league president.

**play with anybody** To win with confidence and consistency, regardless of the quality of the opposition. Early in the 1997 season, a Florida Marlins outfielder was quoted: "We feel like we can play with anybody."

**plenty of wood** Said of a team that has several power hitters. **1st Use.** 1910. (*American Magazine,* July; Edward J. Nichols).

**plow-jockey** *arch.* A country boy, from a time when many players entered baseball directly from the farm.

**plug** **1.** *arch.* To bat a ball hard. **1st Use.** 1910.

(*Baseball Magazine,* May; Edward J. Nichols). **2. obs.** To put a runner out by hitting him with the ball. Plugging was allowed in the Massachusetts game, but not allowed by the rules drafted by Alexander Cartwright and the other members of the Knickerbocker Base Ball Club in 1845 for the New York game. Syn. *soak,* 2.

**plugged bat** A baseball bat that has been doctored.

**plugger 1.** A fan who roots for his or her team. **2.** *arch.* A dumb play.

**plunk** *arch.* A base hit. See also *plunket.* **Etymology.** Gerald Cohen notes that the term has an onomatopoeic origin: "the ball lands plunk on the ground." Cohen found several examples from 1889 in *The World* (New York), including this one (Oct. 19): "In a puree of silence that was painful, the Brooklyns came in from the field on the players' bench with nine subdued 'plunks.'"

**plunker** A *Texas Leaguer.* **Usage Note.** Herbert Simons (*Baseball Magazine,* Jan. 1943) has an interesting note on this term: "Curiously, there aren't any Texas Leaguers ever hit in the Texas League. There, low flies that drop safely in the short outfield, too far for the infielders to reach and yet too near for the outfielders to get to, are known as 'plunkers.'" **1st Use.** 1937. (*New York Daily News,* Sept. 5; Edward J. Nichols).

**plunket** Diminutive of *plunk.*

**pneumonia ball** A fastball that supposedly passes the batter with such speed that he catches cold from the draught. "Walter Johnson's 'high swift' was admiringly dubbed the pneumonia ball by sluggers who caught cold from the steady draught across their throats and chests" (William G. Brandt, *Baseball Magazine,* Oct. 1932).

**PO** Abbrev. for *putout.*

**pochismo** Bastardized Spanish and English, which is neither Spanish nor English. The Mexican Academy began crusading against it in 1945, but according to an article in *American Speech* (Oct. 1945), could not find suitable equivalents for "jonrun" (home run), "estraic" (strike), "jit" (hit), and "béisbol" (baseball).

**pocket** The formed hollow part of the fielder's glove or mitt between the thumb and index finger into which the ball can be caught and securely held. Although all gloves come with a pocket, a traditional part of the glove breaking-in process has been to reshape and deepen the pocket.

**point 1.** An element of high skill and sophistication. Henry Chadwick wrote about the "special points of play in the game which occur most generally in first class matches"; i.e., those "points" alluded to when someone talks of the "finer points of the game." **2.** See *percentage point.*

**poisoned ball** An early 19th-century (and, perhaps, earlier) forerunner of baseball played in France on a diamond-shaped field whose four points must be touched by runners in succession. Its major characteristic is the rule that a player is "out" when touched with the "poisoned ball" before he reaches a base. Poisoned ball is described in a book of boys' games published in Paris about the year 1810, entitled *les jeux des jeunes garçons, représentés par vingt-quatre estampes, accompagnés de l'explication détaillée des régles, d'anecdotes historiques.* (Robert W. Henderson, *Ball, Bat and Bishop,* 1947).

**poisoned bat** *arch.* The bat held by a hard hitter.

**poison pen** A player's clubhouse term for a member of the press (Atlanta Braves pitcher Jim Nash, quoted in *The Sporting News,* Apr. 1, 1972). Sometimes *old poison pen.*

**poke** *v.* **1.** To bat the ball; to get a hit. **1st Use.** 1880. (Chicago *Inter-Ocean,* May 15; Edward J. Nichols). **2.** *n.* A base hit, esp. a home run. **1st Use.** 1908. (*Brooklyn Daily Eagle,* May 25; Edward J. Nichols).

**poke hitter** A hitter whose specialty is placing or pushing balls through holes in the infield. "A ball player like Mikes had to be able to run, for he was a poke hitter, a man who pushed singles and doubles where he could get them" (William Brashler, *The Bingo Long Traveling All-Stars and Motor Kings,* 1973; Charles D. Poe).

**poke off** A well-hit ball that goes a long distance, usually a home run.

**Polaroid** A player caught looking at a third strike, in the candid vernacular of Reggie Jackson.

**pole 1.** *n.* A baseball bat. **2.** *v.* To hit with power; e.g., "Smith poled one over the fence." **1st Use.**

1905. "At a tight spot in the game [Danny] Hoffman poled out a vicious liner" (Charles Dryden, *The Athletics of 1905;* David Shulman).

**poleax** To hit with a swinging-down motion, as if wielding a poleax. "[Robby] Thompson poleaxed a fat 2-0 fastball from [Les] Lancaster for a two-run homer" (*Tampa Tribune,* Oct. 4, 1989).

**police the parade grounds** *arch.* To maintain a baseball field; to groundskeep. **Etymology.** A term brought back from World War II by players who had been in the armed forces.

**polished deception** The use of style and grace by a pitcher to mask his mechanical weaknesses.

**polish off** To defeat an opposing team or retire an opposing batter. **1st Use.** 1871. (*New York Herald,* July 29; Edward J. Nichols).

**Polo Grounds** The name for four different ballparks in New York City, none of which exist

**Polo grounds.** *The ballpark in 1887.*

currently. The first two were adjoining parks used for the Metropolitans and the Giants in the 1880s. The third and fourth were primarily used by the New York Giants. The final park was built when its namesake burned down in 1911; it was used not only by the New York Giants (1911–57), but also by the New York Yankees (1913–22) and the fledgling New York Mets (1962–63).

**PONY League** The nickname for the Pennsylvania–Ontario–New York Class D minor league from 1939 to 1956.

**Pony League baseball** An advanced baseball program for youths ages 5–17 in which the complete game of baseball (stealing bases, pitching from the stretch, etc.) and other baseball techniques are taught to children.

**pool cue shot** A batted ball that comes off the end of the bat like a pool or billiard ball being hit by a cue.

**pool table** A smooth infield. **1st Use.** 1937. (*New York Daily News,* Jan. 21; Edward J. Nichols).

**pooper** A *Texas Leaguer.*

**pop 1.** *n.* The extra speed, hop, and sound of the most effective fastball. "[David] Clyde admits his fastball doesn't 'pop' like it once did" (*San Francisco Chronicle,* Mar. 14, 1977; Peter Tamony). **2.** *v.* To throw a fastball; to throw hard. "Ron Guidry had begun popping the ball" (Roger Angell, *The New Yorker,* Aug. 15, 1983). The term refers to the sound made when a fastball hits the catcher's mitt; e.g., "It's good to hear that mitt popping" (*USA Today,* Feb. 24, 1987). **3.** *n.* A hitter's power; e.g., "Jones has a lot of pop in his bat." **4.** *v.* To hit a baseball; e.g., "Smith popped a home run in the third." **5.** *v.* Syn. of *pop up.* **6.** *n.* A *pop fly.* **1st Use.** 1895. "We've got a strong infield—one that can handle the pops and grounders they are sure to get when Kirk is in the box" (Herbert Bellwood, *The Rivals of Riverwood;* David Shulman).

**popcorn 1.** An easily caught fly ball. **2.** A fastball, in reference to high microwave "heat."

**pop fly** A high, but short, fly ball that usually comes down in, or just behind, the infield and is usually (or should be) caught by a fielder. "Profes-

OH! YOU POP FLY

Copyright, 1909, by O. D. Williams, Boston
Boston Baseball Series, No. 108

*Pop fly.*

sional ball players hate to be embarrassed by a simple pop fly, but in the crazy pattern of Candlestick's cross currents they can't do anything else but suffer and curse under their breath" (*San Francisco Examiner,* Apr. 14, 1966; Peter Tamony). Syn. *pop,* 6; *popper; pop-up; pot-fly.* **1st Use.** 1870. (*New York Herald,* June 29; Edward J. Nichols).

**pop foul** A pop fly batted into foul territory.

**pop-off 1.** A player with a mean spirit and a short temper; one who baits an umpire. Syn. *rebel.* **1st Use.** 1939. (Gordon S. "Mickey" Cochrane, *Baseball: The Fan's Game;* David Shulman). **2.** A vociferous or arrogant player; a braggart.

**pop out** *v.* To be retired on a pop fly.

**pop-out** *n.* A pop fly that is caught for an out.

**popper** Syn. of *pop fly.*

**poppycock season** *arch.* Spring training.

**pop the ball** See *pop,* 2.

**pop up** *v.* To bat the ball high into the air over the infield; e.g., "[They kept] popping up balls among the infielders which dropped into their hands most naturally and gracefully" (*Detroit Advertiser and Tribune,* July 27; Peter Morris). Syn. *pop,* 5. **1st Use.** 1867. (*New York Herald,* Aug. 10; Edward J. Nichols).

**pop-up** *n.* Syn. of *pop fly.* Also spelled "popup."

**pop-up slide** A slide in which the baserunner comes into the base feet first and, in the same fluid movement, pushes himself back up onto his feet to a standing position. The runner attempts the slide when he feels that he may have the opportunity to take another base on the play. Syn. *down-and-up.*

**porcelain decorations** Teeth; "what an infielder leaves on the field when he's hit in the teeth by a bad-hop grounder" (*Padres Magazine,* 1993).

**porch** An outfield bleacher, grandstand, or wall that is not far from home plate. See also *short porch; pennant porch.*

**Porkopolis** An early nickname for baseball cities with meatpacking industries, such as Cincinnati (since about 1840) and St. Louis.

**portsider** A left-hander, usually a pitcher. Variations using the term "port" seem limitless and include "portpaw" (a confusing synonym for "southpaw"), "portside thrower," "portside slinger," and "port flinger." **1st Use.** 1860. (*New York Clipper,* Oct. 6). **Etymology.** The term "port" is the left side of a naval vessel when facing forward.

**posish** Slang for *position,* 1. **1st Use.** 1884. "Herkleback has been compelled to relinquish his 'posish' in the Cincinnati team through illness and has returned to Philadelphia" (*Sporting Life,* July 23; Barry Popik).

**position 1.** *n.* A player's assigned place on a team, both in the field and in the batting order. Syn. *posish.* **1st Use.** 1858. (*Brooklyn Daily Times,* June 18; Edward J. Nichols). **2.** *n.* The condition with reference to the pitcher standing on the mound and facing the batter. See also *windup position; set position.* **3.** *v.* To station oneself at a particular spot defensively; e.g., "The manager positioned the outfielders near the wall with Smith coming to bat."

**position player** One of the defensive fielders other than the pitcher. It is the 16 position players that the fans elect in the All-Star voting, not the pitchers or reserves who are picked by the two managers. "He [Jose Canseco] may be the best looking position player in the league, but he's got a lot of growing up to do" (Northwest League Medford A's manager Dennis Rogers, quoted in *Baseball America,* Aug. 15, 1983).

**positive subtraction** The art of improving a team by trading or releasing a poor player. The term was coined by baseball executive Branch Rickey. See also *Rickeyism.*

**post** To record a baseball statistic; e.g., "Smith posted his 100th career victory."

**postponement** The act of rescheduling a game on the same day or on a future day. Games are postponed because of bad weather or technical problems. With the exception of games played late in the season, after first place in the standings has been determined, major-league games are never canceled.

**postseason** The period after the end of the regular season when the divisional playoffs, league championships, and World Series are staged.

**postseason game** A game played following the end of the regular season; e.g., a League Championship Series game or a World Series game.

**pot** To hit a pitched ball.

**potato 1.** The baseball. **1st Use.** 1942. "[Lou] Gehrig clouting the potato out of the ballyard" (Paul Gallico, *Lou Gehrig, Pride of the Yankees*). **2.** A player brought up from a farm club; e.g., "Every one of us potatoes came out of the Cardinal farm" (Johnny Hopp, quoted in *Baseball Digest,* Dec. 1983). **3.** A home run. See also *long potato; tater.*

**potential** Latent ability that may or may not be developed. The baseball meaning of the term is the same as that found in a standard dictionary, but it carries with it a certain negative connotation. Jim Henneman (*Baltimore Sun,* Apr. 28, 1995) commented: "In baseball, that's a nasty word that too often translates into 'could've, would've, should've.' A lot of managers have lost jobs waiting for potential to develop. And some have found the unemployment line because they weren't patient enough to allow it to happen."

**potential tying run**  A batter or runner who, if he succeeds in scoring, will tie the game.

**potential winning run**  A batter or runner who, if he succeeds in scoring, will win the game.

**pot-fly**  *obs.* Syn. of *pop fly.* **1st Use.** 1888. "It looked like an easy pot-fly as it graciously sailed up to me" (Thomas W. Lawson, *The Krank: His Language and What It Means;* David Shulman).

**pots and pans**  The part of the batter's *kitchen* where a jamball is thrown; e.g., "Smith threw an inside pitch and rattled the batter's pots and pans."

**pound 1.**  To get many hits off a single pitcher; e.g., "After being pounded for six straight hits, the manager removed the pitcher." **1st Use.** 1890. (*New York Press,* July 6; Edward J. Nichols). **2.** To hit a pitched baseball hard; e.g., "Smith pounded the 3-0 pitch into the stands." **1st Use.** 1873. (*New York Herald,* Aug. 10; Edward J. Nichols). **3.** To throw a pitched ball hard and inside; e.g., "He pounded the ball inside" or "He pounded the hitters inside."

**pound the air**  To swing at and miss a pitched ball.  **1st Use.** 1908. (*Baseball Magazine,* Oct.; Edward J. Nichols).

**powder 1.**  *v.* To hit a pitched ball so hard that it travels at a high rate of speed; e.g., "Smith powdered the ball so hard that the shortstop did not see it." **2.** *n.* The speed with which a pitcher delivers the ball from the mound. "They like to refer to an excessive amount of speed as 'powder.' Maybe this is a derivative of the term 'fireball.'" (William G. Brandt, *Baseball Magazine,* Oct. 1932). See also *smoke,* 1. **3.** *n.* A fastball.

**powder-puff ball**  An illegal pitch in which the ball is covered with resin powder extracted from the rosin bag by the pitcher. It is a doctored ball that confuses the batter because it arrives at the plate trailing a cloud of white dust. As with other similar innovations, Gaylord Perry has been widely credited with the creation of this pitch. Syn. *puff ball.*

**power 1.**  *n.* The ability to hit the long ball. **2.** *v.* To hit a pitched baseball with force; e.g., "Jones powered the 2-0 pitch 430 feet over the fence." **3.** *n.* The ability to pitch fastballs or to throw hard. **4.** *v.* To pitch or throw the ball with force; e.g., "Brown powered the ball past the batter." **5.** *v.* To play winning baseball; e.g., "Two doubles and a bases-loaded homer combined to power the Astros win" or "Smith's home runs power the home team to doubleheader victory."

**power alley**  One of the two areas between the outfielders in left-center field and in right-center field. Since most powerful hitters naturally tend to drive the ball to the power alleys, home run balls more often travel through these corridors than to straightaway right, center, or left fields. Jim Bouton (*Ball Four,* 1970) defined the term as the place "where the sluggers put away knuckleballs that don't knuckle." See also *alley,* 1.

**power game**  Offensive play characterized by sluggers who swing for home runs. "[Babe] Ruth's natural power was responsible for making baseball what it has been ever since—a power game" (Red Barber, *Christian Science Monitor,* May 23, 1984).

**power hitter**  A hitter known for his home run hitting ability; a hitter who drives the ball for a long distance, often swinging from the heels. Jimmy Cannon's definition: "A muscular player who strikes out a lot." Compare *contact hitter.* Syn. *powerhouse,* 1.

**powerhouse 1.**  Syn. of *power hitter.* **1st Use.** 1937. (Red Barber, World Series broadcast, Oct. 10; Edward J. Nichols). **2.** A team with several home run hitters.

**power outage**  A lack of home runs by a player or team over a protracted period. See also *power shortage.*

**power pitcher**  A pitcher who throws hard and strikes out many batters; e.g., Roger Clemens. *Newsweek* (Aug. 28, 1989) referred to Nolan Ryan as "the greatest power pitcher in the history of baseball." Compare *finesse pitcher.*

**power shortage**  A deficiency, often temporary, of offensive production by a team's power hitters. See also *power outage.*

**power zone** That area of the strike zone from which a power hitter generates long balls; e.g., "Smith threw a pitch into Brown's power zone."

**pow wow** A meeting on the playing field, usually involving several players and a coach or manager; e.g., a meeting on the pitcher's mound to discuss strategy or a gathering at the scene of a disputed play.

**PR** Abbrev. for *pinch runner.*

**prayer ball** A pitch with nothing on it; one which the pitcher "prays" will not be hit. There are many variations of the term, including *glove and a prayer.* One of the odder examples appears in a 1912 article on player slang, which contains the line: "Christian Science stuff is the only thing you ever get on the ball" (*Sporting Life,* May 18, 1912).

**PRC** Abbrev. for *Player Relations Committee.*

**premium free agent** A free agent who is given an exceptionally large financial incentive to sign with a club; e.g., Darrell Evans was the first "premium free agent" ever signed by the Detroit Tigers.

**pre-rookie card** A baseball card of a player issued while he was still in the minor leagues before his rookie card is issued.

**preseason** That period of time before the opening of a regular baseball season. See also *spring training,* 2.

**present the ball** [softball term] For the pitcher to stand with both feet on the pitcher's plate and ground with the ball in both hands just prior to beginning the pitching motion.

**pre-shower epigram** Roger Angell's tongue-in-cheek term for the words exchanged on the mound when a manager relieves a pitcher. Angell's article (*The New Yorker,* 1987) discussed the proliferation of baseball books: he wrote that there were so many being published that he soon expected to see an anthology of "pre-shower epigrams."

**press** To try harder to get a hit by swinging the bat at almost every pitch, regardless of its type or location; e.g., "Smith began to press when opposing pitchers began to pitch around him."

**press box** An area within the ballpark reserved for sportswriters and broadcasters. Press boxes have evolved from boxed-off wooden areas to the plush, electronics-heavy quarters that in most major-league parks are located on the mezzanine level behind home plate. **1st Use.** 1892. (*New York Press,* Aug. 13; Edward J. Nichols).

**press pin** A colorful identifying pin given to a member of the working press during the World Series and other major baseball events. Dating back to the 1911 World Series, press pins are quite attractive and eagerly sought as collector's items.

**pretty** Said of an easily injured player, such as a "tissue-paper Tom."

**pretzel** A curveball. **Etymology.** Tim Considine (*The Language of Sport,* 1982) gives two derivations for the term: "one from the curved shape of a pretzel, and the other from the fact that a curveball can 'tie a batter up in a knot' like a pretzel."

**pretzel bender** A curveball. **1st Use.** 1908. (*New York Evening Journal,* Apr. 18; Edward J. Nichols).

**prima donna** A temperamental player.

**principal owner** The title used by George M. Steinbrenner to describe his role with the New York Yankees. "What was left to talk about except the ways in which the principal owner had degraded the great American game?" (Lewis H. Lapham, *Washington Post,* Apr. 21, 1984).

**pro** **1.** *n.* A professional ballplayer who plays and behaves accordingly. The term carries the clear connotation of a player who is highly experienced and capable, likely to pull through in a pinch. **2.** *adj.* Professional as opposed to amateur; e.g., "pro ball." **Etymology.** Short for "professional."

**probable pitcher** The pitcher who is expected to start the next game.

**pro baseball** Professional baseball as played in the major leagues and minor leagues.

**project** *n.* A player with raw skills who needs instruction and experience. "In his first six years of pro ball, he [Kenny Lofton] vaulted from crude project to major league star" (*Sports Illustrated,* May 1, 1995).

**Promotion.** *Players in alternative uniforms as a promotion.*

**projection signing** The signing of a prospective player to a contract on the basis of a scout's report that he will mature into a qualified player.

**promised land** The *World Series.*

**promoter** An owner or club official who stages events, stunts, and other sideshow attractions and/or gives away free souvenirs to draw crowds. The most famous and flamboyant of the game's promoters was William L. "Bill" Veeck Jr. who at different points in his career owned the St. Louis Browns, Cleveland Indians, and Chicago White Sox. Veeck's most famous promotional stunt was using 3-foot, 7-inch midget Eddie Gaedel to pinch hit in a 1951 Browns–Detroit Tigers game. Veeck also pioneered promotional notions ranging from exploding scoreboards to free baby-sitting.

**promotion** An event used to attract people to the ballpark; e.g., Bat Day, Old-Timers' Day, Seat Cushion Night, Fan Appreciation Day, Knothole Day, Senior Citizens' Day, Cap Day, Hot Pants Day, Poster Day, T-Shirt Night, and Nun's Day (which Steve Garvey recalled in his biography as a day on which nuns got in for a dollar to watch the Dodgers play the Cardinals).

**promotions schedule** A schedule distributed by teams that lists the special events and giveaways of-fered during the season. For instance, the Baltimore Orioles 1987 promotion schedule listed no less than 24 special days and nights, including three on which bags were to be given out (Toyota Travel Bag Day, Chase Bank of Maryland Sports Bag Night, and Chevron School Tote Bag Day). That same season also witnessed the Seattle Mariners host Natural Gas Seat Cushion Night. The oddest promotion schedules are posted by the minor leagues; e.g., the 1990 Triple-A Calgary Cannons 200-foot ice-cream sundae and the Single-A Clearwater Phillies "Dynamite Lady" Blows Herself Up. A planned June 7, 1997, free vasectomy in honor of Father's Day offered by the Charleston River Dogs, a Tampa Bay Devil Rays' Class A farm team, was canceled due to fan disapproval.

**prospect** A farm hand or rookie with apparent talent. The term has been used so widely that it is regarded with some skepticism. Oakland A's owner Charlie Finley once said: "Prospects are a dime a dozen." In the pecking order of the minor leagues, the next rung down the ladder for a faltering young player from "prospect" is "suspect."

**protect 1.** To place a good hitter into the lineup so that the batter before him (usually also a good hitter) will see good pitches and not be walked; e.g., Barry Bonds, a capable third batter in the San

Francisco Giants lineup, drew many walks because the Giants did not have a competent cleanup hitter to "protect" Bonds. **2.** For a pitcher to throw at (or hit) a batter after the opposing pitcher hit a batter on the pitcher's team. **3.** To keep an allotted number of players out of the expansion draft when new teams draft players from existing rosters. The number protected in the 1992 and 1997 drafts was 15.

**Protective Association** An early union of baseball players, founded in 1900 when discontented National League players united with former player-turned-lawyer Harry Taylor as advisor. It demanded an end to trading or selling player contracts without prior consent or compensation, a ban on unreasonable pay cuts and fines, and changes to the reserve clause. However, the leadership could not persuade players to resist tempting American League salaries, and it collapsed when the National Agreement ended the trade war between the major leagues and the minor leagues in 1903. Full name: Protective Association of Professional Baseball Players. Commonly known as *Players Protective Association.*

**protector** Short for *chest protector.* **1st Use.** 1908. (*Baseball Magazine,* Nov.; Edward J. Nichols).

**protect the plate 1.** To swing at a pitched ball with the intent to foul it off. It usually occurs when, with two strikes in the count, a batter will foul off a pitch that appears headed for the strike zone but not good enough to hit. Jimmy Cannon (*Baseball Digest,* Nov.–Dec. 1956) insisted that such protecting was actually "a series of foul tips by a completely fooled batter who intends to hit every one out of the park." **2.** For a catcher to stand fast and effectively block home plate in anticipation of a close play with a runner trying to score.

**protect the runner** To swing at a given pitch to prevent a runner, who is attempting to steal a base or initiate a hit-and-run play, from being thrown out by the catcher. At a minimum the batter is trying to distract the catcher and hamper him from throwing out the runner.

**protest** *n.* **1.** An official complaint filed with the league president by the manager of a team who claims that an umpire's decision is a violation or misapplication of the rules. A protest will not be recognized on the field unless the umpires are notified at the time the play under protest occurs and before the next pitch is made or a runner is retired. If a protest is upheld by the league president, whose decision is final, the umpire's call is declared invalid and the game may be replayed from the point at which the call was made (the game may not be replayed if the violation did not adversely affect the protesting team's chance of winning the game). No protest is permitted on judgment decisions by the umpire. (*Official Baseball Rules,* rule 4.19).

An example of a successful protest occurred in the game between the St. Louis Cardinals and Pittsburgh Pirates on June 16, 1986. The game was ended after rain delays of 17 and 22 minutes and the Cardinals, who were winning 4–0, were declared the winners. The Pirates appealed on the basis that the game was called too quickly, citing rule 3.10(c), which states that the umpire-in-chief must wait at least 30 minutes before calling a game. National League president Chub Feeney upheld the protest, ruling that the game had to be completed at a later date. **2.** *v.* To lodge a formal protest.

**prove a box score** To balance a box score by verifying that the total of the team's times at bat, bases on balls received, hit batters, sacrifice bunts, sacrifice flies, and batters awarded first base because of interference or obstruction equals the total of that team's runs, players left on base, and the opposing team's putouts. [*Official Baseball Rules,* rule 10.03(c)]

**prune** To trim a team's roster to meet the player limit.

**prune picker** A common nickname (ca. 1950) for a player from California.

**psycho** An easily rattled or disturbed player.

**psych out** To gain a real or imagined psychological edge over another player or team; e.g., "Smith psyched out Jones by his intimidating presence on the mound." The term appeared in many sports around 1920. Syn. "psyche out."

**psych up** To ready oneself or become readied for a game; e.g., "Smith psyched himself up by reliving last week's victory." The term appeared in many sports around 1920. Syn. "psyche up."

**PTBNL** Abbrev. for *player to be named later.*

**PTNL** Abbrev. for *player to be named later.*

**public enemy #1** A curveball.

**pud** A padded mitt or glove. **Etymology.** The term is likely a variation of *pad,* 1.

**puff ball** See *powder-puff ball.*

**puff hitter** A weak hitter, without power. **1st Use.** 1909. (Zane Grey, *The Short-Stop;* Edward J. Nichols).

**pugball** [softball term] A form of softball played on a small diamond.

**pugger** [softball term] One who played pugball.

**pull 1.** *v.* To hit the ball early in the swing for greater power. A right-handed batter will pull the ball toward left field; a left-handed batter will pull the ball toward right field. Pulling is the opposite of hitting to the opposite field. Compare *slice,* 1. **1st Use.** 1908. (*American Magazine,* May; Edward J. Nichols). **2.** *n.* The act or instance of pulling a pitched ball. **3.** *v.* To cause a baseman to remove his foot from a base. **4.** *v.* To remove a player from the game.

**pull a bone** To err; to commit a boner.

**pull a brenegan 1.** To get hit hard in the hand by the ball. **2.** To embarrass oneself in a debut. **Etymology.** From Olaf Selmer "Sam" Brenegan who played in his one and only game for the Pittsburgh Pirates in 1914 with no official at-bats. Brenegan, a catcher, was hit on the back of the hand with the ball and thereby allowed a runner to move from second base to third base. For reasons unclear, this player, whose time in the majors was counted in minutes, was remembered in this phrase for years to come. Not to be confused with *Brannigan.*

**pull a Casey** Syn. of *do a Casey.*

**pull a pitch** For a catcher to move his mitt quickly after catching the ball to give the illusion that the ball was actually received in the strike zone. Ron Luciano (*The Umpire Strikes Back,* 1982) noted: "This is something umpires really dislike."

**pull a pitcher** To remove a pitcher from the game. **1st Use.** 1891. (*Chicago Herald,* May 10; Edward J. Nichols).

**pull a rock** To commit a boner. **1st Use.** 1936. (*New York Herald Tribune,* May 21; Edward J. Nichols).

**pulled hamstring** A common baseball injury in which the tendons attached to the hollow of the knee are damaged and the back of the thigh is affected.

**puller** A batter who pulls away from the plate; a pull hitter. **1st Use.** 1932. (*Baseball Magazine;* Edward J. Nichols).

**pull for** To root for; to support a team. **1st Use.** 1905. (*Sporting Life,* Oct. 7; Edward J. Nichols).

**pull hitter** A hitter who mainly hits to the same side of the field on which he stands; one who habitually hits a bit early or "ahead" of the ball. A right-handed batter naturally pulls toward left field and a left-handed batter naturally pulls toward right field. Sometimes spelled "pull-hitter." **1st Use.** 1937. (*Philadelphia Record,* Sept. 2; Edward J. Nichols).

**pull off the bag** To legally lure a runner off the base he occupies.

**pull off the ball** For a batter to open his stance and allow his head to follow suit, going away from the plate, often resulting in a weak ground ball, a swinging strike, or a hook foul. "When you pull off the ball, you can't go the other way and you can't keep your hands in. It's a matter of concentration." (Chris Hoiles, quoted in *Baltimore Sun,* June 15, 1997).

**pull out of the fire** To win a game that appeared to have been lost.

**pull the string** To throw a changeup, causing the batter to swing too soon. **1st Use.** 1935. "Change of pace—the substitution of a fast ball for a slow one, or vice versa, by a pitcher, 'pulling the string'" (Ralph H. Barbour, *How to Play Better Baseball;* David Shulman). **Etymology.** Although the term would seem to derive from the idea of a string used to restrain or hold back the ball, Bert Dunne (*Folger's Dictionary of Baseball,* 1958) states it is derived from a trick featuring "a trapped badger" in a box overhead. The rookie releases the "badger" by pulling the string, and, says Dunne, "down come refuse—and worse."

**pull the switch** To substitute a batter or pitcher for one that bats or pitches from the other side, such as switching a right-handed pitcher for a left-hander.

**pull the trigger** To decide to swing at the ball. According to Robert Kemp Adair (*The Physics of Baseball*, 1990), it takes a batter roughly 0.15 seconds to mentally "pull the trigger" and another 0.2 seconds to actually physically wield the bat.

**pull up** To reach a base after making a hit; e.g., "Smith hit a line drive to deep center and pulled up at second."

**pummel 1.** To hit a ball hard. **1st Use.** 1922. (*New York Times,* June 5; Edward J. Nichols). **2.** To bat hard against a pitcher. **1st Use.** 1912. (*New York Tribune,* Oct. 7; Edward J. Nichols).

**pump 1.** *n.* The part of a pitcher's windup in which he swings his arms back and forward over his head. See also *double pump,* 1. **2.** *v.* For a pitcher to swing his arms back and forward at the beginning of the windup. **3.** *v.* To have made mental preparation for an upcoming game; e.g., "Smith spent the evening getting pumped for the first game of the series the next day." **4.** *v.* To bat a ball; e.g., "Smith pumped one to left." **1st Use.** 1920. (*New York Times,* Oct. 7; Edward J. Nichols). **5.** *n.* See *go for the pump.*

**pumpkin ball** [softball term] An early name for softball.

**pump man** A home run hitter.

**pump out hits** To get many hits.

**pump pellet** *arch.* Syn. of *spitball.* **1st Use.** 1907. (*New York Evening Journal,* June 7; Edward J. Nichols).

**pump system** A method of signaling in which the catcher tells the pitcher what he wants by the number of times he moves ("pumps") his fingers rather than with the signal itself.

**pump up** To infuse with enthusiasm, spirit, and inspiration; e.g., "Smith pumped up his pitching staff with competitive excitement."

**punch 1.** *n.* Batting power. A team that produces a lot of hits is said to have "punch" in its lineup. **1st Use.** 1912. (*New York Tribune,* Sept. 6; Ed-

ward J. Nichols). **2.** *n.* Pitching power. **3.** *v.* To hit a long ball.

**Punch-and-Judy hitter** A hitter who tends to hit well-placed but weakly hit balls for singles; one who chokes up and punches at the ball rather than takes a full swing. Syn. *punch hitter; judy; Judy hitter.* **1st Use.** 1965. "[Willie] McCovey didn't hit any cheap one. When he belts a home run, he does it with such authority it seems like an act of God. You can't cry about it. He's not a Punch and Judy belter." (Los Angeles Dodgers manager Walter Alston, quoted in *San Francisco Examiner,* May 3, 1965; Peter Tamony). **Etymology.** An embellishment of "punch" using the image of the slapstick "Punch and Judy" puppet show.

**punch drunk** *arch.* Said of a player who has become overconfident or arrogant as the result of a string of hits. **Etymology.** A direct borrowing from prizefighting for a boxer who appears stunned or "drunk" from too many punches; slap happy.

**punch hitter** Syn. of *Punch-and-Judy hitter.*

**punchless** Said of a team without offensive power.

**punch out** *v.* **1.** Syn. of *strike out,* 1. **2.** For an umpire to call a third strike on a batter.

**punchout** *n.* Syn. of *strikeout,* 2. Sometimes spelled "punch-out."

**punish** To hit a pitcher hard; e.g., "The Yankees punished pitcher Smith in the first inning." **1st Use.** 1867. (*New York Sunday Mercury,* Sept. 7; Edward J. Nichols).

**punk 1.** Syn. of *punk hit.* **2.** An inferior or "worthless player" (Martin Gardner, *Annotated Casey at the Bat,* 1967).

**punk ball** A ball that defies being hit solidly; one that is soft and flabby. "Fellows with unusually strong grips have been able to loosen the cover . . . and thus toss a 'punk' ball" (*San Francisco News* article on illegal deliveries, July 7, 1938; Peter Tamony).

**punker** Syn. of *Texas Leaguer.*

**punk hit** A ball that may have seemed to be well hit, but which drops to the ground. Syn. *punk,* 1. **1st Use.** 1888. "The hardest hit will sometimes go directly into the waiting hands of a fielder, while a little 'punk' hit from the handle or extreme end of the bat may drop lazily into some unguarded spot" (John Montgomery Ward, *Base-Ball: How to Become a Player;* Peter Morris).

**punk hitter** A hitter who beats out poorly hit balls.

**punkin 1.** A ball that has seen much use. **Etymology.** From the word "pumpkin" and an apparent reference to a pumpkin's less-than-perfect roundness. **2.** A pitched ball that is easy to hit.

**purchase** A transaction in which a professional player's contract is bought for cash rather than being obtained in a trade.

**purloin** To steal a base; e.g., "Smith purloined a hassock." **1st Use.** 1896. (Burt L. Standish, *Frank Merriwell's School Days;* Edward J. Nichols).

**purpose pitch 1.** A pitch thrown close to the batter to get him to back away from the plate. It is usually an inside fastball that can act as a knockdown pitch. See also *message pitch.* **Etymology.** Sportscaster Bob Uecker says the term was created by Branch Rickey. If so, it may have originated in the context of Rickey's observation that the purpose of a purpose pitch was to separate a batter's head from his shoulders. Umpire Ron Luciano (*The Umpire Strikes Back,* 1982) noted that the purpose of the purpose pitch was to remind the batter that the pitched ball is a weapon. **2.** A pitch that is not meant to be hit but rather to set up another pitch (George F. Will, *Men at Work,* 1990).

**push 1.** *v.* To hit the ball to the opposite field. **2.** *n.* The forward move made by the pitcher just before the ball is delivered.

**push bunt** A bunt in which the batter tries to place (or "push") the ball past the pitcher while still keeping it in the shallow part of the infield.

**put a bow tie on him** To throw a brushback pitch under the chin. The phrase was used by Nolan Ryan, and believed to have been coined by Satchel Paige.

**"put a new handle on it"** Time-tested advice given to a player who has just broken his bat.

**put away** *v.* Syn. of *put out.* "I got [Jeffrey] Hammonds in a position to put him away to end the game" (Jeff Montgomery, quoted in *Baltimore Sun,* Apr. 3, 1998). **1st Use.** 1881. (*New York Herald,* July 15; Edward J. Nichols).

**put fannies in the seats** To be able to attract paying spectators. See also *put the meat in the seats.*

**put him down** To move a runner from first base to second base on a sacrifice, with "down" indicating an advance from one base to another. **1st Use.** 1937. (*The Sporting News Record Book;* Edward J. Nichols).

**put him on the train** To trade a player.

**"put it over"** A command to the pitcher to throw the ball in the strike zone. The command can come from an opposition batter who wants a good ball to hit or from one of the pitcher's teammates encouraging him to stop throwing bad pitches. **1st Use.** 1901. (Burt L. Standish, *Frank Merriwell's Marvel;* Edward J. Nichols).

**put mustard on the pretzel** To throw a fastball (mustard) immediately after a curveball (pretzel).

**put out** *v.* To cause an opponent to be retired from play or removed from an opportunity to reach a base or score. Syn. *put away.* **1st Use.** 1860. (*Beadle's Dime Base-Ball Player;* Edward J. Nichols).

**putout** *n.* The retirement of a batter or baserunner by a defensive player. The actual putout is credited to the fielder who actually retires the runner by catching a fly or line drive, tagging the runner, or touching a base while in possession of the ball. Strikeouts are credited to the pitcher. There are rare situations where a fielder gets credited with a putout without touching the ball, as when a batted ball strikes a baserunner. Rarely spelled "put-out." Abbrev. *PO.* Syn. *out,* 2. **1st Use.** 1869. (*New York Herald,* July 14; Edward J. Nichols).

**put out the fire** For a relief pitcher to enter the game and stop an offensive rally; e.g., "With no out and two on, Smith put out the fire by retiring the next three batters."

**"put some grass in your hat"** Advice to an outfielder having trouble catching the ball.

**put some mustard on it** To reach back for a little extra velocity on a fastball.

**put something on it** To pitch a ball that will curve, break, float, or otherwise behave unnaturally.

**put the ball in his pocket** For a defensive player, esp. a catcher, to determine that he cannot make a play on a baserunner and does not throw the ball.

**put the ball in play 1.** For a batter to avoid striking out by hitting the ball fair in hopes of driving in a run or getting a hit. See also *in play*, 3. **2.** For a pitcher to coax the batter to hit the ball assuming that the defense will be able to make outs.

**put the ball on the ground** To *bunt*. "It has been noted that [Brady] Anderson has . . . 'put the ball on the ground' more than he has in the past two years. He hasn't been overly successful, but the Orioles continue to encourage him not to abandon the bunt as an offensive [weapon]" (Jim Henneman, *Baltimore Sun,* June 7, 1994).

**put the bat on the ball** To hit the ball; to make contact with a pitched ball.

**put the game away** To close out a victory; e.g., "The Dodgers put the game away, 8–4."

**put the game on ice** To win a game definitively; to remove any chance of victory by the opposing team. Syn. "put the game in the ice box."

**put the game out of reach** To have such a big lead that it is unlikely that the opposing team will catch up.

**put the meat in the seats** To fill the ballpark, a phrase often used boastfully by Reggie Jackson. See also *put fannies in the seats*.

**put the wood to it** To hit the ball solidly. **1st Use.** 1909. (Zane Grey, *The Short-Stop;* Edward J. Nichols).

**putty** An injury-prone player.

**putty arm** A bad, weak, or sore arm. **1st Use.** 1937. (*The Sporting News Record Book;* Edward J. Nichols).

**puzzler** A deceptively pitched ball. **1st Use.** 1880. (Chicago *Inter-Ocean,* June 25; Edward J. Nichols).

**QS** Abbrev. for *quality start.*

**"quack, quack"** Time-honored call made by players to get the attention of the trainer. It is a puckish and obvious play on the notion that his healing skills and nostrums are based in quackery.

**quadruple double** Attaining double figures in doubles, triples, home runs, and stolen bases during a season. See also *triple double*, 2.

**quail shot** Syn. of *dying quail.*

**quality pitch** A good pitch thrown to a precise spot with something on it; a successful pitch.

**quality start** A statistic credited to a pitcher who pitches at least six innings and allows three or fewer earned runs. The term came into use in the mid-1980s (Richard Justice, *Washington Post,* Mar. 19, 1986). Abbrev. *QS.*

**quantitative quality** The art of improving a team by signing or purchasing a lot of players who appear to be good, hoping that some of them will turn out to be good. The term was coined by baseball executive Branch Rickey. See also *Rickeyism.*

**quarter** A loose spinning slider. Compare *dime.*

**quarterback drill** A pregame warm-up exercise in which players jog along in a line, throwing and catching the ball over their shoulders. Pitchers commonly use it to sharpen their reflexes.

**questionable pitch** A pitched ball that is neither a clear ball nor a clear strike and may be ruled as either by the umpire.

**question mark 1.** A player whose immediate future is uncertain because of injury, illness, or any of several other problems. **2.** A rookie or player from another team who is new and untested.

**quick bat** An attribute of a batter with fast reflexes who can swing quickly and not be intimidated by a fastball.

**quick belly button** Paul Waner's expression for the hip action needed to hit line drives.

**quick exit** A very short appearance by a starting pitcher; e.g., San Francisco Giants pitcher Rick Reuschel's two-thirds of an inning against the Chicago Cubs in the second game of the 1989 National League Championship Series.

**quick hook 1.** A manager's tendency to remove a pitcher from a game at the first sign of trouble. **2.** A term used by Bill James for the removal of a starting pitcher before he pitched six innings or gave up four runs. Compare *slow hook.*

**quick look** An opportunity afforded a minor-league player to get the feel of major-league baseball.

**quickness** The ability of a player to react to any and all game situations.

**quick pitch 1.** *n.* Syn. of *quick return pitch.* **2.** *n.* A legal pitch thrown quicker than usual between pitches. **3.** *v.* To try to pitch to a batter when he is not yet ready to bat. Whitey Ford (*Slick,* 1987) confessed: "Occasionally, I would quick pitch a hitter, catch him between practice swings or when he wasn't ready. That was easy. All I did was speed up my motion or instead of going into my big, full windup, I would just get the ball, pump, and I throw, and the hitter wouldn't be ready for it."

**quick return pitch** **1.** An *illegal pitch,* by which the pitcher hurries his throw with the obvious intent of catching the batter off balance. It is thrown before the batter takes his position and becomes reasonably set (in the judgment of the umpire) in the batter's box. When detected by the umpire, it is treated as a ball (with no runners on base) or a balk (with runners on base). Syn. *quick pitch,* 1;

"quick return." **2.** [softball term] A pitch thrown with the obvious attempt to catch the batter off balance. This would be before the batter takes his desired position in the batter's box or while he is still off balance as a result of the previous pitch. When this is attempted the umpire is expected to declare that "no pitch" has been made. However, in many cases it is not called and some pitchers have learned to use it effectively.

**quick release** The speed and effectiveness by which a catcher relays a ball to a baseman on an attempted steal.

# R

R Abbrev. for *run,* 2.

RA Abbrev. for *red ass.*

rabbit 1. A player with great speed. 2. A knuckle-ball; e.g., Stu Miller's "hippity-hopping" knuckle-ball. 3. Syn. of *rabbit ball,* 1. 1st Use. 1915. "The 'rabbit' was a baseball similar in appearance to the ordinary league ball; under its horsehide cover, however, it was remarkably different" (Zane Grey, *The Redheaded Outfield and Other Baseball Stories;* David Shulman).

rabbit ball 1. A baseball that is livelier than an ordinary ball; one that jumps like a rabbit and can be hit for distance. Although the term can be used for a single ball or a small number of them, it is usually applied to the ball in use throughout a particular season. "Has the 1948 horsehide got a rabbit in it?" asked Jack McDonald (*San Francisco Call-Bulletin,* Apr. 28, 1948; Peter Tamony). There have been many rabbit balls described through the years. These range from the ball of 1910, which was the first to have a cork center, to the 1987 ball, which was widely alleged to be "juiced up": "Bugs Bunny Would Enjoy 1987 'Rabbit Ball'" (*The Sporting News,* May 25, 1987). A few of the other alleged rabbit-ball years include 1925, 1950, 1956, 1961, 1969, and 1977. Over the years players and managers have found many ways of expressing their belief that a ball is a rabbit ball. For instance, in 1969, the International League used a ball from the MacGregor-Brunswick Corp. known as the 97. An unnamed player was quoted in *The Sporting News* (May 17, 1969): "The 97 is the only ball that eats lettuce for breakfast." See also *kangaroo ball; lively ball,* 1. Syn. *lettuce ball; rabbit,* 3. 2. The modern baseball that was introduced in 1920 by the American League and adopted in 1921 by the National League. It was brought in to capitalize on the box-office potential of the home run: it was presumed that sluggers such as Babe Ruth would draw larger crowds if a livelier ball produced more home runs. Originally, it was said that there was a "rabbit in the ball." 3. Syn. of *hopper,* 1.

rabbit ears 1. An attribute of a player or umpire who hears everything or is easily distracted by noise. "A physical phenomena that enables a ballplayer or umpire standing in a ball park before a crowd of 50,000 noisy fans to hear his name whispered in the opponent's dugout twenty-five yards away" (Jim Brosnan, *The Long Season,* 1960). 1st Use. 1943. "Those who have or apparently hear everything said about them by [bench] jockeys are said to have 'rabbit ears'" (*Baseball Magazine,* Jan.; David Shulman). 2. An overly sensitive player or umpire who is especially ready to hear and respond to comments and taunts; one who is easily ridden.

rabbitize To enliven a ball. "If Coast League baseballs aren't rabbitized, as Red Kennealy, the Wilson's man, claims they are not, let us at least say they have been traveling with rare vivacity" (Jack McDonald, *San Francisco Call-Bulletin,* June 6, 1956; Peter Tamony).

**rabbit offense** A lineup that features several fast runners.

**RABS** (Pron. "rabs"). A statistical measurement for the number of at-bats it takes to score a run. The best lifetime RABS is 3.87 (achieved by Babe Ruth); the best single-season RABS is 2.85 (achieved by Billy Hamilton in 1894). The term and concept were developed by Richard Zitrin and Jules Tygiel. Compare *TIBS*. See also *on-base percentage*.

**race** See *pennant race*. **1st Use.** 1880. (*Brooklyn Daily Eagle,* July 26; Edward J. Nichols).

**race to the bag** A contest in which a fielder with the ball is trying to beat the runner to a base for the force out.

**radar gun** An electronic device used to measure the velocity of a pitched ball in miles per hour. The "fast" radar gun (*Jugs gun*) measures the wrist speed of the ball as it leaves the pitcher's hand; the "slow" radar gun (*Ra-Gun*) measures the speed of the ball as it crosses home plate. The velocity gap between the two readings diminishes the higher the ball is released, probably because the more downward trajectory reduces the decelerating force that gravity would place on an object moving horizontally. Pitching coach Charlie Puleo (*Orioles Gazette,* July 8, 1993) notes: "So many baseball people rely only on the radar gun and for a guy who doesn't throw 90 [mph], it can be a challenge to make a mark for yourself." Syn. *gun,* 4; *speed gun*.

**radio ball** A fastball that can be heard but supposedly not seen. Syn. *radio pitch,* 1. **Etymology.** Attributed to Roy Sievers who in 1955 or 1956 deemed Herb Score's quick strikes to be radio balls. The term also is attributed to George "Catfish" Metkovich who in the early 1950s deemed Max Surkont's fastballs to be radio balls.

**radio pitch 1.** Syn. of *radio ball.* **2.** [softball term] A pitch in fast pitch softball that batters can hear, but can't see. The term has been used to describe the fastball of Debbie Doom of El Monte, Calif., who dominated play at the Aug. 1991 Pan-American Games in Cuba where she hurled two perfect games in two outings. The Cuban fans called her "La Supersonica" ("The Supersonic").

**radish** The baseball.

**raftman** A slow outfielder who appears to be poling a raft rather than running. The images used to describe slowness on the diamond are often nautical. An example from a 1912 collection of baseball slang: "He couldn't beat a towboat that was tied to the bank" (*Sporting Life,* May 18, 1912).

**rag 1.** *v.* To ride or heckle; to jockey. "Much laughter, too, and not a little ragging of the Indians" (Christy Mathewson, *Catcher Craig,* 1915). Two examples of ragging from an industrial-league game in Montgomery County, Md.: "Number 20—off your knees" (to a short player); and "Hey 12, get the piano off your back" (to a slow player). **2.** *n.* A fielder's glove. **3.** *n./arch.* The pennant. **1st Use.** 1902. (*Sporting Life,* Sept. 13; Edward J. Nichols).

**rag arm 1.** A pitcher whose pitches lack speed and deception; one who pitches with nothing on the ball. The term is used disparagingly. **2.** A loose arm. The 10th commandment in Herb Pennock's "10 Commandments of Pitching" (*The Sporting News,* Apr. 24, 1971): "Work for what is called a rag arm. A loose arm can pitch overhanded, side-arm, three-quarter, underhanded—any old way—to suit the situation at hand."

**ragged fielding** Loose and unreliable defensive play. **1st Use.** 1885. (Chicago *Inter-Ocean,* June 3; Edward J. Nichols).

**rag man** A pitcher whose pitching-arm sleeve is frayed or loose. No player is allowed to wear ragged, frayed, or slit sleeves because they may distract one's vision [*Official Baseball Rules,* rule 1.11(a)(1)(c)(2)].

**Ra-Gun** A *radar gun* used to measure the velocity of a pitched ball as it crosses home plate. The later reading (after the ball has lost some of its speed—about three or four miles per hour slower than that of the *Jugs gun*) is considered more important because home plate is where the issue is settled. The average major-league fastball registers 86 mph on the Ra-Gun.

**rainbow 1.** A wide, sweeping curveball with a rainbowlike arc; a *roundhouse curve*. "[Calvin] Schiraldi breaks off a rainbow" (Vin Scully, NBC-TV

Game of the Week, May 9, 1987). See also *jug-handle*. Syn. *rainbow curve*. **2.** A long, high throw from an outfielder, resembling the arc of a rainbow.

**rainbow curve** Syn. of *rainbow*, 1. **1st Use.** 1891. (*Chicago Herald*, May 25; Edward J. Nichols).

**rainbow drop** Slang syn. of *home run*.

**rain bringer** A high fly ball. **1st Use.** 1932. (*Baseball Magazine,* Oct.; Edward J. Nichols).

**rain check** The detachable part of a ticket to a baseball game, which can be used to gain admission to a future game if the game in question is called because of inclement weather before it becomes a regulation game (4½ or 5 innings, depending on the score). The custom of giving the ticketholder a rain check became institutionalized in 1890 in the constitution of the National League.

It has long been claimed and often published that the first detachable rain check was issued in 1888 in New Orleans by team owner Abner Powell of the minor-league Pelicans. *Joe Reichler's Book of Baseball Records* (1957) quotes Powell on the discovery, noting that many people were getting into Sportsman's Park, where the Pelicans played, for free. When there was rain in that era of reusable tickets, the spectators lined up to pick up a ticket for the next day, reclaiming those that had already been turned in. "Usually," said Powell, "there were more fans in line than there were tickets in the box. All those free riders and fence jumpers joined the line, too. The situation became so acute that, despite weekday crowds of 5,000 and Sunday throngs of 10,000, we were losing money." Powell thought about this for several days in 1889 (according to this account, not 1887 or 1888, as is stated elsewhere) and came up with the rain-check idea. This claim was heavily publicized

in 1953 when Powell died at age 92 in New Orleans and many newspapers carried his obituary. The Associated Press story said the first Powell rain check was issued in 1887, a year earlier than most other accounts and two years earlier than Reichler's claim. The discrepancy may not be all that important because linguistic research conducted by David Shulman points conclusively to earlier use of the term. **1st Use.** 1884. "Rain checks given out on the St. Louis grounds are good for any succeeding championship game" (Spalding Scrapbooks, vol. IV, July 5; David Shulman). **Extended Use.** 1. A postponed or deferred acceptance. To ask for a rain check is to decline while asking to be reinvited later. "Sorry we can't make dinner, but we'd love to take a rain check on the invitation." 2. A coupon guaranteeing a customer the sales price for a future purchase of a sales item that is out of stock. 3. A parole, in criminal slang.

**rain dance** Delaying tactics used when it starts to rain. It is used both by managers losing a game that is not yet official (and will have to be replayed if it is rained out) and by managers winning a game when the required number of innings have been played (and the team will win if the game is called for rain). "You don't think [Los Angeles Dodgers manager Tommy] Lasorda's about to go into his rain dance, do you?" (Harry Caray, WGN telecast, May 6, 1986, with the Dodgers leading the Chicago Cubs).

**rain date** The new date for a game that was rained out.

**rain delay** The official interruption of a game on account of rain. During such a period play is suspended in the hope that the rain will subside and the game can be resumed. Despite the fact that games played in domed stadiums are not supposed to suffer such delays, they are not immune. In Apr. 1986, a game was delayed as water poured through a tear in the roof of the Hubert H. Humphrey Metrodome in Minneapolis. The Astrodome suffered a rain delay of 15 minutes in June 1989 as heavy rains from Tropical Storm Allison delayed the umpires from getting to the ballpark.

**rainmaker** A towering home run; one that seems capable of rupturing a cloud and bringing

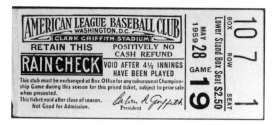

*Rain check.*

rain. "It was a rainmaker shot to left" (Jon Miller describing Ken Gerhart's first major-league home run, WBAL radio, Sept. 19, 1986).

**rain out** *v.* To cause, by raining hard enough, the postponement of a baseball game. The term is usually used in the passive; e.g., "The Friday night game was rained out." **Extended Use. 1.** To rain on any event hard enough to cause its postponement or cancellation. **2.** To fail because of some external event or condition.

**rainout** *n.* A baseball game that is postponed or suspended because of rain or other inclement weather. Sometimes spelled "rain-out."

**rain rippler** *arch.* A *spitball.* **1st Use.** 1907. (*New York Evening Journal,* June 7; Edward J. Nichols).

**rain-shortened game** A game that is called after five innings because of rain.

**raise ball** *arch.* A pitched ball that veers upward as it approaches the batter.

**rake 1.** To hit a home run. "I just want to rake, Cuz" (Colorado Rockies third baseman Vinny Castilla, quoted in *Sports Illustrated,* May 11, 1998). **2.** To get hits; e.g., "The Cardinals raked six pitchers for 17 hits."

**rake in** To field a batted ball. **1st Use.** 1912. (*New York Tribune,* Oct. 13; Edward J. Nichols).

**rally 1.** *n.* Several runs scored together or in rapid succession; a scoring surge. **1st Use.** 1858. (Chadwick Scrapbooks; Edward J. Nichols). **2.** *n.* A run-scoring surge during a half inning for the offensive team that causes it to tie or go ahead. **3.** *v.* To get several hits and runs in one inning. **4.** *v.* To make a comeback in a game, or within a season.

**rally cap** A cap that has been turned inside out, put on backwards, or otherwise oddly displayed by the players on the bench and/or in the bullpen to invoke a rally. The notion began with the Texas Rangers in 1977–79, became popular during the 1986 season as the New York Mets, Houston Astros, and Boston Red Sox, among others, each came up with its own version. The Mets version had the hats worn backwards with the brims turned up, and the Astros simply turned their hats

inside out. The Red Sox ritual, according to *USA Today,* worked this way: "When the count reaches 2-2 with two out on a Red Sox hitter, the players in the bullpen take their hats off and hold them out, upside down."

**rally-killer** That which forestalls or ends a rally, such as a double play, a timely strikeout, or an effective relief pitcher. One statistic published from time to time shows a player's batting average from the seventh inning on, with his team either tied or trailing by a run. A low average in this department is likely to put the glue on the rally-killer label. "But Reggie [Jackson] ranked a mere fifth in rally-killing" (*USA Today,* May 16, 1986).

**ram** To hit the ball.

**ramicack** To hit the ball. **Etymology.** Origin unknown, but the term seems to come with its own suggestions; e.g., "ram" and "crack."

**range 1.** The ability of a fielder (esp. an infielder) to reach batted balls. A player with good range is one who is able to move quickly in front or behind or to either side of his starting position on the field when the ball is hit. **2.** The distance a fielder can be expected to cover in fielding a ball. "For me, range isn't just getting to balls. Range is where you can throw them out from." (Mark McLemore, quoted in *Baltimore Sun,* June 29, 1994).

**range factor** The average number of plays per game successfully made by a fielder (excluding first basemen and catchers), compiled by subtracting errors per game from total chances (putouts, assists, and errors) per game. The statistic has been advanced by baseball statistician Bill James (*The Bill James Historical Baseball Abstract,* 1986) as a more accurate method of rating defensive ability than the standard fielding average. Many consider this to be James's most important contribution to baseball research.

**ranger** A fielder who covers much ground.

**rap 1.** *v.* To hit a ball sharply. **1st Use.** 1888. (Chicago *Inter-Ocean,* July 12; Edward J. Nichols). **2.** *n.* A batted ball. **1st Use.** 1876. "[Joe] Start's rap to short left field" (*Detroit Free Press,* June 20). **3.** *n.* Hitting power.

**raps** *arch.* A turn at bat for a player or a team. **1st Use.** 1898. (*New York Tribune,* May 5; Edward J. Nichols).

**raspberry** Alternate spelling of *razzberry.* After New York Mets outfielder Darryl Strawberry had been booed in 1986, M. Moran (*New York Times*) asked the inevitable: "How to translate [Darryl] Strawberry's raspberries?"

**rattle** For a batter to distract or disorient the pitcher, such as moving close to the plate, changing his batting stance, taking time outs, assuming the bunt position, talking to or kidding the pitcher, or simply getting base hits. **1st Use.** 1880. (*Brooklyn Daily Eagle,* Aug. 17; Edward J. Nichols).

**rattle of tinware** *arch.* The rumored or threatened release of a player from a club. **1st Use.** 1915. (*Baseball Magazine,* Dec.; Edward J. Nichols). **Etymology.** According to Nichols (*An Historical Dictionary of Baseball Terminology,* Ph.D. dissertation, 1939): "Named from association with the phrase 'to tie the can on him.'"

**rattles** *arch.* Nervousness in a player or a team, resulting in ineffectiveness; e.g., "Smith has the rattles because of his uncertain play."

**raw** Said of baseball talent that has not been developed or harnessed; e.g., "The rookie shows signs of raw power."

**rawhide** The baseball.

**Rawlings lobotomy** A *beanball,* so called because Rawlings manufactures the ball and prints its company logo on each one.

**razz** **1.** *v.* To nag or heckle a player or umpire. **2.** *n.* Short for *razzberry.* **Extended Use.** To tease or nag in any realm.

**razzberry** The sound made by sticking one's tongue between one's pressed lips and blowing loudly. The flatulent sound expresses unequivocal contempt. See also *Bronx cheer.* Sometimes spelled *raspberry.* Syn. *razz,* 2. **Etymology.** Commonly believed to be a play on the rasping start of the word "raspberry" or the sound of a metal rasp. Charles Earle Funk gives an alternative etymology (*Hog on Ice,* 1948), after rejecting the notion that it comes

from the metal rasp: "I think that the word should be written 'razzberry,' that it was a humorous extension developed from the slang, 'to razz,' to mock at or make fun of; and that the latter term was originally a contraction of 'to razzle-dazzle,' meaning bamboozle, banter or deceive." Funk notes that the first razzle-dazzle was an amusement-park ride on which one went in circles merry-go-round style while undulating up and down. Citing argot dictionaries, author Lawrence Block suggests (personal communication) that the term is Cockney rhyming slang: "razzberry" = "razzberry tart" = "fart." **Extended Use.** The very same sound and meaning when heard outside the ballpark.

**RBI** **1.** Abbrev. for *run batted in.* **Usage Note.** Charles D. Poe noted from his research: "There is not, apparently, any standardization concerning the abbreviation for the term 'runs batted in.'" Poe found it written "RBIs," "RBI," "rbi's," "RBI's," "R.B.I. 's," "R.B.I.," and "rbi." **2.** Abbrev. for *Reviving Baseball in the Inner Cities.* **3.** Abbrev. for *Research in Baseball Index.*

**RBI man** A hitter adept at driving in runs.

**RBI situation** That time in a game when one or more players are in a scoring position.

**R card** A candy or gum baseball card issued after 1930, the beginning of the "modern" era in baseball cards.

**reach** *n.* **1.** The distance a baseman can stretch his arm without losing contact with the base he is covering. **1st Use.** 1902. (*Sporting Life,* July 12; Edward J. Nichols). **2.** *v.* To get hits and runs off a pitcher; e.g., "The Braves reached Smith for three hits and two runs in the eighth." **3.** *v.* To get to first base; e.g., "[Damion] Easley has reached in 25 straight games" (*Baltimore Sun,* May 22, 1998).

**reach back** For a pitcher able to summon extra speed or deception to get a strike or an out. "[Dwight] Gooden reaches back and gets something extra" (Johnny Bench, CBS radio broadcast, Oct. 14, 1986).

**reaction position** Syn. of *third base,* 2.

**read** **1.** *v.* To decipher a pitcher's movements so closely that a batter can detect what pitch is about to be delivered or a baserunner can decide when to attempt to steal. **2.** *n.* An act or instance of reading a pitcher by a batter or baserunner.

**real estate** A ballpark with large dimensions. When asked how he liked Oriole Park at Camden Yards, with its relatively small dimensions, relief pitcher Lee Smith said: "I like it, but like most pitchers, I like real estate" (*Orioles Gazette,* July 30, 1993).

**realignment** A restructuring of the game, esp. of the makeup of leagues and divisions; e.g., the establishment in 1994 of three divisions (East, Central, and West) in each league and a new system for creating league championships, which included the use of wild cards, or the switch in 1998 of the Milwaukee Brewers to a 16-team National League. A 1992 realignment in the National League proposed by commissioner Fay Vincent, but not implemented, had the Chicago Cubs and St. Louis Cardinals moving to the National League West Division and the Cincinnati Reds and Atlanta Braves moving to the East Division beginning with the 1993 season.

**rebel** Syn. of *pop-off,* 1.

**rebound 1.** *n.* The bounce of the ball off a wall or fence. To catch a ball after such a bounce is to field it "on the rebound." **2.** *v.* For a ball to bounce off a wall or fence.

**recall 1.** *n.* The process of assigning a major-league player to a farm club. It is normally understood that the player who is on recall status may be brought back to the parent club on short notice (such as 24 hours). **2.** *v.* To bring back to a major-league club a player previously optioned to a minor-league club.

**receiver** Syn. of *catcher,* 1. **1st Use.** 1908. (*Baseball Magazine,* Aug.; Edward J. Nichols).

**reconciliation** The new start required to attract fans back to the game after the players' strike that saw a canceled 1994 World Series and a delayed start to the 1995 season.

**record 1.** *n.* Virtually anything for which a claim can be made. On Sept. 14, 1997, for example, the Chicago Cubs tied a major-league record by using

nine pitchers in a nine-inning game. "When Andy Stankiewicz and Mark Grudzielanek hit back-to-back homers . . . it set a record . . . most letters, last names, in consecutive homers, 23. . . . It broke the record of 21 shared by Carl Yastrzemski and Tony Conigliaro in 1970, Yastrzemski and Rico Petrocelli in 1974, and Dom Dallessandro and Swish Nicholson for the 1941 Cubs" (*Boston Globe,* Aug. 31, 1997). **2.** *n.* The standing of a team or player with respect to actions or achievements; e.g., games won and lost, hits made, or an earned run average. **3.** *v.* To attain or add to one's record; e.g., "Smith recorded his 20th victory."

**record book 1.** The official document in which all numbers and statistics of players, clubs, and leagues are kept. The term is often used in the plural. **2.** A mythical document containing such records.

**recovery** The retrieval of a ball after it was momentarily fumbled. **1st Use.** 1880. (Chicago *Inter-Ocean,* June 28; Edward J. Nichols).

**recreation ball** [softball term] An early name for softball.

**recruit** A new player on a ball club; specif., a *rookie.*

**recycled manager 1.** A manager who has served a baseball team on more than one separate occasion; e.g., Billy Martin managed the New York Yankees on five occasions (1975–78, 1979, 1983, 1985, and 1988). **2.** A manager who has managed several teams; e.g., John McNamara, who managed the A's, Padres, Reds, Angels, Red Sox, and Indians between 1969 and 1991.

**red** A short-tempered player; a hot head.

**red ass** A tough, angry player; a player who plays hard. Bill Starr (*Clearing the Bases,* 1989) noted that Earl Whitehill was a "firebrand" when pitching in the 1920s and 1930s, "aptly described in the terminology of those days as a 'red-ass.'" Abbrev. *RA.*

**red-ball express** A fastball. **Etymology.** In railroad and trucking jargon, "red ball" describes a fast-moving vehicle that is on schedule. Traditionally, red balls are given priority over slower-moving units.

**Red Cross walk** Awarding first base to a batter after being hit by a pitched ball, from the obvious association of the Red Cross and injuries suffered from being struck. **1st Use.** 1922. (Ernest J. Lanigan, *Baseball Cyclopedia;* Edward J. Nichols).

**red-hot ball** *arch.* A ball that was hit hard. **1st Use.** 1867. (*New York Sunday Mercury,* Sept. 7; Edward J. Nichols).

**Redlegs** A nickname for the Cincinnati Reds during the 1950s because the "Reds" name might imply some association with communism.

**red light** A sign given to a baserunner not to attempt to steal. Compare *green light,* 2.

**red-light player** A player who performs well when the red light of the television camera is on and he is being watched by a large audience.

**red seats** A section in Cincinnati's Riverfront Stadium where only the most spectacular home runs land. Between the time the stadium opened in 1970 through the 1985 season, only 13 home runs landed in these seats. For those familiar with the feat, the measure is applied elsewhere, even in spring training. " 'Red seats' . . . was the description attached to Dave Parker's home run blast against the Pittsburgh Pirates in Bradenton the other day" (*Tampa Tribune-Times,* Mar. 20, 1986).

**Red Sox Nation** New England. The term was created by Dan Shaughnessy of the *Boston Globe* and adopted by others: "What to do, what to do? Red Sox Nation is in a dither." (Steve Marantz, *The Sporting News,* July 24, 1996).

**reentry draft** See *free-agent reentry draft.*

**re-entry rule** [softball term] A rule in Amateur Softball Association of America that stipulates that any of the starting players may be substituted or replaced and re-entered once, provided players occupy the original positions whenever in the lineup. Nonstarting players may not re-enter; starting players may not re-enter a second time. The starting player and his substitute may not be in the lineup at the same time. The rule encourages coaches to replace first-string players with second-string players during a game since the rule permits a player to re-enter the game if his or her skill is later needed. Under United States Slo-Pitch Association rules, the re-entry rule is applicable only in women's softball.

**refuse the ball** For a pitcher to take himself out of the rotation or turn down a relief assignment. "The thing is, I could have refused the ball any one of those days. . . . They would never have pressured me if I'd said, 'I can't go out today.' " (Tippy Martinez, quoted on his overuse as a reliever for the Baltimore Orioles, in *Washington Post,* Feb. 22, 1987).

**regional franchise** A team that draws from a larger area than its name alone suggests; e.g., the Boston Red Sox long ago established itself as a New England team.

**register** To score a run.

**registry station** *arch.* Syn. of *home plate* (where balls, strikes, and runs are "registered"). **1st Use.** 1915. "Instead of coming accurately, as usual, into the hands of the catcher waiting at the registry station, the ball struck the dirt a dozen feet from the pan" (Burt L. Standish, *Covering the Look-in Corner;* David Shulman).

**regroup** To attempt to bring a struggling team into line. Milwaukee Brewers manager George Bamberger's definition of the verb was quoted in the *New York Times* (June 18, 1985): "You do that by getting more runs and getting better pitching."

**regular** A player who routinely starts at the same position.

**regular player** A player who participates in most of a team's games. **1st Use.** 1866. (Chadwick Scrapbooks; Edward J. Nichols).

**regular season** The period of time during which a championship of the division or league is determined. In the major leagues today, the term refers to 162 games played to determine the six divisional champions and two wild cards.

**regulation game** A game played to official completion. A regulation game consists of nine innings, unless extended because of a tie score, or shortened because a) the home team does not need any of its half of the ninth inning or only a fraction of it or b) the umpire calls the game, in which event a regulation game consists of at least five or more equal innings (4½ if the team batting at the bottom of the inning is in the lead). If the score is tied after nine completed innings, play continues until the visiting team has scored more runs than the home team at the end of a completed inning or the home team has scored the winning run in an uncompleted inning. In the minor leagues, a regulation game may consist of seven innings for one or both games of a doubleheader.

When a game becomes regulation ("official"), individual player performances become part of the record and the rain checks become invalid. A game that does not last for the required 4½ or 5 innings is declared "no game" and must be rescheduled and played from the beginning.

**rehabilitation assignment** Sending a major-league player recovering from an injury or illness to a minor-league team for the purpose of getting him back into playing shape before resuming his place on the major-league roster. The assignment is accomplished with the concurrence of the player coming off the disabled list and can last no more than 20 days. See also *injury rehabilitation assignment.* Compare *conditioning assignment.* Syn. "rehab assignment."

**reinstatement 1.** Returning a player to the active list. **2.** Reestablishing the status of a player who has been banned from the game, even after his playing days are over. A decision to reinstate is made by the Executive Council, organized baseball's governing body. There are no rules governing how great a majority would be needed to approve reinstatement. "Pete Rose will apply for reinstatement to baseball after the World Series and before the end of the year, the lawyer for the all-time hits leader said Friday" (*Milwaukee Journal Sentinel,* Sept. 13, 1997).

**relative performance system** A measurement used by Ralph Horton of a pitcher's performance in 13 statistical categories, with his career point total being the summation of the points earned in each of the seasons he pitched. Abbrev. *RPS.*

**relay 1.** *n.* A throwing maneuver in which the ball is taken by a fielder and thrown to another fielder who acts as an intermediary thrower—or relay—for the ball on its way to its final destination; e.g., a ball caught in deep right field would likely be relayed to the second baseman in hopes of getting the ball to third base for a play. **1st Use.** 1908. (*Brooklyn Daily Eagle,* May 21; Edward J. Nichols). **2.** *v.* To catch a ball thrown by one player and then throw it to a third player. **1st Use.** 1908. (*Baseball Magazine,* Sept.; Edward J. Nichols).

**relay position** The point from which a ball sent in from the outfield can be relayed to a third player.

**relay throw** A throw made from the relay position.

**release 1.** *v.* To cut or drop a player from a team's roster rather than trade or sell his contract or demote him to a minor-league farm team. **1st Use.** 1880. (Chicago *Inter-Ocean,* May 31; Edward J. Nichols). **2.** *n.* The discharge of a player from his contract. A release for most players is a crossroads because it is unlikely that they will ever play at the major-league level again. **1st Use.** 1880. (*New York Herald,* July 5; Edward J. Nichols). **3.** *n.* The final position of a motion as the ball leaves the hand of a pitcher or fielder.

**release point** The arm position at which the pitcher lets go of the ball. If the ball is released too early, it will be high; if released too late, it will be low.

**release time 1.** The time that elapses from the instant the pitcher, in the stretch position, begins his move to the plate (the instant the "discernible stop" at the belt ends) to the moment the ball hits the catcher's mitt. It averages 1.35 to 1.4 seconds. **2.** The time that elapses from the instant a pitched ball hits the catcher's mitt to the instant his throw lands into the glove of a fielder covering the base that a runner is attempting to steal. It averages 2 seconds (to second base).

**relief 1.** The replacement of a pitcher during a ball game, usually because of ineffectiveness. **2.** A period of work by a substitute pitcher; e.g., "Smith pitched three innings of relief."

**relief corps** The entire relief pitching staff of a team.

**relief duty** The work of one or more relief pitchers. Syn. *rescue service.* **1st Use.** 1909. (*Reach's Official Base Ball Guide;* Edward J. Nichols).

**relief man** Syn. of *relief pitcher,* 1. **1st Use.** 1912. (*New York Times,* Oct. 16; Edward J. Nichols).

**relief pitcher** **1.** A substitute pitcher who enters the game, often in a critical situation, to take over for the starting pitcher or another relief pitcher. One of the most dramatic developments in baseball during the 20th century has been the evolution of a typical pitching staff, from no regular relief pitchers early in the century to the first few relief pitchers of the 1920s to the relief staff of today consisting of as many as six pitchers in the bullpen replete with its own awards, specialties (such as middle reliever and closer), conventional wisdom, and body of quotations; e.g., "You can't be thinking about too many things. Relief pitchers have to get into a zone of their own. I just hope I'm stupid enough." (Dan Quisenberry, quoted in *Sports Illustrated,* Sept. 13, 1982). Abbrev. *RP.* Syn. *relief man; relief worker; reliever.* **1st Use.** 1914. (*Harper's Weekly,* May 23; Edward J. Nichols). **2.** A pitcher who regularly fills the role of relief pitcher on a team and who seldom, if ever, starts a game.

**relief points** A scoring system used by Rolaids to determine the effectiveness of a relief pitcher. Three points are credited for a save and two points for a win; but two points each are subtracted for a loss or a blown save. See also *Rolaids Relief Man Award.*

**relief truck** The car, golf cart, or other vehicle recently but not currently used to ferry relief pitchers in from the bullpen. "That really got me pumped, when I came down the sideline in the relief truck" (Ed Whitson, on being given the Ed-DEEE chant at Yankee Stadium, quoted in *USA Today,* Apr. 28, 1986).

**relief worker** Syn. of *relief pitcher,* 1. **1st Use.** 1945. (*Baseball Magazine,* July; David Shulman).

**relieve** To act in the role of a relief pitcher. **1st Use.** 1861. (*New York Sunday Mercury,* Aug. 10; Edward J. Nichols).

**reliever** Syn. of *relief pitcher,* 1.

**remember Wally Pipp** See *Wally Pipp.*

**rent a player** To obtain a key player for the balance of the season. It describes the practice of a team involved in a pennant race trading for a player in the last year of his contract, after which he may become a free agent; thus, the team is "renting" him for the balance of the season in hopes that he will make the difference between a championship and just contending. An example is the Toronto Blue Jays trade for pitcher David Cone on Aug. 27, 1992.

**rep** **1.** A player's ability. Short for "reputation." **1st Use.** 1907. (*New York Evening Journal,* Apr. 30; Edward J. Nichols). **2.** Short for *player representative.*

**repeater rights** A clause in the Basic Agreement whereby a player cannot file for free agency twice within five years of major-league service and a club can retain the player's services if it offers the player salary arbitration within five business days after the end of the World Series. The clause was eliminated in the latest Basic Agreement effective Jan. 1, 1997.

**repertoire** Syn. of *assortment.* **1st Use.** 1910. (*American Magazine,* June; Edward J. Nichols).

**replacement** Syn. of *replacement player.*

**replacement baseball** Games played by replacement players during the early days of the 1995 spring-training season when the 1994–95 players' strike was still on. It began on Mar. 1, 1995, when the California Angels played Arizona State Univ. before about 1,300 fans in Tempe, Ariz.

**replacement player** A player who signed a contract to play in the major leagues when the players' strike of 1994–95 was in effect. Replacement players participated in 1995 spring-training games, but were released before the start of the season. The term did not include a player who was in camp under a minor-league contract. *The Sporting News* (Mar. 20, 1995) ran a guide on "how to spot a replacement player," with five distinctions, including "good periphery work habits: in contrast to the striking players, replacements typically will do menial chores historically left up to coaches and equipment people." *The Sporting News* piece included a line from Pat Jordan's diary: "I saw one

White Sox player who saw a helmet sitting halfway between first base and the dugout during batting practice. Somebody could have tripped over it, so he ran out and picked it up. That's the kind of basic ethics you learn in youth ball that you see with the replacements now." Syn. *replacement*.

**rescue service** *arch.* Syn. of *relief duty*. **1st Use.** 1909. (*Reach's Official Base Ball Guide;* Edward J. Nichols).

**Research in Baseball Index** A computerized catalog/database to "virtually everything" ever published about baseball. It is an ongoing project of the Bibliography Committee of the Society for American Baseball Research to catalog all books, pamphlets, magazine and feature newspaper articles, recordings, musical scores, dissertations, films, and television programs having to do with baseball. Abbrev. *RBI*, 3.

**reserve clause** A traditional provision in a player's contract that bound (or "reserved") the player's services for the following season. It gave the club the right to invoke the expired contract for an additional year even if the player and the team had not come to terms on a new contract by a specific date. It amounted to a "perpetual contract" under which the player was the property of the club, which could elect to keep, trade, or sell his contract. Team owners long insisted that this was needed to keep the leagues from being wrecked in bidding wars. The reserve clause was twice upheld by the Supreme Court (1922 and 1971).

Until the 1970s, owners and players alike behaved as though the reserve clause gave a club perpetual rights to all players it had under contract. After the 1975 season, pitchers Dave McNally and Andy Messersmith, who had never signed contracts for 1975, argued before an arbitrator that the reserve clause gave teams only the right to renew their contracts for one season, after which the club lost its exclusive rights to their services and they were free to negotiate with any club. The arbitrator agreed. The reserve clause was finally overturned by a series of court decisions at lower levels. Its destruction ushered in the free-agent era in baseball. In subsequent Basic Agreements, the players agreed to reinstate the reserve clause, but in a more limited form, which now allows all players with six years of major-league experience to become free agents when their contracts expire. See also *reserve rule*. (Doug Pappas).

**reserved seats** Seating accommodations immediately behind the box seats in a ballpark. These seats are reserved in the sense that the spectator buys a specific seat defined by row and seat number and can buy or reserve it in advance of the day the game in question is played. These seats are in contrast to general admission or bleacher seats, which are filled on the day of the game by the first person to occupy the seat.

**reserve player** A player, usually with a minor-league club, who is not on a major-league club's regular roster of players but who stands ready to be so used on short notice.

**reserve rule** The rule that bound a player to his club from year to year. It was introduced in 1879 as a means of limiting player salaries. Each team was allowed to reserve a number of players on its roster, with all other clubs agreeing not to offer contracts to reserved players. A player under reserve could no longer sign with the highest bidder for his services, but only for the club that had reserved him. At first, the reserve list was limited to five players per team, but it soon grew to include all players on each major-league roster, and later all players in each club's minor-league farm system. The reserve rule was subsequently incorporated into player contracts as the *reserve clause*. (Doug Pappas).

**resin bag** Syn. of *rosin bag*.

**resin ball** An illegal pitch that breaks sharply because of resin powder on the ball and/or the pitcher's hand. **1st Use.** 1925. (*New York Times,* Dec. 20; Edward J. Nichols).

**resin sack** Syn. of *rosin bag*.

**restricted list** A list of players who, for whatever reason, are not active players but who are not to be cut from the roster.

**retire 1.** To put out a batter or baserunner. **Etymology.** The term is used in both cricket and rounders from which it appears to have been borrowed. **2.** To quit playing professional baseball as a career.

**retired number** A uniform number no longer available for active players on a given team because it has been taken out of circulation to honor a key former player or manager who once wore it.

**retire in order** To put out successively all three batters faced in an inning.

**retire the side** Concluding the opposition's turn at bat for its half inning by attaining three putouts. **1st Use.** 1874. (Chicago *Inter-Ocean,* July 6; Edward J. Nichols).

**retouch 1.** *n.* The act of a runner returning to a base, which he must do after a fly ball has been caught. **2.** *v.* To return to a base to make contact with it.

**retread** A player whose career seems to be nearing its end, but who is given a chance with a new team. The term is a direct borrowing from automotive retreads, which are old tires that are given new life when wrapped in a new tread.

**revenue sharing 1.** The formula by which the home and visiting teams share the gate receipts generated by their game. **2.** The collective term for proposals to reduce the disparity between large-market clubs and small-market clubs. Such proposals include giving visiting clubs a greater share of gate receipts, or requiring all clubs to pay part of their income from local television and cable contracts into a central pool, then dividing the pool equally among all clubs. (Doug Pappas).

**reverse curve** A *screwball,* 1.

**reverse force double play** A double play in which the first out is a force play while the second is on a runner who is tagged out. Compare *force double play.*

**Reviving Baseball in the Inner Cities** A program sponsored by Major League Baseball to give urban youth an opportunity to play baseball. Founded in 1988 by John Young, a former major leaguer, it gained full support from Major League Baseball in 1991. By 1997, it had attracted 70,000 participants in 70 cities. Abbrev. *RBI,* 2.

**revolver** *arch.* A player who practiced revolving. Syn. *rounder; shooting star.*

**revolving** *arch.* Moving from one league or team to another without regard to one's contract or club agreement, in search of better positions, better salaries, better teams, or changes of scenery. The term was used in the late 1850s and early 1860s when the practice was widely engaged in by players who yielded to the temptations of larger offers and repudiated their earlier agreements.

**RF 1.** Abbrev. for *right field,* 2. Sometimes "rf." **2.** Abbrev. for *right fielder.* Sometimes "rf."

**RHB** Abbrev. for *right-handed batter.*

**RHP** Abbrev. for *right-handed pitcher.*

**rhubarb** A ruckus with the umpire(s); confusion; a fight between players or between the players and fans; a stew; a noisy argument. Dizzy Dean's definition adds: "Most of the fightin' is done with their mouths." The most complete definition and

**Rhubarb.** *Brooklyn Dodgers manager Leo Durocher leaning into an umpire during one of his many altercations.*

explanation of the term appears in H. Allen Smith's comic novel *Rhubarb* (1946). The title character is a cat, introduced while clawing its way out of a packing crate. "'Look at the son of a bitch go!'" he howled. "'That's what I call tearin' up the pea patch! Look at that rhubarb!'" Smith continues: "Then and there the cat got his name—perhaps the only printable name he ever had—derived from a colloquialism insinuated into the Yankee vernacular by Red Barber, the baseball broadcaster. Mr. Barber in turn picked it up from the prose writings of Garry Schumacher and spread it to the far-wandering winds. In Mr. Barber's lexicon, a rhubarb was a noisy altercation, a broil, a violent emotional upheaval brought on by epical dispute—such as whether one grown man had touched another grown man on the body with a ball the size of a smallish orange." Barber (*Rhubarb in the Catbird Seat*, 1968) adds that Schumacher got the term from Tom Meany, the New York sportswriter. Syn. *dustup; fracas; melee; rumble.* **1st Use.** 1943. "'A rhubarb,' which has become Brooklynese for a heated verbal run-in, especially between players and umpires" (*Baseball Magazine*, Jan.; David Shulman).

**Etymology.** Although there is widespread agreement that Schumacher and Barber first made the term popular in the late 1930s and the 1940s, there is no such agreement as to why "rhubarb" made the leap from the farmyard to the ballpark. There are enough conflicting explanations for a major etymological rhubarb:

1) A popular explanation, which has appeared in several places, including *Reader's Digest* (Apr. 1982), is that the term originated in the early days of radio from the method a director used to create the impression of a menacing, argumentative crowd. To this end, he got a small group of actors to stand together and murmur "rhubarb-rhubarb-rhubarb." From that point on, the story goes, "rhubarb" has meant a heated dispute. If there is an immediate problem with this theatrical explanation, it is that the story is never tied to a time, place, or person. A variation on this idea, which does tie it, conjecturally, to a person, appeared in the letters column of *The Sporting News* (Jan. 21, 1967). James P. Cruger suggested that the term could have come from a German-born baseball man, perhaps Chris Von der Ahe, legendary owner of the St. Louis Browns (1882–91), who recalled an old stage trick from his homeland: German crowd noises were created by actors repeating the word "Rhabarber." John Ciardi (*Good Words to You*, 1987) agrees in principle, noting that it probably comes from "theatrical practice in Brit. use since Shakespeare's time, in which the crowd noises are based on the sound of rhu-bar-bar." An equally speculative notion is that the term came from the old circus cry of "Hey, rube!," which circus hands supposedly used when there was a fire or when they were being attacked by local toughs.

2) Schumacher recalled having first used the term in 1938 at a Dodgers–Reds game in Cincinnati where he was overheard by Barber who used it on the radio. Red Smith later quoted Schumacher in his column (May 21, 1959) as saying that the word fit because it "suggested an untidy mess, a disheveled tangle of loose ends like the fibers of stewed rhubarb."

3) Hy Turkin (*Baseball Almanac*, 1955) wrote that the expression "stems from the old days when rhubarb was used as a purgative and stomach bitter." This fits with an elaborate explanation given by H. Allen Smith, which appeared in Red Smith's aforementioned column (May 21, 1959). H. Allen Smith held that in Schumacher's era the boys growing up in the Greenpoint section of Brooklyn were mothered by women who "held firmly to the belief that rhubarb was essential to the good health of their sons, that several dosages of rhubarb would invigorate them and permit them to fight like bobcats and thus get along in the world." H. Allen Smith claimed that these youngsters were sent out to play with rhubarb sandwiches, which were often used in fights, and it was not uncommon for a boy to find himself with rhubarb in his hair and down his neck. "In time the Greenpoint kids began referring to their happy play as 'rhubarbs'—exclaiming through puffed lips, 'wotta rhubarb.'"

4) It has often been asserted that "rhubarb" was first used in the barrooms of Brooklyn for a brawl, and a variation on this appears in *The Baseball Catalog* (1975) by Dan Schlossberg who claims "winners of fights in Brooklyn would invariably force the losers to swallow terrible tasting rhubarb tonic." Red Barber (*Rhubarb in the Catbird Seat,*

1968) says that it was in a bar that Tom Meany first picked up the word in 1937 or 1938. It seems that there had been a fight between a Giants fan and a Dodgers fan, which resulted in the Giants partisan getting shot in the stomach. To quote Barber: "Well, according to the story as I know it, Tom Meany stopped in a tavern the day after this thing happened—I think it was the very place where the shooting had occurred—and the bartender said, 'We had quite a rhubarb last night, Mr. Meany.' . . . Tom told that to Garry [Schumacher] who fell in love with the word." (In this regard, it seems inevitable that a word like "rhubarb" should have been created to match Brooklyn's long reputation for offbeat behavior. Lee Allen [*The Cincinnati Reds,* 1948] suggests that Brooklyn's reputation for daffiness dated back to June 14, 1870, when the Atlantics of Brooklyn broke the Red Stockings's 130-game winning streak. In the last half of the 11th inning, a Brooklyn fan jumped on the back of a Cincinnati fielder as a fair ball was being picked up. According to Allen: "When order was restored, one Atlantic run had crossed the plate and the tying marker was resting on third. The crowd, of course, promptly went wild, and the spectator responsible for this turn of events was ceremoniously led from the scene by police, the first in a long line of Brooklyn fanatics to be escorted from the premises.").

5) It is also possible that the term owes something to *rhubarbs* (see below).

**Extended Use.** Any noisy and/or heated argument is likely to be called a rhubarb. Red Barber has written on the spread of the term: "World War II was the thing that really popularized it—after all, Brooklyn was in every part of the armed forces. I know that it kept popping up in war communiques and dispatches." The link to Brooklyn, however, took a long time to break. A UPI report on a brawl in Havana on Oct. 28, 1957, identified it as "a Brooklyn-style rhubarb" (Peter Tamony).

**rhubarbs** *arch.* The sticks. **1st Use.** 1915. "Until I came to Hillsboro I never imagined what the game meant as it's played out in the rhubarbs" (Burt L. Standish, *Covering the Look-in Corner;* David Shulman).

**rhythm** Good tempo, form, and consistency in pitching. See also *concentration.*

**rhythm pitcher** A pitcher who usually takes two or three innings to reach his peak effectiveness.

**ribbie** An acronym for "RBI," the abbrev. for *run batted in.* Also spelled "ribby." **Usage Note.** The term tends to be spoken rather than written, but does show up in print on occasion; e.g., "[Steve Kemp's] pre-injury stats project to only 14 homers and 57 ribbies" (*The Village Voice,* Oct. 11, 1983). Willie McCovey was one of the first players to be quoted using the term. When it first began to show up in the early to mid-1960s, it fell roughly on some ears. Leonard Shecter called it an "unimaginative word" and "inane." Syn. *rib-eye; steak; cookie,* 2.

**rib-eye** A 1990s syn. used by players for *ribbie.*

**rib roaster** Syn. of *brushback pitch.*

**Rickeyism** One of a series of terms and aphoristic definitions created by Branch Rickey, one of the most influential baseball executives of all time, who, among other things, created the farm system while with the St. Louis Cardinals and broke the

**Rickeyism.** *Branch Rickey, a front-office man who had a revolutionary effect on the game.*

color bar with the Brooklyn Dodgers. For instance, he came up with the line "luck is the residue of design" to describe his success with farm teams. See also *positive subtraction; quantitative quality.*

**ride** *v.* **1.** To heckle, deride, or bait a player, team, or umpire; to act like a bench jockey. "Any time a new umpire comes to the league, the players—that is, the trouble-makers—try to ride him" (Baum, quoted in *San Francisco Bulletin,* Mar. 28, 1913; Peter Tamony). **1st Use.** 1912. (*New York Tribune,* Oct. 13; Edward J. Nichols). **Etymology.** The conventional explanation is that the term comes from the idea of "riding one's back." Nichols adds that it may also be associated with "horsing," from "horse-play." **2.** *v.* See *ride the bench.* **3.** *v.* To hit a home run; e.g., "Lou [Gehrig] rode one out of the park" (Paul Gallico, *Lou Gehrig, Pride of the Yankees,* 1942). **4.** *n.* The flight of a home run; e.g., "Smith gave that ball a ride."

**ride blindbaggage** *arch.* To advance from one base to another through the aid of a teammate's batted ball. **1st Use.** 1920. (*New York Times,* Oct. 8; Edward J. Nichols). **Etymology.** It is an old railroad term for a free ride.

**rider of the lonesome pine** A *benchwarmer;* one who seldom gets in the game.

**ride the bench** To sit and wait for one's chance to come into the game as a substitute. Syn. "ride the pine; *wear out the wood.*"

**riffle** A hearty swing at a pitched ball, whether or not the ball is hit. "The boys prefer to take 'riffles' this year instead of cuts" (William G. Brandt, *Baseball Magazine,* May 1932). **1st Use.** 1906. (*Sporting Life,* Feb. 10; Edward J. Nichols).

**rifle** **1.** *n.* A strong arm, usually of an outfielder. See also *gun,* 1; *shotgun.* **2.** *v.* To throw the ball quickly and accurately. See also *gun,* 3; *shoot,* 1. **3.** *v.* To hit a hard line drive; e.g., "Smith rifled a liner into left center for a double."

**rifle arm** **1.** An outfielder with a powerful and accurate throwing arm. **2.** The arm of such an outfielder.

**rifle shot** **1.** A swiftly thrown ball. **1st Use.** 1881. (*New York Herald,* July 26; Edward J. Nichols). **2.**

A ball that is hit hard; a *line drive.* **1st Use.** 1890. (*New York Post,* May 10; Edward J. Nichols).

**rig** *obs.* A baseball uniform. The term came directly from cricket. **1st Use.** 1867. (*Philadelphia Sunday Mercury;* Edward J. Nichols).

**right** Short for *right field.* **1st Use.** 1883. (*Sporting Life,* May 6; Edward J. Nichols).

**right base** The correct base toward which an outfielder returns a batted ball. The term occurs in the phrase "throw to the right base"; e.g., with a runner on first base and a single hit to the outfield, the outfielder needs to decide whether to throw to third base to try to put out the runner advancing from second base or to throw to second base to prevent the batter-runner from taking an extra base on a throw to third base. Compare *wrong base.*

**right center** The area of the playing field between right field and center field. Syn. "right-center field."

**right down Broadway** Syn. of *down the middle,* 2. The term was coined by WJSV sportscaster Arch McDonald of Washington, D.C.

**right down the middle** See *down the middle.*

**right field** **1.** The right side of the outfield as viewed from home plate. Syn. *right.* **2.** The position of the player who defends right field. Abbrev. *RF* or *rf.* Syn. *right.* **1st Use.** 1854. (Knickerbocker Rules; Edward J. Nichols).

**right fielder** The defensive player who is positioned in right field. The right fielder often has a strong throwing arm. Abbrev. *RF* or *rf.* Sometimes spelled "rightfielder." **1st Use.** 1883. (*Sporting Life,* May 27; Edward J. Nichols).

**right field foul line** The line extending from home plate to the fence in deep right field that delineates foul from fair playing areas. Syn. *right field line.*

**right field line** The *first base line* extended beyond the infield; the *right field foul line.*

**right-handed** Said of a player who favors the right hand or the right side of the body. Compare *left-handed.* Also spelled "righthanded."

**right-handed batter** A batter who swings from the right and faces the pitcher with the left side of his body as he stands on the left (third base) side of home plate. Abbrev. *RHB.*

**right-handed pitcher** A pitcher who throws with his right arm. Abbrev. *RHP.*

**right-hander** A right-handed player; esp., a pitcher who throws with his right arm. The term is also used for a right-handed batter. Compare *left-hander.* Also spelled "right hander"; "right-hander."

**rightie** Var. of *righty.*

**right in there pitching** Said of a pitcher who is working hard from the mound; a compliment. In this phrase the word "pitching" means pitching with intensity or pitching well. **Extended Use.** Said of one who is putting forth one's best effort.

**right off the bat** Immediately, without ado. The term is an extended metaphor from the speed with which a ball flies off a bat. **1st Use/Extended Use.** 1909. "You see, if there had been any fighting going on here, I'd have got most of them right off the bat" (Rex Beach, *The Silver Horde;* David Shulman).

**right of way** The part of the basepath that a baserunner must yield to infielders attempting to make a play. A runner who fails to avoid an infielder can be called out for interference.

**right short** *obs.* A long-abandoned position between first base and second base for a tenth player. It lasted only a few games into the 1873 season. It mainly lives on as an entry in such reference books as *The Dictionary of American English.*

**right turn at first base** The route taken by a batter who is out on a ground ball or fly. "So for the fourth time, [Dave] Winfield makes a right turn at first base" (Chuck Thompson, Yankees–Orioles telecast, Sept. 6, 1982).

**righty** A right-handed player; one who throws with the right arm or bats from the left side of home plate as he faces the pitcher. Var. *rightie.*

**ring** The circlet awarded to the winners of the World Series, emblematic of a champion, and sup-posedly the ultimate reward for a professional baseball player. See also *World Series ring.*

**ring the bat** [softball term] To check the size of a softball bat to ensure that it is the officially permitted size by an umpire passing the bat through a bat ring.

**ring up 1.** To strike out a batter. **2.** For an umpire to call a strike, esp. a third strike.

**rinky-dink** A player who does not get to play the game very often.

**rip** To hit the ball hard; e.g., "Smith ripped one back through the box."

**ripe** *arch.* Said of a player who is ready to perform at the major-league level. **1st Use.** 1905. (*Sporting Life,* Sept. 9; Edward J. Nichols).

**rise** The upward movement of a fastball as it approaches the batter. **1st Use.** 1896. (Burt L. Standish, *Frank Merriwell's School Days;* Edward J. Nichols).

**rise ball** [softball term] A pitch that rises as it approaches the plate; specif., a fastball that tends to hop as it gets to the plate. "The rise ball is really the pitch that provides the softball pitcher with a great advantage over the hitter. . . . Even when the hitter times the rise ball accurately, he usually hits under the ball and pops it up." (Loren Walsh, *Inside Softball,* 1977). Syn. *riser,* 2; *upshoot,* 2.

**rise-curve** [softball term] A pitch that combines the rise of the fastball with the curve. "Many pitchers use the rise-curve as their best strikeout pitch" (Loren Walsh, *Inside Softball,* 1977).

**riser 1.** Syn. of *rising fastball.* **2.** [softball term] Syn. of *rise ball.*

**rising fastball** A fastball that rises in flight to the batter, who will usually swing under it. It is the opposite of the sinker. Syn. *riser,* 1.

**rite of spring** Spring-training activities and their assorted hoopla. "Fans Flock to Florida for Baseball's Rite of Spring" (*Tampa Tribune* headline, Mar. 5, 1989).

**RO** The letters (for "Rawlings Official") identifying the model ball supplied to the major leagues under contract by Rawlings Sporting Goods.

**road 1.** *n.* The locale of any game not played on a team's home field. **2.** *adj.* Away; not at home.

**road draw** The ability of a team to sell tickets in other teams' home ballparks.

**road game** Syn. of *away game.*

**road grays** The uniform that a team wears for its away games. It is often gray and usually drabber than the *home whites.*

**road record** The statistics of a baseball team for games played away from its home field.

**road schedule** The schedule of baseball games to be played by a team away from home.

**road secretary** Syn. of *traveling secretary.*

**road team** A team that plays well away from its home field yet may do poorly at home. **1st Use.** 1905. (*Sporting Life,* Sept. 9; Edward J. Nichols).

**road trip** A series of games played away from a team's home field.

**roamer** A fielder, usually an outfielder, who covers a lot of territory.

**rob 1.** To deprive a batter of a safe hit through skillful or spectacular fielding. **1st Use.** 1905. (*Sporting Life,* Oct. 7; Edward J. Nichols). **2.** For the umpire to make what appears to be a bad call against a player. **1st Use.** 1905. (*Sporting Life,* Oct. 7; Edward J. Nichols).

**robber** A derogatory term for an umpire. **1st Use.** 1899. (Burt L. Standish, *Frank Merriwell's Double Shot;* Edward J. Nichols).

**Roberto Clemente Award** An annual award given to a player for community involvement and who best represents baseball on and off the field. Termed baseball's most prestigious off-the-field honor, it is named for the Pittsburgh Pirates outfielder (1955–72) who died Dec. 31, 1972, in the crash of a plane taking relief supplies to victims of an earthquake in Managua, Nicaragua.

**Robin Hood league** An outlaw league, such as the Players League of 1890. **1st Use.** 1922.

(Ernest J. Lanigan, *Baseball Cyclopedia;* Edward J. Nichols).

**rock 1.** *n.* A dumb play; a boner; e.g., "Smith pulled a rock in the third inning." Jim Brosnan (*Pennant Race,* 1962) was asked by a young player to explain a "rock"; his answer: "Any time you do something the manager knows you shouldn't, you pull a 'rock.'" **2.** *n.* The backward motion of a pitcher as he prepares to deliver the ball. **3.** *v.* To make several hits off a pitcher; e.g., "The Braves rocked Smith for five straight hits before being relieved." **4.** *n.* The baseball. "Nobody in his right mind throws a rock 90-plus miles an hour at a guy's head." (Bob Gibson, quoted in *New York Times,* July 13, 1986).

**rocker step** The shifting, sideways motion used by a catcher to get positioned for pitches that are low and outside.

**rocket** A hard-hit, fast-moving, low-flying batted ball; e.g., "[Charlie Greene] hit a rocket to the left-field wall" (Ray Miller, quoted in *Baltimore Sun,* Mar. 25, 1998). **1st Use.** 1917. (*New York Times,* Oct. 7; Edward J. Nichols).

**rocking chair** The position of the umpire at third base, presumably because he has so little to do.

**rockpile** A rough infield, esp. one with more than its share of pebbles, or one that is rock hard. A teammate said to Jim Brosnan (*The Long Season,* 1960): "This infield is better than that rockpile in Pittsburgh."

**Rolaids Relief Man Award** An annual award given since 1976 to one relief pitcher in each league by Warner-Lambert Inc., makers of Rolaids antacid tablets ("How do you spell relief?"). Unlike the many awards given on the basis of a vote, this one is determined on a scoring system: two points are credited to a relief pitcher for a win and three for a save, but two points are deducted for each loss and blown save. See also *Fireman of the Year Award; relief points.*

**role player** A nonstarting player who is used during certain specific situations; a player who performs a special function for a team. See also *utility player.*

*Rookie.*

**roll block** *n.* **1.** The maneuver by a baserunner who tries to disrupt the play of the pivot man at second base by tumbling into the player when a double play is being attempted. The roll block is akin to the similar play in football. **2.** *v.* To try to break up a double play by rolling into and blocking the pivot man.

**roller** A slow grounder, such as one that trickles across the field. **1st Use.** 1880. (Chicago *Inter-Ocean,* May 14; Edward J. Nichols).

**romp** An easy victory; a *laugher.* **1st Use.** 1907. (*New York Evening Journal,* May 2; Edward J. Nichols).

**roof-rule double** A *ground-rule double* awarded a batter when the ball is batted onto the roof of a ballpark, into the ceiling material of a roofed ballpark, or (as in the Hubert H. Humphrey Metrodome in Minneapolis) through a drainage hole in the roof of a domed ballpark. Syn. *roof-top double.*

**roofscraper** A towering home run hit in a domed ballpark.

**roof shot** A batted ball (usually a home run) that lands in fair territory on the roof of a ballpark (such as Comiskey Park in Chicago). Syn. *rooftopper.*

**roof-top double** Syn. of *roof-rule double.*

**rooftopper** Syn. of *roof shot.*

**'roo hop** Short for *kangaroo hop.*

**rook** Short for *rookie,* 1.

**rookie** **1.** *n.* A player in his first season; a first-year player. See also *busher,* 1; *gazoonie; green pea; huckleberry; jelly bean; kindergartner; recruit; yannigan.* Syn. *rook; budder; fresh leaguer.* **2.** *n.* The official status (since 1971) of a player eligible for the Rookie of the Year Award; specif., a pitcher who has appeared in fewer than 50 major-league innings during the previous season, or a non-pitcher who has accumulated fewer than 130 at-bats during the previous season, or a player who has been on the roster of a major-league team for less than 45 days during the previous season. **3.** *n.* A player in his first year of eligibility for Hall of

Fame voting. Before a player can become eligible he must be out of baseball for at least five years. "One of the largest rookie crops in years—a total of 24 first-time candidates—helps swell the 1988 Hall of Fame ballot to 45 nominees" (*The Sporting News,* Dec. 7, 1987). **4.** *adj.* Relating to the first season, such as a "rookie manager" or a "rookie owner." **1st Use.** 1908. (*New York Evening Journal,* Aug. 17; Edward J. Nichols). **Etymology.** The term appears to be a corruption of the word "recruit" and may have originated as a derisive term for a fresh recruit in the Army, but this is far from certain. It was listed in the 1903 supplement to *Webster's New International Dictionary of the English Language* as soldier's slang for "recruit" and it was noted that Rudyard Kipling used the word and that its etymology was uncertain. By the time of World War I, it was in common use. In a review of war slang, *Literary Digest* (Mar. 10, 1917) reported: "'Rookie' is soldiers' slang for a raw recruit. The origin of this meaning has been attributed to the name 'rookery,' given, in former military slang, to the quarters occupied by subalterns in barracks." Philip Howard (*A Word in Your Ear,* 1983) notes that the Falklands War of 1982 revived this term in the United Kingdom and that the British had to be reminded that it was not an Americanism but, in fact, made its first literary appearance in Kipling's "Barrack-Room Ballads" (1892) in the line: "So 'ark an' 'eed you rookies, which is always grumblin' sore." Others have suggested: a) a jump from chess where the rook is often the last piece to be used when the game opens; and b) a play on the very old slang word "rook," to cheat, which was applied to new soldiers on the assumption that they would be easily cheated by con men. **Extended Use.** Although "rookie" probably existed in military slang first, its American popularity comes from baseball, from which it spread to other realms. The citations on the word collected by Merriam-Webster include, among others, rookie cook, rookie Senator, rookie cop, CIA rookie, rookie guard (basketball), rookie goalie, rookie priest, rookie astronaut, rookie fireman, rookie starter, rookie year, rookie actor, rookie quarterback, and rookie artist; e.g., "Don't Pair Rookie Pilots, Warns FAA" (*USA Today* headline, Jan. 22, 1988).

**rookie card** The first baseball card that depicts a particular player at the major-league level. In recent years the rookie cards of stars have risen in value much faster than second- and third-year cards, and must be considered the baseball collecting equivalent of a first edition in book collecting. "Don Mattingly seemed amused when told a 3-year-old baseball card picturing him as a rookie was selling for $95. But amusement turned to amazement when he learned people were buying it." (*St. Petersburg Times,* Mar. 14, 1987).

**rookie league** A minor league that is not good enough to meet *Class A* standards; e.g., Appalachian League, Gulf Coast League, and Pioneer League.

**Rookie of the Year Award** An annual award presented by the Baseball Writers Association of America to the outstanding rookie in the major leagues in 1947 and 1948 and to the outstanding rookie in each major league since 1949. Selections

**Rookie of the Year.** *Jackie Robinson was the first-ever recipient of the honor, in 1947; the award now carries his name.*

are made by two writers from each league city. Since 1980, writers name three rookies, with 5 points allotted for each first-place vote, 3 points for each second-place vote, and 1 point for each third-place vote. In 1971, formal guidelines were established for determining rookie status: 130 at-bats, 50 innings pitched, or 45 days on a major-league roster. Since 1987, the award has been officially known as the *Jackie Robinson Award,* to honor the first recipient of the award in 1947. **Extended Use.** Other sports now have "Rookie of the Year" honors. For example, National Hockey League players who have played in "no more than 20 games in the preceding season" are eligible for honors in that sport.

**roomie** Short for "roommate."

**Rooms** A common generic name for a player's roommate on the road.

**room service** *adj.* 1. Said of a batted ball that comes right to the fielder who does not have to move to catch it. **2.** Said of a pitch that is so easy to hit that the batter may as well have ordered it; e.g., a "room-service cheeseburger" is a fastball right down the middle, a juicy offering. "[Wally] Joyner doubled into the right field corner on a room-service fastball" (*Washington Post,* Oct. 8, 1986). **Etymology.** The term is a play on the fact that hotel room service will bring food and drink directly to one's room.

**root** To cheer for or encourage a player or team. **Etymology/1st Use.** 1887. Although it has been stated often that the term comes from the notion of a fan who is so close to his or her team that he or she is "rooted" to it, Gerald Cohen (*Comments on Etymology,* Feb. 1, 1987) has come up with another theory. He traces the term back to Sept. 1887 when it began showing up with regularity in the baseball columns of *The World* (New York). Cohen writes: "The basic meaning of 'root' is clearly 'to dig,' and rooting can be subdivided into the categories of feet-stamping (pedal-music), shouting (chin-music), and hand-clapping. I believe that pedal-music may be the key here; we may deal with the imagery of stamping so hard that it is visualized as digging a hole."

**rooter** An individual who cheers for a team or player; an exuberant fan. **1st Use.** 1890. (*New York Press,* July 8; Edward J. Nichols).

**rope 1.** *n.* A line drive. "I hit ropes against him" (Lee Lacy on pitcher Danny Darwin, quoted in *Washington Post,* June 12, 1986). See also *frozen rope; screaming rope.* **2.** *v.* To hit a line drive. "[Jason] Hackett might walk the next hitter and then somebody would rope a single and he would be in serious trouble" (*Baltimore Sun,* Feb. 23, 1995).

**rosin bag** A small cloth sack containing and covered with sticky resin or rosin that is kept at the back of the pitcher's mound. Pitchers are legally permitted to rub rosin from the bag to dry their hands and improve their grip on the ball. It is illegal to apply rosin to the ball. The rosin bag is used dramatically by some pitchers: Jerry Howarth (*Baseball Lite,* 1986) described it as "constantly being picked up and dropped during the game while occasionally being slammed, kicked, hurled and spat at by angry bilingual pitchers speaking English and Profanity." Syn. *resin bag; resin sack.*

**roster** A list of the active players on a team at any given moment. The length of the roster is set by league rules and changes during the course of the regular season. **1st Use.** 1908. (*New York Evening Journal,* Mar. 3; Edward J. Nichols).

**rotation 1.** The regular order in which a manager will field his starting pitchers. A modern manager wants to leave spring training with his rotation set for, at least, the early weeks of the season. An aspiring starter will try to work his way into the rotation. Commonly, a team has four or five starters in its rotation. Syn. *pitching rotation; starting rotation.* **1st Use.** 1963. "He is expected to instruct the manager on rotation plans" (Ed Richter, *The Making of a Big League Pitcher;* David Shulman). **2.** The spin on a pitched ball. **3.** Syn. of *wheel,* 1. **4.** See *batting rotation.*

**rotator cuff** A tendon structure that encircles, stabilizes, supports, and strengthens the shoulder joint, formed by four muscles attached to the joint capsule. A player may strain or tear his rotator cuff while pitching or throwing, an injury that can have a significant effect on a pitcher's career. Don Drysdale once put a torn one in perspective: "A torn rotator cuff is a cancer for a pitcher. And if a pitcher gets a badly torn one, he has to face the facts: It's all over, baby." Significantly, before the term came into general use, it was said that a pitcher had blown or blown out his arm. A rotator cuff injury used to mean certain retirement, but advances in materials, technology, and technique can return a pitcher (such as Jimmy Key) to the mound. "[Steve] Carlton, 41, is coming back from a 1-8 record and a strained rotator cuff last year" (*St. Petersburg Times,* Mar. 7, 1986).

**Rotisserie League Baseball** A popular armchair baseball game in which participants draft real players for imaginary teams. Players are picked through an open auction in which participants are allowed an amount of cash to purchase players. Standings are determined during the course of the season as the performances of the individuals are added into a collective whole. See Glen Waggoner & Robert Sklars, *Rotisserie League Baseball,* 1987. See also *fantasy baseball league.* **Etymology.** The idea of a statistical baseball league first came up when League founder Daniel Okrent and five other baseball enthusiasts met in Jan. 1980 at a now-defunct French restaurant in New York City called La Rotisserie Française. (Steve Wulf, *Sports Illustrated,* May 14, 1984).

**Rouge Hose** A nickname for the Boston Red Sox.

**rough up** To score, or be scored, against a pitcher. "[Ron] Guidry was roughed up for six runs in the first inning" (*New York Post,* Aug. 13, 1987).

**round** *obs.* An *inning,* 1. **1st Use.** 1870. (*Chicago Evening Journal,* July 25; Skip McAfee). **Etymology.** A term borrowed from boxing.

**round a base** To run across and touch a base in such a manner that the distance and time to reach the next base are minimized.

**round arm delivery** An over-the-shoulder pitching delivery, similar to that of a cricket bowler.

**round ball 1.** A name for various early variations of baseball, including *rounders* and town ball. In 1907, George H. Stoddard (Upton, Mass.) stated that round ball was played by his father in 1820 "and he has the tradition from his parent that two generations before, directly after the Revolution, it was played and was not a novelty even then.

Round Ball was, in fact, the game of the period." (Robert W. Henderson, *Ball, Bat and Bishop,* 1947). **2.** The game of baseball (facetiously) as opposed to football. **3.** A nickname for basketball, a game that lays claim to the term almost universally.

**rounder** Syn. of *revolver.*

**rounders** An ancient British commoners' bat-and-ball game from which most American stick-and-ball games, including baseball, are in part derived. Rounders was popular during the 18th and early 19th centuries in Boston, where it was also called *goal ball, Indian ball, one old cat, round ball, scrub, 2,* and *base-ball.* A British journalist once wrote that baseball was nothing more than "rounders writ large." The game exists in several forms, including those that are played on an individual basis rather than team against team. Robert W. Henderson (*Ball, Bat and Bishop,* 1947) decribes rounders: "Two sides are picked. Usually there is no set number on a side, this being governed by the number of players available, but at one time the number on a side was limited to eleven. The entire side at bat stands in a large batter's box, the other side being in the field, as at baseball. A soft ball is used. A bat is sometimes used, but the ball may be struck with the hand if bats are not available. The pitcher serves and the runners make bases exactly as they do in baseball. In some places if a batter strikes at and misses three balls he is out. But in others, he is allowed to wait until he is served a "good" ball. If a runner is struck by a thrown ball (not touched with it as in baseball) while between bases, he is out. The batsmen circulate around the bases, as in baseball, gradually losing men who have been put out, until no one is left in the batter's box. When this occurs the side is out and the opposing side has its innings. If a batter is caught out in rounders, not only he but his whole team is out. When it is time to change innings the team in the field must rush to the batter's box as quickly as possible, for on the instant a team is out one of their players may seize the ball, throw it at an opposing player, and so put him out." There are no strikes, balls, or fouls. One of the last two players (a "rounder") may opt to be given two tries to circle the bases before the ball is returned: if he makes it, the whole side gets to bat again, if not, the inning is over. Syn. *bass-ball,* 2; *work-up,* 1.

**round heel** A poor player.

**roundhouse curve** A sweeping curveball; one that leaves no doubt that it is arcing. Though impressive to watch, such a pitch has a trajectory that experienced batters can often spot and thus hit the ball. See also *jughandle; rainbow,* 1. Syn. "roundhouse." **1st Use.** 1910. (*American Magazine,* Apr.; Edward J. Nichols). **Etymology.** Probably suggested by the name and shape of the curved track and walls of the railroad structure known as a "roundhouse." Other slang roundhouses include the lavatory on a ship and the full, nothing-held-back swing of the prizefighter. An Associated Press story (Sept. 27, 1938) from London, collected by Peter Tamony, begs to be repeated here in part: "Jack Doyle, handsome Irish heavy weight, knocked himself out tonight in the second round of his fight with Eddie Phillips. Letting go with a 'roundhouse right,' 'the Irish thrush' missed an opponent, fell between the ropes and struck his head on the edge of the ring. He still was prone on the floor outside the ropes when the referee finished the count of ten."

**round-robin** [softball term] A common tournament format in which each team plays every other team at least once. The winner of such a tournament is the team that wins the highest percentage of its games. See also *single elimination; double elimination.* Syn. *league play.*

**round the bases** To trot around the bases, touching each one, after hitting a home run, triple, or double.

**'round the horn** See *around the horn,* 1.

**round-tripper** Syn. of *home run.* Sometimes spelled "round-trip." **1st Use.** 1939. "[Bill] Dickey cracked his round-tripper over Rip Radcliff's reaching glove" (*New York Times,* Sept. 22; David Shulman). **Etymology.** From the rail or air ticket that takes one to a destination and then returns one to the point of origin. The wordplay at work here is a trip from home and then back to home.

**rout 1.** *n.* A defeat, usually a dramatic one. **2.** *v.* To defeat handily or convincingly.

**route** An entire baseball game, commonly applied to a pitcher when he pitches a complete game and is said to have "gone the route."

**rover** [softball term] The 10th player in slow pitch softball who plays at various positions in the field depending on the circumstances; specif., the *short fielder.* Syn. *roving fielder.*

**roving fielder** [softball term] The proper name for *rover.*

**rowdy** Said of a lively, scrappy, and aggressive team (such as the Gashouse Gang of the St. Louis Cardinals of the 1930s) or player (such as 1930s shortstop Dick "Rowdy Richard" Bartell). "If rowdy baseball is to be the fashion, the Giants will be very much present indeed, with Bartell, the most exuberant rowdy of them all" (Stanley Frank, *New York Post,* 1935).

**Royal Rooter** Diehard Boston Red Sox fan of the early 20th century.

**RP** Abbrev. for *relief pitcher.*

**RPS** Abbrev. for *relative performance system.*

**rubber 1.** The rectangular slab of whitened rubber, 24 inches long and 6 inches wide, set into and atop the pitcher's mound so that the distance from the front edge of the rubber to the back point of home plate is 60 feet, 6 inches. The pitcher must come in contact with the rubber while delivering the ball to the batter. The ball is not in play until the pitcher, with the ball in his hand, steps on the rubber. The rubber is the same size at most levels of baseball, although the Little League rubber is 18 inches long and 4 inches wide. Syn. *pitcher's rubber; pitcher's plate; pitching rubber; slab,* 1; *plate,* 4. **1st Use.** 1891. (*Chicago Herald,* May 5; Edward J. Nichols). **2.** obs. Syn. of *home plate.* **1st Use.** 1884. (*DeWitt's Official Base Ball Guide;* Edward J. Nichols).

**rubber arm** A flexible and strong pitching arm, frequently applied to that of a relief pitcher who can work often. Although the term apparently came along later, the all-time rubber arm was attached to Joe "Iron Man" McGinnity (1899–1908), who set a career record that will never be broken let alone attempted: he pitched both games of a doubleheader on five separate occasions (winning both games in three of them). **1st Use.** 1937. (*The Sporting News Record Book;* Edward J. Nichols).

**rubber band** A pitcher with a weak arm.

**rubber bat** A lucky bat used by a player who gets more than his share of fluke or freak hits. The term derives from the fanciful notion of a bat that bends and stretches to make contact with the ball. **1st Use.** 1937. (*The Sporting News Record Book;* Edward J. Nichols).

**rubber chicken circuit** The winter banquet circuit, sarcastically renamed for the poor quality of its mass-produced main courses. Under the headline "He'll Duck Rubber Chicken Circuit," Casey Stengel told *The Sporting News* (Oct. 18, 1950): "I'm 60 years old. I'm too old for that banquet stuff. You get no rest. And, if you don't get rest, how can you keep coming back for such a hard struggle as we've had this year? If you don't feel right, you can't take over a job like this without going batty. And nobody wants to do that."

**rubber-coated baseball** A special ball designed for indoor drills and play.

**rubber game** The last and deciding game of a series when the previous games have been split; e.g., the seventh game of the World Series. **Etymology.** When each side wins one of the first two games in bridge, a card game, the third and deciding game is called the "rubber game." The transfer to baseball makes sense as most regular-season series consist of three games.

**rubbing mud** A mildly abrasive soil that is smeared on baseballs by an umpire before the game to remove their "factory gloss" or shine and make them easier to grip. This procedure dates back many years to a time when tobacco juice or a wad of dirt from the playing field was used. Today both major leagues use a special commercial product known as *Lena Blackburne Rubbing Mud,* named for the Chicago White Sox manager who discovered a mud with just the right qualities on the Delaware River near his home in southern New Jersey. It was introduced to the American League in the late 1930s by Connie Mack and it was adopted by the National League in the 1950s. All teams in major-league baseball use it. See also *baseball mud.*

**rube** *arch.* A player from, or who appears to be from, the country. It was once a very common

*Rubbing mud. Lena "Slats" Blackburne in 1929.*

nickname; more than 25 major-league players have been known as Rube, including Edward "Rube" Waddell, George "Rube" Walberg, Richard "Rube" Marquard, and Ray "Rube" Bressler. **Etymology.** General slang for a farmer or country man, which appears to derive from "Reuben," a name long associated with country bumpkins.

**rubelet** *obs.* A base hit obtained from the pitching delivery of Rube Waddell (1897–1910). (Edward J. Nichols, *An Historical Dictionary of Baseball Terminology,* Ph.D. dissertation, 1939).

**rubinoff** *arch.* A player in need of a haircut.

**rub up** For a pitcher to move his hands with a rotary motion, and some ritualistic intensity, over the baseball to obtain a firmer grip before pitching it.

**rug** The infield grass, esp. if it is synthetic.

**rugball** A tongue-in-cheek term for baseball played on artificial turf.

**rug rat** A small player, from the slang expression for "infant." "Mets Don't Need Babysitter for 'Rug

Rats' [Lenny] Dykstra, [Wally] Backman" (*USA Today* headline, Aug. 14, 1986).

**Rule V draft** A draft of unprotected minor-league players, the order of which is determined by inverse order of finish in each league, with teams from each league choosing alternately. A selected player must remain on the 25-man major-league roster for the entire season or be offered back to the original club for half of the $50,000 draft price.

**rumble** Syn. of *rhubarb*.

**run 1.** *n.* A complete circuit of the bases, from first to second to third to home, in that order. **2.** *n.* The score made by an offensive player. A run is credited to the team and the individual player after he has touched all bases in order and arrives home safely before the third out in the offense's half inning. It is baseball's only unit of scoring. Abbrev. *R.* **Etymology/1st Use.** 1854. The term comes from cricket and appears in the rules of the original Knickerbocker Club. **3.** *v.* To act as a baserunner. **4.** *v.* To manage a baseball team. **5.** *n.* The path of a pitch as it moves across the plate or through the strike zone, or out of the strike zone. **6.** *v.* For an umpire to eject a player, manager, or coach from the game; e.g., "The umpire ran Smith for arguing ball/strike calls."

**run and hit 1.** *n.* Syn. of *run-and-hit play.* **2.** *v.* To attempt to execute the run-and-hit play.

**run-and-hit play** An offensive tactic in which a baserunner is given the green light to steal and the batter has the option of swinging at the pitch. As the runner starts with the pitch, the batter eyes the ball in hopes that it is one he can hit. The runner forces the middle infielder to cover second base, thereby opening a hole for the batter to hit into. If the ball is hit safely, the runner will be able to claim, at least, an extra base. If the ball is not swung at or is swung at and missed, the runner finds himself in the midst of a steal, which he may or may not accomplish depending on his speed and the skill of the catcher. The run-and-hit play differs from the *hit-and-run play* in that the batter chooses whether to swing; i.e., he does not have to protect the runner.

**runaway game** A game in which scoring binges of great magnitude put the game out of reach for the losing team. Some youth leagues have rules concerning the limitation on runaway games; e.g., once the team at bat scores 10 runs in its half of an inning, the sides change regardless of the number of outs at the time (Eastern Area Recreation Baseball Leagues, Montgomery County, Md.).

**run batted in** A run that is caused by a particular batter and that is officially credited to him as part of his record. A run batted in is credited when a runner scores as the result of a base hit, sacrifice or sacrifice fly, hit by pitch, base on balls, infield out (other than a double play), or fielder's choice. The batter himself is counted when he hits a home run. The number of runs batted in that a batter accumulates in a season is an important measure of that player's offensive ability at the plate. See also *ribbie.* Abbrev. *RBI,* 1.

The *Chicago Tribune* invented the run batted in statistic and first published RBI totals for Chicago players in 1880; however, when readers complained that the statistic discriminated against batters at the top of the order, the *Tribune* apologized and stopped publishing the statistic. In 1891, the National League rules committee rejected Henry Chadwick's suggestion that the RBI be recognized in official records and box scores. In 1920, the RBI gained official status, but most newspaper box scores did not show RBIs for another 10 years, when Hack Wilson's season record (190 in 1930) gained widespread acceptance of the RBI in box scores.

**run down** *v.* 1. To tag out a runner who has been caught between two bases. See also *run up,* 1. **1st Use.** 1905. (*Sporting Life,* Sept. 2; Edward J. Nichols). **2.** To catch a fly ball after a long run; e.g., "Smith ran down the fly after a hard sprint."

**rundown** *n.* The act of the defense in an attempt to tag out a runner between bases. It often requires the fielders to throw the ball back and forth several times as the runner tries to avoid being tagged out.

**rundown play** A strategic move in which the offensive team allows one runner to get trapped in a rundown while another runner uses the opportunity to steal home. **1st Use.** 1908. (*Spalding's Official Base Ball Guide;* Edward J. Nichols).

**run his ankles hot** To move swiftly.

**run in 1.** *v.* To pitch close to the batter's body;

e.g., "Smith's pitch ran in on the hands of the batter." "On the first pitch, he ran the ball in on me" (Ray Knight, describing a Calvin Schiraldi pitch, quoted in *Washington Post,* Oct. 26, 1986). **2.** *v.* To score a run. **3.** *n.* A run that has scored.

**run into the box** [softball term] An illegal movement in which the pitcher delivers the ball while running toward the plate.

**run it out** See *run out,* 1. **1st Use.** 1910. (*American Magazine,* Apr.; Edward J. Nichols).

**runner** An offensive player who is advancing toward, touching, or returning to any base; a *baserunner.* **1st Use.** 1845. (Knickerbocker Rules).

**runner in motion** A baserunner who starts to run to the next base as the pitcher delivers the ball on a 3-2 count with two outs.

**runners at the corners** Baserunners at first base and at third base.

**runner's interference** An act by a baserunner that impedes, hinders, or confuses any fielder attempting to make a play; e.g., leaving the baseline for the obvious purpose of crashing into the pivot man on an attempted double play, or intentionally deflecting the course of a batted or thrown ball.

**runners left** The number of baserunners stranded on base at the end of an inning.

**runners left in scoring position 1.** The number of runners on second base and third base stranded by a given batter or team at the end of an inning during a game. **2.** The number of runners on second base and third base stranded by a given batter or team during a game, regardless of the number of outs.

**running catch** A defensive play in which a batted ball is caught on the fly by a swiftly moving fielder. **1st Use.** 1858. (Chadwick Scrapbooks; Edward J. Nichols).

**running game 1.** An offensive strategy that stresses speed, hit-and-run plays, and stealing. "The inability to stop Oakland's running game is killing the [Toronto] Blue Jays" (*Tampa Tribune,* Oct. 6, 1989). **2.** A baseball game characterized by many baserunners and attempted steals.

**run on** To attempt to stretch a hit into extra bases.

**"run on anything"** A command given to a baserunner with two out to run as soon as the ball is hit.

**run out 1.** To run toward first base at maximum speed regardless of where or how the ball has been batted; e.g., "Smith ran it out on the hope that the defense will commit an error." The reward for running out a fly ball comes on those occasions when the ball is dropped or missed and the runner gets to take one or more bases. **2.** To attempt to field a ground ball by running to catch it; e.g., "Jones did not run out the ground ball, he merely trotted toward it." **3.** To put a player in the game.

**run out the string** To wait out the pitcher in the hope of getting a base on balls; to make the pitcher work by not swinging at several pitches. Syn. *run the count.*

**run production** Scoring.

**runs created** An estimate of the number of team runs that would result from a player's offensive statistics, as derived from one of several formulas. (Bill James, *The Bill James Historical Baseball Abstract,* 1986).

**runs produced** A statistical measurement that equals runs scored plus runs batted in minus home runs.

**run the count** Syn. of *run out the string.*

**run through the bag** To be unable to stop and tag up at first because of excessive momentum; e.g., "Smith took off in a flash and ran through the bag."

**run up 1.** To *run down* a runner on the basepath. **2.** To pitch a ball up and in; e.g., "I threw a 2-1 fastball in and he swung at it, so I tried it again and it ran up and in" (Andy Benes, quoted in *Baltimore Sun,* Aug. 11, 1994).

**runway** The basepath. **1st Use.** 1879. "Run ways are to be filled in with clay and pressed" (*Detroit Post and Tribune,* Apr. 27; Peter Morris).

**run with the ball** For an outfielder to take a double step after catching a fly ball.

**ruptured duck** A line drive that drops suddenly and precipitously.

**Ruthian.** *Autographed postcard of George Herman "Babe" Ruth.*

**rush seat** An unreserved general admission or bleacher seat. **Etymology.** The term, rarely used today, originated in the 19th century when such seats were suddenly opened to the onslaught (or "rush") of the crowd as it poured through the gate before a game.

**rusty gate** See *swing like a rusty gate.*

**Ruthian** Colossal, dramatic, prodigious, magnificent; with great power. The term derives from the hitting style and lusty demeanor of Babe Ruth. "He's Ruthian, a tier above superstars today" (Texas Rangers pitching coach Tom House, on pitcher Nolan Ryan, quoted in *Sports Illustrated,* Oct. 4, 1993). The term has been applied to several nouns, such as: Ruthian clout, Ruthian quality, Ruthian smack, Ruthian swat, Ruthian swing, Ruthian proportions, and Ruthian appetite. It sometimes shows up as "Babe Ruthian"; e.g., "a fine Babe Ruthian cameo by Joe Don Baker as the Whammer" (*Newsweek,* on the movie *The Natural,* May 28, 1984). David Shulman found a 1929 citation: "A Negro outfielder . . . had smashed a Ruthian drive against the fence." **1st Use.** 1927. Describing New York Yankees outfielder Bob Meusel's home run on Sept. 16, 1927, against the Chicago White Sox, William Hennigan (*The World* [New York]) wrote: "His Ruthian smash in the fifth was a terrific clout to deep left centre field." **Extended Use.** Mike Capuzzo (*Sports Illustrated,* Dec. 7, 1992): "Babe Ruth's myth is so great that he has entered the American vernacular (Ruthian: larger than life)." John Watters (*Sports Illustrated,* May 2, 1994): "[West Indian cricket batsman Brian] Lara's 375 runs against England last week was, well, Ruthian." When asked if his passing feats had a "Ruthian quality," Miami Dolphins quarterback Dan Marino responded: "Ruthian? You mean the candy bar?" (*Baltimore Sun,* Nov. 26, 1995).

**Ryanesque** In the manner of pitcher Nolan Ryan (1966–93); specif., said of a pitcher's sheer speed and overwhelming power over an extended period of time.

**Ryanitis** A mock disease that "mysteriously struck hitters on the day they were scheduled to face all-time strikeout leader Nolan Ryan" (*USA Today*). The symptoms vary, but the result is that batters try to get out of the lineup rather than face Ryan.

**Ryan Express** The baseball career of pitcher Nolan Ryan (1966–93): "With the suddenness of a crackling fastball, the Ryan Express came to the end of the line" (Mike Dodd, *USA Today,* Sept. 24, 1993).

**Ryan's Express** Nolan Ryan's fastball. The term is a play on the name of the 1965 movie, *Von Ryan's Express.*

# S

**S 1.** Scorecard and box score abbrev. for *sacrifice*, 1. **2.** Abbrev. for *save*. **3.** Abbrev. for successful *steal* of a base.

**SA** Abbrev. for *slugging average*.

**sabermetrician** One who engages in or is a fancier of sabermetrics. A letter soliciting subscribers for *Sabermetric Review* begins with the salutation "Dear Sabermetrician." *Time* magazine (Sept. 5, 1983) referred to sabermetricians as "a small numbers-crunching band of men who call themselves baseball scientists."

**sabermetrics** The study and mathematical analysis of baseball statistics and records. *Insight* magazine (Apr. 7, 1986) noted: "It is a fascinating conglomeration of statistical breakdowns—some basic, others so bizarre and arcane that they almost defy explanation—of baseball's teams and players." The term was coined from the acronym "SABR" by Bill James, who defined it as "the search for objective knowledge about baseball" (*The Bill James Historical Baseball Abstract*, 1986).

**SABR** (Pron. "saber"). Abbrev. for *Society for American Baseball Research*.

**sac** Abbrev. for *sacrifice*, 1.

**sac fly** Short for *sacrifice fly*.

**sack** Any *base*, 2, save for home plate, from the fact that it is a filled canvas bag that resembles a stuffed sack. **1st Use.** 1891. (*Chicago Herald*, May 5; Edward J. Nichols).

**sacker** *arch.* A *baseman*; e.g., "first sacker." **1st Use.** 1911. (*Baseball Magazine*, Oct.; Edward J. Nichols).

**sacks full** Syn. of *bases loaded*.

**sacrifice 1.** *n.* A *sacrifice hit*. Abbrev. *S*, 1; *sac.* **1st Use.** 1880. (Chicago *Inter-Ocean*, June 29; Edward J. Nichols). **2.** *v.* To make a sacrifice hit. **3.** *v.* To advance a baserunner by means of a sacrifice hit. **Etymology.** From the concept of a batter giving himself up for the good of the team by advancing or scoring a teammate.

**sacrifice bunt** A *sacrifice hit* in which a bunted ball with less than two outs advances one or more baserunners and the batter is put out at first base, or would have been put out except for a fielder's error. The batter is not credited with an official at-bat and may be credited with a run batted in if a baserunner scores. A sacrifice bunt is not credited to the batter if any runner is put out attempting to advance one base or when, in the judgment of the official scorer, the batter is bunting primarily for a base hit. Compare *drag bunt*. **1st Use.** 1935. "A sacrifice bunt is a bunted ball laid down for a like purpose" (Ralph H. Barbour, *How to Play Better Baseball*; David Shulman).

**sacrifice fly** A *sacrifice hit* in which a fly ball or line drive, either fair or foul, with less than two outs, is caught but hit deep enough for an outfielder (or an infielder running in the outfield) to handle and to allow one or more baserunners to tag up and score. It has been typified as a "bunt with muscles." The batter is not credited with an official at-bat, but is credited with a run batted in. From 1931 to 1953 (with the exception of 1939), a batter who hit a sacrifice fly was charged with an official at-bat. The ruling was changed in 1954 to help create a few more .300 batters. It was assumed that the rule was worth seven to ten points to a power hitter's batting average. Occasionally two runs score on a sacrifice fly; e.g., on Aug. 8, 1983, Albert Belle's fly to right field was caught over the fence, thereby allowing runners to score from second base and third base. Abbrev. *SF.* Syn. *sac fly.* **1st Use.** 1885. "[Cap] Anson's long sacrifice fly to [Paul] Hines allowed [George] Gore to cross the plate, thus giving the Chicagos the lead" (*Providence Evening Bulletin,* July 30; Fred Ivor-Campbell). The sacrifice fly was formally introduced in 1908: the batter was credited with a sacrifice fly only when a runner scored after the ball was caught. In his summary history of the rule, John Kuenster (*SABR Bulletin,* June 1987) noted that, beginning in 1926, the batter was credited with a sacrifice fly if "any runner advances after the catch."

**sacrifice hit** A batted ball that advances a baserunner at the expense of the batter being put out; specif., *sacrifice bunt* and *sacrifice fly.* Abbrev. *SH.* Syn. *sacrifice,* 1; *sacrifice play.* **1st Use.** 1878. (*Detroit Post and Tribune,* Apr. 20; Peter Morris).

**sacrifice hitter** A hitter who makes a sacrifice bunt or a sacrifice fly. **Extended Use.** The term has seen limited use in politics for a candidate who runs for the good of the party and other candidates, but who is likely to lose. "With a 'sacrifice hitter'—another candidate involved—they can get the 'right to work' monkey off their backs by supporting him" (*San Francisco Call-Bulletin,* Dec. 17, 1957; Peter Tamony).

**sacrifice play** Syn. of *sacrifice hit.* "Alike in the field and at bat, a man may do the most effective work in that branch of baseball technically called 'sacrifice play' and yet not receive a word of credit for it at the hands of many of the reporters" (*Sporting Life,* Mar. 3, 1886; David Shulman).

**safe 1.** Successful in getting on base or advancing to the next base. Compare *out,* 1. **1st Use.** 1862.

**Safe.** *Umpire giving the sign.*

(*New York Sunday Mercury,* July 13; Edward J. Nichols). **2.** The declaration by the umpire that a batter-runner or baserunner is entitled to the base to which he was advancing. The umpire signals the safe sign by holding his hands out with the palms facing and parallel to the ground.

**safe carrier** A slow runner, one who seems as if he is running with a safe on his back.

**safe in the ice box** Said of a game that is out of reach and won. **1st Use.** 1915. "Occasionally Joe went in as a relief pitcher when the game was safe in the ice box" (Lester Chadwick, *Baseball Joe in the Big League*).

**safe hit** A base hit. **1st Use.** 1865. (Chadwick Scrapbooks; Edward J. Nichols).

**safety 1.** A base hit; specif., a single. **1st Use.** 1905. (*Sporting Life,* Sept. 9; Edward J. Nichols). **2.** A reserve player.

**safety set** A series of baseball cards given out by police and fire departments to promote safety. Almost without exception each card contains the image of a player and a safety tip.

**safety squeeze** A *squeeze play* in which the batter bunts and the runner on third base starts or breaks for home if, and only if, it looks like a good bunt. Compare *suicide squeeze.*

**sailer 1.** A fastball that takes off horizontally—as if it had a sail attached—rather than dropping. Ethan Allen (*Baseball Techniques Illustrated,* 1951) notes that it is "gripped with the fingers along the seams and released with pressure on the middle finger." Sailers are notoriously hard to control. **2.** An early name for *slider,* 1.

**St. Louis Browns** The name of the American League franchise in St. Louis, Mo. The team came from Milwaukee in 1902 and moved to Baltimore in 1954, where it became the Orioles. The team spent its life in two ballparks known as Sportsman's Park. It used the latter Sportsman's Park from 1909 to 1953, sharing it for many years with the National League St. Louis Cardinals. Named for the brown trim of the club uniform, many called the team the Brownies.

**St. Louis Cardinals** The name of the National League Central Division franchise in St. Louis, Mo. Once known as the Browns for the color of their stockings, there was a hose change to red in 1899. A reporter covering the team overheard a woman remark that the color was a lovely shade of cardinal. This remark appeared in the paper along with the suggestion that the team adopt the name, which it did in 1900. The cardinal bird was adopted as a symbol for the team.

**salad** A term coined by Dennis Eckersley for a *nothing ball.*

**salami** A *grand slam* home run. **Etymology.** A pure play on the word "slam," which turns it into "s(a)lam(i)."

**salary arbitration** See *arbitration.*

**salary arm** *arch.* A pitcher's throwing arm, so called because a pitcher earns his salary on the strength and effectiveness of his arm. See also *money wing.* Syn. *salary whip.* **1st Use.** 1892. (*New York Press,* Aug. 11; Edward J. Nichols).

**salary cap** A ceiling below which major-league club owners agreed among themselves to keep each club's player salaries. In the 1994 labor negotiations with the players, the owners first demanded a hard salary cap (one with no exceptions), then settled for a form of luxury tax.

**salary drive** A period of good performance and/or behavior, seemingly staged for the benefit of the player's paycheck rather than the benefit of the club. It is commonly mounted during the last month of the season so as to improve the player's statistics for salary negotiations and added leverage in arbitration. Broadcaster and former pitcher Jim Palmer (Home Team Sports, Oct. 1986) defined the term as "a great performance before free agency."

**salary whip** Syn. of *salary arm.*

**salary wing** Syn. of *money wing.* **1st Use.** 1904. "The special implication is that Joe McGinnity is more than a mere star if he is capable of teaching a younger rival how to extend the life of his salary wing" (*Everybody's Magazine,* vol. 10; David Shulman).

**saliva jive**  The loading of a spitball.

**saliva toss**  *arch.* A *spitball.* **1st Use.** 1920. (*New York Times,* Oct. 10; Edward J. Nichols).

**Sally League**  A nickname for the South Atlantic League, founded in 1904 and a Class A minor league since 1980 that traditionally supplies many good players to the major leagues. **1st Use.** 1911. (*Spalding's Official Base Ball Guide;* Edward J. Nichols).

**Sammy Vick**  See *do a Sammy Vick.*

**San Diego Chicken**  An individual outfitted as a chicken who entertained fans as a mascot of the San Diego Padres. Ted Giannoulas, who portrayed the Chicken, commented on his prospect of entering the Baseball Hall of Fame (*Baltimore Sun,* July 3, 1993): "Who knows? I mean, they have a broadcasters wing. They have a players wing. Maybe one day they'll have a chicken wing."

**San Diego Padres**  The name of the National League West Division franchise in San Diego, Calif. The team took the Padres nickname from the city's long-established Pacific Coast League team. It was originally adopted because of the city's Spanish heritage and the fact that padres ("priests" in Spanish) established so many early missions in the area.

**sandlot 1.**  *n.* A vacant lot, playground, pasture, yard, or other such location where youngsters and amateurs play baseball. Robert Smith (*Baseball in America,* 1961), writing on the growth of baseball in the 19th century, captures the spirit of the sandlot: "This was through the seventies and eighties, when boys began to play the game on the outskirts of every major city, in country pastures, and in public parks. The great camp of Manhattan's west side, the prairies on the edges of fire-gutted Chicago, the filled grounds on Boston's Back Bay, the wide meadows on Philadelphia's outskirts, the vacant lots in Indianapolis, in Buffalo, in Patterson, the prairies around St. Louis, the back pastures of New England, the flatlands of New Jersey, the windy reaches of Iowa, even the back yards of

**Sandlot.** *Typical sandlot scene on the site of what is now Doubleday Field in Cooperstown, N.Y.*

San Francisco's Telegraph Hill saw baseball diamonds of every size scratched where boys would play the new game." Sometimes spelled "sand lot." Syn. *lot,* 2. **2.** *adj.* Relating to a class of amateur players, teams, and leagues whose games are played on sandlots. The term is generic and seldom specifically applies to a "sand lot," but rather to a lack of sophistication and organization. It has been said that college baseball, American Legion baseball, Little League Baseball, and other organized programs have all but made sandlot baseball obsolete. In 1964, newspaper columnist Jack McDonald reported that "sandlots have virtually dried up as a reservoir for future talent." Some sandlot leagues have survived, however. John Kelliher (*Boston Globe,* May 22, 1988), manager of one of the clubs in the Boston Park League, commented: "You might say that our league's longevity [beginning its 59th season] is a modern miracle, one of sandlot baseball's very few survivors." Before about 1960, however, it was rare to pick up a baseball player's biography that did not contain a line on the dust jacket concerning "his rise from sandlot baseball to the big leagues." For several years, the Hearst newspapers sponsored its own "sandlot program"; in 1965, newspapers in the chain noted that seven graduates of the program were appearing in the major-leagues All-Star Game. In 1993, the movie *The Sandlot* brought the term back to a new generation. **1st Use.** 1887. "A team called the Joe Gerhardt's of which comedian Pete Daily is pitcher, will tackle the City Island team on the sand lots tomorrow. They will play for a basket of clams." (*New York World,* July 3; from Gerald Cohen, *Comments on Etymology,* Feb. 1, 1987). **Etymology.** Peter Tamony did extensive research on the term, culminating in his article "Sandlot Baseball" in *Western Folklore* (Nov. 1968). He traces the term back to 1850 in San Francisco when a cemetery was created from a "triangular piece of land crested by a hill of sand," which is now the site of the Civic Center. Some 5,000 people were interred at the spot from 1850 to 1860, when the board of supervisors ordered the dead moved, had the hill leveled, and opened the 17 acres as a park. In 1870, the city demanded the spot for a new City Hall. While the building was going up, the demagogue Denis Kearney led his attacks on Chinese labor there, and the name "Sand Lot" was "cabled all over the English-speaking world." Tamony cites several examples in which the term jumped from the name for a specific city lot to a general and extended usage.

Tamony found the term clearly relates to baseball in the "Base Ball Supplement" to *Breeder and Sportsman* (June 7, 1890): "Why such players are overlooked . . . and 'skates' and 'walters' are kept in the team simply because at one time they were alleged good players by some sand lot critic." **Extended Use.** Rough and untutored in other sports and other walks of life. "NFC Salvages Pro Bowl Triumph with 'Sandlot Plays'" (*San Francisco Examiner* headline, Feb. 7, 1983; Peter Tamony).

**Sand Lot Kid** The name of a bronze sculpture by Victor Salvatore depicting a barefooted farm boy that stands outside the gates to Doubleday Field in Cooperstown, N.Y. Since it was put in place in 1939, it has become one of the true icons of the game.

**sandlotter** *arch.* A sandlot or amateur player; a graduate of the lower realms of the game. **1st Use.** 1911. (*Baseball Magazine,* Oct.; Edward J. Nichols).

**sandpaper ball** An illegally pitched ball that has been defaced with sandpaper. "The National League today suspended Kevin Gross of the Philadelphia Phillies for 10 days for having sandpaper glued to his glove" (*Washington Post,* Aug. 12, 1987). **1st Use.** 1914. (*New York Tribune,* Sept. 23; Edward J. Nichols).

**San Francisco Giants** The name of the National League West Division franchise in San Francisco, Calif. The nickname was established by the New York Giants and was carried with the team when it moved to San Francisco in 1958.

**sanitaries** Short for *sanitary socks.* "Underneath you wear long white socks that are called sanitaries" (Jim Bouton, *Ball Four,* 1970; Charles D. Poe).

**sanitary hose** Syn. of *sanitary socks.*

**sanitary socks** The long white socks worn under the outer colored *stirrup socks* to prevent blood poisoning in the event that a player is spiked. "Willie

McGee sat quietly in front of his . . . locker . . . and fiddled with his equipment. First, his long white sanitary socks had to be just so. Then it was time for his cardinal-red stirrup socks to be pulled high and taut." (Don Banks, *St. Petersburg Times,* Mar. 28, 1987). Syn. *sanitaries; sannies; sanitary hose; athletic hose.* **Usage Note.** The term appears to come in and out of fashion. Bill Freehan (*Behind the Mask,* 1970) tells of Al Kaline calling out for a pair of "undersocks." A younger player asks him what he's talking about and Kaline replies: "You aren't old enough to know. That's what we called sanitary socks in the mid-fifties" (Charles D. Poe). **Etymology.** The term is a direct reference to the fact that the white socks are not dyed, like one's outer socks, and that they would provide a cleaner and more sanitary dressing in the event of a spiking.

**sannies** Syn. of *sanitary socks.*

**satchelfoot** A player with large feet requiring large brogans. The term reportedly was the source of Leroy "Satchel" Paige's nickname, which began as "Satchelfoots" in deference to his size-12 shoes (*Time* magazine, June 3, 1940).

**save** The credit given to one relief pitcher for ensuring his team's victory by protecting the lead in a given game. To receive a save the pitcher cannot be taken from the game and must finish it. Even though the starting or other relief pitcher receives credit for the win, the save is the formal recognition of the closer's role in the victory. Only one save can be credited in a game.

To be credited with a save, a pitcher must meet all three of the following conditions (*Official Baseball Rules,* rule 10.20): 1) he is the finishing pitcher in a game won by his club; 2) he is not the winning pitcher; and 3) he qualifies under one of the following conditions: a) he enters the game with a lead of no more than three runs and pitches for at least one inning, b) he enters the game with the potential tying run either on base, at bat, or on deck, or c) he pitches effectively for at least three innings.

According to *Sports Illustrated* (June 8, 1992), the save concept was invented by Chicago baseball writer Jerome Holtzman in 1960 to credit a relief pitcher who enters the game with the tying or go-ahead run on base or at the plate and finishes the game with the lead. The save was officially adopted in 1969, but the reliever had to protect a lead until the end of the game or until he was lifted for a pinch hitter or pinch runner; if more than one pitcher qualified, the official scorer judged which of the pitchers was more effective. In 1973, the reliever had to pitch three innings or enter the game with the tying run on base or at the plate. The current rule was adopted in 1975. Abbrev. *SV; S,* 2.

**save opportunity** A statistic for a relief pitching appearance in which the pitcher has the chance to be credited with a save. It is used to give perspective to the save statistic in that two pitchers with 12 saves may have had vastly different save opportunities (e.g., 14 vs. 24). See also *hold,* 4; *squander,* 2.

**sawed-off bat** A baseball bat shaved flat on the end to reduce air resistance.

**saw off** To pitch on the inside of the plate, causing the batter to hit with the bat handle, figuratively "sawing off" the barrel of the bat.

**"say hey!"** The verbal trademark of Hall of Famer outfielder Willie Mays, the "Say Hey Kid."

**"say it ain't so, Joe!"** The oft-heard lament that came to represent the 1919 Black Sox scandal in which the World Series was "fixed" to accommodate gamblers. On Sept. 28, 1920, a young boy supposedly walked up to Shoeless Joe Jackson (the most famous player accused in the case) in front of the Cook County Courthouse and delivered the famous line. According to an account of the incident in the *Chicago Herald and Examiner,* Jackson replied: "Yes, kid, I'm afraid it is." The boy was then reported to have said: "Well, I never would've thought it."

As with other elements of baseball lore, there is reason to question the veracity of the quotation and the response to it. David Shulman (*New York Daily News Sunday Magazine,* May 1, 1988) wrote: "To his dying day, Jackson never admitted guilt in the Black Sox scandal and denied saying anything after he left the Grand Jury room. It is dubious that any newsboy could have approached him then, as he was carefully guarded." Responding to the claim of eyewitnesses, Shulman adds that they were all reporters and "it is a fact that sometimes reporters contrive their own stories."

**THE CHANGING WORLD**

[Copyright: 1920: By The Chicago Tribune.]

"THE BEAUTY ABOUT BASE BALL IS THAT IT'S ALWAYS BEEN KEPT STRAIGHT AND CLEAN"

POLITICS    HIGH FINANCE

PUGILISM    HORSE RACING    BASE BALL

*Our national sport as it has been regarded.*            *It now joins the "Black Eye club."*

**"Say it ain't so, Joe!"** *The disillusion of the "Say it ain't so" catchphrase is mirrored in this 1920 Chicago* Tribune *cartoon.*

Jackson was quoted in Harvey Frommer's *Shoeless Joe and Ragtime Baseball* (1992): "No such word 'Say it ain't so' was ever said. The fellow [Hugh S. Fullerton] who wrote that just wanted something to say. When I came out of the courthouse that day, nobody said anything to me. The only one who spoke was a guy who yelled at his friend 'I told you the big son of a bitch wore shoes.' I walked right out of there and stepped into my car and drove off." See also *Black Sox.*

**Extended Use.** Used broadly as an expression of disbelief or hoped-for denial. It was given a brief and specific workout when Senator Joseph Biden of Delaware dropped out of the race for the Democratic nomination for the Presidency in 1987. Biden was alleged to have plagiarized the speeches of other politicians. In 1988, the line came into play again when Ben Johnson, the Canadian runner, was stripped of his Olympic gold medal for testing positively for steroid use. This time the cry was, "Say it ain't so, Ben."

**SB** Scorecard and box score abbrev. for *stolen base.*

**scald** To hit a ball hard.

**scalped field** A playing surface with little or no turf.

**scatter** For a pitcher to spread the small number of hits given up over several innings throughout a game so that few or no runs are scored; e.g., "Smith scattered four hits for a 3–0 win." **1st Use.** 1892. (*Chicago Herald,* May 25; Edward J. Nichols).

**scatter arm 1.** A pitcher or fielder given to wild pitches and throwing errors. **1st Use.** 1937. (*The Sporting News Record Book;* Edward J. Nichols). **2.** The throwing arm of a player given to wild pitches or throws; e.g., Buck Weaver had a "scatter arm" when he was a rookie.

**scatter-armed** Given to wild throws and bad relays. The term is more often applied to fielders than pitchers.

**scatter hitter** A hitter whose hits follow no apparent pattern.

**schedule** The list of games that a team will play during a season. Normally, the schedule specifies the date, location, and time of day on which games will be played. Each major-league team plays 162 regular season games, of which 81 are away and 81 are at home.

**schneid** A game, series of games, or period during which a team has been shut out or a batter has gone hitless. See also *off the schneid; on the schneid.*

**schneider** *v.* To shut out. **Etymology.** According to Harold Wentworth & Stuart Berg Flexner (*Dictionary of American Slang,* 1960), the term came originally from the German and Yiddish "schneider" for one who cuts cloth, a tailor. On its way to baseball, it appears to have become a gin rummy term for preventing an opponent from scoring a point in a game or match.

**schoolboy** A rookie or new player.

**school of slug** A class of hitters who "major" in long balls. **1st Use.** 1902. (*Sporting Life,* July 12; Edward J. Nichols).

**science** The collective body of strategy and techniques accruing to the sport of baseball.

**scientific baseball** A term used by Baltimore Orioles manager Ned Hanlon (1892–98) for the collective use of the bunt, Baltimore chop, hit-and-run play, and the cutoff man to win baseball games. See also *inside baseball.*

**scissors** A positioning technique in which the plate umpire (esp. in the National League) spreads his legs as if he's ready to start a race. Compare *slot,* 3.

**scissors slide** A slide in which both legs clamp the bag. Syn. "scissors glide."

**scoop** 1. *n.* A catch of a low batted ball. **1st Use.** 1876. "Myers fouled out on a capital 'run and scoop' by Brown" (*Detroit Free Press,* July 30). **2.** *v.* To dig down to field a low batted or thrown ball. **1st Use.** 1874. (Chicago *Inter-Ocean,* July 7; Edward J. Nichols).

**scorch** 1. To pitch a hard fastball; e.g., "Smith scorched one over for a called strike." **2.** To hit a ball hard; e.g., "Jones scorched the pitch for a line drive to deep center."

**scorcher** 1. A hard-hit, low line drive. **1st Use.** 1876. "Hawes batted a scorcher into Terwilliger's hands" (*Detroit Free Press,* July 30). **2.** A hard fastball.

**scorchers** *arch.* Syn. of *bleachers,* 1. **1st Use.** 1931. "The term 'scorchers' applies to the bleachers where the fans sit and burn in the sun" (W. Clifford Harvey, *Baseball Magazine,* Jan.).

**score** 1. *v.* To touch home plate for a run; e.g., "Smith scored the fifth run." **1st Use.** 1858. (Walt Whitman, *Brooklyn Daily Times,* June 18; Edward J. Nichols). **2.** *v.* To bring a baserunner safely to home; e.g., "Jones scored Brown with a double to left." **3.** *n.* The tally in a game, expressed exclusively in runs. **1st Use.** 1858. (Walt Whitman, *Brooklyn Daily Times,* June 18; Edward J. Nichols). **4.** *v.* To create a record of a baseball game, including runs, hits, errors, and other events. **5.** *v.* For the official scorer to make a judgment call; e.g., "The ground ball was scored as a hit by the official scorer."

**scoreboard** A signboard erected for the benefit of the spectators that, at a minimum, shows each team's inning-by-inning scoring as well as the total number of hits, runs, and errors credited to each team. Many scoreboards give other relevant details of the game (such as the ball/strike count) as well as scores of other games being played concurrently. Scoreboards appear at every level of the game and range from manually operated wooden structures to elaborate electronic screens replete with special effects and moving images. Syn. *board,* 3; *blackboard.* **1st Use.** 1898. (*New York Tribune,* June 28; Edward J. Nichols).

**scorebook** A bound collection of scorecards. **1st Use.** 1872. (*Boston Daily Globe,* Mar. 27, 1872; Peter Morris).

**scorecard** 1. A card, chart, or sheet of paper on which the offensive and defensive plays of a game are noted using the special shorthand of the game. Sometimes spelled "score card." **1st Use.** 1902. (*Sporting Life,* Apr. 26; Edward J. Nichols). **2.** A magazine-style program sold at the ballpark, containing ads, articles, and other information about the home team, including a score sheet bound in the middle as its center spread. It also contains the rosters of both teams with each player's position and number. The vendors who sell them often have a one-line sales pitch that they shout repeatedly. Ken Abrahams at Al Lang Stadium in St. Petersburg, Fla., sold St. Louis Cardinals and New York Mets Grapefruit League scorecards with this simple line: "Get the names and numbers of all the millionaires, just 50 cents."

| It's going to be a good game. | Ha! What did I tell you. | Ah ha! Got them on the run | Well, I'll be \_\_\_\_!!!! | That's a little better. | Ha, ha, ha! That's going some. | Hip! Hip! Hurrah! All over but the shouting. | What the ??!!!?x--!?! | They always were a lot of dubs. |

*Scoreboard.*

**scorekeeper** An official who keeps a record of the score of a game; technically, the umpire-in-chief who conducts the game. Not to be confused with *scorer*.

**scoreless tie** A game or part of a game in which neither team has scored a run.

**scorer** An individual who is given the job of ruling on the plays in a baseball game; specif., *official scorer*. Not to be confused with *scorekeeper*. **1st Use.** 1902. (*Sporting Life,* Apr. 26; Edward J. Nichols).

**scoring** A system of recording the events of a game. It uses its own shorthand; e.g., every defensive player has a number (1 for pitcher, 2 for catcher, 3 for first baseman, 4 for second baseman, 5 for third baseman, 6 for shortstop, 7 for left fielder, 8 for center fielder, and 9 for right fielder). An out is noted by listing all the numbers of the players who touch the ball. A ground ball that is hit to the shortstop who throws it to first base for an out is noted as 6-3. Fly balls are noted by the player who catches the ball. A strikeout is a K, but if the batter is called out the K is reversed. Base hits are 1B (single), 2B (double), 3B (triple), and HR (home run).

There are many variations on standard scoring, both public and private. Writing about a system he developed, Kenneth Ikenberry (*Washington Post,* Aug. 7, 1982) noted that he tried to record every nuance of the game up to and including whether the pitcher was thinking about his stock portfolio when he threw the hanging curve. "I buy score-books of such ancient lineage that they spell base-ball as two words on the cover, and I fill them with tiny symbolic letters, arrows, chevrons, circles, stars—the stuff of the cabals. When they are full I throw them in the back of the car."

**scoring position** Second base and third base when occupied by a baserunner who should be able to score on an outfield hit. A runner who attempts to steal second base is trying to get into scoring position. Having a runner or runners in scoring position is what puts a pitcher in a jam.

**scout 1.** *n.* An individual who evaluates and recommends or signs players at lower levels of the game; an individual who observes and reports on existing talent at any level of the game. **1st Use.** 1905. (*Sporting Life,* Sept. 2; Edward J. Nichols). **2.** *n.* An individual who observes a team's future opponent and reports on its potential strengths and weaknesses. **3.** *v.* To act as a scout. **4.** *obs.* A second catcher in the Massachusetts game who played far to the rear of the regular catcher, grabbed passed balls and wild pitches, and fielded batted balls that landed nearby ("foul balls" were then unknown and batters could run on hits behind the plate as well as in front of it). (Dan Schlossberg, *The Baseball Catalog,* 1975).

**scouting report** A detailed written evaluation of a player of potential worth to the scout's club or an evaluation of a team's future opponent.

**scratch 1.** *v.* To score runs with a series of plays, such as singles, walks, steals, and sacrifices, instead of scoring runs with power, such as home runs. **2.** *v.* To have difficulty in scoring or hitting; e.g., "The Cubs scratched for runs" and "Smith scratched out a hit to shortstop." **1st Use.** 1908. (*Brooklyn Daily Eagle,* May 22; Edward J. Nichols). **3.** *n.* Syn. of *scratch hit.* **1st Use.** 1876. (Chicago *Inter-Ocean,* May 1; Edward J. Nichols). **4.** *v.* To remove a player from the lineup or pitching rotation. **5.** *n.* A player removed from the lineup or pitching rotation. **6.** *n./obs.* Home plate. The term "toe the scratch" first appeared in the *New York Herald* (Aug. 20, 1881) for a batter taking his position at home plate, facing the pitcher (Edward J. Nichols, *An Historical Dictionary of Baseball Terminology,* Ph.D. dissertation, 1939). "Buck Ewing, bat in hand, walked up to the scratch and faced [Charlie] Buffinton, the premier pitcher of the Quakers" (*The World* [New York], Aug. 3, 1889; Gerald Cohen).

**scratch hit** A ball that is not hit solidly but that results, nevertheless, in a hit; a lucky or fluke hit, often an infield grounder. See also *seagull.* Syn. *scratch, 3; scratch single; dime hit.* **1st Use.** 1880. (*New York Press,* June 2; Edward J. Nichols).

**scratch run** A run scored because of a scratch hit.

**scratch single** Syn. of *scratch hit.*

**scratch the diamond** For the ground crew to smooth the basepaths. Frank Gibbons (*Baseball Digest,* May 1959) wrote: "This is an oldie, brought around by Joe Sewell and it means drag the field."

**scratchy** In the nature of scratch hits.

**screamer** A hard-hit ball; a line drive. "Tommy Davis pulled a low two-base screamer just inside the bag at third, apparently fossilizing Joe Foy, the young Boston third baseman" (Roger Angell, *The Summer Game,* 1972; Charles D. Poe). **1st Use.** 1895. (*New York Press,* Aug. 1; Edward J. Nichols).

**screaming meemie** A vicious, low line drive that seems to "scream," probably due to a high rate of spin on the ball. **Etymology.** The term is a bit of slang that has been applied to a variety of things. Peter Tamony noted that the "screaming mimis" were the jitters (as in the 1942 film *Balls of Fire,* starring Gary Cooper and Barbara Stanwyck). During World War II, it was used as slang for German artillery shells.

**screaming rope** An extraordinarily hard-hit *rope.*

**screen 1.** A wire or net barrier erected in front of spectators to protect them from batted balls (esp. behind home plate). **1st Use.** 1879. "It is intended to put up a wire screen behind the catcher instead of the unsightly boards generally used" (*Detroit Post and Tribune,* Apr. 28; Peter Morris). **2.** See *batting-practice screen.* **3.** A baserunner who gets between the ball and the fielder.

**screw arm** The left arm.

**screw armer** A left-handed pitcher.

**screwball** *n.* **1.** A pitched ball that is held the same as a fastball or curveball but is thrown with an inward rotation of the hand and arm. It is spun out of the hand between the middle finger and the fourth and fifth fingers with the middle finger and wrist providing the spin. Unlike the curveball, the wrist is snapped a quarter turn inward and the ball breaks less and with less speed than a curveball. When thrown by a right-handed pitcher, the screwball breaks down and in to a right-handed batter and down and away to a left-handed batter. Because it is difficult to master, the screwball is not a popular pitch. The pitch was first made famous by Christy Mathewson, who called it the *fade-away,* and later revived by Carl Hubbell as the "screwball." Hubbell developed three speeds for the pitch. According to Frank Graham (*McGraw of the Giants,* 1944), Ty Cobb did not sign Hubbell because he thought the screwball would ruin Hubbell's arm, to which New York Giants manager John McGraw snorted: "That's a joke. Screw ball! When Matty was pitching it, they called it a fadeaway—and it never hurt his arm." Also spelled "screw ball." Archaic syn. *incurve.* Syn. *reverse curve; scroogie; screwgie; corkscrew.* **1st Use.** 1928. (*New York Times,* Oct. 7; Edward J. Nichols found the term in print and associated with Hubbell as early as 1928, the same year that Hubbell began his 16-year career with the New York Giants.) **Etymology.** George Vecsey interviewed Hubbell (*New York Times,* July 9, 1984). After establishing the fact that Hubbell first threw the pitch in the minor leagues, Vecsey concluded: "If the pitch was thrown before Hubbell, it certainly had no mystique until a catcher in Oklahoma City—Hubbell says his name was Earl Walgamot—warmed him up before a game and said: 'That's the screwiest thing I ever saw.'" **2.** *n.* A zany player. See also *nervous breakdown.* **3.** *adj.* Eccentric; odd. "Giants Try to Stop Screwball Errors" (*San Francisco Examiner* headline, May 16, 1974; Peter Tamony). **Extended Use. 1.** *n.* Since the 1930s, an eccentric. "The spirit of the screwball is neither national nor mortal but transcends time itself, and, like love's fragrant essence, is everywhere" (Nunnally Johnson, introduction to Stanley Walker, *Mrs. Astor's Horse,* 1935; Peter Tamony). **2.** *adj.* Eccentric, zany, or insane; e.g., "screwball comedy," a form of romantic comedy films that thrived between 1929 and 1948 and featured madcap plots, odd pranks, and slapstick. **3.** *adj.* Said of jazz or crazy, wide-open swing music. "The music of hot bands . . . is referred to as 'swing' or 'jive' of which in turn there are several kinds. Accepted meanings vary according to locale, and the terms overlap, but, roughly, the most-used designations, in order of their increasing hotness are 'gut-bucket,' 'screwball,' and 'whacky,' the last

being the wildest, most unbridled kind of swing." (Benny Goodman, *The New Yorker,* Apr. 17, 1937).

**screwballer** One who throws the screwball pitch. "The prime screwballer of our time is Fernando Valenzuela" (Roger Angell, *The New Yorker,* May 4, 1987).

**screwbeenie** Var. of *scrubeenie.*

**screwgie** A *screwball,* 1. "Without the benefit of a tape measure, my ego will not permit me to believe that there is any way Luis could hit my screwgie" (Bill Lee, *The Wrong Stuff,* 1984). See also *scroogie.*

**screwjack** *arch.* **1.** A player who is notoriously whacky. **2.** A player who is notoriously lucky.

**scribe** A sportswriter. Babe Ruth (*Babe Ruth's Own Book of Baseball,* 1928) noted that scribes are not just any writers but "the newspaper men who accompany a big league ball club on the road." **1st Use.** 1887. (*Base Ball Tribune,* May 23; Edward J. Nichols).

**scrimmage 1.** *n.* An informal intra- or inter-squad game. The term seems to have been borrowed from football and applied only at the amateur level. From a report on a high-school team: "The Whalers' first scrimmage of the season will take place at the high school field Saturday when they'll play a doubleheader against a team from Montville, Connecticut" (Steve Sheppard, *Nantucket Inquirer and Mirror,* Apr. 2, 1987). **2.** *v.* To conduct a scrimmage.

**scroogie** A *screwball,* 1. This slang term is also spelled *screwgie;* although this is the less-common spelling, Charles D. Poe notes that "since the root word is 'screw' and not 'Scrooge,' it seems to me that 'screwgie' should be the preferred spelling. 'Scroogie' has a misleading Dickensian flavor to it." **1st Use.** 1953. "Mickey Mantle coined a new word to describe the pitch he hit for [a] home run—'It was some sort of a scroogie.' [Preacher] Roe confirmed Mantle's description: 'It was a changeup screwball'" (Associated Press, Oct. 2; Harold Wentworth & Stuart Berg Flexner, *Dictionary of American Slang,* 1960).

**scrub** **1.** A substitute or member of the B or second team; a backup player on the bench. The term tends to be used in a derogatory manner. See also *scrubeenie.* Syn. *scrubbie.* **2.** Syn. of *rounders.* **3.** A game played by children in the United States and Canada, as described by Bill Kirwin (editor of *NINE: A Journal of Baseball History and Social Policy Perspectives*): "Since I am old enough to have played the game before Little League, I remember playing this game until enough kids appeared to constitute a real game. The version we usually played used just one base with two batters and any number of fielders. We would then expand the game to two bases (first and third using three batters) and finally to all bases, although this rarely happened."

**scrubbie** Syn. of *scrub,* 1.

**scrubbini** Var. of *scrubeenie.*

**scrubeenie** A modern variation on *scrub,* 1, which seems a touch more affectionate than the original. "Hell, I wasn't even a regular with the Yankees, I was just a 'scrubeenie,' as Phil Linz and Johnny Blanchard and the rest of us substitutes called ourselves, and these racket guys made me feel like I was a star" (Joe Pepitone, *Joe, You Coulda Made Us Proud,* 1975; Charles D. Poe). Var. *scrubbini; screwbeenie.* **1st Use.** 1954. No citation is given, but the term appears in a list of new words for the year 1954 in Kenneth Versand, *Polyglot's Lexicon 1943–1966* (1973).

**scrub game** An informal baseball game, usually between members of the same club, in which the players choose sides and no records are kept.

**scrub nine** A team of rookies and/or substitutes. **1st Use.** 1868. (*New York Herald,* Aug. 11; Edward J. Nichols).

**scrub team** A team composed of scrub players.

**scuff** **1.** *v.* To doctor a baseball by roughening its surface. **2.** *v.* To rub shiny white baseballs with mud to remove their gloss. **3.** *n.* A rough spot or mark on the ball, which causes it to break when pitched.

**scuffball** Syn. of *scuffed ball.* "The [New York] Mets whining about whether [Houston Astros pitcher] Mike Scott's scuffball in the playoffs actually was a scuffball" (*USA Today,* Oct. 24, 1986).

**scuffed ball** A ball that has been illegally marked or roughed up to give it an unnatural trajectory. Pitcher Mike Flanagan once gave this explanation of how the pitch works (quoted by Thomas Boswell, *How Life Imitates the World Series,* 1982): "Any time I want four new pitches, I got 'em, because I can make a scuffed ball break in, out, up, or down. It's the same principle as one of those flat-sided Wiffle Balls. You hold the ball with the scuffed side opposite to the direction you want it to break. It takes no talent whatsoever. You just throw it like a mediocre fastball. The scuff gives the break." Syn. *scuffer; scuffball.*

**scuffer** Syn. of *scuffed ball.*

**scuffgate** A controversy involving scuffed balls; specif., the discussion surrounding the alleged illegal pitching technique of Houston Astros hurler Mike Scott during the 1986 National League Championship Series against the New York Mets, who claimed that Scott put marks on the ball that were the size of 25-cent pieces. **Etymology.** The term is one of many that play off the Watergate scandal of the 1970s by using the suffix "-gate."

**scuffing** **1.** Roughing up or marking a ball prior to pitching it. **2.** The act of making a ball grippable without changing its natural flight.

**scullion** A very ugly player (John Maffei, *Padres Magazine,* 1993). See also *mullion.*

**seagull** *arch.* A *scratch hit* in which the bat is broken.

**Seagull Incident** An incident that occurred in Exhibition Stadium in Toronto on Aug. 5, 1983, when New York Yankees outfielder Dave Winfield killed a seagull when he tossed a warmup ball toward the bullpen and was charged with cruelty to animals (the charges were later dropped).

**sea level** A won-loss mark of .500. A team can be said to be above or below "sea level."

**seam** The curved line formed by the raised, heavy stitching of the baseball. Although the two pieces of leather covering the ball are actually held together by one continuous seam, the stitching is almost always referred to in the plural. The seams are used by pitchers to gain added control over the ball; e.g., a pitcher will grip the ball across the seams to help his fastball rise, while a sidearm pitcher will grasp a ball along the seams to help his fastball sink.

**seamer** A pitch thrown by gripping the ball either along or across the seams.

**season** The days from Apr. (now, late Mar.) to early Oct. when major-league teams play out their regularly scheduled games. **1st Use.** 1880. (*Brooklyn Daily Eagle,* July 22; Edward J. Nichols).

**season ticket** A seat, usually a box seat, bought by an individual or corporation for every home game. The ticket is only good for the regular season but it usually entitles its owner to an option to buy that seat or one like it for postseason play should the home team make it to the playoffs. In 1934, the Cincinnati Reds was the first team to offer season-long ticket plans to fans (Donald Dewey & Nicholas Acocella, *Encyclopedia of Major League Baseball Teams,* 1993). **1st Use.** 1870. "There are one hundred and fifty honorary members, who . . . get a season ticket" (*Lakeside Monthly;* David Shulman).

**seat-boomer** Slang syn. of *home run.*

**seats** Where spectators sit; e.g., "Swing for the seats."

**Seattle Mariners** The name of the American League West Division franchise in Seattle, Wash. Formed in 1977, the Mariners was the second American League expansion team to locate in Seattle (after the Pilots in 1969). The name was suggested in a newspaper contest. The team is often referred to as the *M's.*

**Seattle Pilots** The name of the American League expansion team established in Seattle, Wash., in 1969. It slid into quick bankruptcy and moved to Milwaukee the following year where it survives as the Brewers.

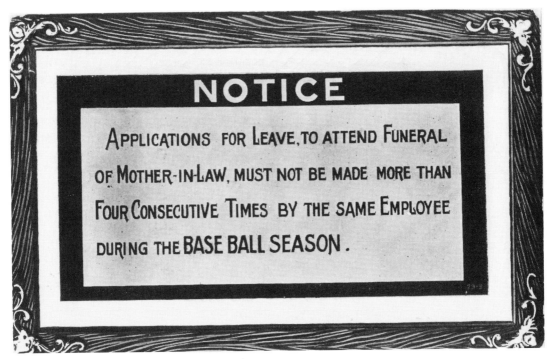

*Season.*

**second 1.** *n.* Short for *second base.* **1st Use.** 1862. (Chadwick Scrapbooks clipping, Aug. 3; Edward J. Nichols). **2.** *n.* The second inning. **3.** *adv.* Said of the second position in the batting order; e.g., "Smith is batting second."

**second bagger** Syn. of *second baseman.*

**second base 1.** The base located 90 feet from first base on the opposite corner of the infield diamond from home plate; the halfway point on the trip around the bases. Abbrev. *2B.* Syn. *second,* 1; *keystone,* 1; *keystone bag; keystone sack; middle bag; middle station; midway; second station.* **1st Use.** 1845. (Knickerbocker Rules). **2.** The defensive position given to the player who normally stands to the first base side of second base. Abbrev. *2B.* Syn. *second,* 1.

**second baseman** One of two defensive infield players (the other being the shortstop) who covers second base. As seen from the plate, the second baseman is normally positioned to the right of the shortstop and to the left of the first baseman. He normally covers first base on a bunt and is likely to be involved when a ball is being relayed in from the outfield. Abbrev. *2B.* Syn. *second bagger; second sacker; keystoner.* **1st Use.** 1880. (*New York Herald,* July 12; Edward J. Nichols).

**second division** *obs.* The bottom half of a league's standings (the last four teams in an eight-team league or the last five teams in a ten-team league) before 1969, when each of the two major leagues was broken into two Divisions. Compare *first division.* **1st Use.** 1907. (*Lajoie's Official Base Ball Guide;* Edward J. Nichols).

**second guess** To use hindsight in criticizing the manager or players either generally or in regard to specific decisions or plays.

**second guesser** One who is habitually criticizing the players and their manager for specific actions. **1st Use.** 1937. (*The Sporting News Record Book,* Edward J. Nichols).

**second half 1.** That part of a regular baseball season following the All-Star break in mid-July. Some pitchers are known as "second-half pitchers" because they do better in the second half of the season. Compare *first half,* 1. **2.** That part of the inning when the home team gets its turn at bat. Compare *first half,* 2. Syn. *bottom,* 1; *bottom half; home half; last half; lower half,* 1.

**second infield** Infield practice before the game, after the starting infielders have practiced.

**second-look free agency** Syn. of *new-look free agency.*

**second sacker** Syn. of *second baseman.* **1st Use.** 1911. (*Spalding's Official Base Ball Guide;* Edward J. Nichols).

**second season** The last two months of the 1981 season, which was bifurcated by a 50-day players' strike. It was a short season (48 to 54 games, depending on each team's remaining schedule) that began on Aug. 10. The term was applied laughingly by some.

**second station** Syn. of *second base.*

**second-story drive** A long, high fly ball.

**second string** *n.* The collection of players on a team who are not regularly given playing assignments. Compare *first string.* **1st Use.** 1912. (*New York Tribune,* Sept. 16; Edward J. Nichols).

**second-string** *adj.* Said of a player who is not given a regular playing assignment. **Etymology.** Borrowed from the realm of the bow and arrow. Alfred H. Holt (*Phrase and Word Origins,* 1961) discusses this term under the entry for "two strings to his bow." Holt writes: "The Elizabethans were very fond of this old archery figure for having something in reserve in case of accident. It is not often heard today, but its two children, first-string and second-string, are well known on every athletic field, though almost nobody thinks to pay homage to their sturdy old father."

**seed** A pitched or batted ball that is moving so fast that it appears smaller than it actually is. It is said to look like a seed; e.g., "They're having trouble with Smith throwing seeds at them." See also *pea.*

**seeing-eye ball** A batted ball that eludes fielders as if it had the power of vision. **1st Use.** 1974. "It's a ball that seems to find the right hole" (Floyd

Richards, WTIC radio broadcast, Hartford, Conn., Sept. 4). **Etymology.** From "Seeing Eye," the trademark used by the trainers of dogs for the blind.

**seeing-eye bat** The figurative bat of a hitter in a streak when seemingly routine grounders become hits; a bat that for a period seems to be able to connect with every pitched ball for a hit. **1st Use.** 1952. "I got a seeing-eye bat, one of those Murine jobs" (*San Francisco Examiner,* July 17; Peter Tamony). **Etymology.** From "Seeing Eye," the trademark used by the trainers of dogs for the blind.

**seeing-eye single** A single when the ball eludes fielders as if it had the power of vision. "Davey Concepcion . . . broke our hearts with a seeing-eye single up the middle that knotted the game up" (Bill Lee, *The Wrong Stuff,* 1984; Charles D. Poe). See also *ball with eyes on it.*

**seesaw game** A game in which runs are scored alternately by the teams so that first one team, then the other, is ahead. **1st Use.** 1892. (*Chicago Herald,* May 21; Edward J. Nichols).

**see the ball** To take a good swing at the ball because it looks bigger than normal. When hitters "see the ball" they say it "looks as big as a grapefruit, . . . a melon, . . . the moon. When they aren't seeing it, the ball looks like a pea or an aspirin tablet" (Bill Littlefield, *Baseball Days,* 1993). "I'm just trying to see the ball and hit it hard" (Brady Anderson, quoted in *Baltimore Sun,* Apr. 5, 1996).

**see the barrels** To experience a good omen. **Etymology.** According to Joseph McBride (*High and Inside,* 1980): "'Turkey Mike' Donlin of the New York Giants arrived for a game at the Polo Grounds in the early 1900s and noted a wagon load of empty barrels going by. On that day, he got three hits but on the following day he went hitless and blamed this on the fact that he had not seen any barrels before the game. His manager, the crafty John McGraw, hired a wagon loaded with barrels to circle the grounds every day and Donlin went on a hitting spree."

**seeya** A home run. **Etymology.** Asked about this term, Atlanta Braves pitcher Jim Nash (*The Sporting News,* Apr. 1, 1972) said: "Yep, that's what you say as it goes out of the park. Seeya!"

**sell 1.** To get a batter to go after a pitch; e.g., a pitcher may be said to be having a difficult time "selling" his curveball. **2.** For an umpire to convince the players of a close call by making his decision in an emphatic manner.

**sell out 1.** To throw a game. **1st Use.** 1874. (Chicago *Inter-Ocean,* July 4; Edward J. Nichols). **2.** To sell all available seats for a game.

**sellout crowd** A situation in which all available seats are sold and some fans may be standing.

**semi-pro** Said of the status of a player who is paid to play the game, but who must depend on another occupation to make a living. Sometimes the fee given to such a player is a mere token of $10 or $20. Semi-pro teams in the early part of the 20th century and through World War II were formed by firehouses, police departments, towns (the town's merchants supported teams), industrial leagues, independent players (play for whoever would pay), barnstorming teams (under contract), and professional Negro leagues (which were called "semi-pro" in the 1930s and 1940s). Syn. "semi-professional." **1st Use.** 1908. (*Spalding's Official Base Ball Guide;* Edward J. Nichols).

**semi-swing** A less-than-a-full cut at the ball. Complaining about the plethora of home runs hit early in the 1987 season, California Angels manager Gene Mauch commented: "Baseball's getting ridiculous. I've never seen such semi-, semi-, semi-swings, and the ball going out in my life." (*Iowa City Press-Citizen,* May 29, 1987).

**send 1.** To signal a runner to try to advance to the next base. **2.** To bat a ball, usually hard; e.g., "Smith sent one down to third." **1st Use.** 1899. (Burt L. Standish, *Frank Merriwell's Double Shot;* Edward J. Nichols).

**send down** To assign a major-league player to a minor-league team for further training and experience. Paul Wilborn (*Tampa Tribune,* Mar. 26, 1989) writes: "[To be] 'sent down' means going back to Indianapolis, or Albuquerque, or Jacksonville. It means another year of buses, tight budgets and no permanent address." Syn. *send out.*

**send in 1.** To replace a player in the lineup; e.g., "Smith sent Jones in to bat for Brown." **2.** To instruct a baserunner on third to go home; e.g., "The third base coach sent Wilson in."

**send out** Syn. of *send down*.

**send to the rubber** To put a relief pitcher into the game.

**send to the shelf** To strike out. The term comes from the notion of the batter going back to place his batting helmet on the shelf in the dugout.

**send to the showers 1.** To remove a player (esp. a pitcher) during the game, usually because of ineffectiveness. The player presumably heads for the clubhouse and a hot shower. Syn. *shower.* **Extended Use.** To remove from any activity. Here is an early example alluding to World War I: "No doubt Pershing and Foch has got the game sewed up tight or they would never take a chance and send me to the showers whilst they was more innin's to play" (H. C. Witwer, *A Smile a Minute,* 1919; David Shulman). **2.** To cause a pitcher to be replaced during a game; e.g., "Smith's home run sent Jones to the showers." Syn. *knock out of the box.* **1st Use.** 1914. (*New York Tribune,* Sept. 19; Edward J. Nichols).

**senior circuit** Traditional nickname for the *National League* because it is 25 years older than the American League. Compare *junior circuit.*

**Senior Professional Baseball Association** A short-lived (1989–90), eight-team Florida league of former major leaguers at least 35 years old (32 for catchers). Abbrev. *SPBA.*

**sensational** Said of a particularly great or outstanding fielding play; e.g., "Smith made a sensational catch against the right-field wall." The term was used frequently in the 1950s.

**September callup** A minor-league player brought up to a major-league club when his season is over and the major-league roster expands from 25 to 40 in Sept.

**series** A scheduled set of games between two teams. The term can refer to a regular group of games (e.g., a three-game series in Cleveland), a postseason playoff, or the World Series itself. **1st Use.** 1866. (*New York Herald,* June 17; Edward J. Nichols).

**Series, the** Short for *World Series.*

**Series burnout** A term used in the 1980s for the problems (injuries, contract disputes, quarrels, etc.) that can accrue to a team after it has been in the World Series. "Red Sox Still Smoking from Series Burnout" (*Washington Post* headline, Mar. 24, 1987).

**serve** *v.* To pitch. The term clearly implies the idea that the pitcher presents the ball to the batter in the way that a waiter serves a meal or a drink. "[Ken] Dixon Serves 3 Homers Before Orioles Fly Home" (*Washington Post* headline, Apr. 5, 1987). **1st Use.** 1913. (*Spalding's Official Base Ball Guide;* Edward J. Nichols). **Etymology.** Nichols identified the term as borrowed from tennis.

**serve us ball** [softball term] An early name for softball.

**session** Syn. of *inning,* 1. **1st Use.** 1908. (*Brooklyn Daily Eagle,* May 24; Edward J. Nichols).

**set 1.** *n.* The motionless position taken by a pitcher before beginning his delivery. A pitcher who holds his arms high above his head is said to have a "high set." **2.** *adj.* Established or fixed in place. "Our infield is pretty much set, it's just a matter of who's going to play" (Cincinnati Reds manager Pete Rose on the uncertainty of his lineup, quoted in *USA Today,* Jan. 1, 1987).

**set down** To retire one or more batters; e.g., "Smith set down the Cubs in order" or "Jones set down the top of the order." **1st Use.** 1912. (*New York Tribune,* Oct. 17; Edward J. Nichols).

**set one down** To retire a single batter.

**set oneself** For a fielder to get in position to throw the ball after fielding it.

**set position** One of two legal pitching positions, taken when the pitcher attempts to hold a runner on base. The pitcher faces the batter with his entire pivot foot on or in front of, and in contact with, the rubber and his stepping foot in front of the rubber, and holds the ball with both hands in front of his body and coming to a complete stop. [*Official Baseball Rules,* rule 8.01(b)]. From this position, the pitcher may deliver the ball to the batter, throw to a base, or step back and off the rubber with his pivot foot. Compare *windup position*. Syn. *stretch position*.

**set tag** A tag in which the fielder holds his glove with the ball in it on the ground in front of the base and waits for the runner to slide into it for an out.

**set the table 1.** To get on base to start an inning offensively; e.g., "At 39 he [Rickey Henderson] can still set the table—49 runs scored in 208 at-bats, a .430 on-base percentage, and 15 stolen bases in 16 attempts through Thursday" (*Milwaukee Journal Sentinel*, 1997). See also *table-setter*. **2.** To get a baserunner in scoring position. "The O's have the table set" (Jon Miller, radio broadcast, June 6, 1987). **3.** To serve as a setup man; e.g., "[Norm Charlton's] main job will be to set the table for [closer] Armando Benitez" (*Sports Illustrated*, Mar. 23, 1998).

**settle down** For a pitcher to regain control after several bad pitches; e.g., a pitcher who cannot "settle down" will begin to surrender runs. Often, the catcher will stroll out to the mound to "settle the pitcher down" by urging him to concentrate or take more time between pitches.

**settle under** For a fielder to get ready to catch a fly ball or pop-up.

**set up 1.** To insert a setup man before the closer; to get to a point in a game at which the setup man can enter. **2.** To lead a batter into thinking that there is a pattern to the pitches he is seeing and then deliver an unexpected pitch. "If you are the man with the ball, you are trying to 'set up' the man with the bat, meaning you set up his expectations or thinking and then try to take advantage of any preconceptions he has" (Tom Seaver, quoted in *New York Times*, May 7, 1986). **3.** To increase the chance to turn a double play by intentionally walking the batter with first base open and a runner on second base and/or third base. Jim Murray once observed: "Overlooked is the fact that this also sets up the three-run homer."

**setup man** A relief pitcher who tries to hold the lead, usually in the seventh or eighth innings, before turning the game over to the closer. Compare *short reliever*. Syn. *caddy*.

**7** The scorekeeper's designation for the left fielder.

**seven-inning pitcher** A starting pitcher who regularly requires relief help after about seven innings of work.

**seven-o'clock hitter** A player who hits well in batting practice and poorly during the game. See also *ten-o'clock hitter; one-o'clock hitter; two-o'clock hitter; five-o'clock hitter; six-o'clock hitter*. **Etymology.** From the fact that batting practice is likely to be in full swing at seven o'clock for a night game beginning at eight o'clock.

**seventh 1.** *n.* The seventh inning. **2.** *adv.* Said of the seventh position in the batting order; e.g., "Smith is batting seventh."

**seventh-inning stretch** A time-honored baseball custom in which the fans ritualistically stand and stretch before their team comes to bat in the seventh inning. This is done not only to relieve muscles that have begun to stiffen, but also to bring luck to one's team (perhaps from the association of the number 7 with good luck).

The simple ritual has different meanings to different people. Charles Einstein (*New York Times*, Apr. 21, 1985) described his experience: "My own initial contact with it came in the seventh inning of the first game I ever saw, as a 6-year-old taken to Fenway Park in Boston by my father. 'Did you know I was a magician?' he said. 'Stand up.' I stood up. So did all the other spectators, to the farthest cranny of the bleachers. Two minutes later, his voice even softer than before, my father said 'Sit down.' Everybody sat." Einstein added that his grandfather had done this to his father and that, a generation later, he had done it to his own son.

**Etymology/1st Use.** The origin of the custom is probably lost in the earliest days of the game. Baseball historian Dan Daniel is quoted by Zander Hollander (*Baseball Lingo*, 1967): "It probably originated as an expression of fatigue and tedium, which seems to explain why the stretch comes late in the game instead of at the halfway point."

The earliest reference that has surfaced appears in an 1869 letter from Harry Wright of the Cincinnati Red Stockings to a friend: "The spectators all arise between halves of the seventh inning, extend their legs and arms and sometimes walk about. In so doing they enjoy the relief afforded by relaxation from a long posture upon hard benches." David Shulman found this example by Christy Mathewson (*Won in the Ninth,* 1910): "In the stand-up session (Oh yes! seventh inning), however, the tonsorial artists made the Lowell hair stand up."

The most popular story of its origin is much more colorful. It was created in 1910 when President William Howard Taft, on a visit to Pittsburgh, went to a baseball game and stood up to stretch during the seventh inning. The crowd, thinking the Chief Executive was about to leave, stood up out of respect for the office.

Another story has been published several times. This incident occurred in 1882 at Manhattan College in New York City during a game between the college and a semipro club called the New York Metropolitans. According to a Manhattan College press release on file at the National Baseball Library and Archives in Cooperstown, N.Y., the inventor of the ritual was Brother Jasper, the school's first "moderator of athletics" and source of the Manhattan "Jaspers" nickname. Quoting from the college's news release:

"Whenever there was a home game, the entire student body marched to the field and stayed in a section of the stands. Brother Jasper, since he was both the coach and the Prefect of Discipline, had to watch both the players on the field and the students in the stands. Before each game, he sharply admonished the students not to leave their seats or move about until the game was over and they were ready to return to the college for the evening meal. Then, the good Brother went down to the bench to direct the play of the team. . . .

"Then, on a hot sticky day in the spring of 1882, Manhattan was playing the Metropolitans. . . . The game, it turned out, was a long, drawn-out affair. As the game passed the mid-way mark, Brother Jasper noticed the youngsters in the stands were getting restless and unruly. So as the team came to bat in the seventh inning, he went over to the stands and told his charges to stand, stretch and move about for a minute or two. This eased the tension and unrest, and so Brother Jasper repeated it in the next few games. . . .

"Soon the student body made it a practice 'to give it the old seventh inning stretch.' Since Man-

hattan played many of its games in the old Polo Grounds, the seventh inning stretch passed along to the Giant fans and eventually throughout the world of baseball, the unintentional invention of Brother Jasper."

Despite the claims of this story, the term itself may not have come along until much later. Edward J. Nichols traces it back no further than 1920 (*New York Times,* Oct. 10).

**sew up** To score the winning run; e.g., "Smith's homer in the bottom of the ninth sewed up the game."

**SF** Scorecard and box score abbrev. for *sacrifice fly.*

**SH** Scorecard and box score abbrev. for *sacrifice hit.*

**shackle** To pitch effectively; to keep opposing batters from making hits; to *handcuff,* 3.

**shade** 1. For an outfielder to move slightly toward the part of the field where the batter is expected to hit the ball; e.g., "Smith shaded to the left when Jones came to bat." 2. For the shortstop to move a little closer to third base, or the second baseman to move a little closer to first base, in anticipation of where the batter is expected to hit the ball; e.g., "Shortstop Smith shaded in the hole for Jones, a right-handed batter." 3. To win by one run; e.g., "The Orioles shaded the Indians, 4–3."

**shadow** To remain close to a base for defensive reasons; e.g., "Smith shadowed the bag to remain close to the baserunner."

**shadow ball** 1. A crowd-pleasing pantomime stunt in which a team plays without the benefit of a ball. It calls for a lot of action, including brilliant leaping catches. Connie Johnson (*Baltimore Sun,* June 27, 1982) said that Satchel Paige threw the ball so fast that it seemed like he was playing shadow ball. Johnson recalled saying to himself: "They're not supposed to play 'shadow ball' until the fourth inning. Was Satch playing 'shadow ball' already?" 2. A metaphor for the Negro leagues. Ken Burns underscored the term by subtitling the "Fifth Inning" of *Baseball* (PBS television series, 1994) "Shadow Ball." Steve Wulf (*Sports Illustrated,* Sept. 19, 1994) commented: "On one level, shadow ball was the amazingly realistic pantomime of baseball—without the ball—often performed by Negro leaguers before their games. But it is also a metaphor for the black baseball that shadowed the segregated major leagues."

**shag** To chase and catch fly balls as a part of batting practice; to retrieve foul balls. "Dipsy Ruggles, our first baseman, wore sneakers instead of cleats and was able to shag foul balls over the ledge with the grace of a mountain sheep, but then he would fall down running bases" (John Gould, *Christian Science Monitor*, Apr. 26, 1985). **1st Use.** 1911. "Gradually, however, I became interested in it, and before long, I was allowed to stand behind the catcher when the Factoryville team was playing, and 'shag' foul balls, or carry the bats or the water" (Carl H. Claudy, *St. Nicholas Magazine*, Apr.–Oct.; David Shulman). **Etymology.** The term appears to have begun as "shack," which was a variation on "shake" (as in, to "shake it"), which became "shag." **Extended Use.** To chase and retrieve, such as shagging golf or tennis balls.

**shagger** [softball term] A youngster who is hired to retrieve over-the-fence home runs in slow pitch softball tournaments and bring them back for reuse.

**shake off** *v.* For a pitcher to indicate his refusal to deliver the type of pitch called for by the catcher; to veto a pitch. The term is so called because the pitcher commonly shakes his head from side to side to clearly indicate that he will not throw the pitch called for and wants a new signal. Some pitchers shake off a sign with another gesture such as a move of the glove rather than the head. Syn. *throw off.* **1st Use.** 1932. (*Baseball Magazine*, Oct.; Edward J. Nichols).

**shake-off** *n.* The act of indicating a refusal from a pitcher to a catcher who has called for a specific pitch. Shake-offs underscore a difference in approach between the two.

**shake the catcher around** For a pitcher to shake off all the signs and return to the original sign. Joe Garagiola (*Baseball is a Funny Game*, 1960) explained: "A pitcher does that to confuse the hitter as to what the pitcher is going to throw."

**shake the jinx** To win a game after several defeats.

**shakeup** A rearrangement of team personnel to obtain improved play. **1st Use.** 1902. (*Sporting Life*, Apr. 26; Edward J. Nichols).

**shaky start** A bad beginning for a pitcher.

**shallow 1.** *adj.* Said of that part of the outfield closest to the infield; e.g., Dom DiMaggio played a "shallow center field" or "Smith hit a pop fly into shallow right." Compare *deep*, 2. **2.** *adv.* Close to home plate; e.g., the infield is playing "shallow" to cut off a run on a ground ball. Compare *deep*, 1.

**shank 1.** *v.* To hit the ball off the handle of the bat. **2.** *n.* A ball hit off the handle of the bat.

**sharpen one's spikes** To strongly imply that one is preparing to injure another player with the aid of spikes. The term can also be defined in the same manner as did Hugh S. Fullerton (*American Magazine*, June 1912): "The pretense of a player to sharpen the triangular toe and heel plates he wears on his shoes, is a threat to 'cut his way around,' or spike certain antagonists if they attempt to stop or touch him. Chiefly a form of braggadocio, and seldom carried into effect."

Legend has it that Ty Cobb was a spike sharpener, but he claimed otherwise. He insisted (*The Saturday Evening Post*, 1958) that it was two other players ("neither of them regulars") who sharpened their spikes to unnerve the New York Yankees. Prescott Sullivan (*San Francisco Examiner*, June 12, 1958; Peter Tamony) quoted Cobb: "These two fellows decided to practice some amateur psychology. So . . . as the Yankees came on the field, the two sat on the bench filing their spikes. Neither of them played in the game. But the press had to have a 'name' to go with the story, so they chose 'Cobb.'"

**sharpshooter 1.** An effective *place hitter;* a hitter who can put the ball where he wants it to go. **1st Use.** 1912. (*New York Tribune*, Sept. 21; Edward J. Nichols). **2.** A pitcher with good control.

**shave 1.** *v.* To pitch high and inside; to brush a batter back as if the ball was being used to shave the batter's face. **2.** *v.* To pitch to the edges of the strike zone; e.g., "Smith shaved the corners with his breaking pitches." **3.** *n.* A ball that is pitched close to a batter's face. "Tornay walked several steps towards the mound and verbally challenged the statuesque Oakland righthander when he was treated to a 'shave' in the ninth inning" (*San Francisco News,* July 31, 1953; Peter Tamony).

**she** *n.* An injured player, esp. one who may be favoring himself. **Usage Note.** The term is a derogatory remark that somehow equates being or playing injured with femininity or hints that someone who cannot tolerate pain is effeminate.

**Shea Stadium** Home field of the New York Mets since 1964. It is located in Flushing Meadows, Queens, and is named for attorney William Shea, who headed the special committee that successfully brought National League baseball back to New York after the city's loss of the Dodgers and Giants in 1958.

**sheeny mike** *arch.* A *Texas Leaguer.* **Usage Note.** "Sheeny" is a highly derogatory term for a Jew. Whether, or how, this fits into the etymology of the term is not as important as the fact that it is regarded as highly offensive. Given this, however, one possible etymological link is that "sheeny" implies a miser (Harold Wentworth & Stuart Berg Flexner, *Dictionary of American Slang,* 1960). The hit could be aptly described as miserly, a "cheap" hit. **1st Use.** 1937. (*New York Daily News,* Jan. 31; Edward J. Nichols).

**sheepherder** An umpire.

**shell 1.** To bat so well and so hard that the pitcher must be removed, as if he had been attacked ("shelled") by a barrage of hard-hit baseballs (also known as rockets); e.g., "The Marlins shelled Smith in his last two outings" or "The Cubs shelled Jones off the hill." **2.** To defeat a team by many runs; e.g., "The Braves shelled the Reds, 14–0."

**shellack** To defeat soundly.

**shelling** The act of getting many hits. "Gooden Rebounds in Scoreless Stint—Makes Up For Shelling" (*New York Times* headline, Mar. 14, 1987).

**shelve** To take a player out of action; to put a player on the disabled list. "White Sox Shelve [Neil] Allen" (*Washington Post* headline, Apr. 22, 1987).

**shepherd** *arch.* The manager of a baseball team.

**Shibe Park** A major-league ballpark from 1909 to 1970 in Philadelphia. At various times it was the home field for the American League Athletics and the National League Phillies. It was named for Ben Shibe, stockholder in the Athletics, and known as Connie Mack Stadium from 1953 to 1970. It was damaged in a 1971 fire and torn down in 1976.

**shift 1.** *v.* To change fielding position; to move defensive players from their traditional positions in the field to compensate for a batter's proclivities and/or to be in a better position for a double play. Fielders generally shift to their left for left-handed batters (because they tend to hit in that direction) and vice versa. **2.** *n.* The act of moving players for defensive reasons, often phrased as "the shift is on," usually accomplished by moving outfielders to areas where a hitter is apt to hit the ball. Occasionally, a radical shift is named for the player the shift is created to defend against, such as the *Williams shift,* employed to stop Ted Williams. A more recent example: "The Boggs Shift Works" (*Boston Globe* headline, July 30, 1988). In this case the Milwaukee Brewers brought center fielder Robin Yount into the infield to defend against Wade Boggs (then hitting .359) with two runners on base (Boggs then struck out). **3.** *v.* For the catcher to move in front of the path of a pitched ball so that he will be able to maintain his balance for catching and throwing. Bob Bennett (*On the Receiving End: The Catcher's Guidebook,* 1982) wrote: "In shifting, the basic idea is to step into the path of the ball. If the ball is thrown to the left, the step should be to the left with the left foot. If the ball is to the right, a step to the right should be taken with the right foot."

**shifter** A manager of a baseball team. **1st Use.** 1908. "Manager [John] McGraw, always a quick shifter, yanked him at once and substituted Leon Ames" (*Cincinnati Enquirer,* May 17, 1908; Peter Morris).

**shillelagh** The baseball bat as an instrument of power. Syn. "shillalah." **1st Use.** 1937. (*Philadelphia Record,* Oct. 11; Edward J. Nichols). **Etymology.** From the Irish fighting club or cudgel.

**shinburger 1.** A leg bruise that is commonly inflicted by a bad hop; a barked shin. **2.** A ball batted through the pitcher's box that ricochets off his shins.

**shine ball** A ball that the pitcher renders esp. smooth by rubbing it hard on his glove or clothing or doctoring it with a foreign substance such as talcum powder. Such shining or polishing, which helps the ball curve as it slips from the fingers more easily when thrown, has been illegal since 1920. Eddie Cicotte is said to have developed the shine ball in 1915 when he discovered that the ball did funny things after he rubbed it to a shine on his uniform. Hod Eller, who won 20 games for Cincinnati's 1919 world championship team, was known as a "shine-ball pitcher." Syn. *shiner.* **1st Use.** 1917. (*New York Times,* Oct. 6; Edward J. Nichols). **Etymology.** Gerald Secor Couzens (*A Baseball Album,* 1980) reports: "Probably invented by Dave Danforth in 1915 while pitching for Louisville in the American Association. Oil was used on the field to control the dust problem, and the innovative Danforth discovered that by rubbing the oil-and-dirt-covered ball on his trouser leg the ball became smooth and shiny and hopped when he pitched it."

**shiner** Syn. of *shine ball.*

**shin guard** A piece of protective (molded plastic) equipment, strapped to the leg, worn by catchers, plate umpires, and some batters to prevent injury from foul tips and pitches in the dirt. **1st Use.** 1908. (*Spalding's Base Ball Record;* Edward J. Nichols). **Etymology.** Invented and first donned by New York Giants catcher Roger Bresnahan in 1907, according to most accounts. However, Philadelphia Phillies catcher Charley "Red" Dooin claims (*The Sporting News,* Mar. 5, 1936) he was the first catcher to use shin guards, under his stockings, in 1906: made of rattan at first, he switched to papier-mâché. Bresnahan got the idea from Dooin and in 1907, was the first to wear them outside the stockings.

**shin-skimmer** A hard-hit ground ball. **1st Use.** 1908. (*New York Evening Journal,* Aug. 21; Edward J. Nichols).

**ship** To trade a player; e.g., "The Padres shipped Ozzie Smith to St. Louis for Garry Templeton."

*Shin guards. New York Giants catcher Roger Bresnahan.*

**ShO** Scorecard and box score abbrev. for *shutout,* 1.

**shoehorn** To enter a relief pitcher into the game just to pitch to one batter, usually with runners on base and the game on the line.

**shoemaker** *arch.* A player who is awkward, but not necessarily ineffective, at his position. **Etymology.** The term has drawn many comments along the lines of the following (Herbert Simons, *Baseball Magazine,* 1943): "We've always considered that usage a libel against our many friends of the bootmaking profession, who are some of the most polished artisans we know." One can only suggest that the baseball usage might derive from the image of a shoemaker bent over at his workbench. Edward J. Nichols (*An Historical Dictionary of Baseball Terminology,* Ph.D. dissertation, 1939) traces it to a player who makes frequent errors and "boots" the ball. **1st Use.** 1907. (*New York Evening Journal,* May 2; Edward J. Nichols).

**shoestring catch** A catch made by a running fielder just before the ball hits the ground. It is caught in the vicinity of the player's feet (or shoestrings) and can be quite spectacular to witness. "He took the ball off his shoe-strings and without apparently slackening his pace hurled the sphere on a line to third for an easy double killing" (*National Police Gazette*, Jan. 14, 1928; Peter Tamony). **1st Use.** 1912. (*New York Tribune*, Oct. 12; Edward J. Nichols). **Extended Use.** A similar catch in other games, such as football.

**shoot 1.** *v.* To throw a baseball hard. See also *rifle, 2; gun, 3.* **2.** *n.* A 19th-century term for a type of curveball. See *inshoot; double shoot; offshoot; outshoot; down shoot; upshoot.* **1st Use.** 1887. (*Harper's Weekly*, Sept. 10; Edward J. Nichols).

**shooting star** Syn. of *revolver.*

**shoot out** For an umpire to call a player out by pointing to him as if he were being shot with a revolver. This unorthodox signal became the trademark of umpire Ron Luciano, who came upon it accidentally during the 1972 season. Luciano (*The Umpire Strikes Back,* 1982) wrote he was having a difficult time calling Amos Otis safe in close plays during the latter's first years with the Kansas City Royals. At the start of the 1972 season, he consciously worked on calling Otis safe, but soon found he had overdone it again and was now having a hard time calling him out. Finally, Otis hit into a play in which he was out by a full 15 feet and Luciano was so pleased that he pointed his index finger at him and cocked his thumb. The rest of the Royals began yelling "Shoot him, shoot him!" Luciano realized what he had done and played it to its conclusion. He pretended to shoot him and then as he brought his hand back he blew imaginary smoke away from his index finger and pretended to put his hand in a holster.

**shoot the ball** To hit the ball through the infield to the opposite field; e.g., for a right-handed batter to hit (aim) the ball between first base and second base.

**shop** To offer a player in a possible trade to ascertain his value; e.g., "The team let it be known that Smith was available by shopping him around the league."

**short 1.** *n.* Short for *shortstop,* 1. **1st Use.** 1858. (*Brooklyn Daily Times,* June 18; Edward J. Nichols).

**2.** *adj.* Relatively close to the plate; e.g., the infielder played "short" in anticipation of a bunt. **3.** *adj.* Said of the area in the outfield behind one of the bases and in front of the usual playing position of the outfielder; e.g., "short center" is the area behind second base and in front of the center fielder. **4.** [softball term] *adj.* Said of a pitch that drops in front of a batter in slow pitch softball, analogous to "low" in baseball or fast pitch softball. Compare *deep,* 5.

**short-arm 1.** *adj.* Relating to a throw made with the arm close to the body as opposed to a full throw with the arm extended. Short-arm throws are made for short distances, such as between infielders. **2.** *v.* To throw with the arm close to, rather than extended from, the body. **3.** *v.* To pitch without windup, with an abbreviated delivery.

**short center 1.** The area behind second base and in front of the center fielder. **2.** [softball term] The tenth or extra player in Chicago-style 16-inch softball, so called because he or she plays in what can be best described as short center field just outside the infield.

**shortened game 1.** A game in which the home team is winning and does not need to bat for all or a fraction of its half of the ninth inning. **2.** A game called by the umpire for whatever reason. If a game is called before it becomes a regulation game, it is declared "No Game" and not considered a shortened game. See also *called game.*

**shortened season** A baseball season other than a full one; e.g., the 1981 season which was curtailed by the players' strike.

**shorten up 1.** To move one's hands up on the bat handle to get more control on the swing, esp. when the batter has two strikes against him. **2.** To move one's hands along the bat when preparing to bunt.

**short fastball** A fastball lacking some velocity.

**short field 1.** The area between second base and third base where the shortstop normally plays. **2.** The playing territory behind the infield. **1st Use.** 1854. (Knickerbocker Rules; Edward J. Nichols).

**short fielder 1.** *obs.* Syn. of *shortstop,* 2. **2.** [softball term] The *rover* in slow pitch softball, usually positioned in the shallow part of the outfield.

**short fuse** The temperament of an umpire who is quick to eject a player or manager from a game. **Etymology.** From the image of an explosive equipped with a fuse that makes it blow up quickly. It links the human blowup (temper) with the blowup of dynamite and other explosives.

**short-handed rule** [softball term] A provision in slow pitch softball that allows a player to leave the game without causing the game to end.

**short-hop** *v.* **1.** For a fielder to snatch the ball just as it bounces off the ground; e.g., "Third baseman Smith short-hopped the grounder and threw to first for the out." **2.** For a fielder to throw a ball that hits the ground just before another fielder catches it; e.g., "Third baseman Smith short-hopped two throws to first."

**short hop** *n.* **1.** A batted or thrown ball that hits the ground and is caught low before it can take a sharp, unpredictable bounce. **2.** A ball that seems to die on the first bounce.

**short leg** *arch.* A derogatory term for a player who lets his teammates go after balls that he himself should get. **1st Use.** 1937. (*New York Daily News*, Feb. 14; Edward J. Nichols).

**short man** **1.** Syn. of *short reliever.* **2.** The infielder who backs up the cutoff man in a relay play, in the event of an overthrow.

**short park** A ballpark with a notably short outfield fence. "Brewers to Cancel Short-Park Solons" (*San Francisco Chronicle*, Aug. 22, 1975) was the headline for an article about the Milwaukee Brewers canceling their agreement with the minor-league Sacramento Solons because the short left-field fence at the team's park "had impeded the development of many promising young players."

**short porch** A right- or left-field wall, barrier, or upper deck that is unusually near home plate; a friendly target to a batter. The term derives from the design of older ballparks, which often featured overhanging roofs that made outfield spectators look like they were sitting on a porch. "If the porch is close to home plate like left field at Fenway Park or right field in Detroit's Tiger Stadium, it's a 'short porch' and hitters 'love' it" (Tim Horgan, *Baseball Digest*, June 1964).

**short relief** **1.** The replacement of a pitcher late in the game. **2.** A period of relief pitching, usually two innings or less, late in the game.

**short reliever** A relief pitcher who works in short relief. Because of the brevity of the assignment, a short reliever may appear in several consecutive games. Occasionally a short reliever is called on to face only one or a few batters in one inning. Compare *long reliever; middle reliever; setup man.* Syn. *short man.*

**short route** The relatively few stops taken by a player with little or no minor-league experience before he reaches the major leagues.

**short score** The results of a game that show only the total runs, hits, and errors for each team, as opposed to the box score or inning-by-inning tabulation.

**short-season league** A minor league that has a significantly shorter season than that of the major leagues.

**shortstop** **1.** The infield position that is normally to the left of second base as viewed from home plate. By most accounts, it is the most physically demanding position in the field. Abbrev. *SS* or "ss." Originally spelled "short stop." Syn. *short,* 1. **1st Use.** 1859. "Short stop is . . . [Charles S. De Bost's] post next to that of catcher" (report of the match between the Empire and Knickerbocker clubs, *New York Clipper*, Aug. 27; Tom Shieber). **Etymology.** The term is clearly a blend of "short" and "stop," probably created to better describe the defensive function of the job performed in the short field. Dr. Daniel L. Adams, former Knickerbocker Base Ball Club player, recalled in an interview (*The Sporting News*, Feb. 29, 1896): "I used to play shortstop, and I believe I was the first to occupy that place, as it had formerly been left uncovered." John Thorn (*Total Baseball*, 3rd ed., 1993) noted that the position was created in 1849 or 1850 by Adams "not to bolster the infield but to assist in relays from the outfield. The early Knickerbocker ball was so light that it could not be thrown even 200 feet; thus the need for a short fielder to send the ball in to the pitcher's point." **2.** The player who plays the shortstop position. The shortstop and the second baseman together cover second base. A main element of the short-stop's job is to create double plays. Abbrev. *SS* or "ss." Syn. *short fielder,* 1.

**short toss** A throw of limited distance without velocity. See also *soft toss.*

**short windup** The abbreviated windup used by a pitcher when there are one or more baserunners. The arm movement is condensed to give the runner(s) less time in which to steal.

**shot 1.** An especially hard-hit ball, usually a line drive. **1st Use.** 1880. (*New York Herald,* Aug. 20; Edward J. Nichols). **2.** A home run; e.g., "Smith hit a three-run shot." **3.** A strong throw. **1st Use.** 1910. (*Baseball Magazine,* Apr.; Edward J. Nichols). **4.** A chance to play in a game. "He'll get a shot, whether it's a one-inning shot, two-inning shot or three-inning shot" (Baltimore Orioles manager Ray Miller, on pitcher Rick Krivda, quoted in *Baltimore Sun,* Mar. 11, 1998).

**shotgun** A powerful throwing arm. See also *rifle,* 1. Syn. *gun,* 1; *slingshot,* 1; "shotgun arm." **1st Use.** 1937. (*New York Daily News,* Jan. 17, Edward J. Nichols).

**"Shot Heard 'Round the World"** The famous three-run home run hit by Bobby Thomson off Ralph Branca on Oct. 3, 1951, to win the pennant for the New York Giants in the ninth inning of the third game of the playoffs against the Brooklyn Dodgers. Thomson has been called "The Scot Heard 'Round the World." See also *Miracle of Coogan's Bluff.* **Etymology.** From a line by Ralph Waldo Emerson which he wrote as part of his "Hymn Sung at the Completion of the Battle Monument, Concord" (July 4, 1837). He used the term to describe the beginning of the American Revolution: "Here once the embattled farmers stood,/And fired the shot heard round the world."

**shove along** *n./arch.* The act of stealing a base; e.g., "Smith did the shove along in the fourth inning." **1st Use.** 1907. (*New York Evening Journal,* May 2; Edward J. Nichols).

**shovel** To toss the ball underhand for a short distance. The motion suggests throwing dirt with a shovel, and it is what the shortstop often does when he throws the ball to the second baseman on a force play.

**shovel throw** A short, underhand toss. "Chambers . . . made a backhanded pickup and shovel throw to Wheelrock, covering, to nab Samba" (Michael Schiffer, *Ballpark,* 1982).

**Show, the** Syn. of *major leagues.* In 1995, Major League Baseball adopted the slogan "Welcome to the Show." Sometimes spelled "the show."

**showboat 1.** *v.* To show off. **2.** *n.* A player who is clearly playing to the crowd with a fancy style; an exhibitionist. "A player who never catches a ball with two hands that he can catch with one" (Fresco Thompson, *Every Diamond Doesn't Sparkle,* 1964). "The term 'showboat' is synonymous with exhibitionism in baseball" (Bob Feller, *Strikeout Story,* 1947). See also *cap-tipper.* **1st Use.** 1942. "There will be an all-star team of 'showboats' in the Pacific Coast League" (*San Francisco News,* July 20, 1942; Peter Tamony). **Etymology.** An article on Peanuts Nyasses (*Liberty,* Sept. 19, 1942) suggests that this well-known black player and baseball clown helped popularize the term in the context of baseball. The article explains that Nyasses dubbed himself the "Showboat King of Baseball."

**showboat catch** Syn. of *circus catch.*

**shower** To remove from the game; to *send to the showers.* "Now they'll shower him" (Al Michaels, on a pitcher about to be removed from the game, ABC telecast, Oct. 12, 1986).

**showers** The figurative place where a player (esp. a pitcher) goes after being removed during a game. Fred Schwed Jr. (*How to Watch a Baseball Game,* 1957) relates a story, which had been told to him by Charles Einstein, that underscores the extent to which this meaning of "showers" has become unique to America. "It seems that a number of years ago another reporter took Fred Perry of England, then the best tennis player in the world, to his first American baseball game. Mr. Perry was suspicious of the whole affair, and when in the second inning the losing pitcher was shelled off the mound, and started his lugubrious trudge over second base and the outfield, Perry asked, 'Where is he going?' The reporter said, 'To the showers.' 'It's a hot day,' said Perry, 'I imagine he will feel famously when he comes back.'"

**Show-Me Series** The 1985 World Series, which pitted the Kansas City Royals against the St. Louis Cardinals, two teams from Missouri, the Show-Me State. See also *I-70 Series*.

**show spikes** To slide into a base with one spiked foot held high enough to intimidate the fielder covering the base. **1st Use.** 1928. (*New York Times,* Oct. 6, Edward J. Nichols).

**show up 1.** To humiliate an opponent; e.g., to steal a base when leading by 12 runs. Ira Berkow (*New York Times,* Aug. 14, 1986) described a fight between the St. Louis Cardinals and San Francisco Giants: "The fight started after [Cardinals outfielder] Vince Coleman was first brushed back with a pitch and then hit with a pitch on the foot in the seventh inning. It was apparently intentional. Coleman had stolen second and third in the fifth inning, with the score 10–2, and the Giants felt, according to [manager] Roger Craig, that Coleman was trying to 'show up' the Giants—one of the cotton-headed clichés that abound in baseball." **2.** To humiliate an umpire. "[Catcher Jim] Hegan could tell you off pretty good. But he never turned around to show you up. He always said it over his shoulder while he was down in his crouch." (Bill McKinley, quoted in Larry R. Gerlach, *Men in Blue,* 1980).

**show your colors** To display courage.

**shut down 1.** For a pitcher to dominate the opposing team. **2.** To bench a player temporarily because of injury; e.g., "The manager shut down Smith because of his shoulder bursitis."

**shut off** To defeat; to allow the opposing team few or no runs. "Astros Shut Off Braves" (*Buffalo News* headline, Sept. 28, 1986).

**shut out** *v.* To prevent one's opponents from scoring. The term is normally used to describe a pitcher who deprives the other team of scoring any runs. Syn. *skunk,* 1. **1st Use.** 1881. (*New York Herald,* July 17; Edward J. Nichols). **Etymology.** A borrowing from horse racing where it has long

referred to a bettor who arrives at the window too late to wager a bet and is "shut out." **Extended Use.** To prevent scoring in other endeavors, from football to politics.

**shutout 1.** *n.* A game in which the losing team does not score. It is a particular achievement that is credited to the winning pitcher (if he pitches a complete game). Shutouts are often described by the number of hits made by the losers; e.g., a "two-hit shutout." The lifetime leader in pitching shutouts is Washington Senators hurler Walter Johnson, with 110. Abbrev. *ShO; SO,* 2. **1st Use.** 1889. (*Trenton Times,* July 18; Edward J. Nichols). **2.** *adj.* Describing a period in which there are no runs; e.g., three innings of "shutout relief."

**shut the door** To pitch exceptionally well in either stopping or preventing a rally; to retire the side. "You've got to tip your hat to him [Bret Saberhagen]. He threw an outstanding game. He shut the door." (Al Nipper, quoted in *USA Today,* Apr. 17, 1986). See also *close the door.* Syn. *slam the door.*

**Shuttle Series** The 1986 World Series between the Boston Red Sox and the New York Mets, representing two cities linked by commuter air-shuttle routes. Both shuttle operators (Eastern and Pan American) attempted to capitalize on the nickname.

**shuttle system** The process of moving players back and forth between the major leagues and the minor leagues.

**side 1.** One of the two teams in a game. When a half inning is over, it is common to say that the "side has been retired." **1st Use.** 1864. (*Brooklyn Daily Eagle,* Sept. 9; Edward J. Nichols). **2.** A location for a player not in the game; e.g., "Smith threw on the side to test his arm."

**sidearm** Said of any delivery, pitch, or throw with a sweeping forward motion of the arm from the side of the body at or below shoulder level, more or less parallel with the ground. It is neither *overhand* nor *underhand.* Syn. *sidewheel.* **1st Use.** 1908. (*Baseball Magazine,* June; Edward J. Nichols).

**sidearmer** A pitcher who habitually throws from the sidearm position. Syn. *sidewheeler; sidewinder.*

**sideline** *v.* To remove a player temporarily from the lineup because of a minor injury or some other reason; e.g., "The team sidelined Smith for three days because of his twisted ankle."

**sidelines** *n.* A mythical location where a player is kept out of the game; a place literally outside the foul lines.

**side out** The situation when three players have been retired.

**sidewheel** Syn. of *sidearm*. **1st Use.** 1910. (*Baseball Magazine,* Dec.; Edward J. Nichols).

**sidewheeler** Syn. of *sidearmer.* Var. "sidewheel pitcher"; "side-wheeling pitcher." **1st Use.** 1911. (*Spalding's Official Base Ball Guide;* Edward J. Nichols).

**sidewinder** Syn. of *sidearmer.*

**siege gun** A strong, excellent player.

**sieve infield** A poor defensive infield; one with many "holes."

**sign 1.** *n.* A secret motion, gesture, or sound that conveys information, such as the flashing fingers of a catcher or a vocal communication by a coach. A catcher employs signs constantly in calling for specific pitches from the pitcher. A coach uses them to call for offensive plays, such as bunts and steals. "Giving, getting and carrying out signs win close games. Signs are given by word of mouth and movement." (Joe Cronin, quoted in *San Francisco News,* July 22, 1940; Peter Tamony). Syn. *signal,* 1; *wig-wag.* **1st Use.** 1888. "As to the question of 'signs.' Every battery, by which is meant a pitcher and catcher, must have a perfectly understood private code of signals, so that they may make known their intentions and wishes to another without at the same time apprising the opposing players. . . . Until within a few years this sign was always given by the pitcher, but now it is almost the universal practice for the catcher to give it to the pitcher, and if the latter doesn't want to pitch the ball asked for he changes the sign by a shake of the head." (John Montgomery Ward, *Base-Ball: How to Become a Player;* Peter Morris). **2.** *v.* To send a signal. "I wanted to give him a spitter but Schalk signs me for the fast one and I give it to him"

(Ring W. Lardner, *You Know Me Al,* 1914). **3.** *v.* To put one's signature on a contract. **1st Use.** 1887. (*Base Ball Tribune,* May 23; Edward J. Nichols). **4.** *n.* One given to signing an autograph or contract; e.g., "Smith was a tough sign."

**signal 1.** *n.* Syn. of *sign,* 1. **1st Use.** 1888. (John Montgomery Ward, *Base-Ball: How to Become a Player;* Skip McAfee). **2.** *v.* To make a sign.

**sign a pass** To issue a base on balls. Syn. "sign a ticket." **1st Use.** 1912. (*New York Tribune,* Sept. 6; Edward J. Nichols).

**signing bonus** A *bonus* given to a player for agreeing to sign a contract with a team. The practice of offering signing bonuses was common up to 1965 and the first amateur player draft, created to end bidding wars that led to large bonuses. Young players are still paid signing bonuses and the amounts are not insignificant.

**sign stealing** A tactic by which a team spots and deciphers its opponent's signs. For this reason, teams work to keep their signs as cryptic and confusing as possible. With a runner at second base, the pitcher and catcher usually change signs because the catcher's signs to the pitcher are clearly visible to the batting team. Some have attached great significance to the practice. "Of all the skills wrapped up in the complex game of big-league baseball, none is practiced with more ingenuity and less publicity than the fine art of diamond larceny. From the days of the old Orioles to Durocher's Giants, sign-stealers have been surreptitiously deciding crucial ball games and winning world championships." (Martin Abramson, *The American Weekly,* June 5, 1955; Peter Tamony).

There are many stories that underscore the extensiveness of sign stealing. Tristram Potter Coffin (*The Old Ball Game,* 1971) insists: "The most famous is the one usually told about Charlie Dressen at a now half-forgotten All-Star Game. Supposedly the All-Stars were together before the game attempting to come up with a series of signals for the day. Dressen, who was a noted sign-stealer, is [thought] to have said, 'Forget it, I'll give each of you the ones used on your own team.'" A new wrinkle to the practice came into play in the 1997 season when it was claimed that the New York

Mets were using video cameras to steal signs, but no charges were filed and the league office took no action.

**Silver Bullets** The first all-women's professional baseball team. Formed in 1993 as the Colorado Silver Bullets, the team played its first guaranteed schedule of games in the Northern League. The team ceased play after the 1997 season because it was unable to find a sponsor after Coors Brewing Co. bowed out as chief sponsor.

**Silver Slugger Award** An award instituted in 1980 and given by Hillerich & Bradsby Co. (manufacturers of the Louisville Slugger bat) in conjunction with *The Sporting News* to the top hitters in both major leagues at their respective positions, including pitchers in the National League. The awards are chosen by managers and coaches.

**silver sombrero** A mythical award given to a batter who strikes out four times in a game. Syn. *golden sombrero.*

**simulated game** A routine in which a pitcher throws to a catcher as if he were pitching a real game. It is used for pitchers recovering from injury or coming off the disabled list. After throwing to three or more batters the pitcher takes about five minutes off to simulate the period when his team is at bat.

**simulated play-by-play** A broadcast that apes the live action of a real game. It can occur after the game or be created from telegraph or teletype reporting of a game in progress, or, as was common during the 1981 baseball strike, be of an imaginary or fantasy game. The process is also used to re-create games from the past.

**single 1.** *n.* A base hit on which the batter reaches first base safely. Abbrev. *1B*, 3. Syn. *one-base hit; one-bagger; one-sacker; bingle,* 1. **1st Use.** 1858. (Chadwick Scrapbooks; Edward J. Nichols). **2.** *v.* To hit a single; e.g., "Smith singled to center." **Etymology.** The term is used in cricket where it originated.

**Single A** Syn. of *Class A.*

**single elimination** [softball term] A tournament format in which one defeat eliminates a team from further play. It is the speediest way of reaching a champion, but is unpopular at the higher levels of the game (where the top team can be eliminated after a round or two). See also *round-robin; double elimination.* Syn. *straight elimination.*

**singleheader** A facetious name for one game of a day-night doubleheader with separate admissions.

**single in a run** To score a baserunner by hitting a single.

**singles hitter** A player who seldom hits a ball for extra bases. See also *parachute hitter.*

**singleton** A lone run scored in any inning.

**sinker 1.** A pitched ball that drops sharply as it nears the plate, making it nearly impossible to hit it in the air. It is a fastball that moves laterally and downward because it is delivered with a downward movement and an inward roll of the wrist. When thrown by a right-handed pitcher, the sinker breaks down and in to a right-handed batter and down and away to a left-handed batter. Syn. *drop,* 1; *sinkerball.* **1st Use.** 1937. (*Philadelphia Record,* Oct. 6; Edward J. Nichols). **2.** Syn. of *downer.* **3.** A batted ball that drops sharply, usually between the infield and the outfield. **1st Use.** 1928. "A sinker—a fly ball that has a back spin which causes it to sink to the ground quickly" (Babe Ruth, *Babe Ruth's Own Book of Baseball;* David Shulman).

**sinkerball** Syn. of *sinker,* 1.

**sinkerballer** A pitcher who is adept at throwing the sinker; e.g., Wilcy Moore, New York Yankees relief pitcher for the 1927 world championship team, who was one of the first sinkerballers, who are notorious for inducing batters to hit ground balls.

**sinking fastball** A pitch that behaves like a sinker but has the velocity of a fastball, often described in terms of its speed; e.g., "an 89-mph sinking fastball" (*Washington Post,* June 11, 1986).

**sinking liner** A line drive that drops suddenly in midflight.

**Sir Charles** The superb curveball thrown by Dwight Gooden (*Washington Post,* Oct. 19, 1987). See also *Uncle Charlie; Lord Charles.*

**sit dead-red** To wait for a fastball. "After a 1-0 count, I'm sitting dead-red, looking for a fastball

all the way" (Chipper Jones, quoted in *Baltimore Sun,* May 10, 1998).

**sit down 1.** For a pitcher to retire a batter; e.g., "Smith sat Jones down with a strikeout." **2.** To take a player out of the lineup; e.g., "The manager had no feelings about sitting down nonproductive players."

**sit in the catbird seat** To be in an advantageous position, such as a batter with a 3-0 count. See also *catbird seat.*

**sit on 1.** For a batter to anticipate or wait for a specific pitch. "I knew he [Eric Plunk] had to come after me. So, I was just sitting on his fastball." (Jeffrey Hammonds, quoted in *Baltimore Sun,* Sept. 16, 1997). **2.** For a team to protect a lead.

**sitting duck** A runner who is in a position to be put out by a wide margin by a defensive player; e.g., a baserunner who attempts to steal on a pitchout is usually a sitting duck. **Etymology.** From the long-established simile used to express an easy shot, "as easy as hitting a sitting duck."

**situational hitter** A hitter who can produce the type of hit needed for a given situation, such as a single or sacrifice fly with runners in scoring position or a home run to tie or win the game.

**6** The scorekeeper's designation for the shortstop.

**6-4-3** Scorecard notation for a double play in which the ball goes from the shortstop (6) to the second baseman (4) to the first baseman (3). It is the most common double play combination. After the 1988 Orioles had hit into double plays in 24 consecutive games, Tim Kurkjian of the *Baltimore Sun* wrote that manager Frank Robinson "manages Team 6-4-3." Compare *4-6-3.*

**600 Home Run Club** An imaginary and exclusive club with only three members: Hank Aaron, Babe Ruth, and Willie Mays, the only players to have hit 600 or more home runs.

**six-o'clock hitter** A player who hits well in batting practice and poorly during the game. See also *ten-o'clock hitter; one-o'clock hitter; two-o'clock hitter; five-o'clock hitter; seven-o'clock hitter.* **Etymol-**

ogy. From the fact that batting practice is likely to be in full swing at six o'clock for a night game beginning at seven o'clock or later. When day games were the norm, the six-o'clock hitter was likely to be called a "two-o'clock hitter."

**sixth 1.** *n.* The sixth inning. **2.** *adv.* Said of the sixth position in the batting order; e.g., "Smith is batting sixth."

**6-12 movement** The motion of a thrown ball when it is rotating clockwise from six o'clock to twelve o'clock. A catcher throwing to second base wants this kind of movement so that the "ball's not tumbling in all different directions" (Andy Etchebarren, quoted in *Baltimore Sun,* Feb. 23, 1997).

**61-in-'61** The feat of New York Yankees outfielder Roger Maris who hit 61 home runs in 1961. "Mantle Honors Maris' 61-in-'61 Feat" (*USA Today* headline, Apr. 19, 1991).

**size up** To spot a player's strengths and weaknesses; e.g., "Smith sizes up the batter before pitching to him."

**sizzle** To be doing very well on the mound, at the plate, or as a team. "[Jeffrey] Leonard's bat still sizzling as Giants topple Cubs 6–2" (*USA Today,* Apr. 29, 1987). "Baseball's Boston Red Sox are sizzling like no other Red Sox team has sizzled since '46" (*USA Today,* June 6, 1986).

**sizzler 1.** A fastball. **1st Use.** 1911. (*Baseball Magazine,* Oct.; Edward J. Nichols). **2.** A hard-hit ball, such as a searing ground ball or a fast, low line drive. **1st Use.** 1908. (*New York Evening Journal,* May 14; Edward J. Nichols).

**sked** Short for the printed regular-season schedule of baseball games to be played. The term is used by collectors of baseball cards and other baseball novelties and commonly shows up in the magazine *Sports Collectors Digest.*

**skid 1.** A losing streak; e.g., "The Tigers's sixth consecutive loss is their longest skid in four years." **2.** A hitless streak; e.g., "Mark Grace ended a two-day, 0-for-8 skid in the first inning with his seventh home run" (*Baltimore Sun,* May 29, 1998).

**skillet** A fielder's glove, esp. an unwieldy one or one on the hand of a fielder who doesn't catch very well.

**skimmer** A low batted ball, often a ground ball, that skims over the grass or the ground. See also *daisy cutter; grass clipper.* **1st Use.** 1868. "Hatfield . . . ran in on Fisler's 'skimmer' to left field" (Chadwick Scrapbooks; David Shulman).

**skin** The dirt portion of the infield, which is intentionally kept free of grass or artificial turf.

**skin diamond** An infield devoid of grass.

**skinned** [softball term] Said of the proper condition and description of a softball infield that is devoid of grass.

**skip** **1.** The intentional miss of a base by a canny baserunner when the umpire's attention was on the ball or other runners. **1st Use.** 1883. "The 'skip' from second base to home plate while the umpire was engaged in some astrological calculations" (*Grand Rapids* [Mich.] *Evening Leader,* Aug. 7; Peter Morris). **2.** Short for *skipper.*

**skipper** **1.** An affectionate name for the manager of a baseball team. Syn. *skip,* 2. **Etymology.** From the Dutch "schipper," which is pronounced "skipper." The term has a long history as a form of address for the captain or master of a ship. **2.** A ball batted along the ground with a slight bounce. **1st Use.** 1895. "Once more the Riversides seemed trying to see who could make the greatest number of errors, and the way they muffed easy flies, let skippers go through them, and throw wild to bases, was painful to witness" (Herbert Bellwood, *The Rivals of Riverwood;* David Shulman).

**skip rope** **1.** To jump up quickly to avoid being hit by a low, inside pitch. **2.** For a pitcher to jump out of the way of a ball hit back through the box.

**skip the dew** To run exceptionally well. **1st Use.** 1937. (*New York Daily News,* Feb. 14; Edward J. Nichols).

**skirt** A player who avoids a ground ball or who won't play on a given day. Researcher Kenneth Forehand (letter, Apr. 29, 1994) writes: "I have heard speculation that this may . . . have originated from a player who would 'skirt' around a ball instead of getting in front of it."

**skull** **1.** *v.* To bean or hit a batter in the head with a pitched ball. "Don't skull these boys. You'll kill one of them and we'll never get out of here." (William Brashler, *The Bingo Long Traveling All-Stars and Motor Kings,* 1973; Charles D. Poe). **2.** *n.* A dumb play or an error caused by faulty judgment; e.g., "Smith pulled a skull on that grounder."

**skuller** *A batting helmet.*

**skull practice** A club meeting where the manager, coaches, and players "put their heads together" to discuss strategy before a game. Syn. "skull session." **1st Use.** 1917. (*New York Times,* Oct. 6; Edward J. Nichols).

**skunk** **1.** *v.* Syn. of *shut out.* See also *Chicago.* **2.** *n.* Zero. "We beat them three to skunk" (Herbert Simons, *Baseball Magazine,* Jan. 1943). **3.** *n./obs.* An inning in which a team does not score. **1st Use.** 1862. (*New York Sunday Mercury,* Sept. 21; Edward J. Nichols). **Etymology.** The term applies in several sports and games. It plays an important role in the card game of cribbage, signifying loss by a large margin.

**skunk rule** [softball term] The proviso in many Over the Line encounters in which a game is ended if a team is ahead by a certain number of runs at the end of an inning. The number of runs is usually 11, but is sometimes changed.

**sky** To hit a very high fly ball; e.g., "Smith skies to center" or "Jones skies out to left" or "Brown skies one to right." **1st Use.** 1905. (*Montrose* [Pa.] *Independent Republican,* June 30; Edward J. Nichols).

**sky ball** Syn. of *skyscraper.* **1st Use.** 1863. (*New York Sunday Mercury,* Aug. 9; Edward J. Nichols).

**skybox** A luxury seating accommodation, usually enclosed, high above the playing surface. The annual cost of skyboxes at Oriole Park at Camden Yards was as much as $175,000 in 1998. **1st Use.** 1965. "Wealthy Texans snapped up five-year $15,000 leases on every last Skybox, as they were called, before a game was ever played [in the Astrodome]" (John Helyar, *Lords of the Realm,* 1994).

**SkyDome** Home field since June 1989 of the Toronto Blue Jays, a $500 million showcase stadium with a 9,000-ton, 310-foot-high retractable roof that takes 20 minutes to close and a 348-room luxury hotel in center field.

**skyer** *arch.* A towering fly ball. **1st Use.** 1862. "Manolt was the fifth striker, and he hit a 'skyer' which fell into Abrams' hands" (*New York Sunday Mercury,* Oct. 12; David Shulman).

**sky rocket 1.** A long, hard-hit fly ball that goes high into the air; e.g., "[Ron] Kittle stroked a sky rocket in the . . . Comiskey Park bleacher area" (*Baseball Digest,* Oct. 1983). **2.** Syn. of *skyscraper.* **1st Use.** 1861. (*New York Sunday Mercury,* Aug. 10; Edward J. Nichols).

**skyscraper** A fly ball that goes straight up from the plate and is usually pursued by the catcher in the area between the foul lines and the stands. "Fourteen times the Bostons hit what the small boy calls skyscrapers, and fourteen times a pair of big New York hands squeezed the ball" (*The World* [New York], May 11, 1889; Gerald Cohen). Syn. *sky rocket,* 2; *sky ball;* "sky chaser"; "sky searcher." **1st Use.** 1866. (*New York Herald,* June 27; Edward J. Nichols).

**slab 1.** The pitcher's *rubber,* 1. "One of the star hurlers of the year, Joe Benz, was on the slab" (James Crusinberry, *Chicago Tribune,* Aug. 1914). **Usage Note.** The term has a certain honorific aspect to it. On the eve of the tainted 1919 World Series, Chicago White Sox second baseman Eddie Collins was quoted as saying: "[Eddie] Cicotte and [Lefty] Williams are two of the greatest pitchers who ever planted a foot on the slab, and our gang can field and hit." **1st Use.** 1892. (*Chicago Herald,* June 13; Edward J. Nichols). **2.** Syn. of *home plate.*

**slab artist** A pitcher. "In recent years the 'slab artist' has been given the advantage, and the complaint grows that there is not batting enough" (Albert G. Spalding, *Base Ball: America's National Game,* 1911; Peter Tamony). **1st Use.** 1905. "He was a wonder, and the year following, as a slab artist . . . made an excellent record" (National Association of Professional Base Ball Leagues, *1905 Official Guide;* David Shulman).

**slabber** A pitcher.

**slabbist** A pitcher.

**slabman** A pitcher. **1st Use.** 1905. "The team developed the league's leading slabman" (National Association of Professional Base Ball Leagues, *1905 Official Guide;* David Shulman).

**slabster** A pitcher. "George Foster and Ernie Shore were a couple of Red Sox slabsters who never regained the winning knack after chucking no hitters" (Red Foley, *The Sporting News,* May 23, 1956). **1st Use.** 1910. (*Baseball Magazine,* Apr.; Edward J. Nichols).

**slam 1.** *v.* To hit with great power. **1st Use.** 1905. (*Sporting Life,* Oct. 7; Edward J. Nichols). **2.** *n.* A hard-hit ball. **1st Use.** 1907. (*Reach's Official Base Ball Guide;* Edward J. Nichols). **3.** *n.* Short for *grand slam,* 1. "Bo Jackson's 2 Homers Include Slam, 7 RBI" (*Washington Post* headline, Apr. 15, 1987). **4.** *n.* A *sweep,* 3. "Atlanta First in Southern Ass'n to Make 'Slam' in Dixie Series; Crackers, in Addition to Winning League Championship, Took Play-off and Then Beat Beaumont Four Straight" (*The Sporting News* headline, Oct. 13, 1938). See also *grand slam,* 2.

**slamfest** A *slugfest.* "Jays Run Down Phils in 15–14 Slamfest" (*Baltimore Sun* headline, Oct. 21, 1993).

**slammer** Syn. of *grand slam,* 1.

**slam the door** Syn. of *shut the door.*

**slant 1.** A pitch; esp., a curveball. The term is often used in the plural; e.g., "The Sox downed New York, 8 to 3, behind the slants of Dickie Kerr" (Irving Stein, *The Ginger Kid,* 1992). **1st Use.** 1902. (*Sporting Life,* July 12; Edward J. Nichols). **2.** [softball term] A pitched ball, esp. in the fast pitch softball parlance of the 1930s and 1940s.

**slap 1.** *v.* To hit a pitch sharply with a quick jab rather than a full swing. **1st Use.** 1912. (*New York Tribune,* Oct. 12; Edward J. Nichols). **2.** *n.* A quick jab at a pitched ball; e.g., "Many of Smith's hits are opposite-field slaps."

**slap hit 1.** A base hit in which the ball is characteristically placed between, or just over the heads of, the infielders with a quick jab of the bat rather than with a full swing. **2.** [softball term] A maneuver in fast pitch softball in which a left-handed batter will take a step toward first base as the ball leaves the pitcher's hand. While this step is being taken the batter jabs the ball to the left side of the infield with a slapping motion. With the shorter basepath and what is essentially a legal lead off the plate and good timing, the batter has a fairly good chance of making it safely to first base.

**slap hitter** A hitter who specializes in slap hits; e.g., Brett Butler and John Cangelosi. Syn. *slapper,* 1.

**slapper 1.** Syn. of *slap hitter.* **2.** An infielder who takes swipes at the ball or who uses his glove like a flyswatter.

**slap tag** A putout accomplished by an infielder who hits the baserunner with a gloved ball.

**slash** To hit the ball sharply, usually to the opposite field. **1st Use.** 1901. (Burt L. Standish, *Frank Merriwell's Marvel;* Edward J. Nichols).

**slasher** A hitter who slashes the ball.

**slaughter** A decisive defeat.

**slaughter rule** A rule in softball and high school baseball in which a team that is ahead by a given number of runs after a given number of innings (e.g., ten runs after five innings) is declared the winner. Syn. *mercy rule.*

**sleeper rabbit play** A rare bit of baseball skullduggery that is brought into play with baserunners on second and third. The runner on second, who gets the attention of the catcher, is noticeably slow in returning to his base after the first pitch. He repeats this lazy act until the catcher is lured into throwing to second at which time the runner on second breaks for third and the runner on third dashes toward home. **Etymology.** The play was invented by George Moriarity in the early 1900s. It would seem that this might be a reversal on the fable of the tortoise and the hare. Unlike the original story in which the rabbit sleeps, allowing the tortoise to win, the baseball play has the rabbit pretending to sleep to trip up the opposition.

**slewfoot** An awkward player.

**slice 1.** *v.* To hit the ball with a late swing. A ball sliced by a right-handed batter takes off spinning and curving in the direction of right field, while a left-handed batter will slice a ball that veers toward left field. Compare *pull,* 1. **Etymology.** Possibly borrowed from golf, where the curve is more common and pronounced. **2.** *n.* A late swing at a pitched ball. **3.** *n.* A batted ball that has been sliced.

**slicer** A batted ball that veers off in the opposite direction.

**slice hitter** Syn. of *opposite-field hitter.*

**slide 1.** *v.* To throw oneself along the ground toward a base to avoid being tagged out or overrunning the base. Contact with the base is made with a hand or a foot, which offers a much smaller target for the defender to tag. **2.** *n.* The act of sliding. Slides are performed either feet first or, more daringly, headfirst. **1st Use.** 1866. "[Butler] Ives obtained his run by a tremendous jump and slide on to the base under the pitcher's hands" (*Detroit Advertiser and Tribune,* Oct. 18). **3.** *n.* A slump; e.g., "With 0 for 20, Smith's batting average took a slide."

**"Slide, Kelly, Slide"** Chant and motto aimed at Mike "King" Kelly (1878–93), the player widely credited with turning base stealing into an art. It was also a popular song copyrighted in 1889. The phrase tends to emphasize one side of his reputation. He was in fact a remarkable player whom Connie Mack later compared to Ty Cobb. The handsome, well-dressed Kelly was the first player to get "important" money (he was paid $5,000 in 1887 when Boston of the National League bought him for $10,000) and the first to inspire fan adulation—it has been said that he was the first player to be targeted by autograph seekers. See also *Chicago slide.*

**slider 1.** A modified curveball that is rolled—or slid—out of the hand, rather than spun hard. It has less motion than a pure curveball and breaks slightly but sharply just as it crosses the plate; i.e., it starts out like a fastball and then breaks late without warning, like a curveball (but not as much as a curve). It can break up to 6 inches horizontally or vertically. The slider is more effective the harder

**"Slide, Kelly, Slide."** *Mike "King" Kelly was credited with turning base stealing into an art.*

it is thrown; e.g., Steve Carlton threw a vicious hard slider. Thrown by a right-hander, the slider breaks down and away to a right-handed batter and down and in to a left-handed batter. It creates a strong illusion, which once caused Willie Stargell to compare hitting a slider to "trying to drink coffee with a fork."

Tim McCarver (*New York Times,* June 29, 1986) described Carlton's slider (which he termed the best in baseball): "The tighter you grip the ball, the more spin you can get on it. And with his forearm strength, he could grip it tighter than anyone else. With that tight grip, his slider had a gyroscope-type downward movement that often spun it into the dirt. But to the batter and to the umpire it had the illusion of a strike."

Jim Brosnan (*The Long Season,* 1960) defined the slider as "a pitch that is not quite so fast as a good fast ball, nor curves so much as a good curve-ball; but which is easier to throw and control than either of them." Charlie Dressen (*Baseball Digest,* Aug. 1961) considered the slider "the worst pitch in baseball: it slides over the plate—and slides out of the ballpark." **Etymology.** The origin of the pitch has been obscured by time, but the first pitchers to make a name for themselves throwing the slider worked in the 1930s. They were George Uhle of the Detroit Tigers and George Blaeholder of the St. Louis Browns. Uhle said that he invented the pitch in 1929: "Harry Heilmann and I were just working [on the sidelines to catcher Eddie] Phillips. It just came to me all of a sudden, letting the ball go along my index finger and using my ring finger and pinky to give it just a little bit of a twist. It was a sailing fastball, and that's how come I named it the slider. The real slider is a sailing fastball. Now they call everything a slider." (John Thorn & John Holway, *The Pitcher,* 1987). The term has been in use since the 1930s; earlier names for the pitch included *nickel curve* and *sailer.* The pitch came into widespread use in the 1950s, and was made famous by Carlton and others in the 1970s.

**2.** A sliding injury in which a patch of skin has been scraped from the leg or thigh. "Many players suffer much from these injuries, often having the skin torn off their limbs in patches four or five inches square" (Hugh S. Fullerton, *American Magazine,* June 1912). **1st Use.** 1910. (*American Magazine,* Apr.; Edward J. Nichols). **3.** A baserunner who slides.

**slide short** To stop one's slide before the base is actually reached. Though this usually results in the runner being tagged out, Marty Barrett used it on occasion to avoid a sure tag at second base, scrambling to safety in the confusion.

**slide step** A move by the pitcher whose front leg steps quickly down the mound toward home plate rather than lifts as in the normal delivery, designed to delay a baserunner attempting to steal. The move reduces base stealing, but makes for a less-effective pitch to the plate.

**sliding catch** A catch in which the fielder throws his body on the ground and slides under the ball.

**sliding pad** Stuffed padding worn as protective equipment on the hips under a player's pants to prevent injuries to the hips and thighs when sliding. **1st Use.** 1888. (John Montgomery Ward, *Base-Ball: How to Become a Player;* Peter Morris).

**sliding pit 1.** The dirt surrounding a base on a field that has a synthetic surface. **2.** A large, three-sided, boxed structure filled with sand used for practicing sliding, as, e.g., during spring training. **1st Use.** 1940. "The sliding pit was in deep right field behind the foul lines, and Gabby stood at the side explaining and pointing out each man's faults as he came into the bag" (John R. Tunis, *The Kid from Tomkinsville*).

**sling** To pitch a baseball. **1st Use.** 1907. (*New York Evening Journal,* May 22; Edward J. Nichols).

**slinger** A pitcher. **1st Use.** 1908. (*New York Evening Journal,* May 9; Edward J. Nichols).

**slingshot 1.** A strong throwing arm; a *shotgun.* **1st Use.** 1937. (*New York Daily News,* Jan. 21; Edward J. Nichols). **2.** [softball term] A delivery in fast pitch softball in which the arm, gripping the ball, leaves its position at the waist and is whipped backward to the stretching point, then moved forward with as much speed and force as possible. The ball is released at its furthest point forward, with as much drive as possible. It is a single powerful stroke rather than a circular delivery producing more control but less speed than the windmill delivery. See also *figure eight; windmill.*

**slingshot delivery** A pitching delivery that imparts considerable initial momentum to a pitched ball.

**slip one by** To get a strike by throwing the ball toward the edges of the strike zone. Bob Uecker's eulogy for one-time American League batting champion (1959) and former Milwaukee Brewers manager Harvey Kuenn contained these lines: "The last couple of years Harvey lived with a 3-2 count on him, but every time they tried to slip one by him on the corner he fouled it off. To get Harvey looking they must have wanted him awful bad." (*St. Petersburg Times,* Mar. 6, 1988).

**slippery elm** A mucilaginous substance from the inner bark of the elm (*Ulmus rubra*), once used by pitchers to give the ball the same effect as a spitball. **1st Use.** 1908. (*New York Evening Journal,* May 22; Edward J. Nichols).

**slip pitch** A pitched ball that comes toward the plate with diminished velocity and a sudden drop. It is thrown like the *palm ball* except that the pitcher's fingers are raised above the surface of the ball. Paul Richards claimed he learned it from Fred "Deacon" Jones in the Southern Association in the late 1930s. Richards brought the pitch to prominence while managing the Chicago White Sox and Baltimore Orioles in the 1950s; it was used successfully by Skinny Brown, Dick Hall, Harry Dorish, and Jim Wilson.

**slobberer** An artless and clumsy spitball pitcher. Gaylord Perry (*Me and the Spitter,* 1974) noted that slobberers not only showed "no respect for a delicate art" but also actually triggered a 1968 rule change that ended finger-licking on the mound. (Charles D. Poe).

**slo-pitch softball** [softball term] Syn. of *slow pitch softball.*

**slot 1.** *n.* A player's position on the team, both in the field and in the batting order. **2.** *v.* To be put in a position; e.g., "Smith is slotted second in the batting order." **3.** *n.* The area in which the plate umpire (esp. in the American League) positions himself, over the catcher's shoulder nearest the batter. Compare *scissors.* **4.** *n.* The area between first base and second base or between second base and third base. See also *alley,* 4. **5.** *n.* A place in the pitching rotation. **6.** *n.* Syn. of *on-deck circle.*

**slow ball** A pitch delivered with the same motion as a fastball but with much less speed; a *change of pace.* It is intended to throw off the batter's timing, causing him to swing too soon. **Usage Note.** This entirely accurate term has drifted out of fashion and today's "slow ball" is almost universally referred to as the *changeup.* **1st Use.** 1893. (*Harper's Weekly,* July 8; Edward J. Nichols).

**slow bat** The bat of a hitter who hits bloopers and does not overswing or who swings late. Catchers late in the season often have slow bats because they are tired after catching many games.

**slow-breaking curve** A pitch that slowly enters its curving course.

**slow hook** A term used by Bill James for the removal of a starting pitcher after he has pitched more than nine innings, has given up seven or more runs, or has a combined total of at least 13 runs and innings pitched. Compare *quick hook, 2.*

**slow pitching** [softball term] An earlier term for *slow pitch softball.* Leo H. Fischer (*Winning Softball,* 1940) wrote: "A type of softball which has attained popularity in many sections of the country and which is gaining in others is the variety known as 'slow-pitching.'" It was played with a 16-inch ball.

**slow pitch softball** [softball term] One of the two major branches of softball, characterized by ten players on each team (including a short fielder), bunting and base stealing are not allowed, a hit batter is not awarded first base, and the ball must be pitched underhand at a moderate speed in an arc that peaks above the batter's head. Amateur Softball Association of America rules specify that the arc be between 6 and 12 feet, while United States Slo-Pitch Softball Association rules call for a pitching arc of between three and ten feet. Compare *fast pitch softball.* Also called "slow pitch." Syn. *slow pitching.* **Usage Note.** The term is often spelled *slo-pitch softball,* most notably by the United States Slo-Pitch Softball Association.

**slow roller** A slow-moving ground ball.

**slow roller pitch** A pitch with less speed than usual so that the batter can observe its rotation.

**slud** The past tense for the verb "to slide" in the parlance of Dizzy Dean. The term may have been the most famous in Dean's lexicon. Jack Smith (*San Francisco Examiner and Chronicle,* Mar. 23, 1975; Peter Tamony) wrote: "I have written to the big dictionary publishers suggesting that the word 'slud' be included in their next editions, and now I am receiving just what they will want to see—public support." Smith embarked on this campaign after he used the word in a column and some readers had the gall to write in and say that he had made an error.

**slug** To hit a baseball hard; to hit the long ball.

"Sometimes we slug and run. Other times we run and slug. Then there are times when we slug and slug. When we slug and slug, it works." (Baltimore Orioles slugger Eric Davis, quoted in *Baltimore Sun,* May 10, 1998). **1st Use.** 1888. (Chicago *Inter-Ocean,* July 6; Edward J. Nichols). **Etymology.** As early as 1756 "slug" was a slang term for a drink of strong liquor. Not much later it also took on the meaning of a punch or heavy blow, and thus passed into baseball usage.

**slug bunt** A slap hit past an invisible charging infielder during batting practice with no fielders.

**slugfest** A game characterized by heavy and repeated hitting by one or both teams. Syn. *slamfest; slugging match.* **Etymology.** From the nickname for a boxing match in which offense rather than defense or strategy dominates.

**slugger 1.** A hitter with a high percentage of extra-base hits; one likely to hit the long ball. Sluggers tend to be placed at the third, fourth, or fifth positions in the batting order. Syn. *slugsmith; sockdolager; socker; swatter; swatsmith; swatsman.* **Usage Note.** The term amounts to an unofficial title and is used with some discretion; there are only a few dozen players in the history of the game who wear it well. A gallery of sluggers appears in Ted Williams's *Science of Hitting* (1971), including Hack Wilson, Hank Greenberg, Babe Ruth, Lou Gehrig, Ralph Kiner, Mickey Mantle, Roger Maris, and Johnny Mize. **1st Use.** 1883. (*Sporting Life,* Apr. 22; Edward J. Nichols). **2.** A large, imposing baseball bat. **1st Use.** 1901. (Burt L. Standish, *Frank Merriwell's Marvel;* Edward J. Nichols). **3.** Short for *Louisville Slugger.* **Etymology.** The term was applied to a boxer (alternatively, "slogger") before its use in baseball. A reckless batter in cricket has been known as a "slogger" since the 19th century. **Extended Use. 1.** A term of endearment, often applied by an adult to a little kid who is anything but. **2.** A boxer who wins on punches rather than on defense or tactics. **3.** A heavy-handed reporter.

**Sluggersville** The figurative hometown of sluggers. **1st Use.** 1891. "Then he was as frisky as a young colt and a slugger from Sluggersville" (*Sporting Times,* July 11, 1891; David Shulman).

**slugging average** A statistical representation of a batter's ability to make extra-base hits. It is determined by dividing the player's total times at bat into his total bases. Hence, a batter with a home run, a triple, a double, and a single (10 total bases) in 20 at-bats has a slugging average of .500. During the 1920 season Babe Ruth's slugging average was an astonishing .847 (388 bases in 458 at-bats). It would be possible to have a slugging average of greater than 1.000 if one averaged more than one base per at-bat; a slugger who hit a home run with every at-bat would have a 4.000 slugging average. Abbrev. is *SA*. Syn. *slugging percentage.*

**slugging match** Syn. of *slugfest*. Also expressed as "slugging contest" and "slugging duel."

**slugging percentage** Syn. of *slugging average.*

**slugsmith** Syn. of *slugger*, 1. **1st Use.** 1920. "Good old Rufe, the slugsmith! The crowd was imploring him to bring Tapland home" (Burt L. Standish, *The Man on First;* David Shulman).

**slump 1.** *n.* A period of poor or below-normal performance. A team is said to be in a slump when it loses games, while an individual may go into a batting, pitching, or even a fielding slump. "The truest definition of a slump is you're not feeling well, you're not seeing the ball well, things aren't going well" (Cal Ripken Jr., quoted in *Baltimore Sun,* Aug. 19, 1997). Jimmy Cannon's definition (*Baseball Digest,* Nov.–Dec. 1956): "Any time in the season when the Yankees are leading by less than eight games." **1st Use.** 1895. (*New York Press,* July 1; Edward J. Nichols). See also *drought; dry spell,* 1. **2.** *n.* A downward trend. In extreme cases, the game of baseball can be on the skids: "Baseball fell into a slump this week" (*Maine Sunday Telegram,* Aug. 10, 1986) after the owners fired arbitrator Tom Roberts. **3.** *v.* To be in a slump.

**slump-ridden** Said of a team in which many of its players are in slumps at the same time.

**slurve 1.** *n.* A pitch that slides and curves. It curves more than a slider, is faster than a curveball, and breaks at the very last instant without warning. **2.** *v.* To pitch the slurve. "Kaat 'Slurves' Yanks" (*San Francisco Examiner* headline, July 19, 1973; Peter Tamony). **Etymology.** A combina-tion of "slider" plus "curve" equals "slurve." However, sources for the term vary in specific applications. "Among batsmen of the National League, the favorite pitch of Don Drysdale was known as the 'slurve.' This comprised one part slobber and two parts curve." (Mel Durslag, *San Francisco Examiner,* July 24, 1970; Peter Tamony).

**smack** To hit the ball hard. **1st Use.** 1902. (*Sporting Life,* July 5; Edward J. Nichols).

**small ball** Playing the game by paying attention to the "little" things, such as sacrifice hits, bunt plays, hit-and-run plays, advancing or hitting behind the runner, pickoffs, stolen bases, and taking advantage of walks and errors. "[Colorado Rockies] will play 'small ball,' moving runners rather than waiting for the bombs" (*Sports Illustrated,* Mar. 31, 1997). See also *little ball,* 3.

**small baseball** A term used by Casey Stengel for a "very fast ball" (Red Barber, NPR's "Morning Edition," May 30, 1986).

**small market club** A low-revenue major-league club (such as the Montreal Expos and Pittsburgh Pirates). The term includes other low-revenue clubs, regardless of their market size (such as the Detroit Tigers and Philadelphia Phillies). Compare *large market club.*

**smash** To hit a ball powerfully. **1st Use.** 1888. (*New York Press,* Apr. 19; Edward J. Nichols).

**smell hit** *arch.* A *Texas Leaguer.*

**smoke 1.** *n.* Speed in pitching. Usually stated as "throwing smoke," the term figuratively alludes to a ball that comes in so fast, it leaves a trail of smoke. It would appear that this was the source of several baseball nicknames, including that of Smoky Joe Wood, who was also called "Smoke" by Tris Speaker. As Dwight Gooden emerged from a drug rehabilitation center in Apr. 1987, attendants yelled out the windows, "Throw smoke, Dwight"; in reply, he thrust a fist into the air. (*New York Times,* Apr. 30, 1987). See also *powder,* 2. **1st Use.** 1912. (*New York Tribune,* Sept. 8; Edward J. Nichols). **2.** *n.* A fastball; heat. **3.** *v.* To bear down with a fastball; e.g., "Smith smoked one by Jones." **4.** *v.* To hit the ball very hard; e.g.,

"Brown smoked the ball past the third baseman." Mike Shropshire (*Seasons in Hell*, 1996) states: "A big leaguer doesn't simply hit an occasional pitcher hard. He 'smokes his tits,' one of the milder expressions that color conversational patterns of players." **5.** *v.* To hit a batter with a thrown ball. Asking about a Japanese custom after hitting a batter, Roger Clemens said: "If I smoke somebody, do I have to tip my hat?" A Japanese interpreter laughed and said: "If Rocket-san smokes someone, there might not be anything left to tip his hat to." (*Orioles Gazette*, Dec. 1992).

**smoke ball** A ball that is pitched very fast. **1st Use.** 1912. (*New York Tribune*, Sept. 26; Edward J. Nichols).

**smoker** A fastball. **1st Use.** 1914. "That Lewis expected a smoker and had every intention of lacing it out, was perfectly evident from his action" (Burt L. Standish, *Brick King, Backstop;* David Shulman).

**smother in leather** To field the ball effectively; to kill an offensive threat. Syn. "smother the ball." **1st Use.** 1896. (Burt L. Standish, *Frank Merriwell's School Days;* Edward J. Nichols).

**snag** To reach out and catch a batted or thrown ball; e.g., "The throw was high but Smith was able to snag it."

**snake 1.** A curveball. One does not merely "throw the snake," but usually something on the order of "a nasty snake." "[Paul] Hopkins delivered the slowest, prettiest snake that he had thrown [Babe] Ruth yet" (William Nack, *Sports Illustrated*, Aug. 24, 1998). **1st Use.** 1908. (*Spalding's Official Base Ball Guide;* Edward J. Nichols). **2.** A pitched ball that changes directions and actually undulates on its way to the plate. Despite reports of the snake at the turn of the 20th century, the experts claimed it never existed. Walter Camp (*Book of College Sports*, 1901) said that it "exists in the imagination only, unless the ball be blown out of its course by the wind."

**snake-bit** Unlucky; said of a player or team with extremely bad luck. In 1984, when his record was 2-9, Pittsburgh Pirates relief pitcher Kent Tekulve was asked if he had been snake-bit; his reply: "I feel like I've had a cobra wrapped around my neck." **Etymology.** In his section of the *Encyclopedia of Sports Talk* (edited by Zander Hollander, 1976), Phil Pepe writes: "Origin is unknown, but since baseball was a game played by country boys who know of such things as snakes, that probably was the derivation. Being bitten by a snake is about as bad luck as one can have."

**snap 1.** *v.* To throw a breaking ball; to release a curveball. **2.** *n.* The sharp breaking action of a curveball. **3.** *v.* To break a losing or winning streak or break up a tie game; e.g., "Smith's double drove in two runs and snapped a 2–2 tie." **4.** *n.* The energy of a player or team. **1st Use.** 1890. (*New York Evening Post*, May 5; Edward J. Nichols).

**snapper** A good curveball that "snaps off" with a sharp breaking action.

**snap throw 1.** *n.* A quick, short toss made with a flick of the wrist, used chiefly by infielders. **1st Use.** 1896. (Burt L. Standish, *Frank Merriwell's School Days;* Edward J. Nichols). **2.** *v.* To throw the ball with a flick of the wrist.

**snatch catch** A catch characterized by a swift downward movement of the glove as the ball settles into it. It was popularized by outfielder Rickey Henderson.

**sneaker 1.** A deceptive fastball. "A pitch that is faster than it appears to be and figuratively sneaks up on the batter" (H. G. Salsinger, *Baseball Digest*, Aug. 1945). **2.** An athletic canvas shoe with a rubber or synthetic sole. **1st Use.** 1909. "He dressed his feet in a pair of rubber soled, canvas shoes—call 'em 'sneakers' now—and journeyed to Fall River" (*Baseball Magazine*, Aug. 1909; David Shulman). **Etymology.** There are two common theories on how this term originated: 1) from British thieves who found them useful in their work; or 2) from baseball players who found them useful in stealing bases. The shoes themselves predated the name by several years. "The first sneaker hit the market in 1868, according to historian William Rossi" (*Chicago Tribune*, 1987).

**sneaky 1.** Said of the inexplicable. The term is used when players try to explain what they don't understand. "He's [New York Yankees relief pitcher Mariano Rivera] sneaky. Because he's small and because his delivery is so free and easy, so smooth, his stuff doesn't look as if it's coming at you as fast as it is. Then it's by you." (Catcher Joe Girardi, quoted in *Sports Illustrated*, Mar. 24, 1997). **2.** Said of a fastball or other pitch that for whatever reason does not look as fast as it really is.

**sno-cone** Var. of *snow cone*.

**Snodgrass Muff** A muff or boner, named for the hapless New York Giants outfielder Fred Snodgrass who dropped an easy fly ball hit by Boston Red Sox pinch hitter Clyde Engle in the tenth inning of the final game (Oct. 12) of the 1912 World Series. The Giants had been leading 2–1 but the error (dubbed the "$30,000 muff") put the tying run on second base and the Red Sox went on to win the game, 3–2, and the Series. Ironically, the batter following Engle, Harry Hooper, was robbed of a hit by Snodgrass, who made a great catch in deep center field.

**snow cone** A catch in which the ball is caught in the top of the glove webbing and when held up resembles a scoop of frozen confection in a cone. See also *ice-cream cone,* 2. Var. *sno-cone.*

**snowman** The numeral eight. When a team "builds a snowman," it means it scored eight runs. "[The Angels] dropped a snowman early on us and we built a snowman early too" (*Baltimore Sun,* June 3, 1996).

**snuff out** To stop a rally; e.g., "Smith's relief pitching snuffed out the White Sox rally."

**snyder** A groundout to the second baseman.

**snyder out** To ground out routinely to the second baseman. The term may be a bit of slang primarily used by one team, the Baltimore Orioles, and named for outfielder Russ Snyder, who often "snydered out" during his years (1960–67) with the Orioles. The term was used by broadcaster Brooks Robinson (WMAR-TV, Aug. 20, 1982) who noted that it was commonly used by the Orioles, even by those who were unaware of its background.

**SO 1.** Abbrev. for *strikeout,* 1. **2.** Abbrev. for *shutout,* 1.

**soak 1.** To bat the ball hard. "There is wild de-

**Snodgrass Muff.** *Fred Snodgrass of the New York Giants.*

mand that 'Shorty, soak 'er home!'" (Charles S. Brooks, *Journeys to Bagdad,* 1915). **1st Use.** 1896. (Burt L. Standish, *Frank Merriwell's School Days;* Edward J. Nichols). **2.** *obs.* To put out a runner in town ball and other early variations of baseball by throwing the ball at and hitting him. Syn. *plug,* 2.

**soak ball** Baseball with soaking. **1st Use.** 1900. "Soak ball was at this time my favorite sport" (Adrian C. "Cap" Anson, *A Ball Player's Career*).

**soaker 1.** *arch.* A solid hit. **1st Use.** 1895. "You hit a soaker, and I'll bet you've taken some of the sand out of Flood" (Herbert Bellwood, *The Rivals of Riverwood;* David Shulman). **2.** A fastball.

**soaking** The action by which a runner is put out in town ball and other early variations of baseball by hitting him with a thrown ball.

**Society for American Baseball Research** An organization headquartered in Cleveland, Ohio, of researchers and fans with an interest in the history and statistics of baseball. The mission of the Society is "to foster the study of baseball as a significant American institution." It publishes several periodicals, supports many research committees, and holds regional meetings and a national convention. It was the brainchild of L. Robert "Bob" Davids of Washington, D.C., who formed it along with 15 other baseball historians at a 1971 meeting in Cooperstown, N.Y. Abbrev. *SABR.*

**sock 1.** *v.* To hit a pitched ball hard; e.g., "Smith socked a liner to deep center." **2.** *n.* Offensive power of a baseball team or player.

**sockamayock** A second-string or mediocre pitcher in the Negro leagues. "We had pitchers that we never would have pitched in league games. Sockamayocks, we used to call 'em. . . . Those fellas I was talking about who weren't first-stringers, they might be Class-B or -C or -D ballplayers." (Buck Leonard, quoted in Robert Person, *Only the Ball was White,* 1970).

**sockdolager** *obs.* A *slugger* in the mid-19th century.

**socker** *arch.* A *slugger,* 1. **1st Use.** 1907. (*Lajoie's Official Base Ball Guide;* Edward J. Nichols).

**sodfather** A puckish nickname for a head groundskeeper, a punning play on *The Godfather.* When the *Washington Post* (Apr. 6, 1983) carried a profile of Baltimore's Pasquale Santarone, it was headlined "The Sodfather of Memorial Stadium." Some weeks later the *Post* published a letter from a reader who termed the use of the nickname for an Italian American a "demeaning slur."

**soft 1.** Lacking velocity or power; e.g., "Smith hit a soft liner that was fielded easily" or "Jones throws a soft breaking pitch." Compare *hard.* **2.** Said of a defense that does not hold runners on. **3.** Said of a player or team lacking competitive fire. **1st Use.** 1880. (*Brooklyn Daily Eagle,* July 25; Edward J. Nichols).

**softball** [softball term] **1.** An offshoot of baseball played with a larger, softer ball, which pitchers throw underhand and, depending on the league, throw fast or slow. The field is similar to the baseball diamond but smaller (bases are 60 feet apart for fast pitch and 65 feet apart for slow pitch) and a game is only seven innings. The game is played with the same equipment and most of the same rules. The emphasis in fast pitch is on pitching while slow pitch players concentrate on both hitting and fielding. Softball is totally dominated by amateur play. Early names for the game of softball include: army ball, big ball, church ball, diamond ball, indoor-outdoor, kitten ball, lightning ball, night ball, panty waist, playground ball, recreation ball, serve us ball, and twilight ball. See also *mush ball,* 2.

The game dates back to 1887 when it was created as *indoor baseball,* 1. It received a major boost about 1910 when the Playground Society of America acknowledged it as a good game for kids (and suggested the addition of a tenth player known as a rover). Its major leap forward occurred in the 1930s after a national tournament at the 1933 Century of Progress Exposition in Chicago. *Time* magazine (Sept. 26, 1939) said of the game: "A product of the Depression, softball has grown into a major U.S. mania."

In 1939, the game was brought back indoors when a short-lived attempt was made to promote it as a winter alternative to baseball, organized along the same lines as major-league baseball. Under the name National Professional Indoor Baseball League, franchises were sold in New York, Brooklyn, Boston, Cleveland, Chicago, Philadelphia, Cincinnati, and St. Louis.

The game has undergone modifications and changes, including the distance from the pitching mound to the plate, which was set at 37 feet, 8 inches in 1933, dropped back to 40 feet in 1940, 46 feet in 1950, and 50 feet (slow pitch only) in 1985.

**2.** The ball used to play softball. It is 12 inches in circumference and weighs 6¼ to 7 ounces. There are variations on the standard ball, including a ball 16 inches in circumference used in a form of slow pitch, and a ball 11 inches in circumference used in women's games. "Softball" is a misnomer in the sense that the ball is not soft, but rather heavier and larger than a baseball and just about as hard. Traditionally, the softball was made of a core of tightly packed and molded kapok, wound tightly with cotton winding, dipped in rubber cement, covered with horsehide, and then hand-stitched. **Etymology.** The history of the term as a name for the game begins long after the game itself had been created. The term "softball" was first used to describe the game in 1926 when a meeting was held in Colorado to standardize that state's rules under a common name. The term "softball" was suggested by Walter C. Hakanson, the YMCA director for Denver and former commissioner and president of the Amateur Softball Association of America.

It took a while for the term to spread even in Colorado and it may have found its first popular application in Canada. The earliest printed reference in the collection of the many citations in the extensive file on the term "softball" at Merriam-Webster, the dictionary company in Springfield, Mass., is not in fact from Colorado but from a headline in the *Guelph* [Ont.] *Evening Mercury* (Aug. 26, 1927): "Guelph Softball Champions Eliminate Supremes of Galt." There are articles on both men's and women's softball. These were high-spirited, high-scoring games. One of the women's games was described as "a heavy hitting affair with lots of good baseball injected into the fray." A team known as the Woolworths defeated St. James, 16–11, with the aid of four home runs. **1st Use.** The Merriam-Webster dictionaries use the 1927 Canadian citation as the moment of origin. The *Oxford English Dictionary* carries a 1926 Canadian citation for its point of origin (*Victoria* [B.C.] *Daily Colonist,* July 2) in which the term appears but as two words: "The remainder of the morning was occupied by the younger members of the party in playing soft ball and other less strenuous games." **Extended Use.** It is worth noting that softball has a few meanings outside the game. In tennis, a "softball" is a ball lobbed at low velocity for tactical reasons; e.g., a player may "softball" a shot to slow the pace of a volley or throw the other player off balance. The term has seen limited use for a changeup pitch in baseball; e.g., "Harry Brecheen . . . was having a wonderful time on the mound for the Cardinals. Inning after inning he screwballed and softballed the Dodgers into submission." (*Negro Digest,* Nov. 1947).

According to the *Oxford English Dictionary* (2nd ed.), the oldest meaning of "softball" in English (usually written as "soft ball" or "soft-ball") refers to the process of making candy, in which a soft globule of sugar is formed by dropping hot sugar into cold water. The soft ball is created to test the degree to which the sugar has been cooked. The term is very much still in use, and it is the "soft ball" that shows up in James Beard's *American Cookery* (1972). It is also defined in various cooking dictionaries as the stage at which syrup reaches 234 to 240 degrees F.

The most recent and currently popular use of the term is as an adjective or noun meaning "easy and not at all provocative." It is a clear play on the "soft" of "softball." A question that is easy to field and handle, such as one asked by a member of a Congressional committee of a witness, has become known as a "softball." "Practically all of the questions thrown at [Jimmy] Carter were softballs that allowed him, in many cases, just to repeat much of his 1976 campaign oratory" (*San Francisco Examiner,* Mar. 17, 1977).

The antonym of playing political softball is playing "hardball." The earliest example of "softball" so used in print (*Saturday Review,* Dec. 1979) occurs when Tim O'Brien alleges that Justice Warren Burger will only grant in-depth interviews to those "who clear the subject matter with him in advance, promise to throw softballs, and then let the chief justice edit the finished product himself."

There are many other examples of the term applied to other situations. For instance, asking a movie star "What makes a sex symbol?" is a "softball query" (*People,* Mar. 1, 1982), while allowing a company to "persistently misrepresent itself" is "softball media coverage" (*Fortune,* Aug. 9, 1982) and an easily discharged issue is a "political softball" (*U.S. News and World Report,* Apr. 18, 1988). On the other hand, a "softball interview" is a television phenomenon in which the camera is turned on and "letting the stars talk" (*People,* Aug. 20, 1984). In some cases, the softball question or query becomes simply "softball." A writer for *U.S. News and World Report* (Jan. 25, 1988), discussing the performance of Sen. Robert Dole as he began his drive for the Republican nomination, noted after a student asked him how a Dole administration could help him finance a college education: "This, in the currently fashionable vernacular, was a 'softball'—which Dole swung on and missed, never looking the student in the eye and rambling on in unfathomable generalities."

**softballer** [softball term] One who plays softball. A *Time* magazine (Sept. 26, 1939) feature on the game is simply titled "Softballers."

**softball loop** [softball term] A league of teams that play softball. The term appears as early as 1934 in Maurice H. Weseen's *Dictionary of American Slang.* It was favored by headline writers, as in this 1940 banner: "New Pitcher Discovered in Softball Loop."

**softball throw** A track and field event in which individuals compete by throwing a softball for distance.

**soft hands 1.** The hands of a fielder who is able to handle the ball with ease and seldom makes an error; esp., the hands of a fielder who can effortlessly absorb the force of a batted ball. "He's got soft hands. That ball was a pea hit at him and you don't even hear it hit the glove." (Ray Miller, on third baseman Ryan Minor, quoted in *Baltimore Sun,* Mar. 7, 1998). Shortstop Ernie Banks was known for having soft hands. **2.** The hands of a catcher who is quick to release the ball and flexible to make last-second adjustments as the pitch comes in.

**softie** [softball term] *arch.* A softball player. "Police Softies Defeat Firemen" (*San Francisco News* headline, Aug. 26, 1937; Peter Tamony).

**soft liner** A line drive without much force behind it.

**soft toss** A throw made without exertion, as in batting practice or sideline catch and throw. Pitchers recovering from injury are often limited to soft tosses. See also *long toss, 3; short toss.*

**soft tosser** A pitcher who throws off-speed pitches (*Baltimore Sun,* July 18, 1993).

**soft tossing** Light throwing exercise employed when rehabilitating a sore arm; e.g., "The Kansas City Royals said the [arthroscopic] surgery [to repair a tear in his right shoulder] was successful and that Kevin Appier is expected to begin soft tossing

in six weeks" (*Baltimore Sun,* Mar. 25, 1998). See also *long tossing.* Sometimes spelled "soft-tossing."

**soldier** A derogatory term for a batter given to keeping the bat on his shoulder.

**sold out 1.** Syn. of *bases loaded.* **2.** Said of a situation in which there are no more seats available for sale at the ballpark.

**solid hitter** A hitter who is usually able to get a hit when one is needed.

**solid performance** Consistently good to excellent playing.

**solid season** A good season during which a player does everything right and makes a meaningful contribution to the success of his team.

**solid up the middle** Said of a team that has excellent players at catcher, starting and relief pitching, second base, shortstop, and center field.

**solo** Syn. of *solo home run.*

**solo home run** A home run hit with no runners on base. Syn. *solo; solo shot,* 1; *bases-empty home run.*

**Solons** A nickname for the *Washington Senators,* 2.

**solo shot 1.** Syn. of *solo home run.* **2.** A single.

**solve a pitcher** To begin getting hits off a pitcher, presumably after determining the trajectory and speed of his pitches and the way they are mixed. **1st Use.** 1898. (*New York Tribune,* Apr. 22; Edward J. Nichols).

**sombrero** See *golden sombrero.*

**sophomore** A player in his second season in the major leagues.

**sophomore jinx** Bad luck or a poor showing in the season after a successful rookie or freshman year. Perhaps the most famous modern example of a player suffering from this condition was Joe Charboneau, who was the American League Rookie of the Year at Cleveland in 1980 and back in the minor leagues in 1981. Baltimore Orioles pitcher Rocky Coppinger: "After the success I had in '96 [10-6], I was scared of failing. You hear so much about the sophomore jinx and all that. I had never failed before in this game. People say it happens to everybody eventually. It got me last year" (*Baltimore Sun,* Feb. 14, 1998). "Commissioner [Bowie] Kuhn, it can be seen, had a difficult second year in office, and should probably be listed as another victim of the legendary 'sophomore jinx'" (Roger Angell, *The Summer Game,* 1972; Charles D. Poe).

**sophomore year** Second year in the major leagues.

**sore arm** A generic term formerly used for the injured arm of a player, especially a pitcher. Many sore arms are due to injuries to the rotator cuff. Syn. *bugaboo.*

**soupbone** *arch.* The throwing arm of a player, esp. that of a pitcher. "Tim had been a star thrower in his day, but the soupbone had slowed up and he was clinging to his job with his finger-nails" (*Collier's,* July 19, 1930; Peter Tamony). Syn. *souper.* **1st Use.** 1910. (*American Magazine,* Apr.; Edward J. Nichols). **Etymology.** The term seems to have arisen in recognition of the importance of the pitcher's throwing arm, which is to his performance what a soupbone is to a soup.

**soupboner** A pitcher.

**soupboning** Pitching.

**souper** Syn. of *soupbone.*

**southpaw 1.** *n.* A left-handed player; esp. a *left-handed pitcher.* Compare *northpaw.* **2.** *adj.* Left-handed; e.g., "southpaw slants" refers to the pitches of a left-handed pitcher. **3.** *v.* To throw with the left hand. "[Hal Newhouser] hooked up with the Detroit Tigers and he quickly southpawed his way into the baseball headlines" (Bill Stern, *Bill Stern's Favorite Baseball Stories,* 1949). **4.** *n.* The left hand of a left-handed pitcher. **1st Use.** 1885. "Morris and Carroll had never seen the St. Louis team play ball, and as they had always been accustomed to having their opponents hug their bases pretty close, out of respect for Morris' quick throw over to first with that south-paw of his, they were supremely disgusted by the reckless manner in which the Mound City gang ran the lines on them" (*Sporting Life,* Jan. 14; David Shulman). **Etymology.** The oft-repeated etymology of

the term is that it derives from the "fact" that ballparks were once laid out with home plate to the west, which meant that a left-handed pitcher faced the west and threw with his southern limb. This westward orientation kept the sun out of the batter's eyes and out of the eyes of the customers in the more expensive seats behind the plate during an afternoon game. The story is that the term was created by Finley Peter Dunne or Charles Seymour of the *Chicago Herald* and used by them as early as July 1891. H. L. Mencken (*The American Language; Suppl. II,* 1948) reported that Richard J. Finnigan, publisher of the *Chicago Times,* attributed the term to Seymour. As Finnigan put it in a 1945 letter to Mencken: "The pitchers in the old baseball park on the Chicago West Side faced the west and those who pitched left-handed did so with their southpaws."

But does the sun theory work—or did it before most games were played at night? When Happy Felton mentioned the sun theory on his postgame television show from Ebbets Field in 1951, sportswriter Harry Grayson decided to investigate. In his NEA dispatch (*San Francisco News,* July 12, 1951; Peter Tamony), Grayson sided with the sun and reported: "All parks, save one in Lancaster, Pa., are laid out so the sun is not in the batter's eyes. Consequently, the lefthanded pitcher throws from the south side. At Stumpf Field, home of the Lancaster Red Roses of the Class B Interstate League, 25 minutes or so have to be taken out of a late afternoon, or until the sun sinks below the horizon. It is remindful of the English dropping everything for tea in the middle of a cricket match."

A different theory from Charley Dryden, an early sportswriter, has attracted few converts. In this version, an unnamed left-hander from Southpaw, Ill., tries out for the Cubs at spring training in New Orleans, thus inspiring the Chicago writers to start calling all portsiders "southpaws." The reason why it is hard to muster enthusiasm for this theory is that no maps of Illinois or of any other state reveal a town by the name of Southpaw. Illinois does have a South Pekin and a South Park. **Extended Use. 1.** By extension, any left-handed person. **2.** A boxer who stands with his right foot and right hand extended and who counterpunches with his left; also, the left hand itself. "This boxer was Gene Tunney, who had just been whipped by Harry Greb. He was one of the few who discovered what a left hand meant, both offensively and defensively, and worked away hour after hour building up his own southpaw." (*Colliers*, Apr. 12, 1930; Peter Tamony). **3.** A member of the political left wing. Citations on file at Merriam-Webster indicate that this meaning of the term began showing up in print in 1938. The earliest appearance was in Paul Mallon's "News Behind the News" column in the *Schenectady* [N.Y.] *Gazette* (Feb. 10, 1938): "House southpaws are generally known in the House as the 'mavericks,' not only because Texas Congressman Maury Maverick is the leader but because *Webster's New International Dictionary* defines a maverick as 'a motherless calf.'" Damon Runyon, Walter Winchell, and other newspaper columnists were noted for calling Communists "southpaws."

**southpaw disease** The common inability of left-handed batters to hit left-handed pitchers.

**southpawing** Left-handed pitching.

**Southside** The White Sox in Chicago. Compare *Northside.* Syn. "Southsiders"; "South Sides."

**Southside Hit Men** The 1977 Chicago White Sox.

**souvenir** A foul ball or home run hit into the stands and kept by a spectator.

**Sox 1.** Short for *Chicago White Sox.* **2.** Short for *Boston Red Sox.*

**SP** Abbrev. for *starting pitcher.*

**space cadet** An eccentric player; a flake who seems to have come from another planet or outer space. The name of pitcher Bill "Spaceman" Lee is likely to come to mind when the term is used. **Etymology.** The term may have survived from a television serial (1950–52) called *Tom Corbett, Space Cadet.*

**spaceshot** A long home run.

**"Spahn and Sain and two days of rain"** The motto of the Boston Braves of the late 1940s. Much of the team's success derived from the abilities of pitchers Warren Spahn and Johnny Sain. In an interview with Frederick C. Klein (*Wall Street Journal,* Aug. 2, 1985), Spahn commented: "It's not so much my pitching people know, but that little poem about me and Johnny Sain with the '48 Braves. . . . Guys who were kids 40 years ago learned it as a nursery rhyme. Now they meet me and say, 'Oh, you're *that* Spahn.' I used to think that rhyme was silly, but I guess it's how I'll be remembered. Life's funny, huh?" **Etymology/1st Use.** 1948. Gerald V. Hern created the phrase in the form of a poem (*Boston Post,* Sept. 14): "First we'll use Spahn, then we'll use Sain, / Then an off day, followed by rain, / Back will come Spahn, followed by Sain / And followed, we hope, by two days of rain." Hern told the *Boston Globe* in 1967: "The piece resulted from the wonderful statement by [Boston Braves manager] Billy Southworth the previous day that he had made up his mind about his pitchers: 'From here on I will rotate my pitching staff. Spahn on one day. Sain the next.'"

**spaldeen** The hollow, pink, rubber ball used in such baseball variations as stickball and stoopball. The name is a "sweetened" form of the name of Albert Goodwill Spalding, whose company made the spaldeen until 1980 (Harvey Frommer, *Sports Roots,* 1979). *Newsweek* (Oct. 22, 1984) noted the ball's passing as "a victim of the trend toward giving boys a place to play where there are no windows." The term is deeply embedded in the minds of many. "To this day, when I see 'Spalding' I consider it a misspelling" (Leonard Shecter, *The Jocks,* 1969).

**Spalding** *arch.* The baseball during the time it was manufactured by the A. G. Spalding Co. **1st Use.** 1890. (*New York Press,* July 25; Edward J. Nichols).

**Spalding Guide** *arch.* A player whose every move seems posed, as if he were being photographed for the popular *Spalding Base Ball Guides* of yore. The books, published beginning in the 1870s, were illustrated guidebooks featuring records and team profiles.

**spangles** *arch.* A player's uniform. **1st Use.** 1906. (*Sporting Life,* Mar. 3; Edward J. Nichols).

**Spanish home run 1.** *arch.* A ball that is misjudged by a fielder and therefore allows the batter to score but which, if properly played, might have been a single or double. **2.** Any cheap or easy home run. **Etymology.** The term appears in Franklin P. Huddle's (*American Speech,* Apr. 1943) article on baseball jargon and elsewhere, but no suggestion is made of its origin. Implied, however, is Spanish fielding ineptitude. The expression may have died out as Latin players showed their skill in the field.

**spank** To bat the ball sharply. **1st Use.** 1891. (*Chicago Herald,* May 16; Edward J. Nichols).

**spare bat** A dependable player normally assigned to the bench but put in the game when a hit is needed.

**spark** The animating influence in getting a rally started. See also *igniter.* Syn. *trigger.*

**spark plug** A player or manager with a fiery temper, one with the ability to spark the team.

**spasm** An *inning,* 1. "With the third inning faded into the dim and forgotten past, the fourth spasm in the afternoon's matinee of Dementia Baseballitis hopped into the glare of the calcium glim" (*Baseball Magazine,* Sept. 1909). **1st Use.** 1907. (*New York Evening Journal,* Apr. 12; Edward J. Nichols).

**SPBA** Abbrev. for *Senior Professional Baseball Association.*

**spear** To catch a ball, usually a line drive, with a sudden reach of the arm fully extended, as if throwing a spear. **1st Use.** 1902. (*Sporting Life,* July 5; Edward J. Nichols).

**special** *arch.* A term once used in the Eastern League (ca. 1933) for a *Texas Leaguer.*

**special assignment scout** A scout who follows a specific team. Compare *cross-checker.*

**special day** A day featuring any of several inducements to boost attendance at the game. Special days range from discounts (Ladies Day and $3 Night) to giveaways (Helmet Day and Photo Album Night).

**spectator interference** An act by a spectator that prevents a fielder from making a play on a batted or thrown ball; e.g., when a spectator reaches out of the stands, or goes on the playing field, and touches a live ball. The ball is dead at the moment of interference and the umpire shall impose such penalties that will nullify the act of interference. The spectator can expect to be ejected from the ballpark. Syn. *fan interference.*

**speed 1.** The ability of an individual or a team to run the bases. **2.** The ability to field the ball expeditiously. **3.** The ability to throw the fastball. **1st Use.** 1887. (*Base Ball Tribune,* May 23; Edward J. Nichols). **4.** See *arm speed.* **5.** See *bat speed.*

**speedball** The fastball. **Extended Use.** The term "speedballing" is used by drug addicts for injecting heroin and cocaine. "The dangers of speedballing: [John] Belushi killed by 'treacherous' combination of drugs, medic says" (*San Francisco Examiner,* Mar. 11, 1982; Peter Tamony).

**speed game** Baseball strategy that is highlighted by the speed of certain baserunners; e.g., "The manager could not execute his speed game because the batters were not getting on base."

**speed gun** Syn. of *radar gun.*

**speed merchant 1.** A particularly fast runner who is likely to steal bases. **1st Use.** 1910. (*Baseball Magazine,* May; Edward J. Nichols). **2.** A fastball pitcher.

**speedster** A faster-than-usual baserunner.

**spell** To relieve a pitcher or another player.

**spellbinder** A glib, talkative player.

**sphere** The baseball.

**spheroid** The baseball. **1st Use.** 1874. (Chicago *Inter-Ocean,* July 9; Edward J. Nichols).

**spike 1.** *n.* A metal, rubber, or plastic projection on the bottom of a player's shoes to give him greater traction. The term is something of a misnomer for baseball spikes are not sharp and pointed like those which are found on track shoes. **2.** *v.* To cut or otherwise injure another player with one's spikes. It commonly occurs when a player is sliding into a base feet first and the defensive player gets in the way. "Nudge him with rubber—don't spike him with steel" (B. F. Goodrich advertisement for

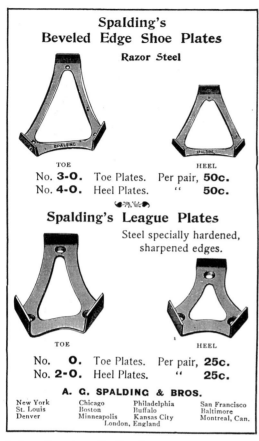

**Spikes.** *Shoe plates offered in the 1904* Spalding Baseball Guide. *Street shoes could be turned into athletic shoes by attaching these plates.*

rubber spikes, *Time* magazine, Apr. 22, 1940; Peter Tamony). **1st Use.** 1885. (Chicago *Inter-Ocean,* May 17; Edward J. Nichols).

**spikes 1.** *n.* The array of metal, rubber, or plastic projections on the bottom (sole and heel) of a player's shoes, used to improve traction. See also *cleats,* 1. **1st Use.** 1866. "The uniform [of the Minerva Club of Philadelphia, organized June 10, 1857] consists of gray pants with cord on the side, plaid shirt with rolling collar, leather shoes with spikes, white navy cap trimmed with blue, german-text M on top of cap, and blue silk belt" (Charles A. Peverelly, *The Book of American Pastimes;* Peter Tamony). **2.** Syn. of *baseball shoe.* **3.** See *sharpen one's spikes.* **4.** See *hang up one's spikes.*

**spikes high** Describing aggressive baserunning tactics; specif., characterizing a slide in which a baserunner attempts to gain advantage by imperiling the fielder with his spikes. The term is often associated with the rough and belligerent Ty Cobb, but one infielder who did not fear him was Buck Weaver, the Chicago White Sox third baseman, who once warned Cobb: "If you ever come in with your spikes high, I'll stomp all over you" (Irving M. Stein, *The Ginger Kid,* 1992).

**spin 1.** *n.* The turning of a pitched ball that keeps it on its intended trajectory. All pitches have spin except for the knuckleball. **2.** *v.* To cause the ball to turn as it moves through the air. **3.** *v.* To pitch; e.g., "Smith will spin the first game of the doubleheader."

**spin ball** A name for softball.

**spin his cap** To brush back a batter; to intimidate with a high, inside pitch.

**spine** Syn. of *middle defense.*

**spinner** A pitched baseball that spins in flight; a breaking ball.

**spitball 1.** *n.* A pitch made with a ball that has been spat upon or otherwise moistened, causing it to break more sharply. It is thrown like a fastball but with a stiff wrist, squirting the ball out of the fingers like a watermelon seed. It was once legal, and used commonly. "The American League, during the early days of the 'spitball,' used it so much that Charlie Dryden, angler and scribe, remarked that: 'The American League consists of Ban Johnson, the "spitball," and the Wabash Railroad'" (William Patten & J. W. McSpadden, *The Book of Baseball,* 1913; Peter Tamony).

The spitball was banned before the 1920 season; however, 17 pitchers who were already using it were allowed to continue to do so for the remainder of their playing years under what amounted to a "grandfather clause." The last legal spitball pitcher was Burleigh Grimes, who retired in 1934 after 19 years in the major leagues.

The spitball is still thrown despite the fact that the rule against it has been made tougher. For instance, in 1968, a stricter anti-spitball rule was added that prohibited any contact between the

**Spitball.** *Burleigh Grimes was the last pitcher to throw spitballs legally.*

pitcher's throwing hand and his mouth. However, the attitude toward the pitch seems to be summed up by one-time pitching coach and manager George Bamberger, as quoted by Thomas Boswell (*Washington Post,* Aug. 8, 1987): "A guy who cheats in a friendly game of cards is a cheater. A pro who throws a spitball to support his family is a contender."

Few baseball terms have as many odd and diverse synonyms as "spitball." They include: *aqueous toss, brown spitter, bubble-gum ball, country sinker, Cuban forkball, Cuban palmball, cuspidor curve, damp sling, drooler, humidity dispenser, moist ball, perspiration pellet, pump pellet, rain rippler, saliva toss, spitter, Staten Island sinker, wet ball, wet one, wet pitch,* and *wet wipe.* Sometimes spelled "spit ball." **1st Use.** 1905. "There is one way the prevalent 'spit ball' can be neutralized to some extent, and clever batsmen have already figured it out" (*Sporting Life,* May 13; Peter Tamony). **Etymology.** Hugh S. Fullerton claims Tom Bond threw the first spitball in New Bedford in 1876 using glycerine, which he carried in his pocket.

Most others insist it came later. There are many who have attributed it to Elmer Stricklett, who started experimenting with it in 1902 and 1903. However, Stricklett himself threw water on this notion. In an interview (*San Francisco Call-Bulletin,* July 2, 1940; Peter Tamony) he had this to say: "I never discovered the spitball. In countless magazine articles, radio skits and even in some of the baseball records I've been called the originator of the spitter though I never claimed credit for it. A fellow named Frank Corridon really discovered the spitball. Back in 1902 Corridon by chance let a ball leave his pitching hand that was wet with saliva. The ball performed some weird antics en route to the plate." Corridon told George Hildebrand about it and he passed it along to Stricklett on a train trip.

If Stricklett did not invent the pitch, he developed it, taking it from Corridon (who seldom used it), and turning it into a major weapon in the pitcher's arsenal. And Stricklett may have named it, or at least that is the claim made by Gustav W. Axelson (*"Commy": The Life of Charles A. Comiskey,* 1919). The incident takes place in 1904 at the Chicago White Sox camp, where hitters were swinging at and missing Stricklett's pitches, sometimes by a foot or more. Catcher Billy Sullivan found the ball wet and slippery and asked Stricklett what he was throwing. "Don't know," was Stricklett's answer. "I suppose 'spitball' explains it as well as anything."

An interesting light on the subject was given by Billy Hart, a veteran pitcher from the 1890s, who was quoted (*New York Sun,* Feb. 10, 1908; Peter Morris): "I notice they claim [Jack] Chesbro and Stricklett were the first to discover the 'spit ball.' Well, back in 1896, when I was pitching for St. Louis, I met Catcher [Frank] Bowerman, who was with Baltimore that year. Calling me aside in St. Louis one day, he took the ball and requested me to get back of the catcher and watch his curves. I did so and was surprised to see how the ball acted as it neared the catcher. I asked Bowerman what made the ball act so. He explained that he simply spit on the ball, held onto it with his thumb at the seam and let it go. The odd part of it was that there was no speed to the ball that Bowerman pitched, whereas today they claim that the 'spit ball' can only be delivered with speed. I mastered it after a while, but found that it injured my arm, as it brought into play muscles not generally used. I advise any pitcher with good speed and curves to let the 'spit ball' severely alone. It will ruin an arm of steel in due time." **2.** *n.* A generic term for a baseball that has been altered by the pitcher or catcher by the application of illegal substances, such as saliva, sweat, grease, hair tonic, oil, and any substance that will stick to the cover of the ball. **Extended Use.** An act of deception; a dirty trick. "As Joe Biden knows, it would not be the first spitball the Dukakis campaign has thrown" (*National Review*, Feb. 5, 1988; Charles D. Poe). **3.** *v.* To throw the spitball. **Extended Use.** William Safire (*On Language*, 1980) notes: "Because an old-time baseball pitcher never knew which way his spitball would break, the verb 'to spitball' now means 'to speculate.'"

**spitballer** A pitcher noted for throwing the spitball.

**spitter** Syn. of *spitball*, 1. The term has been around for many years, but it was given new prominence with the 1974 publication of Gaylord Perry's audacious, tell-all autobiography, *Me and The Spitter*. **1st Use.** 1908. (*Baseball Magazine*, July; Edward J. Nichols).

**Splendid Splinter** A nickname for Ted Williams, a splendid hitter who was deceptively thin for a power hitter.

**splinters** Syn. of *splinter squad.*

**splinter squad** Players on the bench. Syn. *splinters.*

**split 1.** *v.* To win one game and lose the other in a doubleheader; e.g., "The Yankees split a pair." **2.** Short for *split-fingered fastball.*

**split-admission doubleheader** A modern doubleheader in which the ballpark is cleared after the first game to collect new admission tickets for the second game. See also *split doubleheader.*

**split contract** A contract in which a player will receive a stipulated salary while on the roster of a major-league team but a different (usually lower) salary for time spent on a minor-league roster.

*Splendid splinter.*

**split doubleheader** A doubleheader in which there is a period of several hours between games, such as a morning game followed later by an afternoon game; thus, there are two separate tickets and gates. See also *split-admission doubleheader.*

**split-finger** Syn. of *split-fingered fastball.*

**split-fingered fastball** A fastball thrown much like a *forkball*, traveling straight but dropping suddenly just before reaching the plate. The pitcher's grip is on "top of the ball" and close to the fingertips, and it is thrown with the middle and index fingers spread wide (forming a V) along the seams. The ball appears to "tumble" out from between the fingers, having the effect of slowing the ball's velocity without altering the pitcher's fastball arm speed or motion. The ball sinks after falling out of the strike zone. A good split-fingered fastball results in "missed swings and ground balls" (Tom Verducci, *Sports Illustrated*, Mar. 31, 1997).

Roger Craig, a former pitcher, pitching coach, and manager, invented the pitch and began teaching it at a boy's camp in 1974. Dubbed the *pitch of the 1980s,* the split-fingered fastball was used by Bruce Sutter, Mike Scott, and Jack Morris. The extent to which Craig taught his San Francisco Giants the pitch was reflected in the 1987 spring-training line that the "SF" on the players' hats actually stood for "split-fingered."

The pitch has created some confusion, as others in the game periodically declare that it is "nothing more than a [fill in the blank]." Jerry Howarth (*Baseball Lite,* 1986) defines it as: "A pitch five major-league pitching coaches call a fork ball, five others call a spitter, six more recognize as a changeup, and ten others won't recognize at all." Joe Garagiola has termed it a "fast forkball." Billy Martin (*Billyball,* 1987) insisted that it is nothing new, just a "variation of the forkball." Syn. *split,* 2; *splitter,* 1; *split-finger.* Sometimes spelled "split-finger fastball."

**split squad** A spring-training team composed of part of a team's roster, esp. when the team plays exhibition games in two different locales on the same day. Abbrev. *SS3.*

**splitter 1.** Syn. of *split-fingered fastball.* **2.** A forkball.

**split the plate** To pitch a ball over the middle of home plate. **1st Use.** 1909. (Zane Grey, *The Short-Stop;* Edward J. Nichols).

**split time** To play a position on an alternating basis with another player.

**spoiler 1.** One who gets in the way of a victory or an important personal achievement, such as a batter who gets a hit to break up a no-hitter. **2.** A team with no chance of winning a division title that defeats a team vying for the title.

**sportscaster** One who announces baseball and other games on radio and television. The term is a blend of "sports" and "broadcaster."

**Sportsman's Park** The former home field for the St. Louis Browns (1909–53) and the St. Louis Cardinals (1920–66).

**'Spos** Shortened name for the Montreal Expos.

**spot 1.** *v.* To pitch the ball to a particular part of the strike zone; to throw a particular pitch at a given time. "He's trying to spot everything" (George Brett on Ron Guidry, *Washington Post,* Aug. 24, 1986). **2.** *n.* The location of a pitched ball as it passes

through the strike zone. A good spot is one that keeps the batter off balance, such as one thrown to a corner of the strike zone. "Frustrating [Frank] Tanana is Finding the 'Good Spots'" (*The Sporting News* headline, Aug. 17, 1987). **3.** *n.* A position in the batting order.

**spot pitcher** A pitcher with the ability to place the ball at different points in and around the strike zone.

**spot reliever** A relief pitcher who is used for a specific, usually short, assignment, such as one finishing an inning or a left-hander facing a left-handed batter.

**spot starter** A pitcher who is not in the regular pitching rotation but is available to start on an irregular or interim basis.

**spot-throw** A throw to a particular spot rather than to another fielder. **1st Use.** 1935. "A throw made to a place rather than a player" (Ralph H. Barbour, *How to Play Better Baseball;* David Shulman).

**spray** To hit the ball in any direction; e.g., "Smith sprays to all fields."

**spray hitter** A hitter who is able to place the ball unpredictably to any part of the field as opposed to one who tends to hit to one part of the field; e.g., Tony Gwynn.

**spray paint** To be able to hit to different parts of the field. "Yesterday, he [Carl Yastrzemski] drove in five runs with a two-run homer and a bases-loaded double, the kind of spray painting Yaz hasn't done since Jimmy Carter gave up the peanut farm to run for president" (Larry Whiteside, *Boston Globe,* July 10, 1983).

**spring training 1.** A program of conditioning, preparation, and exhibition play in warm climates that begins in late Feb. and ends a day or two before Opening Day. Teams conduct spring training in camps located in Florida or Arizona and play their games in small ballparks in those states. **2.** The period during which such a program occurs. See also *preseason.* **1st Use.** 1905. (*Sporting Life,* Sept. 9; Edward J. Nichols). **Etymology.** Although teams barnstormed in the South before 1870,

Harold Seymour (*Baseball: The Early Years,* 1960) pinpoints that year as the time when the Chicago White Stockings and the Cincinnati Red Stockings started the first formal camps for spring training in New Orleans, La. The first Florida encampment was made by the National League Washington Senators in 1888. **Extended Use.** A metaphor for a preliminary event or period that does not count in the final outcome. "Spring training is not very important," was Hubert H. Humphrey's response to questions about the 1968 Presidential primaries (*New York Times,* May 30, 1968).

**spy in the sky** A baseball scout who operates from a seat high behind home plate or from the press box.

**squab squad** A team of rookies and substitutes. **1st Use.** 1911. "While on the road with the 'squab squad' he slept for two nights in a Pullman berth with his right arm in the hammock, which he had been told was put there for the particular benefit of the baseball players" (Charles E. Van Loan, *The Big League;* David Shulman).

**squander 1.** *v.* For a relief pitcher to come in with a lead and leave or end the game with his team behind or the game tied. **2.** *n.* A *save opportunity* credited to a relief pitcher who allows the opponent to tie or go ahead. Compare *hold,* 4. See also *Miller-Brown System.*

**square** To prepare to bunt.

**square around** To attempt to bunt in which the batter turns toward the pitcher and holds his bat parallel to an imaginary line connecting his feet.

**square stance** A batting position in which the batter's feet are in a line parallel to home plate and with the pitcher's mound. Syn. *parallel stance; straightaway stance.*

**squawk 1.** *v.* To protest. **2.** *n.* A protest. A section in Otto Vogel's book (*Ins and Outs of Baseball,* 1952) is titled "The Fine Art of the Squawk." He makes this point: "The wise coach or captain seldom protests in the hope that an umpire might change a decision; his objective generally is to cultivate the ground for a better break the next time. This is a definite part of the game, and certainly not illegal or unsporting."

*Square around.*

**squeaker** *n.* A low-scoring game won by one run, usually in a late inning; a pitcher's duel.

**squeak past** To win a low-scoring game by one run, usually in a late inning.

**squeeze 1.** *n.* Syn. of *squeeze play.* **1st Use.** 1908. (*Spalding's Official Base Ball Guide;* Edward J. Nichols). **2.** *v.* To attempt or make the squeeze play. **1st Use.** 1907. (*New York Evening Journal,* May 14; Edward J. Nichols). **3.** *v.* For the plate umpire seemingly to reduce the size of the strike zone; e.g., "The plate umpire . . . squeezed him [Mike Mussina] so tightly . . . that Mussina and catcher Chris Hoiles took turns questioning the strike zone" (*Baltimore Sun,* Mar. 22, 1998). See also *pinch,* 3. **4.** *v.* To catch a fly ball.

**squeeze bunt** Syn. of *squeeze play.*

**squeeze off** To execute; e.g., "Smith squeezed off a perfect one-hop throw to the plate."

**squeeze play** An offensive play in which the batter attempts to score the runner on third base by bunting neatly to avoid or delay a play at the plate. It is usually attempted with less than two outs. See also *suicide squeeze; safety squeeze.* Syn. *squeeze,* 1; *squeeze bunt; bunt and run,* 1. **1st Use.** 1905.

*Squeeze play.*

"Kitty Bransfield and [Red] Dooin on Saturday succeeded in working the 'squeeze' play" (*Sporting Life*, Apr. 22). **Etymology.** Hy Turkin (*Baseball Almanac*, 1955) states that the squeeze play was first used by two Yale men (George Case and Dutch Carter) in a game against Princeton on June 16, 1894. He adds that it was introduced to the major leagues by New York Highlanders manager Clark Griffith in 1904. Another version says that Joe Yeager introduced it in Brooklyn in 1898.

**squib 1.** *v.* To bloop or hit the ball without much force, usually off the handle or end of the bat. **2.** *n.* A ball hit off the end of the bat. See also *squibb,* 2. **1st Use.** 1943. "A 'squib' is a ground ball which, generally hit with the end of the bat, has so much spring or English that instead of rolling true

it dodges through the grass" (*Baseball Magazine,* Jan.; David Shulman).

**squibb 1.** A substitute; a poor player. **1st Use.** 1917. (*Spalding's Official Base Ball Guide;* Edward J. Nichols). **2.** An early version of *squibber.* See also *squib,* 2.

**squibber** A blooper or ground ball that is difficult to field and often becomes an infield base hit; a scratch hit. Rod Kanehl is quoted by Leonard Shecter (*The Jocks,* 1969): "Baseball is a lot like life. The line drives are caught, the squibbers go for base hits. It's an unfair game." See also *squibb,* 2; *squibbler; dribbler.*

**squibbler** An earlier synonym for *squibber,* which has replaced it. **1st Use.** 1930. "The sports writers call those little flies over the infield . . . 'squibblers'" (*Country Home,* Aug.; David Shulman).

**squirrely** Descriptive of an eccentric player or flake. **Etymology.** Perhaps a borrowing from car racing, where the term has been used to describe a car that is erratic or hard to handle.

**SS 1.** Abbrev. for *shortstop,* 1. Sometimes "ss." **2.** Abbrev. for *shortstop,* 2. Sometimes "ss." **3.** Abbrev. for *split squad.*

**stab 1.** *v.* To make a spectacular or difficult catch of a batted ball; e.g., "Smith stabbed the ball after a long run." **1st Use.** 1908. (*New York Evening Journal,* May 27; Edward J. Nichols). **2.** *n.* An attempt to make a play; e.g., "Jones made a stab at fielding the line drive but it got away from him."

**stab and grab** Descriptive of a defensive move in which a fielder makes a desperate attempt ("stab") to catch ("grab") the ball. "Pete instinctively lunged to his right, stretching his gloved left hand across his body. It was simply a stab and grab attempt; on a ball that was hit that swiftly, an infielder could do little more than reach and hope it bounced right." (Dick Friendlich, *Relief Pitcher,* 1964; Charles D. Poe).

**stadium** A large ballpark, open or domed, and oval, round, or U-shaped, surrounded by tiers of seats for thousands of spectators; e.g., Yankee Stadium.

**stair step** *v.* To throw a series of higher and higher pitches. See also *up the ladder,* 1; *climb the ladder.*

**stair-stepping** The process by which a pitcher throws a series of higher and higher pitches. The idea is to keep throwing pitches higher in the strike zone until the umpire calls a ball and/or the batter swings at a pitch out of the strike zone. Syn. *stair-stuffing.*

**stair-stuffing** Syn. of *stair-stepping.*

**stake** 1. *n.* A piece of wood projecting $4\frac{1}{2}$ feet out of the ground, representing one of the four bases set 60 feet apart in a rectangle in the Massachusetts game. Syn. *base,* 3. 2. *v.* To provide a lead; e.g., "The Red Sox staked Smith to a five-run lead in the second inning."

**staketender** An infielder stationed near one of the four wooden stakes used as bases in the Massachusetts game. Syn. *basetender.*

**stance** See *batting stance.*

**stand in** 1. To come to the plate to bat; to face the pitcher. 2. To hold a batting stance without bailing out or stepping into the bucket; e.g., "There aren't many left-handed batters who like to stand in against a southpaw coming from the side."

**standing O** An ovation given by fans who stand and applaud a player who has distinguished himself.

**standings** The ranking of teams in a division based on their won-lost percentages at any given time. It also includes the number of games or half-games a team is behind the first-place team. Sometimes expressed as "standing." **1st Use.** 1881. (*New York Herald,* Sept. 12; Edward J. Nichols).

**standing up** Said of a runner coming into a base or scoring without sliding; e.g., "Smith came into second standing up." **1st Use.** 1908. (*New York Evening Journal,* Apr. 16; Edward J. Nichols).

**stand on your ear** To be off balance.

**stands** 1. The raised seating area for the fans at a ballpark. Short for *grandstand.* **1st Use.** 1881. (*New York Press,* June 1; Edward J. Nichols). 2. The fans in the grandstand. **1st Use.** 1907. (Burt

L. Standish, *Dick Merriwell's Marvel;* Edward J. Nichols).

**stand-up** Said of a hit in which the batter is able to reach base without sliding; e.g., a "stand-up double" or a "stand-up triple."

**stand-up slide** A short slide into a base in which the runner immediately bounces up to a standing position.

**stanza** Syn. of *inning,* 1. This is clearly sportswriter jargon brought in when the word "inning" has been used once too often. See also *canto.* **1st Use.** 1909. (*New York Evening Journal,* July; Edward J. Nichols).

**star** 1. *n.* A player with clear preeminence. There is no official star designation in baseball, but those who are stars seem able to make it evident. See also *superstar.* **1st Use.** 1880. (*Brooklyn Daily Eagle,* Aug. 12; Edward J. Nichols). 2. *v.* To assume the role of an outstanding player; e.g., to "star" in a series. **1st Use.** 1890. (*New York Evening Post,* May 12; Edward J. Nichols).

**starboard** Descriptive of a right-handed pitcher. From the nautical term for the right forward side of a boat. **1st Use.** David Shulman traces "starboard flinger" to 1913 and Edward J. Nichols traces "starboard slinger" to 1908 (*New York Evening Journal,* Mar. 11).

**starboarder** A right-handed pitcher.

**stare** For a player holding the ball to look at a baserunner in such a manner as to convince him that he probably would not be able to take the next base and that he should head back toward the base he is occupying. "Dwight Evans bounced back to the mound, where [Ron] Darling made the play to first base after staring [Jim] Rice back to second" (*New York Times,* Oct. 20, 1986).

**start** 1. *v.* To be in the lineup at the beginning of the game. 2. *n.* The appearance of a starting pitcher. 3. *n.* The beginning part of a baseball season for a player or team, usually characterized as being either "fast" or "slow," or "good" or "bad," in relation to a given number of games.

**starter** 1. A player who begins the game in the

starting lineup. **2.** A team's regular player at a given position. **3.** Syn. of *starting pitcher.* **1st Use.** 1912. (*New York Tribune,* Oct. 8; Edward J. Nichols).

**starting lineup** The players who begin a game and remain in place until the first substitute is brought into the game.

**starting pitcher** The pitcher who starts the game for his team and who cannot legally be replaced until he has finished with the first batter (retired him or put him on base) unless the umpire determines that the pitcher has become incapacitated. Abbrev. *SP.* Syn. *starter,* 3.

**starting rotation** See *rotation,* 1.

**Staten Island sinker** A *spitball,* 1. Credit for this coinage is generally given to pitching coach and manager George Bamberger.

**station 1.** A *base,* 2. **1st Use.** 1860. (*Beadle's Dime Base-Ball Player;* Edward J. Nichols). **2.** The defensive position assigned to a player.

**station keeper** Syn. of *baseman.* **1st Use.** 1914. "This throw was so high that the station keeper was forced to stretch for it" (Burt L. Standish, *Brick King, Backstop;* David Shulman).

**station-to-station** Said of a baseball strategy that puts runners on base and moves them *one base at a time,* while eschewing the long ball. Syn. *base-to-base.*

**statistics** Numerical facts and data, the lifeblood of baseball. As the most statistical of sports, baseball is awash in both amateur and professional statisticians. All teams and both major leagues maintain their own statistical records. Syn. *stats.*

**statistorian** One who studies baseball by combining statistics and history. The term, coined by L. Robert "Bob" Davids, SABR founder, is a blend of "statistician" and "historian."

**stats** Short for *statistics.*

**Statue of Liberty** A batter who stands at the plate and takes a called third strike. See also *wooden Indian,* 1. **1st Use.** 1937. (*Pittsburgh Press,* Jan. 11; Edward J. Nichols).

**stay alive** To be able to continue playing; e.g., "Smith stayed alive at the plate by fouling off many pitches" or "The Yankees stayed alive by winning the sixth game of the World Series" or "The Rangers will stay alive if it can keep the rally going."

**stay on the ball** For a batter to concentrate and focus on the pitched ball. "As long as I have the approach I have right now, I'll stay on the ball long enough" (Rafael Palmeiro, quoted in *Baltimore Sun,* Mar. 16, 1998).

**stay within yourself** To keep your balance; to know what you can do and cannot do on the field. The phrase "is baseball's first commandment. It means: Do not try to do things that strain your capacities and distort the smooth working of your parts—what players call 'mechanics'" (George F. Will, *Men at Work,* 1990).

**steady a pitcher** To calm a pitcher's nerves; to settle him down, usually by the catcher, a coach, or the manager talking to him on the mound. **1st Use.** 1914. (*New York Tribune,* Oct. 11; Edward J. Nichols).

**steak** A 1990s syn. used by players for *ribbie* (*Sports Illustrated,* June 15, 1998).

**steal 1.** *v.* To advance safely to the next base by running as the pitcher goes into his delivery; to achieve a stolen base. **1st Use.** 1862. (*New York Sunday Mercury,* July 13; Edward J. Nichols). **2.** *n.* The act of advancing a base by stealing. **3.** *n.* A *stolen base.* Abbrev. *S,* 3. **1st Use.** 1880. (*Chicago Inter-Ocean,* June 29; Edward J. Nichols). **4.** *v.* To sight and decipher a sign between two members of the opposing team.

**steal and slam** A variation of the *hit-and-run play.* John McGraw (*My Thirty Years in Baseball,* 1923) described the play: "The man on first would take a lead to actually steal the base. In that case, if the ball was a good one, the batter would slam at it. If the pitcher, expecting a hit and run, pitched out, the batter would simply let it go and take a chance on the runner stealing the base. The batter then would be in a better position than ever."

**stealing** See *base stealing.*

**steam 1.** The velocity of a pitch. **1st Use.** 1896. (Burt L. Standish, *Frank Merriwell's School Days;* Edward J. Nichols). **2.** The endurance of a pitcher.

**steamer** A fastball.

**steamroll** For a baserunner to make crushing body contact with a fielder while sliding into a base; e.g., "Smith steamrolled the catcher with his hard slide."

**Stengelese** The colorful vocabulary, fractured English, and implausible brand of double-talk spoken by Hall of Fame manager Casey Stengel. "By talking in the purest jabberwocky he has learned that he can avoid answering questions and at the same time leave his audience struggling against a mild form of mental paralysis" (Gayle Talbot, *San Francisco Call-Bulletin,* Feb. 1, 1954; Peter Tamony).

Stengelese is difficult to capture (sportswriter Red Smith once likened it to "picking up quicksilver with boxing gloves") but here is an example from a 1958 Congressional hearing on baseball when Sen. Langer asked whether Stengel intended to keep monopolizing the world's championship in New York City (*The Congressional Record,* July 9, 1958):

"Well, I will tell you. I got a little concern yesterday in the first three innings when I saw the three players I had gotten rid of, and I said when I lost nine what am I going to do and when I had a couple of my players I thought so great of that did not do so good up to the sixth inning I was more confused but I finally had to go and call on a young man in Baltimore that we don't own and the Yankees don't own him, and he is doing pretty good, and I would actually have to tell you that I think we are more the Greta Garbo type now from success.

"We are being hated, I mean, from the ownership and all, we are being hated. Every sport that gets too great or one individual—but if we made 27 cents and it pays to have a winner at home, why would not you have a good winner in your own park if you were an owner? That is the result of baseball. An owner gets most of the money at home and it is up to him and his staff to do better or they ought to be discharged."

**Stengelese.** *President Richard Nixon talks baseball with Casey Stengel, longtime Yankees manager, at a White House reception in 1969.*

Stengelese has been applied to others. "Giants manager Tom 'Clancy' Sheehan is from the old school of ambiguity in naming names. Clancy's Stengelese often out-Stengels Casey." (Art Rosenbaum, *San Francisco Chronicle,* July 11, 1960; Peter Tamony).

**step in the bucket** To step back or pull away from home plate with one's front foot while batting. A right-handed batter so afflicted will step toward third base. Though normally considered poor form as a way of batting, some good batters have gotten away with it. "You can't hit very well if you step in the bucket" (Morris Shirts, *Warm Up For Little League Baseball,* 1971, 1976). However, most stepping in the bucket occurs when the batter is fooled by an off-speed pitch and shifts his weight and foot in anticipation of a fastball. See also *foot in the bucket,* 1.

**stepoff** *n.* The act of a pitcher who backs off the rubber to keep a runner close to his base.

**step off the rubber** For a pitcher to remove himself from the act of pitching. A pitcher must have his pivot foot in contact with the rubber while pitching, but he takes his foot off it as the pitch is delivered, to attempt to pick off a base runner, to take a time out, or to confer with other players or the manager.

**step on the plate 1.** To score. A baserunner who touches home plate gains a run for the offensive team. **2.** For a batter to commit an infraction and be declared out by the plate umpire when hitting a ball (either fair or foul) while one or both feet are in contact with home plate.

**step out of the box** For a batter to remove himself from the batter's box. If this is done with the umpire's approval before the pitcher begins his windup, the pitcher must wait until the batter returns to the box. If the batter steps out after the windup has begun or without approval from the umpire, the pitcher can deliver the ball and it will count as an official pitch and be called a strike or a ball.

**stepping foot** The front foot that a pitcher uses to advance his delivery, as contrasted with the *pivot foot* which stays in contact with the rubber. The stepping foot of a right-handed pitcher is his left foot and that of a left-handed pitcher is his right foot. Syn. *striding foot, 3.*

**steps on his toes** Said of a pitcher who cannot field bunts.

**step up to the plate** For a batter to enter the batter's box. **Extended Use.** The phrase is applied to anyone who is willing to enter the fray or to get into the action; e.g., "Are you going to keep talking about it or are you willing to step up to the plate?"

**Stetson hitter** A derogatory term for a bad hitter; one who hits his hat size.

**Steve Blass disease** Sudden inability for a pitcher to throw strikes or inexplicably to issue an extraordinary number of bases on balls; fear of home plate for a pitcher; complete loss of control. Named for the Pittsburgh Pirates pitcher who lost his control in 1973 by issuing 84 walks and hitting 12 batters in 88⅔ innings. In 1972, it took him 249⅔ innings to issue 84 walks.

**stick 1.** A baseball bat. "I was going up there with a stick when Callahan calls me back and sends Easterly up" (Ring W. Lardner, *You Know Me Al,* 1914). **1st Use.** 1868. (*New York Herald,* Aug. 4; Edward J. Nichols). **2.** The batter's ability at the plate; e.g., a batter may be known as a "good stick" or a "weak stick."

**Stick, The** A nickname for *Candlestick Park* (now renamed 3Com Park at Candlestick Point) in San Francisco. It has been called "The Stick" since it opened in 1960 because, according to local fans, "the wind blew out the Candle." "I can remember one time in the early seventies when The Stick was being expanded for football that he [Willie McCovey] hit one completely out of the park over the scaffolding that was stacked a mile high beyond right field" (Norman Clow, *Anderson Valley* [Cal.] *Advertiser,* Apr. 9, 1986).

**stick a fork in him** To determine that a pitcher is to be relieved. According to Frank Gibbons (*Baseball Digest,* May 1959): "It means the man is done for the day. Bushed. Tired. Exhausted." The term is based on the culinary practice of sticking a fork in a turkey or roast to determine if it is done.

**stickball** A variant of baseball commonly played on city streets with a broomstick or similar piece of wood and a rubber ball. The game usually requires an elaborate and very specific set of ground rules, along the order of: "The blue Ford is a double if you hit it on the fly, but an out if the ball hits it on the bounce." Home plate is usually either a manhole cover or a plate chalked on the pavement. A game requires at least two players. The distance of a long ball is measured in sewers; e.g., passing two sewers is good and three is fantastic. Reminiscing on Willie Mays's custom of playing stickball outside the Polo Grounds in New York, an old-timer told sportswriter Dave Anderson: "I used to play stickball with Willie up on the hill. He used to hit five sewers." (*San Francisco Chronicle,* May 17, 1972; Peter Tamony). Mays expressed his nostalgia for New York in 1959 when he told sportswriter Jimmy Cannon about the odd customs of San Francisco: "The kids don't play stickball here. The streets are too hilly" (*San Francisco Call-Bulletin,* May 15; Peter Tamony). **1st Use.** "Stick ball is a new name to me. . . . [It] is a third cousin to baseball, played with a soft ball and a broomstick on the streets of New York. It is one of the most popular pastimes of boys gathered in various settlement houses. With sand lots getting scarcer and scarcer the youth still find a way to emulate Babe Ruth and get their start in baseball."

(George Daley, *New York Herald-Tribune,* Apr. 19, 1934; Peter Morris).

**sticker** *arch.* Syn. of *batter.* **1st Use.** 1888. (*New York Press,* Apr. 7; Edward J. Nichols).

**"stick it in his ear"** Nasty but common advice of the bench jockey to his teammate on the mound to hit the batter in the head. It is stronger than "dust him off." **Usage Note.** The phrase is not to be used lightly. Joe Williams (syndicated column, Oct. 12, 1953) wrote: "The Yankees came out of the Series with reduced respect for Jackie Robinson. They claim the Brooklyn star deliberately tried to foment ill feelings when he hung the 'stick-it-in-his-ear' crack on [Casey] Stengel. Pressed for details, Robinson finally had to admit the information came to him second hand from several players." (Peter Tamony). **Extended Use.** Used impolitely in other walks of life.

**stickman** *arch.* Syn. of *batter.* **1st Use.** 1914. "But what helped him to this and even more than his natural ability as a stickman, was a cool, indomitable determination" (Burt L. Standish, *Brick King, Backstop;* David Shulman).

**stickpin** A batter who chokes up on the bat. The term was used frequently by Casey Stengel to the point that it was identified as part of his "private lexicon" (Fred Lieb, *Comedians and Pranksters of Baseball,* 1958).

**sticks** The minor leagues, in reference to the less-populous areas of the country where the lower-level teams played. **1st Use.** 1914. (Ring W. Lardner, *You Know Me Al;* Edward J. Nichols). **Etymology.** The term appears to have originated in either baseball or show business as a derogatory reference to the flora of the countryside. It stems from that same urge to label as was behind the terms "bush" and "bush league."

**sticksmith** *arch.* Syn. of *batter.* **1st Use.** 1910. (*Baseball Magazine,* May; Edward J. Nichols).

**stickwork** Hitting ability; skill in using a baseball bat. **1st Use.** 1890. (*New York Press,* July 4; Edward J. Nichols).

**stiff back** The excuse of an infielder who does not or cannot bend down to field a grounder.

**stile** Short for *turnstile.*

**sting** To hit the ball hard or sharply; e.g., "Smith stung one for a triple to deep center." **1st Use.** 1906. (*Sporting Life,* Mar. 10; Edward J. Nichols).

**sting ball** A ball thrown so hard it stings the glove hand of the player catching it; e.g., "Smith throws sting balls because his arm is so strong."

**stinger** A hard-hit ball. **1st Use.** 1868. "He drove a stinger to Howe, who stopped it, picked it up, and threw it to Gould, making a beautiful play" (Chadwick Scrapbooks; David Shulman).

**stinker** A ball hit between the infield and outfield; a *Texas Leaguer.*

**stir a breeze** To strike out.

**stirrup socks** The team-colored socks with a loop at the bottom that are worn over the white *sanitary socks.* Most players in the 1990s wear their pants down to their ankles so that the stirrup socks are seldom visible.

**stitch-ball** A slowly pitched ball. **1st Use.** 1915. "[The] third [pitch] was Rube's wide, slow, tantalizing 'stitch-ball,' as we call it, for the reason that it came so slow a batter could count the stitches" (Zane Grey, *The Redheaded Outfield and Other Stories;* David Shulman).

**stolen base** A base gained by a runner advancing to it while the pitcher is in his motion, unaided by a base hit, putout, error, force out, fielder's choice, passed ball, wild pitch, or balk. The success of the play hinges on catching the defensive team off guard. A stolen base is officially credited to the runner. Abbrev. *SB.* Syn. *steal,* 3. **1st Use.** 1889. (*Trenton Times,* July 8; Edward J. Nichols).

**stone glove** A poor defensive player.

**stone hands** The hands of a poor fielder. "The innings flew by to the accompaniment of . . . a flurry of witticisms in the press rows about Willie Davis's attack of stone hands in Los Angeles" (Roger Kahn, *The Boys of Summer,* 1972; Charles D. Poe).

**stonewall** *arch.* An unusually tight infield from which very few batted balls escape. The archetypi-

**Stolen base.** *Ty Cobb steals home for the Philadelphia Athletics (1927) against the Boston Red Sox. Catcher Grover Hartley makes a futile attempt of the tag.*

cal stonewall was that of the 1880s Chicago White Stockings, comprising first baseman Cap Anson, second baseman Fred Pfeffer, shortstop Ned Williamson, and third baseman Tom Burns. **1st Use.** 1888. (Chicago *Inter-Ocean,* July 13; Edward J. Nichols).

**stoolball** A primitive stick-and-ball game dating from the 12th century in England. A local adaptation of ancient pagan rites and a direct forbear of cricket and baseball, stoolball was characterized by a) constant association with the Church and the churchyard as the field of play, b) association with the Easter season, c) always played by young men and maidens, and d) use of flavored cakes (usually tansy, a bitter herb) as prizes. According to Robert W. Henderson (*Ball, Bat and Bishop,* 1947), a batter, either bare-handed or with some form of a bat, stood before an upended three-legged stool: he was "out" if a ball hit the stool or was caught after being struck, and another player took his place at the stool. The winner was the player with

the greatest number of hits. The game was brought to America by the Pilgrims: Gov. William Bradford (1621) discovered men of Plymouth Plantation "frolicking in ye street, at play openly; some at pitching ye ball, some at stoole ball and shuch-like sport." Over time, the game became more complicated as more stools were stationed around the field. In 1916, an attempt was made to revive the game, using a small square target instead of a stool, and a stoolball association was formed in 1927 which had more than 3,000 clubs in 1947. The game of "bittle-battle," a form of stoolball, was mentioned in the *Domesday Book* (1086), the survey of England made by command of William the Conqueror.

**stoopball** A variation of baseball played without a bat. A rubber ball is thrown against a set of steps (or stoop) by the player on offense, while the defense tries to catch the ball on the fly as it comes off the stoop. A ball caught on the fly is an out. Hits and runs are registered by the number of bounces the ball takes or by the distance it flies.

**stop 1.** *v.* To knock down, slow, smother, or otherwise bring a ball under control so that it can be played. **2.** *n.* A defensive play on a batted ground ball. **1st Use.** 1864. (*Brooklyn Daily Eagle,* Sept. 20; Edward J. Nichols).

**stop at the junk yard** A jibe directed at players having trouble holding onto the ball; e.g., "I'm stopping at the junk yard on the way home. Want me to pick you up some new hands." (*The Sporting News,* Mar. 6, 1982).

**stopper 1.** A starting pitcher who can be counted on to win a crucial game; a team's top pitcher, one who can stop a losing streak. During his career with the Boston Red Sox (1984–96), Roger Clemens won 111 times after a team loss. **1st Use.** 1948. "I had been known as the 'stopper' for the [Boston Red] Sox for a long time and I really had to be on September 13, 1946, in Cleveland, the day we clinched the American League championship" (Tex Hughson, quoted in *San Francisco Examiner,* Mar. 10; Peter Tamony). **2.** A relief pitcher who can be counted on to stop the opposition from scoring; a *closer,* 2. "The 'stoppers,' usually the most dependable on the staff, are apt to get the nod most any time" (Arthur Richman & Milton Richman, on the bullpen, *Collier's,* July 9, 1954; Peter Tamony). **3.** The catcher.

**stop position** That part of a pitcher's motion in the set position before releasing the ball to the plate. See also *discernible stop.*

**stop sign** A coach's signal to hold up a baserunner from advancing. "[Chicago Cubs third base coach Tom] Gamboa waved [Sammy] Sosa home, then put on the stop sign too late after Sosa had rounded third . . . [and] was thrown out" (*Baltimore Sun,* May 29, 1998). "I'm not going to run through a stop sign. He [Baltimore Orioles third base coach Sam Perlozzo] threw his hands up and I got stopped." (Lenny Webster, quoted in *Baltimore Sun,* Aug. 18, 1997). Compare *green light,* 2.

**stove league** See *hot stove league.* **1st Use.** 1915. (*Baseball Magazine,* Dec.; Edward J. Nichols).

**straight as a string** Said of a fastball without a hop.

**straightaway** *adj.* Pertaining to an orthodox defensive position, neither to the right nor to the left. A center fielder is playing straightaway if he is in the center of the outfield in line with home plate and second base. Also spelled "straight away."

**straightaway hitter** A hitter who hits the ball to the part of the field according to where it is pitched; e.g., a right-handed batter will hit an outside pitch to right field, an inside pitch to left field, and a pitch over the plate to center field.

**straightaway stance** Syn. of *square stance.*

**straight elimination** [softball term] Syn. of *single elimination.*

**"straighten it out"** A rally cry to encourage a batter who has hit one or more foul balls.

**straighten one out** To hit a line drive. **1st Use.** 1907. (*New York Times,* Oct. 9; Edward J. Nichols).

**strand 1.** For a batter to leave one or more runners on base at the end of the team's half inning. **2.** For a pitcher to retire the side with one or more runners on base. Syn. *hang,* 2.

**stranded** Syn. of *left on base,* 1. **1st Use.** 1905. (*Sporting Life,* Sept. 2; Edward J. Nichols).

**Strat-O-Matic Baseball** A tabletop baseball board game using dice and cards, and a closely guarded method of rating players, developed by Strat-O-Matic Game Co., Great Neck, N.Y.

**strawberry** A red skin abrasion with the texture and hue of a strawberry, produced on the upper leg, thigh, or buttocks of a sliding baserunner. Syn. *hustle blister.* **1st Use.** 1937. (*Pittsburgh Press,* Jan. 11; Edward J. Nichols).

**straw that stirs the drink, the** A phrase used by Reggie Jackson soon after joining the New York Yankees in 1977 to describe where he fit in the metaphoric scheme of things; i.e., the most important member of the team. "You know, this team . . . it all flows from me. I've got to keep it going. I'm the straw that stirs the drink." (Jackson, quoted by Robert Ward, *Sport,* June 1977). The image was strong enough to inspire many parallels. To quote from a letter to the *Baltimore Sun* (May 25, 1986): "If there is a drink to be stirred in Baltimore this baseball season, you can bet that Eddie Murray will be the straw that does it."

Sensational
# JOE DIMAGGIO
Will Seek To Hit Safely In His
## 49th
Consecutive Game.
## Thur. Nite, July 10
AT ST. LOUIS

## Browns vs. Yankees
Sportsman's Park--8:30 P. M.

Tickets Now on Sale at Browns Arcade Ticket
Office--Phone, CHestnut 7900.

*Streak. From 1941, this St. Louis Browns poster turned Joe DiMaggio's hitting streak into a promotional event.*

**streak 1.** *n.* An uninterrupted string of accomplishments or failures by a player or a team; e.g., a "winning streak," a "losing streak," and a "hitting streak." The term is also applied to such achievements as Cal Ripken Jr.'s consecutive-innings streak of 8,243 innings, which ended in Sept. 1987 and his consecutive-game playing streak of 2,632, which ended on Sept. 20, 1998. Unquestionably, before Ripken's consecutive-game playing streak, the most famous streak in baseball history was Joe DiMaggio's feat of hitting in 56 consecutive games in 1941. Both the term and the concept have a high degree of significance. Among other things, they can help give a particular season its character. A key line in Bill Wolle's summary of the 1987 season (*Houston Post*, Oct. 6, 1987; Charles D. Poe): "The season began with a record 13-game winning streak by the Milwaukee Brewers and wound up with San Diego's Benito Santiago fashioning a 34-game hitting streak, a record for rookies and catchers."

Significantly, there is a special section (10.24) of the *Official Baseball Rules* that sets forth the criteria for establishing consecutive hitting streaks,

consecutive-game hitting streaks, and consecutive-game playing streaks. Another major streak was established on Sept. 28, 1988, when Los Angeles Dodgers hurler Orel Hershiser pitched the longest string of scoreless innings (59) in the history of the game. Syn. *string.* **2.** *v.* To be on a streak.

**Streak, The** The name given to Cal Ripken Jr.'s consecutive-game playing streak of 2,632 games, which began on May 30, 1982 and ended Sept. 20, 1998.

**streak hitter** A player who gets base hits in clusters, which alternate with slumps.

**streaky** Occurring in streaks; uneven in accomplishments. "Streaky Brewers Count Their Blessings in Fans" (*Washington Post* headline, Aug. 27, 1987).

**strength against strength** The situation in which a pitcher's best pitch is also the batter's preferred pitch; "a pitcher challenging a hitter with his best pitch, even if it's the hitter's favorite type" (Orel Hershiser, *Out of the Blue,* 1989).

**stretch 1.** *n.* The phase of a pitcher's delivery during which his arms are raised above and behind his head. Its function is to loosen the arm and back muscles. **2.** *n.* A modified or short windup, used esp. by a pitcher to keep baserunners from taking too long a lead and to decrease the length of time it takes to pitch the ball. It starts with the pitcher keeping his hands together at the waist, then raising them to or above his head, then bringing his hands slowly back to the waist, then resting or stopping in the set position to check the runner's lead, before delivering the pitch. To go through the stretch without a discernible stop is to commit a balk. Compare *windup.* **3.** *n.* The position taken by a baseman (esp. the first baseman) as he keeps one foot on the bag while reaching as far as he can to catch the ball thrown by another fielder before the runner touches the base. **4.** *v.* To take an extra base on a hit, usually due to fast, bold running; e.g., "Smith stretched his double into a triple." **1st Use.** 1897. (*New York Tribune,* Sept. 9; Edward J. Nichols). **5.** *n.* The late season when divisional races heat up; the last few games, or last four to five weeks, of the season, usually starting after Labor Day. The term is short for *homestretch,* which is borrowed from horse racing. **6.** *n.* A series of baseball games. **7.** *n.* See *seventh-inning stretch.*

**stretch drive** The effort made during the last few games of the season when a contending team is striving for a division championship. Syn. *stretch run.*

**stretch position** Syn. of *set position.*

**stretch run** Syn. of *stretch drive.*

**stride 1.** *v.* To step into and give power to one's swing when batting. Not all batters stride and some of the best (such as Joe DiMaggio) stride only a few inches. Batters who do not stride are described as flat-footed. To stride to excess, as younger or less-experienced players tend to do, is to overstride. **2.** *n.* The forward foot movement of a batter when swinging at a pitch. **3.** *v.* For a pitcher to raise one foot as the ball is about to be delivered. **4.** *n.* The forward movement of a pitcher as he is about to deliver the pitch.

**stride in step with the pitch** To judge the exact speed of the pitch and hit the ball squarely; to time the pitch perfectly. "When batters are striding in pace with the pitch, the pitcher is in for a drubbing" (H. G. Salsinger, *Baseball Digest,* Aug. 1945).

**striding foot 1.** The forward foot that the batter uses to step into and swing at the ball. **2.** The front foot that a fielder uses to step forward to give strength to his throw. **3.** The *stepping foot* of a pitcher.

**strike 1.** A legally pitched ball that is called as such by the umpire because it is either a) swung at and missed, b) in the strike zone and not swung at, c) fouled off but not caught with less than two strikes, d) a bunted foul with two strikes, or e) a foul tip that is caught by the catcher with two strikes. A batter is out after three strikes. A strike is announced as such by the plate umpire, who also signals it by raising his right hand. **1st Use.** 1845. (Knickerbocker Rules). **Extended Use.** A disadvantage or mistake; e.g., "Her attitude is a strike against her." This usage can even be applied to baseball: "[Commissioner Peter] Ueberroth Makes It Clear: Two Drug Strikes and You're Out" (*St. Petersburg Times* headline, Apr. 2, 1987). **2.** A highly accurate throw from the outfield. **Extended Use.** Something perfectly delivered, such as a "touchdown strike." **3.** A work stoppage or walkout by the players. Much was made during the 1981 players' strike of the irony that the word "strike" was so important to the game itself. This prompted a reader (Phillip Coe) of *The Sporting News* (July 18, 1981) to redefine other terms; e.g., a "walk" was changed to "walkout" in order "to complement the new definition of 'strike!'" As of this writing baseball has had seven strikes or work stoppages: 1972 (13 days), 1976 (17-day spring lockout by owners), 1980 (one week during spring training), 1981 (50 days), 1985 (two days), 1990 (32-day lockout), and 1994–95 (232 days, no 1994 World Series, and 1995 season started late).

**strike out** *v.* **1.** To retire from the plate as a result of three strikes; e.g., "Smith strikes out swinging." Syn. *punch out,* 1. **1st Use.** 1866. (*New York Herald,* Aug. 28; Edward J. Nichols). **Extended Use.** To fail completely. **2.** To put a batter out as a result of three strikes; e.g., "Jones strikes out Smith on a curveball." Syn. *fan,* 1; *K,* 3.

**strikeout** *n.* **1.** An out made by a batter charged with three strikes. Abbrev. *SO.* **1st Use.** 1862. (*New York Sunday Mercury,* June 29; Edward J. Nichols). **2.** An out recorded by a pitcher when the batter has been charged with three strikes. The number of strikeouts achieved by a pitcher in a game, season, or career is a barometer of his effectiveness. Symbol *K,* 1. Abbrev. *SO.* Syn. *K,* 2; *punchout.*

**strikeout artist** A pitcher who strikes out many batters.

**strikeout king 1.** The pitcher with the most strikeouts during any given season. Nolan Ryan holds the single-season strikeout record of 383 in 1973. **2.** The pitcher with the most strikeouts in baseball history. Nolan Ryan became the current strikeout king on Apr. 27, 1983, by passing Walter Johnson's previous record of 3,508 strikeouts. Ryan retired after the 1993 season with 5,714 strikeouts. **1st Use.** 1922. "Thomas Ramsey, eminent strike-out king [of the Louisville Colonels in the late 1880s]" (Ernest J. Lanigan, *Baseball Cyclopedia;* Edward J. Nichols).

**strike out looking** To take a called third strike. See also *catch looking.* Syn. *go down looking.*

**strikeout rule** [softball term] A slow pitch rule in Amateur Softball Association of America that the batter must hit the ball fair if he or she has two strikes; otherwise, it is an out should the batter hit the ball foul. In United States Slo-Pitch Softball Association (USSSA) play, a batter can hit one foul after the second strike, but the second foul is ruled an out. The USSSA rule gives the batter a decided advantage.

**strike out swinging** To swing at and miss a pitch for the third strike. Syn. *go down swinging.*

**strike out the side** To retire three batters in one inning by striking them out.

**striker** *obs.* Syn. of *batter.* **1st Use.** 1854. (Knickerbocker Rules).

**striker to the line** "Batter up," per 1854 Knickerbocker Rules.

**strike zone 1.** The imaginary rectangle over home plate that defines a called strike. It has varied over the years. Since 1995, the *Official Baseball Rules* (rule 2.00) defines the strike zone's upper limit as "a horizontal line at the midpoint between the top of the shoulders and the top of the uniform pants" and the lower level as "a line at the hollow beneath the kneecap." The strike zone is determined from the batter's stance as he is about to swing at a pitched ball; it also depends on the size of the batter and the proclivity of the umpire calling strikes.

A pitch thrown in the strike zone will be called a strike if it is not swung at. One given of the game is that, despite the explicit designation of the rules, the strike zone is in reality a subjective area and its dimensions will vary from umpire to umpire and from league to league. "Over the years, the strike zone has gotten smaller and slightly wider. Umpires are more likely to call pitches on the corner strikes, but anything above the waist or below the knee is usually a ball." (Brad Snyder, *Baltimore Sun,* Apr. 27, 1996).

From 1887 to 1949 and from 1963 to 1968, the strike zone was from the top of the batter's shoulders to the bottom of his knees; from 1950 to 1962, it was from the armpits to the top of the knees; in 1969, the upper limit was lowered from the shoulders to the armpits; and in 1988, the upper limit was the midpoint between the top of the shoulders and the top of the uniform pants. Syn. *zone,* 1. **2.** [softball term] That space over any part of home plate between the batter's armpits and the top of the knees (fast pitch softball) and between the batter's back shoulder and front knee (slow pitch softball).

**string** Syn. of *streak,* 1.

**stringbean** A tall, thin player.

**strings** See *pitching to the strings.*

**stroke 1.** *n.* An even, smooth swing, which often results in a batted ball. **2.** *v.* To hit the ball well and with apparent ease; e.g., "Smith stroked the pitch for a double." **3.** *n./arch.* A batted ball.

**stroker** A batter with a controlled swing.

**stroll 1.** To draw a base on balls. **1st Use.** 1908. (*New York Evening Journal,* Sept. 11; Edward J. Nichols). **2.** To take a lead off first base.

**'Stros** Shortened nickname for the Houston Astros.

**struggle 1.** To be in a slump. A common cliché of the game is to say that a batter is "struggling at the plate" or a pitcher is "struggling from the mound." **2.** For a team to have a difficult time winning enough games to be considered a contender, owing to bad luck, injuries, and slumps.

**stuff 1.** A pitcher's assortment or repertoire of pitches collectively, together with his ability to deliver and control them in the proper sequence at the right velocity to the desired area of the strike zone. Syn. *dope,* 2; *equipment,* 2. **1st Use.** 1905. (*Sporting Life,* Sept. 9; Edward J. Nichols). **2.** The spin or break and the speed that a pitcher imparts to (puts on) the ball. The term originally referred to the spin on the ball, but has subsequently broadened to include other movements of the ball, its speed, and control.

**stun** To overwhelm an opposing team with many runs.

**stunner** A key base hit. **1st Use.** 1868. "Hatfield sends [him] home by a 'stunner' to right field" (Chadwick Scrapbooks; David Shulman).

**stunt** An act designed to be different and to attract the attention of the fans. A classic example is using one player to play all nine positions within a single game, as was done by Bert Campaneris of the Kansas City Athletics in 1965 and Cesar Tovar of the Minnesota Twins in 1968. The *New York Times* (May 29, 1978) asserted: "These are the only two such stunts in major-league history."

**stuntman** An honorific name for a reserve or nonstarter, which implies far greater involvement than the traditional "benchwarmer" nickname. **Etymology.** The term was first applied during the 1988 season by Los Angeles Dodgers manager Tommy Lasorda. It was borrowed from the stuntmen of Hollywood fame and explained by Mickey Hatcher, one of Lasorda's stuntmen, as a proper name for "the doubles, the guys who fill in, the guys who do the dirty work" (*The Sporting News,* June 27, 1988).

**styler** A player who always looks good. At bat, a styler looks good before, during, and after he swings.

**stylin'** Said of a batter who uses up time at the plate for grooming, such as adjusting his batting glove or uniform. "Some veterans . . . think that the proper reward for a 'stylin'' player is a fastball in the ribs" (Thomas Boswell, *Washington Post,* Aug. 30, 1981).

**sub** Short for *substitute,* 1. **1st Use.** 1889. (*Trenton Times,* July 24; Edward J. Nichols).

**submarine 1.** *adj.* Said of a pitch, delivery, or style of pitching characterized by an underhand or sidearm motion. **1st Use.** 1919. (*American Magazine,* June; Edward J. Nichols). **2.** *v.* To pitch using the submarine delivery. **Etymology.** Derived from the underwater vessel.

**submarine pitch** A pitch thrown lower than the usual sidearm delivery.

**submariner** A pitcher who uses the submarine-style delivery; e.g., Carl Mays, whose underhand pitch killed Cleveland Indians shortstop Ray Chapman in 1920. Syn. *subway slinger.*

**substation** A term used by relief pitchers for the bullpen, who see the dugout as the "main terminal."

**substitute 1.** *n.* Any player not in the original lineup who is subsequently brought into the game. Syn. *sub.* **Usage Note.** Although "substitute" is a legitimate and useful term in baseball, it is usually too general to cover specific situations. The preferred form is to specify the exact role of the substitute; e.g., a pinch runner or a short reliever. **2.** *v.* To put a player into a game in progress by replacing a player already in the lineup.

**suburbanite** An outfielder.

**suburbs 1.** The destination of the long ball; the area where monstrous home runs land. Compare *downtown,* 1. **2.** *arch.* The outfield. **1st Use.** 1911. (*Baseball Magazine,* Oct.; Edward J. Nichols).

**subway series 1.** A World Series in which the two opposing clubs could travel between their home fields by using the New York City subway system. Traditionally, it referred to a World Series played between the New York Yankees and the Brooklyn Dodgers (the last one took place in 1956), but today it is most commonly used when a Yankees vs. New York Mets World Series might be in the offing. "Subway series is a synonym for civil war" (Samuel G. Freedman, *New York Times,* Oct. 19, 1986). See also *All-City Series.* **2.** An interleague series during the regular season between the New York Yankees and the New York Mets. "Subway Series Excites Fans More Than Players; Scalpers getting $600 for Yankees–Mets tickets" (*Baltimore Sun* headline, June 27, 1998). **Extended Use.** As other sports have fielded two New York City–area teams, the term has come to refer figuratively to pairings of the Rangers and Islanders in hockey and the Jets and the Giants in football (even though some of these teams are not reached by subway).

**subway slinger** Syn. of *submariner.* **Etymology.** From the concept of a subway being underground.

**sucker** A blooper, esp. one that makes the fielders trying to get to it look foolish; a *Texas Leaguer.* **1st Use.** 1868. "Al Reach sent a sucker to right, which gave him first" (Chadwick Scrapbooks; David Shulman).

**sucker pitch** [softball term] A short pitch that a player throws with exaggerated motion, hoping that the batter will mistime his or her swing.

**Suds Series** A nickname for the 1982 World Series between the St. Louis Cardinals and Milwaukee Brewers, representing two cities with ties to beer ("suds"). The Milwaukee team is named for that city's production of beer and the St. Louis team was owned by the Busch family (of Anheuser-Busch breweries).

**suicide squeeze** A *squeeze play* in which the runner on third base breaks for the plate with the pitch as the batter attempts to lay down a bunt. If the bunt is unsuccessful, the runner is almost always out, a "suicide." Compare *safety squeeze*.

**suit up** To change from street clothes to a baseball player's uniform. Syn. *dress*.

**sullivan** One who sits up all night; a player who will not sleep in a train. See also *Sullivan sleeper*.

**Sullivan sleeper** *arch.* A railroad day coach on which there are no sleeping accommodations. This is a late 19th-century term, which sometimes showed up as *O'Sullivan sleeper* in later references. **1st Use.** 1886. "I did not indulge in a Pullman, but took what ball-players call a 'Sullivan sleeper'—that is, I sat up all night in the smoker" (*Lippincott's Magazine,* Aug.; David Shulman). **Etymology.** Almost certainly from Ted Sullivan, 1888 manager of the Washington Senators, who was notoriously stingy when it came to providing the more expensive sleeping berths; e.g., when he took the team to Florida, he provided 14 day-coach seats for the 14 players but only seven Pullman berths.

**Sultan of Swat 1.** A nickname for Babe Ruth. There have been many puckish plays on this title. "A spring season sloth, [Bob] Horner is the sultan of slow starters" (Roy Cummings, *Tampa Tribune,* Apr. 3, 1988). **2.** An award named in honor of Babe Ruth, a native Baltimorean, given by the Maryland Professional Baseball Players Association. **Etymology.** John Thorn (*The Armchair Book of Baseball,* 1985) traces the title to the Indian state of Swat that once had a sultan or akhond. When the sultan died in 1878 his obituary appeared in the *Times* (London). It inspired Edward Lear to write a ditty called "The Akond of Swat." Thorn says the poem was "surely some sportswriter's inspiration for Ruth's 'title.'" In baseballese, a swat is a long hit—something Ruth specialized in.

**summer classic** Syn. of *All-Star Game,* 1. Sometimes spelled "Summer Classic."

**summer game** The game of baseball. "Just hearing the sounds of the summer game, either in person or on the TV news, makes you feel as if you are stealing time" (John Eisenberg, *Baltimore Sun,* Feb. 15, 1998). See also Roger Angell's *The Summer Game* (1972).

**summer spectacle** Syn. of *All-Star Game,* 1.

**Sunday ball** Baseball played on the Sabbath. Once the most divisive of issues, this was a red flag to those who believed that baseball, especially the professional version, should not take place on the Sabbath.

**Sunday best** Syn. of *Sunday pitch.*

**Sunday pitch** A pitcher's most effective offering; his out pitch. "Well, a pitcher out there, if he's a fast ball pitcher, his best pitch, what we call a Sunday Pitch, would be his fast ball" (Dizzy Dean, *Dizzy Baseball,* 1952). Syn. *Sunday best.*

**Sunday pitcher** An old pitcher who works only one day a week.

**sun field** That part of the playing field where there is the most sun in the fielders' eyes during an afternoon game. To many, the most notorious sun field in baseball is left field at Yankee Stadium, especially the late afternoon sun of Oct., when the World Series is played. Other sun fields include right field at Fenway Park in Boston and left field at the Polo Grounds in New York. The proliferation of night games has given this term a whiff of nostalgia. **1st Use.** 1905. (*Sporting Life,* Sept. 9; Edward J. Nichols).

**sunflower seed finger** Pain caused as three fingers are used to grab the sunflower seeds from the packet. As the pinky finger spreads the packet, it causes stress between the third and fourth fingers. Philadelphia Phillies team doctor Phillip Marone and trainer Jeff Cooper reported on and named the phenomenon in the June 1995 newsletter of the professional baseball athletic trainers.

**sunglasses** Dark-tinted eyeglasses used as a protection from the sun. Sunglasses are part of the uniform of many players, esp. outfielders, during day games. Modern baseball sunglasses differ from other sunglasses in that the lens portion rests against the bottom of the bill of the hat and is flipped down over the eyes as needed.

**sun hit** A batted ball that falls in for a hit because the fielder loses track of it in the sun. **1st Use.** 1897. (*New York Tribune,* Aug. 9; Edward J. Nichols).

**sunshine game** The game of baseball. "It's hard to see how any of this constitutes a menace to the sunshine game" (Roger Angell, *The Summer Game,* 1972).

**superscout** An unofficial title for a scout who locates more than his share of talented players; e.g., Jim Russo of the Baltimore Orioles.

**superstar** An exceptionally outstanding and competent baseball player. See also *star,* 1.

**support** 1. Fielding aid to the pitcher in retiring batters. **1st Use.** 1867. (Chadwick Scrapbooks; Edward J. Nichols). **2.** Run production that gives the pitcher a chance to win the game.

**sure out** 1. A predictable putout; e.g., throwing to first base on an infield play. Often with a runner on base, the sure out will be made to first base rather than risking a throw to get an advancing baserunner with a play that may not be made successfully. **2.** A batter who is not likely to get a base hit. See also *easy out,* 1.

**surprise bunt** A bunt that is attempted when the circumstances of the game do not suggest one. **1st Use.** 1935. "There are two types, the sacrifice bunt and the surprise bunt" (Ralph H. Barbour, *How to Play Better Baseball;* David Shulman).

**surrender** For a pitcher to give up hits and runs; e.g., "Smith surrendered two consecutive doubles and one run."

**surveyor** A player with a good eye at the plate; one who walks frequently by not swinging at balls out of the strike zone.

**survival drive** The effort made by a player to maintain his overall effectiveness.

**suspend** 1. To stop temporarily a baseball game because of inclement weather or some unforeseen condition. **2.** To deny a manager, player, coach, or other person the privilege of participating for a stated period of time because of an infraction of the rules. "The [Pittsburgh] Pirates are going so badly that their mascot, the Parrot, was suspended for a game after throwing a Nerf Ball at umpire [Fred] Brocklander" (Richard Justice, *Washington Post,* May 3, 1987).

**suspended game** A *called game* that is to be completed at a later date. A suspended game shall be resumed at the exact point of suspension of the original game, immediately preceding the next scheduled single game between the two clubs on the same field, if possible. A game terminated for any of the following reasons will be a suspended game if it has progressed far enough to be an official game: a curfew imposed by law; a prearranged time limit; darkness where local law prohibits turning on the lights or where lights are not available; a light failure or malfunction of a mechanical device under the control of the home team; and weather while an inning is in progress and before it is completed and if the visiting team has scored one or more runs to tie the game or take the lead and the home team has not scored or taken the lead. However, if a legal game is tied when called because of weather and neither of the above situations prevails, it is a tie game and must be replayed in its entirety.

**suspension** 1. The temporary stopping of play, for such game-related occurrences as an injured player or dead ball. External causes for a suspension of play primarily come from bad weather. **2.** A period of time during which a player, manager, coach, or other person is ordered from the field of play because of a flagrant violation of the rules. Typically, suspension is the punishment for doctoring the bat or ball, refusing to obey the umpire, or touching an umpire during an argument.

**SV** Abbrev. for *save.*

**swan dive** A line drive that suddenly takes a downward plunge and cannot be caught on the fly, usually going for a hit.

**swang** According to Dizzy Dean, who had his own patent on the term, "this is what a guy has done after he has took a cut and missed." *Time magazine* (Apr. 24, 1950) commented on Dean's creative way with the word "swing": "The fans also noted, for future reference, that the Arkansas-born announcer conjugates the verb 'to swing' as 'swing, swanged, swunged.'"

**swap** *n.* A trade.

**swat** **1.** *v.* To hit the ball with power and for distance. **1st Use.** 1891. (*Chicago Herald,* Aug. 25; Edward J. Nichols). **2.** *n.* A long hit, good for extra bases. **1st Use.** 1907. (*New York Evening Journal,* Apr. 25; Edward J. Nichols). **Usage Note.** Over time, the word "swat" has been put into a number of other baseball constructions. Maurice H. Weseen (*Dictionary of American Slang,* 1934) lists, among others, "swatfest," "swat parade," and "swat streak." **Etymology.** The term has long signified a knock, hit, or hard rub. **Extended Use.** This fascinating item appeared in *American Notes & Queries* (July 1948): "FLY SWATTER: a term coined by Dr. Samuel J. Crumbine, who in 1904 was appointed head of the Kansas State Board of Health; he was taking a bulletin—on flies as typhoid carriers—to the printer one day, and stopped off to watch a ball game, where he heard 'sacrifice fly' and 'swat the ball,' etc., and immediately decided to call the bulletin 'Swat the Fly.' Only a few months later a man came to him with an instrument that he wanted to call a 'fly bat' and Dr. Crumbine persuaded him to call it a 'fly-swatter.'" The man in question was Frank Rose whose son, Bob, retold the story in *Reminisce* magazine (Sept. 1992), adding that his father was a schoolteacher in Weir, Kans., when he read of Crumbine's antifly crusade. The doctor's literature gave him an idea. "My father was a scoutmaster at the time, so he had plenty of help for any civic project he chose to take on. He acquired some yardsticks and screen wire from the local lumberyard. Then he had his scouts saw the yardsticks in half, cut the wire into small squares and nail them together. The scouts decided to call their creations 'fly bats.'"

**swatsman** Syn. of *slugger,* 1. "[Dick Kerr] worked the first game against major league swatsmen and pitched brilliantly" (Hugh S. Fullerton, *Chicago Tribune,* 1919).

**swatsmith** Syn. of *slugger,* 1. **1st Use.** 1908. (*New York Evening Journal,* May 5; Edward J. Nichols).

**swatstick** A baseball bat in the hands of a swat-smith or slugger. **1st Use.** 1908. "With his swatstick, too, [Fred] Tenney has a record to be proud of" (*New York Evening Journal,* Aug. 27; Peter Morris).

**swat team** A team's collection of home run hitters, following the use of the term for a quasimilitary police unit. "Infield 'Swat Team' Adds Leo Hernandez" (*Baltimore Sun* headline, Mar. 31, 1983). Sometimes spelled "SWAT team."

**swatter** Syn. of *slugger,* 1. **1st Use.** 1908. (*Spalding's Official Base Ball Guide;* Edward J. Nichols).

**sweat ball** A variation of the spitball, employing a player's sweat.

**sweep** **1.** *v.* To win all of the games in a series. Fans have been known to wave whisk brooms as they chant "Sweep! Sweep!" when the home team bids to complete a winning series. **2.** *v.* To win both games of a doubleheader. **3.** *n.* A series of wins; e.g., "a three-game sweep." See also *grand slam,* 2; *slam,* 4. **4.** *v.* For a batter to swing his arms too far from his body, thereby subtracting from the power and accuracy of his swing.

**sweep tag** A tag on a sliding baserunner in which the fielder's arm holding the ball is moved down in a continuous arc to intersect the path of the runner. It is commonest in a situation where a runner is attempting to steal. Syn. *swipe tag.*

**sweetheart** A player whose steady hitting, fielding, and morale building year after year wins the respect of the other players; esp., such a player who comes through in a pinch. **1st Use.** 1937. (*Fortune* magazine, Aug.; Edward J. Nichols). **Usage Note.** The term is reserved for those players who are the greatest assets to their clubs, although they may not, in fact, grab the headlines. Lou Gehrig, Hank Aaron, and Mike Schmidt are three who fit the description to a tee.

**sweet spot** The approximately 10-inch-long section on the barrel of a baseball bat where the ball most likely can be hit solidly and for maximum power, giving it the best ride. It is the center of percussion, which, when hit by the ball, produces no recoil of the wrists other than a twisting action. The extent of the sweet spot varies; e.g., Houston

Astros bunting coach Bunny Mick advised "never bunt with the sweet spot: the meat of the bat, from four to eight inches from the end" (quoted by Thomas Boswell, *Why Time Begins on Opening Day,* 1984). A profile of batmaker Dave Cook (*Chicago Tribune,* June 15, 1993) notes: "He wanted to make a bat that would have a hard, heavy sweet spot—baseball lingo for a bat's business area—but would have a light handle and top. So he made the sweet spot out of hickory, the handle out of ash and the top end out of maple." Syn. *joy spot; joy zone.*

**sweet swing** An easy, fluid, seemingly effortless but effective swing; a graceful, unforced swing in which the batter has good balance.

**swing 1.** *v.* To move the bat in a full arc in an attempt to hit a pitched ball. A batter who swings and misses is credited with a strike even if the ball is thrown outside the strike zone. This is important when a batter attempts to stop his swing. If the umpire decides that the batter stopped before making a bona fide attempt to meet the ball, it is not considered a swing and the pitch will be ruled a ball. **2.** *n.* A cut at the ball; the action of a batter in attempting to hit the ball. **1st Use.** 1905. (*Sporting Life,* Oct. 7; Edward J. Nichols). **Extended Use.** To undertake some endeavor is to "take a swing at it."

**swing a big bat** To have a high batting average.

**swing and miss** To swing at a pitch and not hit it; to fan.

**swing away** To take a full cut at the ball. See also *hit away.*

**swinger 1.** A batter who takes a full cut at the ball, rather than choking up on the bat and simply trying to meet the ball. In pre-Ruthian times, Hugh S. Fullerton (*American Magazine,* June 1912) wrote: "The 'swinger' is a type of player not wanted in finished ball clubs. They usually are long distance hitters, but uncertain and usually finish with low averages." This opinion does not prevail today. **1st Use.** 1910. (*American Magazine,* July; Edward J. Nichols). **2.** A batter who, in the words of Jim Brosnan (*The Long Season,* 1960), "will try to hit any pitch that doesn't hit him." See also *free swinger.*

**swing for the fences** To attempt to hit a home run by swinging with maximum force. Syn. "swing for the seats." **Extended Use.** To go all out.

**swing from the heels** To swing with all of one's power, which involves rocking back on one's heels for added leverage. It contrasts with a simple, level swing, which is often more effective. "The [Pittsburgh] Pirates, a notorious swing-from-the-heels bunch [five Pirates had 10 or more hits in the Series, a record], seemed to delight in adversity" (a special advertising insert, *Time* and other magazines, just prior to the 1981 World Series).

**swinging bunt** A poorly hit ball that rolls a short distance from the batter in much the same way a bunt would roll. Though sometimes claimed to be intentional, a swinging bunt is commonly the result of a pitch being hit on a check swing, usually one that is topped and bounces slowly into the infield. It is not scored as a bunt even though it has the characteristic roll of one. "[New York] Yankees third baseman Charlie Hayes led off by hitting a swinging bunt, topping a ball that rolled slowly down the third-base line and stayed in fair territory" (*Baltimore Sun,* Oct. 24, 1996).

**swing late** To swing at the ball as it crosses the plate and is thus difficult to hit.

**swing like a rusty gate** To look inept and perform badly at the plate; to swing wildly at a pitch.

**swingman** A pitcher who is both a spot starter and a reliever; a pitcher who can enter the starting rotation when the regular starter is not able to play. Also spelled "swing man."

**swing the bat** To come to the plate to be a batter. Earl Weaver (*Weaver on Strategy,* 1984) wrote: "I knew that Eddie Murray [as a rookie] was a guy I wanted to see swing the bat." Ray Miller (quoted in *Baltimore Sun,* May 15, 1998) said: "Not only is he [Mike Bordick] swinging the bat with authority, but he's swinging at strikes." **Extended Use.** To confront a difficult situation. Television actor Matthew Perry said he got hooked on the painkiller Vicodin after having his wisdom teeth removed and falling off a Jet Ski. "I took them for the right reasons, at first. It was a very tumultuous and difficult time and it's strange to say, but it's probably the thing I'm most proud of in my life. I know that given a really difficult situation, I stepped up and swung the bat and helped myself. Anything can come at me now and I feel like I can take it because I got myself through that" (*TV Guide,* quoted in *Baltimore Sun,* Apr. 28, 1998).

**swipe 1.** *n.* A stolen base. **2.** *v.* To steal a base; e.g., "to swipe a hassock." **3.** *v.* To go through the sweeping motions of tagging out a baserunner; e.g., "They just swipe the ball in there and half the time they don't touch 'em."

**swipe tag** Syn. of *sweep tag.*

**swish 1.** *n.* A hard swing of the bat that makes no contact with the ball. **2.** *v.* To swing hard and miss.

**switch-hit** To be able to bat from either the right-handed or left-handed side of the plate. **1st Use.** 1942. "[Dave] Bancroft and [Max] Carey switch-hit over a long period of years" (*Baseball Magazine,* July; David Shulman).

**switch-hitter** A batter who can hit from either side of the plate. A player with this skill tends to bat right-handed against left-handed pitchers and vice versa. This ability was rare in earlier decades: "Switch-hitting appears to be dying out in baseball, bearing out Andy High's contention that the noble athletes, despite lingering ideas to the contrary, can do better by confining their activities to one side of the plate" (Jerry Brondfield, *San Francisco News,* July 4, 1938; Peter Tamony). However, more players have developed the ability to hit both ways since a switch-hitter named Mickey Mantle first came to both sides of the plate in 1951. Pete Rose, Eddie Murray, Howard Johnson, Tony Fernandez, Tim Raines, Ozzie Smith, and Roberto Alomar are examples of post-Mantle-era switch-hitters. The first professional switch-hitter, according to a conclusion on file at the National Baseball Library and Archives, was Robert V. Ferguson, captain of the Brooklyn Atlantics, who switch-hit on June 14, 1870, when the Atlantics handed the Cincinnati Red Stockings their first defeat. Also spelled "switch hitter." Syn. *turn-over hitter.* **Extended Use.** Any

person who radically alternates his or her orientation. The term is commonly applied to a person who "swings both ways" (i.e., one who is bisexual).

**switch-pitch 1.** *n.* A changeup. "American Leaguers who had batted against him said he was tough when he kept the ball low, especially his change-up or switch-pitch" (*San Francisco Examiner,* Apr. 10, 1963; Peter Tamony). **2.** *v.* To be able to pitch both right- and left-handed in the same game, an extremely rare ability.

**swoon** A slump; specif., *June swoon.*

**syndicate baseball** A situation that occurs when one person or a small group working together might have interests in more than one baseball club in a league; e.g., Frank and Stanley Robinson owned both the St. Louis and Cleveland teams in the National League in 1899. It is a bygone evil that was once very real. During the winter of 1898–99, it was announced that much of the Baltimore club, including its manager, would be transferred to Brooklyn by a man who owned the Baltimore team and had a part interest in the Brooklyn club. There had been a decline in attendance in Baltimore and the talent of the two teams was to be pooled, with Brooklyn getting the best players. "The respectable public won't stand for 'frame ups,' 'syndicate ball,' or a suspicion of crookedness" (S. Dewitt Clough, *Letters from a Baseball Fan to His Son,* 1910; Peter Tamony). Syn. "syndicalism."

**synthetic turf** Syn. of *artificial turf.*

**Syracuse Car** A railroad car in which the rookies ride. **1st Use.** 1928. "The Pullman in which the rookies and substitutes ride. Originated with the Giants who used to play an exhibition game in Syracuse each year. Usually the second string men would play the game and their car would be shunted off at Syracuse while the others went off to the next big league town to enjoy a day off." (Babe Ruth, *Babe Ruth's Own Book of Baseball;* David Shulman).

# T

**T 1.** Box score abbrev. for *time of game.* **2.** Abbrev. for *triple,* 1.

**TA** Abbrev. for *total average.*

**tab** To select a player; e.g., "The manager tabbed Smith to start the game."

**tabasco** Vigor, as exhibited by a player or a team. **1st Use.** 1895. (*New York Press,* July 8; Edward J. Nichols). **Etymology.** From the trade name of the hot and spicy pepper sauce produced by the McIlhenny Co. of Louisiana.

**table 1.** See *set the table.* **2.** See *off the table.*

**table-setter** A player whose role is to get on base and/or advance others to set up a scoring opportunity. A table-setter is usually the leadoff batter or the next following batter. See also *set the table,* 1. Also spelled "tablesetter."

**tack-on baseball** Scoring one run an inning to catch up or to build a lead gradually.

**tag 1.** *n.* The touching by a fielder on a nonforce play of a baserunner with the ball or with the fielder's hand or glove while holding the ball securely and firmly. **2.** *v.* To touch a baserunner with the ball, or with the hand or glove holding the ball securely, resulting in a putout. **1st Use.** 1907. (Burt L. Standish, *Dick Merriwell's Magnetism;* Edward J. Nichols). **3.** *n.* The touching by a fielder of a base with his body while holding the ball securely and firmly in his hand or glove. **4.** *v.* To touch a base with any portion of the body while in firm

**Tag.** *At second base.*

possession of the ball in the hand or glove, resulting in a putout. **5.** *v.* To hit the ball hard. **1st Use.** 1917. (*American Magazine,* July; Edward J.

Nichols). **6.** *v.* See *tag up.* **7.** *v.* To charge a pitcher with a loss; e.g., "The Yankees tagged Smith for his third straight loss." **8.** *v.* To make base hits or score runs off a pitcher; e.g., "The Braves tagged Smith for six hits and four runs."

**tagger** A player who makes a tag; e.g., "The best 'taggers' among the first basemen in those days were Joe Kuhel and Joe Judge" (Bill Starr, *Clearing the Bases,* 1989; David Shulman).

**tag out** *v.* To put a runner out by touching him with the ball when he is off the base.

**tagout** *n.* A putout in which a fielder with the ball touches a baserunner when he is off the base.

**tag up** **1.** For a baserunner to touch a base before advancing to the next base. With fewer than two outs, a baserunner attempting to gain a base or score on a fly ball can tag up the moment the fielder touches the ball, but not a split second earlier. On a reasonably deep fly ball, a runner on third base will normally have time to tag up and score. **1st Use.** 1935. "Tag-up runner, after a fair or foul ball has been caught" (Ralph H. Barbour, *How to Play Better Baseball;* David Shulman). **2.** For a baserunner to return to a base and touch it before taking another lead.

**tail** *n.* The lateral move of a few inches of a pitch (such as a fastball) as it crosses the plate.

**tail away** **1.** For a pitched ball to move down and away from the batter. **2.** For a batted ball (such as a line drive) to move down and away from the fielder.

**tail-ender** A team at or near the bottom of the standings. Syn. *tail-end team.* **1st Use.** 1886. "Even the 'coming champions' will have their turns of ill-fortune, while the lives of the 'tail-enders' are awful to contemplate" (*Lippincott's* magazine, Aug.; David Shulman).

**tail-end team** Syn. of *tail-ender.* "In 1902 and 1903 Tacoma gained the reputation of being the best losing town in the circuit, giving tailend teams loyal, enthusiastic support" (National Association of Professional Base Ball Leagues, *Official Guide,* 1905; David Shulman).

**tailing fastball** A fastball that moves laterally away from the batter as it approaches the plate. It

moves a few inches to the left for a left-handed pitcher and a few inches to the right for a right-handed pitcher.

**tail-off** *n.* A decline in the batting average of a hitter.

**tailspin** A losing streak.

**take** **1.** *v.* To refrain from swinging at a pitched ball; to permit one strike to be thrown before swinging at the ball; to look at a pitch. Batters often "take a pitch" or "take a strike" to get an idea of what a pitcher is throwing. Taking is most common when the count is 3-0. A batter may be told to "take" by his manager, which occasioned Jim Brosnan (*The Long Season,* 1960) to give this definition of taking: "A batter being forced to watch a pitch cross the plate that he obviously would have hit out of the ball park if the manager had only permitted him to swing." **1st Use.** 1854. (Knickerbocker Rules, rule 13; Edward J. Nichols). **2.** *n.* An instance of taking a pitch. **3.** *v.* To defeat an opponent. **1st Use.** 1880. (Chicago *Inter-Ocean,* June 11; Edward J. Nichols). **Etymology.** Named by shortening the phrase "take into camp" or "take the measure of" (Edward J. Nichols, *An Historical Dictionary of Baseball Terminology,* Ph.D. dissertation, 1939). **4.** *v.* To field ground balls; e.g., "Smith took several grounders at third." **5.** *v.* See *take deep.*

**take a cut** To swing hard at a pitch. **1st Use.** 1932. (*Baseball Magazine,* Oct.; Edward J. Nichols).

**take a drink** To strike out. The term is a play on the presumption that the batter has time to go back to the dugout for a sip of water after failing at the plate. **1st Use.** 1914. (Ring W. Lardner, *You Know Me Al;* Edward J. Nichols).

**take a lead** To move off a base in the direction of the next base to get a head start when the pitch is delivered or a ball is batted.

**take a little off** Syn. of *take something off.*

**take all the way** To let a pitch go by, having had no intention to swing regardless of the pitch's location.

**take a nap** To get picked off a base.

**take a pitch** See *take,* 1.

**take a strike** See *take,* 1.

**take a stroll downtown** To hit a home run.

**take deep** To hit a long ball, esp. a home run, off a pitcher; e.g., "Smith took Jones deep in the fourth." Correspondingly, a pitcher will say a given batter "took me deep." See also *go deep.*

**"take him out!"** Traditional call from the stands for the manager to remove an ineffective player, almost always a pitcher. **1st Use.** 1908. (*Baseball Magazine,* Dec.; Edward J. Nichols).

**take it with you** To hit a drag bunt for a base hit.

**"Take Me Out to the Ball Game"** Baseball's unofficial anthem, written in 1908 by Jack Norworth, a vaudeville performer and songwriter, who was honored with a special day at Ebbets Field in 1942—his first time at the ballpark. The song was an immediate hit on the vaudeville circuit and in sheet-music stores. The music was written by Albert Von Tilzer, who had collaborated with Norworth on "Shine on Harvest Moon."

**take off 1.** For a pitched ball to suddenly rise or deviate laterally as it nears the plate. **2.** To leave a base in a hurry, such as in an attempted steal.

**take-off sign** A sign given to a baserunner to rescind a previous sign to steal.

**take one for the team** To allow oneself to be hit by a pitched ball. See also *team,* 3.

**take one on the meat** To be hit by a pitched ball.

**take out** For a baserunner to block or slide into an infielder, usually done to disrupt the infielder's throw to another base.

**take-out slide** An offensive move in which a baserunner slides into a fielder in such a way as to attempt to prevent him from making a pivot for a double play.

**take sign** A sign from a coach telling a batter not to swing at the next pitch. An alternative definition from Jimmy Cannon (*Baseball Digest,* Nov.–Dec. 1956): "How a manager tells a hitter he hasn't any confidence in him." **1st Use.** 1937. (*Philadelphia Record,* Oct. 9; Edward J. Nichols).

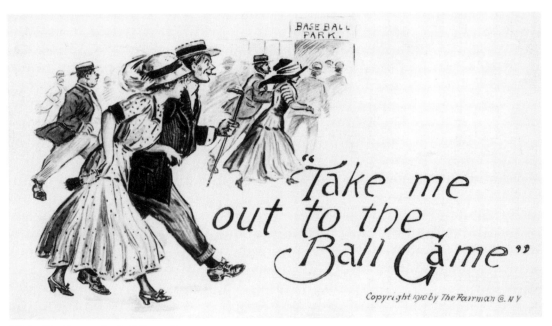

*"Take Me Out to the Ball Game."*

**take something off** To throw a changeup or slow ball after a fastball or series of fastballs; e.g., "Smith took something off on that pitch." Syn. *take a little off.*

**take the ball** For a manager or coach to remove a pitcher from the game by literally and figuratively taking the baseball out of his hands.

**take the bat out of his hands 1.** To keep a batter from hitting, either by pitching with great effectiveness or intentionally walking the batter. **2.** To attempt to steal a base with two outs and a good hitter at the plate, which creates the option (if the steal was successful) of intentionally walking the batter or (if the steal was unsuccessful) of ending the inning when the hitter could have perhaps driven in a run. **3.** For the manager to give the take sign to a batter.

**"take the blood off it"** Advice to a player who has just gotten a weak hit, an obvious play on the fact that such hits are sometimes called "bleeders."

**take the button off his hat** To pitch a ball that comes close to the batter's head.

**take the extra base** To strive to advance as far as possible on a base hit. "Even the guys who don't run well, we've got to take the extra base. Last year we lost a lot of games by one run, and we never took the extra base, and that cost us." (Rafael Palmeiro, quoted in *Baltimore Sun,* Apr. 4, 1996).

**take the mound** To be the starting pitcher; e.g., "The Chicago Cubs rookie [Kerry Woods] took the mound for his first start" (*Baltimore Sun,* May 13, 1998).

**take the throw** To receive a baseball being thrown to make a play.

**take the trainer to dinner** For a player to enter the trainer's room on a frequent basis.

**"take three and sit down"** A jeering admonition to a batter, likely to come from the stands or the bench of the opposing team.

**"take two" 1.** To instruct a batter to allow two strikes to be called with the hope that the pitcher will issue a walk. **1st Use.** 1909. (*American Magazine,* May; Edward J. Nichols). **2.** To instruct the batter-runner to reach second base on a hit.

**"take two and hit to right"** Traditional instruction to a struggling batter that calls for him to let two pitches go by (take two) and then hit the ball to the right side of the field. Raymond V. Curiale (letter, Feb. 16, 1990) recalls the advice from a time more than 40 years earlier: "We would use the term for an inept batter. It was said in a derisive tone, being meant more as an insult rather than to be helpful." **Extended Use.** A phrase of encouragement. The column signed by the anonymous Jupiter (*San Francisco Examiner,* May 31, 1989) talks about the use of the term by Frank McCullough, managing editor of the newspaper, who uses it to encourage the troops in the newsroom by saying, "take two and hit to right." Asked where he picked it up, he said: "I've been hearing it all my life. It's one of those old baseball phrases . . . But I haven't the slightest idea how it got started. Maybe I'd better quit saying it."

**"take your base"** Traditional instruction by the plate umpire to a batter who has just been given a base on balls or has been hit by a pitch to advance to first base. **1st Use.** 1867. (*New York Sunday Mercury;* Edward J. Nichols).

**talcum ball** A ball doctored with talcum powder, giving it the same illegal advantages as a spitball.

**talesman** *obs.* The official scorer in some circles in the very early days of baseball.

**tall grass** *arch.* A low-level minor league, or bush, where the grass grows tall. Syn. *tall timber;* "tall uncut"; "tall weed." **1st Use.** 1910. (*Baseball Magazine,* Apr.; Edward J. Nichols).

**tall timber** *arch.* Syn. of *tall grass.* **1st Use.** 1905. (*Sporting Life,* Sept. 9; Edward J. Nichols).

**tally 1.** *n.* A run. **1st Use.** 1858. (Rules of the Massachusetts Association of Base Ball Players, rules 15 and 17). **2.** *v.* To score a run.

**tallykeeper** The scorekeeper, per 1845 Knickerbocker Rules and through most of the 19th century.

**tallyman** The scorekeeper, per 1858 Rules of the Massachusetts Association of Base Ball Players.

**Tampa Bay Devil Rays** The American League East Division expansion team in Tampa Bay, Fla., that began play in 1998.

**tampering** Unauthorized and illegal discussions with free agents at improper times and places.

**tank out** To recognize a losing situation and not do one's best.

**tank town** *arch.* A small town to old-time barnstormers and minor leaguers, probably from the fact that a train normally stopped in such a place only to take on water from a water tank.

**tap 1.** *n.* A lightly batted ball. **1st Use.** 1901. (Burt L. Standish, *Frank Merriwell's Marvel;* Edward J. Nichols). **2.** *v.* To hit a pitch lightly or without power; e.g., "Smith tapped the ball back to the pitcher." **1st Use.** 1922. (*New York Times,* June 2; Edward J. Nichols).

**tape-measure home run** A very long home run; one that calls for measurement. At the major-league level, the term "tape measure" is linked to blasts in the vicinity of 500 feet. "[Steve] Balboni . . . earned the nickname 'Bye, Bye Balboni' in the minor leagues for his tape-measure home runs" (*St. Petersburg Times,* Mar. 16, 1986). Mark McGwire in the late 1990s attracted many to the stands early to watch him hit tape-measure shots in batting practice. Syn. "tape-measure shot"; "tape-measure job." **Etymology.** The expression and the custom it refers to date to a spectacular home run hit by New York Yankees slugger Mickey Mantle on Apr. 17, 1953, off Washington Senators pitcher Chuck Stobbs. The ball cleared the left-center field bleachers at Griffith Stadium. Yankees public relations director Red Patterson immediately got up, left the ballpark, found a neighborhood kid who had retrieved the ball, and measured the distance to the spot at 565 feet (the actual distance in the air was about 510 feet), one of the longest on record. Led by Mantle, the term attaches itself to only a few names in the game, including Willie Stargell, who became the first player to clear the bleachers at Dodgers Stadium on Aug. 5, 1969, with a 506-foot, 6-inch home run.

**tapper** A lightly hit ball, without power, but perhaps well placed. "[Bob] Forsch . . . got [Dave] Parker on a tapper" (*St. Louis Post-Dispatch,* June 2, 1987).

**tapperitis hitter** *arch.* A hitter who hits tappers.

**tap-tap play** A close play in which the runner is out. Compare *bang-bang play.*

**target 1.** The positioning of the catcher's hands prior to the pitcher's delivery. The catcher places his mitt at the exact point where the ball should be pitched. **2.** The outstretched catcher's mitt, which the pitcher is trying to hit with the ball.

**tarp** Short for "tarpaulin," the covering used to protect the playing field during a downpour. Baseball's oddest tarp incident came in the midst of the 1985 National League Championship Series when St. Louis Cardinals outfielder Vince Coleman was injured by a moving motorized tarp that caught his leg. Like everything else in baseball, some tarps are now covered with advertising. **Etymology.** From the nautical canvas used to cover hatches.

**Tartan Turf** A brand name of *artificial turf.* "This is a very good hitting ballpark. The Tartan Turf permits many balls to skip through the infield and through the outfield as well for extra bases." (Edwin Silberstang, on Royals Stadium, *Playboy's Guide to Baseball Betting,* 1982; Charles D. Poe).

**tarzan** "A slovenly, frowzy baseball player" (Maurice H. Weseen, *Dictionary of American Slang,* 1934).

**tater** A *home run.* "I'm a line-drive hitter, and if it happens to be up in the air, then I have a tater" (Lloyd Moseby, quoted in *St. Petersburg Times,* Mar. 11, 1987). "Taters," Reggie Jackson has been quoted as saying on more than one occasion, "that's where the money is." See also *long tater.* **Etymology.** The term may have originated in the Negro leagues as *potato* and *long potato* but took on new life when George Scott made a habit of calling them "taters" when he came to the Boston Red Sox in 1966; one observer wrote in 1971 that the term "will probably die when he is given his final release." Scott last played in 1978 but the term is still in use, with variations, such as "tater trot" for "home run tally." "Their tater trot has been led by the 27 . . . off left-hander [Eric] Bell" (*New York Post,* June 29, 1987).

**tattoo 1.** To get several hits off a pitcher; e.g., "The Braves tattooed Smith for seven hits in less than two innings." **2.** To hit a baseball; e.g., "Jones tattooed the ball for a double."

**tattooed man** A pitcher who has been hit hard or off whom several hits have been made.

**TB** Abbrev. for *total bases.*

**T-ball 1.** A game played mostly by very young children in which there is no pitching and the batter hits a rubber ball placed on top of an adjustable, stationary tee at home plate. Syn. *tee-ball.* **2.** Batting practice using a tee.

**TC 1.** Insignia for "Twin Cities" that appeared on the Minnesota Twins caps for their first 23 years until 1987 when it was replaced by an "M" for Minnesota. The TC insignia was moved to the Twins uniform sleeve. Outside the Minneapolis–St. Paul area, the TC initials have left fans guessing. **2.** Abbrev. for *total chances.*

**T-card** Syn. of *tobacco card.*

**teacher** The manager of a baseball team. **1st Use.** 1917. (*New York Times,* Oct. 6; Edward J. Nichols).

**teacup end** The scooped-out, concave top end of a *cupped bat,* believed by many to improve bat speed over the traditional round end.

**team 1.** The nine players (ten when the designated hitter is allowed) in a game. **2.** The entire uniformed congregation of a baseball *club,* including players, coaches, and the manager. **1st Use.** 1868. (*New York Herald,* July 24; Edward J. Nichols). **3.** Short for *take one for the team.* The term is used by players who shout it when they want a teammate to allow himself to be hit by an inside pitch.

**team effort** A group activity in which everyone contributes. The term is used when a manager fears that one player is getting too much publicity.

**team game** [softball term] A sobriquet for fast pitch softball in which pitching was not so dominant that other members of the team had an effect on the outcome. Compare *pitcher's game.*

**teammate** A fellow member of a team.

**team player** A player who works with others for the benefit of the team rather than playing for his own recognition; e.g., a player who hits to right field to advance a runner.

**team rules** Regulations that obtain at a particular ballpark and for a particular team. Paul I. Fagan, who owned the minor-league San Francisco Seals from 1945 to 1963, is an example of an owner who made several team rules. His obituary recounted: "Fagan banned billboard ads and insisted players shave before games, quit swearing, and [quit] chewing tobacco. At one time he even banned the sale of peanuts at the park." (Associated Press, Dec. 19, 1960; Peter Tamony).

**teamwork** Working together as a unit. **Etymology/1st Use.** 1902. "Teamwork when expressed in horseology, means two or more horses that pull as one and when expressed in base ball phraseology it means nine players that act as one" (*The Sporting News,* Jan. 25; Barry Popik).

**tear** A winning streak for a team or a hot period for an individual; e.g., "The Yankees are on a tear during the current road trip."

**teaser** An especially deceptive pitcher. **1st Use.** 1883. (Chicago *Inter-Ocean,* May 27; Edward J. Nichols).

**tee** See *batting tee.*

**tee-ball** Syn. of *T-ball,* 1.

**tee off 1.** To hit a ball hard, an obvious borrowing from golf where the tee shot is the power shot. Players generally "tee off a pitcher's delivery," which William G. Brandt (*Baseball Magazine,* Oct. 1932) described as to "step right up and swing from their ankles instead of crouching carefully and taking a good look before making a pass at anything tossed towards the plate." **1st Use.** 1932. (*Baseball Magazine,* Oct.; Edward J. Nichols). **2.** To make many hits in a game or off a specific pitcher; e.g., "The Diamondbacks teed off on Smith for four hits in four at-bats."

**tee party 1.** A game or portion of a game in which batters tee off against a pitcher. **2.** A batting streak. **1st Use.** 1932. (*Baseball Magazine,* Oct.; Edward J. Nichols).

**telegraph** *v.* For a pitcher to suggest through his mannerisms the type of pitch he is about to throw or for the catcher to tip off a pitch by giving an identifiable sign to the pitcher. Slower arm speed, when discernible to the batter, is a common way by which a changeup is telegraphed. See also *tip,* 3. **1st Use.** 1916. (*American Magazine,* Aug.; Edward J. Nichols).

**Temple Cup** A trophy awarded to the champions of a postseason best-of-seven series played from 1894 through 1897 between the first- and second-place finishers in the National League. Named for William C. Temple who once owned (1892) the Pittsburgh Pirates. See also *Dauvray Cup.*

**ten-and-five player** A major-league player who has been in the majors for ten years and with the same team for the last five years. Under current rules, such a player has the right to veto any trade involving him. Syn. *five-and-ten player; 10-five man;* "ten-and-five man"; "10-and-5 player."

**tenant** A baserunner.

**10-five man** Syn. of *ten-and-five player.*

**tenney** *arch.* A padded fielder's glove at the turn of the 20th century. According to Joseph McBride (*High and Inside,* 1980), it referred to first baseman Fred Tenney and his fat, circular glove.

**ten-o'clock hitter** A player who hits well during morning practice sessions, but poorly during the game. See also *one-o'clock hitter; two-o'clock hitter; five-o'clock hitter; six-o'clock hitter; seven-o'clock hitter.*

**ten-run rule** A rule in some amateur leagues in which a game is stopped and a winner declared after seven innings if one team is ten or more runs ahead.

**tenth man 1.** The loyal supporters of a team; the crowd in the sense that it can help or hinder a team. "Cleveland fans supported their team tremendously. They were a 10th man, and [the Indians] got a lot of inspiration from them." (Baltimore Orioles outfielder Eric Davis, quoted in *Baltimore Sun,* Oct. 15, 1997). **2.** An umpire who seems to be favoring one team. **3.** Syn. of *designated hitter.*

**territory 1.** The general area of a playing field for which a given fielder is responsible. **2.** Fair or foul ground; a ball is said to land in "fair territory" or "foul territory."

**Texas League 1.** *n.* A minor league since 1902: Class D (1902–06), Class C (1907–10), Class B (1911–20), Class A (1921–35), Class A1 (1936–42), and Class AA (since 1946). **2.** *v./arch.* To bloop the ball. **1st Use.** 1912. "If you can't shoot 'em, Texas League 'em" (*Sporting Life,* May 18).

**Texas League grip** A nickname for *The Sporting News.* Charley Graham in an interview (*San Francisco News,* Aug. 31, 1948; Peter Tamony) published just after his death discussed the term while recalling the life of a minor-league player at the turn of the 20th century: "Our reading matter was *The Sporting News* or the 'Texas League grip.' You wrapped your shirt, collar and underwear in it and that was your suitcase."

**Texas Leaguer** A poorly hit ball that loops meekly over the infield and lands for a hit; a fly ball just out of reach of the infielders, but too close in for an outfielder to catch it. Defined by H. L. Mencken as "a pop fly which nevertheless takes the batter to first base." Harwell E. West (*The Baseball Scrapbook,* 1938) noted that the "term [is] current everywhere but in Texas League." Other names for the same hit include: *awful; banjo hit,* 2; *bloop,* 1; *blooper,* 1; *drooper; dunker; flare,* 1; *Japanese liner; lazy,* 2; *leaping Lena; lollipop,* 2; *looper; parachute,* 1; *percentage sinker; plunker; pooper; punker; sheeny mike; smell hit; special; stinker; sucker;* and *Texas League single.* **Usage Note.** This term is always being tagged as archaic or old-fashioned but, nevertheless, retains its currency. Here is how Damon Runyon used it in 1933 (*San Francisco Examiner,* Oct. 7; Peter Tamony): "[Joe] Cronin, with two and two on him, drops a lucky hit back of third. It is of the variety that used to be called 'Texas Leaguers.' It is too far back for [Hughie] Critz, and not far enough for [Mel] Ott to get." **1st Use.** 1903. "[Jimmy Sebring's home run to center field came] from a Texas Leaguer; [Chick] Stahl thinking the ball would roll into the crowd" (*Boston Globe,* Oct. 2; Peter Morris). **Etymology.** Hugh

S. Fullerton (*American Magazine,* June 1912) says such hits are usually accidental but are sometimes accomplished on purpose "by good batters who merely tap the ball and float it safe." He goes on to say: "The term originated from the fact that Ted Sullivan, the veteran player-manager-magnate, had a team in the Texas League that was noted for that kind of batting."

However, Hy Turkin (*Baseball Almanac,* 1955) states that the term originated much earlier: "First used to describe the kind of hits that enabled Arthur Sunday, fresh out of the defunct Texas League, to finish with a .398 batting average at Toledo in 1889." This version ends with a quote from a Toledo sportswriter that Sunday had hit another of those "Texas League hits."

Equally common is the version that traces the term to either the major-league debut of Ollie Pickering in 1896 or his earlier debut in Houston of the Texas League. There are various versions of the story, but the earliest version (1906) tells of him showing up in Houston where he is given a trial with the team. He gets seven hits in his first seven at-bats, all of them bloopers. An unidentified news clipping of Apr. 2, 1906 (on file at the Baseball Hall of Fame), states that as word of the feat spread, these hits became known as "Texas Leaguers," since they had been made in the Texas League.

Zander Hollander (*The Encyclopedia of Sports Talk,* 1976) offers this theory: "So called because before the turn of the century the parks in the Texas League were particularly small." This contrasts dramatically with the theory Bill Brandt proposed on his "Inside Sports" radio show (Sept. 9, 1946; recorded by Peter Tamony): "In former days, the fences in the Texas baseball parks were away out in the wide open spaces, far from home plate. The outfielders had to play deep, and the consequence was that many short flies went for hits."

Finally, there is the Gulf Stream theory that E. V. Durling (*San Francisco Examiner,* 1948; Peter Tamony) attributed to New York Giants infielder Larry Doyle. According to Doyle: "The strong winds from the Gulf Stream greatly affected fly balls in most of the cities of the Texas League. A hard hit fly would seem certain to reach an outfielder and be too far out for an infielder. Then the wind would stop the ball's progress and cause it to drop for a hit between the outfielder and infielder."

**Texas League single** Syn. of *Texas Leaguer.*

**Texas Rangers** The name of the American League West Division franchise in Arlington, Tex. The team was once the expansion Washington Senators (1961–71) before moving to Texas where it was named for the state's most famous law-enforcement group.

**"that one'll bring rain"** Expression sometimes used to describe a very high fly ball.

**the** The definite article has had a peculiar role in baseball. As explained by Leonard Shecter (*Baseball Digest,* June 1963): "'The' is the most used word in baseball. No one knows why, but one does not simply say, 'He is a good hitter.' The expression is: 'He's got THE good bat.' One doesn't say anybody is a poor fielder; rather 'He's got THE bad hands.'" Shecter included other examples: "He's got the tools" and "He's got the good wheels." From *Sporting Life* (Sept. 10, 1884): "Base ball is 'the' sport at the Sandwich Islands."

**The Book** See *book,* 2.

**theft** A stolen base.

**"there goes the ball game"** A phrase spoken when a run or play wins a baseball game.

**"they ought to pay their way into the ballparks"** Long-established taunt made by pitchers about outfielders and by outfielders about pitchers.

**"they show movies on a flight like that"** A comment on a long or well-hit home run. **1st Use.** 1983. (broadcaster Tom Marr, about a John Lowenstein home run, WTOP, Aug. 28; Joseph C. Goulden).

**thief** Syn. of *base stealer.* **1st Use.** 1910. (*Baseball Magazine,* Dec.; Edward J. Nichols).

**thievery** Syn. of *base stealing.*

**thimble** A small fielder's glove.

**thin** Said of a team or pitching staff short on talent or rendered so because of a trade.

**think tank** The brain; the contents of a player's or manager's cap. **1st Use.** 1909. "But 'Blondy' Moeller got things twisted in his think tank and allowed the ball to ooze through his dinner tongs" (Edward M. Thierry, *Baseball Magazine*, Sept.). **Extended Use.** Many years after its original use as baseball slang, this term became general slang for "brain" and then for a policy research institute, such as the Rand Corporation.

**third 1.** *n.* Short for *third base.* **2.** *n.* The third inning. **3.** *adv.* Said of the third position in the batting order; e.g., "Smith is hitting third."

**third bagger** Syn. of *third baseman.*

**third base 1.** The base located to the left side of and 90 feet from home plate, which is three-quarters of the way around the bases on the way to scoring a run. Abbrev. *3B.* Syn. *third,* 1; *coffin corner; hot corner; far corner; far turn.* **2.** The position played by the third baseman. Abbrev. *3B.* Syn. *third,* 1; *reaction position.* **1st Use.** 1854. (Knickerbocker Rules; Edward J. Nichols).

**third base coach** A member of the managerial staff who stands in the coach's box adjacent to third base. He normally decides whether a baserunner should stop at third or head home, and commonly gives signals to the batter. Syn. *yodeler.*

**third base hole** The area between the shortstop and third baseman, near the outfield grass. Syn. *hole,* 1.

**third base line** The line extending from home plate to third base. See also *left field line.*

**third baseman** The defensive player stationed at third base. Abbrev. *3B.* Syn. *third bagger; third sacker.* **1st Use.** 1883. (*Sporting Life,* May 27; Edward J. Nichols). **Extended Use.** A blackjack term for the player on the left-hand side of the table who is the last player to be able to ask for a hit. (Donald I. Collyer, *Scientific Blackjack and Complete Casino Guide,* 1966).

**third sacker** Syn. of *third baseman.* **1st Use.** 1905. (*Sporting Life,* Oct. 7; Edward J. Nichols).

**third strike dropped** See *dropped third strike.*

**30-30 club** A mythical group of players who have hit 30 or more home runs and stolen 30 or more bases in a single season. First to do it: Ken Williams of the St. Louis Browns in 1922, with 39 home runs and 37 stolen bases. Compare *40-40 club; 50-50 club.*

**Thomas Edison** *arch.* A pitcher who is continually experimenting with new pitches. See also *Edison.*

**thousand-mile bus ride** The fabled condition endured by players in the Mexican League.

**thread the needle** To pitch with skill and precision; to keep the batter from hitting the ball.

**threat 1.** A team that is likely to contend for first place. **2.** A player likely to hit or steal.

**3** The scorekeeper's designation for the first baseman.

**three and two** A count of three balls and two strikes on the batter; a full count. Unless the batter fouls it off, the next pitch will determine if the batter is out or gets on base. **1st Use.** 1908. (*Baseball Magazine,* July; Edward J. Nichols).

**3B 1.** Abbrev. for *third base.* **2.** Abbrev. for *third baseman.* **3.** Abbrev. for *triple,* 1.

**three-bagger** Syn. of *triple,* 1.

**three-base hit** Syn. of *triple,* 1. Defined by Milton Richman (*Baseball Digest,* May 1947) as "the poke invented to test your wind." **1st Use.** 1879. (*Spirit of the Times,* Aug. 23; Edward J. Nichols).

**three blind mice** A derogatory term for a three-man umpiring crew. Before the fourth umpire was added to the crew, the phrase was used to heckle the umpires as they came out of the dugout. One oft-told tale had Leo Durocher leading thousands of fans in greeting the umpiring crew, on the day after a series of disputed calls, with: "Three blind mice, see how they come!" At Ebbets Field in Brooklyn, a zany band of musicians known as the Dodger Sym-Phoney used to play "Three Blind Mice" when the umpires appeared. It has since been picked up by ballpark organists who have been known to play a few bars of the song after a disputed call. In 1985, an organist for the Class A Clearwater Phillies was ejected for playing the song. See also *blind mice.*

**three-decker** A towering home run capable of landing in the real or imagined third and uppermost deck of a large ballpark.

**Three-Eye League** *arch.* A Class B minor league that began in 1902 and ceased play in 1961, composed primarily of teams from Illinois, Iowa, and Indiana. The term is used in a derogatory manner when referring to the ineptness of minor-league players. Also spelled "Three-I League." **1st Use.** 1902. (*Sporting Life,* Oct. 4; Edward J. Nichols).

**three-foot line** A baseline that marks the last half of the distance to first base, situated parallel to and three feet to the right of the first base foul line, thereby forming a three-foot lane with the foul line, within which the batter-runner must run while the ball is being fielded to first base. If the batter-runner runs outside (to the right of) the three-foot line or inside (to the left of) the foul line, the umpire may call interference if the batter-runner interferes with the fielder taking the throw at first base or attempting to field a batted ball. See also *45-foot lane.*

**.300 hitter** A player whose batting average is .300 or higher. The term is one of high distinction, as an average above, or even close to, .300 is remarkable in any league.

**300/.300 club** A mythical and exclusive club composed of players who have hit 300 or more home runs with a lifetime batting average of .300 or higher. The term was invented by Bill Deane (*Baseball Digest,* Apr. 1984) when discussing Jim Rice's candidacy (Rice eventually hit 382 home runs but had a lifetime batting average of .298).

**300th victory** A major mark of accomplishment

for a pitcher. "I sent Gaylord Perry a telegram early last week about his 300th victory" (Early Wynn, quoted in *New York Times,* May 4, 1982).

**three o'cat** Syn. of *three old cat.*

**three old cat** A variant of *one old cat,* using six players. Syn. *three o'cat.*

**three-quarters delivery** A pitching delivery in which the arm is between the sidearm and overhand deliveries. Sometimes spelled "three-quarter delivery." Syn. "¾."

**3RH + WPG = WINS** An equation advocated by Baltimore Orioles manager Earl Weaver, which translates to "three-run homers plus well-pitched games equal victories" (*Baltimore Sun,* May 25, 1986).

**three-sacker** Syn. of *triple,* 1. **1st Use.** 1870. "Barnes hit a three-sacker, bringing Deming in" (*The Yale Courant,* Oct. 5; David Shulman).

**three-six game** A game in which three players produce six of a team's hits. Many such games will make a team successful over the long run.

**3-6-3** Scorecard notation for a double play in which the ball goes from the first baseman (3) to the shortstop (6) for the force at second base and back to the first baseman (3) for the second out.

**three strikes** A strikeout. **Extended Use.** "Three Strikes" legislation is meant to send third-time felons (in some places, violent felons; in other places, all felons) to jail for life without parole. The first of the Three Strikes proposals passed a Washington state referendum in 1993. A second variation on the law went into effect in California in 1994. It mandates 25 years to life or triple the usual sentence, whichever is more.

Ellen Goodman (syndicated column, Mar. 25, 1994) voiced her objection: "I have never been a fan of jocktalk in political life. The endless campaign lingo about slam-dunking opponents and hitting questions out of the ballpark has left me on the sidelines. But I am even more uncomfortable when sporting life stops being a metaphor and starts becoming public policy. This is exactly

**Three strikes.**

what is happening with the new favorite anti-crime legislation known as 'three strikes and you're out.' This is criminology according to Abner Doubleday."

**three-two count** A count of three balls and two strikes on the batter; a *full count.*

**three up, three down** Said of an inning in which the three batters are retired in order.

**throat cutter** Syn. of *knockdown pitch.*

**throttle** To defeat an opponent.

**through the hole** Said of a ball that is hit through the space between two infielders, esp. the shortstop and third baseman. **1st Use.** 1935. "A batsman hitting past an unguarded area of the infield is said to hit 'through the hole'" (Ralph

H. Barbour, *How to Play Better Baseball;* David Shulman).

**through the slot** Said of a pitch thrown over home plate.

**through the wickets** Said of a batted ball that goes between the legs (wickets) of a fielder, often those of the pitcher.

**throw 1.** *v.* To propel a baseball by a forward motion of the hand and arm to a given objective. **1st Use.** 1845. "The ball must be pitched, not thrown, for the bat" (Knickerbocker Rules, 9th rule). **2.** *n.* The act of throwing, as distinguished by the rules of baseball from the act of pitching. Whereas a pitch is a ball delivered to the batter by the pitcher, a throw covers all other deliveries by one player to another. Hence, a pitcher throws to first base but pitches to the batter. **3.** *n.* A thrown ball. **4.** *v.* To use a pitcher; e.g., "Smith's great, but I can't throw him every game."

**throw a game** To deliberately allow the opposing team to win the game. **1st Use.** 1874. (*New York Herald,* Sept. 10; Edward J. Nichols). **Etymology.** To "throw a race" was a horse racing term as early as 1868.

**throw a glove** To attempt to stop a batted or thrown ball by throwing a glove at it. There is no penalty for this action if the glove misses the ball but if it hits a batted ball the batter is granted three bases and if it hits a thrown ball each runner is granted two bases from the moment of the infraction.

**throw away** To lose a game by poor pitching or poor throwing; e.g., "Smith threw that game away by walking three batters" or "Jones threw away a game by making that error." **1st Use.** 1902. (*Sporting Life,* July 12; Edward J. Nichols).

**throwback** A player who plays like a player from a previous era; e.g., Pete Rose was a "throwback" to the days of Ty Cobb. "Cal Ripken Jr. and Kirby Puckett are throwbacks to an era when players stayed with one team their entire careers, and became a symbol of the city where they put on the home team uniform" (*Baltimore Sun,* July 5, 1995).

"[Matt Williams is] a throwback player, one who'll get his uniform dirty, do whatever it takes to win" (*Milwaukee Journal Sentinel*, Oct. 24, 1997).

**throw darts** To pitch with great control.

**throw-down** *arch.* A throw from the catcher to a player covering second base. **1st Use.** 1916. "Smith made the other [error] when he fumbled Sam's throw-down and let the runners steal second" (Christy Mathewson, *First Base Faulkner*; David Shulman).

**thrower 1.** A pitcher without finesse; one who relies on speed and power as opposed to deceptive pitching. "The thing that disturbs me is when they're drafting pitchers, they're really not drafting pitchers. They're drafting throwers. They want somebody who throws 90 to 95 miles an hour. I feel I'm a pitcher. I throw 86 to 88, and my ball moves." (college pitcher Mike Loynd, quoted in *New York Times*, June 1, 1986). Compare *pitcher*, 2. **1st Use.** 1880. (*Brooklyn Daily Eagle*, July 26; Edward J. Nichols). **2.** The pitcher in the Massachusetts game and other early forms of baseball. The modern distinction between pitcher and thrower is nearly opposite the original one.

**throw for the cycle** To throw a player out at each base and home plate during a game. It is the defensive equivalent of *hit for the cycle*, 1. Charles Einstein quoted Walter Alston on Willie Mays (*The Sporting News*, Jan. 17, 1970): "It happened—or darn near happened—in May of 1966, when the Giants were playing the Dodgers at Los Angeles, and Mays threw out one man at home, another at first, another at third. He had a fourth one nailed at second, but the second baseman, his back to the oncoming runner, turned the wrong way and missed the tag."

**throw ground balls** To pitch balls that tend to yield grounders.

**throw his glove in the box** Said of a pitcher who has another team so completely dominated that all he has to do is to throw his glove on the mound to win. **1st Use.** 1914. (Ring Lardner, *You Know Me Al*; Edward J. Nichols).

**throw-in 1.** A marginal player included in a trade, often to complete a trade. Bill Veeck (*Veeck—as in Wreck*, 1962) opined: "The throw-in players can turn out to be more important in the long run than the guys you each set out to get." **2.** A throw made from an outfielder to one of the basemen or the catcher. **1st Use.** 1881. (*New York Herald*, July 23; Edward J. Nichols).

**throwing error** An error resulting from a wild throw.

**throw it away** To make a wild throw.

**throw Laredo** To throw underhand. Glen Waggoner & Robert Sklars (*Rotisserie League Baseball*, 1987) explained the term geographically: "The term is derived from the fact that Laredo is in the lower left-hand corner of Texas, which is where Kent Tekulve and Dan Quisenberry seem to be throwing from." Writer Stephen Banker suggested that right-handed submariners pitch from Port Arthur in southeast Texas. The term also has been applied to sidearm pitchers.

**thrown ball** Any delivery of the ball, other than a pitch, by one player to another. Compare *batted ball.*

**throw off** Syn. of *shake off.*

**throw on top** *n.* An overhand pitch.

**throw out 1.** To put a runner out by a throw or relay; to field a batted ball and throw it to a baseman before the batter reaches that base. **1st Use.** 1880. (*Brooklyn Daily Eagle*, Oct. 10; Edward J. Nichols). **2.** For an umpire to eject a player, manager, or coach from the game.

**throw out the first ball** To toss a ball as part of a pregame ceremony. Traditionally, a political figure throws out the *first ball*, 1, from a place in the stands or, increasingly, from a place on the field, formally opening the baseball season in the ballpark of the home team.

**throw-over** A throw from the pitcher to the first baseman to hold a runner close.

**throws left** Said of a player (esp. a pitcher) who throws left-handed. Abbrev. *TL.*

**throws right** Said of a player (esp. a pitcher) who throws right-handed. Abbrev. *TR.*

**throw the mask 1.** To end an inning, as signaled by the catcher doffing his protective face mask. **2.** For the catcher to prepare to catch a pop fly by tossing aside the face mask, which may obstruct his vision.

**thumb** *v.* **1.** For an umpire to banish a player, manager, or coach from the playing field or the bench for the remainder of the game. Umpires often make a gesture of ejection with the thumb raised. **1st Use.** 1937. (National League Service Bureau file clipping, May 6; Edward J. Nichols). **2.** *n.* The ejection from a game by an umpire of a player, manager, or coach. "Bobo [Newsom] Given Thumb" (*San Francisco Call-Bulletin* headline, Aug. 29, 1949; Peter Tamony). **3.** *v.* To hit a pitch with the handle of the bat; e.g., "Smith thumbed one, a pop fly to short."

**thumber** A slow pitched ball that seems to slide off the thumb. **1st Use.** 1910. (*American Magazine,* June; Edward J. Nichols).

**thumb happy** Said of an umpire who ejects more than a normal number of participants from a game.

**thumbing** An ejection. On the removal of minor-league manager Joe Gordon: "He was tossed out of an Opening Day game for the first time in his long career which includes few 'thumbings' from umpires on any day" (*San Francisco News,* Apr. 2, 1952; Peter Tamony).

**thumb on** To reach base safely by hitting a ball on the bat handle, close to the thumb. The term is a play on hitchhiking or "thumbing a ride." **1st Use.** 1943. "Thumbed on . . . [is] getting on base by way of a hit close to the thumb" (*Baseball Magazine,* Jan.; David Shulman).

**thump 1.** *v.* To defeat. **2.** *v.* To hit the ball. **3.** *n.* A batted ball. **1st Use.** 1920. (*New York Times,* Oct. 3; Edward J. Nichols).

**thunder round** Batting practice finale in which the batters try to hit the ball out of the park.

"Mike Young is the Thunder Round champion" (Richard Justice, *Washington Post,* Apr. 4, 1986).

**tibbies** Syn. of *TIBS.*

**TIBS** (Pron. "tibbs") A statistical measurement for the number of teammates batted in, expressed as runs batted in minus home runs. The best lifetime TIBS is 1,836 (achieved by Ty Cobb); the best single-season TIBS is 143 (achieved by Hank Greenberg in 1937). The term and concept were developed by Richard Zitrin and Jules Tygiel. Compare *RABS.* Syn. *tibbies.*

**ticket** *v.* To bat a ball; e.g., "Smith ticketed the ball for right field but it was caught by the first baseman."

**ticket to first** Syn. of *base on balls.*

**ticket to the minors** A demotion to the minor leagues.

**tickie-hitter** A hitter who "ticks," or makes only partial contact with, the ball rather than hits it with good wood.

**tie 1.** *v.* To score one or more runs so that both teams have the same number of runs at a given moment during a game. "There is an old saying that you play to tie on the road and win at home" (Steve Kluger, *Changing Pitches,* 1984; Charles D. Poe). **1st Use.** 1875. (*New York Herald,* Sept. 9; Edward J. Nichols). **2.** *v.* To win and lose the same number of games during a series, road trip, or other stretch of games. **3.** *n.* Syn. of *tie game.* **1st Use.** 1856. (Knickerbocker Rules; Edward J. Nichols).

**tie game** A regulation game that is called and ruled official, with each team having scored the same number of runs; e.g., a game called because of rain after six innings with each team having scored the same number of runs. The term tends to show up in a major-league context in exhibition games. In Japanese major-league baseball, if a game is tied after 12 innings, it's a tie game. Writing about the Japanese game, Gary A. Warner (*Advocate & Greenwich Time,* Aug. 24, 1997) notes: "Fans love the rare tie—it's a well-played contest in which no one 'loses face' by being defeated."

**tie-breaker 1.** A run that breaks the tie in a game. **2.** A one-game playoff that occurs when two teams are tied for first place in their division at the end of the regular season. The site is determined by a coin flip weeks ahead of the need for such a game.

**tie up** To pitch a ball inside so that the batter cannot get his bat around fast enough to hit the ball.

**tight 1.** Referring to closeness to the batter; e.g., "Smith throws the pitch in tight." **2.** Said of a defense or infield in which no ground balls escape. Compare *loose,* 1.

**tighten up 1.** To become more effective defensively, esp. pitching. **1st Use.** 1910. (*New York Tribune,* July 5; Edward J. Nichols). **2.** To become less effective; to choke. **Usage Note.** The fact that this term can have diametrically opposed meanings is noted with the observation that this is a prime example of why nonnative speakers of English often find it so confusing.

**tight pitch** A pitch thrown inside or close to the batter.

**tight slider** A slider with a minor break.

**tight spin** The sharp rotation of a pitch. Tom Verducci (*Sports Illustrated,* Mar. 31, 1997) noted that Kevin Brown throws a sinker 93 mph and "with the tightest spin in the game, giving the ball a wicked sinking action in the last five feet before the plate."

**tight spot** Any difficult moment in a game, commonly applied to pitchers, as when the bases are loaded and there is a 3-0 count on the batter.

**timber** A baseball bat. **1st Use.** 1868. (*New York Herald,* Sept. 27; Edward J. Nichols).

**"time"** The announcement or call by an umpire of a legal interruption of play, during which the ball is dead. When a player is injured, "time" cannot be called until the umpire considers the play to be completed; e.g., if two fielders collide while attempting to catch a fly ball, another player must retrieve the ball and it must be returned to the pitcher before "time" can be called and the ball deemed dead. See also *time out.*

**time at bat** Syn. of *at-bat,* 1.

**time of game** The length of the game expressed in hours and minutes. Abbrev. *T,* 1.

**time out** A temporary suspension of play called by the umpire. It can be initiated by the umpire or called in response to a request by a player, manager, or coach. See also *"time."*

**time the pitch** For a batter to judge the speed of a pitched ball and initiate the swing of his bat so that it makes contact with the ball.

**timing** The ability of a batter to judge the speed and path of a pitched ball in correlation with his swing.

**timothy trimmer** Syn. of *daisy cutter.* **1st Use.** 1869. (*New York Herald,* Sept. 16; Edward J. Nichols).

**tin cup** A derogatory term for an *umpire,* alluding to the cup used by a sterotypical blind beggar.

**Tinker to Evers to Chance** The double-play combination of the Chicago Cubs from 1902 to 1912: shortstop Joe Tinker, second baseman Johnny Evers, and first baseman Frank Chance. The term has become synonymous with precision teamwork (even though Tinker and Evers rarely spoke to each other). **Etymology/1st Use.** 1902. Frank Graham (*Baseball Extra,* 1954) wrote:
"On Sept. 15, 1902 at the old West Side Park in Chicago, where the Cubs were playing the Cincinnati Reds, a forgotten scorer set down on the sheet before him:
"'Double play: Tinker to Evers to Chance.'
"He didn't know it, but he was linking on paper for the first time in that fashion the names of a double-play combination which, if not the greatest of all time, certainly was the most colorful."
The fame of the combination got a gigantic boost when columnist Franklin P. Adams featured them in the poem "Baseball's Sad Lexicon," which

M. BROWN. J. PFEISTER A. HOFMAN C.G. WILLIAMS O. OVERALL. E. REULBACH. J. KLING.
H. GESSLER. J. TAYLOR. H. STEINFELDT. J. McCORMICK. F. CHANCE. J. SHECKARD. P. MORAN. F. SCHULTE
C. LUNDGREN. T. WALSH. J. EVERS. J. SLAGLE. J. TINKER.

CHICAGO NATIONAL LEAGUE BALL CLUB 1906    THE "CUBS"—PENNANT WINNERS

"*Tinker - Evers to Chance*".     1906

V. O. HAMMON PUB. CO., CHICAGO

**Tinker to Evers to Chance.**

appeared in the *New York Globe* in 1908. The poem contained one of the most repeated lines in American light verse: "These are the saddest of possible words:/Tinker to Evers to Chance."

**tip 1.** *v.* To make incomplete contact of the bat with the ball; to hit a pitched ball a glancing blow; e.g., "Smith tipped the ball for a foul." **2.** *n.* A ball that has barely made contact with the bat; a ball that glances off the bat. **1st Use.** 1845. (Knickerbocker Rules, 12th rule). **3.** *v.* For a pitcher or catcher to reveal what is about to be pitched; e.g., "Smith had a tendency to tip off his pitches when he displayed his grip on the ball" or the catcher's signs "tipped" the runner at second base regarding the next pitch. The pitcher can tip his pitches in several ways; e.g., an open glove may indicate a forkball, a closed glove, a fastball; or elbows together may indicate a curveball, but elbows separated, a different pitch. "When [right-hander Hideo] Nomo was throwing a fastball, his left pinkie was visible at the height of his exaggerated windup. When he threw a split[-fingered fastball],

his pinkie was stuck in his glove" (*Baltimore Sun,* June 8, 1998). See also *telegraph.*

**tip-foul** *n./arch.* Syn. of *foul tip.* **1st Use.** 1874. (Chicago *Inter-Ocean,* July 7; Edward J. Nichols).

**tipped bat** A swinging bat that has come into contact with the catcher's mitt. A tipped bat can result in the umpire awarding the batter first base.

**tire** A player's foot. A player who cannot get moving quickly is said to have "two flat tires." See also *wheel,* 2.

**tissue bat** A weak turn at the plate, replete with a strikeout. **1st Use.** 1876. "Brannock followed with a tissue bat" (*Detroit Free Press,* July 29; Peter Morris).

**tissue-paper Tom** *arch.* An athlete who is easily injured. See also *paper mache.* **1st Use.** 1937. (*New York Daily News,* Jan. 17; Edward J. Nichols).

**titan** A traditional term for a team that "clashes in the fall classic" (World Series).

**titanic** *arch.* A sinking liner, from the name of the British luxury ocean liner that sank after colliding with an iceberg in the North Atlantic on its maiden voyage in Apr. 1912.

**title** A baseball championship.

**Title IX** [softball term] An educational amendment that became law in 1979, designed to outlaw sex discrimination in collegiate athletics. The initial act ordered schools to provide reasonable competitive athletic outlets for female students. It was a once and future boost for women's softball and has become a term of reference for women who play softball. Stephanie Salter (*Women's Sports and Fitness,* July 1987) wrote: "My problem, you see, is that I adore the game of softball but play it so badly I could die of shame. When people insist I play, I tell them I am 37 years old, that I grew up before Title IX, and it is simply too late for me to emulate Joan Joyce."

**titty-high** Said of a pitched ball that comes in at chest level. **Usage Note.** Edward J. Nichols (*An Historical Dictionary of Baseball Terminology,* Ph.D. dissertation, 1939) puts this term in historic context: "The term is obviously not likely to appear in print, but its common use has been attested for the writer by an interview with Honus Wagner."

**TL** Abbrev. for *throws left.*

**tobacco card** A baseball card issued with tobacco. Syn. *T-card.*

**tobasco tap** A hard-hit ground ball. The term is a variant of "Tabasco," the trade name for a hot and spicy pepper sauce. **1st Use.** 1907. (*New York Evening Journal,* Apr. 30; Edward J. Nichols).

**toehold** A firm position in the batter's box effected by the batter digging in with his spikes. **1st Use.** 1912. "Get a toe-hold and make the best of it" (*Sporting Life,* May 18).

**toe plate** An extra piece of leather on the shoe of the pitcher's pivot foot that protects the shoe as it is dragged across the mound.

**toe the rubber** **1.** To prepare to pitch by having the pitcher's pivot foot touching or in contact with the rubber. **1st Use.** 1901. (Burt L. Standish, *Frank Merriwell's Marvel;* Edward J. Nichols). **2.** To pitch in the abstract. "Now I'm going up

against the studs. It's going to be awesome toeing the rubber against those guys." (Baltimore Orioles pitcher Rick Krivda, quoted in *Baltimore Sun,* Aug. 8, 1995).

**"to hell with Babe Ruth!"** A refrain used by Japanese troops to goad American soldiers during World War II, which began for the United States six years after Ruth's retirement in 1935. The name "Babe Ruth" was synonymous with America. The refrain may have been the magazine and Hollywood film version of much cruder goads in which Ruth's name was used.

**tomahawk** To take a high swinging chop at the ball with a bat. Syn. "tommy-hawk."

**tomahawk chop** The chopping motion made by Atlanta Braves fans, often with a toy tomahawk in their hands.

**tomato** The baseball.

**Tommy John operation** A surgical operation, first performed on pitcher Tommy John on Sept. 25, 1974, in which a tendon from the nonpitching forearm is transplanted to replace a torn or damaged ligament in the elbow of the pitching arm. The operation was developed and refined by Los Angeles orthopedic specialists Dr. Robert Kerlan and Dr. Frank Jobe. The operation saved and lengthened John's career, as well as those of many other pitchers. Syn. "Tommy John surgery."

**tonk** A home run. **Etymology.** The term was associated with Roger Maris (*The Sporting News,* July 7, 1974).

**too hot to handle** Said of a hard-batted ball that eludes capture. **1st Use.** 1932. (*Baseball Magazine,* Oct.; Edward J. Nichols).

**Tony Conigliaro Award** An annual award presented by the Boston baseball writers to a player who has overcome adversity. It is named for the Boston Red Sox outfielder who made a dramatic comeback from a 1967 beaning that sidelined him for the entire 1968 season.

**tools** **1.** The basic skills of a baseball player (nonpitcher): hitting for power, hitting for average, throwing, running, and fielding. Compare *fundamentals.* **2.** The specific talents or abilities of a baseball player. "Your tools—let's break that out.

You have speed, movement, placement. I never had speed. I have movement and placement. If you have two of the three you can be outstanding. If you have all three, you're Sandy Koufax." (pitcher Tommy John, quoted in *New York Times,* Sept. 11, 1983). **3.** *arch.* Physical strength and size. Leonard Shecter (*Baseball Digest,* June 1963) put the term's shifting meaning in context: "'He's got the tools' means he's big enough, now if he only had some talent. Today it would mean that the player had talent, but, perhaps, was not big enough."

**tools of ignorance** The catcher's equipment: shin guards, chest protector, helmet, mask, and mitt. Bruce Lowitt (*St. Petersburg Times,* Mar. 27, 1988) wrote: "A first baseman with warning-track power or an outfielder one step too slow to make that one final step out of obscurity. If he is wise, he will pick up the tools of ignorance." **1st Use.** 1937. (*New York Daily News,* Jan. 17; Edward J. Nichols). **Etymology.** The term is based on the notion that catching is a grueling, painful job that a smart player would try to avoid. Hy Turkin (*Baseball Almanac,* 1955) insists that the term was "coined by Muddy Ruel, a college graduate and a lawyer, in disgust at his catching chores." Charles C. Meloy (*Baseball Magazine,* Aug. 1939) gives a conflicting attribution: "The ballplayers love phrases that are pungent and redolent with meaning. Thus, Bill Dickey, Yankee catcher, coined a phrase that was greeted with whoops of joy and at once included in the language. Brooding over the fate that made him a catcher on a blazing July day, Bill spoke of the catcher's armor as 'the tools of ignorance.'"

**toothpick** A baseball bat.

**too true** Said of a pitcher who cannot get the ball over the corners or who can only throw over the heart of the plate.

**top 1.** *n.* The *first half* of an inning. **2.** *v.* To bat a ball with a downward motion and hit its upper part, which usually results in a ground ball; e.g., "Smith topped a slow roller toward short." **3.** *v.* To win. **4.** *n.* The upper part of the strike zone. **5.** *n.* See *top of the order.*

**top-flight** Said of a first-rate team. **1st Use.** 1939. "When the heat is on in a close race, the championship club is the team which holds its own with the top-flight teams and annihilates the lesser clubs" (Gordon S. "Mickey" Cochrane, *Baseball: The Fans' Game;* David Shulman).

**top half** The *first half* of an inning.

**topnotcher** *arch.* A first-class or excellent player. "In the major leagues there are three classes of players designated in the picturesque language of the game as 'bushers,' 'bone-heads' and 'topnotchers'" (Hugh S. Fullerton, *Collier's,* Sept. 11, 1909). **1st Use.** 1889. "Today both of them rank with the top notchers in their respective positions" (*Cincinnati Times-Star,* Feb. 19; David Shulman). **Extended Use.** Anyone at the highest level. Elbert Hubbard (*Concerning Slang,* 1920) noted: "A topnotcher is an individual who works for the institution of which he is a part, not against it."

**top of the order 1.** The first batter in the batting order. **2.** The first three batters in the batting order.

**topped ball** A ball that is hit slightly above its center.

**top spin** The overhand rotation on a pitched ball.

**Tools of ignorance.** *Robert DeNiro as the dying catcher, Bruce Pearson, in the 1973 movie of Mark Harris's* Bang the Drum Slowly.

**Toronto Blue Jays** The name of the American League East Division franchise in Toronto, Ont., Canada. The team took its name from more than 4,000 submitted by potential fans. Not one, but 154, picked Blue Jays, a bird common to southern Canada.

**torpedo 1.** *n.* A baseunner who knocks down or attempts to knock down the infielder covering second base in an attempt to break up a double play. **2.** *v.* To act as a torpedo.

**toss 1.** *n.* A short, soft, usually underhand throw. See also *long toss; short toss; soft toss.* **1st Use.** 1881. (*New York Herald,* Aug. 19; Edward J. Nichols). **2.** *v.* To throw the ball a short distance. **1st Use.** 1887. (Chicago *Inter-Ocean,* Apr. 8; Edward J. Nichols). **3.** *v.* To pitch a baseball game. **4.** *v.* To pitch a baseball to a batter. **5.** *v.* For an umpire to eject a participant from the game.

**tosser** A pitcher. **1st Use.** 1880. (Chicago *Inter-Ocean,* May 27; Edward J. Nichols).

**toss out 1.** To throw out a baserunner. **1st Use.** 1920. (*Spalding's Official Base Ball Guide;* Edward J. Nichols). **2.** To eject a participant from the game.

**tossup** *adj.* A game or series between equally matched teams; a game or series whose outcome could as easily be determined by the "toss up" of a coin. **1st Use.** 1891. (*Harper's Weekly,* Apr. 18; Edward J. Nichols).

**total average** A ratio between the number of bases a player gains for his team and the number of outs he makes. It equals: (total bases + stolen bases + walks + hit by pitches) divided by (at-bats − hits + caught stealing + grounded into double plays). Grounding into a double play equals two outs. The total average for the major leagues is about .666. Abbrev. *TA.* **Usage Note.** The statistic was advocated by writer Thomas Boswell (*How Life Imitates the World Series,* 1982), who has termed himself its "proprietor and purveyor." A Boswellian rule of thumb is that any player with a TA over .900 will end up in the Hall of Fame and any player with a TA below .500 should not be allowed on a major-league field unless he is a top-flight shortstop. The highest lifetime TA is Babe Ruth's 1.432. "This simple stat . . . cleanly combines the virtues of batting average, slugging average, on-base percentage,

and stolen-base proficiency" (Thomas Boswell, *The Washington Post,* Feb. 17, 1983).

**total bases** A statistic for the total number of bases created by base hits, credited to a batter as a means of computing his worth as a batter. One base is credited for a single, two for a double, three for a triple, and four for a home run. The statistic was created as an alternative accounting to the batting average, in which all hits count as one. The single-season record for total bases is 457 by Babe Ruth in 1921; the lifetime record for total bases is 6,856 by Hank Aaron. Abbrev. *TB.*

**total chances** A statistic for the total number of a fielder's opportunities, arrived at by adding putouts, assists, and errors. See also *chance,* 1. Abbrev. *TC.*

**touch 1.** To contact any part of the body, clothing, or equipment of a player or umpire. **2.** To

*Touch.*

contact a base with the ball securely held in a fielder's hand or glove to record a putout. **3.** To get several hits and runs off a pitcher; e.g., "The Brewers touched Smith for five hits and three runs." Syn. *touch up.* **1st Use.** 1887. (Chicago *Inter-Ocean,* May 9; Edward J. Nichols).

**touch all bases** To assure that contact is made with each base on one's way around the basepath. **Extended Use.** To cover a large variety of things; to explore all avenues. "Reagan and Press: Touching all Bases" (*USA Today* headline, Feb. 12, 1986).

**touch 'em all** To hit a home run; e.g., "Smith touched 'em all with two on."

**touch up 1.** Syn. of *touch,* 3. **2.** To reach a base; e.g., "Jones touched up at third on Smith's single." **3.** To return to a base after taking a lead.

**tough 1.** Said of a pitcher who refuses to give the batter anything good to hit; "Smith pitched Jones tough." **2.** Said of a hitter who fouls off several pitches waiting to get a good pitch to hit; e.g., "Jones was tough to retire."

**tough out** A batter who is not easily retired, such as one who is difficult to strike out, or one who

does not hit into double plays, or one who can attract a base on balls.

**tourist** A player who performs on several different teams.

**towel** A piece of cloth that, when thrown onto the field from the dugout, is a rare but dramatic means of showing displeasure with an umpire's decision. Bert Dunne (*Folger's Dictionary of Baseball,* 1958) reported: "Umpire usually interprets towel as white flag—symbol of personal cowardice—and may even clean bench." **Etymology.** Throwing in the towel has long been the means by which a boxer's handlers surrender for him in a prizefight; by extension, to surrender or quit any activity or pursuit, usually in defeat.

**towering fly** A fly ball hit high into the air.

**town ball 1.** *obs.* An early variation of baseball, played on the day of a town meeting. It employed a box-shaped field and four 4½-foot-high wooden stakes as "bases," with the batter's box midway between two bases. A baserunner did not make a complete circuit. The batter could wait until he judged that he had a good pitch to hit and he could be put out by being struck with the ball be-

**Town team baseball.** *Maine town ball team, circa 1950.*

tween stakes. "In the rural context during the 1820 to 1840 period, ballplaying was commonly reserved for market days or holidays, such as the July 4th celebration. On a typical market day in rural New England, farmers and villagers would gather on a town common to barter food produce and craft goods. While the women and girls tended to these business matters, the men and boys might strike up an informal ball game which often lasted through the afternoon until dusk. This tradition is thought to have given rise to the term 'town ball.'" (Leatherstocking Base Ball Club, Cooperstown, N.Y., 1992). The first organized town ball team was the Olympic Ball Club of Philadelphia in 1820. Town ball continued to be played in New England until 1860, where it was known as the *Massachusetts game.* **2.** Syn. of *town team baseball.*

**town team baseball** Baseball competition at the level at which villages, towns, and small cities field a team, usually featuring players of various ages; e.g., the Pine Tree League in Maine. Syn. *town ball,* 2.

**TP** Abbrev. for *triple play.*

**TR** Abbrev. for *throws right.*

**track it down** To pursue and catch a fly ball in the outfield.

**trade 1.** *v.* To exchange and/or sell the contracts of one or more players with another club. **1st Use.** 1898. (*New York Tribune,* May 15; Edward J. Nichols). **2.** *n.* The exchange of one or more players between two clubs. **1st Use.** 1911. (William Patten & J. W. McSpadden, *The Book of Base Ball;* Edward J. Nichols).

**trade bait** A player or players used as an inducement to effect a trade with another team or to attract trade offers from other teams.

**trademark** The printed or embossed manufacturer's logo and name that appears on the barrel of a bat. If a ball is hit on the trademark, the bat usually breaks.

**trading block** The status of a player being offered for trade or sale.

**trading card** One of a set or series of cards sold separately or included as a premium with packages of bubble gum or other products and that is collected and traded; specif., a *baseball card.*

**trading deadline** The last moment at which two teams are allowed to trade players. The concept is fast losing all meaning as teams now use waivers to trade at almost any time. As recently as the 1970s, the deadline for interleague trading was at midnight on the final day of the winter meetings, the early Dec. get-together of team and league officials. The regular season trading deadline is July 31.

**traffic cop 1.** The third base coach. **2.** A ball that is "difficult to handle," like a traffic cop.

**traffic director** A pitcher who moves defensive players around the infield and outfield.

**tragic number** The *magic number,* as seen from the perspective of the team about to be eliminated from contention.

**trail** To be behind in runs in a game or in games won in the standings.

**trainer** A member of a team's staff who gives first aid and physical therapy to injured players

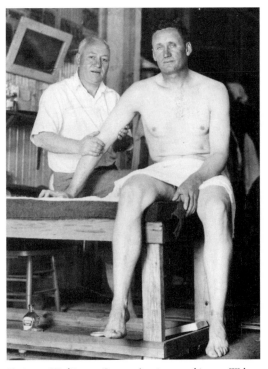

***Trainer.*** *Washington Senators' trainer working on Walter Johnson's fabled right arm.*

510 • training camp

and tends to their physical well-being, and who may also supervise exercise and weight-control programs.

**training camp** The place where a team prepares itself for the regular season. **1st Use.** 1906. (*Sporting Life,* Mar. 3; Edward J. Nichols).

**training trip** Exhibition games played on the road in preparation for the regular season. Such trips were common before World War II. **1st Use.** 1910. (*Baseball Magazine,* May; Edward J. Nichols).

**trampoline effect** [softball term] The action that occurs when a softball is hit from bats made of thin-walled aircraft aluminum. The ball is literally launched off the surface of the bat, much like a person bouncing off a trampoline.

**trampoline turf** An artificial playing surface with a high degree of bounce, as in the Hubert H. Humphrey Metrodome in Minneapolis where many hard-hit, bouncing balls quickly turn into singles.

**transfer** To move a franchise from one city to another.

**trap 1.** To field a ball on a short hop rather than catch it on the fly. **2.** To catch a runner on the basepath between two fielders. **1st Use.** 1863. (Chadwick Scrapbooks clipping, Aug. 9; Edward J. Nichols).

**trap a ball** *obs.* To deliberately drop an infield fly with less than two outs and runners at second base and first base. The ball is muffed to trick the runners into advancing and getting thrown out. Now illegal, the infield fly rule is invoked by the umpire under such a condition. **1st Use.** 1892. (*Chicago Herald,* May 16; Edward J. Nichols).

**trap ball** A children's game in colonial United States, a forerunner of baseball.

**trapped ball** A batted ball that is ruled to have been caught after it has hit the ground or fence. Sometimes a fielder will try to make it look as if a trapped ball is a legally caught fly ball.

**trapped runner** A baserunner caught between two or more fielders.

**trapper's mitt** The modern, shovel-like first

baseman's glove, composed of three large sections: one for the thumb, one for the fingers, and one in the middle that serves as a pocket. Syn. "trapper."

**trap play** A defensive maneuver in which a batted ball is short-hopped. "One of the toughest plays for an umpire is the trap play in the outfield" (Ron Luciano, *The Umpire Strikes Back,* 1982; Charles D. Poe).

**trash bag** The flabby plastic "walls" at the Hubert H. Humphrey Metrodome in Minneapolis, which appear to have the characteristics of a mammoth trash-can liner. A player catching a ball off this surface is said to "play the trash bag." Syn. *Hefty bag.*

**traveling secretary** A member of a club's front-office staff who attends to the team's hotel accommodations, transportation, and other arrangements while away from home. Syn. *road secretary.*

**trial** A period during which a player from a lower level is given a chance to succeed at a higher level. See also *tryout.* **1st Use.** 1902. (*Sporting Life,* Sept. 20; Edward J. Nichols).

**tribe** Any baseball team.

**Tribe** A common alternative nickname for a team whose primary nickname relates to Indians; specif., the Cleveland Indians. "Most members of the Cleveland press corps and the Tribe's front office would not be so ambiguous as [Alvin] Dark" (Pat Jordan, *The Suitors of Spring,* 1973).

**trickle in** To score by making one base at a time.

**trickler** A slow ground ball. See also *bleeder,* 1. **1st Use.** 1922. (*New York Times,* June 2; Edward J. Nichols).

**trigger 1.** See *pull the trigger.* **2.** Syn. of *spark.*

**trim** To win a close game. "Cubs Trim Pirates, 3–2" (*Tampa Tribune* headline, Sept. 24, 1989).

**trimmer** A ball hit along the ground; one that "trims" the grass. **1st Use.** 1870. (*New York Herald,* June 19; Edward J. Nichols).

**Tripartite Agreement** The accord signed by the National League (NL), American Association (AA), and Northwestern League prior to the 1883 season that brought peace between the two warring major leagues (NL and AA), created the first recognized minor league, and established the framework under which the game prospered. The mutual recognition of the contracts and the blacklists of all teams led to a stable business climate. See also *National Agreement.*

**triple 1.** *n.* A base hit on which the batter reaches third base safely. Joe Garagiola once said that Willie Mays's glove was where triples went to die. Abbrev. *T, 2; 3B, 3.* Syn. *three-base hit; three-bagger; three-sacker; triple bagger; triplet.* **1st Use.** 1880. (*New York Press,* June 3; Edward J. Nichols). **2.** *v.* To hit a triple; e.g., "Smith tripled in the gap." **3.** *v.* To complete a triple play.

**Triple A** Syn. of *Class AAA.*

**triple bagger** Syn. of *triple,* 1. **1st Use.** 1880. (Chicago *Inter-Ocean,* June 29; Edward J. Nichols).

**Triple Crown 1.** The rare distinction by which a player ends the season leading his league in batting average, runs batted in, and home runs. The only players to win the Triple Crown more than once were Rogers Hornsby (1922 and 1925) and Ted Williams (1942 and 1947); the last to achieve the distinction was Carl Yastrzemski in 1967. **2.** *obs.* The distinction of leading the league in batting average, runs, and hits. The term was applied to Ty Cobb's efforts in the early 20th century: he achieved the distinction in 1909, 1911, and 1915. **3.** The distinction by which a pitcher ends the season leading his league in games won, earned run average, and strikeouts. Roger Clemens, Sandy Koufax, Lefty Grove, and Grover Cleveland Alexander are "the only pitchers to win back-to-back pitching Triple Crowns" (Tom Verducci, *Sports Illustrated,* Oct. 5, 1998).

**triple double 1.** The achievement by a player of leading his league in doubles for three consecutive years. The term came into play in late 1986 when Don Mattingly was successful in repeating Tris Speaker's triple double of 1920–22 (Speaker also lead the American League in doubles in 1923). **2.** Attaining double figures in doubles, triples, and home runs during a season. Compare *quadruple double.* **Etymology.** Borrowed from basketball where

it means to post double-digit numbers in three statistical categories (such as points, assists, and rebounds, or points, rebounds, and blocked shots) in a single game.

**tripleheader** A set of three games played in succession on the same day between the same two teams. The only tripleheader in the 20th century occurred on Oct. 2, 1920, when the Cincinnati Reds defeated the Pittsburgh Pirates in the first two games but the Pirates won the third game, which was called after six innings because of darkness.

**triple play** A defensive play in which three players are put out as a result of continuous action, providing there are no errors committed between putouts. Though rare today (many ardent fans have never seen one), Hugh S. Fullerton (*American Magazine,* June 1912) wrote: "There are records of eight triple plays made by one man unassisted, and about twenty triple plays are made in each league every season." A modern player, Brooks Robinson, holds the record for hitting into the most triple plays: four. Abbrev. *TP.* **1st Use.** 1867. "Gus Stillwagner, on first base, made a handsome triple play, by catching a fly ball, and putting two men out running their bases" (*Detroit Advertiser and Tribune,* Oct. 30; Peter Morris).

**triple steal 1.** A maneuver in which three baserunners each simultaneously steal the next base. **2.** A feat in which a player steals second base, third base, and home in the same inning. Milwaukee Brewers infielder Paul Molitor accomplished such a feat in July 1987.

**triplet** A 19th-century term for *triple,* 1.

**triple threat** An unofficial title for a pitcher who, in one season, wins 20 or more games, has 200 or more strikeouts, and maintains an earned run average of 3.00 or less.

**triple up** To make or be the third out in a triple play.

**trip to the plate** A turn at bat; an *at-bat,* 1. **Usage Note.** The term is almost always used retrospectively; e.g., "One hit in three trips to the plate."

**Trolley Dodgers** The nickname of the Brooklyn

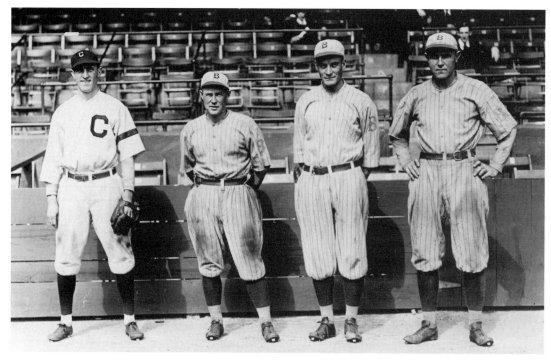

***Triple play.*** *Bill Wambsganss with (l. to r.) Pete Kilduff, Clarence Mitchell, and Otto Miller. Wambsganss caught Mitchell's line drive for the first out, stepped on second base before Kilduff could get back for the second out, and tagged Miller who was running from first.*

entry in the American Association from 1884 to 1889. The name referred to the great maze of streetcars in the bustling borough of Brooklyn. The Brooklyn entry in the National League (beginning in 1890) was known by several names until it adopted the shortened version "Dodgers."

**trolley league** *obs.* A minor or bush league, esp. one made up of teams close enough together to be reached by interurban trolley cars. **1st Use.** 1899. (Burt L. Standish, *Frank Merriwell's Double Shot;* Edward J. Nichols).

**trouble** The state of a pitcher who gets behind in the count or puts runners on base; e.g., "Smith continued to pitch in trouble throughout the evening."

**trounce** To defeat soundly.

**truck horse** *arch.* A particularly slow baserunner.

**True Blue Brew Crew** A nickname for the blue-uniformed Milwaukee Brewers.

**tryout** A playing session in which aspiring, young baseball players without credentials perform under the watchful eyes of scouts who are looking for outstanding new talent. See also *trial.* **1st Use.** 1905. (*Sporting Life,* Sept. 2; Edward J. Nichols).

**tryout camp** A playing session held to a) sign players to professional contracts and b) get leads on good young players whose progress can be followed in the future (Edwin Howsam, *Baseball Graffiti,* 1995).

**tumble bug 1.** An acrobatic player given to crashing and diving in the field. **2.** A grandstand player. **1st Use.** 1932. (*Baseball Magazine,* Oct.; Edward J. Nichols).

**tunnel** An underground passageway leading from

**Tunnel.** *Jackie Robinson and Sam Jethroe pose outside the tunnel at the old Braves field, circa 1950.*

the clubhouses and the umpires' dressing room to the dugouts.

**tunneler** A player who takes on managerial airs and begins giving orders to other players.

**turf toe** An injury occurring on artificial turf where the sole of the shoe sticks to the turf and the big toe is jammed into the front of the shoe. "Yes it does hurt and yes it can end careers" (*USA Today,* July 19, 1991).

**turkey** *obs.* Syn. of *home plate.* **1st Use.** 1889. "[Mike] Tiernan . . . slammed a tall and ornamental fly into left field for two bases, bringing [George] Gore across the turkey" (*The World* [New York], July 13; Gerald Cohen). **Etymology.** This 19th-century term showed up repeatedly in Gerald Cohen's research into baseball slang in *The World.* He speculates that the 19th-century home plate was likened in shape to a turkey.

**turn 1.** See *turn at bat.* **1st Use.** 1863. (Chadwick Scrapbooks clipping, Aug. 9; Edward J. Nichols). **2.** A pitcher's start in the normal rotation. **1st Use.** 1905. (*Sporting Life,* Sept. 9; Edward J. Nichols).

**turn a double play** To execute a defensive play in which two offensive players are put out in continuous action. See *turn two.*

**turn around 1.** To be in a losing position in a game or series but able to score enough runs or win enough games to overcome. **2.** To have a winning season following a losing one; e.g., "The team, a noncontender, turned its season around so much that it is now considered a contender" or "Smith turned his season around by changing from a defensive player to an aggressive offensive player." **3.** To force a switch-hitter to hit from one side of the plate to another by bringing in a relief pitcher. **4.** To pull a ball; e.g., "Smith turned the fastball around with his hit down the line." See also *turn on.*

**turn at bat** A player's opportunity to bat the ball, from the moment he enters the batter's box until he is either put out or becomes a baserunner.

**turn away 1.** To retire a side without allowing it

to score; e.g., "Smith turned away the Cubs in the top of the fifth." **2.** To strike out three batters in succession.

**turn back** To defeat an opposing team; e.g., "The Padres turned back the Cubs."

**turn in** To complete; e.g., "Smith turns in another fine pitching performance."

**turn it into a souvenir** To hit a home run into the stands or out of the park, with the ball being claimed by a fan.

**turn on** To pull the ball on an inside pitch; to get a good swing and make good contact by using one's legs and hips to hit with power. "[Alex Ochoa] has a solid line-drive stroke but also can turn on inside pitches and pull them" (*Baltimore Sun*, June 14, 1995). See also *turn around*, 4.

**turn on the big guns** To use the best players, esp. pitchers.

**turn on the heat** To play well and with intensity; to bear down. Syn. "turn on the current."

**turn over 1.** To complete a double play; e.g., "The Cubs turned it over when Smith touched second and threw to first." **2.** See *turn the ball over*.

**turn-over hitter** *arch.* Syn. of *switch-hitter*. **1st Use.** 1928. (*New York Times*, Oct. 7; Edward J. Nichols).

**turnstile** A device for counting spectators as they enter the ballpark. Syn. *stile*.

**turnstile count** Total attendance at a ballpark. **1st Use.** 1902. (Timothy H. Murnane, *Official Guide of the National Association of Professional Baseball Leagues;* Edward J. Nichols).

**turnstiler** *arch.* A spectator at a baseball game. **1st Use.** 1932. (*All Sports Record Book;* Edward J. Nichols).

**turn the ball over 1.** To throw the ball and turn one's hand over the top of the ball in the process; specif., to throw the screwball. The term derives from the fact that the ball has been turned to give it a reverse spin. **2.** For a pitcher to rotate his wrist

as he releases the ball, causing it to stay low in the strike zone; e.g., "Jones turned the ball over as he pulled down during the pitch."

**turn the order** To make more than one defensive change simultaneously so as to change the order in which the new players will come to bat. "I have always suspected it was Dallas Green who first saw that a hidden purpose of the designated hitter rule lay not in getting an extra good bat into the lineup but an extra bad glove out of it. His opposite number in the 1980 World Series, Jim Frey, perhaps forgetting that this time the DH rule was not in effect, used up all his pinch hitters and wound up having to let his pitcher bat for himself." (Charles Einstein, letter, Mar. 5, 1990).

**turn two** Syn. of *turn a double play*.

**turn up the dial** To pitch with increased velocity.

**turtleback** Syn. of *mound*, 1.

**tweener** A base hit that falls between two outfielders or between two infielders. When he was denying his ability as a power hitter, Vada Pinson was once asked to account for the doubles and triples he was hitting: "Oh, those were just 'tweener' hits, those that light between outfielders" (*San Francisco Call-Bulletin*, May 16, 1959; Peter Tamony). Sometimes spelled " 'tweener." See also *in-betweener*.

**twelve o'clock high** A straight overhand pitch.

**12-to-6** Said of a pitch that drops straight down, as if on a clock, from top to bottom. "David Wells has a 12-to-6-o'clock curve that dips, wiggles and does a fair rendition of Chuck Berry's duck strut" (Franz Lidz, *Sports Illustrated*, Sept. 8, 1997).

**twenty-eighty system** A rating system used by scouts when evaluating a player, with 20 points accorded the maximum for each of the five tools that scouts look for (fielding, throwing, running, hitting, and hitting with power). An 80 rating indicates a blue-chip major leaguer; a 50 rating indicates an average major leaguer.

**25-man roster** The standard list and number of regular players allowed on a major-league team, from Opening Day until Sept. 1, after which the limit is 40.

**24-man roster** The list and number of regular players allowed on a major-league team beginning in 1986. The reason for the change from 25 to 24 was to save money, but, by all accounts, it was a detriment to a team's ability to make strategic moves in the late innings of a game. "The new 24-man roster limit claimed another victim Tuesday when the Chicago Cubs released veteran pinch-hitter Richie Hebner, who came up in 1968" (*USA Today,* Apr. 2, 1986). In 1990, teams were given the option of going with a 24- or 25-man roster (most opted for 25).

**20-game winner** A pitcher who has won 20 or more games in a single season. Winning 20 games in a season is a common standard of excellence for pitchers.

**20-second rule** A rule that allows the pitcher 20 seconds between pitches to deliver the ball when there is nobody on base and no time outs are called. If the pitcher violates this rule, the umpire shall call "ball" (*Official Baseball Rules,* rule 8.04). With one or more baserunners, there is no time limit.

**twight** A game played from twilight through the night. The term was created by the Brooklyn Dodgers in 1942 as a blend of "twilight" and "night." Ed Danforth (*Baseball Digest,* Sept. 1942) opposed the "twend" and noted: "If baseball is going baby talk and wadio announcers are going to give out: 'Weese twipled to wight scoring Wizzo. Wiggs drew four balls and Weiser sacwificed him to second,' then lets suspend baseball for the duwation." See also *twilight baseball.*

**twilight ball** [softball term] An early name for softball.

**twilight baseball** A game played too late for a day game and too early for a night game. An Acme wire photo (June 15, 1942) contains this caption: "Twilight Baseball. The Brooklyn Dodgers inaugurated a modified form of night baseball at Ebbets Field . . . The game, which started in the daylight at 7:00 PM, and finished under the arc-

lights two hours later, drew a crowd of 15,157 fans." (Cleveland Public Library Photo Collection). See also *twight.*

**twilight-night** Syn. of *twi-night doubleheader.*

**twin bill** Syn. of *doubleheader.*

**twi-night doubleheader** A *doubleheader* with the first game starting in the late afternoon, usually about 5:30 P.M., and the second game being played at night under the lights. The term is a blend of "twilight" and "night." Syn. *twilight-night; twi-nighter.* **1st Use.** 1949. The term shows up in the context of baseball in Parke Cummings's *Dictionary of Sports* (1950). Research conducted by Mamie Meredith (Univ. of Nebraska) and on file in the Tamony collection reveals that the term may actually date back to the World War II period.

**twi-nighter** Syn. of *twi-night doubleheader.*

**twin killing** Syn. of *double play.* "The term 'twin killing' . . . has taken on a perverse new meaning for the Cubs. Their regular double-play combination, which knocks 'em dead in the best of times, is now left to kill time on the disabled list" (Phil Hersh, *Chicago Tribune,* June 17, 1987). **1st Use.** 1934. "Andy helped Dazz by rapping into a twin killing" (*Philadelphia Evening Bulletin,* Sept. 13; Peter Morris).

**twirl** To pitch. **1st Use.** 1883. (*Sporting Life,* June 3; Edward J. Nichols). **Etymology.** From the fact that a pitcher winds up—or "twirls" his arm—before delivering the ball.

**twirler** A pitcher. "Asa Brainard . . . was one of the first great twirlers" (Alfred H. Spink, *The National Game,* 1910). **1st Use.** 1883. (*Sporting Life,* Apr. 15; Edward J. Nichols).

**twist** *arch.* A curveball. **1st Use.** 1861. (*New York Sunday Mercury,* Aug. 10; Edward J. Nichols).

**twister** A thrown or batted ball that twists and turns in flight. **1st Use.** 1910. (*Baseball Magazine,* Apr.; Edward J. Nichols).

**2** The scorekeeper's designation for the catcher.

**two away** Two out.

**2B 1.** Abbrev. for *second base.* **2.** Abbrev. for *second baseman.* **3.** Abbrev. for *double,* 1.

**two-bagger** Syn. of *double,* 1. **1st Use.** 1881. (*New York Herald,* July 13; Edward J. Nichols). **Extended Use.** A double victory; a repeat success. "Brown 'Two-Bagger' Brings in $132,000,000" (*San Francisco Call-Bulletin* headline, May 27, 1959; Peter Tamony).

**two-base error** A misplay that allows the batter-runner or a baserunner to take two bases. **1st Use.** 1917. (*New York Times,* Oct. 9; Edward J. Nichols).

**two-base hit** Syn. of *double,* 1. **1st Use.** 1872. (*Boston Daily Globe,* Apr. 15; Peter Morris).

**two-baser** Syn. of *double,* 1. **1st Use.** 1874. (Chicago *Inter-Ocean,* July 14; Edward J. Nichols).

**two class** *arch.* The highly select group of pitchers with an earned run average below 2.00. **1st Use.** 1922. (*Spalding's Official Base Ball Guide;* Edward J. Nichols).

**two-cushion shot** Syn. of *double,* 1. **1st Use.** 1912. (*New York Tribune,* Sept. 16; Edward J. Nichols).

**two down** Two out.

**two fingers only** Said of a pitcher whose only deceptive pitch is the curveball. The term alludes to the traditional catcher's sign (two fingers) for a curveball. **1st Use.** 1912. (*American Magazine,* June; Edward J. Nichols).

**two-hopper** A batted ball that bounces twice before it is fielded. "If he can't get the ball up he's going to hit a two-hopper to the second baseman" (Bill Lee, *The Wrong Stuff,* 1984; Charles D. Poe).

**two league** *arch.* A baseball league that plays many doubleheaders.

**two o'cat** Syn. of *two old cat.*

**two-o'clock hitter** *arch.* A player who hits well in batting practice and poorly during the game. The term dates back to when most games started at three o'clock and batting practice at two o'clock.

See also *ten-o'clock hitter; one-o'clock hitter; five-o'clock hitter; six-o'clock hitter; seven-o'clock hitter.* **1st Use.** 1934. "Two o'clock hitter—one who hits line drives during hitting practice but pops up during the game" (Al Abrams, *Pittsburgh Post-Gazette,* Aug. 13; Bill Mead).

**two old cat** A precursor to baseball that differed from *one old cat* in having two batters at opposite stations with the fielders divided so that half faced one batter and the other half faced the other batter. "The process by which . . . Base Ball has grown out of the primeval 'two-old-cat' is very gradual and natural" (*Lakeside Monthly* [Chicago], Apr. 1870; David Shulman). Syn. *two o'cat.* **1st Use.** 1866. (Constitution and By-Laws of Olympic Ball Club of Philadelphia; Edward J. Nichols).

**two-ply killing** Syn. of *double play.* **1st Use.** 1920. (*Spalding's Official Base Ball Guide;* Edward J. Nichols).

**two-sacker** Syn. of *double,* 1. **1st Use.** 1891. (*Chicago Herald,* July 5; Edward J. Nichols).

**two-seam changeup** A changeup thrown with the middle and ring fingers placed along two seams. It is thrown by Tom Glavine. See also *four-seam changeup.*

**two-seamer 1.** A lucky home run, as described by Joe Goddard (*The Sporting News,* Mar. 6, 1982): "One of those duck-hook jobs that barely gets over the fence. It's not awesome. The ball sinks a little and the hitter gets on top of the ball, only getting his bat on two seams." Compare *four-seamer,* 1. **2.** Syn. of *two-seam fastball.*

**two-seam fastball** A sinking fastball in which the ball is gripped along (not across) two seams. It does not run or slide as much as a *four-seam fastball.* Syn. *two-seamer,* 2.

**two time a pitch** To take an extra step forward to swing at an esp. slow-pitched ball.

**Tygers** A nickname for the Detroit Tigers when Ty Cobb was on the roster.

**tying run** A run that ties the score of a game.

**Tygers.** *Detroit's team name took on new meaning when Cobb joined the roster.*

**Type A free agent** A *free agent* ranked among the top 30% of major leaguers at his position as determined by a formula developed by the Elias Sports Bureau. Any club that signs a Type A free agent must surrender a top draft pick to the free agent's former club: its first-round pick in the next summer's amateur draft if the team was in the top half of the standings, otherwise its second-round pick. The club losing a Type A free agent also receives an extra draft pick between the first and second rounds of the amateur draft.

**Type B free agent** A *free agent* ranked among the top half (but not the top 30%) of major leaguers at his position as determined by a formula developed by the Elias Sports Bureau. The club losing a Type B free agent receives the signing club's draft pick, but no extra pick, in the next summer's amateur draft.

**Type C free agent** A *free agent* ranked among the bottom half of major leaguers at his position as determined by a formula developed by the Elias Sports Bureau. The club losing a Type C free agent receives an extra draft pick between the second and third rounds of the next summer's amateur draft.

# U

**U** Scorecard abbrev. for an unassisted putout.

**UA** Abbrev. for *Union Association.*

**UBL** Abbrev. for *United Baseball League.*

**ugly** Describing a game played gracelessly characterized by miscues, wasted leads, and runners thrown out on hits. "The Yankees are even winning the ugly ones these days" (*Milwaukee Journal Sentinel,* July 24, 1997). See also *winning ugly.*

**ugly finder** A foul ball lined into the dugout, so-called because such a ball is believed to seek out a homely player.

**ukulele hitter** A hitter who hits weak ground balls to the infielders; a poor hitter.

**ukulele umpire** The umpire stationed at third base.

**ump** Short for *umpire.* "Playoff Umps Not Chosen Blindly" (*USA Today* headline, Oct. 7, 1986). **1st Use.** 1888. "He wants to ump in some of the minor leagues" (*Cincinnati Times-Star,* Apr. 18; David Shulman).

**umpire** **1.** *n.* An official who is responsible for the conduct of the game on the playing field by administering the official rules of baseball and for maintaining discipline and order; baseball's third-party adjudicator. There are four umpires at a major-league game (one at home plate and one at each base) and an additional two during postseason play (one for each foul line). The *plate umpire* is the *umpire-in-chief* and the *base umpires* are *field um-*

*pires.* The umpires are responsible for individual calls during a game, from the initial instruction of "play ball!" through the announcement of the last out. They determine, among other things, if a given pitch is a ball or strike, if a given baserunner is safe or out, and if the ball is in play or dead. See also *arbiter; arbitrator,* 1; *blind tom; blue; bluecoat; boy blue; Jesse James; Mr. Guess; man in blue; sheepherder; tin cup.* Syn. *ump.* **1st Use.** 1845. (Knickerbocker Rules, 17th rule). **2.** *v.* To act as a judge or umpire. Syn. *ump.* **1st Use.** 1891. (*Harper's Weekly,* May 9; Edward J. Nichols). **Etymology.** From the Middle English "nomper" or "noumper" for an extra person brought in when two individuals disagreed. The Middle English word, in turn, derives from the old French word "nompair," meaning "not paired" (hence, ideally suited to act as the third party to arbitrate a dispute). Umpires are also employed in cricket, field hockey, badminton, polo, tennis, table tennis, and volleyball. John Ciardi (*Goods Words to You,* 1987) notes that the term was "nonced" in Middle English; the letter "n" was dropped from the word and attached itself to the article. This is the same process (also known as nunation) that transformed a "napron" into an "apron."

**umpire-baiting** Consistent bickering with the umpires, perhaps with an eye to getting the benefit of close calls in the future. **1st Use.** 1902. (*Sporting Life,* Oct. 4; Edward J. Nichols).

**umpire-in-chief** The *umpire* positioned behind the plate when there are two or more umpires assigned to a game. He is the official in charge of the

Drawn by E. W. Kemble

A LITTLE ARGUMENT WITH THE UMPIRE

**Umpire.**

game and the only person with the authority to declare a forfeit. He makes all decisions regarding the batter, which includes calling balls, strikes, and foul balls. Compare *crew chief.* See also *plate umpire.* Syn. *chief of staff.*

**umpire school** A commercial enterprise, usually operated by a former and/or current major-league umpire, dedicated to teaching umpiring skills to qualified young aspirants.

**umpire's interference** An act by an umpire that hinders a fielder; e.g., touching a fair ball before it passes a fielder or impeding a catcher's throw attempting to prevent a stolen base. A pitched or thrown ball that hits the umpire is in play, but a batted ball that hits an umpire after it has bounded past the pitcher is dead. Runners may not advance when the plate umpire interferes with the catcher's throw.

**umpiring** The art of judging a game; acting like an umpire. "Anybody can see high and low. It is 'in and out' that is umpiring." (American League umpire Durwood Merrill, quoted by George F. Will, *Washington Post,* Mar. 29, 1987).

**umpiring signal** One of a simple set of hand and arm movements that an umpire uses to indicate calls; e.g., a raised right arm with a clenched fist along the basepaths means that the runner is out, while an emphatic horizontal crossing of the hands with the palms down indicates the runner is safe; and a raised right arm at the plate indicates a called strike.

**ump's broom** The common whisk broom used by the plate umpire to clean or dust off home plate so that it is clearly visible. Before the turn of the 20th century, umpires swept the plate with a long-handled house broom and then tossed the broom toward the visitors' bench. In 1904, Chicago Cubs outfielder Jack McCarthy was running from third base to home when he stepped on the umpire's broom and seriously injured his ankle. The National League president subsequently issued an order banning the long-handled brooms and requiring that umpires carry brooms small enough to put in their pockets. The American League adopted the rule soon thereafter. Syn. *brush.*

**unassisted** Without help; specif., said of a putout without the help of a teammate. **1st Use.**

1884. (*DeWitt's Official Base Ball Guide;* Edward J. Nichols).

**unassisted double play** A double play in which a fielder is credited with both putouts without a teammate touching the ball.

**unassisted triple play** A triple play in which a fielder is credited with three putouts without a teammate touching the ball. On July 8, 1994, Boston Red Sox shortstop John Valentin accomplished this rarest of plays for only the tenth time in major-league history. The most famous unassisted triple play was accomplished by Cleveland Indians second baseman Bill Wambsganss during the fifth inning of the fifth game of the 1920 World Series against the Brooklyn Robins: Wambsganss caught a line drive hit by Clarence Mitchell, touched second to retire Pete Kilduff, and tagged Otto Miller running from first base.

**unbutton your shirt** To take a good swing at the ball. The term is based on the idea that a batter might want to loosen his shirt for maximum freedom in swinging.

**unbreakable** Describing a record that would seem unattainable, such as Rogers Hornsby's modern record of .424 batting average set in 1924 or Joe DiMaggio's 56-game hitting streak set in 1941.

**Uncle Charlie** Syn. of *curveball.* "To the lefties . . . a few sweeping curves can remind you of what a real Uncle Charlie looks like" (Thomas Boswell, *Washington Post,* May 18, 1987). "[Bo Jackson] has great ability, great tools, but he has problems with Uncle Charlie" (Ralph Wiley, *Sports Illustrated,* Dec. 14, 1987). See also *Lord Charles; Sir Charles.* **Etymology.** The origin of the term is elusive, but the two words—"uncle" and "Charlie"—may onomatopoetically suggest a curve. The term was common in citizens band radio slang in the 1970s as slang for the Federal Communications Commission. By extension, *The Dictionary of CB Lingo* (1976) calls the president of the United States "Uncle Charlie's Uncle."

**Uncle Charlie's got him** A phrase that describes a batter who cannot hit the curveball. **1st Use.** 1952. "When she [Laraine Day, wife of Leo Durocher] fastens her eye on a batter and says, 'Uncle Charlie's got him,' she means simply he

**Underhand.** *Kid Nichols was known for his underhand delivery. In a 15-year career he won 301 games and lost 208.*

can't hit curve balls" (*Collier's* magazine article, quoted in *Word Study,* May 1952; Peter Tamony).

**unconditional release** The removal of a player from the roster who has no contract or who is still paid under the terms of his contract but is free to offer his services to another club. **1st Use.** 1897. (*New York Tribune,* July 22; Edward J. Nichols).

**uncork** To throw explosively, like a champagne cork coming out of a bottle. **Usage Note.** The term is sometimes used facetiously. In an account of a game in Boonville, Calif., the *Anderson Valley Advertiser* (June 11, 1986) noted: "G.P. rared back and uncorked a throw that landed about four feet in front of him."

**underground** Said of an ineffective pitch; e.g., "Smith's sinker went underground and he had to rely on his fastball."

**underhand** Said of a pitch or throw delivered with the hand below the elbow, or that begins below the belt. Infielders often throw underhand on close plays because there is not enough time to get positioned for an overhand throw. Underhand pitchers include Dennis Eckersley, Dan Quisenberry, Mark Eichhorn, Ted Abernathy, and Carl Mays. Underhand pitching is mandatory in softball. Compare *overhand; sidearm.* Syn. *underslung.* **1st Use.** 1866. (Henry Chadwick, *Base Ball Player's Book of Reference;* Edward J. Nichols).

**underslung** Syn. of *underhand.* "Carl Mays, Yankee pitcher of the 'underslung' delivery, was waived out of the American League" (*National Police Gazette,* Dec. 22, 1923; Peter Tamony).

**under the big top** In the major leagues.

**under the leg pitch** [softball term] A legal pitch in which the pitcher lifts his leg and throws the ball under it. The pitch is allowed in the United States Slo-Pitch Softball Association.

**undertakers rule** [softball term] The Amateur Softball Association of America rule adopted in 1941 that required all pitchers in both day and night games to wear all-black or all-dark-blue uniforms with no letters or trimming on the front of the uniform. It was so called because it made the players look like undertakers. The rule was repealed in 1947.

**under the lights** Descriptive of a night game.

**undress 1.** To slide into a catcher with such force that, literally, at least one piece of the catcher's equipment (e.g., a shin guard or the chest protector) is jarred loose or knocked out of place. The term is also used in the figurative sense for any hard slide into the catcher, as if the slamming was enough to tear his equipment off. **2.** To hit the ball hard directly at a fielder.

**unearned run** A run that is scored because of an error, catcher's interference, passed ball, or following an error on a play that would have ended the inning. The significance of unearned runs is that they are not charged against a pitcher in computing his earned run average. Compare *earned run.* **1st Use.** 1879. (*Spirit of the Times,* Aug. 23; Edward J. Nichols).

**unhittable 1.** Said of a pitcher off whom it is difficult to get base hits. **2.** Said of a pitched ball that is very difficult to hit.

**uni** Short for *uniform.* "The uni change may be second only to the managerial change in front-office strategy" (*Village Voice,* Oct. 7, 1986). "It's been a long road.... Just being out in a 'uni' again, it feels good." (Kelly Gruber, quoted in *Baltimore Sun,* Feb. 18, 1997).

**unie** Short for *uniform.* "Buck Weaver kept his new unie clean for half of the preliminary practice. After that it looked natural on him." (Irving E. Sanborn, *Chicago Tribune,* 1919).

**uniform** A team's official costume. Major-league teams have two different uniforms: one for home games and another for away games. Syn. *uni; unie.*

**Union Association** A major league that barely lasted but one season: 1884. It was founded on the premise that the reserve clause was invalid. As a

**Uniform.** *John McGraw (left) and Christy Mathewson (right) in the special uniforms adopted for the 1911 World Series.*

result, the new league announced that it would openly and freely contract with players from established teams. The existing teams fought back by luring their players to return, and before the first season was over the upstart league was in shambles. Abbrev. *UA.*

**union hours** A nine-inning ball game.

**United Baseball League** An eight-team league founded in Nov. 1994 by former Congressmen John Bryant and Robert Mrazek, sports agent Dick Moss, and economist Andrew Zimbalist to begin play in 1996 as Major League Baseball's first rival in 80 years; but it never got off the ground. Players would have participated in revenue sharing and the team's pretax profits. Teams were proposed for Bayamon (Puerto Rico), Kissimmee (Fla.), Brentwood (N.Y.), Los Angeles, New Orleans, Portland (Ore.), Vancouver (B.C.), and Washington, D.C. Abbrev. *UBL.*

**United States League** A Negro league in 1945 and 1946, organized by William A. "Gus" Greenlee with the moral support of Branch Rickey of the Brooklyn Dodgers. The 1945 teams included the Brooklyn Brown Dodgers, Toledo Cubs, Hilldale (Philadelphia), Detroit Giants, Chicago Brown Bombers, and Pittsburgh Crawfords. The 1946 teams included the Cleveland Clippers, Boston Blues, Pittsburgh Crawfords, Brooklyn Brown Dodgers, and Milwaukee Tigers. Abbreviation *USL.*

**United States Slo-Pitch Softball Association** An organization based in Petersburg, Va., that promotes the slow pitch version of amateur softball. Abbrev. *USSSA.*

**United States Stickball League** An organization based in Far Rockaway, N.Y., that promotes the stickball version of baseball played with a broomstick and lightweight rubber ball. Among other things, it features a Hall of Fame and a speaker's bureau.

**unleash a barrage** To get many hits in succession.

**unlimber** To prepare to pitch or throw. **1st Use.** 1943. "President and Mrs. Harding attended the opener, the President unlimbering his arm by throwing out the first ball" (*Baseball Magazine,* Jan.; David Shulman).

**unlimited arc** [softball term] The *arc* (in slow pitch softball only) in which a pitcher is able to throw the ball as high as 25 feet or more on its way to the plate. The unlimited arc is not allowed by either the Amateur Softball Association of America or the United States Slo-Pitch Softball Association under current rules, but it is permitted in some unofficial leagues. Michael Ivankovich (*The Strategy of Pitching Slow Pitch Softball,* 1986) points out that the unlimited arc, which had been allowed at various points in the evolution of the slow pitch game, gave the pitcher too much of an advantage, which was akin to the advantage that pitchers claim in the fast pitch game. According to Ivankovich: "Some pitchers were able to drop strikes from 20–25 feet and more making it extremely difficult on the batter." See also *minimum arc; maximum arc.*

**unload 1.** To hit a home run. "I had no idea or intention of trying to unload one. I just wanted to take my cut" (Mickey Mantle, *Playing Major League Baseball,* 1957). **2.** To defeat decisively. "Angels Unload on Yankees, 12–0" (*Tampa Tribune* headline, Aug. 28, 1988).

**unpack the bat bag** For a team to start hitting effectively. **1st Use.** 1917. (*New York Times,* Apr. 2; Edward J. Nichols).

**unsportsmanlike conduct** A catchall term for fighting, use of obscene language, inciting or trying to incite a demonstration by spectators, and other actions that are likely to get a player, manager, or coach ejected from a game; e.g., a fielder taking a position in the batter's line of vision and acting deliberately to distract the batter could be removed from the game for "unsportsmanlike intent" [*Official Baseball Rules,* rule 4.06(b)]. Each umpire has the authority to disqualify any player, manager, or coach for unsportsmanlike conduct or language [*Official Baseball Rules,* rule 9.01(d)].

**untouchable** Said of a player who would not be considered for a trade or sale to another baseball team.

**unwritten rules** [softball term] The standards of different leagues and tournaments as to what will be allowed and not allowed by the umpires and officials; e.g., the extent and passion with which a call by an umpire can be disputed varies considerably.

**up 1.** *adv.* Being the player or team that is batting, or at bat; e.g., "The Yankees are up" or "Batter up!" **1st Use.** 1862. (*New York Sunday Mercury,* July 13; Edward J. Nichols). **Extended Use.** Taking or in a position to take one's turn; e.g., "The keynote speaker is up next." **2.** *prep.* Brought from a minor-league team to the parent club; e.g., "Smith was called up from the minors." **3.** *adj.* Said of a pitch that is high. **4.** *adv.* Toward home plate, such as an infield that is playing close in anticipation of a bunt or a play at home plate. Syn. *in,* 1.

**up-and-down 1.** Describing a player who finds himself being sent back and forth between the major leagues and the minor leagues. **2.** Said of a team that enjoys a winning streak of a few games followed by a losing streak of a few games followed by another winning streak and so forth.

**up-and-down the ladder** Said of pitching a sequence of pitches that are high, then low, then high, or vice versa. "Sid Fernandez is the classic up-and-down-the-ladder pitcher. Tom Seaver, Nolan Ryan, a lot of great pitchers get you to chase the high fastball, then the low breaking ball, the high fastball . . . The batter can make an out against these guys and never swing at a pitch in the strike zone. Frustrating" (Keith Hernandez, *Pure Baseball,* 1994). Compare *up the ladder,* 1.

**up and in** Syn. of *high and inside.*

**update set** A special series of supplemental baseball cards issued at the end of the season to represent rookies and players who were traded after the regular set of cards was printed.

**up in his neck** Said of a player who does not come through in the pinch (*The Sporting News Record Book,* 1937).

**up in the air** Unnerved or excited. Hugh S. Fullerton (*American Magazine,* June 1912) wrote: "A term used to describe the condition of a pitcher who loses his courage or presence of mind at critical stages of a contest." **1st Use.** 1898. (*New York Tribune,* May 31; Edward J. Nichols).

**uppercut 1.** *n.* An upward batting stroke that commonly yields fly balls. It is generally regarded as a flaw. **2.** *v.* To swing at the ball with an upward motion of the bat. **Etymology.** A boxing term for a punch that comes up from the waist toward the head of an opponent.

**upper deck** The top tier of seats in a ballpark.

**upper-downer** A fictional pitch thrown by Burt L. Standish's Dick Merriwell, which broke down and then up on its way to the plate. Compare *inner-outer.*

**upper half 1.** The *first half* of an inning. **2.** The baseball player as a public person. Compare *lower half,* 2.

**uprising** A rally in which several runs are scored.

**upset** An unexpected defeat.

**upshoot 1.** A pitched ball that rises as it reaches the plate. Compare *down shoot.* **1st Use.** 1883. "[Dick Burns] is developing an upshoot that is a beauty" (*Detroit Free Press,* Apr. 5; Peter Morris). **2.** [softball term] Syn. of *rise ball.*

**upstairs 1.** *adv.* To or on the upper grandstands; to or on any tier of seats above those at ground level. The term is most commonly used to describe the destination of foul pop flies; e.g., "Smith fouled one upstairs." **2.** *n.* The location of a ball that is pitched high. Compare *downstairs.* **3.** *n.* The brain; e.g., "His problems are all upstairs."

**up the chute** Said of any ball that is hit straight up. Syn. *up the shaft; up the silo.*

**up the ladder 1.** Said of pitching a series of pitches progressively higher in the strike zone. Compare *up-and-down the ladder.* See also *climb the ladder; stair step.* **2.** Said of a fielder going high to get a line drive or bouncing ball.

**up the middle 1.** Around and over second base. A ball that is hit straight up the center of the playing field is said to be "up the middle." **2.** Said of the players at catcher, second base, shortstop, and center field, collectively. A team is said to be strong or weak "up the middle." See also *down the middle,* 1.

**up the shaft** Syn. of *up the chute.*

**up the silo** Syn. of *up the chute.*

**use the whole field** To be able to hit the ball to any part of the field or to place it in any direction. Syn. "use the entire yard."

**USL** Abbrev. for *United States League.*

**USSSA** [softball term] Abbrev. for *United States Slo-Pitch Softball Association.*

**utility man** Syn. of *utility player.* "He used to be Dave Concepcion, All-Star shortstop. Now he's Dave Concepcion, utility man" (*St. Petersburg Times,* Mar. 24, 1987). Cleveland Indians infielder Lou Camilli once punned: "They ought to change our name to the Cleveland Light Company. We don't have anything but utility men."

**utility player** A substitute who can play any one of several positions as needed. Utility players tend to be grouped into three categories: the rookie trying to break into the everyday lineup; the mid-level player backing up a superstar; or the veteran extending his career. See also *role player.* Syn. *utility man.* **1st Use.** 1868. (Chadwick Scrapbooks; Edward J. Nichols).

**Utility player.** *Jerry Downs as a Detroit utility player, 1908.*

# V

**vacuum cleaner** An excellent fielder; a *Hoover*, 1.

**Valhalla** **1.** The place where baseball greats go after death. The term is part of the pumped-up prose of early 20th-century sportswriting. "Years of pain, torture and misery finally came to an end for one-legged Joe Tinker, who on his sixty-eighth birthday [July 27, 1948] decided it was time to join his teammates in Valhalla" (Bill Stern, *Bill Stern's Favorite Baseball Stories*, 1949). The image was boosted when Lou Gehrig was buried at Kensico Cemetery in Valhalla, N.Y., in 1941. **2.** See *Baseball's Valhalla*, a syn. of *Cooperstown*, 1. **Etymology.** From the banqueting hall of the gods and the dwelling place of slain warriors in Norse mythology.

**Van Heusen** *arch.* A day at the plate without a hit; a *collar*, 1. The term is often prefaced by the adjective "big." **Etymology.** From the name of the collar- and shirtmaker.

**vanilla** Said of a team without vitality or fire.

**vapor lock** Failure to perform on the field due to lack of concentration; e.g., "[Infielder Manny Alexander] was given coverages [on attempted steals] and didn't cover. That's what we call in baseball 'vapor lock.'" (Davey Johnson, quoted in *Baltimore Sun*, July 17, 1996). See also *brain cramp*. **Etymology.** From the obstruction to the flow of fuel to a gasoline engine due to bubbles in the fuel as a result of overheating.

**variable chance deviation theory** A mock scientific notion, invented and named by pitcher Jim Palmer, that a little wildness on the mound can be an asset; or, by aiming for the middle of the plate, a pitcher might hit the corners.

**varsity** **1.** *n.* The first or senior team competing for a school, college, or university. **2.** *adj.* Pertaining to first-level athletes. **Etymology.** According to Richard D. Mallery (*Our American Language*, 1947), the term comes from the shortening and 19th-century pronunciation of "university."

**Vaseline ball** A variation on the illegal spitball that is fueled by the famous petroleum product. The application of the Vaseline is facilitated by the fact that it can be used as a hair dressing and easily get on a pitcher's fingers when he is fussing with or tugging at his hat. **1st Use.** 1964. Although one must assume that the Vaseline ball was thrown secretly for years before this date, the pitch was announced as new by Arno Goethel (*The Sporting News*, May 16), who had originally written about it in the *St. Paul Pioneer Press:* "In a conversation that sounded more like a commercial for hair dressing, a member of the [Minnesota] Twins pitching staff said that the trickier twirlers around the American League have come up with a new illegal delivery. It's called the Vaseline ball and rapidly is replacing its predecessor, the spitball."

**vaya** Said of the destination of a home run. The term is Spanish for "gone."

**velocity** The speed of a pitch; that which determines a good fastball. It is a quality of a pitcher who can throw hard. "It takes three components to win, and I had 'em all going tonight—velocity, location, and movement" (Roger Clemens, quoted by Garry Brown, *Springfield* [Mass.] *Union-News,* Sept. 1, 1989). **Usage Note.** The term "velocity" has become a modern term for what used to be called *speed,* 3.

**verbal signal** A sign expressed in coded expressions and words.

**verse** Syn. of *inning,* 1.

**vest-pocket catch** A catch of a high fly ball with the glove close to the body at, or just above, the waist. See also *basket catch.*

**vet** Short for *veteran.* **1st Use.** 1902. (*Sporting Life,* Apr. 26; Edward J. Nichols).

**veteran** An experienced professional baseball player. Syn. *vet.* **1st Use.** 1880. (*New York Herald,* Aug. 23; Edward J. Nichols).

**Veterans Committee** A group of baseball men empowered to elect members to the Baseball Hall of Fame who have eluded or failed to appear on the normal ballot of the Baseball Writers Association of America (BBWAA). Candidates may include managers, executives, umpires, and former players. The players include those from the Negro leagues and those major-league players who have been overlooked or passed over by the BBWAA election.

**VI** Abbrev. for *village idiot.*

**vicinity play** Syn. of *neighborhood play.*

**video replay** A play recorded on videotape for use in running instant replays.

**village idiot** A player who says or does foolish things, or makes a fool of himself. "You try to protect guys, shade the truth a bit, but there's a term players use . . . when a player starts believing fantasy. He's a 'village idiot.'" (Tony LaRussa, quoted in *San Francisco Chronicle,* May 31, 1995). Abbrev. *VI.*

**vines** Street clothes.

**vintage base ball** Presenting the game of baseball as it was played during its formative years in the mid-19th century in accordance with the rules, equipment, uniforms, field specifications, customs, practices, language, and behavioral norms of the period. Games are played today under the leadership of the Vintage Base Ball Association, a national organization of individual clubs organized to preserve, perpetuate, and promote vintage base ball. Syn. *historic baseball; period baseball.*

**vintage pitcher** A pitcher with many years of pitching experience.

**violinist** A batter with an especially smooth swing.

**visiting team** The traveling club, or the team on the road, which always comes up to bat in the top of an inning. Syn. "visitors."

**vitamins** See *make vitamins.*

**voice** An announcer; the person at the microphone.

**Voodoo ball** A nickname for a baseball assembled and stitched in Haiti.

**vultch** A save by a relief pitcher. **Etymology.** According to Tim Considine (*The Language of Sport,* 1982): "From the word 'vulture.' In the 1960s, pitchers likened relievers, who came into well-pitched games in the late innings and got credit for saves and sometimes wins, to vultures, figuratively picking over the bones of starting pitchers."

**vulture** A relief pitcher. Los Angeles Dodgers reliever Phil Reagan was nicknamed "The Vulture" by teammate Claude Osteen in 1966.

**vulture-bait** A pitcher with a dead arm.

# W

**W 1.** Abbrev. for *win*, 4. "[Dave] Schmidt Counting Ws Not HRs" (*USA Today* headline, Apr. 17, 1987). **2.** Box score abbrev. for *winning pitcher.* **3.** Abbrev. for *walk*, 1.

**wabble** *arch.* To lose control of the ball while pitching.

**Wacks Museum** Nickname for *Ebbets Field.*

**waft** To hit a ball hard, usually for a home run. "Hank Aaron has wafted nineteen [home runs]" (Roger Angell, *The Summer Game,* 1972; Charles D. Poe).

**Wagner card** The most valuable baseball card of all. It dates from 1909, carries the likeness of Honus Wagner, and has fetched $640,500 in mint condition. Legend has it that the extreme rarity of this card stems from the fact that Wagner was opposed to smoking and the card was issued by Sweet Caporal cigarettes. When Wagner found that he was depicted on a tobacco premium, he demanded that his image be taken out of circulation. Only a handful are known to exist.

**wagon spoke** A baseball bat.

**wagon tongue** An early term for a large baseball bat. **1st Use.** 1891. (*Chicago Herald,* May 27; Edward J. Nichols).

**waist ball** A pitched ball that comes in at the batter's waist. Syn. *waister.* **1st Use.** 1908. (*Baseball Magazine,* June; Edward J. Nichols).

**waister** Syn. of *waist ball.* **1st Use.** 1914. "After the high balls came 'waisters' and then low ones" (Christy Mathewson, *Pitcher Pollock;* David Shulman).

**wait-and-see** Not anticipating the opposition; not hitting, or not scoring runs.

**waiter 1.** A batter who attempts to get on base by waiting for a base on balls. **2.** A batter who swings only at strikes. **1st Use.** 1909. (*Baseball Magazine,* Nov.; Edward J. Nichols). **3.** A batter who swings late.

**wait on** Syn. of *wait out.* "Looking to drive a fastball to left field . . . [Rafael] Palmeiro was able to wait on a breaking pitch that hung inside" (*Baltimore Sun,* Mar. 16, 1998).

**wait out** To make the pitcher keep throwing by staying in the batter's box until the pitcher throws the kind of pitch the batter wants. To accomplish this feat requires fouling off several pitches. "They wait you out in the Series. You've got to put it over the plate or else" (*San Francisco Call-Bulletin,* Oct. 12, 1949; Peter Tamony). Syn. *wait on.* **1st Use.** 1908. (*American Magazine,* Aug.; Edward J. Nichols).

**"wait 'til next year"** The plaintive motto of fans whose team has once again fallen short of expectations. The refrain was long associated with the Brooklyn Dodgers and their fans. It achieved its greatest play in those years (1941, 1947, 1949, 1952, 1953, and 1956) when the Dodgers lost to the New York Yankees in the World Series. The term is now applied to other teams; e.g., "There is no light in the Old North Church tonight. Boston is dark and despairing, waiting, as always, until next year." (Tony Kornheiser, *Washington Post,* Oct. 28, 1986). The term and its variations are the titles of books written by Carl Rowan (with Jackie Robinson, 1960) and Christopher Jennison (1974). Var. "wait till next year"; "wait until next year." Acronym *WUNY.* **1st Use.** 1884. "Visitors at Mason's headquarters are met with the legend— 'Wait till next year'" (*Sporting Life,* Nov. 5, 1884; Barry Popik). A later application in 1939 may have done much to popularize the phrase.

A Willard Mullin cartoon shows a New York Giants character singing "Wait 'till next year!" A character in a Brooklyn Dodgers uniform says, "That's my act! He's stealin' m' stuff! That's my theme song! I wrote it!" On the ground is a piece of sheet music on which is written, "Wait 'Till Next Year: A Torch Ballad in One Flat. Words and Music by The Dodgers." (*New York World Telegram,* Aug. 9, 1939; Barry Popik). In 1941, the term first achieved prominent display as a headline in the *Brooklyn Eagle,* after the Dodgers were beaten by the Yankees in the World Series. **Extended Use.** The line has been used as a battle cry in a host of areas and situations; e.g., see Doris Kearns Goodwin's 1997 book *Wait Till Next Year,* the story of a young girl growing up in the suburbs of New York City in the 1950s.

**waive** To refrain from claiming a player whose contract is offered for sale by a major-league team.

**waivers** The abandonment by a major-league team of its right to purchase the contract of another team's player for a stipulated price. It amounts to a system by which all the teams in a league have a chance to bid on a player about to be released or to be included in a trade. Before a player can be released, waivers must be granted by all teams in the league in reverse order of their standings (and then by all teams in the other league in reverse order of their standings). If the rights to that player are claimed (not waived) by one of those teams, his contract must be sold at a standard waiver price. The team offering the player can decide to retain him at this point. The rules are complex. Murray Chass (*New York Times,* Aug. 29, 1993) wrote:

"Baseball's waiver rules are only slightly better understood than the plans for the design and operation of the $1 billion dollar Mars Observer spacecraft." See also *outright waivers; irrevocable waivers; major-league waivers.* **1st Use.** 1908. (*New York Evening Journal,* Feb. 26; Edward J. Nichols).

**wake up** To go into action; specif., to get a team's hitters to get base hits. "[Pat] Hentgen pitched his butt off. Hentgen didn't give the bats a chance to wake up." (Bobby Bonilla, quoted in *Baltimore Sun,* Sept. 21, 1996).

**wakeup call** Syn. of *calling card.*

**walk 1.** *n.* A *base on balls;* the taking of first base by a batter to whom four balls have been pitched. "There is no defense against a walk" is Joe Garagiola's oft-quoted remark on the subject. Abbrev. *W,* 3. **1st Use.** 1866. (*New York Herald,* Aug. 28; Edward J. Nichols). **2.** *v.* To advance to first base after the fourth ball; to receive a base on balls from the pitcher; e.g., "Smith walks on four wide ones from Jones." **3.** *v.* To advance a batter to first base by pitching four balls; to give a base on balls to a batter; e.g., "Jones walks Smith by throwing four wide ones." **4.** *v.* To force in a run by issuing a base on balls with the bases loaded; e.g., "Jones walked in the winning run."

**walk all over** To defeat a team decisively; e.g., "The Tigers walked all over the Indians."

**walk-away** Syn. of *walkover.*

**walker** Syn. of *walking man.* **1st Use.** 1911. (*Spalding's Official Base Ball Guide;* Edward J. Nichols).

**walkfest** A game or part of a game in which there is an unusual number of bases on balls.

**walking man** A batter who receives many bases on balls. Eddie Yost, who led the American League in bases on balls six times, was nicknamed "The Walking Man." Syn. *walker.*

**walking step** The movement of a pitcher's pivot (push-off) foot placed in front of the rubber, not in contact with it, when he delivers the pitch. Nolan Ryan and Harry Brecheen were known to "cheat" in this manner.

**walk-off** A term coined by Dennis Eckersley for that lonely stroll from the mound after giving up the winning run (*Sports Illustrated,* Oct. 4, 1993).

**walk-off piece** A game-winning home run. Dennis Eckersley created the term to describe the fact that the pitcher walks off the field after one is hit. Buster Olney (*San Diego Tribune,* Apr. 11, 1994) commented: "Kirk Gibson's game-winning homer off Eckersley in the 1988 World Series is one of the most memorable walk-off pieces of all time."

**walk-off pitch** A pitch that results in a game-winning home run. When Steve Howe threw such a pitch to lose 3–2, he said: "It was a walk-off pitch. You throw the ball and walk off the mound. It was a sinker that didn't sink." (*Baltimore Sun,* May 15, 1995).

**walkover** An easy victory; a game, series, or division race that is easily won by a superior team. Syn. *walk-away.* **1st Use.** 1881. (*New York Herald,* Sept. 24; Edward J. Nichols).

**walk the ballpark** To issue many bases on balls; to pitch a walkfest.

**walk the bases full** To give a base on balls that loads the bases.

**walk the Dixie Highway** To leave the game. The term was used by sportscaster Bob Uecker.

**walk-up** A fan who makes a single-game ticket purchase at the box office on the day of the game.

**walk year** The last year of a player's contract, with the player becoming a free agent the next season. Increasingly, players are being traded, or offered in trade, during their walk year so that the club can get some value from them before they are lost to the open market.

**wall** The outfield fence. A ball hit over the wall is a home run.

**Wall, The** Syn. of *Green Monster.*

**wallop 1.** *v.* To hit the ball with great power. **1st Use.** 1908. (*New York Evening Journal,* Feb. 25; Edward J. Nichols). **2.** *n.* A hard-hit ball. **1st Use.** 1908. (*Baseball Magazine,* July; Edward J. Nichols).

**3.** *n.* A long base hit. **4.** *v.* To thrash an opponent. **1st Use.** 1888. (*New York Press,* Apr. 7; Edward J. Nichols). **Etymology.** Pre-baseball slang: to beat or thrash.

**wall-scraper 1.** A home run that barely clears the fence. **2.** A base hit where the ball glances off the outfield wall.

**Wally Pipp 1.** *n.* A player who takes himself out of the lineup, such as for illness or injury; one who makes a bad move. When a player takes a day off, he is reminded "remember Wally Pipp." "[Jim] Traber was still hitting when [Eddie] Murray got hurt, so he got the call. After a week or so, his Oriole mates began calling Murray 'Wally Pipp'" (*Boston Globe,* Aug. 10, 1986). **2.** *v.* To lose one's job. "[Gregg] Olson thought that, in locker room vernacular, he'd been Wally Pipped. That means somebody else has been given a full shot at your job, and, unless he fails, you can't get it back again even if you regain your normal form." (Thomas Boswell, *Washington Post,* May 1, 1993). "Wally

**Wally Pipp.** *Walter Clement Pipp, who went on to play in Cincinnati after losing his job in New York to Lou Gehrig.*

Pipp has become a tragicomic actor in a cautionary tale, the victim of cruel fate and a false sense of security, the first person ever to be Wally Pipped" (Neal McCabe & Constance McCabe, *Baseball's Golden Age,* 1993). See also *Pipp.* **Etymology.** New York Yankees first baseman Wally Pipp, according to a story told a million times, got a headache on June 2, 1925, took himself out of the lineup, and was replaced by Lou Gehrig, who went on to play in a then-record 2,130 consecutive games. (Gehrig's consecutive-game streak began a day earlier when he went in as a pinch runner.) However, there is another version to the story. Eleanor Gehrig (Lou's wife) reports (*My Luke and I,* 1976): "They said that Pipp had a headache and couldn't make it that day. The real thing was that Pipp was slowing down and hadn't been hitting, so he just decided that a day's relaxation at the racetrack might help his state of mind and his bankroll. So Wally went to the racetrack that June 2 and Lou Gehrig went to first base." (Charles D. Poe).

**Wally World** The area of Anaheim Stadium where Wally Joyner's home runs landed. The name comes from a place made famous in the comedy movie, *National Lampoon's Vacation* (1983), and the fact that Disneyland is also in Anaheim.

**wami** *arch.* A curse. William G. Brandt (*Baseball Magazine,* Oct. 1932) quotes a player: "The breaks have been on us ever since the bell rang. Got a wami I guess." "Wami" appears to have evolved into *whammy.*

**wand** A baseball bat. **1st Use.** 1910. (*New York Tribune,* July 2; Edward J. Nichols).

**war club** A baseball bat.

**warehouse power** The ability of a batter to hit a ball against the Baltimore and Ohio Railroad warehouse 446 feet from home plate down the right-field line at Oriole Park at Camden Yards, Baltimore. The first to exhibit such power was Ken Griffey Jr. during a home run derby before the 1993 All-Star Game.

**warm the bench** To sit on the bench. Syn. *warm the pine.* **1st Use.** 1907. (Burt L. Standish, *Dick Merriwell's Magnetism;* Edward J. Nichols).

**warm the pine** Syn. of *warm the bench.* "He is too valuable a player to warm the pine, no matter who is serving the cocktails" (Bill Croum, *Fort Worth Star Telegram,* 1934).

**warm up** *v.* To throw the ball in practice before the game begins. See also *limber up.* **1st Use.** 1883. (Chicago *Inter-Ocean,* June 27; Edward J. Nichols).

**warmup** *n.* Pregame routine for stretching and limbering up the body. Sometimes spelled "warm-up."

**warm-up jacket** A windbreaker used by a player as he warms up or sits on the bench. To prevent his arm from getting cold, a pitcher tends to wear the jacket any time he is not actually on the mound or in the batter's box.

**warm-up mound** The pitcher's mound in the bullpen.

**warm-up pitch** One of the pitches allowed before an inning begins; one of the pitches that a relief pitcher is allowed to make from the mound before the batter steps into the batter's box. Between innings, pitchers are allowed eight warm-up pitches.

**warm-up swing** A preliminary swing taken by a batter before the ball is pitched.

**warning track** An ungrassed area about 10 feet wide, encircling the outfield just inside the wall, that alerts an outfielder that he is approaching the wall. Its purpose is to protect the outfielder from crashing into the wall as he backs up to catch a ball. With his eyes fixed on the ball, the outfielder knows he is nearing the wall as he senses the granular texture of the warning track with his feet. According to a *New York Times* article (July 19, 1982), the track was conceived when Brooklyn Dodgers outfielder Pete Reiser was seriously hurt in 1947 after he crashed into the wall at Ebbets Field. In 1948, the Dodgers covered the walls with foam rubber and, soon after, warning tracks began to appear. The first parks to use them were Wrigley Field in Chicago, Braves Field in Boston, and Shibe Park in Philadelphia. Syn. "warning path."

**warning-track power** The ability of a batter

*Washington Senators.*

with enough strength to hit a ball to the warning track but not enough to hit a home run. A player with warning-track power is useful when a sacrifice fly is called for; however, the term often refers to a long-ball hitter who has lost some of his power.

**washed up** Said of a player who is no longer considered to be a major leaguer. "Jimmy Callahan considered [Babe Adams] . . . washed up and let him go to St. Joseph in 1917" (Harry Grayson, *They Played the Game,* 1944).

**Washington Senators 1.** The name of the National League franchise in Washington, D.C., from 1886 to 1889 and from 1892 to 1899. **2.** The name of the American League franchise in Washington, D.C., from 1901 to 1960; it moved to Minnesota at the end of the 1960 season and became the Minnesota Twins. The team was also known as the *Nationals,* the *Solons,* and the *Griffmen* and "Griffs" (after owner Clark C. Griffith). The Senators were the target of the old line on Washington: "First in war, first in peace, and last in the American League." **3.** The name of the American League expansion team from 1961 to 1971; it moved to the Dallas area after the 1971 season and became the Texas Rangers. The team was also known as the *Nats.*

**washout** A game called because of rain.

**waste** To deliberately pitch outside and wide of the plate in an effort to head off a steal or prevent a hit-and-run play. **1st Use.** 1909. (*Baseball Magazine,* Dec.; Edward J. Nichols).

**waste ball** Syn. of *waste pitch.* **1st Use.** 1942. "Most pitchers in the minors throw a lot of bad balls and even waste balls" (*Baseball Magazine,* Nov.; David Shulman).

**waste hits** *v.* To make base hits that do not help in the scoring of runs. **1st Use.** 1902. (*Sporting Life,* Sept. 13; Edward J. Nichols).

**waste pitch** A pitch deliberately thrown out of the strike zone, usually with an 0-2 count on the batter. The pitch is commonly thrown in an attempt to get the batter to swing at a bad pitch, to head off a steal by giving the catcher a high pitch on which to make a play on a baserunner, or to prevent a hit-and-run play by making the pitch unhittable. Syn. *waste ball.*

**waster** A pitcher who habitually tries to get batters to swing at balls out of the strike zone. **1st Use.** 1909. (*American Magazine,* May; Edward J. Nichols).

**"watch your lips"** A phrase used to warn of a bumpy or rough infield, one on which the ball is likely to take a bad hop. A phrase of the late 1980s, it may be a play on the popular "read my lips" cliché.

**wave** For an infielder to make a halfhearted attempt to field a ground ball.

**wave, the** An activity in which fans in sections of the grandstand rise to their feet with arms raised, in sequence, giving the appearance of an undulating ocean wave. **Usage Note.** The wave is decried by many purists. "One more reason seeing a game at Wrigley Field is a special experience: According to Cubs publicist Ned Coletti, Cubs fans have never done the wave" (*USA Today,* May 29, 1987).

**wave howdy** For a fielder to let a hard-hit ball pass rather than risk injury. Syn. "wave howdy-do."

**wave on** For a coach to signal a runner to continue to the next base.

**wax** To hit a pitcher hard. **Usage Note.** The

term seems to be used almost exclusively in reference to pitchers. Thomas Boswell (*Washington Post*) quoted Scott McGregor, who, when asked how Don Mattingly struck him, replied: "All over the place. He just waxes you and goes home."

**wax pack** Baseball cards wrapped entirely in opaque wax paper. Compare *cello pack.*

**weaken** To lose one's pitching effectiveness over the course of a game. **1st Use.** 1905. (*Sporting Life,* Sept. 2; Edward J. Nichols).

**weak end of the batting order** The last batters in the batting order. They usually hold this position because they are the least effective hitters and are likely to get one less at-bat in a game than those at the top of the order. **1st Use.** 1899. (Burt L. Standish, *Frank Merriwell's Double Shot;* Edward J. Nichols).

**weak grounder** A lightly hit ground ball that infielders are never supposed to miss. **Extended Use.** Figuratively, something that one should not misplay. "With big Ed Pauley ducking pop bottles, and Harry Truman's Missouri infield bobbling weak grounders, the President's critics were ready to boo almost anyone he sent in" (*Time* magazine, Mar. 11, 1946; Peter Tamony).

**weakness** An area in or around the strike zone with which a batter has trouble.

**weapon** A baseball bat.

**wear a size . . .** To go without a hit for the stated number of at-bats in a game; e.g., "Smith wore a size 4 for four hitless at-bats." This is a play on the term "collar" for a hitless performance.

**wear out the pitcher** For a batter to continuously foul off pitches; e.g., "Smith wore out the pitcher with 12 foul balls."

**wear out the wood** To *ride the bench.* **1st Use.** 1914. (Ring W. Lardner, *You Know Me Al;* Edward J. Nichols).

**wear the horns** To have a serious lapse in performance; be the goat.

**Weaverism** Any one of a multitude of pronouncements on winning baseball games uttered by Baltimore Orioles manager Earl Weaver; e.g., "The way to win is with pitching and three-run homers" or "The hit and run is the worst and dumbest play in baseball." A few Weaverisms are saved for the nature of the game itself: "This ain't a football game. We do this every day."

**web** The leather patch or stitching sewn between the thumb and forefinger of a fielder's glove or mitt.

**webbing** The array of laces and leather panels that connect the thumb and finger sections of a fielder's glove or mitt.

**weed-eater** A ground ball that hugs the ground.

**weigh in** To contribute to the outcome; e.g., "Smith weighed in with a triple."

**Wells Fargo pitch** A fastball that is not overpowering. The term is a play on the fact that it appears to come at the batter in stages, alluding to the Wells Fargo stagecoaches of the 19th-century American West. **Etymology.** Created by San Francisco Giants public relations director Garry Schumacher to describe Stu Miller's fastball, and attested to by Joe Garagiola (*Baseball is a Funny Game,* 1960).

**West Division 1.** See *American League West.* **2.** See *National League West.*

**western swing** A road trip through the western states by an eastern or midwestern club.

**West Vest** An umpire's *chest protector* developed by National League umpire Joe West that features high-impact plastic plates which conform to the umpire's body shape.

**Westrum's dictum** The comment by catcher and manager Wes Westrum on the game of baseball as most fans understand it: "It's like church. Many attend but few understand."

**wet ball** Syn. of *spitball,* 1.

**wet grounds** A playing field deemed unfit for play because of rainwater on the ground. **1st Use.**

1912. (*New York Tribune,* Sept. 19; Edward J. Nichols).

**wet one** Syn. of *spitball,* 1.

**wet pitch** Syn. of *spitball,* 1.

**wet wipe** Syn. of *spitball,* 1.

**"we want a hit!"** A crowd plea for a rally. See also *"CHARGE!"*

**whack** To hit the ball. **1st Use.** 1896. "He is whacking the ball also with unusual vim and success" (*The Sporting News,* May 24; David Shulman).

**whale** To bat a ball hard. **1st Use.** 1905. (*Sporting Life,* Sept. 9; Edward J. Nichols).

**whale belly** An overweight player.

**whammy** A *jinx;* bad luck brought on a player by what another says. "Nearly every player in the game engages in some little practice which he believes will bring him good luck or put the whammy on the other fellow" (Jim Hurley, *American Legion Monthly,* Feb. 1937). See also *hoodoo.* **Etymology.** From *wami.*

**whang** To bat a ball hard. **1st Use.** 1883. "A new ball was put in as the old one had ripped, and Lewis whanged it nicely to center field" (*Sporting Life,* Apr. 15).

**whangdoodle** *obs.* A good play or hit. **1st Use.** 1902. (*Sporting Life,* Oct. 4; Edward J. Nichols).

**wheel 1.** A defensive play in which all four infielders move ("rotate") to prevent a runner from advancing or scoring on a bunt. "[Bud] Harrelson . . . ordered the 'wheel,' a play in which the shortstop covers third, the second baseman covers first, and the two cornermen charge the plate in an effort to field a bunt and throw out the baserunner at third" (*New York Times,* June 4, 1990; David Shulman). Second base is left unguarded. Syn. *wheel play; rotation,* 3. **2.** A player's leg. A "bad wheel" is a leg injury and a "flat wheel" is a bad foot. A decrease in a player's number of stolen bases is often attributed to "a case of bad wheels." See also *tire.*

**wheel and deal** For a pitcher to wind up and throw.

**wheelhouse** That part of the strike zone in which the batter swings with the most power or strength; the path of a batter's best swing. A pitcher tries not to "hang one" in the batter's wheelhouse; to do so is to invite a home run. "[Ken] Dixon put a fastball in [Charlie] Moore's wheelhouse . . . and dared Moore to hit it" (*Washington Post,* June 7, 1987). See also *crush zone.* **1st Use.** 1959. "It just seems he's not seeing 'em the way he used to. . . . He had a couple that came right into the wheelhouse—the kind he used to knock out of sight—and he fouled 'em off." (Bill Rigney, on Orlando Cepeda's slump, *San Francisco Chronicle,* May 11, 1959; Peter Tamony). **Etymology.** Peter Tamony suggested that batters "wheel" at the ball ("take good, level 'roundhouse' swings") and that such wheels "probably suggested the word association, 'wheelhouse.'" In nautical terms, a wheelhouse is the pilothouse or the place from which a vessel is controlled.

**wheelman** A 19th-century term for a pitcher.

**wheel play** Syn. of *wheel,* 1.

**wheels came off** Describing a situation in which a lead evaporated or the other team started to score many runs.

**Wheeze Kids** A nickname for the 1983 Philadelphia Phillies, who won the National League pennant with a roster that included several older players. The term is a clear play on the Phillies's *Whiz Kids* team of 1950.

**"when does the balloon go up?"** Traditional greeting for a player who shows up overweight, such as on the first day of spring training.

**whiff 1.** *v.* For a pitcher to strike out a batter. "I whiffed eight men in five innings in Frisco yesterday and could of done better than that if I had of cut loose" (Ring W. Lardner, *You Know Me Al,* 1914; Peter Tamony). **2.** *v.* For a batter to strike out. "Mickey Mantle tied the New York Yankees club strikeout record today when he whiffed for the 111th time this season" (United Press International

*Whiff.*

dispatch, Sept. 3, 1958; Peter Tamony). **3.** *v.* To swing at a pitch without touching the ball. **4.** *n.* A strikeout. **1st Use.** 1908. (*New York Evening Journal,* Apr. 18; Edward J. Nichols).

**whiffle ball 1.** A called strike. **2.** Incorrect syn. of *Wiffle ball.*

**whiff list** A pitcher's record of strikeouts.

**whip 1.** *n.* The throwing arm. **1st Use.** 1898. "Ren Mulford reports that Harry Steinfeldt has the most phenomenal 'whip' in the Western League, and will tie any of the seasoned major leaguers in distance and accuracy as a thrower" (*Detroit Free Press,* Feb. 1; Peter Morris). **2.** *n.* A quick throw. **3.** *v.* To throw the ball fast. **1st Use.** 1905. (*Sporting Life,* Oct. 7; Edward J. Nichols). **4.** *v.* To defeat decisively. **5.** *v.* To bat a ball. **1st Use.** 1908. (*Brooklyn Daily Eagle,* May 28; Edward J. Nichols). **6.** *n.* A championship pennant. **1st Use.** 1872. "Both clubs . . . met at the Capitol grounds, Washington . . . with the privilege of flying the 'whip' pennant from the White House" (George C. Small, *A Presidential Base-Ball Match;* David Shulman).

**whisker trimmer** An inside pitch. **1st Use.** 1914. "The pitcher sneaked over a fast 'whisker trimmer,' catching the batter napping" (Burt L. Standish, *Brick King, Backstop;* David Shulman).

**whisperette** A batted ball with little power. **1st Use.** 1909. (*New York Evening Journal,* July 1; Edward J. Nichols).

**whistle** To throw a fastball.

**whistler 1.** A fastball. **1st Use.** 1883. "His swift ball is a whistler" (*Detroit Free Press,* Apr. 3; Peter Morris). **2.** A batted ball that moves with great speed; e.g., "Smith hit a whistler down the third base line."

**White Elephants** A nickname for the Philadelphia Athletics. The nickname derived from John McGraw's comment early in the 1902 season that the owner of the Philadelphia team had a "white elephant" on his hands, alluding to a costly possession out of proportion to its value. The Athletics went on to win the pennant and the McGraw insult was turned into a nickname and a team symbol.

**white lines** The literal and figurative confines of the game of baseball. "Once I step between the white lines, I can't control what people think of me, but I can hit home runs, drive in some runs, steal a few bases and make a couple of spectacular catches. That's all I'm concerned about." (Chicago White Sox outfielder Albert Belle, quoted in *Baltimore Sun*, Feb. 21, 1997). See also *between the white lines*. **Usage Note.** Implied in the term is baseball isolationism. "At the conclusion of every baseball storm—be it a strike or rash of drug busts or the latest contract hassle—players and executives fall back on that old bromide: 'All that really matters is what goes on between the white lines'" (*Sports Illustrated*, Feb. 27, 1987).

**whites** See *home whites*.

**whitewash 1.** *v.* To shut out a team. **1st Use.** 1851. (*Short Oxford Dictionary*; Edward J. Nichols). **2.** *n.* A defeat in which the loser fails to score. **Etymology.** It is easy to see how the term might derive from both the obliterating quality of the white stain and the laundered purity of a pitcher's shutout.

**whittle 1.** To catch up gradually with an opponent who is ahead in a game; e.g., "The Royals whittled away the Red Sox lead." **1st Use.** 1912. (*New York Tribune*, Sept. 29; Edward J. Nichols). **2.** For a pitcher to attempt to lure batters with pitches just off the corners of the plate. **1st Use.** 1928. (Babe Ruth, *Babe Ruth's Own Book of Baseball*; David Shulman).

**whittler** A pitcher who throws the ball just outside the strike zone and lures the batter into swinging at bad pitches. "A good whittler can drive a batter screwy in no time with his tantalizing offerings that aren't quite good enough" (Charles C. Meloy, *Baseball Digest*, Aug. 1939). **1st Use.** 1928. "A pitcher who mixes up balls with strikes and carries a batter along to a two-two or three-two count

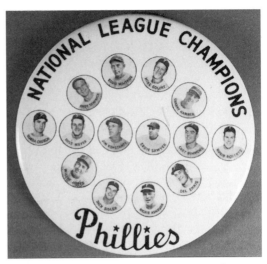

**Whiz Kids.** *The cast of the 1950 Phillies, all under 30.*

before making him hit" (Babe Ruth, *Babe Ruth's Own Book of Baseball*; David Shulman).

**whiz chuck** *arch.* A swiftly pitched ball. **1st Use.** 1908. (*New York Evening Journal*, Aug. 21; Edward J. Nichols).

**Whiz Kids** A nickname for the 1950 Philadelphia Phillies, who took the National League pennant with a starting lineup of players all under the age of 30. Compare *Wheeze Kids*.

**whizzer** A fast-moving baseball. "He sent a whizzer away 'over the fence'" (*New York Sunday Mercury*, Oct. 16, 1861; David Shulman). **1st Use.** 1861. (*New York Sunday Mercury*, Aug. 10; Edward J. Nichols).

**whole ball of wax** The pennant and/or world championship. **Etymology.** From a general slang term that emerged in the 1950s for the "whole thing" or "whole deal." Peter Tamony toyed with the notion that this started out as the "whole bailiwick."

**whole field** See *use the whole field*.

**whole new ball game** A new start, such as a sudden turn of events in a game. See also *new ball game, 1*. **Extended Use.** Any new start. James Rogers (*The Dictionary of Clichés*, 1985) quotes a passage from a 1971 issue of *The New Yorker*: "If this were to happen [Chinese entry into the Vietnam War], some official of our government would no doubt announce that we were in a 'whole new ballgame,' which would mean that none of the policies or promises made in the past were binding any longer, including the prohibition against the use of nuclear weapons."

**"Who's on First?"** The title of the 1939 radio comedy skit supposedly written by Irving Gordon and made famous by Bud Abbott and Lou Costello, who included the pitter-patter sketch in their 1945 film, *The Naughty Nineties*. The comedians estimated that they performed the skit about 10,000 times in radio and television appearances and in live performances. The full lineup: Who (1b), What (2b), I Don't Care (ss), I Don't Know (3b), Why (lf), Because (cf), [omitted] (rf), Tomorrow (p), and Today (c).

**wicket** A player's leg. When a ball passes through a player's legs it is said to have gone "through the wickets." **Etymology.** The wicket is a prime piece of equipment in both croquet and cricket. Whereas the cricket ball cannot go through the wicket, the croquet ball is supposed to go through the wicket; hence, croquet is most certainly the inspiration for the baseball usage.

**wide 1.** *adj.* Off target; far to one side or the other of a base or, in the case of a pitch, home plate. **2.** *n.* A ball thrown wide of home plate. **1st Use.** 1874. (Chicago *Inter-Ocean*, July 7; Edward J. Nichols).

**wide one** A ball pitched too far outside home plate for the batter to hit it. Syn. "wide ball."

**wield a wicked bat** To bat well.

**Wiffle ball 1.** A lightweight, hollow plastic ball perforated by holes with which it is easy to make trick pitches ("the curvingist ball in the world"). It was invented in 1953 by David N. Mullany (Fairfield, Conn.). **2.** A game played like baseball with a plastic bat (no longer than 38 inches, no heavier than 24 ounces, and no thicker than 2 inches in diameter) and a Wiffle ball. Since the ball cannot be hit too far, it makes a good game for a restricted area. Each team has no more than five players (a pitcher, outfielders, and a catcher) who go up against a batter. There is no baserunning: the runners are imaginary and advance depending on where the balls are hit. The World Wiffle Ball Association organized adult leagues in 1977. **Etymology.** David A. Mullany (son of the inventor) said: "You swung and missed so much, it just seemed logical"; dropping the "h" in "whiffle" was his idea—"I told my dad it would be cheaper to make signs with fewer letters" (*Sports Illustrated*, July 28, 1997). Incorrect syn. *whiffle ball*, 2. Sometimes spelled "wiffle ball."

**wig-wag** Syn. of *sign*, 1. **1st Use.** 1917. (*New York Times*, Oct. 9; Edward J. Nichols).

**wig-wagger** A *base coach*.

**wild 1.** Lacking consistent accuracy; esp. said of a pitcher who issues many bases on balls. **2.** Said of a ball that is thrown or pitched far from its intended target. **1st Use.** 1883. (*Sporting Life*, May 20; Edward J. Nichols).

**wild card** A team given a berth in the Division Series (beginning in 1995) by virtue of having the best record among the three second-place teams in the three divisions in each major league. The Florida Marlins were the first wild-card team to win a World Series (in 1997). **Etymology.** From card playing where a given card, such as an ace, can be played as if it were any other card.

**wild-card standings** A chart since 1995 showing the standing of each major league's potential wild-card teams.

**wild in the strike zone** Said of a pitcher who throws strikes but without pinpoint location; e.g., "I was wild in the strike zone. I was throwing strikes, but they weren't quality ones." (Mark Eichhorn, quoted in *Baltimore Sun*, June 19, 1994).

**wild pitch** *n.* A legally delivered pitched ball that is so high, wide, or low that the catcher cannot control or stop it with ordinary effort, thereby allowing one or more baserunners to advance. A wild pitch is charged if the ball touches the ground before reaching home plate and is not handled by

**Wild Pitch.**

the catcher, permitting a runner to advance. The distinction between a wild pitch and a *passed ball* is made by the official scorer. A wild pitch is charged against the pitcher only if a runner advances a base. Abbrev. *WP,* 1. **1st Use.** 1880. (Chicago *Inter-Ocean,* June 28; Edward J. Nichols). **Extended Use.** A careless statement or action. "At midweek the Republican campaign was bolstered by an innovation—the 'truth squad'—a team of senators who trailed whistle-stopping Harry Truman to field what they denounced as his wild pitches" (*Life* magazine, Oct. 13, 1952).

**wild-pitch** *v.* To pitch a ball without control and be charged with a wild pitch.

**wild throw** A ball thrown by a fielder to another fielder beyond his reach, allowing the batter-runner or one or more baserunners to advance, resulting in

an error. **1st Use.** 1861. (*New York Sunday Mercury,* Oct. 2; Edward J. Nichols).

**Williamsburg** The right-field bullpen area at Fenway Park in Boston when Ted Williams was using it as a target for line drives.

**Williams shift 1.** A strategical defensive move created by Cleveland Indians manager Lou Boudreau on July 14, 1946, during the second game of a doubleheader to deal with the particular pull-hitting strength of Boston Red Sox left-handed slugger Ted Williams. The shift placed the third baseman behind second base, the shortstop halfway between first base and second base, the first baseman hugging the line behind first base, the second baseman closer to first base and on the grass in short right field, the right fielder on the right-field line, the center fielder playing the right fielder's position, and the left fielder (the only player covering the left side of the field) about 30 feet behind the skin of the infield. The intent was to dare Williams to hit singles to left field rather than doubles or home runs to right field. During the game, Williams walked twice and lined a one-hopper to the second baseman in short right field, who threw Williams

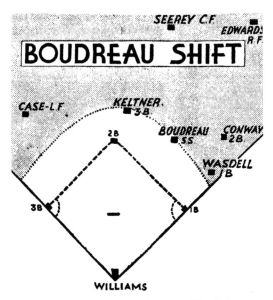

**Williams Shift.** *A newspaper diagram of the shift—here termed the Boudreau Shift.*

out. The shift was originally known as the *Boudreau shift* for its inventor. See also *Averill shift*. **2.** A defensive move in which the shortstop is moved to the right side of the infield to deal with a powerful pull hitter. The term was used by Bob Uecker on an Oct. 3, 1997, telecast to describe the move against Chicago White Sox slugger Frank Thomas.

**William Tell** An easy, head-high bounding ball. **Etymology.** From the legendary archer who shot an apple off his son's head with an arrow. The term is used in the context of baseball because the ball bounces head high or close to the head, as if it could knock an apple off the fielder's head.

**willow** A baseball bat. **1st Use.** 1870. "[The Water Sprites Club of Ypsilanti are juniors but] seniors both in wielding the willow and lively handling of the ball" (*Detroit Advertiser and Tribune*, July 19; Peter Morris).

**Wilson Pickett** A skillful infielder who makes sharp defensive plays. The term is a rather elaborate pun on the name of rock musician Wilson Pickett, whereby the infielder uses his trademarked Wilson glove to "pick it" (the ball) (John Hall, *Baseball Digest*, Dec. 1973). First baseman Bill Buckner, among others, named his glove "Wilson Pickett."

**wilted lily** A batter who lets his bat droop as he awaits the pitch.

**win 1.** *v.* To score the most runs in a baseball game. **2.** *n.* A victory. **Usage Note.** As recently as 1934, this particular use of a verb as a noun was noted as an oddity of American sportswriting by J. Willard Ridings (*Journalism Quarterly*, Dec. 1934). **1st Use.** 1905. (*Sporting Life*, Sept. 2; Edward J. Nichols). **3.** *v.* To pitch a winning baseball game. **4.** *n.* That which is credited against a winning pitcher and is counted both in his single-season and career records. In giving this statistic, the wins always appear before the number of losses; e.g., a season record of 18–8 means 18 wins and 8 losses. Abbrev. *W,* 1.

**wind** For a pitcher to swing his pitching arm preparatory to pitching the ball. See also *wind up*.

**windage** [softball term] The effect of wind on a pitched ball. Eddie Feigner (*What Little I Know About Pitching and Hitting,* 1980) describes the importance of windage in the fast pitch game: "In pitching, technically, you lead the target. Often, you'll be working against a wind that will move the ball. You'll also be throwing a ball straight in the strike zone that, with the spin, will move up or out or down or away from the strike zone. This is windage and ahead-of-target practice that you must work at. From the 46-foot mound, softball pitchers really have to learn windage. They will not be able to throw the ball by the batter unless they are very strong and very tall. When I pitch from second base, there are times in a wind that I throw a ball just out of dead reckoning, as far as fifteen feet to the right or left of home plate, and the ball comes down in the strike zone from the spin on the wind."

**wind-blown home run** A home run in which the ball goes over the fence with the real or imagined help of the wind.

**wind down** To play the last few games of spring training or of the season.

**wind is holding it up** Said of a batted ball that flies into the wind and not only is prevented from going for a home run, but also is easier for the fielder to reach because the wind keeps the ball longer in the air.

**windmill** [softball term] A delivery in fast pitch softball that begins with a full circle *windmill windup*. It results in fastballs of the highest momentum and speed and is used by pitchers with a high level of skill. Edward Claflin (*Irresistible American Softball Book,* 1978) states: "The first windmill pitch ever seen in softball was at a picnic game in Detroit in 1922. It was thrown by Mike Lutomski, a school principal, and was declared illegal by Hubert Johnson, the unofficial rules boss in Detroit. So many playground kids adopted the windmill style that Johnson had to reverse his decision and declare it legal in 1926." See also *slingshot, 2*; *figure eight*.

**windmill windup** [softball term] A windup in which the pitcher makes a full vertical circle with his arm before delivering the ball; the force behind the *windmill* delivery. Harry D. Wilson (*Play Softball*, 1942) described it as follows (for a right-handed pitcher): "The left foot swings back, thereby throwing the weight on the right leg as the arm goes up overhead. The left foot starts forward on the second twirl and the weight goes forward on the left leg as the ball is released. Balance is maintained by the left arm. A slight hesitation as the ball is released may deceive the batter and cause him to swing too soon."

**window-wearer** A player who wore eyeglasses on the field. The term was popular in the 1930s and 1940s for players such as Bill Dietrich, Walter Beck, Dom DiMaggio, and Paul Waner.

**wind pad** Syn. of *chest protector*. **1st Use.** 1905. "Each had a mask and a mitt, but the wind pad was common property worn on alternative days" (Charles Dryden, *The Athletics of 1905;* David Shulman).

**wind paddist** Syn. of *catcher,* 1. Sometimes spelled "windpaddist." **1st Use.** 1905. (*Sporting Life,* Oct. 7; Edward J. Nichols).

**wind up** *v.* For a pitcher to execute a windup before delivering the ball. See also *wind.* **1st Use.** 1912. (*New York Tribune,* Sept. 22; Edward J. Nichols).

**windup** *n.* The preliminary movements of the pitcher's arm prior to pitching the ball. It involves taking a step back from the rubber, raising one's hands together over one's head, and then stepping forward to deliver the ball. Compare *no windup; stretch,* 2. **1st Use.** 1906. (*Lajoie's Official Base Ball Guide;* Edward J. Nichols).

**windup position** One of two legal pitching positions, taken when the pitcher faces the batter with his entire pivot foot on or in front of, and in contact with, the rubber and his stepping foot free, and holds the ball with both hands in front of his body. [*Official Baseball Rules,* rule 8.01(a)]. From this position, any natural movement associated with the delivery of the ball commits the pitcher to throw without interruption or alteration. Compare *set position.*

**wing 1.** *n.* The throwing arm, esp. that of a pitcher. "Talk about pitchers with a good wing!" (*Yankees* magazine, Aug. 31, 1981). **1st Use.** 1904. "The special implication is that Joe McGinnity is more than a mere star if he is capable of teaching a younger rival how to extend the life of his salary wing" (*Everybody's Magazine,* v. 10; David Shulman). **2.** *v.* To throw the ball; e.g., "to wing a baserunner" is to retire him by throwing the ball to the base before he reaches it. **1st Use.** 1908. (*Spalding's Official Base Ball Guide;* Edward J. Nichols). **3.** *v.* To hit a batter with a pitched ball. **1st Use.** 1914. (*New York Tribune,* Oct. 11; Edward J. Nichols). **4.** *v.* To get moving, to hustle, to run; e.g., "Smith winged it from first to third." **5.** *n.* An irregularity on the surface of the ball created when a pitcher uses his fingernails to illegally raise a piece of the cover. The term is usually used in the plural.

**wingy ball** *arch.* A ball with a rough, loose cover.

**wink-out 1.** *v.* To go berserk and attack someone or something, such as a watercooler or the clubhouse wall. **2.** *n.* A berserk attack. Bill Lee (*The Wrong Stuff,* 1984) notes that sometimes two players will wink-out at the same time and attack each other. He adds puckishly that this is called a "twin wink-out," better known as a "twinkie." (Charles D. Poe).

**winner 1.** Syn. of *winning pitcher.* **2.** The team that wins a game.

**winning pitcher** The pitcher who is given official credit for his team's victory. It can be the starting pitcher (if he pitches at least five complete innings) or a relief pitcher who comes in with his team tied or behind and is the pitcher when his team scores the winning run. Compare *losing pitcher.* Abbrev. *WP,* 2. Box score abbrev. *W,* 2. Syn. *winner,* 1.

**winning run** The run, when scored, that gives the winning team a lead that it never relinquishes.

**winning streak** Two or more games won in succession by either a pitcher or a team. **1st Use.** 1897. (*New York Tribune,* Aug. 3; Edward J. Nichols).

**winning ugly** Winning a game despite violating many of the fundamentals of baseball. The term was first used by Texas Rangers manager Doug Rader in reference to the West Division–winning 1983 Chicago White Sox. See also *ugly*.

**winter ball** Organized off-season play for major leaguers and minor leaguers desiring added experience and retaining their skills or remaining fine-tuned. Winter ball is played in the Caribbean area, Central America, and South America (e.g., Venezuela, Dominican Republic, Mexico, and Puerto Rico). "[Brad] Havens looked great in winter ball. Course, they'll chase the breaking ball in the dirt in Puerto Rico." (Earl Weaver, quoted in *Washington Post,* Feb. 9, 1986).

**winter book** A list of major-league players playing winter ball.

**winter instructional league** An off-season *instructional league* that usually starts in Sept. and has a 48-game schedule.

**winter league** Any of several leagues outside the United States where baseball is played during the off-season.

**winter meetings** Traditional annual gathering, discontinued since 1993 due to lack of activity, of baseball team owners, general managers, and associated officials, usually held in early Dec. in a warm locale, for the purpose of conducting league business and discussing and/or making trades. The importance of the winter meetings declined with the decline of rigid trading deadlines; until the 1970s, the deadline for interleague trading was the final night of the winter meetings.

**winter season** That period following one baseball season and before the next when baseball cannot be played.

**wipe-off sign** A sign that nullifies another sign to mystify anyone trying to steal signs. Keith Hernandez (*Pure Baseball,* 1994) notes: "The wipe-off sign on every team I played on was the same: a hand swiped across the chest. Is this the universal wipe-off sign? I sometimes wondered." Compare *indicator,* 2.

**wipe out** *v.* To win a one-sided game; e.g., "The Dodgers wiped out the Padres, 10–2."

**wipeout** *n.* A one-sided baseball game.

**"wipe the blood off it"** Syn. of *"take the blood off it."*

**wire cage** *arch.* The catcher's mask. **1st Use.** 1908. (*New York Evening Journal,* Aug. 26; Edward J. Nichols).

**wire-to-wire** From the beginning of a season to its end; specif., said of a team that spent every day of the season in first place. Only seven major-league teams have accomplished this feat: 1998 Cleveland Indians, 1997 Baltimore Orioles, 1927 New York Yankees, 1984 Detroit Tigers, 1923 New York Giants, 1955 Brooklyn Dodgers, and 1990 Cincinnati Reds.

**wish ball** A pitch that is thrown with the hope that the batter doesn't hit it. It is a specialty of pitchers who have "lost their stuff."

**within oneself** Said of a player who does not do more than he is capable of doing, or does not try "to do things that strain . . . [his] capacities and distort the smooth working of . . . [his] parts—what players call 'mechanics'" (George F. Will, *Men at Work,* 1990); said of a player whose reach should not exceed his grasp, such as "I stay within myself" or "He is pitching within himself."

**wobble** To falter or lose one's pitching effectiveness. **1st Use.** 1912. (*New York Tribune,* Sept. 11; Edward J. Nichols).

**wolf 1.** *v.* For a spectator to heckle and complain. **1st Use.** 1902. (*Sporting Life,* July 12; Edward J. Nichols). **2.** *n.* A spectator who constantly heckles a player or a team. William G. Brandt (*Baseball Magazine,* Oct. 1932) quotes a dejected player: "Even our wolves have quit us."

**won-lost percentage** A number expressed to the nearest thousandth that shows a team's relative standing in its league or division. It is created by dividing the total number of wins by the total number of wins and losses.

**won-lost record** The record of a club or pitcher stated with the number of wins followed by the number of losses.

**wood** The baseball bat. The term is used in describing the contact made between the bat and the pitched ball; e.g., "Smith put more wood on the pitch to drive the ball farther." Milwaukee Brewers catcher Kelly Stinnett, protesting the plate umpire's call that a pitch nicked the batter, said, "I thought I heard it hit wood" (*Milwaukee Journal Sentinel*, Sept. 29, 1997). See also *good wood*.

**wood-carrier** A batter who often strikes out; one who carries his bat to and from the plate. **1st Use.** 1932. "The day Ed gets a drink of water for every at-bat he's just a 'wood-carrier' instead of an 'apple-crasher'" (William G. Brandt, *Baseball Magazine*, Oct.).

**wooden Indian 1.** A batter who does not swing at the ball; one who waits on the pitcher. See also *Statue of Liberty*. **2.** A base coach who does not give a signal to a baserunner. **Etymology.** From the impassive image of the carved wooden American Indian traditionally placed in front of cigar stores.

**woodman** A skilled hitter. Sometimes spelled "wood man."

**woodpile** A row of bats, such as in a bat rack or laid out in front of the dugout. Sometimes spelled "wood pile." **1st Use.** 1917. (*American Magazine*, Aug.; Edward J. Nichols).

**wood player** A good hitter who cannot field. Compare *leather player*. See also *lumber man*. **1st Use.** 1937. (*New York Daily News*, Jan. 21; Edward J. Nichols).

**woods** Syn. of *bushes*. **1st Use.** 1902. (*Sporting Life*, July 12; Edward J. Nichols).

**word sign** A sign that is passed along verbally, perhaps encoded in a seemingly meaningless bit of chatter.

**work 1.** To pitch in a game; e.g., "Smith worked the fourth through the seventh innings." **1st Use.** 1908. (*Brooklyn Daily Eagle*, May 29; Edward J. Nichols). **2.** To take part in a game. **1st Use.** 1862. (*New York Sunday Mercury*, Aug. 3; Edward J. Nichols). **3.** To umpire; e.g., "to work the plate" is to serve as the plate umpire. **1st Use.** 1909. (*Baseball Magazine*, July; Edward J. Nichols).

**work a pitcher for a pass** Syn. of *coax a pass*. **1st Use.** 1902. (*Sporting Life*, Apr. 26; Edward J. Nichols).

**worker** A pitcher; e.g., "A fast worker wastes no time between pitches whereas a slow worker usually makes more pitches."

**workhorse** An honorific term for a pitcher who appears in many games or a large number of innings during a season; e.g., "You think of [Scott] Erickson as a workhorse guy who is going to throw a lot of innings" (Ray Miller, quoted in *Baltimore Sun*, Mar. 25, 1998). See also *horse*, 1.

**work on a batter** For a pitcher to try to get a batter out by tempting him with pitches just outside the strike zone. **1st Use.** 1899. (Burt L. Standish, *Frank Merriwell's Double Shot*; Edward J. Nichols).

**work the corners** To pitch to the edges of the strike zone. **1st Use.** 1901. (Burt L. Standish, *Frank Merriwell's Marvel*; Edward J. Nichols).

**work the count** For a batter to attempt to get the count in his favor by taking pitches and fouling off potential strikes to get a good pitch to hit, such as a fastball over the plate or a hanging curve. See also *coax a pass*.

**work-up 1.** Syn. of *rounders*. **2.** A children's baseball game in which a player stays at bat until he or she is retired, at which point everyone else moves up a position. "Players start in the outfield, working their way up with each out—from the outfield to third base, from third base to shortstop, and so on, until finally getting an opportunity to hit" (Benjamin G. Rader, *Baseball*, 1992).

**world champion** The winner of the World Series.

**World Series** The series of games played in Oct. between the pennant winners of the American League and the National League to decide the "world championship." The first team to win four games is the champion. The modern World Series first took place in 1903, but before then the name had been attached to other championship contests. In 1994, for the first time in 90 years, Oct. came

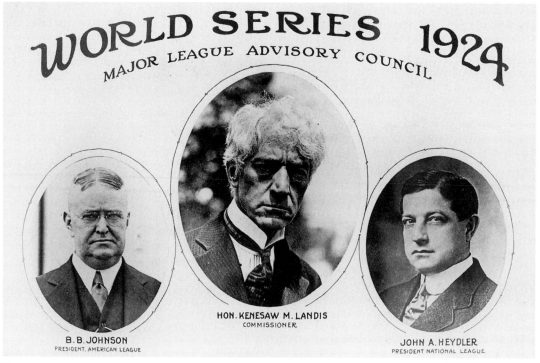

World Series.

and went with no World Series because of a play-ers' strike. See also *World's Series; World Serious.* Ab-brev. *WS.* Syn. *autumn classic; fall classic; big classic; big series; Commissioner's Games; promised land; Se-ries, the.* **Usage Note.** The term "World Series" has been used for other baseball championship series, such as the Triple-A World Series, the NCAA Col-lege World Series, the Little League World Series, the American Legion World Series, and the World Series in the Negro leagues. **1st Use.** 1884. First "World's Championship Series" held in New York, according to research conducted by the National Baseball Library and Archives. Edward J. Nichols (*An Historical Dictionary of Baseball Terminology,* Ph.D. dissertation, 1939) finds the term "World Series" in the *Spalding's Official Base Ball Guide* for 1887. **Extended Use.** The term has been applied to high-level contests in other sports, games, and activities; e.g., "The World Series of Poker."

**World Series ring** The prize given to the play-ers, manager, and coaches of the team that wins

the World Series. Players often say that the fore-most reason they play baseball is not to attain per-sonal records but to earn "the *ring.*"

**World Serious** A cynical and facetious name for *World Series* that pokes fun at the self-importance surrounding the event. "It was the first time in world serious history that a man named Wambs-ganss had ever made a triple play assisted by con-sonants only" (Ring W. Lardner, quoted in Mike Sowell, *The Pitch That Killed,* 1989). Also spelled "world serious."

**world's largest saloon** A nickname for Dodger Stadium in Los Angeles, Calif. "People in the con-cession business refer to Dodger Stadium as 'the world's largest saloon'" (Howard Cosell, *I Never Played the Game,* 1985; Charles D. Poe).

**World's Series** An early term for *World Series.* "In a number of world's series the final result has been greatly influenced by some one situation that was not reckoned with as even a probability"

(American League umpire Billy Evans, Newspaper Enterprise Association syndicated column, Sept. 23, 1919). Also spelled "world's series."

**worm burner** **1.** A hard-hit ball that rolls quickly across the ground without bouncing. Syn. "worm killer." **2.** [softball term] A low, hard pitch, esp. in Over the Line and fast pitch softball. Stephanie Salter (*Women's Sports and Fitness,* July 1987) noted that the pitch, thrown extremely fast and so low that it scrapes over the plate, "appears at crucial moments in [a] game, usually when [the] pitcher has lost her 'stuff' [and it is] hazardous to animals, plant life, catcher's shins, and umpire's feet."

**wounded duck** Syn. of *dying quail.*

**WP** **1.** Scorecard and box score abbrev. for *wild pitch.* **2.** Abbrev. for *winning pitcher.*

**wrapper** A cellophane or wax-paper enclosure for a baseball card that has become a collectible in its own right.

**wrap up** To win a division or series title.

**wrecking crew** A group of heavy hitters. "The 1932 Yankees . . . a great wrecking crew" (broadcaster Vin Scully, "Game of the Week," Aug. 30, 1986).

**Wrigley Field** Home field of the Chicago Cubs since 1916, located at the corner of Clark and Addison on Chicago's North Side. It opened in 1914 as Weeghman Park, the home field of the Chicago Whales of the Federal League, and was known as Cubs Park from 1916 to 1925; it was renamed Wrigley Field in 1926 for longtime owner William F. Wrigley Jr., the heir to the Wrigley chewing gum fortune. Noted for day baseball (until 1988 when lights were installed), natural grass, wind conditions (the breeze may or may not blow in from Lake Michigan), and, since 1937, an outfield wall of Boston ivy. A ground-rule double is granted when the ball sticks in the ivy.

**Wrigleyville** A nickname for Wrigley Field and its immediate neighborhood in Chicago. The day after the first night game was completed there, the lead sentence in an Associated Press report read: "Wrigleyville looked no different Tuesday" (*Bangor Daily News,* Aug. 10, 1988).

**wrinkle** **1.** A curveball with little break. **1st Use.** 1908. (*New York Evening Journal,* May 24; Edward J. Nichols). **2.** A little break of a curveball.

**wrist hitter** A hitter who obtains added power from a quick, timely turn of the wrists, rather than relying on pure body strength. Ernie Banks and Hank Aaron were wrist hitters.

**write out a pass** To issue a base on balls. **1st Use.** 1910. (*New York Tribune,* July 13; Edward J. Nichols).

**wrong armer** *arch.* A left-handed pitcher. Syn. "wrong sider."

**wrong base** The incorrect base toward which an outfielder returns a batted ball. The term occurs in the phrase "throw to the wrong base"; e.g., with a runner on first base and a single hit to the outfield, the outfielder throws to third base in a vain attempt to put out the runner advancing from second base, thereby allowing the batter-runner to reach second base on his single. Compare *right base.*

**wrong field** Syn. of *opposite field.*

**wrong turn** A move to the left of first base made by the batter-runner. A batter-runner who has made a move toward second base on an overrun of first base can be tagged out.

**WS** Abbrev. for *World Series.*

**WUNY** Acronym for *wait [un]'til next year.*

# X

**x  1.** The symbol used in club standings to indicate that a team has clinched its division title. **2.** The symbol used in box scores to indicate something out of the ordinary, such as an extraordinary play or occurrence. It is used rarely and only when the box-score compiler feels compelled to append a note to the summary of a game.

**X-ray test** An examination using X-ray equipment of baseball bats for possible corking. The test was first employed when the bat used by New York Mets infielder Howard Johnson to hit his 27th home run of the 1987 season was impounded and X-rayed. According to the official results, the test did not reveal cork or other foreign substance. This was not the first time an X-ray machine made baseball headlines. According to Jerry Howarth (*Baseball Lite,* 1986), the day after Dizzy Dean was beaned, a headline read: "X-rays of Dean's head show nothing."

# Y

**yack attack** A cluster of yakkers.

**"ya gotta believe"** The slogan of and for the 1973 New York Mets, a team that was in last place on Aug. 30 but still managed to win the National League pennant. The rallying cry was originated by pitcher Tug McGraw.

**yakker 1.** A sharp-breaking curveball. See also *yellow hammer.* **2.** A hard fastball. "If he [Dennis Eckersley] threw a 'yakker for your coolu' it meant you were going to get nailed in the ass with a fastball" (Bill Lee, *The Wrong Stuff,* 1984; Charles D. Poe). **Etymology.** Mike Whiteford (*How to Talk Baseball,* 1983) and Patrick Ercolano (*Fungoes, Floaters and Fork Balls,* 1987) maintain that the term is derived from "yawker," a name for the flicker (yellow-shafted woodpecker).

**Yallerhammer** Syn. of *yellow hammer.*

**yan** Short for *yannigan.*

**yank 1.** To remove a pitcher from a game. "[Scott] Kamieniecki was yanked shortly after his 75th pitch" (*Baltimore Sun,* May 13, 1998). See also *derrick.* **1st Use.** 1914. (*Lippincott's Magazine,* Sept.; Edward J. Nichols). **2.** To hit a home run; e.g., "Wade Boggs got to yank a two-run homer for a 3–0 Devil Rays' lead" (*Baltimore Sun,* May 11, 1998).

**Yankee Doodle game** The game of baseball, the national pastime. **1st Use.** 1902. (*Sporting Life;* Apr. 26; Edward J. Nichols).

**Yankee-Doodle hitter** A weak hitter.

**Yankee hater** One who has a long-standing aversion to the New York Yankees. "We hated the Yankees, of course, the whole country did" (Pete Hamill, *Washington Post,* Mar. 9, 1981). William B. Mead (*The Official New York Yankees Hater's Handbook,* 1983) writes: "We hate the New York Yankees for many reasons. They're spoiled rotten. They think they're such Hot Stuff. Their owner is obnoxious. They pout, sulk and whine, no matter how much they're paid and pampered. Their fans are gross and crude. . . . Most all good Americans hate the Yankees. It is a value we cherish and pass along to our children." Mead also noted: "The first Yankee haters were New Yorkers. They were fans of the New York Giants."

**Yankee killer** A player who performs well against the New York Yankees; e.g., Detroit Tigers pitcher Frank Lary. Joel Lewis (Hoboken, N.J.) relates: "This was a term I heard in the early sixties on radio broadcasts, on the backs of baseball cards, and in the pages of *Baseball Digest.* It refers to a mediocre ballplayer, usually a pitcher, who managed to catch fire against the then-invincible Yankees."

**Yankee Stadium** Home field of the New York Yankees since 1923. It is also known as *The House That Ruth Built* because of Babe Ruth's influence in its creation. It went through a major renovation between the end of the 1973 season and the opening of the 1976 season. The Yankees played at Shea Stadium during the rebuilding.

**yannigan** A *rookie,* not a regular player; a player on the second team in a spring-training camp game. "The Yannigans hooked it on to the Regulars in great style this afternoon. Yannigans 9, Regulars 5." (*San Francisco Examiner,* Mar. 24, 1912; Peter Tamony). Syn. *yan.* **1st Use.** 1898. "Charlie thinks so well of McCloskey's 'yannigans' that the Louisville colors will be his colors" (*Sporting Life,* Jan. 18; David Shulman). **Usage Note.** The term received national publicity in 1906. According to Bill James (*The Bill James Historical Baseball Abstract,* 1986), Brooklyn held a benefit game for the survivors of the 1906 San Francisco earthquake, pitting the Yannigans against the Regulars; the Yannigans won. **Etymology.** The term appears in other slang contexts; e.g., the "yannigan bags" that lumberjacks, prospectors, and others used to carry their clothing. Joseph McBride (*High and Inside,* 1980) states that the baseball term derived from the carpetbag, and was a reference to the disreputability of rookies and subs. McBride adds: "According to Lee Allen, Jerry Denny, a third baseman for Providence in 1884, was responsible for dumping the name 'yannigan' on rookies." There is no clear link between this term and a word in another language or an earlier form of English or an English dialect; e.g., no word close to "yannigan" appears in John S. Farmer and W. E. Henley's *Slang and Its Analogues* (1905). James Stevens (*American Speech,* Dec. 1925) suggested that the word was born in American lumber camps: "Like such old terms as 'cross-cut,' 'bitted,' 'yannigan,' and 'snubline' they had the ringing life of the timber in them."

**yard 1.** A baseball park or field; e.g., "Catch One at the Yard" (Baltimore Orioles promotion to attend a game at Oriole Park at Camden Yards in Baltimore, 1998). **2.** See *go yard.*

**yardbird** A home run. **1st Use.** 1986. "Today, you go to the suburbs, just go deep or leave the yard. A home run is sometimes also referred to as a yardbird" (Scripps Howard News Service article reporting on current player terms used and heard by Pittsburgh Pirates outfielder R. J. Reynolds, Sept. 17).

**Year of the Asterisk** The 1981 major-league season, which was interrupted and disoriented by a players' strike. See also *asterisk,* 1.

**Year of the Family** The 1986 major-league season, so proclaimed by baseball commissioner Peter Ueberroth. Teams took action to appeal to the family trade; e.g., the Pittsburgh Pirates opened special seating sections where the sale of beer was prohibited.

**Year of the Hitter** The 1930 major-league season in which the collective batting average of National League hitters was .303 and that of American League hitters was .288.

**Year of the No-Hitter** The 1990 major-league season, which saw seven no-hitters. There were also seven no-hitters during the 1991 season.

**Year of the Rookie** The 1986 major-league season. "[Jose] Canseco, [Wally] Joyner, [Pete] Incaviglia, [Todd] Worrell, [Barry] Bonds, [Mark] Eichhorn. The fresh names and faces that stamped the 1986 baseball season 'The Year of the Rookie' are growing more familiar and famous each day." (*St. Petersburg Times,* Mar. 22, 1987). "Not since the early '50s have so many splendid kids arrived at once" (Thomas Boswell, *Washington Post,* Oct. 5, 1986).

**Year without a World Series** 1994.

**yellow game** *arch.* A game characterized by inexcusably bad play. **1st Use.** 1890. (*New York Press,* July 6; Edward J. Nichols).

**yellow hammer** Syn. of *curveball.* "Watching the ballgame today someone broke off a real good curve and I said, 'That was a real yellow hammer'" (Jim Bouton, *Ball Four,* 1970; Charles D. Poe). See also *yakker,* 1. Syn. *Yallerhammer.* **Etymology.** Almost every reference made to this term in print notes that the person uttering the term has no idea where it came from or how it became a name for a curveball. "Don't ask me where it came from," said Steve Garvey, a language major at Michigan State Univ., in *Baseball Digest.* "Maybe it started with a Chinese right-hander." Several sources assert that it was used by Satchel Paige for an overhand curve. Mike Whiteford (*How to Talk Baseball,* 1983) and

Patrick Ercolano (*Fungoes, Floaters and Fork Balls,* 1987) claim the term is derived from the flicker (yellow-shafted woodpecker), a bird that travels in an undulating manner that resembles a curveball.

**yellow team** A late 19th-century team characterized by sloppy play.

**yield** For a pitcher to give up runs; e.g., "Smith yielded three runs on five hits."

**yodeler** The *third base coach,* esp. a noisy one who may be trying to unnerve the pitcher or who shouts instructions to the runner on second base. **1st Use.** 1937. (*The Sporting News Record Book;* Edward J. Nichols).

**Yogiism** One of a series of aphorisms and comments issued by catcher, coach, and manager Lawrence Peter "Yogi" Berra, some of which have woven themselves into folklore status. Some are gaffs, some are syntactical errors, but many of them contain their own special logic. A small sampling:

On a player's permission to steal: "He can run anytime he wants. I'm giving him the red light."

On whether he would make a good manager: "I've been playing for 18 years, and you can observe a lot by watching."

On how many slices he wanted to have his pizza cut into: "Better make it four, I don't think I can eat eight."

On a popular restaurant: "Nobody goes there any more, it's too crowded."

On a pennant race: "It's not over until it's over."

On declining attendance in Kansas City, Mo.: "If people don't want to come to the ballpark, how are you gonna stop them?"

On explaining baseball: "Ninety percent of this game is half mental."

On Yogiisms: "I really didn't say everything I said."

Also spelled "Yogism"; "Yogi-ism." Syn. *Berraism.*

**"you can't steal first"** An expression signifying that baseball has its precise limits. It is also practical advice in that it is the one base a player must earn and cannot steal, whether it be from home or from second base. **Etymology.** An old baseball cliché with a fascinating history. After Herman "Germany" Schaefer stole second base and then went back and stole first base to disrupt the pitcher's concentration, rule 7.08(i) of the *Official Baseball Rules* was created in 1920 to declare any runner out who runs the bases in reverse order.

**"you can't win 'em all"** A philosophical expression to mitigate the effects of a defeat. Someone else undoubtedly said it earlier, but the expression has attached itself to Boston Braves pitcher Cliff Curtis who said, "Oh well. You can't win 'em all," after losing his 23rd consecutive game during the 1910–11 seasons. It has also been associated with Philadelphia Athletics manager Connie Mack, who reportedly uttered it after losing 117 games during the 1916 season. **Extended Use.** The phrase long ago was generalized to other sports and endeavors. It is often invoked as understatement after a severe defeat or series of defeats.

**"you could look it up!"** A verbal punctuation used by Casey Stengel to let listeners know that he was not merely making things up and that the point he was making was doubtlessly written down somewhere.

**youneverknow** Pitcher Joaquin Andujar's "favorite English word" (Ron Fimrite, *Sports Illustrated,* Mar. 17, 1986) that has attached itself to baseball. Its meaning is summed up in a story (*USA Today,* Apr. 2, 1986) about California Angels pitcher Don Sutton, who asked his teammates for "the one word that sums up baseball perfectly." As no one knew the magic word, Sutton gleefully provided it, quoting Andujar: "youneverknow."

"I understand baseball. It's a profession that one day you can be here and the next day be there. I never thought I was going to be traded from San Diego. But I was traded to Toronto. You never know." (Roberto Alomar, quoted in *Baltimore Sun,* May 28, 1998). **Etymology.** All of this stems from a quote attributed to Andujar when he was with the Houston Astros: "There is one word in America that says it all, and that one word is, 'Youneverknow.'"

**younger game** [softball term] A term used by

softball partisans for the game during its pre–World War II period of expansion. Compare *older game.*

**young hopeful** A newly acquired player with promise.

**youth baseball** A collective term for various national and local programs for boys and girls under 18 years of age who play baseball as part of an organized team and league. Babe Ruth Baseball and Little League are two of many participants. An interesting use of the term was found on coupons attached to meat sold under the Oscar Mayer label in 1987; they stated that "for every coupon re-

deemed, Oscar Mayer will donate 5 cents to youth baseball, up to $1 million . . . to help kids in communities like yours" (Charles D. Poe).

**youth movement** The process of releasing old players and bringing up highly promising rookies from the minor leagues. "First baseman Bill Buckner, who has more than 2,500 major-league hits and one unforgettable World Series error, was waived Thursday as part of the Boston Red Sox' youth movement" (*Lewiston* [Maine] *Daily Sun,* July 24, 1987).

# Z

**z** The symbol used in club standings to indicate that a team has been mathematically eliminated from the divisional race.

**Zackyzooky** The minor leagues. According to Mike Gonring (*Baseball Digest,* June 1979), the term is peculiar to the Milwaukee Brewers, derived somehow from Sacramento, where the Brewers used to have a Triple-A club: "You don't want to be sent . . . to Zackyzooky."

**Zamboni** Trade name for a machine used to clean Astroturf and other artificial playing surfaces. **Etymology.** The original and dominant Zamboni was used to resurface the ice on hockey rinks. It is named for Frank Zamboni, who introduced his ice-resurfacing machine in 1947. On Zamboni's death, the *Boston Herald* (July 30, 1988) reported that he had been an ice supplier who was forced out of that business in the 1930s by the growth of mechanical refrigeration. He invented his first machine after he opened a skating rink and discovered that it took five men 90 minutes each night to create a new layer of ice.

**zebra** A very fast outfielder. The term is not to be confused with the zebra of football, who is a referee.

**zigzagger** A curveball or erratic throw. **1st Use.** 1915. "Keith swung his right arm in a wide sweep, balancing himself on his right foot, and shot over a zigzagger which Manny missed by

inches" (Burt L. Standish, *Courtney of the Center Garden;* David Shulman).

**zimmerman** *arch.* A bonehead play, in reference to New York Giants third baseman Heinie Zimmerman, who chased Eddie Collins of the Chicago White Sox across the plate rather than throwing the ball for a tagout during the sixth game of the 1917 World Series. Prescott Sullivan (*San Francisco Examiner,* May 8, 1957) tried to exonerate the man behind the eponym, pointing out that it is misused: "Zimmerman had to chase Collins because home plate was left uncovered and there was nobody he could throw the ball to" (Peter Tamony).

**zip** 1. *v.* To shut out. "Tigers Zip Yanks in 10 Innings, 1–0" (*The Buffalo News* headline, Sept. 28, 1986). 2. *v.* To move with the sound and character of the fastball. "I gave them nothing but fast ones but they sure were fast ones and you could hear them zip" (Ring W. Lardner, *You Know Me Al,* 1914). 3. *n.* Speed. **1st Use.** 1920. (*New York Times,* Oct. 7; Edward J. Nichols).

**zone** 1. Syn. of *strike zone.* 2. A mythical place where a player feels he cannot fail (such as a batter who cannot miss hitting the ball) yet cannot explain his situation; e.g., "I got into a zone . . . and I couldn't get out of it" (Jeff Manto, quoted in *Baltimore Sun,* Apr. 10, 1995). "Randy [Myers] is in a league all by himself . . . He gets in his own little zone." (Davey Johnson, quoted in *Baltimore*

*Sun,* Mar. 3, 1996). "I was in a zone today. I just hope it's not the no-parking zone." (Andy Van Slyke, quoted in *Baltimore Sun,* May 15, 1994).

**zone rating** A statistic of fielding efficiency compiled by STATS Inc. that compares the number of plays a fielder makes to the number of balls hit into the area he patrols.

**zurdo** Spanish for *lefty.*

# THESAURUS

If you don't understand the game you won't enjoy it. I'll explain it to you. The first guy gets up to take his cut. Maybe he whiffs, maybe he gets on. Let's say he gets on. So then there is a guy on first. Then the second guy comes up to take his cut. Maybe he whiffs, maybe he gets on. Let's say . . .

—Cab driver explaining the game in a Nunnally Johnson story retold in Fred Schwed's *How to Watch a Baseball Game* (1957)

The ability of baseball writers, fans, and players to come up with synonyms is astonishing. Consider, for instance, the fact that newspapers have come up with a seemingly infinite variety of choices in announcing that one team has beaten another.

Using real headlines from real newspapers, one finds that Team A can:

batter, beat, beat up, belt, best, blank, blast, blow away, blow out, blow past, bomb, brawl past, breeze past, breeze to a victory, burn, bury, cage (works well with avian names, such as "Orioles cage Blue Jays, 8–0), can, catch, claw, claw apart, clip, clobber, come from behind, cream, cruises past, crush, darns (works only with Red and White Sox as in "Guzman darns Sox again, 5–3"), deal a loss, deep six, defeat, deflate, derail, devour, discard, dispose of, douse, down, drill, drop, drown (especially when beating the Mariners), drub, dump, edge, explode, fall, fend off, finish off, flatten, flog, fly past, foil, foiled by, frustrate, gain a victory over, gang up on, get by, get past, give the boot, go the distance, gun down, halt, hand a loss, handle, hang 10 (for a team posting a 10th victory in a row), harpoon, haunt, hold off, hose, jar, jolt, knock down, knock off, KO, lick, lifts, manhandle, master, maul, mows down, nick, nip, notch, oust, outbattle, outclass, outduel, outlast, outmuscle, outscore, overcome, overpower, overrun, overtake, past, pick on, polish off, post a victory, pounce on (as in "Pirates pounce on pitiful Padres"), pound, pound out, power over, power past, prevail over, pull away from, pull out, pummel, punch out, put away, quell, race past, rally by, rally for, rally past, rip, rock, roll, roll by, roll over, roll past, roll through, romp over, rough up, rout, rule, rule over, run past, save face, shackle, shade, shakedown, shellack, shock, shoot down, shut down, shut out, silence, sink, skin, slip past, slips by, slug it out with, smash, snap a losing streak, sneak by, spank, spill, spoil, squash, squeak by, squak past, steal, stifles, stop, stops, stun, subdue, surprise, stymie, swallow, swindle, take, take care of, tame (often used when Detroit Tigers are defeated), tattoo, throttle, thump, thunder, tie up, tip, tips, tiptoes past, top, topple, trap, trim, trip, trip up, triumph, triumph over, trounce, turn back, unplug, upend, upset, victimize, wallop, wash (as in "Indians wash Sox"), wear down, whip, whitewash, wilt, win, win over, and zip over team B.

There are more, many more, but the point is made that the game relishes alternative expressions. With this in mind, here is a thesaurus which does not even attempt to be comprehensive but offers the reader synonyms in key areas—all of which are defined in the dictionary.

## ballpark
**Used for:** baseball park, park
**Related term:** sandlot
**Synonyms:** ball field, ballyard, baseball field, diamond, field, green cathedral, grounds, lot, orchard, pasture, peapatch, yard
**Narrower terms:** backlot, back yard, bandbox, cigar box, concrete ashtray, cookie-cutter, cow pasture, crackerbox, dome, donut, flea-box, friendly confines, hitter's park, Hogan's brickyard, home, home field, home grounds, home orchard, home pasture, launching pad, pitcher's paradise, pitcher's park, real estate, short park, stadium

## base
**Related term:** stake
**See also:** first base, second base, third base
**Synonyms:** anchorage, bag, cushion, hassock, hazard, pillow, sack, station
**Narrower terms:** audible signal base, empty base, extra base, open base, right base, wrong base

## baseball (the ball)
**Used for:** ball
**Synonyms:** agate, apple, aspirin, bulb, bun, cantaloupe, casaba, cowhide, egg, globe, globule, grapefruit, hand grenade, hardball, hide, horsehide, leather, lemon, marble, nugget, onion, orange, pellet, pelota, pill, potato, radish, rawhide, rock, sphere, spheroid, tomato
**Narrower terms:** autographed ball, balata ball, balloon, batted ball, BB, brick, commando, dead ball, doctored ball, fast pellet, game ball, jackrabbit, juiced ball, kangaroo ball, lettuce ball, live ball, lively ball, low-impact ball, marked ball, mud ball, mush bag, nickel-brick, nickel rock, pea, peewee, Phillips 99 ball, punk ball, punkin, rabbit, rabbit ball, rubber-coated baseball, seed, Spalding, thrown ball, Voodoo ball, wingy ball

## baseball (the game)
**Synonyms:** America's pastime, ball, base, base ball, base-ball, beisbol, field of dreams, game, game of inches, Grand Ol' Game, hardball, Mudville, national game, national pastime, old ball game, round ball, summer game, sunshine game, Yankee Doodle game
**Forerunners:** ante-over, barn ball, base-ball, bass-ball, baste ball, Boston ball, Boston game, cat, cat ball, choose up, club ball, cricket, feeder, four old cat, goal ball, Indian ball, Massachusetts game, New England game, New York Game, old-cat, one-cornered cat, one-hole cat, one o'cat, one old cat, poisoned ball, round ball, rounders, scrub, soak ball, stoolball, three o'cat, three old cat, town ball, trap ball, two o'cat, two old cat, work-up
**Tactics and strategy:** inner game, inside ball, inside baseball, inside game, inside work, little ball, old army game, outside baseball, percentage baseball, scientific baseball, small ball
**Variants:** baseball-rounders, burn ball, burnout, corkball, donkey baseball, fudge, half-rubber, indoor baseball, kickball, move up, One Eye Jim Bats, one, two, three, pickle, pick-up game, scrub, stickball, stoopball, T-ball, Wiffle ball, work-up

## baseball card
**Broader term:** trading card
**Related terms:** cello pack, factory set, safety set, update set, wax pack, wrapper
**Narrower terms:** arcade card, bubble-gum card, chase card, checklist card, cigarette card, combination card, common card, E-card, exhibit card, leader card, mini, pre-rookie card, R card, rookie card, T-card, tobacco card, Wagner card

## baseball player
**Related term:** Boys of Summer
**Synonyms:** ballgame, ballist, ballplayer, baseballeer, baseballer, baseballist, baseplayer, diamond artist, diamondeer, horsehider, player

## base hit
**Use:** hit

**base on balls**
> **Synonyms:** Annie Oakley, casualty pass, four wide ones, free check, free pass, free passage, free ride, free ticket, free transit, free transportation, free trip, furlough, gift, handout, life, pass, phantom hit, ticket to first, walk
> **Narrower terms:** bases-loaded walk, intentional base on balls, intentional pass, intentional walk

**baserunner**
> **Used for:** runner
> **Synonym:** tenant
> **Narrower terms:** backward runner, base clogger, batter-runner, base-sticker, blocker, courtesy runner, deer, designated runner, flyer, ghost runner, inherited runner, invisible man, kangaroo, leading lady, lead runner, leadoff runner, man in the middle, man overboard, pickle, pinch runner, player running bases, runner in motion, safe carrier, screen, sitting duck, slider, speed merchant, speedster, torpedo, trapped runner, truck horse

**bases loaded**
> **Synonyms:** bags clogged, bags full, bases bulging, bases choked, bases crowded, bases drunk, bases full, bases jammed, bases juiced, bases tenanted, bases waterlogged, full house, sacks full, sold out

**bat**
> **Used for:** baseball bat
> **Synonyms:** ash, ball club, biff stick, bludgeon, chopstick, club, cudgel, dues collector, fagot, hickory, log, lumber, mace, oak, pencil, pole, shillelagh, stick, timber, toothpick, wagon spoke, wand, war club, weapon, willow, wood
> **Narrower terms:** aluminum bat, banana stalk, Big Bertha, Black Betsy, bottle bat, cheater, cold bat, corked bat, crack, cupped bat, doctored bat, dynamite bat, fat bat, fungo, fungo bat, gamer, graphite bat, helicopter, hollow bat, hot bat, iron bat, lead bat, live bat, Louisville slugger, magic wand, morning journal, piece of iron, pine tar bat, plugged bat, poisoned bat, rubber bat, sawed-off bat, seeing-eye bat, slow bat, slugger, swatstick, tipped bat, wagon tongue

**batter**
> **See also:** hitter
> **Synonyms:** apple-knocker, baton swinger, batsman, biffer, bludgeon wielder, goal tender, sticker, stickman, sticksmith, striker
> **Narrower terms:** anchor man, automatic out, checker, cripple shooter, cutter, dead batter, fish, fisherman, free swinger, hacker, hit batsman, hit batter, Hoover, human rain delay, leading lady, leadoff, leadoff batter, leadoff man, left-handed batter, looker, monkey, "no-batter," peeker, pitcher reader, puller, right-handed batter, soldier, Statue of Liberty, stickpin, stroker, sure out, surveyor, swinger, table-setter, tough out, violinist, waiter, walker, walking man, wilted lily, wood-carrier, wooden Indian

**bunt**
> **Related terms:** fake bunt, slug bunt, swinging bunt
> **Synonyms:** baby act, baby hit
> **Narrower terms:** dead fish, drag bunt, foul bunt, individual offensive bunt, push bunt, sacrifice bunt, squeeze bunt, surprise bunt

**catch** (noun)
> **Related term:** Catch, The
> **Narrower terms:** basket catch, breadbasket catch, circus catch, clamshell catch, diving catch, Dunlap, fly catch, ice-cream cone, Jawn Titus, one-hand catch, running catch, scoop, sensational catch, shoestring catch, showboat catch, sliding catch, snatch catch, sno-cone, snow cone, vest-pocket catch

**catcher**
> **Synonyms:** backstop, backstopper, battery mate, behind, blocker, catch, hind snatcher, mask man, paddist, pegger, plate blocker, receiver, stopper, wind paddsit
> **Narrower terms:** battlin' backstop, bullpen catcher, one-handed catcher, scout

**curveball**
> **Broader terms:** breaking ball, hammer
> **Synonyms:** around the horn, Aunt Susie, bender, corkscrew-er, corkscrew twist, crook, crooked pitch, curve, deuce, equalizer, fish hook, hipper-dipper, hook, hoopdy-scoop,

mystifier, number 2, outcurve, out drop, out-shoot, pretzel, public enemy #1, shoot, slant, snake, snapper, twist, Uncle Charlie, yakker, Yallerhammer, yellow hammer, zigzagger

**Narrower terms:** barrelhoop curve, bulge, dipsy-doodle, double curve, double shoot, downer, down shoot, fall away, fast-breaking curve, hanger, hanging curve, inner-outer, inshoot, jughandle, Lord Charles, nickel curve, offshoot, Old Sal, rainbow, round-house curve, sinker, Sir Charles, slider, slow-breaking curve, upper-downer, wrinkle

## double

**Synonyms:** double bagger, keystone hit, two-bagger, two-base hit, two-baser, two-cushion shot, two-sacker

**Narrower terms:** ground-rule double, roof-rule double, roof-top double

## doubleheader

**Related terms:** curtain raiser, nightcap

**Synonyms:** bargain bill, double bill, holiday, twin bill

**Narrower terms:** day-night doubleheader, high mass, split doubleheader, split-admission dou-bleheader, twilight-night, twi-night double-header, twi-nighter

## double play

**Related terms:** double-play combination, grounded into a double play, Tinker to Evers to Chance

**Synonyms:** deuce, double, double killing, pitcher's best friend, twin killing, two-ply killing

**Narrower terms:** force double play, phantom double play, reverse force double play, unas-sisted double play

## error

**Related terms:** bobble, foozle

**Synonyms:** bonehead play, boot, bungle, clinker, E, fumble, miscue, misplay, muff, muffed ball

**Narrower terms:** dropped third strike, gift, mental error, two-base error

## fan

**Related terms:** the faithful, fandom, knothole club, knothole gang, stands

**Synonyms:** ant, ballite, baseballeer, baseballite, baseball nut, bug, crank, diamond bug, floper, krank, turnstiler

**Narrower terms:** Baseball Annie, Baseball Sadie, baseball widow, baseball widower, bleacher bum, bleacher critic, bleacherite, bobo, boo bird, Chicago Shirley, crankess, crankette, dyed-in-the-wool fan, fair-weather fan, fly, foul screecher, front runner, gate crasher, grandstander, grandstand manager, green fly, hooter, John fan, knothole cus-tomer, kranklet, leather lungs, pest, plugger, rooter, walk-up, wolf

## fastball

**Synonyms:** alto queso, blazer, breezer, bump, buzzer, cannon shot, cheddar, cheese, dart, dead-red, fireball, flameball, fog, gas, good cheese, good express, hard cheese, hard one, heat, heater, high cheese, high hard one, hot rock, hummer, Linda Ronstadt, Louisiana, low lead, mustard, number 1, popcorn, pow-der, red-ball express, scorcher, sizzler, smoke, smoke ball, smoker, soaker, speedball, whistler, yakker

**Narrower terms:** batting-practice fastball, cross-seamer, cross-seam fastball, cut fastball, darting hummer, four-seamer, four-seam fastball, hopper, jammer, keyhole fastball, little ball, muscle heat, Peggy Lee fastball, pitch of the 1980s, pneumonia ball, radio ball, radio pitch, riser, rising fastball, room-service cheeseburger, Ryan's Express, sailer, short fastball, sinking fastball, small baseball, sneaker, split-fingered fastball, two-seamer, two-seam fastball

## first base

**Synonyms:** corner, first, gateway, getaway bag, initial bag, initial corner, initial cushion, ini-tial hassock, initial sack

## fly ball (caught for an out)

**Used for:** fly, flyout

**Narrower terms:** air ball, balloon, balloon flier, can of corn, Chinese line drive, cloud buster, dinky fly, fungo, fungo hit, high flier, high fly, high pop, home run in an elevator shaft, infield fly, loop, palomita, pop, popcorn, pop fly, pop foul, popper, pop-up, pot fly, rain bringer, sacrifice fly, second-story drive, sinker, sky ball, skyer, sky rocker, skyscraper, towering fly

**foul ball**
   **Synonyms:** cackle clout, foul, foul strike, hen house hoist
   **Narrower terms:** Chinese home run, foul bound, foul bunt, foul fly, foul-out, foul tick, foul tip, long strike, loud foul, pop foul, tip-foul, ugly finder

**glove** (fielder's)
   **Synonyms:** eagle claw, leather, mitt, rag
   **Narrower terms:** basket glove, Big Bertha, big mitt, board, bushel basket, catcher's mitt, D&M glove, first baseman's mitt, gamer, H glove, iron glove, lead glove, lobster net, lobster trap, orange crate, pancake, pad, pud, skillet, tenney, thimble, trapper's mitt

**grand slam**
   **Broader term:** home run
   **Synonyms:** bases-loaded home run, demolition derby, four aces, grand salami, grand slammer, grannie, jackpot, salami, slam, slammer

**ground ball**
   **Synonyms:** grasser, grounder
   **Narrower terms:** alabaster blaster, ant killer, Arlie Latham hit, ball with eyes on it, base on stones, Bill Hassemer Bounce, billiard, bleeder, bounceout, bouncer, bounder, brander, bug bruiser, bug on the rug, charity hop, chop, chopper, comeback, cozy roller, daisy clipper, daisy cutter, dirter, double-play ball, dribbler, drizzler, gopher hunter, grass burner, grass clipper, grass cutter, handle, high chopper, high school hop, hopper, hot grounder, infield roller, lawn mower, nibbler, one-hopper, rabbit ball, roller, shin-skimmer, sizzler, skimmer, skipper, slow roller, snyder, squib, swinging bunt, tobasco top, timothy trimmer, trickler, trimmer, two-hopper, weak grounder, weed-eater, William Tell, worm burner

**hit**
   **Used for:** base hit

   **See also:** double, home run, single, Texas Leaguer, triple
   **Synonyms:** bang, base knock, blow, drive, knock, safe hit, safety
   **Narrower terms:** Arlie Latham hit, Baltimore chop, banjo hit, base on stones, bat-handle blooper, Big Bertha, big hit, bleeder, bloop, blooper, broken-bat hit, can't teach that, cheap hit, Chinese blow, chink hit, Cincinnati base hit, clean hit, cue ball shot, daisy hit, dilly, dime hit, doozy marooney, dropper, ducksnort, dying quail, dying seagull, dying swan, excuse-me hit, extra-base hit, fair-foul hit, fall-in, flare, fluke hit, fungo, gapper, gorker, grenade, hand grenade, handle hit, in-betweener, infield hit, key hit, knubber, leg hit, lick, line-hit, long-hit, nail, nubber, old timer, one cushion shot, pebble hit, percentage hit, pinch hit, Pittsburgh chopper, place hit, plunk(et), poke, punk, punk hit, quail shot, rubelet, scratch, scratch hit, seagull, slap hit, soaker, squibb, squibber, squibbler, stunner, sun hit, tweener, wounded duck

**hit a home run**
   **Synonyms:** adios, clean the bases, clear the bases, clear the fences, clout, connect, deposit the pill in the seats, dial 8, downtown, get all of the ball, get it all, go deep, go downtown, go yard, homer, jack, jerk, knock the ball over the fence, label for four, leave the yard, lose a baseball, park, rake, ride

**hitter**
   **See also:** batter
   **Synonym:** hitsman
   **Narrower terms:** aggressive hitter, All-American out, alley hitter, baby boomer, bad-ball hitter, banger, banjo hitter, basher, bat breaker, Bible hitter, big bat, Big Bertha, big stick, bucket hitter, buttercup hitter, cannon, cherry pie, choke hitter, circuit slugger, cleanup hitter, clouter, clout king, clutch hitter, contact hitter, country-fair hitter, cousin, cream-puff hitter, cripple hitter, cripple shooter, day at the beach, dead-pull hitter, designated hitter, easy out, fence-buster, first-ball hitter, five-o'clock hitter, fluid hitter, .400 hitter, free swinger, front-foot hitter, fungo hitter, gap hitter,

get-up-off-the-bench hitter, glove man, golf hitter, guess hitter, ham hitter, heavy hitter, high-ball hitter, hitsmith, human whiff machine, inside hitter, judy, Judy hitter, larruper, leadoff hitter, legger, leg hitter, line hitter, live hitter, locust hitter, long-ball hitter, low-ball hitter, lumberjack, lumber man, mistake hitter, money hitter, morning glory, natural hitter, no day at the beach, number-four hitter, off-speed hitter, one-ball hitter, one-o'clock hitter, opposite field hitter, option batter, out man, parachute hitter, pinch hitter, pinch-hitting specialist, place hitter, poke hitter, power hitter, powerhouse, puff hitter, pull hitter, pump man, Punch-and-Judy hitter, punch hitter, punk hitter, RBI man, sacrifice hitter, scatter hitter, seven-o'clock hitter, sharpshooter, situational hitter, six-o'clock hitter, slap hitter, slapper, slasher, slice hitter, slugger, slugsmith, sockdolager, socker, solid hitter, spray hitter, Stetson hitter, straightaway hitter, streak hitter, swatsman, swatsmith, swatter, switch-hitter, tapperitis hitter, ten-o'clock hitter, tenth man, tickle-hitter, turnover hitter, two-o'clock hitter, ukulele hitter, woodman, wood player, wrist hitter, Yankee-Doodle hitter

**hit the ball hard**
> **Synonyms:** air it out, bash, baste, belt, biff, bing, blast, blaze, blow, boom, bust, clip, clobber, clock, clout, cork, crash, cream, crush, dent, drill, drive, hammer, hit a ton, jar, juice, jump on, kiss, knock the cover off the ball, lace, ladle, lam, lambaste, land on, larrup, lash, lean against it, line, nail, ozone, pack a punch, paste, pickle, pile into, plank, plaster, plug, pole, pound, powder, power, pummel, put the wood to it, rap, rifle, rip, scald, scorch, send, slam, slug, smack, smash, smoke, soak, sock, spank, sting, swat, tee off, waft, wallop, whale, whang

**home plate**
> **Synonyms:** counting house, dish, hearth stone, home, home base, home turkey, marble, pan, pay station, plate, platter, registry station, rubber, scratch, slab, turkey

**home run**
> **Synonyms:** Babe Ruth, Baker, Ballantine blast, belt, big fly, big hit, big knock, big swat, blast, bomb, boundary belt, bye-bye ball, circuit belt, circuit blow, circuit clout, circuit drive, circuit smash, circuit tripper, circuit wallop, clout, dinger, Dr. Longball, dong, downtowner, five dollar ride in a yellow cab, four-bagger, four-master, four-ply wallop, get-small-quick ball, gopher ball, home bagger, homer, jack, jonrun, long ball, long potato, long tater, master fly, moon shot, poke, poke off, potato, rainbow drop, rainmaker, round-tripper, seat-boomer, seeya, shot, tater, tonk, wallop, yardbird
>
> **Narrower terms:** bases-empty home run, bases-loaded home run, batboy shot, called shot, Chinese home run, dome dong, domerun, down the line, four-seamer, grand slam, inside-the-park home run, monster shot, opposite-field home run, Pekinese poke, roofscraper, roof shot, rooftopper, solo, solo home run, solo shot, space shot, Spanish home run, tape-measure home run, three-decker, two-seamer, walk-off piece, wall-scraper, wind-blown home run

**infield** (physical space)
> **Synonyms:** diamond, inner garden, inner works
>
> **Narrower terms:** ash heap, contractor's back yard, Hogan's brickyard, pool table, rockpile, skin diamond

**infielder**
> **Related term:** keystone combination
>
> **Barrier terms:** ancient mariner, Arlie Latham, bagman, baseman, bookend, cutoff man, dime player, first baseman, Hoover, matador, middle infielder, pickpocket, pivot man, right short, sacker, second baseman, short man, shortstop, slapper, station keeper, third baseman, vacuum cleaner, Wilson Pickett

**inning**
> **Synonyms:** canto, chapter, chucker, frame, heat, loop, round, session, spasm, stanza, verse
>
> **Narrower terms:** big inning, blank, blind, extra inning, go-ahead inning, half inning, late inning, lucky seventh, nightcap, overtime, skunk

## knuckleball

**Synonyms:** bob-and-weave, butterfly, butterfly ball, dancer, fingertip pitch, knuckle, knuckler, mariposa, rabbit

**Narrower terms:** fingernail ball, fingertip ball, flutterball, forkle

## left-handed pitcher

**Broader term:** pitcher

**Synonyms:** forkhander, hook arm, left-hander, lefty, loony Joe, off-side pitcher, portpaw, portsider, screw armer, southpaw, wrong armer, zurdo

## line drive

**Synonyms:** bolt, linea, line ball, liner, line-hit, line shot

**Narrower terms:** at 'em ball, atom ball, bee liner, blue dart, blue darter, bullet, clothesline, darter, frozen rope, hemp, humpbacked liner, line-out, nuclear fission ball, rifle shot, rocket, rope, ruptured duck, scorcher, screamer, screaming meemie, screaming rope, shot, sinking liner, sizzler, soft liner, swan dive, titanic

## manager

**Synonyms:** brains, field general, field manager, maestro, the man, mastermind, Old Man, pilot, shepherd, shifter, skip, skipper, teacher

**Narrower terms:** interim manager, miracle man, percentage manager, player-manager, player's manager, recycled manager

## outfield (physical space)

**Synonyms:** daisies, field, garden, orchard, outer garden, outer patch, outer works, outpost, pasture, suburbs

**Narrower terms:** alley, center field, death valley, left field, no-man's land, power alley, right field, short center, sun field

## outfielder

**Related term:** picket line

**Synonyms:** ball hawk, flycatcher, fly chaser, flyhawk, gardener, grazer, hawk, orchardman, pastureman, pastureworker, roamer, suburbanite

**Narrower terms:** bookend, center fielder, corner outfielder, left fielder, middle gardener, raftman, rifle arm, right fielder, zebra

## pitch (noun)

**See also:** curveball, fastball, knuckleball, screwball, sinker, slider, spitball

**Synonyms:** chuck, heave, offering, slant

**Best pitch:** ace, bastard pitch, bread-and-butter pitch, do-fer pitch, money pitch, out pitch, quality pitch, Sunday best, Sunday pitch

**Breaking ball:** backspinner, breaker, dipsy-doodle, down shoot, drop pitch, forkball, foshball, fush ball, hammer, helicopter, palm ball, raise ball, slurve, spinner, split-fingered fastball, splitter, upshoot

**Control pitch:** beball, corner clipper, cripple, cripple pitch

**Easy to hit:** barn door, cherry, cookie, cream puff, Cuban sandwich, fat one, fat pitch, gimme, groover, ham-and-cheese, lollipop, meatball, my pitch, pay ball, punkin, room-service pitch

**Fictional pitch:** double curve, double shoot, hop ball, inner-outer, upper-downer

**Full-count pitch:** action pitch, decision pitch, payoff pitch

**Hit for home run:** gopher ball, homer ball, home run ball, money ball, walk-off pitch

**Illegal pitch:** alternative pitch, belt-buckle pitch, cut ball, dry spitter, emery ball, grease ball, jellyball, licorice ball, mud ball, paraffin ball, phonographic needle ball, pine tar ball, powder-puff ball, puff ball, quick pitch, quick return pitch, resin ball, sandpaper ball, scuffball, scuffed ball, scuffer, shine ball, shiner, talcum ball, Vaseline ball

**Intimidate batter:** beanball, beaner, blow-down pitch, bow tie, brushback pitch, buzzball, calling card, chin music, duster, ear duster, face ball, flip, Gillette, hit-batter pitch, jamball, jam shot, Kentucky wonder, knee-knocker, knockdown pitch, loosener, message pitch, neck ball, payback pitch, purpose pitch, Rawlings lobotomy, rib roaster, throat cutter, tight pitch, wakeup call, whisker trimmer

**Out of strike zone or badly thrown pitch:** bad ball, dirt pitch, FDR pitch, 55-footer, golf ball, high ball, high pitch, Lady Godiva pitch, low ball, low pitch, mistake, mistake pitch, nudist pitch, over-pitch, pass ball, prayer ball, waste ball, waste pitch, wild pitch, wish pitch

**Slowly pitched ball:** balloon ball, blooper, blooper ball, cambio, change, change of pace, changeup, circle change, dead fish, dead mackerel, ecology pitch, eephus, floater, folly floater, foshball, four-seam changeup, freaky floater, fush ball, gondola, La Lob, Leephus ball, letup, letup ball, letup pitch, load of coal, mackerel, nothing ball, nothing pitch, nuthin' ball, off-speed pitch, palm ball, parachute, salad, slip pitch, slow ball, stitch-ball, thumber, two-seam changeup

**Type of pitch:** Borough Hall, combination ball, crossfire, dead fish, extra pitch, first ball, first pitch, hesitation pitch, junk ball, overhand pitch, purpose pitch, puzzler, questionable pitch, quick pitch, seamer, sidearm pitch, submarine pitch, throw on top, twelve o'clock high, underhand pitch, waist ball, waister, warm-up pitch

## pitch (verb)

**Synonyms:** chuck, crank, deliver, face, fling, go, heave, hurl, offer, serve, sling, spin, toss, twirl, work

**Narrower terms:** air it out, back off, bean, blow smoke, bring it, brush back, burn a hole, burn over, bust, climb the ladder, clip the corner, come in, count the stitches, cut the corner, cut the plate, deal from the bottom, dink, drive the yellow bus, drop down, dust off, find his pots and pans, flip, fog it through, force, go all the way, go nine, go the distance, go the route, groove, hit the black, hit the corners, hook, jam the batter, knock down, low bridge, move the ball around, nick the corner, paint (the black), pitch around, pitch out, pitch to spots, pop the ball, pound the ball inside, power, pull the string, put a bow tie on him, put mustard on the pretzel, put out the fire, put some mustard on it, put something on it, quick pitch, relieve, run in, run up, saw off, scorch, shave (the corner), short-arm, skull, slurve, smoke, snap, spin his cap, split the plate, spot, spot-throw, stair step, submarine, take the button off his hat, thread the needle, throw darts, throw ground balls, throw Laredo, tie up, turn the ball over, turn up the dial, waste, whittle, wild-pitch, work the corners

## pitcher

**See also:** left-handed pitcher, relief pitcher, right-handed pitcher

**Synonyms:** arm, artillerist, battery, battery mate, box artist, boxman, chucker, elbow bender, fifth infielder, flinger, flipper, giver, hand grenader, heaver, hurler, man on the firing line, moundsman, pill slinger, slab artist, slabber, slabbist, slabman, slabster, slinger, soupboner, souper, tosser, twirler, worker

**Narrower terms:** ace, alleged flinger, artist, barber, batting-practice pitcher, beamer, bellcow, bellwether, blower, brushback pitcher, bulldog, cat, closer, control artist, control pitcher, count, cousin, curveballer, cutey, cyclone pitcher, Cy Younger, dipsy-doodler, double duty pitcher, Edison, electronic pitcher, expectoration exhibitor, fastballer, fiddle hitcher, finesse pitcher, fireballer, flamethrower, flyball pitcher, fogger, game winner, George Stallings pitcher, glass arm, good arm, grinder, gun pitcher, hammer, headhunter, Houdini, iron man, junkballer, knuckleballer, knuckler, knuckles, lamb, losing pitcher, Lowdermilk, meal ticket, Michelangelo, near beer pitcher, nibbler, note-book pitcher, nothin' baller, no-wood-on-the-ball pitcher, number 1, paint master, peeker, Picasso, pin pointer, pitcher of record, power pitcher, probable pitcher, rag arm, rhythm pitcher, rubber band, scatter arm, screwballer, seven-inning pitcher, sharpshooter, sidearmer, sidewheeler, sidewinder, sinkerballer, slobberer, soft tosser, speed merchant, spitballer, spot pitcher, spot starter, starter, starting pitcher, stopper, strikeout artist, strikeout king, submariner, subway slinger, Sunday pitcher, swingman, tattooed man, teaser, Thomas Edison, thrower, traffic director, 20-game winner, vintage pitcher, vulture-bait, waster, wheelman, whittler, winning pitcher, workhorse

## play, defensive

**Narrower terms:** appeal play, bastard play, be-there play, Concepcion play, cutoff play, daylight play, double play, fielder's choice, force play, hidden-ball trick, "I'll be there" play, in-the-vicinity play, neighborhood play, pickoff play, pitcher covering first, rotation (play), rundown play, triple play, vicinity play, wheel (play)

**play, offensive**
> **Narrower terms:** bunt and run, contact play, hit-and-run play, run-and-hit play, sacrifice hit, safety squeeze, sleeper rabbit play, squeeze play, steal and slam, suicide squeeze

**relief pitcher**
> **Broader terms:** pitcher
> **Synonyms:** activity, fireman, hoser, ice man, insurance man, mound savior, 'penner, relief man, relief worker, reliever, vulture
> **Narrower terms:** bullpen ace, caddy, closer, closing reliever, cork, early reliever, finisher, game-ender, ham-and-egg reliever, holder, late reliever, long man, long reliever, middle man, middle reliever, mop-up man, setup man, short man, short reliever, spot reliever, stopper

**right-handed pitcher**
> **Broader terms:** pitcher
> **Synonyms:** northpaw, right-hander, righty, starboarder

**rookie**
> **Synonyms:** budder, busher, bush leaguer, cub, donkey, fresh leaguer, gazoonie, green pea, huckleberry, jelly bean, kindergartner, recruit, rook, schoolboy, yan, yannigan
> **Narrower terms:** April Cobb, early bloomer, ivory, June bug, nail, pheenom, phenom, prospect, question mark

**run** (noun)
> **Synonyms:** ace, counter, marker, tally
> **Narrower terms:** earned run, equalizer, gamer, game winner, go-ahead run, insurance run, potential tying run, potential winning run, scratch run, singleton, tie-breaker, tying run, unearned run, winning run

**scout**
> **Narrower terms:** advance scout, bird dog, checker, commission scout, cradle-snatcher, cross-checker, eye-in-the-sky, ivory hunter, special assignment scout, spy in the sky, superscout

**screwball**
> **Synonyms:** corkscrew, fadeaway, incurve, reverse curve, screwgie, scroogie

**second base**
> **Synonyms:** keystone, keystone bag, keystone sack, middle bag, middle station, midway, second, second station

**series**
> **See also:** World Series
> **Narrower terms:** All-City Series, all-New York Series, American League Championship Series, National League Championship Series, playoff, subway series

**shut out** (verb)
> **Synonyms:** apply the whitewash, Chicago, schneider, skunk, whitewash, zip

**single**
> **Synonyms:** bagger, base hit, baser, bingle, bingo, one-bagger, one-base hit, one-sacker, safety, solo shot
> **Narrower terms:** bloop single, broken-bat single, groundskeeper single, Jesse James single, scratch single, seeing-eye single, Texas League single

**sinker**
> **Synonyms:** drop, dropball, heavy ball, sinkerball

**slide**
> **Narrower terms:** backdoor slide, belly slide, belly whopper, bent-leg slide, break-up slide, Chicago slide, fadeaway, fallaway slide, half gainer, headfirst slide, hook slide, pop-up slide, scissors slide, stand-up slide, take-out slide

**slider**
> **Synonyms:** dry spitter, five-cent curve, nickel, nickel curve, sailer
> **Narrower terms:** backdoor slider, backup slider, cut fastball, cutter, dime, little cutter, quarter, tight slider

**softball**
> **Forerunners:** army ball, big ball, church ball, diamond ball, indoor baseball, indoor-outdoor, kitten ball, kitty-ball, lightning ball, night ball, panty waist, playground ball, playground

baseball, recreation ball, serve us ball, twilight ball

**Synonym:** spin ball

**Narrower terms:** alley softball, baseball (modified), fast pitch softball, modified pitch, mush ball, original softball, Over the Line, pitcher's game, slo-pitch softball, slow pitch softball, team game

## spitball

**Synonyms:** aqueous toss, country sinker, Cuban forkball, Cuban palmball, cuspidor curve, damp sling, drooler, humidity dispenser, moist ball, perspiration pellet, pump pellet, rain rippler, saliva toss, spitter, Staten Island sinker, wet ball, wet one, wet pitch, wet wipe

**Narrower terms:** brown spitter, bubble-gum ball, mud ball, sweat ball

## stolen base

**Synonyms:** bag, steal, swipe, theft

## strike out [batter] (verb)

**Synonyms:** Casey, do a Casey, fan, pull a Casey, punch out, take a drink

**Narrower terms:** admire a third strike, go down looking, go down swinging, strike out looking, strike out swinging, stir a breeze, whiff

## strike out [pitcher] (verb)

**Synonyms:** bury, erase, fan, K, ring up, send to the shelf, whiff

**Narrower term:** catch looking

## strikeout (noun)

**Synonyms:** breeze, Casey act, dipsy-doodle, fan, fandango, gate, K, Navy Yard home run, punchout, three strikes, whiff

**Narrower terms:** KY, line drive to the catcher

## swing (noun)

**Synonym:** cut

**Narrower terms:** backswing, big cut, butcher-boy stroke, check, check(ed) swing, clean swing, cowtail swing, early swing, emergency swing, excuse-me swing, fishing trip, full swing, hack, half swing, healthy, home run swing, inside-out swing, level swing, loose swing, Moriarty, riffle, semi-swing, slice, stroke, sweat swing, swish, uppercut, warm-up swing

## Texas Leaguer

**Synonyms:** awful, banjo hit, bloop, blooper, drooper, dunker, flare, Japanese liner, lazy, leaping Lena, lollipop, looper, parachute, percentage sinker, plunker, pooper, punker, sheeny mike, smell hit, special, squibber, squibbler, stinker, sucker, Texas League single

## third base

**Synonyms:** coffin corner, corner, far corner, far turn, hot corner, third

## triple

**Synonyms:** three-bagger, three-base hit, three-sacker, triple bagger, triplet

## umpire

**Related terms:** blind mice, boys in blue, crew, men in blue, three blind mice

**Synonyms:** arbiter, arbitrator, blind tom, blue, bluecoat, boy blue, dog robber, guesser, Jesse James, man in blue, Mr. Guess, robber, sheepherder, tin cup, ump

**Narrower terms:** ball-and-strike umpire, base umpire, chief of staff, crew chief, field umpire, home plate umpire, homer, home umpire, Pete Homer, plate umpire, rabbit ears, rocking chair, tenth man, ukulele umpire, umpire-in-chief

## World Series

**Related terms:** College World Series, Junior World Series, Little World Series, Year without a World Series

**Synonyms:** autumn classic, big classic, big series, classic, Commissioner's Games, fall classic, promised land, the Series, World Serious, World's Series

**Narrower terms:** All-City Series, all-New York Series, backyarder, Bay Bridge World Series (1989), Fast Food Fall Classic (1984), Hairs vs. Squares (1972), hometown series, I-95 Series (1983), I-70 Series (1985), Klutz World Series (1945), local World Series, Nickel Series, Show-Me Series (1985), Shuttle Series (1986), subway series, Suds Series (1982)

# ABBREVIATIONS AND SYMBOLS

There are a number of abbreviations in baseball and softball that are used most commonly when scoring a game and/or in box scores that appear in the newspapers.

| Abbreviation | Term |
| --- | --- |
| A | Assist, Attendance |
| AA | American Association |
| AAABA | All-American Amateur Baseball Association |
| AAGPBL | All-American Girls Professional Baseball League |
| AB | At-bat |
| ABC | American Baseball Congress |
| ABCA | American Baseball Coaches Association |
| AIBS | All-Important Box Score |
| AILC | All-important loss column |
| AK | Ant Killer |
| AL | American League, Active List |
| ALCS | American League Championship Series |
| APBPA | Association of Professional Baseball Players of America |
| ASA | Amateur Softball Association of America |
| AVG | Average |
| B | Bunt |
| BA | Batting Average |
| BAT | Baseball Assistance Team |
| BB | Base on Balls, Batboy, Baseball |
| BBWAA | Baseball Writers Association of America |
| BK | Balk |
| BL | Bats Left |
| BP | Batting Practice |
| BS | Blown Save |
| BWAA | Baseball Writers Association of America |
| C | Catcher |
| CBA | Collective Bargaining Agreement |
| CERA | Catcher's Earned Run Average |
| CF, cf | Center Field, center fielder |
| CG | Complete Game |
| cp and nc | Can't play and no chance |
| CS | Caught Stealing |
| CWS | College World Series |
| D | Defense, Double |
| DP | Double Play, Designated Player |
| DH | Designated Hitter, Doubleheader |
| DL | Disabled List |
| E | Error |
| EP | Extra Player |
| ER | Earned Run |
| ERA | Earned Run Average |
| F | Fly, Flyout, Foul Fly |
| FC | Fielder's Choice |
| FO | Force Out |
| FP | Fielding Percentage |
| G | Game |
| GB | Games Behind |
| GDP/GIDP | Grounded into a Double Play |
| GF | Games Finished |
| GM | General Manager |
| GOM | Grand Old Man |
| GS | Games Started, Grand Slam |

| | | | | |
|---|---|---|---|---|
| GWRBI | Game-Winning Run Batted In | | OB | Organized Baseball |
| H | Hit, Hold | | OBA | On-Base Average |
| HB | Hit Batter | | OBP | On-Base Percentage |
| HBP | Hit by Pitch, Hit By Pitcher | | obs | Obstruction |
| HOF | Hall of Fame | | OF | Outfield, Outfielder |
| HP | Hit by Pitch | | OS | Official Scorer |
| HR | Home Run | | OTL | Over the Line |
| I | Interference | | P | Pitcher |
| IBA | International Baseball Association | | PA | Plate Appearance |
| IBB | Intentional Base on Balls | | PB | Passed Ball |
| IF | Infield, Infielder, Infield Fly | | PCL | Pacific Coast League |
| IL | International League | | PH | Pinch Hitter |
| IP | Innings Pitched | | PO | Putout |
| IW | Intentional Walk | | PR | Pinch Runner |
| K | A Strikeout | | PRC | Player Relations Committee |
| Ʞ | Strikeout, called | | PTBNL | |
| KC | Strikeout, called | | /PTNL | Player to Be Named Later |
| KS | Strikeout, swinging | | QS | Quality Start |
| L | Line Drive, Loss, Losing Pitcher | | R | Run(s) |
| LCS | League Championship Series | | RA | Red Ass |
| LF, lf | Left Field, left fielder | | RBI | Run(s) Batted In, Reviving |
| LHB | Leff-Handed Batter | | | Baseball in the Inner Cities, |
| LHP | Left-Handed Pitcher | | | Research in Baseball Index |
| LIPS | Late-Inning Pressure Situation(s) | | RF, rf | Right Field, right fielder |
| LL | Little League | | RHB | Right-Handed Batter |
| LO | Left On | | RHP | Right-Handed Pitcher |
| LOB | Left on Base | | RO | Rawlings Official |
| LP | Losing Pitcher | | RP | Relief Pitcher |
| ML | Major League | | RPS | Relative Performance System |
| MLB | Major League Baseball | | S | Sacrifice, Successful Steal of a |
| MLBP | Major League Baseball Properties | | | Base, Save |
| MLBPA | Major League Baseball Players | | SA | Slugging Average |
| | Association | | SABR | Society for American Baseball |
| MLBPAA | Major League Baseball Players | | | Research |
| | Alumni Association | | sac | Sacrifice |
| MVP | Most Valuable Player | | SB | Stolen Base |
| NABBP | National Association of Base Ball | | SF | Sacrifice Fly |
| | Players | | SH | Sacrifice Hit |
| NAL | Negro American League | | ShO | Shutout |
| NAPBL | National Association of | | SO | Strikeout, Shutout |
| | Professional Baseball Leagues | | SP | Starting Pitcher |
| NL | National League | | SPBA | Senior Professional Baseball |
| NLCS | National League Championship | | | Association |
| | Series | | SS, ss | Split Squad, shortstop |
| NNL | Negro National League | | SV | Save |
| NP | Number of Pitches | | T | Time taken to play game, Triple |
| NRI | Non-Roster Invitee | | TA | Total Average |
| O | Ovation | | TB | Total Bases |

| | | | |
|---|---|---|---|
| TC | Total Chances | W | Walk, Win, Winning Pitcher |
| TL | Throws Left | WP | Wild Pitch, Winning Pitcher |
| TP | Triple Play | WS | World Series |
| TR | Throws Right | X | Clinched division title, something |
| U | Unassisted Putout | | out of the ordinary |
| UA | Union Association | z | Mathematically eliminated |
| UBL | United Baseball League | 1B | First Base, First Baseman, Single |
| USL | United States League | 2B | Second Base, Second Baseman, |
| USSSA | United States Slo-Pitch Softball | | Double |
| | Association | 3B | Third Base, Third Baseman, |
| VI | Village Idiot | | Triple |

# ACKNOWLEDGMENTS

The writer wishes to acknowledge his indebtedness to the Mayo brothers, Ringling Brothers, Smith brothers, Rath brothers, the Dolly sisters, and former President Buchanan for their aid in instructing him in the technical terms of baseball, such as "bat," "ball," "pitcher," "foul," "sleeping car," and "sore arm."
— Ring Lardner, from his Preface to the 1925 edition of *You Know Me Al*

An All-Star team—including a dh, a pinch hitter, relief pitchers, and a manager—of help and information sources was absolutely essential to the researching of this book. Collectively, their influence and inspiration are felt on practically every page. These are:

The late James W. Darling who had been working on his own dictionary when the first edition of this book was published. He wrote on May 15, 1989: "Congratulations! Your *DBD* beat me to it. The dictionary is a book which has long been needed and I have been working on one for more than ten years—with no outside help. . . . My purpose in writing to you is to ask if you would be interested in trading an autographed copy of your book for my collection of what would have been entries in my book—more than 3,000 of them."

Joseph C. Goulden who, ever since I first thought about starting the first version of this project through the ninth inning of the second edition, has been feeding me a steady diet of clippings and radio notes with examples of baseballese carefully marked and annotated.

Robert "Skip" McAfee of the Society for American Baseball Research and Columbia, Maryland, was kind enough to come in the late innings of the first edition to spot missing entries and help with last-minute corrections and for hundreds of hours of expert help with the second edition. His devotion to this project has been extraordinary.

Ron Menchine, for unlimited access to his one-of-a-kind collection of early baseball material.

Peter Morris, who provided a host of early citations representing an amazing amount of work and dedication.

Bob Perkins, who came in as a closer to help find scores of citations from the 1997 baseball season ensuring that the book was as up-to-date as possible.

The late Charles D. Poe of Houston, who spent many, many hours finding examples for both editions of this book.

Barry A. Polik of New York City, the lexicographer/etymologist who is eager to share the results of his enormous labors with others.

David Shulman of New York City, who allowed me to use his collection of unpublished citations on the earliest use of certain terms. His generosity and guidance through both editions of this work are acknowledged with the deepest admiration.

The late Peter Tamony of San Francisco and the people at the University of Missouri who now administer his one-of-a-kind collection on the American language. Tamony spent most of his life collecting and writing about slang. One of his particular passions was the language of sport and the information he collected on baseball terms is without parallel. I am especially indebted to Randy Roberts who cataloged the Tamony Collection as its first curator for the organization that administers it under the full name of the Joint Collection University of Missouri (Columbia) Western Historical Manuscript Collection and State Historical Society of Missouri Manuscripts.

Dave Kelly, the sports authority at the Library of Congress, who has helped this book at every juncture.

The staff of the National Baseball Library at Cooperstown, New York, really know how to help a guy. I also must express my special indebtedness to one Edward J. Nichols, whose 1939 thesis, "An Historical Dictionary of Baseball Terminology," has proven to be invaluable.

Finally, every team needs a manager who in this case has been Vicki Austin-Smith, who has piloted this book through extra innings.

Other people who have made important contributions to this work are listed here. I thank them all for their help and enthusiasm:

### A

Frank R. Abate, Bruce Adams, Lane Akers, Thomas L. Altherr, John V. Alviti, Reinhold A. Aman, Russell Ash, Andy Ayers

### B

Roger A. Ballou, Steve Banker, Michael Bein, Fr. Gerry Beirne, C. P. Benoit, Albert P. Blair, Lawrence Block, Steve Boren, Lou Botti, Q. David Bowers, John S. Bowman, Darryl Brown, Patrick Brown, Robert Bryce, Tom Burns, David Bussan

### C

Bob Carr, David Cataneo, Robert L. Chapman, Gordon Christy, Irwin Chusid, Paul Clancy, Gerald Cohen, Stanley A. Cohen, Bonnie Copper, Philip J. Costopoulos, Bruce Coyne, Cliff Crown, Raymond V. Curiale

### D

Tom "Slangman" Dalzell, Ev Daniels, Jon Daniels, Ed Dashman, Bob Davids, Karen Davis, Bob Davis, Jay Davis, Percy Dean, Bill Deane, David

Demsey, the late Charles F. Dery, Donald Dewey, Alex, Andrew, and Nancy Dickson, Royal Duncan, Floyd and Elsa Dunn

### E

Dawn Eason, Connie Eble, C. F. Eckhardt, Morris Eckhouse, Ross Eckler, Charles Einstein, Michael Esserman, Douglas Evelyn

### F

Joe Faletta, Steve Fiffer, Jerome Finster, Keith B. Fleeman, Kenneth Forehand, Matt Frederick, Jeff Freedman, Fumihiro "Fuchan" Fujisawa, Warner Fusselle

### G

Martin Gardner, Jim Gates, Mike Gershman, Walt Giachini, Elizabeth Gibbon, George Gibson, Steve Gietschier, Thomas E. Gill, E. Ward Gilman, Wayne Grady, Robert Greenman, Dan Gutman

### H

John F. Hagemann, Douglas W. Hall, Alex Harary, Kelsie Harder, Robert G. Harding, Bryan Harris, Bill Heath, Bob Heilman, Thomas R. Heitz, Robert Hendrickson, Bill Hickman, Philip H. Hochberg, George S. Hobart, John B. Holway, David Hubler, Truxton Hulbert

### I

Bob Ingraham, Fred Ivor-Campbell

### J

Jake Jacobson, Blair Jett, David A. Jewell, Skip Jewett, Hal Johnson, W. Lloyd Johnson, Clifford Jordan

### K

Cliff Kachline (who helped get the project started), Pat Kelly, John Kenyon, Kevin Kerrane, Harry Kies, Albert Kilchesty, Bill Kirwin, Linda Kittell, Norbert Kraich, John Kuchera, Norman E. Kurland

### L

Bruce C. Ladd Jr., Brian L. Laughlin, Nancy Jo Leachman, Richard Lederer, Jean M. LeMire, Joel Lewis, Matthew E. Lieff, Ed Lindhurst

## M

Norman L. Macht, Jack Mangus, Ed Margolis, Andy McCue, Thomas P. McDonald, Joe McGillen, Bill Mead, Christopher Mead, Doug Meyer, Kenneth Miller, Richard L. Miller, Rick Minch, Frederick C. Mish, Howard R. Morgan, John M. Morse, Russell Mott, Eldon Myers

## N

Joe B. Naiman, Kara Noble

## O

Dan O'Brien, Keith Olbermann, Charles A. Owen Jr.

## P

Brett Palmer, Bill Page, Herbert H. Paper, Murray R. Pearce, Marc Picard, Tom Pitoniak, Bill Plummer III (Amateur Softball Association of America), Gregory Pokrass, Howard A. Pollock M.D., Frank Potter

## Q

Evan Quenon

## R

Rick Randahl, Lawrence Ritter, Randy Roberts, Walter Robertson, Jason Rouby, John Rush

## S

Joseph St. George, Joseph St. Paul, Alice Schaeffer, George H. Scheetz, Aaron Schmidt, John Schwartz, Mike Shannon, Tom Shieber, Donald F. Sisson, Bob Skole, the late Robert Smith, Michael A. Stackpole, David Staffin, John Sullivan

## T

Bill Tammeus, Blair D. Tarr, Dean W. Terlinden, Ralph Testa, the late James L. Thorpe III, Phil Turner

## V

Cullen P. Vane, Alex Van Schuylen, Edwin D. Van Woert, David Vincent, Jay Voke

## W

Richard Wagner, Verlon Wagner, Tim Wendell, Sally F. Whitenack, Tim Wiles, Tom Williams, Charles P. Wilson III, Pete Wilson, Nick Wolf, Daniel Woodhead

## Z

Steve Zane, Richard Zitrin, Larry Zmolik

# AFTERWORD

"... a certain ancient game, played with a ball, hath come up again, yet already are all mouths filled with the phrases that describe its parts and movement; insomuch, indeed, that the ears of the sober and such as would busy themselves with weightier matter are racked with the clack of the same till they do ache with anguish."

—Mark Twain's "An Extract from Methuselah's Diary"

It goes without saying that this book is already out of date and has been for many months. There is no shame in this because the same can be said about virtually any book that attempts to capture an element of a living language.

However, one must always strive for currency and comprehensiveness, and it is with this in mind that the author announces here that he is most interested in hearing from the readers of this book as they encounter new terms. I am, of course, also interested in hearing of errors, omissions, alternative theories on the origins of terms, and earlier dating of a term's earliest appearance in print. Such correspondence will be acknowledged immediately and consulted for future editions of this dictionary. I can be reached directly at Box 80, Garrett Park, MD 20896.

# ANNOTATED BIBLIOGRAPHY

**I. An annotated collection of works that are specifically related to baseball terminology in whole or in part:**

Allen, Ethan. *Baseball Play and Strategy.* New York: Ronald Press, 1969. (Both this book and the next two by Allen contain excellent glossaries.)

————. *Baseball: Major League Technique and Tactics.* New York: Macmillan, 1953.

————. *Baseball Techniques Illustrated.* New York: A. S. Barnes, 1951.

Allen, Lee. *The Hot Stove League.* New York: Barnes, 1955. (Significant work on history of key terms by former Cooperstown librarian.)

Archibald, Joe. *Baseball Talk for Beginners.* New York: Julian Messner, 1969.

Baker, Russell. "Come Back, Dizzy." *New York Times,* October 9, 1979. (Essay in which Baker takes the position that the language of baseball was becoming arid and lifeless.)

Barber, Red, and Robert Creamer. *Rhubarb in the Catbird Seat.* Garden City, N.Y.: Doubleday, 1968. (Barber explains his role in the origin and spread of several key terms including the two in the title.)

Barbour, Ralph Henry. *How to Play Better Baseball; for Junior Players and Their Coaches.* New York: Appleton-Century Co., 1935. (Glossary.)

Berrey, Lester V., and Melvin Van Den Bark. *The American Thesaurus of Slang.* New York: Thomas Y. Crowell, 1942. (Extensive section on baseball slang. Essential.)

Birtwell, Roger. "Three R's Taught in Diamond Lingo." *Baseball Digest,* September 1948.

Borden, Marian Edelman. "Terms for Parents of Little Leaguers." *New York Times,* n.d.

Brandt, William G. "That Unrecognized Language—Baseballese." *Baseball Magazine,* October 1932. (An extremely valuable article in which the author distinguishes play jargon, baseballese, from the baseball slang encountered in pulp fiction. He also makes the point that baseballese is precise and economical; comparable to the verbal shorthand of surgeons.)

Brosnan, Jim. *The Long Season.* New York: Harper and Row, 1960. (This book, which Jimmy Cannon termed "the greatest baseball book ever written," opens with a glossary of words and phrases heard by the player/author during the 1959 season. It is a key to the player jargon of the time.)

Bryson, Bill. "Why We Say It." *Baseball Digest,* April 1948.

Cannon, Jimmy. "Sport Page Dictionary." *Baseball Digest,* November–December 1956. (Certainly the best set of comic baseball terms ever defined in one place. Samples: "*Clubhouse boy* A man who is a valet for a lot of boys" and "*Rabid fan* A guy who screams for fair play after he heaves a bottle at the umpire.")

Chadwick, Henry. *Technical Terms of Baseball.* New York: American Sports Publishing Co., 1887. (Because the British-born Chadwick was responsible for naming or renaming a number of elements of baseball—e.g., he replaced "striker" with "batter"—this small booklet is particularly important.)

Cochrane, Gordon S. *Baseball: The Fan's Game.* New York: Funk and Wagnalls Company, 1939.

Coffin, Tristram Potter. *The Old Ball Game: Baseball in Folklore and Fiction.* New York: Herder and Herder, 1971. (An extremely valuable overall reference. Contains a key chapter on "Baseball Talk.")

Cohen, Gerald. "Old baseball columns as a repository of slang; reading through *The World.*" *Comments on Etymology,* April 1/15, 1986, Part II; *Comments on Etymology,* February 1/15, 1987. (Important commentary on nineteenth-century baseball slang as well as offering several fascinating discoveries; e.g., an account of the first ground rule double.)

Cold Spring Publishers. *1957 Baseball Schedules.* (A giveaway from the East River Savings Bank of New York City containing "Baseball Terms to Know.")

Considine, Tim. *The Language of Sport.* New York: Facts On File, 1982.

Couzens, Gerald Secor. *A Baseball Album.* New York: Lippincott and Crowell, 1980. (Contains a most useful glossary.)

Cummings, Parke. *Dictionary of Baseball.* New York: A. S. Barnes, 1950.

Dean, Jerome H. "Dizzy." *Dizzy Baseball: A Gay and Amusing Glossary of Baseball Terms Used by Radio Broadcasters, with Explanations to Aid the Uninitiated.* New York: Greenberg, 1952.

———. *The Dizzy Dean Dictionary.* St. Louis: Falstaff Brewing Company, 1943 and 1949.

———. "Dizzy's Dictionary." *Baseball Digest,* November 1943.

Dionne, E. J., Jr. "Chattering Class." *Washington Post,* October 19, 1997.

Dunne, Bert. *Folger's Dictionary of Baseball.* San Francisco: Folger's Coffee and Stark-Rath Printing Co., 1958. (Solid booklet collection that mixes official terms with the slang of the period. Many terms appear here that do not appear elsewhere. This is a particularly hard reference to find, but several copies appear in the Peter Tamony Collection.)

Edwards, Bob. *Fridays with Red: A Radio Friendship.* New York: Simon and Schuster, 1993. (Retelling of Red Barber's contributions to the language of baseball.)

Ercolano, Patrick. *Fungoes, Floaters and Fork Balls: A Colorful Baseball Dictionary.* Englewood Cliffs, N.J.: Prentice-Hall, 1987.

Falletta, Joe. "Here's a Look at Some Baseball Jargon of the '80s." *Baseball Digest,* December 1983.

Farine, Michael. "Coming to Terms with Baseball Lingo." *The Potomac Almanac,* April 22, 1987.

Flexner, Stuart Berg. *Listening to America.* New York: Simon and Schuster, 1982. (Contains a lively and most useful chapter on baseball language and how it has changed through the years.)

Foster, John B. "Glossary of Base Ball Terms," an appendix to *Collier's New Dictionary of the English Language.* New York: P. F. Collier & Son, 1908. (An important and often overlooked glossary written by the editor of the Spalding baseball record and guide books of the time. The note that Peter Tamony attached to his copy of this work: "Filed to show small number of terms thought to be peculiar to this field of sport in its early period.")

Frank, Lawrence. *Playing Hardball. The Dynamics of Baseball Folk Speech.* New York: Peter Lang Publishing, 1984. (Based on the author's years playing for the semipro Novato Knicks of Novato, California; it is a study of the language on the field itself.)

Frommer, Harvey. *Sports Lingo.* New York: Atheneum, 1979.

———. *Sports Roots.* New York: Atheneum, 1979.

Fullerton, Hugh S. "The Baseball Primer." *The American Magazine,* June 1912. (An extremely important glossary in which certain terms are defined in print for the first time.)

Gast, Carol R. *Skill on the Diamond.* Omaha: Douglas Publishing Co., 1953.

Gibbons, Frank. "Handy Guide to 'Fieldese'!" *Baseball Digest,* May 1959.

Gibbs, C. M. "Gibberish." *Baltimore Sun,* January 1, 1935.

Goddard, Joe. "Hoover, Mr. Kodak, Salami, Yakker." *Sporting News,* March 6, 1982.

Gonring, Mike. "Baseball Still Has Its Own Special Lingo." *Baseball Digest,* June 1979.

Grieve, Curley. "Baseball Slang Growing Fast." *San Francisco Examiner,* March 11, 1937.

Hall, John. "How's Your Baseball Lingo?" *Baseball Digest,* December 1973.

Hartt, Rollin Lynde. "The National Game." *Atlantic,* August 1908.

Harvey, W. Clifford. "The Fascinating Language of Baseballese." *Baseball Magazine,* January 1931.

Heck, Henry J. "Baseball Terminology." *American Speech,* April 1930.

Hernandez, Keith, with Mike Bryan. *Pure Baseball: Pitch by Pitch for the Advanced Fan.* New York: HarperCollins, 1994.

Hershiser, Orel, with Jerry B. Jenkins. *Out of the Blue.* New York: Charter Books, 1989. (Good contemporary glossary.)

*Holiday,* Editors of. "Baseball Words." *Holiday,* March 1955.

Hollander, Zander. *Baseball Lingo.* New York: W. W. Norton, 1967.

Horgan, Tim. "Smoke Over the Short Porch." *Baseball Digest,* June 1964.

Howarth, Jerry. *Baseball Lite.* Toronto: Protocol Books, 1986. (A book of funny definitions that really is funny.)

Huddle, Franklin P. "Baseball Jargon." *American Speech,* April 1943.

Joyce, Joan, John Anquillare, and Dave Klein. *Winning Softball.* Chicago: NTC/Contemporary Publishing Company, 1975. (Contains a glossary of softball terms.)

Kiernan, John. "The Sportsman's Lexicon." *Saturday Review of Literature,* July 22, 1933.

Klump, C. M. *Who's Who and What's What in Baseball.* Philadelphia: Klump and Co., 1910. (Important, well-written glossary.)

Lawson, Thomas W. *The Krank: His Language and What It Means.* Boston: Rand Avary Co., 1888. (The first attempt to put baseball slang in one volume, this small book is now dated and very rare, but it is essential to any attempt at deciphering the baseball slang of the nineteenth century.)

Lee, Gretchen. "In Sporting Parlance." *American Speech,* April 1926. (An inventory of baseball terminology of the '20s.)

Levinson, Bill. "My Wife's Own Dictionary of Baseball." *San Francisco Examiner,* September 6, 1959. (Comic baseball glossary—better than most.)

Lieb, Frederick G. "How the Big League Clubs Got Their Nick Names." *Baseball,* February 1922.

Lindop, Al. "The Names of Summer." *Indianapolis Star,* April 5, 1981.

Lipsyte, Robert. "Sportspeak Without Tears." *New York Times,* May 30, 1968.

*Literary Digest,* Editors of. "Peril of the Baseball Lingo." *Literary Digest,* September 6, 1913.

Litwhiler, Danny. *The Glossary of International Baseball Terms.* Hamilton Square, N.J.: The United States Baseball Federation, 1961. (Terms in Italian, Spanish, Dutch, and English.)

Logan, Mrs. John A. *The Home Manual. Everybody's Guide in Social, Domestic and Business Life.* Philadelphia: H. J. Smith and Co., 1889. (This book contains everything from rules of etiquette to recipes for such things as toast water and tamarind whey, but it also contains a very early and ambitious glossary of baseball terms prepared by George A. Stackhouse, who was described as an authority on baseball. Commenting on this glossary in the December 1937 issue of *American Speech,* J. Louis Kueth of the Johns Hopkins University Library wrote, "Nearly all of the terms given in this list are still in use.")

Lukas, J. Anthony. "How Mel Allen Started A Lifelong Love Affair." *New York Times Magazine,* September 12, 1971.

Masin, Herman L. "Diamond Definitions You Won't Find in the Dictionary." *Baseball Digest,* June 1959.

McBride, Joseph. *High and Inside: The Complete Guide to Baseball Slang.* New York: Warner Books, 1980.

McCullough, Bill. "Baseball Slang Inconsistent in Various Loops." *Brooklyn Eagle,* September 5, 1937.

McDonald, Jack. "Sandwiches and Flies." *San Francisco Examiner,* April 11, 1966.

McGlone, Joe. Column in the *Providence* (Rhode Island) *Evening Bulletin,* August 2, 1946.

Meloy, Charles C. "Diamond Jargon." *Baseball Magazine,* August 1939.

Merriam-Webster, Editors of. *Webster's Sports Dictionary*. Springfield, Mass.: G. and C. Merriam and Co., 1976.

Miller, John H. "The Jargon of the Diamond." *Baseball,* October 1916.

Minshew, Wayne. "Dugout Lingo Has a Flavor of Its Own." *Baseball Digest,* June 1972.

———. "Players' Lexicon Unique Like Tweener, Chin Music." *The Sporting News,* April 1, 1972.

Moreland, Keith. "Talkin' Baseball Is What Makes It Quite Interesting." *Vineline,* August 1987. (Excellent glossary written from the players' standpoint.)

Murnane, T. H. *How to Umpire, How to Captain a Team, How to Manage a Team, How to Coach, How to Organize a League, How to Score, and the Technical Terms of Base Ball;* Spalding Athletic Library. New York: American Sports Publishing Co., 1915. (Six special and detailed glossaries [pitching terms, umpiring terms, etc.] make this an especially important source.)

*The Nation,* Editors of. "English and Baseball." *The Nation,* August 21, 1913.

*New York Sun.* "Baseball Slang and an Englishman." October 9, 1929.

———. "Have a Language All of Their Own." June 23, 1932.

Nichols, Edward J. *An Historical Dictionary of Baseball Terminology.* Ann Arbor: University Microfilms, 1939.

Nugent, William Henry. "The Sports Section." *The American Mercury,* March 1929. (Shows the seldom-acknowledged influence of Pierce Egan, an English writer of the early nineteenth century, whom Nugent deems "the father of newspaper sports slang.")

Ostler, Scott. "Baseball Lingo Throws Curve for Dudes Trying to Stay Hip." *Binghamton* (New York) *Press and Sun Bulletin,* May 4, 1986.

Paley, Steve. "In There Pitching For Arms Control." *New York Times,* September 6, 1987.

Parrott, Harold. "Bewildering are Slang Terms Used in Talk of Baseball Players." *Brooklyn Eagle,* August 9, 1936.

Povich, Shirley. "Baseball No Longer Speaks Same Language." *Washington Post,* March 20, 1996. (Important debunking of the excesses of modern terminology. "They now also talk of 'a semi-slider.' What is a semi-slider, and how does the play-by-play man know that it is a semi-slider? Half the time the batter himself confesses he doesn't know what kind of pitch he hit or whiffed at, but the men with the microphones from their vantage points in the sky pretend to know the full nature of the pitch. Come off it.")

Powers, Jimmy. "Dugout Slang." *New York Daily News,* January 10, 1937.

Reichler, Joe. *Joe Reichler's Great Book of Baseball Records,* No. 2. New York: Dell, 1957.

Remmers, Mary. *Ducks on the Pond: A Lexicon of Little League Lingo.* Austin, Tex.: Shoal Creek Publishers, 1981.

Richman, Milton. "Rookie Diction-err-y." *Baseball Digest,* May 1947.

Ridings, J. Willard. "Use of Slang in Newspaper Sports Writing." *Journalism Quarterly,* December 1934.

Rose, Howard N. *A Thesaurus of Slang.* New York: Macmillan, 1934.

Rosenbaum, Art. "Sports Terms Have Enriched Our Language." *San Francisco Examiner,* July 30, 1985.

Rothan, Martin. *New Baseball Rules and Decisions Book.* Lexington, Ky.: Baseball Decisions Co., 1947.

Rush, Red. "Red Rush's Dictionary of Baseball Slang." *San Francisco Examiner,* August 12, 1979.

Ruth, George Herman. *Babe Ruth's Own Book of Baseball.* New York: G. P. Putnam, 1928. (Contains a glossary with bygone bits of slang that do not appear elsewhere. Peter Tamony noted in his file on baseball terms that the text of the book is also useful, "for usage of practically all words and terms used in the play of the game of baseball.")

Ryan, Calvin T. "Sports Writers' Semantics." *Word Study,* February 1952.

Safire, William. *I Stand Corrected.* New York: Times Books, 1984. (Key section on "out in left field," pp. 232–35.)

————. *What's The Good Word?* New York: Avon, 1983. (Very important section on the word "fungo," pp. 69–75.)

Salak, John S. *Dictionary of American Sports.* New York: Philosophical Library, 1961.

Salsinger, H. G. "Dugout Dictionary." *Baseball Digest,* January–February 1957.

————. "Jargon of the Field." *Baseball Digest,* August 1945.

Samuels, V. "Baseball Slang." *American Speech,* February 1927. (Published as a letter, it amends Gretchen Lee's "In Sporting Parlance.")

Sargent, Lester L. "Novel Baseball Inventions." *Baseball,* March 1914.

Scheiber, Dave. "Talk Like a Fan." *St. Petersburg Times,* March 5, 1987. (Solid report on the slang heard during spring training.)

Schlossberg, Dan. *The Baseball Book of Why.* Middle Village, N.Y.: Jonathan David Publishers, 1984.

————. *The Baseball Catalog.* Middle Village, N.Y.: Jonathan David Publishers, 1980.

Scholl, Richard. *The Running Press Glossary of Baseball Language.* Philadelphia: Running Press, 1977.

Schoor, Gene, ed. *The Giant Book of Sports.* Garden City, N.Y.: Garden City Publishing Co., 1948. (Useful, slangy section entitled "Familiar Terms Connected with Baseball.")

Schwed, Fred, Jr. *How to Watch a Baseball Game.* New York: Harper and Row, 1957. (Fascinating chapter on baseball semantics.)

Scripps Howard News Service. "Reynolds Guide to Baseball Jive." September 17, 1986.

Shea, Thomas P. *Baseball Nicknames.* Hingham, Mass.: Gates-Vincent Publications, 1946.

Shecter, Leonard. "Baseball Spoken Here." *Baseball Digest,* June 1963.

Sherwood, R. E. "Breezy Bits of Baseball Humor." *Baseball Magazine,* September 1913. (Comic treatment of pre–World War I baseball slang.)

Shirts, Morris A. *Warm Up for Little League Baseball.* New York: Pocket Books, 1971, 1976. (Contains a good, small glossary with certain terms that do not appear elsewhere.)

Shulman, David. "Baseball's Bright Lexicon." *American Speech,* February 1951.

Simons, Herbert. "Do You Speak the Language?" *Baseball Magazine,* January 1943.

————. "Here's Some More Slang." *Baseball Magazine,* April 1943.

Smith, Chester L. "Diamond Slang Goes G.I." *Baseball Digest,* May 1946. (The only reference on the influence of the slang and terminology of the Second World War on baseball slang that I could find.)

Smith, Ken. "How They Express Themselves." *Baseball,* August 1939.

Smith, Red. "Sportspeak and Stuff." *New York Times,* July 1, 1981.

Spector, Robert Donald. "Baseball, Inside Out and Upside Down." *American Speech,* December 1956.

————. "Compound Words in Baseball." *American Speech,* May 1955.

————. "Little Words in the Big League." *Word Study,* May 1955.

Sperling, Dan. *A Spectator's Guide to Baseball.* New York: Avon, 1983.

Spink, C. C. & Son. *The Sporting News Record Book.* St. Louis: *The Sporting News,* 1933 and 1937 editions. (Both contain important sections on the game in slang.)

Spink, C. C. Johnson. "Sports in Our Language." *The Sporting News,* June 10, 1978.

Spink, J. G. Taylor, Fred Lieb, Les Biederman, and Bob Burnes. *Comedians of Baseball Down the Years.* St. Louis: Charles C. Spink and Son, 1958. (Contents include a rich and very important slang dictionary.)

*Sporting Life,* Editors of. "Many Gems of Slang Heard on Ball Field." *Sporting Life,* May 18, 1912.

Sullivan, Frank. "The Cliché Expert Testifies on Baseball." *New Yorker,* August 27, 1949.

Tamony, Peter. "Baseball." *Newsletter and Wasp,* April 14, 1939.

————. "Baseball and its Fans." *Words,* March 1939.

————. "Break," *Newsletter and Wasp.* October 6, 1939.

————. "Championship of the World." *Newsletter and Wasp,* October 13 and 20, 1939.

————. "Dick Smith." *Newsletter and Wasp.* September 15, 1939.

————. "Downtown: A Baseball Nickname." *Comments on Etymology,* May 1, 1983.

————. "Fungo and Bingo Again." *American Speech,* October 1937.

————. "Sandlot Baseball." *Western Folklore,* October 1968.

Thierry, Edward M. "Slang of the Sporting Writers." *Baseball,* September 1909.

Thompson, Fresco. *Every Diamond Doesn't Sparkle.* New York: David McKay, 1964. (Contains a very useful glossary of diamond argot including a handful of slang terms that are not found in other compilations.)

Turkin, Hy. *The Baseball Almanac.* New York: A. S. Barnes, 1955. (Particularly interesting glossary because he attributes a number of slang coinages to particular players.)

Vidmer, Richard. "Down in Front: Native Tongue." *New York Herald Tribune,* June 7, 1941.

Vogel, Otto. *Ins and Outs of Baseball.* St. Louis: C. V. Mosby, 1952.

Wagner, Honus. *Baseball Grins.* Pittsburgh: Laurel House, Inc., 1933. (Contains glossary of "Players' Lingo.")

Walker, Henry. *Illustrated Baseball Dictionary for Young People.* Englewood Cliffs, N.J.: Prentice-Hall, 1970.

Walsh, Edward R. "Baseballese: Truth Stranger Than Diction." *USAir* (inflight magazine), September 1982.

Ward, John Montgomery. *Base-Ball: How to Become a Player, with the Origin, History, and Explanation of the Game,* Philadelphia: The Athletic Publishing Co., 1888.

Weseen, Maurice H. *A Dictionary of American Slang.* New York: Thomas Y. Crowell, 1938. (The grand-daddy of topical slang books does a great job collecting and summarizing baseball slang.)

West, Harwell E. *The Baseball Scrap Book.* Chicago: Diamond Publishing Co., 1938. (Good section on baseball slang on the eve of World War II.)

Whiteford, Mike. *How to Talk Baseball.* New York: Dembner Books, 1983. (Fascinating and insightful work, but one that must be watched for its attribution of coinages which in several cases are made to terms and phrases that were already well-established.)

Will, George F. *Men at Work: The Craft of Baseball.* New York: Macmillan, 1990. (Work that pays particular attention to the talk and phraseology of the game.)

Winchell, Walter. "On Broadway." *San Francisco Call-Bulletin,* May 4, 1933.

Wolpow, Edward R. "Baseballese." *Word Ways,* August 1983. (A very small but revealing article on the troubles the editors of *Webster's Second New International Dictionary* had in classifying baseball terms. Wolpow points out that there are many inconsistencies in tabbing terms "ordinary" vs. cant, slang, or colloquialism.)

**II. These works on baseball and sports were especially useful in providing examples and insights into baseball terminology. Many more books were consulted, but these are the core collection with the most examples:**

Andreano, Ralph. *No Joy in Mudville: The Dilemma of Major League Baseball.* Cambridge, Mass.: Schenkman, 1965.

Angell, Roger. *Five Seasons.* New York: Simon and Schuster, 1977.

————. *Late Innings.* New York: Simon and Schuster, 1982.

————. *The Summer Game.* New York: Popular Library, 1972.

Asinof, Eliot. *Eight Men Out.* New York: Ace, 1963.

Bancroft, Jessie H., and William Dean Pulvermacher. *Handbook of Athletic Games.* New York: Macmillan, 1917.

Barber, Red. *1947—When All Hell Broke Loose in Baseball.* New York: Doubleday, 1982.

Bennett, Bob. *On the Receiving End: The Catcher's Guidebook.* Fresno, Calif.: Mid-Cal, 1982.

Blackwell's Durham Tobacco Co., *The Bull Durham Baseball Guide,* Vol. 2. New York, 1911.

Boswell, Thomas. *How Life Imitates the World Series,* Garden City, N.Y.: Doubleday, 1982.

Bouton, Jim. *Ball Four,* Twentieth Anniverary Edition. New York: Macmillan, 1990.

Brashler, William. *The Bingo Long Traveling All Stars and Motor Kings.* New York: Harper and Row, 1973.

Brosnan, Jim. *The Long Season.* New York: Harper and Row, 1960.

———. *Pennant Race.* New York: Harper and Row, 1962.

Chadwick, Henry. *DeWitt's Base-Ball Guide for 1874.* New York: Robert M. DeWitt, 1874.

Clark, Steve. *The Complete Book of Baseball Cards.* New York: Grosset & Dunlap, 1976.

Conner, Anthony J. *Baseball for the Love of It.* New York: Macmillan, 1982.

Creamer, Robert W. *Babe . . . the Legend Comes to Life.* New York: Simon and Schuster, 1974.

———. *Stengel: His Life and Times.* New York: Simon and Schuster, 1984.

Crepeau, Richard C. *Baseball: America's Diamond Mind, 1919–1941.* Orlando, Fla.: University of Central Florida, 1980.

Dolan, Edward F., Jr. *Calling the Play.* New York: Atheneum, 1982.

Einstein, Charles. *The Fireside Book of Baseball.* New York: Simon and Schuster, all three volumes 1956, 1958, and 1968.

Evans, Billy. *Simplified Base Ball Rules.* N.p.: Billy Evans, 1923 edition.

Freehan, Bill. *Behind the Mask.* Cleveland: World Publishing Company, 1970.

Frick, Ford C. *Games, Asterisks, and People.* New York: Crown, 1973.

Friendlich, Dick. *Relief Pitcher.* New York: Scholastic Book Services, 1966.

Frommer, Harvey. *New York City Baseball.* New York: Macmillan, 1980.

———. *Rickey and Robinson.* New York: Macmillan, 1982.

Garagiola, Joe. *Baseball Is a Funny Game.* New York: Bantam, 1962.

Gardner, Martin. *The Annotated Casey at the Bat.* New York: Bramhall House, 1967.

Graham, Frank. *Baseball Extra.* New York: A. S. Barnes, 1954.

Graham, Frank, and Dick Hyman. *Baseball Wit and Wisdom.* New York: David McKay, 1962.

Grey, Zane. *The Shortstop.* New York: Grosset and Dunlap, 1937 (reprint of 1909 original).

Jordan, Pat. *The Suitors of Spring.* New York: Dodd, Mead, 1973.

Kahn, Roger. *A Season in the Sun.* New York: Harper and Row, 1977.

———. *Good Enough to Dream.* New York: Doubleday, 1985.

———. *The Boys of Summer.* New York: Harper & Row, 1972.

Koppett, Leonard. *A Thinking Man's Guide to Baseball.* New York: Dutton, 1967.

Lardner, Ring. *You Know Me Al.* Cleveland: World Publishing Company, 1945 (reprint of 1914 ed.).

Lee, Bill, with Dick Lally. *The Wrong Stuff.* New York: Viking, 1986.

Lomax, Stan, and Dave Stanley. *A Treasury of Baseball Humor.* New York: Lantern Press, 1950.

Lowry, Phillip J. *Green Cathedrals.* Cooperstown, N.Y.: Society for American Baseball Research, 1986.

Lyle, Sparky, and Peter Golenbock, *The Bronx Zoo.* New York: Crown, 1979.

Maikovich, Andrew J. *Sports Quotations.* Jefferson, N.C.: McFarland, 1984.

Marazzi, Rich. *The Rules and Lore of Baseball.* New York: Stein and Day, 1980.

Mathewson, Christy. *Catcher Craig.* New York: Grosset and Dunlap, 1915.

McCarver, Tim. *Oh, Baby, I Love It.* New York: Dell, 1988.

McCue, Andy. *Baseball By the Books.* Dubuque, Iowa: Brown & Benchmark, 1991.

Mead, William B. *Even the Browns.* Chicago: Contemporary Books, 1978.

Mitchell, Jerry. *The Amazing Mets.* New York: Grosset & Dunlap, 1970.

Murray, Jim. *The Best of Jim Murray.* Garden City, N.Y.: Doubleday, 1965.

Nelson, Kevin. *Baseball's Greatest Quotes.* New York: Fireside Books, Simon and Schuster, 1982.

Offit, Sidney, ed. *The Best of Baseball.* New York: Putnam, 1956.

Peterson, Harold. *The Man Who Invented Baseball*. New York: Scribners, 1973.

Quigley, Martin. *The Crooked Pitch: The Curveball in American Baseball History*. Chapel Hill, N.C.: Algonquin Books, 1984.

Reichler, Joseph L., ed. *The Baseball Encyclopedia*. New York: Macmillan, 1969, revised, updated, and expanded editions through 1996.

Rice, Grantland. *The Tumult and the Shouting: My Life in Sport*. New York: A. S. Barnes, 1954.

Richter, Francis C. *The Millennium Plan of Sporting Life*. Philadelphia: Sporting Life Publishing Co., 1888.

Ritter, Lawrence S. *The Glory of Their Times*. New York: Macmillan, 1966.

Robinson, Jackie, with Charles Dexter. *Baseball Has Done It*. Philadelphia: Lippincott, 1964.

Schiffer, Michael. *Ballpark*. New York: Signet, 1982.

Smith, H. Allen. *Low and Inside*. Garden City, N.Y.: Doubleday, 1949.

Smith, Myron J. *Baseball: A Comprehensive Bibliography*. Jefferson, N.C.: McFarland, 1986.

Smith, Robert. *Baseball*. New York: Simon and Schuster, 1947.

Stern, Bill. *Favorite Baseball Stories*. New York: Pocket Books, 1949.

United States Congress, House of Representatives, Committee on the Judiciary, *Organized Baseball*. Washington, D.C.: GPO, 1952.

Veeck, Bill, with Ed Linn. *Veeck—As in Wreck*. New York: New American Library, 1962.

Vogel, O. H. *Ins and Outs of Baseball*. St. Louis: C. V. Mosby, 1952.

Waggoner, Glen, ed. *Rotisserie League Baseball*. New York: Bantam, 1984.

Wallop, Douglas. *Baseball: An Informal History*. New York: Norton, 1969.

———. *The Year the Yankees Lost the Pennant*. New York: Norton, 1954.

Williams, Ted, with John Underwood. *The Science of Hitting*. New York: Simon and Schuster, 1970.

Wills, Maury, with Don Freeman. *How to Steal a Pennant*. New York: Putnam, 1976.

### III. Works on words and language and general works that were especially useful in the preparation of this dictionary.

Ciardi, John. *A Browser's Dictionary*. New York: Harper and Row, 1980.

———. *A Second Browser's Dictionary*. New York: Harper and Row, 1983.

———. *Good Words to You*. New York: Harper and Row, 1987.

Colcord, Joanna Carver. *Sea Language Comes Ashore*. New York: Cornell Maritime Press, 1945.

Evans, Bergen. *Comfortable Words*. New York: Random House, 1962.

Farmer, John S. *Americanisms*. London: Thomas Poulter and Sons, 1889; republished by Gale Research Co., Detroit, 1976.

Farmer, John S., and W. E. Henley. *Slang and Its Analogues*. New York: Arno Press, 1970; reprint of the original multivolume series of 1890–1904.

Funk, Charles Earle. *Heavens to Betsy!* New York: Harper, 1955.

Hendrickson, Robert. *The Facts On File Encyclopedia of Word and Phrase Origins*. New York: Facts On File, 1987.

———. *Salty Words*. New York: Hearst Marine Books, 1984.

Holt, Alfred H. *Phrase and Word Origins*. New York: Dover, 1961.

Howard, Philip. *A Word in Your Ear*. New York: Oxford University Press, 1983.

Mallery, Richard D. *Our American Language*. New York: Halcyon House, 1947.

Marckwardt, Albert H. *American English*. New York: Oxford University Press, 1958.

Mathews, Mitford M. *Americanisms*. Chicago: University of Chicago Press, 1966.

Morris, William, and Mary Morris. *Morris Dictionary of Word and Phrase Origins*. New York: Harper and Row, 1977.

Partridge, Eric. *A Dictionary of Catch Phrases*. New York: Stein and Day, 1977.

————. *A Dictionary of Slang and Unconventional English.* 8th ed. Edited by Paul Beale. London: Routledge & Kegan Paul, 1984.

Plunkett, E. R. *Folk Names and Trade Diseases.* Stamford, Conn.: Barrett, 1978.

Rogers, James. *The Dictionary of Clichés.* New York: Facts On File, 1985.

Shipley, Joseph T. *Dictionary of Word Origins.* New York: Philosophical Library, 1945.

Smith, Logan Piersall. *Words and Idioms.* London: Constable Company, 1925.

Sullivan, Mark. *Pre-War America,* Vol. III of *Our Times.* New York: Scribner, 1930.

Vallins, G. H. *The Making and Meaning of Words.* London: Adam and Charles Black, 1949.

Versand, Kenneth. *Polyglot's Lexicon 1943–1966.* New York: Links Books, 1973.

Weingarten, Joseph A. *An American Dictionary of Slang.* Privately published. New York, 1954.

Wentworth, Harold, and Stuart Berg Flexner. *Dictionary of American Slang.* New York: Thomas Y. Crowell, 1960.

## IV. Newspapers:

Certain newspapers were consulted with regularity. The reason for this is either because a researcher/helper had access to that paper, the paper was well indexed on the Internet, or it was in the CD-ROM holdings of the Library of Congress.

*The Baltimore Sun*
*The Boston Globe*
*The Dallas Morning News*
*Milwaukee Journal Sentinel*
*San Diego Union-Tribune*
*The Sporting News*
*Tampa Tribune*
*USA Today*
*USA Today Baseball Weekly*
*The Washington Post*

# PHOTO CREDITS